# PRINCIPLES of
# Finance with Excel®

# PRINCIPLES of
# Finance with Excel®

## SECOND EDITION

**Simon Benninga**

New York   Oxford
OXFORD UNIVERSITY PRESS
2011

Oxford University Press, Inc., publishes works that further Oxford University's
objective of excellence in research, scholarship, and education.

**Oxford University Press**

Oxford   New York
Athens   Auckland   Bangkok   Bogotá   Buenos Aires   Cape Town
Chennai   Dar es Salaam   Delhi   Florence   Hong Kong   Istanbul   Karachi
Kolkata   Kuala Lumpur   Madrid   Melbourne   Mexico City   Mumbai   Nairobi
Paris   São Paulo   Shanghai   Singapore   Taipei   Tokyo   Toronto   Warsaw

With offices in
Argentina   Austria   Brazil   Chile   Czech Republic   France   Greece
Guatemala   Hungary   Italy   Japan   Poland   Portugal   Singapore
South Korea   Switzerland   Thailand   Turkey   Ukraine   Vietnam

Published by Oxford University Press, Inc.
198 Madison Avenue, New York, New York 10016
http://www.oup.com

Oxford is a registered trademark of Oxford University Press

All references to Excel in this text are understood to be "Microsoft® Excel®," a trademark of
the Microsoft Corporation. The Microsoft Corporation is in no way affiliated with or endorses
this publication. The publisher and author have made every effort to make this book as complete and
accurate as possible, but no warranty or fitness is implied. The information herein is provided on an
"as is" basis. The author and the publisher shall have neither liability nor responsibility to any person or
entity with respect to any loss or damages arising from the information contained in the book or
from the use of the CD or programs accompanying it.

Library of Congress Cataloging-in-Publication Data
Benninga, Simon.
   Principles of Finance with Excel / Simon Benninga.—2nd ed.
      p. cm.
   ISBN 978-0-19-975547-9 (acid-free paper)
   1. Finance—Data processing. 2. Microsoft Excel (Computer file)
3. Capital assets pricing model.   I. Title.
HG173.B463 2011
332.0285'554—dc22                                                2010009514



Printing number: 9 8 7 6 5

Printed in the United States of America
on acid-free paper

*I dedicate this book to the*
*memory of my parents*
*Helen Benninga*
*(1913–2008)*
*and*
*Noach Benninga*
*(1909–1993)*

# CONTENTS

# Preface

Finance is the study of financial decision making. Individuals and companies make financial decisions every day, and it's important to make them wisely. *Principles of Finance with Excel* (PFE) will teach you how to make these decisions—both the theory and the implementation of wise financial decision making—and how to express your decisions using Excel. Learning to do finance with Excel serves two purposes: It teaches you an important academic and practical subject (finance), and it teaches you how to implement financial analysis using the most important tool (in most cases, the *only* tool) for financial analysis (Excel). Your knowledge of both finance and Excel will be enhanced by carefully working through the examples and exercises in each chapter.

Finance is a very practical discipline. Most readers of this book will study finance not only to increase their understanding of the valuation process, but also to get answers to practical problems. You will find that the extensive computation required in this book will not only enable you to get numerical answers to important problems (although that alone would justify the Excel-centered focus of this book)—but also deepen your understanding of the concepts involved.

## Changes from the First Edition

Thanks to feedback solicited from the first-edition adopters, colleagues, and students, the second edition of *Principles of Finance with Excel* incorporates a number of important changes:

- The structure of the book has been streamlined so that the reader goes straight into the heart of finance—time value of money and discounting. Based on reviewer comments, Chapters 1, 2, and 3 from the first edition have been removed, with the most important material integrated in other places in the text where necessary.
- Nearly every example in every chapter—a centerpiece of the text—has been updated. Most now refer to the post-2008-crash financial world.
- Every chapter and spreadsheet has been thoroughly reviewed for accuracy. Every page of text has been revisited and, where appropriate, refined for clarity and conciseness.
- The second edition now uses Excel 2007 throughout the book.[1] The disk that comes with PFE includes chapter and exercise files for the whole book, so that it can easily be used for self-teaching. As in the first edition, we include an Excel "primer" at the end of the book. Note that all the examples and spreadsheets can be used with previous versions of Excel.

## Prerequisites—What Excel Background Is Required for *Principles of Finance with Excel?*

This book will teach you—alongside finance—all of the Excel concepts needed for finance. However, you should not expect the book to be a complete Excel text. I expect that, before you

---

[1] If you are using an earlier version of Excel, download a free compatibility pack by typing "Office 2007 compatibility pack" into the search box at http://www.microsoft.com. The Excel files are fully compatible with Excel 2010.

start your finance course, you will know how to do the following in Excel (just in case, many of these topics are covered in Chapter 24):

- Open and save an Excel workbook.
- Use basic Excel functions, for example: **Sum( )**....
- Format numbers: Here's an example of something that is usually not explained in the text.

| | C | D | E | F | G |
|---|---|---|---|---|---|
| 6 | ($6,144.57) | <-- =PV(10%,10,1000) | | | |
| 7 | | | | | |
| 8 | | | | | |
| 9 | -6,144.57 | <-- In many cases I prefer this format | | | |

- Use absolute and relative values in copying and formulas.
- Graphing—building the basic Excel charts. The favorite chart format for PFE is Excel's XY graph. You should know how to do the basics of graphing in Excel: label axes, add chart titles, and format axes.

## Somewhat More Advanced Excel Concepts

Chapters 25–29 cover a grab bag of other Excel concepts used in PFE. You can refer to these chapters as you need them:

- **Charts in Excel**: More advanced charting techniques are explained in Chapter 25.
- **Excel functions**: Most of the Excel functions required for this book are explained the first time they occur. Chapter 26 is a compendium of these explanations and may be useful for reference.
- **Data tables**: "Data table" is Excel jargon for "sensitivity table." The data table technique is a little tricky, but it is well worth learning (for some reason, data tables are often not covered in introductory Excel courses). Although the early chapters of PFE avoid the use of data tables, their use is required in later chapters of the book. Chapter 27 will teach you how to use data tables.
- **Goal Seek and Solver**: Excel's optimization tools are discussed in Chapter 28.
- **Dates in Excel**: Many finance computations require the use of dates. This topic is covered in Chapter 29.

## PFE's CD-ROM

Each chapter is accompanied by two spreadsheets, which are on the enclosed CD-ROM. One spreadsheet, typically called **PFE2, chapter01.xlsm** or **PFE2, chapter15.xlsm**, presents all the examples covered in Chapter 1 or Chapter 15. A second spreadsheet, called something like **PFE2, exercise15.xlsm**, gives the answers to the end-of-chapter exercises.[2]

When you open a PFE spreadsheet, you will see the following message informing you that there is a macro attached to the spreadsheet.

---

[2] Instructors can contact the author for a separate set of exercises to use in classes or exams. PowerPoints for most chapters are also available.

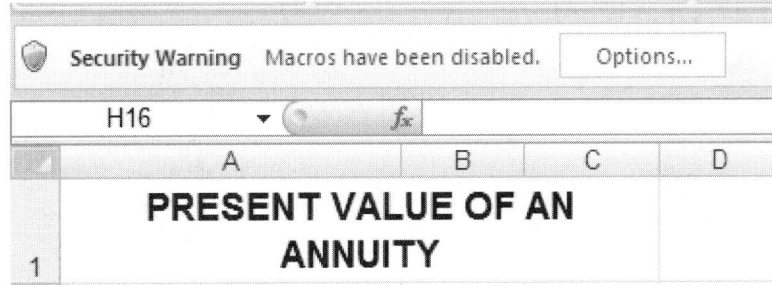

This message refers to a little program (in Excel jargon, a "macro") that dynamically updates cell references, so output like the following will automatically retain the correct cell references even if you move things around or add rows.

|  | A | B | C | D |
|---|---|---|---|---|
| 1 | **CALCULATING PRESENT VALUES WITH EXCEL** | | | |
| 2 | | | | |
| 3 | X, future payment | 100 | | |
| 4 | n, time of future payment | 3 | | |
| 5 | r, interest rate | 6% | | |
| 6 | Present value, $X/(1+r)^n$ | 83.96 | <-- =B3/(1+B5)^B4 | |
| 7 | | | | |
| 8 | **Proof** | | | |
| 9 | Payment today | 83.96 | | |
| 10 | Future value in *n* years | 100 | <-- =B9*(1+B5)^B4 | |

Clicking the **Options...** button gives you another box, in which you can safely click **Enable this content**.

You can safely enable this macro.[3]

---

[3] There is a document (**GetFormula.doc**) on the CD-ROM showing you how to put this macro into any spreadsheet you will want to create.

## A Final Word

Writing *Principles of Finance with Excel* was a lot of fun! I hope you enjoy the book. If you have comments or suggestions, feel free to contact me.

Simon Benninga
simon@simonbenninga.com

## Acknowledgments

During the years of writing *Principles of Finance with Excel*, I've gotten many wonderful comments from readers of the many versions of the Web draft of the book. University instructors, financial professionals, and students have all chipped in to make PFE a better book. Students at a number of colleges and universities have been unwitting guinea pigs for the materials: The Wharton School of the University of Pennsylvania, Tel Aviv University, Gonzaga University, Otago University, Rutgers University, Rider University, Tulane University, University of Amsterdam, University of Groningen.

This edition of PFE has benefited from the careful comments of a number of academic colleagues, and I am grateful for their insight:

William Arndt (Northwestern University), Jon Bakija (Williams College), David Carter (Oklahoma State University), Brent Dalrymple (University of Central Florida), Joseph J. French (University of Northern Colorado), Iordanis Karagiannidis (Michigan State University), Merouane Lakehal Ayat (Rochester Institute of Technology), Paul Laux (University of Delaware), David Mercurio (Northwestern University), Gary L. Mingle (Golden Gate University), Bruce Niendorf (University of Wisconsin-Oshkosh), Dror Parnes (University of South Florida), Glenn Pederson (University of Minnesota), Spuma Rao (University of Louisiana at Lafayette), Kemal Saatcioglu (Özyeğin University), Ozlem Sayilir (Anadolu University), Gökçe Soydemir (University of Texas-Pan American), Alasdair Turnbull (Clarkson University), Shawn Tysiak (University of Toledo), Matthew Will (University of Indianopolis), and Jack Zimmerman (Zayed University).

I've tried to carefully note all the readers who've been helpful in the editorial/writing process (if I've forgotten someone, there's always the next printing of the book...):

**Second edition**: Meni Aboudy, Brian Adams, Olaf Alex, Andrei Belgolov, Noaam Blum, Savio Braganza, Kenrick Chatman, Yaron Chechick, Sushil Dudani, Michael Ezewoko, Eugene Floyd, Yilmaz Guney, Mikael Steve Hackman, Hanan, Loo Choo Hong, Patrick Johnson, Michael Kesner, Susan Kleinmann, Joe Klunder , Ken Kotansky, , Mingsheng Li, Jason Manoharan, Juan Mendoza, Carlos Morais, Nathan Mott, Andrew Naporano, Michelle O'Neill, Joseph Pagliari Jr., Warren Palmer, Art Prunier, Csoma Róbert, Gerald Strever, Ilya Talman, Richard Teplick, Richard Trainer, Bin Xi, Brent Yarkin, and Mike Zystra. I owe special thanks to Sergey Popov and Eran Vodevoz, who read and commented on the revised manuscript.

**First edition**: Meni Aboudy, Ilan Adam, Gil Aharony, Mazin A. M. Al Janabi, Thomas C. Altman, Clifford S. Ang, Tom Arnold, Chana Arnon, Naftali Arnon, Almaz Asylbek, Dan Atzmon, Erik Austin, Daniel Bachner, Robert Balik, Keshav Baljee, Naomi Belfer, Helen Benninga, Ricardo Botero, Reider Bratvold, Lucas Brown, Yoshua Carhuamaca, P. J.

Carroll, Lydia Cassorla, Elizabeth Caulk, David Centeno, Le Chang, Peter Chepets, Nikolai Chuvakhin, Marcus Cole, Robin Desman, Daniel Diamant, Ian Dickson, Bjarne Eggesbo, Patricia A. Ellenburg, Etune Emelieze, Jon Fantell, Yiktat Fung, Brian Fusco, Denis Gaiovy, Terry Garden, Glenn Gaston, Fan Ge, Gary Glassie, Kobi Glazer, Randy Gordon, Kenji Goto, Michael Grant, Jonathan Gray, Pallav Gupta, George Guzzi, Kim Hale, Mark Helmantel, Raoul Hermens, Charlyn Ho, Reginald Holden, James W. B. Hole, Cesar Hurtado, Mafaz Ishaq, Ryan Scott Jackson, Youngsoo Kim, Itzik Kleschelski, Pierre Kohn, Timo Korkeamaki, Krushna Kumaar, Jeff S. Lee, Rowan Legg, Ross Leimberg, Björn Leonardz, Shai Leshkowitz, Daniel Leung, Hui Li, Shulin Liu, Paul Malherbe, Ariela Markel, Carlos Martinez, William Matthaei, Walter McGuire, Steve Medwin, Michael Miles, Kirill Mokh, Tal Mofkadi, Igor Morais, Eran Mordechai, Sviatoslav Moskalev, Joshua Nabatian, Bharat Pardasani, Dror Parnes, Jayesh Patel, Langston Payne, David Piccardi, Yong-Xuan Qiu, Justin Rapp, Ravinder Rayu, Roberto Rivalta, Jamie Adler Rodriguez, Bas Röling, Yashwant Sankpal, Roderik Schlösser, Jason Scott, Hanan Shahaf, Yaffa Shalit, Benny Sharvit, Teslim K. Shitta-Bey, Dmitry Shklovsky, Wayne Smith, José Arnaldo Ribeiro Soares, Nagaratnam Sreedharan, Yossi Steinblatt, Nathaniel V. Stevens, Lisa Sun, Maurry Tamarkin, Zoltan Till, Masahiro Tokoro, Efrat Tolkowsky, Jake Vachal, Rafael Paschoarelli Veiga, Shally Venugopal, Torben Voetmann, Simon Wang, Michael Wassermann, James L. Williams, Jared Work, Mark Yoffe, Jumana Zahalka, Aziza Zakhidova, Fan Zhang.

Finally, my thanks go to Marianne Paul, Patrick Lynch, Adam Tyrrell, and Terry Vaughn, my wonderful editors at the Oxford University Press.

# 1

# CAPITAL BUDGETING
# AND VALUATION

C$_{\text{HAPTER}}$ 1 OF *PRINCIPLES OF FINANCE WITH EXCEL* is an introductory chapter that discusses the aims of this book: What is finance all about? What is the relation of risk to financial decision making? Why Excel as the computational engine of a finance book?

Chapters 2 – 7 of *Principles of Finance with Excel* contain the core of most introductory of finance courses. These chapters are wholly self-contained. They teach:

- Time value of money—net present value (NPV), internal rate of return (IRR)
- Pricing using IRR—real-world examples
- Capital budgeting
- Determining the discount rate
- Using the weighted average cost of capital (WACC)
- Financial planning models and valuation

## Details and Outline

Chapter 2 addresses the basics of time value of money. We introduce the concepts of present and future value, net present value (NPV), and internal rate of return (IRR). Excel has functions that make all of these calculations easier to do, and Chapter 5 both illustrates the concepts and shows you how to use the relevant Excel functions.

Chapter 3 is entitled "What Does It Cost?" This chapter stresses the uses of discounting and present value in making effective financial decisions. The examples are taken primarily from consumer math, and cover credit cards, mortgages, and auto leasing. Along the way we also discuss multiple IRRs and continuous compounding—all motivated by simple examples.

"Capital budgeting" is finance jargon for whether to spend money on a specific project. Chapter 4 covers basic capital budgeting calculations. This chapter deals with the classic questions: making decisions using IRR versus NPV, choosing between projects with different life spans, mid-year versus end-year discounting, sunk costs, and reinvestment rates.

Chapter 5 discusses more advanced issues in capital budgeting. This chapter discusses several problems with using IRR as a decision criterion. It also shows you how to choose between projects with different lifetimes and how to discount cash flows that don't occur at year end (we call this "mid-year discounting"). Chapter 5 shows you how to incorporate taxes and inflation into the capital budgeting process.

A critical factor in time-value-of-money computations is the choice of the discount rate. Chapter 6 discusses how to compute a discount rate appropriate to both risk and tax considerations. This chapter will show you how to use the weighted average discount rate to calculate the value of a project.

Chapter 7 shows how to construct a financial planning model and how to use this model to value a firm. This is a topic that integrates much of the material in Chapters 2 – 6: A financial planning model combines both accounting and finance concepts to arrive at the valuation of the firm and its shares. This highly useful tool is the core of most business plans and valuations.

# 1 Introduction to Finance

## CHAPTER CONTENTS

## 1.1. What Is Finance?

Finance is the study of financial decision making. Individuals and companies make financial decisions every day, and it's important to make them wisely. *Principles of Finance with Excel* discusses how to make these decisions. The book covers the theory and the implementation of wise financial decision making and how to express your decisions using Excel.

Learning to do finance with Excel serves two purposes: It teaches you an important academic and practical subject (finance), and it teaches you how to implement financial analysis using the most important tool (in most cases, the *only* tool) for financial analysis (Excel).

## Individual Financial Decision Making

People are constantly called on to make financial decisions in their personal lives. Here are examples of decisions we will examine in this book:

- How much should you save to attain a specific goal in the future? For example, you're starting a savings plan today to save for your college education. How much should you put away each month for you to have the money to pay for your education?

- You're thinking about buying a house and renting it out for the income. How should you evaluate this decision?

- You have some money saved from working, and you'd like to invest it. How should you choose your financial portfolio? Investors big and small have to decide whether to invest in stocks, bonds, or other assets such as real estate, art, and gold. They also have to decide how to choose the *investment proportions*: What percentage of your financial portfolio should you invest in stocks (and what percentage in *which* stocks), what percentage in bonds, real estate, and so on?

- How should you finance a purchase, a project, or some other undertaking? Here are some examples: You're about to buy a new car. Should you borrow the money from the bank or should you accept the car dealer's "zero interest loan" alternative? That piece of real estate you're buying—should you finance it with a mortgage? If so, how large should the mortgage be?

- What is financial risk and how can it be measured? Financial risk can be measured using statistical tools. This book will show you which tools you need and how to apply them. When you're comfortable applying these tools, you will be better able to compare the riskiness of two assets or two investments. Comparing risks is critical to making optimal financial decisions.

- What is the fair value for stocks and bonds and other financial assets? This book will show you how to compute the value of stocks and bonds. It will also discuss the role of financial markets in incorporating available financial information into prices. If financial markets do this well, you may not need to determine these values yourself: You can let the financial markets tell you what the value should be.

- How can you value options? Options are securities that give you the right to buy a stock in the future. If you work in a corporate environment, your employers are likely, at some point, to offer you some options on the company's stock instead of a regular salary. If you're trying to regulate the risk of your financial portfolio, your investment advisor may try to sell you some options. In this book you'll learn what an option is, how to use it to regulate financial risk, and how to value it.

As these examples show, the study of finance can benefit you in many areas of your personal life by enabling you to make better financial decisions.

## Financial Decisions in a Business Environment

You only have to turn on the TV, log onto the Internet, or read a newspaper to hear about the financial decisions made every day by businesses. Some of these financial decisions are huge and dramatic, like Kraft's $16.7 billion bid to buy Cadbury; some are smaller but nonetheless very important for the company, like Courier Corporation's purchase of a new press for $12 million (Figure 1.1).

# Kraft wants to eat Cadbury for $16.7 billion

Posted Sep 7th 2009 1:00PM by Tom Taulli
Filed under: Hershey Co (HSY), Kraft Foods 'A' (KFT)

 More

 2 tweets

retweet

Over the past year, M&A has been on a starvation diet. Then again, with a terrible recession and credit crunch, what do you expect?

Yet, while it is still toot soon to tell, there are signs that things are beginning to improve. Just look at what's cooking between Kraft Foods (NYSE: KFT) and Cadbury (NYSE: CBY). Both global giants are involved in, well, an M&A food fight.

Kraft, which is the number two food company, made a $16.7 billion offer for rival Cadbury, which rejected the bid. But this is no deterrent. Kraft isn't going to give up on its pursuit.

# Courier Purchases Second High-Capacity Press

Business Wire, Oct 29, 2004

NORTH CHELMSFORD, Mass. -- Courier Corporation (Nasdaq: CRRC), one of America's leading book manufacturers and specialty publishers, today announced an agreement to purchase its second MAN Roland Lithoman four-color press in two years. The new press, representing a capital investment of approximately $12 million, will be installed next to an identical press placed in operation earlier this year at Courier's Kendallville, Indiana plant, significantly boosting Courier's capacity as a producer of high-quality four-color books for the education and trade markets.

"A year ago, when many book manufacturers were hedging their bets on capacity, Courier invested aggressively to expand by offering our customers state-of-the-art printing technology from MAN Roland," said Courier Chairman and CEO James F. Conway III. "That investment was a vote of confidence in the market, in our customers, and in the ability of our workforce. Six months after the press's startup last spring, that confidence has been rewarded, as the new press has rapidly approached 100% utilization thanks to strong demand for four-color textbooks and growing commitments from key customers. As a result, we have ordered a second one with identical capabilities while undertaking additional investments in prepress and bindery operations that will enhance our service even more. We expect to have this second new press installed and ready to run by late 2005."

FIGURE 1.1 Two financial decisions. Finance provides the tools to value Kraft's offer for Cadbury and to decide whether Courier's purchase of a new press is worthwhile.

Dramatic business decisions like mergers and acquisitions make the news, but "run-of-the-mill" business decisions that are critical to the financial health of the firm are made by all businesses, big or small. Here are some typical decisions businesses make:

- A company wants to replace its current production line with a line of new, improved machines. The new machines cost more but are more efficient. Should the company buy the new machines or leave the old ones in place?

- A firm needs to acquire a particular kind of machine. Should it buy a cheap machine with a relatively short life or an expensive machine with a longer lifespan?

- When a company wants to develop and produce a new product, how can it integrate the marketing forecasts for the new product with the financial requirements of the development and production processes? How can the company deal with the fact that the biggest costs of development and production will be incurred before any revenues have been realized from the sale of the product?

- How should the financial officers of a corporation plan for a new or existing business? A *financial planning model* can provide a systematic approach to making many of the financial decisions in a new or existing business. Perhaps you're thinking of setting up a laundromat on the corner of Main and Pine Streets. Perhaps you're starting a real estate business. Or perhaps you're trying to finance a new high-tech idea. In each case your ability to get financing from financial institutions—whether banks or venture capital funds or your Uncle Joe—will depend on your ability to make a financial model for the new business. This financial model will show your thoughts about how the business will develop, how much equipment you'll need to purchase, and how you will finance sales. Most important, the financial model will project future earnings from the business.

- All companies must decide how to finance their activities. This is true for multinational conglomerates, mom-and-pop convenience stores, and the new taxi company you're about to start with your cousin Sarah. In all cases someone has to decide whether to borrow the money from others or use shareholder funds (equity, in the terminology of finance) to finance the company.

## Wealth Maximization and Risk

This book is primarily about making *sensible financial decisions*. Sometimes a sensible financial decision is also an *optimal* financial decision. Optimal financial decisions make you better off than all the other relevant alternatives, including doing nothing at all. Economists call this property of optimal financial decisions *wealth maximization*. Not every case of money management boils down to making a wealth-maximizing decision; sometimes we will be able to only point to a *sensible set of financial alternatives* from which you can choose a final decision.

Making sensible or wealth-maximizing financial decisions always involves two elements.

- **Defining the parameters of the decision**: Financial decisions can always be defined in terms of numbers. The outcomes of a financial decision almost always depend on the *decision parameters*, the inputs that define the results of the financial decision.

Here's an example: You've been given $100 for your birthday, and you decide to save it toward your summer vacation next year. You have two choices: You can leave the money in your checking account or you can put the money in a savings account. The two parameters of this decision are the amount you're saving ($100) and the interest paid on the account—the checking account pays 1% interest, whereas the savings account pays 4% interest. The *financial outcomes* are that one year from now, you will have $101 if you leave the money in your checking account and $104 if you put the money in a savings account. This decision is, of course, a no-brainer: You always prefer earning 4% to earning 1% on your money.[1]

This book will help you distinguish between the parameters of financial decisions and the outcomes of financial decisions.

- **Recognizing the risks of financial decisions**: Financial decisions should be made within a framework that takes into account the risks associated with them.

Let's go back to the $100 you intend to save for your summer vacation. In addition to the two alternatives (1% on your checking account and 4% on your savings account), your Uncle Joe suggests that you might want to buy shares in his new hot dog stand. Investors in Joe's previous hot dog stands have earned as much as 40% on their investment.

If you put your money in Uncle Joe's hot dog stand, you *might* have $140 at the end of the year, instead of $104, but if the hot dog stand does poorly, you could lose your $100 investment and end up with nothing. Uncle Joe's hot dog stand is *much more risky* than a bank account—although some investors have made as much as 40%, others have lost all their money with Joe. Comparing an investment in the hot dog stand with a deposit in a savings account must take into account the differences in their risks. This book will show you how to account for risks inherent in making financial decisions.

## 1.2. Microsoft Excel: Why This Book and Not Another?

There are dozens of introductory finance texts out there. Many of them are very good. So why this one? In a word: **Excel**. Finance is the study of financial decision making and is therefore inherently a topic requiring lots of computation. In this book the computation is done in, and illustrated with, Excel, the premier business computational tool. Excel gives you the flexibility to change the elements of an example and to immediately get a new answer. We will use this flexibility extensively throughout *Principles of Finance with Excel*.

Finance is a very practical discipline. Most of you are studying finance not only to increase your understanding of the valuation process, but also to *get answers to practical problems*. You will find that the extensive computation required in this book will not just enable you to get numerical answers to important problems (although that alone would justify the Excel-centered focus of this book)—it will also deepen your understanding of the concepts involved.

Using Excel enables us to discuss many more real-life examples than is possible using a calculator. Your knowledge of both finance and Excel will be enhanced by carefully working through the examples and exercises in each chapter.[2]

Most college students will be coming to a finance course after having taken an initial computing course that covers the basics of Excel used in this book. If you want an Excel review, the last six chapters of this book cover the essential Excel concepts that are used in this book. In

---

[1]Of course there may be other things going on: Checking account balances are always available, whereas the balance in your savings account might need to be there for a minimum period of time before you earn interest. These *liquidity considerations* are discussed in Chapter 14.

[2]If you're a finance student at a college or university, this combination of Excel and finance will also enhance your employment opportunities. Excel is practically the only financial tool used by business today.

addition, throughout the book you will find explanations of Excel functions and their application to financial problems. When things get really rough, you'll find little boxes called "Excel Notes," which explain difficult concepts. Here is an example of such a box.

---

## EXCEL NOTE

The Excel function **Sum** can often be used to simplify calculations. Here's an example based on the computation of a profit-and-loss statement:

| | A | B | C |
|---|---|---|---|
| 1 | USING SUM TO COMPUTE THE PROFIT AND LOSS | | |
| 2 | Profit and loss | | |
| 3 | Sales | 1,000 | |
| 4 | Cost of goods sold | -500 | |
| 5 | Depreciation | -100 | |
| 6 | Interest | -35 | |
| 7 | Profit before taxes | 365 | <-- =SUM(B3:B6) |
| 8 | Taxes (40%) | -146 | <-- =-40%*B7 |
| 9 | Profit after taxes | 219 | <-- =SUM(B7:B8) |

Cells B7 and B9 use the **Sum** function to add multiple cells. An alternative to using **Sum** in cell B7 would be to use the formula **=B3+B4+B5+B6**. As you can see, **Sum** is more concise.

---

## Excel Versions: Excel 2007 versus Excel 2003 and Excel 2010

*Principles of Finance with Excel* illustrates all its examples using Excel 2007, but the spreadsheets are fully compatible with earlier versions of Excel and with the forthcoming Excel 2010. A slightly fuller discussion of compatibility issues is in Section 5 of this chapter.

## What Are the Excel Prerequisites for This Book?

You do not have to be an Excel expert to use this book. Almost all the Excel concepts needed to do finance are explained in the text itself. Although this book will teach you the Excel concepts needed for finance, it is not a complete Excel text. Before you start Chapter 2, you should know how to do the following in Excel (all are covered in Chapter 24):

- Open and save an Excel notebook.
- Format numbers: You can make numbers appear in different forms. In the example below, the number 2313.88 is shown in three different ways. You should know how to do this formatting. In this case, we've chosen an appropriate format from the drop-down list on the **Format** section of the **Home** tab of Excel and indicated the appropriate formatting.

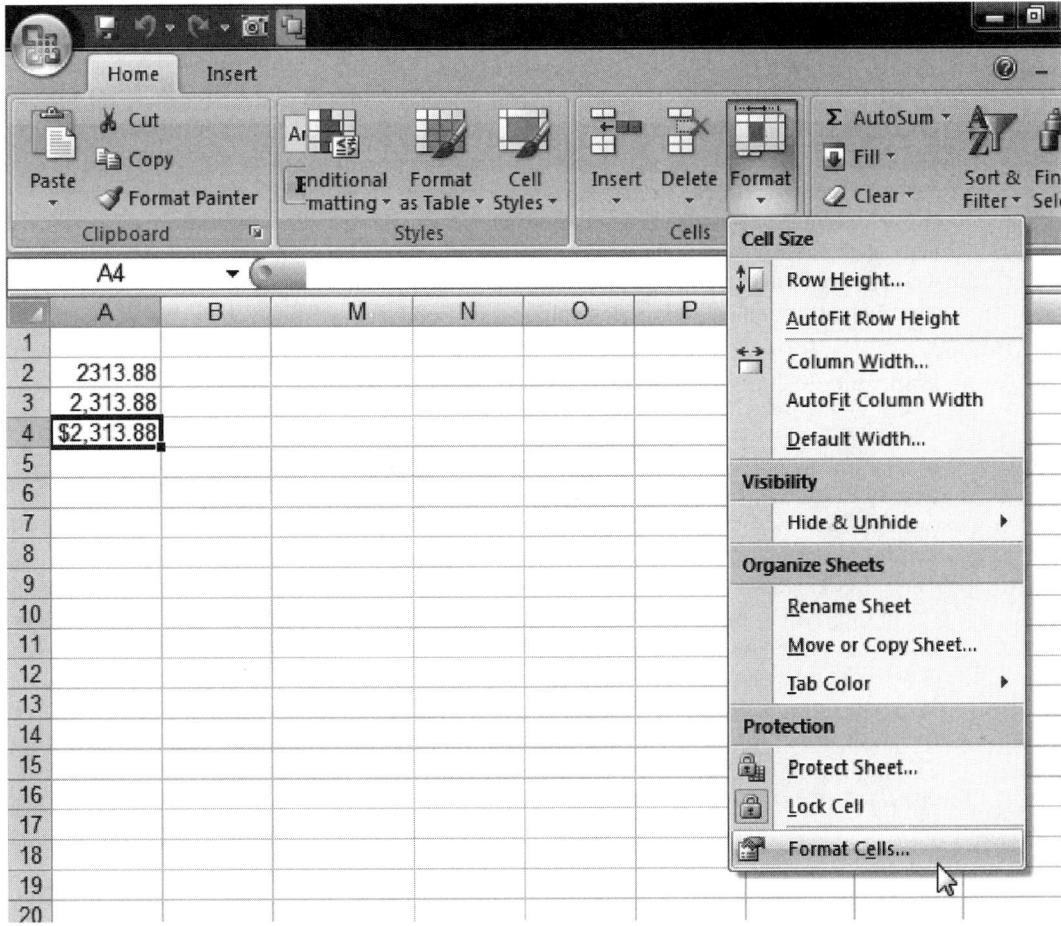

- Use absolute and relative values in copying and formulas: When you copy in Excel, you can use either *relative* or *absolute* copying. As explained in Chapter 24, relative copying changes the cell reference addresses, whereas absolute copying leaves them the same.[3]
- Build basic Excel charts to graph data. You should know how to label axes, put in chart titles, format axes, and so on.

## 1.3. Eight Principles of Finance

In this section we look at eight unifying principles of finance. At this stage you may not understand them all or even find them convincing, but we introduce them here to give you an overview of what finance is all about. They will be more fully explained in the rest of *Principles of Finance with Excel.*

---

[3]If you find this sentence mysterious, look at Section 24.3.

## Principle 1: Buy Assets That Add Value; Avoid Buying Assets That Don't

On the simplest level, making optimal financial decisions has to do with buying assets that add value and avoiding those that don't. For example, you need to decide whether to keep using your old, inefficient photocopying machine or buy an expensive new one that works faster, doesn't break down as often, and uses less ink and energy. The finance question about these two alternatives is which—keeping the old photocopier or buying a new one—adds more value to your business. To make a determination about how valuable things (such as stocks, bonds, machines, and companies) are, you need to be sure that you are comparing apples with apples and oranges with oranges. This sounds like a simple principle to follow, but it can be surprisingly tricky to implement!

## Principle 2: Cash Is King

The value of an asset is determined by the *cash flows it produces over its life*. The cash flow of an asset is the *after-tax cash* that the asset produces at a given point in time.

Although it is too early in the book to give you the full flavor of the difference between a cash flow and a profit number, we can give a small example. Suppose your pizza parlor sells $500 of pizzas on Tuesday night, and suppose the same day you bought $300 worth of ingredients. Looking in the cash register at the end of the day, you expect to find $200, but instead you're surprised to find $300. The explanation: Of the $500 of pizzas sold, you only collected $400—the other $100 were sold to a campus fraternity that maintains an account with you that they settle at the end of each month. Of the $300 of ingredients you bought, you only paid for $100—the other $200 will be billed to you for payment in 10 days.

Cash flows are different from accounting profits or sales receipts. The pizza parlor's *accounting profit* for the day is $200, but its *cash flow* for the day is $300 ($400 collected from sales minus $100 paid for supplies). The difference between the two is caused by the *timing difference* between inflows and outflows. (Of course, 10 days from now the pizza parlor will have a negative cash flow of $200 as a result of paying for the ingredients.)

In finance, *cash flow is all-important*. Most corporate financial data come from accountants, who—despite the bad press they've gotten in the past few years—do a very good job at representing the economic realities of corporate activities. When making financial decisions, we have to translate the accounting data to their cash equivalents. Much of finance involves first translating accounting information into cash flows.[4]

## Principle 3: The Time Dimension of Financial Decisions Is Important

Many financial decisions have to do with comparing cash flows at different points in time. As an example, you pay for that new photocopy machine *today* (a cash *outflow*), but you save money in the *future* (a cash *inflow*). Finance has to do with correctly dealing with this time dimension of cash flows.

## Principle 4: Know How to Compute the Cost of Financial Alternatives

Financial alternatives are often bewildering: Is it more expensive to buy or lease a photocopier? When your credit card charges you "daily interest," is it more or less expensive than the bank

---

[4]Not familiar with basic accounting? See the book's Web site, http://www.simonbenninga.com, for a review of basic accounting principles.

loan that charges you "monthly interest?" In making financial decisions you need to know how to compute the cost of two or more competing alternatives. This book will teach you how.

### Principle 5: Minimize the Cost of Financing

Many financial decisions have to do with choosing the right alternative. Should you finance that photocopier with a loan from the dealer or with a loan from the bank? Should you buy a new car or lease it?

Choosing the right financial alternative is, in many cases, a decision made separately from the investment decision: You've decided to purchase the copier (the investment decision), and now you have to choose whether to finance it through a bank loan or by accepting the dealer's "zero interest financing" (the financing decision).

### Principle 6: Take Risk into Account

Many financial alternatives cannot be directly compared without taking into account their risk. Should you take money out of the bank and invest it in the stock market? On the one hand, people who invest in the stock market *on average* earn more than those who leave their money in the bank. On the other hand, a bank deposit is safe, whereas a stock market investment is much less safe (riskier).

"Risk" is the magic word in finance. This book will show you how to quantify risk so you can compare financial alternatives.

### Principle 7: Markets Are Efficient and Deal Well with Information

Financial markets are awash in information. In making a financial decision, how can we possibly know or obtain all the information we need to make a sensible, well-informed decision? The bad news is that we probably can't incorporate all available information into our decision-making process. The good news is that we may not have to: The confluence of many market participants striving to make use of what information they have leads markets to work to eliminate riskless profitable opportunities. In many cases financial markets work so well that we can't add anything to their information-gathering abilities. In short, it may well be that the stock market's valuation of XYZ stock is correct given all the information available about the stock. This *market efficiency* can simplify the way you think about assets and their prices when making financial decisions.

### Principle 8: Diversification Is Important

"Don't put all your eggs in one basket." The financial equivalent of this hackneyed expression is diversify the assets you hold; don't hold just a few stocks or bonds, buy a portfolio. *Principles of Finance with Excel* will show you how to analyze portfolios of assets and how to choose the individual assets in your portfolio wisely.

## 1.4. An Excel Note—Building Good Financial Models

We've chosen this place in the chapter to tell you a bit about financial modeling. A few simple rules will help you create better and neater Excel models.

**Modeling rule 1: Put all the variables that are important (the fashionable jargon is "value drivers") at the top of your spreadsheet.** In the "Saving for College" spreadsheet below, the three value drivers—the interest rate, the annual deposit, and the annual cost of college—are in the top left corner of the spreadsheet.

| | A | B | C | D | E | F | G | H | I |
|---|---|---|---|---|---|---|---|---|---|
| 1 | | SAVING FOR COLLEGE | | | | | | | |
| 2 | Interest rate | 8% | | | Critical parameters (some times called "value | | | | |
| 3 | Annual deposit | 12,000.00 | ← | | drivers") are in the upper left corner. The | | | | |
| 4 | Annual cost of college | 35,000 | | | actual cost of saving for a college education is | | | | |
| 5 | | | | | discussed in Chapter 2. | | | | |
| 6 | Birthday | In bank on birthday, before deposit/withdrawal | Deposit or withdrawal at beginning of year | End of year before interest | End of year with interest | | | | |
| 7 | 10 | 0.00 | 12,000.00 | 12,000.00 | 12,960.00 | | | | |
| 8 | 11 | 12,960.00 | 12,000.00 | 24,960.00 | 26,956.80 | | | | |
| 9 | 12 | 26,956.80 | 12,000.00 | 38,956.80 | 42,073.34 | | | | |
| 10 | 13 | 42,073.34 | 12,000.00 | 54,073.34 | 58,399.21 | | | | |
| 11 | 14 | 58,399.21 | 12,000.00 | 70,399.21 | 76,031.15 | | | | |
| 12 | 15 | 76,031.15 | 12,000.00 | 88,031.15 | 95,073.64 | | | | |
| 13 | 16 | 95,073.64 | 12,000.00 | 107,073.64 | 115,639.53 | | | | |
| 14 | 17 | 115,639.53 | 12,000.00 | 127,639.53 | 137,850.69 | | | | |
| 15 | 18 | 137,850.69 | -35,000.00 | 102,850.69 | 111,078.75 | | | | |
| 16 | 19 | 111,078.75 | -35,000.00 | 76,078.75 | 82,165.05 | | | | |
| 17 | 20 | 82,165.05 | -35,000.00 | 47,165.05 | 50,938.25 | | | | |
| 18 | 21 | 50,938.25 | -35,000.00 | 15,938.25 | | | | | |
| 19 | | | | | | | | | |
| 20 | | NPV of all payments | | 6,835.64 | <-- =C7+NPV(B2,C8:C18) | | | | |

**Modeling rule 2: Never use a number where a formula will also work.** Using formulas instead of "hard-wiring" numbers means that when you change a parameter value, the rest of the spreadsheet changes appropriately. As an example, cell C20 in the above spreadsheet contains the formula **=C7+NPV(B2,C8:C18)**. We could have written this as **=C7+NPV(8%,C8:C18)**. But this means that changing the entry in cell B2 will not go through the whole model.

**Modeling rule 3: Avoid the use of blank columns to accommodate cell "spillovers."** Here's an example of a potentially bad model.

| | A | B | C |
|---|---|---|---|
| 1 | Interest rate | | 6% |

Because "Interest rate" has spilled over to column B, the author of this spreadsheet has decided to put the "6%" in column C. This could be confusing. A better way is to make column A wider and put the 6% in column B.

| | A | B |
|---|---|---|
| 1 | Interest rate | 6% |

Widening the column is simple: Put the cursor on the break between columns A and B.

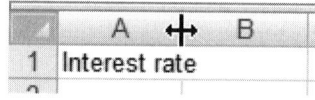

Double clicking the left mouse button will expand the column to accommodate the widest cell. You can also "stretch" the column by holding the left mouse button down and moving the column width to the right.

**Modeling rule 4: Make your Excel default one sheet.** Excel's default is to open notebooks with three spreadsheets, but 99% of the time you'll only need one sheet. So set your default to one sheet, and if you need more, you can always add. In Excel 2007, go to the **Office Button → Excel Options → Popular**.

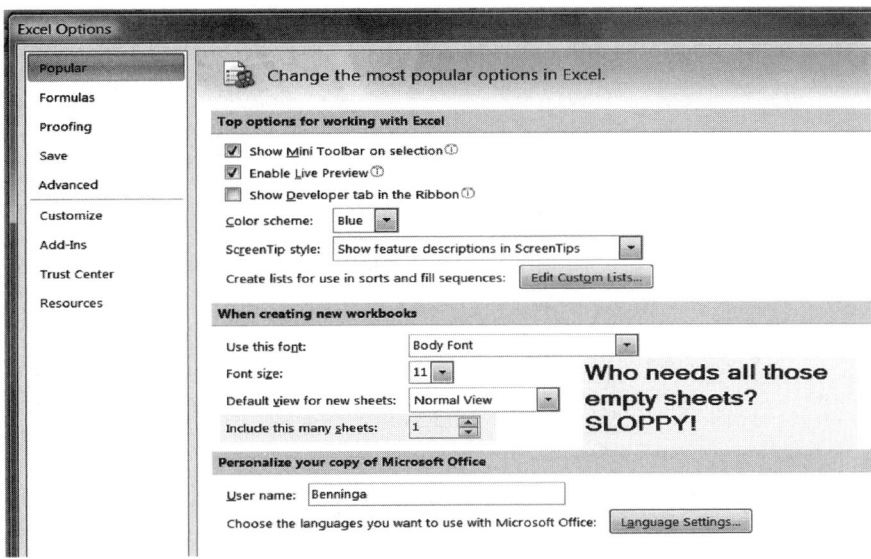

**Modeling Rule 5**: **Turn off the "auto jump down" feature**. The Excel default is that when you click **Enter**, the cursor jumps down to the next cell. But in financial modeling we need to look at the formulas we've written to make sure that they make sense! So turn off this feature! Go to the **Office Button → Excel Options → Advanced**:

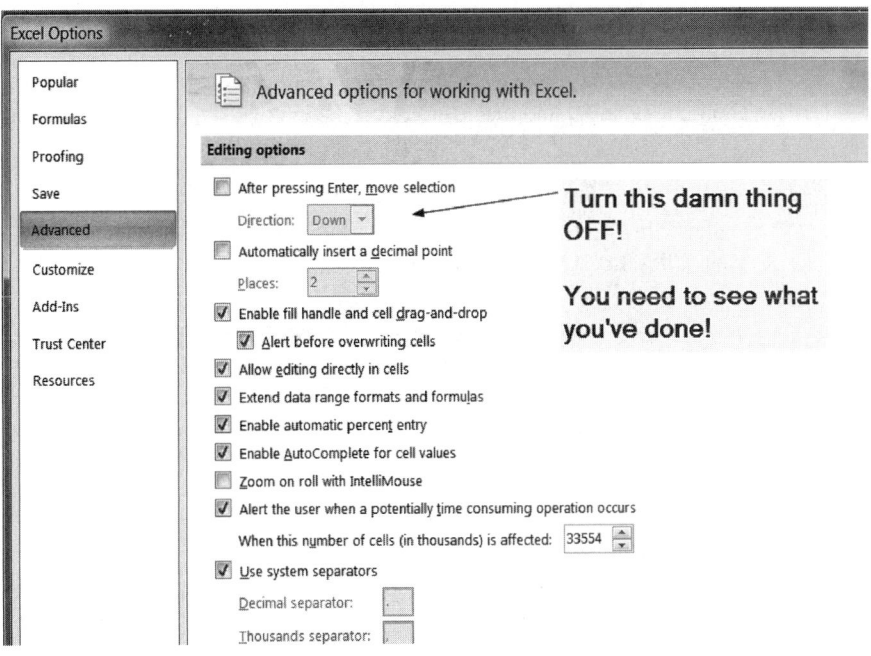

## 1.5. A Note about Excel Versions

This book uses Excel 2007 but the spreadsheets are compatible with both Excel 2003 and the newly-arrived Excel 2010. All spreadsheets are saved in Excel 2007's "xlsm" format. If this format does not open on your computer, you are probably using an older version of Excel and need to download the free converter. The box below shows how to do this.

- Users who use an earlier version of Excel can also download the Microsoft office Compatibility Pack for 2007 Office Word, Excel and PowerPoint File Formats to install updates and converters for the earlier version of Excel. This allows them to open, edit, and save an Excel 2007 workbook in the earlier version of Excel, without having to save it to that version's file format first or without having to upgrade the earlier version of Excel to Excel 2007.

Compatibility with Excel 2003: The clip above is taken from http://office.microsoft.com/en-au/excel/HA100141071033.aspx. Downloading the Compatibility Pack allows you to open Excel 2007 files in Excel 2003.

## 1.6. Adding "Getformula" to Your Spreadsheet

The spreadsheets that accompany *Principles of Finance with Excel* all include a short macro called **Getformula** that tracks the cell contents. I've found **Getformula** to be extraordinarily useful in my work—it allows me to explain (to myself and to my readers) what I've done in my spreadsheets. The macro is *dynamic*: When you change a spreadsheet by moving something (for example, by adding rows or columns), **Getformula** automatically updates the formulas.

### Setting the Excel Security Level

To use **Getformula**, you have to first set the security level of Excel to medium. This allows you to choose to open (or not) macros in Excel. Doing this is a two-step procedure.

**Step 1**: In Excel 2007, go to the Office Button  and then to **Excel Options|Trust Center**. Click **Trust Center Settings**.

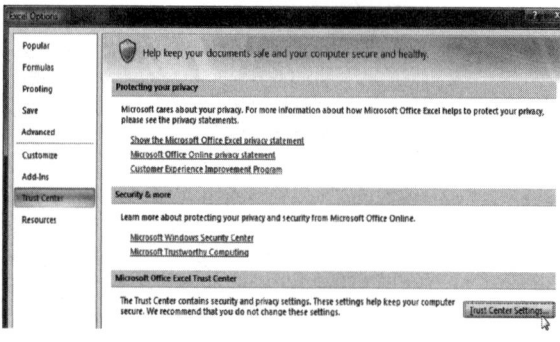

**Step 2**: Go to the **Macro Settings** tab and click **Disable All Macros with Notification**. This is a backhanded way of saying that Excel will ask whether you want to open macros.

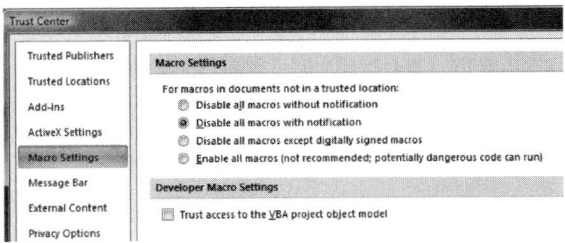

These steps need be done only once. Now, when you open a spreadsheet from *Principles of Finance with Excel*, you will be asked whether to open the macros.

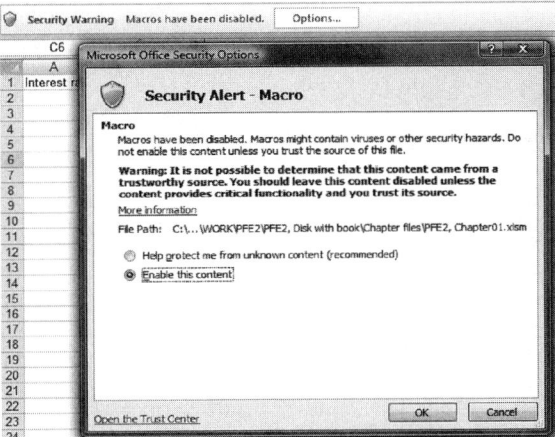

## Summary

The combination of finance concepts with an Excel implementation is a "killer app"! *Principles of Finance with Excel* is the only finance principles book on the market that contains this combination.

Enjoy!

## CHAPTER CONTENTS

## Overview

This chapter deals with the most basic concepts in finance: future value, present value, net present value, and internal rate of return. These concepts tell you how much your money will grow if deposited in a bank (future value), how much promised future payments are worth today (present value), what an investment is worth (net present value), and what percentage rate of return you're getting on your investments (internal rate of return).

Financial assets and financial planning always have a time dimension. Here are some simple examples:

- You put $100 in the bank today in a savings account. How much will you have in 3 years?

- You put $100 in the bank today in a savings account and plan to add $100 every year for the next 10 years. How much will you have in the account in 20 years?

- XYZ Corporation just sold a bond to your mother for $860. The bond will pay her $20 per year for the next 5 years. In 6 years she gets a payment of $1020. Has she paid a fair price for the bond?

- Your Aunt Sara is considering making an investment. The investment costs $1,000 and will pay back $50 per month in each of the next 36 months. Should she do this or should she leave her money in the bank, where it earns 5%?

This chapter discusses these and similar issues, all of which fall under the general topic of *time value of money*. You will learn how compound interest causes invested income to grow (*future value*) and how money to be received at future dates can be related to money in hand today (*present value* and *net present value*). You will also learn how to calculate the compound rate of return earned by an investment (*internal rate of return*). The concepts of future value, present value, net present value, and internal rate of return underlie much of the financial analysis that will appear in the following chapters.

As always, we use Excel, the best financial analysis tool!

### Finance Concepts Discussed

- Future value
- Present value
- Net present value
- Internal rate of return
- Pension and savings plans and other accumulation problems

### Excel Functions Used

- Excel functions: **FV, PV, NPV, IRR, PMT, NPER**
- Goal seek

## 2.1. Future Value

Future value is the value at some future date of a payment (or payments) made before this future date. The future value includes the interest earned on the payments.

Future value (FV) is a concept that relates the value in the future of money deposited in a bank account today and over time and left in the account to draw interest. Suppose, for example, that you put $100 in a savings account in your bank today and the bank pays you 6% interest at the end of every year. If you leave the money in the bank for 1 year, you will have $106 after 1 year: $100 of the original savings balance + $6 in interest. The $106 is the *future value after 1 year of the initial deposit of $100 at 6% annual interest.*

Now suppose you leave the money in the account for a second year: At the end of this year, you will have the following:

| | |
|---|---|
| $106 | The savings account balance at the end of the first year |
| + | |
| 6%*$106 = $6.36 | The interest on this balance for the second year |
| = $112.36 | Total in account after 2 years |

The $112.36 is the *future value after 2 years of the initial deposit of $100 at 6% annual interest.* Another way to express this is $112.36 = $100*(1+6\%)^2$:

$$\underbrace{\underbrace{\underbrace{\$100}_{\substack{\uparrow \\ \text{Initial deposit}}} * \underbrace{1.06}_{\substack{\uparrow \\ \text{Year 1's future} \\ \text{value factor at 6\%}}}}_{\substack{\uparrow \\ \text{Future value of \$100 after} \\ \text{one year} = \$100*1.06}} * \underbrace{1.06}_{\substack{\uparrow \\ \text{Year 2's} \\ \text{future value factor}}}}_{\substack{\uparrow \\ \text{Future value of \$100 after two years}}} = \$100 * (1+6\%)^2 = \$112.36$$

Note that the future value uses the concept of *compound interest*: The interest earned in the first year ($6) itself earns interest in the second year. To sum up,

*The future value of $X deposited today in an account paying r% interest annually and left in the account for n years is $FV = X*(1+r)^n$.*

---

## NOTATION

In this book we will often match our mathematical notation to that used by Excel. Because in Excel multiplication is indicated by an asterisk, "*", we will sometimes write 6%*$106 = $6.36, even though this is not necessary. Similarly, we will sometimes write $(1.10)^3$ as 1.10^3.

---

Future value calculations are easily done in Excel.

| | A | B | C |
|---|---|---|---|
| 1 | \multicolumn{2}{c}{**CALCULATING FUTURE VALUES WITH EXCEL**} | |
| 2 | Initial deposit | 100 | |
| 3 | Interest rate | 6% | |
| 4 | Number of years, n | 2 | |
| 5 | | | |
| 6 | Account balance after n years | 112.36 | <-- =B2*(1+B3)^B4 |

Note the use of the carat (^) to denote the exponent: In Excel $(1+6\%)^2$ is written as $(1+B3)\text{^}B4$, where cell B3 contains the interest rate and cell B4 the number of years.

We can use Excel to make a table of how the future value grows with the years and then use Excel's graphing abilities to graph this growth.

| | A | B | C | D | E | F | G |
|---|---|---|---|---|---|---|---|
| 1 | **THE FUTURE VALUE OF A SINGLE $100 DEPOSIT** | | | | | | |
| 2 | Initial deposit | 100 | | | | | |
| 3 | Interest rate | 6% | | | | | |
| 4 | Number of years, n | 2 | | | | | |
| 5 | | | | | | | |
| 6 | Account balance after n years | 112.36 | <-- =B2*(1+B3)^B4 | | | | |
| 7 | | | | | | | |
| 8 | Year | Future value | | | | | |
| 9 | 0 | 100.00 | <-- =$B$2*(1+$B$3)^A9 | | | | |
| 10 | 1 | 106.00 | <-- =$B$2*(1+$B$3)^A10 | | | | |
| 11 | 2 | 112.36 | <-- =$B$2*(1+$B$3)^A11 | | | | |
| 12 | 3 | 119.10 | <-- =$B$2*(1+$B$3)^A12 | | | | |
| 13 | 4 | 126.25 | <-- =$B$2*(1+$B$3)^A13 | | | | |
| 14 | 5 | 133.82 | | | | | |
| 15 | 6 | 141.85 | | | | | |
| 16 | 7 | 150.36 | | | | | |
| 17 | 8 | 159.38 | | | | | |
| 18 | 9 | 168.95 | | | | | |
| 19 | 10 | 179.08 | | | | | |
| 20 | 11 | 189.83 | | | | | |
| 21 | 12 | 201.22 | | | | | |
| 22 | 13 | 213.29 | | | | | |
| 23 | 14 | 226.09 | | | | | |
| 24 | 15 | 239.66 | | | | | |
| 25 | 16 | 254.04 | | | | | |
| 26 | 17 | 269.28 | | | | | |
| 27 | 18 | 285.43 | | | | | |
| 28 | 19 | 302.56 | | | | | |
| 29 | 20 | 320.71 | | | | | |

Future Value of $100 at 6% Annual Interest

**EXCEL NOTE**

Note that the formula in cells B9:B29 in the table has $ signs on the cell references (for example, **=$B$2*(1+$B$3)^A9**). This use of the *absolute references* feature of Excel is explained in Chapter 24.

In the spreadsheet below, we present a table and graph that show the future value of $100 for three different interest rates: 0, 6, and 12%. As the spreadsheet shows, future value is *very* sensitive to the interest rate! Note that when the interest rate is 0%, the future value doesn't grow.

| | A | B | C | D | E |
|---|---|---|---|---|---|
| 1 | | **FUTURE VALUE OF A SINGLE DEPOSIT AT DIFFERENT INTEREST RATES** **How $100 at time 0 grows at 0%, 6%, 12%** | | | |
| 2 | Initial deposit | 100 | | | |
| 3 | Interest rate | 0% | 6% | 12% | |
| 4 | | | | | |
| 5 | **Year** | **FV at 0%** | **FV at 6%** | **FV at 12%** | |
| 6 | 0 | 100.00 | 100.00 | 100.00 | <-- =$B$2*(1+D$3)^$A6 |
| 7 | 1 | 100.00 | 106.00 | 112.00 | <-- =$B$2*(1+D$3)^$A7 |
| 8 | 2 | 100.00 | 112.36 | 125.44 | |
| 9 | 3 | 100.00 | 119.10 | 140.49 | |
| 10 | 4 | 100.00 | 126.25 | 157.35 | |
| 11 | 5 | 100.00 | 133.82 | 176.23 | |
| 12 | 6 | 100.00 | 141.85 | 197.38 | |
| 13 | 7 | 100.00 | 150.36 | 221.07 | |
| 14 | 8 | 100.00 | 159.38 | 247.60 | |
| 15 | 9 | 100.00 | 168.95 | 277.31 | |
| 16 | 10 | 100.00 | 179.08 | 310.58 | |
| 17 | 11 | 100.00 | 189.83 | 347.85 | |
| 18 | 12 | 100.00 | 201.22 | 389.60 | |
| 19 | 13 | 100.00 | 213.29 | 436.35 | |
| 20 | 14 | 100.00 | 226.09 | 488.71 | |
| 21 | 15 | 100.00 | 239.66 | 547.36 | |
| 22 | 16 | 100.00 | 254.04 | 613.04 | |
| 23 | 17 | 100.00 | 269.28 | 686.60 | |
| 24 | 18 | 100.00 | 285.43 | 769.00 | |
| 25 | 19 | 100.00 | 302.56 | 861.28 | |
| 26 | 20 | 100.00 | 320.71 | 964.63 | |

## Terminology: What's a Year? When Does It Begin?

Although these questions may seem obvious, this is not the case. There's a lot of semantic confusion on this subject in finance courses and texts.

Throughout this book we will use the following as synonyms:

| Year 0 | Year 1 | Year 2 |
|--------|--------|--------|
| | End of | End of |
| Today | year 1 | year 2 |
| Beginning of year 1 | Beginning of year 2 | Beginning of year 3 |
| 0 | 1 | 2 |

To reiterate, the words "Year 0," "Today," and "Beginning of year 1" are synonyms. For example, "$100 at the beginning of year 2" is the same as "$100 at the end of year 1." If you're at a loss to understand what someone means, ask for a drawing; better yet, ask for an Excel spreadsheet.

## Accumulation—Savings Plans and Future Value

In the previous example you deposited $100 and left it in your bank. Suppose you intend to make 10 annual deposits of $100, with the first deposit made in year 0 (today) and each succeeding deposit made at the end of years 1, 2,..., 9. The *future value* of all these deposits at the end of year 10 tells you how much you will have accumulated in the account. If you are saving for the future (whether to buy a car at the end of your college years or to finance a pension at the end of your working life), this is obviously an important and interesting calculation.

So how much will you have accumulated at the end of year 10? There's an Excel function for calculating this answer, which we will discuss later; for the moment we will set this problem up in Excel and do our calculation the long way, by showing how much we will have at the end of each year.

| | A | B | C | D | E | F |
|---|---|---|---|---|---|---|
| 1 | | **FUTURE VALUE WITH ANNUAL DEPOSITS** at beginning of year | | | | |
| 2 | Interest | 6% | | | | |
| 3 | =E5 | | | | | =(C6+B6)*$B$2 |
| 4 | Year | Account balance, beg. year | Deposit at beginning of year | Interest earned during year | Total in account at end of year | |
| 5 | 1 | 0.00 | 100.00 | 6.00 | 106.00 | <-- =B5+C5+D5 |
| 6 | 2 | 106.00 | 100.00 | 12.36 | 218.36 | <-- =B6+C6+D6 |
| 7 | 3 | 218.36 | 100.00 | 19.10 | 337.46 | |
| 8 | 4 | 337.46 | 100.00 | 26.25 | 463.71 | |
| 9 | 5 | 463.71 | 100.00 | 33.82 | 597.53 | |
| 10 | 6 | 597.53 | 100.00 | 41.85 | 739.38 | |
| 11 | 7 | 739.38 | 100.00 | 50.36 | 889.75 | |
| 12 | 8 | 889.75 | 100.00 | 59.38 | 1,049.13 | |
| 13 | 9 | 1,049.13 | 100.00 | 68.95 | 1,218.08 | |
| 14 | 10 | 1,218.08 | 100.00 | 79.08 | 1,397.16 | |
| 15 | | | | | | |
| 16 | | Future value using Excel's FV function | $1,397.16 | <-- =FV(B2,A14,-100,,1) | | |

For clarity, let's analyze a specific year: At the end of year 1 (cell E5) you've got $106 in the account. This is also the amount in the account at the beginning of year 2 (cell B6). If you now deposit another $100 and let the whole amount of $206 draw interest during the year, it will earn $12.36 interest. You will have $218.36 = (106+100)*1.06 at the end of year 2.

|   | A | B | C | D | E |
|---|---|---|---|---|---|
| 6 | 2 | 106.00 | 100.00 | 12.36 | 218.36 |

Finally, look at rows 13 and 14: At the end of year 9 (cell E13) you have $1,218.08 in the account; this is also the amount in the account at the beginning of year 10 (cell B14). You then deposited $100 and the resulting $1,318.08 earns $79.08 interest during the year, accumulating to $1,397.16 by the end of year 10.

|   | A | B | C | D | E |
|---|---|---|---|---|---|
| 13 | 9 | 1,049.13 | 100.00 | 68.95 | 1,218.08 |
| 14 | 10 | 1,218.08 | 100.00 | 79.08 | 1,397.16 |

## The Excel FV Function

The spreadsheet of the previous subsection illustrates in a step-by-step manner how money accumulates in a typical savings plan. To simplify this series of calculations, Excel has a **FV** function that computes the future value of any series of constant payments. This function is illustrated in cell C16.

|   | B | C | D | E |
|---|---|---|---|---|
| 16 | Future value using Excel's FV function | $1,397.16 | <-- =FV(B2,A14,-100,,1) | |

The **FV** function and the inputs required can be computed using a dialog box—an important feature that comes with each Excel function. The Excel note that follows illustrates how to generate the dialog box for the computation in cell C16. If you already know how to use a dialog box, here it is for this example.

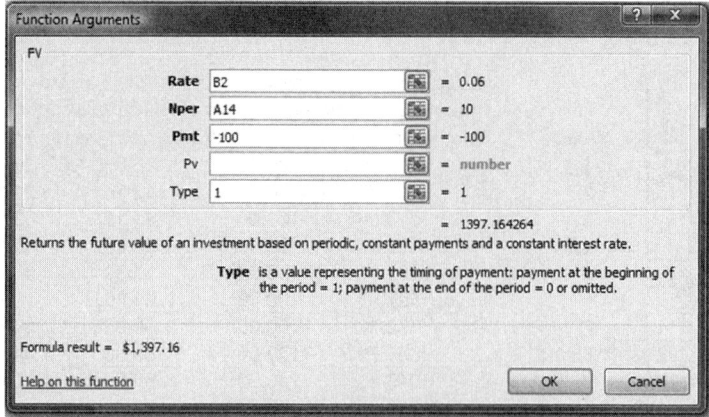

The **FV** function requires as inputs the **Rate** of interest, the number of periods, **Nper**, and the annual payment, **Pmt**. You can also indicate the **Type**, which tells Excel whether payments are made at the beginning of the period (type **1** as in our example) or at the end of the period (type **0**).[1]

## EXCEL NOTE

### FUNCTIONS AND DIALOG BOXES

Cell C16 of the previous example contains the function **FV(B2,A14,-100,,1)**. In this note we illustrate the use of the dialog box for **FV** to generate this function.

The last part of this Excel note discusses why the payment of $100 is entered into this function as a negative number. This is a peculiarity of the **FV** function shared by many other Excel financial functions.

### Going Through the Function Wizard

Suppose you're in cell C16 and you want to put the Excel function for future value in the cell. With the cursor in C16, you move your mouse to the $f_x$ icon on the tool bar.

| | A | B | C | D | E | F |
|---|---|---|---|---|---|---|
| | | Clipboard | Font | | | Alignment |
| | | C16 | $f_x$ | | | |
| 1 | | FUTURE VA Insert Function ANNUAL DEPOSITS at beginning of year | | | | |
| 2 | Interest | | 6% | | | |
| 3 | =E5 | | | | | =(C6+B6)*$B$2 |
| 4 | Year | Account balance, beg. year | Deposit at beginning of year | Interest earned during year | Total in account at end of year | |
| 5 | 1 | 0.00 | 100.00 | 6.00 | 106.00 <-- =B5+C5+D5 | |
| 6 | 2 | 106.00 | 100.00 | 12.36 | 218.36 <-- =B6+C6+D6 | |
| 7 | 3 | 218.36 | 100.00 | 19.10 | 337.46 | |
| 8 | 4 | 337.46 | 100.00 | 26.25 | 463.71 | |
| 9 | 5 | 463.71 | 100.00 | 33.82 | 597.53 | |
| 10 | 6 | 597.53 | 100.00 | 41.85 | 739.38 | |
| 11 | 7 | 739.38 | 100.00 | 50.36 | 889.75 | |
| 12 | 8 | 889.75 | 100.00 | 59.38 | 1,049.13 | |
| 13 | 9 | 1,049.13 | 100.00 | 68.95 | 1,218.08 | |
| 14 | 10 | 1,218.08 | 100.00 | 79.08 | 1,397.16 | |
| 15 | | | | | | |
| 16 | | Future value using Excel's FV function | | | | |

---

[1] Exercises 2 and 3 at the end of the chapter illustrate both cases.

Clicking the 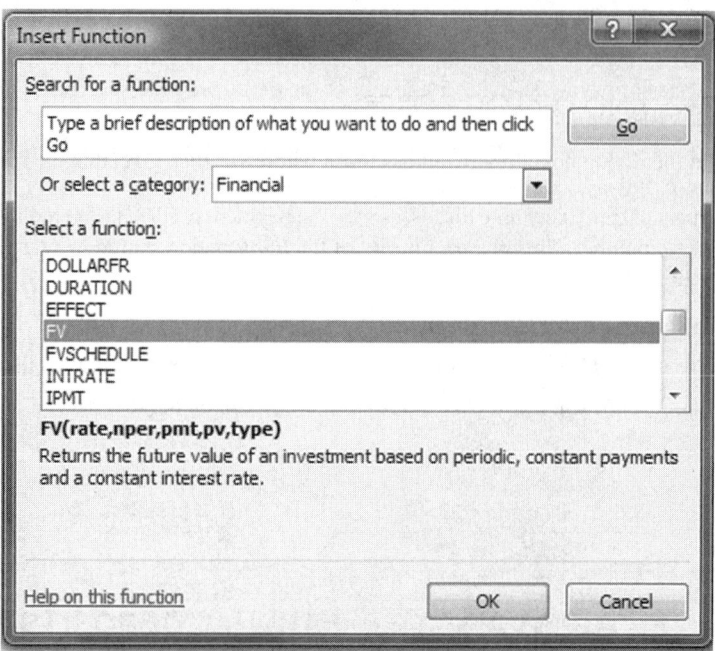 icon brings up the dialog box below. We've chosen the **category** to be the **Financial** functions, and we've scrolled down in the next section of the dialog box to put the cursor on the **FV** function.

Clicking OK brings up the dialog box for the **FV** function, which can now be filled in as illustrated below.

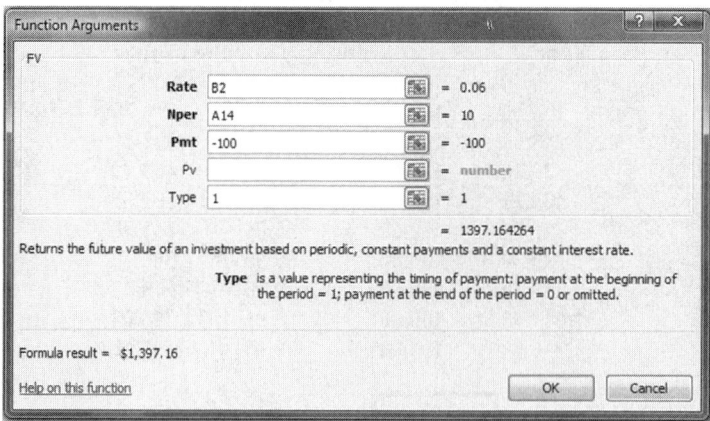

Excel's function dialog boxes have room for two types of variables.

- **Boldface** variables must be filled in—in the **FV** dialog box these are the interest, **Rate**, the number of periods, **Nper**, and the payment, **Pmt**. (Read on to see why we wrote a negative payment.)

- Variables that are not boldface are optional. For example, **Type** refers to when the payments are made and so has only two options—**1** when the payments are made at the beginning of the period and **0** when they are made at the end of the period. In the example above we've indicated a **1** for the **Type**; this indicates (as shown in the dialog box itself) that the future value is calculated for payments made at the beginning of the period. Had we *omitted this variable* or put in **0**, Excel would compute the future value for a series of payments made at the end of the period; see the subsection of Section 2.1 entitled "Beginning versus End of Period" for an illustration.

Note that the dialog box already tells us (even before we click **OK**) that the future value of $100 per year for 10 years compounded at 6% is $1,397.16.

## A Short Way to Get to the Dialog Box

If you know the name of the function you want, you can just write it in the cell and then click the ƒx icon on the toolbar. As illustrated below, you have to write

$$=\textbf{FV(}$$

and then click the ƒx icon—note that we've written an **equal sign**, the **name of the function**, and the **opening parenthesis**.

Here's how the spreadsheet looks in this case.

| | A | B | C | D | E | F |
|---|---|---|---|---|---|---|
| 1 | | | **FUTURE VALUE WITH ANNUAL DEPOSITS** at beginning of year | | | |
| 2 | Interest | 6% | | | | |
| 3 | =E5 | | | | | =$B$2*(C6+B6) |
| 4 | Year | **Account balance, beg. year** | **Deposit at beginning of year** | **Interest earned during year** | **Total in account at end of year** | |
| 5 | 1 | 0.00 | 100.00 | 6.00 | 106.00 | <-- =B5+C5+D5 |
| 6 | 2 | 106.00 | 100.00 | 12.36 | 218.36 | <-- =B6+C6+D6 |
| 7 | 3 | 218.36 | 100.00 | 19.10 | 337.46 | |
| 8 | 4 | 337.46 | 100.00 | 26.25 | 463.71 | |
| 9 | 5 | 463.71 | 100.00 | 33.82 | 597.53 | |
| 10 | 6 | 597.53 | 100.00 | 41.85 | 739.38 | |
| 11 | 7 | 739.38 | 100.00 | 50.36 | 889.75 | |
| 12 | 8 | 889.75 | 100.00 | 59.38 | 1,049.13 | |
| 13 | 9 | 1,049.13 | 100.00 | 68.95 | 1,218.08 | |
| 14 | 10 | 1,218.08 | 100.00 | 79.08 | 1,397.16 | |
| 15 | | | | | | |
| 16 | | Future value using Excel's FV function | =FV( | | | |
| 17 | | | FV(**rate**, nper, pmt, [pv], [type]) | | | |
| 18 | | | | | | |

Look in the text displayed by Excel below cell C16: As illustrated here, some versions of Excel show the format of the function when you type it in a cell.

## One Further Option

You don't have to use a dialog box! If you know the format of the function then just type in its variables and you're all set. In the example of Section 2.1 you could just type = FV(B2,A14,-100,,1) in the cell. Pressing [Enter] would give the answer.

## Why Is the Pmt Variable a Negative Number?

In the **FV** dialog box we've entered in the payment, **Pmt,** as a negative number, -100. The **FV** function has the peculiarity (shared by some other Excel financial functions) that a *positive* deposit generates a *negative* answer. We won't go into the (strange?) logic that produced this thinking; whenever we encounter it we just put in a negative deposit.

## Beginning versus End of Period

In the preceding example you make deposits of $100 at the *beginning* of each year. In terms of timing, your deposits are made at dates 0, 1, 2, 3,..., 9. Here's a schematic way of looking at this, showing the future value of each deposit at the end of year 10.

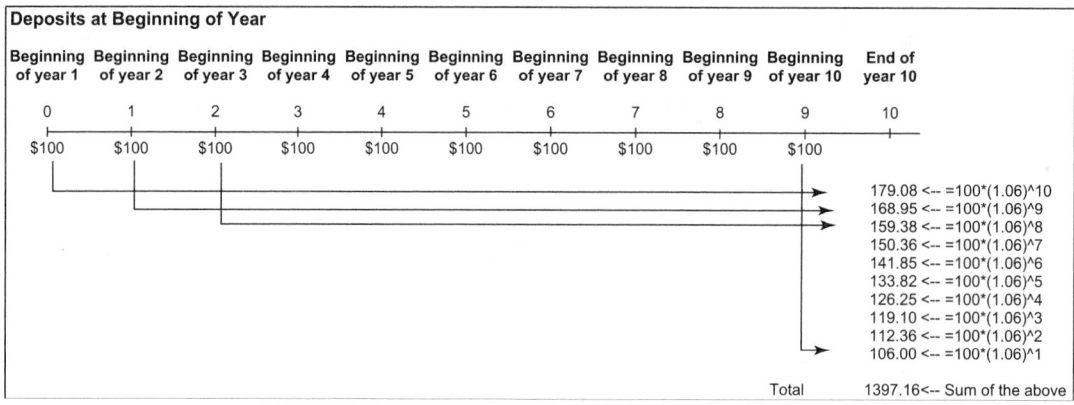

Suppose you made 10 deposits of $100 at the *end of each year*. How would this affect the accumulation in the account at the end of 10 years? The schematic diagram below illustrates the timing and accumulation of the payments.

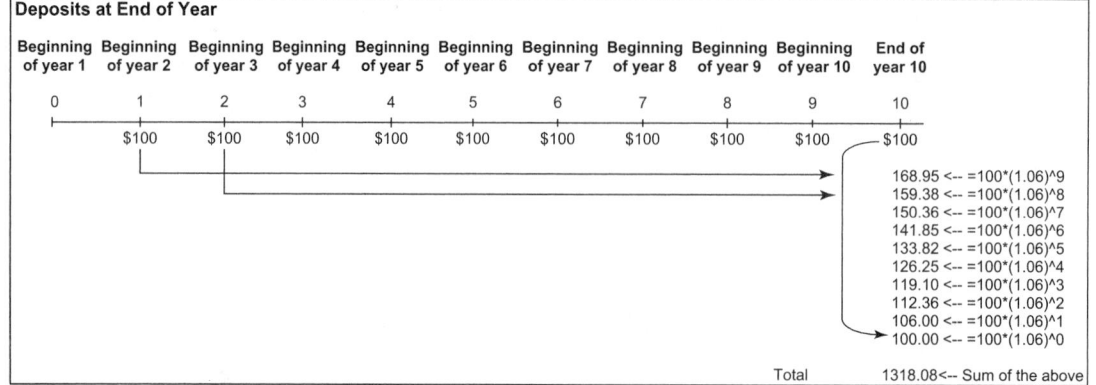

The account accumulation is less when you deposit at the end of each year than in the previous case, where you deposit at the beginning of the year. When you deposit at the end of each year, each deposit is in the account 1 year less and consequently earns 1 year's less interest. In a spreadsheet, this looks like the following.

| | A | B | C | D | E | F |
|---|---|---|---|---|---|---|
| 1 | | | **FUTURE VALUE WITH ANNUAL DEPOSITS** at end of year | | | |
| 2 | Interest | | 6% | | | |
| 3 | | | | | =$B$2*B6 | |
| 4 | =E5 / Year | **Account balance, beg. year** | **Deposit at end of year** | **Interest earned during year** | **Total in account at end of year** | |
| 5 | 1 | 0.00 | 100.00 | 0.00 | 100.00 | <-- =B5+C5+D5 |
| 6 | 2 | 100.00 | 100.00 | 6.00 | 206.00 | <-- =B6+C6+D6 |
| 7 | 3 | 206.00 | 100.00 | 12.36 | 318.36 | |
| 8 | 4 | 318.36 | 100.00 | 19.10 | 437.46 | |
| 9 | 5 | 437.46 | 100.00 | 26.25 | 563.71 | |
| 10 | 6 | 563.71 | 100.00 | 33.82 | 697.53 | |
| 11 | 7 | 697.53 | 100.00 | 41.85 | 839.38 | |
| 12 | 8 | 839.38 | 100.00 | 50.36 | 989.75 | |
| 13 | 9 | 989.75 | 100.00 | 59.38 | 1,149.13 | |
| 14 | 10 | 1,149.13 | 100.00 | 68.95 | 1,318.08 | |
| 15 | | | | | | |
| 16 | | Future value | $1,318.08 | <-- =FV(B2,A14,-100) | | |

Cell C16 illustrates the use of the Excel **FV** formula to solve this problem. Here's the dialog box for the **FV** function in cell C16.

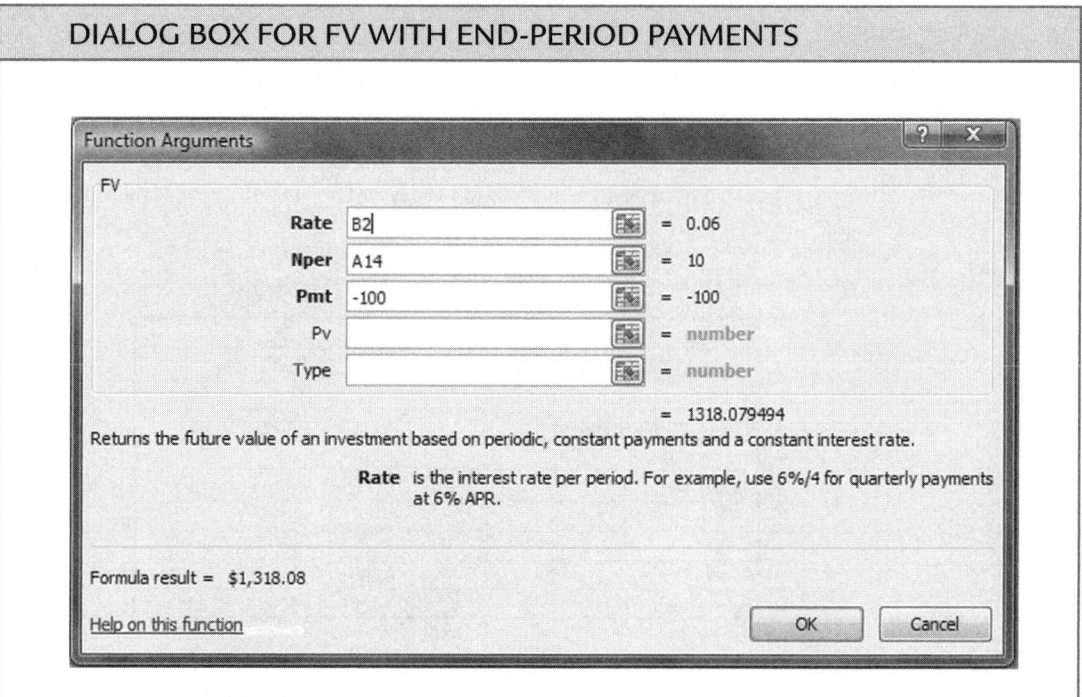

DIALOG BOX FOR FV WITH END-PERIOD PAYMENTS

In this example we've omitted any entry in the **Type** box. We could have also put a 0 in the **Type** box and gotten the same result.

### Some Finance Jargon and the Excel FV Function

An *annuity* is a series of *equal* periodic payments made over a specified amount of time. Examples of annuities are widespread:

- The allowance your parents give you ($1,000 per month for your next 4 years of college) is a monthly annuity with 48 payments.
- Pension plans often give a retiree a fixed annual payment for as long as he lives. This is a bit more complicated because the number of payments is uncertain.
- Certain kinds of loans are paid off in fixed, periodic (usually monthly, sometimes annual) installments. Mortgages and student loans are two examples.

An annuity with payments at the end of each period is often called a *regular annuity*. As you've seen in this section, the value of a regular annuity is calculated with **=FV(B2,A14,-100)**. An annuity with payments at the beginning of each period is often called an *annuity due* and its value is calculated with the Excel function **=FV(B2,A14,-100,,1)**.

## 2.2. Present Value

The present value is the value today of a payment (or payments) that will be made in the future.

Here's a simple example: Suppose that you anticipate getting $100 in 3 years from your Uncle Simon, whose word is as good as a bank's. Suppose that the bank pays 6% interest on savings accounts. *How much is the anticipated future payment worth today?* The answer is $83.96 = \dfrac{100}{(1.06)^3}$; if you put $83.96 in the bank today at 6% annual interest, then in 3 years you would have $100 (see the "proof" in rows 8 and 9).[2] The value of $83.96 is also called the *discounted or present value of $100 in 3 years at 6% interest.*

|   | A | B | C |
|---|---|---|---|
| 1 | SIMPLE PRESENT VALUE CALCULATION | | |
| 2 | X, future payment | 100 | |
| 3 | n, time of future payment | 3 | |
| 4 | r, interest rate | 6% | |
| 5 | Present value, $X/(1+r)^n$ | 83.96 | <-- =B2/(1+B4)^B3 |
| 6 | | | |
| 7 | Proof | | |
| 8 | Payment today | 83.96 | |
| 9 | Future value in n years | 100 | <-- =B8*(1+B4)^B3 |

---

[2] Actually, $100/(1.06)^3 = 83.96193$, but we've used **Home|Cells|Format|Format Cells|Number** to show only two decimals.

To summarize,

The present value of $X to be received in *n* years when the appropriate interest rate is *r*% is

$$\frac{X}{(1+r)^n}.$$

The interest rate *r* is also called the *discount rate*. We can use Excel to make a table of how the present value decreases with the discount rate. As you can see, higher discount rates make for lower present values.

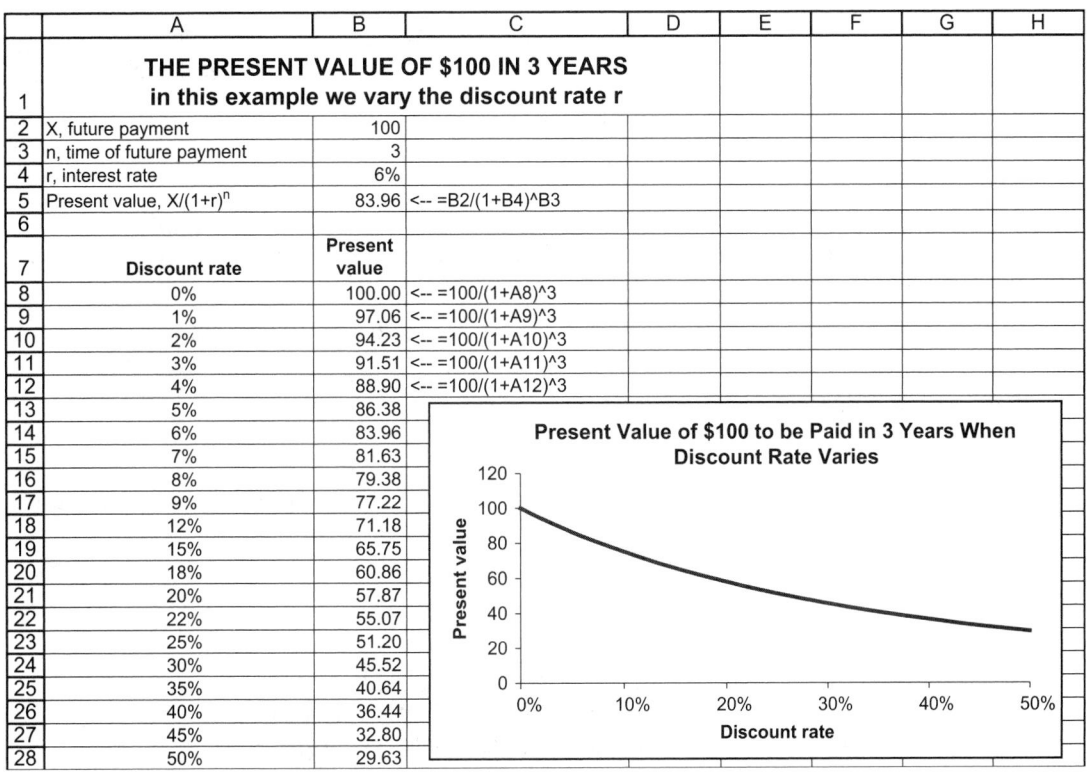

| | A | B | C | D | E | F | G | H |
|---|---|---|---|---|---|---|---|---|
| 1 | **THE PRESENT VALUE OF $100 IN 3 YEARS**<br>**in this example we vary the discount rate r** | | | | | | | |
| 2 | X, future payment | 100 | | | | | | |
| 3 | n, time of future payment | 3 | | | | | | |
| 4 | r, interest rate | 6% | | | | | | |
| 5 | Present value, X/(1+r)ⁿ | 83.96 | <-- =B2/(1+B4)^B3 | | | | | |
| 6 | | | | | | | | |
| 7 | Discount rate | Present value | | | | | | |
| 8 | 0% | 100.00 | <-- =100/(1+A8)^3 | | | | | |
| 9 | 1% | 97.06 | <-- =100/(1+A9)^3 | | | | | |
| 10 | 2% | 94.23 | <-- =100/(1+A10)^3 | | | | | |
| 11 | 3% | 91.51 | <-- =100/(1+A11)^3 | | | | | |
| 12 | 4% | 88.90 | <-- =100/(1+A12)^3 | | | | | |
| 13 | 5% | 86.38 | | | | | | |
| 14 | 6% | 83.96 | | | | | | |
| 15 | 7% | 81.63 | | | | | | |
| 16 | 8% | 79.38 | | | | | | |
| 17 | 9% | 77.22 | | | | | | |
| 18 | 12% | 71.18 | | | | | | |
| 19 | 15% | 65.75 | | | | | | |
| 20 | 18% | 60.86 | | | | | | |
| 21 | 20% | 57.87 | | | | | | |
| 22 | 22% | 55.07 | | | | | | |
| 23 | 25% | 51.20 | | | | | | |
| 24 | 30% | 45.52 | | | | | | |
| 25 | 35% | 40.64 | | | | | | |
| 26 | 40% | 36.44 | | | | | | |
| 27 | 45% | 32.80 | | | | | | |
| 28 | 50% | 29.63 | | | | | | |

## Why Does Present Value Decrease as the Discount Rate Increases?

The Excel table above shows that the $100 Uncle Simon promises you in 3 years is worth $83.96 today if the discount rate is 6% but worth only $40.64 if the discount rate is 35%. The mechanical reason for this is that taking the present value at 6% means dividing by a smaller denominator than taking the present value at 35%:

$$83.96 = \frac{100}{(1.06)^3} > \frac{100}{(1.35)^3} = 40.64$$

The economic reason relates to future values: If the bank is paying you 6% interest on your savings account, you would have to deposit $83.96 today to have $100 in 3 years. If the bank pays 35% interest, then $40.64 today will grow to $100 in 3 years because $40.64 * (1.35)^3 = $100.

What this short discussion shows is that the *present value is the inverse of the future value.*

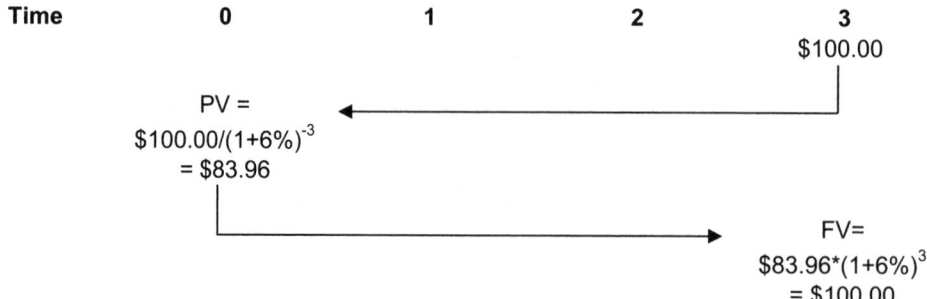

## Present Value of an Annuity

Recall that an *annuity* is a series of equal periodic payments. The *present value* of an annuity tells you *the value today* of all the future payments on the annuity.

The present value of an annuity of $X$ to be received at the end of years 1, 2, 3,..., $N$ when

the appropriate interest rate is $r$% is $\dfrac{X}{(1+r)} + \dfrac{X}{(1+r)^2} + \dfrac{X}{(1+r)^3} + ... + \dfrac{X}{(1+r)^N}$.

Here's an example: Suppose you've been promised $100 at the end of each of the next 5 years. Assuming that you can get 6% at the bank, this promise is worth $421.24 today.

|  | A | B | C | D |
|---|---|---|---|---|
| 1 | PRESENT VALUE OF AN ANNUITY: FIVE ANNUAL PAYMENTS OF $100 EACH | | | |
| 2 | Annual payment | 100 | | |
| 3 | r, interest rate | 6% | | |
| 4 | | | | |
| 5 | Year | Payment at end of year | Present value of payment | |
| 6 | 1 | 100 | 94.34 | <-- =B6/(1+$B$3)^A6 |
| 7 | 2 | 100 | 89.00 | <-- =B7/(1+$B$3)^A7 |
| 8 | 3 | 100 | 83.96 | |
| 9 | 4 | 100 | 79.21 | |
| 10 | 5 | 100 | 74.73 | |
| 11 | | | | |
| 12 | Present value of all payments | | | |
| 13 | Summing the present values | | 421.24 | <-- =SUM(C6:C10) |
| 14 | Using Excel's PV function | | 421.24 | <-- =PV(B3,5,-B2) |
| 15 | Using Excel's NPV function | | 421.24 | <-- =NPV(B3,B6:B10) |

The preceding example shows three ways of getting the present value of $421.24:

- You can sum the individual discounted values. This is done in cell C13.
- You can use Excel's **PV** function, which calculates the present value of an annuity (cell C14).
- You can use Excel's **NPV** function (cell C16). This function calculates the present value of any series of periodic payments (whether they're flat payments, as in an annuity, or nonequal payments).

We devote separate subsections to the **PV** function and the **NPV** function.

## The Present Value of a Perpetuity

A perpetuity is an annuity that goes on forever. In Appendix 2.1 at the end of this chapter we show that

The present value of a perpetuity of $X$ to be received at the end of years 1, 2, 3,..., when the appropriate interest rate is $r\%$ is

$$\frac{X}{(1+r)} + \frac{X}{(1+r)^2} + \frac{X}{(1+r)^3} + \cdots = \frac{X}{r}.$$

Suppose, for example, that you were offered a payment of $100 per year at the end of years 1, 2, 3,.... Suppose that the appropriate interest rate is $r = 5\%$. As the following spreadsheet shows, the present value of this perpetuity is $2,000.

|  | A | B | C |
|---|---|---|---|
| 1 | **PRESENT VALUE OF AN ANNUITY** | | |
| 2 | Payment at end of each year | 100 | |
| 3 | Interest rate | 5% | |
| 4 | Perpetuity present value | 2,000 | <-- =B2/B3 |

## The Excel PV Function

The **PV** function calculates the present value of an *annuity* (a series of equal payments). It looks a lot like the **FV** discussed above, and like **FV**, it also has the peculiarity that positive payments give negative results (which is why we set **Pmt** equal to –100). As in the case of the **FV** function, **Type** denotes whether the payments are made at the beginning or the end of the year. Because end-year is the default, you can either enter **0** or leave the **Type** entry blank (if the payment is at the beginning of the period you have to enter **1** in the **Type** box).

## DIALOG BOX FOR THE PV FUNCTION

Function Arguments

PV

| | | | | |
|---|---|---|---|---|
| **Rate** | B3 | | = | 0.06 |
| **Nper** | 5 | | = | 5 |
| **Pmt** | -100 | | = | -100 |
| Fv | | | = | number |
| Type | | | = | number |

= 421.2363786

Returns the present value of an investment: the total amount that a series of future payments is worth now.

**Type** is a logical value: payment at the beginning of the period = 1; payment at the end of the period = 0 or omitted.

Formula result = 421.24

Help on this function        OK        Cancel

The "Formula result" in the dialogue box shows that the answer is $421.24.

### The Excel NPV Function

The **NPV** function computes the present value of a series of payments. The payments need not be equal, although in the current example they are. The ability of the **NPV** function to handle nonequal payments makes it one of the most useful of all Excel's financial functions. We will make extensive use of this function throughout this book. In the current example, because the annual payments are equal, the result is the same ($421.24) whether we use the **PV** function or the **NPV** function.

## DIALOG BOX FOR THE NPV FUNCTION

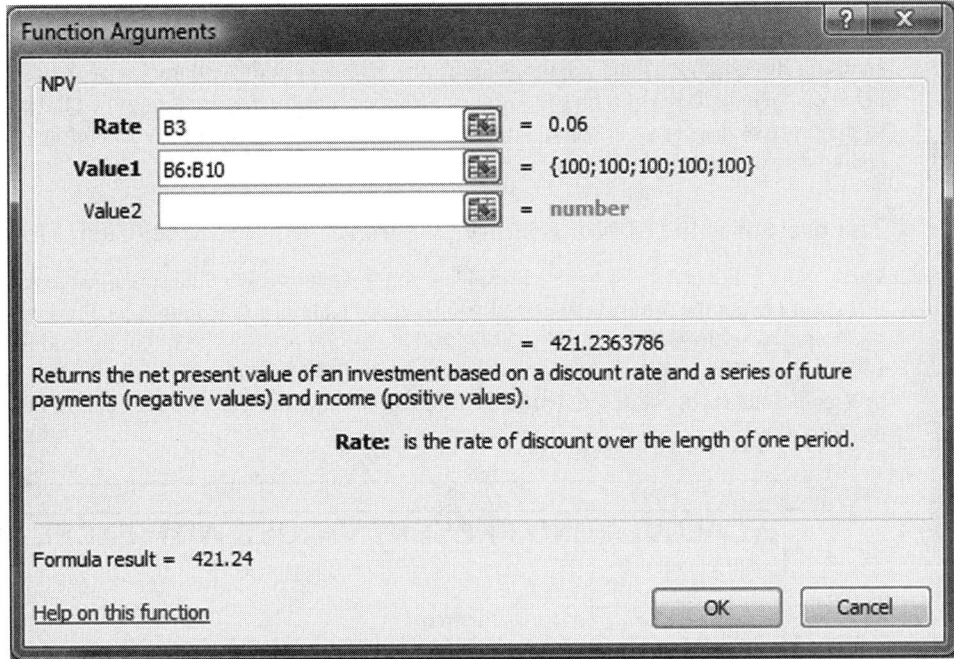

Excel's **NPV** function computes the present value of a series of payments. You can either enter the payments separately (as **Value1**, **Value2**, . . .), or—as illustrated above—you can enter a range of payments into the **Value1** box.

## IMPORTANT NOTATION NOTE

Finance professionals use "NPV" to mean "net present value," a concept we explain in the next section. Excel's **NPV** function actually calculates the *present value* of a series of payments. Almost all finance professionals and textbooks would call the number computed by the Excel **NPV** function PV. Thus, the Excel use of NPV differs from the standard usage in finance, which is explained in Section 2.3.

## Choosing a Discount Rate

We've defined the present value of $X to be received in $n$ years as $\dfrac{X}{(1+r)^n}$. The interest rate $r$ in the denominator of this expression is also known as the *discount rate*. Why is 6% an appropriate discount rate for the money promised you by Uncle Simon? The basic principle is to choose a discount rate that is appropriate to the *riskiness* and the duration of the cash flows being discounted. Uncle Simon's promise of $100 per year for 5 years is assumed to be as good as the promise of your local bank, which pays 6% on its savings accounts. Therefore, 6% is an appropriate discount rate.[3]

## The present value of Nonannuity (Meaning Nonconstant) Cash Flows

The present value concept can also be applied to nonannuity cash flow streams, meaning cash flows that are not the same every period. Suppose, for example, that your Aunt Terry has promised to pay you $100 at the end of year 1, $200 at the end of year 2, $300 at the end of year 3, $400 at the end of year 4, and $500 at the end of year 5. This is not an annuity, and so it cannot be accommodated by the **PV** function. But we can find the present value of this promise using the **NPV** function.

|   | A | B | C | D |
|---|---|---|---|---|
| 1 | **CALCULATING PRESENT VALUES WITH EXCEL** | | | |
| 2 | r, interest rate | 6% | | |
| 3 | | | | |
| 4 | **Year** | **Payment at end of year** | **Present value** | |
| 5 | 1 | 100 | 94.34 | <-- =B5/(1+$B$2)^A5 |
| 6 | 2 | 200 | 178.00 | <-- =B6/(1+$B$2)^A6 |
| 7 | 3 | 300 | 251.89 | |
| 8 | 4 | 400 | 316.84 | |
| 9 | 5 | 500 | 373.63 | |
| 10 | | | | |
| 11 | **Present value of all payments** | | | |
| 12 | Summing the present values | | 1,214.69 | <-- =SUM(C5:C9) |
| 13 | Using Excel's NPV function | | 1,214.69 | <-- =NPV($B$2,B5:B9) |

The example shows that the present value of Aunt Terry's promised series of payments over the next 5 years is $1,214.69:

$$\frac{\$100}{1.06} + \frac{\$200}{(1.06)^2} + \frac{\$300}{(1.06)^3} + \frac{\$400}{(1.06)^4} + \frac{\$500}{(1.06)^5} = \$1,214.69$$

[3] There's more to be said on the choice of a discount rate, but we postpone the discussion until Chapters 5 and 6.

## EXCEL NOTE

Excel's **NPV** function allows you to input up to 29 payments directly in the function dialogue box. Here's an illustration for the example above.

**Function Arguments** ? X

NPV

| **Value1** | 100 | = 100 |
| Value2 | 200 | = 200 |
| Value3 | 300 | = 300 |
| Value4 | 400 | = 400 |
| Value5 | 500 | = 500 |

= 1214.691247

Returns the net present value of an investment based on a discount rate and a series of future payments (negative values) and income (positive values).

**Value5:** value1,value2,... are 1 to 254 payments and income, equally spaced in time and occurring at the end of each period.

Formula result = 1214.691247

Help on this function       OK       Cancel

## 2.3. Net Present Value

The net present value (NPV) of a series of future cash flows is their present value minus the initial investment required to obtain the future cash flows. The NPV = PV of future cash flows – initial investment. The NPV of an investment represents the increase in wealth that you get if you make the investment.

Here's an example based on the spreadsheet on page 34. Would you pay $1,500 today to get the series of future cash flows in cells B5:B9? Certainly not—they're worth only $1,214.69, so why pay $1,500? If asked to pay $1,500, the NPV of the investment would be

$$NPV = \underbrace{-\$1,500}_{\substack{\text{Cost of the}\\\text{investment}}} + \underbrace{\frac{100}{1.06} + \frac{200}{(1.06)^2} + \frac{300}{(1.06)^3} + \frac{400}{(1.06)^4} + \frac{500}{(1.06)^5}}_{\substack{\text{Present value of}\\\text{investment's future}\\\text{cash flows at discount}\\\text{rate of 6\%}}}$$

$$= -\$1,500 + \$1,214.69 = \underbrace{-\$285.31}_{\text{Net present value}}$$

If you paid $1,500 for this investment, you would be overpaying $285.31 for the investment, and you would be poorer by the same amount. That's a bad deal!

On the other hand, if you were offered the same future cash flows for $1,000, you'd snap up the offer because you would be paying $214.69 less for the investment than it's worth:

$$NPV = \underbrace{-\$1,000}_{\substack{\text{Cost of the} \\ \text{investment}}} + \underbrace{\$1,214.69}_{\substack{\text{Present value of} \\ \text{investment's future} \\ \text{cash flows at discount} \\ \text{rate of 6\%}}} = \underbrace{\$214.69}_{\text{Net present value}}$$

In this case the investment would make you $214.69 richer. As we said before, the NPV of an investment represents the increase in your wealth if you make the investment.

To summarize,

The net present value (NPV) of a series of cash flows is used to make investment decisions: An investment with a positive NPV is a good investment and an investment with a negative NPV is a bad investment. An investment with a zero NPV is a "fair game"—the future cash flows of the investment exactly compensate you for the investment's initial cost.

Net present value is a basic tool of financial analysis. It is used to determine whether a particular investment ought to be undertaken; in cases where we can make only one of several investments, it is the tool of choice to determine which investment to undertake.

Here's another NPV example: You've found an interesting investment—If you pay $800 today to your local pawnshop, the owner promises to pay you $100 at the end of year 1, $150 at the end of year 2, $200 at the end of year 3,..., and $300 at the end of year 5. You feel that the pawnshop owner is as reliable as your local bank, which is currently paying 5% interest. The following spreadsheet shows the NPV of this $800 investment.

| | A | B | C | D |
|---|---|---|---|---|
| 1 | **CALCULATING NET PRESENT VALUE (NPV) WITH EXCEL** | | | |
| 2 | r, interest rate | 5% | | |
| 3 | | | | |
| 4 | Year | **Payment** | **Present value** | |
| 5 | 0 | -800 | -800.00 | |
| 6 | 1 | 100 | 95.24 | <-- =B6/(1+$B$2)^A6 |
| 7 | 2 | 150 | 136.05 | <-- =B7/(1+$B$2)^A7 |
| 8 | 3 | 200 | 172.77 | |
| 9 | 4 | 250 | 205.68 | |
| 10 | 5 | 300 | 235.06 | |
| 11 | | | | |
| 12 | NPV | | | |
| 13 | Summing the present values | | 44.79 | <-- =SUM(C5:C10) |
| 14 | Using Excel's NPV function | | 44.79 | <-- =B5+NPV($B$2,B6:B10) |

The spreadsheet shows that the value of the investment—the *NPV* of its payments, including the initial payment of -$800—is $44.79:

$$NPV = -800 + \underbrace{\frac{100}{(1.05)} + \frac{150}{(1.05)^2} + \frac{200}{(1.05)^3} + \frac{250}{(1.05)^4} + \frac{300}{(1.05)^5}}_{\substack{\text{The } present\ value \text{ of the future payments:} \\ \text{Calculated with Excel NPV function} = 844.79}} = 44.97$$

At a 5% discount rate, you should make the investment because its NPV is $44.79, which is positive.

## EXCEL NOTE

As mentioned on page 33, the Excel **NPV** function's name does **not correspond** to the standard finance use of the term NPV.[4] In finance, present value usually refers to the value today of future payments (in the previous example, the present value is

$$\frac{100}{(1.05)} + \frac{150}{(1.05)^2} + \frac{200}{(1.05)^3} + \frac{250}{(1.05)^4} + \frac{300}{(1.05)^5} = 844.79).$$ Finance professionals use NPV to mean

the *present value* of future payments *minus the cost of the initial payment*; in the previous example this is $844.79 – $800 = $44.79. In this book we use the term NPV to mean its true finance sense. The Excel function **NPV** will always appear in boldface. We trust that you will rarely be confused.

## NPV Depends on the Discount Rate

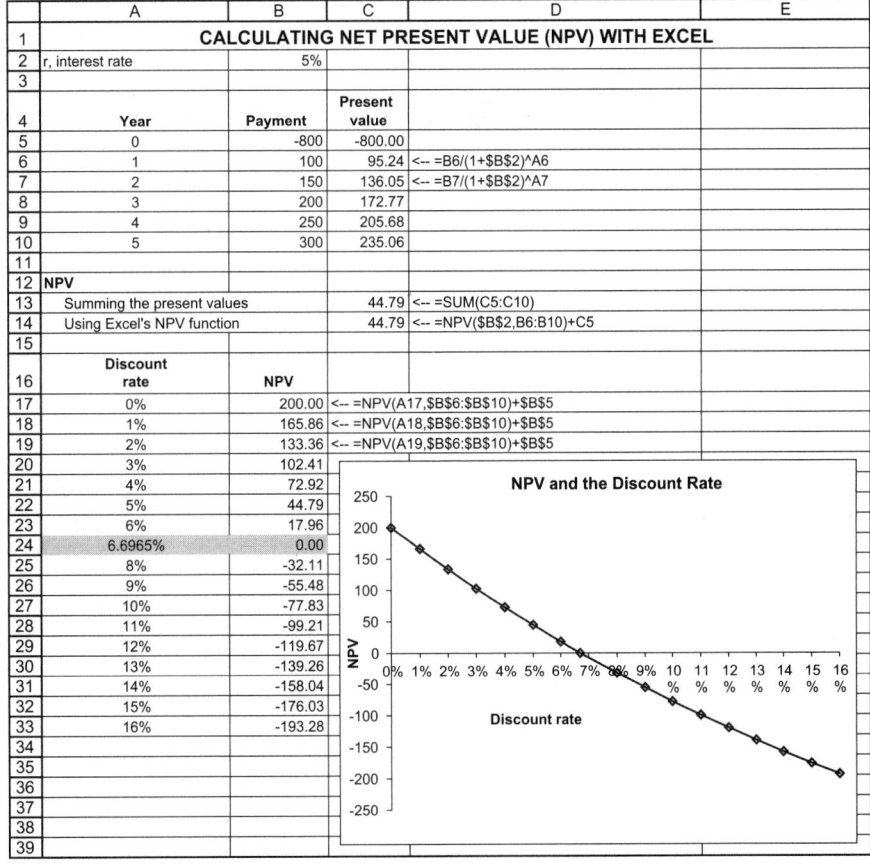

|    | A | B | C | D | E |
|----|---|---|---|---|---|
| 1 | | | CALCULATING NET PRESENT VALUE (NPV) WITH EXCEL | | |
| 2 | r, interest rate | 5% | | | |
| 3 | | | | | |
| 4 | Year | Payment | Present value | | |
| 5 | 0 | -800 | -800.00 | | |
| 6 | 1 | 100 | 95.24 | <-- =B6/(1+$B$2)^A6 | |
| 7 | 2 | 150 | 136.05 | <-- =B7/(1+$B$2)^A7 | |
| 8 | 3 | 200 | 172.77 | | |
| 9 | 4 | 250 | 205.68 | | |
| 10 | 5 | 300 | 235.06 | | |
| 11 | | | | | |
| 12 | NPV | | | | |
| 13 | Summing the present values | | 44.79 | <-- =SUM(C5:C10) | |
| 14 | Using Excel's NPV function | | 44.79 | <-- =NPV($B$2,B6:B10)+C5 | |
| 15 | | | | | |
| 16 | Discount rate | NPV | | | |
| 17 | 0% | 200.00 | <-- =NPV(A17,$B$6:$B$10)+$B$5 | | |
| 18 | 1% | 165.86 | <-- =NPV(A18,$B$6:$B$10)+$B$5 | | |
| 19 | 2% | 133.36 | <-- =NPV(A19,$B$6:$B$10)+$B$5 | | |
| 20 | 3% | 102.41 | | | |
| 21 | 4% | 72.92 | | | |
| 22 | 5% | 44.79 | | | |
| 23 | 6% | 17.96 | | | |
| 24 | 6.6965% | 0.00 | | | |
| 25 | 8% | -32.11 | | | |
| 26 | 9% | -55.48 | | | |
| 27 | 10% | -77.83 | | | |
| 28 | 11% | -99.21 | | | |
| 29 | 12% | -119.67 | | | |
| 30 | 13% | -139.26 | | | |
| 31 | 14% | -158.04 | | | |
| 32 | 15% | -176.03 | | | |
| 33 | 16% | -193.28 | | | |
| 34 | | | | | |
| 35 | | | | | |
| 36 | | | | | |
| 37 | | | | | |
| 38 | | | | | |
| 39 | | | | | |

NPV and the Discount Rate

---

[4]There's a long history to this confusion, and it doesn't start with Microsoft. The original spreadsheet—Visicalc—(mistakenly) used NPV in the sense that Excel still uses today; this misnomer has been copied ever since by all other spreadsheets: Lotus, Quattro, and Excel.

Let's revisit the pawnshop example on page 36 and use Excel to create a table that shows the relation between the discount rate and the NPV. As the graph on page 37 shows, the higher the discount rate, the lower the NPV of the investment.

Note that we've highlighted a special discount rate: When the discount rate is 6.6965%, the net present value of the investment is zero. The 6.6965% rate is referred to as the *internal rate of return (IRR)*. For discount rates less than the IRR, the NPV is positive, and for discount rates greater than the IRR the NPV is negative. We discuss the IRR in more detail in Section 2.4.

## Using NPV to Choose between Investments

In the examples discussed thus far, we've used NPV only to choose whether to undertake a particular investment. But NPV can also be used to choose between investments. Look at the following spreadsheet: You have $800 to invest, and you've been offered the choice between Investment A and Investment B. The spreadsheet shows that at an interest rate of 15%, Investment A has an NPV = $219.06 and Investment B has an NPV = $373.75. If the investments are not mutually exclusive, you would want to invest in both A and B because they each have a positive NPV. But if you are forced to choose only one investment, you should choose Investment B because it has a higher NPV. Investment A will increase your wealth by $219.06, whereas Investment B increases your wealth by $373.75.

|  | A | B | C | D |
|---|---|---|---|---|
| 1 | USING NPV TO CHOOSE BETWEEN INVESTMENTS | | | |
| 2 | Discount rate | 15% | | |
| 3 | | | | |
| 4 | Year | Investment A | Investment B | |
| 5 | 0 | -800 | -800 | |
| 6 | 1 | 250 | 600 | |
| 7 | 2 | 500 | 200 | |
| 8 | 3 | 200 | 100 | |
| 9 | 4 | 250 | 500 | |
| 10 | 5 | 300 | 300 | |
| 11 | | | | |
| 12 | NPV | 219.06 | 373.75 | <-- =NPV(B2,C6:C10)+C5 |

## TERMINOLOGY—IS IT A DISCOUNT RATE OR AN INTEREST RATE?

In some of the preceding examples we've used *discount rate* instead of *interest rate* to describe the rate used in the NPV calculation. As you will see in further chapters of this book, the rate used in the NPV has several synonyms: discount rate, interest rate, cost of capital, opportunity cost—these are but a few of the names for the rate that appears in the denominator of the NPV:

$$\frac{Cash\ flow\ in\ year\ t}{(1+r)^t}$$
$$\uparrow$$

*Discount rate*
*Interest rate*
*Cost of capital*
*Opportunity cost*

To summarize,

*In using the NPV to choose between two mutually exclusive positive NPV investments, we choose the investment with the higher NPV.*

## 2.4. The Internal Rate of Return (IRR)

The internal rate of return (IRR) of a series of cash flows is the discount rate that sets the net present value of the cash flows equal to zero.

Before we explain in depth (in the next section) why you want to know the IRR, we explain how to compute it. Let's go back to the example on page 36: If you pay $800 today to your local pawnshop, the owner promises to pay you $100 at the end of year 1, $150 at the end of year 2, $200 at the end of year 3, $250 at the end of year 4 , and $300 at the end of year 5. Discounting these cash flows at rate $r$, the NPV can be written as follows:

$$NPV = -800 + \frac{100}{(1+r)} + \frac{150}{(1+r)^2} + \frac{200}{(1+r)^3} + \frac{250}{(1+r)^4} + \frac{300}{(1+r)^5}$$

In cells B16:B32 of the spreadsheet below, we calculate the NPV for various discount rates. As you can see, somewhere between $r = 6\%$ and $r = 7\%$, the NPV becomes negative.

| | A | B | C | D |
|---|---|---|---|---|
| 1 | | CALCULATING THE IRR WITH EXCEL | | |
| 2 | r, interest rate | 6.6965% | | |
| 3 | | | | |
| 4 | Year | Payment | | |
| 5 | 0 | -800 | | |
| 6 | 1 | 100 | | |
| 7 | 2 | 150 | | |
| 8 | 3 | 200 | | |
| 9 | 4 | 250 | | |
| 10 | 5 | 300 | | |
| 11 | | | | |
| 12 | NPV | 0.00 | <-- =NPV(B2,B6:B10)+B5 | |
| 13 | IRR | 6.6965% | <-- =IRR(B5:B10) | |
| 14 | | | | |
| 15 | Discount rate | NPV | | |
| 16 | 0% | 200.00 | <-- =NPV(A16,$B$6:$B$10)+$B$5 | |
| 17 | 1% | 165.86 | <-- =NPV(A17,$B$6:$B$10)+$B$5 | |
| 18 | 2% | 133.36 | <-- =NPV(A18,$B$6:$B$10)+$B$5 | |
| 19 | 3% | 102.41 | | |
| 20 | 4% | 72.92 | NPV and the Discount Rate | |
| 21 | 5% | 44.79 | | |
| 22 | 6% | 17.96 | | |
| 23 | 7% | -7.65 | | |
| 24 | 8% | -32.11 | | |
| 25 | 9% | -55.48 | | |
| 26 | 10% | -77.83 | | |
| 27 | 11% | -99.21 | | |
| 28 | 12% | -119.67 | | |
| 29 | 13% | -139.26 | | |
| 30 | 14% | -158.04 | | |
| 31 | 15% | -176.03 | | |
| 32 | 16% | -193.28 | | |
| 33 | | | | |
| 34 | | | | |
| 35 | | | | |

In cell B13, we use Excel's **IRR** function to calculate the exact discount rate at which the NPV becomes 0. The answer is 6.6965%; at this interest rate, the NPV of the cash flows equals zero (look at cell B12). We can use the dialog box for the Excel **IRR** function.

## DIALOG BOX FOR IRR FUNCTION

Note that we haven't used the second option (Guess) to calculate our IRR. We discuss this option in Chapter 5.

| Function Arguments | | ? X |
| --- | --- | --- |
| IRR | | |
| **Values** B5:B10 | ▦ = | {-800;100;150;200;250;300} |
| **Guess** | ▦ = | number |
| | = | 0.066965491 |

Returns the internal rate of return for a series of cash flows.

**Values** is an array or a reference to cells that contain numbers for which you want to calculate the internal rate of return.

Formula result = 6.6965%

Help on this function          OK     Cancel

## What Does the IRR Mean?

Suppose you could get 6.6965% interest at the bank and suppose you wanted to save today to provide yourself with the future cash flows of the example on page 39:

- To get $100 at the end of year 1, you would have to put the present value $\frac{100}{1.06965} = 93.72$ in the bank today.
- To get $150 at the end of year 2, you would have to put its present value $\frac{150}{(1.06965)^2} = 131.76$ in the bank today.
- And so on…(see the picture on page 41)

The total amount you would have to save is $800, exactly the cost of this investment opportunity. This is what we mean when we say that

The IRR is the compound interest rate you earn on an investment.

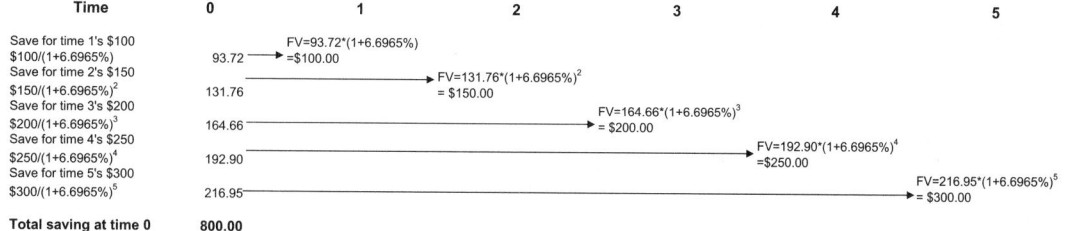

## Using IRR to Make Investment Decisions

The IRR is often used to make investment decisions. Suppose your Aunt Sara has been offered the following investment by her broker: For a payment of $1,000, a reputable finance company will pay her $300 at the end of each of the next 4 years. Aunt Sara is currently getting 5% on her bank savings account. Should she withdraw her money from the bank to make the investment? To answer the question, we compute the IRR of the investment and compare it with the bank interest rate:

|   | A | B | C |
|---|---|---|---|
| 1 | **USING IRR TO MAKE INVESTMENT DECISIONS** | | |
| 2 | **Year** | **Cash flow** | |
| 3 | 0 | -1,000 | |
| 4 | 1 | 300 | |
| 5 | 2 | 300 | |
| 6 | 3 | 300 | |
| 7 | 4 | 300 | |
| 8 | | | |
| 9 | IRR | 7.71% | <-- =IRR(B3:B7) |

The IRR of the investment, 7.71%, is greater than the 5% Sara can earn on her alternative investment (the bank account). Thus, she should make the investment.

To summarize,

In using the IRR to make investment decisions, an investment with an IRR greater than the alternative rate of return is a good investment and an investment with an IRR less than the alternative rate of return is a bad investment.

## Using IRR to Choose between Two Investments

We can also use the internal rate of return to choose between two investments. Suppose you've been offered two investments. Both Investment A and Investment B cost $1,000, but they have different cash flows. If you're using the IRR to make the investment decision, then you would choose the investment with the *higher* IRR. Here's an example.

| | A | B | C | D |
|---|---|---|---|---|
| 1 | USING IRR TO CHOOSE BETWEEN INVESTMENTS | | | |
| 2 | Year | Investment A cash flows | Investment B cash flows | |
| 3 | 0 | -1,000.00 | -1,000.00 | |
| 4 | 1 | 450.00 | 550.00 | |
| 5 | 2 | 425.00 | 300.00 | |
| 6 | 3 | 350.00 | 475.00 | |
| 7 | 4 | 450.00 | 200.00 | |
| 8 | | | | |
| 9 | IRR | 24.74% | 22.26% | <-- =IRR(C3:C7) |

We would choose Investment A, which has the higher IRR.
To summarize,

In using the IRR to choose between two comparable investments, we choose the investment that has the higher IRR. This assumes that: (1) both investments have an IRR greater than the alternative rate and (2) the investments are of comparable risk.

## USING NPV AND IRR TO MAKE INVESTMENT DECISIONS

In this chapter we have now developed two tools, NPV and IRR, for making investment decisions. We've also discussed two kinds of investment decisions. Here's a summary.

| | "Yes or No": Choosing whether to undertake a single investment | "Investment ranking": Comparing two investments that are mutually exclusive |
|---|---|---|
| NPV criterion | The investment should be undertaken if its NPV > 0: | Investment A is preferred to investment B if NPV(A) > NPV(B) |
| IRR criterion | The investment should be undertaken if its IRR > r, where r is the appropriate discount rate. | Investment A is preferred to investment B if IRR(A) > IRR(B). |

In Chapter 4 we discuss further implementation of these two rules and two decision problems.

## 2.5. What Does IRR Mean? Loan Tables and Investment Amortization

In the previous section we gave a simple illustration of what we meant when we said that *the IRR is the compound interest rate that you earn on an asset*. This short sentence underlies a slew of finance applications: When finance professionals discuss the "rate of return" on an investment or the "effective interest rate" on a loan, they are almost always referring to the IRR. In this section we explore some meanings of the IRR. Almost the whole of Chapter 3 is devoted to this topic.

## A Simple Example

Suppose you buy an asset for $200 today, and suppose that the asset will pay you $300 in 1 year. Then the asset's IRR is 50%. To see this, recall that the IRR is the interest rate that makes the NPV zero. Because the investment NPV $= -200 + \dfrac{300}{1+r}$, this means that the NPV is zero when $1 + r = \dfrac{300}{200} = 1.5$. Solving this equation gives $r = 50\%$.

Here's another way to think about this investment and its 50% IRR:

- At time 0 you pay $200 for the investment.

- At time 1, the $300 investment cash flow repays the initial $200. The remaining $100 represents a 50% return on the initial $200 investment. This is the IRR.

The IRR is the rate of return on an investment; it is the rate that repays, over the life of the asset, the initial investment in the asset and that pays interest on the outstanding investment balances.

## A More Complicated Example

We now give a more complicated example, which illustrates the same point. This time, you buy an asset costing $200. The asset's cash flow is $130.91 at the end of year 1 and $130.91 at the end of year 2. Here's our IRR analysis of this investment.

| | A | B | C | D | E | F |
|---|---|---|---|---|---|---|
| 1 | \multicolumn{5}{c}{THE IRR AS A RATE OF RETURN ON AN INVESTMENT} | |
| 2 | IRR | 20.00% | <-- =IRR({-200,130.91,130.91}) | | | |
| 3 | Year | Investment at beginning of year | Payment at end of year | Part of payment which is interest | Part of payment which is repayment of principal | |
| 4 | 1 | 200.00 | 130.91 | 40.00 | 90.91 | |
| 5 | 2 | 109.09 | 130.91 | 21.82 | 109.09 | |
| 6 | 3 | 0.00 | | | | |
| 7 | | | | | | |
| 8 | =B4-E4 | | | =$B$2*B4 | =C4-D4 | |
| 9 | | | | | | |
| 10 | | | =B5-E5 | | =$B$2*B5 | =C5-D5 |
| 11 | | | | | | |

- The IRR for the investment is 20.00%. Note how we calculated this—we simply typed into cell B2 the formula **=IRR({-200,130.91,130.91})** (if you're going to use this method of calculating the IRR in Excel, you have to put the cash flows in the curly brackets).

- Using the 20% IRR, $40.00 (=20%*$200) of the first year's payment is interest, and the remainder—$90.91—is repayment of principal. Another way to think of the $40.00 is to consider that to buy the asset, you gave the seller the $200 cost of the asset. When he pays you $130.91 at the end of the year, $40 (=20%*$200) is interest—your payment for allowing someone else to use your money. The remainder, $90.91, is a partial repayment of the money lent out.

- This leaves the outstanding principal at the beginning of year 2 as $109.09. Of the $130.91 paid out by the investment at the end of year 2, $21.82 (=20%*109.09) is interest, and the rest (*exactly* $109.09) is repayment of principal.

- The outstanding principal at the beginning of year 3 (the year *after* the investment finishes paying out) is *zero*.

As in the first example of this section, the IRR is the rate of return on the investment, defined as the rate that repays, over the life of the asset, the initial investment in the asset and that pays interest on the outstanding investment balances.

---

## USING FUTURE VALUE, NET PRESENT VALUE, AND INTERNAL RATE OF RETURN—THE REST OF THE CHAPTER

In the remaining sections we apply the concepts learned in the chapter to solve several common problems:
Sections 2.6–2.8. Saving for the future
Section 2.9. Paying off a loan with "flat" payments of interest and principal
Section 2.10. How long does it take to pay off a loan?

---

# 2.6. Computing Annual "Flat" Payments on a Loan—Excel's PMT Function

You've just graduated and you have 10 years to pay off your student loan of $100,000. The loan has an annual interest rate of 10% and payment is in "even payments," meaning that you pay the same amount each year. How much will you have to pay off?

Suppose we denote the annual payment by $X$. The correct $X$ has the property that the present value of all the payments equals the loan principal:

$$100,000 = \frac{X}{1.10} + \frac{X}{(1.10)^2} + \frac{X}{(1.10)^3} + \ldots + \frac{X}{(1.10)^{10}}$$

Rewriting the right side slightly, you can see that

$$X = \frac{100,000}{\frac{1}{1.10} + \frac{1}{(1.10)^2} + \frac{1}{(1.10)^3} + \ldots + \frac{1}{(1.10)^{10}}}$$

This expression can be calculated using Excel's PV function

Here's all this in an Excel spreadsheet.

|   | A | B | C |
|---|---|---|---|
| 1 | LOAN PAYMENT | | |
| 2 | Loan principal | 100,000 | |
| 3 | Loan interest | 10% | |
| 4 | Years to pay off loan | 10 | |
| 5 | Annual payment | 16,274.54 | <-- =B2/PV(B3,B4,-1) |
| 6 | | 16,274.54 | <-- =PMT(B3,B4,-B2) |

In cell B6 we use Excel's **PMT** function, which does the calculation of the loan payment directly (see box below).

## DIALOG BOX FOR PMT FUNCTION

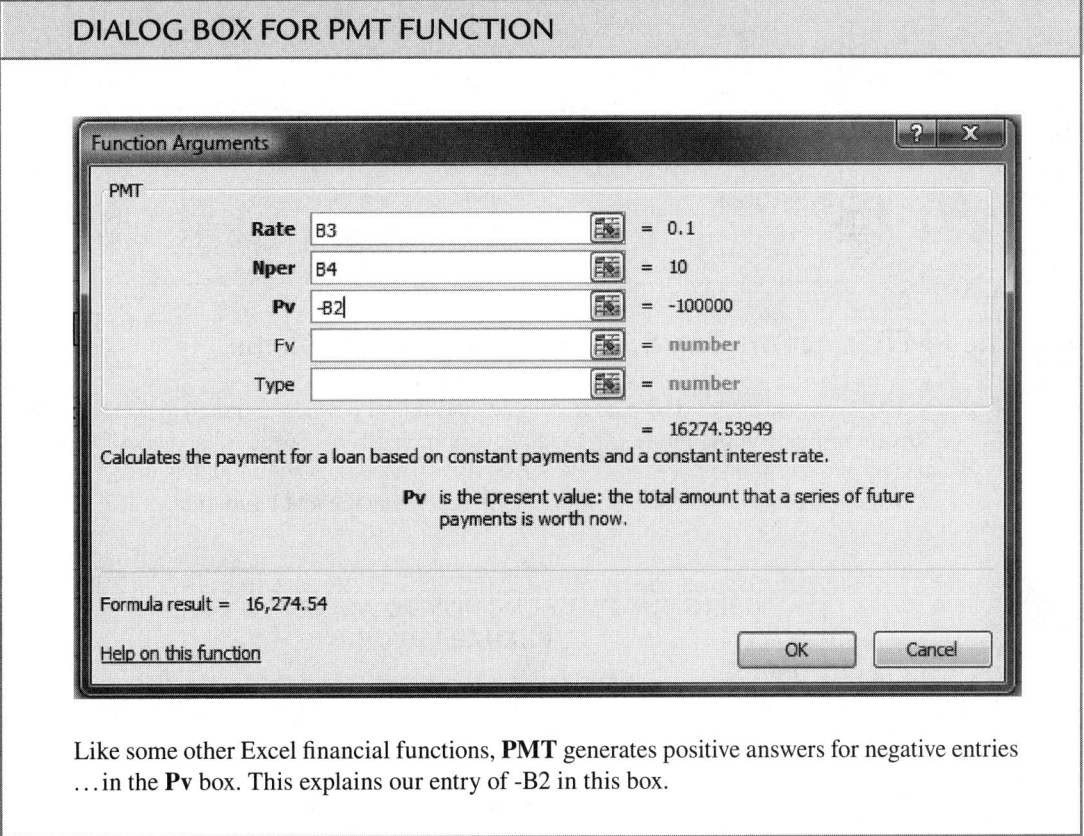

Like some other Excel financial functions, **PMT** generates positive answers for negative entries …in the **Pv** box. This explains our entry of -B2 in this box.

## Loan Amortization Tables

"Amortize" means to pay off something over time. A *loan amortization table* shows how the payments on a loan are split between interest and repayment of the loan principle. Here's the previous example, with the amortization table attached (rows 9–18).

When we put all the payments in a loan table (rows 9–18 of the following spreadsheet) you can see the split of each end-year payment between interest on the outstanding principal at the beginning of the year and repayment of principal. If you were reporting to the Internal Revenue Service, the interest column (column D) is deductible for tax purposes; the repayment of principal column (column E) is not.

|   | A | B | C | D | E | F |
|---|---|---|---|---|---|---|
| 1 | | | **LOAN PAYMENT** | | | |
| 2 | Loan principal | 100,000 | | | | |
| 3 | Loan interest | 10% | | | | |
| 4 | Years to pay off loan | 10 | | | | |
| 5 | Annual payment | 16,274.54 | <-- =B2/PV(B3,B4,-1) | | | |
| 6 | | 16,274.54 | <-- =PMT(B3,B4,-B2) | | | |
| 7 | | | | | | =$B$3*B9 |
| 8 | Year | Principal at beginning of year | Payment at end of year | Part of payment that is interest | Part of payment that is principal | |
| 9 | 1 | 100,000.00 | 16,274.54 | 10,000.00 | 6,274.54 | <-- =C9-D9 |
| 10 | 2 | 93,725.46 | 16,274.54 | 9,372.55 | 6,901.99 | |
| 11 | 3 | 86,823.47 | 16,274.54 | 8,682.35 | 7,592.19 | |
| 12 | 4 | 79,231.27 | 16,274.54 | 7,923.13 | 8,351.41 | |
| 13 | 5 | 70,879.86 | 16,274.54 | 7,087.99 | 9,186.55 | |
| 14 | 6 | 61,693.31 | 16,274.54 | 6,169.33 | 10,105.21 | |
| 15 | 7 | 51,588.10 | 16,274.54 | 5,158.81 | 11,115.73 | |
| 16 | 8 | 40,472.37 | 16,274.54 | 4,047.24 | 12,227.30 | |
| 17 | 9 | 28,245.07 | 16,274.54 | 2,824.51 | 13,450.03 | |
| 18 | 10 | 14,795.04 | 16,274.54 | 1,479.50 | 14,795.04 | |
| 19 | | | | | | |
| 20 | =B9-E9 | | The principal due at the beginning of year | | | |
| 21 | | | 10 equals the principal paid off at the end | | | |
| 22 | | | of the year. **Meaning**: The loan is paid | | | |
| 23 | | | off over 10 years. | | | |

## 2.7. The PMT Function Can Solve Future Value Problems

The PMT function can also be used to compute the annual payment required to achieve a given accretion of funds in the future. As the following spreadsheet shows, if you deposit $5,087.87 annually at the beginning of each of 10 years, this will accumulate to $100,000 at 12% interest. In cell B20, we do this computation in one step, using the **PMT function**.

|   | A | B | C | D | E |
|---|---|---|---|---|---|
| 1 | | | **USING THE PMT FUNCTION TO ACHIEVE A GIVEN FUTURE VALUE** | | |
| 2 | Interest rate | 12% | | | |
| 3 | Years | 10 | | | |
| 4 | Annual deposit | 5,087.872 | | | |
| 5 | Desired future value | 100,000 | | | |
| 6 | | | | | |
| 7 | Year | In account at beginning of year | Deposit at beginning of year | Total in account at end of year | |
| 8 | 1 | 0.00 | 5,087.87 | 5,698.42 | <-- =(B8+C8)*(1+$B$2) |
| 9 | 2 | 5,698.42 | 5,087.87 | 12,080.64 | <-- =(B9+C9)*(1+$B$2) |
| 10 | 3 | 12,080.64 | 5,087.87 | 19,228.74 | |
| 11 | 4 | 19,228.74 | 5,087.87 | 27,234.60 | |
| 12 | 5 | 27,234.60 | 5,087.87 | 36,201.17 | |
| 13 | 6 | 36,201.17 | 5,087.87 | 46,243.73 | |
| 14 | 7 | 46,243.73 | 5,087.87 | 57,491.39 | |
| 15 | 8 | 57,491.39 | 5,087.87 | 70,088.78 | |
| 16 | 9 | 70,088.78 | 5,087.87 | 84,197.85 | |
| 17 | 10 | 84,197.85 | 5,087.87 | 100,000.00 | |
| 18 | | | | | |
| 19 | Solve this in one step using PMT | | | | |
| 20 | Annual payment | 5,087.872 | <-- =PMT(B2,B3,,-B5,1) | | |

The dialog box for cell B20 is given below.

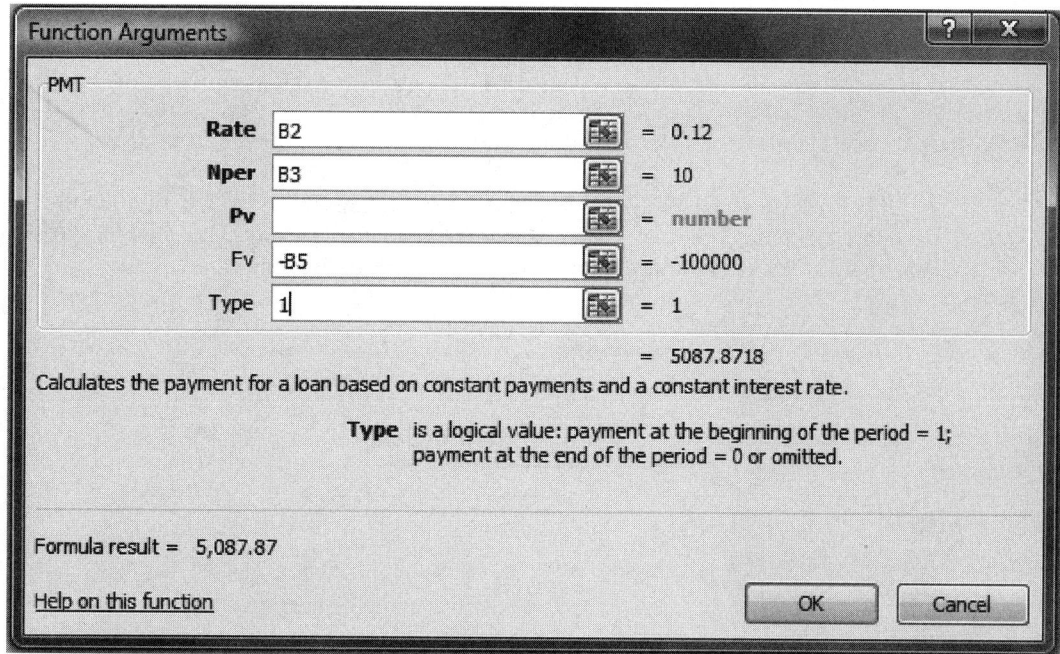

## 2.8. Saving for the Future—Buying a Car for Mario

Mario has his eye on a car that costs $20,000. He wants to buy a car in 2 years. He plans to open a bank account and to deposit $X today and $X in 1 year. Balances in the account will earn 8%. How much does Mario need to deposit so that he has $20,000 in 2 years? In this section we'll show you that

To finance future consumption with a savings plan, the net present value of all the cash flows has to be zero. In the jargon of finance, the future consumption plan is fully funded if the net present value of all the cash flows is zero.

To see this, start with a graphical representation of what happens.

| 0 | 1 | 2 |
|---|---|---|
| X | X | -20,000 |

$X*(1.08)$

$X*(1.08)^2$

In year 2 Mario will have accumulated $X*(1.08)+X*(1.08)^2$. This should finance the $20,000 car, so that

$$\underbrace{X*(1.08)+X*(1.08)^2}_{\substack{\uparrow \\ \text{Future value of} \\ \text{deposits in 2 years}}} = \underbrace{20,000}_{\substack{\uparrow \\ \text{Desired accumulation}}}$$

Now subtract the $20,000 from both sides of the equation and divide through by $(1.08)^2$:

$$X + \frac{X}{(1.08)} - \underbrace{\frac{20,000}{(1.08)^2} = 0}_{\substack{\text{Net present value} \\ \text{of all cash flows}}}$$

If you were to actually solve this equation, you would find that $X = \$8,903.13$. To fully fund the future purchase of the car, Mario has to deposit $8,903.13 today and another $8,903.13 a total of 1 year from now. If he does this, the NPV of all the payments is zero:

$$\underbrace{\underbrace{\$8,903.13}_{\substack{\text{The PV of the} \\ \text{deposit made} \\ \text{today}}} + \underbrace{\frac{\$8,903.13}{(1.08)}}_{\substack{\text{The PV of the} \\ \text{deposit made 1} \\ \text{year from now}}} - \underbrace{\frac{20,000}{(1.08)^2}}_{\substack{\text{The PV of the cost} \\ \text{of the car in 2 years}}} = 0}_{\substack{\text{The NPV of the 2 deposits} \\ \text{and the cost of the car in} \\ \text{year 2}}}$$

### Excel Solution

Of course, this same solution is easily reached using Excel.

|   | A | B | C | D | E |
|---|---|---|---|---|---|
| 1 | | **HELPING MARIO SAVE FOR A CAR** | | | |
| 2 | Deposit, X | 8,903.13 | | | |
| 3 | Interest rate | 8.00% | | | |
| 4 | Year | In bank, before deposit | Deposit or withdrawal | Total at beginning of year | End of year with interest |
| 5 | 0 | 0.00 | 8,903.13 | 8,903.13 | 9,615.38 |
| 6 | 1 | 9,615.38 | 8,903.13 | 18,518.52 | 20,000.00 |
| 7 | 2 | 20,000.00 | (20,000.00) | 0.00 | 0.00 |
| 8 | | | | | |
| 9 | | NPV of all deposits and payments | | $0.00 <-- =C5+NPV(B3,C6:C7) | |

If Mario deposits $8,903.13 in years 0 and 1, then the accumulation in the account at the beginning of year 2 will be exactly $20,000 (cell B7). The NPV of all the payments (cell C9) is zero.

In the next section we discuss three methods for solving Mario's savings problem.

## 2.9. Solving Mario's Savings Problem—Three Solutions

We can solve Mario's savings problem using one of three methods: trial and error, using Excel's **Goal Seek**, and using Excel's PMT function. Each of these three methods is illustrated in this section.

## Method 1: Trial and Error

You can "play" with the spreadsheet, adjusting cell B2 until cell C9 equals zero. For example, if you put $5,000 into cell B2, you see that the NPV in cell C9 is negative, indicating that Mario is saving too little.

| | A | B | C | D | E |
|---|---|---|---|---|---|
| 1 | | **HELPING MARIO SAVE FOR A CAR** | | | | |
| 2 | Deposit, X | 5,000.00 | | | |
| 3 | Interest rate | 8.00% | | | |
| 4 | Year | In bank, before deposit | Deposit or withdrawal | Total at beginning of year | End of year with interest |
| 5 | 0 | 0.00 | 5,000.00 | 5,000.00 | 5,400.00 |
| 6 | 1 | 5,400.00 | 5,000.00 | 10,400.00 | 11,232.00 |
| 7 | 2 | 11,232.00 | (20,000.00) | (8,768.00) | (9,469.44) |
| 8 | | | | | |
| 9 | | NPV of all deposits and payments | ($7,517.15) <-- =C5+NPV(B3,C6:C7) | | |

If you put 10,000 into cell B2, cell C9 will be positive; this indicates that the answer is somewhere between 5,000 and 10,000. By trial and error you can reach the correct solution.

## Method 2: Using Excel's Goal Seek

**Goal Seek** is an Excel function that looks for a specific number in one cell by adjusting the value of a different cell (for a discussion of how to use **Goal Seek**, see Chapter 28). To solve Mario's problem, we can use **Goal Seek** to set cell C9 equal to 0. The Excel 2007 menu selection is **Data|Data Tools|What-If Analysis|Goal Seek.**

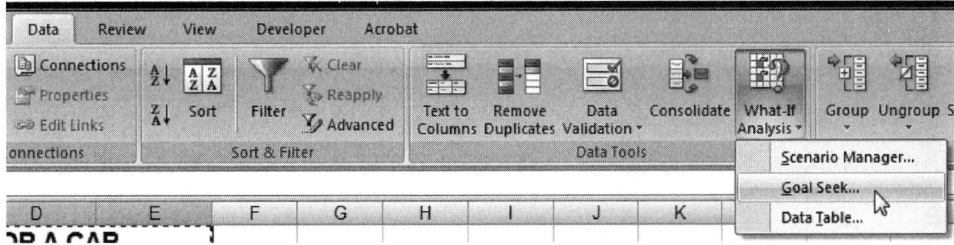

Having chosen **Goal Seek**, we fill in the dialog box as shown below.

| | A | B | C | D | E | F | G |
|---|---|---|---|---|---|---|---|
| 1 | | **HELPING MARIO SAVE FOR A CAR** | | | | | |
| 2 | Deposit, X | 5,000.00 | | | | | |
| 3 | Interest rate | 8.00% | | | | | |
| 4 | Year | In bank, before deposit | Deposit or withdrawal | Total at beginning of year | | | |
| 5 | 0 | 0.00 | 5,000.00 | 5,000 | | | |
| 6 | 1 | 5,400.00 | 5,000.00 | 10,400 | | | |
| 7 | 2 | 11,232.00 | (20,000.00) | (8,768 | | | |
| 8 | | | | | | | |
| 9 | | NPV of all deposits and payments | -7,517.15 <-- =C5+NPV(B3,C6:C7) | | | | |
| 10 | | | | | | | |

Goal Seek dialog box:
Set cell: $C$9
To value: 0
By changing cell: $B$2
OK    Cancel

When we click **OK**, **Goal Seek** will find the solution of 8,903.13.

## Method 3: Using the Excel PMT Function

Excel's PMT function can solve Mario's problem directly, as illustrated by the following spreadsheet.

| | A | B | C |
|---|---|---|---|
| 1 | | **HELPING MARIO SAVE FOR A CAR** using Excel PMT function | |
| 2 | Goal | 20,000.00 | <-- The cost of the car |
| 3 | When to reach the goal? | 2 | <-- The year in which Mario wants to buy the car |
| 4 | Interest rate | 8.00% | |
| 5 | Deposit, X | 8,903.13 | <-- =PMT(B4,B3,,-B2,1) |

The dialog box for this function is given below.

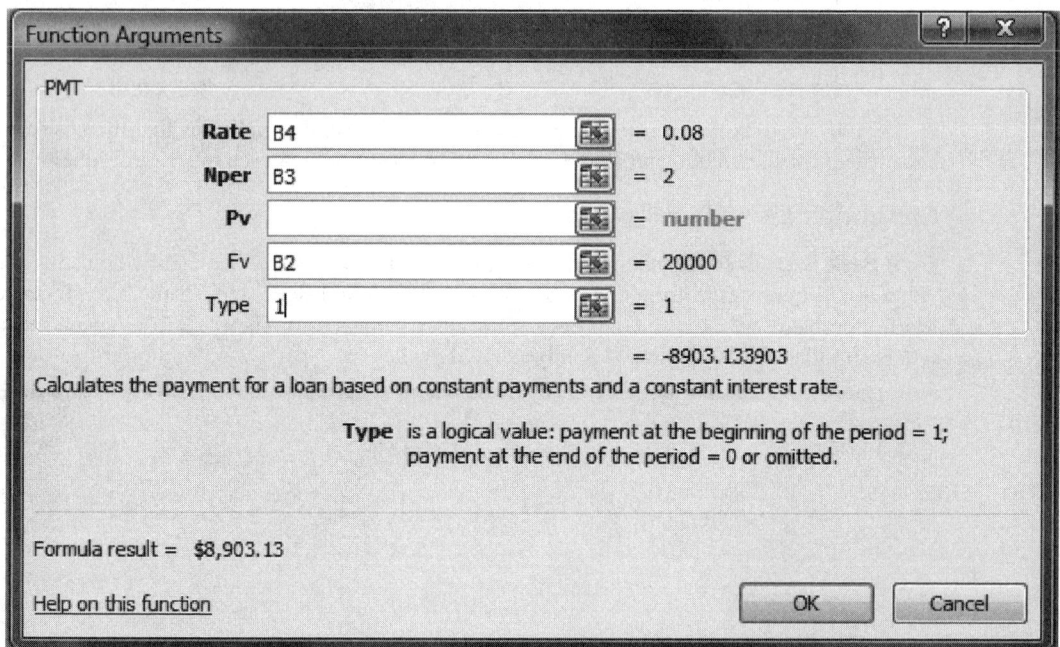

## 2.10. Saving for the Future—More Complicated Problems

In this section we present two more complicated versions of Mario's problem from Section 2.8. We start by trying to determine whether a young girl's parents are putting enough money aside to save for her college education. Here's the problem:

- On her 10th birthday Linda Jones's parents decide to deposit $4,000 in a savings account for their daughter. They intend to put an additional $4,000 in the account each year on her 11th, 12th,..., 17th birthdays.

- All account balances will earn 8% per year.
- On Linda's 18th, 19th, 20th, and 21st birthdays, her parents will withdraw $20,000 to pay for her college education.

Is the $4,000 per year sufficient to cover the anticipated college expenses? We can easily solve this problem in a spreadsheet.

|  | A | B | C | D | E |
|---|---|---|---|---|---|
| 1 | | SAVING FOR COLLEGE | | | |
| 2 | Interest rate | 8% | | | |
| 3 | Annual deposit | 4,000.00 | | | |
| 4 | Annual cost of college | 20,000 | | | |
| 5 | | | | | |
| 6 | Birthday | In bank on birthday, before deposit/withdrawal | Deposit or withdrawal at beginning of year | Total | End of year with interest |
| 7 | 10 | 0.00 | 4,000.00 | 4,000.00 | 4,320.00 |
| 8 | 11 | 4,320.00 | 4,000.00 | 8,320.00 | 8,985.60 |
| 9 | 12 | 8,985.60 | 4,000.00 | 12,985.60 | 14,024.45 |
| 10 | 13 | 14,024.45 | 4,000.00 | 18,024.45 | 19,466.40 |
| 11 | 14 | 19,466.40 | 4,000.00 | 23,466.40 | 25,343.72 |
| 12 | 15 | 25,343.72 | 4,000.00 | 29,343.72 | 31,691.21 |
| 13 | 16 | 31,691.21 | 4,000.00 | 35,691.21 | 38,546.51 |
| 14 | 17 | 38,546.51 | 4,000.00 | 42,546.51 | 45,950.23 |
| 15 | 18 | 45,950.23 | -20,000.00 | 25,950.23 | 28,026.25 |
| 16 | 19 | 28,026.25 | -20,000.00 | 8,026.25 | 8,668.35 |
| 17 | 20 | 8,668.35 | -20,000.00 | -11,331.65 | -12,238.18 |
| 18 | 21 | -12,238.18 | -20,000.00 | -32,238.18 | -34,817.24 |
| 19 | | | | | |
| 20 | | NPV of all payments | -13,826.4037 | <-- =NPV(B2,C8:C18)+C7 | |

By looking at the end-year balances in column E, the $4,000 is *not* enough—Linda and her parents will run out of money somewhere between her 19th and 20th birthdays.[5] By the end of her college career, they will be $34,817 "in the hole" (cell E18). Another way to see this is to look at the NPV calculation in cell C20: As we saw in the previous section, a combination savings/withdrawal plan is fully funded when the NPV of all the payments/withdrawals is zero. In cell C20 we see that the NPV is negative—Linda's plan is *underfunded*.

How much should Linda's parents put aside each year? There are several ways to answer this question, which we explore below. These methods are basically the same as the three methods for solving Mario's problem presented in the previous section, but for completeness we present them again.

## Method 1: Trial and Error

Assuming that you have put the correct formulas in the spreadsheet, you can "play" with cell B3 until cell E18 or cell C20 equals zero. Doing this shows that Linda's parents should have planned to deposit $6,227.78 annually.

---

[5]At the end of Linda's 19th year (row 16), there is $8,668.35 remaining in the account. At the end of the following year, there is a negative amount in the account.

|  | A | B | C | D | E |
|---|---|---|---|---|---|
| 1 | | SAVING FOR COLLEGE | | | |
| 2 | Interest rate | 8% | | | |
| 3 | Annual deposit | 6,227.78 | | | |
| 4 | Annual cost of college | 20,000 | | | |
| 5 | | | | | |
| 6 | Birthday | In bank on birthday, before deposit/withdrawal | Deposit or withdrawal at beginning of year | Total | End of year with interest |
| 7 | 10 | 0.00 | 6,227.78 | 6,227.78 | 6,726.00 |
| 8 | 11 | 6,726.00 | 6,227.78 | 12,953.77 | 13,990.08 |
| 9 | 12 | 13,990.08 | 6,227.78 | 20,217.85 | 21,835.28 |
| 10 | 13 | 21,835.28 | 6,227.78 | 28,063.06 | 30,308.10 |
| 11 | 14 | 30,308.10 | 6,227.78 | 36,535.88 | 39,458.75 |
| 12 | 15 | 39,458.75 | 6,227.78 | 45,686.52 | 49,341.45 |
| 13 | 16 | 49,341.45 | 6,227.78 | 55,569.22 | 60,014.76 |
| 14 | 17 | 60,014.76 | 6,227.78 | 66,242.54 | 71,541.94 |
| 15 | 18 | 71,541.94 | -20,000.00 | 51,541.94 | 55,665.29 |
| 16 | 19 | 55,665.29 | -20,000.00 | 35,665.29 | 38,518.52 |
| 17 | 20 | 38,518.52 | -20,000.00 | 18,518.52 | 20,000.00 |
| 18 | 21 | 20,000.00 | -20,000.00 | 0.00 | 0.00 |
| 19 | | | | | |
| 20 | | NPV of all payments | | 0.0000 | <-- =NPV(B2,C8:C18)+C7 |

Note that the net present value of all the payments (cell C20) is zero when the solution is reached. The future payouts are fully funded when the NPV of all the cash flows is zero.

## Method 2: Using Excel's Goal Seek

We can use **Goal Seek** to set E18 equal to zero. After hitting **Data|What-If Analysis|Goal Seek**, we fill in the dialog box.

|  | A | B | C | D | E | F | G | H |
|---|---|---|---|---|---|---|---|---|
| 1 | | SAVING FOR COLLEGE | | | | | | |
| 2 | Interest rate | 8% | | | | | | |
| 3 | Annual deposit | 4,000.00 | | | | | | |
| 4 | Annual cost of college | 20,000 | | | | | | |
| 5 | | | | | | | | |
| 6 | Birthday | In bank on birthday, before deposit/withdrawal | Deposit or withdrawal at beginning of year | Total | End with | | | |
| 7 | 10 | 0.00 | 4,000.00 | 4,000.00 | | | | |
| 8 | 11 | 4,320.00 | 4,000.00 | 8,320.00 | | | | |
| 9 | 12 | 8,985.60 | 4,000.00 | 12,985.60 | | | | |
| 10 | 13 | 14,024.45 | 4,000.00 | 18,024.45 | | | | |
| 11 | 14 | 19,466.40 | 4,000.00 | 23,466.40 | | | | |
| 12 | 15 | 25,343.72 | 4,000.00 | 29,343.72 | | | | |
| 13 | 16 | 31,691.21 | 4,000.00 | 35,691.21 | | | | |
| 14 | 17 | 38,546.51 | 4,000.00 | 42,546.51 | 45,950.23 | | | |
| 15 | 18 | 45,950.23 | -20,000.00 | 25,950.23 | 28,026.25 | | | |
| 16 | 19 | 28,026.25 | -20,000.00 | 8,026.25 | 8,668.35 | | | |
| 17 | 20 | 8,668.35 | -20,000.00 | -11,331.65 | -12,238.18 | | | |
| 18 | 21 | -12,238.18 | -20,000.00 | -32,238.18 | -34,817.24 | | | |
| 19 | | | | | | | | |
| 20 | | NPV of all payments | | -13,826.4037 | <-- =NPV(B2,C8:C18)+C7 | | | |
| 21 | | | | | | | | |

Goal Seek dialog box:
Set cell: $C$20
To value: 0
By changing cell: $B$3
OK    Cancel

When we click OK, Goal Seek looks for the solution. The result is the same as before: $6,227.78.

## Method 3: Using the Excel PV and PMT Formula

We can use the Excel **PV** and **PMT** functions to solve this problem directly, as illustrated in the following spreadsheet screen.

| | A | B | C |
|---|---|---|---|
| 1 | | SAVING FOR COLLEGE Using PV and PMT functions | |
| 2 | Interest rate | 8% | |
| 3 | Linda's age today | 10 | |
| 4 | Age at starting college | 18 | |
| 5 | Years of college | 4 | |
| 6 | | | |
| 7 | Annual cost of college | 20,000 | |
| 8 | | | |
| 9 | PV of college at 18 | 71,541.94 | <-- =PV(B2,B5,-B7,,1) |
| 10 | Annual payment | 6,227.78 | <-- =PMT(B2,B4-B3,,-B9,1) |

Explanation: Cell B9 is the present value of the college tuitions at the start of the 18th year. The **PMT** function computes the annual payment required so that the future value of the payments (compounded at 8% for 8 years) will be equal to $71,541.94.

We can, of course, integrate the PV function into the PMT function, so that the result is even simpler.

| | A | B | C |
|---|---|---|---|
| 1 | | SAVING FOR COLLEGE PV function is inside the PMT function | |
| 2 | Interest rate | 8% | |
| 3 | Linda's age today | 10 | |
| 4 | Age at starting college | 18 | |
| 5 | Years of college | 4 | |
| 6 | | | |
| 7 | Annual cost of college | 20,000 | |
| 8 | | | |
| 9 | Annual payment | 6,227.78 | <-- =PMT(B2,B4-B3,,PV(B2,B5,B7,,1),1) |

## Pension Plans

The savings problem of Linda's parents is exactly the same as that faced by an individual who wishes to save for his retirement. Suppose that Joe is 20 today and wishes to start saving so that when he's 65 he can have 20 years of $100,000 annual withdrawals. Adapting the previous spreadsheet, we get the following.

In the table in rows 12–27 you see the power of compound interest: If Joe starts saving at age 20 for his retirement, an annual deposit of $2,540.23 will grow to provide him with his retirement needs of $100,000 per year for 20 years at age 65. On the other hand, if he starts saving at age 35, it will require $8,666.90 per year.

| | A | B | C |
|---|---|---|---|
| 1 | | SAVING FOR RETIREMENT | |
| 2 | Joe's age today | 20 | |
| 3 | Joe's age at last deposit | 64 | |
| 4 | Number of deposits | 45 | <-- =B3-B2+1 |
| 5 | Number of withdrawals | 20 | |
| 6 | Annual withdrawal from age 65 | 100,000 | |
| 7 | Interest rate | 8% | |
| 8 | | | |
| 9 | Annual deposit | 2,540.23 | <-- =(B6/(1+B7)^(B4-1))*PV(B7,B5,-1)/PV(B7,B4,-1,,1) |
| 10 | | | |
| 11 | Joe's age today | Annual amount deposited | |
| 12 | 20 | 2,540.23 | <-- =($B$6/(1+$B$7)^($B$3-A12))*PV($B$7,$B$5,-1)/PV($B$7,$B$3-A12+1,-1,,1) |
| 13 | 22 | 2,978.96 | <-- =($B$6/(1+$B$7)^($B$3-A13))*PV($B$7,$B$5,-1)/PV($B$7,$B$3-A13+1,-1,,1) |
| 14 | 24 | 3,496.73 | <-- =($B$6/(1+$B$7)^($B$3-A14))*PV($B$7,$B$5,-1)/PV($B$7,$B$3-A14+1,-1,,1) |
| 15 | 26 | 4,109.02 | |
| 16 | 28 | 4,834.85 | |
| 17 | 30 | 5,697.73 | |
| 18 | 32 | 6,727.03 | |
| 19 | 34 | 7,959.85 | |
| 20 | 35 | 8,666.90 | |
| 21 | 38 | 11,239.91 | |
| 22 | 40 | 13,430.03 | |
| 23 | 42 | 16,123.53 | |
| 24 | 44 | 19,471.60 | |
| 25 | 46 | 23,688.86 | |
| 26 | 48 | 29,090.61 | |
| 27 | 50 | 36,159.79 | |
| 28 | | | |
| 29 | | | |

Annual Deposit Required to Fund 20 Years of $100,000 When Joe is 65

Joe's age at start of plan

## 2.11. How Long Will It Take to Pay Off a Loan?

You're getting a $1,000 loan from the bank at 10% interest. The maximum payment you can make is $250 per year. How long will it take you to pay off the loan? There's an Excel function that answers this question, which we'll show you in a bit. But first let's do this the long way so we can understand the question. In the spreadsheet below we look at a loan table like the one considered in Section 2.5.

| | A | B | C | D | E |
|---|---|---|---|---|---|
| 1 | HOW LONG TO PAY OFF THIS LOAN? | | | | |
| 2 | Loan amount | 1,000 | | | |
| 3 | Interest rate | 10% | | | |
| 4 | Annual payment | 250 | | | |
| 5 | | | | | |
| 6 | Year | Principal at beginning of year | Payment at end of year | Interest | Return of principal |
| 7 | 1 | 1,000.00 | 250.00 | 100.00 | 150.00 |
| 8 | 2 | 850.00 | 250.00 | 85.00 | 165.00 |
| 9 | 3 | 685.00 | 250.00 | 68.50 | 181.50 |
| 10 | 4 | 503.50 | 250.00 | 50.35 | 199.65 |
| 11 | 5 | 303.85 | 250.00 | 30.39 | 219.62 |
| 12 | 6 | 84.24 | 250.00 | 8.42 | 241.58 |
| 13 | | | | | |
| 14 | | | | | |
| 15 | | Year 6 is the first year in which the return of principal | | | |
| 16 | | at the end of the year > principal at the beginning of | | | |
| 17 | | the year--meaning that sometime during year 6 you | | | |
| 18 | | will have paid off the loan. | | | |
| 19 | | | | | |

As you can see from row 12, year 6 is the first year in which the return of principal at the end of the year is bigger than the principal at the beginning of the year. Thus, sometime between 5 and 6 years you pay off the loan.

Excel's **NPER** function, illustrated in cell B22, provides an exact answer to this question.

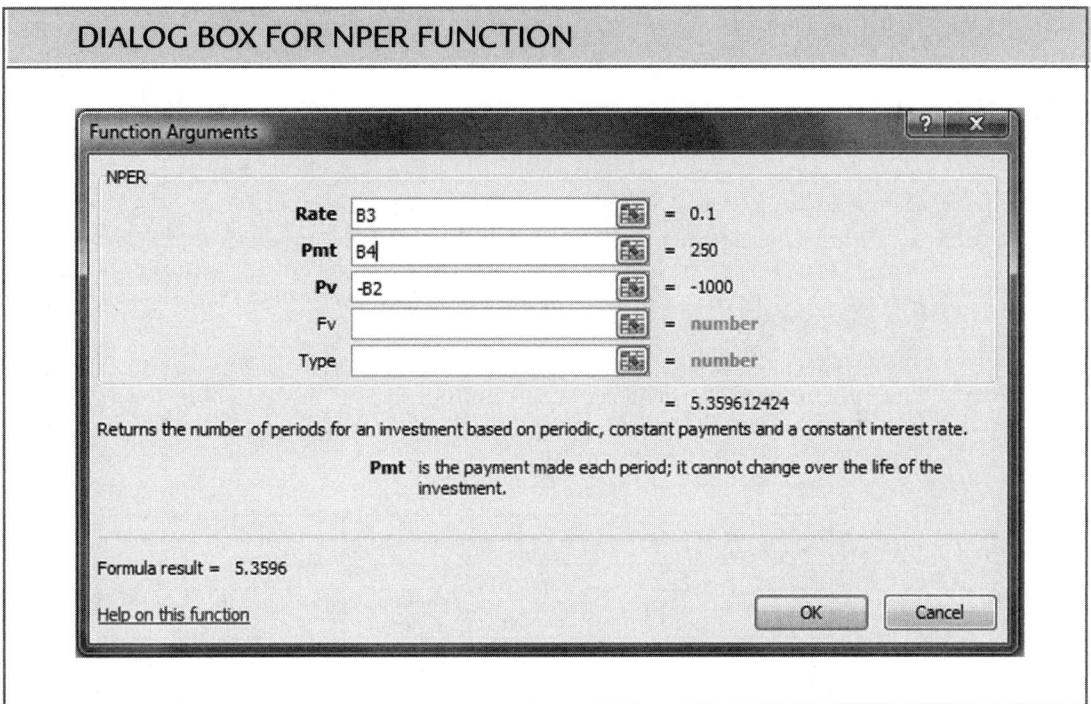

**DIALOG BOX FOR NPER FUNCTION**

Like the functions **PMT**, **PV**, and **FV** discussed elsewhere in this chapter, the **NPER** function requires you to make the amount owed negative to get a positive answer.

## Summing Up

In this chapter we have covered the basic concepts of the time value of money:

- Future value (FV): The amount you will accumulate at some future date from deposits made in the present.
- Present value (PV): The value today of future anticipated cash flows.
- Net present value (NPV): The value today of a series of future cash flows, including the cost of acquiring these cash flows.
- We've gone to great pains to point out the difference between the finance concept of NPV and the Excel **NPV** function. The Excel **NPV** function calculates the present value of the future cash flows, whereas the finance concept of NPV computes the present value of the future cash flows *minus* the initial cash flow.

- Internal rate of return (IRR): The compound interest rate paid by a series of cash flows, including the cost of their acquisition.

- NPER: The number of periods to pay off the investment.

We have also showed you the Excel functions (**FV, PV, NPV, IRR,** and **NPER**) that perform these calculations and discussed some of their peculiarities. Finally, we have showed you how to do these calculations using formulas.

## EXERCISES

1. You just put $600 in the bank and you intend to leave it there for 10 years. If the bank pays you 15% interest per year, how much will you have at the end of 10 years?

2. Your generous grandmother has just announced that she's opened a savings account for you with a deposit of $10,000. Moreover, she intends to make nine more similar gifts, at the end of this year, next year, etc. If the savings account pays 8% interest, how much will you have accumulated at the end of 10 years (1 year after the last gift)?

   **Suggestion:** Do this problem two ways, as shown below: (a) take each amount and calculate its future value in year 10 (as illustrated in cells C4:C13) and then sum them; (b) use Excel's **FV** function, noting that here the amounts come at the *beginning* of the year (you'll need to enter "1" in the **Type** option as described in Section 2.1).

|   | A | B | C | D |
|---|---|---|---|---|
| 1 | Interest rate | 8.00% | | |
| 2 | | | | |
| 3 | Year | Gift | Future value in year 10 | |
| 4 | 0 | 10,000 | 21,589.25 | <--=B4*(1+$B$1)^(10-A4) |
| 5 | 1 | 10,000 | | |
| 6 | 2 | 10,000 | | |
| 7 | 3 | 10,000 | | |
| 8 | 4 | 10,000 | | |
| 9 | 5 | 10,000 | | |
| 10 | 6 | 10,000 | | |
| 11 | 7 | 10,000 | | |
| 12 | 8 | 10,000 | | |
| 13 | 9 | 10,000 | | |
| 14 | | | | |
| 15 | Total (summing C4:C13) | | | |
| 16 | Using FV function | | | |

3. Your uncle has just announced that he's going to give you $10,000 per year at the end of each of the next 4 years (he's less generous than your grandmother...). If the relevant interest rate is 7%, what's the value today of this promise? (If you're going to use **PV** to do this problem, note that the **Type** option is 0 or omitted.)

4. What is the present value of a series of four payments, each $1,000, to be made at the end of years 1, 2, 3, and 4? Assume that the interest rate is 14%.

**Suggestion:** Do this problem two ways, as shown in rows 9 and 10 below.

| | A | B | C | D |
|---|---|---|---|---|
| 1 | Interest rate | 14% | | |
| 2 | | | | |
| 3 | Year | Payment | PV | |
| 4 | 1 | 1,000 | 877.19 | <-- =B4/(1+$B$1)^A4 |
| 5 | 2 | 1,000 | | |
| 6 | 3 | 1,000 | | |
| 7 | 4 | 1,000 | | |
| 8 | | | | |
| 9 | Total of C4:C7 | | | |
| 10 | Using NPV function | | | |

5. Screw-'Em-Good Corp. (SEG) has just announced a revolutionary security: If you pay SEG $1,000 now, you will get back $150 at the end of each of the next 15 years. What is the IRR of this investment?

   **Suggestion:** Do this problem two ways—once using Excel's **IRR** function and once using Excel's RATE function (illustrated below).

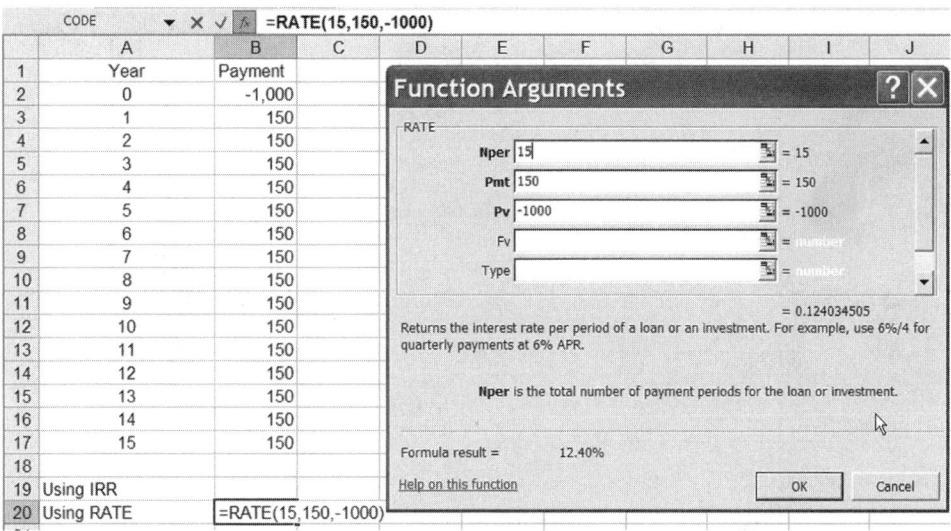

6. Make-'Em-Happy Corp. (MEH) has a different security for sale: You pay MEH $1,000 today and the company will give you back $100 at the end of the first year, $200 at the end of year 2,…, $1,000 at the end of year 10.

   a. Calculate the IRR of this investment.

   b. Show an amortization table for the investment.

7. You are thinking about buying a $1,000 bond issued by the Appalachian Development Authority. The bond will pay $120 interest at the end of each of the next 5 years. At the end of year 6, the bond will pay $1,120 (this is its face value of $1,000 plus the interest). If the relevant discount rate is 7%, how much is the present value of the bond's future payments?

8. Anuradha Dixit just turned 55. Anuradha is planning to retire in 10 years, and she currently has $500,000 in her pension fund. Based on the longevity pattern of her family, she assumes that she will live 20 years past her retirement rate; during each of these years she desires to withdraw

$100,000 from her pension fund. If the interest rate is 5% annually, how much will Anuradha have to save annually for the next 10 years? Assume that the first deposit to her pension fund will be today, followed by nine more annual deposits, and that the annual withdrawals from age 65 will occur at the beginning of each year.

Use the following spreadsheet (the numbers are not correct) and Goal Seek to find an answer.

| | A | B | C | D | E | F |
|---|---|---|---|---|---|---|
| 1 | | SAVING FOR THE FUTURE | | | | |
| 2 | Annual desired pension payout | 100,000 | | | | |
| 3 | Annual payment | 10,000 | | | | |
| 4 | Interest rate | 5% | | | | |
| 5 | | | | | | |
| 6 | Your age | Account balance, beginning of year | Deposit or withdrawal beginning of year | Interest earned during year | Total in account end of year | |
| 7 | 55 | 500,000 | 10,000 | 25,500 | 535,500 | <-- =D7+C7+B7 |
| 8 | 56 | 535,500 | 10,000 | 27,275 | 572,775 | <-- =D8+C8+B8 |
| 9 | 57 | 572,775 | 10,000 | 29,139 | 611,914 | |
| 10 | 58 | 611,914 | 10,000 | 31,096 | 653,009 | |
| 11 | 59 | 653,009 | 10,000 | 33,150 | 696,160 | |
| 12 | 60 | 696,160 | 10,000 | 35,308 | 741,468 | |
| 13 | 61 | 741,468 | 10,000 | 37,573 | 789,041 | |
| 14 | 62 | 789,041 | 10,000 | 39,952 | 838,993 | |
| 15 | 63 | 838,993 | 10,000 | 42,450 | 891,443 | |
| 16 | 64 | 891,443 | 10,000 | 45,072 | 946,515 | |
| 17 | 65 | 946,515 | (100,000) | 42,326 | 888,841 | |
| 18 | 66 | 888,841 | (100,000) | 39,442 | 828,283 | |
| 19 | 67 | 828,283 | (100,000) | 36,414 | 764,697 | |
| 20 | 68 | 764,697 | (100,000) | 33,235 | 697,932 | |
| 21 | 69 | 697,932 | (100,000) | 29,897 | 627,829 | |
| 22 | 70 | 627,829 | (100,000) | 26,391 | 554,220 | |
| 23 | 71 | 554,220 | (100,000) | 22,711 | 476,931 | |
| 24 | 72 | 476,931 | (100,000) | 18,847 | 395,778 | |
| 25 | 73 | 395,778 | (100,000) | 14,789 | 310,566 | |
| 26 | 74 | 310,566 | (100,000) | 10,528 | 221,095 | |
| 27 | 75 | 221,095 | (100,000) | 6,055 | 127,150 | |
| 28 | 76 | 127,150 | (100,000) | 1,357 | 28,507 | |
| 29 | 77 | 28,507 | (100,000) | (3,575) | (75,068) | |
| 30 | 78 | (75,068) | (100,000) | (8,753) | (183,821) | |
| 31 | 79 | (183,821) | (100,000) | (14,191) | (298,012) | |
| 32 | 80 | (298,012) | (100,000) | (19,901) | (417,913) | |
| 33 | 81 | (417,913) | (100,000) | (25,896) | (543,808) | |
| 34 | 82 | (543,808) | (100,000) | (32,190) | (675,999) | |
| 35 | 83 | (675,999) | (100,000) | (38,800) | (814,799) | |
| 36 | 84 | (814,799) | (100,000) | (45,740) | (960,539) | |

9. Solve the previous problem using functions **PV** and **Pmt** and the template below.

| | A | B | C |
|---|---|---|---|
| 1 | SAVING FOR THE FUTURE | | |
| 2 | Pension savings today | 500,000 | |
| 3 | Annual desired pension payout | 100,000 | |
| 4 | Number of years until retirement | 10 | |
| 5 | Number of payout years after retirement | 20 | |
| 6 | Interest rate | 5% | |
| 7 | | | |
| 8 | Present value today of all future retirement payments | | |
| 9 | Annual payment until retirement | | |

10. If you deposit $25,000 today, Union Bank offers to pay you $50,000 at the end of 10 years. What is the interest rate?

11. Assuming that the interest rate is 5%, which of the following is more valuable?

    a. $5,000 today

    b. $10,000 at the end of 5 years

    c. $9,000 at the end of 4 years

    d. $300 a year in perpetuity (meaning forever), with the first payment at the end of this year

12. You receive a $15,000 signing bonus from your new employer and decide to invest it for 2 years. Your banker suggests two alternatives, which both require a commitment for the full 2 years. The first alternative will earn 8% per year for both years. The second alternative earns 6% for the first year and 10% for the second year. Interest compounds annually.

    Which should you choose?

13. Your annual salary is $100,000. You are offered two options for a severance package. Option 1 pays you 6 months' salary now. Option 2 pays you and your heirs $6,000 per year forever (first payment at the end of this year). If your required return is 11%, which option should you choose?

14. Today is your 40th birthday. You expect to retire at age 65 and actuarial tables suggest that you will live to be 100. You want to move to Hawaii when you retire. You estimate that it will cost you $200,000 to make the move (on your 65th birthday). Starting on your 65th birthday and ending on your 99th birthday, your annual living expenses will be $25,000 a year. You expect to earn an annual return of 7% on your savings.

    a. How much will you need to have saved by your retirement date?

    b. You already have $50,000 in savings. How much would you need to save today and at age 41, … 64 to be able to afford this retirement plan?

    c. If you did not have any current savings and did not expect to be able to start saving money for the next 5 years (that is, your first savings payment will be made on your 45th birthday), how much would you have to set aside each year after that to be able to afford this retirement plan?

15. You have just invested $10,000 in a new fund that pays $1,500 at the end of each of the next 10 years. What is the compound rate of interest being offered in the fund? (**Suggestion**: Do this problem two ways: Using Excel's **IRR** function and using Excel's **Rate** function.)

16. John is turning 13 today. His birthday resolution is to start saving toward the purchase of a car that he wants to buy on his 18th birthday. The car costs $15,000 today, and he expects the price to grow at 2% per year.

    John has heard that a local bank offers a savings account that pays an interest rate of 5% per year. He plans to make six contributions of $1,000 each to the savings account (the first contribution to be made today); he will use the funds in the account on his 18th birthday as a down payment for the car, financing the balance through the car dealer.

    He expects the dealer to offer the following terms for financing: seven equal yearly payments (with the first payment due 1 year after he takes possession of the car); an annual interest rate of 7%.

    a. How much will John need to finance through the dealer?

    b. What will be the amount of his yearly payment to the dealer?

    (Hint: This is like the college savings problem discussed in Section 2.8.)

17. Mary has just completed her undergraduate degree from Northwestern University and is already planning to enter an MBA program 4 years from today. The MBA tuition will be $20,000 per year for 2 years, paid at the beginning of each year. In addition, Mary would like to retire 15 years from today and receive a pension of $60,000 every year for 20 years, with the first pension payment paid out 15 years from today. Mary can borrow and lend as much as she likes at a rate of

7%, compounded annually. To fund her expenditures, Mary will save money at the end of years 0–3 and at the end of years 6–14.

- Calculate the constant annual dollar amount that Mary must save at the end of each of these years to cover all of her expenditures (tuition and retirement). (Hint: It might be helpful to use **Goal Seek**.)

Note: Just to remove all doubts, here are the cash flows:

|   | A | B | C | D | E | F |
|---|---|---|---|---|---|---|
| 1 | **MARY** | | | | | |
| 2 | Year | Balance at beginning of year before withdrawal | Withdrawal beginning of year | Net balance beginning of year | Savings at end of year | Account end of year |
| 3 | 0 | 0 | | | $X | |
| 4 | 1 | | | | $X | |
| 5 | 2 | | | | $X | |
| 6 | 3 | | | | $X | |
| 7 | 4 | | $ (20,000.00) | | | |
| 8 | 5 | | $ (20,000.00) | | | |
| 9 | 6 | | | | $X | |
| 10 | 7 | | | | $X | |
| 11 | 8 | | | | $X | |
| 12 | 9 | | | | $X | |
| 13 | 10 | | | | $X | |
| 14 | 11 | | | | $X | |
| 15 | 12 | | | | $X | |
| 16 | 13 | | | | $X | |
| 17 | 14 | | | | $X | |
| 18 | 15 | | $ (60,000.00) | | | |
| 19 | 16 | | $ (60,000.00) | | | |
| 20 | 17 | | $ (60,000.00) | | | |
| 21 | 18 | | $ (60,000.00) | | | |
| 22 | 19 | | $ (60,000.00) | | | |
| 23 | 20 | | $ (60,000.00) | | | |
| 24 | 21 | | $ (60,000.00) | | | |
| 25 | 22 | | $ (60,000.00) | | | |
| 26 | 23 | | $ (60,000.00) | | | |
| 27 | 24 | | $ (60,000.00) | | | |
| 28 | 25 | | $ (60,000.00) | | | |
| 29 | 26 | | $ (60,000.00) | | | |
| 30 | 27 | | $ (60,000.00) | | | |
| 31 | 28 | | $ (60,000.00) | | | |
| 32 | 29 | | $ (60,000.00) | | | |
| 33 | 30 | | $ (60,000.00) | | | |
| 34 | 31 | | $ (60,000.00) | | | |
| 35 | 32 | | $ (60,000.00) | | | |
| 36 | 33 | | $ (60,000.00) | | | |
| 37 | 34 | | $ (60,000.00) | | | 0 |

18. You are the CFO of Termination, Inc. Your company has 40 employees, each earning $40,000 per year. Employee salaries grow at 4% per year. Starting from next year, and every second year thereafter, 8 employees retire and no new employees are recruited. Your company has in place a retirement plan that entitles retired workers to an annual pension, which is equal to their annual salary at the moment of retirement. Life expectancy is 20 years after retirement, and the annual pension is paid at year end. The return on investment is 10% per year. What is the total value of your pension liabilities?

19. You are 30 today and are considering studying for an MBA. You just received your annual salary of $50,000 and expect it to grow by 3% per year. MBAs typically earn $60,000 upon graduation, with salaries growing by 4% per year.

   The MBA program you're considering is a full-time, 2-year program that costs $20,000 per year, payable at the end of each study year. You want to retire on your 65th birthday. The relevant discount rate is 8%.[6] Is it worthwhile for you to quit your job to do an MBA (ignore income taxes)? What is the internal rate of return of the MBA?

20. You're 55 years old today, and you wish to start saving for your pension. Here are the parameters:

   - You intend to make a deposit today and at the beginning of each of the next 9 years (that is, on your 55th, 56th, . . . , 64th birthdays).
   - Starting from your 65th birthday until your 84th, you would like to withdraw $50,000 per year (no plans after that).
   - The interest rate is 12%.
     a. How much should you deposit in each of the initial years to fully fund the withdrawals?
     b. If you start saving at age 45, what is the answer?
     c. (More difficult) Set up the formula for the savings amount so that you can solve for various starting ages. Do a sensitivity analysis that shows the amount you need to save as a function of the age at which you start saving.

21. Section 2.8 of this chapter discusses the problem of Linda Jones's parents, who wish to save for Linda's college education. The setup of the problem implicitly assumes that the bank will let the Jones's borrow from their savings account and will charge them the same 8% it was paying on positive balances. This is unlikely!

   In this problem you are asked to program the following spreadsheet: In it you will assume that the bank pays Linda's parents 8% on positive account balances but charges them 10% on negative balances.

   If Linda's parents can only deposit $4,000 per year in the years preceding college, how much will they owe the bank at the beginning of year 22 (the year after Linda finishes college)?

|  | A | B | C | D | E |
|---|---|---|---|---|---|
| 1 | | SAVING FOR COLLEGE | | | |
| 2 | Interest rates | | | | |
| 3 | On positive balances | 8% | | | |
| 4 | On negative balances | 10% | | | |
| 5 | Annual deposit | 4,000.00 | | | |
| 6 | Annual cost of college | 20,000 | | | |
| 7 | | | | | |
| 8 | Birthday | In bank on birthday, before deposit/withdrawal | Deposit or withdrawal at beginning of year | Total | End of year with interest |
| 9 | 10 | | 4,000.00 | | |
| 10 | 11 | | 4,000.00 | | |
| 11 | 12 | | 4,000.00 | | |
| 12 | 13 | | 4,000.00 | | |
| 13 | 14 | | 4,000.00 | | |
| 14 | 15 | | 4,000.00 | | |
| 15 | 16 | | 4,000.00 | | |
| 16 | 17 | | 4,000.00 | | |
| 17 | 18 | | -20,000.00 | | |
| 18 | 19 | | -20,000.00 | | |
| 19 | 20 | | -20,000.00 | | |
| 20 | 21 | | -20,000.00 | | |
| 21 | 22 | | | | |

[6]Meaning: Your MBA is an investment, like any other investment. On other investments you can earn 8% per year; the MBA has to be judged against this standard.

**Excel note:** To set up this spreadsheet you will need to use the Excel If function (if you are not familiar with this function, see Chapter 26).

22. A fund of $10,000 is set up to pay $250 at the end of each year indefinitely. What is the fund's IRR? (There's no Excel function that answers this question—use some logic!)

23. In the spreadsheet below we calculate the FV of 5 deposits of $100, with the first deposit made at time 0. As shown in Section 2.1, this calculation can also be made using the Excel function **=FV(interest,periods,-amount,,1)** .

    a. Show that you can also compute this by **=FV(interest,periods,-amount)*(1+interest)**.

    b. Can you explain why **FV(r,5,-100,,1)=FV(r,5,-100)*(1+r)**?

| | A | B | C | D | E | F |
|---|---|---|---|---|---|---|
| 1 | | | FUTURE VALUE | | | |
| 2 | Interest | 6% | | | | |
| 3 | | | | | | |
| 4 | Year | Account balance, beginning of year | Deposit at beginning of year | Interest earned during year | Total in account at end of year | |
| 5 | 1 | 0.00 | 100.00 | 6.00 | 106.00 | <-- =B5+C5+D5 |
| 6 | 2 | 106.00 | 100.00 | 12.36 | 218.36 | <-- =B6+C6+D6 |
| 7 | 3 | 218.36 | 100.00 | 19.10 | 337.46 | |
| 8 | 4 | 337.46 | 100.00 | 26.25 | 463.71 | |
| 9 | 5 | 463.71 | 100.00 | 33.82 | 597.53 | |

24. Abner and Maude are both in their eighties. They're thinking of selling their house for $500,000 and moving into an apartment complex for seniors. The apartment will cost $50,000 per year, payable in full at the beginning of each year.

    a. If they can earn 6% annually on the proceeds from their house and if they live for 10 more years, how much will they be able to leave to their children as inheritance?

    b. What is the longest they can live from the apartment proceeds before the money runs out?

25. What are your answers to the question above assuming that the interest rate is 7%? 5%?

26. Michael is considering his consumption habits, trying to figure out how to save money. He realizes that he could save $2 every day by ordering regular coffee instead of a latte at the local coffee shop. Because he buys a cup of coffee every work day, this works out to $10 per week, which amounts to a saving of $520 per year.

    a. If Michael is 25 today and retires at age 65, how much money will he have accumulated from savings on coffee versus latte? Assume that the annual interest rate is 4% and that the $520 savings occur at the end of each year.

    b. Michael was astounded at the answer to part (a) of this problem. He realized he had more wasteful habits, and he made a list of possible savings to see how much richer he could be at age 65. What are the rewards to Michael's frugality?

| | A | B | C | D |
|---|---|---|---|---|
| 1 | MICHAEL SAVES MONEY<br>By changing his consumption habits | | | |
| 2 | Annual interest rate | 4% | | |
| 3 | Item | Weekly<br>savings | Yearly<br>savings | Future value at<br>age 65 |
| 4 | | | | |
| 5 | Latte versus regular coffee | $ 10.00 | $ 520.00 | |
| 6 | Deli versus brown bag lunch | $ 25.00 | $ 1,300.00 | |
| 7 | Excess alcohol | $ 10.00 | $ 520.00 | |
| 8 | Cigarettes | $ 11.00 | $ 572.00 | |
| 9 | Candy | $ 5.00 | $ 260.00 | |
| 10 | Excess junk food | $ 10.00 | $ 520.00 | |
| 11 | Cell phone (chat vs. needed calls) | $ 6.00 | $ 312.00 | |
| 12 | Wasted groceries | $ 7.00 | $ 364.00 | |
| 13 | Restaurants.fast food vs. eat at home | $ 30.00 | $ 1,560.00 | |
| 14 | Wasted energy: heat, AC, lights | $ 12.00 | $ 624.00 | |
| 15 | Movies versus books | $ 10.00 | $ 520.00 | |
| 16 | Expensive cable TV | $ 13.00 | $ 676.00 | |
| 17 | Wasted gasoline on excessive trips, etc. | $ 8.00 | $ 416.00 | |
| 18 | Wasteful spending at mall | $ 10.00 | $ 520.00 | |
| 19 | Money saved by time Michael is 65 | | | |

# APPENDIX: ALGEBRAIC PRESENT VALUE FORMULAS

MOST OF THE COMPUTATIONS IN THE CHAPTER CAN also be done with one basic bit of high-school algebra relating to the sum of a geometric series. Suppose you want to find the sum of a geometric series of $n$ numbers $a + aq + aq^2 + aq^3 + \cdots + aq^{n-1}$. In the jargon of geometric series,

$a$  is the *first term*
$q$  is the *ratio* between terms (the number by which the previous term is multiplied to get the next term)
$n$  is the *number of terms*

Denote the sum of the series by $S$: $S = a + aq + aq^2 + aq^3 + \cdots + aq^{n-1}$. In high school you learned a trick to find the value of $S$:

1. Multiply $S$ by $q$:

$$qS = \qquad aq \ + \ aq^2 \ + \ aq^3 \ + \ \cdots \ + \ aq^{n-1} \ + \ aq^n$$

2. Subtract $qS$ from $S$:

$$S = \ a \ + \ aq \ + \ aq^2 \ + \ aq^3 \ + \ \cdots \ + \ aq^{n-1}$$
$$-qS = -( \qquad aq \ + \ aq^2 \ + \ aq^3 \ + \ \ldots \ + \ aq^{n-1} \ + \ aq^n )$$

$$(1-q)S = a - aq^n \Rightarrow S = \frac{a(1-q^n)}{1-q}$$

In the remainder of this appendix we apply this formula to a variety of situations covered in the chapter.

## Future Value a Constant Payment

This topic is covered in Section 2.1. The problem there is to find the value of $100 deposited annually over 10 years, with the first payment today:

$$S = 100 * (1.06)^{10} + 100 * (1.06)^9 + \cdots + 100 * (1.06) = ???$$

For this geometric series,

$$a = \text{first term} = 100 * 1.06^{10}$$

$$q = \text{ratio} = \frac{1}{1.06}$$

$$n = \text{number of terms} = 10$$

The formula gives $S = \dfrac{a(1 - q^n)}{1 - q} = \dfrac{100 * 1.06^{10}\left(1 - \left(\dfrac{1}{1.06}\right)^{10}\right)}{1 - \dfrac{1}{1.06}} = 1397.16$, where we have done

the calculation in Excel.

|  | A | B | C |
|---|---|---|---|
| 1 | **FUTURE VALUE FORMULA** | | |
| 2 | First term, a | 179.0848 | <-- =100*1.06^10 |
| 3 | Ratio, q | 0.943396 | <-- =1/1.06 |
| 4 | Number of terms, n | 10 | |
| 5 | | | |
| 6 | Sum | 1,397.16 | <-- =B2*(1-B3^B4)/(1-B3) |
| 7 | Excel PV function | 1,397.16 | <-- =FV(6%,B4,-100,,1) |

Substituting symbols for the numerical values we get

$$\begin{array}{c} \text{Future value of n payments} \\ \text{at end of year n, at interest r} = \\ \text{first payment today} \end{array} \frac{Payment * (1 + r)^n\left(1 - \left(\dfrac{1}{1+r}\right)^n\right)}{1 - \dfrac{1}{1+r}} = \underbrace{FV(r,n,-1,,1)}_{\substack{\uparrow \\ \text{The Excel function}}}$$

## PV of an Annuity

We can also apply the formula to find the present value of an annuity. Suppose, for example, that we want to calculate the PV of an annuity of $150 per year for 5 years:

$$\frac{150}{(1.06)} + \frac{150}{(1.06)^2} + \frac{150}{(1.06)^3} + \frac{150}{(1.06)^4} + \frac{150}{(1.06)^5}.$$

For this annuity,

$$a = first\ term = \frac{150}{1.06}.^7$$

$$q = ratio = \frac{1}{1.06}$$

$$n = number\ of\ terms = 5.$$

Thus, the present value of the annuity becomes

$$S = \frac{a(1-q^n)}{1-q} = \frac{\frac{150}{1.06}\left(1-\left(\frac{1}{1.06}\right)^5\right)}{1-\frac{1}{1.06}} = 631.85 = \underbrace{PV(6\%,5,-150)}_{\underset{\text{The Excel function}}{\uparrow}}.$$

We can work this out in a spreadsheet.

| | A | B | C |
|---|---|---|---|
| 1 | **ANNUITY FORMULAS** | | |
| 2 | First term, a | 141.5094 | <-- =150/1.06 |
| 3 | Ratio, q | 0.9434 | <-- =1/1.06 |
| 4 | Number of terms, n | 5 | |
| 5 | | | |
| 6 | Sum | 631.85 | <-- =B2*(1-B3^B4)/(1-B3) |
| 7 | Excel PV function | 631.85 | <-- =PV(6%,5,-150) |

## Cleaning Up the Formula (a Bit)

Textbooks often manipulate the annuity formula to make it look "better." Here's an example of something you might see in a textbook.

$$S = \frac{a(1-q^n)}{1-q} = \frac{\frac{annual\ payment}{(1+r)}\left(1-\left(\frac{1}{1+r}\right)^n\right)}{1-\frac{1}{1+r}}$$

$$= \frac{annual\ payment}{r}\left(1-\left(\frac{1}{1+r}\right)^n\right)$$

This is not a different annuity formula—it's just an algebraic simplification of the formula we've been using. If you put it in Excel you'll get the same answer (and in our opinion, there's no point in the simplification).

---

[7]If you're like most of the rest of humanity, you (mistakenly) thought that the first term was $a = 150$. But look at the series—the first term actually is $\frac{150}{1.06}$. So there you are.

## The Present Value of Series of Growing Payments

Suppose we're trying to apply the formula to the following series:

$$\frac{150}{(1.06)}+\frac{150*(1.10)}{(1.06)^2}+\frac{150*(1.10)^2}{(1.06)^3}+\frac{150*(1.10)^3}{(1.06)^4}+\frac{150*(1.10)^4}{(1.06)^5}$$

Here there are five payments, the first of which is $150; this payment grows at an annual rate of 10%. We can apply the formula

$$a = first\ term = \frac{150}{1.06}.$$

$$q = ratio = \frac{1.10}{1.06}$$

$n = number\ of\ terms = 5.$

In the following spreadsheet, you can see that the formula and the Excel **NPV** function give the same answer for the present value:

|   | A | B | C |
|---|---|---|---|
| 1 | **A CONSTANT-GROWTH CASH FLOW** | | |
| 2 | First term, a | 141.5094 | <-- =150/1.06 |
| 3 | Ratio, q | 1.0377 | <-- =1.1/1.06 |
| 4 | Number of terms, n | 5 | |
| 5 | | | |
| 6 | Sum | 763.00 | <-- =B2*(1-B3^B4)/(1-B3) |
| 7 | | | |
| 8 | | Year | Payment |
| 9 | | 1 | 150.00 |
| 10 | | 2 | 165.00 | <-- =B9*1.1 |
| 11 | | 3 | 181.50 | <-- =B10*1.1 |
| 12 | | 4 | 199.65 |
| 13 | | 5 | 219.62 |
| 14 | | | |
| 15 | Present value | | 763.00 | <-- =NPV(6%,B9:B13) |

Note that the formula in cell B6 is more compact than Excel's **NPV** function. **NPV** requires you to list all the payments, whereas the formula in cell B6 requires only several lines (think about finding the present value of a very long series of growing payments—clearly the formula is more efficient).

## The Present Value of a Constant Growth Annuity

An annuity is a series of annual payments; a constant growth annuity is an annuity whose payments grow at a constant rate. Here's an example of such a series.

$$\frac{20}{(1.10)}+\frac{20*(1.05)}{(1.10)^2}+\frac{20*(1.05)^2}{(1.10)^3}+\frac{20*(1.05)^3}{(1.10)^4}+\frac{20*(1.05)^4}{(1.10)^5}+...$$

We can fit this into our formula:

$$a = \textit{first term} = \frac{20}{1.10}$$

$$q = \textit{ratio} = \frac{1.05}{1.10}$$

$n = \textit{number of terms} = \infty.$
The formula gives

$$S = \frac{a(1-q^n)}{1-q} = \frac{\frac{20}{1.10}\left(1-\left(\frac{1.05}{1.10}\right)^n\right)}{1-\frac{1.05}{1.10}}.$$

When $n \to \infty$, $\left(\frac{1.05}{1.10}\right)^n \to 0$, so that

$$S = \frac{a(1-q^n)}{1-q} = \frac{\frac{20}{1.10}\left(1-\left(\frac{1.05}{1.10}\right)^n\right)}{1-\frac{1.05}{1.10}} = \frac{\frac{20}{1.10}}{1-\frac{1.05}{1.10}} = \frac{20}{0.10-0.05} = 400$$

**Warning**: You have to be careful! This version of the formula only works because the growth rate of 5% is smaller than the discount rate of 10%. The discounted sum of an infinite series of constantly growing payments only exists when the growth rate $g$ is less than the discount rate $r$.

Here's a general formula:

$$\begin{aligned}\text{sum of}\\ \text{constant-growth} \\ \text{annuity}\end{aligned} = \frac{CF}{(1+r)} + \frac{CF*(1+g)}{(1+r)^2} + \frac{CF*(1+g)^2}{(1+r)^3} + \ldots = \frac{\frac{CF}{(1+r)}\left(1-\left(\frac{1+g}{1+r}\right)^\infty\right)}{1-\frac{1+g}{1+r}}$$

$$= \begin{cases} \dfrac{CF}{r-g} & \textit{when } |g| < |r| \\ \textit{undefined} & \textit{otherwise} \end{cases}$$

To summarize,

The present value of a constant-growth annuity—a series of cash flows with first term CF that grows at rate g—that is discounted at rate r is $\dfrac{CF}{r-g}$ , provided g < r.

We use this formula in Chapter 6 when we discuss the valuation of stocks using discounted dividends (the "Gordon dividend model").

# 3 What Does It Cost? IRR and the Time Value of Money

## CHAPTER CONTENTS

## Overview

In Chapter 2 we introduced the basic tools of financial analysis—present value (PV), net present value (NPV), and internal rate of return (IRR). In Chapters 3–7 we use these tools to answer two basic types of questions:

- *What is it worth*? Presented with an asset—this could be a stock, a bond, a real estate investment, a computer, or a used car—we would like to know *how to value* the asset. The finance tools used to answer this question are mostly related to the concept of present value (PV) and net present value (NPV). The basic principle is that the value of an asset is the present value of its future cash flows. Comparing this present value to the asset's price tells us whether we should buy it. We introduced PV and NPV in Chapter 2 and we return to them and their applications in Chapter 4.

- *What does it cost?* This sounds like an innocuous question—after all, you usually know the price of the stock, bond, real estate investment, or used car you're trying to value. But many interesting questions of *financing alternatives* depend on the relative interest costs of each alternative. For example, should you pay cash for a car or borrow money to pay for it (and hence make a series of payments over time)? Should you lease that new computer you want or buy it outright? Or perhaps borrow money from the bank to buy it? It's all clearly a question of *cost*—you'd like to pick the alternative that costs the least.

The tools used for the second question—What does it cost?—are mostly derived from the concept of internal rate of return (IRR). This concept—introduced in Chapter 2—measures the compound rate of return of a series of cash flows. In this chapter we'll show you that rate of return, when properly used, can be used to measure the cost of financing alternatives. The main concept presented in this chapter is the *effective annual interest rate* (EAIR), a concept based on the annualized IRR that you can use to compare financing alternatives.

Much of the discussion in this chapter relates to calculating the EAIR and showing its relation to the IRR. We show that the EAIR is a much better gauge of the financing costs than the *annualized percentage rate* (APR), the financing cost often quoted by many lenders such as banks and credit card companies. We show you how to apply this concept to credit-card borrowing, mortgages, and auto leasing. A case that comes with this book applies the concept to student loans.

## Finance Concepts Discussed

- Effective annual interest rate (EAIR)
- Internal rate of return (IRR)
- Annual percentage rate (APR)
- Loan tables
- Mortgage points
- Lease versus purchase

## Excel Functions Used

- **IRR**
- **PMT, IPMT, and PPMT**
- **Rate**
- **NPV**
- **PV**
- **Exp**
- **Ln**
- **Sum**
- **Goal Seek**

# 3.1. Don't Trust the Quoted Interest Rate—Three Examples

To set the stage for the somewhat more complicated examples in the rest of the chapter, we start with three simple examples. Each example shows why *quoted interest rates* are not necessarily representative of costs.

We use the three examples in this section to introduce the concept of EAIR.

> The effective annual interest rate (EAIR) is the annualized internal rate of return (IRR) of the cash flows of a particular credit arrangement or security.

## Example 1: Borrowing from a Bank

In finance "cost" often refers to an interest rate: "I'm taking a loan from the West Hampton Bank because it's cheaper—West Hampton charges 8% instead of the 9% charged by the East Hampton Bank." This is a sentence we all understand—8% interest results in lower payments than 9% interest.

But now consider the following alternatives. You want to borrow $100 for 1 year, and you've investigated both the West Hampton Bank and the East Hampton Bank:

- West Hampton Bank is lending at 8% interest. If you borrow $100 from them today, you'll have to repay them $108 in 1 year.

- The East Hampton Bank is willing to lend you any amount you want at a 6% rate. BUT: East Hampton Bank has a "loan initiation charge" of 4%. What this means is that for each $100 you borrow, you'll get only $96, even though you'll pay interest on the full $100.[1]

Obviously the cost of West Hampton's loan is 8%. But is this cheaper or more expensive than the East Hampton loan? You reason as follows: To actually get $100 in your hands from East Hampton, you'll have to borrow $104.17; after they deduct their 4% charge, you'll be left with $100 in hand, which is exactly what you need (96% * 104.17 = 100). At the end of a year, you'll owe East Hampton Bank $104.17 + 6% interest = $110.42. So the actual interest rate they're charging you (the effective annual interest rate) is $EAIR = \dfrac{110.42}{100} - 1 = 10.42\%$.

| | A | B | C | D |
|---|---|---|---|---|
| 1 | CHEAPER LOAN: WEST HAMPTON OR EAST HAMPTON? | | | |
| 2 | | West Hampton | East Hampton | |
| 3 | Quoted interest rate | 8% | 6% | |
| 4 | Initial charges | 0% | 4% | |
| 5 | Amount borrowed to get $100 today | 100.00 | 104.17 | <-- =100/(1-C4) |
| 6 | | | | |
| 7 | Date | Cash flow | Cash flow | |
| 8 | Date 1, get loan | 100.00 | 100.00 | |
| 9 | Date 2, pay it back | -108.00 | -110.42 | <-- =-C5*(1+C3) |
| 10 | Effective annual interest rate, EAIR | 8.00% | 10.42% | <-- =IRR(C8:C9) |

---

[1]Such charges are common in many kinds of bank loans, especially mortgages. They're obviously a way to increase the cost of the loan and befuddle the customer.

This makes everything easier—West Hampton's 8% loan (EAIR = 8%) is actually cheaper than East Hampton's "6%" loan (EAIR = 10.42%).

Note in this example that the EAIR is just an IRR, adjusted for the cost of taking the loan from East Hampton. EAIR is *always an interest rate*, but usually with some kind of adjustment.

**The lesson of Example 1:** When calculating the cost of financial alternatives, *you must include the fees*, even if the lender (in our case East Hampton Bank) fudges this issue.

## Example 2: Monthly versus Annual Interest

You want to buy a computer for $1,000. You don't have any money, so you'll have to finance the computer by taking out a loan for $1,000. You've got two financing alternatives:

- Your bank will lend you the money for 15% annual interest. When you ask the bank what this means they assure you that they will give you $1,000 today and ask you to repay $1,150 at the end of 1 year.

- Loan Shark Financing Company will also lend you the $1,000. Their ads say "14.4% annual percentage rate (APR) on a monthly basis." When you ask them what this means, it turns out that Loan Shark charges 1.2% *per month* (they explain to you that $\frac{14.4\%}{12} = 1.2\%$). This means that each month Loan Shark adds 1.2% to the loan balance outstanding at the end of the previous month:

| | A | B | C | D | E | F | G | H |
|---|---|---|---|---|---|---|---|---|
| 1 | HOW LOAN SHARK CHARGES: 14.4% PER YEAR ON A MONTHLY BASIS = 1.2% PER MONTH | | | | | | | |
| 2 | | | | | | | | |
| 3 | Loan balance outstanding at the end of each month | | | | | | | |
| 4 | Month 0 | Month 1 | Month 2 | Month 3 | Month 4 | Month 5 | Month 6 | |
| 5 | $ 1,000.00 | | | | | | | |
| 6 | | $ 1,012.00 | <-- =A5*(1+1.2%) | | | | | |
| 7 | | | $ 1,024.14 | <-- =B6*(1+1.2%) | | | | |
| 8 | | | | $ 1,036.43 | <-- =C7*(1+1.2%) | | | |
| 9 | | | | | $ 1,048.87 | <-- =D8*(1+1.2%) | | |
| 10 | | | | | | $ 1,061.46 | <-- =E9*(1+1.2%) | |
| 11 | | | | | | | $ 1,074.19 | <-- =F10*(1+1.2%) |
| 12 | | | | | | | | |
| 13 | Month 7 | Month 8 | Month 9 | Month 10 | Month 11 | Month 12 | | |
| 14 | $ 1,087.09 | <-- =G11*(1+1.2%) | | | | | | |
| 15 | | $ 1,100.13 | <-- =A14*(1+1.2%) | | | | | |
| 16 | | | $ 1,113.33 | <-- =B15*(1+1.2%) | | | | |
| 17 | | | | $ 1,126.69 | <-- =C16*(1+1.2%) | | | |
| 18 | | | | | $ 1,140.21 | <-- =D17*(1+1.2%) | | |
| 19 | | | | | | $ 1,153.89 | <-- =E18*(1+1.2%) | |

By the end of the year, you will owe Loan Shark $1,153.89.

$$\$1,153.89 = \$1,500 * \left(1 + \underbrace{\frac{14.4\%}{12}}\right)^{12}$$

Loan Shark's loan is "compounded monthly." This means that the 14.4% annual interest translates to 1.2% per month.

Because this is more than the $1,150 you will owe the bank, you should prefer the bank loan.

The effective annual interest rate (EAIR) of each loan is the *annualized interest rate* charged by the loan. The bank charges you 15% annually and the loan shark charges you 15.39% annually:

| | A | B | C | D |
|---|---|---|---|---|
| 1 | | THE BANK OR LOAN SHARK? | | |
| 2 | | Bank | Loan Shark | |
| 3 | Quoted interest rate | 15.0% | 14.4% | |
| 4 | Borrow today | 1,000.00 | 1,000.00 | |
| 5 | Repay in one year | -1,150.00 | -1,153.89 | <-- =-C4*(1+C3/12)^12 |
| 6 | Effective annual interest rate, EAIR | 15.00% | 15.39% | <-- =-C5/C4-1 |
| 7 | | | | |
| 8 | A second way to compute the EAIR | | | |
| 9 | Monthly interest rate | | 1.20% | <-- =C3/12 |
| 10 | EAIR Annualized monthly rate | | 15.39% | <-- =(1+C9)^12-1 |

Cells C9 and C10 show another way to compute the 15.39% EAIR charged by the loan shark. Cell C9 computes the monthly rate charged by the loan shark as 1.20%, and cell C10

annualizes this rate $\left(1+\dfrac{14.4\%}{12}\right)^{12}-1=15.39\%$. Thus, there are two ways to compute the EAIR:

$$EAIR = 15.39\% = \begin{cases} \dfrac{\textit{Payment at end of year}}{\textit{Loan taken out beginning of year}} - 1 = \dfrac{\$1,153.89}{\$1,000.00} - 1 & \leftarrow \text{Cell C6} \\[2em] \left(1+\dfrac{14.4\%}{12}\right)^{12} - 1 & \leftarrow \text{Cell C10} \end{cases}$$

**The lesson of Example 2:** The annual percentage rate (APR) does not always correctly reflect the costs of borrowing. To compute the true cost, calculate the effective annual interest rate (EAIR).

## Example 3: An "Interest Free" Loan

You're buying a used car. The Junkmobile your heart desires has a price tag of $2,000. You have two financing options:

- The dealer explains that if you pay cash you'll get a 15% discount. In this case you'll pay $1,700 for the car today. Because you don't have any money now, you intend to borrow the $1,700 from your Uncle Frank, who charges 10% interest.

- On the other hand, the dealer will give you "0% financing": You don't pay anything now, and you can pay the dealer the full cost of the Junkmobile at the end of the year.

Thus, you have two choices: The dealer's 0% financing and Uncle Frank's 10% rate. Which is cheaper?

A little thought will show that the dealer is actually charging you an effective annual interest rate (EAIR) of 17.65%: His "0% financing" essentially involves a loan to you of $1,700 with an end-year repayment of $2,000:

| | A | B | C | D | E |
|---|---|---|---|---|---|
| 1 | **FINANCING THE JUNKMOBILE** | | | | |
| 2 | **Year** | **Pay cash** | **Dealer's "0% financing"** | **Differential cash flow** | |
| 3 | 0 | -1,700 | 0 | 1,700 | <-- =C3-B3 |
| 4 | 1 | | -2,000 | -2,000 | <-- =C4-B4 |
| 5 | | | | | |
| 6 | Effective annual interest rate (EAIR) charged by dealer | | | 17.65% | <-- =IRR(D3:D4) |

Uncle Frank's EAIR is 10%: He will loan you $1,700 and have you repay only $1,870. So you're better off borrowing from him.

**The lesson of Example 3:** Free loans are usually not free! To compute the cost of a "free" loan, calculate the EAIR of the differential cash flows.

# 3.2. Calculating the Cost of a Mortgage

Now that we've set the stage, we'll proceed to a series of somewhat more complicated examples. We start with a mortgage. Housing is most often the largest personal asset an individual owns. Financing housing with a mortgage is something almost every reader of this book will do in his or her lifetime. Calculating the cost of a mortgage is thus a useful exercise. In this chapter mortgages will be one of the examples we use to illustrate the problems encountered in computing the cost of financial assets.

## A Simple Mortgage

We start with a simple example. Your bank has agreed to give you a $100,000 mortgage, to be repaid over 10 years at 8% interest. For simplicity, we assume that the payments on the mortgage are annual.[2] The bank calculates the annual payment as $14,902.95, using Excel's **PMT** function.

The **PMT** function calculates an annuity payment (a constant periodic payment) that pays off a loan:

$$100,000 = \sum_{t=1}^{10} \frac{14,902.95}{(1.08)^t} = \frac{14,902.95}{(1.08)} + \frac{14,902.95}{(1.08)^2} + \frac{14,902.95}{(1.08)^3} + \cdots + \frac{14,902.95}{(1.08)^{10}}$$

---

[2]In the real world payments are probably monthly; see the example in Section 3.3.

## DIALOG BOX FOR PMT FUNCTION

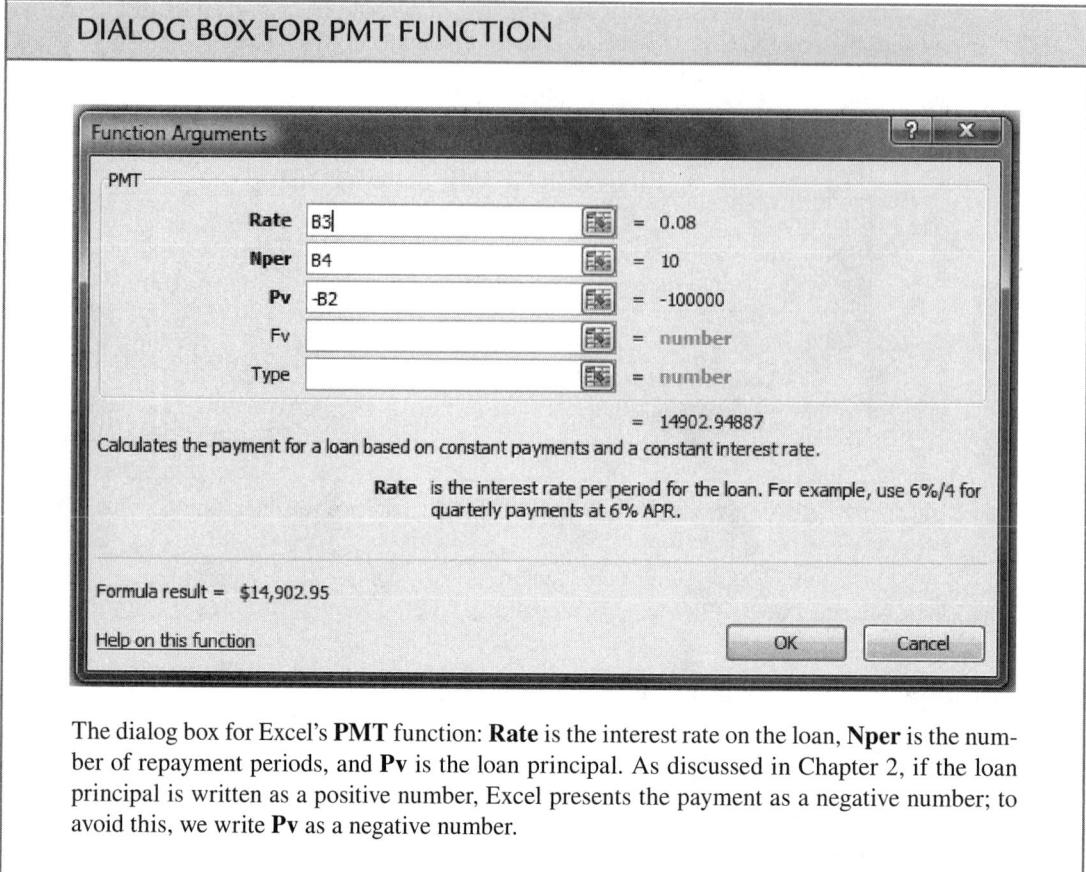

The dialog box for Excel's **PMT** function: **Rate** is the interest rate on the loan, **Nper** is the number of repayment periods, and **Pv** is the loan principal. As discussed in Chapter 2, if the loan principal is written as a positive number, Excel presents the payment as a negative number; to avoid this, we write **Pv** as a negative number.

We can summarize all of this in an Excel spreadsheet:

|    | A | B | C |
|----|---|---|---|
| 1 | **A SIMPLE MORTGAGE** | | |
| 2 | Mortgage principal | 100,000 | |
| 3 | Interest rate | 8% | |
| 4 | Mortgage term (years) | 10 | |
| 5 | Annual payment | $14,902.95 | <-- =PMT(B3,B4,-B2) |
| 6 | | | |
| 7 | Year | Mortgage cash flow | |
| 8 | 0 | 100,000.00 | |
| 9 | 1 | -14,902.95 | <-- =-$B$5 |
| 10 | 2 | -14,902.95 | |
| 11 | 3 | -14,902.95 | |
| 12 | 4 | -14,902.95 | |
| 13 | 5 | -14,902.95 | |
| 14 | 6 | -14,902.95 | |
| 15 | 7 | -14,902.95 | |
| 16 | 8 | -14,902.95 | |
| 17 | 9 | -14,902.95 | |
| 18 | 10 | -14,902.95 | |
| 19 | | | |
| 20 | Effective annual interest rate (EAIR) | 8.00% | <-- =IRR(B8:B18) |

The EAIR of this particular mortgage is simply the internal rate of return of its payments. Because the payments on the mortgage are annual, the IRR in cell B20 is already in annual terms.

## The Bank Charges "Mortgage Points"

As in the previous example, you've asked the bank for a $100,000 mortgage. They've agreed to give you this mortgage, and they've explained that you'll be asked to repay $14,902.95 per year for the next 10 years. However, when you get to the bank, you learn that the bank has deducted "1.5 points" from your mortgage. What this means is that you only get $98,500 ($100,000 minus 1.5%). Your payments, however, continue to be based on a principal of $100,000.[3] You realize immediately that this mortgage is more expensive than the mortgage discussed in the previous subsection. The question is: by *how much* is it more expensive? By calculating the EAIR on the mortgage we can answer this question. The calculation below shows that you're actually paying 8.34% interest annually.

| | A | B | C |
|---|---|---|---|
| 1 | **A MORTGAGE WITH POINTS** | | |
| 2 | Mortgage principal | 100,000 | |
| 3 | "Points" | 1.50% | |
| 4 | Quoted interest | 8.00% | |
| 5 | Mortgage term (years) | 10 | |
| 6 | Annual payment | $14,902.95 | <-- =PMT(B4,B5,-B2) |
| 7 | | | |
| 8 | Year | Mortgage cash flow | |
| 9 | 0 | 98,500.00 | <-- =B2*(1-B3) |
| 10 | 1 | -14,902.95 | <-- =-$B$6 |
| 11 | 2 | -14,902.95 | |
| 12 | 3 | -14,902.95 | |
| 13 | 4 | -14,902.95 | |
| 14 | 5 | -14,902.95 | |
| 15 | 6 | -14,902.95 | |
| 16 | 7 | -14,902.95 | |
| 17 | 8 | -14,902.95 | |
| 18 | 9 | -14,902.95 | |
| 19 | 10 | -14,902.95 | |
| 20 | | | |
| 21 | Effective annual interest rate (EAIR) | 8.34% | <-- =IRR(B9:B19) |

Note that the EAIR of 8.34% is the IRR of the stream of payments consisting of the actual loan amount ($98,500) versus the actual payments you're making ($14,902.95 annually). Here's the calculation:

$$98,500 = \sum_{t=1}^{10} \frac{14,902.95}{(1.0834)^t} = \frac{14,902.95}{(1.0834)} + \frac{14,902.95}{(1.0834)^2} + \frac{14,902.95}{(1.0834)^3} + \cdots + \frac{14,902.95}{(1.0834)^{10}}$$

---

[3]Some banks and mortgage brokers also charge an "origination fee," defined as a payment to cover the initial cost of processing the mortgage. The net effect of "points" and the "origination fee" is the same—you are charged interest on more money than you actually get in hand.

At the end of each year, you will report to the Internal Revenue Service the amount of interest paid on the mortgage. Because this interest is an expense for tax purposes, it's important to get it right. To calculate this interest, we need a loan table, which allocates the each year's payment made between interest and repayment of principal (see Section 2.5, page 42). This table is sometimes called an "amortization table" ("amortize" means to repay with a series of periodic payments):

| | A | B | C | D | E | F |
|---|---|---|---|---|---|---|
| 21 | Effective annual interest rate | 8.34% | <-- =IRR(B9:B19) | | | |
| 22 | | | | | | |
| 23 | **MORTGAGE AMORTIZATION TABLE** | | | | | |
| 24 | Year | Mortgage principal at beginning of year | Payment at end of year | Part of payment that is interest (expense for taxes!) | Part of payment that is repayment of principal (not an expense for tax purposes) | |
| 25 | 1 | 98,500.00 | $14,902.95 | $8,211.41 | 6,691.54 | <-- =C25-D25 |
| 26 | 2 | 91,808.46 | $14,902.95 | $7,653.58 | 7,249.37 | |
| 27 | 3 | 84,559.09 | $14,902.95 | $7,049.23 | 7,853.71 | |
| 28 | 4 | 76,705.38 | $14,902.95 | $6,394.51 | 8,508.44 | |
| 29 | 5 | 68,196.94 | $14,902.95 | $5,685.21 | 9,217.74 | |
| 30 | 6 | 58,979.20 | $14,902.95 | $4,916.78 | 9,986.17 | |
| 31 | 7 | 48,993.03 | $14,902.95 | $4,084.28 | 10,818.66 | |
| 32 | 8 | 38,174.37 | $14,902.95 | $3,182.39 | 11,720.56 | |
| 33 | 9 | 26,453.81 | $14,902.95 | $2,205.31 | 12,697.64 | |
| 34 | 10 | 13,756.17 | $14,902.95 | $1,146.78 | 13,756.17 | |

(Annotations: B25-E25 points to the Payment column; $B$21*B25 points to the Part of payment that is interest column.)

Column D of the table gives the interest expense for tax purposes. If you report interest payments on your tax return, this is the payment you'd be allowed to report. Note that the interest portion of the annual $14,902.95 payments gets smaller over the years, whereas the repayment of the principal portion (which is not deductible for tax purposes) gets larger.

## Calculating the Individual Payments with IPMT and PPMT

The above spreadsheet gives the intuition behind the loan table and the split between interest and principal of each payment. The interest and repayment-of-principal payments can be computed directly using the Excel functions **IPMT** and **PPMT**. This is illustrated below.[4]

---

[4]Note that **IPMT** and **PPMT** work only when the loan payments are equal.

| | A | B | C | D | E | F | G |
|---|---|---|---|---|---|---|---|
| 1 | | **COMPUTING THE MORTGAGE PAYMENTS USING IPMT AND PPMT** | | | | | |
| 2 | Loan principal | 100,000 | | | | | |
| 3 | Points | 1.50% | | | | | |
| 4 | Quoted interest | 8.00% | | | The interest rate from the previous spreadsheet has been formatted to show only two decimal places. The actual interest rate is 8.336459884% | | |
| 5 | Term (years) | 10 | | | | | |
| 6 | Effective interest rate | 8.34% <-- ='Mortgage with points'!B21 | | | | | |
| 7 | Annual payment | $14,902.95 <-- =PMT(B6,B5,-B2*(1-B3)) | | | | | |
| 8 | | | | | | | |
| 9 | **MORTGAGE AMORTIZATION TABLE** | | | | | | |
| 10 | Year | Mortgage principal at beginning of year | Payment at end of year | Part of payment that is interest | Part of payment that is repayment of principal | | |
| 11 | 1 | 100,000.00 | $14,902.95 | $8,336.46 | 6,793.44 | | |
| 12 | 2 | 93,206.56 | $14,902.95 | $7,770.13 | 7,359.77 | | |
| 13 | 3 | 85,846.79 | $14,902.95 | $7,156.58 | 7,973.31 | | |
| 14 | 4 | 77,873.48 | $14,902.95 | $6,491.89 | 8,638.01 | | |
| 15 | 5 | 69,235.47 | $14,902.95 | $5,771.79 | 9,358.11 | | |
| 16 | 6 | 59,877.36 | $14,902.95 | $4,991.65 | 10,138.24 | | |
| 17 | 7 | 49,739.12 | $14,902.95 | $4,146.48 | 10,983.42 | | |
| 18 | 8 | 38,755.70 | $14,902.95 | $3,230.85 | 11,899.04 | | |
| 19 | 9 | 26,856.66 | $14,902.95 | $2,238.89 | 12,891.00 | | |
| 20 | 10 | 13,965.66 | $14,902.95 | $1,164.24 | 13,965.66 | | |
| 21 | | | | | | | |
| 22 | | =IPMT($B$6,A11,$B$5,-$B$2) | | | | | |
| 23 | | | | | | | |
| 24 | | | | =PPMT($B$6,A11,$B$5,-$B$2) | | | |

Here is the dialog box for **IPMT** in cell D9 (the syntax of **PPMT** is similar). Note that **Per** specifies the specific period for which the interest is calculated:

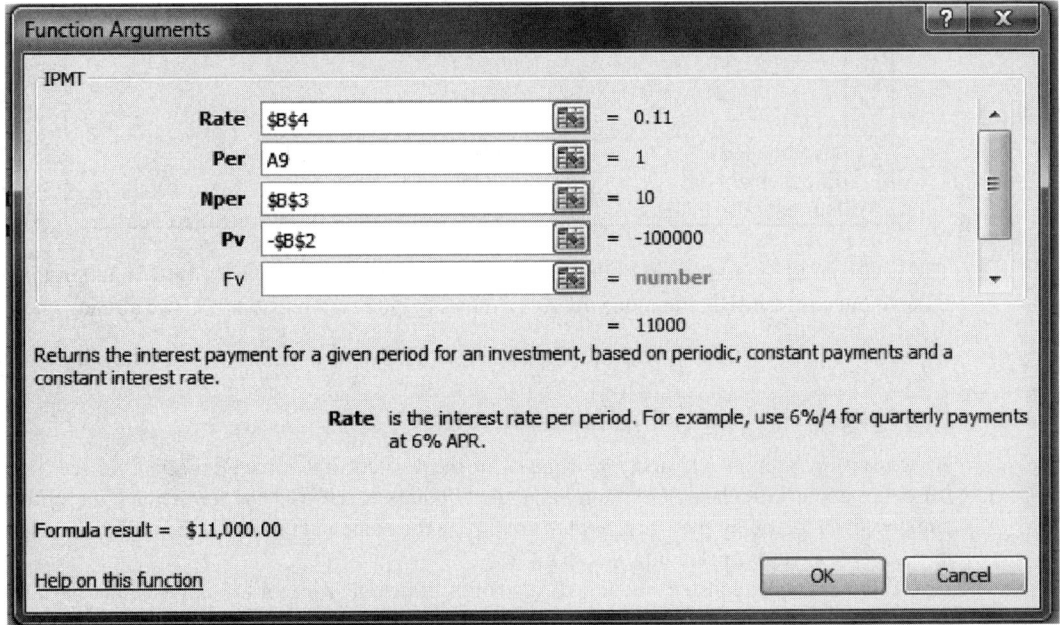

## 3.3. Mortgages with Monthly Payments

We continue with the mortgage examples from Section 3.2. This time we introduce the concept of monthly payments. Suppose you get a $100,000 mortgage with an 8% interest rate, payable monthly, and suppose you have to pay the mortgage back over 1 year (12 months).[5] Many banks interpret the combination of 8% annual interest and "payable monthly" to mean that the monthly interest on the mortgage is $\frac{8\%}{12} = 0.667\%$. This is often referred to as "monthly compounding," although the usage of this term is not uniform. To compute the monthly repayment on the mortgage, we use Excel's **PMT** function:

|    | A | B | C |
|----|---|---|---|
| 1  | **MORTGAGE WITH MONTHLY PAYMENTS** | | |
| 2  | Loan principal | 100,000 | |
| 3  | Loan term (years) | 1 | |
| 4  | Quoted interest rate | 8% | |
| 5  | | | |
| 6  | **Month** | **Cash flow** | |
| 7  | 0 | 100,000.00 | |
| 8  | 1 | -8,698.84 | <-- =PMT($B$4/12,$B$3*12,$B$2) |
| 9  | 2 | -8,698.84 | |
| 10 | 3 | -8,698.84 | |
| 11 | 4 | -8,698.84 | |
| 12 | 5 | -8,698.84 | |
| 13 | 6 | -8,698.84 | |
| 14 | 7 | -8,698.84 | |
| 15 | 8 | -8,698.84 | |
| 16 | 9 | -8,698.84 | |
| 17 | 10 | -8,698.84 | |
| 18 | 11 | -8,698.84 | |
| 19 | 12 | -8,698.84 | |
| 20 | | | |
| 21 | Monthly IRR | 0.667% | <-- =IRR(B7:B19) |
| 22 | Effective annual interest rate, EAIR | 8.30% | <-- =(1+B21)^12-1 |

The EAIR on the mortgage in the example is computed by using Excel's **IRR** function (cell B21). In our case the **IRR** function will give a monthly interest rate of 0.667% (we already knew this because $\frac{8\%}{12} = 0.667\%$). Annualizing this gives $8.30\% = \left(1 + \frac{8\%}{12}\right)^{12} - 1$ (cell B22).

## Mortgages: A More Complicated Example

As we saw in Section 3.1, many mortgages in the United States have "origination fees" or "discount points" (the latter are often just called "points"). All of these fees reduce the initial amount given to you by the bank, *without reducing* the principal on which the bank computes its payments (sounds misleading, doesn't it?).

As an example, consider the above 12-month mortgage with an 8% annual rate, payable monthly, but with an origination fee of 0.5% and 1 point. This means that you actually get

---

[5] Most mortgages are, of course, for a much longer term. But 12 months enables us to fit the example comfortably within a page. Later we'll consider longer terms, but the principles will be the same.

$98,500 ($100,000 minus $500 for the origination fee and $1,000 for the point), but that your monthly repayment remains $8,698.84:

| | A | B | C |
|---|---|---|---|
| 1 | **MORTGAGE EXAMPLE WITH POINTS AND ORIGINATION FEE** | | |
| 2 | Loan principal | 100,000.00 | |
| 3 | Loan term (years) | 1 | |
| 4 | Quoted interest rate | 8% | |
| 5 | Discount points | 1 | |
| 6 | Origination fee | 0.5% | |
| 7 | | | |
| 8 | **Month** | **Cash flow** | |
| 9 | 0 | 98,500.00 | <-- =B2*(1-B5/100-B6) |
| 10 | 1 | -8,698.84 | <-- =PMT($B$4/12,$B$3*12,$B$2) |
| 11 | 2 | -8,698.84 | |
| 12 | 3 | -8,698.84 | |
| 13 | 4 | -8,698.84 | |
| 14 | 5 | -8,698.84 | |
| 15 | 6 | -8,698.84 | |
| 16 | 7 | -8,698.84 | |
| 17 | 8 | -8,698.84 | |
| 18 | 9 | -8,698.84 | |
| 19 | 10 | -8,698.84 | |
| 20 | 11 | -8,698.84 | |
| 21 | 12 | -8,698.84 | |
| 22 | | | |
| 23 | Monthly IRR | 0.9044% | <-- =IRR(B9:B21) |
| 24 | EAIR | 11.41% | <-- =(1+B23)^12-1 |
| 25 | | | |
| 26 | Monthly IRR using Excel's **Rate** function | 0.9044% | <-- =RATE(12,8698.84,-98500) |

The monthly IRR (cell B23) is the interest rate that sets the present value of the monthly payments equal to the initial $98,500 received:

$$\$98,500 = \frac{\$8,698.94}{(1+0.9044\%)} + \frac{\$8,698.94}{(1+0.9044\%)^2} + \frac{\$8,698.94}{(1+0.9044\%)^3} + \ldots + \frac{\$8,698.94}{(1+0.9044\%)^{12}}.$$

$EAIR = 11.41\% = (1+0.9044\%)^{12} - 1$ is the annualized cost of the mortgage payments.

As you can see in cell B26, Excel's **Rate** function will also calculate the monthly IRR that we've calculated in cell B23.

## EXCEL NOTE: CALCULATING THE MONTHLY IRR WITH RATE

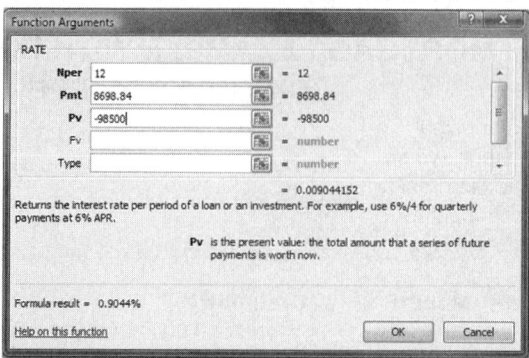

The **Rate** function computes the IRR of a series of constant (the financial jargon is "flat" or "even") payments so that the discounted value equals the **PV** indicated. Note that in the **Rate** function the signs of the payments (indicated by **Pmt**) and the **Pv** of these payments must be different. This is a feature **Rate** shares with Excel functions like **PMT** and **PV,** discussed in Chapter 2.

## Longer-Term Mortgages

Suppose the mortgage in the previous example has a 30-year term (meaning: 360 = 30 * 12 repayments). Each repayment would be $733.76 and the EAIR would be 8.4721%:

| | A | B | C |
|---|---|---|---|
| 1 | **30-YEAR MORTGAGE**<br>**with points and origination fee** | | |
| 2 | Loan principal | 100,000.00 | |
| 3 | Loan term (years) | 30 | |
| 4 | Quoted interest rate | 8% | |
| 5 | Discount points | 1 | |
| 6 | Origination fee | 0.5% | |
| 7 | | | |
| 8 | Initial amount of loan, net of fees | 98,500.00 | <-- =B2*(1-B5/100-B6) |
| 9 | Monthly repayment | 733.76 | <-- =PMT(B4/12,B3*12,-B2) |
| 10 | | | |
| 11 | **Calculating the EAIR** | | |
| 12 | Monthly interest rate | 0.6800% | <-- =RATE(B3*12,B9,-B8) |
| 13 | Effective annual interest rate (EAIR) | 8.4721% | <-- =(1+B12)^12-1 |

We've used **PMT** to calculate the payment and **Rate** to compute the monthly interest rate. The EAIR is computed in the usual manner—by compounding the monthly payments (cell B13).

Note that the effect of the initial mortgage fees on mortgage EAIR declines when the mortgage is longer term:

- For the 1-year mortgage discussed previously, the 1.5% initial fee increased the EAIR of the mortgage from 8 to 11.41%.

- For the 30-year mortgage, the same initial fees increase the EAIR from 8 to 8.4721%.

- The reason that the fees have a smaller effect for the second mortgage is that they are spread out over a much longer term.

# 3.4. Lease or Purchase?

This section uses the concepts of present value and internal rate of return to explore the relative advantages of leasing versus buying an asset. As you will see, the choice between leasing and buying basically comes down to choosing the cheaper of two methods of financing.

Here's our terminology: A *lease* is a rental agreement; in our examples leases will usually be for equipment (we discuss a computer lease and a car lease), but the analysis for real estate is virtually the same. The party that rents the asset and uses it is called the *lessee* and the owner of the asset is called the *lessor*.

## A Simple Lease Example

You need a new computer, but you can't decide whether you should buy it or lease it. The computer costs $4,000. The lessor is your neighborhood computer leasing company, which offers to lease you the computer for $1,500 per year. The lessor's conditions are that you make four payments of $1,500: the first payment at the start of the lease (time 0) and subsequent payments at the end of years 1, 2, and 3. Based on past experience, you know that you will keep your new computer for about 3 years. One additional fact: you can borrow from your bank at 15%.

Here is a spreadsheet with the cash flows for the lease and for the purchase:

| | A | B | C | D |
|---|---|---|---|---|
| 1 | | **BASIC LEASE VERSUS PURCHASE** | | |
| 2 | Asset cost | 4,000.00 | | |
| 3 | Annual lease payment | 1,500.00 | | |
| 4 | Bank rate | 15% | | |
| 5 | | | | |
| 6 | Year | **Purchase cash flow** | **Lease cash flow** | |
| 7 | 0 | 4,000.00 | 1,500.00 | |
| 8 | 1 | | 1,500.00 | |
| 9 | 2 | | 1,500.00 | |
| 10 | 3 | | 1,500.00 | |
| 11 | | | | |
| 12 | PV of costs | 4,000.00 | 4,924.84 | <-- =C7+NPV($B$4,C8:C10) |
| 13 | Lease or purchase? | purchase | | <-- =IF(B12<C12,"purchase","lease") |

To decide whether the lease is preferable, we discount the cash flows from both the lease and the purchase at the 15% bank lending rate. We write the outflows as positive numbers, so that the PV in row 12 is the *present value of the costs*. As you can see in cell B12, the PV of the lease costs is $4,924.84, which is more than the $4,000 cost of purchasing the computer. Thus, you prefer the purchase, which is less costly.

There's another way of doing this same calculation. We compute the IRR of the *differential* cash flows—subtracting the lease cash flow from the purchase cash flow in each of the years:

| | A | B | C | D | E |
|---|---|---|---|---|---|
| 1 | | BASIC LEASE VERSUS PURCHASE<br>THE DIFFERENTIAL CASH FLOWS | | | |
| 2 | Asset cost | 4,000 | | | |
| 3 | Annual lease payment | 1,500 | | | |
| 4 | Bank rate | 15% | | | |
| 5 | | | | | |
| 6 | Year | Purchase cash flow | Lease cash flow | Differential cash flow | |
| 7 | 0 | 4,000 | 1,500 | 2,500 | <-- =B7-C7 |
| 8 | 1 | | 1,500 | -1,500 | <-- =B8-C8 |
| 9 | 2 | | 1,500 | -1,500 | <-- =B9-C9 |
| 10 | 3 | | 1,500 | -1,500 | <-- =B10-C10 |
| 11 | | | | | |
| 12 | IRR of differential cash flows | | | 36.31% | <-- =IRR(D7:D10) |
| 13 | Lease or purchase? | | | purchase | <-- =IF(D12>B4,"purchase","lease") |
| 14 | | | | | |
| 15 | Explanation: The lease is like a loan--you save 2,500 in year 0 and pay back 1,500 in each of years 1-3. The IRR of this "loan" is 36.31%. | | | | |

The computer lease is equivalent to paying $1,500 for the computer in year 0 and taking a loan of $2,500 from the computer leasing company. The computer leasing "loan" has three equal repayments of $1,500 and an IRR of 36.31%. Because you can borrow money from the bank at 15%, you would prefer to purchase the computer with borrowed money from the bank (at 15%) rather than "borrowing" $2,500 from the leasing company, which charges 36.31%.

In the spreadsheet below you can see another way to make this same point. If you borrowed $2,500 from the bank at 15%, you'd have to pay back $1,094.94 per year for each of the next 3 years (assuming the bank asked for a flat repayment schedule). This is substantially less than the $1,500 that the computer lessor asks for on the same loan.

$$2,500 = \frac{1,094.94}{1.15} + \frac{1,094.94}{(1.15)^2} + \frac{1,094.94}{(1.15)^3}.$$

The conclusion is that if you decide to borrow $2,500 to purchase the computer, you should do so from the bank rather than from the computer leasing company. In the spreadsheet, we've used the Excel **PMT** function to compute the repayment:

| | A | B | C | D | E |
|---|---|---|---|---|---|
| 17 | What if you borrowed $2,500 from the bank? | | | | |
| 18 | Year | Money saved by leasing | | Same amount from bank | |
| 19 | 0 | 2,500 | | 2,500.00 | |
| 20 | 1 | -1,500 | | -1,094.94 | <-- =PMT($B$4,3,$D$19) |
| 21 | 2 | -1,500 | | -1,094.94 | |
| 22 | 3 | -1,500 | | -1,094.94 | |

## What Have We Assumed about Leasing versus Purchasing?

The leasing example we've considered above illustrates the spirit of lease/purchase analysis. The example makes some simplifying assumptions that are worth noting:

- No taxes: When corporations lease equipment, the lease payments are expenses for tax purposes; when these corporations buy assets, the depreciation on the asset is an expense for tax payments. Taxes complicate the analysis somewhat; the case of leasing with taxes is considered in Chapter 5.

- Operational equivalence of lease and purchase: In our analysis we don't ask whether you need a computer—we assume that you've already answered this question positively, so that only the method of acquisition is in question. Our analysis also assumes that any maintenance or repairs that need to be done on the computer will be done by you, whether you lease or buy the computer.

- No residual value: We've assumed that the asset (in this case, the computer) is worthless at the end of the lease term.

We explore the last point briefly. Suppose you think that the computer will be worth $800 at the end of year 3. Then—as shown below—the purchase cash flows change, so that owning the computer gives you an inflow of $800 in year 3.[6] The cost of purchasing the computer is reduced (the present value of the purchase is now $3,304) and the lease alternative becomes even less attractive than the purchase. Another way of seeing this is to look at the IRR of the differential cash flows, which is now 45.07% (cell B23).[7]

| | A | B | C | D |
|---|---|---|---|---|
| 1 | **LEASE VERSUS PURCHASE WITH RESIDUAL VALUE** | | | |
| 2 | Asset cost | 4,000.00 | | |
| 3 | Annual lease payment | 1,500.00 | | |
| 4 | Residual value, yr. 3 | 800 | <-- Value of computer at end year 3 | |
| 5 | Bank rate | 15% | | |
| 6 | | | | |
| 7 | Year | **Purchase cash flow** | **Lease cash flow** | |
| 8 | 0 | 4,000.00 | 1,500.00 | |
| 9 | 1 | | 1,500.00 | |
| 10 | 2 | | 1,500.00 | |
| 11 | 3 | -800.00 | 1,500.00 | |
| 12 | | | | |
| 13 | PV of costs | 3,304.35 | 4,924.84 | <-- =C8+NPV($B$5,C9:C11) |
| 14 | Lease or purchase? | | purchase | <-- =IF(B13<C13,"purchase","lease") |
| 15 | | | | |
| 16 | Calculating the IRR of the differential cash flow | | | |
| 17 | Year | | **Money saved by leasing** | |
| 18 | 0 | | 2,500.00 | <-- =B8-C8 |
| 19 | 1 | | -1,500.00 | <-- =B9-C9 |
| 20 | 2 | | -1,500.00 | |
| 21 | 3 | | -2,300.00 | |
| 22 | | | | |
| 23 | IRR of differential | | 45.07% | <-- =IRR(C18:C21) |
| 24 | Lease or purchase? | | purchase | <-- =IF(C23>B5,"purchase","lease") |

[6]Note that because we're writing *outflows* (like the cost of the computer) as *positive numbers*, we have to write the inflows as negative numbers.

[7]A caveat is in order here: We're treating the computer's residual value as if it has the same certainty as the rest of the cash flows, whereas clearly it is less certain. The finance literature has a technical solution to this: We find the *certainty equivalent* of the residual value. For example, it may be that we expect the residual value to be $1,200, but that—recognizing the uncertainty of getting this value—we treat this as equivalent to getting an $800 residual with certainty.

## 3.5. Auto Lease Example

Here's a slightly more realistic (and more complicated) example of leasing: You've decided to get a new car. You can either lease the car or buy it; if you decide to buy the car, you can finance with a 3% bank loan. The relevant facts are given in the spreadsheet that follows, but we'll summarize them here:

- The manufacturer's suggested retail price (MSRP) for the car is $24,550, but you've been able to negotiate a price of $22,490 with the dealer.[8] In the jargon of the car leasing business, the $22,490 is referred to as the "capitalized cost." To this price must be added a destination charge of $415, so that you end up paying $22,905 if you purchase the car. This price represents your alternative purchase cost if you decide to buy instead of lease the car.

- The dealer has offered you the following lease terms:

  - You pay $1,315 at the signing of the lease. The dealer explains that this is the total of $415 "destination charge," $450 "acquisition fee," and a $450 security deposit. The security deposit will be refunded at the end of the lease.

  - You will pay $373.43 per month for the next 24 months. In month 24 you get your security deposit of $450 back.

  - You guarantee that the car will have a residual value of $13,994 at the end of the lease. The dealer has based this value on 57% of the MSRP. What this means is that if the car is worth less than $13,994 at the end of the 24th month, the lessee (you) will make up the difference.[9] The end-lease payment associated with this residual can be written as:

$$End\text{-}lease\ residual\ payment = \begin{cases} 13,994 - market\ value & if\ market\ value\quad 13,994 \\ 0 & otherwise \end{cases}$$

Another way of writing this payment is $Max(13,994 - market\ value, 0)$. The $max(A,B)$ notation means that you pay the larger of $A$ or $B$. Conveniently, **Max** is also a function in Excel.

The residual value turns out to be an important factor in the way you view leasing versus purchase. We'll devote more time to it later. For the moment, let's assume that you think the car will actually be worth $15,000 at the end of 2 years so your last payment on the lease is zero:

$$End\text{-}lease\ residual\ payment = Max(13,994 - market\ value, 0)$$
$$= Max(13,994 - 15,000, 0) = Max(-1,006, 0) = 0$$

All of the lease costs are listed in column C of the following spreadsheet. To evaluate these costs, look at column D, which shows the costs associated with buying the car; there are only

---

[8] The "manufacturer's suggested retail price" (MSRP—also referred to as the car's "sticker price"—is the price the auto manufacturer suggests as an appropriate price for the car. In reality it's a kind of official fiction and forms the basis for negotiation between the dealer and the car purchaser. In our example the MSRP is used in the residual value computation, but the actual price paid for the car is less.

[9] According to *www.edmunds.com*: "The lease-end fees are generally reasonable, unless the car has 100,000 miles on it, a busted-up grille and melted chocolate smeared into the upholstery. Dealers and financial institutions want you to buy or lease another car from them, and can be rather lenient regarding excess mileage and abnormal wear. After all, if they hit you with a bunch of trumped-up charges you're not going to remain a loyal customer, are you?...But keep in mind that if you take your business elsewhere, you're going to be facing a bill for items like worn tires, paint chips, door dings, and the like."

two: the initial purchase price of the car ($22,490 + the destination cost of $415 = $22,905) and what you anticipate will be the market value of the car at the end of the lease term (in the example below, you think the car will actually be worth $15,000). Because we've used the convention of making costs positive numbers, the inflow from selling the car is a negative number.

This last number bears some examination: If you lease, your last payment is

$$last\ lease\ payment = last\ month's\ rental - return\ of\ security\ deposit$$
$$+ end\text{-}of\text{-}lease\ residual\ payment$$
$$= 373.43 - 450 + Max(13,994 - market\ value, 0)$$

If you're right, and the actual market value of the car is $15,000, then your last "payment" is −$76.57 (meaning that you'll get $76.57 back from the lease company).

| | A | B | C | D | E | F |
|---|---|---|---|---|---|---|
| 1 | | AUTO LEASE VERSUS PURCHASE | | | | |
| 2 | MSRP | 24,550 | <-- Manufacturer's suggested retail price | | | |
| 3 | Capitalized cost | 22,490 | <-- Negotiated price | | | |
| 4 | Destination charge | 415 | <-- Paid both by the lessee and the buyer | | | |
| 5 | Acquisition fee | 450 | <-- Paid only by the lessee | | | |
| 6 | Security deposit | 450 | <-- refunded at end of lease | | | |
| 7 | | | | | | |
| 8 | Payment due at signing | 1,315 | <-- =SUM(B4:B6) | | | |
| 9 | Monthly payment | 373.43 | <-- Dealer's lease offer | | | |
| 10 | | | | | | |
| 11 | | | | | | |
| 12 | Residual value after 2 years as % of MSRP | 57% | | | | |
| 13 | Lease residual value after 2 years | 13,994 | <-- =B12*B2--lessee guarantees this value | | | |
| 14 | Your estimated residual value | 15,000 | <-- Your guess | | | |
| 15 | | | | | | |
| 16 | | | | | =B3+B4 | |
| 17 | | Month | Payment | Purchase | Difference | |
| 18 | | 0 | 1,315.00 | 22,905.00 | 21,590.00 | <-- =D18-C18 |
| 19 | =B8 | 1 | 373.43 | | -373.43 | <-- =D19-C19 |
| 20 | | 2 | 373.43 | | -373.43 | <-- =D20-C20 |
| 21 | | 3 | 373.43 | | -373.43 | |
| 22 | | 4 | 373.43 | | -373.43 | |
| 23 | | 5 | 373.43 | | -373.43 | |
| 24 | | 6 | 373.43 | | -373.43 | |
| 25 | | 7 | 373.43 | | -373.43 | |
| 26 | | 8 | 373.43 | | -373.43 | |
| 27 | | 9 | 373.43 | | -373.43 | |
| 28 | | 10 | 373.43 | | -373.43 | |
| 29 | | 11 | 373.43 | | -373.43 | |
| 30 | | 12 | 373.43 | | -373.43 | |
| 31 | | 13 | 373.43 | | -373.43 | |
| 32 | | 14 | 373.43 | | -373.43 | |
| 33 | | 15 | 373.43 | | -373.43 | |
| 34 | | 16 | 373.43 | | -373.43 | |
| 35 | | 17 | 373.43 | | -373.43 | |
| 36 | | 18 | 373.43 | | -373.43 | |
| 37 | | 19 | 373.43 | | -373.43 | |
| 38 | | 20 | 373.43 | | -373.43 | |
| 39 | | 21 | 373.43 | | -373.43 | |
| 40 | | 22 | 373.43 | | -373.43 | |
| 41 | | 23 | 373.43 | | -373.43 | |
| 42 | | 24 | -76.57 | -15,000.00 | -14,923.43 | <-- =D42-C42 |
| 43 | | | | | | |
| 44 | =$B$9-B6+MAX(B13-B14,0) | | Monthly IRR | | 0.44% | <-- =IRR(E18:E42) |
| 45 | | | EAIR | | 5.39% | <-- =(1+E44)^12-1 |
| 46 | | | | | | |
| 47 | | | Buy or lease? | | | |
| 48 | | | Alternative financing | | 7% | |
| 49 | | | Buy or lease? | | lease | <-- =IF(E48>E45,"lease","buy") |

Column E in the spreadsheet subtracts the lease from the purchase cash flows. Initially, the lease saves you $21,590; in months 1–23, the lease costs you $373.43 more than the purchase, and at the end of month 24 the lease costs you $14,923.43 more than the purchase.

The monthly IRR of the differential cash flows is 0.44%, which gives an EAIR of 5.39% (cells E44 and E45).

Should you buy or should you lease? It depends on your alternative cost of financing. If you can finance at a bank for less than 5.39%, then you should buy the car; otherwise, the lease looks like a good deal. In our case you can finance at the bank for 3% (cell B48), so you should buy the car with a bank loan instead of leasing it.

## The Role of the Residual

The residual value of the car is very important in determining the cost of the lease. To illustrate this we use the **Data|Data Tools|What-if Analysis|Data Table** feature of Excel (see Chapter 27) to run a sensitivity table that shows the EAIR and the lease/buy decision as a function of your estimated end-lease market value of the car:

| | A | B | C | D | E | F | G |
|---|---|---|---|---|---|---|---|
| 52 | Data table: The EAIR of the lease as a function of the market value of car at end of lease | | | | | | |
| 53 | Estimated market value of car at end-lease | EAIR | Lease or buy? | | | | |
| 54 | | | | <-- Data table header has been hidden | | | |
| 55 | 10,000 | 2.6% | lease | | | | |
| 56 | 10,500 | 2.6% | lease | | | | |
| 57 | 11,000 | 2.6% | lease | | | | |
| 58 | 11,500 | 2.6% | lease | | | | |
| 59 | 12,000 | 2.6% | lease | | | | |
| 60 | 12,500 | 2.6% | lease | | | | |
| 61 | 13,000 | 2.6% | lease | | | | |
| 62 | 13,500 | 2.6% | lease | | | | |
| 63 | 14,000 | 2.6% | lease | | | | |
| 64 | 14,500 | 4.0% | lease | | | | |
| 65 | 15,000 | 5.4% | lease | | | | |
| 66 | 15,500 | 6.7% | lease | | | | |
| 67 | 16,000 | 8.1% | buy | | | | |
| 68 | 16,500 | 9.4% | buy | | | | |
| 69 | 17,000 | 10.7% | buy | | | | |
| 70 | 17,500 | 11.9% | buy | | | | |
| 71 | 18,000 | 13.2% | buy | | | | |
| 72 | | | | | | | |

Lease EAIR As a Function of the Car's Market Value at Lease-End

As the data table shows, leasing is preferable if you think that the actual market value at the end of the lease term will be low relative to the lease residual of $13,994. The lease is based on your "reselling" the car to the dealer for $13,994; if you think that the actual market value of the car will be much higher, then you would be selling it to the dealer at a loss, and you're better off buying the car and reselling it yourself.[10] The break-even market value—the estimated market value for which you are indifferent between leasing the car or financing it at the bank at 3%—is

---

[10] Some leases actually give you the option of buying the car for the residual value at the end of the lease term. This effectively locks in the lease EAIR, because if the car is worth more than the lease residual value, you can always buy it for the residual and resell the car on the open market.

somewhere between $14,000 and $14,500; in this range the EAIR of the lease is 3%, which is equal to the cost of the alternative financing.[11]

## Financing the Purchase of a Car with a Bank Loan: Cheaper or More Expensive?

In our preceding analysis we concluded that the annual cost of the 2-year lease (cell E45) is an EAIR of 5.39%. So it stands to reason that if you can get a cheaper loan from a bank, you should take the bank loan and use the proceeds to buy the car. And yet...suppose the bank offers you a 3% loan (with monthly compounding, so that the monthly interest rate is 3%/12 = 0.25%), and suppose that we have the same amount to finance (namely, the car cost of $22,905 minus the money down of $1,315). The spreadsheet below shows that the monthly payments on this bank loan are much *larger* than those of the car lease:

| | H | I | J |
|---|---|---|---|
| 2 | Financing with a bank loan | | |
| 3 | Cost of car | 22,905 | <-- =B3+B4 |
| 4 | Money down | 1,315 | |
| 5 | Amount to finance | 21,590 | <-- =I3-I4 |
| 6 | | | |
| 7 | Bank rate | 3% | |
| 8 | Monthly loan payment | 927.96 | <-- =-PMT(I7/12,24,I5) |
| 9 | Monthly lease payment | 373.43 | |
| 10 | | | |
| 11 | **Note**:  The PMT function in cell H8 calculates the | | |
| 12 | monthly payment on a $21,590 loan (cell H5) given for 24 | | |
| 13 | months at monthly interest 0.25% (cell H7/12). | | |

Now this is confusing: Borrowing from the bank at 3% to buy the car involves a much higher monthly payment ($926.96) than the monthly lease payment ($373.43). Yet in our first analysis of the lease on page 86, we concluded that a loan rate of 3% is preferable to the lease EAIR of 5.39%. To resolve this apparent contradiction, recall that the difference between the two—the lease and the loan—is the residual value built into the lease: This residual value—essentially a guarantee that you, the lessee, extend to the auto lessor—both reduces your monthly lease payments *and* increases your stake in the residual value of the car. Compared with the bank loan, the lease gives you lower payments in return for bearing the higher risk of guaranteeing the residual value of the car. There is no free lunch.

To see that the loan is actually cheaper, assume that you take a separate bank loan to finance the car's residual value of $15,000 in 2 years:

$$PV \ of \ residual \ value = \frac{\$15,000}{\left(1+\dfrac{3\%}{12}\right)^{24}} = \$14,127.53.$$

---

[11] The exact residual value for which you are indifferent is $14,134.

We can now divide the purchase price of $22,905 into two parts:

$$\$22,905 = \underbrace{\$14,127.53}_{\substack{\uparrow \\ \dfrac{\$15,000}{\left(1+\dfrac{3\%}{12}\right)^{24}}}} + \$8,777.47$$

The total cost of $8,777.47 is the cost of using the car for the next 2 years. Of this amount, you have to pay an immediate down payment of $1,315, which leaves $7,462.47 to finance. Financing this amount with a lease will cost $373.43 per month, whereas financing with a bank loan will cost $320.75 per month:

| | A | B | C |
|---|---|---|---|
| 1 | **AUTO LEASE VERSUS PURCHASE**<br>**COMPARING BANK LOAN TO LEASE PAYMENT** | | |
| 2 | MSRP | 24,550.00 | <-- Manufacturer's suggested retail price |
| 3 | Capitalized cost | 22,490.00 | <-- Negotiated price |
| 4 | Destination charge | 415.00 | <-- Paid both by the lessee and the buyer |
| 5 | Acquisition fee | 450.00 | <-- Paid only by the lessee |
| 6 | Security deposit | 450.00 | <-- refunded at end of lease |
| 7 | | | |
| 8 | Payment due at signing | 1,315.00 | <-- =SUM(B4:B6) |
| 9 | Monthly payment | 373.43 | <-- Dealer's lease offer |
| 10 | | | |
| 11 | Residual value after 2 years as % of MSRP | 57% | |
| 12 | Lease residual value after 3 years | 13,993.50 | <-- =B11*B2--lessee guarantees this value |
| 13 | Your estimated residual value | 15,000.00 | <-- Your guess |
| 14 | | | |
| 15 | **Financing with a bank loan** | | |
| 16 | Bank rate | 3% | |
| 17 | Monthly rate | 0.25% | <-- =B16/12 |
| 18 | | | |
| 19 | Cost of car | 22,905.00 | <-- =B3+B4 |
| 20 | Money down | 1,315.00 | |
| 21 | Amount to finance | 21,590.00 | <-- =B19-B20 |
| 22 | | | |
| 23 | Loan principal to finance residual in 2 years | 14,127.53 | <-- =B13/(1+B17)^24 |
| 24 | Loan principal to finance car lease for 2 years | 7,462.47 | <-- =B19-B20-B23 |
| 25 | | | |
| 26 | Monthly loan payment to finance<br>car lease for 2 years | 320.75 | <-- =PMT(B17,24,-B24) |
| 27 | Monthly lease payment | 373.43 | |

The bank loan is cheaper. We've summarized our logic in Figure 3.1.

## THINKING ABOUT A CAR LEASE VERSUS A CAR LOAN FROM A BANK

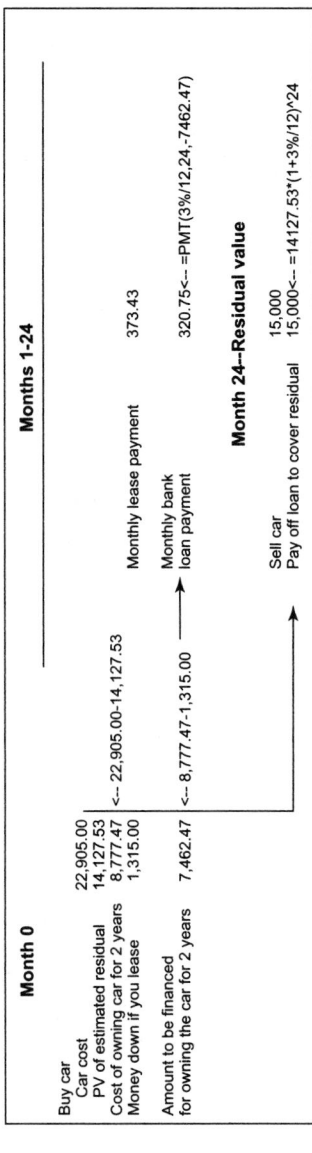

**Month 0**

Buy car
Car cost                                    22,905.00
PV of estimated residual                    14,127.53
Cost of owning car for 2 years               8,777.47   <-- 22,905.00-14,127.53
Money down if you lease                      1,315.00

Amount to be financed
for owning the car for 2 years   7,462.47   <-- 8,777.47-1,315.00

**Months 1-24**

Monthly lease payment                        373.43

Monthly bank
loan payment                   320.75 <-- =PMT(3%/12,24,-7462.47)

**Month 24--Residual value**

Sell car                          15,000
Pay off loan to cover residual    15,000 <-- =14127.53*(1+3%/12)^24

Explanation: The cost of the car is $22,905. You estimate the residual value of the car in 2 years at $15,000, which has a present value of $14,127.53. The cost of owning the car for 2 years is therefore $8,777.47. If you lease the car you are required to put down $1,315.

Assume that you finance the remaining cost of $7,462.47 with a bank loan. This loan will cost you $320.75 per month, compared with the $373.43 per month for the car lease. It's thus cheaper to finance with a car loan from the bank.

FIGURE 3.1  Car lease versus car loan.

## 3.6. More-Than-Once-a-Year Compounding and the EAIR

Suppose you are charged interest on a monthly basis, but you want to compute the annual interest cost. Here's an example: XYZ Bank says that it charges an annual percentage rate (APR) of 18% on your credit card balances, with "interest computed monthly." Suppose that what the bank means is that it charges 1.5% per month on the outstanding balance at the beginning of the month. To determine what this means in practice, you should ask yourself "If I have a credit balance of $100 outstanding for 12 months, how much will I owe at the end of the 12-month period?" If we set this up in Excel, we get the following:

| | A | B | C | D |
|---|---|---|---|---|
| 1 | MONTHLY COMPOUNDING OF CREDIT CARD BALANCES | | | |
| 2 | "Annual" rate | 18% | | |
| 3 | Monthly rate | 1.5% | <-- =B2/12 | |
| 4 | | | | |
| 5 | Month | Balance at beginning of month | Interest for month | Balance at end of month |
| 6 | 1 | 100.00 | 1.50 | 101.50 |
| 7 | 2 | 101.50 | 1.52 | 103.02 |
| 8 | 3 | 103.02 | 1.55 | 104.57 |
| 9 | 4 | 104.57 | 1.57 | 106.14 |
| 10 | 5 | 106.14 | 1.59 | 107.73 |
| 11 | 6 | 107.73 | 1.62 | 109.34 |
| 12 | 7 | 109.34 | 1.64 | 110.98 |
| 13 | 8 | 110.98 | 1.66 | 112.65 |
| 14 | 9 | 112.65 | 1.69 | 114.34 |
| 15 | 10 | 114.34 | 1.72 | 116.05 |
| 16 | 11 | 116.05 | 1.74 | 117.79 |
| 17 | 12 | 117.79 | 1.77 | 119.56 |
| 18 | | | | |
| 19 | Effective annual interest rate (EAIR) | 19.56% | <-- =D17/B6-1 | |
| 20 | | 19.56% | <-- =(1+B3)^12-1 | |

At the end of 12 months you would owe $119.56—the initial $100 balance plus $19.56 in interest. Cells B19 and B20 show two ways of calculating the effective annual interest rate:

- In cell B19, we take the end-year balance that results from the initial $100 credit card balance and divide it by the initial balance to calculate the interest rate:

$$EAIR = \frac{End\text{-}year\ balance}{Initial\ balance} - 1$$
$$= \frac{119.56}{100} - 1 = 19.56\%$$

- In cell B20 we take the monthly interest rate and compound it:

$$EAIR = (1 + monthly\ rate)^{12} - 1$$
$$= (1.015)^{12} - 1 = 19.56\%$$

*When the annual interest rate r is compounded n times per year, the* $EAIR = \left(1+\dfrac{r}{n}\right)^{n} - 1.$

## APR and EAIR

By an act of Congress ("The Federal Truth in Lending Act") lenders are required to specify the annual percentage rate (APR) charged on loans. Unfortunately, the Truth in Lending Act does not specify how the APR is to be computed, and the use of the term by lenders is not uniform. Although "APR" is legal terminology designed to help the consumer understand the true cost of borrowing, in practice the APR is not well-defined and may not represent the actual cost of borrowing. Sometimes the APR is the effective annual interest rate (EAIR), but in other cases—like the credit card example in this section—the APR is something else. The result is much convoluted wording and a lot of confusion.[12]

## The EAIR and the Number of Compounding Periods per Year n

In the preceding example, the credit card company takes its 18% "annual" interest rate charge and turns it into a 1.5% monthly interest rate. As we saw, the resulting EAIR is 19.56%.

In Figure 3.2 we compute the effect of the number of compounding periods on the EAIR The EAIR grows with the number of compounding periods. The EAIR is

$$EAIR = \left(1 + \frac{stated\ annual\ interest\ rate}{number\ of\ annual\ compounding\ periods}\right)^{number\ of\ compounding\ periods\ per\ year} - 1$$

When we do this in Excel, we see that the EAIR grows as the number of compounding periods increases. For a very large number of compounding periods, the EAIR approaches a limit of 19.722% (cell C20 below in the following spreadsheet).

There are two important things to note about the EAIR computation:

- As the number of compounding periods per year *n* increases, the $EAIR = \left(1+\dfrac{r}{n}\right)^{n} - 1$ gets higher.

- The rate at which the EAIR increases gets smaller as the number of annual compounding periods gets larger. There is very little difference between the EAIR when interest is compounded 36 times per year (EAIR = 19.668%) and the EAIR when we compound 365 times per year (EAIR = 19.716%).

---

[12] A case that accompanies this book gives three actual APR examples and the resulting EAIR. In each case the definition of APR used by the lender is different. In only one of the three cases does the APR correspond to the EAIR.

## THE EFFECTIVE ANNUAL INTEREST RATE (EAIR) AND THE NUMBER OF COMPOUNDING PERIODS

The stated annual interest rate is 18%

| Number of compounding periods per year | EAIR formula | EAIR (%) |
|---|---|---|
| 1 | $(1+18\%)-1$ | 18.00 |
| 2 (Semiannual compounding) | $\left(1+\dfrac{18\%}{2}\right)^{2}-1$ | 18.81 |
| 4 (Quarterly compounding) | $\left(1+\dfrac{18\%}{4}\right)^{4}-1$ | 19.252 |
| 12 (Monthly compounding) | $\left(1+\dfrac{18\%}{12}\right)^{12}-1$ | 19.562 |
| 24 (Semimonthly compounding) | $\left(1+\dfrac{18\%}{24}\right)^{24}-1$ | 19.641 |
| 52 (Weekly compounding | $\left(1+\dfrac{18\%}{52}\right)^{52}-1$ | 19.685 |
| 365 (Daily compounding) | $\left(1+\dfrac{18\%}{365}\right)^{365}-1$ | 19.716 |

FIGURE 3.2: The EAIR when an annual interest rate of 18% is compounded for various times per year.

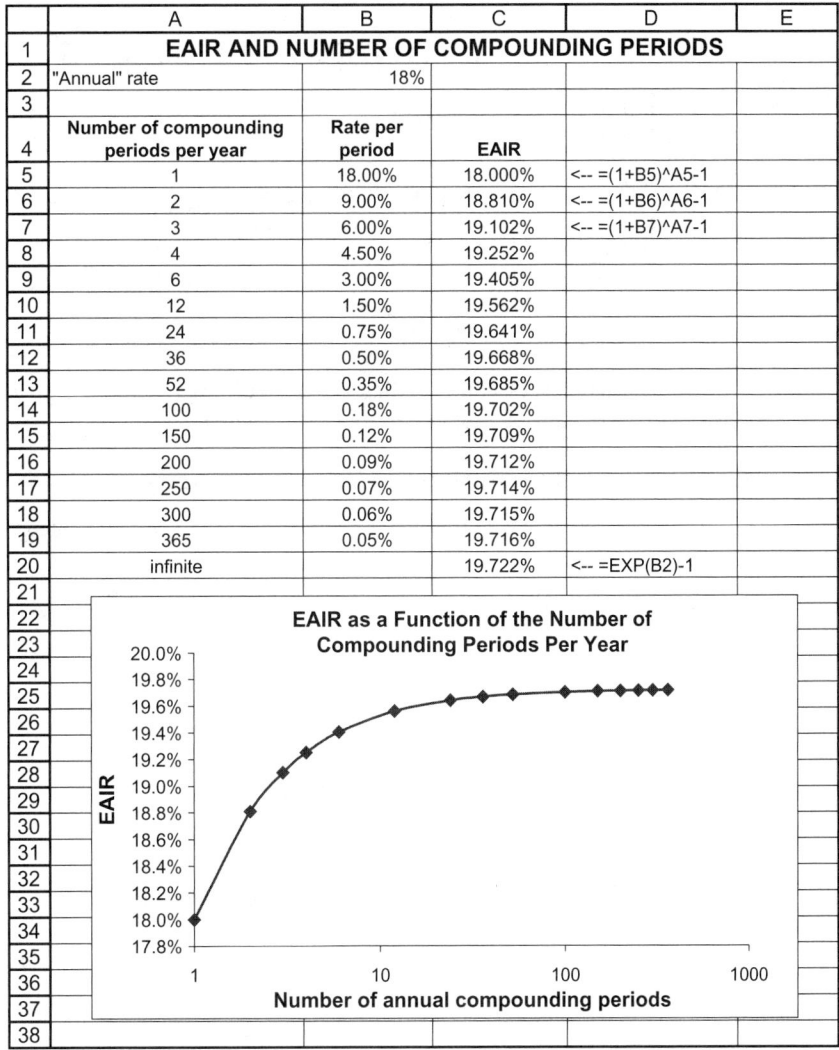

|   | A | B | C | D | E |
|---|---|---|---|---|---|
| 1 | **EAIR AND NUMBER OF COMPOUNDING PERIODS** | | | | |
| 2 | "Annual" rate | 18% | | | |
| 3 | | | | | |
| 4 | **Number of compounding periods per year** | **Rate per period** | **EAIR** | | |
| 5 | 1 | 18.00% | 18.000% | <-- =(1+B5)^A5-1 | |
| 6 | 2 | 9.00% | 18.810% | <-- =(1+B6)^A6-1 | |
| 7 | 3 | 6.00% | 19.102% | <-- =(1+B7)^A7-1 | |
| 8 | 4 | 4.50% | 19.252% | | |
| 9 | 6 | 3.00% | 19.405% | | |
| 10 | 12 | 1.50% | 19.562% | | |
| 11 | 24 | 0.75% | 19.641% | | |
| 12 | 36 | 0.50% | 19.668% | | |
| 13 | 52 | 0.35% | 19.685% | | |
| 14 | 100 | 0.18% | 19.702% | | |
| 15 | 150 | 0.12% | 19.709% | | |
| 16 | 200 | 0.09% | 19.712% | | |
| 17 | 250 | 0.07% | 19.714% | | |
| 18 | 300 | 0.06% | 19.715% | | |
| 19 | 365 | 0.05% | 19.716% | | |
| 20 | infinite | | 19.722% | <-- =EXP(B2)-1 | |
| 21 | | | | | |

**EAIR as a Function of the Number of Compounding Periods Per Year**

# 3.7. Continuous Compounding and Discounting (Advanced Topic)

In cell C20 we compute the limit of the EAIR when the number of compounding periods gets very large. This limit is called *continuous compounding*. For *n* annual compounding periods per year, the $EAIR = \left(1 + \dfrac{r}{n}\right)^n - 1$. When the number of annual compounding periods *n* gets very large, the EAIR becomes close to $e^r - 1$. The number $e = 2.71828182845904$ is the base of natural logarithms and is included in Excel as the function **Exp( )**. In the jargon of finance, $e^{rT}$ is called the *continuously compounded future value after T years at annual interest rate r*. In the spreadsheet below you can see the difference between the *discretely compounded* future value and the *continuously compounded* future value.

| | A | B | C |
|---|---|---|---|
| 1 | **CONTINUOUS COMPOUNDING** | | |
| 2 | "Annual" rate | 18% | |
| 3 | Number of compounding periods per year | 250 | |
| 4 | Number of years, T | 3 | |
| 5 | Effective annual interest rate, EAIR | | |
| 6 | | 19.71% | |
| 7 | Discretely compounded future value after t years $=(1+\text{EAIR})^T$ | 1.7157 | <-- =(1+B2/B3)^(B3*B4) |
| 8 | Continuously compounded future value $=e^{rT}$ | 1.7160 | <-- =EXP(B2*B4) |

When the number of compounding periods gets very large, the difference between the discrete and continuous interest rate becomes very small.

## The Continuously Compounded Discount Factor

In Chapter 2 we saw that future value and present value are closely related:

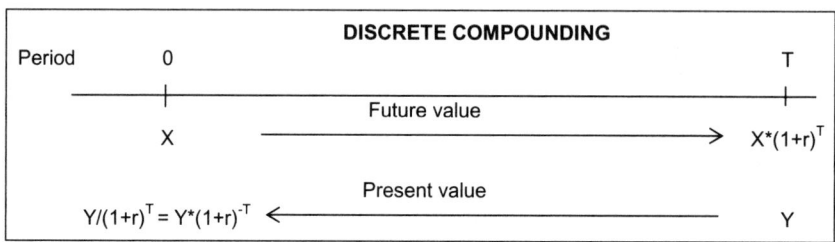

A similar relation holds for continuous compounding:

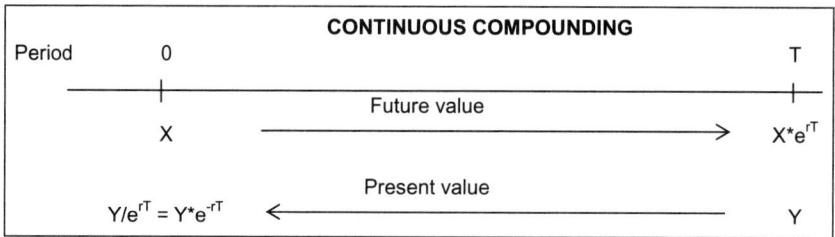

The following spreadsheet summarizes these relations:

| | A | B | C |
|---|---|---|---|
| 1 | **DISCRETE AND CONTINUOUS COMPOUNDING** | | |
| 2 | Interest rate | 10% | |
| 3 | Initial amount, X | 100 | |
| 4 | Terminal date, T | 3 | |
| 5 | Discretely compounded future value, $X*(1+r)^T$ | 133.100 | <-- =B3*(1+B2)^B4 |
| 6 | Continuously compounded future value, $X*e^{rT}$ | 134.986 | <-- =B3*EXP(B2*B4) |
| 7 | | | |
| 8 | Interest rate | 10% | |
| 9 | Terminal amount, Y | 100 | |
| 10 | Terminal date, T | 3 | |
| 11 | Discretely compounded present value, $Y/(1+r)^T$ | 75.131 | <-- =B9/(1+B8)^B10 |
| 12 | Continuously compounded present value, $Y*e^{-rT}$ | 74.082 | <-- =B9*EXP(-B10*B8) |

## An Actual Credit Card Example

Continuously compounded interest may seem like an ethereal concept—highly theoretical but not very useful. The example in this subsection shows how useful continuously compounded interest can actually be. The Columbus State University credit card in the ad below charges a penalty annual percentage rate (APR) of 27.99%.[13] The parentheses in the ad make it clear that the company is actually charging 0.07669% *per day* on outstanding balances. This rate is calculated by taking 27.99% and dividing it by the number of days per year:

$$0.07669\% = \frac{27.99\%}{365}.$$

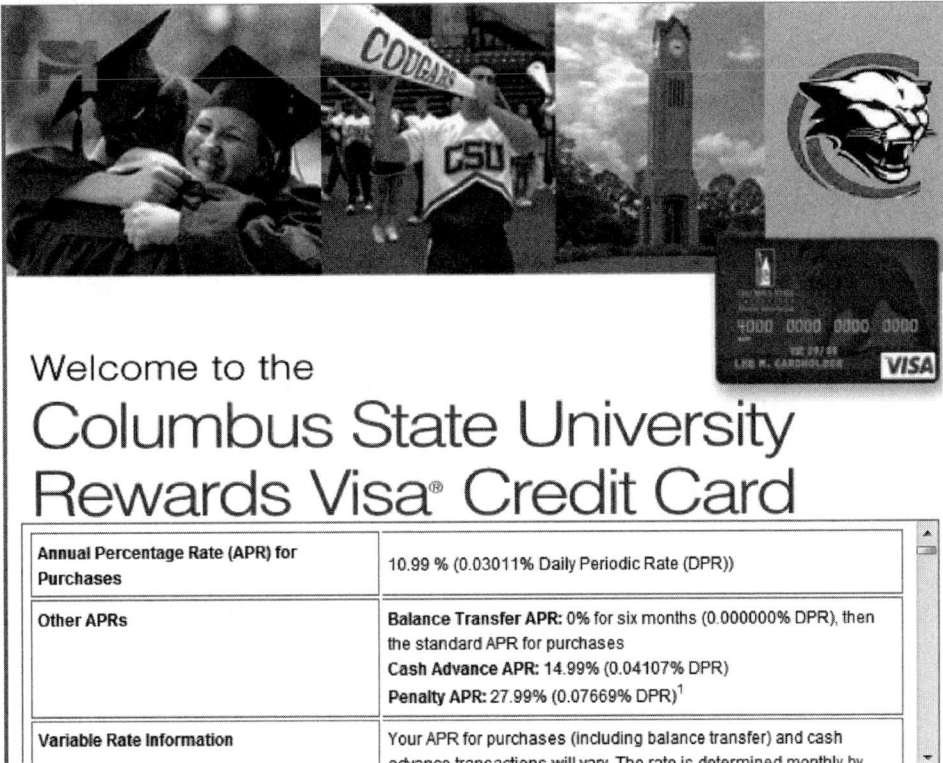

| Welcome to the | |
|---|---|
| **Columbus State University** | |
| **Rewards Visa® Credit Card** | |

| Annual Percentage Rate (APR) for Purchases | 10.99 % (0.03011% Daily Periodic Rate (DPR)) |
|---|---|
| Other APRs | **Balance Transfer APR:** 0% for six months (0.000000% DPR), then the standard APR for purchases<br>**Cash Advance APR:** 14.99% (0.04107% DPR)<br>**Penalty APR:** 27.99% (0.07669% DPR)[1] |
| Variable Rate Information | Your APR for purchases (including balance transfer) and cash advance transactions will vary. The rate is determined monthly by |

If you carried a $100 balance throughout the year, you would owe $100*(1.007668)^{365}$ at the end of the year.[14] As the spreadsheet shows, this translates into a 32.286% EAIR (cell B5):

---

[13]What is the penalty rate? As the card Web site explains: "If you are late making a payment, any rates not exceeding the Penalty Rate may change to the same rate and type as the Penalty Rate." In other words, if you are overdue on *any* payment, the penalty rate applies to all existing balances.

[14]Note the small discrepancy between our Excel and the Visa advertisement: 27.99%/365=0.0766849%. By the normal rules of rounding off, this should be rounded down to 0.07668%, but Columbus State's Visa takes the extra 0.0001%! As they say: "Every little bit helps."

| | A | B | C |
|---|---|---|---|
| 1 | **COLUMBUS STATE VISA CARD** | | |
| 2 | APR | 27.99% | |
| 3 | Daily | 0.07668% | <-- =B2/365 |
| 4 | | | |
| 5 | Effective annual interest rate (EAIR) | 32.286% | <-- =(1+B3)^365-1 |
| 6 | Continuously compounded interest | 32.300% | <-- =EXP(B2)-1 |

As you can see in cell B6, essentially the same interest rate can be computed using continuous compounding. From a computational point of view, using continuous compounding is simpler than discretely compounding a daily interest rate.

## CONTINUOUS COMPOUNDING IN THIS BOOK

We rarely use continuous compounding in this book, except in the options chapters (Chapters 20–23). In other cases we use only discrete compounding, although we may occasionally point out in a footnote the continuously compounded counterpart of a discretely compounded calculation.

## Computing the Continuous Return

In past subsections we have measured discrete versus continuous compounding. In this section we show how to measure discrete versus continuous rates of return. Suppose that an investment grows from $X$ at time zero to $Y$ at time $T$. Then the *discretely compounded annual return* on the investment is $r = \left(\dfrac{Y}{X}\right)^{1/T} - 1$. The *continuously compounded annual return* is given by $r = \dfrac{1}{T} Ln\left(\dfrac{Y}{X}\right)$. In the example below, an investment of $100 grows to $200 over a period of 4 years.[15] The spreadsheet computes both the discretely compounded and the continuously compounded annual returns:

| | A | B | C |
|---|---|---|---|
| 1 | **COMPUTING DISCRETE AND CONTINUOUS RETURNS** | | |
| 2 | Investment at time 0 | 100 | |
| 3 | Value at time T | 200 | |
| 4 | T (years) | 4 | |
| 5 | | | |
| 6 | Discretely compounded annual return | 18.92% | <-- =(B3/B2)^(1/B4)-1 |
| 7 | Continously compounded annual return | 17.33% | <-- =(1/B4)*LN(B3/B2) |
| 8 | | | |
| 9 | **Why is this true: Compounding the initial investment to get the future value** | | |
| 10 | Discrete compounding | 200 | <-- =B2*(1+B6)^B4 |
| 11 | Continuous compounding | 200 | <-- =B2*EXP(B7*B4) |

---

[15] The Excel function **Ln** computes the natural logarithm of a number. If $Ln(a)=b$, then $e^b = a$.

The discretely compounded annual return (cell B6) is 18.92%; this is proved in cell B10, where we show that $200 = 100*(1 + 18.92\%)^4$. In other words, over 4 years the discretely compounded future value of $100 at 18.92% annually is $200.

The continuously compounded annual return is 17.32% (cell B7); this is proved in cell B11, where we show that $200 = 100*\exp(17.32\%*4)$. Over 4 years the continuously compounded future value of $100 at 17.32% annually is $200.

Note that you would be indifferent in choosing between an annual discretely compounded return of 18.92% and an annual continuously compounded return of 17.32%. Over any given time frame, both rates make an initial investment grow to the same final result!

## Summing Up

In this chapter we've applied the time value of money (PV, NPV, and IRR) to a number of relevant problems:

- Finding the effective annual interest rate (EAIR): This is the compound annual interest rate implicit in a specific financial asset; another way to think about this is that it's the annualized IRR. We've given a number of examples—leases, mortgages, credit cards— all of which illustrate that the only way to evaluate the financing cost is by calculating the EAIR.

- The effect of nonannual compounding periods: Many interest rates are calculated on a monthly or even a daily basis. The EAIR demands that we annualize these interest rates so that we can compare them. When the number of compounding periods gets very large (like our Columbus State University example), the EAIR = $er$, where $e$ = 2.71828182845905 (computed by **=Exp( )** in Excel) and $r$ is the stated interest rate.

## Exercises

1. You are considering buying the latest stereo system model. The dealer in "The Stereo World" store has offered you two payment options. You can either pay $10,000 now, or you can take advantage of their special deal and "buy now and pay a year from today," in which case you will pay $11,100 in 1 year. Calculate the effective annual interest rate (EAIR) of the store's special deal.

2. You have two options of paying for your new dishwasher: You can either make a single payment of $400 today, or you can pay $70 for the next 6 months, with the first payment made today. What is the effective annual interest rate (EAIR) of the second option?

3. Your lovely wife has decided to buy you a vacuum cleaner for your birthday (she always supports you in your hobbies . . . ). She called your best friend, a manager of a vacuum cleaner store, and he has suggested one of two payment plans: She can either pay $100 now or make 12 monthly payments of $10 each, starting from today. What are the monthly IRR and the EAIR of the payment-over-time plan?

4. Your local bank has offered you a mortgage of $100,000. There are no points, no origination fees, and no extra initial costs (meaning you get the full $100,000). The mortgage is to be paid back over 10 years in annual payments, and the bank charges 12% annual interest.

   a. Calculate the annual mortgage payments

   b. What is the mortgage EAIR?

5. Your local bank has offered you a 20-year, $100,000 mortgage. The bank is charging 1.5 points and "processing" costs of $750; both points and processing costs are deducted from the mortgage when it is given. Payments on the mortgage are annual and are based on a 10% interest rate on the full amount of the mortgage (that is, $100,000).

   a. Calculate the annual mortgage payment

   b. Calculate the EAIR

   c. Compute an amortization table that shows the amount of interest you can report for taxes each year.

6. Your local bank has offered you a 10-year, $100,000 mortgage with monthly payments. The bank is charging 1.5 points and "processing" costs of $750; both points and processing costs are deducted from the mortgage when it is given. Monthly payments on the mortgage are based on the 12% annual interest rate on the full amount of the mortgage (that is, $100,000).

   a. Calculate the monthly payment on the mortgage, show the amortization table, and compute the EAIR.

   b. Will the EAIR of the mortgage change if the loan period is 6 years?

   c. Compute the total interest paid in each of the years of the mortgage. You can base your answer on the amortization table or investigate the Excel function **Cumipmt**.

7. You just bought the first floor of the famous "Egg-Plant" Building for $250,000. You plan to rent the space to convenience stores. Your banker has offered you a mortgage with the following terms:

   • The mortgage is for the full amount of $250,000.

   • The mortgage will be repaid in equal monthly payments over 36 months, starting 1 month from now.

   • The annual interest rate on the mortgage is 8%, compounded monthly (meaning: $\frac{8\%}{12} = 2/3\%$ per month).

   • You have to pay the bank an initiation charge of $1,500 and 1 point.

   a. What is the monthly payment you will pay the bank?

   b. What is the EAIR of the mortgage?

   c. Compute an amortization table that shows the amount of interest you can report for taxes each month.

8. Your local bank has offered you a 5-year, $100,000 mortgage. The bank is charging 1.5 points and "processing" costs of $750. If the interest rate is 12% compounded monthly (meaning: 1% per month):

   a. Calculate the monthly mortgage payment.

   b. Calculate the EAIR.

   c. Compute an amortization table that shows the amount of interest you can report for taxes each month and use it to compute the annual mortgage interest you can report for tax purposes.

9. You're considering buying an asset that has a 3-year life and costs $15,000. As an alternative to buying the asset, you can lease it for $4,000 per year (four annual payments, the first due on the day you sign the lease). If you can borrow from your bank at 10%, should you lease or buy?

10. You're considering buying an asset that has a 3-year life and costs $2,000. As an alternative to buying the asset, you can lease it for $600 per year (four annual payments, the first due today). Your bank is willing to lend you money for 15%.

   a. Should you lease or purchase the asset?

   b. What is the largest lease payment you would be willing to make?

11. You're considering leasing or purchasing an asset with the following cash flows.

    a. Calculate the present value of the lease versus the purchase. Which is preferable?

    b. What is the largest annual lease payment you would be willing to pay?

| | A | B | C | D |
|---|---|---|---|---|
| 1 | **LEASE VERSUS PURCHASE WITH RESIDUAL VALUE** | | | |
| 2 | Asset cost | 20,000 | | |
| 3 | Annual lease payment | 5,500 | | |
| 4 | Residual value, year 3 | 3,000 | <-- Value of asset at end year 3 | |
| 5 | Bank rate | 15% | | |
| 6 | | | | |
| 7 | Year | Purchase cash flow | Lease cash flow | |
| 8 | 0 | 20,000 | 5,500 | |
| 9 | 1 | | 5,500 | |
| 10 | 2 | | 5,500 | |
| 11 | 3 | -3,000 | 5,500 | |

12. You intend to buy a new laptop computer. Its price at electronic shops is $2,000, but your next-door neighbor offered to lease you the same computer for monthly payments of $70 for a 24-month period, with the first payment made today. Assuming you can sell the computer at the end of 2 years at $500 and the interest rate in the market is 20%, should you buy or lease?

13. You're considering leasing or purchasing a car. The details of each method of financing are given below. The lease is for 24 months. What should you do?

| | A | B | C | D | E | F |
|---|---|---|---|---|---|---|
| 1 | **AUTO LEASE VERSUS PURCHASE** | | | | | |
| 2 | MSRP | 50,000.00 | <-- Manufacturer's suggested retail price | | | |
| 3 | Capitalized cost | 45,000.00 | <-- Negotiated price | | | |
| 4 | Destination charge | 415.00 | <-- Paid both by the lessee and the buyer | | | |
| 5 | Acquisition fee | 450.00 | <-- Paid only by the lessee | | | |
| 6 | Security deposit | 450.00 | <-- refunded at end of lease | | | |
| 7 | | | | | | |
| 8 | Payment due at signing | 1,315.00 | | | | |
| 9 | Monthly payment | 600.00 | <-- Dealer's lease offer | | | |
| 10 | | | | | | |
| 11 | Residual value after 2 years as % of MSRP | 60% | | | | |
| 12 | Lease residual value after 3 years | 30,000.00 | <-- =B11*B2 | | | |
| 13 | Your estimated residual value | 35,000.00 | <-- Your guess | | | |
| 14 | | | | | | |
| 15 | Bank loan cost (annual) | 7.00% | | | | |

14. You are considering buying a new, very expensive, FancyCar. The details of your negotiation for a 48-month lease are given below.

    a. If your alternative cost of financing is 6%, should you buy or lease?

    b. If you financed the purchase through the bank at 6%, what would be your monthly loan payment?

    c. As your estimated residual value (cell B15) gets larger, does leasing or buying become more advantageous? Explain.

d. What is the estimated residual value for which you are indifferent between buying and leasing?

| | A | B | C |
|---|---|---|---|
| 1 | **AUTO LEASE VERSUS PURCHASE: 48-MONTH LEASE** | | |
| 2 | MSRP | 50,000 | <-- Manufacturer's suggested retail price |
| 3 | Capitalized cost | 45,000 | <-- Negotiated price |
| 4 | Destination charge | 415 | <-- Paid both by the lessee and the buyer |
| 5 | Acquisition fee | 450 | <-- Paid only by the lessee |
| 6 | Security deposit | 450 | <-- refunded at end of lease |
| 7 | | | |
| 8 | Payment due at signing | 1,315 | |
| 9 | Monthly payment | 400 | <-- Dealer's lease offer |
| 10 | | | |
| 11 | | | |
| 12 | Residual value after 4 years as % of MSRP | 60% | |
| 13 | Lease residual value after 4 years | 30,000 | |
| 14 | Your estimated residual value | 35,000 | <-- Your guess |

15. You're considering buying a new top-of-the-line luxury car. The car's list price is $99,000. The dealer has offered you two alternatives for purchasing the car:

   • You can buy the car for $90,000 in cash and get a $9,000 discount in the bargain.

   • You can buy the car for the list price of $99,000. In this case the dealer is willing to take $39,000 as an initial payment. The remainder of $60,000 is a "zero-interest loan" to be paid back in equal installments over 36 months.

   Alternatively, your local bank is willing to give you a car loan at an annual interest rate of 10%, compounded monthly (that is, 10%/12 per month).

   Decide how to finance the car: bank loan, zero-interest loan with the dealer, or cash payment.

16. You've been offered two credit cards:

   • Credit card 1 charges 19% annually, on a monthly basis.

   • Credit card 2 charges 19% annually, on a weekly basis.

   • Credit card 3 charges 18.90% annually, on a daily basis.

   Rank the cards on the basis of EAIR.

17. You plan to put $1,000 in a savings plan and leave it there for 5 years. You can choose between various alternatives. How much will you have in 5 years under each alternative?

   a. Bellon Bank is offering 12% stated annual interest rate, compounded once a year.

   b. WNC Bank is offering 11% stated annual interest rate, compounded twice a year.

   c. Plebian Bank is offering 10% stated annual interest rate, compounded monthly.

   d. Byfus Bank is offering 11.5% stated annual interest rate, compounded continuously.

18. Assuming that the interest rate is 5%, compounded semiannually, which of the following is more valuable?

   a. $5,000 today.

   b. $10,000 at the end of 5 years.

   c. $9,000 at the end of 4 years.

   d. $450 at the end of each year (in perpetuity) commencing in 1 year.

19. You plan to put $10,000 in a savings plan for 2 years. How much will you have at the end of 2 years with each of the following options?

   a. Receive 12% stated annual interest rate, compounded monthly.

   b. Receive 12.5% stated annual interest rate, compounded annually.

   c. Receive 11.5% stated annual interest rate, compounded daily.

   d. Receive 10% stated annual interest rate in the first year and 15% stated annual interest rate in the second year, compounded annually.

   How much will you have at the end of 2 years in each option?

20. Michael Smith was in trouble: He was unemployed and living on his monthly disability pay of $1,200. His credit card debts of $19,000 were threatening to overwhelm this puny income. Every month in which he delayed paying the credit card debt cost him 1.5% on the remaining balance. His only asset was his house, on which he had a $67,000 mortgage.

    Then Michael got a phone call from Uranus Financial Corporation: The company offered to refinance Michael's mortgage. The Uranus representative explained to Michael that, with the rise in real-estate values, Michael's house could now be remortgaged for $90,000. This amount would allow Michael to repay his credit card debts and even leave him with some money.

    Here are some additional facts:

    - The new mortgage would be for 25 years and would have an annual interest rate of 9.23%. The mortgage would be repayable in equal monthly payments over this term, at a monthly interest rate of $9.23\% / 12 = 0.76917\%$. The fees on the mortgage are $8,000.

    - There are no penalties involved in repaying the $67,000 existing mortgage.

    Answer the following questions:

    a. What will Michael's monthly payments be on the new mortgage?

    b. After repaying his credit card debts, how much money will Michael have left?

    c. What is the effective annual interest rate (EAIR) on the Uranus mortgage?

21. A note from the author's credit card company included the following statement.

    **Annual Percentage Rate for Cash Advances:**

    Your annual percentage rate for cash advances is the U.S. Prime Rate plus 14.99%, but such cash advance rate will never be lower than 19.99%. As of August 1, 2004, this cash advance ANNUAL PERCENTAGE RATE is 19.99%, which corresponds to a daily periodic rate of 0.0548%. A daily periodic rate is the applicable annual percentage rate divided by 365.

    As of August 1, 2004, what is the effective annual interest rate (EAIR) charged by the credit card on cash advances?

22. WindyRoad is an investment company that has two mutual funds. The WindyRoad Dull Fund invests in boring corporate bonds and its Lively Fund invests in "high-risk, high-return" companies. The returns for the two funds in the 5-year period 2001–2005 are given below.

    a. Suppose you had invested $100 in each of the two funds at the beginning of 2001. How much would you have at the end of 2005?

    b. What was the EAIR paid by each of the funds over the 5-year period 2001–2005?

    c. Is there a conclusion you can draw from this example?

|   | A | B | C | D |
|---|---|---|---|---|
| 1 | \multicolumn{4}{c|}{**DULL FUND OR LIVELY FUND?**} | | | |
| 2 | **Year** | **Dull Fund return** | **Lively Fund return** | |
| 3 | 2001 | 9.20% | 11.50% | |
| 4 | 2002 | 5.20% | -14.50% | |
| 5 | 2003 | 4.30% | -23.40% | |
| 6 | 2004 | 3.30% | 42.40% | |
| 7 | 2005 | 7.00% | 13.60% | |
| 8 | | | | |
| 9 | Average return | 5.80% | 5.92% | <-- =AVERAGE(C3:C7) |

23. (Advanced).

   a. Compute the annual continuous returns for Dull Fund and Lively Fund (exercise 22) for each of the years 2001–2005. What is the average continuous return $r_{average}^{continuous}$ for each fund?

   b. Suppose you had invested $100 in each of the two funds at the beginning of 2001. Show that the total amount you would have in each fund (see Exercise 22.a) can be written as $\$100 * e^{5*r_{average}^{continuous}}$. Note that this makes computations much simpler.

24. Capital Star Motors of Canberra, Australia, has the following lease offer for a Smart car:

   • Lease term: 48 months.

   • No initial deposit, $8,995 balloon payment at end of lease.

   • Daily payment: $9.95 per day, payable monthly.

   • Smart car cash cost: $18,800.

   a. Assuming 30 days per month, compute the effective annual interest rate (EAIR) in the lease.

   b. Compute the balloon payment that gives a 7% EAIR.

25. Ten years ago Reem and Forsan took out a $150,000 mortgage to buy their new house. The mortgage was a 20-year, 10% mortgage with annual payments. Today their bank offers similar mortgages at 8% interest; however, when the young couple went to the bank to inquire about the possibility of refinancing the remainder of their mortgage with a 10-year, 8% mortgage, they were informed that the bank has a $15,000 "exit fee" for the refinancing.[16] Should they still refinance the mortgage?

   We offer some hints:

   • The remaining mortgage principal at any point is the present value of the future payments on the mortgage. Further hint: Use Excel's PV function.

   • Excel's Rate function can compute the IRRs of fixed payment loans.

---

[16]This question was inspired by an article in the *Melbourne Age* on 12 August 2009. High exit fees are common in Australia; they are also called "early termination fees," "deferred establishment fees," or "early repayment fees."

- A convenient template to solve this problem might be the following:

| | A | B | C |
|---|---|---|---|
| 1 | MORTGAGE EXIT FEE | | |
| 2 | Initial mortgage | | |
| 3 | Principal | 150,000.00 | |
| 4 | Term (years) | 20 | |
| 5 | Interest rate | 10.00% | |
| 6 | Annual payment | | <-- |
| 7 | Term remaining | 10 | |
| 8 | Remaining mortgage principal | | <-- |
| 9 | Exit fee | 15,000.00 | |
| 10 | | | |
| 11 | New mortgage | | |
| 12 | Principal | | <-- |
| 13 | Term (years) | 10 | |
| 14 | Interest rate | 8.00% | |
| 15 | Annual payment | | <-- |
| 16 | Effective annual cost (EAIR) | | <-- |

# 4 Introduction to Capital Budgeting

## CHAPTER CONTENTS

# Overview

*Capital budgeting* is finance jargon for the process of deciding whether to undertake an investment project. Two standard concepts are used in capital budgeting: net present value (NPV) and internal rate of return (IRR). Both concepts were introduced in Chapter 2; in this chapter we discuss their application to capital budgeting. Here are some of the topics covered:

- Should you undertake a specific project? We call this the "yes–no" decision, and we show how both NPV and IRR answer this question.
- Ranking projects: If you have several alternative investments, only one of which you can choose, which should you undertake?
- Should you use IRR or NPV? Sometimes the IRR and NPV decision criteria give different answers to the yes–no and the ranking decisions. We discuss why this happens and which criterion should be used for capital budgeting (if there's disagreement).
- Sunk costs. How should we account for costs incurred in the past?
- The cost of foregone opportunities.
- Salvage values and terminal values.
- Incorporating taxes into the valuation decision. This issue is dealt with briefly in Section 6.7. We return to it at greater length in Chapters 7–9.

## Finance Concepts Discussed

- IRR
- NPV
- Project ranking using NPV and IRR
- Terminal value
- Taxation and calculation of cash flows
- Cost of foregone opportunities
- Sunk costs

## Excel Functions Used

- **NPV**
- **IRR**
- **Data table**

# 4.1. The NPV Rule for Judging Investments and Projects

In the preceding chapters we introduced the basic NPV and IRR concepts and their application to capital budgeting. We start off this chapter by summarizing each of these rules—the NPV rule in this section and the IRR rule in the following section.

Here's a summary of the decision criteria for investments implied by the net present value (NPV):

**The NPV rule for deciding whether a specific project is worthwhile:** Suppose we are considering a project that has cash flows $CF_0$, $CF_1$, $CF_2$,..., $CF_N$. Suppose that the appropriate discount rate for this project is $r$. Then the NPV of the project is

$$NPV = CF_0 + \frac{CF_1}{(1+r)} + \frac{CF_2}{(1+r)^2} + ... + \frac{CF_N}{(1+r)^N} = CF_0 + \sum_{t=1}^{N} \frac{CF_t}{(1+r)^t}.$$

**Rule:** A project is worthwhile by the NPV rule if its NPV > 0.

**The NPV rule for deciding between two mutually exclusive projects:** Suppose you are trying to decide between two projects $A$ and $B$, each of which can achieve the same objective. For example, your company needs a new widget machine, and the choice is between machine $A$ or machine $B$. You will buy either $A$ or $B$ (or perhaps neither machine, but you will certainly not buy both machines). In finance jargon these projects are "mutually exclusive."

Suppose Project A has cash flows $CF_0^A, CF_1^A, CF_2^A, ..., CF_N^A$ and Project B has cash flows $CF_0^B, CF_1^B, CF_2^B, ..., CF_N^B$.

**Rule:** Project $A$ is preferred to Project $B$ if

$$NPV(A) = CF_0^A + \sum_{t=1}^{N} \frac{CF_t^A}{(1+r)^t} > CF_0^B + \sum_{t=1}^{N} \frac{CF_t^B}{(1+r)^t} = NPV(B)$$

The logic of both NPV rules presented above is that the *present value* of a project's cash flows, $PV = \sum_{t=1}^{N} \frac{CF_t}{(1+r)^t}$, is the economic value today of the project. Thus—if we have correctly chosen the discount rate $r$ for the project—the PV is what we ought to be able to sell the project for in the market.[1] The net present value is the *wealth increment* produced by the project, so NPV > 0 means that a project adds to our wealth:

$$NPV = \underbrace{CF_0}_{\substack{\text{Initial cash} \\ \text{flow required} \\ \text{to implement} \\ \text{the project.} \\ \text{This is usually} \\ \text{a negative number.}}} + \underbrace{\sum_{t=1}^{N} \frac{CF_t}{(1+r)^t}}_{\substack{\text{Market value} \\ \text{of future cash} \\ \text{flows.}}}.$$

## An Initial Example

To set the stage let's assume that you're trying to decide whether to undertake one of two projects. Project $A$ involves buying expensive machinery that produces a better product at a lower cost. The machines for Project $A$ cost $1,000 and, if purchased, you anticipate that the project will produce cash flows of $500 per year for the next 5 years. Project $B$'s machines are cheaper, costing $800, but they produce smaller annual cash flows of $420 per year for the next 5 years. We'll assume that the correct discount rate is 12%.

---

[1] This assumes that the discount rate is "correctly chosen," by which we mean that it is appropriate to the riskiness of the project's cash flows. For the moment we fudge the question of how to choose discount rates; this topic is discussed in Chapter 6.

Suppose we apply the NPV criterion to Projects *A* and *B*.

| | A | B | C | D |
|---|---|---|---|---|
| 1 | | **TWO PROJECTS** | | |
| 2 | Discount rate | 12% | | |
| 3 | | | | |
| 4 | **Year** | **Project A** | **Project B** | |
| 5 | 0 | -1000 | -800 | |
| 6 | 1 | 500 | 420 | |
| 7 | 2 | 500 | 420 | |
| 8 | 3 | 500 | 420 | |
| 9 | 4 | 500 | 420 | |
| 10 | 5 | 500 | 420 | |
| 11 | | | | |
| 12 | NPV | 802.39 | 714.01 | <-- =C5+NPV($B$2,C6:C10) |

Both projects are worthwhile because each has a positive NPV. If we have to choose between the projects, then Project *A* is preferred to Project *B* because it has the higher NPV.

## EXCEL'S NPV FUNCTION VERSUS THE FINANCE DEFINITION OF NPV

We reiterate our Excel note from Chapter 2 (page 37): Excel's **NPV** function computes the PV of *future* cash flows; this does not correspond to the *finance notion* of NPV, which includes the initial cash flow. To calculate the finance NPV concept in the spreadsheet, we have to include the initial cash flow. Hence, in cell B12, the NPV is calculated as =NPV($B$2,B6:B10)+B5 and in cell C12 the calculation is =NPV($B$2,C6:C10)+C5.

## 4.2. The IRR Rule for Judging Investments

An alternative to using the NPV criterion for capital budgeting is to use the internal rate of return (IRR). Recall from Chapter 2 that the IRR is defined as the discount rate for which the NPV equals zero. It is the compound rate of return you get from a series of cash flows.

Here are the two decision rules for using the IRR in capital budgeting:

**The IRR rule for deciding whether a specific investment is worthwhile:** Suppose we are considering a project that has cash flows $CF_0, CF_1, CF_2, \ldots, CF_N$.

*IRR is an interest rate such that:*

$$CF_0 + \frac{CF_1}{(1+IRR)} + \frac{CF_2}{(1+IRR)^2} + \cdots + \frac{CF_N}{(1+IRR)^N} = CF_0 + \sum_{t=1}^{N} \frac{CF_t}{(1+k)^t} = 0 \, .$$

**Rule:** If the appropriate discount rate for a project is *r*, you should accept the project if its IRR > *r* and reject it if its IRR < *r*.

The logic behind the IRR rule is that the IRR is the compound return you get from the project. Because *r* is the project's required rate of return, it follows that if IRR > *r*, you get more than you require.

**The IRR rule for deciding between two competing projects:** Suppose you are trying to decide between two mutually exclusive projects, $A$ and $B$ (meaning both projects are ways of achieving the same objective, and you will choose at most one of the projects). Suppose Project A has cash flows $CF_0^A, CF_1^A, CF_2^A, ..., CF_N^A$ and Project B has cash flows $CF_0^B, CF_1^B, CF_2^B, ..., CF_N^B$.

**Rule:** Project A is preferred to Project B if IRR(A) > IRR(B).

Again the logic is clear: Because the IRR gives a project's compound rate of return, if we choose between two projects using the IRR rule, we prefer the higher compound rate of return.

Applying the IRR rule to our Projects $A$ and $B$, we get

|    | A | B | C | D |
|----|---|---|---|---|
| 1  | |  |  |  |
| 2  | Discount rate | 12% |  |  |
| 3  |  |  |  |  |
| 4  | Year | Project A | Project B |  |
| 5  | 0 | -1000 | -800 |  |
| 6  | 1 | 500 | 420 |  |
| 7  | 2 | 500 | 420 |  |
| 8  | 3 | 500 | 420 |  |
| 9  | 4 | 500 | 420 |  |
| 10 | 5 | 500 | 420 |  |
| 11 |  |  |  |  |
| 12 | IRR | 41.04% | 44.03% | <-- =IRR(C5:C10) |

Row 1 spans: **TWO PROJECTS**

Both Project $A$ and Project $B$ are worthwhile because each has an IRR > 12%, which is our relevant discount rate. If we have to choose between the two projects using the IRR rule, Project $B$ is preferred to Project $A$ because it has a higher IRR.

## 4.3. NPV or IRR—Which to Use?

We can sum up the NPV and the IRR rules as follows:

|  | **"Yes or no":** Choosing whether to undertake a single project | **"Project ranking":** Comparing two mutually exclusive projects |
|---|---|---|
| NPV criterion | The project should be undertaken if its NPV > 0. | Project $A$ is preferred to Project $B$ if NPV(A) > NPV(B). |
| IRR criterion | The project should be undertaken if its IRR > $r$, where $r$ is the appropriate discount rate. | Project $A$ is preferred to Project $B$ if IRR(A) > IRR(B). |

Both the NPV rules and the IRR rules look logical. In many cases your investment decision—to undertake a project or not, or which of two competing projects to choose—will be the same whether you use NPV or IRR. There are some cases, however (such as that of Projects $A$ and $B$ illustrated above), where NPV and IRR give different answers. In our net present value analysis Project $A$ won out because its NPV was greater than that of Project $B$. In our IRR analysis of the same projects, Project $B$ was chosen because it had the higher IRR. In such cases we should always use the NPV to decide between projects. The logic is that if individuals are interested in maximizing their wealth, they should use NPV, which measures the incremental wealth from undertaking a project.

## 4.4. The "Yes–No" Criterion: When Do IRR and NPV Give the Same Answer?

Consider the following project: The initial cash flow of –$1,000 represents the cost of the project today, and the remaining cash flows for years 1–6 are projected future cash flows. The discount rate is 15%.

| | A | B | C |
|---|---|---|---|
| 1 | SIMPLE CAPITAL BUDGETING EXAMPLE | | |
| 2 | Discount rate | 15% | |
| 3 | | | |
| 4 | Year | Cash flow | |
| 5 | 0 | -1,000 | |
| 6 | 1 | 100 | |
| 7 | 2 | 200 | |
| 8 | 3 | 300 | |
| 9 | 4 | 400 | |
| 10 | 5 | 500 | |
| 11 | 6 | 600 | |
| 12 | | | |
| 13 | PV of future cash flows | 1,172.13 | <-- =NPV(B2,B6:B11) |
| 14 | NPV | 172.13 | <-- =B5+NPV(B2,B6:B11) |
| 15 | IRR | 19.71% | <-- =IRR(B5:B11) |

The NPV of the project is $172.13, meaning that the present value of the project's future cash flows ($1,172.13) is greater than the project's cost of $1,000.00. Thus, the project is worthwhile.

| | A | B | C | D | E | F | G |
|---|---|---|---|---|---|---|---|
| 18 | Discount rate | NPV | | | | | |
| 19 | 0% | 1,100.00 | <-- =$B$5+NPV(A19,$B$6:$B$11) | | | | |
| 20 | 3% | 849.34 | <-- =$B$5+NPV(A20,$B$6:$B$11) | | | | |
| 21 | 6% | 637.67 | | | | | |
| 22 | 9% | 457.83 | NPV of Cash Flows | | | | |
| 23 | 12% | 304.16 | | | | | |
| 24 | 15% | 172.13 | | | | | |
| 25 | 18% | 58.10 | | | | | |
| 26 | 21% | -40.86 | | | | | |
| 27 | 24% | -127.14 | | | | | |
| 28 | 27% | -202.71 | | | | | |
| 29 | 30% | -269.16 | | | | | |
| 30 | | | | | | | |
| 31 | | | | | | | |
| 32 | | | | | | | |
| 33 | | | | | | | |
| 34 | | | | | | | |
| 35 | | | | | | | |
| 36 | | | | | | | |
| 37 | | | | | | | |
| 38 | | | | | | | |

NPV of Cash Flows

If we graph the project's NPV we can see that the IRR—the point where the NPV curve crosses the $x$-axis—is very close to 20%. As you can see in cell B15, the actual IRR is 19.71%.

### Accept or Reject? Should We Undertake the Project?

It is clear that the above project is worthwhile:

- Its NPV > 0, so that by the NPV criterion the project should be accepted.
- Its IRR of 19.71% > the project discount rate of 15%, so that by the IRR criterion the project should be accepted.

### A General Principle

We can derive a general principle from this example:

For conventional projects, projects with an initial negative cash flow and subsequent non-negative cash flows ( $CF_0 < 0, CF_1 \geq 0, CF_2 \geq 0,..., CF_N \geq 0$ ), the NPV and IRR criteria lead to the same "yes–no" decision: If the NPV criterion indicates a "yes" decision, then so will the IRR criterion (and vice versa).

## 4.5. Do NPV and IRR Produce the Same Project Rankings?

In the previous section we saw that for conventional projects, NPV and IRR give the same "yes–no" answer about whether to invest in a project. In this section we'll see that NPV and IRR do not necessarily *rank* projects the same, even if the projects are both conventional.

Suppose we have two projects and can choose to invest in only one. The projects are *mutually exclusive*: They are both ways to achieve the same end, and thus we would choose only one. In this section we discuss the use of NPV and IRR to rank the projects. To sum up our results before we start:

- Ranking projects by NPV and IRR can lead to possibly contradictory results. Using the NPV criterion may lead us to prefer one project, whereas using the IRR criterion may lead us to prefer the other project.
- Where a conflict exists between NPV and IRR, the project with the larger NPV is preferred. That is, the NPV criterion is the correct criterion to use for capital budgeting. This is not to impugn the IRR criterion, which is often very useful. However, NPV is preferred over IRR because it indicates the *increase in wealth* that the project produces.

### An Example

Next we show the cash flows for Project *A* and Project *B*. Both projects have the same initial cost of $500, but have different cash flow patterns. The relevant discount rate is 15%.

|   | A | B | C | D |
|---|---|---|---|---|
| 1 | **RANKING PROJECTS WITH NPV AND IRR** | | | |
| 2 | Discount rate | 15% | | |
| 3 | | | | |
| 4 | Year | **Project A** | **Project B** | |
| 5 | 0 | -500 | -500 | |
| 6 | 1 | 100 | 250 | |
| 7 | 2 | 100 | 250 | |
| 8 | 3 | 150 | 200 | |
| 9 | 4 | 200 | 100 | |
| 10 | 5 | 400 | 50 | |
| 11 | | | | |
| 12 | NPV | 74.42 | 119.96 | <-- =C5+NPV(B2,C6:C10) |
| 13 | IRR | 19.77% | 27.38% | <-- =IRR(C5:C10) |

**Comparing the projects using IRR:** If we use the IRR rule to choose between the projects, then *B* is preferred to *A* because the IRR of Project *B* is higher than that of Project *A*.

**Comparing the projects using NPV:** Here the choice is more complicated. When the discount rate is 15% (as illustrated above), the NPV of Project *B* is higher than that of Project *A*. In this case the IRR and the NPV agree: Both indicate that Project *B* should be chosen. Now suppose that the discount rate is 8%; in this case the NPV and IRR rankings conflict.

|   | A | B | C | D |
|---|---|---|---|---|
| 1 | **RANKING PROJECTS WITH NPV AND IRR** | | | |
| 2 | Discount rate | 8% | | |
| 3 | | | | |
| 4 | Year | **Project A** | **Project B** | |
| 5 | 0 | -500 | -500 | |
| 6 | 1 | 100 | 250 | |
| 7 | 2 | 100 | 250 | |
| 8 | 3 | 150 | 200 | |
| 9 | 4 | 200 | 100 | |
| 10 | 5 | 400 | 50 | |
| 11 | | | | |
| 12 | NPV | 216.64 | 212.11 | <-- =C5+NPV(B2,C6:C10) |
| 13 | IRR | 19.77% | 27.38% | <-- =IRR(C5:C10) |

In this case we have to resolve the conflict between the ranking on the basis of NPV (*A* is preferred) and ranking on the basis of IRR (*B* is preferred). As we stated in the introduction to this section, the solution to this question is that you should choose on the basis of NPV. We explore the reasons for this later on, but first we discuss a technical question.

## Why Do NPV and IRR Give Different Rankings?

Next we construct a table and graph that show the NPV for each project as a function of the discount rate.

| | A | B | C | D | E | F | G |
|---|---|---|---|---|---|---|---|
| 1 | RANKING PROJECTS WITH NPV AND IRR | | | | | | |
| 2 | Discount rate | 15% | | | | | |
| 3 | | | | | | | |
| 4 | Year | Project A | Project B | | | | |
| 5 | 0 | -500 | -500 | | | | |
| 6 | 1 | 100 | 250 | | | | |
| 7 | 2 | 100 | 250 | | | | |
| 8 | 3 | 150 | 200 | | | | |
| 9 | 4 | 200 | 100 | | | | |
| 10 | 5 | 400 | 50 | | | | |
| 11 | | | | | | | |
| 12 | NPV | 74.42 | 119.96 | <-- =C5+NPV(B2,C6:C10) | | | |
| 13 | IRR | 19.77% | 27.38% | <-- =IRR(C5:C10) | | | |
| 14 | | | | | | | |
| 15 | TABLE OF NPVs AND DISCOUNT RATES | | | | | | |
| 16 | | Project A NPV | Project B NPV | | | | |
| 17 | 0% | 450.00 | 350.00 | <-- =$C$5+NPV(A17,$C$6:$C$10) | | | |
| 18 | 2% | 382.57 | 311.53 | <-- =$C$5+NPV(A18,$C$6:$C$10) | | | |
| 19 | 4% | 321.69 | 275.90 | | | | |
| 20 | 6% | 266.60 | 242.84 | | | | |
| 21 | 8% | 216.64 | 212.11 | | | | |
| 22 | 10% | 171.22 | 183.49 | | | | |
| 23 | 12% | 129.85 | 156.79 | | | | |
| 24 | 14% | 92.08 | 131.84 | | | | |
| 25 | 16% | 57.53 | 108.47 | | | | |
| 26 | 18% | 25.86 | 86.57 | | | | |
| 27 | 20% | -3.22 | 66.00 | | | | |
| 28 | 22% | -29.96 | 46.66 | | | | |
| 29 | 24% | -54.61 | 28.45 | | | | |
| 30 | 26% | -77.36 | 11.28 | | | | |
| 31 | 28% | -98.39 | -4.93 | | | | |
| 32 | 30% | -117.87 | -20.25 | | | | |
| 33 | | | | | | | |
| 34 | | | | | | | |
| 35 | | | | | | | |

From the graph you can see why contradictory rankings occur:

- Project B has a higher IRR (27.38%) than Project A (19.77%). (Remember that the IRR is the point at which the NPV curve cuts the x-axis.)

- When the discount rate is low, Project A has a higher NPV than Project B, but when the discount rate is high, Project B has a higher NPV. There is a crossover point (in the next subsection you will see that this point is 8.51%) that marks the disagreement/agreement range.

- Project A's NPV is more sensitive to changes in the discount rate than Project B. The reason for this is that Project A's cash flows are more spread out over time than those of Project B; another way of saying this is that Project A has substantially more of its cash flows at later dates than Project B.

Summing up,

|  | Discount rate < 8.51% | Discount rate = 8.51% | Discount rate > 8.51% |
|---|---|---|---|
| NPV criterion | A preferred:<br>NPV(A) > NPV(B) | Indifferent between A and B:<br>NPV(A) = NPV(B) | B preferred:<br>NPV(B) > NPV(A) |
| IRR criterion | B always preferred to A because<br>IRR(B) > IRR(A) | | |

## Calculating the Crossover Point

The crossover point—which we claimed earlier was 8.51%—is the discount rate at which the NPV of the two projects is equal. A bit of formula manipulation will show you that *the crossover point is the IRR of the differential cash flows*. To see what this means, consider the following example.

|  | A | B | C | D | E |
|---|---|---|---|---|---|
| 36 | **Calculating the crossover point** | | | | |
| 37 | Year | Project A | Project B | Differential cash flows:<br>cash flow(A) - cash flow(B) | |
| 38 | 0 | -500 | -500 | 0 | <-- =B38-C38 |
| 39 | 1 | 100 | 250 | -150 | <-- =B39-C39 |
| 40 | 2 | 100 | 250 | -150 | |
| 41 | 3 | 150 | 200 | -50 | |
| 42 | 4 | 200 | 100 | 100 | |
| 43 | 5 | 400 | 50 | 350 | |
| 44 | | | | | |
| 45 | | | IRR | 8.51% | <-- =IRR(D38:D43) |

Column D in this example contains the differential cash flows—the difference between the cash flows of Project *A* and Project *B*. In cell D43 we use the Excel **IRR** function to compute the crossover point.

A bit of theory (can be skipped): To see why the crossover point is the IRR of the differential cash flows, suppose that for some rate *r*, NPV(A) = NPV(B):

$$NPV(A) = CF_0^A + \frac{CF_1^A}{(1+r)} + \frac{CF_2^A}{(1+r)^2} \ldots + \frac{CF_N^A}{(1+r)^N}$$

$$= CF_0^B + \frac{CF_1^B}{(1+r)} + \frac{CF_2^B}{(1+r)^2} \ldots + \frac{CF_N^B}{(1+r)^N} = NPV(B)$$

Subtracting and rearranging shows that *r* must be the IRR of the differential cash flows:

$$CF_0^A - CF_0^B + \frac{CF_1^A - CF_1^B}{(1+r)} + \frac{CF_2^A - CF_2^B}{(1+r)^2} \ldots + \frac{CF_N^A - CF_N^B}{(1+r)^N} = 0$$

## What to Use? NPV or IRR?

Let's go back to the initial example and suppose that the discount rate is 8%.

| | A | B | C | D |
|---|---|---|---|---|
| 1 | RANKING PROJECTS WITH NPV AND IRR | | | |
| 2 | Discount rate | 8% | | |
| 3 | | | | |
| 4 | Year | Project A | Project B | |
| 5 | 0 | -500 | -500 | |
| 6 | 1 | 100 | 250 | |
| 7 | 2 | 100 | 250 | |
| 8 | 3 | 150 | 200 | |
| 9 | 4 | 200 | 100 | |
| 10 | 5 | 400 | 50 | |
| 11 | | | | |
| 12 | NPV | 216.64 | 212.11 | <-- =C5+NPV(B2,C6:C10) |
| 13 | IRR | 19.77% | 27.38% | <-- =IRR(C5:C10) |

In this case we know there is disagreement between the NPV (which would lead us to choose Project A) and the IRR (by which we choose Project B). Which is correct?

The answer to this question is that we should—for the case where the discount rate is 8%—choose using the NPV (that is, choose Project A). This is just one example of the general principal discussed in Section 3 that *using the NPV is always preferred* because the NPV is the additional *wealth* that you get, whereas IRR is the compound rate of return. The economic assumption is that consumers maximize their wealth, not their rate of return.

## WHERE IS THIS CHAPTER GOING?

Until this point in the chapter, we've discussed general principles of project choice using the NPV and IRR criteria. The following sections discuss some specifics:

- Ignoring sunk costs and using marginal cash flows (Section 4.6)
- Incorporating taxes and tax shields into capital budgeting calculations (Section 4.7)
- Incorporating the cost of foregone opportunities (Section 4.9)
- Incorporating salvage values and terminal values (Section 4.11)

## 4.6. Capital Budgeting Principle: Ignore Sunk Costs and Consider Only Marginal Cash Flows

This is an important principle of capital budgeting and project evaluation: Ignore the cash flows you can't control and look only at the *marginal cash flows*—the outcomes of financial decisions you can still make. In the jargon of finance, ignore *sunk costs*, costs that have already been incurred and are thus not affected by future capital budgeting decisions.

Here's an example: You recently bought a plot of land and built a house on it. Your intention was to sell the house immediately, but it turns out that the house is really badly built and cannot be sold in its current state. The house and land cost you $100,000, and a friendly local contractor has offered to make the necessary repairs, which will cost $20,000. Your real estate broker estimates that even with these repairs you'll never sell the house for more than $90,000. What should you do? There are two approaches to answering this question:

- "My father always said 'Don't throw good money after bad.'" If this is your approach, you won't do anything. This attitude is typified in column B below, which shows that if you make the repairs you will have lost 25% on your money.

- "My mother was a finance prof, and she said 'Don't cry over spilt milk. Look only at the marginal cash flows.'" These turn out to be pretty good. In column C below you see that making the repairs will give you a 350% return on your $20,000.

|   | A | B | C | D |
|---|---|---|---|---|
| 1 | **IGNORE SUNK COSTS** | | | |
| 2 | House cost | 100,000 | | |
| 3 | Fix up cost | 20,000 | | |
| 4 | | | | |
| 5 | Year | **Cash flow wrong!** | **Cash flow right!** | |
| 6 | 0 | -120,000 | -20,000 | |
| 7 | 1 | 90,000 | 90,000 | |
| 8 | IRR | -25% | 350% | <-- =IRR(C6:C7) |

Of course your father was wrong and your mother right (this often happens): Even though you made some disastrous mistakes (you never should have built the house in the first place), you should—at this point—ignore the sunk cost of $100,000 and make the necessary repairs.

## 4.7. Capital Budgeting Principle: Don't Forget the Effects of Taxes— Sally and Dave's Condo Investment

In this section we discuss the capital budgeting problem faced by Sally and Dave, two business-school grads who are considering buying a condominium and renting it out for the income.

We use Sally and Dave and their condo to emphasize the place of taxes in the capital budgeting process. No one needs to be told that taxes are very important.[2] In the capital budgeting process, the cash flows that are to be discounted are *after-tax cash flows*. We postpone a fuller discussion of this topic to Chapters 6 and 7, where we define the concept of *free cash flow*. For the moment we concentrate on a few obvious principles, which we illustrate with the example of Sally and Dave's condo investment.

Sally and Dave—fresh out of business school with a little cash to spare—are considering buying a nifty condo as a rental property. The condo will cost $100,000, and (in this example at least) they're planning to buy it with all cash. Here are some additional facts:

- Sally and Dave figure they can rent out the condo for $24,000 per year. They'll have to pay property taxes of $1,500 annually and they're figuring on additional miscellaneous expenses of $1,000 per year.

---

[2] Will Rogers: "The difference between death and taxes is death doesn't get worse every time Congress meets."

- All the income from the condo has to be reported on their annual tax return. Currently Sally and Dave have a tax rate of 30%, and they think this rate will continue for the foreseeable future.

- Their accountant has explained to them that they can depreciate the full cost of the condo over 10 years—each year they can charge $10,000 depreciation $(= \dfrac{condo\ cost}{10\text{-}year\ depreciable\ life})$ against the income from the condo.[3] This means that they can expect to pay $3,450 in income taxes per year if they buy the condo and rent it out and have net income from the condo of $8,050.

|  | A | B | C |
|---|---|---|---|
| 1 | **SALLY & DAVE'S CONDO** | | |
| 2 | Cost of condo | 100,000 | |
| 3 | Sally & Dave's tax rate | 30% | |
| 4 | | | |
| 5 | Annual reportable income calculation | | |
| 6 | Rent | 24,000 | |
| 7 | Expenses | | |
| 8 | Property taxes | -1,500 | |
| 9 | Miscellaneous expenses | -1,000 | |
| 10 | Depreciation | -10,000 | |
| 11 | Reportable income | 11,500 | <-- =SUM(B6:B10) |
| 12 | Taxes (rate = 30%) | -3,450 | <-- =-B3*B11 |
| 13 | Net income | 8,050 | <-- =B11+B12 |

## SIDEBAR: WHAT IS DEPRECIATION?

In computing the taxes they owe, Sally and Dave get to subtract expenses from their income. Taxes are computed on the basis of the *income before taxes* (=income−expenses−depreciation −interest). When Sally and Dave get the rent from their condo, this is *income*—money earned from their asset. When Sally and Dave pay to fix the faucet in their condo, this is an *expense*—a cost of doing business.

The cost of the condo is neither income nor an expense. It's a *capital investment*—money paid for an asset that will be used over many years. Tax rules specify that each year part of the capital investments can be taken off the income ("expensed," in the accounting jargon). This reduces the taxes paid by the owners of the asset and accounts for the fact that the asset has a limited life.

There are many depreciation methods in use. The simplest method is *straight-line depreciation*. In this method the asset's annual depreciation is a percentage of its initial cost. In the case of Sally and Dave, for example, we've specified that the asset is depreciated over 10 years. This results in annual depreciation charges of

$$straight\text{-}line\ depreciation = \frac{initial\ asset\ cost}{depreciable\ life\ span} = \frac{\$100,000}{10} = \$10,000\ annually$$

---

[3] You may want to read the sidebar on depreciation before going on.

In some cases depreciation is taken on the asset cost minus its salvage value: If you think that the asset will be worth $20,000 at the end of its life (this is the salvage value), then the annual straight-line depreciation might be $8,000:

$$\begin{matrix} \text{straight-line depreciation} \\ \text{with salvage value} \end{matrix} = \frac{\text{initial asset cost} - \text{salvage value}}{\text{depreciable life span}}$$

$$= \frac{\$100,000 - \$20,000}{10} = \$8,000 \; annually$$

## Accelerated Depreciation

Although historically depreciation charges are related to the life span of the asset, in many cases this connection has been lost. Under U.S. tax rules, for example, an asset classified as having a 5-year depreciable life (trucks, cars, and some computer equipment are in this category) will be depreciated over 6 years (yes *6*) at 20, 32, 19.2, 11.52, 11.52, and 5.76% in each of the years 1, 2, ... , 6. Note that this method *accelerates* the depreciation charges—more than one sixth of the depreciation is taken annually in years 1–3 and less in later years. Because—as we show in the text—depreciation ultimately saves taxes, this benefits the asset's owner, who now gets to take more of the depreciation in the early years of the asset's life.

## Two Ways to Calculate the Cash Flow

In the previous spreadsheet you saw that Sally and Dave's net income was $8,050. In this section you'll see that the *cash flow produced by the condo* is much more that this amount. It all has to do with depreciation: Because the depreciation is an expense for tax purposes but not a cash expense, the *cash flow* from the condo rental is different. So even though the net income from the condo is $8,050, the annual cash flow is $18,050—you have to add back the depreciation to the net income to get the cash flow generated by the property.

|     | A | B | C |
| --- | --- | --- | --- |
| 16 | Cash flow, method 1:<br>Add back depreciation | | |
| 17 | Net income | 8,050 | <-- =B13 |
| 18 | Add back depreciation | 10,000 | <-- =-B10 |
| 19 | Cash flow | 18,050 | <-- =B18+B17 |

In the above calculation, we've added the depreciation back to the net income to get the cash flow.

> An asset's *cash flow* (the amount of cash produced by an asset during a particular period) is computed by taking the asset's net income (also called profit after taxes or sometimes just "income") and adding back noncash expenses like depreciation.[4]

## Tax Shields

There's another way of calculating the cash flow that involves a discussion of *tax shields*. A tax shield is a tax saving that results from being able to report an expense for tax purposes.

---

[4]In Chapter 6 we introduce the concept of *free cash flow*, which is an extension of the cash flow concept discussed here.

In general, a tax shield just reduces the cash cost of an expense—in the preceding example, because Sally and Dave's property taxes of $1,500 are an expense for tax purposes, the after-tax cost of the property taxes is

$$(1 - 30\%)* \$1,500 = \$1,500 - \underbrace{30\% * 1,500}_{\substack{\uparrow \\ \text{This \$450 is the} \\ \text{tax shield}}} = \$1,050.$$

The tax shield of $450 ( = 30% * $1,500) has reduced the cost of the property taxes.

Depreciation is a special case of a *noncash expense* that generates a tax shield. A little thought will show you that the $10,000 depreciation on the condo generates $3,000 of cash. Because depreciation reduces Sally and Dave's reported income, each dollar of depreciation saves them $0.30 (30 cents) of taxes, without actually costing them anything in out-of-pocket expenses (the $0.30 comes from the fact that Sally and Dave's tax rate is 30%). Thus, $10,000 of depreciation is worth $3,000 of cash. This $3,000 *depreciation tax shield* is a cash flow for Sally and Dave.

In the spreadsheet below we calculate the cash flow in two stages:

- We first calculate Sally and Dave's net income ignoring depreciation (cell B29). If depreciation were not an expense for tax purposes, Sally and Dave's net income would be $15,050.

- We then add to this figure the depreciation tax shield of $3,000. The result (cell B32) gives the cash flow for the condo.

| | A | B | C | D |
|---|---|---|---|---|
| 21 | Cash flow, method 2: Compute after-tax income without depreciation, then add depreciation tax shield | | | |
| 22 | Rent | 24,000 | | |
| 23 | Expenses | | | This is what the net income would have been if depreciation were not an expense for tax purposes. |
| 24 | Property taxes | -1,500 | | |
| 25 | Miscellaneous expenses | -1,000 | | |
| 26 | Depreciation | 0 | | |
| 27 | Reportable income | 21,500 | <-- =SUM(B22:B26) | |
| 28 | Taxes (rate = 30%) | -6,450 | <-- =-B3*B27 | |
| 29 | Net income without depreciation | 15,050 | <-- =B27+B28 | |
| 30 | | | | The effect of depreciation is to add a $3,000 tax shield. |
| 31 | Depreciation tax shield | 3,000 | <-- =B3*10000 | |
| 32 | Cash flow | 18,050 | <-- =B31+B29 | |
| 33 | | | | |

## Is Sally and Dave's Condo Investment Profitable?— A Preliminary Calculation

At this point Sally and Dave can make a preliminary calculation of the NPV and IRR on their condo investment. Assuming a discount rate of 12% and assuming that they only hold the condo for 10 years, the NPV of the condo investment is $1,987 and its IRR is 12.48%.

| | A | B | C |
|---|---|---|---|
| 1 | SALLY & DAVE'S CONDO--PRELIMINARY VALUATION | | |
| 2 | Discount rate | 12% | |
| 3 | | | |
| 4 | Year | Cash flow | |
| 5 | 0 | -100,000 | |
| 6 | 1 | 18,050 | |
| 7 | 2 | 18,050 | |
| 8 | 3 | 18,050 | |
| 9 | 4 | 18,050 | |
| 10 | 5 | 18,050 | |
| 11 | 6 | 18,050 | |
| 12 | 7 | 18,050 | |
| 13 | 8 | 18,050 | |
| 14 | 9 | 18,050 | |
| 15 | 10 | 18,050 | |
| 16 | | | |
| 17 | Net present value, NPV | 1,987 | <-- =B5+NPV(B2,B6:B15) |
| 18 | Internal rate of return, IRR | 12.48% | <-- =IRR(B5:B15) |

## Is Sally and Dave's Condo Investment Profitable?—Incorporating Terminal Value into the Calculations

A little thought about the previous spreadsheet reveals that we've left out an important factor: the value of the condo at the end of the 10-year horizon. In finance an asset's value at the end of the investment horizon is called the asset's *salvage value* or *terminal value*. In the above spreadsheet we've assumed that the terminal value of the condo is zero, but this assumption is implausible.

To make a better calculation about their investment, Sally and Dave will have to make an assumption about the condo's terminal value. Suppose they assume that at the end of the 10 years they'll be able to sell the condo for $80,000. The taxable gain relating to the sale of the condo is the difference between the condo's sale price and its book value at the time of sale—the initial price minus the sum of all the depreciation since Sally and Dave bought it. Because Sally and Dave have been depreciating the condo by $10,000 per year over a 10-year period, its book value at the end of 10 years will be zero.

In cell E10 below you can see that the sale of the condo for $80,000 will generate a cash flow of $56,000.

| | A | B | C | D | E | F |
|---|---|---|---|---|---|---|
| 1 | SALLY & DAVE'S CONDO: PROFITABILITY AND TERMINAL VALUE | | | | | |
| 2 | Cost of condo | 100,000 | | | | |
| 3 | Sally & Dave's tax rate | 30% | | | | |
| 4 | | | | | | |
| 5 | Annual reportable income calculation | | | Terminal value | | |
| 6 | Rent | 24,000 | | Estimated resale value, year 10 | 80,000 | |
| 7 | Expenses | | | Book value | 0 | |
| 8 | Property taxes | -1,500 | | Taxable gain | 80,000 | <-- =E6-E7 |
| 9 | Miscellaneous expenses | -1,000 | | Taxes | 24,000 | <-- =B3*E8 |
| 10 | Depreciation | -10,000 | | Net after-tax cash flow from terminal value | 56,000 | <-- =E8-E9 |
| 11 | Reportable income | 11,500 | <-- =SUM(B6:B10) | | | |
| 12 | Taxes (rate = 30%) | -3,450 | <-- =-B3*B11 | | | |
| 13 | Net income | 8,050 | <-- =B11+B12 | | | |
| 14 | | | | | | |
| 15 | Cash flow, method 1 Add back depreciation | | | | | |
| 16 | Net income | 8,050 | <-- =B13 | | | |
| 17 | Add back depreciation | 10,000 | <-- =-B10 | | | |
| 18 | Cash flow | 18,050 | <-- =B17+B16 | | | |

To compute the rate of return of Sally and Dave's condo investment, we put all the numbers together.

| | A | B | C | D |
|---|---|---|---|---|
| 20 | Discount rate | 12% | | |
| 21 | | | | |
| 22 | **Year** | **Cash flow** | | |
| 23 | 0 | -100,000 | | |
| 24 | 1 | 18,050 | <-- =B18, Annual cash flow from rental | |
| 25 | 2 | 18,050 | | |
| 26 | 3 | 18,050 | | |
| 27 | 4 | 18,050 | | |
| 28 | 5 | 18,050 | | |
| 29 | 6 | 18,050 | | |
| 30 | 7 | 18,050 | | |
| 31 | 8 | 18,050 | | |
| 32 | 9 | 18,050 | | |
| 33 | 10 | 74,050 | <-- =B32+E10 | |
| 34 | | | | |
| 35 | NPV of condo investment | 20,017 | <-- =B23+NPV(B20,B24:B33) | |
| 36 | IRR of investment | 15.98% | <-- =IRR(B23:B33) | |

Assuming that the 12% discount rate is the correct rate, the condo investment is worthwhile: Its NPV is positive and its IRR exceeds the discount rate.[5]

## BOOK VALUE VERSUS TERMINAL VALUE

The *book value* of an asset is its initial purchase price minus the accumulated depreciation. The *terminal value* of an asset is its assumed market value at the time you "stop writing down the asset's cash flows." This sounds like a weird definition of terminal value, but often when we do present value calculations for a long-lived asset (like Sally and Dave's condo or the company valuations we discuss in Chapters 6 and 7), we write down only a limited number of cash flows.

Sally and Dave are reluctant to make predictions about condo rents and expenses beyond a 10-year horizon. Past this point, they're worried about the accuracy of their guesses. So they write down 10 years of cash flows; the terminal value is their best guess of the condo's value at the end of year 10. Their thinking is, "Let's examine the profitability of the condo if we hold on to it for 10 years and sell it."

This is what we mean when we say that "the terminal value is what the asset is worth when we stop writing down the cash flows."

Taxes: If Sally and Dave are right in their terminal value assumption, they will have to account for taxes. The tax rules for selling an asset specify that the tax bill is computed on the *gain over the book value*. So, in the example of Sally and Dave,

$$Terminal\ value - taxes\ on\ gain\ over\ book =$$
$$Terminal\ value - tax\ rate * (Terminal\ value - book\ value)$$
$$= 80,000 - 30\% * (80,000 - 0) = 56,000$$

---

[5]When we say that a discount rate is "correct," we usually mean that it is appropriate to the riskiness of the cash flows being discounted. In Chapter 6 we have our first discussion in this book on how to determine a correct discount rate. For the moment, let's assume that the discount rate is appropriate to the riskiness of the condo's cash flows.

## Doing Some Sensitivity Analysis (Advanced Topic)

A sensitivity analysis can show how the IRR of the condo investment varies as a function of the annual rent and the terminal value. Using Excel's **Data Table** (see Chapter 27) we build a sensitivity table.

| | A | B | C | D | E | F | G | H |
|---|---|---|---|---|---|---|---|---|
| 38 | Data table--Condo IRR as function of annual rent and terminal value | | | | | | | |
| 39 | | | Rent | | | | | |
| 40 | | 15.98% | 18,000 | 20,000 | 22,000 | 24,000 | 26,000 | 28,000 |
| 41 | Terminal value --> | 50,000 | 9.72% | 11.45% | 13.15% | 14.82% | 16.47% | 18.10% |
| 42 | | 60,000 | 10.26% | 11.93% | 13.59% | 15.22% | 16.84% | 18.44% |
| 43 | | 70,000 | 10.77% | 12.40% | 14.01% | 15.61% | 17.19% | 18.76% |
| 44 | =B36 | 80,000 | 11.25% | 12.84% | 14.42% | 15.98% | 17.54% | 19.08% |
| 45 | | 90,000 | 11.71% | 13.27% | 14.81% | 16.34% | 17.87% | 19.38% |
| 46 | | 100,000 | 12.15% | 13.67% | 15.19% | 16.69% | 18.19% | 19.68% |
| 47 | | 110,000 | 12.58% | 14.06% | 15.55% | 17.02% | 18.50% | 19.96% |
| 48 | | 120,000 | 12.98% | 14.44% | 15.90% | 17.35% | 18.80% | 20.24% |
| 49 | | 130,000 | 13.37% | 14.80% | 16.23% | 17.66% | 19.09% | 20.51% |
| 50 | | 140,000 | 13.75% | 15.15% | 16.56% | 17.96% | 19.37% | 20.78% |
| 51 | | 150,000 | 14.11% | 15.49% | 16.87% | 18.26% | 19.65% | 21.03% |
| 52 | | 160,000 | 14.46% | 15.82% | 17.18% | 18.55% | 19.91% | 21.28% |
| 53 | | | | | | | | |
| 54 | | | Note: The data table above computes the IRR of the condo investment for combinations of rent (from $18,000 to | | | | | |
| 55 | | | $26,000 per year) and terminal value (from $50,000 to $160,000). | | | | | |
| 56 | | | Data tables are very useful though not trivial to compute. See Chapter 27 for more information. | | | | | |

The calculations in the data table aren't that surprising: For a given rent, the IRR is higher when the terminal value is higher, and for a given terminal value, the IRR is higher given a higher rent.

## Building the Data Table[6]

Here's how the data table was set up:

- We build a table with terminal values in the left-hand column and rent in the top row.
- In the top left-hand corner of the table (cell B40), we refer to the IRR calculation in the spreadsheet example (this calculation occurs in cell B36).

At this point the table looks like this:

| | A | B | C | D | E | F | G | H |
|---|---|---|---|---|---|---|---|---|
| 38 | Data table--Condo IRR as function of annual rent and terminal value | | | | | | | |
| 39 | | | Rent | | | | | |
| 40 | | 15.98% | 18,000 | 20,000 | 22,000 | 24,000 | 26,000 | 28,000 |
| 41 | Terminal value --> | 50,000 | | | | | | |
| 42 | | 60,000 | | | | | | |
| 43 | | 70,000 | | | | | | |
| 44 | =B36 | 80,000 | | | | | | |
| 45 | | 90,000 | | | | | | |
| 46 | | 100,000 | | | | | | |
| 47 | | 110,000 | | | | | | |
| 48 | | 120,000 | | | | | | |
| 49 | | 130,000 | | | | | | |
| 50 | | 140,000 | | | | | | |
| 51 | | 150,000 | | | | | | |
| 52 | | 160,000 | | | | | | |

Using the mouse, we now mark the whole table. We use the **Data|What-If Analysis|Data Table** command.

---

[6] This subsection doesn't replace Chapter 27, but it may help you recall what we said there.

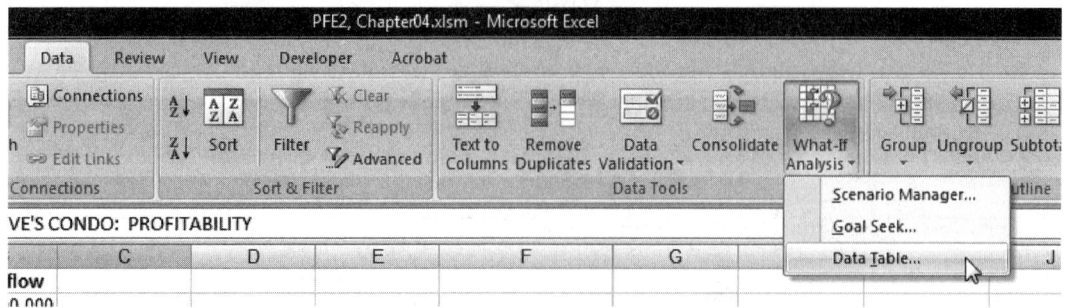

We can now fill in the cell references from the original example.

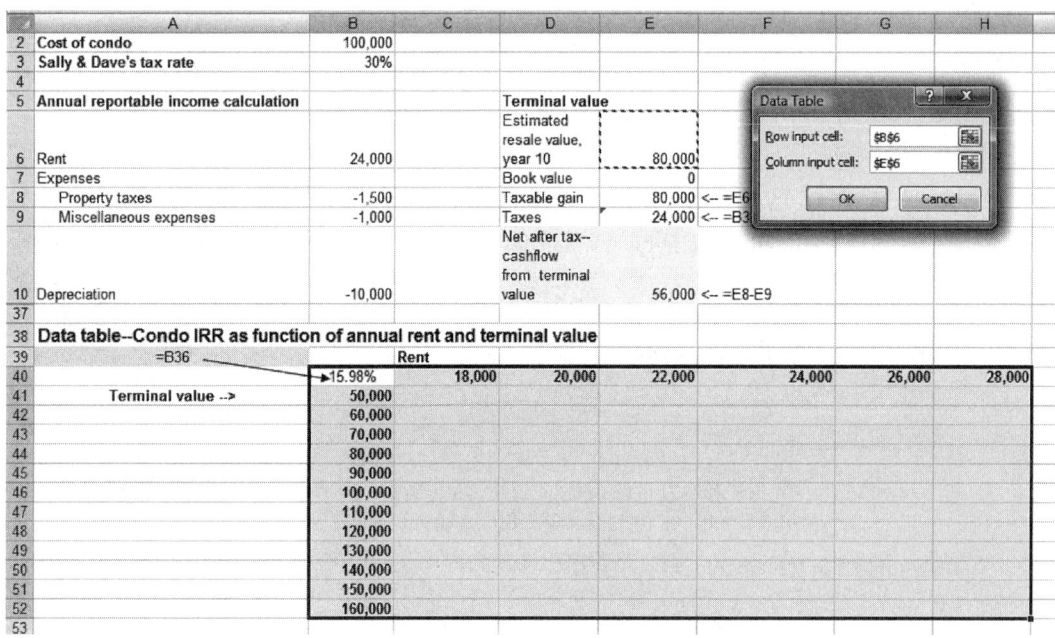

The dialog box tells Excel to repeat the calculation in cell B36, varying the rent number in cell B6 and varying the terminal value number in cell E6. Pressing **OK** does the rest.

---

**MINI CASE**

A mini case for this chapter looks at Sally and Dave's condo once more—this time under the assumption that they take out a mortgage to buy the condo. Highly recommended!

---

## 4.8. Capital Budgeting and Salvage Values

In the Sally–Dave condo example we've focused on the effect of noncash expenses on cash flows: Accountants and the tax authorities compute earnings by subtracting certain kinds of expenses from sales, even though these expenses are *noncash expenses*. To compute the cash flow, we add back these noncash expenses to accounting earnings. We showed that these non-cash expenses create *tax shields*—they create cash by saving taxes.

In this section's example we consider a capital budgeting example in which a firm sells its asset before it is fully depreciated. We show that the asset's book value at the date of the terminal value creates a tax shield and we look at the effect of this tax shield on the capital budgeting decision.

Here's the example. Your firm is considering buying a new machine. Here are the facts:

- The machine costs $800.
- Over the next 8 years (the life of the machine) the machine will generate annual sales of $1,000.
- The annual cost of the goods sold (COGS) is $400 per year and other costs; selling, general, and administrative expenses (SG&A) are $300 per year.
- Depreciation on the machine is straight-line over 8 years (that is, $100 per year).
- At the end of 8 years, the machine's salvage value (or terminal value) is zero.
- The firm's tax rate is 40%.
- The firm's discount rate for projects of this kind is 15%.

Should the firm buy the machine? Here's the analysis in Excel.

| | A | B | C | D | E | F | G |
|---|---|---|---|---|---|---|---|
| 1 | | | BUYING A MACHINE--NPV ANALYSIS | | | | |
| 2 | Cost of the machine | 800 | | | | | |
| 3 | Annual anticipated sales | 1,000 | | | | | |
| 4 | Annual COGS | 400 | | | | | |
| 5 | Annual SG&A | 300 | | | NPV Analysis | | |
| 6 | Annual depreciation | 100 | | | Year | Cash flow | |
| 7 | | | | | 0 | -800 | <-- =-B2 |
| 8 | Tax rate | 40% | | | 1 | 220 | <-- =$B$23 |
| 9 | Discount rate | 15% | | | 2 | 220 | |
| 10 | | | | | 3 | 220 | |
| 11 | Annual profit and loss (P&L) | | | | 4 | 220 | |
| 12 | Sales | 1,000 | | | 5 | 220 | |
| 13 | Minus COGS | -400 | | | 6 | 220 | |
| 14 | Minus SG&A | -300 | | | 7 | 220 | |
| 15 | Minus depreciation | -100 | | | 8 | 220 | |
| 16 | Profit before taxes | 200 | <-- =SUM(B12:B15) | | | | |
| 17 | Subtract taxes | -80 | <-- =-B8*B16 | | NPV | 187 | <-- =F7+NPV(B9,F8:F15) |
| 18 | Profit after taxes | 120 | <-- =B16+B17 | | | | |
| 19 | | | | | | | |
| 20 | Calculating the annual cash flow | | | | | | |
| 21 | Profit after taxes | 120 | | | | | |
| 22 | Add back depreciation | 100 | | | | | |
| 23 | Cash flow | 220 | | | | | |

Note that we first calculate the profit and loss (P&L) statement for the machine (cells B12:B18) and then turn this P&L into a cash flow calculation (cells B21:B23). The annual cash flow is $220. Cells F7:F15 show the table of cash flows, and cell F17 gives the NPV of the project. The NPV is positive, and we would therefore buy the machine.

## Salvage Value—A Variation on the Theme

Suppose the firm can sell the machine for $300 at the end of year 8. To compute the cash flow produced by this salvage value, we must make the distinction between *book value* and *market value*.

| Book value | An accounting concept: The book value of the machine is its initial cost minus the accumulated depreciation (the sum of the depreciation taken on the machine since its purchase). In our example, the book value of the machine in year 0 is $800, in year 1 it is $700,..., and at the end of year 8 it is zero. |
| Market value | The market value is the price at which the machine can be sold. In our example the market value of the machine at the end of year 8 is $300. |
| Taxable gain | The taxable gain on the machine at the time of sale is the difference between the market value and the book value. In our case the taxable gain is positive ($300), but it can also be negative (see an example at the end of this chapter). |

Here's the NPV calculation including the salvage value.

| | A | B | C | D | E | F | G |
|---|---|---|---|---|---|---|---|
| 1 | | | BUYING A MACHINE--NPV ANALYSIS with salvage value | | | | |
| 2 | Cost of the machine | 800 | | | | | |
| 3 | Annual anticipated sales | 1,000 | | | | | |
| 4 | Annual COGS | 400 | | | | | |
| 5 | Annual SG&A | 300 | | | NPV Analysis | | |
| 6 | Annual depreciation | 100 | | | Year | Cash flow | |
| 7 | | | | | 0 | -800 | <-- =-B2 |
| 8 | Tax rate | 40% | | | 1 | 220 | <-- =$B$23 |
| 9 | Discount rate | 15% | | | 2 | 220 | |
| 10 | | | | | 3 | 220 | |
| 11 | Annual profit and loss (P&L) | | | | 4 | 220 | |
| 12 | Sales | 1,000 | | | 5 | 220 | |
| 13 | Minus COGS | -400 | | | 6 | 220 | |
| 14 | Minus SG&A | -300 | | | 7 | 220 | |
| 15 | Minus depreciation | -100 | | | 8 | 400 | <-- =$B$23+B30 |
| 16 | Profit before taxes | 200 | <-- =SUM(B12:B15) | | | | |
| 17 | Subtract taxes | -80 | <-- =-B8*B16 | | NPV | 246 | <-- =F7+NPV(B9,F8:F15) |
| 18 | Profit after taxes | 120 | <-- =B16+B17 | | | | |
| 19 | | | | | | | |
| 20 | Calculating the annual cash flow | | | | | | |
| 21 | Profit after taxes | 120 | | | | | |
| 22 | Add back depreciation | 100 | | | | | |
| 23 | Cash flow | 220 | | | | | |
| 24 | | | | | | | |
| 25 | Calculating the cash flow from salvage value | | | | | | |
| 26 | Machine market value, year 8 | 300 | | | | | |
| 27 | Book value, year 8 | 0 | | | | | |
| 28 | Taxable gain | 300 | <-- =B26-B27 | | | | |
| 29 | Taxes paid on gain | 120 | <-- =B8*B28 | | | | |
| 30 | Cash flow from salvage value | 180 | <-- =B26-B29 | | | | |

Note the calculation of the cash flow from the salvage value (cell B30) and the change in the year 8 cash flow (cell F15).

## One More Example

Suppose we change the example slightly:

- The annual sales, SG&A, COGS, and depreciation are still as specified in the original example. The machine will still be depreciated on a straight-line basis over 8 years.

- However, we think we will sell the machine at the *end of year 7* for an estimated salvage value of $450. At the end of year 7 the book value of the machine is $100.

Here's how our calculations look now.

| | A | B | C | D | E | F | G |
|---|---|---|---|---|---|---|---|
| 1 | BUYING A MACHINE--NPV ANALYSIS<br>with salvage value<br>Machine sold at end of year 7 | | | | | | |
| 2 | Cost of the machine | 800 | | | | | |
| 3 | Annual anticipated sales | 1,000 | | | | | |
| 4 | Annual COGS | 400 | | | | | |
| 5 | Annual SG&A | 300 | | | NPV Analysis | | |
| 6 | Annual depreciation | 100 | | | Year | Cash flow | |
| 7 | | | | | 0 | -800 | <-- =-B2 |
| 8 | Tax rate | 40% | | | 1 | 220 | <-- =$B$23 |
| 9 | Discount rate | 15% | | | 2 | 220 | |
| 10 | | | | | 3 | 220 | |
| 11 | **Annual profit and loss (P&L)** | | | | 4 | 220 | |
| 12 | Sales | 1,000 | | | 5 | 220 | |
| 13 | Minus COGS | -400 | | | 6 | 220 | |
| 14 | Minus SG&A | -300 | | | 7 | 530 | <-- =$B$23+B30 |
| 15 | Minus depreciation | -100 | | | | | |
| 16 | Profit before taxes | 200 | <-- =SUM(B12:B15) | | NPV | 232 | <-- =F7+NPV(B9,F8:F15) |
| 17 | Subtract taxes | -80 | <-- =-B8*B16 | | | | |
| 18 | Profit after taxes | 120 | <-- =B16+B17 | | | | |
| 19 | | | | | | | |
| 20 | **Calculating the annual cash flow** | | | | | | |
| 21 | Profit after taxes | 120 | | | | | |
| 22 | Add back depreciation | 100 | | | | | |
| 23 | Cash flow | 220 | | | | | |
| 24 | | | | | | | |
| 25 | **Calculating the cash flow from salvage value** | | | | | | |
| 26 | Machine market value, year 7 | 450 | | | | | |
| 27 | Book value, year 7 | 100 | | | | | |
| 28 | Taxable gain | 350 | <-- =B26-B27 | | | | |
| 29 | Taxes paid on gain | 140 | <-- =B8*B28 | | | | |
| 30 | Cash flow from salvage value | 310 | <-- =B26-B29 | | | | |

Note the subtle changes from the previous example:

- The *cash flow from salvage value* is

$$Salvage\ value - tax * \underbrace{\left( Salvage\ value - Book\ value \right)}_{\substack{\text{Taxable gain at time} \\ \text{of machine sale}}}$$

In our example this is $310 (cell B30).

- Another way to write the cash flow from the salvage value is

$$\underbrace{Salvage\ value * \left( 1 - tax \right)}_{\substack{\text{After-tax proceeds from machine} \\ \text{sale } if \text{ the whole salvage value is} \\ \text{taxed}}} + \underbrace{tax * book\ value}_{\substack{\text{Tax shield on book} \\ \text{value at time of machine} \\ \text{sale}}}$$

Using this example, you can see the role taxes play even if we sell the machine at a loss. Suppose, for example, that the machine is sold in year 7 for $50, which is less than the book value:

| | A | B | C | D | E | F | G |
|---|---|---|---|---|---|---|---|
| 1 | | BUYING A MACHINE--NPV ANALYSIS with salvage value Machine sold at end of year 7 | | | | | |
| 2 | Cost of the machine | 800 | | | | | |
| 3 | Annual anticipated sales | 1,000 | | | | | |
| 4 | Annual COGS | 400 | | | | | |
| 5 | Annual SG&A | 300 | | NPV Analysis | | | |
| 6 | Annual depreciation | 100 | | Year | Cash flow | | |
| 7 | | | | | 0 | -800 | <-- =-B2 |
| 8 | Tax rate | 40% | | | 1 | 220 | <-- =$B$23 |
| 9 | Discount rate | 15% | | | 2 | 220 | |
| 10 | | | | | 3 | 220 | |
| 11 | Annual profit and loss (P&L) | | | | 4 | 220 | |
| 12 | Sales | 1,000 | | | 5 | 220 | |
| 13 | Minus COGS | -400 | | | 6 | 220 | |
| 14 | Minus SG&A | -300 | | | 7 | 290 | <-- =$B$23+B30 |
| 15 | Minus depreciation | -100 | | | | | |
| 16 | Profit before taxes | 200 | <-- =SUM(B12:B15) | | NPV | 142 | <-- =F7+NPV(B9,F8:F15) |
| 17 | Subtract taxes | -80 | <-- =-B8*B16 | | | | |
| 18 | Profit after taxes | 120 | <-- =B16+B17 | | | | |
| 19 | | | | | | | |
| 20 | Calculating the annual cash flow | | | | | | |
| 21 | Profit after taxes | 120 | | | | | |
| 22 | Add back depreciation | 100 | | | | | |
| 23 | Cash flow | 220 | | | | | |
| 24 | | | | | | | |
| 25 | Calculating the cash flow from salvage value | | | | | | |
| 26 | Machine market value, year 7 | 50 | | | | | |
| 27 | Book value, year 7 | 100 | | | | | |
| 28 | Taxable gain | -50 | <-- =B26-B27 | | | | |
| 29 | Taxes paid on gain | -20 | <-- =B8*B28 | | | | |
| 30 | Cash flow from salvage value | 70 | <-- =B26-B29 | | | | |

In this case, the negative taxable gain (cell B28, the jargon often heard is "loss over book") produces a "tax shield"—the negative taxes of -$20 in cell B29. This tax shield is really a reduction in your total taxes attributable to the $50 loss in cell B28. It is added to the market value to produce a salvage value cash flow of $70 (cell B30). Thus, even selling an asset at a loss can produce a positive cash flow.

## 4.9. Capital Budgeting Principle: Don't Forget the Cost of Foregone Opportunities

This is another important principle of capital budgeting. An example: You've been offered the following project, which involves buying a widget-making machine for $300 to make a new product. The cash flows in years 1–5 have been calculated by your financial analysts.

|   | A | B | C |
|---|---|---|---|
| 1 | | **DON'T FORGET THE COST OF FOREGONE OPPORTUNITIES** | |
| 2 | Discount rate | 12% | |
| 3 | | | |
| 4 | **Year** | **Cash flow** | |
| 5 | 0 | -300 | |
| 6 | 1 | 185 | |
| 7 | 2 | 249 | |
| 8 | 3 | 155 | |
| 9 | 4 | 135 | |
| 10 | 5 | 420 | |
| 11 | | | |
| 12 | NPV | 498.12 | <-- =NPV(B2,B6:B10)+B5 |
| 13 | IRR | 62.67% | <-- =IRR(B5:B10) |

Looks like a fine project! But now someone remembers that the widget process makes use of some already existing but underused equipment. Should the value of this equipment be somehow taken into account?

The answer to this question has to do with whether the equipment has an alternative use. For example, suppose that, if you don't buy the widget machine, you can sell the equipment for $200. Then the true year 0 cost for the project is $500, and the project has a lower NPV.

|   | A | B | C |
|---|---|---|---|
| 16 | Discount rate | 12% | |
| 17 | | | |
| 18 | **Year** | **Cash flow** | |
| 19 | 0 | -500 | The $300 direct cost + $200 <-- value of the existing machines |
| 20 | 1 | 185 | |
| 21 | 2 | 249 | |
| 22 | 3 | 155 | |
| 23 | 4 | 135 | |
| 24 | 5 | 420 | |
| 25 | | | |
| 26 | NPV | 298.12 | |
| 27 | IRR | 31.97% | |

Although the logic here is clear, the implementation can be murky: What if the machine is to occupy space in a building that is currently unused? Should the cost of this space be taken into account? It all depends on whether there are alternative uses, now or in the future.[7]

# 4.10. In-House Copying or Outsourcing? A Mini Case Illustrating Foregone Opportunity Costs

Your company is trying to decide whether to outsource its photocopying or continue to do it in-house. The current photocopier won't do anymore—it has to be either sold or thoroughly

---

[7]There's a fine Harvard case on this topic: "The Super Project," Harvard Business School case 9-112-034.

fixed up. Here are some details about the two alternatives:

- The company's tax rate is 40%.
- Doing the copying in-house requires an investment of $17,000 to fix up the existing photo-copy machine. Your accountant estimates that this $17,000 can be immediately booked as an expense, so that its after-tax cost is $(1-40\%)*17,000 = 10,200$. Given this invest-ment, the copier will be good for another 5 years. Annual copying costs are estimated to be $25,000 on a before-tax basis; after-tax this is $(1-40\%)*25.000 = 15,000$.
- The photocopy machine is on your books for $15,000, but its market value is in fact much less—it could only be sold today for $5,000. This means that the sale of the copier will generate a loss for tax purposes of $10,000; at your tax rate of 40%, this loss gives a tax shield of $4,000. Thus, the sale of the copier will generate a cash flow of $9,000.
- If you decide to keep doing the photocopying in-house, the remaining book value of the copier will be depreciated over 5 years at $3,000 per year. Because your tax rate is 40%, this will produce a tax shield of 40% * $3,000 = $1,200 per year.
- Outsourcing the copying will be $33,000 per year—$8,000 more expensive than doing it in-house on the rehabilitated copier. Of course this $33,000 is an expense for tax pur-poses, so that the net savings from doing the copying in-house is

$$\left(1 - tax\,rate\right)*\,outsourcing\,\cos ts = \left(1 - 40\%\right)*\,\$33,000 = \$19,800\,.$$

- The relevant discount rate is 12%.

We will show you two ways to analyze this decision. The first method values each of the alternatives separately. The second method looks only at the differential cash flows; while this produces a somewhat "cleaner" set of cash flows that take explicit account of foregone opportunity costs, we recommend the first method—it's simpler and leads to fewer mistakes.

## Method 1: Write Down the Cash Flows of Each Alternative

This is often the simplest way to do things; if you do it correctly, this method takes care of all the foregone opportunity costs without your thinking about them. Below we write down the cash flows for each alternative.

| | IN HOUSE | OUTSOURCING |
|---|---|---|
| **Year 0** | $-\left(1 - tax\,rate\right)*\,machine\,rehab\,cost$ <br> $= -\left(1 - 40\%\right)*\,17,000 = -\$10,200$ | *Sale price of machine* <br> $+tax\,rate*loss\,over\,book\,value$ <br> $= \$5,000 + 40\%*\left(\$15,000 - 5,000\right)$ <br> $= \$9,000$ |
| **Years 1–5 annual cash flow** | $-\left(1 - tax\,rate\right)*\,in\text{-}house\,costs$ <br> $+\,tax\,rate*depreciation$ <br> $= -\left(1 - 40\%\right)*\,\$25,000$ <br> $+ 40\%*\$3,000 = -\$13,800$ | $-\left(1 - tax\,rate\right)*\,outsourcing\,costs$ <br> $= -\left(1 - 40\%\right)*\,\$33,000$ <br> $= -\$19,800$ |

Putting these data in a spreadsheet and discounting at the discount rate of 12% shows that it is cheaper to do the in-house copying. The NPV of the in-house cash flows is -$59,946, whereas the NPV of the outsourcing cash flows is -$62,375. Note that both NPVs are negative; but the in-house alternative is less negative (meaning more positive) than the outsourcing alternative; therefore, the in-house method is preferred.

|  | A | B | C |
|---|---|---|---|
| 1 | **SELL THE PHOTOCOPIER OR FIX IT UP?** | | |
| 2 | Annual cost savings (before tax) after fixing up the machine | 8,000 | |
| 3 | Book value of machine | 15,000 | |
| 4 | Market value of machine | 5,000 | |
| 5 | Rehab cost of machine | 17,000 | |
| 6 | Tax rate | 40% | |
| 7 | Annual depreciation if machine is retained | 3,000 | |
| 8 | Annual copying costs | | |
| 9 | In-house | 25,000 | |
| 10 | Outsourcing | 33,000 | |
| 11 | Discount rate | 12% | |
| 12 | | | |
| 13 | **Alternative 1:  Fix up machine and do copying in-house** | | |
| 14 | Year | Cash flow | |
| 15 | 0 | -10,200 | <-- =-B5*(1-B6) |
| 16 | 1 | -13,800 | <-- =-$B$9*(1-$B$6)+$B$6*$B$7 |
| 17 | 2 | -13,800 | |
| 18 | 3 | -13,800 | |
| 19 | 4 | -13,800 | |
| 20 | 5 | -13,800 | |
| 21 | NPV of fixing up machine and in-house copying | -59,946 | <-- =B15+NPV(B11,B16:B20) |
| 22 | | | |
| 23 | **Alternative 2:  Sell machine and outsource copying** | | |
| 24 | Year | Cash flow | |
| 25 | 0 | 9,000 | <-- =B4+B6*(B3-B4) |
| 26 | 1 | -19,800 | <-- =-(1-$B$6)*$B$10 |
| 27 | 2 | -19,800 | |
| 28 | 3 | -19,800 | |
| 29 | 4 | -19,800 | |
| 30 | 5 | -19,800 | |
| 31 | NPV of selling machine and outsourcing | -62,375 | <-- =B25+NPV(B11,B26:B30) |

## Method 2: Discounting the Differential Cash Flows

In this method we subtract the cash flows of Alternative 2 from those of Alternative 1.

|  | A | B | C |
|---|---|---|---|
| 34 | **Subtract Alternative 2 CFs from Alternative 1 CFs** | | |
| 35 | Year | Cash flow | |
| 36 | 0 | -19,200 | <-- =B15-B25 |
| 37 | 1 | 6,000 | <-- =B16-B26 |
| 38 | 2 | 6,000 | |
| 39 | 3 | 6,000 | |
| 40 | 4 | 6,000 | |
| 41 | 5 | 6,000 | |
| 42 | NPV(Alternative 1 - Alternative 2) | 2,429 | <-- =B36+NPV(B11,B37:B41) |

The NPV of the differential cash flows is positive. This means that Alternative 1 (in-house) is better than Alternative 2 (outsourcing):

$$NPV\left(In\text{-}house - Outsourcing\right) = NPV\left(In\text{-}house\right) - NPV(Outsourcing) > 0$$
This means that
$$NPV\left(In\text{-}house\right) > NPV(Outsourcing)$$

If you look carefully at the differential cash flows, you'll see that they take into account the cost of the foregone opportunities.

|  | Differential cash flow | Explanation |
|---|---|---|
| Year 0 | -$19,200 | This is the after-tax cost of rehabilitating the old copier (-$10,200) and the foregone opportunity cost of selling the copier (-$9,000). In other words: This is the cost in year 0 of deciding to do the copying in house. |
| Years 1–5 | $6,000 | This is the after-tax saving of doing the copying in house: If you do it in house, you save $8,000 pretax (= $4,800 after tax) and you get to take depreciation on the existing copier (= tax shield of $1,200). Relative to in house copying, the outsourcing alternative has a foregone opportunity cost of the loss of the depreciation tax shield. |

If you examine the convoluted prose in the table above ("the outsourcing alternative has a foregone opportunity cost of the loss of the depreciation tax shield") you'll agree that it might just be simpler to list each alternative's cash flows separately.

## 4.11. Accelerated Depreciation

As you know by now, the *salvage value* for an asset is its value at the end of its life; another term sometimes used is *terminal value*. Here's a capital budgeting example that illustrates the importance of accelerated depreciation in computing the cash:

- Your company is considering buying a machine for $10,000.

- If bought, the machine will produce annual cost savings of $3,000 for the next 5 years; these cash flows will be taxed at the company's tax rate of 40%.

- The machine will be depreciated over the 5-year period using the accelerated depreciation percentages allowable in the United States. At the end of the 5th year, the machine will be sold; your estimate of its terminal value at this point is $4,000, even though for accounting purposes its book value is $576 (cell B19 below).

You have to decide what the NPV of the project is, using a discount rate of 12%. Here are the relevant calculations.

| | A | B | C | D | E | F | G |
|---|---|---|---|---|---|---|---|
| 1 | | | CAPITAL BUDGETING WITH ACCELERATED DEPRECIATION | | | | |
| 2 | Machine cost | 10,000 | | | | | |
| 3 | Annual materials savings, before tax | 3,000 | | | | | |
| 4 | Salvage value, end of year 5 | 4,000 | | | | | |
| 5 | Tax rate | 40% | | | | | |
| 6 | Discount rate | 12% | | | | | |
| 7 | | | | | | | |
| 8 | Accelerated depreciation schedule (ACRS) | | | | | | |
| 9 | Year | ACRS depreciation percentage | Actual depreciation | Depreciation tax shield | | | |
| 10 | 1 | 20.00% | 2,000 | 800 | <-- =$B$5*C10 | | |
| 11 | 2 | 32.00% | 3,200 | 1,280 | <-- =$B$5*C11 | | |
| 12 | 3 | 19.20% | 1,920 | 768 | <-- =$B$5*C12 | | |
| 13 | 4 | 11.52% | 1,152 | 461 | <-- =$B$5*C13 | | |
| 14 | 5 | 11.52% | 1,152 | 461 | | | |
| 15 | 6 | 5.76% | 576 | 230 | The book value at the end of year 5 is the initial cost of the machine ($10,000) *minus* the sum of all the depreciation taken on the machine through year 5 ($9,424). | | |
| 16 | | | | | | | |
| 17 | Terminal value, end of year 5 | | | | | | |
| 18 | End-year 5 sale price, estimated | 4,000 | <-- =B4 | | | | |
| 19 | End-year 5 book value | 576 | <-- =B2-SUM(C10:C14) | | | | |
| 20 | Taxable gain | 3,424 | <-- =B18-B19 | | | | |
| 21 | Taxes | 1,370 | <-- =B5*B20 | | | | |
| 22 | Net cash flow from terminal value | 2,630 | <-- =B18-B21 | The net cash flow from the terminal value equals the end-year 5 sale price minus applicable taxes. | | | |
| 23 | | | | | | | |
| 24 | | | | | | | |
| 25 | Net present value calculation | | | | | | |
| 26 | Year | Cost | After-tax cost savings | Depreciation tax shield | Terminal value | Total cash flow | |
| 27 | 0 | -10,000 | | | | -10,000 | |
| 28 | 1 | | 1,800 | 800 | | 2,600 | <-- =SUM(B28:E28) |
| 29 | 2 | | 1,800 | 1,280 | | 3,080 | |
| 30 | 3 | | 1,800 | 768 | | 2,568 | |
| 31 | 4 | | 1,800 | 461 | | 2,261 | |
| 32 | 5 | | 1,800 | 461 | 2,630 | 4,891 | |
| 33 | | | | | | | |
| 34 | Net present value | | 817 | <-- =F27+NPV(B6,F28:F32) | | | |
| 35 | IRR | | 15.01% | <-- =IRR(F27:F32) | | | |

The annual after-tax cost saving is $1,800 = (1–40%) * $3,000. The depreciation tax shields are determined by the accelerated depreciation schedule (rows 10–15). When the asset is sold at the end of year 5, its book value is $576. This leads to a taxable gain of $3,424 (cell B20) and to taxes of $1,370 (cell B21). The net cash flow (cell B22) from selling the asset at the end of year 5 is its sale price of $4,000 minus the taxes (cell B21). The NPV of the asset is $817 and the IRR is 14.36% (cells B34 and B35).

# 4.12. Conclusion

In this chapter we've discussed the basics of capital budgeting using NPV and IRR. Capital budgeting decisions can be crudely separated into "yes–no" decisions ("Should we undertake a given project?") and into "ranking" decisions ("Which of the following list of projects do we prefer?"). We've concentrated on two important areas of capital budgeting:

- The difference between NPV and IRR in making the capital budgeting decision. In many cases these two criteria give the same answer to the capital budgeting question. However, there are cases—especially when we rank projects—where NPV and IRR give different answers. Where they differ, NPV is the preferable criterion to use because the NPV is the additional wealth derived from a project.

• Every capital budgeting decision ultimately involves a set of anticipated cash flows, so when you do capital budgeting, it's important to get these cash flows right. We've illustrated the importance of sunk costs, taxes, foregone opportunities, and salvage values in determining the cash flows.

## EXERCISES

1. You are considering a project with the cash flows given below.

|    | A             | B         |
|----|---------------|-----------|
| 3  | Discount rate | 25%       |
| 4  |               |           |
| 5  | Year          | Cash flow |
| 6  | 0             | -1,000    |
| 7  | 1             | 100       |
| 8  | 2             | 200       |
| 9  | 3             | 300       |
| 10 | 4             | 400       |
| 11 | 5             | 500       |
| 12 | 6             | 600       |

a. Calculate the present value of the future cash flows of the project.

b. Calculate the project's net present value.

c. Calculate the project's internal rate of return.

d. Should you undertake the project?

2. Your firm is considering two projects with the following cash flows:

|   | A             | B         | C         |
|---|---------------|-----------|-----------|
| 1 | Discount rate | 12%       |           |
| 2 |               |           |           |
| 3 | Year          | Project A | Project B |
| 4 | 0             | -500      | -500      |
| 5 | 1             | 167       | 200       |
| 6 | 2             | 180       | 250       |
| 7 | 3             | 160       | 170       |
| 8 | 4             | 100       | 25        |
| 9 | 5             | 100       | 30        |

a. If the appropriate discount rate is 12%, rank the two projects.

b. Which project is preferred if you rank by IRR?

c. Calculate the crossover rate—the discount rate $r$ in which the NPVs of both projects are equal.

d. Should you use NPV or IRR to choose between the two projects? Give a brief discussion.

3. Your uncle is a proud owner of an up-market clothing store. Because business is down, he is considering replacing the languishing tie department with a new sportswear department. To examine the profitability of such a move he has hired a financial advisor to estimate the cash flows of the new department. After 6 months of hard work, the financial advisor came up with the following calculation:

| Investment (at t = 0) | |
|---|---|
| Rearranging the shop | 40,000 |
| Loss of business during renovation | 15,000 |
| Payment for financial advisor | 12,000 |
| Total | 67,000 |

| Annual profits (from t = 1 to infinity) | |
|---|---|
| Annual earnings from the sport department | 75,000 |
| Loss of earnings from the tie department | -20,000 |
| Loss of earnings from other departments* | -15,000 |
| Additional worker for the sport department | -18,000 |
| Municipal taxes | -15,000 |
| Total | 7,000 |
| *Some of your uncle's stuck-up clients will not buy in a shop that sells sportswear. | |

The discount rate is 12%, and there are no additional taxes. Thus, the financial advisor calculated the NPV as follows.

$$-67,000 + \frac{7,000}{0.12} = -8,667$$

Your surprised uncle asked you (a promising finance student) to go over the calculations. What are the correct NPV and IRR of the project?

4.  You are the owner of a factory that supplies chairs and tables to schools in Denver. You sell each chair for $1.76 and each table for $4.40 based on the following calculation:

|  | Chair department | Table department |
|---|---|---|
| No. of units | 100,000 | 20,000 |
| Cost of material | 80,000 | 35,000 |
| Cost of labor | 40,000 | 20,000 |
| Fixed cost | 40,000 | 25,000 |
| Total cost | 160,000 | 80,000 |
| Cost per unit | 1.60 | 4.00 |
| Plus 10% profit | 1.76 | 4.40 |

You have received an offer from a school in Colorado Springs to supply an additional 10,000 chairs and 2,000 tables for the price of $1.05 and $3.50, respectively. Your financial advisor advises you not to take the offer because the price does not even cover the cost of production. Is the financial advisor correct?

5. A factory is considering the purchase of a new machine for one of its units. The machine costs $100,000. The machine will be depreciated on a straight-line basis over its 10-year life to a salvage value of zero. The machine is expected to save the company $50,000 annually, but to operate it the factory will have to transfer an employee (with a salary of $40,000 a year) from one of its other units. A new employee (with a salary of $20,000 a year) will be required to replace the transferred employee. What is the NPV of the purchase of the new machine if the relevant discount rate is 8% and corporate tax rate is 35%?

| Year | EBDT (Earnings before depreciation and taxes) |
|---|---|
| 0 | -10,500 |
| 1 | 3,000 |
| 2 | 3,000 |
| 3 | 3,000 |
| 4 | 2,500 |
| 5 | 2,500 |
| 6 | 2,500 |
| 7 | 2,500 |

6. You are considering the following investment:

The discount rate is 11% and the corporate tax rate is 34%.

a. Calculate the project NPV using straight-line depreciation.

b. What will be the company's gain if it uses a 7-year modified accelerated depreciation (MACRS) schedule, given below?

| MACRS depreciation | |
|---|---|
| Year | Percentage |
| 1 | 14.29% |
| 2 | 24.49% |
| 3 | 17.49% |
| 4 | 12.49% |
| 5 | 8.93% |
| 6 | 8.93% |
| 7 | 8.93% |
| 8 | 4.45% |

7. A company is considering buying a new machine for one of its factories. The cost of the machine is $60,000 and its expected life span is 5 years. The machine will save the cost of a worker estimated at $22,500 annually. The book value of the machine at the end of year 5 is $10,000 but the company estimates that the market value will be only $5,000. Calculate the NPV of the machine if the discount rate is 12% and the tax rate is 30%. Assume straight-line depreciation over the 5-year life of the machine.

8. The ABD Company is considering buying a new machine for one of its factories. The machine cost is $100,000 and its expected life span is 8 years. The machine is expected to reduce the production cost by $15,000 annually. The terminal value of the machine is $20,000 but the company believes

that it would only manage to sell it for $10,000. If the appropriate discount rate is 15% and the corporate tax is 40%,

a. Calculate the project NPV.

b. Calculate the project IRR.

9. You are the owner of a factory located in a hot tropical climate. The monthly production of the factory is $100,000 except during June–September, when it falls to $80,000 because of the heat in the factory. In January 2010 you get an offer to install an air-conditioning system in your factory. The cost of the air-conditioning system is $150,000 and its expected life span is 10 years. If you install the air-conditioning system, the production in the summer months will equal the production in the winter months. However, the cost of operating the system is $9,000 per month (only in the 4 months that you operate the system). You will also need to pay a maintenance fee of $5,000 annually in October. What is the NPV of the air-conditioning system if the interest rate is 12% and the corporate tax rate is 35% (the depreciation costs are recognized in December of each year)?

10. The "Cold and Sweet" (C&S) company manufactures ice-cream bars. The company is considering the purchase of a new machine that will top the bar with high-quality chocolate. The cost of the machine is $900,000.

Depreciation and terminal value: The machine will be depreciated over 10 years to zero salvage value. However, the company intends to use the machine for only 5 years. Management thinks that the sale price of the machine at the end of 5 years will be $100,000.

The machine can produce up to 1 million ice cream bars annually. The marketing director of C&S believes that if the company will spend $30,000 on advertising in the first year and another $10,000 in each of the following years, the company will be able to sell 400,000 bars for $1.30 each. The cost of producing of each bar is $0.50; and other costs related to the new products are $40,000 annually. C&S's cost of capital is 14% and the corporate tax rate is 30%.

a. What is the NPV of the project if the marketing director's projections are correct?

b. What is the minimum price that the company should charge for each bar if the project is to be profitable? Assume that the price of the bar does not affect sales.

c. The C&S marketing vice president suggested canceling the advertising campaign. In his opinion, the company sales will not be reduced significantly because of the cancellation. What is the minimum quantity that the company needs to sell to be profitable if the vice president's suggestion is accepted?

d. The marketing vice president would like some sensitivity analysis done. He asks what the NPV of the project would be if annual unit sales vary from 300,000, 350,000, ..., 700,000 and if the unit price per bar varies from $1.20, $1.30, ..., $1.70. Show the **Data Table** that answers his question.

11. The "Less Is More" company manufactures swimsuits. The company is considering expanding to the bathrobe market. The proposed investment plan includes the following:

   - Purchase of a new machine: The cost of the machine is $150,000 and its expected life span is 5 years. The terminal value of the machine is 0, but the chief economist of the company estimates that it can be sold for $10,000.

   - Advertising campaign: The head of the marketing department estimates that the campaign will cost $80,000 annually.

   - The fixed cost of the new department will be $40,000 annually.

   - Variable costs are estimated at $30 per bathrobe but because of the expected rise in labor costs they are expected to rise at 5% per year.

- Each of the bathrobes will be sold at a price of $45 the first year. The company estimates that it can raise the price of the bathrobes by 10% in each of the following years.

The "Less Is More" discount rate is 10% and the corporate tax rate is 36%.

a. What is the break-even point of the bathrobe department?

b. Plot a graph in which the NPV is the dependent variable of the annual production.

12. The Car Clean company operates a car wash business. The company bought a machine 2 years ago at the price of $60,000. The life span of the machine is 6 years and the machine has no disposal value; the current market value of the machine is $20,000. The company is considering buying a new machine. The cost of the new machine is $100,000 and its life span is 4 years. The new machine has a disposal value of $20,000. The new machine is faster than the old one; thus, the company believes the revenue will increase from $1 million annually to $1.03 million. In addition, the new machine is expected to save the company $10,000 in water and electricity costs.

The discount rate of Car Clean is 15% and the corporate tax rate is 40%. What is the NPV of replacing the old machine?

13. A company is considering whether to buy a regular or color photocopier for the office. The cost of the regular machine is $10,000, its life span is 5 years, and the company has to pay another $1,500 annually in maintenance costs. The color photocopier's price is $30,000, its life span is also 5 years, and the annual maintenance costs are $4,500. The color photocopier is expected to increase the revenue of the office by $8,500 annually. Assume that the company is profitable and pays 40% corporate tax; the relevant interest rate is 11%. Which photocopy machine should the firm buy?

14. The Coka company is a soft drink company. Until today the company bought empty cans from an outside supplier that charges Coka $0.20 per can. In addition the transportation cost is $1,000 per truck that transports 10,000 cans. The Coka company is considering whether to start manufacturing cans in its plant. The cost of a can machine is $1 million and its life span is 12 years. The terminal value of the machine is $160,000. The machine will be straight-line depreciated over 12 years to its terminal value. Maintenance and repair costs will be $150,000 for every 3-year period. The additional space for the new operation will cost the company $100,000 annually. The marginal cost of producing a can in the factory is $0.17.

The cost of capital of Coka is 11% and the corporate tax rate is 40%.

a. What is the minimum number of cans that the company has to sell annually to justify self-production of cans? Start by assuming that annual production is 3 million cans and then use **Goal Seek** to find a breakeven point.

b. Advanced: Use data tables to show the NPV and IRR of the project as a function of the number of cans.

15. The ZZZ Company is considering investing in a new machine for one of its factories. The company can choose either Machine A or Machine B. The life span of each machine is 5 years; depreciation for each machine is straight-line to zero salvage value. ZZZ sells each unit for a price of $6. The company has a cost of capital of 12% and its tax rate is 35%.

a. If the company manufactures 1 million units per year, which machine should it buy?

| | Machine A | Machine B |
|---|---|---|
| Cost | $4,000,000 | $10,000,000 |
| Annual fixed cost per machine | $300,000 | $210,000 |
| Variable cost per unit | $1.20 | $0.80 |
| Annual production | 400,000 | 550,000 |

b. Plot a graph showing the profitability of investment in each machine type depending on the annual production.

16. The Easy Sight company manufactures sunglasses. The company has two machines, each of which produces 1,000 sunglasses per month. The book value of each of the old machines is $10,000 and their expected life span is 5 years. The machines are being depreciated on a straight-line basis to zero salvage value. The company assumes it will be able to sell a machine today (January 2011) for the price of $6,000. The price of a new machine is $20,000 and its expected life span is 5 years. The new machine will save the company $0.85 for every pair of sunglasses produced.

    Demand for sunglasses is seasonal. During the 5 summer months (May–September) demand is 2,000 sunglasses per month, whereas during the winter months it falls to 1,000 per month.

    Assume that because of insurance and storage costs it is uneconomical to store sunglasses at the factory. Should Easy Sight replace its two old machines with new ones if its discount rate is 10% and its corporate tax rate is 40%?

17. Poseidon is considering opening a shipping line from Athens to Rhodes. To open the shipping line Poseidon will have to purchase two ships that cost 1,000 gold coins each. The life span of each ship is 10 years, and Poseidon estimates that he will earn 300 gold coins in the first year and the earnings will increase by 5% per year. The annual costs of the shipping line are estimated at 60 gold coins annually, Poseidon's interest rate is 8%, and Zeus's tax rate is 50%.

    a. Will the shipping line be profitable?

    b. Because of Poseidon's good connections on Olympus, he can get a tax reduction. What is the maximum tax rate at which the project will be profitable?

18. At the board meeting on Olympus, Hera tried to convince Zeus to keep the 50% tax rate intact because of the budget deficit. According to Hera's calculations, the shipping line will be more profitable if Poseidon will buy only one ship and sell tickets only to first-class passengers. Hera estimated that Poseidon's annual costs will be 40 gold coins.

    a. What are the minimum annual average earnings required for the shipping line to be profitable assuming that earnings are constant throughout the 10 years?

    b. Zeus, who is an old-fashioned god, believes that "blood is thicker than money." He agreed to give Poseidon a tax reduction if he will only buy one ship. Use data tables to show the profitability of the project as dependent on the annual earnings and the tax rate.

19. Kane Running Shoes is considering the manufacturing of a special shoe for race walking that will indicate whether an athlete is running (this happens if neither of the walker's legs is touching the ground). The chief economist of the company presented the following calculation for the Smart Walking Shoes (SWS):

    • Research and development (R&D) $200,000 annually in each of the next 4 years.

        The manufacturing project:

    • Expected life span: 10 years

    • Investment in machinery: $250,000 (at $t = 4$); expected life span of the machine 10 years

    • Expected annual sales: 5,000 pairs of shoes at the expected price of $150 per pair

    • Fixed cost $300,000 annually

    • Variable cost: $50 per pair of shoes

    Kane's discount rate is 12%, the corporate rate is 40%, and R&D expenses are tax deductible against other profits of the company. Assume that at the end of project (that is, after 14 years) the new technology will have been superseded by other technologies and therefore have no value.

a. What is the NPV of the project?

b. The International Olympic Committee (IOC) decided to give Kane a loan without interest for 6 years to encourage the company to take on the project. The loan will have to be paid back in six equal annual payments. What is the minimum loan that the IOC should give for the project to be profitable?

20. The Aphrodite company is a manufacturer of perfume. The company is about to launch a new line of products. The marketing department has to decide whether to use an aggressive or a regular campaign.

## Aggressive Campaign

Initial cost (production of commercial advertisement using a top model): $400,000

First month profit: $20,000

Monthly growth in profit (months 2–12): 10%

After 12 months the company is going to launch a new line of products and it is expected that the monthly profits from the current line would be $20,000 forever.

## Regular Campaign

Initial cost (using a less famous model): $150,000

First month profit: $10,000

Monthly growth in profits (months 2–12): 6%

Monthly profit (month 13– ∞ ): $20,000

a. The annual cost of capital is 7%. Calculate the NPV of each campaign and decide which campaign the company should undertake.

b. The manager of the company believes that because of the recession expected next year, the profit figures for the aggressive campaign (both first-month profit and 2- to 12-month profit growth) are too optimistic. Use a data table to show the differential NPV as a function of the first-month payment and the growth rate of the aggressive campaign.

21. The Long-Life Company has a new vaccine. The company estimates that it has a 10-year monopoly for the production of the vaccine, and it is trying to estimate how many vaccines it should try to sell annually.

   Machines to produce the new vaccine cost $70 million and have a 5-year life, straight-line depreciation, and a zero salvage value. Each machine is capable of producing 75,000 vaccines annually. Annual fixed costs for producing the vaccine are $120 million, and the variable cost per vaccine is $1,000. The company's discount rate for this type of vaccine is 15%, and its corporate tax rate is 30%. The total market for the vaccine is 250,000 annually.

   Use the template below (on the disk with *Principles of Finance with Excel*) to answer the following questions:

a. If the annual sales are 200,000, what will be the NPV of the product over its 10-year life?

b. Fill in the data table at the bottom of the template. At a 16% discount rate, how many vaccines should the company aim to sell?

| | A | B | C | D | E | F | G | H | I | J | K | L |
|---|---|---|---|---|---|---|---|---|---|---|---|---|
| 1 | | | | | LONG-LIFE COMPANY | | | | | | | |
| 2 | Discount rate | 15% | | | | | | | | | | |
| 3 | Tax rate | 30% | | | | | | | | | | |
| 4 | Mahcine cost | 70,000,000 | | | | | | | | | | |
| 5 | Annual depreciation | 14,000,000 | | | | | | | | | | |
| 6 | Annual vaccines per machine | 75,000 | | | | | | | | | | |
| 7 | Variable cost per vaccine | 1,000 | | | | | | | | | | |
| 8 | Annual fixed costs | | | | | | | | | | | |
| 9 | | | | | | | | | | | | |
| 10 | Annual vaccines sold | 400,000 | | | | | | | | | | |
| 11 | Price per vaccine | 1,500 | | | | | | | | | | |
| 12 | Annual revenue | 600,000,000 | <-- =B11*B10 | | | | | | | | | |
| 13 | Number of machines needed | 5 | <-- =ROUND(B10/B6,0) | | | | | | | | | |
| 14 | | | | | | | | | | | | |
| 15 | | | | | | | | | | | | |
| 16 | Year | 0 | 1 | 2 | 3 | 4 | 5 | 6 | 7 | 8 | 9 | 10 |
| 17 | Machine purchase | | | | | | | | | | | |
| 18 | Revenue | | | | | | | | | | | |
| 19 | Fixed costs | | | | | | | | | | | |
| 20 | Cost of vaccines | | | | | | | | | | | |
| 21 | Depreciation | | | | | | | | | | | |
| 22 | Profits before taxes | | | | | | | | | | | |
| 23 | Taxes | | | | | | | | | | | |
| 24 | Profits after taxes | | | | | | | | | | | |
| 25 | Add back depreciation | | | | | | | | | | | |
| 26 | Cash flow | | | | | | | | | | | |
| 27 | | | | | | | | | | | | |
| 28 | Net present value | | | | | | | | | | | |
| 29 | Internal rate of return | | | | | | | | | | | |
| 30 | | | | | | | | | | | | |
| 31 | | | | | | | | | | | | |
| 32 | DATA TABLE: sensitivity of NPV to number of vaccines sold and to discount rate | | | | | | | | | | | |
| 33 | | | | | | Number of vaccines sold annually | | | | | | |
| 34 | | | 100,000 | 150,000 | 160,000 | 180,000 | 200,000 | 220,000 | 250,000 | | | |
| 35 | WACC--> | 10% | | | | | | | | | | |
| 36 | | 12% | | | | | | | | | | |
| 37 | | 14% | | | | | | | | | | |
| 38 | | 16% | | | | | | | | | | |
| 39 | | 18% | | | | | | | | | | |
| 40 | | 20% | | | | | | | | | | |
| 41 | | 22% | | | | | | | | | | |
| 42 | | 24% | | | | | | | | | | |
| 43 | | 26% | | | | | | | | | | |
| 44 | | 28% | | | | | | | | | | |
| 45 | | 30% | | | | | | | | | | |

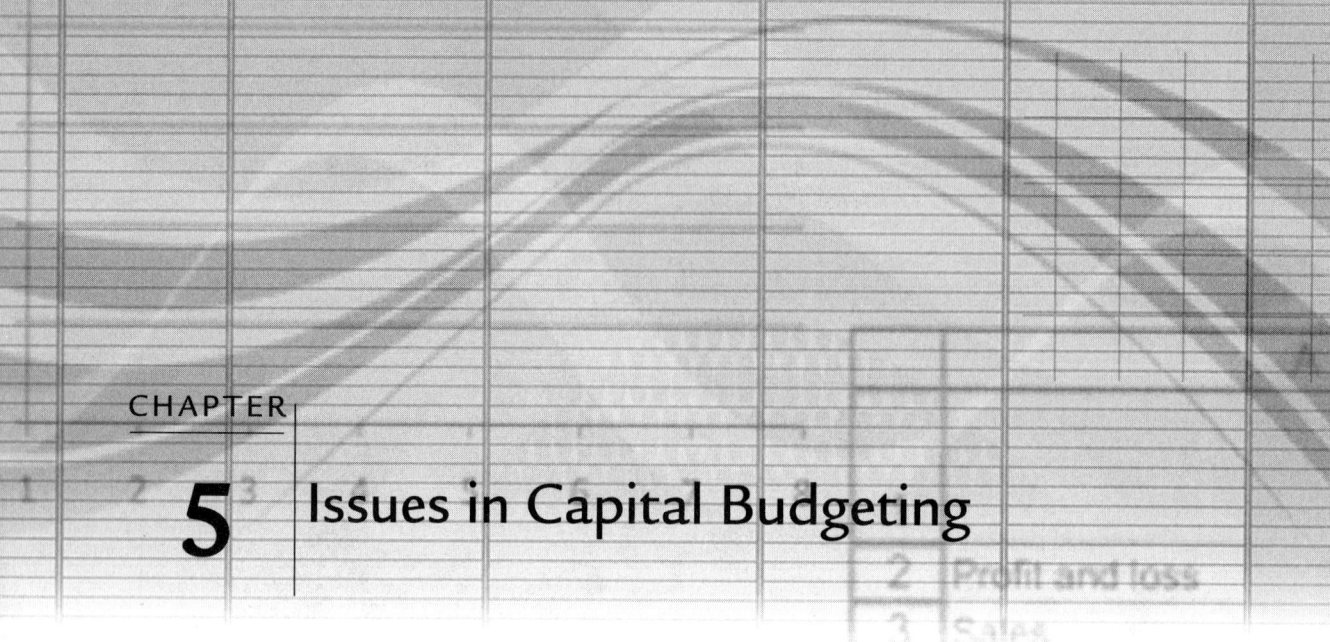

# 5 | Issues in Capital Budgeting

## CHAPTER CONTENTS

# Overview

The capital budgeting decisions we examined in Chapter 4 were all pretty cut and dried: The NPV and IRR criteria always indicated which investment was worthwhile for the individual or the company. As you might expect, in real life the decisions of where and how to spend your investment dollars are not always so clear cut.

In this chapter we expand on the discussion of capital budgeting started in Chapter 4 and examine a number of issues that often cause confusion.

## Finance Concepts Discussed

- Problems with IRR as a decision criterion
  - IRR can't distinguish between borrowing and lending
  - Multiple IRRs
- Choosing between projects with different lifetimes
- Discounting cash flows that don't occur at year end ("mid-year discounting")
- Incorporating tax considerations into the lease vs. purchase problem
- Incorporating inflation into capital budgeting—discounting nominal versus real cash flows

## Excel Functions Used

- **IRR**, **NPV**
- **Sum**
- **PMT**
- **If**
- **XNPV**, **XIRR**

# 5.1. A Problem with IRR: You Can't Always Tell Good Projects from Bad Ones

Sometimes it's hard to tell from the IRR whether a project is good or bad. Here's a simple example: You've decided to buy a car; the list price is $11,000, and the dealer has offered you two purchase options:

- You can pay the dealer cash and get a $1,000 discount, thus paying only $10,000.
- You can pay $5,000 now and pay $2,000 in each of the next 3 years. The dealer calls this his "zero-interest car loan" plan. The bank is giving car loans at 9% interest, so the dealer claims that his plan is much cheaper.

Which offer is better? Having learned a bit of finance, you set up the following Excel spreadsheet.

| | A | B | C | D | E |
|---|---|---|---|---|---|
| 1 | | | **BUYING A CAR** | | |
| 2 | List price of car | 11,000.00 | | | |
| 3 | Downpayment | 5,000.00 | | | |
| 4 | Cash cost of car | 10,000.00 | | | |
| 5 | | | | | |
| 6 | Year | **Payment in cash** | **Payment with credit** | **Cash spent or saved with credit plan** | |
| 7 | 0 | -10,000.00 | -5,000.00 | 5,000.00 | <-- =C7-B7 |
| 8 | 1 | | -2,000.00 | -2,000.00 | <-- =C8-B8 |
| 9 | 2 | | -2,000.00 | -2,000.00 | |
| 10 | 3 | | -2,000.00 | -2,000.00 | |
| 11 | | | | | |
| 12 | Internal rate of return | | | 9.70% | <-- =IRR(D7:D10) |
| 13 | | | | | |
| 14 | Bank rate of interest | 9% | | | |
| 15 | NPV of cash saved | -62.59 | <-- =D7+NPV(B14,D8:D10) | | |

The critical element in the spreadsheet is column D, which compares the annual cash outlays of the credit plan with those of the cash payment plan. Column D shows that if you pay with the credit plan instead of paying cash, you'll spend $5,000 *less* in year 0. On the other hand, you'll spend $2,000 *more* in years 1, 2, and 3. The IRR of this column is 9.70%. Because the bank is lending money at 9%, you should take a bank loan instead of using the dealer's credit plan.

To understand this further, note that the pattern of the cash flows in column D is like the pattern of cash flows from taking a loan. When you take a loan, there is an initial positive cash flow (this is when you get the loan) and subsequent negative cash flows (the loan repayments). When you buy the car using the dealer's credit plan, the cash flow pattern is the same: There is an initial positive cash flow (the savings from paying only $5,000 instead of $10,000) and subsequent negative cash flows (the additional $2,000 annual cost of the credit plan). Thus, the IRR of 9.70% represents the *cost* of the dealer's credit plan. Because the bank lends at a cost of 9%, it is cheaper to borrow through the bank.

What if you don't have the $10,000 cash for the cash payment plan? Then you should take a bank loan (read on for details).

Cell B15 discounts the differential payment flow of column D at the bank interest rate. This shows that this flow has a negative NPV, another indication that you shouldn't undertake this project: You should opt for the cash payment plan.

## How Will You Pay for the Car?

So you're better off paying the dealer cash. If you don't have the $10,000 cash, you could borrow $5,000 from the bank. This plan would have the following cash flows (assuming equal annual payments of principal and interest, calculated using Excel's **PMT** function).

| | A | B | C | D | E |
|---|---|---|---|---|---|
| 18 | **Borrowing the money from the bank** | | | | |
| 19 | Year | **Payment in cash** | **Bank loan cash flows** | **Total cash flow to car owner** | |
| 20 | 0 | -10,000.00 | 5,000.00 | -5,000.00 | |
| 21 | 1 | | -1,975.27 | -1,975.27 | <-- =PMT(9%,3,C20) |
| 22 | 2 | | -1,975.27 | -1,975.27 | |
| 23 | 3 | | -1,975.27 | -1,975.27 | |

The cash flows in cells D20:D23 are an improvement over those in cells C7:C10, which shows (again) that it's better to buy the car in cash and borrow the money from the bank than to take the dealer's financing offer.

## The Dealer's Cash Flows

To see how confusing the IRR can be, consider the dealer's cash flows. He's offered you the choice of paying $10,000 in cash or $5,000 down with three equal payments of $2,000.

| | A | B | C | D | E |
|---|---|---|---|---|---|
| 1 | | IRR VERSUS NPV--THE DEALER'S PROBLEM | | | | |
| 2 | List price of car | 11,000.00 | | | |
| 3 | Downpayment | 5,000.00 | | | |
| 4 | Cash cost of car | 10,000.00 | | | |
| 5 | | | | | |
| 6 | Year | Payment in cash | Payment with credit | Differential dealer cash flow | |
| 7 | 0 | 10,000.00 | 5,000.00 | -5,000.00 | <-- =C7-B7 |
| 8 | 1 | | 2,000.00 | 2,000.00 | <-- =C8-B8 |
| 9 | 2 | | 2,000.00 | 2,000.00 | |
| 10 | 3 | | 2,000.00 | 2,000.00 | |
| 11 | | | | | |
| 12 | Internal rate of return | | | 9.70% | <-- =IRR(D7:D10) |
| 13 | | | | | |
| 14 | Bank rate of interest | 9% | | | |
| 15 | NPV of cash saved | 62.59 | <-- =D7+NPV(B14,D8:D10) | | |

Column D shows that between the two plans, the dealer has a negative cash flow of $5,000 in year 0, but then has a positive cash flow of $2,000 in each of the 3 subsequent years. Effectively, the dealer is acting like a bank giving a loan, and the 9.70% represents the interest earned by the dealer on the loan; if he can borrow the $5,000 in cell D8 from the bank at 9%, he's better off—his NPV on the loan is $62.59.

## What's the Point?

The dealer's IRR and your IRR are the same. But this turns out to mean that the payment plan is bad for you and good for the dealer: The IRR of the dealer's cash flows represents the interest he earns on the loan he's giving you; the IRR of your cash flows is the cost of the loan you're taking. To tell whether you're getting a good deal or a bad deal, use the NPV of the differential payments discounted at the bank's loan rate; this NPV clearly shows that the payment plan is bad for you (negative NPV of $62.59) and good for the dealer (positive NPV of $62.59).

# 5.2. Multiple Internal Rates of Return

A project has a "conventional cash flow pattern" when all the positive and negative cash flows are bunched together. If this condition is not met, then we'll call the cash flow pattern of the project "nonconventional." Here are some examples of conventional and nonconventional cash flows.

|   | A | B | C | D | E | F | G |
|---|---|---|---|---|---|---|---|
| 1 | | CONVENTIONAL AND NON CONVENTIONAL CASH FLOW PATTERNS | | | | | | |
| 2 | Year | Cash flow Project A | Cash flow Project B | Cash flow Project C | Cash flow Project D | Cash flow Project E | Cash flow Project F |
| 3 | 0 | -100 | -100 | 100 | 25 | -25 | -250 |
| 4 | 1 | 200 | -50 | 55 | 35 | 80 | 35 |
| 5 | 2 | 500 | 60 | 35 | -200 | -100 | 145 |
| 6 | 3 | 50 | 80 | 50 | 33 | 200 | 330 |
| 7 | 4 | 60 | 99 | -100 | 55 | 55 | 55 |
| 8 | 5 | 35 | 100 | -35 | 155 | -250 | -250 |
| 9 | | ↑ Conventional cash flow pattern | ↑ Conventional cash flow pattern | ↑ Conventional cash flow pattern | ↑ Nonconventional cash flow pattern | ↑ Nonconventional cash flow pattern | ↑ Nonconventional cash flow pattern |
| 10 | | Initial negative cash flow followed by positive cash flows | Two initial negative cash flows followed by positive cash flows | Initial positive cash flows followed by negative cash flows | Two positive cash flows, then negative, then three positive cash flows | Initial negative cash flow, then positive, then negative, positive, negative cash flows | Negative cash flows at beginning and end, other cash flows positive |

In Section 3.4 of Chapter 3 we showed that for projects with conventional cash flows, the NPV and the IRR criteria give the same answers to the "yes–no" capital budgeting question (the question of whether a particular project is worthwhile). In this section we discuss the IRR of projects with nonconventional cash flows. Such projects often have multiple IRRs, which makes our analysis of a nonconventional project using the IRR confusing. We will ultimately conclude that NPV is a better decision tool.

Consider the case of a company that operates sanitary landfills. A "landfill" is basically a big hole in the ground where lots of garbage is dumped until the hole is filled in.

Here are the cash flows anticipated by the company for a new landfill:

- The initial cost of the landfill is $800,000: This covers the expense of digging the hole, fencing it, and providing appropriate truck access.

- The annual net cash inflows from the landfill are $450,000. These represent the fees the company collects in return for giving trash collection companies the right to dump their trash in the landfill. These cash inflows are the net of any costs incurred by the landfill company.

- After 5 years the landfill will be full. The costs of closing the landfill, incurred at the end of year 6, are $1,500,000. This includes the costs of abiding by various ecological regulations, etc.

In the next spreadsheet, the cash flows for the landfill are given in cells B3:B9. In columns E and F we have created a table that computes the net present value of these cash flows at various discount rates. The graph shows that the cash flows have *two* internal rates of return: These are the two points at which the graph cuts the x-axis.

In cells B14 and B15 we identify both of these IRRs using Excel's **IRR** function. We have used the **Guess** option for this function. This option allows you to identify the *approximate* IRR (we used the graph to identify this number); Excel then computes an IRR close to this approximation. In the following spreadsheet we use 25% as a **Guess** in cell B15. Excel's **IRR** function then shows that the actual IRR that is close to this **Guess** is 27.74%.

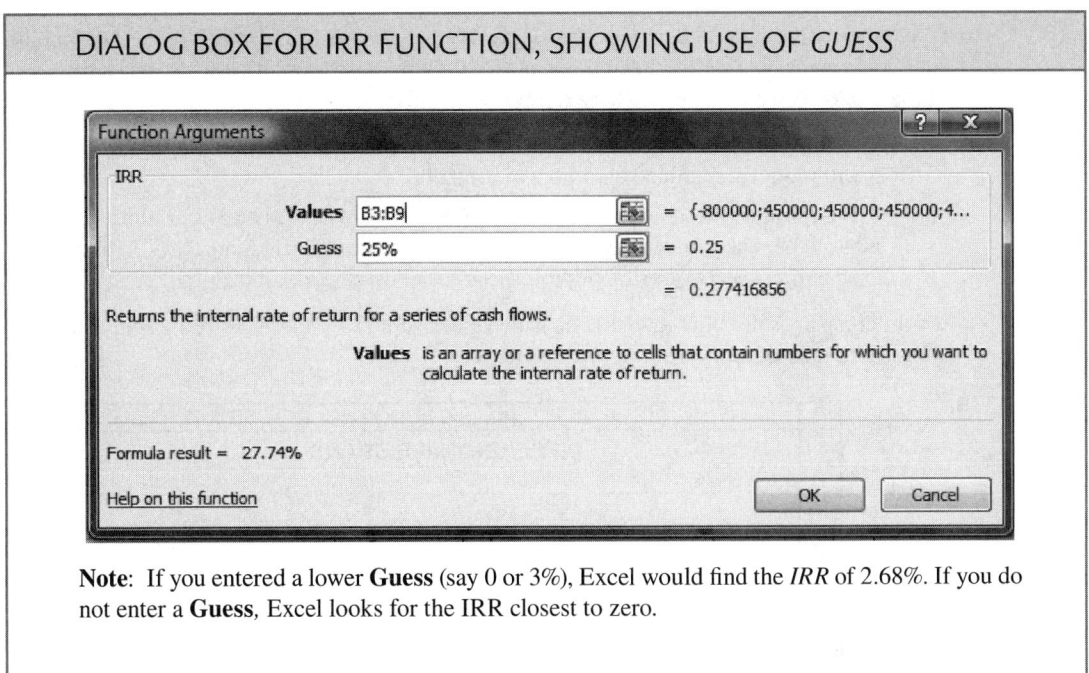

| | A | B | C | D | E | F | G | H | I | J | K |
|---|---|---|---|---|---|---|---|---|---|---|---|
| 1 | SANITARY LANDFILL, INC. | | | | | | | | | | |
| 2 | Year | Cash flow | | | Discount rate | NPV | | | | | |
| 3 | 0 | -800,000 | | | 0% | -50,000 | <-- =NPV(E3,$B$4:$B$9)+$B$3 | | | | |
| 4 | 1 | 450,000 | | | 2% | -10,900 | <-- =NPV(E4,$B$4:$B$9)+$B$3 | | | | |
| 5 | 2 | 450,000 | | | 4% | 17,848 | <-- =NPV(E5,$B$4:$B$9)+$B$3 | | | | |
| 6 | 3 | 450,000 | | | 6% | 38,123 | | | | | |
| 7 | 4 | 450,000 | | | 8% | 51,465 | | | | | |
| 8 | 5 | 450,000 | | | 10% | 59,143 | | | | | |
| 9 | 6 | -1,500,000 | | | 12% | 62,203 | | | | | |
| 10 | | | | | 14% | 61,507 | | | | | |
| 11 | Sum of cash flows | -50,000 | | | 16% | 57,769 | | | | | |
| 12 | | | | | 18% | 51,580 | | | | | |
| 13 | | | | | 20% | 43,428 | | | | | |
| 14 | First IRR | 2.68% | <-- =IRR(B3:B9,0) | | 22% | 33,721 | | | | | |
| 15 | Second IRR | 27.74% | <-- =IRR(B3:B9,25%) | | 24% | 22,793 | | | | | |
| 16 | | | | | 26% | 10,923 | | | | | |
| 17 | | | | | 28% | -1,658 | | | | | |
| 18 | | | | | 30% | -14,758 | | | | | |
| 19 | | | | | 32% | -28,219 | | | | | |
| 20 | | | | | 34% | -41,912 | | | | | |
| 21 | | | | | 36% | -55,727 | | | | | |

## DIALOG BOX FOR IRR FUNCTION, SHOWING USE OF *GUESS*

Function Arguments

**IRR**

**Values** B3:B9    = {-800000;450000;450000;450000;4...

Guess 25%    = 0.25

= 0.277416856

Returns the internal rate of return for a series of cash flows.

          **Values** is an array or a reference to cells that contain numbers for which you want to calculate the internal rate of return.

Formula result = 27.74%

Help on this function       OK    Cancel

**Note**: If you entered a lower **Guess** (say 0 or 3%), Excel would find the *IRR* of 2.68%. If you do not enter a **Guess**, Excel looks for the IRR closest to zero.

## Two IRRs. What Does This Mean?

This business of two IRRs is confusing! Suppose we're trying to decide whether to undertake the landfill project. As you saw in Chapter 4, there are two traditional rules for accepting or rejecting a project:

- NPV rule: A project is acceptable if its NPV > 0. In the case of the sanitary landfill, the NPV rule says that the project is acceptable if the discount rate is larger than 2.68% and smaller than 27.74%.

- IRR rule: A project is acceptable if its IRR > appropriate discount rate. Because there are two IRRs in this case, the IRR rule is impossible to apply. In practical terms, this means that when a project has more than one IRR, you should determine its attractiveness only by the NPV rule.

### How Many IRRs Are There?

For a given set of cash flows, there are potentially as many IRRs as there are changes in sign of the cash flow. The cash flow pattern of a conventional project has an initial negative cash flow and thereafter only positive cash flows; there is only one change of sign (from negative to positive) and hence only one possible IRR. The previous cash flow example has two changes in sign (and hence two possible IRRs): from −800,000 in year 0 to 450,000 in year 1 and then again from 450,000 in year 5 to −1,500,000 in year 6.[1]

## 5.3. Choosing between Projects with Different Life Spans

Sometimes our capital budgeting choices involve projects with different life spans. Suppose your company is considering buying one of two tank trucks to haul high-tech liquid materials. The company is trying to decide between two alternatives:

- Truck *A* is a relatively cheap truck. It costs $100,000 and has a 6-year life, during which it will produce an annual cash flow of $150,000.

- Truck *B* is much more expensive. It costs $250,000 and has only a 3-year life, after which it has to be replaced. However, Truck *B* is much more efficient than Truck *A*, and during each of the 3 years of its life it produces a cash flow of $300,000.

If your company's discount rate is 12%, which truck should it choose? Here's a simple (and, as it turns out, misleading) way of doing the analysis.

| | A | B | C | D |
|---|---|---|---|---|
| 1 | DIFFERENT LIFE SPANS | | | |
| 2 | Discount rate | 12% | | |
| 3 | | | | |
| 4 | Year | Truck A | Truck B | |
| 5 | 0 | -100 | -250 | |
| 6 | 1 | 150 | 300 | |
| 7 | 2 | 150 | 300 | |
| 8 | 3 | 150 | 300 | |
| 9 | 4 | 150 | | |
| 10 | 5 | 150 | | |
| 11 | 6 | 150 | | |
| 12 | | | | |
| 13 | NPV | 516.71 | 470.55 | <-- =C5+NPV($B$2,C6:C11) |

Using this analysis you might conclude that Truck *A* is preferable to Truck *B* because its NPV is higher. But because the two trucks have different life spans, there's a problem concluding

---

[1]Exercises 2 and 3 at the end of this chapter show examples with three IRRs.

that *A* is preferred to *B*. To make them comparable, we assume that at the end of year 3 we will replace Truck *B* with another, similar truck. This makes the year 3 cash flow

$$Year\ 3\ cash\ flow: \underbrace{300}_{\substack{\text{year 3 cash flow}\\\text{from truck}}} - \underbrace{250}_{\substack{\text{purchase price}\\\text{of new truck}}} = 50.$$

Once we've replaced Truck *B* in year 3, the cash flows in years 4, 5, and 6 will be $300. We can put this into a spreadsheet.

|  | A | B | C | D |
|---|---|---|---|---|
| 1 | | DIFFERENT LIFE SPANS<br>at end of year 3, Truck B is replaced | | |
| 2 | Discount rate | 12% | | |
| 3 | | | | |
| 4 | Year | Cash flow (A) | Cash flow (B) | |
| 5 | 0 | -100 | -250 | |
| 6 | 1 | 150 | 300 | |
| 7 | 2 | 150 | 300 | |
| 8 | 3 | 150 | 50 | <-- =300-250 |
| 9 | 4 | 150 | 300 | |
| 10 | 5 | 150 | 300 | |
| 11 | 6 | 150 | 300 | |
| 12 | | | | |
| 13 | NPV | 516.71 | 805.48 | <-- =C5+NPV($B$2,C6:C11) |

As you can see in cells B13 and C13, the NPV from the two (now comparable) projects indicates that *B* is preferred to *A*.

There's another way to reach this same conclusion: Look at the following calculations:

$$NPV(A) = -100 + \frac{150}{(1.12)} + \frac{150}{(1.12)^2} + \frac{150}{(1.12)^3} + \frac{150}{(1.12)^4} + \frac{150}{(1.12)^5} + \frac{150}{(1.12)^6} = 516.71$$

$$= \sum_{t=1}^{6} \frac{125.68}{(1.12)^t}$$

$$NPV(B) = -250 + \frac{300}{(1.12)} + \frac{300}{(1.12)^2} + \frac{300}{(1.12)^3} = 470.55$$

$$= \sum_{t=1}^{3} \frac{195.91}{(1.12)^t}$$

What these calculations show is that Truck *A* is equivalent to getting a constant cash flow of $125.68 per year for each of the 6 years of its life, whereas Truck *B* is equivalent to getting a constant cash flow of $195.91 for each of its 3 years of life. We call these cash flow the *equivalent annuity cash flow* (EAC). Because every time you buy Truck *B* you get $195.91 per year and every time you buy Truck *A* you get $125.68 per year, it is clear that Truck *B* is preferred.

The EAC is easy to compute. It is defined as a constant future cash flow whose present value is equal to the net present value of the project.

$$NPV = CF_0 + \sum_{t=1}^{N} \frac{CF_t}{(1+r)^t} = \sum_{t=1}^{N} \frac{equivalent\ annuity\ cash\ flow\ (EAC)}{(1+r)^t}, \text{ where } N \text{ is the project life}$$

We rearrange this equation a bit and use the Excel function **PMT** to compute the EAC.

$$EAC = \frac{NPV = CF_0 + \sum_{t=1}^{N} \frac{CF_t}{(1+r)^t}}{\sum_{t=1}^{N} \frac{1}{(1+r)^t}} = -\mathbf{PMT}(r, N\ periods, NPV)$$

$$\uparrow$$

*Excel function*

We implement this formula in the following spreadsheet.

| | A | B | C | D |
|---|---|---|---|---|
| 1 | **DIFFERENT LIFE SPANS**<br>**Computing the equivalent annuity cash flow (EAC)** | | | |
| 2 | Discount rate | 12% | | |
| 3 | | | | |
| 4 | **Year** | **Cash flow (A)** | **Cash flow (B)** | |
| 5 | 0 | -100 | -250 | |
| 6 | 1 | 150 | 300 | |
| 7 | 2 | 150 | 300 | |
| 8 | 3 | 150 | 300 | |
| 9 | 4 | 150 | | |
| 10 | 5 | 150 | | |
| 11 | 6 | 150 | | |
| 12 | | | | |
| 13 | NPV | 516.71 | 470.55 | <-- =C5+NPV($B$2,C6:C11) |
| 14 | EAC--Equivalent annuity cash flow | 125.68 | 195.91 | <-- =-PMT(B2,3,C13) |
| 15 | | | | |
| 16 | =-PMT(B2,6,B13) | | | |

## A Nontrivial Example of Different Life Spans: Choosing a Light Bulb

This business of the EAC may seem somewhat academic and ethereal, but it's not. In this section we offer a real-life example that can only be solved using the EAC.

You're considering replacing the light bulbs in a hotel you own. Currently you're using 100-watt incandescent bulbs, which cost $1 each and have an average lifetime of 1,000 hours. You're thinking of replacing them with compact fluorescent bulbs. These are much more expensive, costing $5 each. But they produce the same luminescence, use only 15 watts, and last for 10,000 hours. Here are some additional facts:

- A kilowatt of electricity costs $0.10.
- You tend to burn a light bulb 250 hours per month.
- The interest rate is 8%. In the computations below we translate this to a monthly interest rate of $0.643\% = (1 + 8\%)^{1/12} - 1.$

Should you replace the bulbs?

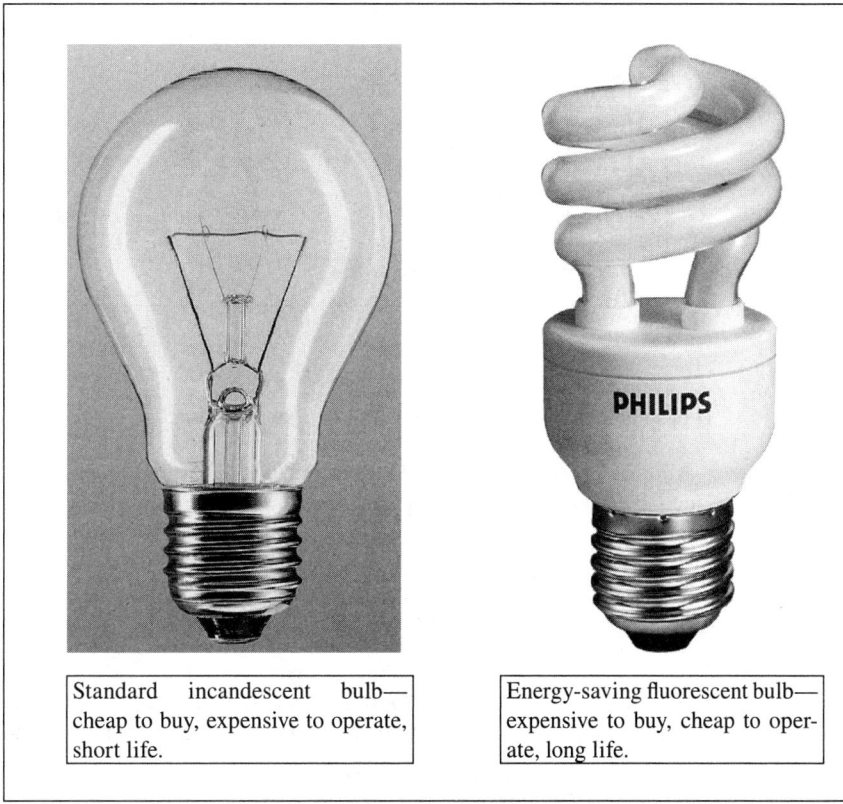

| Standard incandescent bulb—cheap to buy, expensive to operate, short life. | Energy-saving fluorescent bulb—expensive to buy, cheap to operate, long life. |

FIGURE 5.1 Standard bulbs versus energy-saving fluorescents.

This problem can be readily solved using the EAC.

| | A | B | C |
|---|---|---|---|
| 1 | **LIGHT BULBS**<br>**Choosing between cheap incandescents and**<br>**expensive fluorescents** | | |
| 2 | Annual discount rate | 8% | |
| 3 | Monthly discount rate | 0.643% | <-- =(1+B2)^(1/12)-1 |
| 4 | Electric cost per kilowatt<br>(a kilowatt = 1,000 watts) | 0.10 | |
| 5 | | | |
| 6 | **Incandescent bulb** | | |
| 7 | Watts | 100 | |
| 8 | Cost | $1.00 | |
| 9 | Hours per month used | 250 | |
| 10 | Lifetime of bulb (hours) | 1,000 | |
| 11 | Lifetime in months | 4 | |
| 12 | Monthly cost | 2.50 | <-- =B9*$B$4*B7/1000 |
| 13 | NPV of lifetime use | 10.84 | <-- =B8+PV(B3,B11,-B12) |
| 14 | Monthly equivalent annuity cash flow<br>(EAC) for cheap incandescent | 2.75 | <-- =-PMT(B3,B11,B13) |
| 15 | | | |
| 16 | **Equivalent fluorescent bulb** | | |
| 17 | Watts | 15 | |
| 18 | Cost | $5.00 | |
| 19 | Hours per month used | 250 | |
| 20 | Lifetime of bulb (hours) | 10,000 | |
| 21 | Lifetime in months | 40 | |
| 22 | Monthly cost | 0.38 | <-- =B19*$B$4*B17/1000 |
| 23 | NPV of lifetime use | 18.19 | <-- =B18+PV(B3,B21,-B22) |
| 24 | Monthly equivalent annuity cash flow<br>(EAC) for expensive fluorescent | 0.52 | <-- =-PMT(B3,B21,B23) |

This spreadsheet requires some additional explanation:

- An incandescent bulb costs $1.00 to buy and $2.50 per month to operate. As shown in cell B13, the NPV of buying and operating one incandescent bulb during its 4-month life is

$$1.00 + \frac{2.50}{1+0.643\%} + \frac{2.50}{\left(1+0.643\%\right)^2} + \frac{2.50}{\left(1+0.643\%\right)^3} + \frac{2.50}{\left(1+0.643\%\right)^4} = 10.84$$

- A fluorescent bulb costs $5.00 to buy and $0.38 per month to operate. As shown in cell B23, the NPV of buying and operating one fluorescent bulb during its 40-month life is

$$5.00 + \frac{0.38}{1+0.643\%} + \frac{0.38}{\left(1+0.643\%\right)^2} + \ldots + \frac{0.38}{\left(1+0.643\%\right)^{40}} = 18.19$$

- To find the monthly equivalent annuity cash flow (EAC) of each bulb, we divide the NPV of the bulb's cost and operation by the appropriate PV factor:

$$Incandescent\ EAC = \frac{10.84}{\displaystyle\sum_{t=1}^{4} \frac{1}{(1.00684)^t}} = -\textbf{PMT}(0.643\%, 4, 10.84) = 2.75/month$$

$$Fluorescent\ EAC = \frac{18.19}{\displaystyle\sum_{t=1}^{40} \frac{1}{(1.00684)^t}} = -\textbf{PMT}(0.643\%, 40, 18.19) = 0.52/month$$

- As you can see, the monthly equivalent annuity cash flow (EAC) of the incandescent light bulb is $2.75, whereas the monthly EAC of the fluorescent bulb is $0.52. The EAC tells you that it's *much cheaper* to switch to the fluorescent!

## 5.4. Lease versus Purchase When Taxes Are Important

We dealt with leasing in Section 3.4, but there we assumed that taxes were not a factor. This is often true for individuals—when you're considering leasing a computer or buying one, the tax considerations are secondary, because you cannot usually subtract either your computer lease payment or any part of the purchase price of the computer from your taxes.

On the other hand, for a business tax considerations are very important. Firms can subtract depreciation from their pretax profits as a cost (as we showed in Chapter 4, this means that depreciation gives rise to a *tax shield*). Furthermore, firms that finance with debt can subtract their interest costs from their pretax profits; thus, the *after-tax* cost of an interest rate $r\%$ paid by a firm with a tax rate of $T$ is $(1 - T) * r\%$.

In the example below we introduce tax considerations into the lease-versus-purchase decision. We use the same example introduced in Chapter 3 (page 81), but provide additional information about the firm's tax rate and depreciation policy.

### An Example

Your business has decided that it needs another computer. Here are the facts:

- The business has a tax rate of 40% and can borrow from the bank at 15%.
- You can buy the computer for $4,000 and depreciate it on a straight-line basis over 3 years. This means annual depreciation of $\$4,000/3 = \$1,333$. Because you're taxed at a 40% rate, this depreciation will save you $40\% * \$1,333 = \$533$ per year in taxes. This *tax shield* is the cash savings from the depreciation deduction and must be taken into account in deciding between the lease and the purchase.
- You can lease the computer for $1,500 a year, payable in advance for 4 years. This means that if you lease the computer, you'll pay $1,500 today and $1,500 at the end of each of years 1, 2, and 3. The lease payment is an expense for tax purposes, so that its net after-tax cost to the firm is $(1 - 40\%) * 1,500 = \$900$.

Here's a spreadsheet describing these cash flows.

| | A | B | C | D | E | F |
|---|---|---|---|---|---|---|
| 1 | | LEASE OR PURCHASE? | | | | |
| | | Costs are negative numbers and inflows positive numbers | | | | |
| 2 | Asset cost | 4,000.00 | | | | |
| 3 | Annual depreciation if asset is purchased | 1,333.33 | <-- =B2/3 | | | |
| 4 | Annual lease payment | 1,500.00 | | | | |
| 5 | Bank rate | 15% | | | | |
| 6 | Tax rate | 40% | | | | |
| 7 | | | | | | |
| 8 | Year | 0 | 1 | 2 | 3 | |
| 9 | **Purchase cash flows** | | | | | |
| 10 | Cost of machine | -4,000 | | | | |
| 11 | Depreciation tax shield | | 533 | 533 | 533 | <-- =$B$3*$B$6 |
| 12 | Total | -4,000 | 533 | 533 | 533 | <-- =E11+E10 |
| 13 | | | | | | |
| 14 | **After-tax lease payments** | -900 | -900 | -900 | -900 | <-- =-$B$4*(1-$B$6) |
| 15 | | | | | | |
| 16 | The lease saves | 3,100 | -1,433 | -1,433 | -1,433 | <-- =-E12+E14 |
| 17 | | | | | | |
| 18 | IRR of lease savings | 18.33% | <-- =IRR(B16:E16) | | | |
| 19 | Alternative cost (after-tax bank interest) | 9.00% | <-- =B5*(1-$B$6) | | | |
| 20 | | | | | | |
| 21 | Lease or purchase? | buy | <-- =IF(B18>B19,"buy","lease") | | | |

Row 12 describes the after-tax cash flows associated with the purchase and row 14 the after-tax cash flows from the lease. The lessee loses the depreciation tax shield that he would have had if he had purchased and additionally bears the cost of the lease payments, which after tax amount to $900 per year. Row 16 shows that, taking account of these two items, leasing the computer is like taking a loan of $3,100 with after-tax repayments of $1,433 in years 1–3. The IRR of this "loan" is 18.33% (cell B18).

Should you lease or buy? If the bank is willing to lend you money at 15% and if interest costs are deductible expenses for tax purposes, then the after-tax cost of a bank loan is $(1-40\%) * 15\% = 9\%$. This means that the bank is a cheaper source of financing than the leasing company. The conclusion (cell B21): Buy the computer.

Another way to reach the conclusion that a purchase is better than a lease is to think of financing the machine with a 3-year bank loan of $3,100.

| | A | B | C | D | E | F |
|---|---|---|---|---|---|---|
| 24 | | Alternative: Borrow $3,100 from the bank and buy the computer | | | | |
| 25 | Year | 0 | 1 | 2 | 3 | |
| 26 | Loan at beginning of year | | 3,100.00 | 2,207.27 | 1,180.63 | <-- =D26-D30 |
| 27 | Payment at end of year | | 1,357.73 | 1,357.73 | 1,357.73 | <-- =PMT(B5,3,-$C$26) |
| 28 | Of this payment | | | | | |
| 29 | Interest | | 465.00 | 331.09 | 177.10 | <-- =$B$5*E26 |
| 30 | Repayment of principal | | 892.73 | 1,026.64 | 1,180.63 | <-- =E27-E29 |
| 31 | Remaining principal at end of year | | 2,207.27 | 1,180.63 | 0.00 | <-- =E26-E30 |
| 32 | | | | | | |
| 33 | After-tax interest | | 279.00 | 198.65 | 106.26 | <-- =(1-$B$6)*E29 |
| 34 | Net after-tax loan cash cost | | 1,171.73 | 1,225.29 | 1,286.89 | <-- =E33+E30 |
| 35 | | | | | | |
| 36 | **Machine + loan** | | | | | |
| 37 | Cost of machine | -4,000.00 | | | | <-- =B10 |
| 38 | Depreciation tax shield | | 533.33 | 533.33 | 533.33 | <-- =E12 |
| 39 | After-tax loan cash flow | 3,100.00 | -1,171.73 | -1,225.29 | -1,286.89 | <-- =-E34 |
| 40 | Total: Buy machine + take loan | -900.00 | -638.40 | -691.96 | -753.56 | <-- =SUM(E37:E39) |
| 41 | | | | | | |
| 42 | Compare this to the after-tax lease payments | -900.00 | -900.00 | -900.00 | -900.00 | <-- =E14 |

Rows 26–31 are a standard loan table discussed in Chapter 2 (page 46). Because interest is an expense for tax purposes, the after-tax interest cost to the firm is $(1-40\%)*$ *Interest*; in row 33 we compute this cost. The net after-tax cost of the loan to the firm (row 34) is the sum of the after-tax interest (row 33) and the annual repayment of principal (row 30).

In rows 37–40 we compute the total after-tax cash flows from buying the loan-financed machine. Comparing these to the after-tax lease payments (row 42 is just a copy of row 14)—you can see that in each year the cost of buying the machine with the loan is less than or equal to the cost of the after-tax lease payments, which is why the loan is preferable to the lease.

## What's the Maximum Lease Payment We'll Pay?

The above analysis shows that $1,500 per year is too much to pay for the lease. How much would we be willing to pay? To do this calculation, we use **Goal Seek** to find the lease payment for which the IRR of the differential cash flows (cell B18) is 9%. To get to the correct screen on Excel 2007, click **Data|What-If Analysis|Goal Seek**.

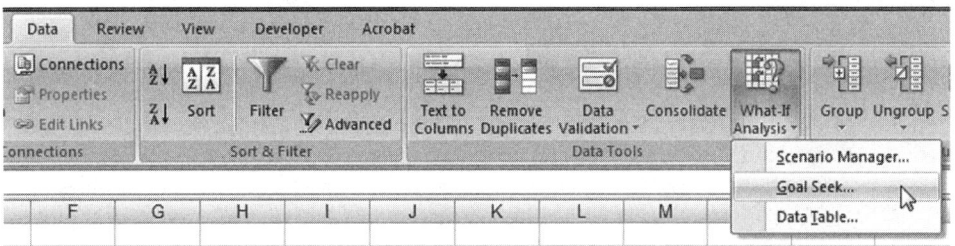

Clicking on **Goal Seek** brings up the following dialog box, which we have filled in with the relevant entries.

| | A | B | C | D | E | F |
|---|---|---|---|---|---|---|
| | | CORPORATE LEASING | | | | |
| 1 | | Costs are negative numbers and inflows positive numbers | | | | |
| 2 | Asset cost | 4,000.00 | | | | |
| 3 | Annual depreciation if asset is purchased | 1,333.33 | <-- =B2/3 | | | |
| 4 | Annual lease payment | 1,500.00 | | | | |
| 5 | Bank rate | 15% | | | | |
| 6 | Tax rate | 40% | | | | |
| 7 | | | | | | |
| 8 | Year | 0 | 1 | | | |
| 9 | Purchase cash flows | | | | | |
| 10 | Cost of machine | -4,000 | | | | |
| 11 | Depreciation tax shield | | 533 | | | |
| 12 | Total | -4,000 | 533 | | | |
| 13 | | | | | | |
| 14 | After-tax lease payments | -900 | -900 | -900 | -900 | <-- =-$B$4*(1-$B$6) |
| 15 | | | | | | |
| 16 | The lease saves | 3,100 | -1,433 | -1,433 | -1,433 | <-- =-E12+E14 |
| 17 | | | | | | |
| 18 | IRR of lease savings | 18.33% | <-- =IRR(B16:E16) | | | |
| 19 | Alternative cost (after-tax bank interest) | 9.00% | <-- =B5*(1-$B$6) | | | |
| 20 | | | | | | |

Goal Seek dialog box:
Set cell: $B$18
To value: 9%
By changing cell: $B$4

The conclusion is that a lease payment of $1,250.72 is the largest lease payment the lessee would be willing to pay.

|   | A | B | C | D | E | F |
|---|---|---|---|---|---|---|
| 1 | | **CORPORATE LEASING** | | | | |
| | | **Costs are negative numbers and inflows positive numbers** | | | | |
| 2 | Asset cost | 4,000.00 | | | | |
| 3 | Annual depreciation if asset is purchased | 1,333.33 | <-- =B2/3 | | | |
| 4 | Annual lease payment | 1,250.72 | | | | |
| 5 | Bank rate | 15% | | | | |
| 6 | Tax rate | 40% | | | | |
| 7 | | | | | | |
| 8 | **Year** | **0** | **1** | **2** | **3** | |
| 9 | **Purchase cash flows** | | | | | |
| 10 | Cost of machine | 4,000 | | | | |
| 11 | Depreciation tax shield | | -533 | -533 | -533 | <-- =-$B$3*$B$6 |
| 12 | Total | 4,000 | -533 | -533 | -533 | <-- =E11+E10 |
| 13 | | | | | | |
| 14 | **After-tax lease payments** | -750 | -750 | -750 | -750 | <-- =-$B$4*(1-$B$6) |
| 15 | | | | | | |
| 16 | The lease saves | 3,250 | -1,284 | -1,284 | -1,284 | <-- =E12+E14 |
| 17 | | | | | | |
| 18 | IRR | 9.00% | <-- =IRR(B16:E16) | | | |
| 19 | Alternative cost | 9.00% | <-- =B5*(1-$B$6) | | | |

# 5.5. Capital Budgeting Principle: Think about Mid-year Discounting

We could have called this section "Think about the timing of cash flows," but "mid-year discounting" is catchier. To show what we mean, we present two examples. In our first example, a company is thinking about spending $10,000 to produce an annual cash flow of $3,000 per year for the next 5 years. If the discount rate is 15% and the cash flows occur at year end, then the NPV of the project is $56.47.

|   | A | B | C |
|---|---|---|---|
| 1 | | **NPV, CASH FLOWS OCCUR** **AT YEAR END** | |
| 2 | Initial cost | 10,000.00 | |
| 3 | Annual cash flow | 3,000.00 | |
| 4 | Discount rate | 15% | |
| 5 | | | |
| 6 | **Year** | **Cash flow** | |
| 7 | 0 | -10,000.00 | |
| 8 | 1 | 3,000.00 | |
| 9 | 2 | 3,000.00 | |
| 10 | 3 | 3,000.00 | |
| 11 | 4 | 3,000.00 | |
| 12 | 5 | 3,000.00 | |
| 13 | | | |
| 14 | NPV of year-end cash flows | 56.47 | <-- =B7+NPV(B4,B8:B12) |

The NPV of $56.47 assumes that the cash flow for each year occurs at the end of the year:

$$NPV = -10,000 + \frac{3,000}{(1.15)} + \frac{3,000}{(1.15)^2} + \frac{3,000}{(1.15)^3} + \frac{3,000}{(1.15)^4} + \frac{3,000}{(1.15)^5} = 56.47 .$$

For many capital budgeting situations, this end-year cash flow assumption is not realistic. Think of a company buying a machine and getting cash flows by selling the machine's products—in this case the cash flows are likely to occur as a stream throughout the year rather than a single, end-year, cash flow. Because it's always better to get cash earlier, the NPV of the project will be higher than $56.47.

To get some feeling for whether this is important, suppose that the $3,000 annual cash flow is actually received as $750 at the end of each quarter. Then, as the spreadsheet below shows, the NPV would increase significantly.

| | A | B | C |
|---|---|---|---|
| 1 | NPV, CASH FLOWS OCCUR EACH QUARTER | | |
| 2 | Initial cost | 10,000.00 | |
| 3 | Annual cash flow | 3,000.00 | |
| 4 | Discount rate | 15% | |
| 5 | Quarterly discount rate | 3.56% | <-- =(1+B4)^(1/4)-1 |
| 6 | | | |
| 7 | Quarter | Quarterly cash flow | |
| 8 | 0 | -10,000.00 | |
| 9 | 1 | 750.00 | |
| 10 | 2 | 750.00 | |
| 11 | 3 | 750.00 | |
| 12 | 4 | 750.00 | |
| 13 | 5 | 750.00 | |
| 14 | 6 | 750.00 | |
| 15 | 7 | 750.00 | |
| 16 | 8 | 750.00 | |
| 17 | 9 | 750.00 | |
| 18 | 10 | 750.00 | |
| 19 | 11 | 750.00 | |
| 20 | 12 | 750.00 | |
| 21 | 13 | 750.00 | |
| 22 | 14 | 750.00 | |
| 23 | 15 | 750.00 | |
| 24 | 16 | 750.00 | |
| 25 | 17 | 750.00 | |
| 26 | 18 | 750.00 | |
| 27 | 19 | 750.00 | |
| 28 | 20 | 750.00 | |
| 29 | | | |
| 30 | NPV, quarterly cash flows | 605.68 | <-- =B8+NPV(B5,B9:B28) |

Note that in calculating the NPV of the quarterly cash flows (cell E29), we've used the *quarterly discount rate,* which is equivalent to the annual discount rate of 15% (3.56%, cell E4). This quarterly discount rate is calculated by

$$(1+ quarterly\ discount\ rate)=(1+ annual\ discount\ rate)^{1/4}$$

So far, the message of this section is clear and uncontroversial: When you discount you should take the timing of the cash flows into account. The problem is that for many capital budgeting problems we project annual cash flows, even though the actual flows occur throughout the year.[2] In many cases it is difficult to project the precise timing of the cash flows throughout the year, even though our example shows that this timing is very important.

---

[2] This has a lot to do with most firms' accounting cycles, which are annual. (There we go again—blaming the accountants!)

## Mid-year Discounting—An Elegant Compromise

On the one hand the timing of cash flows is important, but on the other hand it's difficult to deviate from end-year cash flow projections and project the precise timing of each cash flow. An elegant compromise is to project annual cash flow numbers but to assume that they occur mid-year. Here's how this looks in Excel.

| | A | B | C | D |
|---|---|---|---|---|
| 1 | | **MID-YEAR DISCOUNTING** | | |
| 2 | Initial cost | 10,000.00 | | |
| 3 | Annual cash flow | 3,000.00 | | |
| 4 | Discount rate | 15% | | |
| 5 | | | | |
| 6 | **Year** | **Cash flow** | **Discounted value** | |
| 7 | 0 | -10,000.00 | -10,000.00 | <-- =B7 |
| 8 | 1 | 3,000.00 | 2,797.51 | <-- =B8/(1+$B$4)^(A8-0.5) |
| 9 | 2 | 3,000.00 | 2,432.62 | <-- =B9/(1+$B$4)^(A9-0.5) |
| 10 | 3 | 3,000.00 | 2,115.32 | |
| 11 | 4 | 3,000.00 | 1,839.41 | |
| 12 | 5 | 3,000.00 | 1,599.49 | |
| 13 | | | | |
| 14 | NPV, midyear | | 784.36 | <-- =SUM(C7:C12) |
| 15 | | | 784.36 | <-- =B7+NPV(B4,B8:B12)*(1+B4)^0.5 |

The spreadsheet shows two ways to do the calculation:

- In cells B8:B12, each cash flow has been discounted by a factor $(1+r)^{year-0.5}$. This is equivalent to calculating the following NPV:

$$NPV = -10,000 + \frac{3,000}{(1.15)^{0.5}} + \frac{3,000}{(1.15)^{1.5}} + \frac{3,000}{(1.15)^{2.5}} + \frac{3,000}{(1.15)^{3.5}} + \frac{3,000}{(1.15)^{4.5}} = \underset{\underset{\text{Cell C43}}{\uparrow}}{784.36}$$

- In cell B15, we show a simple Excel formula that produces the same result: Simply take the Excel **NPV** formula and multiply by $(1+r)^{0.5}$.

## Using the XNPV Function

We can also do the mid-year NPV calculation using Excel's **XNPV** function.[3] To use **XNPV** you have to indicate the dates on which the cash flows will be received. The spreadsheet below shows an implementation of the function to our problem.

| | A | B | C |
|---|---|---|---|
| 1 | | **CALCULATING THE MID-YEAR** **NPV WITH EXCEL'S XNPV FUNCTION** | |
| 2 | Annual discount rate | 15% | |
| 3 | | | |
| 4 | **Date** | **Cash flow** | |
| 5 | 1-Jan-02 | -10,000 | |
| 6 | 1-Jul-02 | 3,000 | |
| 7 | 1-Jul-03 | 3,000 | |
| 8 | 1-Jul-04 | 3,000 | |
| 9 | 1-Jul-05 | 3,000 | |
| 10 | 1-Jul-06 | 3,000 | |
| 11 | | | |
| 12 | NPV | 788.43 | <-- =XNPV(B2,B5:B10,A5:A10) |

---

[3] If this function does not appear in your list of Excel functions, go to **Tools|Add-ins** on the Excel menu and check **Analysis Toolpak**.

## USING THE XNPV FUNCTION

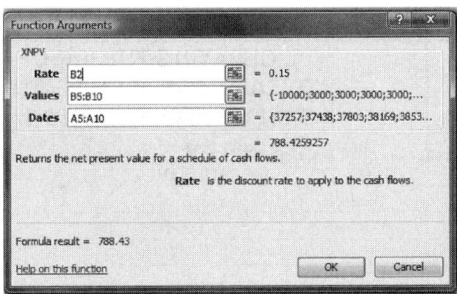

As the dialog box shows, **XNPV** requires you to input the *annual* discount rate, the values to be discounted, and the dates on which these values occur. The function then finds the net present value on the first date of the series (in our example: 1-Jan-02). The **XNPV** function differs from the **NPV** function in one very important aspect: In Chapter 2 (page 37) we stressed that Excel's **NPV** calculates the present value of future cash flows; to calculate the true net present value, you have to add in the initial cash flow separately. The **XNPV** function has *all* the cash flows as inputs (including the initial cash flow) and has as output the true net present value.

The **XNPV** function (and its cousin, the **XIRR** function discussed later) are part of the standard Excel package, but they have to be separately installed as an add-in. Here's what you do:

**Step 1: Click on the Office Button  and go to Excel Options**

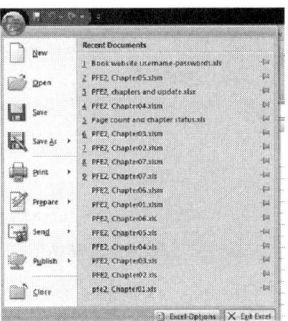

**Step 2: Go to Add-Ins, find the appropriate entry under Manage, and click Go:**

**Step 3: Click Analysis ToolPak**

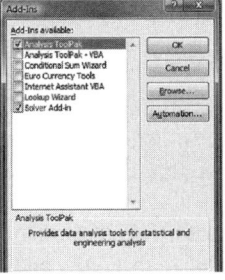

## Calculating the Mid-year IRR

What if you want to compute the IRR of the cash flows, taking into account the fact that they occur mid-year? The easiest way to do this is to use the Excel function **XIRR**, as shown below.

|  | A | B | C |
|---|---|---|---|
| 1 | CALCULATING THE IRR OF MIDYEAR CASH FLOWS WITH EXCEL'S XIRR FUNCTION | | |
| 2 | Date | Cash flow | |
| 3 | 1-Jan-02 | -10,000 | |
| 4 | 1-Jul-02 | 3,000 | |
| 5 | 1-Jul-03 | 3,000 | |
| 6 | 1-Jul-04 | 3,000 | |
| 7 | 1-Jul-05 | 3,000 | |
| 8 | 1-Jul-06 | 3,000 | |
| 9 | | | |
| 10 | IRR | 19.06% | <-- =XIRR(B3:B8,A3:A8) |

## AN EXCEL NOTE: THE XIRR FUNCTION

The **XIRR** function requires you to put in a list of dates at which the cash flows occur. The syntax of the function is given in the dialog box below.

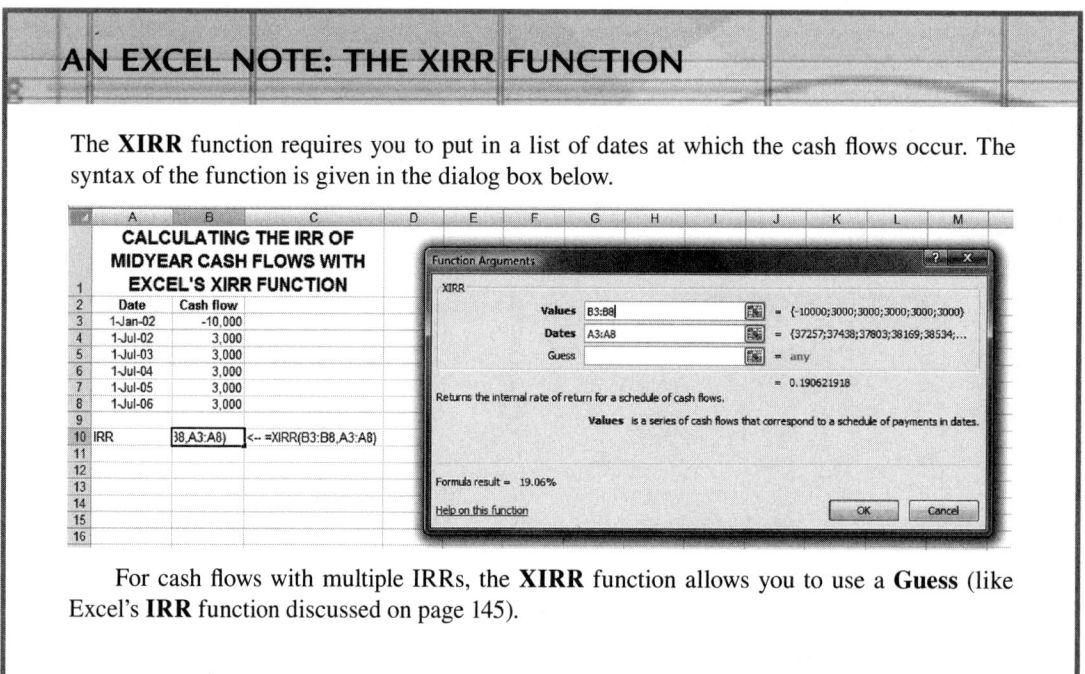

For cash flows with multiple IRRs, the **XIRR** function allows you to use a **Guess** (like Excel's **IRR** function discussed on page 145).

## Applying Mid-year Cash Flows to Sally and Dave's Condo

In this section we have stressed the importance of cash flow timing in determining the NPV of a project. We have also suggested that—rather than try to determine the precise timing of each cash flow—it may be roughly equivalent to assume that the cash flows occur mid-period.

The implementation of this simple idea can be complicated. Take Sally and Dave's condo, for example, which was discussed in Chapter 4 (page 115). Recall that Sally and Dave's annual cash flow of $18,050 from the condo rental was computed as follows:

- The annual rent of $24,000 is taxable income, and the annual property taxes ($1,500) and maintenance ($1,000) are expenses for tax purposes. Because Sally and Dave's tax rate is 30%, these three items produce $(1-30\%)*(\$24,000-1,000-1,500)=\$15,050$ of after-tax income per year.
- The condo's annual depreciation of $10,000 produces a tax shield of $30\%*\$10,000=\$3,000$. Adding this tax shield to the $15,050 gives Sally and Dave's annual cash flow of $18,050 in years 1–10.
- Sally and Dave plan to sell the condo for $100,000 after 10 years. At this point the condo will be fully depreciated, so that all the money they receive from the sale will be income. Thus, the after-tax terminal value of the condo is $(1-30\%)*\$100,000=\$70,000$. Adding this to the condo's year-10 cash flow produces a total year-10 cash flow of $88,050.

Our initial calculation gave us an IRR of 16.69% on Sally and Dave's investment (cell B37 below).

| | A | B | C |
|---|---|---|---|
| 1 | **SALLY & DAVE'S CONDO** **Example from Section 4.7** | | |
| 2 | **Cost of condo** | 100,000 | |
| 3 | **Sally & Dave's tax rate** | 30% | |
| 4 | | | |
| 5 | **Annual reportable income calculation** | | |
| 6 | Rent | 24,000 | |
| 7 | Expenses | | |
| 8 | Property taxes | -1,500 | |
| 9 | Miscellaneous expenses | -1,000 | |
| 10 | Depreciation | -10,000 | |
| 11 | Reportable income | 11,500 | <-- =SUM(B6:B10) |
| 12 | Taxes (rate = 30%) | -3,450 | <-- =-B3*B11 |
| 13 | Net income | 8,050 | <-- =B11+B12 |
| 14 | | | |
| 15 | Annual cash flow | 18,050 | <-- =B13-B10 |
| 16 | | | |
| 17 | **Terminal value** | | |
| 18 | Estimated resale value, year 10 | 100,000 | |
| 19 | Book value | 0 | |
| 20 | Taxable gain | 100,000 | <-- =B18-B19 |
| 21 | Taxes | 30,000 | <-- =0.3*B20 |
| 22 | Net after tax--cash flow from terminal value | 70,000 | <-- =B20-B21 |
| 23 | | | |
| 24 | **Year** | **Cash flow** | |
| 25 | 0 | -100,000 | |
| 26 | 1 | 18,050 | <-- =$B$15 |
| 27 | 2 | 18,050 | |
| 28 | 3 | 18,050 | |
| 29 | 4 | 18,050 | |
| 30 | 5 | 18,050 | |
| 31 | 6 | 18,050 | |
| 32 | 7 | 18,050 | |
| 33 | 8 | 18,050 | |
| 34 | 9 | 18,050 | |
| 35 | 10 | 88,050 | <-- =$B$15+B22 |
| 36 | | | |
| 37 | IRR | 16.69% | |

## Incorporating the Timing of Cash Flows

Now suppose we try to incorporate the timing of the cash flows into our analysis of the condo IRR. We make the following assumptions:

- The annual rent of $24,000 occurs mid-year. This is an approximation to the fact that the renters pay their rent monthly.
- Miscellaneous expenses of $1,000 also occur mid-year.
- Property taxes and income taxes occur at the end of each year.
- The resale of the property (which produces a cash flow of $70,000) occurs at the end of year 10.

These assumptions lead to the cash flows given in cells E4:E44 below. The IRR of these cash flows (9.59%, cell E46) is the *semiannual IRR* (remember that our cash flows are now semiannual). The *annualized IRR* is $(1 + 9.59\%)^2 - 1 = 20.10\%$, which is significantly higher than the 16.69% we calculated earlier assuming that all cash flows occur at year end. Because the IRR gets higher when positive cash flows occur earlier, this is not surprising.

| | A | B | C | D | E | F |
|---|---|---|---|---|---|---|
| 1 | | SALLY & DAVE'S CONDO--INCORPORATING MID-YEAR CASH FLOWS | | | | |
| 2 | Tax rate | 30% | | Return on the condo--Taking into account mid-year cash flows | | |
| 3 | | | | Year | Cash flow | |
| 4 | **Midyear cashflows** | | | 0 | -100,000 | |
| 5 | Rent | 24,000 | | 0.5 | 23,000 | <-- Rent + miscellaneous expenses |
| 6 | Miscellaneous expenses | -1,000 | | 1 | -4,950 | <-- Property and income taxes |
| 7 | Sum of midyear cash flows | 23,000 | <-- =SUM(B5:B6) | 1.5 | 23,000 | |
| 8 | | | | 2 | -4,950 | |
| 9 | **End-year cash flows** | | | 2.5 | 23,000 | |
| 10 | Depreciation | 10,000 | | 3 | -4,950 | |
| 11 | Property taxes | -1,500 | | 3.5 | 23,000 | |
| 12 | Reported income | 11,500 | | 4 | -4,950 | |
| 13 | Income taxes | -3,450 | <-- =-B2*B12 | 4.5 | 23,000 | |
| 14 | Sum of end-year cash flows | -4,950 | <-- =B11+B13 | 5 | -4,950 | |
| 15 | | | | 5.5 | 23,000 | |
| 16 | Annual cash flow | 18,050 | <-- =B7+B14 | 6 | -4,950 | |
| 17 | | | | 6.5 | 23,000 | |
| 18 | | | | 7 | -4,950 | |
| 19 | | Note: Some rows have | | 7.5 | 23,000 | |
| 33 | | been hidden. For full | | 14.5 | 23,000 | |
| 34 | | version see disk with book. | | 15 | -4,950 | |
| 35 | | | | 15.5 | 23,000 | |
| 36 | | | | 16 | -4,950 | |
| 37 | | | | 16.5 | 23,000 | |
| 38 | | | | 17 | -4,950 | |
| 39 | | | | 17.5 | 23,000 | |
| 40 | | | | 18 | -4,950 | |
| 41 | | | | 18.5 | 23,000 | |
| 42 | | | | 19 | -4,950 | |
| 43 | | | | 19.5 | 23,000 | |
| 44 | | | | 20 | 65,050 | <-- Sale of condo + taxes |
| 45 | | | | | | |
| 46 | | | | IRR (semiannual) | 9.59% | <-- =IRR(E4:E44) |
| 47 | | | | IRR (annualized) | 20.10% | <-- =(1+E46)^2-1 |

## Two "Reality" Notes

**Note 1**: Sally and Dave's condo example shows that getting the dates of the cash flows right is important, but it also shows that this can be cumbersome. As a compromise, perhaps we should have gone back to the mid-year IRR. In the spreadsheet below we use the **XIRR** function in cell B37 to compute the IRR on the assumption that all the condo cash flows occur mid-year.

| | A | B | C |
|---|---|---|---|
| 1 | **SALLY & DAVE'S CONDO--MIDYEAR CASH FLOWS** | | |
| 2 | **Cost of condo** | 100,000 | |
| 3 | **Sally & Dave's tax rate** | 30% | |
| 4 | | | |
| 5 | **Annual reportable income calculation** | | |
| 6 | Rent | 24,000 | |
| 7 | Expenses | | |
| 8 | Property taxes | -1,500 | |
| 9 | Miscellaneous expenses | -1,000 | |
| 10 | Depreciation | -10,000 | |
| 11 | Reportable income | 11,500 | <-- =SUM(B6:B10) |
| 12 | Taxes (rate = 30%) | -3,450 | <-- =-B3*B11 |
| 13 | Net income | 8,050 | <-- =B11+B12 |
| 14 | | | |
| 15 | Annual cash flow | 18,050 | <-- =B13-B10 |
| 16 | | | |
| 17 | **Terminal value** | | |
| 18 | Estimated resale value, year 10 | 100,000 | |
| 19 | Book value | 0 | |
| 20 | Taxable gain | 100,000 | <-- =B18-B19 |
| 21 | Taxes | 30,000 | <-- =0.3*B20 |
| 22 | Net after tax--cash flow from terminal value | 70,000 | <-- =B20-B21 |
| 23 | | | |
| 24 | **Date** | **Cash flow** | |
| 25 | 1-Jan-02 | -100,000 | |
| 26 | 1-Jul-02 | 18,050 | <-- =$B$15 |
| 27 | 1-Jul-03 | 18,050 | |
| 28 | 1-Jul-04 | 18,050 | |
| 29 | 1-Jul-05 | 18,050 | |
| 30 | 1-Jul-06 | 18,050 | |
| 31 | 1-Jul-07 | 18,050 | |
| 32 | 1-Jul-08 | 18,050 | |
| 33 | 1-Jul-09 | 18,050 | |
| 34 | 1-Jul-10 | 18,050 | |
| 35 | 1-Jul-11 | 88,050 | <-- =$B$15+B22 |
| 36 | | | |
| 37 | IRR | 18.69% | <-- =XIRR(B25:B35,A25:A35) |

**Note 2**: In this book we often ignore mid-year discounting—not because we don't believe it's important, but because it's cumbersome to explain this, along with all the other myriad capital budgeting problems. In this case our advice to you is "Do as we say, don't do as we do."

## 5.6. Inflation: Real and Nominal Interest Rates and Cash Flows

Prices tend to rise and because they do, money loses its value over time. What else is new? This section discusses the terminology of inflation. When you finish the section, you should understand the difference between real and nominal interest rates and real and nominal cash flows. We'll illustrate these concepts with several "real world" examples, so that hopefully you'll have a better idea of the impact of inflation. In Section 5.7 we apply the concepts of this section to a number of capital budgeting problems.

First some facts. The following spreadsheet shows the purchasing power of $1 from 1980 through 2009. All the numbers in column B are in terms of 2009 dollars. As the spreadsheet shows, the goods you could buy with $1 in 1980 would cost you $2.62 in 2009. Adjusting for inflation, $1 in 1990 would be worth $1.65 in 2009.

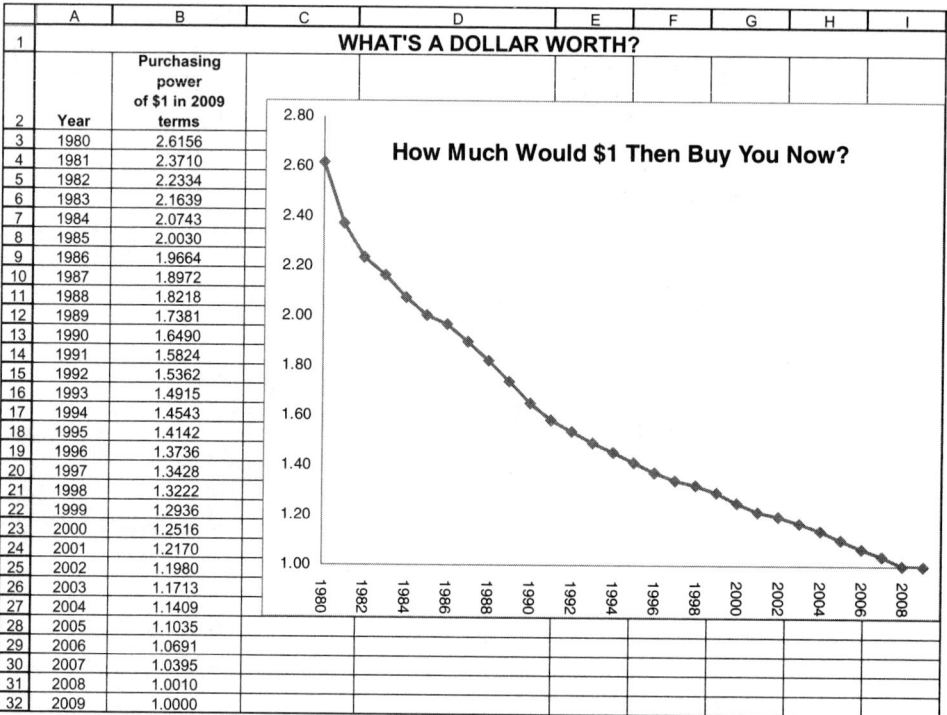

| | A | B |
|---|---|---|
| 1 | | WHAT'S A DOLLAR WORTH? |
| 2 | Year | Purchasing power of $1 in 2009 terms |
| 3 | 1980 | 2.6156 |
| 4 | 1981 | 2.3710 |
| 5 | 1982 | 2.2334 |
| 6 | 1983 | 2.1639 |
| 7 | 1984 | 2.0743 |
| 8 | 1985 | 2.0030 |
| 9 | 1986 | 1.9664 |
| 10 | 1987 | 1.8972 |
| 11 | 1988 | 1.8218 |
| 12 | 1989 | 1.7381 |
| 13 | 1990 | 1.6490 |
| 14 | 1991 | 1.5824 |
| 15 | 1992 | 1.5362 |
| 16 | 1993 | 1.4915 |
| 17 | 1994 | 1.4543 |
| 18 | 1995 | 1.4142 |
| 19 | 1996 | 1.3736 |
| 20 | 1997 | 1.3428 |
| 21 | 1998 | 1.3222 |
| 22 | 1999 | 1.2936 |
| 23 | 2000 | 1.2516 |
| 24 | 2001 | 1.2170 |
| 25 | 2002 | 1.1980 |
| 26 | 2003 | 1.1713 |
| 27 | 2004 | 1.1409 |
| 28 | 2005 | 1.1035 |
| 29 | 2006 | 1.0691 |
| 30 | 2007 | 1.0395 |
| 31 | 2008 | 1.0010 |
| 32 | 2009 | 1.0000 |

Here's another way to understand this phenomenon. The following table gives the consumer price index (CPI) for the United States from 1980 to 2009.[4] The index has been normalized so that the average CPI for 1982–1984 is 100. A basket of goods that cost $100 in 1984 would have cost $79.31 in 1980, $87.49 in 1981, and so on. The same basket would cost $207.43 in 2001.

---

[4] The consumer price index measures the market prices of a standard basket of goods. For (much) more information look at the Web site of the Bureau of Labor Statistics, http://www.bls.gov/cpi/, or the Minneapolis Federal Reserve Bank, http://minneapolisfed.org/Research/data/us/calc/index.cfm.

| | K | L | M |
|---|---|---|---|
| 3 | Computations | | |
| 4 | $100 in 1984 in 1980 prices | 79.31 | <-- =100*B3/B7 |
| 5 | $100 in 1984 in 1981 prices | 87.49 | <-- =100*B4/B7 |
| 6 | $100 in 1984 in 2009 prices | 207.43 | <-- =100*B32/B7 |

In column C we've used Excel to compute the *annual inflation rates* from these data:

$$Inflation\ rate\ in\ year\ t = \frac{CPI_t}{CPI_{t-1}} - 1.$$

As you can see from the graph, the inflation rate at the beginning of the 1980s was considerably higher than in the 1990s. Nevertheless, even throughout the relatively low inflation decade of

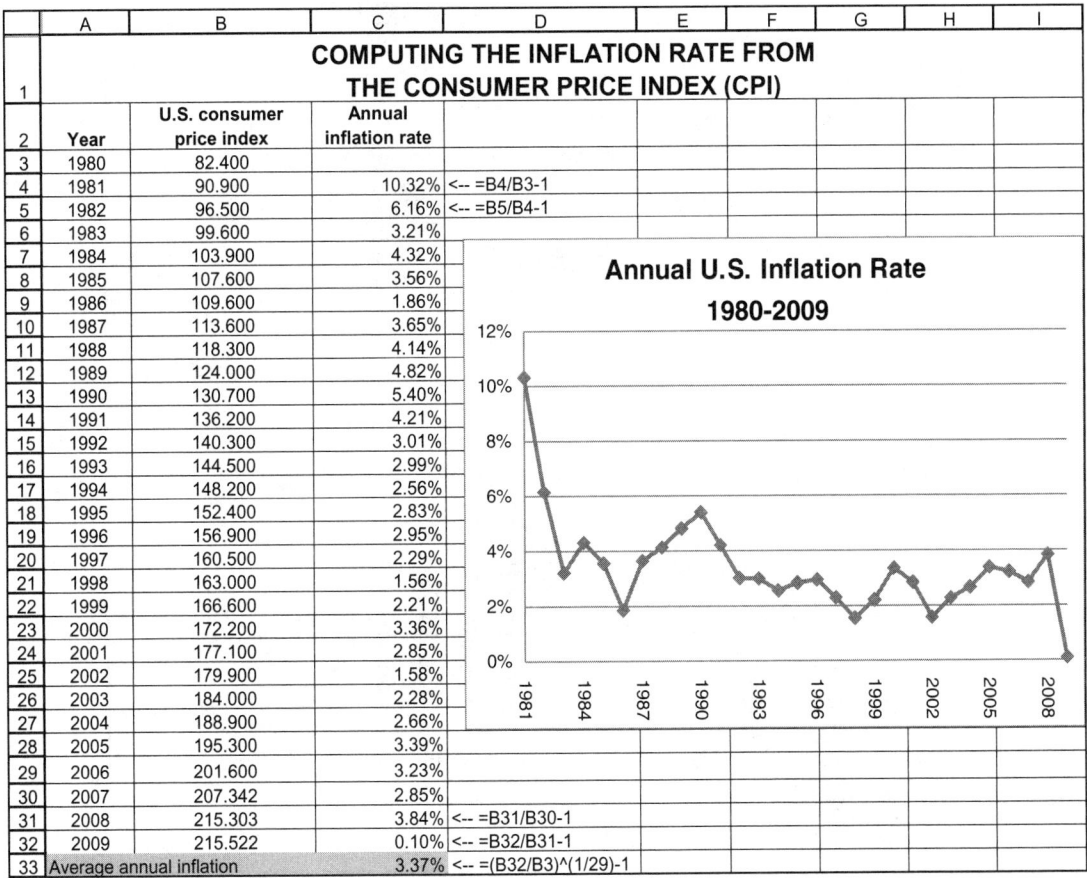

| | A | B | C | D | E | F | G | H | I |
|---|---|---|---|---|---|---|---|---|---|
| 1 | COMPUTING THE INFLATION RATE FROM THE CONSUMER PRICE INDEX (CPI) | | | | | | | | |
| 2 | Year | U.S. consumer price index | Annual inflation rate | | | | | | |
| 3 | 1980 | 82.400 | | | | | | | |
| 4 | 1981 | 90.900 | 10.32% | <-- =B4/B3-1 | | | | | |
| 5 | 1982 | 96.500 | 6.16% | <-- =B5/B4-1 | | | | | |
| 6 | 1983 | 99.600 | 3.21% | | | | | | |
| 7 | 1984 | 103.900 | 4.32% | | | | | | |
| 8 | 1985 | 107.600 | 3.56% | | | | | | |
| 9 | 1986 | 109.600 | 1.86% | | | | | | |
| 10 | 1987 | 113.600 | 3.65% | | | | | | |
| 11 | 1988 | 118.300 | 4.14% | | | | | | |
| 12 | 1989 | 124.000 | 4.82% | | | | | | |
| 13 | 1990 | 130.700 | 5.40% | | | | | | |
| 14 | 1991 | 136.200 | 4.21% | | | | | | |
| 15 | 1992 | 140.300 | 3.01% | | | | | | |
| 16 | 1993 | 144.500 | 2.99% | | | | | | |
| 17 | 1994 | 148.200 | 2.56% | | | | | | |
| 18 | 1995 | 152.400 | 2.83% | | | | | | |
| 19 | 1996 | 156.900 | 2.95% | | | | | | |
| 20 | 1997 | 160.500 | 2.29% | | | | | | |
| 21 | 1998 | 163.000 | 1.56% | | | | | | |
| 22 | 1999 | 166.600 | 2.21% | | | | | | |
| 23 | 2000 | 172.200 | 3.36% | | | | | | |
| 24 | 2001 | 177.100 | 2.85% | | | | | | |
| 25 | 2002 | 179.900 | 1.58% | | | | | | |
| 26 | 2003 | 184.000 | 2.28% | | | | | | |
| 27 | 2004 | 188.900 | 2.66% | | | | | | |
| 28 | 2005 | 195.300 | 3.39% | | | | | | |
| 29 | 2006 | 201.600 | 3.23% | | | | | | |
| 30 | 2007 | 207.342 | 2.85% | | | | | | |
| 31 | 2008 | 215.303 | 3.84% | <-- =B31/B30-1 | | | | | |
| 32 | 2009 | 215.522 | 0.10% | <-- =B32/B31-1 | | | | | |
| 33 | Average annual inflation | | 3.37% | <-- =(B32/B3)^(1/29)-1 | | | | | |

the 1990s, the inflation rate in the United States has generally been between 2 and 4% per year. Through the period surveyed, the average inflation rate (cell C33) was 3.37%.

Inflation of 3.37% per year may not seem like much, but it adds up. Suppose, for example, that we had 3% inflation per year for 10 years. As the Excel spreadsheet that follows shows, this means that the *cumulative inflation* over the decade would have been $(1+3\%)^{10}-1=34.39\%$. Another way to think about this is that in every 10 years, $1 loses 26% of its value—an end-of-the-decade dollar is worth only $1/(1+3\%)^{10} = 0.7441$ in terms of a beginning-of-the-decade dollar.

|   | A | B | C |
|---|---|---|---|
| 1 | **ANNUAL INFLATION RATES AND CUMULATIVE INFLATION** | | |
| 2 | Annual inflation rate | 3% | |
| 3 | Cumulative inflation over 10 years | 34.39% | <-- =(1+B2)^10-1 |
| 4 | End-decade $ worth in terms of beginning of decade $ | 0.7441 | <-- =1/(1+B2)^10 |

We can put this into a table.

| | A | B | C | D |
|---|---|---|---|---|
| 1 | **WHAT'S A DOLLAR WORTH?** | | | |
| 2 | Annual inflation rate | End-decade $ worth in terms of beginning of decade $ | Cumulative inflation over 10 years | |
| 3 | 0% | 1.00 | 0.00% | |
| 4 | 1% | 0.91 | 10.46% | |
| 5 | 2% | 0.82 | 21.90% | |
| 6 | 3% | 0.74 | 34.39% | |
| 7 | 4% | 0.68 | 48.02% | |
| 8 | 5% | 0.61 | 62.89% | =1/(1+B14)^10 |
| 9 | 6% | 0.56 | 79.08% | |
| 10 | 7% | 0.51 | 96.72% | |
| 11 | 8% | 0.46 | 115.89% | |
| 12 | 9% | 0.42 | 136.74% | |
| 13 | 10% | 0.39 | 159.37% | <-- =(1+A13)^10-1 |
| 14 | | | | |

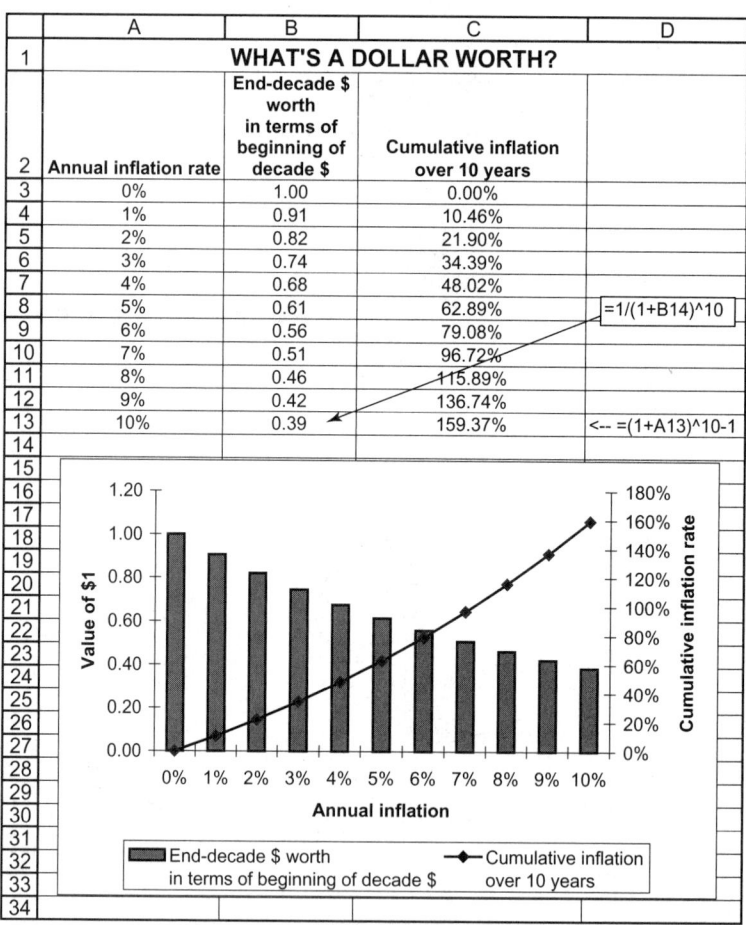

## Nominal and Real Interest Rates

Inflation not only affects the prices of goods—it also affects interest rates. Financial economists distinguish between *nominal* interest rates and *real* interest rates. The nominal interest rate is the rate quoted on a loan or a bank deposit and the real interest rate is the loan or bank deposit rate in purchasing-power terms (that is, after adjusting for inflation). In this section we explore and define these concepts.

Suppose you lend your friend Martha $100 with the agreement that she'll repay you next year. How much interest should you ask for? Martha suggests a 4% interest rate, but thinking about it, you realize that you anticipate 5% inflation over the year—meaning goods worth $100 today will cost $100 * (1.05) = $105 next year when the money is repaid. So if Martha repays you $100 * (1.04) = $104, she's not even repaying you the purchasing power of the loan. In this case,

$$\begin{array}{l} next\ year's \\ repayment\ in \\ terms\ of\ this \\ year's\ dollars \end{array} = \frac{Amount\ repaid}{1+inflation} = \frac{100*(1+interest)}{1+inflation} = \frac{104}{1.05} = 99.048$$

In the jargon of finance, the 4% interest rate is called the *nominal interest rate*; the word "nominal" indicates that the interest paid has not been adjusted for the effects of inflation. This is another way of saying that Martha will repay you $104 regardless of how much prices increase over the year. Quoted interest rates (whether on mortgages, credit cards, or government bonds) are almost always nominal interest rates ("lend me $100 today and I'll pay you back next year with 10% interest").

The *real interest rate* is defined as the interest rate in terms of purchasing power of money. In our example, you can see that you loan Martha $100 but get back (in purchasing power terms) $99.048. Thus, the real interest paid by Martha is -0.952%:

$$\begin{array}{l} real\ interest \\ on\ one\text{-}year\ loan \end{array} = \frac{purchasing\ power\ repaid}{purchasing\ power\ lent} - 1 = \frac{99.048}{100} - 1 = -0.952\%\ .$$

From the above formula, you can see that

$$real\ interest = \frac{1+nominal\ interest}{1+inflation} - 1 = \frac{1+4\%}{1+5\%} - 1 = -0.952\%$$

An equivalent and easier way to define the real interest rate is

---

## TERMINOLOGY REVIEW

**Inflation:** We almost always associate "inflation" with a decrease in the purchasing power of money (and an increase in the price level). Historically there have also been periods of *deflation*—increases in the purchasing power of money caused by decreases in the price level.[5]

**Nominal interest rate or nominal cash flow:** An interest rate or cash flow that has not been adjusted for the effects of inflation. Example: You borrow $100 today and agree to repay $120 at the end of the year. The *nominal interest rate* is 20% and the $120 repayment (which will be in next year's dollars, irrespective of the inflation over the next year) is a *payment in nominal dollars*.

**Real interest rate or real cash flow:** An interest rate or cash flow adjusted for inflation. To calculate the real cash flow, decide on a base year and compute all the cash flows in units of that base year. The cash flows so computed are *real cash flows* (cash flows in *constant dollars*) and the interest rates resulting from them are *real interest rates*.

$$1 + nominal\ interest = (1 + real\ interest) * (1 + inflation\ rate).$$

This equation is often called the Fisher equation, after the famous American economist Irving Fisher (1867–1947).

## Nominal and Real Cash Flows

In the previous subsection we showed the relation between the real and nominal interest rates. The nominal interest rate is the quoted interest rate, unadjusted for inflation, and the real interest rate is the interest rate adjusted for the change in the purchasing power of money.[5]

In this section we show the relation between real and nominal cash flows. We start with a 1-year example: You make an investment $100 in year 0 and get back $120 at the end of year 1; over this period the consumer price index increases from 131 to 138.

|   | A | B | C | D |
|---|---|---|---|---|
| 1 | **REAL AND NOMINAL CASH FLOWS** | | | |
| 2 | | Year 0 | Year 1 | |
| 3 | Nominal cash flow | -100 | 120 | |
| 4 | Consumer price index (CPI) | 131 | 138 | |
| 5 | | | | |
| 6 | Inflation | | 5.34% | <-- =C4/B4-1 |
| 7 | | | | |
| 8 | Real cash flow in year 0 dollars | -100 | 113.913 | <-- =C3*B4/C4 |
| 9 | | | | |
| 10 | Nominal return | | 20.00% | <-- =C3/-B3-1 |
| 11 | Real return | | 13.91% | <-- =C8/-B8-1 |

The *real year-1 cash flow* (defined in this case as the year-1 cash flow in year-0 dollars) is computed as

$$year\text{-}1\ real\ cash\ flow = \frac{year\text{-}1\ cash\ flow}{1 + inflation\ rate\ over\ period}$$

$$= \frac{year - 1\ cash\ flow}{\dfrac{CPI_{end\text{-}period}}{CPI_{beginning\text{-}period}}} = \frac{120}{(138/131)} = 113.913$$

To compute the real return on the investment,

$$1 + real\ investment\ return = \frac{year\text{-}1\ real\ cash\ flow}{year\text{-}0\ real\ cash\ flow} - 1$$

$$= \frac{113.913}{100} - 1 = 13.91\%$$

Equivalently, we can calculate the real return using the *nominal rate of return* and deflating it by the inflation rate:

$$1 + real\ return = \frac{1 + nominal\ return}{1 + inflation\ rate} - 1 = \frac{\dfrac{End - period\ nominal\ cash\ flow}{Beginning - period\ nominal\ cash\ flow}}{\dfrac{CPI_{end\text{-}period}}{CPI_{beginning\text{-}period}}}$$

$$= \frac{\dfrac{120}{100}}{\dfrac{138}{131}} - 1 = \frac{1 + 20\%}{1 + 5.34\%} = 1 + 13.91\%$$

---

[5]During the 1990s, Japan had prolonged periods of declining prices. See next page.

## Investment Analysis: How Much Did You Really Earn?

Suppose that the end of 1995 you invested $1,000 in a security that subsequently paid you $150 at the end of each year from 1996, 1997,..., 2004. At the end of 2005, you sold the security for $1,150. Looking back, you realize that the CPI went from 133 in 1995 to 195 in 2004. What was your real rate of return? To do this calculation, we translate each of the investment's nominal cash flows into real cash flows, using the cumulative inflation rate.

| | A | B | C | D | E | F | G |
|---|---|---|---|---|---|---|---|
| 1 | | | **HOW MUCH DID YOU REALLY EARN?** | | | | |
| 2 | Year | Nominal cash flow | CPI | Cumulative inflation rate | | Real cash flow | < -- This is the cash flow in 1995 dollars |
| 3 | 1995 | -1,000 | 133 | | | -1,000.00 | |
| 4 | 1996 | 150 | 138 | 3.76% | <-- =C4/$C$3-1 | 144.57 | <-- =B4/(1+D4) |
| 5 | 1997 | 150 | 142 | 6.77% | <-- =C5/$C$3-1 | 140.49 | <-- =B5/(1+D5) |
| 6 | 1998 | 150 | 145 | 9.02% | <-- =C6/$C$3-1 | 137.59 | |
| 7 | 1999 | 150 | 148 | 11.28% | | 134.80 | |
| 8 | 2000 | 150 | 153 | 15.04% | | 130.39 | |
| 9 | 2001 | 150 | 166 | 24.81% | | 120.18 | |
| 10 | 2002 | 150 | 172 | 29.32% | | 115.99 | |
| 11 | 2003 | 150 | 180 | 35.34% | | 110.83 | |
| 12 | 2004 | 150 | 191 | 43.61% | | 104.45 | |
| 13 | 2005 | 1,150 | 195 | 46.62% | <-- =C13/$C$3-1 | 784.36 | |
| 14 | | | | | | | |
| 15 | Nominal IRR | 15.00% | <-- =IRR(B3:B13) | | Real IRR | 10.93% | <-- =IRR(F3:F14) |

As you can see, your 15% nominal rate of return was reduced by inflation to a 10.93% real rate of return (the rate of return adjusted for changes in the purchasing power of money).

## Do Prices Always Go Up?

It seems like it, but the example below (Japan from 1990 to 2007) shows that prices can also go down.

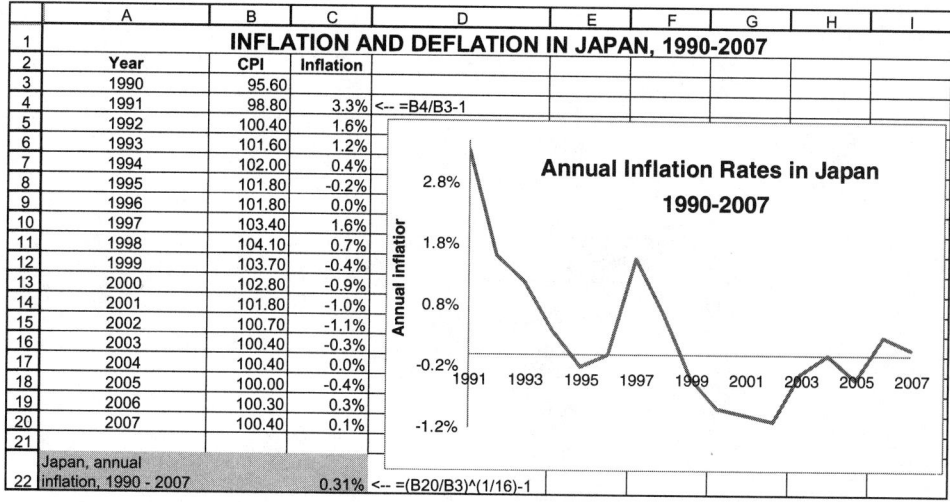

| | A | B | C | D | E | F | G | H | I |
|---|---|---|---|---|---|---|---|---|---|
| 1 | | | **INFLATION AND DEFLATION IN JAPAN, 1990-2007** | | | | | | |
| 2 | Year | CPI | Inflation | | | | | | |
| 3 | 1990 | 95.60 | | | | | | | |
| 4 | 1991 | 98.80 | 3.3% | <-- =B4/B3-1 | | | | | |
| 5 | 1992 | 100.40 | 1.6% | | | | | | |
| 6 | 1993 | 101.60 | 1.2% | | | | | | |
| 7 | 1994 | 102.00 | 0.4% | | | | | | |
| 8 | 1995 | 101.80 | -0.2% | | | | | | |
| 9 | 1996 | 101.80 | 0.0% | | | | | | |
| 10 | 1997 | 103.40 | 1.6% | | | | | | |
| 11 | 1998 | 104.10 | 0.7% | | | | | | |
| 12 | 1999 | 103.70 | -0.4% | | | | | | |
| 13 | 2000 | 102.80 | -0.9% | | | | | | |
| 14 | 2001 | 101.80 | -1.0% | | | | | | |
| 15 | 2002 | 100.70 | -1.1% | | | | | | |
| 16 | 2003 | 100.40 | -0.3% | | | | | | |
| 17 | 2004 | 100.40 | 0.0% | | | | | | |
| 18 | 2005 | 100.00 | -0.4% | | | | | | |
| 19 | 2006 | 100.30 | 0.3% | | | | | | |
| 20 | 2007 | 100.40 | 0.1% | | | | | | |
| 21 | | | | | | | | | |
| 22 | Japan, annual inflation, 1990 - 2007 | | 0.31% | <-- =(B20/B3)^(1/16)-1 | | | | | |

## Is Oil Cheap or Expensive?

In the 56 years between 1947 and 2009, the nominal price of a barrel of oil in the United States increased from $1.93 in 1947 to $73.19 per barrel in 2009. This is an annual increase of 6.10% per year: $(73.19/1.93)^{(1/61)} - 1 = 6.14\%$. The annual price increase in *real dollars* is much lower: The purchasing power, in terms of 2009 dollars, of the $1.93 that a barrel of oil cost in 1947 is equivalent to $15.36. The real price increase over the period was 2.59% per year. This is less than the overall cost-of-living increase of 3.46% per year.

|  | A | B | C | D | E |
|---|---|---|---|---|---|
| 1 | **NOMINAL AND REAL INCREASE IN U.S. OIL PRICES 1947-2009** | | | | |
| 2 | Nominal price increase | | | | |
| 3 | 1947 price per barrel | 1.93 | | | |
| 4 | 2009 price per barrel | 73.18 | | | |
| 5 | Annual increase | 6.14% | <-- =(B4/B3)^(1/61)-1 | | |
| 6 | | | | | |
| 7 | Real price increase | | | | |
| 8 | 1947 price per barrel in 2009 dollars | 15.36 | 1947 price index | 15.51 | |
| 9 | 2009 price per barrel in 2009 dollars | 73.18 | 2009 price index | 123.43 | |
| 10 | Annual increase | | | | |
| 11 | Oil prices | 2.59% | General cost of living | 3.46% | <-- =(D9/D8)^(1/61)-1 |

Of course comparing two points in time doesn't tell the whole story. Here's a chart of the real and nominal cost of oil throughout the period.

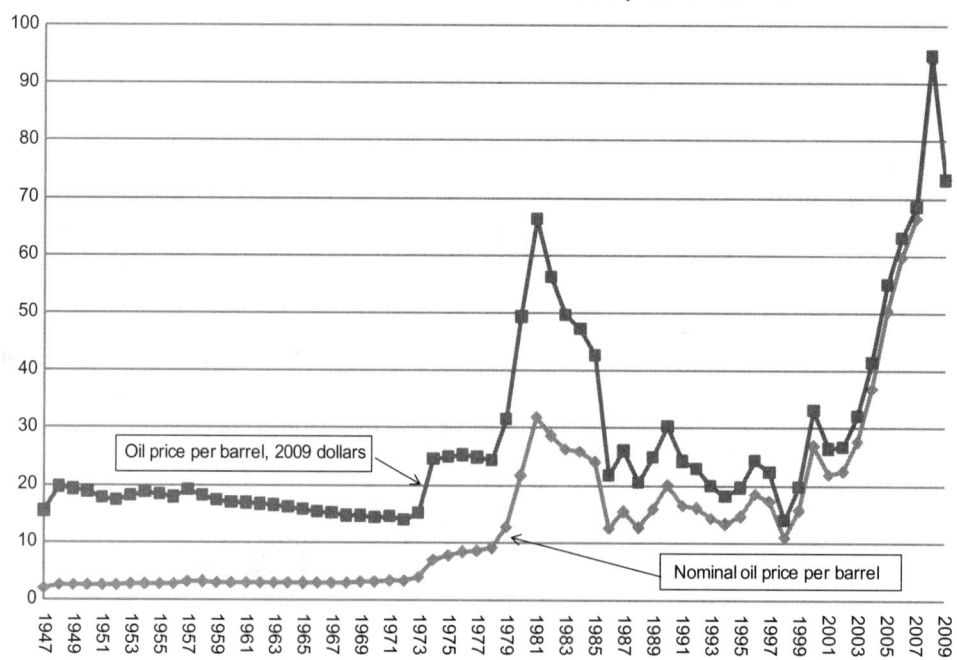

**Real and Nominal Oil Prices, 1947-2009**

Data provided by James L. Williams of WTRG Economics
http://www.wtrg.com

## 5.7. Understanding TIPS

The U.S. Treasury department issues securities called Treasury Inflation Protected Security (TIPS).[6] These securities promise a real rate of interest on your initial investment adjusted for increases in the consumer price index. Here's an example to show how this works:

- You invest $1,000 today in a 1-year TIPS that has a real interest rate of 4%. The consumer price index today is 120.

- In 1 year the Treasury will pay you $1,000 * \dfrac{CPI_{1\ year\ from\ now}}{CPI_{today}} * (1 + 4\%).$

Your investment in TIPS is fully inflation protected. To see this, break up the TIPS repayment into two factors:

$$\underbrace{\$1,000 * \frac{CPI_{1\ year\ from\ now}}{CPI_{today}}}_{\substack{\uparrow \\ \text{Maintains the purchasing} \\ \text{power of \$1,000 today}}} * \underbrace{\left(1 + 4\%\right)}_{\substack{\uparrow \\ \text{Return of initial investment} \\ \text{adjusted for inflation} \\ \text{PLUS} \\ \text{Interest on the inflation-adjusted} \\ \text{investment}}}$$

To analyze TIPS, suppose you think that the CPI will rise from 120 today to 126 in 1 year. As the spreadsheet below shows, you'll anticipate a repayment of $1,092.00.

| | A | B | C |
|---|---|---|---|
| 1 | **ANALYZING A 1-YEAR TREASURY INFLATION-PROTECTED SECURITY (TIPS)** | | |
| 2 | | | |
| 3 | Initial investment | 1,000.00 | |
| 4 | TIPS real interest rate | 4.00% | |
| 5 | Current CPI | 120 | |
| 6 | Anticipated CPI in one year | 126 | |
| 7 | | | |
| 8 | TIPS repayment in one year | 1,092.00 | <-- =B3*(B6/B5)*(1+B4) |
| 9 | | | |
| 10 | **Further analysis** | | |
| 11 | Anticipated inflation rate | 5.00% | <-- =B6/B5-1 |
| 12 | TIPS repayment of inflation-adjusted investment | 1,050.00 | <-- =B3*(1+B11) |
| 13 | TIPS interest on inflation-adjusted investment | 42.00 | <-- =B4*B12 |
| 14 | Total TIPS repayment in one year | 1,092.00 | <-- =B13+B12 |
| 15 | | | |
| 16 | TIPS interest on inflation-adjusted investment (this is the *real* interest rate paid by the TIPS) | 4.00% | <-- =B13/B12 |

In rows 11–16 we show an alternative analysis of the 1-year TIPS repayment of $1,092.00:

- Your anticipated inflation rate is $\dfrac{CPI_{1\ year\ from\ now}}{CPI_{today}} - 1 = \dfrac{126}{120} - 1 = 5.$

- The TIPS always repays you the initial investment, adjusted for the inflation. In this case, this is $\$1,000 * (1 + anticipated\ inflation) = \$1,000 * (1.05) = \$1,050.$

- In addition, the TIPS pays you the real interest rate (4% in this case) on the inflation-adjusted initial investment. As you can see in cell B13, this is $42.

---

[6] The U.S. Treasury Web site offers good explanations of these securities and current prices: http://www.treasurydirect.gov/instit/annceresult/tipscpi/tipscpi.htm.

The result is that the TIPS *maintains the purchasing power of your investment* ($1,000 * (1.05) = $1,050) and *pays you interest on the inflation-adjusted investment* (4% * $1,050 = $42).

## Understanding a 10-Year TIPS

Suppose you've got $1,000 to save, and you're considering buying a 10-year TIPS with the same conditions as above. What will be the nominal payment on the TIPS you can expect in 10 years? In the spreadsheet below, we assume an annual inflation rate of 3%; this brings the total anticipated TIPS repayment to $1,989.32. A little analysis (rows 10–16) shows the breakdown of this payment into return of inflation-adjusted investment ($1,343.92) and interest ($645.41).

| | A | B | C |
|---|---|---|---|
| 1 | **ANALYZING A 10-YEAR TREASURY INFLATION-PROTECTED SECURITY (TIPS)** | | |
| 2 | | | |
| 3 | Initial investment | 1,000.00 | |
| 4 | TIPS real interest rate | 4.00% | |
| 5 | Anticipated annual inflation rate | 3.00% | |
| 6 | | | |
| 7 | TIPS repayment in 10 years | 1,989.32 | <-- =B3*(1+B5)^10*(1+B4)^10 |
| 8 | | | |
| 9 | **Further analysis** | | |
| 10 | Anticipated cumulative inflation rate over 10 years | 34.39% | <-- =(1+B5)^10-1 |
| 11 | TIPS repayment of inflation-adjusted investment | 1,343.92 | <-- =B3*(1+B10) |
| 12 | TIPS interest on inflation-adjusted investment | 645.41 | <-- =B11*((1+B4)^10-1) |
| 13 | Total TIPS repayment in one year | 1,989.32 | <-- =B12+B11 |
| 14 | | | |
| 15 | TIPS interest on inflation-adjusted investment (this is the *real* interest rate paid by the TIPS) | 48.02% | <-- =B12/B11 |
| 16 | Annualized TIPS interest on inflation-adjusted investment | 4.00% | <-- =(1+B15)^(1/10)-1 |
| 17 | | | |
| 18 | Anticipated *nominal* return on TIPS | 7.12% | <-- =(B7/B3)^(1/10)-1 |
| 19 | Another way of computing the nominal return: (1+TIPS real rate)*(1+inflation rate)-1 | 7.12% | <-- =(1+B4)*(1+B5)-1 |

In cells B18:B19 we calculate the TIPS anticipated nominal return. As suggested in the previous section,

$$1 + nominal\ interest = (1 + real\ interest) * (1 + inflation\ rate)$$
$$= (1 + 4\%) * (1 + 3\%) = 1.0712$$

## Comparing TIPS and a Bank Certificate of Deposit

You have $1,000 extra cash that you don't think you'll need for the next 5 years. You're considering two alternatives:

- You can put the money in a bank certificate of deposit. This is a security you buy from the bank (in this case for $1,000). The bank has agreed to pay you 8% per year, so that you anticipate receiving $1,000 * (1 + 8\%)^5 = \$1,469.33$ in 5 years.

- On the other hand, you're considering buying a 5-year U.S. TIPS. This security costs $1,000 and promises you 3.5% annual interest on your initial $1,000 investment, adjusted for the CPI.

How should you make your decision? The spreadsheet below shows the nominal payment made by the TIPS in 5 years. The graph compares these payments to the $1,469.33 you will get from the CD. As you can see from the table in cells A11:C19, if the anticipated inflation rate is more than 4.3478%, the TIPS will pay off more than the CD.

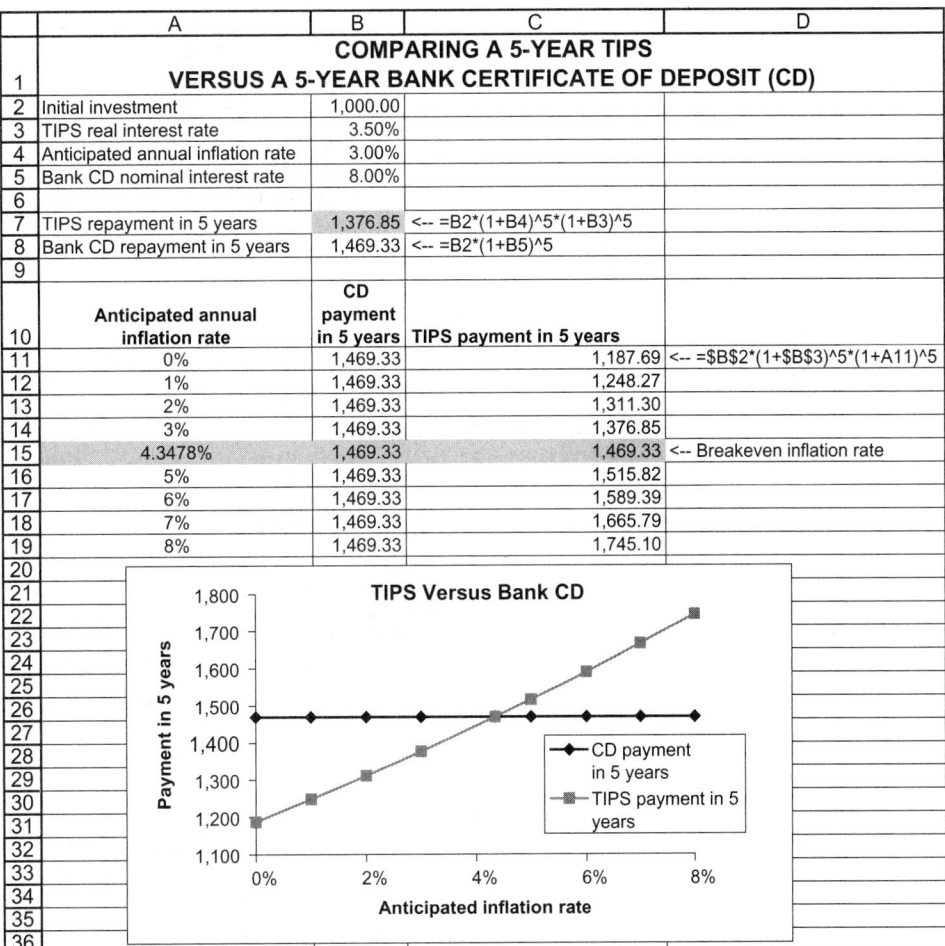

| | A | B | C | D |
|---|---|---|---|---|
| 1 | | | COMPARING A 5-YEAR TIPS VERSUS A 5-YEAR BANK CERTIFICATE OF DEPOSIT (CD) | | |
| 2 | Initial investment | 1,000.00 | | |
| 3 | TIPS real interest rate | 3.50% | | |
| 4 | Anticipated annual inflation rate | 3.00% | | |
| 5 | Bank CD nominal interest rate | 8.00% | | |
| 6 | | | | |
| 7 | TIPS repayment in 5 years | 1,376.85 | <-- =B2*(1+B4)^5*(1+B3)^5 | |
| 8 | Bank CD repayment in 5 years | 1,469.33 | <-- =B2*(1+B5)^5 | |
| 9 | | | | |
| 10 | Anticipated annual inflation rate | CD payment in 5 years | TIPS payment in 5 years | |
| 11 | 0% | 1,469.33 | 1,187.69 | <-- =$B$2*(1+$B$3)^5*(1+A11)^5 |
| 12 | 1% | 1,469.33 | 1,248.27 | |
| 13 | 2% | 1,469.33 | 1,311.30 | |
| 14 | 3% | 1,469.33 | 1,376.85 | |
| 15 | 4.3478% | 1,469.33 | 1,469.33 | <-- Breakeven inflation rate |
| 16 | 5% | 1,469.33 | 1,515.82 | |
| 17 | 6% | 1,469.33 | 1,589.39 | |
| 18 | 7% | 1,469.33 | 1,665.79 | |
| 19 | 8% | 1,469.33 | 1,745.10 | |

## Nominal Return Certainty versus Real Return Certainty

The comparison of the CD and TIPS in the above spreadsheet shows you that whereas the TIPS nominal return depends on the inflation rate, the CD nominal return is fixed. In some ways this might make it look as if the CD is preferred to the TIPS. But wait! In the following spreadsheet we compute the CD and TIPS real rate of returns. This time the tables are turned: The TIPS always returns 3.5% in real terms, whereas the CD's real rate of return depends on the inflation rate.

| | A | B | C | D |
|---|---|---|---|---|
| 1 | REAL RETURN ON TIPS VERSUS 5-YEAR CD | | | |
| 2 | Initial investment | 1,000.00 | | |
| 3 | TIPS real interest rate | 3.50% | | |
| 4 | Anticipated annual inflation rate | 3.00% | | |
| 5 | Bank CD nominal interest rate | 8.00% | | |
| 6 | | | | |
| 7 | TIPS repayment in 5 years | 1,376.85 | <-- =B2*(1+B4)^5*(1+B3)^5 | |
| 8 | Bank CD repayment in 5 years | 1,469.33 | <-- =B2*(1+B5)^5 | |
| 9 | | | | |
| 10 | TIPS year 5 repayment in year 0 dollars | 1,187.69 | <-- =B7/(1+B4)^5 | |
| 11 | CD year 5 repayment in year 0 dollars | 1,267.46 | <-- =B8/(1+B4)^5 | |
| 12 | | | | |
| 13 | TIPS annual real rate of return | 3.50% | <-- =(B10/B2)^(1/5)-1 | |
| 14 | CD annual real rate of return | 4.85% | <-- =(B11/B2)^(1/5)-1 | |
| 15 | | | | |
| 16 | Anticipated annual inflation rate | CD real return | TIPS real return | |
| 17 | 0% | 8.00% | 3.50% | <-- =(B10/B2)^(1/5)-1 |
| 18 | 1% | 6.93% | 3.50% | |
| 19 | 2% | 5.88% | 3.50% | |
| 20 | 3% | 4.85% | 3.50% | |
| 21 | 4.3478% | 3.50% | 3.50% | <-- Breakeven inflation rate |
| 22 | 5% | 2.86% | 3.50% | |
| 23 | 6% | 1.89% | 3.50% | |
| 24 | 7% | 0.93% | 3.50% | |
| 25 | 8% | 0.00% | 3.50% | |
| 26 | | | | |

TIPS Versus Bank CD, Real Returns

## TIPS or CD? What's the answer?

Like all good finance questions, the answer depends on your assumptions. If you believe that the inflation rate will be higher than 4.3478% per year, then the TIPS is preferred; otherwise, you should choose the CD.

# 5.8. Using TIPS to Predict Inflation

We can use the interest data from TIPS and from Treasury bills to derive the market's prediction of future inflation. Here's an example: On 21 August 2009, a 5-year nominal Treasury security sold in the market to yield an annual interest rate of 2.58%. On the same date, a 5-year TIPS was yielding 1.22% annually. Because the TIPS yield is in real interest, we can surmise that the market is predicting an inflation rate of 1.36% annually (=2.58–1.22%) over the 5-year horizon.

Using available data for all maturities, here are the market's predicted inflation rates on the same date.

| | A | B | C | D | E | F | G | H | I | J | K | L |
|---|---|---|---|---|---|---|---|---|---|---|---|---|
| 1 | NOMINAL AND REAL INTEREST RATES ON 21 AUGUST 2009 | | | | | | | | | | | |
| 2 | Treasury interest | 1 mo | 3 mo | 6 mo | 1 yr | 2 yr | 3 yr | 5 yr | 7 yr | 10 yr | 10 yr | 30 yr |
| 3 | Nominal interest | 0.10% | 0.10% | 0.26% | 0.45% | 1.10% | 1.65% | 2.58% | 3.21% | 3.56% | 4.32% | 4.36% |
| 4 | | | | | | | | | | | | |
| 5 | TIPS data | | | | | | | 5 yr | 7 yr | 10 yr | 10 yr | |
| 6 | Real interest | | | | | | | 1.22% | 1.41% | 1.69% | 2.10% | |
| 7 | | | | | | | | | | | | |
| 8 | Implied inflation | -1.12% | -1.12% | -0.96% | -0.77% | -0.12% | 0.43% | 1.36% | 1.80% | 1.87% | 2.22% | 2.26% |

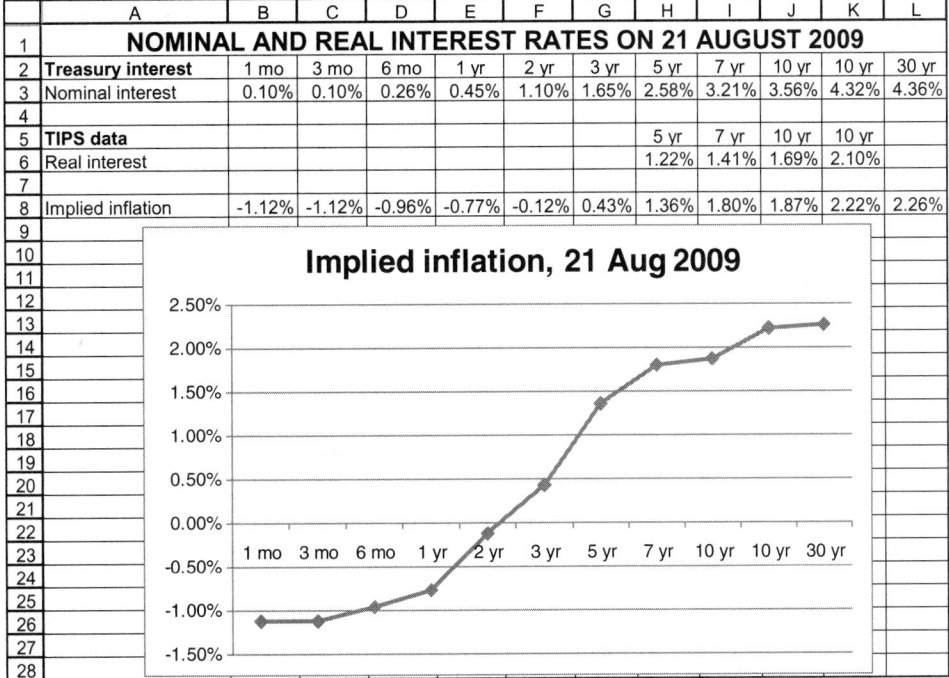

The data predict negative inflation over the 2-year horizon and positive inflation afterward. On the date of these data, the world was in a financial crisis, and the negative inflation rates are indicative of an expectation that this crisis will continue for the next few years.[7]

# 5.9. Inflation-Adjusted Capital Budgeting

You're considering an investment in a new widget machine. The machine will cost $9,500 today; cells B9:B14 give the widget sales forecasts for years 1–6. Widgets today sell for $15 each (cell B3), and the widget price in the future is expected to rise at the inflation rate of 4% (cell B2). Your nominal discount rate is 12% (cell B4).

---

[7]We've had to make some compromises to derive the inflation curve. See the spreadsheet with this chapter (on the CD-ROM for *Principles of Finance with Excel*) for details on the computations and the data sources.

|  | A | B | C | D | E | F | G |
|---|---|---|---|---|---|---|---|
| 1 | CAPITAL BUDGETING FOR THE WIDGET MACHINE | | | | | | |
| 2 | Inflation rate | 4.00% | | | | | |
| 3 | Widget price today | 15.00 | | | | | |
| 4 | Nominal discount rate | 12.00% | | | | | |
| 5 | Equivalent real discount rate | 7.69% | <-- =(1+B4)/(1+B2)-1 | | | | |
| 6 | | | | | | | |
| 7 | Year | Widgets sold | Anticipated nominal widget price | Anticipated nominal cash flow | | Anticipated real cash flow in year 0 dollars | |
| 8 | 0 | | | -9,500.00 | | -9,500.00 | |
| 9 | 1 | 100 | 15.60 | 1,560.00 | <-- =C9*B9 | 1,500.00 | <-- =D9/(1+$B$2)^A9 |
| 10 | 2 | 125 | 16.22 | 2,028.00 | <-- =C10*B10 | 1,875.00 | <-- =D10/(1+$B$2)^A10 |
| 11 | 3 | 150 | 16.87 | 2,530.94 | | 2,250.00 | |
| 12 | 4 | 160 | 17.55 | 2,807.66 | | 2,400.00 | |
| 13 | 5 | 170 | 18.25 | 3,102.46 | | 2,550.00 | |
| 14 | 6 | 200 | 18.98 | 3,795.96 | | 3,000.00 | |
| 15 | | | | | | | |
| 16 | NPV calculations | | | =$B$3*(1+$B$2)^A9 | | | |
| 17 | Discounting nominal cash flows at nominal discount rates | | 778.93 | <-- =NPV(B4,D9:D14)+D8 | | | |
| 18 | Discounting real cash flows at real discount rates | | 778.93 | <-- =NPV(B5,F9:F14)+F8 | | | |
| 19 | | | | | | | |
| 20 | IRR calculations | | | | | | |
| 21 | Nominal IRR | 14.47% | <-- =IRR(D8:D14) | | | | |
| 22 | Real IRR | 10.06% | <-- =IRR(F8:F14) | | | | |
| 23 | (1+nominal IRR)/(1+inflation)-1 | 10.06% | <-- =(1+B21)/(1+B2)-1 | | | | |

- Assuming a nominal discount rate of 12%, an equivalent real discount rate is given in cell B5. This rate is computed by the formula

$$real\ discount\ rate = \frac{1+nominal\ rate}{1+inflation\ rate}-1 = \frac{1+12\%}{1+4\%}-1 = 7.69\%$$

- Column C of the spreadsheet shows the anticipated widget price in each of years 1–6. We've computed this price by computing the *nominal widget price* in each of years 1–6 using the formula

$$nominal\ time\text{-}t\ price = price\ today * (1+inflation)^t$$

- Column D shows the nominal cash flow.[8] Discounting these cash flows at 12% gives the NPV of $778.93 in cell B17. Because the NPV is positive, you should invest in the new machine.

- Assuming that the increase in widget prices and the increase in general prices are the same, we can compute the real cash flows as in column F:

$$real\ cash\ flow,\ year\ t = (widgets\ sold) * widget\ price\ today$$

Column F actually shows a different formula, which gives the same result:

$$real\ cash\ flow,\ year\ t = \left( \frac{nominal\ value\ of\ widgets\ sold}{(1+inflation\ rate)^t} \right)$$

---

[8] We've assumed that it won't cost you anything to produce the widgets once you buy the machine. (Alternatively, you can assume that the widget price is the net of production costs.)

- The NPV of these real cash flows, computed in cell B18, is the same as the $778.93 computed in B17.

  Discounting nominal cash flows at a nominal discount rate and discounting real cash flows at a real discount rate gives the same net present value in year-0 dollars.

## Computing the Real and Nominal IRR

We can compute the real and nominal IRR for the widget machine as follows:

- Taking the IRR of the nominal cash flows (cell B22) gives a nominal IRR of 14.47%. Because the nominal IRR is greater than the nominal discount rate of 12%, the widget machine is a good investment.
- Computing the IRR of the real cash flows (cell B23) gives a real IRR of 10.06%. The investment decision given by the real IRR is the same as the investment decision given by the nominal IRR: Because the real IRR is greater than the real discount rate of 7.69%, the machine is a good investment. Note that we've computed the real discount rate in cell B5 using the formula

$$real\ discount\ rate = \frac{1+nominal\ discount\ rate}{1+anticipated\ inflation\ rate} = \frac{1+12\%}{1+4\%} - 1 = 7.69\%$$

---

### TWO WAYS OF COMPUTING THE REAL IRR

The real IRR can be computed by either

- Taking the IRR of the projected real cash flows (direct calculation of the real IRR) or
- Taking the IRR of the nominal cash flows, dividing by (1 + inflation rate), and subtracting 1.

To see that these two are the same, note that the nominal NPV is computed by

$$Nominal\ NPV = CF_0 + \frac{CF_1(real)*(1+inflation\ rate)}{(1+real\ interest\ rate)*(1+inflation\ rate)}$$

$$+ \frac{CF_2(real)*(1+inflation\ rate)^2}{\left[(1+real\ interest\ rate)*(1+inflation\ rate)\right]^2}$$

$$+ \frac{CF_2(real)*(1+inflation\ rate)^3}{\left[(1+real\ interest\ rate)*(1+inflation\ rate)\right]^3}$$

$$+ \ldots$$

Throughout this formula the (1 + inflation rate) term cancels out, so that

$$Nominal\ NPV = CF_0 + \frac{CF_1(real)}{(1+real\ interest\ rate)} +$$

$$+ \frac{CF_2(real)}{(1+real\ interest\ rate)^2} + \frac{CF_3(real)}{(1+real\ interest\ rate)^3} + \ldots$$

$$= Real\ NPV$$

• The real IRR can also be computed by the formula

$$real\ IRR = \frac{1+nominal\ IRR}{1+inflation\ rate}-1 = \frac{1+14.47\%}{1+4\%}-1 = 10.06\%$$

## Widget Prices Have a Different Inflation Rate Than the General Inflation Rate

In the previous problem the anticipated increase in widget prices was the same as the inflation rate. Suppose this isn't true—in the spreadsheet below, we assume that inflation (understood as the increase in the CPI) will be 4% per year, but that widget prices will increase at 8% per year. (Widget demand is expected to rise sharply, causing a big increase in prices.)

The analysis for this case is shown below. Although in principle it is not different than the analysis for Problem 5, the results are, of course, different—making widgets an even more profitable business.

| | A | B | C | D | E | F | G |
|---|---|---|---|---|---|---|---|
| 1 | | | **CAPITAL BUDGETING FOR THE WIDGET MACHINE**<br>**Widget prices increase at a different rate than the inflation rate** | | | | |
| 2 | Inflation rate | 4.00% | | | | | |
| 3 | Widget price today | 15.00 | | | | | |
| 4 | Annual increase in widget prices | 8.00% | | | | | |
| 5 | Nominal discount rate | 12.00% | | | | | |
| 6 | Equivalent real discount rate | 7.69% | <-- =(1+B5)/(1+B2)-1 | | | | |
| 7 | | | | | | | |
| 8 | Year | Widgets sold | Anticipated nominal widget price | Anticipated nominal cash flow | | Anticipated real cash flow in year 0 dollars | |
| 9 | 0 | | | -9,500.00 | | -9,500.00 | |
| 10 | 1 | 100 | 16.20 | 1,620.00 | <-- =C10*B10 | 1,557.69 | <-- =D10/(1+$B$2)^A10 |
| 11 | 2 | 125 | 17.50 | 2,187.00 | <-- =C11*B11 | 2,022.00 | <-- =D11/(1+$B$2)^A11 |
| 12 | 3 | 150 | 18.90 | 2,834.35 | | 2,519.73 | |
| 13 | 4 | 160 | 20.41 | 3,265.17 | | 2,791.08 | |
| 14 | 5 | 170 | 22.04 | 3,746.79 | | 3,079.59 | |
| 15 | 6 | 200 | 23.80 | 4,760.62 | | 3,762.39 | |
| 16 | | | | | | | |
| 17 | **NPV calculations** | | | =$B$3*(1+$B$4)^A10 | | | |
| 18 | Discounting nominal cash flows at nominal discount rates | 2,320.31 | <-- =NPV(B5,D10:D15)+D9 | | | | |
| 19 | Discounting real cash flows at real discount rates | 2,320.31 | <-- =NPV(B6,F10:F15)+F9 | | | | |
| 20 | | | | | | | |
| 21 | **IRR calculations** | | | | | | |
| 22 | Nominal IRR | 18.87% | <-- =IRR(D9:D15) | | | | |
| 23 | Real IRR | 14.30% | <-- =IRR(F9:F15) | | | | |
| 24 | (1+nominal IRR)/(1+inflation)-1 | 14.30% | <-- =(1+B22)/(1+B2)-1 | | | | |

Compare this spreadsheet to the calculations we did in the previous example: Because widget prices increase faster than the inflation rate, both the nominal and the real anticipated cash flows are greater every year. Thus, the project is more profitable, whether measured by real or nominal NPV or real or nominal IRR.

# Conclusion

This chapter has dealt with a variety of issues in NPV and IRR analysis. Some of these issues dealt with problems associated with using the IRR: IRR may not always give you explicit answers (there can be multiple IRRs, and complicated cash flows can have IRRs that make it difficult to understand if you're borrowing or lending). We also examined the problem of choosing between short-lived and long-lived assets that are alternatives, and we looked again at the lease/purchase problem first introduced in Chapter 2; this time we introduced taxes into the problem and discussed how corporations should choose between leasing and purchasing an asset.

Finally, we discussed how inflation should be incorporated into our analysis of capital budgeting.

## EXERCISES

1. You are considering building a hotel in northern Alaska. Your plan is to build the hotel and then sell it. You've been offered an immediate planning grant of $500,000 from the Alaskan Tourist Authority, and you estimate that to complete the hotel you'll need to make an investment next year of $1,700,000. Once built, you think you can sell the hotel at the end of year 2 for $1,400,000, so that your cash flow pattern looks like the following.

|   | A | B |
|---|---|---|
| 1 | ALASKAN HOTEL PROJECT | |
| 2 | Year | Cash flow |
| 3 | 0 | 500,000 |
| 4 | 1 | -1,700,000 |
| 5 | 2 | 1,400,000 |

   a. Identify the two IRRs of this project.

   b. If the discount rate is 28%, should you undertake the project?

2. Here's an example of a cash flow with three changes in sign.

   a. Graph the NPV of the cash flows using discount rates between 0 and 100%. Use this graph to approximately identify the three IRRs.

   b. Use Excel's **IRR** function with its **Guess** option to identify the three IRRs exactly.

   c. Can you "spin" a story about why a project might have such a complicated cash flow pattern?

|   | A | B |
|---|---|---|
| 1 | CASH FLOW WITH 3 IRRs | |
| 2 | Year | Cash flow |
| 3 | 0 | -350,000 |
| 4 | 1 | 2,500,000 |
| 5 | 2 | -3,000,000 |
| 6 | 3 | 500,000 |
| 7 | 4 | 500,000 |
| 8 | 5 | 500,000 |
| 9 | 6 | 500,000 |
| 10 | 7 | -14,000,000 |
| 11 | 8 | 3,500,000 |
| 12 | 9 | 3,500,000 |
| 13 | 10 | 3,500,000 |
| 14 | 11 | 3,500,000 |
| 15 | 12 | 3,500,000 |
| 16 | 13 | 3,500,000 |
| 17 | 14 | 3,500,000 |
| 18 | 15 | -11,000,000 |

3. You are considering a project with the following cash flows.

|   | A | B |
|---|---|---|
| 2 | Year | Cash flow |
| 3 | 0 | -300 |
| 4 | 1 | 5,000 |
| 5 | 2 | -20,000 |
| 6 | 3 | 8,000 |
| 7 | 4 | 6,000 |
| 8 | 5 | 3,500 |

a. What is the NPV of the project when the discount rate is 0%?

b. What is the NPV of the project when the discount rate grows to infinity?

c. Find all project IRRs.

4. Your firm is considering two projects with the following cash flows.

|    | A | B | C |
|----|---|---|---|
| 3  | Year | Project A | Project B |
| 4  | 0 | -22,500 | -50,000 |
| 5  | 1 | 8,000 | 15,000 |
| 6  | 2 | 8,000 | 15,000 |
| 7  | 3 | 8,000 | 15,000 |
| 8  | 4 | 8,000 | 15,000 |
| 9  | 5 | 8,000 | 15,000 |
| 10 | 6 | 8,000 | 15,000 |

In which discount rate range will the company prefer Project $A$, in which discount rate range will the company prefer Project $B$, and in which discount rate range will the company not invest?

5. You bought a house in January 1996 for $100,000, and you sold the house at the end of 2002 for $185,000. The CPI rose in the period from 118 to 155.

a. What was your annualized nominal rate of return?

b. Calculate your annualized real rate of return.

6. The bank is offering you a new savings account that will give you a 2% real annual interest rate. If the inflation rate is 5% annually, how long will it take you to double your money both in nominal and in real terms?

7. You are considering purchasing a machine to produce golf balls. The cost of the machine is $100,000 and its expected life span is 8 years. The machine will have an annual production of 550,000 balls. The price of a golf ball is today $0.20, and it's expected to rise by 10% each year. The material used to produce a golf ball costs $0.08 and it's expected to rise by 2% a year. To operate the machine you'll need two workers, each earning an annual salary of $30,000. According to their contracts their salaries will rise by 7% a year starting in the third year.

The real discount rate is 4%, the expected inflation is 5%, and the corporate tax rate is 40%.

a. Calculate the NPV of the project using nominal values.

b. Repeat the calculation using real values.

8. A soft drink company is considering whether to use television or radio in its campaign for a new line of products. According to the company's estimates, the TV campaign will cost $205,000 initially (at $t = 0$) and another $100,000 annually. The campaign will generate an annual income of $300,000 for 3 years.

The radio campaign will cost $48,000 and an additional cost of $20,000 annually. The radio campaign will generate an annual income of $150,000 for 3 years. If the company's discount rate is 18% and the tax rate is 30%:

a. Calculate the NPV of the television and the radio campaigns.

b. Repeat your calculation using mid-year discounting and explain the difference in results.

9. A factory is considering purchasing a new machine. It has two alternatives.

|   | A | B | C |
|---|---|---|---|
| 1 | Discount rate | 8% | |
| 2 | Tax rate | 30% | |
| 3 | | | |
| 4 | | **Machine A** | **Machine B** |
| 5 | Cost | 15,000 | 50,000 |
| 6 | Annual costs | 3,000 | 1,000 |
| 7 | Life span | 3 | 7 |

If the company chooses one machine, it will have to continue to choose the same machine forever. Which machine should the company choose if the interest rate is 8% and the corporate tax is 30%? Assume straight-line depreciation to zero salvage value over the life of each machine.

10. Your firm has to replace one of its fender-bender machines. One of your financial wizards has determined that the appropriate discount rate for the machine cash flows is 10%. Your firm has two alternatives.

a. Fender-bender Machine A costs $400,000 and produces annual cash flows of $200,000 at the end of each of its 6 years of life.

b. Fender-bender Machine B costs $200,000 but has only a 2-year life. However, it produces a $300,000 annual cash flow at the end of each of these 2 years.

|   | A | B | C |
|---|---|---|---|
| | | **Cash flow** | **Cash flow** |
| 3 | Year | (A) | (B) |
| 4 | 0 | -400 | -200 |
| 5 | 1 | 200 | 300 |
| 6 | 2 | 200 | 300 |
| 7 | 3 | 200 | |
| 8 | 4 | 200 | |
| 9 | 5 | 200 | |
| 10 | 6 | 200 | |

Calculate the equivalent annuity cash flow (EAC) and determine which machine is preferable.

11. You are the owner of a 5-year-old taxi. Your doctor has advised you to quit driving because of a health problem. You are considering two alternatives:

a. Selling the taxi for $15,000. Because the taxi's book value is 0, you will have to pay tax.

b. Renting your taxi to your cousin. Your cousin will pay you $4,000 today and at *the beginning* of each of the next 4 years. You estimate that in 4 years the taxi can be sold for $300.

Which is the more profitable alternative if your tax bracket is 25% and your discount rate is 5%?

12. A firm is considering the purchase of a machine for one of its factories. The machine's cost is $300,000 and it is expected to save the factory $100,000 annually. The machine's life span is 4 years, the company discount rate is 15%, and the corporate tax rate is 35%.

a. Under the above conditions is it worth buying the new machine?

b. Another supplier of the same machine suggested that instead of buying the machine, the firm should lease it. If the leasing fee for the machine is 80,000 annually and it is an expense for tax purposes, what is the NPV of the leasing offer?

c. The original supplier suggested lending the firm $210,000 that will be returned in three equal payments without interest. What is the NPV of this offer?

13. In Section 5.2 we considered a project called Sanitary Landfill. Now consider a project called Stranger Sanitary Landfill, which has the following cash flows.

|   | A | B |
|---|---|---|
| 4 | Year | Cash flow |
| 5 | 0 | 800,000 |
| 6 | 1 | -450,000 |
| 7 | 2 | -450,000 |
| 8 | 3 | -450,000 |
| 9 | 4 | -450,000 |
| 10 | 5 | -450,000 |
| 11 | 6 | 1,500,000 |

Show that you would accept this project for a suitably *low* or a suitably *high* discount rate, but not for discount rates in the middle. Explain.

14. You have a factory that produces light bulbs. Your old machine is costing a lot of money lately in repairs and you are considering replacing it. You have two offers.

|   | A | B | C |
|---|---|---|---|
| 1 | Discount rate | 12% | |
| 2 | Corporate tax rate | 40% | |
| 3 | | | |
| 4 | Annual production | 1,000,000 | |
| 5 | Price of light bulbs | 0.40 | |
| 6 | | | |
| 7 | | Machine A | Machine B |
| 8 | Cost | 500,000 | 200,000 |
| 9 | Variable cost per light bulbs | 0.12 | 0.25 |
| 10 | Fixed costs | 100,000 | 75,000 |
| 11 | Life span | 10 | 4 |

You sell each light bulb for $0.40, the discount rate is 12%, and the corporate tax rate 40%.

a. Which machine would you prefer to buy if your annual production is 1,000,000 light bulbs?

b. At what level of production will you change your answer?

15. ABC Corp. is trying to decide whether to buy or lease a new egg-scrambling machine. Here are some relevant facts:

• The new machine costs $120,000 and will be depreciated over a 5-year horizon to zero salvage value on a straight-line basis.

• ABC Corp. has a 30% corporate tax rate.

• The company can lease the machine from a reputable lessor for $29,941 per year; payments will be made on dates 0, 1, 2,..., 5 (in other words, six payments).

• ABC Corp. has a line of credit at its local bank. The bank is currently offering loans up to 6 years at 12%.

a. Should ABC Corp. lease or buy the machine? Justify your answer.

b. Suppose that the leasing company offers to sell the machine to ABC for $1 at the end of the lease term. The company feels that the machine can be profitably sold at this point for $25,000. Will this make the lease more or less attractive? (Give a qualitative rather than a numerical answer.)

16. Wharton Waste Disposal (WWD) is trying to decide whether to replace its aged trash compactor with a new, more efficient model. Here are the relevant facts:

    - The new trash compactor costs $400,000. If introduced, the company estimates that it will save $60,000 annually on a before-tax basis (assume that this cash flow occurs at year end).

    - The old trash compactor has a book value of $100,000. Its market value is $50,000. The remaining book value of the old compactor is being depreciated on a straight-line basis to zero salvage value at the rate of $20,000/year.

    - WWD has a corporate tax rate of 40% and is wildly profitable. The company uses a 15% discount rate for all cash flows.

    - Trash compactors never die—they have an essentially infinite life. However, the new compactor will be straight-line depreciated on a 10-year life to zero salvage value.

    - To encourage the replacement of smelly old trash compactors with shiny new ones, the state Environmental Protection Agency is offering a *replacement subsidy*. The subsidy is paid 1 year after the new compactor is put in use.

    What is the minimum subsidy that will make the replacement of the old compactor a break-even proposition?

17. Hunter Brothers Inc. needs to buy printers for its offices. It can buy expensive laser printers or much cheaper (but shorter-lived) inkjets. Here are some relevant facts:

    - A laser printer costs $1,000 and an inkjet costs $250.

    - A laser printer has an anticipated life of 6 years, but an inkjet has an anticipated life of only 2 years. Printers are assumed to have zero market value at the end of their lives.

    - The cost per page for a laser printer is $0.03, whereas the cost per page for an inkjet is $0.10.

    - Each printer purchased is anticipated to print 10,000 pages per year.

    If Hunter Brothers has a discount rate of 12% and a tax rate of zero, which printers should it buy? Assume that the whole year's cost of printing falls at year end.

18. Torreo Coffee Roaster is considering replacing one of its existing machines with a new, more automated and efficient machine. Torreo bought the machine 4 years ago for $87,500. It is being depreciated on a straight-line basis over a 14-year life. The machine could be sold today, 1 January 2000, for $20,000.

    The new machine costs $95,000. The new machine's depreciable life is 10 years with a salvage value of $13,000 in real terms. However, in accordance with U.S. tax law, the asset will be depreciated to zero over 10 years via the straight-line method.

    In 1999 Torreo's current coffee roasting machine accounted for annual revenues of $50,000 and has annual costs of $25,000. The new machine will increase this revenue to $65,000 per year (in real terms, that is, in 1999 dollars). The machine will also increase operating costs by $3,000 per year in real terms.

    The nominal discount rate is 14% per annum. The corporate tax rate for both operating income and capital gains is 40%. The annual anticipated inflation rate is 5%. All cash flows are riskless and they occur at the end of the year. Taxes are also paid at the end of the same year. Torreo has profitable ongoing operations that can be used to offset losses.

    Should Torreo Coffee Roaster replace the old machine with the new machine?

19. One Stop Golf Inc. is considering building a plant to manufacture a child's putter. The initial outlay (year 0) for the plant will be $5 million. At the end of year 1 a further outlay of $1 million on the plant is required. The plant will be built on land that could otherwise be rented out in any of the years for $500,000, before taxes.

The company anticipates producing this specialty item for only 3 years, in years 2, 3, and 4. At the end of year 4, the company will close and sell the plant. It expects to produce and sell 500,000 putters in year 2, 400,000 in year 3 and 100,000 in year 4. Each putter can be sold for $30 in year 2, and this price is expected to increase at a rate of 6% per year in years 3 and 4. The raw materials required for each putter are expected to cost $15 on average for those putters produced in year 2 and to increase at a rate of 3% per year in years 3 and 4. The cost of labor for each putter produced in year 2 is $5 and is expected to increase at the rate of 5% per year in the subsequent 2 years. Advertising the new putters will cost $500,000 in year 1, $220,000 in year 2, and $50,000 in year 3. No other inputs are required for the production of the child's putter.

The firm uses straight-line depreciation and the plant has a depreciable life of 6 years. Starting at the end of year 1, the company will depreciate the plant's total cost of $6 million to a salvage value of zero. The anticipated sale price of the plant at the end of year 4 is anticipated to be $4 million. The firm can offset any losses against other profitable ongoing projects.

The appropriate discount rate for the project is 12%. Assume all cash flows occur at the end of the year. The corporate tax rate is 34%.

a. Calculate the project's incremental cash flows.

b. Calculate the NPV of the project.

20. Grandma Helen was reminiscing with her grandson Noah. "When I married Grandpa in 1937," she recalled, "his monthly salary was $300. We had to scrimp and save. Now here it is 2008, and you're telling me that your first job out of college is going to pay you $4,500 per month. Why, that's *fifteen times* as much as Grandpa made!"

To compare the two salaries, Noah went to the Minneapolis Federal Reserve Web site and dug out the consumer price index (CPI) figures for 1913–2008. Whose salary was larger—in inflation-adjusted terms—Noah's or Grandpa's? (See the table of CPIs on disk with this book.)

21. Using the CPI data on the disk with this book, answer the following questions:

a. In 1803 the administration of President Thomas Jefferson purchased 800,000 square miles of North American territory from the French government for $15,000,000. The Louisiana Purchase doubled the size of the United States. Use the CPI series to adjust this price to 2009 dollars.[9]

b. There are 640 acres per square mile. What was the price of the Louisiana Purchase per acre in 2009 dollars?

**Some perspective:** A random search of the Internet in 2009 reveals the following land prices in the area of the Louisiana Purchase:

- 755 acres in Avoyelles Parish, Louisiana: $1,661,000
- 106 acres in Independence County, Arkansas: $119,900
- 5 acres in Pike County, Mississippi: $50,000
- 51 acres in Itasca County, Minnesota: $1,000,000

22.

a. On 1 January 2004, the Fluffy Finance Company made a $1,000,000 loan to one of its clients. The loan interest was 12%, to be paid monthly (meaning 1% per month), with full repayment of the loan on 1 January 2005. Because the client anticipated significant cash flow problems during July and August, Fluffy Loan agreed to forego interest payments during these months. Use XIRR to compute the annualized rate of return earned by Fluffy Finance on the loan.

---

[9]For historical details and a map, please visit http://gatewayno.com/history/LaPurchase.html.

b. Another Fluffy Finance client has asked for a similar loan, but has asked to forego interest payments in May and June. If Fluffy can make only one of the loans, which should it make?

23. For each of the projects below, compute all the IRRs.

| | A | B | C | D | E | F | G |
|---|---|---|---|---|---|---|---|
| 1 | **CONVENTIONAL AND NONCONVENTIONAL CASH FLOW PATTERNS** | | | | | | |
| 2 | Year | **Cash flows Project A** | **Cash flows Project B** | **Cash flows Project C** | **Cash flows Project D** | **Cash flows Project E** | **Cash flows Project F** |
| 3 | 0 | -100 | -100 | 100 | 25 | -25 | -250 |
| 4 | 1 | 200 | -50 | 55 | 35 | 80 | 35 |
| 5 | 2 | 500 | 60 | 35 | -200 | -100 | 145 |
| 6 | 3 | 50 | 80 | 50 | 33 | 200 | 330 |
| 7 | 4 | 60 | 99 | -100 | 55 | 55 | 55 |
| 8 | 5 | 35 | 100 | -35 | 155 | -250 | -250 |
| 9 | | ↑ Conventional cash flow pattern | ↑ Conventional cash flow pattern | ↑ Conventional cash flow pattern | ↑ Nonconventional cash flow pattern | ↑ Nonconventional cash flow pattern | ↑ Nonconventional cash flow pattern |
| 10 | | Initial negative cash flow followed by positive cash flows | Two initial negative cash flows followed by positive cash flows | Four initial positive cash flows followed by negative cash flows | Two positive cash flows, then negative, then three positive cash flows | Signs of cash flows change several times | Negative cash flows at beginning and end, other cash flows positive |

24. The disk that comes with *Principles of Finance with Excel* gives the CPI and inflation in Japan from 1990 to 2007. Compute the annual inflation over this period in Japan and compare it with the annual inflation in the United States.

# 6 Choosing a Discount Rate

## CHAPTER CONTENTS

## Overview

When you use either net present value (NPV) or internal rate of return (IRR) to make investment decisions, you have to choose a discount rate $r$. Just to remind you:

- In the case of the NPV, the discount rate $r$ is used to discount the future cash flows of the investment. If the NPV is positive when cash flows are discounted at $r$, then the investment is a good one. An investment with a negative NPV should be rejected.

- In the case of the IRR, the discount rate $r$ is the standard of comparison for the investment choice. If the rate $r$ is less than the IRR of the investment, the investment is a good one; if $r >$ IRR, we should reject the investment.[1]

---

[1] Recall from Chapter 5 that the IRR is not always the appropriate rule to use (for example, when there are multiple IRRs). In these cases we should use the NPV.

As you can see, the choice of a discount rate is very important! This chapter discusses how to choose the discount rate. The main principles we stress are as follows:

- The rate you choose should be appropriate to the riskiness of the cash flows being discounted. The riskier the cash flows being discounted, the higher should be the discount rate used in the NPV or IRR computations.

- In many cases the "funding cost" is a good choice for the discount rate. The funding cost is the rate of return demanded by the provider of the funds for the project.

- In a large number of cases involving investments by firms, the appropriate discount rate is the weighted average cost of capital (WACC). The WACC is the *average funding cost* for a firm. The bulk of this chapter is devoted to defining the WACC and showing you how to use it to value a firm.

Figure 6.1 summarizes the uses of NPV and IRR to make investment decisions. Despite the extensive discussion of Chapters 2–5, there are two NPV/IRR questions we haven't answered:

- What is the meaning of the cash flows that are discounted in the NPV and IRR computations? Suppose we're considering an investment that costs $100 today and promises $120 in 1 year. What does this promise of a future cash flow actually mean?

  - One possibility is that the $120 is *riskless*: In this case there is no doubt that the $120 will be paid 1 year from now. The $120 future cash flow is *certain*. Government bonds and bank accounts are two examples of investments that offer riskless cash flows.

  - Another possibility is that the $120 is an *anticipated* or *expected* cash flow, but is not riskless. In this case the $120 is *risky* or *uncertain*. For example, it could be that the investment's cash flow 1 year from now is determined by the flip of a coin: If the coin comes up heads, the cash flow will be $140 and if it comes up tails, the cash flow will be $100. The average future cash flow is $120, but the actual cash flow is uncertain.

- How do we pick the proper discount rate $r$ for the investment? In the NPV and IRR calculations of Chapters 2–5, $r$ is the rate of return that we require from the investment. Once you realize that the cash flow figures you're quoted mask the uncertainty behind the numbers, you'll agree that $r$ should be *risk adjusted*: Investors dislike risk; therefore, the *greater the uncertainty* about the cash flows, the *higher* the rate of return $r$ investors demand. To go back to the investment considered in the previous bullet:

  - If the $120 is a *riskless* cash flow, then the appropriate discount rate $r$ is the *riskless interest rate*. Good examples of riskless interest rates are the interest rates on government bonds or bank accounts.

| USING NPV AND IRR TO MAKE INVESTMENT DECISIONS | | |
|---|---|---|
| | **"Yes or no":** **Choosing whether to undertake a single project** | **"Project ranking":** **Comparing two mutually exclusive projects** |
| NPV criterion | The project should be undertaken if its NPV > 0. | Project A is preferred to Project B if NPV(A) > NPV(B). |
| IRR criterion | The project should be undertaken if its IRR > $r$, where $r$ is the appropriate discount rate. | Project A is preferred to Project B if IRR(A) > IRR(B). |

FIGURE 6.1 Summarizing the use of NPV and IRR for investment decisions. The critical question discussed in this chapter: How to determine the appropriate discount rate $r$?

- If the $120 is a *risky* cash flow, then the return investors demand will be higher. This means that the appropriate discount rate $r$ is a *risk-adjusted discount rate* (RADR).

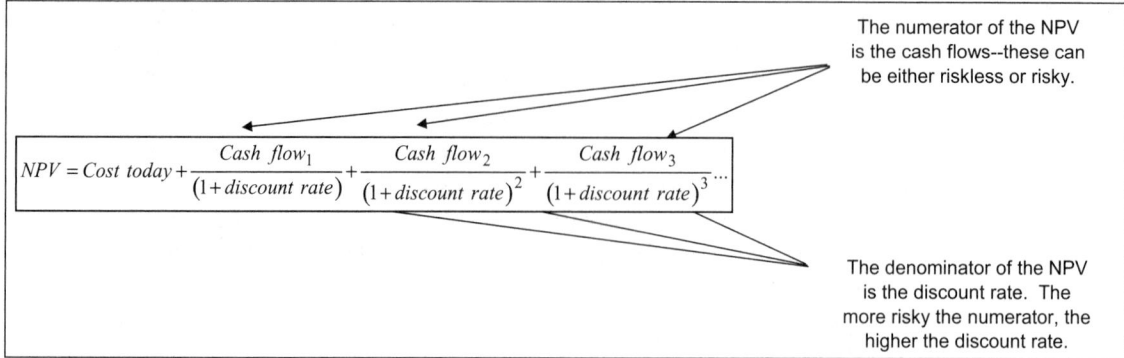

FIGURE 6.2 The "numerator" and the "denominator" of the NPV. The cash flow in the numerator is the anticipated investment cash flow; the discount rate in the denominator is adjusted for the riskiness of the cash flow in the numerator. This chapter discusses the determination of the discount rate.

*Risk*: At a later point in the book (Chapters 8–13), we'll give more formal definitions of risk and how to measure it. For the moment we'll rely on your intuitive understanding of risk. You understand that investing in a government bond is less risky than investing in stocks. You also understand that a real-estate investment is more risky than putting your money in a savings account (but perhaps less risky than buying a race horse).

The main characteristic of the riskiness of a cash flow is its future variability: Some cash flows are known almost with certainty; if your bank promises you 6% interest, you can be certain that $100 today will grow to $106 in 1 year. Other kinds of cash flows are much more uncertain; past experience shows that a $1,000 investment in stocks gives an average annual return of 12%, but you also know that in some years this return has been as low as –20% and in other years it has been as high as 35%. In general, the higher the variability of an investment's return, the higher its risk.

## TERMINOLOGY

The finance literature is full of synonyms for discount rates. Here are some terms you're likely to encounter; all of them are sometimes used to denote the appropriate discount rate for a series of cash flows:

- Discount rate
- Cost of capital
- Opportunity cost
- Interest rate
- Risk-adjusted discount rate (RADR)

## Finance Concepts Discussed

- Funding cost
- Cost of capital
- Cost of equity, $r_E$
- Cost of debt, $r_D$
- Free cash flow (FCF)

- Gordon dividend model
- Mid-year discounting

## Excel Functions Used

- **NPV**
- **IRR**
- **PMT**

# 6.1. Funding Cost as the Discount Rate

The *funding cost* is the cost of raising the money needed for an investment. The funding cost is often the appropriate candidate to use as the discount rate. The idea behind using the funding cost as a discount rate is that we identify the cost of the funds used and use this cost to discount the future investment cash flows. We'll start with an example that illustrates the proper use of the funding cost as the discount rate.

## Example 1: Taking Money Out of a Savings Account to Buy a Bank Certificate of Deposit (CD)

You've got $10,000 in a savings account at the bank that earns 4% per year, and you have no intention of using this money for the next couple of years. Your bank has offered you an alternative investment: a 2-year certificate of deposit (CD) that earns 5%. This CD is like a bond issued by the bank: You pay the bank $10,000 today and the CD will pay you $500 in 1 year ($500 = 5% * $10,000) and $10,500 in 2 years.

The CD looks like a good investment—instead of earning 4%, you'll now earn 5%. Another way to think about this investment is that it will cost you 4% (the foregone interest rate on your savings account) to earn the 5% interest on the CD. Using the 4% rate as the appropriate discount rate, the NPV of the CD is $188.61.

| | A | B | C |
|---|---|---|---|
| 1 | | **BANK CD** | |
| 2 | Savings account interest rate | 4.00% | |
| 3 | CD rate | 5.00% | |
| 4 | | | |
| 5 | Year | CD cash flow | |
| 6 | 0 | -10,000.00 | |
| 7 | 1 | 500.00 | |
| 8 | 2 | 10,500.00 | |
| 9 | | | |
| 10 | NPV | 188.61 | <-- =B6+NPV(B2,B7:B8) |

The $188.61 is the additional wealth you will gain from taking your money out of the savings account and putting it into the CD.

**Warning:** Markets aren't stupid, so you have to ask yourself why the bank is offering you 5% on the CD and only 4% on the savings account. What are the *risks* involved in taking your money out of the savings account and putting it into the CD?

- Lock-in risk: The money in the CD is locked in and is not available for 2 years, whereas the money in the savings account is available at any time.

- Interest rate risk: If interest rates go up, the bank will probably raise the interest rate on the savings account (other banks will raise their savings interest rate and competitive pressure will probably force your bank to raise its interest rate). On the other hand, the CD is a 2-year contract between you and the bank during which the interest rate will not change. (Of course there's another aspect to the interest rate risk: If interest rates go down, then the savings account interest will decrease, but not the interest paid on the CD.)

- Default risk: It is possible that the bank will not be able to keep the promises it made with the CD. Most American bank CDs are guaranteed by the U.S. government, so this is not really a factor.

The bottom line on this example is that if you think that the riskiness of the bank savings account and the CD is not substantially different, you should use the savings bank rate of 4% to discount the investment in the CD. The funding cost is an appropriate discount rate.

## Example 2: When Is the Funding Cost Not a Good Discount Rate?

In the previous example the riskiness of a bank savings account is not substantially different from the riskiness of a CD. This makes the savings account interest rate a good discount rate for evaluating the purchase of the CD. When the risks of funding finance differ substantially from the risks of the investment, the funding cost is not a good choice for a discount rate. Suppose you're thinking about buying a 1-year Evelyn Wyer lipstick franchise. This franchise allows you to sell the prestigious Evelyn Wyer lipsticks on your campus for 1 year. Evelyn's lipstick comes in all colors, but this year's favorite among college students is vomit yellow. The franchise costs $1,000 and is good for 1 year. At the end of this year, you expect to earn $1,500 from the franchise.

If you make the investment, you'll have to take this $1,000 out of your savings account, which pays 4% interest. The 4% is thus the funding cost for the Evelyn Wyer franchise.

If you use the 4% as a discount rate, then the lipstick franchise is a very good investment. It has NPV = $442 and an IRR of 50%:

|  | A | B | C |
|---|---|---|---|
| 1 | EVELYN WYER LIPSTICK FRANCHISE | | |
| 2 | Year | Franchise cash flow | |
| 3 | 0 | -1,000 | |
| 4 | 1 | 1,500 | |
| 5 | | | |
| 6 | Discount rate | 4% | |
| 7 | NPV | 442 | <-- =B3+B4/(1+B6) |
| 8 | IRR | 50% | <-- =IRR(B3:B4) |

However, to decide whether the 4% funding cost is really the appropriate discount rate, you have to consider the relative risks of the lipstick franchise and the bank savings account.

- If you are certain that you will earn $1,500 from the lipstick franchise, then 4% (the funding cost) is the appropriate discount rate.

- If, on the other hand, the $1,500 is uncertain and hence risky, then the 4% rate is *too low* a discount rate. In this case you have to decide whether the 50% IRR is large enough to compensate you for the riskiness of the investment.[2]

---

[2] At this point in the book we use only an intuitive concept of risk. In Chapters 8–13 we define risk more formally and show how the discount rate and risk are related.

## Example 3: If Taxes Are a Factor, Use the After-Tax Funding Cost

Your company needs a new computer. The alternatives are to buy the computer for $4,000 or to lease it. A leasing company has offered you a lease that involves a payment of $1,500 now and $1,500 at the end of each of years 1–3. An alternative financing method is to borrow the money from the bank, which is charging 15%. Your company has a tax rate of 40%; if it buys the computer it can depreciate it over 3 years, giving an annual depreciation tax shield of $\frac{\$4,000}{3} * 40\% = \$533.33$. If the company leases the computer instead of buying it, the $1,500 annual cost of leasing can be deducted from its taxable income. The annual *after-tax cost* of the lease payment is thus $(1-40\%) * \$1,500 = \$900$.

Here's the solution we offer to this problem in Chapter 5.

| | A | B | C | D | E | F | G |
|---|---|---|---|---|---|---|---|
| 1 | | | | LEASE VERSUS PURCHASE WITH TAXES | | | |
| 2 | Asset cost | 4,000.00 | | | | | |
| 3 | Annual lease payment | 1,500.00 | | | | | |
| 4 | Bank rate | 15% | | | | | |
| 5 | After-tax bank rate | 9% | <-- =B4*(1-B6) | This is the depreciation tax shield | | | |
| 6 | Tax rate | 40% | | if you buy the computer. | | | |
| 7 | | | | | | | |
| 8 | Year | Purchase cash flows | | Lease cash flows | | The differential cash flows: Lease minus purchase | |
| 9 | 0 | -4,000.00 | | -900.00 | <-- =-$B$3*(1-$B$6) | 3,100.00 | <-- =D9-B9 |
| 10 | 1 | 533.33 | <-- =$B$2/3*$B$6 | -900.00 | | -1,433.33 | |
| 11 | 2 | 533.33 | | -900.00 | | -1,433.33 | |
| 12 | 3 | 533.33 | | -900.00 | | -1,433.33 | |
| 13 | NPV | -2,649.98 | | -3,178.17 | <-- =D9+NPV(B5,D10:D12) | 18.33% | <-- =IRR(F9:F12) |
| 14 | | | | | | | |
| 15 | Explanation: The lease is like a loan--an inflow of $3,100.00 in year 0, and an after-tax outflow of $1,433.33 in year 1, $1,433.33 in year 2, and $1,433.33 in year 3. The IRR of these cash flows is 18.33%. Thus the lease is more expensive than borrowing the money from the bank, since the after-tax cost of a bank loan is 9.00%. | | | | | | |

Leasing instead of purchasing the asset saves you $3,100 in year 0 but costs you an additional $1,433.33 in years 1–3. The IRR of the differential cash flows (column F) is 18.33%.

**Choosing a discount rate:** In this case we can still use the alternative funding cost as the discount rate. However, we have to take into account the fact that the interest on the bank loan is an expense for tax purposes. Assuming that the riskiness of the lease and purchase cash flows is similar to the riskiness of a bank loan, the appropriate discount rate is the after-tax bank discount rate: $(1-40\%) * 15\% = 9\%$.

It now follows that we should purchase the asset instead of leasing it because the IRR of the lease minus purchase cash flows is higher than the after-tax cost of a bank loan. Another way to see this is to compare the cash flows of a $3,100 bank loan to the cash flows saved by purchasing. As you can see below, the bank loan costs substantially less in each of years 1–3 than the lease minus purchase cash flows.

| | A | B | C | D |
|---|---|---|---|---|
| 17 | What if you borrowed $3,100 from the bank? | | | |
| 18 | Year | After-tax money saved by leasing | Same amount from bank | |
| 19 | 0 | 3,100.00 | 3,100.00 | |
| 20 | 1 | -1,433.33 | -1,224.67 | <-- =PMT(B5,3,C19) |
| 21 | 2 | -1,433.33 | -1,224.67 | |
| 22 | 3 | -1,433.33 | -1,224.67 | |
| 23 | | | | |
| 24 | IRR | 18.33% | 9.00% | <-- =IRR(C19:C22) |

## FUNDING COST AS A DISCOUNT RATE—SUMMING UP

The leasing example illustrates the use of the *funding cost* as a way to find the discount rate: Because your alternative financing for the computer is a bank loan (rather than the lease), we've used the cost of the bank loan as a discount rate.

You have to be careful in applying this method: The funding cost is only an appropriate discount rate if the cash flows being funded have the same riskiness as the source of the funding.

- If you use a bank loan to finance a set of *almost certain* cash flows, then the bank loan rate can be the discount rate. You *know* that you'll repay the loan, and you're convinced that the cash flows being financed will occur with certainty. This is the case for the lease discussed in this section.

- For corporations, the cost of bank loans is an expense for tax purposes; in this case the *after-tax funding cost* should be used as a discount rate.

- If you use a bank loan to finance the purchase of a race horse, then the riskiness of the cash flows is much greater than the loan cash flows (you're almost certain to repay the loan, but you're much less certain about the cash flows from the race horse).

## 6.2. The Weighted Average Cost of Capital as the Firm's Funding Cost

In the previous section we've illustrated why the funding cost—the cost of raising the money for a given project—is often a good choice for the discount rate. The funding cost is a good choice for a project's discount rate when it is commensurate with the project's risk.

The funding cost for a company is often called the company's weighted average cost of capital (WACC). Companies raise funds in two primary ways, either by raising funds from their shareholders or by borrowing. The WACC is determined by averaging the funding costs of these two methods.

- A company can raise funds from its shareholders either by selling additional shares on the stock market or by using earnings to finance new projects instead of paying shareholders dividends. The *funding cost* of a company's raising money from its shareholders is called the *cost of equity*. Symbolized by $r_E$, the cost of equity is the rate of return demanded by a company's shareholders. In Section 6.3 we show you how to compute $r_E$.

- A company can raise funds either by borrowing from banks or by selling bonds. The funding cost of borrowing, symbolized by $r_D$, is called the *cost of debt* and is the interest rate charged by lenders, be they banks or the purchasers of a company's bonds. The interest on a company's borrowing is an expense for tax purposes; denoting the corporate tax rate by $T_C$, the *after-tax cost of borrowing* is $(1-T_C) * r_D$.

The WACC is the *average funding cost of a company's equity and debt*. Another way of putting this is that the WACC is the *average after-corporate-tax return shareholders and debtholders expect to receive from the company*.[3] The definition of the WACC is

---

[3] In finance the *expected return*, the *required return*, the *cost of capital* (be it *cost of equity* or *cost of debt*), and the *required rate of return* are all synonyms. They all represent the market-adjusted rate that investors get (or demand) on various investments or securities.

$$WACC = r_E * \underbrace{\frac{E}{E+D}}_{\substack{\text{the percentage} \\ \text{of equity used to} \\ \text{finance the firm}}} + r_D(1-T_C) * \underbrace{\frac{D}{E+D}}_{\substack{\text{the percentage} \\ \text{of debt used to} \\ \text{finance the firm}}}$$

where

$r_E$ = *the firm's cost of equity – the return required by the firm's shareholders*
$r_D$ = *the firm's cost of debt – the return required by the firm's debtholders*
$E$ = *market value of the firm's equity*
$D$ = *market value of the firm's debt*
$T_C$ = *the firm's tax rate*

Here's a simple example to show what we mean: United Transport Inc. has 3 million shares outstanding; the current market price per share is $10. The company thinks its shareholders want an annual return on their investment of 20%; this 20% return is the company's cost of equity $r_E$.[4] The company has also borrowed $10 million from its banks at a rate of 8%; this is the company's cost of debt, $r_D$. United Transport has a tax rate of $T_C = 40\%$.[5] To compute United Transport's WACC we use the formula

$$WACC = r_E * \frac{E}{E+D} + r_D(1-T_C) * \frac{D}{E+D}$$
$$= 20\% * \frac{30}{30+10} + 8\% * (1-40\%) * \frac{10}{30+10} = 16.20\%$$
$$r_E = 20\%$$
$$r_D = 8\%$$
$$E = 3,000,000 \text{ shares each worth } \$10 = \$30,000,000$$
$$D = \$10,000,000$$
$$T_C = 40\%$$

Here are the computations in a spreadsheet.

| | A | B | C |
|---|---|---|---|
| 1 | UNITED TRANSPORT–WACC | | |
| 2 | Number of shares | 3,000,000 | |
| 3 | Market price per share | 10 | |
| 4 | | | |
| 5 | E, market value of equity | 30,000,000 | <-- =B3*B2 |
| 6 | D, market value of debt | 10,000,000 | |
| 7 | | | |
| 8 | $r_E$, cost of equity | 20% | |
| 9 | $r_D$, cost of debt | 8% | |
| 10 | $T_C$, firm's tax rate | 40% | |
| 11 | | | |
| 12 | WACC, weighted average cost of capital: WACC=$r_E$*E/(E+D)+$r_D$*(1-TC)*D/(E+D) | 16.20% | <-- =B8*B5/(B5+B6)+B9*(1-B10)*B6/(B5+B6) |

The United Transport WACC computation shows you that the WACC depends on five critical variables.

---

[4] How did United Transport come to the conclusion that its shareholders want a 20% return? This is *the* question in the computation of the WACC, and we will spend a lot of this chapter discussing the answer. So be patient!

[5] We use the symbol $T_C$ to indicate the *corporate* tax rate.

- $r_E$, the cost of equity. $r_E$ is the return required by the firm's shareholders. Of the five parameters in the WACC calculation, $r_E$ is the most difficult to calculate. A model for calculating $r_E$ is given in Section 6.3.

- $E$, the market value of a firm's equity. We will usually take $E$ to equal the number of shares of the firm times the market price per share.

- $r_D$, the cost of debt. $r_D$ is the cost of borrowing for the firm. In most cases we will take $r_D$ to be the firm's marginal interest rate—the interest rate at which the firm could borrow additional funds from its banks or sell bonds. Alternatively, we will sometimes take $r_D$ to be the company's average borrowing rate on its current debt. A detailed example of the calculation of $r_D$ for an actual firm is given in Section 6.5.

- $D$, the market value of the firm's debt. In most cases we will take $D$ to be the total value of the firm's financial obligations. An actual example of a calculation for $D$ is given below in Section 6.5.

- $T_C$, the firm's tax rate. Most often we calculate $T_C$ by computing the average tax rate of the firm; see Section 6.5 for an example.

## The WACC

The weighted average cost of capital is the average rate of return the firm has to pay its shareholders and its lenders. The WACC is the funding cost for a company's projects, and it is widely used as the appropriate risk-adjusted discount rate for a company's investment cash flows. Two of the three examples that follow illustrate the use of the WACC in evaluating investments. The third example indicates when the WACC is not an appropriate discount rate for a corporate investment.

- White Water Rafting Corp. is considering buying a new type of raft. The raft is more expensive than the existing rafts operated by the company because it is self-sealing— holes in the raft are automatically and permanently fixed by a new technology. During the rafting season, White Water's existing rafts spend a considerable amount of down time having their punctures fixed, and the company anticipates that the new self-sealing rafts will improve its profitability by increasing efficiency and decreasing costs. By being the first rafting company on the river to have the self-sealing rafts, White Water hopes to attract business away from other rafting companies—customers naturally hate to have their trips interrupted by "flat rafts" (the rafting equivalent of a flat tire), and when they hear of White Water's new rafts, they will prefer White Water over its competitors.

The White Water financial analyst has derived the set of anticipated cash flows for the new raft. To complete the NPV analysis, the company needs to decide on an appropriate discount rate. Here's where the WACC comes in: Because the riskiness of the cash flows from the new rafts is similar to the riskiness of White Water Rafting's existing cash flows, the WACC is an appropriate discount rate.

- Gorgeous Fountain Water Company (GF) sells bottled water from the Gorgeous Fountain natural spring. The company is considering buying Dazzling Cascade Water Company. Dazzling Cascade (DC) operates in a neighboring area to that dominated by GF, and its operations, sales, and anticipated cash flows have been thoroughly analyzed by the GF financial analysis staff.

To value DC, GF has to decide on an appropriate discount rate for the anticipated DC cash flows. Here's where the weighted average cost of capital comes in. GF's WACC is the average return demanded by its investors, taking into account the fact that debt interest is an expense for corporate taxes. Assuming that the riskiness of DC's cash flows is similar to that of GF, the WACC is an appropriate discount rate for the GF cash flows. Discounting the DC cash flows at GF's WACC allows Gorgeous Fountain to establish a bid price for DC.

- We conclude with an example where the WACC is not an appropriate discount rate. Delicious Licorice (DL) is a candy company whose WACC is $WACC_{DL} = 22\%$. To diversify, DL is considering the purchase of Cheap Talk, a regional cell phone operator. The cash flows of the potential purchase have been carefully analyzed by the DL financial staff. They realize that the WACC of DL is not the appropriate rate for analyzing the purchase of Cheap Talk—the risks that are included in the DL weighted average cost of capital are entirely different from the risks of the Cheap Talk cash flows. To use the WACC as a discount rate, it must be appropriate to the riskiness of the cash flows being evaluated.

## Some Important Terminology before We Start

When we talk about "firms" in this book we generally mean corporations, companies that have shareholders and debtholders.[6] A typical firm is *incorporated*, which means that it is a legal entity that is separate from its shareholders and debtholders. The income of a corporation is taxed at the corporate income tax rate.

The shareholders own stock in the firm. When the firm is profitable, management may decide to pay dividends to the shareholders, but these dividend payments are not guaranteed. Shareholders can also sell their shares and in doing so may make a profit (called a "capital gain") or a loss. As you can see, the cash flows of a shareholder in a firm are uncertain. The shareholders in the firm have *limited liability*; they are not responsible for repaying the debtholders if the firm cannot do so out of its cash flows.

The *cost of equity*, denoted $r_E$, is the discount rate applied by shareholders to their expected future cash flows from the firm. It goes without saying that this cost of equity depends on the riskiness of the shareholder cash flows. The higher the riskiness of the shareholder's expected future cash flows, the higher the cost of equity $r_E$.

The firm's *debtholders* are its lenders. Debtholders are promised a predetermined return (interest) on their lending to the firm. Although most lending is at a fixed interest rate, it is also common to find debt with interest rates that periodically reset to market rates or that are tied to the inflation rate.

The debtholders may be banks that have lent money to the firm or they may be individuals or pension funds that have bought the firm's bonds. The interest payments to the firm's debtholders are expenses for tax purposes. The interest payments on the firm's debt and the firm's tax rate determine the *after-tax cost of debt* for the firm, which we denote $r_D(1-T)$.

# 6.3. The Gordon Dividend Model: Discounting Anticipated Dividends to Derive the Firm's Cost of Equity, $r_E$

In this section we present a formula for computing the firm's cost of equity $r_E$. This formula is called the *Gordon dividend model*, in honor of Myron Gordon, who first set out the model in 1959.[7] This section has two subsections:

---

[6] Equivalent terminology for shareholders: stockholders, equity owners; for debtholders: lenders, bondholders.

[7] The model is sometimes simply called the Gordon model; others call it the dividend discount model.

- In the first subsection we derive a model for calculating the value of a firm's shares based on their future anticipated dividends.

- In the second subsection, we use the share valuation model of the first section to derive the cost of equity $r_E$.

## Valuing the Firm's Shares as the Present Value of the Future Anticipated Dividends

We start by computing the fair market value of a stock that pays a growing dividend stream. Here is an example that presents most of the logic of our model: It is 2 March 2000, and you are thinking of purchasing a share of XYZ Corp. Here are some facts about the company and its stock:

- XYZ is a steady payer of dividends; in the past it has paid dividends annually, and these dividends have tended to grow at an annual rate of 7%.

- The company just paid a dividend of $10 per share. This dividend was paid on March 1, the company's traditional dividend payment date.

You want to value XYZ shares by discounting the stream of future anticipated dividends. In predicting the future dividends of XYZ Corp., you assume that the dividends will grow at a rate of 7% per year. Then the future anticipated dividends per share are

$$Dividend\ today = Div_0 = \$10.00$$
$$Dividend\ next\ year = Div_1 = Div_0\left(1+g\right)=\$10*\left(1+7\%\right)=\$10.70$$
$$Div_2 = Div_1\left(1+g\right)= Div_0\left(1+g\right)^2 = \$10*\left(1+7\%\right)^2 = \$11.45$$
$$Div_3 = Div_2\left(1+g\right)= Div_0\left(1+g\right)^3 = \$10*\left(1+7\%\right)^3 = \$12.25$$
$$\vdots \qquad \vdots$$
$$Div_t = Div_0\left(1+g\right)^t$$

The three dots ( ... ) indicate that you think that the dividend stream is *very long* (when we write the actual model, we will assume that the dividend stream goes on forever).

Suppose you think that the appropriate discount rate for the dividend stream is XYZ's cost of equity $r_E = 15\%$. Using $r_E$ to discount the future anticipated dividends, you get the fair value of the XYZ Corp.'s stock today (we will denote this by $P_0$):

$$Valuing\ XYZ\ Corp.\ stock:$$

$$Fair\ share\ value\ today, P_0 = \frac{Div_1}{\left(1+r_E\right)}+\frac{Div_2}{\left(1+r_E\right)^2}+\frac{Div_3}{\left(1+r_E\right)^3}+\ldots$$
$$= \frac{Div_0\left(1+g\right)}{\left(1+r_E\right)}+\frac{Div_0\left(1+g\right)^2}{\left(1+r_E\right)^2}+\frac{Div_0\left(1+g\right)^3}{\left(1+r_E\right)^3}+\ldots$$
$$= \frac{Div_0\left(1+g\right)}{r_E-g}$$

The last line of the above formula uses a formula for the present value of a constant-growth annuity developed in Chapter 2 (page 67): The present value of the cash flows $Div_0(1 + g)$, $Div_0(1 + g)2$, $Div_0(1 + g)^3$, ... at the discount rate $r_E$ is

$$P_0 = \sum_{t=1}^{\infty}\frac{Div_0\left(1+g\right)^t}{\left(1+r_E\right)^t}=\frac{Div_0\left(1+g\right)}{r_E-g}, when\ |g|<|r_E| \quad [8]$$

_____

[8] The condition $|g|<|r_E|$ means that the absolute value of $g$ is less than the absolute value of $r_E$. If a firm's dividends have positive growth, then this is the same as assuming that $0 < g < r_E$.

Applying the valuation model to XYZ stock gives

$$\textit{Fair share value today}, P_0 = \frac{10(1.07)}{(1.15)} + \frac{10(1.07)^2}{(1.15)^2} + \frac{10(1.07)^3}{(1.15)^3} + \dots$$

$$\underset{\substack{\uparrow \\ \text{This is } r_E - g}}{= \frac{\overset{\substack{\text{This is } Div_0(1+g) \\ \downarrow}}{\overbrace{10(1.07)}}}{0.15 - 0.07}} = 133.75$$

Here's a spreadsheet implementation of the Gordon dividend model.

|   | A | B | C |
|---|---|---|---|
| 1 | **VALUING XYZ CORP. SHARES** | | |
| 2 | Current dividend, $D_0$ | 10 | |
| 3 | Dividend growth rate, g | 7% | |
| 4 | Cost of equity, $r_E$ | 15% | |
| 5 | Share value | 133.75 | <-- =B2*(1+B3)/(B4-B3) |

## Using the Gordon Dividend Model to Calculate the Cost of Equity, $r_E$

In the previous subsection we derived the value of a share $P_0$ based on the current dividend per share $Div_0$, the anticipated growth rate of dividends $g$, and the cost of equity $r_E$. In this section we turn this formula around: We derive the cost of equity $r_E$, based on the current value of a share $P_0$, the current dividend per share $Div_0$, and the anticipated growth rate of dividends $g$.

According to the Gordon dividend model of the previous subsection, the stock price is given by $P_0 = Div_0(1+g)/(r_E - g)$. Turning this formula around to solve for the cost of equity $r_E$ gives

$$r_E = \frac{Div_0(1+g)}{P_0} + g \ .$$

This is the *Gordon dividend model cost of equity formula*. In the Gordon dividend model the cost of equity $r_E$—the discount rate to be applied to equity cash flows—is the sum of two terms:

- $\frac{Div_0(1+g)}{P_0}$ This is the *anticipated dividend yield* of the stock. Suppose you buy the stock today, paying $P_0$. Then you anticipate getting a next-period dividend of $Div_0(1 + g)$, where $g$ is the anticipated future growth rate of dividends. The term $\frac{Div_0(1+g)}{P_0}$ is the anticipated next period dividend return.

- $g$. This the *growth rate of all future dividends paid on the stock.*

## Applying the Gordon Dividend Model Cost of Equity Formula—A Simple Example

Consider a firm for which the current share price is $P_0 = \$25.00$ and that has just paid a per-share dividend of $Div_0 = \$3.00$. Shareholders of the firm believe that dividends will grow at a rate $g = 8\%$ per year. In this case the Gordon model cost of equity is $r_E = 20.96\%$.

| | A | B | C |
|---|---|---|---|
| 1 | **USING THE GORDON MODEL TO COMPUTE THE COST OF EQUITY $r_E$** | | |
| 2 | Current dividend, $Div_0$ | 3.00 | |
| 3 | Current share price, $P_0$ | 25.00 | |
| 4 | Anticipated dividend growth rate, g | 8% | |
| 5 | Gordon model cost of equity, $r_E$ | 20.96% | <-- =B2*(1+B4)/B3+B4 |

Note that the Gordon model's cost of equity $r_E$ is very sensitive to the parameter values. If, for example, the dividend growth rate in the above example is 5%, then $r_E = 17.60\%$.

| | A | B | C |
|---|---|---|---|
| 1 | **USING THE GORDON MODEL TO COMPUTE THE COST OF EQUITY $r_E$** | | |
| 2 | Current dividend, $Div_0$ | 3.00 | |
| 3 | Current share price, $P_0$ | 25.00 | |
| 4 | Anticipated dividend growth rate, g | 5% | |
| 5 | Gordon model cost of equity, $r_E$ | 17.60% | <-- =B2*(1+B4)/B3+B4 |

## 6.4. Applying the Gordon Cost of Equity Formula—Courier Corp.

Courier Corp. (stock symbol CRRC) is a book manufacturer that has experienced rapid growth of sales and profits. Courier's financial year ends September 30. We use the Gordon dividend model to calculate Courier's cost of equity at the end of September 2002.

Here's a spreadsheet that gives the relevant data and the calculations.

| | A | B | C |
|---|---|---|---|
| 1 | **COURIER CORPORATION (CRRC) Calculation of cost of equity using Gordon model** | | |
| 2 | **Year ended 30 Sept** | **Dividend per share** | |
| 3 | 1998 | 0.2533 | |
| 4 | 1999 | 0.2667 | |
| 5 | 2000 | 0.3200 | |
| 6 | 2001 | 0.3700 | |
| 7 | 2002 | 0.4000 | |
| 8 | | | |
| 9 | g, growth rate of dividends | 12.10% | <-- =(B7/B3)^(1/4)-1 |
| 10 | $Div_0$, current dividend | 0.40 | <-- =B7 |
| 11 | $Div_0*(1+g)$, dividend anticipated in 2003 | 0.45 | <-- =B10*(1+B9) |
| 12 | $P_0$, stock price, 30 Sept. 2002 | 37.99 | |
| 13 | | | |
| 14 | $r_E$, Gordon dividend model cost of equity | 13.28% | <-- =B11/B12+B9 |

To use the Gordon model to calculate the cost of equity in cell B14, we need the following assumptions:

- **The price of the share $P_0$ is known.** In this case $P_0$ is the stock price on the date of the calculation (30 September 2002). On this date $P_0 = \$37.99$.

- **The current dividend per share $Div_0$ is known**. By "current dividend" we mean the last dividend paid by the firm, which in this case is the year 2002 Courier dividend $Div_0$ = \$0.40 per share.

- **The average growth rate of the dividends, g, can be derived**. We derive this below from the dividend series in cells B3:B8. Our assumption is that the average dividend growth rate $g$ can be calculated from the following assumption:

$$Div_{1998} = 0.2533$$
$$Div_{1999} = Div_{1998}(1+g)$$
$$Div_{2000} = Div_{1998}(1+g)^2$$
$$Div_{2001} = Div_{1998}(1+g)^3$$
$$Div_{2002} = Div_{1998}(1+g)^4 = 0.4000$$

This means that $g = \sqrt[4]{\dfrac{Div_{2002}}{Div_{1998}}} - 1 = \sqrt[4]{\dfrac{0.4000}{0.2533}} - 1 = 12.10\%$

Given these assumptions, the cost of equity $r_E$ for Courier is given by

$$r_E = \frac{Div_0(1+g)}{P_0} + g = \frac{0.40*(1+12.10\%)}{37.99} + 12.10\% = 13.28\%$$

This is the calculation performed in cell B14.

## Alternative Calculations of the Growth Rate

The implementation of the Gordon model illustrated above uses the geometric growth rate $g = \sqrt[4]{\dfrac{D_{2002}}{D_{1998}}} - 1$ to calculate the $g$ in the Gordon model. Here are two alternative ways to compute the growth rate, $g$:

- *Alternative 1: Use a different time period.* In the preceding example, we've assumed that the future expected growth rate of dividends is predicted by the dividends between 1998 and 2002. However, we could—after some thought—decide that we need an extra year of data and that the dividends are better predicted by the period 1997–2002. In this case the dividend growth rate is

$$g = \sqrt[5]{\frac{Div_{2002}}{Div_{1997}}} - 1 = \sqrt[5]{\frac{0.40}{0.21}} - 1 = 13.75\%$$

This changes the cost of equity because anticipated dividend growth $g$ is higher in this alternative than before, the cost of equity $r_E = \dfrac{Div_0(1+g)}{P_0} + g$ will be higher, as shown below.

| | A | B | C |
|---|---|---|---|
| 1 | **COURIER CORPORATION (CRRC)**<br>**Alternative 1: Using a different base year** | | |
| 2 | Year ended<br>30 Sept | Dividend<br>per share | |
| 3 | 1997 | 0.2100 | |
| 4 | 1998 | 0.2533 | |
| 5 | 1999 | 0.2667 | |
| 6 | 2000 | 0.3200 | |
| 7 | 2001 | 0.3700 | |
| 8 | 2002 | 0.4000 | |
| 9 | | | |
| 10 | g, growth rate of dividends | 13.75% | <-- =(B8/B3)^(1/5)-1 |
| 11 | $Div_0$, current dividend | 0.40 | <-- =B8 |
| 12 | $Div_0$*(1+g), dividend anticipated in 2001 | 0.46 | <-- =B11*(1+B10) |
| 13 | $P_0$, stock price, 30 Sept. 2000 | 37.99 | |
| 14 | | | |
| 15 | $r_E$, Gordon dividend model cost of equity | 14.95% | <-- =B12/B13+B10 |

- *Alternative 2: Ignore historical dividends altogether.* You might decide that the past history of Courier dividends is not indicative of its future dividend payouts. In this case, you might want to use a different number altogether for the anticipated dividend growth rate *g*. In the example below you've decided that the growth rate for Courier's future dividends is 15%. This gives a cost of equity of 16.21%.

| | A | B | C |
|---|---|---|---|
| 1 | **COURIER CORPORATION (CRRC)**<br>**Alternative 2: Making up a future growth rate of dividends** | | |
| 2 | g, growth rate of dividends | 15.00% | |
| 3 | $Div_0$, current dividend | 0.40 | |
| 4 | $Div_0$*(1+g), dividend anticipated in 2001 | 0.46 | <-- =B3*(1+B2) |
| 5 | $P_0$, stock price, 30 Sept. 2000 | 37.99 | |
| 6 | | | |
| 7 | $r_E$, Gordon dividend model cost of equity | 16.21% | <-- =B4/B5+B2 |

## A Final Alternative to Computing the Cost of Equity $r_E$: Using the Total Equity Payout Instead of Per-Share Data

In some of the years 1998–2002, Courier purchased stock from its shareholders in open-market repurchase transactions. In many ways a share repurchase is like a dividend—both dividends and repurchases represent money paid by the firm to its shareholders. The following Excel spreadsheet computes the total dividends plus share repurchases in each of the years 1998–2002 and uses this "total equity payout" to compute the Gordon dividend model cost of equity $r_E$.

The data in column C are for the total dividend paid out by Courier (*total dividend = dividend per share * number of shares*); in column D we see the amount of cash paid out to shareholders for the repurchase of their shares. Column E gives the *total equity payout*: the sum of the dividends + repurchases. In column F we compute the year-on-year growth rates of total equity payouts. As you can see, these are quite variable, especially when compared to the relatively smooth growth of the cash dividends (columns B and C). In cell B14, we've decided to use

| | A | B | C | D | E | F | G |
|---|---|---|---|---|---|---|---|
| 1 | COURIER CORPORATION (CRRC) Computing the total equity payout | | | | | | |
| 2 | Year ended 30 Sept | Dividend per share | Total dividends | Share repurchases | Total equity payout: Dividends + repurchases | Annual growth of total dividend payout | |
| 3 | 1998 | 0.2533 | 1,205,000 | 0 | 1,205,000 | | |
| 4 | 1999 | 0.2667 | 1,354,000 | 455,000 | 1,809,000 | 50.12% | <-- =E4/E3-1 |
| 5 | 2000 | 0.3200 | 1,572,000 | 114,000 | 1,686,000 | -6.80% | <-- =E5/E4-1 |
| 6 | 2001 | 0.3700 | 1,824,000 | 0 | 1,824,000 | 8.19% | <-- =E6/E5-1 |
| 7 | 2002 | 0.4000 | 2,086,000 | 0 | 2,086,000 | 14.36% | <-- =E7/E6-1 |
| 8 | | | | | | | |
| 9 | Stock price, 30 Sept. 2002 | 37.99 | | | | | |
| 10 | Number of shares, 30 Sept. 2002 | 5,215,000 | | | | | |
| 11 | Market value of equity, 30 Sept. 2002 | 198,117,850 | <-- =B10*B9 | | | | |
| 12 | | | | | | | |
| 13 | 2002 total dividend | 2,086,000 | <-- =E7 | | | | |
| 14 | Anticipated dividend growth rate | 11.27% | <-- =AVERAGE(F6:F7) | | | | |
| 15 | | | | | | | |
| 16 | Gordon model cost of equity, $r_E$ | 12.45% | <-- =B13*(1+B14)/B11+B14 | | | | |

the average of the last 2 years of total cash payout growth rates as our prediction of the future growth rate $g$. This gives us a cost of equity $r_E$ of 12.45% (cell B16):

*Gordon dividend model for cost of equity using all payouts to equity holders :*

$$r_E = \frac{\begin{bmatrix} Total\ current \\ equity\ payout = \\ total\ dividends + \\ repurchases\ of\ stock \end{bmatrix} \left( 1 + \underset{\substack{\text{The anticipated} \\ \text{growth rate} \\ \text{of total equity} \\ \text{payouts}}}{g} \right)}{Total\ equity\ value\ today} + g$$

$$= \frac{2{,}086{,}000 * (1 + 11.27\%)}{198{,}117{,}850} + 11.27\% = 12.45\%$$

Although there is some controversy attached to the use of total equity payouts to compute the cost of equity $r_E$, we think it is the correct method. In the examples for Courier Corp. that follow, we will assume that the $r_E$ for Courier is 12.45%.

## WHY DO FIRMS REPURCHASE STOCK?

In recent years share buybacks have exceeded dividends as a form of distribution to shareholders. Firms repurchase stock instead of paying extra dividends for several reasons:

- Repurchases are used to "soak up" extra cash and keep dividend growth predictable. Most dividend-paying firms think their shareholders want to see a steady pattern of dividend growth. So if they have extra cash, they'll use it to buy back shares instead of increasing the dividend paid to shareholders.

- Repurchases help reduce shareholder taxes on cash paid out to shareholders. When a dividend is paid, all the shareholders receiving the dividend pay taxes on it at their ordinary income tax rate. Stock repurchases are voluntary (you don't have to sell your stock back to the company). If you let your stock be repurchased, the gain in most cases is taxed at your capital gains tax rate (lower than the ordinary income tax rate).

• Stock repurchases benefit both the shareholder who is bought out and the shareholder who does not let his shares be repurchased. Why? When some of the shares of the firm are repurchased, those shareholders who "stay in" the firm will get a larger share of its income and dividend payments in the future. So all parties gain.

## 6.5. Calculating the WACC for Courier

So far we've calculated Courier's cost of equity as $r_E = 12.45\%$. This is the return demanded by the company's shareholders, taking into account their expectations of cash dividend growth and stock repurchases. Now we want to calculate Courier's weighted average cost of capital $WACC = r_E \frac{E}{E+D} + r_D(1-T_C)\frac{D}{E+D}$. Before we can do this, however, we need to compute the values of the following variables:

• $E$: the market value of Courier's equity. As you can see from the previous spreadsheet, on 30 September 2002, Courier had 5,215,000 shares worth $37.99 per share. This gives $E = 5,215,000 * $37.99 = $198,117,850$.

• $D$: The value of Courier's debt. On 30 September 2002, Courier had debt of $752,000. This information comes from the company's annual report (see Figure 6.3). Courier's **debt** includes both the *current portion of long-term debt* and the *long-term debt* itself.[9] Note that Courier's debt has declined significantly from the previous year: 2001 debt for the company was $16,577,000.

|  | September 28, 2002 | September 29, 2001 |
|---|---|---|
| **Liabilities and Stockholders' Equity** | | |
| Current liabilities: | | |
| Current maturities of long-term debt | $ 78,000 | $ 76,000 |
| Accounts payable (Note A) | 6,708,000 | 11,933,000 |
| Accrued payroll | 7,642,000 | 6,652,000 |
| Accrued taxes | 6,965,000 | 6,092,000 |
| Other current liabilities | 6,362,000 | 6,789,000 |
| Total current liabilities | 27,755,000 | 31,542,000 |
| Long-term debt (Notes A and D) | 674,000 | 16,501,000 |
| Deferred income taxes (Note C) | 4,658,000 | 2,801,000 |
| Other liabilities | 2,652,000 | 2,446,000 |
| Total liabilities | 35,739,000 | 53,290,000 |

FIGURE 6.3 Courier's liabilities from its balance sheet. The financial debt items are marked. The company repaid significant amounts of debt during the financial year.

[9]The calculation of the WACC actually calls for the *market value* of the firm's debt. However, this is a number that is very difficult to calculate; instead it is standard practice to use the book value of the debt as illustrated.

- $r_D$, the cost of Courier's borrowing. In theory $r_D$ ought to be the marginal cost of debt—the borrowing rate of the company for additional debt. However, this rate is usually difficult to derive. A plausible alternative is to use information about the current borrowing rate of the company. In Figure 6.3 you can see what the company reports about its debt and from Courier's profit and loss statement (Figure 6.4) you can learn about its interest paid. We use the average borrowing rate of 5.54% (the rate applicable to most of the debt) as the company's cost of debt $r_D$.

|   | A | B | C | D |
|---|---|---|---|---|
| 1 | **COURIER CORPORATION (CRRC)** | | | |
|   | **Analysis of interest paid** | | | |
| 2 | **Year ending 30 September** | **2002** | **2001** | |
| 3 | Total debt | 752,000 | 16,577,000 | |
| 4 | Interest paid | 480,000 | | |
| 5 | | | | |
| 6 | Average interest rate, $r_D$ | 5.54% | <-- =B4/AVERAGE(B3:C3) | |

| For the Years Ended | September 28, 2002 | September 29, 2001 | September 30, 2000 |
|---|---|---|---|
| Net sales (Note A) | $202,184,000 | $211,943,000 | $192,226,000 |
| Cost of sales | 137,991,000 | 150,572,000 | 144,132,000 |
| Gross profit | 64,193,000 | 61,371,000 | 48,094,000 |
| Selling and administrative expenses | 39,602,000 | 39,258,000 | 31,406,000 |
| Amortization of goodwill (Note A) | - | 1,410,000 | 596,000 |
| Interest expense | 480,000 | 1,899,000 | 325,000 |
| Other income (Note J) | - | (1,230,000) | (119,000) |
| Income before taxes | 24,111,000 | 20,034,000 | 15,886,000 |
| Provision for income taxes (Note C) | 7,936,000 | 6,817,000 | 5,249,000 |
| Net income | $ 16,175,000 | $ 13,217,000 | $ 10,637,000 |

FIGURE 6.4 Courier's income statements, showing interest of $480,000 paid in 2002. Computing the interest paid on the average debt outstanding over the year (see Figure 6.3) gives $r_D = \dfrac{480,000}{(752,000+16,577,000)/2} = 5.54\%$. By dividing the company's year 2002 taxes of $7,936,000 by its income before taxes, we arrive at a tax rate of $T_C = \dfrac{7,936,000}{24,111,000} = 32.91\%$.

- $T_C$, Courier's tax rate. We can calculate Courier's tax rate from its provision for income taxes. Courier's provision for income taxes in 2002 was $T_C = \dfrac{7,936,000}{24,111,000} = 32.91\%$. We use this as an estimate for the firm's tax rate $T_C$.

|   | A | B | C | D |
|---|---|---|---|---|
| 1 | **COURIER CORPORATION (CRRC)** | | | |
|   | **Analysis of taxes paid** | | | |
| 2 | **Year ending 30 September** | **2002** | **2001** | **2000** |
| 3 | Income before taxes | 24,111,000 | 20,034,000 | 15,886,000 |
| 4 | Provision for income taxes | 7,936,000 | 6,817,000 | 5,249,000 |
| 5 | | | | |
| 6 | Average tax rate | 32.91% | 34.03% | 33.04% |

## So What's Courier's WACC?

Here's our calculation for Courier's WACC.

| | A | B | C |
|---|---|---|---|
| 1 | COURIER CORPORATION (CRRC) Calculating the WACC, Sept. 2002 | | |
| 2 | Cost of equity, $r_E$ | 12.45% | <-- Computed from total equity payouts |
| 3 | Cost of debt, $r_D$ | 5.54% | <-- From Courier Corp. financial statements |
| 4 | | | |
| 5 | Sept. 2002 equity value, E | 198,117,850 | <-- Number of shares times current share price |
| 6 | Sept. 2002 debt value, D | 752,000 | <-- From Courier Corp. financial statements |
| 7 | Total: Equity + Debt, E+D | 198,869,850 | <-- =SUM(B5:B6) |
| 8 | | | |
| 9 | Percentage of equity, E/(E+D) | 99.62% | <-- =B5/B7 |
| 10 | Percentage of debt, D/(E+D) | 0.38% | <-- =B6/B7 |
| 11 | | | |
| 12 | Tax rate, $T_C$ | 32.91% | <-- From Courier Corp. financial statements |
| 13 | | | |
| 14 | WACC | 12.41% | <-- =B2*B9+B3*(1-B12)*B10 |

In the next section we'll use the WACC of 12.41% for Courier to value the company.

# 6.6. Two Uses for the WACC

The weighted average cost of capital is the weighted average rate of return required by a company's shareholders and debtholders. We presume that this rate of return reflects the average risk of shareholder and debtholder future cash flows. This is plausible because we have derived the cost of equity $r_E$ from anticipated future payouts to shareholders, and we have derived the cost of debt $r_D$ from the rate demanded on the firm's debts by its lenders. Thus, the WACC represents a weighted average of the riskiness of shareholder and debtholder cash flows.

When the riskiness of a stream of cash flows is similar to the riskiness of the cash flows received by shareholders and debtholders, the WACC is the appropriate risk-adjusted discount rate. There are two important cases where this is often true:

- In capital budgeting situations. When a company is considering investing in a project whose risk is comparable to the riskiness of the company as a whole, the WACC is an appropriate discount rate for the project's cash flows. We've previously illustrated this use of the WACC in the White Water Rafting example of Section 6.2.

- To value the company as a whole. Later we define the concept of FCF. The value of the Courier is the discounted value of its future anticipated FCFs, where the WACC is the discount rate. The Gorgeous Fountain Water Company example of Section 6.2 gave a preliminary discussion of this use of the WACC.

In this section we illustrate both these uses of the WACC for Courier.

## Using the WACC as a Discount Rate for Projects

The WACC of Courier Corp. is 12.41%—this is the weighted average return demanded by the firm's shareholders and bondholders. Recall that Courier is in the book-printing business. Suppose the company is thinking of investing in a project whose riskiness is like the riskiness of its current business. This could be something as simple as another printing press to print more books or a warehouse to house them, but it could also be something much more complicated—like the acquisition of another printing company.

In all of these cases, the WACC is the natural starting point as a discount rate. What we mean by "starting point" is that—in discounting the cash flows of the project—Courier should assume that initial discount rate is 12.41% and then "tweak" the discount rate a bit to adjust for perceived risks.

Let's say that the company is considering buying a machine that will allow them to print more books. The cash flows, NPV, and IRR of the machine are given below. If the riskiness of the machine's cash flows is similar to the riskiness of Courier's overall cash flows, then the WACC is a reasonable discount rate. The analysis below shows that the company should not undertake the investment—the investment's NPV is negative (-$11,777) and its IRR (7.80%) is less than the WACC of 12.41%:

| | A | B | C |
|---|---|---|---|
| 1 | **COURIER CORPORATION (CRRC)** **Using the WACC as a discount rate** | | |
| 2 | WACC | 12.41% | |
| 3 | | | |
| 4 | **Year** | **Cash flows** | |
| 5 | 0 | -100,000 | |
| 6 | 1 | 15,000 | |
| 7 | 2 | 22,000 | |
| 8 | 3 | 33,000 | |
| 9 | 4 | 44,000 | |
| 10 | 5 | 12,000 | |
| 11 | | | |
| 12 | NPV | -11,777 | <-- =B5+NPV(B2,B6:B10) |
| 13 | IRR | 7.80% | <-- =IRR(B5:B10) |
| 14 | | | |
| 15 | **Extreme case:  Cash flow riskiness same as Courier debt** | | |
| 16 | Cost of debt | 5.54% | |
| 17 | Courier tax rate | 32.91% | |
| 18 | After-tax cost of debt | 3.72% | <-- =(1-B17)*B16 |

Of course there's always room for adjustment because some of the assumptions we made may not be as accurate as we thought. Suppose, for example, that the machine's cash flows are perceived to be much less risky than the overall cash flows of Courier. As an extreme case we might consider the case where the machine cash flows are only as risky as Courier's debt. Because the company's after-tax cost of debt is 5.54% * (1–32.91%) = 3.72%, this would then be an appropriate discount rate for the project and the company should accept it (because the IRR of 7.80% is higher than 3.72%).

## Valuing Courier Corporation Using Its WACC and Predicted Free Cash Flows (FCFs)

In the previous subsection we used the WACC to value a typical project of the firm. The second major use of the WACC is to value companies. A complete explanation of this use of the WACC will have to wait until Chapter 7, where we explain the use of the free cash flow (FCF) in detail. For our purposes in this chapter, the FCF is the amount of cash generated by the company's business activities, by its operations as opposed to its financing activities. The FCF is "free" in the sense that it can be used to provide cash to the firm's shareholders and debtholders in the form of dividends and share repurchases (payments to shareholders) and interest payments (to debtholders).

To accurately define the FCF, you need some familiarity with accounting. Here's the definition of the FCF.

| Defining the Free Cash Flow (FCF) | |
|---|---|
| Profit after taxes | This is the basic measure of the profitability of the business, but it is an accounting measure that includes financing flows (such as interest), as well as noncash expenses such as depreciation. Profit after taxes does not account for either changes in the firm's working capital or purchases of new fixed assets, both of which can be important cash drains on the firm. The FCF definition takes changes in working capital and purchases of new fixed assets into account separately. |
| + Depreciation | This noncash expense is added back to the profit after tax. |
| **The sum of the next two items is the** *change in net working capital*, **often denoted by ΔNWC** | |
| - Increase in current assets related to the firm's operations. | When the firm's sales increase, more investment is needed in inventories, accounts receivable, etc. This increase in current assets is not an expense for tax purposes (and is therefore ignored in the profit after taxes), but it is a cash drain on the company. For purposes of calculating the FCF, the increase in current assets does not include changes in cash and marketable securities. |
| + Increase in current liabilities related to the firm's operations | An increase in sales often causes an increase in financing related to sales (such as accounts payable or taxes payable). This increase in current liabilities—when related to sales— provides cash to the firm. The FCF includes all current liability items related to operations; it does not include financial items such as short-term borrowing, the current portion of long-term debt, and dividends payable. |
| - Capital expenditures (CAPEX) | An increase in fixed assets (the long-term productive assets of the company) is a use of cash, which reduces the firm's FCF. |
| + After-tax interest payments (net) | FCF measures the cash produced by the business activity of the firm. It is a flow to both debtholders and equity holders and should therefore be cash before any distributions to the providers of financing. In particular we need to neutralize the effect of interest payments that appear in the firm's profit after taxes. We do this by: <br> • Adding back the after-tax cost of interest on debt (*after-tax* because interest payments are tax deductible), <br> • Subtracting out the after-tax interest payments on cash and marketable securities. |
| FCF = sum of the above | |

In 2002 Courier Corp. had an FCF of $22,519,493. Cell B9 in the following spreadsheet shows how this number is derived using the company's consolidated statement of cash flows.

| | A | B | C |
|---|---|---|---|
| 1 | COURIER CORPORATION<br>Calculation of free cash flow for 2002 | | |
| 2 | Profit after taxes | 16,175,000 | <-- =F11 |
| 3 | Add back depreciation | 10,687,000 | <-- =B16 |
| 4 | Changes in working capital | | |
| 5 | Subtract increases in current assets | 4,515,000 | <-- =SUM(B17:B19) |
| 6 | Add increases in current liabilities | -2,411,000 | <-- =B22+B21+B23 |
| 7 | Subtract out capital expenditures | -6,739,000 | <-- =B27+B28 |
| 8 | Add back after-tax interest | 292,493 | <-- =(1-B50)*B44 |
| 9 | **Free cash flow (FCF)** | **22,519,493** | <-- =SUM(B2:B8) |
| 10 | | | |
| 11 | | | |
| 12 | CONSOLIDATED STATEMENT OF CASH FLOWS | 2002 | Note that the change in current assets is positive and the change in current liabilities is negative:  Courier actually decreased CA (leading to an inflow in cash) and increased CL (ditto). |
| 13 | Operating activities | | |
| 14 | Net income | 16,175,000 | |
| 15 | Adjustments to reconcile net income to cash provided from operating activities | | |
| 16 | Depreciation and amortization | 10,687,000 | |
| 17 | Change in accounts receivable | 2,914,000 | |
| 18 | Change in inventory | 728,000 | |
| 19 | Change in accrued taxes | 873,000 | |
| 20 | | | |
| 21 | Change in accounts payable | -5,225,000 | |
| 22 | Deferred income taxes | 1,531,000 | |
| 23 | Other changes in current liabilities | 1,283,000 | |
| 24 | Cash provided from operating activities | 28,966,000 | |
| 25 | | | |
| 26 | Investment activities | | |
| 27 | Capital expenditures | -4,918,000 | |
| 28 | Prepublication costs | -1,821,000 | |
| 29 | Cash used for investment activities | -6,739,000 | |
| 30 | | | |
| 31 | Financing activities | | |
| 32 | Scheduled long-term debt repayments | -76,000 | |
| 33 | Repayments of debt, net | -15,750,000 | |
| 34 | Cash dividends | -2,058,000 | |
| 35 | Stock repurchases | 0 | |
| 36 | Proceeds from stock plans | 1,114,000 | |
| 37 | Cash provided from financing activities | -16,770,000 | |
| 38 | | | |
| 39 | Increase (decrease) in cash and equivalents | 5,457,000 | |
| 40 | Cash and equivalents at beginning of period | 173,000 | |
| 41 | Cash and equivalents at end of period | 5,630,000 | |
| 42 | | | |
| 43 | Supplemental information | | |
| 44 | Interest paid | 436,000 | |
| 45 | | | |
| 46 | Income before taxes | 24,111,000 | |
| 47 | Provision for income taxes | 7,936,000 | |
| 48 | Net income | 16,175,000 | |
| 49 | | | |
| 50 | Tax rate =B47/B46 | 32.91% | |

## Using FCFs and WACC to Value Courier

In finance theory, the *enterprise value* of a company's debt and equity is the value of its free cash flows discounted at its weighted average cost of capital:

*Enterprise value = Present Value value of future FCFs, discounted at WACC*

The enterprise value represents the value today of the cash flows produced by the firm's future business activities. Suppose that you've performed a careful analysis of Courier Corp. and you think the future growth of Courier's FCF is 4% per year. Because Courier's WACC is 12.41%, its enterprise value is

*Courier enterprise value* $= PV\left(FCFs, discounted\ at\ WACC\right)$

$$= \sum_{t=1}^{\infty} \frac{FCF_t}{(1+WACC)^t} = \sum_{t=1}^{\infty} \frac{FCF_{2002} * (1+FCF\ growth\ rate)^t}{(1+WACC)^t}$$

$$= \sum_{t=1}^{\infty} \frac{22,519,493 * (1+4\%)^t}{(1+12.41\%)^t} = \frac{22,519,493 * (1+4\%)}{12.41\% - 4\%} = 278,376,871$$

Note that this valuation—like the Gordon dividend model of Section 6.3—makes use of the constant-growth annuity formula developed in Chapter 2 (page 67):

$$\sum_{t=1}^{\infty} \frac{FCF_{2002} * (1+FCF\ growth\ rate)^t}{(1+WACC)^t} = \frac{FCF_{2002} * (1+FCF\ growth\ rate)}{WACC - FCF\ growth\ rate}$$

To get from this enterprise valuation to a valuation of the company's shareholder equity, we have to make two additional adjustments:

- We add in the cash and marketable securities balances of $5,630,000 that Courier has on hand in 2002. The enterprise value measures the value today of Courier's future FCFs. The cash and marketable securities that the company has on hand today are not part of these future FCFs, but they belong to the company, so they must be added. In cell B8 of the next spreadsheet, you can see that adding in the cash balances gives an estimated asset value of $284,006,871.

- We subtract out the company's debt of $752,000 in 2002. In cell B10, you can see that subtracting out the debt value gives an estimated equity valuation of $283,254,871.

Here's our valuation with these two adjustments.

| | A | B | C |
|---|---|---|---|
| 1 | **VALUING COURIER** | | |
| 2 | Year 2002 FCF | 22,519,493 | |
| 3 | Anticipated FCF growth | 4% | |
| 4 | WACC | 12.41% | |
| 5 | | | |
| 6 | Enterprise value | 278,376,871 | <-- =B2*(1+B3)/(B4-B3) |
| 7 | Initial cash and marketable securities | 5,630,000 | From 2002 balance <-- sheet |
| 8 | Asset value | 284,006,871 | <-- =B6+B7 |
| 9 | Debt value | 752,000 | |
| 10 | Equity value | 283,254,871 | <-- =B8-B9 |
| 11 | | | |
| 12 | Number of shares | 5,215,000 | |
| 13 | Per-share valuation | 54.32 | <-- =B10/B12 |

Our per-share valuation of Courier is $54.32: Because there are 5,215,000 shares, each share is worth $\dfrac{\$283,254,871}{5,125,000} = \$54.32$. This compares favorably with the current share price of Courier, $37.99, so this makes Courier (in the parlance of stock market analysts) a "buy" recommendation.

## Valuing Courier Using Mid-year Discounting

We introduced this topic in Chapter 5 (page 154). The idea was that because most cash flows occur throughout the year, the appropriate discounting process should discount them as if they occur mid-year. In terms of the computation just done for Courier, instead of calculating

$$Enterprise\ value = \frac{FCF_{2002}\left(1+FCF\ growth\right)}{\left(1+WACC\right)} + \frac{FCF_{2002}\left(1+FCF\ growth\right)^2}{\left(1+WACC\right)^2} + \dots$$
$$= \frac{FCF_{2002}\left(1+FCF\ growth\right)}{WACC-FCF\ growth}$$

we should be calculating the

$$Enterprise\ value_{Mid\text{-}year\ discounting} = \frac{FCF_{2002}\left(1+FCF\ growth\right)}{\left(1+WACC\right)^{0.5}} + \frac{FCF_{2002}\left(1+FCF\ growth\right)}{\left(1+WACC\right)^{1.5}}$$
$$= \left[\frac{FCF_{2002}\left(1+FCF\ growth\right)}{WACC-FCF\ growth}\right] * \left(1+WACC\right)^{0.5}$$

As explained in Chapter 5, mid-year discounting raises our valuation of cash flows because the earlier a cash flow occurs, the more it is worth. If we use mid-year discounting for Courier, then our valuation of Courier's shares increases from $54.32 to $56.45.

|    | A | B | C |
|----|---|---|---|
| 1  | **VALUING COURIER** <br> **Using midyear discounting** | | |
| 2  | Year 2002 FCF | 22,519,493 | |
| 3  | Anticipated FCF growth | 4% | |
| 4  | WACC | 12.41% | |
| 5  | | | |
| 6  | Enterprise value | 295,149,271 | <-- =(1+B4)^0.5*B2*(1+B3)/(B4-B3) |
| 7  | Initial cash and marketable securities | 5,630,000 | <-- From 2002 balance sheet |
| 8  | Asset value | 300,779,271 | <-- =B6+B7 |
| 9  | Debt value | 752,000 | |
| 10 | Equity value | 300,027,271 | <-- =B8-B9 |
| 11 | | | |
| 12 | Number of shares | 5,215,000 | |
| 13 | Per-share valuation | 57.53 | <-- =B10/B12 |

## One Further Note: Doing Some Sensitivity Analysis

No valuation is complete without doing some sensitivity analysis on the main parameters. For example, what happens to the per-share valuation if Courier's WACC is 15% instead of the 12.41% we have used? What happens to the per-share valuation if Courier's FCF growth rate is 5% instead of the 4% we used above? With Excel's **Data Table** (Chapter 27) this is easy.

|   | A | B | C |
|---|---|---|---|
| 1 | **VALUING COURIER**<br>**Sensitivity analysis**<br>**Still using mid-year discounting** | | |
| 2 | Year 2000 FCF | 22,519,493 | |
| 3 | Anticipated FCF growth | 5% | <-- 5% instead of 4% |
| 4 | WACC | 15.00% | <-- 15% instead of 12.41% |
| 5 | | | |
| 6 | Enterprise value | 253,569,392 | <-- =(1+B4)^0.5*B2*(1+B3)/(B4-B3) |
| 7 | Initial cash and marketable securities | 5,630,000 | <-- From 2002 balance sheet |
| 8 | Asset value | 259,199,392 | <-- =B6+B7 |
| 9 | Debt value | 752,000 | |
| 10 | Equity value | 258,447,392 | <-- =B8-B9 |
| 11 | | | |
| 12 | Number of shares | 5,215,000 | |
| 13 | Per-share valuation | 49.56 | <-- =B10/B12 |

|   | A | B | C | D | E | F | G | H |
|---|---|---|---|---|---|---|---|---|
| 1 | **Courier Valuation--Sensitivity Analysis** | | | | | | | |
| 2 | Year 2000 FCF | 22,519,493 | | | | | | |
| 3 | Anticipated FCF growth | 5% | | | | | | |
| 4 | WACC | 15.00% | | | | | | |
| 5 | | | | | | | | |
| 6 | Enterprise value | 253,569,392 | <-- =(1+B4)^0.5*B2*(1+B3)/(B4-B3) | | | | | |
| 7 | Initial cash and marketable securities | 5,630,000 | | | | | | |
| 8 | Asset value | 259,199,392 | <-- =B6+B7 | | | | | |
| 9 | Debt value | 752,000 | | | | | | |
| 10 | Equity value | 258,447,392 | <-- =B8-B9 | | | | | |
| 11 | | | | | | | | |
| 12 | Number of shares | 5,215,000 | | | | | | |
| 13 | Per-share valuation | 49.56 | <-- =B10/B12 | | | | | |
| 14 | Current share value | 37.99 | | | | | | |
| 15 | | | | | | | | |
| 16 | =IF(B4>B3,B13,"nmf") | | **Data table:  share value of Courier for various assumptions on WACC and FCF growth rates** | | | | | |
| 17 | | | FCF growth rate ↓ | | | | | |
| 18 | | 49.56 | **0%** | **2%** | **4%** | **6%** | **8%** | **10%** |
| 19 | | 6% | 75.03 | 114.31 | 232.12 | nmf | nmf | nmf |
| 20 | WACC --> | 8% | 57.03 | 77.22 | 117.61 | 238.78 | nmf | nmf |
| 21 | | 10% | 46.23 | 58.68 | 79.44 | 120.95 | 245.50 | nmf |
| 22 | | 12% | 39.02 | 47.55 | 60.34 | 81.67 | 124.32 | 252.28 |
| 23 | | 14% | 33.87 | 40.13 | 48.89 | 62.03 | 83.93 | 127.73 |
| 24 | | 16% | 30.00 | 34.82 | 41.24 | 50.23 | 63.72 | 86.20 |
| 25 | | 18% | 27.00 | 30.84 | 35.78 | 42.37 | 51.60 | 65.43 |
| 26 | | 20% | 24.59 | 27.74 | 31.68 | 36.75 | 43.51 | 52.97 |
| 27 | | 22% | 22.62 | 25.26 | 28.49 | 32.53 | 37.73 | 44.66 |
| 28 | | 24% | 20.97 | 23.23 | 25.94 | 29.25 | 33.39 | 38.72 |
| 29 | | | | | | | | |
| 30 | | | **Note**:  The valuation formula in cell B6 is correct only when the WACC (cell B4) > growth rate (cell B3).  Therefore we've put a formula into cell B18 which indicates that when B3 exceeds B4, the data table prints out "no meaningful figure" (nmf). | | | | | |
| 31 | | | | | | | | |
| 32 | | | **Note**:  The highlighted cells are combinations of WACC and FCF growth for which the Courier valuation exceeds the current share value of $37.99.  We've used Excel's **Conditional Formatting** to color these cells. | | | | | |

A more extensive sensitivity analysis can be performed by using the **Data Table** feature of Excel explained in Chapter 27. In cells C19:H28 in the preceding spreadsheet you can see the valuation of Courier for various combinations of WACC and FCF growth. The highlighted cells are those combinations of WACC and FCF growth for which the per-share valuation exceeds the current market value of $37.99.

## Summing Up

In this chapter we have calculated the firm's weighted average cost of capital (WACC). The WACC is the risk-adjusted discount rate (RADR) for the firm's free cash flows (FCFs). It is often used to value projects with riskiness that is similar to the riskiness of the firm's existing activities, and it is also used to derive the value of the firm. Both of these uses have been illustrated in this chapter.

The WACC is defined as

$$WACC = r_E \frac{E}{E+D} + r_D \left(1 - T_C\right)\frac{D}{E+D}$$

In the table below we summarize how we derived each of the elements of this formula.

| Cost of equity $r_E$ | We've used the Gordon model to determine the cost of equity: $$r_E = \frac{Div_0\left(1+g\right)}{P_0} + g\,,$$ where $Div_0$ = total dividends + stock repurchases of the current year<br>$g$ = anticipated growth rate of dividends + repurchases<br>$P_0$ = total equity value on current date |
|---|---|
| Cost of debt $r_D$ | In principle, this should be the firm's marginal borrowing rate, but this is often difficult to determine. For Courier, we used a number representative of the firm's cost of borrowing. An alternative is to use the firm's average borrowing cost over the previous year: $$r_D = \frac{Interest\ paid\ in\ current\ year}{Average\ debt, this\ year\ and\ last}$$ |
| Market value of equity $E$ | Current number of shares * current market price per share |
| Market value of debt $D$ | The market value of a firm's debt is difficult to calculate. We almost always substitute the *book value* of the firm's debt for this number. In the Courier example we showed how to determine this book value from the firm's balance sheets. |
| Firm's tax rate $T_C$ | $T_C$ ought to be the firm's *marginal tax rate*. In practice we usually use either of the following:<br><br>a.    The firm's average tax rate, measured by: $$average\ tax\ rate = \frac{Taxes\ from\ Profit\ and\ Loss\ Statement}{Profit\ before\ taxes} = 33.04\%$$ <br><br>b.    The firm's *statutory tax rates*. Courier's statutory Federal tax rate is 34%. State taxes are another 2.98% of its income. Another estimate of its tax rates might thus be 36.98% . |

## A Final Warning

Cost of capital calculations are critical for valuations. Because cost of capital calculations involve a mixture of theory and judgment, they are quite often controversial. Almost every number in the preceding WACC calculation can be determined in several ways. In many cases professionals do extensive sensitivity analysis on the WACC and the FCF growth to establish a *price range*—the range of valuations that appears to be reasonable, given the variation in plausible assumptions.

The most important modification you might want to make to the WACC calculation above involves the cost of equity $r_E$. An important competing model to the Gordon model is the capital asset pricing model (CAPM). In Chapter 13 we will show you how to use this model to calculate the cost of equity.

# Exercises

1. Compute the weighted average cost of capital (WACC) for a company with the following:

   | | |
   |---|---|
   | Market value of debt | $200,000 |
   | Market value of equity | $300,000 |
   | Cost of debt, $r_D$ | 7.5% |
   | Cost of equity, $r_E$ | 13% |
   | Tax rate, $T_C$ | 40% |

2. Calculate the cost of equity $r_E$ for a company with the following:

   | | |
   |---|---|
   | Market value of debt | $2,500,000 |
   | Market value of equity | $1,000,000 |
   | Cost of debt, $r_D$ | 5% |
   | Tax rate, $T_C$ | 25% |
   | WACC | 10% |

3. Aboudy Corp.'s stock price is currently $22.00 per share. The company has just paid a dividend of $0.55 per share, and shareholders anticipate that this dividend will grow in the future at a rate of 6% per year. Use the Gordon model to calculate the company's cost of equity $r_E$.

4. You wish to estimate the share price of Softy, your favorite underwear company. You know that tomorrow the company will pay its annual dividend of $1.50 per share, and you anticipate that the company's futures dividends will grow at a rate of 4% per year. As an experienced investor, you demand a yield of 12% on your investment in the company. What should be the company's share price?

5. XYZ Corp. has just paid a dividend of $5 per share. You think this dividend will grow at 8% per year.

   a. If you think the correct discount rate for the dividend stream of XYZ is 25%, how much should you be willing to pay for the stock?

   b. Show in an Excel graph the share's price as a function of the XYZ dividend growth rate (let the growth rate be 0, 2, 4, ..., 20% ).

6. You just bought a share of ABC Corp. for $28. The company has just paid a dividend of $2 per share, and you anticipate that this dividend will grow at a rate of 12% per year. What is your implied cost of equity for ABC?

7. Gradcom's anticipated next-year dividend is $1.20. Analysts anticipate that this dividend will grow at a 4% annual rate.

    a. If the stock's current share price is $30, what is its cost of equity $r_E$ according to the Gordon Model?

    b. Show in an Excel graph the cost of equity as a function of the dividend growth rate (let the growth rate be 0, 2, 4, ..., 20%).

8. You are considering purchasing a stock of ABC Corp, which has just paid a $3 annual dividend per share. The company does not repurchase any of its shares. You anticipate that the company's dividends will grow at a rate of 20% per year for the next 5 years. After this time, you think that the growth of the annual dividends will slow to 5% per year. If your cost of equity for ABC is 10%, what price should you be prepared to pay for the stock?

9. Assume that Gradcom (from Exercise 7) has changed its dividend growth forecasts. The year-1 dividend is still anticipated to be $1.20, but the growth rate in the following 2 years is expected to be 6 and 4%. After this, the annual dividend growth rate is expected to be 3%. If Gradcom's cost of equity is 10%, what will be its share price?

10. Consider the following data regarding Cinema Company.

| | A | B | C | D | E | F |
|---|---|---|---|---|---|---|
| 1 | Cinema Company | | | | | |
| 2 | Year | Dividend per share | Total dividends | Number of share repurchases | Payments from share repurchases | Total |
| 3 | 1995 | 0.25 | ??? | 0 | 0 | ??? |
| 4 | 1996 | 0.25 | ??? | 115,000 | 140,000 | ??? |
| 5 | 1997 | 0.3 | ??? | 0 | 0 | ??? |
| 6 | 1998 | 0.31 | ??? | 200,000 | 260,000 | ??? |
| 7 | 1999 | 0.35 | ??? | 120,000 | 180,000 | ??? |
| 8 | 2000 | 0.37 | ??? | 0 | 0 | ??? |
| 9 | 2001 | 0.39 | ??? | 0 | 0 | ??? |
| 10 | 2002 | 0.42 | ??? | 120,000 | 220,000 | ??? |
| 11 | | | | | | |
| 12 | Stock price, end of 2002 | 1.83 | | | | |
| 13 | Number of shares, January 1995 | 4,300,000 | | | | |

    a. Complete the ??? in the spreadsheet above (assume that the dividend payment was before the share repurchase).

    b. Find the cost of equity $r_E$ of Cinema using the Gordon dividend model for the total equity payout.

    c. What would be Cinema's cost of equity if we consider only the dividend payments without the share repurchases?

11. It is 1 January 2005 and you are interested in finding the cost of equity $r_E$ of your company. After a quick search you have found the following data:

    • The company currently has 1,600,000 shares outstanding. The current share price is $3.

    • The company's earnings for 2004 were $2,000,000. The company policy has just paid out $300,000 in dividends, and it intends to continue this 15% dividend payout from earnings in the future.

    • During 2004 the company spent $600,000 on share repurchases. It is the company's intention to increase the amount spent on share repurchases at the same growth rate as the amount spent on dividends.

    • Projected earnings growth is 2% per year.

Using the Gordon model for the total equity payout, what is the company's cost of equity $r_E$?

12. Suppose that a firm is financed with 70% equity and 30% debt. The interest rate on debt is 8%, and the expected return on the common stocks is 17%. The firm's tax rate is 40%. What is the firm's WACC?

13. Your boss asked you to find the WACC of Welcome to Paradise company, based on the following data:
    - The company has 1,600,000 shares, currently sold for $2 per share.
    - The company's debt is $2,500,000. The interest paid last year by the company was $300,000.
    - The corporate tax rate is 40%.
    - The cost of capital requested by the investors is 13%.

14. You are interested in calculating the cost of capital of Lion Company, based on the average WACC of its industry, which is 11%. You know that the company stock price is $11, and it has 5,500,000 shares. The company cost of debt is 9%, its debt is $4,000,000, and the company's tax rate is 40%. What is the company's cost of equity?

15. You want to compute the WACC of ABC Company. The company's stock price is $8, and it has a debt-to-equity ratio of 1. ABC's cost of debt is 9%, its cost of equity is 12%, and the company's tax rate is 40%. What is the company's WACC?

16. Assume the following data concerning ZZZ Company and use it to compute the company's WACC:
    - The company has 2,000,000 shares, currently sold for $2.5 per share.
    - The company's debt is 3,000,000 from the company market value. The interest rate paid last year by the company was $250,000.
    - The company paid total dividend of $600,000 last year, and its expected dividend growth is 3%. In addition, the company repurchases 150,000 of its shares.
    - The corporate tax rate is 30%.

17. You have come up with the following data concerning Zion Company.
    - The company has 2,500,000 shares.
    - The company's debt is 90% from the company market value. The interest rate paid last year by the company was $500,000.
    - The company paid total dividends of $800,000 last year, which is 25% of its pretax profit, and its expected growth next year is $50,000 more.
    - The company paid taxes of $950,000.
    - The cost of capital requested by the investors is 13%.
    What is the company's WACC?

18. You have come up with the following data concerning your sister's company.
    - The company market value is $6,000,000.
    - The company's debt is 75% from the company market value. The interest rate paid last year by the company was $450,000.
    - The company paid total dividends of $600,000 last year, which is 20% of its pretax profit, and its expected growth next year is $45,000 more.
    - The company paid taxes in the amount of $1,200,000.
    What is the company's WACC?

19.
    a. You are considering a new project for your firm. This project requires investment of $500,000 and generates cash flow of $70,000 for the next 10 years. You think that these cash flows are completely riskless. You know that your company's WACC is 14% and that the risk-free rate is 6%. Should you take this project?
    b. Should you take the project if its risk is comparable to the overall riskiness of the company's other activities?

20.

    a. Sauce, a well-known pizza factory, has asked you to evaluate the factory FCF. You estimate that the FCF of the factory is $4,500,000, its WACC is 12.5%, and its estimated growth is 5% each year. If you know that Sauce's debt is $19,000,000 and it has 6,500,000 outstanding shares, what should be its share price?

    b. Repeat the question using mid-year discounting.

21. You are given the following information for Twin, Inc.

| | |
|---|---|
| Long-term debt outstanding: | $300,000 |
| Current debt yield to maturity ($r_D$): | 8% |
| Number of shares of common stock: | 10,000 |
| Price per share: | $50 |
| Book value per share: | $25 |
| Expected rate of return on stock ($r_E$): | 15% |

    a. Calculate Twin, Inc.'s, WACC (assuming that the firm pays no taxes).

    b. How would $r_E$ and the WACC change if Twin, Inc.'s, stock price falls to $25 because of declining profits? Assume that the business risk is unchanged.

# 7 Using Financial Planning Models for Valuation

## CHAPTER CONTENTS

## Overview

This chapter explains how to build spreadsheet models that allow you to predict the future performance of a firm. These models are called *financial planning models* or *pro forma models*. Recall that accounting statements—the firm's income statement, its balance sheet, and its consolidated statement of cash flows—report what *happened* to the firm in the past. On the other hand, a financial planning model *predicts* what the firm's accounting statements will look like in the future. In accounting jargon something that looks like an accounting statement but that is *forward looking* is sometimes called a "pro forma" statement.

Financial planning models have a variety of uses:

- Projecting future financing needs of the firm: Building a financial planning model helps you predict whether the firm will need financing in the future. It also helps you tie the firm's financing needs to its future performance. For example, does an increase in the growth rate of sales create cash or use cash? The answer is not always clear: More sales produce more profits (and hence produce more cash). However, an increase in the growth rate of sales may also require more capital investment (machines, land, etc.) and may require greater working capital (inventories, credit to clients, etc.). A financial planning model can help us sort out these two opposing trends.

- Creating business plans: When you make a business plan (which you then take to investors to get financing or to a bank to explain why you need a loan and can pay it back), you'll often need to build a pro forma model of your firm. The model you build illustrates your assumptions about the financial and business environment in which your firm will operate in the future.

- Valuing a firm: Financial planning models can be used to predict the future free cash flows (FCF), dividends, and profits of a firm. This chapter shows how to use the pro forma prediction of FCF to value a firm. The valuation technique we employ—called *discounted cash flow* (DCF) *valuation*—is the valuation technique universally favored by the finance profession. When a financial planning model is used to do a DCF valuation, it is also used to do much of the sensitivity analysis that helps determine whether the valuation is reasonable.

## Finance Concepts Used

- Present value and net present value
- Free cash flow (FCF)
- Gordon model
- Terminal value
- Mid-year valuation

## Excel Functions Used

- **NPV**
- **Sum**
- **If**
- Relative versus absolute copying
- Circular references
- **Data tables**

# 7.1. Initial Accounting Statements for a Financial Planning Model

Financial planning models are predictions of what a firm's *future* financial statements will look like. To build such a model we start with the *present*—the firm's current financial statements.

To illustrate the process by which financial planning models are constructed, in the next section we will project 5 years of financial statements for Whimsical Toenails, a company that runs a chain of toenail-painting parlors. Whimsical's management and bankers want to project the firm's future performance, and we will help them by constructing a financial planning model.

Our starting point is Whimsical Toenail's current income statement and balance sheet for year-end 2004.

### WHIMSICAL TOENAILS INCOME STATEMENT 31 December 2004

| | |
|---|---|
| Sales | 10,000,000 |
| Cost of goods sold | -5,000,000 |
| Depreciation | -1,000,000 |
| Interest payments on debt | -320,000 |
| Interest earned on cash | 64,000 |
| Profit before tax | 3,744,000 |
| Taxes (40% tax rate) | -1,497,600 |
| Profit after tax | 2,246,400 |
| Dividends | -898,560 |
| Retained earnings | 1,347,840 |

### WHIMSICAL TOENAILS BALANCE SHEET 31 December 2004

| Assets | | Liabilities and equity | |
|---|---|---|---|
| Cash | 800,000 | Current liabilities | 800,000 |
| Current assets | 1,500,000 | Debt | 3,200,000 |
| Fixed assets | | | |
| Fixed assets at cost | 10,700,000 | Equity | |
| Accumulated depreciation | -3,000,000 | Stock (paid-in capital) | 4,500,000 |
| Net fixed assets | 7,700,000 | Accumulated retained earnings | 1,500,000 |
| **Total assets** | **10,000,000** | **Total liabilities and equity** | **10,000,000** |

## Accounting versus Financial Planning Model Concepts

In the next section we build the Whimsical Toenails financial planning model. However, before we do this, it is important to point out some differences between the use of certain concepts used by accountants and their adaptation to financial modeling. Although most of the terminology in this chapter follows the standard accounting classification, some changes are necessary to accommodate the structure of financial planning models. For example, whereas accountants use "current assets" to denote both operating current assets (like inventories and accounts receivable—as yet unpaid customer bills) and financial short-term assets (like cash and marketable securities), financial planning models use "current assets" to mean only operating short-term assets. To emphasize this point, the terminology "operating current assets" is sometimes used. Similarly, in the accounting framework "current liabilities" includes both operational items (like accounts payable—bills that are as yet unpaid by the firm) and financial items (like short-term debt and current portion of long-term debt). Financial planning models use "current liabilities" to denote operational items only. To emphasize this point, we sometimes use the terminology "operating current liabilities."

The next two subsections discuss these differences between accounting and financial concepts of current assets and current liabilities in more detail.

## Current Assets—What's Included in the Financial Planning Model and What's Not?

In financial planning models the "current assets" category contains only items that are related to the operations of the firm. Here are several typical items that would be included in the financial planning model definition of current assets.

- Accounts receivable: These are payments due from customers and are generated by the operations of the firm. Because accounts receivable are generated by the firm's sales, they are included in the operating current assets of the financial planning model.
- Inventories: Inventories include both raw materials to be used for production and unsold finished products. Inventories are part of the operating current assets of the financial planning model.
- Prepaid expenses: Prepaid expenses are costs that the firm pays before it actually receives the associated services. An example might be rent paid by the firm for future periods: If the firm pays this rent in advance (for example, not month by month, but 6 months in advance), then this prepayment of the rent is recorded by the accountant as a prepaid expense, which is part of current assets. For our financial planning model, we assume that prepaid expenses are part of *operating* current assets.

Two important examples of accounting current assets that are not included in the financial planning model definition of current assets are cash and marketable securities:

- Cash: The "cash" item on the balance sheet refers to money kept in the firm's bank accounts. Sometimes the accounting line item is called "cash and equivalents," with the second term denoting assets like certificates of deposit and money market accounts that can be easily converted into cash. Cash is an operating current asset to the extent that it is needed by the firm for its daily operations. In most cases, however, the cash accounts on the balance sheets simply refer to nonoperating assets that are kept in liquid form by the firm.
- Marketable securities: This item on the balance sheet refers to other financial assets—such as stocks and bonds—bought by the firm. Marketable securities are not needed for the firm's operations and are thus not an operating current asset.

The distinction between cash as an operating asset and cash as a store of value is usually obvious once you understand the business of the firm. A taxi driver needs to keep some cash on hand to make change for his customers, and a supermarket needs to keep some cash in the till for the same reason; in these cases at least some of the cash is an operating current asset (although even for a taxi or supermarket, most of the cash is likely to be a financial, nonoperating current asset). On the other hand, in March 2003, Microsoft reported having $4.3 billion in cash and another $41.9 billion in marketable securities. It is unlikely that almost any of this $46.2 billion is needed for daily operations. It is not an operating current asset, but rather a financial current asset. In a financial planning model financial current assets—cash and marketable securities not needed for the operations of the firm—are not included in the current assets.

## Current Liabilities

For purposes of the financial planning model, "current liabilities" contains only items that are related to the operations of the firm. Here are two typical items that would be included in the current liabilities of our financial planning model:

- Accounts payable: These are unpaid bills the firm owes to its suppliers. Because this item is related to the operations of the firm, we include it in the financial planning model definition of current liabilities.
- Taxes payable: When a firm's payment of taxes does not coincide with the accounting period, the taxes owed are entered into the balance sheet as a current liability. For example, for the year ending 31 December 2005, XYZ Corp. owes $2,000 in taxes, but it won't pay this tax bill until 15 January 2006. The financial statements of XYZ Corp. for 2005 will report taxes of $2,000 in the income statement statement; the firm's balance sheet will report taxes payable of $2,000 in the current liabilities. Taxes payable relate to the firm's operations and are included in the financial planning model definition of current liability.

Accounting current liability items that are not included in the financial planning model definition of current liabilities are typically financial items. Here are two examples:

- Short-term debt: These are borrowings by the firm that are due within 1 year. A bank overdraft (a credit line on a business's checking account) is a good example of a short-term debt. Accountants include this item in current liabilities, but financial planning models include them as *debt*.
- Current portion of long-term debt: This is the portion of the firm's debt that is due for payment within the current financial year. Accountants include this item in current liabilities; financial planning models include the current portion of long-term debt in the *debt* category.

## 7.2. Building a Financial Planning Model

Now that we have our terminology straight, we can build our financial planning model for Whimsical Toenails. A typical financial planning model has three major components:

- The model parameters. Also called the *value drivers*, a financial planning model's parameters include the major assumptions of the model. For example, we might assume that the *sales growth* parameter is 10% per year. Or we might assume that the *current assets to sales* parameter is 15%—meaning that an increase of $1,000 in sales requires an additional $150 of current assets. Typically, financial statement models are *sales driven*; this term means that many of the most important financial statement value drivers are assumed to be functions of the firm's sales.
- The financial policy assumptions. We will make assumptions about how the firm finances itself in the future. What is the mix between debt and new equity issued? Does excess cash produced by the firm go toward repaying debt, is it distributed as payments

to shareholders, or does it end up in the firm's cash balances? These assumptions are important determinants of the firm's future financial statements.

- The pro forma financial statements. Once we decide on the financial model's parameters, we will build the pro forma financial statements for the firm we are modeling—the income statement, balance sheets, and free cash flows (FCF).

When we've used the model's parameters and the financing assumptions to project the future financial statements of the firm, we can then use the model. By varying the model's assumptions, we can use the financial planning model to build different scenarios of how the firm will perform in the future. In Sections 7.6–7.8 we use the financial planning model to project the future FCFs of the firm to value the firm. We might also want to use the model to evaluate the ability of the firm to repay its debts (there's an end-of-chapter exercise that illustrates this use).

## The Model's Parameters—The Value Drivers

The *sales growth* parameter is usually the most important parameter of the financial planning model. In our example Whimsical Toenails current (year 0) level of sales is $10,000,000. Over the 5-year horizon of the financial planning model, the firm expects its sales to grow at a rate of 10% per year.

Other model parameters are derived from the following financial statement relations.[1]

- Current assets: We assume that Whimsical's end-year current assets on the balance sheet will be 15% of the annual firm sales.
- Current liabilities: We assume that Whimsical's end-year current liabilities on the balance sheet will be 8% of the annual firm sales.
- Net fixed assets: End-year net fixed assets are assumed to be 77% of annual sales.
- Depreciation: The annual depreciation charge is 10% of the average cost of the fixed assets on the books during the year.
- Cost of goods sold: Assumed to be 50% of sales.
- Interest rate on debt: 10%.
- Interest earned on cash: Whimsical Toenails earns 8% on the average balances of cash.
- Tax rate: 40% of the firm's profit before taxes.
- Dividends paid: We assume that Whimsical Toenails pays out 40% of its profits after taxes as dividends to shareholders.

## The Model's Financial Policy Assumptions

The second component of a financial planning model is the model's financial policy assumptions. In this initial financial planning model we make the following assumptions:

- Debt: Whimsical currently has debt of $3,200,000 on its balance sheet. The company's agreement with the bank specifies that it will repay $800,000 of this debt in each of the next 4 years. Once the debt is fully repaid, the company intends to stay debt free.

---

[1] In practice the model's parameters are often derived from an analysis of the company's historic financial statements.

- Stock: Company management does not intend to either issue new stock or repurchase stock over the 5-year model horizon. The stock item in the firm's balance sheets thus remains at its 2004 level of $4,500,000.

- Cash. In our model this item is the *plug*: The cash item is defined so that the left-hand side of the balance sheet always equals the right-hand side of the balance sheet:

$$Cash = Total \; liabilities \; and \; equity - Current \; assets - Net \; fixed \; assets$$

The plug is the balance sheet item that guarantees the equality of the future projected total assets and the future projected total liabilities and equity. Every financial planning model has a plug, and the plug is almost always cash (as in this case), debt, or stock.

To see how the plug fits into our model, consider the projected future balance sheets.

### WHIMSICAL TOENAILS balance sheet model assumptions

| Assets | Liabilities and equity |
| --- | --- |
| Cash [PLUG] | Current liabilities [8% of sales] |
| Current assets [15% of sales] | Debt [repaid by $800,000/year until zero] |
| Fixed assets Fixed assets at cost-Accumulated | Equity Stock (paid in capital) [constant] |
| depreciation [10% of average assets] Net fixed assets | Accumulated retained earnings [previous year's |
| [77% of sales] | accumulated retained + this year's retained from |
|  | income statement] |
| **Total assets** | **Total liabilities and equity** |

The plug assumption has two meanings:

1. The *mechanical* meaning of the plug: By defining cash to equal the total liabilities and equity minus current assets and minus net fixed assets, we guarantee that future projected assets and liabilities will always be equal. This is important, because the two sides of the balance sheet must always be equal. As mentioned previously, cash is not the only candidate to plug the financial model; we could also use either stock or debt (there are some examples of this in the end-of-chapter exercises). However, no matter what your plug, its "mechanical" function is the same—to guarantee that the two sides of the financial model's balance sheet are equal.

2. The *financial* meaning of the plug: Whimsical Toenails sells no additional stock and is locked into a debt repayment schedule. By defining the plug to be cash, we are also making a statement about how the firm finances itself. For the case of Whimsical Toenails, this means that all incremental financing (if needed) for the firm will come from the cash; it also means that if the firm has additional cash, it will go into this account.

## Projecting the 2005 Balance Sheet and Income Statement

Given Whimsical Toenails' financial statements and our assumptions, we can now develop the pro forma model and project the financial statements for 2005.

|  | A | B | C | D |
|---|---|---|---|---|
| 1 | **WHIMSICAL TOENAILS**<br>**SETTING UP THE FINANCIAL STATEMENT MODEL**<br>**for 2005** | | | |
| 2 | Sales growth | 10% | | |
| 3 | Current assets/Sales | 15% | | |
| 4 | Current liabilities/Sales | 8% | | |
| 5 | Net fixed assets/Sales | 77% | | |
| 6 | Costs of goods sold/Sales | 50% | | |
| 7 | Depreciation rate | 10% | | |
| 8 | Interest rate on debt | 10.00% | | |
| 9 | Interest earned on cash balances | 8.00% | | |
| 10 | Tax rate | 40% | | |
| 11 | Dividend payout ratio | 40% | | |
| 12 | | | | |
| 13 | **Year** | **2004** | **2005** | |
| 14 | **Income statement** | | | |
| 15 | Sales | 10,000,000 | 11,000,000 | <-- =B15*(1+$B$2) |
| 16 | Costs of goods sold | (5,000,000) | (5,500,000) | <-- =-C15*$B$6 |
| 17 | Depreciation | (1,000,000) | (1,166,842) | <-- =-$B$7*(C30+B30)/2 |
| 18 | Interest payments on debt | (320,000) | (280,000) | <-- =-$B$8*(B36+C36)/2 |
| 19 | Interest earned on cash and marketable securities | 64,000 | 57,595 | <-- =$B$9*(B27+C27)/2 |
| 20 | Profit before tax | 3,744,000 | 4,110,753 | <-- =SUM(C15:C19) |
| 21 | Taxes | (1,497,600) | (1,644,301) | <-- =-C20*$B$10 |
| 22 | Profit after tax | 2,246,400 | 2,466,452 | <-- =C21+C20 |
| 23 | Dividends | (898,560) | (986,581) | <-- =-$B$11*C22 |
| 24 | Retained earnings | 1,347,840 | 1,479,871 | <-- =C23+C22 |
| 25 | | | | |
| 26 | **Balance sheet** | | | |
| 27 | Cash | 800,000 | 639,871 | <-- =C39-C28-C32 |
| 28 | Current assets | 1,500,000 | 1,650,000 | <-- =C15*$B$3 |
| 29 | Fixed assets | | | |
| 30 | At cost | 10,700,000 | 12,636,842 | <-- =C32-C31 |
| 31 | Depreciation | (3,000,000) | (4,166,842) | <-- =B31-$B$7*(C30+B30)/2 |
| 32 | Net fixed assets | 7,700,000 | 8,470,000 | <-- =C15*$B$5 |
| 33 | **Total assets** | 10,000,000 | 10,759,871 | <-- =C32+C28+C27 |
| 34 | | | | |
| 35 | Current liabilities | 800,000 | 880,000 | <-- =C15*$B$4 |
| 36 | Debt | 3,200,000 | 2,400,000 | <-- =B36-800000 |
| 37 | Stock | 4,500,000 | 4,500,000 | <-- =B37 |
| 38 | Accumulated retained earnings | 1,500,000 | 2,979,871 | <-- =B38+C24 |
| 39 | **Total liabilities and equity** | 10,000,000 | 10,759,871 | <-- =SUM(C35:C38) |

# EXCEL NOTE: RELATIVE VERSUS ABSOLUTE REFERENCING

The dollar signs within a formula indicate that when the formulas are copied the cell references to the model parameters should not change. The technical jargon for this in Excel is *absolute referencing* as opposed to the *relative referencing* when variables are indicated without dollar signs. The distinction between absolute and relative copying is critical for financial planning models—if you fail to put the dollar signs correctly in the model, it will not copy correctly when you project years 2 and beyond.

Two cells in the previous spreadsheet have been highlighted to stress this important distinction:

- Cell B15: Sales in 2005 equal sales in the previous year times 1 + sales growth rate. Because we want to copy this definition to subsequent cells, cell B15's formula is **=B15*(1+$B$2)**. "$B$2" is the sales growth rate parameter, which stays the same as we copy the cell contents.

- Cell B16: Cost of goods sold in 2005 equal 50% of 2005 sales. The 50% parameter is in cell B6 and will stay the same as we copy the B16 formula to subsequent cells. Therefore, we write the formula in cell B16 as **=C15*$B$6**.

The use of relative versus absolute referencing is explained in Chapter 24.

## Income Statement Equations

Here are the relations for our financial planning model, with model parameters in boldface. These relations will end up as the formulas in the cells of our Excel model.

- Sales($t$) = Sales($t-1$)*(1 + **Sales growth**)
- Costs of goods sold = Sales * **Costs of goods sold/Sales**

We assume that Whimsical's only expenses related to sales are costs of goods sold. Most companies also book an expense item called selling, general and administrative expenses (SG&A). Exercise 2 at the end of this chapter illustrates how you would introduce SG&A into the model.

- Interest payments on debt = **Interest rate on debt** * Average debt over the year. We use this formula to estimate Whimsical's interest payments on the debt. For example, if the company's debt at the end of 2004 is $3,200,000 and its debt at the end of 2005 is $2,400,000, the financial planning model estimates its 2005 interest payments as

$$10\% * \frac{3,200,000 + 2,400,000}{2} = 10\% * \underbrace{2,800,000}_{\substack{\uparrow \\ \text{Whimsical's} \\ \text{average debt} \\ \text{in year 1}}} = 280,000$$

- Interest earned on cash = **Interest rate on cash** * Average cash over the year. This is the same logic used for the interest payments on debt. Whimsical earns 8% on its average cash balances over the year. If end-2004 cash balances are $800,000 and end-2005 cash balances are $639,871, then the firm earned $57,595 on its cash balances:

$$8\% * \frac{800,000 + 639,871}{2} = 8\% * \underbrace{719,935}_{\substack{\uparrow \\ \text{Whimsical's} \\ \text{average cash} \\ \text{in year 1}}} = 57,595$$

- Depreciation = **Depreciation rate** * Average fixed assets at cost over the year. This assumes that all new fixed assets are purchased more or less evenly throughout the year. We also assume that there is no disposal of fixed assets. Looking at the financial model may help you understand the calculation of the depreciation: Whimsical's 2004 fixed assets at cost are $10,700,000 and its projected fixed assets at cost for 2005 are $12,636,842. Because the company's depreciation rate is 10%, its year-1 depreciation in the income statement is

$$10\% * \frac{10,700,000 + 12,636,842}{2} = 10\% * \underbrace{11,668,411}_{\substack{\text{Average fixed} \\ \text{assets at cost} \\ \text{in year 1}}} = 1,166,842$$

- Profit before taxes = Sales − Costs of goods sold − Interest payments on debt + Interest earned on cash & marketable securities − Depreciation.
- Taxes = **Tax rate** * Profit before taxes
- Profit after taxes = Profit before taxes − Taxes
- Dividends = **Dividend payout ratio** * Profit after taxes.

Whimsical Toenails has a policy of paying out a fixed percentage of its profits as dividends. In the exercises for this chapter we explore some alternative dividend policies.

- Retained earnings = Profit after taxes − Dividends.

## Balance Sheet Equations

- Cash = Total liabilities − Current assets − net fixed assets.

As explained earlier, this definition means that cash is the balance sheet plug.

- Current assets = **Current assets/sales** * Sales
- Net fixed assets = **Net fixed assets/sales** * Sales.
- Accumulated depreciation = Previous year's accumulated depreciation + **Depreciation rate** * average fixed assets at cost over the year.
- Fixed assets at cost = Net fixed assets + accumulated depreciation.

Note that this model does not distinguish among plant, property, and equipment (PP&E) and other fixed assets, such as land.

- Current liabilities = **Current liabilities/Sales** * Sales.[2]
- Debt is assumed to decrease by $800,000 per year. This means that Whimsical Toenails will repay all of its debt by the end of the fourth year of the financial model. An alternative model, which assumes that debt is the balance sheet plug, is the subject of one of the end-of-chapter exercises.
- Stock is assumed to be unchanged. The company is assumed to issue no new stock or repurchase any existing stock.
- Accumulated retained earnings = Previous year's accumulated retained earnings + current year's additions to retained earnings.

---

[2] Some modelers prefer to model current liabilities as a percentage of the firm's cost of goods sold (COGS). The thinking here is that—because current liabilities include the firm's accounts payable (which in turn include the firm's unpaid bills for inventories and the like)—current liabilities are largely dependent on the level of the firm's costs of goods sold. Although it is easy to incorporate this assumption in our model, it doesn't make much difference: If COGS are a percentage of sales and current liabilities are a percentage of sales, then the current liabilities are also a percentage of the COGS.

## EXCEL NOTE—SOLVING CIRCULAR REFERENCES

Financial statement models in Excel always involve cells that are mutually dependent. In our model, for example, the interest earned on cash depends on the profits of the firm, but the profits depend on the interest earned on cash. Another example of mutual dependence in our model involves the fixed asset accounts: Fixed assets at cost are the sum of net fixed assets plus accumulated depreciation, but accumulated depreciation is a function of the fixed assets at cost.

As a result of these inevitable mutual dependencies, the solution of the model depends on the ability of Excel to solve circular references. To make sure your spreadsheet recalculates, you have to set your spreadsheet to allow for iterative calculations (for how to do this, read on in this box). If you open a spreadsheet that involves iteration and the spreadsheet is not set up for iterations, you will see the following Excel error message.

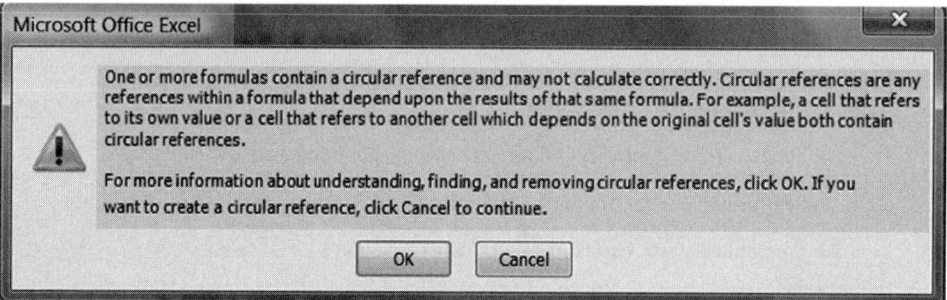

Get out of this message by clicking **Cancel**. Then click the Office button 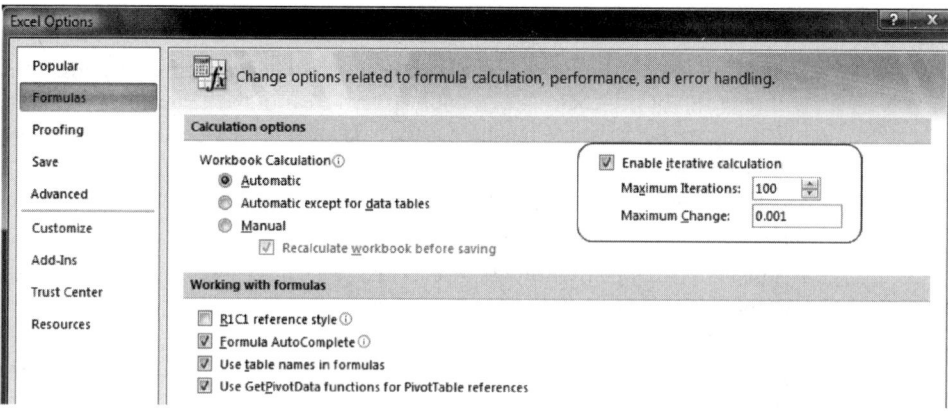. From here go to **Excel Options|Formulas** and click to enable iterative calculations.

Note that we have also clicked the **Automatic** button—this guarantees that the spreadsheet will recalculate every time a new entry is made. If your spreadsheet is very large or your computer somewhat aged, automatic recalculation can really slow you down. In this case it may be wise to click the **Manual** button and recalculate the spreadsheet manually by pressing either the **F9** key or the **[Shift]+F9** keys. (**F9** recalculates the whole spreadsheet, and **[Shift]+F9** recalculates only the current spreadsheet.)

FIGURE 7.1 Solving circular references in Excel.

## 7.3. Extending the Model to Years 2 and Beyond

Now that you have the model set up, you can extend it by copying the columns.

| | A | B | C | D | E | F | G |
|---|---|---|---|---|---|---|---|
| 1 | WHIMSICAL TOENAILS--FINANCIAL MODEL | | | | | | |
| 2 | Sales growth | 10% | | | | | |
| 3 | Current assets/Sales | 15% | | | | | |
| 4 | Current liabilities/Sales | 8% | | | | | |
| 5 | Net fixed assets/Sales | 77% | | | | | |
| 6 | Costs of goods sold/Sales | 50% | | | | | |
| 7 | Depreciation rate | 10% | | | | | |
| 8 | Interest rate on debt | 10.00% | | | | | |
| 9 | Interest earned on cash balances | 8.00% | | | | | |
| 10 | Tax rate | 40% | | | | | |
| 11 | Dividend payout ratio | 40% | | | | | |
| 12 | | | | | | | |
| 13 | Year | 2004 | 2005 | 2006 | 2007 | 2008 | 2009 |
| 14 | Income statement | | | | | | |
| 15 | Sales | 10,000,000 | 11,000,000 | 12,100,000 | 13,310,000 | 14,641,000 | 16,105,100 |
| 16 | Costs of goods sold | -5,000,000 | -5,500,000 | -6,050,000 | -6,655,000 | -7,320,500 | -8,052,550 |
| 17 | Depreciation | -1,000,000 | -1,166,842 | -1,374,773 | -1,613,102 | -1,885,879 | -2,197,668 |
| 18 | Interest payments on debt | -320,000 | -280,000 | -200,000 | -120,000 | -40,000 | 0 |
| 19 | Interest earned on cash and marketable securities | 64,000 | 57,595 | 47,355 | 42,349 | 42,755 | 80,609 |
| 20 | Profit before tax | 3,744,000 | 4,110,753 | 4,522,582 | 4,964,248 | 5,437,376 | 5,935,491 |
| 21 | Taxes | -1,497,600 | -1,644,301 | -1,809,033 | -1,985,699 | -2,174,950 | -2,374,196 |
| 22 | Profit after tax | 2,246,400 | 2,466,452 | 2,713,549 | 2,978,549 | 3,262,426 | 3,561,295 |
| 23 | Dividends | -898,560 | -986,581 | -1,085,420 | -1,191,419 | -1,304,970 | -1,424,518 |
| 24 | Retained earnings | 1,347,840 | 1,479,871 | 1,628,130 | 1,787,129 | 1,957,455 | 2,136,777 |
| 25 | | | | | | | |
| 26 | Balance sheet | | | | | | |
| 27 | Cash | 800,000 | 639,871 | 544,001 | 514,730 | 554,145 | 1,461,078 |
| 28 | Current assets | 1,500,000 | 1,650,000 | 1,815,000 | 1,996,500 | 2,196,150 | 2,415,765 |
| 29 | Fixed assets | | | | | | |
| 30 | At cost | 10,700,000 | 12,636,842 | 14,858,615 | 17,403,417 | 20,314,166 | 23,639,190 |
| 31 | Depreciation | -3,000,000 | -4,166,842 | -5,541,615 | -7,154,717 | -9,040,596 | -11,238,263 |
| 32 | Net fixed assets | 7,700,000 | 8,470,000 | 9,317,000 | 10,248,700 | 11,273,570 | 12,400,927 |
| 33 | Total assets | 10,000,000 | 10,759,871 | 11,676,001 | 12,759,930 | 14,023,865 | 16,277,770 |
| 34 | | | | | | | |
| 35 | Current liabilities | 800,000 | 880,000 | 968,000 | 1,064,800 | 1,171,280 | 1,288,408 |
| 36 | Debt | 3,200,000 | 2,400,000 | 1,600,000 | 800,000 | 0 | 0 |
| 37 | Stock | 4,500,000 | 4,500,000 | 4,500,000 | 4,500,000 | 4,500,000 | 4,500,000 |
| 38 | Accumulated retained earnings | 1,500,000 | 2,979,871 | 4,608,001 | 6,395,130 | 8,352,585 | 10,489,362 |
| 39 | Total liabilities and equity | 10,000,000 | 10,759,871 | 11,676,001 | 12,759,930 | 14,023,865 | 16,277,770 |

The most common Excel mistake to make in the transition between the two-column financial model and this one is the failure to mark the model parameters with dollar signs. We discuss this critical point in the Excel note on page 221. If you commit this error, you will get zeros in places where there should be numbers.[3]

---

[3] If this paragraph is mysterious to you, change the model by putting in the following mistake: In cell C28, write the formula =C15*B3 (instead of the correct formula =C15*$B$3). Then copy cell C28 to D28:G28. Now you will understand the importance of *dollarizing* the correct cell references!

## Understanding the Model by Changing Some of the Value Drivers

The financial model we've built shows that our firm's profits after tax will grow from $2,246,400 in 2004 to $3,561,295 in 2009. The balances of cash grow from $800,000 to $1,461,078, the firm's total assets grow to $16,277,770, and so on....

What would happen if we changed some of the value drivers in the model? For example, what would happen to profits if the growth rate of sales were to be 8% instead of 10% and if the cost of goods sold were to be 55% of sales instead of the 50% currently in the model? Given our Excel model, we simply have to make the relevant changes in the parameters in cells B2 and B6. Our intuition is that these performance changes will make the firm's financial results worse, and this is indeed confirmed in the model, as shown below.

|  | A | B | C | D | E | F | G |
|---|---|---|---|---|---|---|---|
| 1 | WHIMSICAL TOENAILS MODEL WITH SOME CHANGES | | | | | | |
| 2 | Sales growth | 8% <-- Changed from 10% | | | | | |
| 3 | Current assets/Sales | 15% | | | | | |
| 4 | Current liabilities/Sales | 8% | | | | | |
| 5 | Net fixed assets/Sales | 77% | | | | | |
| 6 | Costs of goods sold/Sales | 55% <-- Changed from 50% | | | | | |
| 7 | Depreciation rate | 10% | | | | | |
| 8 | Interest rate on debt | 10.00% | | | | | |
| 9 | Interest earned on cash balances | 8.00% | | | | | |
| 10 | Tax rate | 40% | | | | | |
| 11 | Dividend payout ratio | 40% | | | | | |
| 12 | | | | | | | |
| 13 | Year | 2004 | 2005 | 2006 | 2007 | 2008 | 2009 |
| 14 | Income statement | | | | | | |
| 15 | Sales | 10,000,000 | 10,800,000 | 11,664,000 | 12,597,120 | 13,604,890 | 14,693,281 |
| 16 | Costs of goods sold | (5,500,000) | (5,940,000) | (6,415,200) | (6,928,416) | (7,482,689) | (8,081,304) |
| 17 | Depreciation | (1,000,000) | (1,158,737) | (1,348,145) | (1,562,886) | (1,806,057) | (2,081,118) |
| 18 | Interest payments on debt | (320,000) | (280,000) | (200,000) | (120,000) | (40,000) | - |
| 19 | Interest earned on cash and marketable securities | 64,000 | 55,181 | 39,185 | 26,432 | 16,813 | 42,050 |
| 20 | Profit before tax | 3,244,000 | 3,476,444 | 3,739,840 | 4,012,250 | 4,292,956 | 4,572,909 |
| 21 | Taxes | (1,297,600) | (1,390,578) | (1,495,936) | (1,604,900) | (1,717,182) | (1,829,163) |
| 22 | Profit after tax | 1,946,400 | 2,085,866 | 2,243,904 | 2,407,350 | 2,575,774 | 2,743,745 |
| 23 | Dividends | (778,560) | (834,347) | (897,562) | (962,940) | (1,030,309) | (1,097,498) |
| 24 | Retained earnings | 1,167,840 | 1,251,520 | 1,346,342 | 1,444,410 | 1,545,464 | 1,646,247 |
| 25 | | | | | | | |
| 26 | Balance sheet | | | | | | |
| 27 | Cash | 800,000 | 579,520 | 400,102 | 260,691 | 159,629 | 891,628 |
| 28 | Current assets | 1,500,000 | 1,620,000 | 1,749,600 | 1,889,568 | 2,040,733 | 2,203,992 |
| 29 | Fixed assets | | | | | | |
| 30 | At cost | 10,700,000 | 12,474,737 | 14,488,162 | 16,769,550 | 19,351,589 | 22,270,768 |
| 31 | Depreciation | (3,000,000) | (4,158,737) | (5,506,882) | (7,069,767) | (8,875,824) | (10,956,942) |
| 32 | Net fixed assets | 7,700,000 | 8,316,000 | 8,981,280 | 9,699,782 | 10,475,765 | 11,313,826 |
| 33 | Total assets | 10,000,000 | 10,515,520 | 11,130,982 | 11,850,042 | 12,676,128 | 14,409,446 |
| 34 | | | | | | | |
| 35 | Current liabilities | 800,000 | 864,000 | 933,120 | 1,007,770 | 1,088,391 | 1,175,462 |
| 36 | Debt | 3,200,000 | 2,400,000 | 1,600,000 | 800,000 | 0 | 0 |
| 37 | Stock | 4,500,000 | 4,500,000 | 4,500,000 | 4,500,000 | 4,500,000 | 4,500,000 |
| 38 | Accumulated retained earnings | 1,500,000 | 2,751,520 | 4,097,862 | 5,542,272 | 7,087,736 | 8,733,984 |
| 39 | Total liabilities and equity | 10,000,000 | 10,515,520 | 11,130,982 | 11,850,042 | 12,676,128 | 14,409,446 |

If you compare the model above to our previous version of the model, you'll see that the firm's sales growth has slowed (from 10 to 8%) and that its sales have become more expensive (cost of goods sold is 55% of sales instead of 50%). The result is that profits after taxes (row 22) are lower than before. Cash balances (row 27) are also lower than in the previous version of the model.

# 7.4. FCF: Measuring the Cash Produced by the Firm's Operations

In this section we use our model to measure the firm's projected free cash flow (FCF). We have previously discussed the concept of FCF in Chapter 6. A good way to think of FCF is that it is the amount of cash the firm would produce if it had no debt whatsoever. This is equivalent to the amount of cash produced by the firm if the shareholders have to finance *all* of the operations of the firm. For short, we'll say that the FCF is a measure of the *cash produced by the firm's operations*.

The FCF is the measure on which we base our valuation of the firm. We gave an example of this in Chapter 6 (page 206, where we used the future predicted FCFs of Courier Corp. to value the company). In Section 7.6 we return to this topic and show how a financial planning model's predictions of FCFs can be used to value a company.

In this section we merely use the financial planning model to project the firm's future FCFs. Before we do so, however, let's recap the definition and the terminology we use.

The definition of the free cash flow is as follows.

## Defining the Free Cash Flow (FCF)

| | |
|---|---|
| Profit after taxes | This is the basic measure of the profitability of the business, but it is an accounting measure that includes financing flows (such as interest), as well as noncash expenses such as depreciation. Profit after taxes does not account for changes in the firm's working capital or purchases of new fixed assets, both of which can be important cash drains on the firm. |
| + Depreciation | This noncash expense is added back to the profit after tax. |
| - Increase in current assets | When the firm's sales increase, more investment is needed in inventories, accounts receivable, etc. This increase in current assets is not an expense for tax purposes (and is therefore ignored in the profit after taxes), but it is a cash drain on the company. Note that our use of the term "current assets" is slightly different from the standard accounting usage—see the discussion in Section 7.1. |
| + Increase in current liabilities | An increase in the sales often causes an increase in financing related to sales or purchases (such as accounts payable or taxes payable). This increase in current liabilities—when related to sales—provides cash to the firm. Because it is directly related to sales, we include this cash in the FCF calculations. Note that our use of the term "current liabilities" is slightly different from the standard accounting usage—see the discussion in Section 7.1. |
| - Increase in fixed assets at cost (also called "capital expenditures"—CAPEX) | An increase in fixed assets (the long-term productive assets of the company) is a use of cash, which reduces the firm's FCF. |
| + After-tax interest payments (net) | FCF is an attempt to measure the cash produced by the business activity of the firm. To neutralize the effect of interest payments on the firm's profits, we<br>• Add back the after-tax cost of interest on debt (*after-tax* because interest payments are tax-deductible) and<br>• Subtract out the after-tax interest payments on cash. |
| FCF = sum of the above | The free cash flow measures the cash produced by the firm's operations. |

Here is the FCF calculation for Whimsical Toenails. Note that we have returned to the initial model (sales growth = 10%, cost of goods sold = 50% of sales).

| | A | B | C | D | E | F | G |
|---|---|---|---|---|---|---|---|
| 42 | **Free cash flow calculation** | | | | | | |
| 43 | **Year** | **2004** | **2005** | **2006** | **2007** | **2008** | **2009** |
| 44 | Profit after tax | | 2,466,452 | 2,713,549 | 2,978,549 | 3,262,426 | 3,561,295 |
| 45 | Add back depreciation | | 1,166,842 | 1,374,773 | 1,613,102 | 1,885,879 | 2,197,668 |
| 46 | Subtract increase in current assets | | -150,000 | -165,000 | -181,500 | -199,650 | -219,615 |
| 47 | Add back increase in current liabilities | | 80,000 | 88,000 | 96,800 | 106,480 | 117,128 |
| 48 | Subtract increase in fixed assets at cost | | -1,936,842 | -2,221,773 | -2,544,802 | -2,910,749 | -3,325,025 |
| 49 | Add back after-tax interest on debt | | 168,000 | 120,000 | 72,000 | 24,000 | 0 |
| 50 | Subtract after-tax interest on cash | | -34,557 | -28,413 | -25,410 | -25,653 | -48,365 |
| 51 | **Free cash flow** | | 1,759,895 | 1,881,136 | 2,008,739 | 2,142,733 | 2,283,085 |

The FCFs in row 51 are substantially lower than the firm's profits after taxes in row 44. The major reasons for this are the large capital expenditure (row 48), which outweighs the cash effect of the depreciation (row 45).

The FCF calculations are sensitive to the model assumptions. Suppose that Whimsical Toenail's sales growth is 8% (instead of 10%) and that its cost of goods sold is 55% of sales (instead of 50%). You might suspect that these negative changes in the model assumptions will make Whimsical's future projected FCFs substantially lower, and you're right.

| | A | B | C | D | E | F | G |
|---|---|---|---|---|---|---|---|
| 1 | WHIMSICAL TOENAILS MODEL WITH SOME CHANGES | | | | | | |
| 2 | Sales growth | 8% | <-- Changed from 10% | | | | |
| 3 | Current assets/Sales | 15% | | | | | |
| 4 | Current liabilities/Sales | 8% | | | | | |
| 5 | Net fixed assets/Sales | 77% | | | | | |
| 6 | Costs of goods sold/Sales | 55% | <-- Changed from 50% | | | | |
| 7 | Depreciation rate | 10% | | | | | |
| 8 | Interest rate on debt | 10.00% | | | | | |
| 9 | Interest earned on cash balances | 8.00% | | | | | |
| 10 | Tax rate | 40% | | | | | |
| 11 | Dividend payout ratio | 40% | | | | | |
| 41 | | | | | | | |
| 42 | Free cash flow calculation | | | | | | |
| 43 | Year | 2004 | 2005 | 2006 | 2007 | 2008 | 2009 |
| 44 | Profit after tax | | 2,085,866 | 2,243,904 | 2,407,350 | 2,575,774 | 2,743,745 |
| 45 | Add back depreciation | | 1,158,737 | 1,348,145 | 1,562,886 | 1,806,057 | 2,081,118 |
| 46 | Subtract increase in current assets | | (120,000) | (129,600) | (139,968) | (151,165) | (163,259) |
| 47 | Add back increase in current liabilities | | 64,000 | 69,120 | 74,650 | 80,622 | 87,071 |
| 48 | Subtract increase in fixed assets at cost | | (1,774,737) | (2,013,425) | (2,281,388) | (2,582,040) | (2,919,179) |
| 49 | Add back after-tax interest on debt | | 168,000 | 120,000 | 72,000 | 24,000 | 0 |
| 50 | Subtract after-tax interest on cash | | (33,108) | (23,511) | (15,859) | (10,088) | (25,230) |
| 51 | Free cash flow | | 1,548,758 | 1,614,633 | 1,679,670 | 1,743,160 | 1,804,266 |

## EXCEL NOTE: HIDING AND GROUPING ROWS

In the above example we've hidden rows 12–40 to make more room on the screen. To hide rows in Excel:

- Mark the rows you want to hide.
- Right-click on the mouse and click **Hide.**

Here's what the screen looks like.

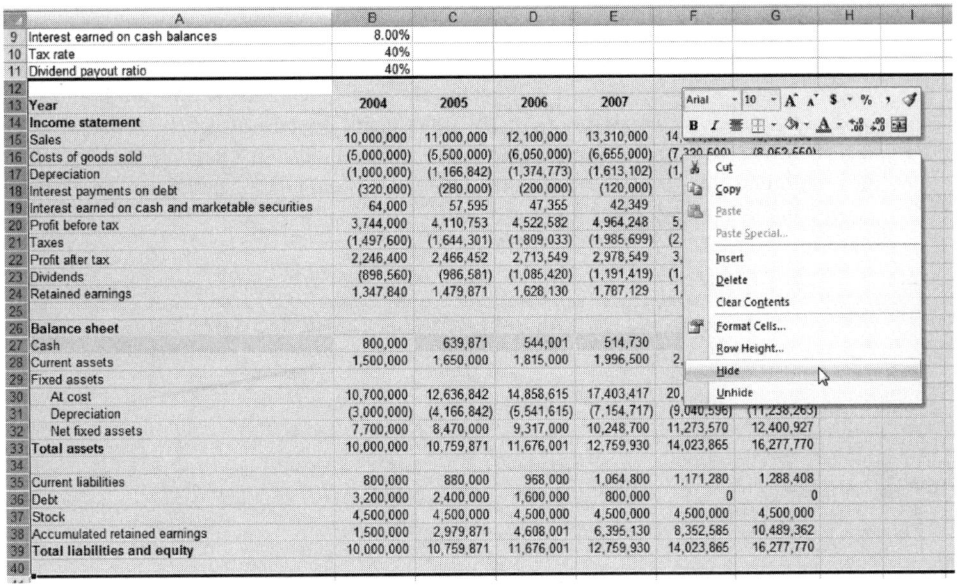

| | A | B | C | D | E | F | G | H | I |
|---|---|---|---|---|---|---|---|---|---|
| 9 | Interest earned on cash balances | 8.00% | | | | | | | |
| 10 | Tax rate | 40% | | | | | | | |
| 11 | Dividend payout ratio | 40% | | | | | | | |
| 12 | | | | | | | | | |
| 13 | Year | 2004 | 2005 | 2006 | 2007 | | | | |
| 14 | Income statement | | | | | | | | |
| 15 | Sales | 10,000,000 | 11,000,000 | 12,100,000 | 13,310,000 | 14, | | | |
| 16 | Costs of goods sold | (5,000,000) | (5,500,000) | (6,050,000) | (6,655,000) | (7,320,500) | (8,052,550) | | |
| 17 | Depreciation | (1,000,000) | (1,166,842) | (1,374,773) | (1,613,102) | (1, | | | |
| 18 | Interest payments on debt | (320,000) | (280,000) | (200,000) | (120,000) | (, | | | |
| 19 | Interest earned on cash and marketable securities | 64,000 | 57,595 | 47,355 | 42,349 | 5, | | | |
| 20 | Profit before tax | 3,744,000 | 4,110,753 | 4,522,582 | 4,964,248 | 5, | | | |
| 21 | Taxes | (1,497,600) | (1,644,301) | (1,809,033) | (1,985,699) | (2, | | | |
| 22 | Profit after tax | 2,246,400 | 2,466,452 | 2,713,549 | 2,978,549 | 3, | | | |
| 23 | Dividends | (898,560) | (986,581) | (1,085,420) | (1,191,419) | (1, | | | |
| 24 | Retained earnings | 1,347,840 | 1,479,871 | 1,628,130 | 1,787,129 | 1, | | | |
| 25 | | | | | | | | | |
| 26 | Balance sheet | | | | | | | | |
| 27 | Cash | 800,000 | 639,871 | 544,001 | 514,730 | | | | |
| 28 | Current assets | 1,500,000 | 1,650,000 | 1,815,000 | 1,996,500 | 2, | | | |
| 29 | Fixed assets | | | | | | | | |
| 30 | At cost | 10,700,000 | 12,636,842 | 14,858,615 | 17,403,417 | 20, | | | |
| 31 | Depreciation | (3,000,000) | (4,166,842) | (5,541,615) | (7,154,717) | (9,040,596) | (11,238,263) | | |
| 32 | Net fixed assets | 7,700,000 | 8,470,000 | 9,317,000 | 10,248,700 | 11,273,570 | 12,400,927 | | |
| 33 | Total assets | 10,000,000 | 10,759,871 | 11,676,001 | 12,759,930 | 14,023,865 | 16,277,770 | | |
| 34 | | | | | | | | | |
| 35 | Current liabilities | 800,000 | 880,000 | 968,000 | 1,064,800 | 1,171,280 | 1,288,408 | | |
| 36 | Debt | 3,200,000 | 2,400,000 | 1,600,000 | 800,000 | 0 | 0 | | |
| 37 | Stock | 4,500,000 | 4,500,000 | 4,500,000 | 4,500,000 | 4,500,000 | 4,500,000 | | |
| 38 | Accumulated retained earnings | 1,500,000 | 2,979,871 | 4,608,001 | 6,395,130 | 8,352,585 | 10,489,362 | | |
| 39 | Total liabilities and equity | 10,000,000 | 10,759,871 | 11,676,001 | 12,759,930 | 14,023,865 | 16,277,770 | | |
| 40 | | | | | | | | | |

(Context menu shown with: Cut, Copy, Paste, Paste Special..., Insert, Delete, Clear Contents, Format Cells..., Row Height..., Hide, Unhide)

Marking the rows and clicking **Unhide** reverses the action.

Another slightly more sophisticated way to accomplish the same result is to **Group** the rows. To do this, first mark the rows as before. Then go to **Data|Outline|Group** as shown below.

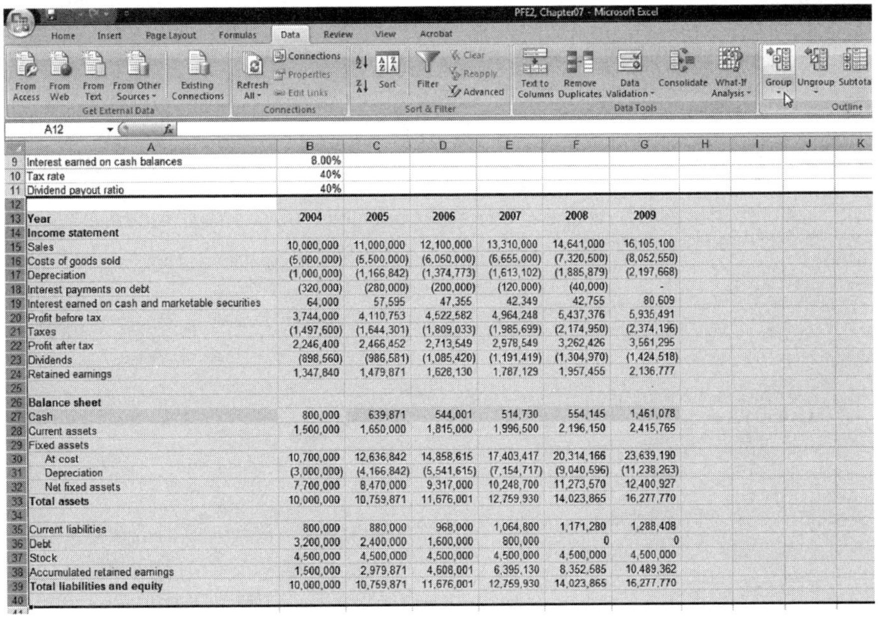

| | A | B | C | D | E | F | G | H |
|---|---|---|---|---|---|---|---|---|
| 9 | Interest earned on cash balances | 8.00% | | | | | | |
| 10 | Tax rate | 40% | | | | | | |
| 11 | Dividend payout ratio | 40% | | | | | | |
| 12 | | | | | | | | |
| 13 | Year | 2004 | 2005 | 2006 | 2007 | 2008 | 2009 | |
| 14 | Income statement | | | | | | | |
| 15 | Sales | 10,000,000 | 11,000,000 | 12,100,000 | 13,310,000 | 14,641,000 | 16,105,100 | |
| 16 | Costs of goods sold | (5,000,000) | (5,500,000) | (6,050,000) | (6,655,000) | (7,320,500) | (8,052,550) | |
| 17 | Depreciation | (1,000,000) | (1,166,842) | (1,374,773) | (1,613,102) | (1,885,879) | (2,197,668) | |
| 18 | Interest payments on debt | (320,000) | (280,000) | (200,000) | (120,000) | (40,000) | - | |
| 19 | Interest earned on cash and marketable securities | 64,000 | 57,595 | 47,355 | 42,349 | 42,755 | 80,609 | |
| 20 | Profit before tax | 3,744,000 | 4,110,753 | 4,522,582 | 4,964,248 | 5,437,376 | 5,935,491 | |
| 21 | Taxes | (1,497,600) | (1,644,301) | (1,809,033) | (1,985,699) | (2,174,950) | (2,374,196) | |
| 22 | Profit after tax | 2,246,400 | 2,466,452 | 2,713,549 | 2,978,549 | 3,262,426 | 3,561,295 | |
| 23 | Dividends | (898,560) | (986,581) | (1,085,420) | (1,191,419) | (1,304,970) | (1,424,518) | |
| 24 | Retained earnings | 1,347,840 | 1,479,871 | 1,628,130 | 1,787,129 | 1,957,455 | 2,136,777 | |
| 25 | | | | | | | | |
| 26 | Balance sheet | | | | | | | |
| 27 | Cash | 800,000 | 639,871 | 544,001 | 514,730 | 554,145 | 1,461,078 | |
| 28 | Current assets | 1,500,000 | 1,650,000 | 1,815,000 | 1,996,500 | 2,196,150 | 2,415,765 | |
| 29 | Fixed assets | | | | | | | |
| 30 | At cost | 10,700,000 | 12,636,842 | 14,858,615 | 17,403,417 | 20,314,166 | 23,639,190 | |
| 31 | Depreciation | (3,000,000) | (4,166,842) | (5,541,615) | (7,154,717) | (9,040,596) | (11,238,263) | |
| 32 | Net fixed assets | 7,700,000 | 8,470,000 | 9,317,000 | 10,248,700 | 11,273,570 | 12,400,927 | |
| 33 | Total assets | 10,000,000 | 10,759,871 | 11,676,001 | 12,759,930 | 14,023,865 | 16,277,770 | |
| 34 | | | | | | | | |
| 35 | Current liabilities | 800,000 | 880,000 | 968,000 | 1,064,800 | 1,171,280 | 1,288,408 | |
| 36 | Debt | 3,200,000 | 2,400,000 | 1,600,000 | 800,000 | 0 | 0 | |
| 37 | Stock | 4,500,000 | 4,500,000 | 4,500,000 | 4,500,000 | 4,500,000 | 4,500,000 | |
| 38 | Accumulated retained earnings | 1,500,000 | 2,979,871 | 4,608,001 | 6,395,130 | 8,352,585 | 10,489,362 | |
| 39 | Total liabilities and equity | 10,000,000 | 10,759,871 | 11,676,001 | 12,759,930 | 14,023,865 | 16,277,770 | |
| 40 | | | | | | | | |

The result is a marker in the left-hand margin of the spreadsheet that allows you to hide or unhide the rows: Clicking on the ▬ in the margin collapses the grouped rows. Clicking on the ⊞ in the margin expands the grouped rows. You can also use **Ungroup** and **Group** on the toolbar.

FIGURE 7.2  Hiding and grouping rows in Excel.

## 7.5. Reconciling the Cash Balances—The Consolidated Statement of Cash Flows

The free cash flow (FCF) calculation is different from the "consolidated statement of cash flows" that is a part of every accounting statement. The FCF calculation shows you how much cash is produced by the firm's operations. On the other hand, the purpose of the accounting statement of cash flows is to explain the increase in the cash accounts in the balance sheet as a function of the cash flows from the firm's operating, investing, and financing activities. Here's the consolidated statement of cash flows for our model.

| | A | B | C | D | E | F | G |
|---|---|---|---|---|---|---|---|
| 1 | **WHIMSICAL TOENAILS–RECONCILING THE CASH BALANCES** Note that the profit and loss statement and FCF statement have been hidden | | | | | | |
| 2 | Sales growth | 10% | | | | | |
| 3 | Current assets/Sales | 15% | | | | | |
| 4 | Current liabilities/Sales | 8% | | | | | |
| 5 | Net fixed assets/Sales | 77% | | | | | |
| 6 | Costs of goods sold/Sales | 50% | | | | | |
| 7 | Depreciation rate | 10% | | | | | |
| 8 | Interest rate on debt | 10.00% | | | | | |
| 9 | Interest earned on cash balances | 8.00% | | | | | |
| 10 | Tax rate | 40% | | | | | |
| 11 | Dividend payout ratio | 40% | | | | | |
| 12 | | | | | | | |
| 25 | | | | | | | |
| 26 | **Balance sheet** | | | | | | |
| 27 | Cash | 800,000 | 639,871 | 544,001 | 514,730 | 554,145 | 1,461,078 |
| 28 | Current assets | 1,500,000 | 1,650,000 | 1,815,000 | 1,996,500 | 2,196,150 | 2,415,765 |
| 29 | Fixed assets | | | | | | |
| 30 | At cost | 10,700,000 | 12,636,842 | 14,858,615 | 17,403,417 | 20,314,166 | 23,639,190 |
| 31 | Depreciation | (3,000,000) | (4,166,842) | (5,541,615) | (7,154,717) | (9,040,596) | (11,238,263) |
| 32 | Net fixed assets | 7,700,000 | 8,470,000 | 9,317,000 | 10,248,700 | 11,273,570 | 12,400,927 |
| 33 | **Total assets** | 10,000,000 | 10,759,871 | 11,676,001 | 12,759,930 | 14,023,865 | 16,277,770 |
| 34 | | | | | | | |
| 35 | Current liabilities | 800,000 | 880,000 | 968,000 | 1,064,800 | 1,171,280 | 1,288,408 |
| 36 | Debt | 3,200,000 | 2,400,000 | 1,600,000 | 800,000 | 0 | 0 |
| 37 | Stock | 4,500,000 | 4,500,000 | 4,500,000 | 4,500,000 | 4,500,000 | 4,500,000 |
| 38 | Accumulated retained earnings | 1,500,000 | 2,979,871 | 4,608,001 | 6,395,130 | 8,352,585 | 10,489,362 |
| 39 | **Total liabilities and equity** | 10,000,000 | 10,759,871 | 11,676,001 | 12,759,930 | 14,023,865 | 16,277,770 |
| 40 | | | | | | | |
| 41 | | | | | | | |
| 54 | **CONSOLIDATED STATEMENT OF CASH FLOWS–RECONCILING THE CASH BALANCES** | | | | | | |
| 55 | **Cash flows from operating activities** | | | | | | |
| 56 | Profit after tax | | 2,466,452 | 2,713,549 | 2,978,549 | 3,262,426 | 3,561,295 |
| 57 | Add back depreciation | | 1,166,842 | 1,374,773 | 1,613,102 | 1,885,879 | 2,197,668 |
| 58 | Adjust for changes in net working capital: | | | | | | |
| 59 | Subtract increase in current assets | | (150,000) | (165,000) | (181,500) | (199,650) | (219,615) |
| 60 | Add back increase in current liabilities | | 80,000 | 88,000 | 96,800 | 106,480 | 117,128 |
| 61 | Net cash from operating activities | | 3,563,294 | 4,011,322 | 4,506,950 | 5,055,135 | 5,656,475 |
| 62 | | | | | | | |
| 63 | **Cash flow from investing activities** | | | | | | |
| 64 | Aquisitions of fixed assets–capital expenditures | | (1,936,842) | (2,221,773) | (2,544,802) | (2,910,749) | (3,325,025) |
| 65 | Purchases of investment securities | | 0 | 0 | 0 | 0 | 0 |
| 66 | Proceeds from sales of investment securities | | 0 | 0 | 0 | 0 | 0 |
| 67 | Net cash used in investing activities | | (1,936,842) | (2,221,773) | (2,544,802) | (2,910,749) | (3,325,025) |
| 68 | | | | | | | |
| 69 | **Cash flow from financing activities** | | | | | | |
| 70 | Net proceeds from borrowing activities | | -800,000 | -800,000 | -800,000 | -800,000 | 0 |
| 71 | Net proceeds from stock issues, repurchases | | 0 | 0 | 0 | 0 | 0 |
| 72 | Dividends paid | | (986,581) | (1,085,420) | (1,191,419) | (1,304,970) | (1,424,518) |
| 73 | Net cash from financing activities | | (1,786,581) | (1,885,420) | (1,991,419) | (2,104,970) | (1,424,518) |
| 74 | =C73+C67+C61 | | | | | | |
| 75 | Net increase in cash and cash equivalents | | -160,129 | -95,870 | -29,271 | 39,415 | 906,933 |
| 76 | Cash balances at end of previous year | =B27 | 800,000 | 639,871 | 544,001 | 514,730 | 554,145 |
| 77 | Cash balances at end of current year | | 639,871 | 544,001 | 514,730 | 554,145 | 1,461,078 |
| 78 | | | | | | | |
| 79 | =C75+C76 . This number should | | | | | | |
| 80 | be equal to cell C27 . | | | | | | |

Row 77 checks that the ending balances in the cash accounts derived through the consolidated statement of cash flows match those derived in row 27 of the balance sheets (which use cash as a plug). The fact that row 77 is the same as row 27 shows that our model correctly accounts for all the accounting relations. To see this, look at cells C75, C76, and C77:

- C76 shows that at the end of year 0 the firm's cash balances were $800,000.
- C75 shows that *everything the firm did during the year*—sales, costs of sales, interest paid, new financing through debt and equity, . . . *everything*—produced a net decrease in cash of $160,129.
- C77 is the sum of the previous two cells: If the firm started off the year with $800,000 in cash and if its total activities produced -$160,129 in cash, then the ending cash balances should be $639,871. And so they are—this is the cash listed in cell C27. Our model accounts for all of the firm's activities!

### What's more useful—The consolidated statement of cash flows or the free cash flow?

What's more useful—the cash increment in row 75 of the consolidated statement of cash flows or the free cash flow we derived in Section 7.4? Although they both have their purposes, there's no doubt that for finance purposes the FCF is a more useful and more widely used number. The FCF measures the cash produced by the firm's business activities. It is the relevant finance measure for the effectiveness of the firm at doing what it was founded to do—make something and sell it. The cash increment in row 75 is also important, however: First, it allows us to check that we've done our calculations correctly by giving a check and balance on the cash line in the balance sheet. Second, it shows us why the cash line in the balance changed.

## 7.6. Valuing Whimsical Toenails Using a DCF Model

The terms "value of a company" or "value of a firm" are often used interchangeably by finance professionals. Even finance professionals, however, can use a confusing variety of meanings for these terms. In finance the definition most often used for "firm value" is the following:

> **The finance definition of firm value**: The value of a firm is the market value of the firm's equity plus the market value of the firm's financial debt.

The finance definition of firm value, which we use in this chapter, is not the only definition of firm value that is in use. Often when individuals discuss the *firm value*, they really mean the *value of its shares*. It is better to use the term *equity value* for the value of a company's shares and to use the term *firm value* (or *company value*) to denote the market value of the firm's equity plus its debt. In our calculations on page 233, we also show you how to compute the value of a firm's shares.

Sometimes the term *firm value* is used to denote the *accounting value* of the firm. Also known as the *book value*, this value is based on the firm's balance sheets. Because accounting statements are based on historical values, people in finance generally prefer not to use this definition. At the end of this section we illustrate why we do not like this valuation method.

In this section we illustrate three methods of computing the finance definition of firm value.

- The simplest valuation method is to value the firm's equity (its shares) using the firm's share price in the market and to add to this the value of the firm's debt.

- A second valuation method, the DCF method, is based on discounted cash flows. This is the method preferred by finance professionals; it is the main method illustrated in this section. In a DCF valuation firm value equals the PV of the firm's futures FCFs *plus* the value of its currently available liquid assets. The discount rate is the firm's WACC, which we have previously discussed in Chapter 6.

- A third valuation method values the firm using the book value of a firm's assets.

## The Share Price Valuation Method: Valuing Whimsical Toenails Using Current Share Price

The simplest way to value Whimsical Toenails is to look at the value of its share. Whimsical Toenails has 1 million shares, which were trading on 31 December 2004 at $10 per share. Thus the market value of the firm's equity is $10 million. In addition, the company's balance sheet shows that it has debt of $3.2 million; we use these balance sheet values (also called book values) of the debt as an approximation of the debt's market value.[4]

Using the current share price, the *firm value* of Whimsical Toenails is $13,200,000.

| | A | B | C |
|---|---|---|---|
| 1 | **WHIMSICAL TOENAILS**<br>**Valuation using share price** | | |
| 2 | Number of shares | 1,000,000 | |
| 3 | Current share price | 10.00 | |
| 4 | Market value of equity | 10,000,000 | <-- =B2*B3 |
| 5 | | | |
| 6 | Debt | 3,200,000 | |
| 7 | | | |
| 8 | **Firm value:  Market Value of Equity + Debt** | 13,200,000 | <-- =B4+B6 |

## The DCF Valuation Method: Valuing Whimsical Toenails by Discounting Its Future Free Cash Flows

The advantage of the share-price valuation method illustrated above is that it is very simple: The firm value equals the market value of the firm's shares plus the book value of its debt. Valuing the company at its current price of $10 per share is perfectly acceptable for someone considering buying a few shares of the company, but it makes less sense if Whimsical Toenails is selling a controlling block of shares. In this case the purchaser would probably have to take the following considerations into account:

- If the purchaser tried to buy a big block of shares of Whimsical shares on the open market, he might have to offer more than the current market price per share. As he bought more and more shares, the price would go up; in addition, the announcement that someone was trying to take over Whimsical Toenails would—in many cases—force the share price up.

- There are benefits to controlling a company that are not included in the market price per share. The market price of a share reflects the value of a company's future dividends to a *passive* shareholder who has no control over the company. In general, the value of a controlling block of shares is larger than the market value because the controlling

---

[4]This is common practice. Most company debt is not traded on financial markets, and therefore there is no easily available market value for the debt. As a first approximation, most finance professionals use the book value of a firm's debt as a proxy for the debt's market value.

shareholder can actually decide what the company will do. He can also derive consider-able *private benefits* from running the company.[5]

To deal with these problems, we use the discounted cash flow (DCF) valuation method to value the shares. DCF valuations are a standard finance methodology, which defines the value of the firm as the present value of the firm's future free cash flows (FCF), discounted at the weighted average cost of capital (WACC), plus the firm's initial cash and marketable securities. Section 7.9 discusses the theory behind this method of valuation, but for the moment we skip all the theory and simply present the formula:

$$DCF \ firm \ value = \frac{Market \ value}{of \ firm's \ debt} + \frac{Market \ value}{of \ firm's \ equity}$$

$$= \underbrace{PV \left( \frac{all \ future \ FCFs}{discounted \ at \ WACC} \right)}_{\substack{\text{Often called the "enterprise value"} \\ \text{of the firm}}} + \frac{Today's \ cash \ and}{marketable \ securities}$$

As you can see in the equation, the present value of the firm's future FCFs is often called the firm's *enterprise value*. Using the financial planning model for Whimsical Toenails, we con-clude that when the WACC is 14%, the shares of Whimsical are worth $20.11.

| | A | B | C | D | E | F | G |
|---|---|---|---|---|---|---|---|
| 1 | WHIMSICAL TOENAILS–DCF VALUATION | | | | | | |
| 2 | Year | 2005 | 2006 | 2007 | 2008 | 2009 | |
| 3 | Estimated free cash flow | 1,759,895 | 1,881,136 | 2,008,739 | 2,142,733 | 2,283,085 | |
| 4 | Terminal value | | | | | 30,250,880 | <-- =F3*(1+B8)/(B7-B8) |
| 5 | Total | 1,759,895 | 1,881,136 | 2,008,739 | 2,142,733 | 32,533,966 | |
| 6 | | | | | | | |
| 7 | Weighted average cost of capital, WACC | 14.00% | | | | | |
| 8 | Long-term FCF growth | 6.00% | | | | | |
| 9 | | | | | | | |
| 10 | Enterprise value, PV of future FCFs + terminal value | 22,512,874 | <-- =NPV(B7,B5:F5) | | | | |
| 11 | Add current cash & marketable securities | 800,000 | | | | | |
| 12 | Firm value | 23,312,874 | <-- =B11+B10 | | | | |
| 13 | | | | | | | |
| 14 | Subtract out debt | -3,200,000 | | | | | |
| 15 | Estimated value of equity | 20,112,874 | <-- =B12+B14 | | | | |
| 16 | | | | | | | |
| 17 | Number of shares | 1,000,000 | | | | | |
| 18 | Estimated value per share | 20.11 | <-- =B15/B17 | | | | |

There are a few things to explain about this valuation:

- We have used the financial planning model of Section 7.4 to project 5 years of future FCFs. At the end of the 5 years, we have projected a *terminal value* for the com-pany. The DCF methodology requires us to estimate the PV of all the future FCFs: $PV \left( \frac{all \ future \ FCFs}{discounted \ at \ WACC} \right)$. However, instead of estimating all future FCFs, we

---

[5] Economists use the term *private benefits* to denote all kinds of financial and nonfinancial benefits asso-ciated with firm ownership. The big car with a driver that the company gives its president is a private benefit of ownership and so is the feeling of ownership—a psychological benefit, perhaps, but nonetheless valuable.

estimate 5 years of FCFs and then estimate the *terminal value*, the value of Whimsical at the end of year 5:

$$Enterprise\ value = PV\left(\begin{array}{c} all\ future\ FCFs \\ discounted\ at\ WACC \end{array}\right)$$

$$= \frac{FCF_{2005}}{(1+WACC)} + \frac{FCF_{2006}}{(1+WACC)^2} + \ldots + \frac{FCF_{2009}}{(1+WACC)^5} + \frac{Terminal\ Value}{(1+WACC)^5}$$

- The terminal value is estimated by assuming that the 2009 FCF of $2,283,085 will grow in years 2010, 2011,... at a long-term FCF growth rate of 6% (cell B8). This means that the terminal value is

$$\begin{aligned} \frac{Terminal\ value}{at\ end\ of\ 2009} &= \frac{FCF_{2010}}{(1+WACC)} + \frac{FCF_{2011}}{(1+WACC)^2} + \frac{FCF_{2012}}{(1+WACC)^3} + \ldots \\ &= \frac{FCF_{2009}*(1+LT\ growth)}{(1+WACC)} + \frac{FCF_{2009}*(1+LT\ growth)^2}{(1+WACC)^2} \\ &\quad + \frac{FCF_{2009}*(1+LT\ growth)^3}{(1+WACC)^3} + \ldots \\ &= \frac{FCF_{2009}*(1+LT\ growth)}{WACC-LT\ growth} \\ &= \frac{\$2,283,085*(1.06)}{14\%-6\%} = \$30,250,880 \end{aligned}$$

The theory behind this is further explained in Section 7.9.

- If the weighted average cost of capital (WACC) is 14%, the enterprise value—the present value of the free cash flows and the terminal value—is $22,512,874 (cell B10 in the previous spreadsheet).[6]
- Adding current balances of cash and marketable securities to the present value of the FCFs and subtracting out the value of the firm's debts gives an *equity valuation* of $20,112,874 (cell B15). Because there are 1 million shares outstanding, this values each share at $20.11 (cell B18).

Thus, the conclusion from this DCF valuation is that the shares of Whimsical Toenails are worth $20.11, more than double their current market value of $10.

## Valuation Using the Firm's Book Value—A Definition We'd Rather Not Use

There's another valuation method that is sometimes used to value a firm: The *accounting definition* of firm value uses the balance sheet to arrive at the value of the firm. For the case of Whimsical Toenails, the balance sheet at the end of 2004 looks like this:

---

[6] See Chapters 6 and 13 for two techniques to compute the WACC.

| | A | B | C | D | E | F |
|---|---|---|---|---|---|---|
| 1 | | WHIMSICAL TOENAILS, BALANCE SHEET 31 December 2004 | | | | | |
| 2 | **Assets** | | | **Liabilities and equity** | | |
| 3 | Cash and marketable securities | 800,000 | | Current liabilities | 800,000 | |
| 4 | Current assets | 1,500,000 | | Debt | 3,200,000 | |
| 5 | Fixed assets at cost | 10,700,000 | | | | |
| 6 | Accumulated depreciation | -3,000,000 | | Common stock | 4,500,000 | |
| 7 | Net fixed assets | 7,700,000 | | Accumulated retained earnings | 1,500,000 | |
| 8 | Total assets | 10,000,000 | <-- =B3+B4++B7 | Total liabilities and equity | 10,000,000 | <-- =SUM(E3:E7) |

By the accounting definition of firm value, the firm is worth

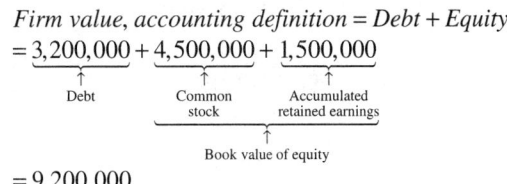

$$Firm\ value,\ accounting\ definition = Debt + Equity$$
$$= \underbrace{3,200,000}_{\text{Debt}} + \underbrace{4,500,000}_{\substack{\text{Common}\\\text{stock}}} + \underbrace{1,500,000}_{\substack{\text{Accumulated}\\\text{retained earnings}}}$$

Book value of equity

$$= 9,200,000$$

The accounting definition of firm value relies on *book values*, the value of the firm's debt and equity as listed in the firm's balance sheet. Recall from Chapter 3 that the accounting definition, which is based on historical values, is a *backward-looking* definition. The finance definition of firm value is a *forward-looking* definition (it discounts the future anticipated values of the cash flows). In general, the accounting definition gives an inappropriate firm valuation.[7] In the case of Whimsical Toenails, the forward-looking DCF valuation of the firm is $23,312,874, whereas the backward-looking accounting definition is $9,200,000.

## 7.7. Using the DCF Valuation—A Summary

The discounted cash flow (DCF) valuation of a firm is based on discounting the firm's future expected free cash flows (FCF), using the weighted average cost of capital (WACC) as the discount rate. In this section we summarize the steps for implementing this valuation.

### Step 1: Estimate the WACC

The WACC is the discount rate for the future FCFs. We discussed the WACC in Chapter 6 and gave an example of how to estimate it.[8] In this chapter we will not go into the details of estimating the WACC; calculating the WACC entails many assumptions and in many cases the calculation itself becomes a topic of controversy among the parties involved in the valuation. For this example, we assume that the WACC is 14%. In Section 7.8 we perform some sensitivity analysis (using an Excel **Data Table**, discussed in Chapters 4 and 27) to show how changes in the WACC affect the valuation.

### Step 2: Project a Reasonable Number of FCFs

A financial planning model's predictions of future FCFs are based on the assumption that the parameters of the model will not change by too much. Most financial analysts define "reasonable"

---

[7] This is not meant to disparage accounting (very important) or accountants (most of whom would readily agree that book values are an inappropriate approximation to market values).

[8] Later in the book, Chapter 13 gives another approach to estimating the WACC.

to mean number of periods over which this basic assumption is not too silly.[9] Everyone recognizes that a firm's environment is dynamic and that the model parameters will change over time, a fact that is usually addressed by doing sensitivity analysis (see Section 7.8). In our valuation we assumed that we can reasonably project the next 5 years of cash flows.

## Step 3: Project the Long-Term FCF Growth Rate and the Terminal Value

Valuation using the DCF method in principle requires us to project an *infinite number* of future FCFs, but in a standard financial planning model we project only a limited number of FCFs. A solution to this problem is to define the firm's terminal value as the firm value at the end of year 5. The definition we use is illustrated in Figure 7.3.

### SCHEMATIC: DCF VALUATION OF THE FIRM

$$DCF\ firm\ value = PV \begin{pmatrix} all\ future\ FCFs \\ discounted\ at\ WACC \end{pmatrix} + \begin{matrix} Current\ cash\ and \\ marketable\ securities \end{matrix}$$

$$= \frac{FCF_1}{(1+WACC)} + \frac{FCF_2}{(1+WACC)^2} + \frac{FCF_3}{(1+WACC)^3} + \ldots + \begin{matrix} Current\ cash\ and \\ marketable\ securities \end{matrix}$$

$$= \frac{FCF_1}{(1+WACC)} + \frac{FCF_2}{(1+WACC)^2} + \frac{FCF_3}{(1+WACC)^3} + \frac{FCF_4}{(1+WACC)^4} + \frac{FCF_5}{(1+WACC)^5} \leftarrow \text{Line 1: We estimate these FCFs with}$$

a financial planning model

$$+ \frac{FCF_6}{(1+WACC)^6} + \frac{FCF_7}{(1+WACC)^7} + \ldots \qquad \leftarrow \text{Line 2: We use the terminal value}$$

in place of these numbers:

$$\frac{1}{(1+WACC)^5} \underbrace{\frac{FCF_5 * (1+long\text{-}term\ FCF\ growth)}{WACC - long\text{-}term\ FCF\ growth}}_{\text{This is the "terminal value"}}$$

$$+ \begin{matrix} Today's\ cash\ and \\ marketable\ securities \end{matrix} \qquad \leftarrow \text{Line 3: The last term in the valuation}$$

FIGURE 7.3  A DCF valuation.

As you can see, there are three parts to this valuation equation:

- Line 1 is the present value of the first 5 years of free cash flows. We projected these cash flows one by one, using our financial planning model.

- Instead of projecting the present value of each of the cash flows in years 6, 7, 8, . . . , infinity, we summarized them in the *present value of the terminal value*. In Line 2 this is given as

$$\frac{1}{(1+WACC)^5} \underbrace{\frac{FCF_5 * (1+long\text{-}term\ FCF\ growth)}{WACC - long\text{-}term\ FCF\ growth}}_{\text{This is the "terminal value"}}.$$

Terminal value is what we project the firm to be worth at the end of the projection horizon. In Section 7.9 we explain how this expression for the terminal value is derived.

- Line 3 gives the value of the cash and marketable securities.

---

[9] The author defines "not too silly" as something he can explain to his mother with a straight face.

The terminal value formula requires us to estimate the long-term FCF growth rate. In the financial planning model for the Whimsical Toenails FCFs, this long-term growth rate is different from the sales growth rate projected for the company's next 5 years. As you saw in Section 7.2, we project a growth rate of sales of 10% for Whimsical over the 5-year horizon of the planning model. Our criterion for choosing the long-term FCF growth rate of the company is that a company's cash flows cannot grow forever at a rate greater than the economy in which it operates. The long-term rate of 6% for Whimsical Toenails is meant to represent an estimate of the company's sustainable FCF growth rate.

Using this model, we estimate that Whimsical's year-5 FCF is $2,283,085. Using the WACC of 14% and the long-term FCF growth rate of 6%, the company's terminal value is $30,250,880:

$$Terminal\ value = \frac{FCF_5 * (1 + long\text{-}term\ FCF\ growth)}{WACC - long\text{-}term\ FCF\ growth} = \frac{\$2,283,085 * (1 + 6\%)}{14\% - 6\%} = \$30,250,880$$

## Step 4: Determine the Value of the Firm

At this point all the elements of the firm valuation formula are in place:

- WACC: the discount rate for the FCFs and the terminal value
- Five years of FCFs projected from the financial planning model
- The terminal value of the firm
- The firm's initial (year 0) balances of cash and marketable securities

We can now value the firm.

| | A | B | C | D | E | F | G |
|---|---|---|---|---|---|---|---|
| 1 | WHIMSICAL TOENAILS–DCF VALUATION | | | | | | |
| 2 | Year | 2005 | 2006 | 2007 | 2008 | 2009 | |
| 3 | Estimated free cash flow | 1,759,895 | 1,881,136 | 2,008,739 | 2,142,733 | 2,283,085 | |
| 4 | Terminal value | | | | | 30,250,880 | <-- =F3*(1+B8)/(B7-B8) |
| 5 | Total | 1,759,895 | 1,881,136 | 2,008,739 | 2,142,733 | 32,533,966 | |
| 6 | | | | | | | |
| 7 | Weighted average cost of capital, WACC | 14.00% | | | | | |
| 8 | Long-term FCF growth | 6.00% | | | | | |
| 9 | | | | | | | |
| 10 | Enterprise value, PV of future FCFs + terminal value | 22,512,874 | <-- =NPV(B7,B5:F5) | | | | |
| 11 | Add current cash & marketable securities | 800,000 | | | | | |
| 12 | Firm value | 23,312,874 | <-- =B11+B10 | | | | |
| 13 | | | | | | | |
| 14 | Subtract out debt | -3,200,000 | | | | | |
| 15 | Estimated value of equity | 20,112,874 | <-- =B12+B14 | | | | |
| 16 | | | | | | | |
| 17 | Number of shares | 1,000,000 | | | | | |
| 18 | Estimated value per share | 20.11 | <-- =B15/B17 | | | | |

The value of the firm is $23,312,874 (cell B10). In cells B15 and B18 we've added two more steps.

## Step 5: Value the Firm's Equity by Subtracting the Value of the Firm's Debt Today from the Firm Value

The firm value is the value of the firm's debt + equity. We are often interested in valuing only the firm's equity—our estimate of the market value of the firm's shares.

$Firm\ value = Debt + Equity = \$23,312,874$
This means that
$Equity = Firm\ value - Debt = \$23,312,874 - \$3,200,000 = \$20,112,874$

Stock market analysts often use the estimate of a firm's equity value to arrive at a per-share valuation of the firm. They then compare this estimated per-share value to the current market price to come up with a buy or sell recommendation for the stock. Because Whimsical Toenails has 1,000,000 shares outstanding, the estimated market value per share is $\frac{\$20,112,874}{1,000,000} = \$20.11$.

This share valuation is much higher than the current market value per share of $10. If the DCF valuation analysis were being used to make recommendations about the stock, we would expect the analyst would make a "buy" recommendation for the shares of Whimsical Toenails.

### Step 6: Adding Mid-year Valuation

In Chapter 5 (page 156) we discussed *mid-year valuation* of cash flows. The idea was that when cash flows occur over the course of the year and not at the end of the year, we should take the standard present value formula and multiply it by $(1 + WACC)^{0.5}$. For Whimsical Toenails, mid-year valuation makes sense, because the company's sales occur throughout the year and not just at year end. In the spreadsheet below you can see how mid-year valuation affects the value of the firm and projected share valuation: Cell B10 shows that the present value of future cash flows and terminal value firm value increases to $24 million. In cell B18 you can see that the projected share value increases to $21.64 from the $20.11 computed without the mid-year valuation.

| | A | B | C | D | E | F | G |
|---|---|---|---|---|---|---|---|
| 1 | WHIMSICAL TOENAILS–DCF VALUATION using mid-year discounting (see cell B10) | | | | | | |
| 2 | Year | 2005 | 2006 | 2007 | 2008 | 2009 | |
| 3 | Estimated free cash flow | 1,759,895 | 1,881,136 | 2,008,739 | 2,142,733 | 2,283,085 | |
| 4 | Terminal value | | | | | 30,250,880 | <-- =F3*(1+B8)/(B7-B8) |
| 5 | Total | 1,759,895 | 1,881,136 | 2,008,739 | 2,142,733 | 32,533,966 | |
| 6 | | | | | | | |
| 7 | Weighted average cost of capital, WACC | 14.00% | | | | | |
| 8 | Long-term FCF growth | 6.00% | | | | | |
| 9 | | | | | | | |
| 10 | PV of future FCFs + terminal value | 24,037,172 | <-- =NPV(B7,B5:F5)*(1+B7)^0.5 | | | | |
| 11 | Add current cash & marketable securities | 800,000 | | | | | |
| 12 | Firm value | 24,837,172 | <-- =B11+B10 | | | | |
| 13 | | | | | | | |
| 14 | Subtract out debt | -3,200,000 | | | | | |
| 15 | Estimated value of equity | 21,637,172 | <-- =B12+B14 | | | | |
| 16 | | | | | | | |
| 17 | Number of shares | 1,000,000 | | | | | |
| 18 | Estimated value per share | 21.64 | <-- =B15/B17 | | | | |

### Step 7: Don't Trust Anything! Do a Sensitivity Analysis

Valuations are based on a formidable number of assumptions! Performing a sensitivity analysis helps us evaluate the effect of changing values of the main variables on the value of the firm. Our "weapon of choice" for sensitivity analysis is the **Data Table** feature of Excel (see Chapter 27). In the next section we demonstrate the use of sensitivity analysis in the DCF valuation of Whimsical Toenails.

## 7.8. Sensitivity Analysis

Given the full-blown financial planning model, there are obviously many sensitivity analyses we can perform. Next we show two data tables. The first table analyzes the effect of the sales

| | A | B | C | D | E | F | G | H | I |
|---|---|---|---|---|---|---|---|---|---|
| 1 | | **WHIMSICAL TOENAILS–FINANCIAL MODEL** | | | | | | | |
| 2 | Sales growth | 10% | | | | | | | |
| 3 | Current assets/Sales | 15% | | | | | | | |
| 4 | Current liabilities/Sales | 8% | | | | | | | |
| 5 | Net fixed assets/Sales | 77% | | | | | | | |
| 6 | Costs of goods sold/Sales | 50% | | | | | | | |
| 7 | Depreciation rate | 10% | | | | | | | |
| 8 | Interest rate on debt | 10.00% | | | | | | | |
| 9 | Interest earned on cash balances | 8.00% | | | | | | | |
| 10 | Tax rate | 40% | | | | | | | |
| 11 | Dividend payout ratio | 40% | | | | | | | |
| 12 | | | | | | | | | |
| 13 | Year | 2004 | 2005 | 2006 | 2007 | 2008 | 2009 | | |
| 14 | Income statement | | | | | | | | |
| 15 | Sales | 10,000,000 | 11,000,000 | 12,100,000 | 13,310,000 | 14,641,000 | 16,105,100 | | |
| 16 | Costs of goods sold | -5,000,000 | -5,500,000 | -6,050,000 | -6,655,000 | -7,320,500 | -8,052,550 | | |
| 17 | Depreciation | -1,000,000 | -1,166,842 | -1,374,773 | -1,613,102 | -1,885,879 | -2,197,668 | | |
| 18 | Interest payments on debt | -320,000 | -280,000 | -200,000 | -120,000 | -40,000 | 0 | | |
| 19 | Interest earned on cash and marketable securities | 64,000 | 57,595 | 47,355 | 42,349 | 42,755 | 80,609 | | |
| 20 | Profit before tax | 3,744,000 | 4,110,753 | 4,522,582 | 4,964,248 | 5,437,376 | 5,935,491 | | |
| 21 | Taxes | -1,497,600 | -1,644,301 | -1,809,033 | -1,985,699 | -2,174,950 | -2,374,196 | | |
| 22 | Profit after tax | 2,246,400 | 2,466,452 | 2,713,549 | 2,978,549 | 3,262,426 | 3,561,295 | | |
| 23 | Dividends | -898,560 | -986,581 | -1,085,420 | -1,191,419 | -1,304,970 | -1,424,518 | | |
| 24 | Retained earnings | 1,347,840 | 1,479,871 | 1,628,130 | 1,787,129 | 1,957,455 | 2,136,777 | | |
| 25 | | | | | | | | | |
| 26 | Balance sheet | | | | | | | | |
| 27 | Cash | 800,000 | 639,871 | 544,001 | 514,730 | 554,145 | 1,461,078 | | |
| 28 | Current assets | 1,500,000 | 1,650,000 | 1,815,000 | 1,996,500 | 2,196,150 | 2,415,765 | | |
| 29 | Fixed assets | | | | | | | | |
| 30 | At cost | 10,700,000 | 12,636,842 | 14,858,615 | 17,403,417 | 20,314,166 | 23,639,190 | | |
| 31 | Depreciation | -3,000,000 | -4,166,842 | -5,541,615 | -7,154,717 | -9,040,596 | -11,238,263 | | |
| 32 | Net fixed assets | 7,700,000 | 8,470,000 | 9,317,000 | 10,248,700 | 11,273,570 | 12,400,927 | | |
| 33 | Total assets | 10,000,000 | 10,759,871 | 11,676,001 | 12,759,930 | 14,023,865 | 16,277,770 | | |
| 34 | | | | | | | | | |
| 35 | Current liabilities | 800,000 | 880,000 | 968,000 | 1,064,800 | 1,171,280 | 1,288,408 | | |
| 36 | Debt | 3,200,000 | 2,400,000 | 1,600,000 | 800,000 | 0 | 0 | | |
| 37 | Stock | 4,500,000 | 4,500,000 | 4,500,000 | 4,500,000 | 4,500,000 | 4,500,000 | | |
| 38 | Accumulated retained earnings | 1,500,000 | 2,979,871 | 4,608,001 | 6,395,130 | 8,352,585 | 10,489,362 | | |
| 39 | Total liabilities and equity | 10,000,000 | 10,759,871 | 11,676,001 | 12,759,930 | 14,023,865 | 16,277,770 | | |
| 40 | | | | | | | | | |
| 41 | | | | | | | | | |
| 42 | Free cash flow calculation | | | | | | | | |
| 43 | Year | 2004 | 2005 | 2006 | 2007 | 2008 | 2009 | | |
| 44 | Profit after tax | | 2,466,452 | 2,713,549 | 2,978,549 | 3,262,426 | 3,561,295 | | |
| 45 | Add back depreciation | | 1,166,842 | 1,374,773 | 1,613,102 | 1,885,879 | 2,197,668 | | |
| 46 | Subtract increase in current assets | | -150,000 | -165,000 | -181,500 | -199,650 | -219,615 | | |
| 47 | Add back increase in current liabilities | | 80,000 | 88,000 | 96,800 | 106,480 | 117,128 | | |
| 48 | Subtract increase in fixed assets at cost | | -1,936,842 | -2,221,773 | -2,544,802 | -2,910,749 | -3,325,025 | | |
| 49 | Add back after-tax interest on debt | | 168,000 | 120,000 | 72,000 | 24,000 | 0 | | |
| 50 | Subtract after-tax interest on cash | | -34,557 | -28,413 | -25,410 | -25,653 | -48,365 | | |
| 51 | Free cash flow | | 1,759,895 | 1,881,136 | 2,008,739 | 2,142,733 | 2,283,085 | | |
| 52 | | | | | | | | | |
| 53 | | | | | | | | | |
| 54 | Valuing the firm | | | | | | | | |
| 55 | Weighted average cost of capital, WACC | 14% | | | | | | | |
| 56 | Long-term growth rate of FCFs, g | 6% | | | | | | | |
| 57 | | | | | | | | | |
| 58 | Year 5 FCF | 2,283,085 | | | | | | | |
| 59 | Terminal value | 30,250,880 | <-- =B58*(1+B56)/(B55-B56) | | | | | | |
| 60 | | | | | | | | | |
| 61 | Year | 2004 | 2005 | 2006 | 2007 | 2008 | 2009 | | |
| 62 | FCF | | 1,759,895 | 1,881,136 | 2,008,739 | 2,142,733 | 2,283,085 | | |
| 63 | Terminal value | | | | | | 30,250,880 | <-- =B59 | |
| 64 | Total | | 1,759,895 | 1,881,136 | 2,008,739 | 2,142,733 | 32,533,966 | | |
| 65 | | | | | | | | | |
| 66 | PV of row 64 | 22,512,874 | <-- =NPV(B55,C64:G64) | | | | | | |
| 67 | Add in initial (year 0) cash and mkt. securities | 800,000 | <-- =B27 | | | | | | |
| 68 | Firm value | 23,312,874 | <-- =B67+B66 | | | | | | |
| 69 | Subtract out value of firm's debt today | -3,200,000 | <-- =-B36 | | | | | | |
| 70 | Equity value | 20,112,874 | <-- =B68+B69 | | | | | | |
| 71 | Per-share equity valuation | 20.11 | <-- =B70/1000000 | | | | | | |
| 72 | | | | | | | | | |
| 73 | Valuing the firm using midyear valuation | | | | | | | | |
| 74 | PV of row 64, with mid-year adjustment | 24,037,172 | <-- =NPV(B55,C64:G64)*(1+B55)^0.5 | | | | | | |
| 75 | Add in initial (year 0) cash and mkt. securities | 800,000 | <-- =B27 | | | | | | |
| 76 | Firm value | 24,837,172 | <-- =B75+B74 | | | | | | |
| 77 | Subtract out value of firm's debt today | -3,200,000 | <-- =-B36 | | | | | | |
| 78 | Equity value | 21,637,172 | <-- =B76+B77 | | | | | | |
| 79 | Per-share equity valuation | 21.64 | <-- =B78/1000000 | | | | | | |
| 80 | | | | | | | | | |
| 81 | Data table: effect of sales growth on share value | **Sales growth** | 21.64 | <-- =B79 | | | | | |
| 82 | | 0% | 20.25 | | | | | | |
| 83 | | 2% | 20.70 | | | | | | |
| 84 | | 3% | 20.89 | | | | | | |
| 85 | | 6% | 21.36 | | | | | | |
| 86 | | 8% | 21.55 | | | | | | |
| 87 | | 10% | 21.64 | | | | | | |
| 88 | | 12% | 21.60 | | | | | | |
| 89 | | 15% | 21.30 | | | | | | |
| 90 | | 20% | 19.98 | | | | | | |
| 91 | | | | | | | | | |

Sales Growth and Share Value

growth assumption (cell B2 of the model) on the share valuation. In our initial model we estimated sales growth of 10% annually for the next 5 years. In rows 81–90, we use the **Data Table** feature of Excel to explore the effect of different rates of sales growth on the share valuation of Whimsical Toenails.

The sales growth assumption produces a surprising result: Up to a point, larger sales growth rates produce large share valuations. But very large growth rates actually reduce the value of the shares.[10]

A second sensitivity analysis examines the effect of the weighted average cost of capital (WACC) and the long-term growth rate (cells B55 and B56) on the per-share valuation. Note that these two parameters affect the valuation in two ways:

- The terminal value calculation in cell G63 is $\dfrac{FCF_5 * (1 + \textit{long-term FCF growth})}{WACC - \textit{long-term FCF growth}}$. This computation is affected by both the long-term growth and the WACC parameters.

- The PV calculation in cell B66 is affected by the WACC.

To examine the effect of these two parameters, we build a two-dimensional data table.

| | A | B | C | D | E | F | G |
|---|---|---|---|---|---|---|---|
| 95 | =IF(B55>B56,B78,"nmf") | | | | | | |
| 96 | | | WACC | | | | |
| 97 | | 21,637,172 | 10% | 14% | 20% | 22% | 24% |
| 98 | | 0% | 20,381,232 | 13,905,234 | 9,073,530 | 8,053,685 | 7,205,794 |
| 99 | Long-term FCF growth | 2% | 24,469,956 | 15,623,442 | 9,743,593 | 8,571,101 | 7,613,120 |
| 100 | | 4% | 31,284,495 | 18,028,934 | 10,581,171 | 9,203,499 | 8,101,912 |
| 101 | | 6% | 44,913,574 | 21,637,172 | 11,658,057 | 9,993,996 | 8,699,323 |
| 102 | | 8% | 85,800,810 | 27,650,902 | 13,093,905 | 11,010,349 | 9,446,088 |
| 103 | | 10% | nmf | 39,678,362 | 15,104,092 | 12,365,487 | 10,406,214 |
| 104 | | 12% | nmf | 75,760,741 | 18,119,373 | 14,262,680 | 11,686,382 |
| 105 | | 14% | nmf | nmf | 23,144,842 | 17,108,469 | 13,478,617 |
| 106 | | 16% | nmf | nmf | 33,195,778 | 21,851,451 | 16,166,970 |
| 107 | | | | | | | |
| 108 | | Note: Data tables are discussed in Chapter 27 | | | | | |

The results produced by this sensitivity analysis are not surprising:

- *Going across rows* shows that as the WACC increases, the value per share decreases. Because a larger WACC means that the present value of a future cash flow is less, this is to be expected.

- *Going down columns* shows that the larger the long-term growth rate expected from Whimsical Toenails, the more the shares are worth. Again, this is not a surprise, because larger long-term growth rates mean higher FCFs after the year-5 model horizon. As noted in the box on the next page, our terminal value model only works when the long-term growth rate is less than the WACC. When this assumption is not true (meaning the long-term growth > WACC), we've had Excel write "nmf" ("no meaningful figure"). The technique for doing this is explained next.

---

[10] The reason for this is probably that large sales growth rates require large amounts of new fixed assets. This reduces the FCFs by enough to also reduce share value.

---

**EXCEL/FINANCE NOTE**

Note our use of the **If** function in cell B97 of the preceding data table. The terminal value formula is

$$Terminal\ value = \frac{FCF_5^*(1 + long\text{-}term\ FCF\ growth\ rate)}{WACC - long\text{-}term\ FCF\ growth\ rate}$$

As noted in Chapter 2 (page 67), this formula is only valid when $WACC > long\text{-}term\ FCF\ growth$. Because some of the combinations of growth and WACC in the data table violate this condition, we've used the **If** function to isolate them. As used in cell B97, this function says

$$If(B55>B56, \quad \underline{B78} \quad , \quad "nmf" \quad )$$

If WACC>long-term FCF growth, put in the valuation as performed in cell B78     If WACC ≤ long-term FCF growth, write "no meaninful figure"

---

## 7.9. Advanced Section: The Theory behind the DCF Model

In this section we explain some theoretical points about the valuation model illustrated in the previous section. Not all of this is easy, and you may (understandably) want to skip this section.[11]

### Why Is the Firm's Value Related to the PV of the Future FCFs?

Our basic valuation formula is

$$Firm\ value = Debt + Equity$$

$$= and\ marketable + \frac{FCF_1}{(1+WACC)^1} + \frac{FCF_2}{(1+WACC)^2} + \frac{FCF_3}{(1+WACC)^3} + ...$$

(Initial cash and marketable securities)

The *enterprise value* of the firm is defined to be the value of the firm's operations. In financial theory, the enterprise value is the present value of the firm's future anticipated cash flows. In this section we explain these concepts.

### The Valuation Process

One way of viewing valuation is through the use of the accounting paradigm, but using market values. We rewrite the balance sheet by moving the current liabilities from the liabilities/equity side to the asset side of the balance sheet.

---

[11] Why would an author put a section like this in this book? Our experience is that ultimately almost all finance professionals are called upon to do valuations. At some point in every valuation, someone is going to question your techniques and theory. That's the time to come back to this section.

| USING THE BALANCE SHEET AS AN ENTERPRISE VALUATION MODEL | | |
|---|---|---|
| **ORIGINAL BALANCE SHEET** | | |
| **Assets** | **Liabilities** | |
| Cash and marketable securities | Operating current liabilities | |
| Operating current assets | Debt | |
| Net fixed assets | Equity | |
| Goodwill | | |
| **Total assets** | **Total liabilities and equity** | |
| | | |
| | | |
| **THE ENTERPRISE VALUATION "BALANCE SHEET"** | | |
| **Assets** | **Liabilities** | |
| Cash and marketable securities | | |
| Operating current assets | Debt | |
| - Operating current liabilities | | =PV(FCFs discounted at WACC) |
| = Net working capital | | |
| Net fixed assets | Equity | |
| Goodwill | | |
| **Firm value** | **Firm value** | |

To value a company, we set

$$Firm\ value = Initial\ cash\ balances + \sum_t \frac{FCF_t}{(1 + WACC)^t}$$
$$= Initial\ cash\ balances + Enterprise\ value$$

If we are valuing the equity of the firm, we subtract the value of the debt:

$$Equity\ value = Firm\ value - Debt$$
$$= Initial\ cash\ balances + \sum_t \frac{FCF_t}{(1 + WACC)^t} - Debt$$
$$= \sum_t \frac{FCF_t}{(1 + WACC)^t} - (Debt - Initial\ cash)$$

Note that this means that we can write the enterprise balance sheet in a slightly different form.

| THE ENTERPRISE VALUATION "BALANCE SHEET" A slight variation (cash netted out from debt) | | |
|---|---|---|
| | | |
| **Assets** | **Liabilities** | |
| Operating current assets | Debt - cash & Mkt. securities | |
| - Operating current liabilities | = Net debt | |
| = Net working capital | | =PV(FCFs discounted at WACC) |
| Net fixed assets | Equity | |
| Goodwill | | |
| **Enterprise Value** | **Enterprise Value** | |
| Note that both variations on the enterprise valuation "balance sheet" give the same equity value. | | |

We can use the FCF projections and a cost of capital to determine the enterprise value of the firm. Suppose we have determined that the firm's weighted average cost of capital (WACC) is 20%.[12] Then the *enterprise value* of the firm is the discounted value of the firm's projected FCFs plus its terminal value.

$$Enterprise\ value = \frac{FCF_1}{(1+WACC)^1} + \frac{FCF_2}{(1+WACC)^2} + ... + \frac{FCF_5}{(1+WACC)^5} + \frac{Year\text{-}5\ Terminal\ Value}{(1+WACC)^5}$$

In this formula, the *Year-5 Terminal Value* is a proxy for the present value of all FCFs from year 6 onward.[13]

## Terminal Value

In determining the terminal value we use a version of the Gordon model described in Chapter 6. We have assumed that—after the year-5 projection horizon—the cash flows will grow at a long-term FCF growth of 6%. This gives the terminal value as

$$Terminal\ Value\ at\ end\ of\ year\ 5 = \sum_{t=1}^{\infty} \frac{FCF_{t+5}}{(1+WACC)^t} = \sum_{t=1}^{\infty} \frac{FCF_5 * (1 + LT\ FCF\ growth)^t}{(1+WACC)^t}$$
$$= \frac{FCF_5 * (1 + LT\ FCF\ growth)}{WACC - growth}$$

The last equality is derived in a manner similar to the dividend valuation of shares (the Gordon model) discussed in Chapter 6.

# Conclusion

In this chapter we've used Excel to construct financial planning models. These models, also called pro forma models or financial planning models, have a variety of uses in finance. Financial planning models are at the heart of most business plans, the financial projections that firms use to persuade banks to loan them money and to persuade investors to buy their shares. Financial planning models are used to value firms (see Chapter 8) and to build scenarios showing how the firm will perform under various operating and financial assumptions.

Building a financial planning model is a powerful intellectual exercise: It forces you to combine accounting statements, a firm's operational parameters, and the firm's financing into one integrated model of the firm.

To do a DCF valuation you have to understand almost all facets of the business:

- How the business works—this affects the financial parameters used in the financial planning model. The composition of the firm's current assets and current liabilities (meaning its net working capital needed to do its business) and the amount of fixed assets (buildings and equipment and land) needed to do this business—all of these factors affect a firm's valuation.
- How to compute the cost of capital. The WACC is the discount rate used to value the future FCFs of the firm. In this chapter we have not discussed its computation (Chapters 6 and 13 give different methods of computing the WACC).
- How to use Excel to do the relevant computations.

---

[12] In Chapter 6 we introduced the topic of the WACC and showed you how to calculate this using the Gordon dividend model. In Chapter 13 we show an alternative calculation of the WACC that uses the security market line. In this chapter we simply assume a value for the WACC.

[13] We don't actually project these cash flows. We determine the terminal value based on year-5 FCF.

# Exercises

Note: The CD-ROM that comes with *Principles of Finance with Excel* contains an Excel notebook entitled **PFE2, chapter07template.xlsm**. Except for Exercise 1, this template can be used as the basis for almost all the problems (although you may have to make some changes in the template).

1. The following data describes the activity of your firm in the previous year:
   - The company's cash at the end of the year was $105,000.
   - The company owes $20,000 to its suppliers.
   - The company bought securities in the amount of $22,000.
   - The company's income during the year was $170,000. Of this amount only 70% was paid.
   - The company was forced to pay damages to one of its clients of $40,000. This amount has still not been paid.
   - The company had materials inventory of $7,500 and product materials of $5,000 at the end of the year.
   - The company has to pay $12,000 to its bank in the following year.
   - The company tax payment is $45,000. Half of the taxes remain unpaid and are due in the current year.
   - The company rented a store for 3 years at the beginning of the year, paying $14,000 for each year in advance for the entire period.

   Calculate the firm's operating current assets and its operating current liabilities.

2. Build a financial model on the following template. Assuming that the WACC is 20%, value the company's equity.

| | A | B | C | D | E | F | G |
|---|---|---|---|---|---|---|---|
| 1 | FINANCIAL MODEL TEMPLATE | | | | | | |
| 2 | Sales growth | 10% | | | | | |
| 3 | Current assets/Sales | 15% | | | | | |
| 4 | Current liabilities/Sales | 8% | | | | | |
| 5 | Net fixed assets/Sales | 77% | | | | | |
| 6 | Costs of goods sold/Sales | 50% | | | | | |
| 7 | Depreciation rate | 10% | | | | | |
| 8 | Interest rate on debt | 10.00% | | | | | |
| 9 | Interest paid on cash and marketable securities | 8.00% | | | | | |
| 10 | Tax rate | 40% | | | | | |
| 11 | Dividend payout ratio | 40% | | | | | |
| 12 | | | | | | | |
| 13 | Year | 0 | 1 | 2 | 3 | 4 | 5 |
| 14 | Income statement | | | | | | |
| 15 | Sales | 1,000 | | | | | |
| 16 | Costs of goods sold | (500) | | | | | |
| 17 | Interest payments on debt | (32) | | | | | |
| 18 | Interest earned on cash and marketable securities | 6 | | | | | |
| 19 | Depreciation | (100) | | | | | |
| 20 | Profit before tax | 374 | | | | | |
| 21 | Taxes | (150) | | | | | |
| 22 | Profit after tax | 225 | | | | | |
| 23 | Dividends | (90) | | | | | |
| 24 | Retained earnings | 135 | | | | | |
| 25 | | | | | | | |
| 26 | Balance sheet | | | | | | |
| 27 | Cash and marketable securities | 80 | | | | | |
| 28 | Current assets | 150 | | | | | |
| 29 | Fixed assets | | | | | | |
| 30 | At cost | 1,070 | | | | | |
| 31 | Depreciation | (300) | | | | | |
| 32 | Net fixed assets | 770 | | | | | |
| 33 | Total assets | 1,000 | | | | | |
| 34 | | | | | | | |
| 35 | Current liabilities | 80 | | | | | |
| 36 | Debt | 320 | | | | | |
| 37 | Stock | 450 | | | | | |
| 38 | Accumulated retained earnings | 150 | | | | | |
| 39 | Total liabilities and equity | 1,000 | | | | | |

3.

   a. The model in Exercise 2 includes costs of goods sold but not selling, general, and administrative (SG&A) expenses. Suppose that the firm has $200 of these expenses each year, irrespective of the level of sales. Change the model to accommodate this new assumption. Show the resulting income statements, balance sheets, the free cash flows (FCF), and the valuation.

   b. Build a data table in which you show the sensitivity of the equity value to the level of SG&A. Let SG&A vary from $0 per year to $600 per year.

4. Suppose that in the model in Exercise 2 the fixed assets *at cost* for years 1–5 are 100% of sales (in the current model, it is *net* fixed assets that are a function of sales). Change the model accordingly. Show the resulting income statements, balance sheets, and free cash flows (FCF) for years 1–5. (Assume that in year 0, the fixed assets accounts are as shown in Section 7.2. Note that because year 0 is given—it is the current situation of the firm, whereas years 1-5 are the predictions for the future—there is no need for the year 0 ratios to conform to the predicted ratios for years 1–5.)

5. Back to the model of Exercise 2. Suppose that the fixed assets at cost follow the following step function:

$$Fixed\ Assets\ at\ Cost = \begin{cases} 100\% * Sales & if\ Sales \leq 1,200 \\ 1,200 + 90\% * (Sales - 1,200) & 1,200 \quad Sales \leq 1,400 \\ 1,380 + 80\% * (Sales - 1,400) & Sales \quad 1,400 \end{cases}$$

Incorporate this function into the model.

6.

   a. Consider the model in Exercise 2. Make two changes in the model: (i) Let debt be the plug and keep cash constant at its year-0 level. (ii) Suppose that the firm has 1,000 shares and that it decides to pay, in year 1, a dividend per share of $0.15. In addition, suppose that it wants this dividend per share to grow in subsequent years by 12% per year. Incorporate these changes into the pro forma model.

   b. Do a sensitivity analysis in which you show the effect on the debt/equity ratio of the annual growth rate of dividends. Vary this rate from 0 to 18%, in steps of 2%.

7. The Excel sheet below presents a firm's balance sheet and income statement.

Assume the following:

- The firm expects its sales growth rate to be 10% per year.
- The current assets at the end of each year are 20% of the annual firm sales.
- The current liabilities at the end of each year are 15% of the annual firm sales.
- The net fixed assets at the end of each year are 320% of annual sales.
- The annual depreciation is 5% of the average of the fixed assets value during the year.
- The cost of goods sold is 50% of sales.
- Interest earned on cash is 5% on the average balances of cash.
- The tax rate is 40%.

Use the above data to project the financial statements for year 1.

| | A | B |
|---|---|---|
| 1 | **BALANCE SHEET AND INCOME STATEMENT** | |
| 2 | Year | 0 |
| 3 | **Income statement** | |
| 4 | Sales | 50,000 |
| 5 | Costs of goods sold | (25,000) |
| 6 | Depreciation | (20,000) |
| 7 | Interest earned on cash | 7,000 |
| 8 | Profit before tax | 12,000 |
| 9 | Taxes (40%) | (4,800) |
| 10 | Profit after tax | 7,200 |
| 11 | Retained earnings | 7,200 |
| 12 | | |
| 13 | **Balance sheet** | |
| 14 | Cash | 140,000 |
| 15 | Accounts receivable | 10,000 |
| 16 | Fixed assets | |
| 17 | At cost | 400,000 |
| 18 | Depreciation | (240,000) |
| 19 | Net fixed assets | 160,000 |
| 20 | **Total assets** | 310,000 |
| 21 | | |
| 22 | Current liabilities | 20,000 |
| 23 | Debt | - |
| 24 | Stock | 275,000 |
| 25 | Accumulated retained earnings | 15,000 |
| 26 | **Total liabilities and equity** | 310,000 |

8.

a. Extend the model of the previous exercise to 5 years.

b. The model in Exercise 8a contains the costs of goods sold (COGS) but doesn't contain selling, general, and administrative expenses (SG&A). Assume that this cost is $2,000 in year 0 and has a growth rate of 7.5%. Make the appropriate adjustment to the model of Exercise 8a.

9. The following sheet presents a firm's balance sheets and income statement.

| | A | B | C | D | E |
|---|---|---|---|---|---|
| 1 | **BALANCE SHEET AND INCOME STATEMENT** | | | | |
| 2 | **Assets** | | | **Liabilities and Equity** | |
| 3 | **Current assets** | | | **Current liabilities** | |
| 4 | Cash | 10,000 | | Accounts payable | 2,000 |
| 5 | Prepaid expenses | 1,500 | | **Total current liabilities** | 2,000 |
| 6 | **Total current assets** | 11,500 | | | |
| 7 | | | | **Long-term liabilities** | |
| 8 | | | | Debt | 10,000 |
| 9 | **Fixed assets** | | | | |
| 10 | At cost | 30,000 | | **Equity** | |
| 11 | Accumulate depreciation | -14,000 | | Equity | 10,500 |
| 12 | **Net Fixed assets** | 16,000 | | Accumulated retained earnings | 5,000 |
| 13 | | | | | |
| 14 | **Total assets** | 27,500 | | **Total liabilities and equity** | 27,500 |
| 15 | | | | | |
| 16 | **Income statement** | | | | |
| 17 | Sales | 20,000 | | | |
| 18 | Cost of Goods Sold (COGS) | -12,000 | | | |
| 19 | Depreciation | -2,000 | | | |
| 20 | Interest on cash | 300 | | | |
| 21 | Interest payments on debt | -400 | | | |
| 22 | Profit before tax | 5,900 | | | |
| 23 | Tax (40%) | -2,360 | | | |
| 24 | Profit after tax | 3,540 | | | |
| 25 | Dividend | -708 | | | |
| 26 | Retained Earnings | 2,832 | | | |

a. You believe that these financial statements are representative of the firm's *value drivers* (For example, if the sales are $20,000 and the COGS are $12,000, then the COGS to sales parameter is 60%). Find and calculate the *value drivers* that can be derived from the firm's balance sheet and P&L statement.

b. Use the following data to project the financial statements for year 1:
   • The sales growth is 12%.
   • The depreciation is 10% of the average of the fixed assets value during the year.
   • The interest rate earned on cash is 5% on the average cash balances.
   • The debt payments are $2,000 each year.
   • The interest rate on debt is 8%.

c. Show in a graph the change in the firm's profit relative to the change in the COGS.

10.

a. Extend the project of the previous exercise to 6 years.

b. The model we are dealing with doesn't contain advertising and marketing costs (these are usually a part of the SG&A). Assume that these costs are $800 in year 0 and 5% of sales in years 1–6. Furthermore, assume that the firm has to pay each year for its license a fixed cost of $1,500. Adjust the model in Exercise 10a to these new assumptions.

c. Show in a graph the change in the firm's profit relative to the change in the license fee.

11. Compute the FCF for the firm model in Exercise 8a and Exercise 10a.

12. Compute the consolidated statements of cash flow for the firm's model of Exercise 8a and Exercise 10a.

13. The following sheet contains data concerning Donna Company's balance sheet, income statement, and its value drivers.

| | A | B | C | D | E | F | G |
|---|---|---|---|---|---|---|---|
| 1 | DONNA'S BALANCE SHEET AND INCOME STATEMENT | | | | | | |
| 2 | **Value Drivers** | | | | | | |
| 3 | Sales growth | 15% | | | | | |
| 4 | Current assets/sales | 20% | | | | | |
| 5 | Current liabilities/sales | 14% | | | | | |
| 6 | Net fixed assets/sales | 80% | | | | | |
| 7 | Costs of goods sold/sales | 45% | | | | | |
| 8 | Depreciation rate | 10% | | | | | |
| 9 | Interest rate on debt | 8% | | | | | |
| 10 | Interest earned on average cash balances | 5% | | | | | |
| 11 | Tax rate | 36% | | | | | |
| 12 | Dividend payout ratio | 30% | | | | | |
| 13 | Annual debt repayments | 6,000 | | | | | |
| 14 | | | | | | | |
| 15 | **Income statement** | | | | | | |
| 16 | **Year** | **0** | **1** | **2** | **3** | **4** | **5** |
| 17 | Sales | 45,000 | | | | | |
| 18 | Cost of goods sold (COGS) | -33,000 | | | | | |
| 19 | Depreciation | -4,000 | | | | | |
| 20 | Interest on cash | 80 | | | | | |
| 21 | Interest payments on debt | -150 | | | | | |
| 22 | Profit before tax | 7,930 | | | | | |
| 23 | Tax (36%) | -2,855 | | | | | |
| 24 | Profit after tax | 5,075 | | | | | |
| 25 | Dividend | -1,523 | | | | | |
| 26 | Retained earnings | 3,553 | | | | | |
| 27 | | | | | | | |
| 28 | **Balance sheet** | | | | | | |
| 29 | **Assets** | | | | | | |
| 30 | Cash | 10,000 | | | | | |
| 31 | Current assets | 4,700 | | | | | |
| 32 | Fixed assets | | | | | | |
| 33 | At cost | 47,000 | | | | | |
| 34 | Accumulated depreciation | -14,000 | | | | | |
| 35 | Net Fixed assets | 33,000 | | | | | |
| 36 | **Total assets** | 47,700 | | | | | |
| 37 | | | | | | | |
| 38 | **Liabilities and Equity** | | | | | | |
| 39 | Current liabilities | 4,000 | | | | | |
| 40 | Debt | 30,000 | | | | | |
| 41 | Equity | | | | | | |
| 42 | Equity | 10,000 | | | | | |
| 43 | Accumulated retained earnings | 3,700 | | | | | |
| 44 | **Total liabilities and equity** | 47,700 | | | | | |

You know that Donna Company pays $6,000 of its debt every year and that the interest rate, paid and earned, is on the average debt and cash balances, respectively, and the depreciation is on the average fixed assets.

Make a model of Donna's balance sheet, income statement, and its FCF evaluation for the following 5 years based on these data.

14. Consider the following changes in the assumptions regarding Donna Company from Exercise 13:

- Assume the debt remains at its current level and the loan is paid back only at the end of year 5.
- The dividend has a constant growth of 15%, irrelevant of the increase in the company sales.
- The company pays a bonus of 5% from sales to its employees if the sales are more than $70,000.

Combine these changes to the pro forma model and the FCF evaluation.

15. How will your answer to Exercise 13 change if you know that Donna Company intends to increase its debt by 6% each year for the next 5 years and that the current liabilities are 25% of COGS?

16. The following sheet presents the balance sheet of your firm.

| | A | B | C | D | E |
|---|---|---|---|---|---|
| 1 | | **BALANCE SHEET** | | | |
| 2 | **Assets** | | | **Liabilities and Equity** | |
| 3 | **Current assets** | | | **Current liabilities** | |
| 4 | Cash | 72,000 | | Accounts payable | 40,000 |
| 5 | Marketable securities | 80,000 | | Tax payable | 35,000 |
| 6 | Accounts receivable | 42,000 | | Short-term debt | 32,000 |
| 7 | Prepaid expenses | 15,000 | | **Total current liabilities** | 107,000 |
| 8 | **Total current assets** | 209,000 | | | |
| 9 | | | | **Long-term liabilities** | |
| 10 | | | | Debt | 420,000 |
| 11 | **Fixed assets** | | | | |
| 12 | At cost | 500,000 | | **Equity** | |
| 13 | Accumulated depreciation | -25,000 | | Equity | 120,000 |
| 14 | **Net fixed assets** | 475,000 | | Accumulated retained earnings | 37,000 |
| 15 | | | | | |
| 16 | **Total assets** | 684,000 | | **Total liabilities and equity** | 684,000 |

What is the firm's value according to the share price valuation model if the share price in the market is $5.50 and there are 90,000 outstanding shares?

17. What is the share value of the firm of Exercise 16 using the book value? How do you explain the difference between this valuation and the per-share market price?

18. The Yahoo! profile for PepsiCo Company (PEP) is given below. What is PEP's firm value according to the share price valuation model? What is the PEP book value?

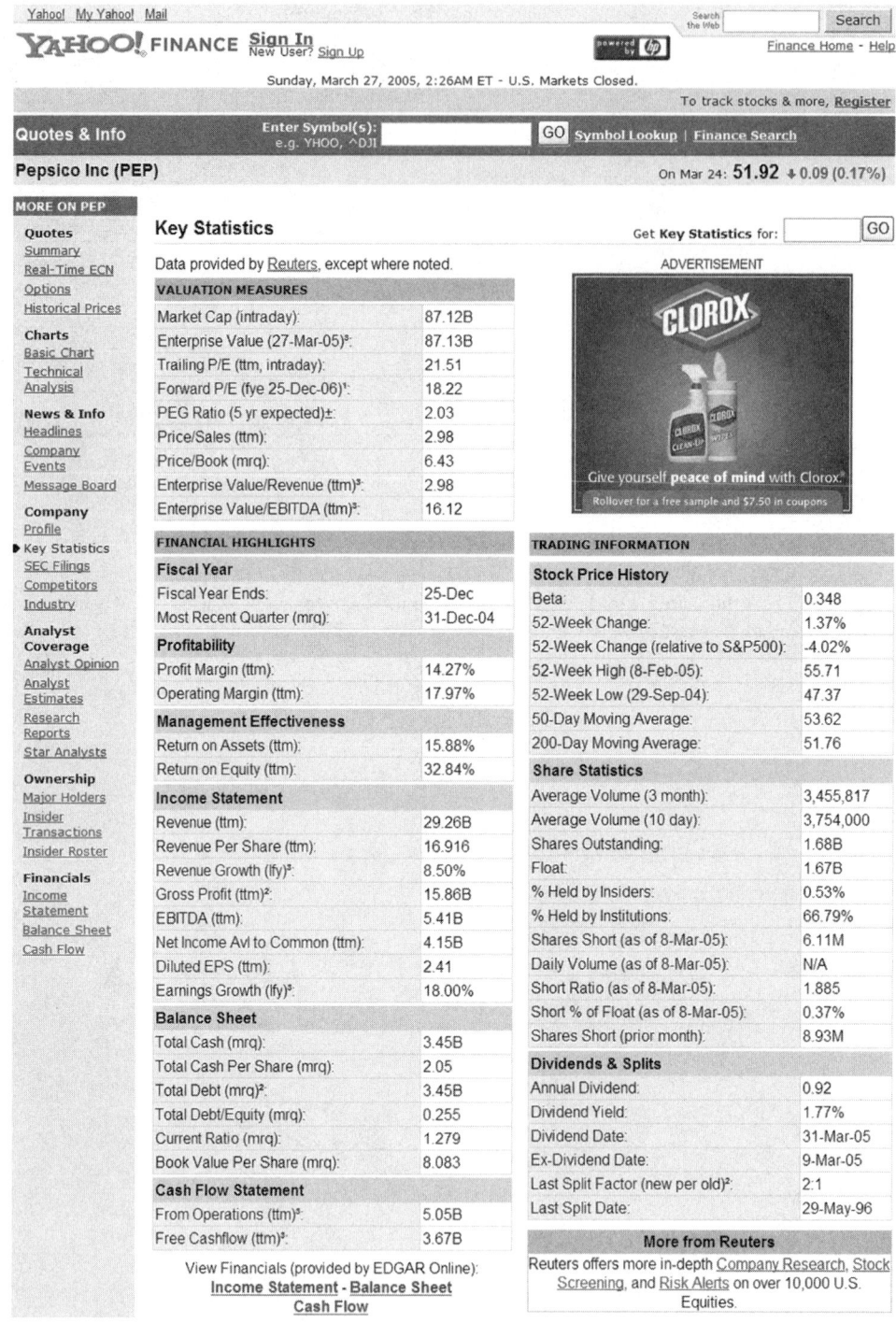

19. The Yahoo! profile for Boeing (BA) is given below. What is BA's firm value according to the share price valuation model? What is BA's book value?

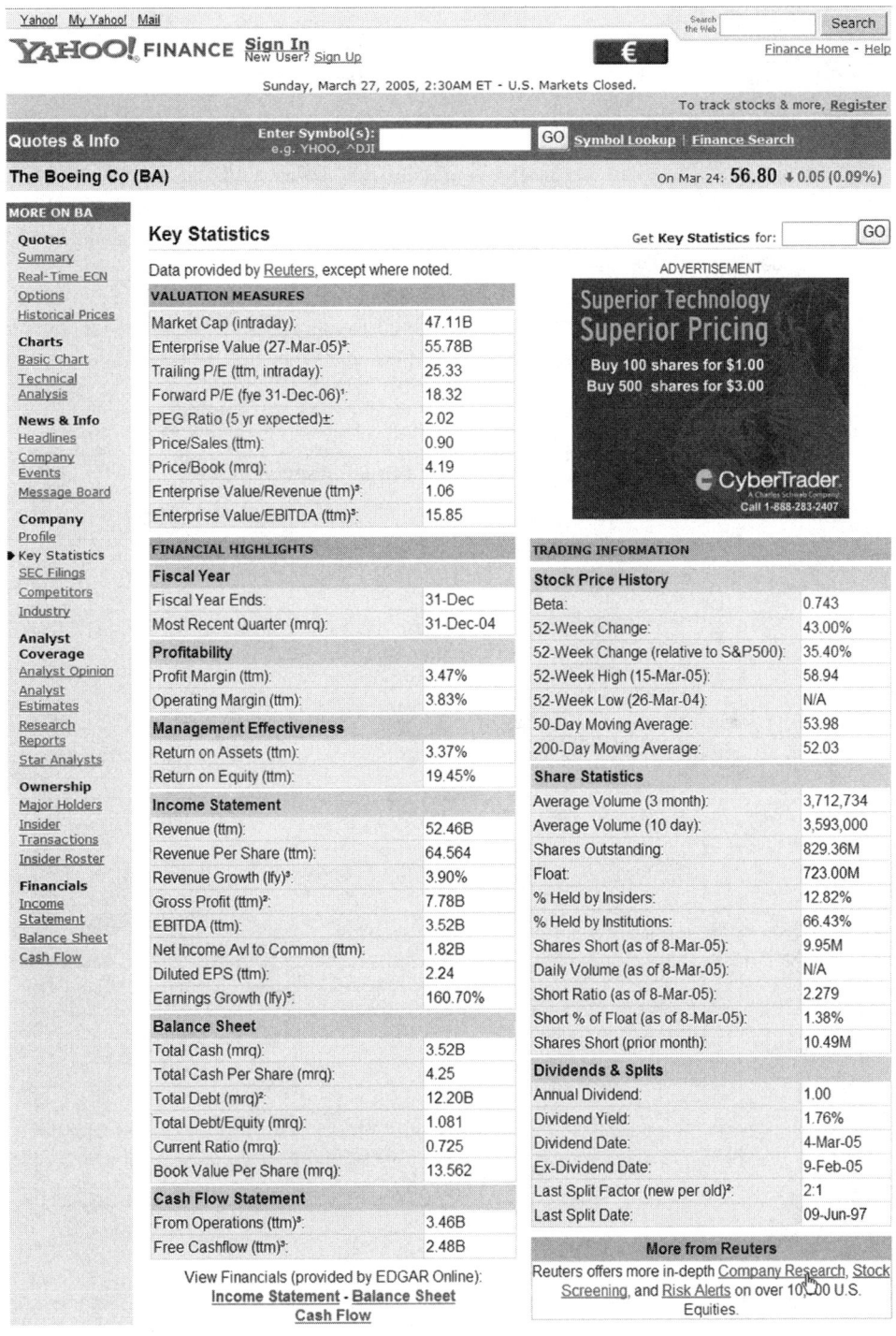

20. Go back to the firm of Exercise 16. In the firm's board meeting it was decided to evaluate the firm using the DCF evaluation, and after performing evaluation you came up with the data described in the following sheet.

| | A | B | C | D | E | F |
|---|---|---|---|---|---|---|
| 1 | DCF VALUATION | | | | | |
| 2 | Year | 1 | 2 | 3 | 4 | 5 |
| 3 | Estimated free cash flow | 220,115 | 232,150 | 274,410 | 315,145 | 316,000 |
| 4 | Terminal value | | | | | 750,456 |
| 5 | Total | 220,115 | 232,150 | 274,410 | 315,145 | 1,066,456 |

What is the firm's equity value, assuming the firm's WACC is 18% and using the firm's balance sheet? What is the equity value per share?

21. Repeat Exercise 20, but instead of using the firm's terminal value, assume that the FCF of the firm from the 6th year will remain constant forever (perpetuity cash flow). Use mid-year discounting.

22. The following sheet presents the balance sheet and value drivers of Yummy Company, which manufactures a very special tomato sauce.

| | A | B | C |
|---|---|---|---|
| 1 | Yummy Company, Financial model | | |
| 2 | Value drivers: | | |
| 3 | Sales growth | 12% | |
| 4 | Current assets/Sales | 22% | |
| 5 | Current liabilities/Sales | 20% | |
| 6 | Net fixed assets | 5% | |
| 7 | Costs of goods sold/Sales | 45% | |
| 8 | Depreciation rate | 20% | |
| 9 | Interest rate on debt | 8.00% | |
| 10 | Interest earned on cash balances | 4.00% | |
| 11 | Tax rate | 36% | |
| 12 | Dividend payout ratio | 25% | |
| 13 | Sales | 2,000,000 | |
| 14 | Weighted average cost of capital | 16% | |
| 15 | Long-term FCF growth rate | 4% | |
| 16 | | | |
| 17 | Balance sheet | | |
| 18 | Cash | 460,000 | |
| 19 | Current assets | 440,000 | |
| 20 | Fixed assets | | |
| 21 | At cost | 4,000,000 | |
| 22 | Depreciation | (500,000) | |
| 23 | Net fixed assets | 3,500,000 | |
| 24 | Total assets | 4,400,000 | |
| 25 | | | |
| 26 | Current liabilities | 400,000 | |
| 27 | Debt | 3,000,000 | |
| 28 | Stock (1,500,000 shares, issued at $0.5 each) | 750,000 | |
| 29 | Accumulated retained earnings | 250,000 | |
| 30 | Total liabilities and equity | 4,400,000 | |
| 31 | | | |

Additional model assumptions are as follows:

• The FCF evaluation is for a 5-year period. In addition, a terminal value should be determined using the long-term FCF growth rate.

- The debt principal repayments are $300,000 each year.
- Cash is a plug in the model.

Make a pro forma model for Yummy and compute the firm value using a DCF valuation model with year-end discounting.

23. Compute the following while referring to Yummy Company from Exercise 22:
    - Show how the company value and its share value change if you use mid-year discounting.
    - Show in a graph the sensitivity of the enterprise value (of the end-year calculation) to the growth in sales.
    - Show in a graph the sensitivity of the enterprise value (of the end-year calculation) to the company's WACC.

24. The following sheet presents the balance sheet and value drivers of Little India, a company that operates Indian food restaurants.

|  | A | B | C |
|---|---|---|---|
| 1 | **Little India, Financial model** | | |
| 2 | **Value drivers:** | | |
| 3 | Sales growth | 25% | |
| 4 | Current assets/Sales | 10% | |
| 5 | Current liabilities/Sales | 30% | |
| 6 | Net fixed assets | 15% | |
| 7 | Costs of goods sold/Sales | 35% | |
| 8 | Depreciation rate | 5% | |
| 9 | Interest rate on debt | 8.00% | |
| 10 | Interest earned on cash balances | 3.00% | |
| 11 | Tax rate | 40% | |
| 12 | Dividend payout ratio | 20% | |
| 13 | Sales | 1,100,000 | |
| 14 | Weighted average cost of capital | 12% | |
| 15 | Long-term FCF growth rate | 3% | |
| 16 | | | |
| 17 | **Balance sheet** | | |
| 18 | Cash | 370,000 | |
| 19 | Current assets | 110,000 | |
| 20 | Fixed assets | | |
| 21 | At cost | 2,000,000 | |
| 22 | Depreciation | (500,000) | |
| 23 | Net fixed assets | 1,500,000 | |
| 24 | **Total assets** | 1,980,000 | |
| 25 | | | |
| 26 | Current liabilities | 330,000 | |
| 27 | Debt | 1,000,000 | |
| 28 | Stock (500,000 shares, issued at $1 each) | 500,000 | |
| 29 | Accumulated retained earnings | 150,000 | |
| 30 | **Total liabilities and equity** | 1,980,000 | |
| 31 | | | |

Additional model assumptions are as follows:

- The FCF evaluation is for a 5-year period. In addition, a terminal value should be determined using the long-term FCF growth rate.
- The debt principal repayments are $200,000 each year.
- Cash is a plug in the model.

Make a pro forma model including a DCF valuation to determine the company value and its estimated share value using a mid-year discounting.

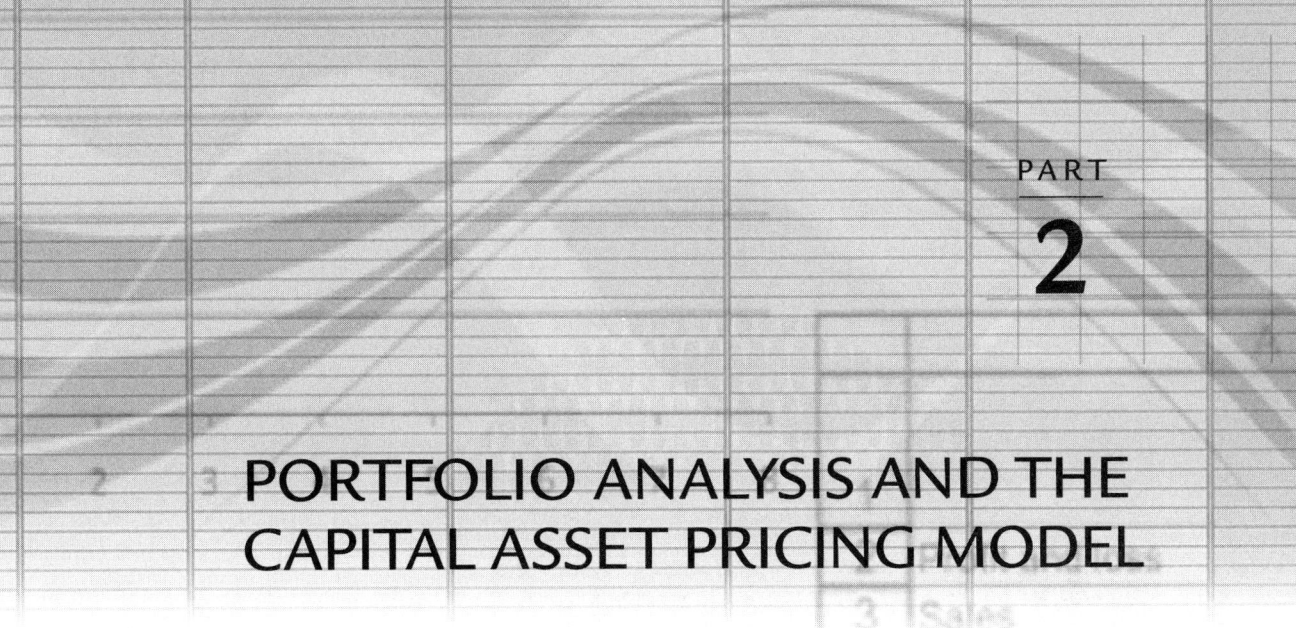

# PORTFOLIO ANALYSIS AND THE CAPITAL ASSET PRICING MODEL

P<small>ART</small> 2 OF *P<small>RINCIPLES OF</small> F<small>INANCE WITH</small> E<small>XCEL</small>* discusses how portfolio composition affects the risk of the combined assets. Most individuals hold investment portfolios composed of multiple stocks and bonds. This means that the risk of the investment portfolio is related to the combined riskiness of the securities in the portfolio, as opposed to the riskiness of the individual portfolio assets.

Chapter 8 starts by introducing and illustrating the concept of financial risk. This chapter examines the three components of an asset's risk: horizon, safety, and liquidity. Using illustrations from the stock and bond markets, we show how even safe assets can be risky. We also show how risk can be measured.

To discuss portfolio risks, you will need some statistical background. Chapter 9 develops the statistical concepts that you need to analyze portfolios. Although many readers of *Principles of Finance with Excel* have had a statistics course, Chapter 9 assumes virtually no background. Of course Excel—with its many mathematical and statistical functions—is extraordinarily helpful in doing portfolio statistics.

Chapters 10 and 11 combine the statistical analysis of portfolios with some basic economics. The result is the capital asset pricing model (CAPM). This model relates portfolio returns to portfolio risks (a concept summarized in the capital market line, the CML). The CAPM also relates the risks of individual assets to their returns, a concept known as the security market line (SML).

Chapters 12 and 13 show how the SML can be used. In Chapter 12 we examine the uses of the SML to measure portfolio performance: How well do portfolio managers perform, given the riskiness of their portfolios? Chapter 13 returns to the concept of the weighted average cost of capital (WACC) first discussed in Chapter 6; this chapter shows how the SML can be used to compute the cost of equity and the WACC.

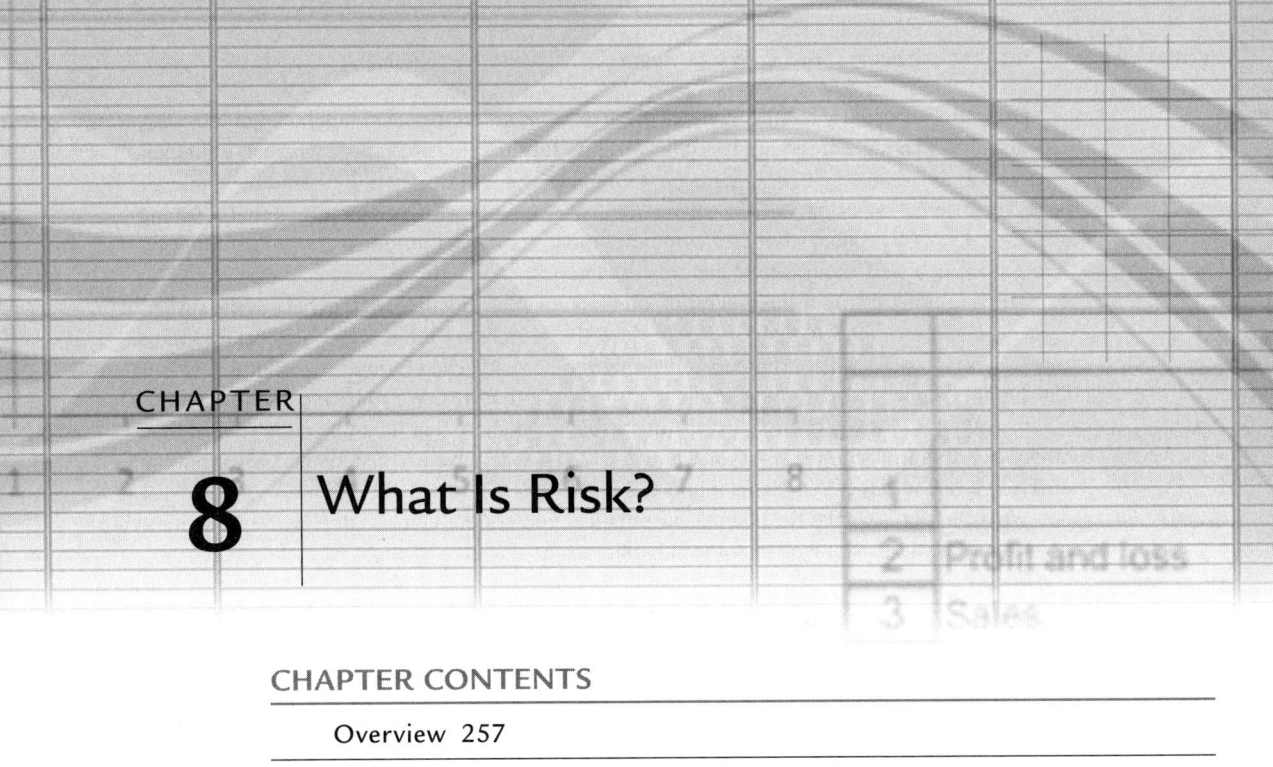

# CHAPTER

# 8 | What Is Risk?

## CHAPTER CONTENTS

## Overview

Risk is the magic word in finance. Whenever finance people can't explain something, we try to look confident and say "it must be the risk." If you want to appear intelligent when hearing a financial presentation, look skeptical and say "Have you considered the risks?" Usually that's enough to score a point or two.[1]

---

[1] I give my students the following hint about taking finance exams: Suppose you have to answer a question to which you absolutely don't know the answer ("What is the zeta function of the annual returns?" "How do you explain the difference between XYZ Corp's annual returns over time?"). If you know nothing about the question, make up a meaningless sentence that includes the word "risk" ("The zeta function of the annual returns relates to the riskiness of the returns." "XYZ's annual returns vary because of the changing risk of the company.") You're bound to get a point or two.

Our intuition usually relates financial risks to *unpredictability*. A financial asset like a savings account is thought to be not risky because its future value is known, whereas a financial asset like a stock is risky because we do not know what it will be worth in the future. Financial assets of different types have different gradations of risk: Our intuitions tell us that a savings account is less risky than a share in a company, and a share in a high-tech start-up is more risky than a share in a well-established blue-chip company.

The intuition that ties unpredictability and risk together is valid, but can have some surprising aspects. For example, in Section 8.2 we show that a Treasury bill ("T-bill"), a certain kind of bond issued by the U.S. government, can sometime be risky, even though it is completely safe. The T-bill becomes risky if you need to sell it before it matures. We illustrate this risk with an example. We also look at the risk of holding a share and show that it can be quantified statistically. This is an important insight for Chapters 12–14, where we use a statistical description of stock price risk to talk about choosing portfolios of stocks.

We have tried to make the chapter unstatistical and nonmathematical. However, inevitably the measurement of risk involves some calculations.[2]

## Finance Concepts Discussed

- Ex post and ex ante returns
- Holding-period returns
- Treasury bond returns
- Return statistics—mean, variance, and standard deviation

## Excel Functions Used

- **Sqrt**
- **Average**
- **Stdevp**
- **Varp**
- **Frequency**
- **Count**
- **Ln**

# 8.1. The Risk Characteristics of Financial Assets

In the course of your life you'll be exposed to many financial assets. You've already been exposed to them, even if you didn't know that they were "financial assets": When you were small, your parents might have opened a savings account for you at the local bank, or your grandparents bought you a few shares of stock. Now that you're a student, you're stuck with student loans, and each month you're trying to decide whether to pay off your credit card balances or let them ride

---

[2]Students reading this book will generally have had a statistics course. This chapter assumes some familiarity with basic statistical concepts and Chapter 9 reviews these concepts in the context of financial assets. In this sense Chapters 8 and 9 are twins.

for another month and pay interest on them. Once you finish school, you'll be taking a car loan, buying a house and taking a mortgage, buying stocks and bonds, . . . .

All financial assets have different characteristics of *horizon*, *safety*, and *liquidity*. As you will see, all three of these terms are in some basic sense indicative of the asset's riskiness. In this section we briefly review these concepts.

## Horizon

Some assets are *short term* and others *long term*. Money deposited in a checking account is a good example of a *very short-term* financial asset; the money can be withdrawn at any time. On the other hand, many savings accounts require you to deposit the money for a given period of time. Look at Figure 8.1, which shows the rates offered on certificates of deposits (CD) by Discover Bank of Delaware. A CD is a time-deposit at a bank—a deposit that cannot be withdrawn for a certain period of time without the payment of a penalty. Not surprisingly, longer-term CDs offer higher interest rates.

You're not always "locked in" to a financial asset with a long horizon. Many long-horizon assets can be sold in the open market. Suppose, for example, that you buy a 10-year government bond. You can "cash out" of the bond at almost any time by selling the bond in the open market, but selling the bond before its 10-year maturity exposes you to the riskiness of an unknown market price. This subject is explored in detail in Section 8.2.

Some assets have a long and indeterminate horizon. A share of stock in a company is a good example. Holding a share of McDonald's stock, for example, entitles you to whatever dividends the company pays its shareholders for as long as you hold the stock and the company exists. You can, of course, sell the stock in the stock market, but this exposes you to the risks of the stock price fluctuations. In Section 8.3 we discuss how to analyze the riskiness of stock holding; this is a topic to which we return in much greater detail in Chapters 9–13.

## Safety

Financial assets differ in the certainty with which you get back your money. The Discover Bank CDs in Figure 8.1 are guaranteed by the Federal Deposit Insurance Corporation, an agency of the U.S. government, up to a limit of $250,000. Up to this limit, the purchaser of a Discover Bank CD will get his money back (including interest), even if the bank fails to meet its obligations.

Figure 8.2 compares the rates offered by Discover Bank to those available to investors in bonds issued by the General Motors Acceptance Corporation (GMAC). The market rates on GMAC bonds are much higher than those of Discover. However, there is a distinct difference in safety between these two types of securities: When this data was collected in May 2009, General Motors, the parent company of GMAC, was close to bankruptcy, and the uncertainty associated with actualizing the GMAC yields was great. Subsequently, the company went into bankruptcy. Clearly an investment in GMAC bonds is much less safe than an investment in a Discover Bank CD.

In general, the less safe an asset, the greater the return investors will demand and expect from the asset. Thus, for example, if Discover Bank's CDs pay interest of between 1 and 4%, intelligent holders of McDonald's stock (less safe and more uncertain than a CD) should expect a return greater than 1 to 4%.

# CD Rates & Calculator

As of: April 28, 2009

| Term | Interest Rate | APY⁴ |
|------|--------------|------|
| 3 months | 1.25% | 1.25% |
| 6 months | 1.74% | 1.75% |
| 9 months | 1.89% | 1.90% |
| **1 year** | **2.33%** | **2.35%** |
| 1½ years | 2.47% | 2.50% |
| 2 years | 2.72% | 2.75% |
| 2½ years | 2.72% | 2.75% |
| 3 years | 3.06% | 3.10% |
| 4 years | 3.25% | 3.30% |
| 5 years | 3.54% | 3.60% |
| 7 years | 3.64% | 3.70% |
| 10 years | 3.93% | 4.00% |

FIGURE 8.1 Discover Bank of Delaware offers certificates of deposit (CD) with varying maturities. The difference between "interest rate" and "APY" (annual percentage yield) stems from the fact that Discover's quoted interest rate is compounded daily. For example, the 10-year interest rate of 3.93% gives an APY of $\left(1+\dfrac{3.93\%}{365}\right)^{365}-1=4\%$. This topic has been previously discussed in Chapter 3.

This business of "expected return" is complicated:

- If you buy a Discover Bank 5-year CD, you are promised an annual return of 3.60%. You will get this annual return with absolute certainty (well, *almost absolutely*: There's always the remote possibility of a catastrophe that prevents both Discover Bank and the U.S. government from honoring their obligations). For the Discover Bank 5-year CD, the *expected return* and the *realized return* (by which we mean the actual return received) are the same. In economists' jargon, the expected return is often called the *ex*

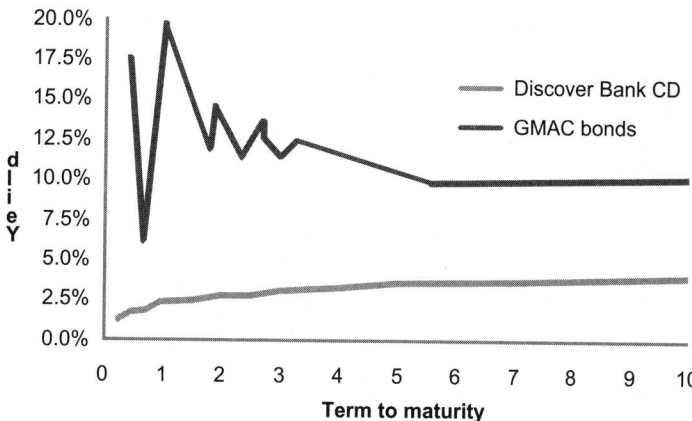

FIGURE 8.2  GMAC bonds are much more risky than Discover Bank CDs! Not surprisingly the promised yield of the GMAC bonds is much higher than that of the (very safe) Discover Bank CDs.

*ante return* and the realized return is often called the *ex post* return (this terminology is derived from Latin words for "before" and "after").

- If you buy a share of McDonald's stock, you will *expect* to get more than 3.60% annual return. However, in this case this *expectation* is merely an *anticipated average future return*. In other words, you would be disappointed but not too surprised if the actual annual return on the stock after 5 years was less than 3.60%.

## Liquidity

The *ease* with which an asset can be bought or sold is the asset's *liquidity*. In general, the more liquid an asset, the easier it is to "get rid of" and the lower its risk.

Listed stocks of major American companies have very high liquidity. For the 10 years between 1999 and 2008, the average daily number of McDonald's shares traded (meaning shares bought and sold) on the New York Stock Exchange was 6.2 million shares. This is the average; the highest number of shares traded daily was almost 87 million and the lowest number of shares was 1.3 million. If you want to buy or sell a single share of stock (or even several thousand shares), you'll have no trouble doing so: McDonald's stock is very liquid.

Liquidity has another aspect, which financial economists call *price impact*. Suppose you decided to sell the 1,000 shares of McDonald's stock your grandmother gave you. You'll have no trouble selling the stock, but will your sale affect the market price? For McDonald's stock the answer is no.

Not all stocks are equally liquid. Audiovox, which trades on the NASDAQ exchange, is a much smaller company than McDonald's. On an average day, around 165,000 shares of Audiovox are bought and sold, but in the 10 years between 1999 and 2008, this number has been as low as 3,600 shares per day. You would have relatively little trouble buying or selling several thousand shares of Audiovox stock, but your action might well affect the market price of the stock. Audiovox is not nearly as liquid as McDonald's and consequently has greater liquidity risk.

## What Now?

*Horizon, safety, and liquidity* all determine the *risk* of a financial asset. In the succeeding sections we'll give some concrete examples. We start by looking at the risks inherent in holding a

U.S. Treasury bill. A T-Bill is completely *safe*, in the sense that the U.S. Treasury will keep its obligation to pay back the money borrowed. It's also very *liquid*—billions of dollars of T-bills are bought and sold every day in the financial market. However, we'll show that the *horizon* of a T-bill means that it is *somewhat risky*—if you try to sell it before it matures, the market price is unpredictable.

From the T-bill we move on to an analysis of the risks inherent in McDonald's stock. McDonald's stock is *not safe* in the sense that the company makes no promises about either the dividends or the future market price of the stock. We'll analyze the returns on McDonald's stock over the decade 1990–2000 and we'll try to make some statistical sense out of these returns.

## IS IT RISK OR UNCERTAINTY?

Frank H. Knight (1885–1972) wrote a dissertation in 1921 called *Risk, Uncertainty and Profit*. Knight used *risk* to mean *randomness with knowable probabilities* and *uncertainty* to mean *randomness that is unmeasurable*. In finance the distinction between these two concepts is often blurred and in this book the words "risk" and "uncertainty" are used interchangeably.

## 8.2. A Safe Security Can Be Risky Because It Has a Long Horizon

Finance people use the words "risk free" and "riskless" to describe an asset whose value in the future is known with certainty. One classic textbook example of a risk-free asset is a bank savings account. If you deposit $100 in your federally insured bank savings account that currently earns 10%, then you *know* that 1 year from now there will be $110 in the account. It's risk free and it's safe.

A U.S. Treasury bill is an example of a safe asset that is not riskless. Treasury bills are short-term bonds issued by the government of the United States.[3] Unlike bank CDs, Treasury bills do not have an explicit interest rate. Instead they are sold at a discount—a bill with a face value of $1,000 that matures 1 year from now might be sold today for $953.04. In this case the purchaser of the bill who holds the bill to maturity would be paid $1,000 by the U.S. Treasury and would thus earn a rate of return of $\frac{1,000}{953.04} - 1 = 4.93\%$. Treasury bills are issued by the U.S. government, and thus at least one kind of risk—default risk—is absent from these instruments: Because the government owns the printing machines that produce dollar bills, they can always run off a few dollars to make good on their promises.

Although Treasury bills are free of default risk, however, they may have elements of *price risk*. The rest of this section illustrates this.

Suppose that on 1 June 2008 you buy a 1-year $1,000 U.S. Treasury bill, intending to hold the bill until its maturity on 1 June 2009. As we said, a Treasury bill doesn't pay any interest; instead, it is bought at a discount—that is, for less than its face value. In the case at hand, suppose you buy the bill for $977.04; because it matures in 1 year after the purchase, you anticipated getting interest of 2.35%:

---

[3]There are many different kinds of bonds. For a more complete discussion, see Chapter 15.

| | A | B | C |
|---|---|---|---|
| 1 | **INTEREST ON THE TREASURY BILL** | | |
| 2 | Purchase price | 977.04 | |
| 3 | Payoff on maturity | 1,000.00 | <-- This is the Treasury bill's face value |
| 4 | Interest | 2.35% | <-- =B3/B2-1 |

Now before we start doing fancier calculations, let's make one thing perfectly clear: *If you hold the Treasury bill from 1 June 2008 until its maturity 1 year later, you will absolutely, definitely earn 2.35% interest.* T-bills are obligations of the U.S. government, which has never defaulted on them.

In finance jargon the *ex ante* return (sometimes called the *anticipated* or *expected* return) is the return you *think* you're going to get. The *ex post* return (also called the *realized* return) is the *actual* return that you get when you sell the asset. For the Treasury bill illustrated here, the ex ante return equals the ex post return *if you hold the bill until maturity.* This is always true for riskless bonds.

## The Price Risk of Treasury Bills

Out of curiosity, you track the market price of the bill on the first of each month during the year. Here's what you find.

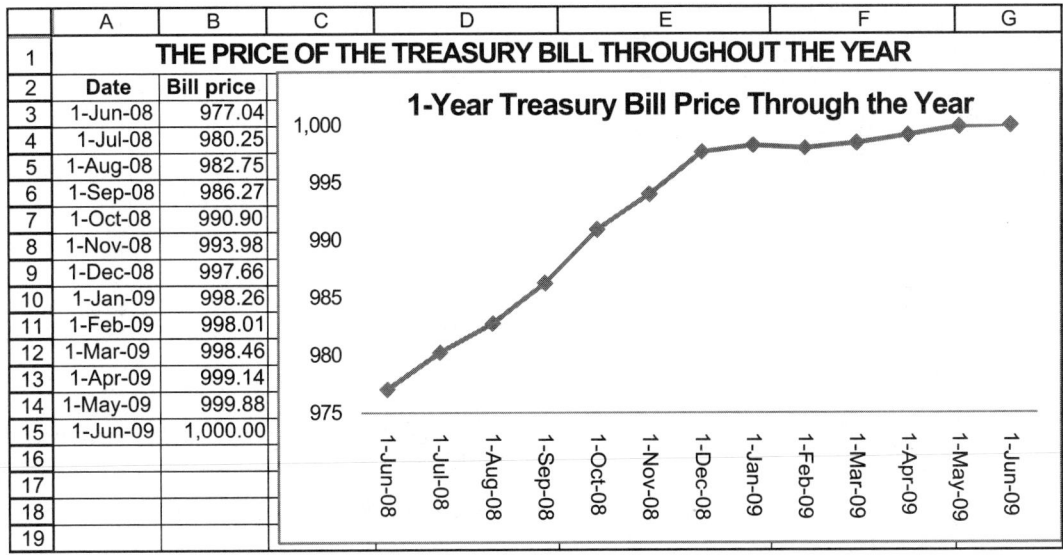

| | A | B | C | D | E | F | G |
|---|---|---|---|---|---|---|---|
| 1 | **THE PRICE OF THE TREASURY BILL THROUGHOUT THE YEAR** | | | | | | |
| 2 | **Date** | **Bill price** | | | | | |
| 3 | 1-Jun-08 | 977.04 | | | | | |
| 4 | 1-Jul-08 | 980.25 | | | | | |
| 5 | 1-Aug-08 | 982.75 | | | | | |
| 6 | 1-Sep-08 | 986.27 | | | | | |
| 7 | 1-Oct-08 | 990.90 | | | | | |
| 8 | 1-Nov-08 | 993.98 | | | | | |
| 9 | 1-Dec-08 | 997.66 | | | | | |
| 10 | 1-Jan-09 | 998.26 | | | | | |
| 11 | 1-Feb-09 | 998.01 | | | | | |
| 12 | 1-Mar-09 | 998.46 | | | | | |
| 13 | 1-Apr-09 | 999.14 | | | | | |
| 14 | 1-May-09 | 999.88 | | | | | |
| 15 | 1-Jun-09 | 1,000.00 | | | | | |
| 16 | | | | | | | |
| 17 | | | | | | | |
| 18 | | | | | | | |
| 19 | | | | | | | |

We use these monthly price data to compute some returns.

## What ex Post Rate of Return Would You Have Earned If You'd Sold the Treasury Bill Early?

Suppose you had sold the T-bill after 3 months on 1 September 2008 for $986.27. What would you have earned? A relatively simple calculation provides the answer. The monthly rate of return—the *ex post* return—is defined by

$$1 + \textit{ex-post monthly rate of return} = \left( \frac{\textit{Price on } 1 \textit{ September } 2008}{\textit{Initial price on } 1 \textit{ June } 2008} \right)^{1/3}$$

$$= \left( \frac{986.27}{977.04} \right)^{1/3} = 1.0031$$

The exponent of 1/3 is there because of the 3-month interval between June and September. If we raise this to the 12th power, we will get an annual rate of return of 3.83%.

|  | A | B | C |
|---|---|---|---|
| 1 | **ANNUALIZED EX-POST RETURN, June-September** | | |
| 2 | Bought 1 June 2008 | 977.04 | |
| 3 | Sold 1 September 2008 | 986.27 | |
| 4 | Monthly return | 0.31% | <-- =(B3/B2)^(1/3)-1 |
| 5 | Annualized return | 3.83% | <-- =(1+B4)^12-1 |

If, instead, you had sold the Treasury bill on August 1, 1 month earlier, you would have made 3.56% in annual terms.

|  | A | B | C |
|---|---|---|---|
| 1 | **ANNUALIZED EX-POST RETURN, June-August** | | |
| 2 | Bought 1 June 2008 | 977.04 | |
| 3 | Sold 1 August 2008 | 982.75 | |
| 4 | Monthly return | 0.29% | <-- =(B3/B2)^(1/2)-1 |
| 5 | Annualized return | 3.56% | <-- =(1+B4)^12-1 |

We can do this exercise for each of the months from July 2008 to May 2009. In the spreadsheet below we calculate the ex post, annualized return from selling the Treasury bill at the beginning of July, August, ... May.

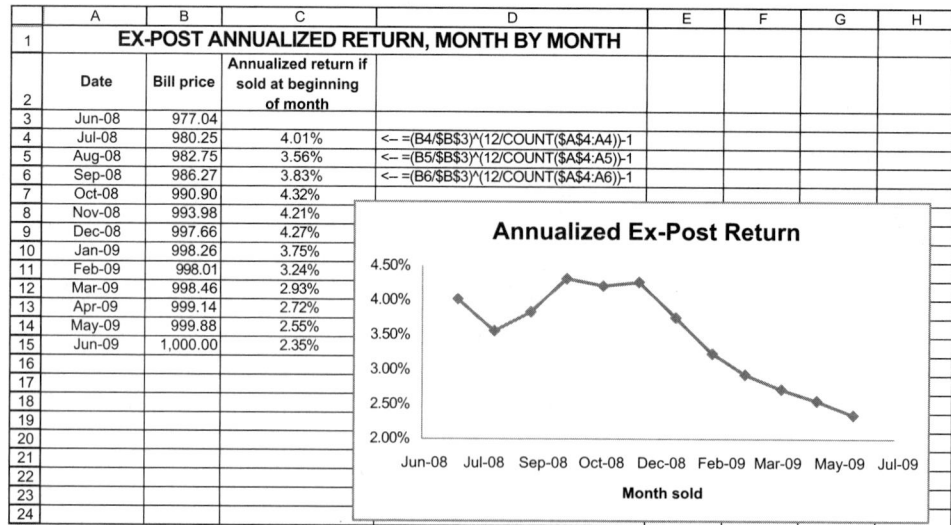

| | A | B | C | D | E | F | G | H |
|---|---|---|---|---|---|---|---|---|
| 1 | **EX-POST ANNUALIZED RETURN, MONTH BY MONTH** | | | | | | | |
| 2 | Date | Bill price | Annualized return if sold at beginning of month | | | | | |
| 3 | Jun-08 | 977.04 | | | | | | |
| 4 | Jul-08 | 980.25 | 4.01% | <-- =(B4/$B$3)^(12/COUNT($A$4:A4))-1 | | | | |
| 5 | Aug-08 | 982.75 | 3.56% | <-- =(B5/$B$3)^(12/COUNT($A$4:A5))-1 | | | | |
| 6 | Sep-08 | 986.27 | 3.83% | <-- =(B6/$B$3)^(12/COUNT($A$4:A6))-1 | | | | |
| 7 | Oct-08 | 990.90 | 4.32% | | | | | |
| 8 | Nov-08 | 993.98 | 4.21% | | | | | |
| 9 | Dec-08 | 997.66 | 4.27% | | | | | |
| 10 | Jan-09 | 998.26 | 3.75% | | | | | |
| 11 | Feb-09 | 998.01 | 3.24% | | | | | |
| 12 | Mar-09 | 998.46 | 2.93% | | | | | |
| 13 | Apr-09 | 999.14 | 2.72% | | | | | |
| 14 | May-09 | 999.88 | 2.55% | | | | | |
| 15 | Jun-09 | 1,000.00 | 2.35% | | | | | |
| 16 | | | | | | | | |
| 17 | | | | | | | | |
| 18 | | | | | | | | |
| 19 | | | | | | | | |
| 20 | | | | | | | | |
| 21 | | | | | | | | |
| 22 | | | | | | | | |
| 23 | | | | | | | | |
| 24 | | | | | | | | |

As you can see, if the T-bill is sold before its maturity, there is a considerable amount of risk—defined here as the possible variation in the ex post rate of return. The Treasury bill—a complete safe security in the sense that the U.S. Treasury will always make good on its obligation—has price risk that translates to risky returns if sold before maturity.

---

## EXCEL NOTE

The interest rate calculations above use the following formula:

$$r_{monthly} = 1 + \text{monthly interest rate} = \left( \frac{\textit{T-bill price, month t}}{\textit{T-bill purchase price}} \right)^{\frac{1}{\textit{number of months held}}}$$

$$r_{annual} = 1 + \text{annual interest rate} = \left( 1 + r_{monthly} \right)^{12}$$

To calculate the number of months the T-bill has been held, we use the Excel function **Count**. For example, to see how many months we've held the T-bill if we buy at the beginning of June 2008 and sell at the beginning of September 2008, we use COUNT($A$4:A6). This counts the number of cells between A6 and A4 (the months July, August, and September). The clever use of the dollar signs ensures that when the formula is copied it always starts counting from July.

---

## What ex Ante Rate of Return Would You Have Earned If You'd Bought the T-Bill During the Year?

In the previous exercise we calculated the ex post rate of return you would have earned if you had bought the T-bill on 1 June 2008 and had sold it before the bill's maturity on 1 June 2009. There's a second "game" we can play with the T-bill prices. Suppose you had bought the bill at the beginning of August for 982.74 and suppose you intended to hold it for 10 months until maturity in June 2009. What's the annualized ex ante return you could expect? We can compute this by first computing the monthly ex ante return and then annualizing this return in a manner similar to our computation for the ex post returns.

$$1 + \textit{ex-ante monthly rate of return} = \left( \frac{1{,}000}{\textit{Price on 01August08}} \right)^{1/10}$$

$$= \left( \frac{1{,}000}{982.75} \right)^{1/10} = 1.00174$$

$$\textit{Annualized ex-ante return} = \left( 1.00174 \right)^{12} - 1 = 2.11\%$$

If we do this for each of the months, we'll see that throughout the year from June 2008 to June 2009 the ex ante rate on Treasury bills fell.

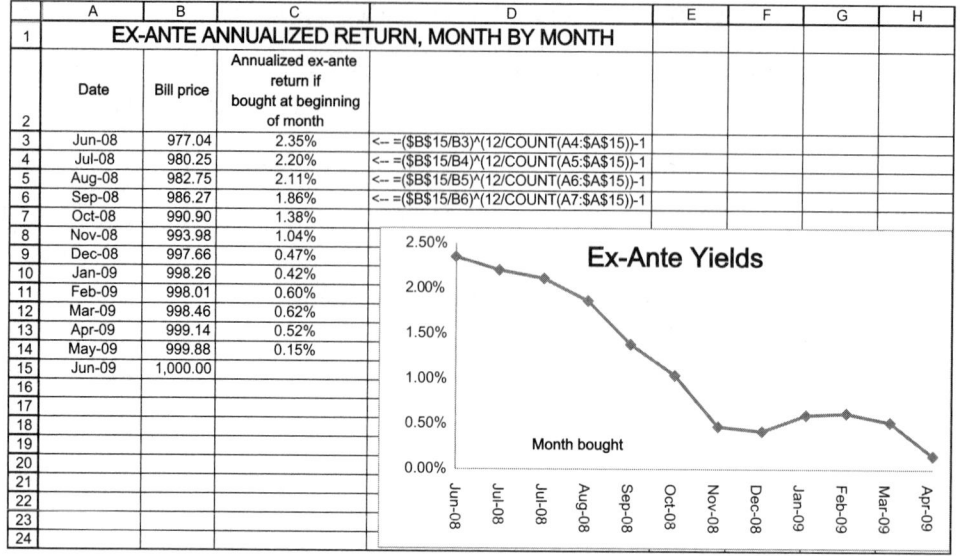

## What's the Message?

This example, which illustrates the riskiness of a "riskless" U.S. Treasury bill, illustrates that financial risk depends on horizon: A financial asset can be riskless over one horizon and risky over another. In our example, buying the Treasury bill at any point during the year and holding it until maturity *guarantees* that the *ex ante* return will equal the *ex post* return. On the other hand, selling the bill before its maturity involves risk—in this case the realized return (the ex post return) varies.

## A Final Word: What Caused the Riskiness of the Treasury Bills?

We've shown that holding a T-bill during June 2008–June 2009 could have been pretty risky—if you were thinking of selling the bill before maturity. The cause of this was, of course, the terrible mayhem in financial markets during this period. To keep the banking system afloat, the Federal Reserve Bank flooded the markets with money. Interest rates declined almost monthly. The results are clear in our discussion of the risks of holding or buying a Treasury bill.

# 8.3. Risk in Stock Prices—McDonald's Stock

A U.S. Treasury bill is a relatively simple security: The issuer is very well-known and has never defaulted, the *ex ante* return can be derived from the price, and this return is guaranteed if you hold the bill until maturity. A stock has none of these properties and is thus in every sense riskier. The problem is how to quantify this risk.

Here's an example—Figure 8.3 shows how the stock price of McDonald's varied from 31 December 1998 to 31 December 2008.

The fact that the stock's price goes up and down is an indication of the stock's riskiness. If we calculate the daily returns, we see a different kind of risk. Below we calculate the *daily return* from holding McDonald's stock—this is what you would earn in percentages if you bought the stock at its closing price on day $t$ and sold it at its closing price on day $t + 1$.

$$Daily\,return,\,day\,t = \frac{P_{t+1}}{P_t} - 1$$

FIGURE 8.3  The stock price of McDonald's, 31 December 1998–31 December 2008. Over the decade the stock price climbed from $31.69 to $60.58 per share, but with considerable volatility. The compound annual growth rate of the share price was 6.69% (this computation assumes that dividends were reinvested to purchase more stock).

If you plot the daily returns for 1 month, you get a very spiky pattern.

| | A | B | C | D |
|---|---|---|---|---|
| 1 | McDONALD'S--DAILY STOCK PRICES DURING DECEMBER 2008 | | | |
| 2 | | Stock price | Daily return | |
| 3 | 28-Nov-08 | 57.23 | | |
| 4 | 1-Dec-08 | 54.71 | -4.40% | <-- =B4/B3-1 |
| 5 | 2-Dec-08 | 55.57 | 1.57% | <-- =B5/B4-1 |
| 6 | 3-Dec-08 | 58.01 | 4.39% | <-- =B6/B5-1 |
| 7 | 4-Dec-08 | 59.26 | 2.15% | <-- =B7/B6-1 |
| 8 | 5-Dec-08 | 61.09 | 3.09% | <-- =B8/B7-1 |
| 9 | 8-Dec-08 | 59.34 | -2.86% | |
| 10 | 9-Dec-08 | 58.13 | -2.04% | |
| 11 | 10-Dec-08 | 60.06 | 3.32% | |
| 12 | 11-Dec-08 | 59.29 | -1.28% | |
| 13 | 12-Dec-08 | 59.02 | -0.46% | |
| 14 | 15-Dec-08 | 59.12 | 0.17% | |
| 15 | 16-Dec-08 | 61.29 | 3.67% | |
| 16 | 17-Dec-08 | 61.01 | -0.46% | |
| 17 | 18-Dec-08 | 59.70 | -2.15% | |
| 18 | 19-Dec-08 | 58.76 | -1.57% | |
| 19 | 22-Dec-08 | 59.81 | 1.79% | |
| 20 | 23-Dec-08 | 59.08 | -1.22% | |
| 21 | 24-Dec-08 | 59.69 | 1.03% | |
| 22 | 26-Dec-08 | 59.48 | -0.35% | |
| 23 | 29-Dec-08 | 58.81 | -1.13% | |
| 24 | 30-Dec-08 | 60.14 | 2.26% | |
| 25 | 31-Dec-08 | 60.58 | 0.73% | |

If you plot the daily returns for all 2,515 data points, you get a very "noisy" pattern.

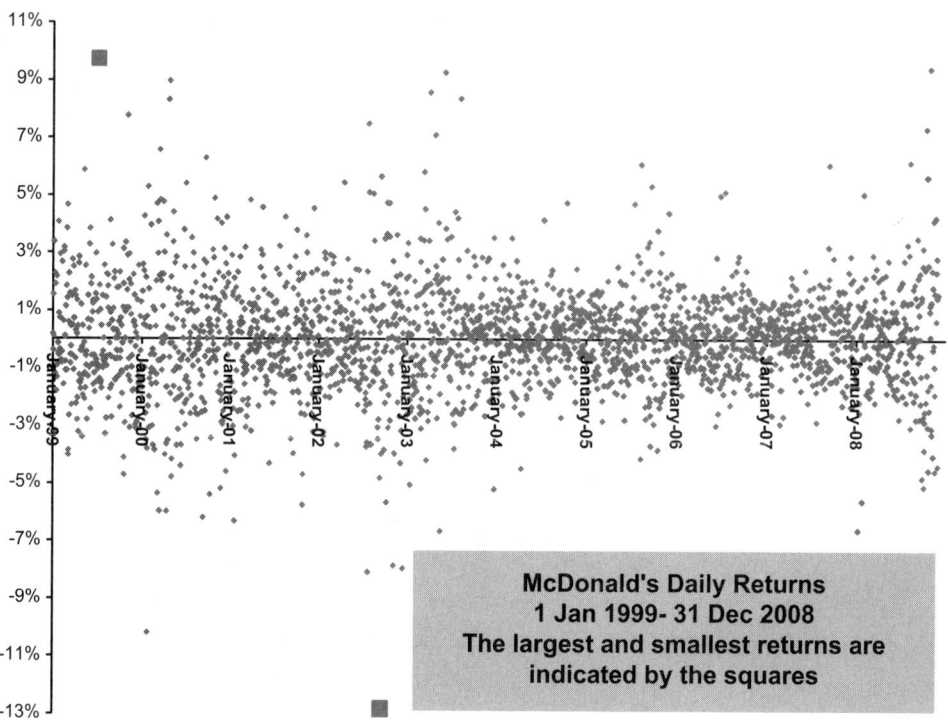

Each dot represents the return on McDonald's stock on a particular day. Although there are dots all over the place, there seem to be slightly more dots above the x-axis than below it, indicating that on average the return on McDonald's stock was positive. The highest and lowest daily returns over the period are indicated by the square markers: On 9 July 1999 the price of McDonald's stock went up by 9.68% and on 17 September 2002 the price went down by 12.82%.

## The Distribution of McDonald's Stock Returns

The previous two graphs show the return on McDonald's stock on each specific date. These graphs clearly show that the stock is risky—the returns vary from day to day—but they don't give much insight into the statistical nature of the riskiness of the stock. A different way to think about the riskiness of McDonald's stock is to look at the frequency distribution of the daily returns: Of the 2,515 daily returns, how many were between 0.5 and 1.25%? The answer turns out to be 429, which is 17.06% of the total number of returns. As another example, 32 of the returns (1.27% of the total) were between −4.00% and −3.25%. In the spreadsheet below we've used Excel's **Frequency** function to calculate the whole frequency distribution of the returns (see the Excel Note on page 270 for more on how to use this function). The plots of the returns look very much like the normal distribution (the "bell curve") you've probably studied in a statistics course.

# McDONALD'S--DAILY STOCK PRICES AND RETURNS, 31 Dec 1998 - 31 Dec 2008

| | A | B | C | D |
|---|---|---|---|---|
| 2 | Date | Stock price | Daily return | |
| 3 | 31-Dec-98 | 31.69 | | |
| 4 | 4-Jan-99 | 31.75 | 0.19% | <-- =B4/B3-1 |
| 5 | 5-Jan-99 | 31.61 | -0.44% | <-- =B5/B4-1 |
| 6 | 6-Jan-99 | 32.1 | 1.55% | <-- =B6/B5-1 |
| 7 | 7-Jan-99 | 32.13 | 0.09% | <-- =B7/B6-1 |
| 8 | 8-Jan-99 | 33.21 | 3.36% | <-- =B8/B7-1 |
| 9 | 11-Jan-99 | 32.13 | -3.25% | |
| 10 | 12-Jan-99 | 31.07 | -3.30% | |
| 11 | 13-Jan-99 | 31.77 | 2.25% | |
| 12 | 14-Jan-99 | 31.38 | -1.23% | |
| 13 | 15-Jan-99 | 31.98 | 1.91% | |
| 14 | 19-Jan-99 | 32.67 | 2.16% | |
| 15 | 20-Jan-99 | 32.08 | -1.81% | |
| 16 | 21-Jan-99 | 31.64 | -1.37% | |
| 17 | 22-Jan-99 | 31.36 | -0.88% | |
| 18 | 25-Jan-99 | 31.3 | -0.19% | |
| 19 | 26-Jan-99 | 32.57 | 4.06% | |
| 20 | 27-Jan-99 | 32.39 | -0.55% | |
| 21 | 28-Jan-99 | 32.23 | -0.49% | |
| 22 | 29-Jan-99 | 32.52 | 0.90% | |
| 23 | 1-Feb-99 | 32.75 | 0.71% | |
| 24 | 2-Feb-99 | 32.62 | -0.40% | |
| 25 | 3-Feb-99 | 33.57 | 2.91% | |
| 26 | 4-Feb-99 | 33.32 | -0.74% | |
| 27 | 5-Feb-99 | 33.14 | -0.54% | |
| 28 | 8-Feb-99 | 33.37 | 0.69% | |
| 29 | 9-Feb-99 | 33.11 | -0.78% | |
| 30 | 10-Feb-99 | 32.95 | -0.48% | |
| 31 | 11-Feb-99 | 33.83 | 2.67% | |
| 32 | 12-Feb-99 | 33.55 | -0.83% | |
| 33 | 16-Feb-99 | 33.75 | 0.60% | |
| 34 | 17-Feb-99 | 33.21 | -1.60% | |
| 35 | 18-Feb-99 | 34.22 | 3.04% | |
| 36 | 19-Feb-99 | 35.3 | 3.16% | |
| 37 | 22-Feb-99 | 35.33 | 0.08% | |
| 38 | 23-Feb-99 | 35.36 | 0.08% | |
| 39 | 24-Feb-99 | 35.07 | -0.82% | |
| 40 | 25-Feb-99 | 34.68 | -1.11% | |
| 41 | 26-Feb-99 | 35.07 | 1.12% | |
| 42 | 1-Mar-99 | 35.71 | 1.82% | |
| 43 | 2-Mar-99 | 37.08 | 3.84% | |

## Some statistics about McDonald's stock prices

| | | |
|---|---|---|
| Number of days | 2515 | <-- =COUNT(C4:C2519) |
| Minimum return | -12.82% | <-- =MIN(C4:C2519) |
| Maximum return | 9.67% | <-- =MAX(C4:C2519) |
| Date of minimum return | 17-Sep-02 | <-- =INDEX(A:A,MATCH(G4,C:C,0)) |
| Date of maximum return | 9-Jul-99 | <-- =INDEX(A:A,MATCH(G5,C:C,0)) |
| Number of zero-return days | 43 | <-- =COUNTIF(C:C,"=0") |

## Computing the frequency distribution

| Bin | How many? | |
|---|---|---|
| -13.00% | 0 | <-- {=FREQUENCY(C4:C2518,F12:F43)} |
| -12.25% | 1 | |
| -11.50% | 0 | |
| -10.75% | 0 | |
| -10.00% | 1 | |
| -9.25% | 0 | |
| -8.50% | 0 | |
| -7.75% | 4 | |
| -7.00% | 0 | |
| -6.25% | 3 | |
| -5.50% | 6 | |
| -4.75% | 9 | |
| -4.00% | 18 | |
| -3.25% | 32 | |
| -2.50% | 83 | |
| -1.75% | 150 | |
| -1.00% | 295 | |
| -0.25% | 456 | |
| 0.50% | 533 | |
| 1.25% | 429 | |
| 2.00% | 232 | |
| 2.75% | 120 | |
| 3.50% | 65 | |
| 4.25% | 30 | |
| 5.00% | 19 | |
| 5.75% | 11 | |
| 6.50% | 6 | |
| 7.25% | 2 | |
| 8.00% | 3 | |
| 8.75% | 3 | |
| 9.50% | 3 | |
| 10.25% | 1 | |

# EXCEL NOTE: THE FREQUENCY FUNCTION

The frequency distribution that gave rise to the bell curve for McDonald's stock returns was calculated with an Excel function called **Frequency**. To use this function, consider the following example, which gives the monthly returns on IBM stock between January 2007 and January 2009:

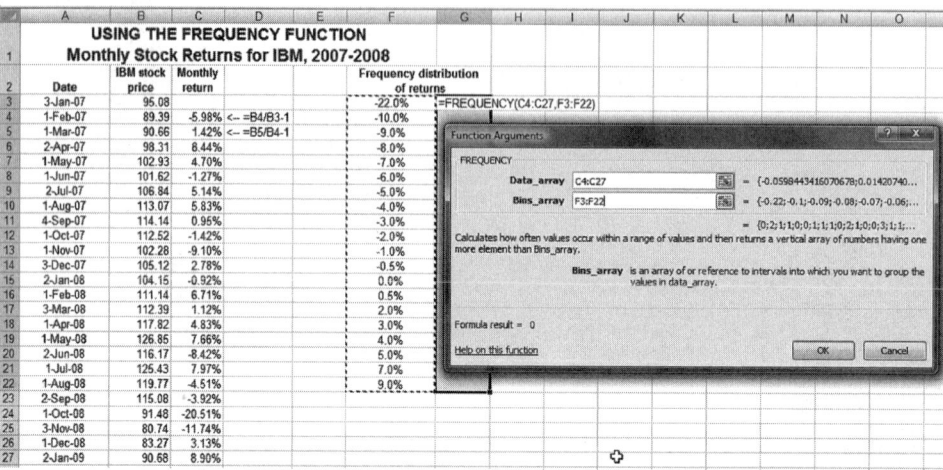

When you finish putting in range C4:C27 and F3:F22 as shown above, *don't click **OK***! Instead, simultaneously press the keys [Ctrl]+[Shift]+[Enter]. This will put the frequency in the spreadsheet as shown below.

|  | F | G |
|---|---|---|
| 2 | **Frequency distribution of returns** | |
| 3 | -22.0% | 0 |
| 4 | -10.0% | 2 |
| 5 | -9.0% | 1 |
| 6 | -8.0% | 1 |
| 7 | -7.0% | 0 |
| 8 | -6.0% | 0 |
| 9 | -5.0% | 1 |
| 10 | -4.0% | 1 |
| 11 | -3.0% | 1 |
| 12 | -2.0% | 0 |
| 13 | -1.0% | 2 |
| 14 | -0.5% | 1 |
| 15 | 0.0% | 0 |
| 16 | 0.5% | 0 |
| 17 | 2.0% | 3 |
| 18 | 3.0% | 1 |
| 19 | 4.0% | 1 |
| 20 | 5.0% | 2 |
| 21 | 7.0% | 3 |
| 22 | 9.0% | 4 |

This table says that in the period January 2007–January 2009:

- There were 2 months when IBM stock had a return between −22 and −10%.

- There was 1 month when IBM stock had a return between −9 and −10%.

and so on . . .

## Computing the Average and Standard Deviation of the McDonald's Returns

In the spreadsheet below we look at the end-year prices of McDonald's between 1999 and 2008. On average, a McDonald's shareholder got an annual return of 10.49% per year over the period January 1999–January 2009. The standard deviation of the annual returns is 26.88%. The standard deviation is a statistical measure of the variation of the stock's returns—the greater the standard deviation, the greater the riskiness of the stock.

| | A | B | C | D | E | F | G | H |
|---|---|---|---|---|---|---|---|---|
| 1 | | | McDONALD'S--BEGINNING-YEAR STOCK PRICES, Jan 1999-Jan 2009 | | | | | |
| 2 | Date | Stock price | Return | | | Statistics | | |
| 3 | 4-Jan-99 | 31.75 | | | | Largest annual return | 52.12% | <-- =MAX(C4:C13) |
| 4 | 3-Jan-00 | 32.85 | 3.46% | <-- =B4/B3-1 | | Smallest annual return | -36.65% | <-- =MIN(C4:C13) |
| 5 | 2-Jan-01 | 27.95 | -14.92% | <-- =B5/B4-1 | | | | |
| 6 | 2-Jan-02 | 22.29 | -20.25% | | | Average annual return | 6.94% | <-- =(B13/B3)^(1/10)-1 |
| 7 | 2-Jan-03 | 14.12 | -36.65% | | | Variance of annual returns | 0.0723 | <-- =VARP(C4:C13) |
| 8 | 2-Jan-04 | 21.48 | 52.12% | | | Standard deviation of annual returns | 26.88% | <-- =STDEVP(C4:C13) |
| 9 | 3-Jan-05 | 28.09 | 30.77% | | | | | |
| 10 | 3-Jan-06 | 30.19 | 7.48% | | | | | |
| 11 | 3-Jan-07 | 40.48 | 34.08% | | | | | |
| 12 | 2-Jan-08 | 55.02 | 35.92% | | | | | |
| 13 | 2-Jan-09 | 62.10 | 12.87% | | | | | |
| 14 | | | | | | | | |
| 15 | | | STATISTICAL REVIEW | | | | | |
| 16 | | MCD return | Return minus average, squared | | | Statistical note: The only consistent way of computing annual average returns is to use the continuously compounded returns, illustrated on page 273. This Excel sheet uses discrete returns, but these give contradictory results. (Compare, for example 10.49% in cell B28 with 6.94% in cell G6 .) | | |
| 17 | 3-Jan-00 | 3.46% | 0.49% | <-- =(B17-$B$28)^2 | | | | |
| 18 | 2-Jan-01 | -14.92% | 6.45% | <-- =(B18-$B$28)^2 | | | | |
| 19 | 2-Jan-02 | -20.25% | 9.45% | | | | | |
| 20 | 2-Jan-03 | -36.65% | 22.22% | | | | | |
| 21 | 2-Jan-04 | 52.12% | 17.34% | | | | | |
| 22 | 3-Jan-05 | 30.77% | 4.11% | | | | | |
| 23 | 3-Jan-06 | 7.48% | 0.09% | | | | | |
| 24 | 3-Jan-07 | 34.08% | 5.57% | | | | | |
| 25 | 2-Jan-08 | 35.92% | 6.47% | | | | | |
| 26 | 2-Jan-09 | 12.87% | 0.06% | | | | | |
| 27 | | | | | | | | |
| 28 | Average | | 10.49% | <-- =AVERAGE(B17:B26) | | | | |
| 29 | Variance | | 0.0723 | <-- =SUM(C17:C26)/10 | | | | |
| 30 | | | 0.0723 | <-- =VARP(B17:B26) | | | | |
| 31 | Standard deviation | | 26.88% | <-- =SQRT(B29) | | | | |

# EXCEL NOTE: EXCEL AND STATISTICAL REVIEW

We delve deeper into statistics in Chapter 9. Here we remind you of the meanings of the terms:
- The *average* (also called the *mean*) return for McDonald's is computed either by summing the annual returns and dividing by 10 or by taking the compound annual return over the 10 years. We've illustrated both ways in cell B28 and in cell G6. Note the inconsistency between B28 and G6—this is caused by our use in this example of discrete returns. In Section 8.4 we use continuously-compounded returns and the inconsistency disappears.
- The *variance* of McDonald's annual returns is computed in three steps: (i) Subtract each return from the average. (ii) Square the result; these "squared deviations from the average" are shown in cells C17:C26. (iii) Average the sum of the squared deviations. This is illustrated in cell B29. Cell G8 shows that the Excel function **Varp** gives the same result.

- Because the returns are in percentages, the variance has units "percent squared." This is a bit difficult to understand. The *standard deviation* of the returns is the square root of the variance (this has units that are in percentages). Informally, you can think of the standard deviation as representing the average percentage variability of the individual returns. Cell B30 used the Excel function **Sqrt** to derive the standard deviation, and cell G9 uses the Excel function **Stdevp**.

## How Risky Are Other Assets?

To give you some feel for how risky different assets are, here is a table of the annualized returns and standard deviations for various assets over the same period for which we computed McDonald's annual returns.

| AVERAGE RETURN VERSUS STANDARD DEVIATION OF RETURNS A somewhat arbitrary list of assets, 1999-2008 | | | | | |
|---|---|---|---|---|---|
| | Average return | Standard deviation | | Average return | Standard deviation |
| Abbott | 4.25% | 21.47% | Marriott | 2.51% | 27.70% |
| Alcoa | -3.43% | 42.03% | McGraw-Hill | 0.71% | 24.05% |
| Altria | 8.65% | 29.51% | Microsoft | -5.79% | 35.88% |
| American Airlines | -8.04% | 75.72% | Nasdaq | -5.11% | 30.98% |
| Boeing | 4.49% | 30.95% | Nicor | 4.06% | 27.34% |
| Cisco | -4.89% | 43.06% | Nordstrom | -1.56% | 42.24% |
| Coca Cola | 0.10% | 24.98% | Northrop | 7.80% | 25.31% |
| Dell | -15.50% | 41.97% | Procter & Gamble | 5.16% | 22.31% |
| Exxon | 10.60% | 18.06% | PPG | 1.24% | 23.08% |
| Ford | -22.92% | 48.67% | S&P 500 | -3.22% | 15.28% |
| GE | -4.89% | 24.22% | Safeway | -8.13% | 28.46% |
| Hershey | 4.40% | 23.17% | TEVA | 21.33% | 29.81% |
| IBM | 0.43% | 30.36% | U.S. Steel | 6.11% | 55.83% |
| Johnson & Johnson | 5.30% | 19.39% | Value Line Equity Fund | -5.14% | 18.09% |
| Kellogg | 3.79% | 20.82% | Vanguard High-Yield | 1.79% | 8.59% |
| Kraft | 0.74% | 21.01% | Vanguard Long-Term Treasury | 5.44% | 13.37% |
| Kroger | -1.42% | 25.22% | Vanguard Windsor | 1.93% | 16.97% |
| Manpower | 4.29% | 32.37% | Walmart | 3.72% | 22.89% |

A closer look at the some of the highlighted financial assets can give you some better intuition on the relation between financial risk and return:

- Vanguard's Long-Term Treasury Fund is a mutual fund that invests in long-term U.S. Treasury bonds. As you saw in Section 8.2, the absence of default risk in these bonds does not mean that they are riskless: Their prices can vary considerably, and as a result the holder of the Vanguard Long-Term Treasury Fund may experience uncertainty in her returns. Nevertheless, our intuition tells us (correctly, as you'll see in the succeeding bullets) that this fund ought to be less risky than most stocks. During the decade of 1999–2008, the Vanguard Long-Term Treasury Fund gave an average annual return of 5.44% and this return had a standard deviation of 13.37%.

- Standard & Poor's (S&P) 500 Index is a broad-based index of the largest U.S. stocks and is often used as a measure of the performance of the U.S. stock markets. During the decade of 1999–2008, the S&P 500 Index had an average annual return of –3.22% and a standard deviation of 15.28%. You might have expected a clearer trade-off between the Vanguard Long-Term Treasury Bond fund and the S&P 500, but in the case, the S&P returned both lower returns with higher risk than the Vanguard Treasury fund. Of course this is all with hindsight: We would generally perceive that the riskiness of the S&P is greater than that of a fund of Treasury bonds, and we might reasonably expect that, going forward, the *ex ante returns* (meaning the expected future returns) of the S&P would be higher than those of Vanguard.[4]

- The riskiest stock in our sample was American Airlines and it was also one of the poorest performers, with an annualized negative return of –8.04%.[5]

There seems little relation between the standard deviation of the returns and the average returns. In Chapter 10 we define another measure of asset risk, called *beta*, which works better as a descriptor of risk.

# 8.4. Advanced Topic: Using Continuously Compounded Returns to Compute Annualized Return Statistics

We discussed continuous compounding in Chapter 3. As explained, the continuously compounded return is calculated using the **Ln** function. For reasons that are beyond the scope of this book, the continuously compounded return is often a better method of computing return statistics (by "better" we mean two things: there's a theory behind the numbers, and this theory gives the same results whether you're computing the annual statistics from daily, weekly, or monthly data). In the spreadsheet below, we've computed the continuously compounded return statistics for McDonald's.

| | A | B | C | D | E | F | G | H |
|---|---|---|---|---|---|---|---|---|
| 1 | | | | McDONALD'S--DAILY STOCK PRICES AND RETURNS, 31 Dec 1998 - 31 Dec 2008 | | | | |
| 2 | Date | Stock price | Daily return | | | Statistics based on continuous returns | | |
| 3 | 31-Dec-98 | 31.69 | | | | Number of days | 2515 | <-- =COUNT(C4:C2519) |
| 4 | 4-Jan-99 | 31.75 | 0.19% | <-- =LN(B4/B3) | | Minimum daily return | -13.72% | <-- =MIN(C4:C2519) |
| 5 | 5-Jan-99 | 31.61 | -0.44% | <-- =LN(B5/B4) | | Maximum daily return | 9.23% | <-- =MAX(C4:C2519) |
| 6 | 6-Jan-99 | 32.1 | 1.54% | <-- =LN(B6/B5) | | | | |
| 7 | 7-Jan-99 | 32.13 | 0.09% | <-- =LN(B7/B6) | | Average daily return | 0.026% | <-- =AVERAGE(C4:C2519) |
| 8 | 8-Jan-99 | 33.21 | 3.31% | <-- =LN(B8/B7) | | Variance of daily returns | 0.0003 | <-- =VARP(C4:C2519) |
| 9 | 11-Jan-99 | 32.13 | -3.31% | | | Standard deviation of daily returns | 1.82% | <-- =SQRT(G8) |
| 10 | 12-Jan-99 | 31.07 | -3.35% | | | | | |
| 11 | 13-Jan-99 | 31.77 | 2.23% | | | Average annual return | 6.49% | <-- =252*G7 |
| 12 | 14-Jan-99 | 31.38 | -1.24% | | | Variance of annual returns | 0.0836 | <-- =252*G8 |
| 13 | 15-Jan-99 | 31.98 | 1.89% | | | Standard deviation of annual returns | 28.91% | <-- =SQRT(G12) |
| 14 | 19-Jan-99 | 32.67 | 2.13% | | | | | |
| 15 | 20-Jan-99 | 32.08 | -1.82% | | | | | |
| 16 | 21-Jan-99 | 31.64 | -1.38% | | | | | |

The average daily continuously compounded return (cell G7) is 0.026%. To *annualize* this return, we multiply by 252, the average number of business days per year.[6] The

---

[4] In the previous decade this was true: The S&P had an average return of 15.09% and the Vanguard Treasury fund an average return of 2.43%; the standard deviations of the two funds were 13.18 and 7.94%, respectively.

[5] In the previous decade the numbers for American Airlines were 9.26 and 29.34%.

[6] Over the 10-year period 1999–2008, there were 2,516 days on which McDonald's stock was transacted. This averages out to 252 days per year.

annualized average continuously compounded return is 6.49% (cell G11). Similarly, the annualized return variance is 0.0053 (cell G12), and the annualized standard deviation of returns is 7.26% (cell G13).[7]

## Conclusion

In this chapter we have tried to give you some intuitions into the nature of financial risk by a series of examples. Risk—the variability of returns from an asset over time—depends on a number of factors. Broadly speaking, the characteristics of an asset's risk are its *horizon*, its *safety*, and its *liquidity*. As we've shown, even default-free assets like U.S. Treasury bills can be risky because their prices can change over the asset's horizon. With our example of McDonald's stock we've shown that some statistical sense can be made of the variability of the stock's return over time—using Excel's **Frequency** function, we were able to show that McDonald's stock returns look very much like the familiar statistical bell curve.

Risk is the most important concept in finance: The variability of financial asset returns is the main fact of financial life, but this risk is not easy to define or measure. In Chapters 10–13 we will develop a model to *price risks*; by this we mean a model that will help us determine the risk-adjusted discount rate. The important innovation of this model is that risk depends on a *portfolio context*—it is not just the asset's returns by themselves that determine the asset's riskiness, but the asset's returns in the context of the portfolio of all the assets held by the investor.

Before we can develop this model, however, you might need a brush-up on your statistics skills. This is the task we set ourselves in Chapter 9.

## EXERCISES

1. Professor Smith was bragging about her abilities as an investor in the stock market: "In the last month, I earned 8% on my portfolio," she told her friends. "That's nothing special," commented Mr. Jackson. "Last month I made 20% on my portfolio, without studying 15 years at university." Did Mr. Jackson really outperform Mrs. Smith?

2. Can a corporate bond have a lower expected return than a government bond? Can it have lower ex post return?

3. It's 1 January 2007 and you're considering buying a $1,000 face-value U.S. Treasury bill that matures in 1 year. The interest rate is 7% annually.
   a. If you buy the T-Bill now, how much will you pay?
   b. If the interest rate remains 7% annually, how much will the bill be worth on 1 February 2007? 1 March? 1 April?…1 December?

4. Diana bought bonds issued by the ZZZ company, a small high-tech company from Newfoundland. The bond is zero-coupon, has a face value of $1,000, and matures in 2 years. Diana intends to keep the bond until maturity.
   a. If the price of the bond is $756.14, what is the annual expected return of Diana's bond?
   b. One day after Diana bought her bond, ZZZ was purchased by the electronic giant ABA, which has a very low default probability. Investors demand only a 6.5% annual return on ABA's

[7]Note that the continuously compounded average return of 6.49% is less than the discretely compounded return of 6.94% computed in cell G6 on page 271. One reason for this is that continuous compounding builds up faster than discretely compounded interest. As noted in Chapter 3, there are legitimate alternative ways to compute returns. To compare the returns of two assets, make sure that the basis of the computation is the same.

bonds. What will be the new price of the ZZZ bonds and how much will Diana gain from the takeover?

5. On 15 March 2002, you purchased a 2-year Treasury bond with face value of $10,000 and a 4% coupon (payable semiannually). The price of the bond was $9,750. The bond promises a coupon of $200 on 15 September 2002, 15 March 2003, 15 September 2003, and 15 March 2004 (on this last date the bond will repay its face value).

   a. Based on the following, compute the annualized IRR of the bond purchase.

   |   | A | B | C |
   |---|---|---|---|
   | 1 | Date | Cash flow | |
   | 2 | 15-Mar-02 | -9,750 | |
   | 3 | 15-Sep-02 | 200 | |
   | 4 | 15-Mar-03 | 200 | |
   | 5 | 15-Sep-03 | 200 | |
   | 6 | 15-Mar-04 | 10,200 | |
   | 7 | | | |
   | 8 | Semiannual IRR | | 2.67% <-- =IRR(B2:B6) |

   b. Immediately after receiving the $200 bond interest payment on 15 September 2002, you sold the bond for $10,000. What was your ex post annualized yield? What was the ex ante annualized yield of the buyer of the bond?

6. During a stamp collector convention the chairman spoke about the profitability of investing in rare stamps. "Last year I invested $150,000 in rare stamps. These stamps are now worth $200,000 according to the catalog, meaning an annual return of 33%. For comparison the average return in the stock market in the last 30 years was only 16%." Find (at least) three problems with the chairman's argument.

7. A basic assumption of economics is that investors are risk averse, meaning when they view Asset *A* as riskier than Asset *B* they will demand a higher expected return.

   A "fair bet" is a bet whose expected return is zero. Here's an example of a fair bet: Pay $1 to get $2 if a coin flip yields heads or to get $0 if the coin flip yields tails. Note that this bet has an expected return of zero.

$$Expected\ payoff = \underset{\substack{\uparrow \\ \text{Probability} \\ \text{of heads}}}{0.5} * \underset{\substack{\uparrow \\ \text{Payoff} \\ \text{if heads}}}{\$2} + \underset{\substack{\uparrow \\ \text{Probability} \\ \text{of tails}}}{0.5} * \underset{\substack{\uparrow \\ \text{Payoff} \\ \text{if tails}}}{\$0} = \$1$$

$$Expected\ return = \frac{Expected\ payoff}{Cost\ of\ bet} - 1 = \frac{\$1}{\$1} - 1 = 0\%$$

Will a risk-aversive investor agree to a fair bet?

8. A risk-neutral investor is willing to make bets with an expected return of zero. Suppose a risk-neutral investor is offered the chance to participate in a die-toss game. If the die comes up 1, the payoff is $1, if the die comes up 2, the payoff is $2, .... What is the maximum price the risk-neutral investor is willing to pay to play this game?

9. On Planet Apathy all investors are indifferent to risk. The annual expected returns of government bonds are 5%. Does that mean that the average stock returns should be 5%?

10. One of the ways in which the United States helps foreign countries is to guarantee their bank loans. Explain (in short) the benefits for foreign countries in getting those guaranties. (Footnote 1 is a good place to start your answer.)

11. During a finance lecture Prof. Johnson explained to his students the relation between higher risk and higher expected returns. At the end of the lecture one of the students asked: "Yesterday I read in the paper that the U.S. stock markets earned higher returns than 15 African stock markets in

the past decade. How is that fact consistent with high risk equaling higher returns?" How would you advise Prof. Johnson to respond to his students? (Your answer should include the words ex ante and ex post.)

12. On 1 January 2005, the U.S. government is issuing two series of bonds. The two series are completely identical except for the fact that the volume of trade in the first series is anticipated to be much higher than the volume in the second series. What do you expect will be the relation between the prices of the two series?

13. DEF is a firm that is traded on NASDAQ. On 1 January 2010 the company issued 10,000 zero-coupon bonds. Each bond has a face value of $100 and matures on 1 January 2015. The bonds are the only debt of the company. A bond-rating company estimated the total value of DEF's assets on 1 January 2015 as follows:

| Probability | Value of DEF assets on 1/1/05 |
|---|---|
| 0.2 | 2,000,000 |
| 0.3 | 1,750,000 |
| 0.4 | 1,200,000 |
| 0.1 | 750,000 |

Two years after the bond issue, on 1 January 2012, the bond-rating agency reexamined the DEF Company and estimated the total value of the firm's assets as follows.

| Probability | Value of DEF assets on 1/1/2015 |
|---|---|
| 0.05 | 2,000,000 |
| 0.25 | 1,750,000 |
| 0.65 | 1,200,000 |
| 0.05 | 750,000 |

a. What will be the influence of the new estimation on the expected return on DEF bonds?

b. What will be the influence of the new estimation on the DEF stock price?

14. Can you think of a risk-based explanation for the following finding? Over the past 40 years "small stocks"—defined as shares of firms with a low market value—had higher returns than big stocks.

15. A well-known finance professor published a paper in which he argued that because of the high volume of stock trade on the Internet, he expects stock returns to decline in future years. What is the basis for the professor's argument?

16. At the end of 1999 an investor bought 10,000 shares of Yakuna Corp. for ¥456 each in the Japanese stock market (¥ is the symbol for Japanese yen). At that time $1 U.S. was worth ¥128.35. The investor sold all the shares at the beginning of 2003 when the stock was worth ¥448; $1 was worth ¥108.33. Calculate the annual return in dollar terms and yen terms.

17. On 1 January 2010 an American investor bought $1,000,000 worth of Swiss francs (SFr) and put it in a savings account for 1 year. The annual interest rate in Swiss francs was 6%. During that period the interest rate in the United States was 2%. On the purchase date the exchange rate was $1 = 1.56 SFr.

a. One year after the start of the savings in Switzerland, the exchange rate was 1.45 Sfr per U.S. dollar. If the investor turned his savings back into dollars, what *dollar rate of return* did he earn?

b. What should be the exchange rate on 1 January 2011 for the investment in SFr to be better than the investment in U.S. dollars?

18. The disk that comes with this book has daily prices for AMD Corp.'s stock from 1 July 1994 through 26 July 2004.

a. Compute the daily stock returns and graph them.

b. Use **Frequency** to build a frequency distribution of the stock returns and graph this distribution.

19. The disk that comes with this book contains data on annual stock prices for Ford Motor Company for 1987–2003. Compute the average annual return and the standard deviation of annual returns for Ford.

| | A | B |
|---|---|---|
| 1 | **FORD MOTOR COMPANY annual stock prices** | |
| 2 | **Date** | **Closing price** |
| 3 | 2-Jan-87 | 0.5900 |
| 4 | 4-Jan-88 | 0.8900 |
| 5 | 3-Jan-89 | 1.3600 |
| 6 | 2-Jan-90 | 1.3500 |
| 7 | 2-Jan-91 | 1.1900 |
| 8 | 2-Jan-92 | 1.5600 |
| 9 | 4-Jan-93 | 2.6800 |
| 10 | 3-Jan-94 | 4.3000 |
| 11 | 3-Jan-95 | 3.4800 |
| 12 | 2-Jan-96 | 4.4100 |
| 13 | 2-Jan-97 | 5.2100 |
| 14 | 2-Jan-98 | 8.8700 |
| 15 | 4-Jan-99 | 25.9000 |
| 16 | 3-Jan-00 | 22.3100 |
| 17 | 2-Jan-01 | 25.1400 |
| 18 | 2-Jan-02 | 14.1800 |
| 19 | 2-Jan-03 | 8.7600 |
| 20 | 2-Jan-04 | 14.4500 |

20. The disk that comes with this book contains data on annual stock prices for Kellogg for 1987–2003. Compute the average annual return and the standard deviation of annual returns for Kellogg.

|  | A | B |
|---|---|---|
| 1 | **KELLOGG annual stock prices** | |
| 2 | **Date** | **Closing price** |
| 3 | 2-Jan-87 | 5.68 |
| 4 | 4-Jan-88 | 5.48 |
| 5 | 3-Jan-89 | 7.66 |
| 6 | 2-Jan-90 | 8.27 |
| 7 | 2-Jan-91 | 11.26 |
| 8 | 2-Jan-92 | 17.91 |
| 9 | 4-Jan-93 | 20.37 |
| 10 | 3-Jan-94 | 18.47 |
| 11 | 3-Jan-95 | 19.90 |
| 12 | 2-Jan-96 | 29.03 |
| 13 | 2-Jan-97 | 27.59 |
| 14 | 2-Jan-98 | 38.01 |
| 15 | 4-Jan-99 | 34.14 |
| 16 | 3-Jan-00 | 20.93 |
| 17 | 2-Jan-01 | 23.52 |
| 18 | 2-Jan-02 | 28.70 |
| 19 | 2-Jan-03 | 32.00 |
| 20 | 2-Jan-04 | 37.35 |

21. Graph the annual stock returns of Kellogg and Ford on the same graph. Is one of the companies more risky than the other? Explain.

# 9 Statistics for Portfolios

## CHAPTER CONTENTS

## Overview

To understand and work through Chapters 10–13, you will need to know some statistics. If you're like a lot of finance students, you've had a statistics course and forgotten much of what you learned there. This chapter is a refresher—it shows you exactly what you need to proceed with the succeeding chapters, using Excel to do all the calculations. (Excel is a great statistical toolbox—someday all business-school statistics courses will use it. In the meantime you're stuck with this chapter.)

### Finance Concepts

- How to calculate stock returns and adjust them for dividends and stock splits
- Return mean, variance, and standard deviation for an asset
- Return mean and variance for a portfolio of two assets
- Regressions

### Excel Functions and Techniques

- **Average**
- **Var** and **Varp**
- **Stdev** and **Stdevp**
- **Covar** and **Correl**
- **Trendlines** (Excel's term for regressions)
- **Slope**, **Intercept**, **Rsq**

## 9.1. Basic Statistics for Asset Returns: Mean, Standard Deviation, Covariance, and Correlation

In this section you will learn to calculate the return on a stock and its statistics: the *mean* (interchangeably referred to as the *average* or *expected* return), the *variance*, and the *standard deviation*.

### Kellogg Stock and Its Returns

The following spreadsheet shows data for Kellogg Company (stock symbol K) stock during the period 1998–2008. For each year, we show the closing price of K stock and the dividend the company paid during the year.[1] We also calculate the annual returns and their statistics; these calculations are explained after the table.

Suppose you bought a share of Kellogg at the end of December 1998 for $34.13 and sold it a year later, at the end of December 1999, for $30.81. During this year, Kellogg paid a per-share dividend of $0.96. Your return from holding K throughout 1999 would have been

$$r_{K,1999} = \frac{P_{K,1999} + Div_{K,1999} - P_{K,1999}}{P_{K,1998}} = \frac{30.81 + 0.96 - 34.13}{34.13} = -6.89\% \ .$$

Here are several notes:

- We use $r_{K,1999}$ to denote the return on K stock in 1999 and we use $Div_{K,1999}$ to denote K's dividend in 1999.
- The numerator of $r_{K,1999}$ is

$$P_{K,1991} + Div_{K,1991} - P_{K,1990} = 30.81 + 0.96 - 34.13 = -2.35$$

---

[1] The "closing price" is the price of the stock at the end of the day.

|    | A | B | C | D | E |
|----|---|---|---|---|---|
| 1  | **PRICE AND DIVIDEND DATA FOR KELLOGG (K) 1998 - 2008** | | | | |
| 2  | **Date** | **Price** | **Dividend** | **Annual return** | |
| 3  | 31-Dec-98 | 34.13 | 0.92 | | |
| 4  | 31-Dec-99 | 30.81 | 0.96 | -6.89% | <-- =(B4+C4)/B3-1 |
| 5  | 29-Dec-00 | 26.25 | 0.99 | -11.59% | |
| 6  | 31-Dec-01 | 30.10 | 1.01 | 18.51% | |
| 7  | 31-Dec-02 | 34.27 | 1.01 | 17.21% | |
| 8  | 31-Dec-03 | 38.08 | 1.01 | 14.06% | |
| 9  | 31-Dec-04 | 44.66 | 1.01 | 19.93% | |
| 10 | 30-Dec-05 | 43.22 | 1.06 | -0.85% | |
| 11 | 29-Dec-06 | 50.06 | 1.14 | 18.46% | |
| 12 | 31-Dec-07 | 52.43 | 1.20 | 7.14% | |
| 13 | 31-Dec-08 | 42.73 | 1.30 | -16.02% | |
| 14 | | | | | |
| 15 | Average return, E(r$_K$) | | | 6.00% | <-- =AVERAGE(D4:D13) |
| 16 | Variance of return, $\sigma^2{}_K$ | | | 0.0171 | <-- =VARP(D4:D13) |
| 17 | Standard deviation of return, $\sigma_K$ | | | 13.06% | <-- =STDEVP(D4:D13) |

This is the gain on holding Kellogg during the year (in this case it's a negative "gain": a loss of $2.35). The denominator of $r_{K,1999}$ is the initial investment from buying Kellogg stock at the beginning of the year.

- In cell D4 of the spreadsheet we've written $r_{K,1999}$, the return for 1999, in a slightly different form as **(C4+B4)/B3–1**:

$$r_{K,1999} = \frac{P_{K,1999} + Div_{K,1999} - P_{K,1998}}{P_{K,1998}} = \frac{P_{K,1999} + Div_{K,1999}}{P_{K,1998}} - 1$$

Cells D15, D16, and D17 give the return statistics for Kellogg:

- Cell D15: The average return over the decade is 6.00% per year. This number is also called the *mean return* and it's calculated with the Excel function **=Average(D4:D13)**. We often use the past returns to predict future returns. When we make this use of the data, we also call the mean the *expected return*, meaning that we use the historic average of Kellogg stock returns as a prediction of what the stock will return in the future. In this book the terms mean, average, and expected return will be used almost interchangeably, and we will sometimes use the notations $E(r_K)$ or $\bar{r}_K$. The formal definition is

$$Mean\ K\ return = E(r_K) = \bar{r}_K = \frac{r_{K,1998} + r_{K,1999} + \ldots + r_{K,2008}}{10}$$

You might wonder at the number of expressions (mean, average, expected return) and the number of symbols $(E(r_K), \bar{r}_K)$ for the same idea. We've introduced them all both for convenience and because, in your further finance studies, you're likely to see them used synonymously.

- Cell D16: The variance of the annual returns is 0.0171. Variance and standard deviation are statistical measures of the variability of the returns. The variance is calculated with the Excel function **=Varp(D4:D13)**. (See the "Excel and Statistical Note" box on page 283 for more information about this function and its cousin, **=Var(D4:D13)**. The variance is often denoted by the Greek symbol $\sigma_K^2$ (pronounced "sigma squared of Kellogg"); sometimes it is written as $Var(r_k)$. The formal definition of the variance is

$$Var(r_K) = \sigma_K^2 = \frac{(r_{K,1999} - \overline{r}_K)^2 + (r_{K,2000} - \overline{r}_K)^2 + \ldots + (r_{K,2008} - \overline{r}_K)^2}{10}$$

- Cell D17: The standard deviation of the annual returns is the square root of the variance: $\sqrt{0.0171} = 13.06\%$. Excel has two functions, **Stdevp** and **Stdev**, to do this calculation directly. Because we usually use **Varp** for the variance, we will use **Stdevp** for the standard deviation. It is common to use the Greek letter sigma for the standard deviation, writing $\sigma_K$ (pronounced "sigma of Kellogg").

## Continuously Compounded Returns (Skip on First Reading)

Advanced finance computations often use the continuously compounded returns discussed in Section 3.9. Using this computation, the return on Kellogg stock in 1999 would be

$$r_{K,1999} = Ln\left(\frac{P_{K,1999} + Div_{K,1999}}{P_{K,1999}}\right) = Ln\left(\frac{30.81 + 0.96}{34.13}\right) = -7.14\%$$

We use this form of return computation in the options chapters of *Principles of Finance with Excel* (Chapters 21–23).

## Downloaded Data from Commercial Sources Are Adjusted for Dividends and Splits

The author's two favorite data sources for stock price information are Yahoo!, which is free, and the Center for Research in Security Prices (CRSP) database that originates from the University of Chicago (many universities subscribe to CRSP—ask your data manager).[2] When you download data from these sources, they automatically adjust the price data to account for dividends and for stock splits. So you don't have to do the dividend adjustments illustrated for Kellogg—the prices from Yahoo! and CRSP assume that dividends are reinvested in buying new stock.[3] In general, you can calculate returns from the adjusted stock price data given by your data provider. They usually do the corrections correctly.

---

[2] For penniless students, Yahoo! is especially useful. An appendix to this chapter shows you how to download financial data from Yahoo!.

[3] If it's all in the downloaded data, why the heck did we do all the work in this section? The answer, of course, is that it helps to understand what the numbers are telling you.

## EXCEL AND STATISTICAL NOTE (SKIP UNTIL LATER, OR PERHAPS FOREVER, IF YOU LIKE)

Excel has two variance functions, **Varp** and **Var**. The former measures the "population variance," and the latter measures the "sample variance." Similarly, Excel has two functions for the standard deviation, **Stdevp** and **Stdev**. In this book we use only the functions **Varp** and **Stdevp**. This box is a reminder but not an explanation of the difference between the two concepts.

If you have return data $\{r_{stock,1}, r_{stock,2}, \ldots, r_{stock,N}\}$ for a *stock*, then the mean return is $\bar{r}_{stock} = \dfrac{1}{N}\sum_{t=1}^{N} r_{stock,t}$. The definitions of the two variance functions are

$$VarP\left(\{r_{stock,1}, r_{stock,2}, \ldots, r_{stock,N}\}\right) = \frac{1}{N}\sum_{j=1}^{N}\left(r_{stock,j} - \bar{r}_i\right)^2$$

$$Var\left(\{r_{stock,1}, r_{stock,2}, \ldots, r_{stock,N}\}\right) = \frac{1}{N-1}\sum_{j=1}^{N}\left(r_{stock,j} - \bar{r}_i\right)^2$$

There's a long story about the difference between these two concepts that we'll leave for someone else (like your statistics instructor) to explain. Suffice it to say that in the examples covered in this book we'll use **VarP** and its standard deviation equivalent **StdevP**.

Finally, you might wonder why there are two expressions—the variance and the standard deviation—that measure variability. The answer has to do with the units of these expressions. Each term in the variance is squared to make everything positive. But this means that the units of the variance are "percent squared," which is a bit difficult to understand. The standard deviation, the square root of the variance, reduces the squared percentages of the variance back to "percent." This way the mean and the standard deviation have the same units.

### Exxon Price and Return Data

Below we compute the returns for Exxon stock over the period 1998–2008.

| | A | B | C | D |
|---|---|---|---|---|
| 1 | **EXXON (XOM) STOCK PRICES** Adjusted for dividends and splits | | | |
| 2 | **Date** | **Price** | **Return** | |
| 3 | 31-Dec-98 | 29.12 | | |
| 4 | 31-Dec-99 | 32.79 | 12.60% | <-- =B4/B3-1 |
| 5 | 29-Dec-00 | 36.15 | 10.25% | |
| 6 | 31-Dec-01 | 33.40 | -7.61% | |
| 7 | 31-Dec-02 | 30.44 | -8.86% | |
| 8 | 31-Dec-03 | 36.72 | 20.63% | |
| 9 | 31-Dec-04 | 47.03 | 28.08% | |
| 10 | 30-Dec-05 | 52.57 | 11.78% | |
| 11 | 29-Dec-06 | 73.11 | 39.07% | |
| 12 | 31-Dec-07 | 90.87 | 24.29% | |
| 13 | 31-Dec-08 | 78.96 | -13.11% | |
| 14 | | | | |
| 15 | Average return, $E(r_{XOM})$ | | 11.71% | <-- =AVERAGE(C4:C13) |
| 16 | Variance of return, $\sigma^2_{XOM}$ | | 0.0267 | <-- =VARP(C4:C13) |
| 17 | Standard deviation of return, $\sigma_{XOM}$ | | 16.34% | <-- =STDEVP(C4:C13) |

## 9.2. Covariance and Correlation—Two Additional Statistics

So far we've looked at statistics—mean, variance, standard deviation—that relate to the returns of an individual stock. In this section we examine two statistics—*covariance* and *correlation*—that relate the returns of two stocks to each other. We use data for Kellogg (K) and Exxon (XOM). In the following spreadsheet, we've put the returns for both stocks on one spreadsheet and calculated the covariance and correlation (cells B17:B19).

|  | A | B | C | D |
|---|---|---|---|---|
| 1 | KELLOGG (K) AND EXXON (XOM) ANNUAL RETURN DATA | | | |
| 2 | Date | Kellogg | Exxon | |
| 3 | 31-Dec-99 | -6.89% | 12.60% | |
| 4 | 29-Dec-00 | -11.59% | 10.25% | |
| 5 | 31-Dec-01 | 18.51% | -7.61% | |
| 6 | 31-Dec-02 | 17.21% | -8.86% | |
| 7 | 31-Dec-03 | 14.06% | 20.63% | |
| 8 | 31-Dec-04 | 19.93% | 28.08% | |
| 9 | 30-Dec-05 | -0.85% | 11.78% | |
| 10 | 29-Dec-06 | 18.46% | 39.07% | |
| 11 | 31-Dec-07 | 7.14% | 24.29% | |
| 12 | 31-Dec-08 | -16.02% | -13.11% | |
| 13 | | | | |
| 14 | Average return $E(r_K)$ and $E(r_{XOM})$ | 6.00% | 11.71% | <-- =AVERAGE(C3:C12) |
| 15 | Variance of returns, $\sigma^2_K$ and $\sigma^2_{XOM}$ | 0.0171 | 0.0267 | <-- =VARP(C3:C12) |
| 16 | Standard deviation of returns, $\sigma_K$ and $\sigma_{XOM}$ | 13.06% | 16.34% | <-- =STDEVP(C3:C12) |
| 17 | Covariance of returns Cov($r_K$,$r_{XOM}$) | 0.0074 | | <-- =COVAR(B3:B12,C3:C12) |
| 18 | Correlation of returns $\rho_{K,XOM}$ | 0.3482 | | <-- =CORREL(B3:B12,C3:C12) |
| 19 | | 0.3482 | | <-- =B17/(B16*C16) |

The *covariance* between two series is a measure of how much the series (in our case, the returns on K and XOM) move up or down together. The formal definition is

$$Cov(r_K, r_{XOM}) = \sigma_{K,XOM} = \frac{1}{10}\left\{\begin{array}{l}(r_{K,1999} - \overline{r}_K)(r_{XOM,1999} - \overline{r}_{XOM}) + (r_{K,2000} - \overline{r}_K)(r_{XOM,2000} - \overline{r}_{XOM}) + \\ \ldots + (r_{K,2008} - \overline{r}_K)(r_{XOM,2008} - \overline{r}_{XOM})\end{array}\right\}$$

The idea behind the formula is to measure the deviations of each data point from its average and to multiply these deviations. As you can see from cell B17, Excel has a function **Covar** that, when applied directly to the returns in columns B and C, calculates the covariance.[4]

Another common measure of how much two data series move up or down together is the *correlation coefficient*. The correlation coefficient is always between −1 and +1, which—as you'll see in the next subsection—makes it possible for us to be more precise about how the two sets of returns move together. Roughly speaking, two sets of returns that have a correlation coefficient of −1 vary *perfectly inversely*, by which we mean that when one return goes up (or down), we can perfectly predict how the other return goes down (or up). A correlation coefficient of +1 means that the returns vary in *perfect tandem*, by which we mean that when one return goes up

---

[4] The covariance is sometimes written as $\sigma_{K,XOM}$. One of the exercises at the end of this chapter has you compute the covariance in the long, tedious way suggested by the formula. You'll see that you get the same result as that returned by Excel's **Covar** function.

(or down), we can perfectly predict how the other return goes up (or down). A correlation coefficient between −1 and +1 means that the two sets of returns vary together less than perfectly.

The correlation coefficient is defined as

$$Correlation\left(r_K, r_{XOM}\right) = \rho_{K,XOM} = \frac{Cov\left(r_K, r_{XOM}\right)}{\sigma_K \sigma_{XOM}}.$$

The Greek letter $\rho$ (pronounced "rho") is often used as a symbol for the correlation coefficient. In the preceding spreadsheet, we calculate the correlation coefficient in two ways: In cell G16 of the previous spreadsheet, we use the Excel function **Correl** to compute the correlation. Cell G17 applies the formula $\frac{Cov\left(r_K, r_{XOM}\right)}{\sigma_K \sigma_{XOM}}$ (and, of course, gets the same result).

## Some Facts about Covariance and Correlation

Here are some facts about covariance and correlation. We state them without much attempt at elaborate explanation or proof.

**Fact 1.** Covariance is affected by units; correlation isn't. Here's an example: In the spreadsheet below, we've presented the annual returns as whole numbers instead of percentages (writing K's 1999 return as −6.89 instead of −6.89%). The covariance (cell B17) is now 74.30, which is 10,000 times our previous calculation. But the correlation coefficient (B18) remains the same as before, 0.3482.

| | A | B | C | D |
|---|---|---|---|---|
| 1 | KELLOGG (K) AND EXXON (XOM) Percentages presented as whole numbers | | | |
| 2 | Date | Kellogg | Exxon | |
| 3 | 31-Dec-99 | -6.89 | 12.60 | |
| 4 | 29-Dec-00 | -11.59 | 10.25 | |
| 5 | 31-Dec-01 | 18.51 | -7.61 | |
| 6 | 31-Dec-02 | 17.21 | -8.86 | |
| 7 | 31-Dec-03 | 14.06 | 20.63 | |
| 8 | 31-Dec-04 | 19.93 | 28.08 | |
| 9 | 30-Dec-05 | -0.85 | 11.78 | |
| 10 | 29-Dec-06 | 18.46 | 39.07 | |
| 11 | 31-Dec-07 | 7.14 | 24.29 | |
| 12 | 31-Dec-08 | -16.02 | -13.11 | |
| 13 | | | | |
| 14 | Average return $E(r_K)$ and $E(r_{XOM})$ | 6.00 | 11.71 | <-- =AVERAGE(C3:C12) |
| 15 | Variance of returns, $\sigma^2_K$ and $\sigma^2_{XOM}$ | 170.55 | 266.96 | <-- =VARP(C3:C12) |
| 16 | Standard deviation of returns, $\sigma_K$ and $\sigma_{XOM}$ | 13.06 | 16.34 | <-- =STDEVP(C3:C12) |
| 17 | Covariance of returns $Cov(r_K,r_{XOM})$ | 74.30 | | <-- =COVAR(B3:B12,C3:C12) |
| 18 | Correlation of returns $\rho_{K,XOM}$ | 0.3482 | | <-- =CORREL(B3:B12,C3:C12) |
| 19 | | 0.3482 | | <-- =B17/(B16*C16) |
| 20 | Correlation is symmetric: $\rho_{K,XOM} = \rho_{XOM,K}$ | 0.3482 | | <-- =CORREL(C3:C12,B3:B12) |

**Fact 2.** The correlation between Kellogg and Exxon is the same as the correlation between Exxon and Kellogg. The same holds for the covariance: $Cov\left(r_K, r_{XOM}\right) = Cov\left(r_{XOM}, r_K\right)$ The technical jargon for this is that "correlation and covariance are symmetric." To see this in Excel, note that cells B18 ( **=Correl(B3:B12,C3:C12)** ) and B20 ( **=Correl(C3:C12,B3:B12)** ) are equal in the above spreadsheet.

**Fact 3**. The correlation will always be between +1 and –1. The higher the correlation coefficient is in absolute value, the more the two series move together. If the correlation is either -1 or +1, then the two series are *perfectly correlated*, which means that knowing one series allows you to predict completely the value of the second series. If the correlation coefficient is between −1 and +1, then the two series move in tandem less than perfectly.

**Fact 4**. If the correlation coefficient is either +1 or –1, this means that the two returns have a linear relation between them. Because this is not easy to understand, we illustrate with a numerical example: Adams Farm and Morgan Sausage are two shares listed on the Farmers Stock Exchange. For reasons that are difficult to determine, each Morgan Sausage's stock return is equal to 60% of that of Adams Farm plus 3%. We can thus write $r_{Morgan\ Sausage,t} = 3\% + 0.6 * r_{Adams\ Farm,t}$. This means that the return on Morgan Sausage stock is *completely predictable* given the return on Adams Farm stock. Thus, the correlation is either −1 or +1. Because when Adams Farm's return moves up so does the return of Morgan Sausage, the correlation is +1.[5]

The Excel spreadsheet that follows confirms that the correlation is +1.

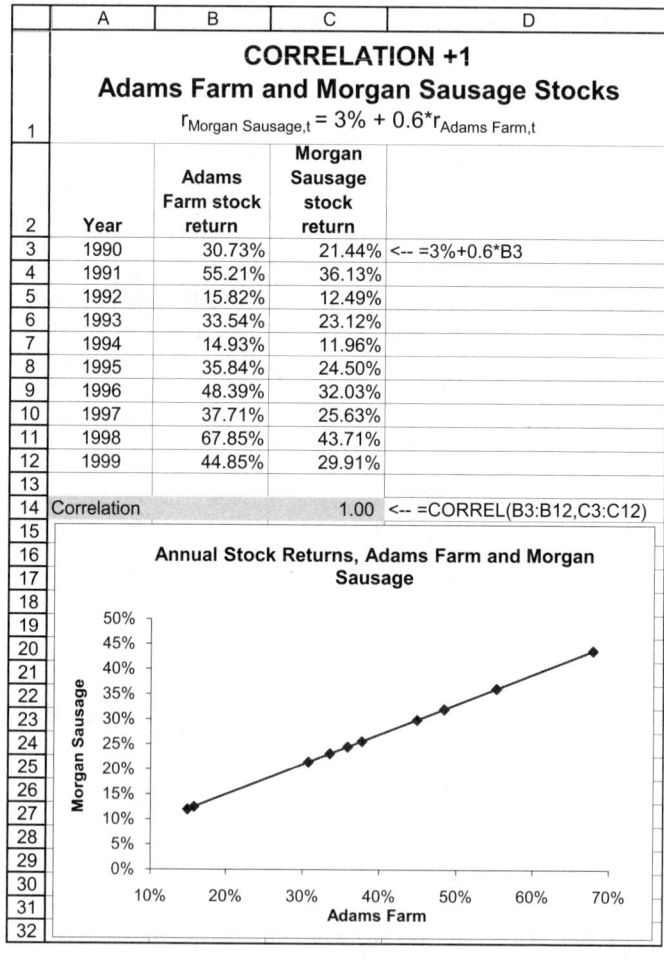

|  | A | B | C | D |
|---|---|---|---|---|
| 1 | | | **CORRELATION +1** Adams Farm and Morgan Sausage Stocks $r_{Morgan\ Sausage,t} = 3\% + 0.6*r_{Adams\ Farm,t}$ | |
| 2 | Year | Adams Farm stock return | Morgan Sausage stock return | |
| 3 | 1990 | 30.73% | 21.44% | <-- =3%+0.6*B3 |
| 4 | 1991 | 55.21% | 36.13% | |
| 5 | 1992 | 15.82% | 12.49% | |
| 6 | 1993 | 33.54% | 23.12% | |
| 7 | 1994 | 14.93% | 11.96% | |
| 8 | 1995 | 35.84% | 24.50% | |
| 9 | 1996 | 48.39% | 32.03% | |
| 10 | 1997 | 37.71% | 25.63% | |
| 11 | 1998 | 67.85% | 43.71% | |
| 12 | 1999 | 44.85% | 29.91% | |
| 13 | | | | |
| 14 | Correlation | | 1.00 | <-- =CORREL(B3:B12,C3:C12) |

Annual Stock Returns, Adams Farm and Morgan Sausage

---

[5] The Farmers Stock Exchange has two other stocks whose returns are related by the equation $r_{Chicken\ Feed,\ t} = 50\% - 0.8 * r_{Poultry\ Delight,t}$. In this case, the negative coefficient (−0.8) tells us that the correlation between the two sets of returns is −1. (See the end-of-chapter exercises.)

Fact 4 can be written mathematically as follows: Suppose Stock 1 and Stock 2 are *perfectly correlated* (meaning that the correlation is either +1 or −1). Then

$$r_{Stock1,t} = a + b * r_{Stock2,t} \Big\} \begin{array}{l} \leftarrow b>0 \text{ if the correlation} = +1 \\ \leftarrow b<0 \text{ if the correlation} = -1 \end{array}$$

## 9.3. Portfolio Mean and Variance for a Two-Asset Portfolio

A *portfolio* is a set of stocks or other financial assets. Most people who own stock own more than one stock; they own portfolios of stocks, and the risks they bear relate to the riskiness of their portfolio. In the next chapter we'll start our economic analysis of portfolios. In this section we'll show you how to compute the mean and variance of a portfolio composed of two stocks. Suppose that between 1998 and 2008 you held a portfolio invested 50% in Kellogg and 50% in Exxon. Column E of the spreadsheet below shows what the annual returns would have been on this portfolio. For example, holding 50% of your portfolio in K and 50% in XOM would have given you a portfolio return of 2.85% in 1999:

$$2.85\% = \underbrace{50\%}_{\substack{\text{proportion of} \\ \text{K stock in} \\ \text{portfolio}}} * \underbrace{-6.89\%}_{\substack{\text{Return on} \\ \text{K stock} \\ \text{in 1999}}} + \underbrace{50\%}_{\substack{\text{proportion of} \\ \text{XOM stock in} \\ \text{portfolio}}} * \underbrace{12.60\%}_{\substack{\text{Return on} \\ \text{XOM stock} \\ \text{in 1999}}}$$

In cells E17:E21 we calculate the portfolio return statistics in the same way we calculated the return statistics for the individual assets K and XOM.

| | A | B | C | D | E | F |
|---|---|---|---|---|---|---|
| 1 | | CALCULATING PORTFOLIO RETURNS AND THEIR STATISTICS | | | | |
| 2 | Proportion of Kellogg | 0.5 | | | | |
| 3 | Proportion of Exxon | 0.5 | <-- =1-B2 | | | |
| 4 | | | | | | |
| 5 | Date | Kellogg return | Exxon return | | Portfolio return | |
| 6 | 31-Dec-99 | -6.89% | 12.60% | | 2.85% | <-- =$B$2*B6+$B$3*C6 |
| 7 | 29-Dec-00 | -11.59% | 10.25% | | -0.67% | |
| 8 | 31-Dec-01 | 18.51% | -7.61% | | 5.45% | |
| 9 | 31-Dec-02 | 17.21% | -8.86% | | 4.17% | |
| 10 | 31-Dec-03 | 14.06% | 20.63% | | 17.35% | |
| 11 | 31-Dec-04 | 19.93% | 28.08% | | 24.00% | |
| 12 | 30-Dec-05 | -0.85% | 11.78% | | 5.46% | |
| 13 | 29-Dec-06 | 18.46% | 39.07% | | 28.76% | |
| 14 | 31-Dec-07 | 7.14% | 24.29% | | 15.71% | |
| 15 | 31-Dec-08 | -16.02% | -13.11% | | -14.56% | |
| 16 | | | | | | |
| 17 | Mean | 6.00% | 11.71% | | 8.85% | <-- =AVERAGE(E6:E15) |
| 18 | Variance | 1.71% | 2.67% | | 0.0147 | <-- =VARP(E6:E15) |
| 19 | Standard deviation | 13.06% | 16.34% | | 12.10% | <-- =STDEVP(E6:E15) |
| 20 | Covariance | | 0.0074 | | | |
| 21 | Correlation | | 0.3482 | | | |
| 22 | | | | | | |
| 23 | Direct calculation of portfolio mean and variance | | | | | |
| 24 | Portfolio mean, $E(r_p)$ | 8.85% | <-- =B2*B17+B3*C17 | | | |
| 25 | Portfolio variance, $Var(r_p)$ | 0.0147 | <-- =B2^2*B18+B3^2*C18+2*B2*B3*C20 | | | |
| 26 | Portfolio standard dev., $\sigma_p$ | 12.10% | <-- =SQRT(B25) | | | |

Cells B24:B26 show that these portfolio statistics can be calculated directly from the statistics for the individual assets. To calculate the portfolio mean using these shortcuts, we first need some notation: Let $x_K$ stand for the proportion of Kellogg stock in the portfolio and let $x_{XOM}$ denote the proportion of Exxon stock in the portfolio. In our example $x_K = 0.5$ and $x_{XOM} = 0.5$ and the portfolio mean return is given by

$$Portfolio\ mean\ return = E(r_p) = x_K E(r_K) + x_{XOM} E(r_{XOM})$$
$$= x_K E(r_K) + (1 - x_K) E(r_{XOM})$$

Note the second line of the formula: If we only have two assets in the portfolio, then the proportion of the second asset is "one minus" the proportion of the first asset: $x_{XOM} = 1 - x_K$.

The formula for the portfolio variance is given by

$$Portfolio\ variance = Var(r_p) = x_K^2 Var(r_K) + x_{XOM}^2 Var(r_{XOM}) + 2x_K x_{XOM} Cov(r_K, r_{XOM}).$$

In the spreadsheet below we've built a table of the portfolio statistics using the formulas. In the table we vary the proportion of Kellogg stock in the portfolio from 0 to 100% (which means, of course, that the proportion of Exxon stock goes from 100 to 0%).

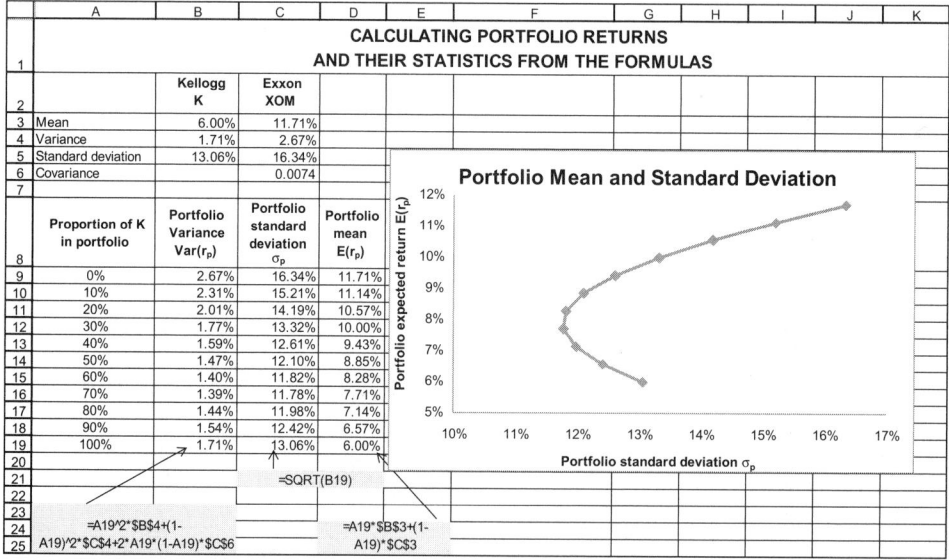

The graph is one that you will see again (lots!) in Chapters 10 and 11. It plots the portfolio standard deviation $\sigma_p$ on the x-axis and the portfolio mean return $E(r_p)$ on the y-axis. The parabolic shape of the graph is the subject of much discussion in finance, but this is a purely technical chapter—the finance part of the discussion will have to wait until the following chapters.

# 9.4. Using Regressions

*Linear regression* (for short, regression) is a technique for fitting a line to a set of data. Regressions are used in finance to examine the relation between data series. In the chapters that follow we often need to use regressions; we introduce the basic concepts here. We do not discuss the statistical theory behind regressions, but instead we show you how to run a regression and how to use it.

We've divided the discussion into three subsections: First we discuss the mechanics of doing a regression in Excel, then we discuss the meaning of the regression, and finally we discuss alternative ways of doing the regression.

## The Mechanics of Doing a Regression in Excel

In this subsection we discuss a simple regression example and make little attempt to explain the economic meaning of the regression. Instead we focus on the mechanics of doing the regression in Excel and leave the economic interpretation for the next subsection.

The table below gives the monthly returns for the S&P 500 Index (stock symbol SPX) and for IBM (stock symbol IBM) for 2007 and 2008. The S&P 500 Index includes the 500 largest stocks traded on U.S. stock exchanges, and its performance is roughly indicative of the performance of the U.S. stock market as a whole. We will use the regression analysis to see whether we can understand the relation between S&P's returns and IBM's returns—that is, if we can understand the effect of the U.S. stock market on the returns of IBM's stock.

Here are the data we examine. Note that we have graphed the data using an Excel XY scatter graph (see Chapter 25 for details).

| | A | B | C | D | E | F | G | H |
|---|---|---|---|---|---|---|---|---|
| 1 | | | | | \multicolumn{4}{c}{**MONTHLY RETURNS ON S&P 500 AND IBM**} |
| | | | | | \multicolumn{4}{c}{**January 2007 - December 2008**} |
| 2 | | Price at beginning of month | | | Return for the month | | | |
| 3 | Date | S&P 500 | IBM | | S&P 500 | IBM | | |
| 4 | 3-Jan-07 | 1438.24 | 95.08 | | | | | |
| 5 | 1-Feb-07 | 1406.82 | 89.39 | | -2.18% | -5.98% | <-- =C5/C4-1 | |
| 6 | 1-Mar-07 | 1420.86 | 90.66 | | 1.00% | 1.42% | <-- =C6/C5-1 | |
| 7 | 2-Apr-07 | 1482.37 | 98.31 | | 4.33% | 8.44% | | |
| 8 | 1-May-07 | 1530.62 | 102.93 | | 3.25% | 4.70% | | |
| 9 | 1-Jun-07 | 1503.35 | 101.62 | | -1.78% | -1.27% | | |
| 10 | 2-Jul-07 | 1455.27 | 106.84 | | -3.20% | 5.14% | | |
| 11 | 1-Aug-07 | 1473.99 | 113.07 | | 1.29% | 5.83% | | |
| 12 | 4-Sep-07 | 1526.75 | 114.14 | | 3.58% | 0.95% | | |
| 13 | 1-Oct-07 | 1549.38 | 112.52 | | 1.48% | -1.42% | | |
| 14 | 1-Nov-07 | 1481.14 | 102.28 | | -4.40% | -9.10% | | |
| 15 | 3-Dec-07 | 1468.36 | 105.12 | | -0.86% | 2.78% | | |
| 16 | 2-Jan-08 | 1378.55 | 104.15 | | -6.12% | -0.92% | | |
| 17 | 1-Feb-08 | 1330.63 | 111.14 | | -3.48% | 6.71% | | |
| 18 | 3-Mar-08 | 1322.70 | 112.39 | | -0.60% | 1.12% | | |
| 19 | 1-Apr-08 | 1385.59 | 117.82 | | 4.75% | 4.83% | | |
| 20 | 1-May-08 | 1400.38 | 126.85 | | 1.07% | 7.66% | | |
| 21 | 2-Jun-08 | 1280.00 | 116.17 | | -8.60% | -8.42% | | |
| 22 | 1-Jul-08 | 1267.38 | 125.43 | | -0.99% | 7.97% | | |
| 23 | 1-Aug-08 | 1282.83 | 119.77 | | 1.22% | -4.51% | | |
| 24 | 2-Sep-08 | 1164.74 | 115.08 | | -9.21% | -3.92% | | |
| 25 | 1-Oct-08 | 968.75 | 91.48 | | -16.83% | -20.51% | | |
| 26 | 3-Nov-08 | 896.24 | 80.74 | | -7.48% | -11.74% | | |
| 27 | 1-Dec-08 | 903.25 | 83.27 | | 0.78% | 3.13% | | |
| 28 | 2-Jan-09 | 825.88 | 90.68 | | -8.57% | 8.90% | | |
| 29 | | | | | | | | |
| 30 | Total decline | | | | -42.58% | -4.63% | <-- =C28/C4-1 | |
| 31 | Largest monthly gain | | | | 4.75% | 8.90% | <-- =MAX(F5:F28) | |
| 32 | Largest monthly loss | | | | -16.83% | -20.51% | <-- =MIN(F5:F28) | |

IBM Monthly Returns vs S&P 500 2007-2008

The months graphed were not happy months for American stocks! During these 2 years, the S&P 500 declined almost 43% and IBM declined by almost 5%.

We want to draw a line through the points above, and we want this line to be to be the "best" line in the sense that it is the closest line you could draw through the points.[6] There are several ways to do this in Excel (as usual). Here's what we do:

- Click on the points of the graph so that Excel marks all of them. If you have a lot of data points, Excel may mark only some of the points; just ignore this and proceed to the next step. After you do this, you'll see a graph like the one below (note that Excel shows us the coordinates of the point we happened to point at—in this case the point where the SPX return is −4.40% and the IBM return is −9.10%):

- With the points marked, right click the mouse and choose **Add Trendline.** This brings up the following box, in which we leave the choice **Linear** regression. Note that we have clicked the two boxes at the bottom of the box—"Display equation on chart" and "Display R-squared value on chart."

---

[6]There's a formal statistical definition of "best" and "closest," but we'll leave that to another course.

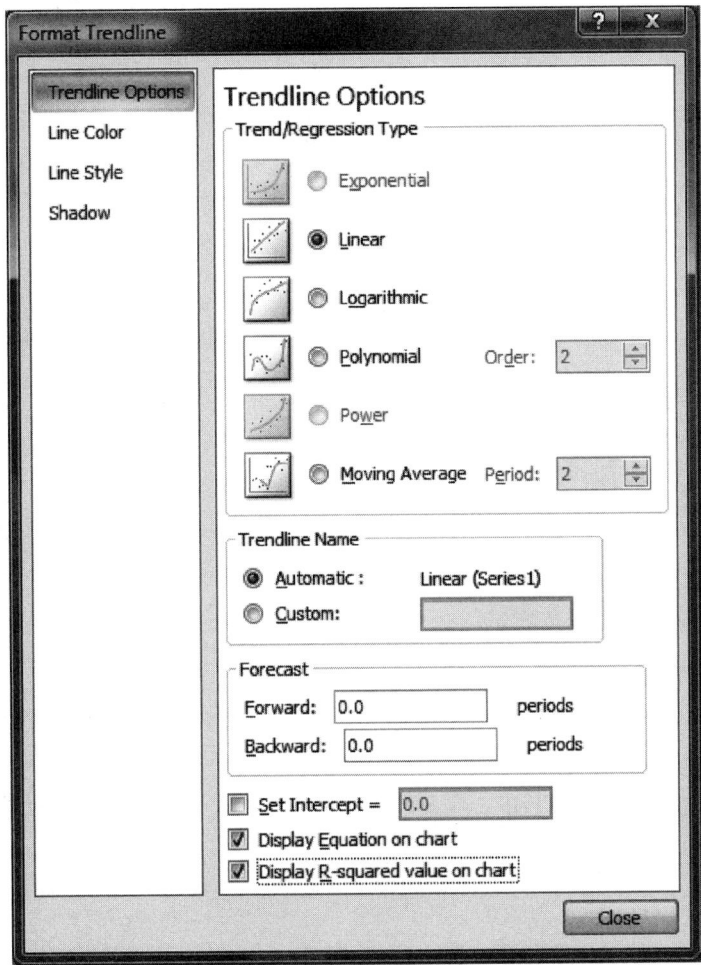

Clicking **Close** brings up the following chart.

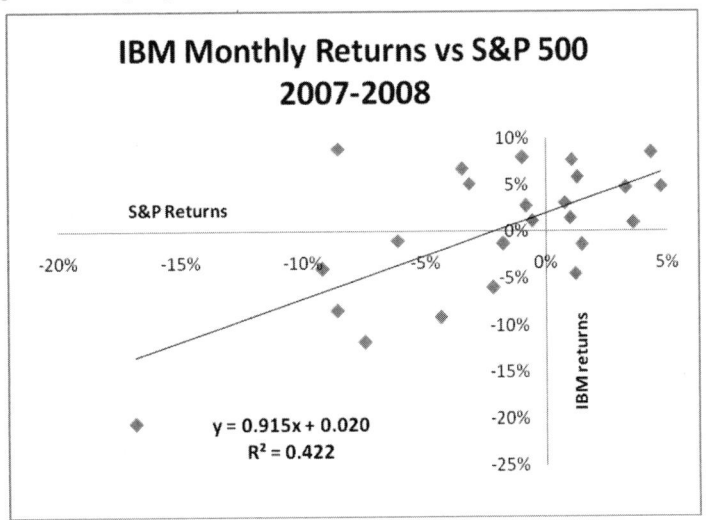

The box with the regression results can be moved with the mouse. The text inside the box can be formatted to the font and the size you desire.

## What Does the Regression Mean?

The graph above shows the regression line as $y = 0.915x + 0.020, R^2 = 0.422$. Because we're trying to understand the effect of the S&P Index on IBM stock, we can attach the following meaning to the variables of the regression line:

- The "$y$" of the regression line stands for the monthly percentage return of IBM and the "$x$" stands for the monthly percentage return of the S&P 500 index.

- The *slope* of the regression line is 0.915. This tells us that, on average, a 1% increase in the S&P monthly return caused a 0.915% increase in the IBM monthly return.[7] Of course this also goes the other direction: On average, a 1% decrease in the S&P is related to a 0.915% decrease in IBM's return.

- The fact that the slope of the regression is less than 1 means that IBM is somewhat less sensitive to the S&P than an average stock: Variations (increases or decreases) in the S&P return cause smaller variations in the IBM return. We return to this topic in Chapter 11.

- The *intercept* of the regression line is 0.02. The intercept tells us that in months when the S&P 500 doesn't "move," IBM's return is 2%. This is a remarkable fact—it indicates that during this period IBM had a "monthly excess return" over the S&P of 2%, which—compounded annually—is $(1 + 2\%)^{12} - 1 = 26.8\%$.

- The $R^2$ (pronounced "r squared") of the regression line says that 42.2% of the variability in the IBM returns is explained by the variability of the S&P 500 returns. The other 58% of the return variability is presumably explained by factors that are unique to IBM. You wouldn't expect much more: If for some strange reason the $R^2$ were 100%, this would mean that *all* of IBM's returns are explained by the S&P returns, which is clearly nonsense.

The regression line thus allows you to make some interesting predictions about the IBM return based on the S&P return. Suppose you're a financial analyst and you think that this month the S&P index will go up by 20%. Based on the regression, you'd expect IBM stock to increase

---

[7] During the period 2007–2008, returns mostly declined! Therefore, another way of understanding the coefficient 0.915 is that a decline of 1% in the S&P 500 was accompanied by a 0.915% decline in IBM returns.

by $0.915*20\%+0.02=20.30\%$. Knowing that the $R^2$ is approximately 42%, only about half of the variability in IBM stock returns is explained by the S&P stock return, and you would thus attach some degree of skepticism to this prediction.

## Other Ways of Doing a Regression in Excel

As you might expect, in Excel there are other methods for calculating the slope, intercept, and $R^2$ of the regression equation. Excel has functions called **Slope**, **Intercept**, and **Rsq**. These functions are illustrated below in cells F30, F33, and F36. Note that in these functions, the IBM returns come before the S&P returns, so that we write, for example, **Slope(IBM returns,S&P returns)**.

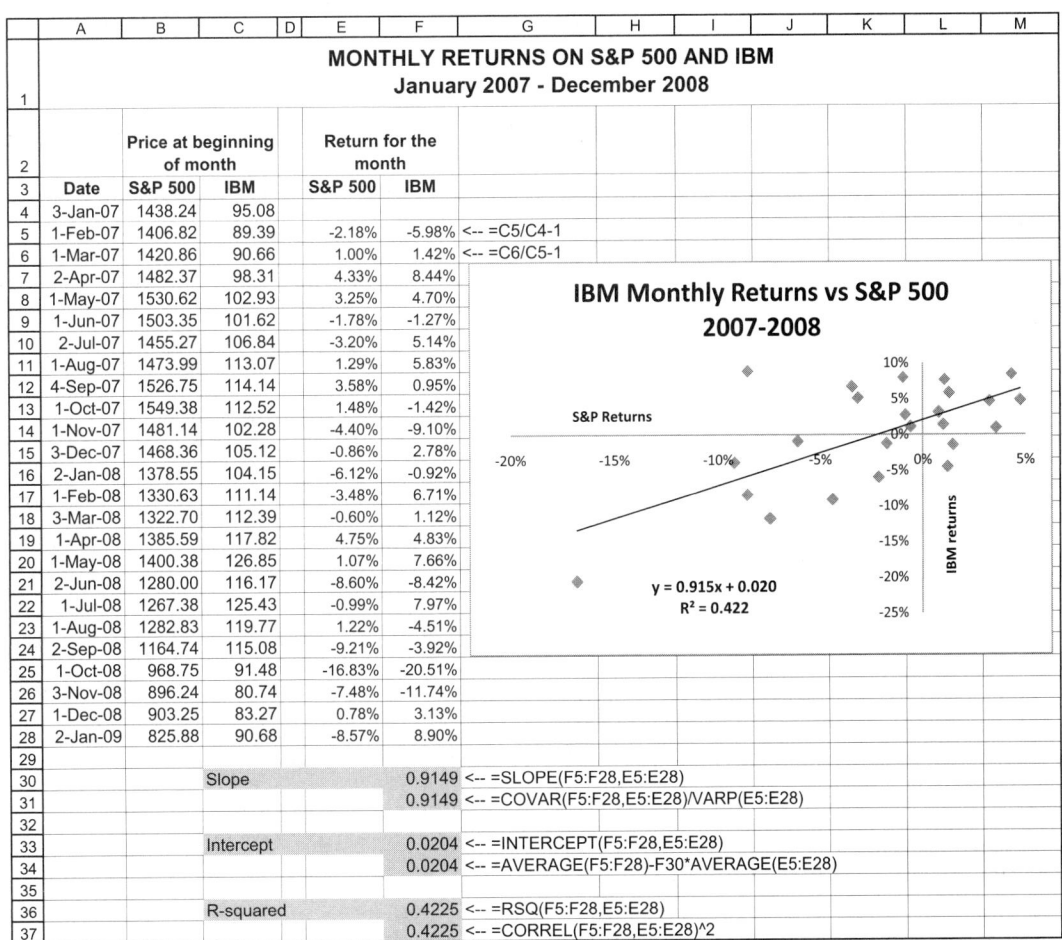

| | A | B | C | D | E | F | G |
|---|---|---|---|---|---|---|---|
| 1 | | | | | | MONTHLY RETURNS ON S&P 500 AND IBM<br>January 2007 - December 2008 | |
| 2 | | Price at beginning of month | | | Return for the month | | |
| 3 | Date | S&P 500 | IBM | | S&P 500 | IBM | |
| 4 | 3-Jan-07 | 1438.24 | 95.08 | | | | |
| 5 | 1-Feb-07 | 1406.82 | 89.39 | | -2.18% | -5.98% | <-- =C5/C4-1 |
| 6 | 1-Mar-07 | 1420.86 | 90.66 | | 1.00% | 1.42% | <-- =C6/C5-1 |
| 7 | 2-Apr-07 | 1482.37 | 98.31 | | 4.33% | 8.44% | |
| 8 | 1-May-07 | 1530.62 | 102.93 | | 3.25% | 4.70% | |
| 9 | 1-Jun-07 | 1503.35 | 101.62 | | -1.78% | -1.27% | |
| 10 | 2-Jul-07 | 1455.27 | 106.84 | | -3.20% | 5.14% | |
| 11 | 1-Aug-07 | 1473.99 | 113.07 | | 1.29% | 5.83% | |
| 12 | 4-Sep-07 | 1526.75 | 114.14 | | 3.58% | 0.95% | |
| 13 | 1-Oct-07 | 1549.38 | 112.52 | | 1.48% | -1.42% | |
| 14 | 1-Nov-07 | 1481.14 | 102.28 | | -4.40% | -9.10% | |
| 15 | 3-Dec-07 | 1468.36 | 105.12 | | -0.86% | 2.78% | |
| 16 | 2-Jan-08 | 1378.55 | 104.15 | | -6.12% | -0.92% | |
| 17 | 1-Feb-08 | 1330.63 | 111.14 | | -3.48% | 6.71% | |
| 18 | 3-Mar-08 | 1322.70 | 112.39 | | -0.60% | 1.12% | |
| 19 | 1-Apr-08 | 1385.59 | 117.82 | | 4.75% | 4.83% | |
| 20 | 1-May-08 | 1400.38 | 126.85 | | 1.07% | 7.66% | |
| 21 | 2-Jun-08 | 1280.00 | 116.17 | | -8.60% | -8.42% | |
| 22 | 1-Jul-08 | 1267.38 | 125.43 | | -0.99% | 7.97% | |
| 23 | 1-Aug-08 | 1282.83 | 119.77 | | 1.22% | -4.51% | |
| 24 | 2-Sep-08 | 1164.74 | 115.08 | | -9.21% | -3.92% | |
| 25 | 1-Oct-08 | 968.75 | 91.48 | | -16.83% | -20.51% | |
| 26 | 3-Nov-08 | 896.24 | 80.74 | | -7.48% | -11.74% | |
| 27 | 1-Dec-08 | 903.25 | 83.27 | | 0.78% | 3.13% | |
| 28 | 2-Jan-09 | 825.88 | 90.68 | | -8.57% | 8.90% | |
| 29 | | | | | | | |
| 30 | | | Slope | | | 0.9149 | <-- =SLOPE(F5:F28,E5:E28) |
| 31 | | | | | | 0.9149 | <-- =COVAR(F5:F28,E5:E28)/VARP(E5:E28) |
| 32 | | | | | | | |
| 33 | | | Intercept | | | 0.0204 | <-- =INTERCEPT(F5:F28,E5:E28) |
| 34 | | | | | | 0.0204 | <-- =AVERAGE(F5:F28)-F30*AVERAGE(E5:E28) |
| 35 | | | | | | | |
| 36 | | | R-squared | | | 0.4225 | <-- =RSQ(F5:F28,E5:E28) |
| 37 | | | | | | 0.4225 | <-- =CORREL(F5:F28,E5:E28)^2 |

IBM Monthly Returns vs S&P 500 2007-2008

$y = 0.915x + 0.020$
$R^2 = 0.422$

The slope, intercept, and $R^2$ can also be calculated directly using the **Average, Covar, Varp,** and **Correl** (cells F31, F34, and F37 above). Look at the alternative definitions of each of the regression variables:

- The regression slope can be computed with the **Slope** function (cell F30), but as shown in cell F31 it is also equal to the $\dfrac{Covariance(S\&P,IBM)}{Var(S\&P)}$.

- The regression intercept can be computed with the **Intercept** function, but as shown in cell F34 it is also equal to $Average(IBM) - slope * Average(S\&P)$.

- The regression $R^2$ can be computed with the **Rsq** function, but as shown in cell F37 it is also equal to the squared correlation between the S&P and IBM: $\left[Correlation(S\&P,IBM)\right]^2$.

## 9.5. Advanced Topic: Portfolio Statistics for Multiple Assets

This section discusses a slightly more advanced topic. You can skip it on your first reading. In Section 9.3 we discussed the calculation of the portfolio mean and variance for a two-asset portfolio. In this section we discuss the calculation for a portfolio composed of more than two assets.

To set the scene, we introduce some notation. Suppose that we have three stocks and that for each stock $i$ ($i = 1,2,3$) we have computed the mean $E(r_i)$ and the variance $\sigma_i^2 = Var(r_i)$ of the stock's returns. Furthermore, suppose that for each pair of stocks $i$ and $j$, we have calculated the covariance of the returns $Cov(r_i,r_j)$. Here's an example.

| | A | B | C | D | E |
|---|---|---|---|---|---|
| 1 | PORTFOLIO RETURNS FOR A THREE-STOCK PORTFOLIO | | | | |
| 2 | Year ending | Boeing BA | Kellogg K | IBM | |
| 3 | 31-Dec-99 | 28.67% | -7.31% | 17.57% | |
| 4 | 29-Dec-00 | 61.21% | -11.38% | -20.83% | |
| 5 | 31-Dec-01 | -40.42% | 18.80% | 43.00% | |
| 6 | 31-Dec-02 | -13.40% | 17.28% | -35.45% | |
| 7 | 31-Dec-03 | 30.43% | 14.56% | 20.49% | |
| 8 | 31-Dec-04 | 24.89% | 20.15% | 7.19% | |
| 9 | 30-Dec-05 | 37.89% | -0.93% | -15.83% | |
| 10 | 29-Dec-06 | 28.40% | 18.60% | 19.77% | |
| 11 | 31-Dec-07 | -0.11% | 7.15% | 12.84% | |
| 12 | 31-Dec-08 | -50.07% | -14.14% | -20.79% | |
| 13 | | | | | |
| 14 | Average | 10.75% | 6.28% | 2.79% | <-- =AVERAGE(D3:D12) |
| 15 | Variance | 0.1152 | 0.0166 | 0.0548 | <-- =VARP(D3:D12) |
| 16 | Sigma | 33.94% | 12.87% | 23.41% | <-- =STDEVP(D3:D12) |
| 17 | | | | | |
| 18 | Covariances | | Correlations | | |
| 19 | Cov($r_{BA}$,$r_K$) | -0.0043 | Corr($r_{BA}$,$r_K$) | -0.0978 | <-- =B19/(B16*C16) |
| 20 | Cov($r_{BA}$,$r_{IBM}$) | -0.0053 | Corr($r_{BA}$,$r_{IBM}$) | -0.0669 | <-- =B20/(B16*D16) |
| 21 | Cov($r_K$,$r_{IBM}$) | 0.0134 | Corr($r_K$,$r_{IBM}$) | 0.4448 | <-- =B21/(C16*D16) |

Now suppose we form a portfolio composed of the following proportions of each of the stocks: $x_{BA} = 20\%$, $x_K = 50\%$, and $x_{IBM} = 1 - x_{BA} - x_K = 30\%$. Cells G3:G12 in the spreadsheet below show you the returns of this portfolio, and cells H16:H18 compute the portfolio's mean return, variance, and standard deviation.

| | A | B | C | D | E | F | G | H | I |
|---|---|---|---|---|---|---|---|---|---|
| 1 | | | | | PORTFOLIO RETURNS FOR A THREE-STOCK PORTFOLIO | | | | |
| 2 | Year ending | Boeing BA | Kellogg K | IBM | | | | Portfolio return | |
| 3 | 31-Dec-99 | 28.67% | -7.31% | 17.57% | | | | 7.35% | <-- =$B$14*B3+$C$14*C3+$D$14*D3 |
| 4 | 29-Dec-00 | 61.21% | -11.38% | -20.83% | | | | 0.30% | <-- =$B$14*B4+$C$14*C4+$D$14*D4 |
| 5 | 31-Dec-01 | -40.42% | 18.80% | 43.00% | | | | 14.21% | |
| 6 | 31-Dec-02 | -13.40% | 17.28% | -35.45% | | | | -4.68% | |
| 7 | 31-Dec-03 | 30.43% | 14.56% | 20.49% | | | | 19.51% | |
| 8 | 31-Dec-04 | 24.89% | 20.15% | 7.19% | | | | 17.21% | |
| 9 | 30-Dec-05 | 37.89% | -0.93% | -15.83% | | | | 2.37% | |
| 10 | 29-Dec-06 | 28.40% | 18.60% | 19.77% | | | | 20.91% | |
| 11 | 31-Dec-07 | -0.11% | 7.15% | 12.84% | | | | 7.40% | |
| 12 | 31-Dec-08 | -50.07% | -14.14% | -20.79% | | | | -23.32% | |
| 13 | | | | | | | | | |
| 14 | Portfolio proportions | 0.20 | 0.50 | 0.30 | | | | | |
| 15 | | | | | | | | | |
| 16 | Average | 10.75% | 6.28% | 2.79% | <-- =AVERAGE(D3:D12) | | Average | 6.13% | <-- =AVERAGE(H3:H12) |
| 17 | Variance | 0.1152 | 0.0166 | 0.0548 | <-- =VARP(D3:D12) | | Variance | 0.0162 | <-- =VARP(H3:H12) |
| 18 | Sigma | 33.94% | 12.87% | 23.41% | <-- =STDEVP(D3:D12) | | Sigma | 12.73% | <-- =STDEVP(H3:H12) |
| 19 | | | | | | | | | |
| 20 | Covariances | | | | | | | Alternative calculation of portfolio statistics | |
| 21 | Cov($r_{BA}$,$r_K$) | | -0.0043 | <-- =COVAR(B3:B12,C3:C12) | | | Average | 6.13% | <-- =$B$14*B16+$C$14*C16+$D$14*D16 |
| 22 | Cov($r_{BA}$,$r_{IBM}$) | | -0.0053 | <-- =COVAR(B3:B12,D3:D12) | | | Variance | 0.0162 | <-- =B14^2*B17+C14^2*C17+D14^2*D17+2*B14*C14*B21+2*B14*D14*B22+2*C14*D14*B23 |
| 23 | Cov($r_K$,$r_{IBM}$) | | 0.0134 | <-- =COVAR(D3:D12,C3:C12) | | | Sigma | 12.73% | <-- =SQRT(H22) |

If you look at cells H21:H23, you'll see that there is a straightforward way of doing the portfolio return calculations, based on the following formulas:

Average portfolio return (cell H21) $= E(r_p) = x_{BA}E(r_{BA}) + x_K E(r_K) + x_{IBM}E(r_{IBM})$

Portfolio variance (cell H22) $= Var(r_p) = x_{BA}^2 Var(r_{BA}) + x_K^2 Var(r_K) + x_{IBM}^2 Var(r_{IBM})$
$$+2x_{BA}x_K Cov(r_{BA},r_K) + 2x_{BA}x_{IBM}Cov(r_{BA},r_{IBM})$$
$$+2x_K x_{IBM}Cov(r_{BA},r_{IBM})$$

Portfolio standard deviation (cell H23) $= \sqrt{Portfolio\ variance\ (cell\ H22)}$

These formulas generalize to any number of assets: If we have a portfolio composed of $N$ assets, and we know all the expected returns, variances, and covariances, then

- The portfolio's expected return is the weighted average of the individual asset returns. Denoting the portfolio weights by $\{x_1, x_2, ..., x_N\}$, the portfolio expected return is

$$E(r_p) = x_1 E(r_1) + x_2 E(r_2) + ... + x_N E(r_N)$$
$$= \sum_{i=1}^{N} x_i E(r_i)$$

- The portfolio's variance of return is the sum of the following two expressions:
  - The sum of each asset's variance, weighted by the *square* of the asset's portfolio proportion: $x_1^2 Var(r_1) + x_2^2 Var(r_2) + ... + x_N^2 Var(r_N)$.
  - The sum of twice each of the covariances, weighted by the *product* of the asset proportions:

$$2x_1x_2Cov(r_1,r_2) + 2x_1x_3Cov(r_1,r_3) + \ldots + 2x_1x_NCov(r_1,r_N)$$
$$+ 2x_2x_3Cov(r_2,r_3) + \ldots + 2x_2x_NCov(r_2,r_N)$$
$$+ \ldots + 2x_{N-1}x_NCov(r_{N-1},r_N)$$

## Conclusion and Summary

Information about stocks—their prices, dividends, and returns—produces mounds of data. Statistics is a way of dealing with these large masses of data. This chapter has given you the necessary statistical techniques to do typical finance computations related to stocks. We've shown how to compute stock returns from basic data about stock prices, dividends, and stock splits. We've also shown how to compute the mean return (also called the average return), the variance and standard deviation of returns, and the covariance between the returns of two different stocks.

Stocks are most often combined into portfolios, and this chapter has shown you how to compute the mean and standard deviation of a portfolio's return. It also introduced you to regression analysis, which allows you to relate the returns of two stocks one to the other.

In succeeding chapters we will use these statistical techniques to do financial analysis of individual stocks and stock portfolios.

## EXERCISES

Note: The data for these problems is included in the CD-ROM that comes with the book.

1. Here is the stock price history of HighTech and LowTech corporations. Calculate the following:

|  | A | B | C |
|---|---|---|---|
| 1 |  | HighTech Corp. Stock price | LowTech Corp. Stock price |
| 2 | 31-Dec-11 | 75.00 | 40.00 |
| 3 | 31-Dec-12 | 86.25 | 45.20 |
| 4 | 31-Dec-13 | 125.32 | 55.60 |
| 5 | 31-Dec-14 | 91.64 | 48.37 |
| 6 | 31-Dec-15 | 100.80 | 32.88 |
| 7 | 31-Dec-16 | 145.93 | 61.64 |
| 8 | 31-Dec-17 | 151.21 | 75.82 |
| 9 | 31-Dec-18 | 196.57 | 97.05 |
| 10 | 31-Dec-19 | 226.05 | 109.66 |
| 11 | 31-Dec-20 | 89.00 | 122.99 |

a. The annual returns for each stock.

b. The mean (average) return for the period of 10 years for each firm. Which stock has the higher average return?

c. The variance and the standard deviation of returns for the period of 10 years for each firm. Which stock is riskier?

d. The covariance and correlation of the returns for each firm. Use two formulas to compute the correlation: The Excel formula **Correl** and the definition

$$Correlation(r_A, r_B) = \frac{Cov(r_A, r_B)}{\sigma_A \sigma_B}.$$

e. If you had to choose between the two stocks, which would you choose? Explain briefly.

2. Below you will find price data for three mutual funds.

|  | A | B | C | D |
|---|---|---|---|---|
| 1 | **DATA ON THREE MUTUAL FUNDS** | | | |
| 2 | Date | **Scudder Development Fund** | **Value Line Leveraged Growth Fund** | **Fidelity Fund** |
| 3 | 4-Jan-93 | 24.34 | 17.47 | 9.47 |
| 4 | 3-Jan-94 | 24.20 | 20.32 | 11.39 |
| 5 | 3-Jan-95 | 20.87 | 19.15 | 11.19 |
| 6 | 2-Jan-96 | 30.35 | 24.45 | 15.25 |
| 7 | 2-Jan-97 | 30.94 | 26.95 | 18.46 |
| 8 | 2-Jan-98 | 31.28 | 32.08 | 23.44 |
| 9 | 4-Jan-99 | 33.32 | 47.19 | 31.04 |
| 10 | 3-Jan-00 | 36.06 | 49.12 | 35.36 |
| 11 | 2-Jan-01 | 33.89 | 47.23 | 33.82 |
| 12 | 2-Jan-02 | 20.01 | 37.31 | 28.46 |
| 13 | 2-Jan-03 | 13.79 | 26.87 | 21.55 |

a. Compute the annual returns on the funds for the period.

b. Compute the mean, variance, and standard deviation of the fund returns.

c. Graph the fund returns and the dates.

d. Calculate the correlations of the fund returns.

e. If the historical information correctly predicts future returns (is this reasonable?), which fund would you choose?

3. Here is the monthly stock price data for Ford Corp. and GM Corp.

|  | A | B | C | D |
|---|---|---|---|---|
| 1 | **PRICES FOR FORD AND GM STOCK** | | | |
| 2 | Date | Ford | GM | |
| 3 | 8-Nov-99 | 24.44 | 66.08 | |
| 4 | 1-Dec-99 | 25.79 | 65.09 | |
| 5 | 3-Jan-00 | 24.32 | 72.14 | |
| 6 | 1-Feb-00 | 20.35 | 68.54 | |
| 7 | 1-Mar-00 | 22.45 | 74.63 | |
| 8 | 3-Apr-00 | 27.00 | 84.37 | |
| 9 | 1-May-00 | 23.95 | 64.02 | |
| 10 | 1-Jun-00 | 22.08 | 52.63 | |
| 11 | 3-Jul-00 | 24.17 | 51.61 | |
| 12 | 1-Aug-00 | 21.95 | 63.97 | |
| 13 | 1-Sep-00 | 23.14 | 59.40 | |
| 14 | 2-Oct-00 | 23.98 | 56.77 | |
| 15 | 1-Nov-00 | 20.89 | 45.64 | |
| 16 | 1-Dec-00 | 21.52 | 46.96 | |
| 17 | 2-Jan-01 | 26.16 | 49.51 | |
| 18 | 1-Feb-01 | 25.30 | 51.77 | |

Calculate the following:

- Monthly returns for each firm.
- Covariance between returns of Ford Corp. and GM Corp.
- Correlation between returns of Ford Corp. and GM Corp.

4. Using the returns of Ford and GM corporations you calculated in the previous question, perform a regression of Ford's returns versus GM's returns. Report the following:

- The slope of the regression.
- The value of the intercept.
- The *r*-squared of the regression.

Is the mutual impact of the two company's returns (one on the other) large or small? Explain.

5. Here are stock price and dividend data for Kellogg Co.

| | A | B | C |
|---|---|---|---|
| 1 | KELLOGG PRICE AND DIVIDEND DATA | | |
| 2 | | Price | Dividend during year |
| 3 | 31-Dec-89 | 64.62 | |
| 4 | 31-Dec-90 | 78.00 | 1.44 |
| 5 | 31-Dec-91 | 56.75 | 2.15 |
| 6 | 31-Dec-92 | 62.12 | 1.16 |
| 7 | 31-Dec-93 | 53.75 | 1.32 |
| 8 | 31-Dec-94 | 55.00 | 1.40 |
| 9 | 31-Dec-95 | 76.62 | 1.50 |
| 10 | 31-Dec-96 | 69.62 | 1.62 |
| 11 | 31-Dec-97 | 46.38 | 1.28 |
| 12 | 31-Dec-98 | 40.62 | 0.90 |
| 13 | 31-Dec-99 | 24.25 | 0.98 |
| 14 | 31-Dec-00 | 26.20 | 1.00 |
| 15 | 31-Dec-01 | 30.86 | 1.00 |
| 16 | 31-Dec-02 | 33.40 | 1.00 |

a. Calculate the dividend-adjusted returns for each of the years, their mean, and their standard deviation.

b. Stock analysts like to talk about the *dividend yield*—the dividend divided into the stock price. Compute the annual dividend yield for Kellogg (define it as $\frac{Dividends\ over\ the\ year}{Stock\ price\ at\ beginning\ of\ year}$) and compute its statistics (mean and standard deviation) over the period.

c. If you bought Kellogg stock and had no intention of ever selling it, why might you be interested in the stock's dividend yield?

6. Below you will find stock price, dividend, and split data for IBM. Calculate the dividend and split-adjusted returns for each of the years, their mean, and their standard deviation.

|  | A | B | C | D |
|---|---|---|---|---|
| 1 | | | IBM PRICE, DIVIDEND, AND SPLIT DATA | |
| 2 | | Closing price | Dividend during year | Other information |
| 3 | 31-Dec-89 | 98.62 | | |
| 4 | 31-Dec-90 | 126.75 | | |
| 5 | 31-Dec-91 | 90.00 | | |
| 6 | 31-Dec-92 | 51.50 | | |
| 7 | 31-Dec-93 | 56.50 | | |
| 8 | 31-Dec-94 | 72.12 | | |
| 9 | 31-Dec-95 | 108.50 | | |
| 10 | 31-Dec-96 | 156.88 | | |
| 11 | 31-Dec-97 | 98.75 | | 2 for 1 split (May 97) |
| 12 | 31-Dec-98 | 183.25 | | |
| 13 | 31-Dec-99 | 112.25 | | 2 for 1 split (May 99) |
| 14 | 31-Dec-00 | 112.00 | | |
| 15 | 31-Dec-01 | 107.89 | | |
| 16 | 31-Dec-02 | 78.20 | 0.30 | |

7. Compute the covariance and correlation coefficient between IBM and Kellogg (previous two questions). Are there any advantages to diversifying between IBM and Kellogg?

8. Here is the stock price and split data for HeavySteel Corp.

|  | A | B | C |
|---|---|---|---|
| 1 | | HEAVYSTEEL CORPORATION | |
| 2 | | Closing stock price | Stock splits |
| 3 | 31-Dec-01 | 11.24 | |
| 4 | 31-Dec-02 | 11.98 | |
| 5 | 31-Dec-03 | 10.23 | |
| 6 | 31-Dec-04 | 11.02 | 2 for 1 |
| 7 | 31-Dec-05 | 12.56 | |
| 8 | 31-Dec-06 | 13.45 | |
| 9 | 31-Dec-07 | 15.36 | 1.5 for 1 |
| 10 | 31-Dec-08 | 16.01 | |
| 11 | 31-Dec-09 | 17.23 | |
| 12 | 31-Dec-10 | 15.23 | |

a. Calculate the split-adjusted returns for each year and its statistics (mean and standard deviation).

b. If you bought 100 shares of this stock in the beginning of 1990 and during the period of 10 years never sold or bought additional shares, how many shares would you have by the end of 2000?

9. A *reverse split* is just like a split, but only in a reverse direction. For example, in a 1 for 2 reverse split, you receive 1 share for every 2 shares you hold. How would your answers to the previous question change if you learned that in 1999 the firm did a 3 for 4 reverse split?

10. Here are two companies: Young Corp. and Mature Corp. Young Corp. grows very rapidly, does not pay any dividends, and retains all its profits. Mature Corp. stopped growing a long time ago, generates sizable cash flows, and pays out dividends.

| | A | B | C | D |
|---|---|---|---|---|
| 1 | | **Young Corp.** | **Mature Corp.** | |
| 2 | | Share price | Share price | Dividend per share |
| 3 | 31-Dec-05 | 32.56 | 78.50 | 0.00 |
| 4 | 31-Dec-06 | 34.50 | 82.50 | 0.00 |
| 5 | 31-Dec-07 | 38.98 | 84.50 | 1.00 |
| 6 | 31-Dec-08 | 44.50 | 81.60 | 0.00 |
| 7 | 31-Dec-09 | 40.20 | 79.60 | 1.50 |
| 8 | 31-Dec-10 | 39.50 | 80.96 | 1.50 |
| 9 | 31-Dec-11 | 38.45 | 82.65 | 0.00 |
| 10 | 31-Dec-12 | 37.50 | 83.69 | 2.00 |
| 11 | 31-Dec-13 | 43.58 | 82.79 | 2.00 |
| 12 | 31-Dec-14 | 50.30 | 81.97 | 0.00 |

Calculate the following:

- Young's yearly returns.
- Mature's yearly returns.
- Which is the better investment of the two? Give a brief explanation.

11. Chicken Feed and Poultry Delight are two stocks traded on the Farmers Stock Exchange. A statistician has determined that the returns on the two stocks are related by the equation $r_{Chicken\ Feed,t} = 50\% - 0.8 * r_{Poultry\ Delight,t}$. Show that the correlation between the two sets of returns is −1. Use the following template.

| | A | B | C |
|---|---|---|---|
| 2 | Year | Poultry Delight stock return | Chicken Feed stock return |
| 3 | 1990 | 30.73% | |
| 4 | 1991 | 55.21% | |
| 5 | 1992 | 15.82% | |
| 6 | 1993 | 33.54% | |
| 7 | 1994 | 14.93% | |
| 8 | 1995 | 35.84% | |
| 9 | 1996 | 48.39% | |
| 10 | 1997 | 37.71% | |
| 11 | 1998 | 67.85% | |
| 12 | 1999 | 44.85% | |
| 13 | | | |
| 14 | Correlation | | |

12. Below you will find the annual returns of two assets. Fill in the blanks and graph the returns of the portfolios (rows 13–27).

| | A | B | C |
|---|---|---|---|
| 1 | | **Asset 1** | **Asset 2** |
| 2 | 31-Dec-90 | 12.56% | 7.56% |
| 3 | 31-Dec-91 | 13.50% | 8.56% |
| 4 | 31-Dec-92 | 14.23% | 4.56% |
| 5 | 31-Dec-93 | 15.23% | 2.12% |
| 6 | 31-Dec-94 | 14.23% | 1.23% |
| 7 | 31-Dec-95 | 12.23% | 0.26% |
| 8 | 31-Dec-96 | 10.23% | 3.25% |
| 9 | 31-Dec-97 | 5.26% | 4.89% |
| 10 | 31-Dec-98 | 4.25% | 5.56% |
| 11 | 31-Dec-99 | 2.23% | 6.45% |
| 12 | | | |
| 13 | Average return | | |
| 14 | Return variance | | |
| 15 | Covariance | | |
| 16 | **Proportion of asset 1** | **Portfolio standard deviation** | **Portfolio mean return** |
| 17 | 0 | | |
| 18 | 0.1 | | |
| 19 | 0.2 | | |
| 20 | 0.3 | | |
| 21 | 0.4 | | |
| 22 | 0.5 | | |
| 23 | 0.6 | | |
| 24 | 0.7 | | |
| 25 | 0.8 | | |
| 26 | 0.9 | | |
| 27 | 1 | | |

13. Below are data on the returns of General Electric, Boeing, and Walmart. Calculate the highlighted cells.

|  | A | B | C | D |
|---|---|---|---|---|
| 1 | MONTHLY RETURNS: BOEING (BA), GENERAL ELECTRIC (GE), WALMART (WMT) | | | |
| 2 | Return for month ending | BA | GE | WMT |
| 3 | 2-Feb-09 | -28.69% | -32.58% | 4.42% |
| 4 | 2-Mar-09 | 12.35% | 17.26% | 6.20% |
| 5 | 1-Apr-09 | 11.83% | 22.44% | -3.33% |
| 6 | 1-May-09 | 12.29% | 6.33% | -0.78% |
| 7 | 1-Jun-09 | -5.36% | -13.18% | -2.64% |
| 8 | 1-Jul-09 | 0.94% | 13.41% | 2.93% |
| 9 | 3-Aug-09 | 15.59% | 3.68% | 2.51% |
| 10 | 1-Sep-09 | 8.64% | 17.23% | -3.56% |
| 11 | 1-Oct-09 | -12.48% | -14.11% | 1.19% |
| 12 | 2-Nov-09 | 10.08% | 11.66% | 9.35% |
| 13 | 1-Dec-09 | 3.23% | -5.09% | -1.54% |
| 14 | 4-Jan-10 | 11.29% | 6.10% | -0.04% |
| 15 | 1-Feb-10 | 4.83% | 0.50% | 1.20% |
| 16 | 1-Mar-10 | 13.93% | 12.53% | 3.35% |
| 17 | 1-Apr-10 | -0.25% | 3.53% | -3.59% |
| 18 | 3-May-10 | -11.51% | -14.26% | -5.33% |
| 19 | 1-Jun-10 | -2.25% | -11.95% | -5.05% |
| 20 | 1-Jul-10 | 3.00% | 3.61% | 2.79% |
| 21 | | | | |
| 22 | Average return | | | |
| 23 | Standard deviation | | | |
| 24 | Covariances | | | |
| 25 | Cov(BA,GE) | | | |
| 26 | Cov(BA,WMT) | | | |
| 27 | Cov(GE,WMT) | | | |
| 28 | | | | |
| 29 | Correlations | | | |
| 30 | Corr(BA,GE) | | | |
| 31 | Corr(BA,WMT) | | | |
| 32 | Corr(GE,WMT) | | | |
| 33 | | | | |
| 34 | Portfolio proportions | | | |
| 35 | BA | 0.5 | | |
| 36 | GE | 0.3 | | |
| 37 | WMT | 0.2 | | |
| 38 | | | | |
| 39 | Portfolio mean return | | | |
| 40 | Portfolio variance | | | |
| 41 | Portfolio standard deviation | | | |

14. Go to http://finance.yahoo.com. Download monthly stock price data for Oracle Corporation (ORCL), Microsoft Corporation (MSFT), Dell Corp. (DELL), and Gateway Corp. (GTW) for 2007 and 2008. Also, download the same data for S&P 500 index (SPX) for the same period.[8] Answer the following questions:

   a. What is the mean return, variance, and standard deviation of a portfolio consisting of the four stocks, where wealth is allocated equally among each stock?

   b. On average, would you be better off investing in this portfolio or investing in S&P 500 index, during the period of 2 years?

---

[8] Recall that when you download data from Yahoo! into Excel, it is already adjusted for stock splits and dividends.

15. Using information provided in the previous problem, perform a regression of the portfolio returns versus S&P 500 index returns for a period of 24 months. Report the following: The slope of the regression, its intercept, and I-squared. Explain what each of these numbers tell you.

16. (This is a hard question!) On the disk that comes with the book, you will find 2 years of monthly unadjusted and adjusted stock price data for AT&T Corp. (symbol: T). Calculate the following:

    a. Cumulative adjustment factor for AT&T stock.

    b. What two interesting things happened in November 2002 and what happened to cumulative adjustment factor in this month? (You will have to do an Internet search.)

17. Explain why each of the following statements is correct or incorrect:

    a. Diversification reduces risk because prices of stocks do not usually move exactly together.

    b. The expected return on a portfolio is a weighted average of the expected returns on the individual securities.

    c. The standard deviation of returns on a portfolio is equal to the weighted average of the standard deviations on the individual securities if these returns are completely uncorrelated.

18. Suppose that the annual returns on two stocks ($A$ and $B$) are perfectly negatively correlated and that $r_A = 0.05$, $r_B = 0.15$, $\sigma_A = 0.1$, and $\sigma_B = 0.4$. Assuming that there are no arbitrage opportunities, what must the 1-year interest rate be?

19. Assume that an individual can either invest all of her resources in one of two securities $A$ or $B$ or, alternatively, she can diversify her investment between the two. The distribution of the returns is as follows.

| | A | B | C | D |
|---|---|---|---|---|
| 1 | Security A | | Security B | |
| 2 | Return | Probability | Return | Probability |
| 3 | -10% | 0.5 | -20% | 0.5 |
| 4 | 50% | 0.5 | 60% | 0.5 |

Assume that the correlation between the returns from the two securities is zero.

a. Calculate each security's expected return, variance, and standard deviation.

b. Calculate the probability distribution of the returns on a *mixed portfolio* composed of equal proportions of securities $A$ and $B$. Also calculate the expected return, variance, and standard deviation.

c. Calculate the expected return and the variance of a mixed portfolio composed of 75% security $A$ and 25% security $B$.

| | A | B | C | D | E | F | G | H |
|---|---|---|---|---|---|---|---|---|
| 1 | Date | Open | High | Low | Close | Volume | Adj. Close* | Cumulative Adjustment factor |
| 2 | Dec 02 | | | $0.19 Cash Dividend | | | | |
| 3 | Dec 02 | 28.54 | 28.88 | 25.11 | 26.11 | 4,932,428 | 26.11 | |
| 4 | Nov 02 | | | $8.48 Cash Dividend | | | | |
| 5 | Nov 02 | | | 1:5 Stock Split | | | | |
| 6 | Nov 02 | 12.94 | 28.25 | 12.84 | 28.04 | 13,146,915 | 28.04 | |
| 7 | Oct 02 | 12.1 | 13.64 | 10.45 | 13.04 | 14,453,869 | 65.2 | |
| 8 | Sep 02 | | | $0.04 Cash Dividend | | | | |
| 9 | Sep 02 | 11.95 | 13.79 | 11.2 | 12.01 | 15,095,745 | 60.05 | |
| 10 | Aug 02 | 10.12 | 12.85 | 8.69 | 12.22 | 17,147,918 | 61.1 | |
| 11 | Jul 02 | 10.5 | 10.55 | 8.2 | 10.18 | 18,639,136 | 50.9 | |
| 12 | Jun 02 | | | $0.04 Cash Dividend | | | | |
| 13 | Jun 02 | 11.85 | 12.4 | 9.09 | 10.7 | 29,520,930 | 53.5 | |
| 14 | May 02 | 13.2 | 14.3 | 11.76 | 11.97 | 17,814,400 | 59.85 | |
| 15 | Apr 02 | 15.74 | 15.85 | 12.66 | 13.12 | 15,936,609 | 65.6 | |
| 16 | Mar 02 | | | $0.04 Cash Dividend | | | | |
| 17 | Mar 02 | 15.8 | 16.48 | 15 | 15.7 | 11,042,700 | 78.5 | |
| 18 | Feb 02 | 17.55 | 17.91 | 14.18 | 15.54 | 16,401,442 | 77.7 | |
| 19 | Jan 02 | 18.48 | 19.25 | 16.65 | 17.7 | 11,919,185 | 88.5 | |
| 20 | Dec 01 | | | $0.04 Cash Dividend | | | | |
| 21 | Dec 01 | 17.35 | 18.75 | 15.8 | 18.14 | 14,846,490 | 90.7 | |
| 22 | Nov 01 | 15.33 | 17.85 | 14.75 | 17.49 | 10,987,857 | 87.45 | |
| 23 | Oct 01 | 19.15 | 20 | 15.17 | 15.25 | 15,015,643 | 76.25 | |
| 24 | Sep 01 | | | $0.04 Cash Dividend | | | | |
| 25 | Sep 01 | 19.01 | 19.64 | 16.5 | 19.3 | 15,798,733 | 96.5 | |
| 26 | Aug 01 | 20.32 | 20.95 | 18.66 | 19.04 | 7,457,491 | 95.2 | |
| 27 | Jul 01 | | | $5.52 Cash Dividend | | | | |
| 28 | Jul 01 | 21.75 | 23 | 18.1 | 20.21 | 16,556,647 | 101.05 | |
| 29 | Jun 01 | | | $0.04 Cash Dividend | | | | |
| 30 | Jun 01 | 21.16 | 22.16 | 19.82 | 22 | 11,332,052 | 110 | |
| 31 | May 01 | 22.58 | 23.1 | 20.48 | 21.17 | 15,562,513 | 105.85 | |
| 32 | Apr 01 | 21.3 | 23.27 | 19.85 | 22.28 | 12,075,000 | 111.4 | |
| 33 | Mar 01 | | | $0.04 Cash Dividend | | | | |
| 34 | Mar 01 | 22.8 | 24.6 | 20.6 | 21.3 | 12,662,459 | 106.5 | |
| 35 | Feb 01 | 23.95 | 24.53 | 20.2 | 23 | 12,220,989 | 115 | |
| 36 | Jan 01 | 17.37 | 25.15 | 17.25 | 23.99 | 20,407,609 | 119.95 | |
| 37 | Dec 00 | | | $0.04 Cash Dividend | | | | |
| 38 | Dec 00 | 19.44 | 22.69 | 16.5 | 17.25 | 23,385,210 | 86.25 | |
| 39 | Nov 00 | 22.62 | 22.94 | 18.25 | 19.62 | 20,863,095 | 98.1 | |
| 40 | Oct 00 | 29 | 30 | 21.25 | 23.19 | 24,254,945 | 115.95 | |
| 41 | Sep 00 | | | $0.22 Cash Dividend | | | | |
| 42 | Sep 00 | 31.62 | 32.94 | 27.25 | 29 | 19,280,690 | 145 | |
| 43 | Aug 00 | 30.94 | 32.94 | 29.62 | 31.62 | 17,828,760 | 158.1 | |
| 44 | Jul 00 | 31.81 | 35.19 | 30.5 | 30.94 | 19,562,070 | 154.7 | |
| 45 | Jun 00 | | | $0.22 Cash Dividend | | | | |
| 46 | Jun 00 | 34.94 | 37.75 | 31.25 | 31.81 | 20,312,436 | 159.05 | |
| 47 | May 00 | 46.31 | 49 | 33.63 | 34.94 | 25,649,081 | 174.7 | |
| 48 | Apr 00 | 56.69 | 58.81 | 45.88 | 45.88 | 12,616,194 | 229.4 | |
| 49 | Mar 00 | | | $0.22 Cash Dividend | | | | |
| 50 | Mar 00 | 49.38 | 61 | 47.5 | 56.31 | 13,692,547 | 281.55 | |
| 51 | Feb 00 | 52.75 | 53 | 44.31 | 49.38 | 10,648,485 | 246.9 | |
| 52 | Jan 00 | 50.81 | 56 | 47.5 | 52.75 | 11,964,045 | 263.75 | |
| 53 | Dec 99 | | | $0.22 Cash Dividend | | | | |
| 54 | Dec 99 | 55.88 | 58.69 | 49.88 | 50.81 | 9,812,559 | 254.05 | |
| 55 | Nov 99 | 47.13 | 61 | 44.94 | 55.88 | 13,277,338 | 279.4 | |
| 56 | Oct 99 | 43.5 | 49.06 | 41.5 | 46.75 | 11,850,266 | 233.75 | |
| 57 | Sep 99 | | | $0.22 Cash Dividend | | | | |
| 58 | Sep 99 | 45.38 | 48.81 | 41.81 | 43.5 | 10,775,514 | 217.5 | |
| 59 | Aug 99 | 52.13 | 52.81 | 44.25 | 45 | 12,892,813 | 225 | |
| 60 | Jul 99 | 55.94 | 59 | 51.75 | 52.13 | 9,257,600 | 260.65 | |
| 61 | Jun 99 | | | $0.22 Cash Dividend | | | | |
| 62 | Jun 99 | 55.5 | 56.88 | 52.38 | 55.81 | 10,673,172 | 279.05 | |
| 63 | May 99 | 51 | 63 | 50.88 | 55.5 | 14,542,265 | 277.5 | |
| 64 | Apr 99 | | | 3:2 Stock Split | | | | |
| 65 | Apr 99 | 79.81 | 89.5 | 50.06 | 50.5 | 13,690,428 | 252.5 | |
| 66 | Mar 99 | | | $0.33 Cash Dividend | | | | |
| 67 | Mar 99 | 82.12 | 89 | 75.87 | 79.81 | 9,906,500 | 266.03 | |
| 68 | Feb 99 | 91.94 | 95.12 | 82.12 | 82.12 | 8,755,210 | 273.73 | |
| 69 | Jan 99 | 76.5 | 96.12 | 76.5 | 90.75 | 10,024,863 | 302.5 | |

20. The correlations between the returns of three stocks $A$, $B$, and $C$ are given in the following table.

| | A | B | C | D |
|---|---|---|---|---|
| 1 | Stock | A | B | C |
| 2 | A | 1.00 | 0.80 | 0.10 |
| 3 | B | | 1.00 | 0.15 |
| 4 | C | | | 1.00 |

The expected rates of return on $A$, $B$, and $C$ are 16, 12, and 15%, respectively. The corresponding standard deviations of the returns are 25, 22, and 25%.

a. What is the standard deviation of a portfolio invested 25% in stock *A*, 25% in stock *B*, and 50% in stock *C*?

b. You plan to invest 50% of your money in the portfolio constructed in Question 20a and 50% in the risk-free asset. The risk-free interest rate is 5%. What is the expected return on this investment? What is the standard deviation of the return on this investment?

21. You believe that there is a 15% chance that stock *A* will decline by 10% and an 85% chance that it will increase by 15%. Correspondingly, there is a 30% chance that stock *B* will decline by 18% and a 70% chance that it will increase by 22%. The covariance between the two stocks is 0.009. Calculate the expected return, the variance, and the standard deviation for each stock. Then calculate the correlation coefficient between their returns.

22. Outdoorsy people know that the crickets chirp faster when the temperature is warmer. Some evidence for this can be found in a book published in 1948 by Harvard physics professor George W. Pierce.[9] Pierce's book includes the table below, which relates the average number of cricket chirps per minute to the temperature at which the data were recorded. Plot the data in an Excel graph and use regression to determine the (approximate) relation between the number of chirps per second and the temperature. If you detect 19 chirps per second, what would you guess the temperature to be? What about 22 chirps a second? (We know this problem has nothing to do with finance, but it's interesting!)

|    | A<br>Chirps per<br>second | B<br>Temperature<br>in Farenheit |
|----|--------------------------|----------------------------------|
| 4  |                          |                                  |
| 5  | 20.0 | 88.60 |
| 6  | 16.0 | 71.60 |
| 7  | 19.8 | 93.30 |
| 8  | 18.4 | 84.30 |
| 9  | 17.1 | 80.60 |
| 10 | 15.5 | 75.20 |
| 11 | 14.7 | 69.70 |
| 12 | 17.1 | 82.00 |
| 13 | 15.4 | 69.40 |
| 14 | 16.2 | 83.30 |
| 15 | 15.0 | 79.60 |
| 16 | 17.2 | 82.60 |
| 17 | 16.0 | 80.60 |
| 18 | 17.0 | 83.50 |
| 19 | 14.4 | 76.30 |

23. Economists have long believed that the more money printed, the higher will be long-term interest rates. Evidence for this view can be found in the following table, which gives long-term government bond rates for 31 countries and the corresponding growth rate of money supply for each country.[10]

  • Plot the data and use a regression to find the relation between the money growth and the long-term bond interest rate.
  • If a country has zero money growth, what is its predicted long-term bond interest rate?
  • The monetary authorities in your country are considering increasing the money growth rate by 1% from its current level. Predict by how much this will increase the long-term bond interest rate.
  • Do you find the evidence in the table convincing? (Discuss briefly the $R^2$ of the regression.)

---

[9]Additional facts: Cricket chirping is produced by the rapid sliding of the cricket's wings one over the other. The higher the temperature, the faster the crickets slide their wings. George W. Pierce's book is called *The Songs of Insects* and was published by Harvard University Press.

[10]The data were first presented in an article entitled "Money and Interest Rates," by Cyril Monnet and Warren Weber in the *Federal Reserve Bank of Minneapolis Quarterly Review*, Fall 2001. My thanks to the authors for providing me with an Excel version of their data.

| | A | B | C | D | E | F | G |
|---|---|---|---|---|---|---|---|
| 38 | MONEY GROWTH AND BOND INTEREST RATES | | | | | | |
| 39 | Country | Average money growth | Average long-term bond interest rate | | Country | Average money growth | Average long-term bond interest rate |
| 40 | US | 5.65% | 7.40% | | New Zealand | 10.29% | 8.81% |
| 41 | Austria | 6.82% | 7.80% | | South Africa | 14.14% | 11.11% |
| 42 | Belgium | 5.20% | 8.22% | | Honduras | 16.20% | 15.57% |
| 43 | Denmark | 9.43% | 10.36% | | Jamaica | 19.88% | 15.35% |
| 44 | France | 8.15% | 8.49% | | Netherlands Antilles | 4.36% | 9.40% |
| 45 | Germany | 8.00% | 7.20% | | Trinidad & Tobago | 12.14% | 9.10% |
| 46 | Italy | 12.07% | 10.66% | | Korea | 15.12% | 16.53% |
| 47 | Netherlands | 7.89% | 7.31% | | Nepal | 15.55% | 8.59% |
| 48 | Norway | 10.64% | 8.00% | | Pakistan | 12.79% | 7.88% |
| 49 | Switzerland | 5.53% | 4.54% | | Thailand | 10.86% | 10.62% |
| 50 | Canada | 8.99% | 8.52% | | Malawi | 20.80% | 17.62% |
| 51 | Japan | 9.07% | 6.16% | | Zimbabwe | 13.49% | 12.01% |
| 52 | Ireland | 9.43% | 10.38% | | Solomon Islands | 15.89% | 12.12% |
| 53 | Portugal | 12.91% | 10.79% | | Western Samoa | 12.90% | 13.17% |
| 54 | Spain | 10.38% | 12.72% | | Venezuela | 28.47% | 28.92% |
| 55 | Australia | 9.15% | 8.95% | | | | |

24. Mabelberry Fruit and Sawyer's Jam are two competing companies. An MBA student has done a calculation and found that the return on Sawyer's Jam stock is completely predictable once the return on Mabelberry Fruit stock is known:

$$r_{Sawyer's,t} = 40\% - 1.5 * r_{Mabelberry,t}.$$

a. Given the Mabelberry Fruit stock returns below, compute the Sawyer's Jam returns.

b. Regress Mabelberry Fruit stock returns on those of Sawyer's Jam. Can you explain the $R^2$?

| | A | B |
|---|---|---|
| 2 | Year | Mabelberry Fruit stock return |
| 3 | 1990 | 30.73% |
| 4 | 1991 | 15.00% |
| 5 | 1992 | -9.00% |
| 6 | 1993 | 12.00% |
| 7 | 1994 | 13.00% |
| 8 | 1995 | 22.00% |
| 9 | 1996 | 30.00% |
| 10 | 1997 | 12.00% |
| 11 | 1998 | 43.00% |
| 12 | 1999 | 16.00% |

# APPENDIX 9.1: DOWNLOADING DATA FROM YAHOO![11]

Y\AHOO! PROVIDES FREE STOCK PRICE AND DATA THAT can be used to calculate returns. In this appendix we show you how to access these data and download them into Excel.

**Step 1:** Go to http://www.yahoo.com and click on Finance.

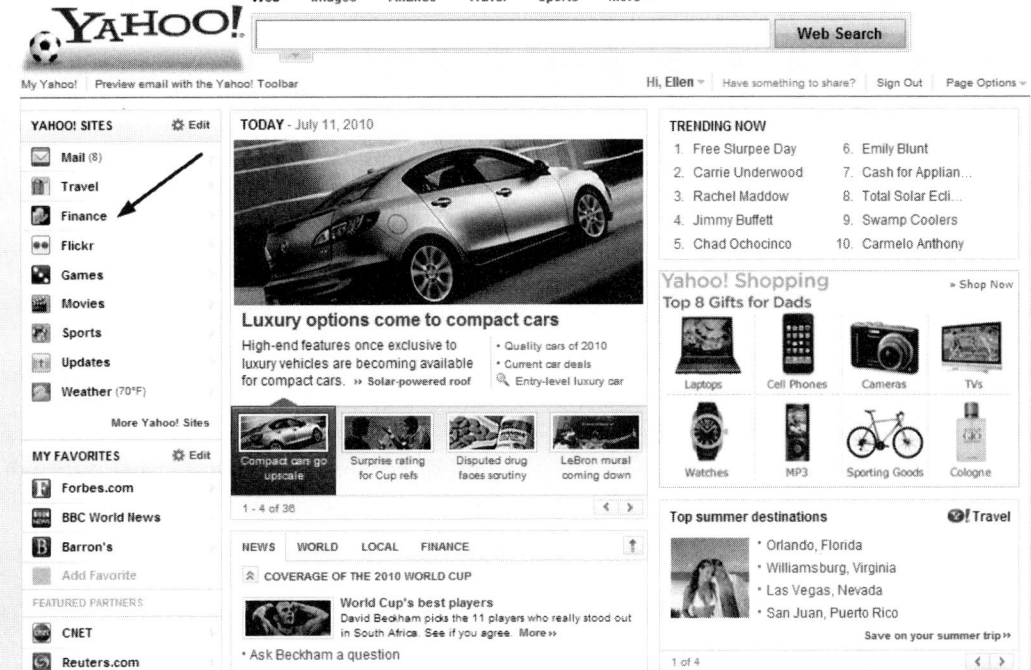

**Step 2:** In the "Enter symbol" box, put in the symbol for the stock you want to look up (we've put in MRK for Merck). You see that you can also look up symbols or put in multiple symbols. When you have put in the symbols, click **Go**.

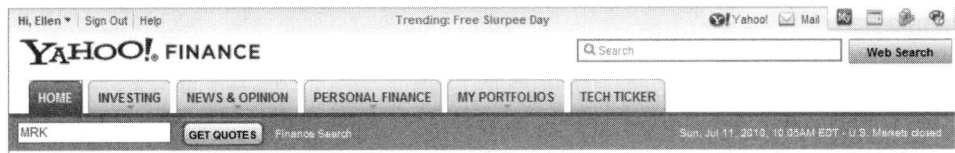

**Step 3:** This brings up the following screen. We choose **Historical Prices** to get Merck's price history.

---

[11] Yahoo! occasionally changes its interface; the information in this appendix is correct as of July 2005.

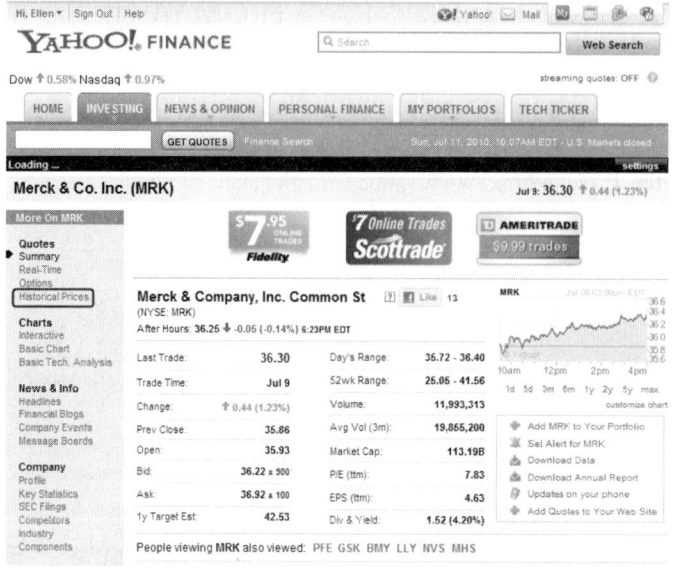

**Step 4:** In the next screen, we indicated the time period and frequency for the data we want. Yahoo! provides a table with stock prices, dividends, and an **Adjusted Closing Stock Price** that accounts for dividends and stock splits.

**Step 5:** The bottom of the above table allows you to download the data in spreadsheet format. In most browsers the Excel spreadsheet opens automatically (see the results in Step 6).

| 21-Apr-05 | 34.97 | 34.98 | 33.95 | 34.28 | 9,455,100 | 33.88 |
|---|---|---|---|---|---|---|
| 20-Apr-05 | 34.40 | 34.56 | 33.60 | 34.07 | 8,629,800 | 33.67 |
| 19-Apr-05 | 34.65 | 34.83 | 34.13 | 34.68 | 8,203,800 | 34.27 |
| 18-Apr-05 | 34.75 | 34.75 | 34.00 | 34.43 | 10,407,000 | 34.03 |
| 15-Apr-05 | 35.24 | 36.26 | 34.76 | 34.80 | 19,490,900 | 34.39 |
| 14-Apr-05 | 34.60 | 34.97 | 34.53 | 34.78 | 14,166,500 | 34.37 |
| 13-Apr-05 | 33.81 | 35.30 | 33.52 | 34.52 | 25,685,600 | 34.12 |
| 12-Apr-05 | 33.05 | 33.82 | 32.95 | 33.81 | 7,908,000 | 33.41 |
| 11-Apr-05 | 33.45 | 33.59 | 33.05 | 33.14 | 4,930,800 | 32.75 |

\* Close price adjusted for dividends and splits.

First | Prev | Next | Last

🖩 Download To Spreadsheet

**Step 6:** In the author's browser Yahoo! offers to save a file called **table.csv**. We changed the name of this file to **Merck.csv** and saved it on our hard disk.

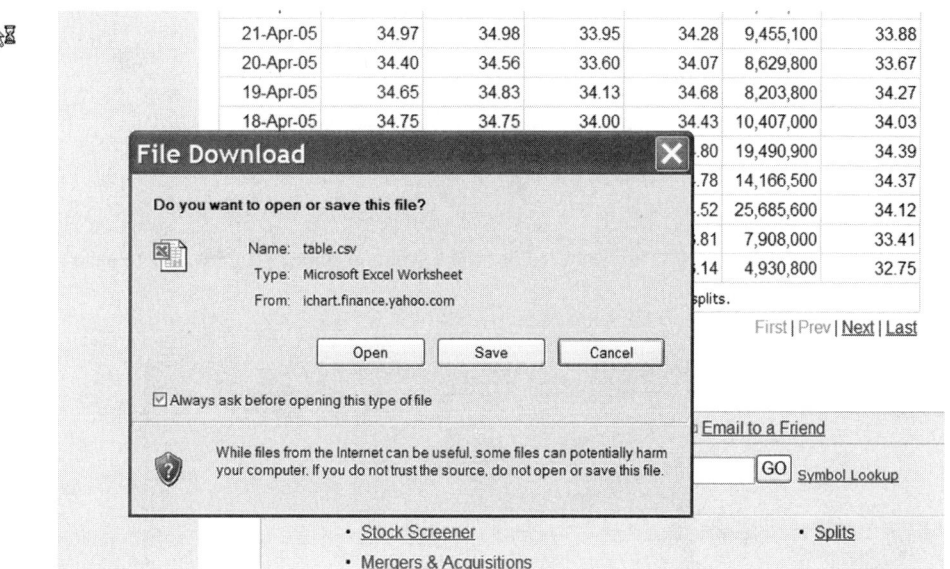

**Step 7:** The author's browser offered to open the file immediately (it will open as an Excel file). Here's the way the opened Excel file looks.

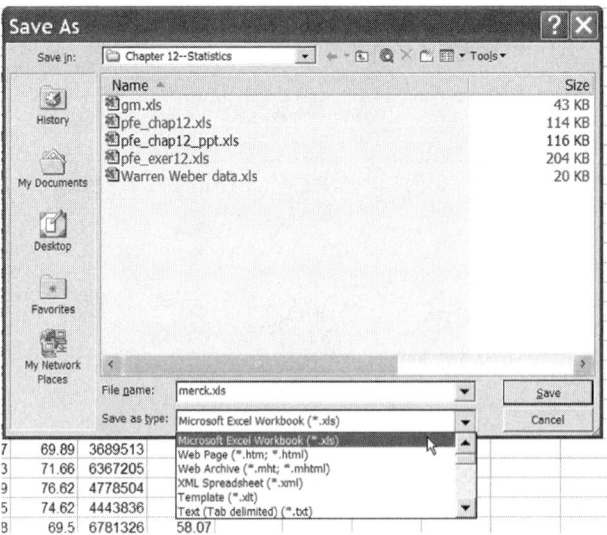

**Step 8:** It is advisable to use the Excel command **File|Save As** to save the file as a standard Excel file.

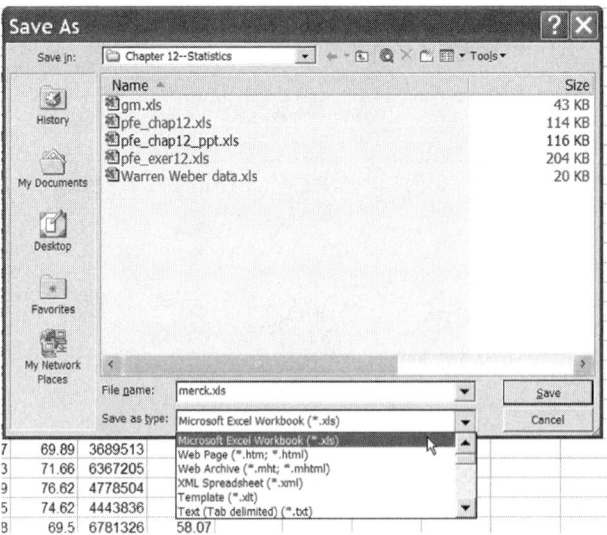

# APPENDIX 9.2: WHY VARP INSTEAD OF VAR?

THROUGHOUT *PRINCIPLES OF FINANCE WITH EXCEL* WE USE the Excel functions **Varp** and **Stdevp** instead of their cousins **Var** and **Stdevp**. This appendix briefly discusses this choice.

Recall that the definition of these two functions relates to whether the data are taken from a *sample* or whether the data are the *whole population*. Suppose we have return data $\{r_1, r_2, ..., r_N\}$ for a stock. Then **Varp** is the population variance and **Var** is the sample variance.

$$\text{Population variance} = Varp = \frac{1}{N} \sum_{t=1}^{N} (r_t - \bar{r})^2$$

$$\text{Sample variance} = Var = \frac{1}{N-1} \sum_{t=1}^{N} (r_t - \bar{r})^2$$

There are two reasons why we choose **Varp** instead of **Var**: The first reason is that in most introductory statistics courses students are taught **Varp** (that is, divide by $N$) instead of **Var** (divide by $N - 1$). Thus, the choice made in *Principles of Finance with Excel* corresponds with what students have been previously taught.

The second reason for choosing **Varp** is that this choice makes the Excel **Slope** function consistent with the definition of $\beta$ that we teach: $\beta_i = \dfrac{Covariance(r_{it}, r_{Mt})}{Variance(r_{Mt})}$. To see this, reconsider the following example from Section 9.5 in which we calculate the $\beta_{Mirage}$ for Mirage from monthly data for Mirage and for the S&P 500 index.

In cells B28:B29 we compute the $\beta_{Mirage}$ using the Excel function **Slope(C3:C26,B3:B26)** and the Excel functions **Covar(C3:C26,B3:B26)/VarP(B3:B26)**. These two definitions give the same (and the correct) answer. In cells B31:B32 we compare the Excel **Slope** function with the answer given by **Covar(C3:C26,B3:B26)/Var(B3:B26)**. Note that the answers are different (the second answer is incorrect).

To drive home this point, we compute $\beta_M$ in cells B34:B36. The **Slope** function gives the correct answer, as does the definition **Covar(B3:B26,B3:B26)/VarP(B3:B26)**. However, using the function **Var** in cell B36 gives the *wrong* answer.

| | A | B | C | D |
|---|---|---|---|---|
| 1 | | **WHY VARP INSTEAD OF VAR?** | | |
| 2 | **Date** | **S&P 500 Index SPX** | **Mirage Resorts MIR** | |
| 3 | Jan-97 | 6.13% | 16.18% | |
| 4 | Feb-97 | 0.59% | 0.00% | |
| 5 | Mar-97 | -4.26% | -15.42% | The S&P index represents the market returns |
| 6 | Apr-97 | 5.84% | -5.29% | |
| 7 | May-97 | 5.86% | 18.63% | |
| 8 | Jun-97 | 4.35% | 5.76% | |
| 9 | Jul-97 | 7.81% | 5.94% | |
| 10 | Aug-97 | -5.75% | 0.23% | |
| 11 | Sep-97 | 5.32% | 12.35% | |
| 12 | Oct-97 | -3.45% | -17.01% | |
| 13 | Nov-97 | 4.46% | -5.00% | |
| 14 | Dec-97 | 1.57% | -4.21% | |
| 15 | Jan-98 | 1.02% | 1.37% | |
| 16 | Feb-98 | 7.04% | -0.54% | |
| 17 | Mar-98 | 4.99% | 5.99% | |
| 18 | Apr-98 | 0.91% | -9.25% | |
| 19 | May-98 | -1.88% | -5.67% | |
| 20 | Jun-98 | 3.94% | 2.40% | |
| 21 | Jul-98 | -1.16% | 0.88% | |
| 22 | Aug-98 | -14.58% | -30.81% | |
| 23 | Sep-98 | 6.24% | 12.61% | |
| 24 | Oct-98 | 8.03% | 1.12% | |
| 25 | Nov-98 | 5.91% | -12.18% | |
| 26 | Dec-98 | 5.64% | 0.42% | |
| 27 | | | | |
| 28 | Mirage β using **VarP** | 1.4693 | <-- =SLOPE(C3:C26,B3:B26) | |
| 29 | | 1.4693 | <-- =COVAR(C3:C26,B3:B26)/VARP(B3:B26) | |
| 30 | | | | |
| 31 | Mirage β using **Var** | 1.4693 | <-- =SLOPE(C3:C26,B3:B26) | |
| 32 | | 1.4080 | <-- =COVAR(C3:C26,B3:B26)/VAR(B3:B26) | |
| 33 | | | | |
| 34 | Market β using **Var** | 1.0000 | <-- =SLOPE(C3:C26,C3:C26) | |
| 35 | | 1.0000 | <-- =COVAR(B3:B26,B3:B26)/VARP(B3:B26) | |
| 36 | | 0.9583 | <-- =COVAR(B3:B26,B3:B26)/VAR(B3:B26) | |
| 37 | | | | |
| 38 | | | The beta of the market should = 1. But using Covar($r_M$,$r_{Mirage}$)/Var($r_M$) produces a beta < 1. | |
| 39 | | | | |
| 40 | | | | |
| 41 | | | | |

Conclusion: Best use **VarP** instead of **Var!**[12]

[12]There's a slightly more cynical answer to the difference between **Var** and **VarP**. "If the difference between $N$ and $N-1$ ever matters to you, then you are probably up to no good anyway—e.g., trying to substantiate a questionable hypothesis with marginal data." This wonderful quote is from the book *Numerical Recipes* by William H. Press, Brian P. Flannery, Saul A. Teukolsky, and William T. Vettering (Cambridge University Press, 1986, page 456).

# 10 Portfolio Returns and the Efficient Frontier

## CHAPTER CONTENTS

## Overview

How should you invest your money? What's the best investment portfolio? How do you maximize your return without losing money? People often ask these knotty questions, and you may even be reading this book to answer them. In this and the next chapter we explore some of the answers to these questions. You will see that—although no one can tell you exactly how to invest—we can shed considerable light on some important general investment principles. We can also show you some rules of thumb about how *not to invest.*

Let's go back to the questions with which we started the previous paragraph:

- How should you invest your money? Finance can't tell you *in what* to invest, but it can give you some guidelines. The most important is this: You should *diversify* your investment—spread it out among many assets to lower the risk. Using simple examples with only two stocks, this chapter will show you how diversification can lower investment risk.

- What is the best investment portfolio? It won't surprise you that the finance answer to this question tells you that there is no single best investment portfolio. It all depends on your willingness to trade off *return* for *additional risk*.[1] What may surprise you, however, is that we can say a lot about how not to invest. In this chapter we develop the notion of the *efficient frontier*—this is the set of all portfolios that you would consider as investment portfolios. Inherent in the concept of the efficient frontier is that there are many portfolios that are not good investments and these portfolios can be described statistically.

- How do you maximize your return without losing money? To some extent the efficient frontier answers this question: It shows us which portfolios are so bad that you can improve both the return and the risk. Once we've gotten on the efficient frontier, however, the risk–return trade-off begins to operate, and higher returns mean larger risks.[2]

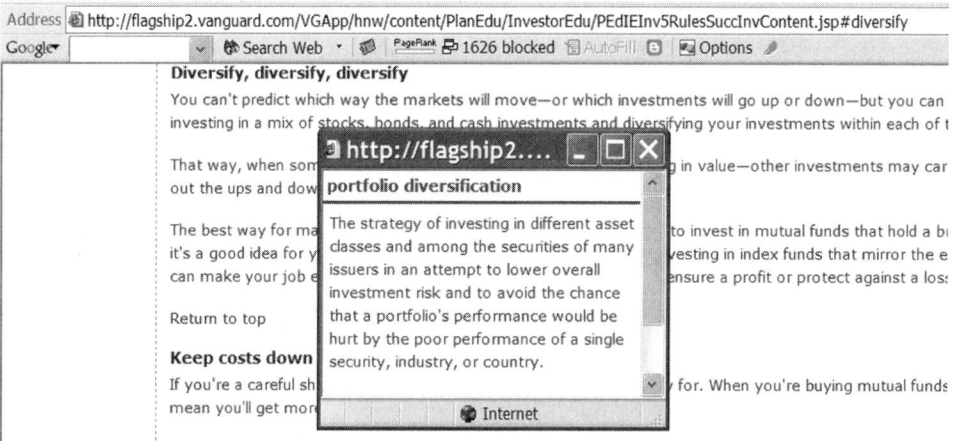

FIGURE 10.1 Vanguard Funds is a major manager of stock and bond funds. Here's how the Vanguard Web site defines *diversification.*

---

[1] As you learned in Chapter 8, nearly all the interesting finance questions involve the word "risk." Portfolio choice is no different!

[2] As the author's father used to say: "It is better to be rich and healthy than poor and sick." The investment interpretation of this is that we would all like to *have more return* and *risk less.* The efficient frontier represents the set of difficult investment choices: Once you're on the efficient frontier, it is impossible to get more return without taking on more risk.

In most of this chapter we examine the risk and return of portfolios composed of two financial assets. By choosing a combination of the two assets, you can achieve significant reductions in risk.[3] Much of the chapter relies on the statistics for portfolios discussed in the previous chapter. Even our main example, which considers portfolios of Exxon (XOM) and Kellogg (K) stock, is one we started in Chapter 9.

The close links in the materials of this chapter and the materials in Chapter 9 should not blind you to their differences. Whereas Chapter 9 develops the statistical concepts necessary for portfolio choice, this chapter looks at portfolio choice as an economic choice. In this chapter we develop concepts that help us think more precisely about acceptable and unacceptable portfolios. In the next chapter we carry this line of thought further.

## Finance Concepts in This Chapter

- Mean and standard deviation of portfolio of two assets
- Portfolio risk and return
- Minimum variance portfolio
- The efficient frontier
- Mean-variance calculations for three-asset portfolios

## Excel Concepts and Functions Used

- **Average( ), Varp( ), Stdevp( )**
- **Regression**
- Sophisticated graphing
- **Solver**

# 10.1. The Advantage of Diversification—A Simple Example

In this section we give an example that illustrates the benefits of diversification. In finance jargon, diversification means investing in several different assets as opposed to putting all of your money in one single asset. In our examples you will see when diversification pays off (and when it doesn't). The examples are much simpler than the real-world examples that follow in the next sections, but they embody many of the intuitions of why investors invest in portfolios. In particular, you will see how the correlation between asset returns is important in determining the amount of risk reduction you can get through portfolio formation.

In each of the following examples you can invest in two assets, A and B. The return on each asset is uncertain and is determined by the flip of a coin: If the coin comes up heads, the return on both assets A and B is 20% and if the coin comes up tails, the assets return –8%. In dollar terms, if you invest $100 in one of the two assets, you'll get back $120 if the coin comes up heads and $92 if it comes up tails.

Our example is largely concerned with the sequencing of the coin flips and the connection between them. In terms of the sequence of coin flips, here's what the asset returns look like.

---

[3] Of course in the real world there are many investment assets. We use the two-asset case to develop the requisite intuitions and ask you to take it on faith that the multiasset case is similar.

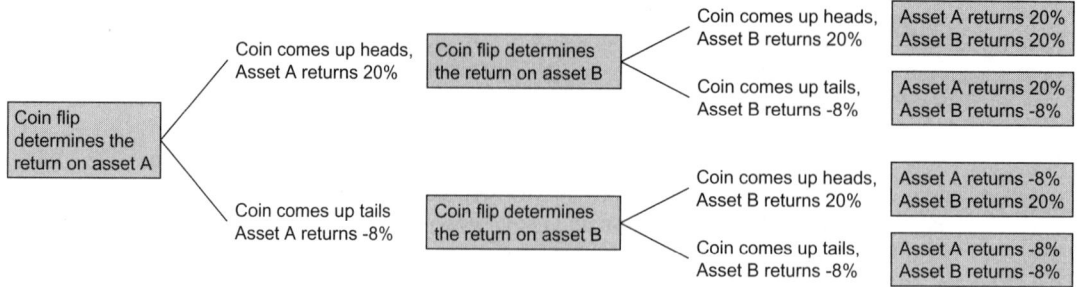

## Case 1: Investing in a Single Risky Asset

Suppose you decide to invest your $100 wholly in asset *A*. If the coin comes up heads, you'll earn 20% on your investment, and if it comes up tails you will lose 8%. Your $100 investment in asset *A* will have the following cash flow and return pattern.

| | A | B | C | D | E | F | G | H | I | J |
|---|---|---|---|---|---|---|---|---|---|---|
| 1 | | | | | **CASE 1: MEAN AND STANDARD DEVIATION OF RETURN FROM A SINGLE COIN FLIP** | | | | | |
| 2 | Coin flip: | | | | | | | | | |
| 3 | heads | | **Cash flow** | | **Return** | | | **Return statistics** | | |
| 4 | | | 120 | | 20% | <-- =C4/A6-1 | | Average return | 6.00% | <-- =AVERAGE(E4,E8) |
| 5 | | | | | | | | Variance | 0.0196 | <-- =VARP(E4,E8) |
| 6 | 100 | | | | | | | Standard deviation | 14.00% | <-- =SQRT(I5) |
| 7 | | | | | | | | | | |
| 8 | | | 92 | | -8% | <-- =C8/A6-1 | | | | |
| 9 | Coin flip: | | | | | | | | | |
| 10 | tails | | | | | | | | | |
| 11 | | | | | | | | | | |

Note the return statistics in column I: Asset *A* has average return of 6% and return standard deviation of 14%.[4]

## Case 2: The Case of the "Fair" Coin: Splitting Your Investment between the Assets

In Case 1 you invested only in one asset. In Cases 2–5 you will invest in both assets *A* and *B*.

In Case 2 we suppose that the coin that determines the returns on asset *A* and the coin that determines the returns on asset *B* are *independent*. In simple terms you can think of a single coin that is flipped twice—once to determine the return of *A* and the second time to determine the return of *B*. If the coin flip is fair then the results of the first coin flip have no influence on the results of the second coin flip.

Now here's the question we want to answer: Should you invest all your money in *A*? in *B*? Or should you split your investment between the two? The answer has to do with the effects of diversification. To examine this question more closely, let's assume that you have decided to invest $50 in each asset. Your final outcomes are given below.

---

[4]You'll note that we've used the Excel function **Varp** to compute the portfolio variance and *not* the function **Var**. The reasons for this choice—which we make throughout the book—were given in Appendix 9.2. Similarly, we would use **StDevp** to compute the standard deviation and not **StDev**. We can also calculate the standard deviation by taking the square root of the variance, which is what we've done in the current example.

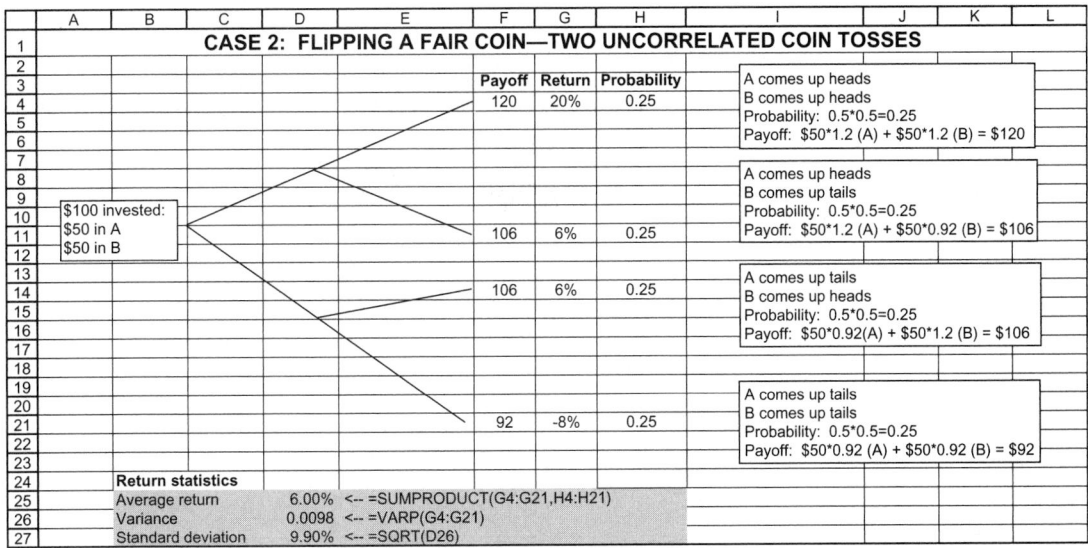

As you can see, the average return from the investment in two assets (6%) is the same as the average return in case 1, where we invested in only one asset. Note, however, that the standard deviation went down from 14 to 9.9%—you earn the same but incur less risk.

Message: Diversification in uncorrelated assets improves your investment returns.

This message—that diversification pays off because it reduces risk—can be explored further. In the next example we explore the returns when you have *correlated* assets.

## Case 3: The Case of the Counterfeit Coin: A Correlation of +1

Now suppose you have the same situation as above; only this time your coin is counterfeit. You do not know whether you will get heads or tails but you do know that whatever the result of the

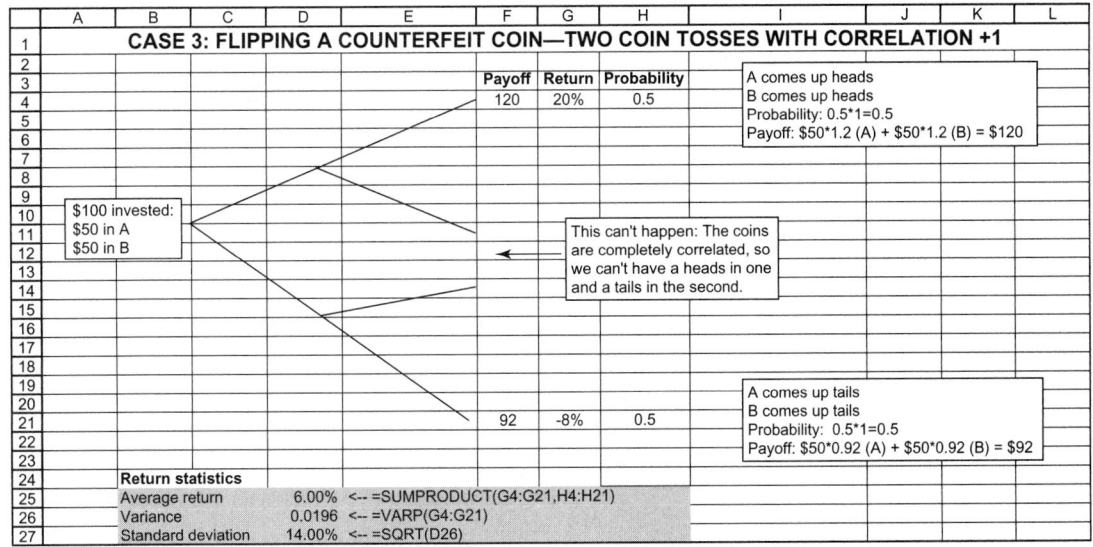

"*A*" coin, the result of the "*B*" coin will be the same. In statistical terms this is a correlation of +1. Will diversification improve your returns in this situation?

As you can see, the returns from splitting your investment between two assets are identical to the return of only investing in one asset (cells D25:D27). Both the average return and the return standard deviation are the same as in case 1, where we flipped only one coin.

> Message: When the asset returns are perfectly positively correlated, diversification will not reduce your risk.

## Case 4: The Case of the Counterfeit Coin—Correlation of –1

We're still on the same example, and our coin is still counterfeit. But this time it's counterfeit with a perfectly negative correlation (–1): If coin "*A*" comes up heads, coin "*B*" will come up tails. In statistical terms, the correlation between the two coins is –1. For this case we can find a portfolio that completely eliminates all risk: By splitting our investment between assets *A* and *B*, we get 6% expected return without any standard deviation.

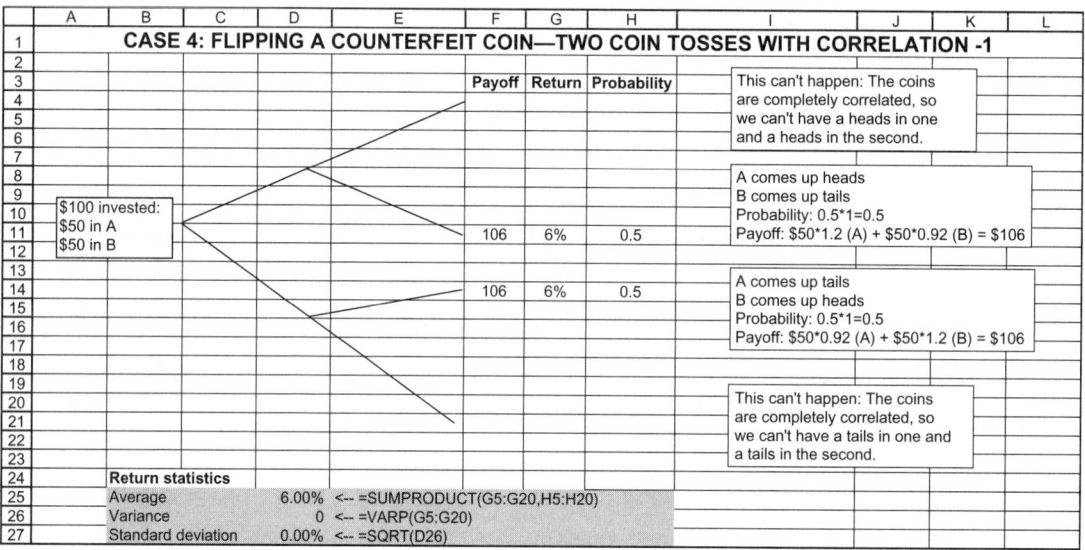

Message: When the asset returns are perfectly negatively correlated, diversification can completely eliminate all risk.

## Case 5: The Partially Counterfeit Coin (the Real World?)

In the real world there's often a connection between the stock prices of one company and those of another. In the most general handwaving[5] way, stock prices reflect two elements:

- How well a particular business is doing: In some industries this element leads to *negative correlation*. For example if Procter & Gamble (a major manufacturer of toothpastes,

---

[5] The Web site http://c2.com defines "handwaving" as follows: "Handwaving is what people do when they don't want to tell you the details, either because they don't want to get bogged down, they don't know, nobody knows, or they have sinister ulterior motives."

laundry soaps, and so on) is gaining market share, it is likely to be at the expense of Unilever (another company in the same industry). This isn't always true, however: If Intel (a major manufacturer of computer chips) is doing well, then it may be that the computer industry is expanding and that AMD (another player in the same industry) is also doing well.

• How well the economy is doing: Stock prices are heavily affected by the performance of the economy. This factor tends to be an across-the-board factor, leading to *positive correlation*: When the stock market as a whole is up, most stock prices tend to be up and vice versa. For stock prices, this factor tends to dominate the first: in general stock prices move together, although their correlation is far from complete.

Note how careful we've been here in our language: We've used words like "tend to go up"—stock prices are only partially, not perfectly, correlated.[6]

To model partial correlation with our coin toss example, we'll assume that the "*A*" coin result influences the result of the "*B*" coin, but not completely. If the "*A*" coin comes up heads (this happens with a probability of 0.5), the probability of the "*B*" coin coming up heads is 0.7. If the "*A*" coin comes up tails (probability 0.5), the probability that the "*B*" coin also comes up tails is 0.7. Here's the spreadsheet that summarizes the returns.

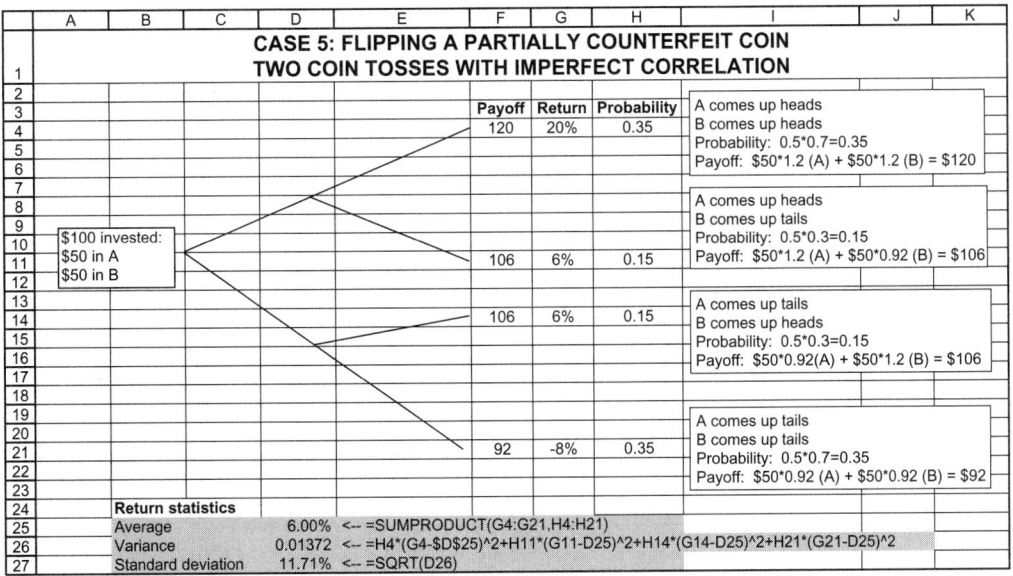

Message: When the asset returns are partially correlated, diversification will reduce risk but not completely eliminate it.

## What's the Point?

Although the two-asset, two-coin examples are simple and farfetched, the lessons you learn from these examples also apply in the "real-world" cases of asset diversification:

---

[6] Negative correlation in stock returns can also happen: See the example of General Motors and Microsoft (Exercise 7 at the end of this chapter).

- If the correlation between asset returns is +1, then diversification will not reduce portfolio risk.

- If the correlation between asset returns is −1, then we can create a risk-free asset—an asset with no uncertainty about its returns (a bank savings account is an example)—using a portfolio of the two assets.

- In the real-world asset returns are almost never fully correlated. When asset returns are partially, but not completely, correlated (meaning that the correlation is between −1 and +1), diversification can lower risk, although it cannot completely eliminate it.

## 10.2. Back to the Real World—Kellogg and Exxon

In Chapter 9 we calculated the data for the annual returns on Kellogg (K) and Exxon (XOM) stock for the 10 years 1999–2008. Here are our calculations.

| | A | B | C | D |
|---|---|---|---|---|
| 1 | KELLOGG (K) AND EXXON (XOM) ANNUAL RETURN DATA | | | |
| 2 | Date | Kellogg | Exxon | |
| 3 | 31-Dec-99 | -6.89% | 12.60% | |
| 4 | 29-Dec-00 | -11.59% | 10.25% | |
| 5 | 31-Dec-01 | 18.51% | -7.61% | |
| 6 | 31-Dec-02 | 17.21% | -8.86% | |
| 7 | 31-Dec-03 | 14.06% | 20.63% | |
| 8 | 31-Dec-04 | 19.93% | 28.08% | |
| 9 | 30-Dec-05 | -0.85% | 11.78% | |
| 10 | 29-Dec-06 | 18.46% | 39.07% | |
| 11 | 31-Dec-07 | 7.14% | 24.29% | |
| 12 | 31-Dec-08 | -16.02% | -13.11% | |
| 13 | | | | |
| 14 | Average return $E(r_K)$ and $E(r_{XOM})$ | 6.00% | 11.71% | <-- =AVERAGE(C3:C12) |
| 15 | Variance of returns, $\sigma^2_K$ and $\sigma^2_{XOM}$ | 0.0171 | 0.0267 | <-- =VARP(C3:C12) |
| 16 | Standard deviation of returns, $\sigma_K$ and $\sigma_{XOM}$ | 13.06% | 16.34% | <-- =STDEVP(C3:C12) |
| 17 | Covariance of returns $Cov(r_K, r_{XOM})$ | 0.0074 | | <-- =COVAR(B3:B12,C3:C12) |
| 18 | Correlation of returns $\rho_{K,XOM}$ | 0.3482 | | <-- =CORREL(B3:B12,C3:C12) |
| 19 | | 0.3482 | | <-- =B17/(B16*C16) |

You can see that the average return of holding Kellogg stock (6% per year) is much lower than the average return of holding Exxon stock (11.71%). On the other hand, the risk of holding XOM—measured by either the variance or the standard deviation of the return—is higher than the risk of Kellogg: This is the trade-off we would expect—K has lower return and lower risk than XOM. Note that K and XOM returns are *positively correlated* (cell B18): On average, an increase in K returns was accompanied by an increase in XOM returns. If you use Excel to plot K returns on the *x*-axis and XOM returns on the *y*-axis, you can detect a slight "southwest to northeast" pattern in the returns.

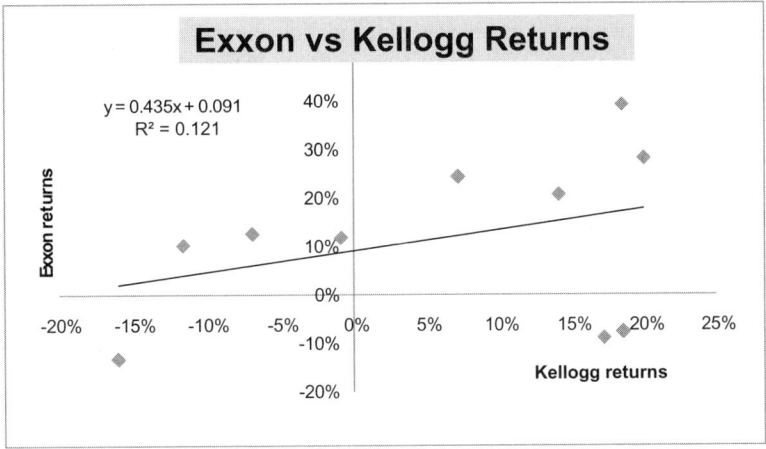

The trendline (which illustrates the regression of XOM on K) shows this trend.[7]

# 10.3. Graphing Portfolio Returns

In this section we graph the returns available to the investor from an investment in a portfolio composed of K and XOM stock. We start by showing you several individual portfolios and end the section by graphing the curve representing all possible portfolio returns.

### Deriving the Risk-Return of an Individual Portfolio

Suppose we form a portfolio composed of 50% K and 50% XOM stock. Cells E8:E17 in the spreadsheet below show the annual returns of this portfolio.

| | A | B | C | D | E | F |
|---|---|---|---|---|---|---|
| 1 | A PORTFOLIO OF K AND XOM STOCK | | | | | |
| 2 | Percentage in K | 50% | | | | |
| 3 | Perecentage in XOM | 50% | <-- =1-B2 | | | |
| 4 | | | | | | |
| 5 | Date | | Stock returns | | Portfolio returns | |
| 6 | | | Kellogg | Exxon | | |
| 7 | 31-Dec-99 | -6.89% | 12.60% | | 2.85% | <-- =$B$2*B7+$B$3*C7 |
| 8 | 29-Dec-00 | -11.59% | 10.25% | | -0.67% | <-- =$B$2*B8+$B$3*C8 |
| 9 | 31-Dec-01 | 18.51% | -7.61% | | 5.45% | <-- =$B$2*B9+$B$3*C9 |
| 10 | 31-Dec-02 | 17.21% | -8.86% | | 4.17% | <-- =$B$2*B10+$B$3*C10 |
| 11 | 31-Dec-03 | 14.06% | 20.63% | | 17.35% | |
| 12 | 31-Dec-04 | 19.93% | 28.08% | | 24.00% | |
| 13 | 30-Dec-05 | -0.85% | 11.78% | | 5.46% | |
| 14 | 29-Dec-06 | 18.46% | 39.07% | | 28.76% | |
| 15 | 31-Dec-07 | 7.14% | 24.29% | | 15.71% | |
| 16 | 31-Dec-08 | -16.02% | -13.11% | | -14.56% | |
| 17 | | | | | | |
| 18 | Average return $E(r_K)$ and $E(r_{XOM})$ | 6.00% | 11.71% | | 8.85% | <-- =AVERAGE(E7:E16) |
| 19 | Variance of returns, $s^2_K$ and $s^2_{XOM}$ | 0.0171 | 0.0267 | | 0.0147 | <-- =VARP(E7:E16) |
| 20 | Standard deviation of returns, $s_K$ and $s_{XOM}$ | 13.06% | 16.34% | | 12.10% | <-- =STDEVP(E7:E16) |
| 21 | Covariance of returns $Cov(r_K, r_{XOM})$ | 0.0074 | <-- =COVAR(B7:B16,C7:C16) | | | |

---

[7]As explained in Chapter 9, the regression $R^2$ indicates the percentage of XOM's return variability explained by the variability in K's returns. $R^2$ is the correlation coefficient squared: $R^2 = 0.121 = [Correlation(Return_{XOM}, Return_K)]^2 = (0.3482)^2$. Although this $R^2$ may appear quite low, it is typical for many pairs of stocks.

As discussed in Chapter 9, the portfolio return statistics in cells E18:E20 can be derived using formulas that involve only information about the individual asset returns, their variances, and the covariance. There's no need to do the extensive calculation in cells E7:E16:

- The average portfolio return of 8.85% is the *weighted* average of the K and the XOM return. Write the percentage weight of K stock by $w_K$ and the percentage weight of XOM stock by $w_{XOM}$; it follows, of course, that $w_{XOM} = 1 - w_K$ because the portfolio proportions must sum to 100%. The formula for the average portfolio return is

$$\text{average  portfolio  return,  } E(r_p) = w_K E(r_K) + w_{XOM} E(r_{XOM})$$
$$= w_K E(r_K) + (1 - w_K) E(r_{XOM})$$

- The variance of the portfolio return, 0.0147, is a more complicated function of the two variances and the portfolio weights:

$$\text{variance of portfolio  return}$$
$$Var(r_p) = w_K^2 Var(r_K) + w_{XOM}^2 Var(r_{XOM}) + \underline{2 w_K w_{XOM} Cov(r_K, r_{XOM})}$$

           ↑                           ↑

| Each portfolio weight is squared and multiplied times the variance | Twice the product of the portfolio weights times the covariance |
|---|---|

Using these two formulas, you avoid the need for the long calculation of the portfolio return, variance, and standard deviation in cells E18:E20. In the spreadsheet below we incorporate these formulas for the portfolio mean, variance, and standard deviation in cells B12:B14.

| | A | B | C | D |
|---|---|---|---|---|
| 1 | **PORTFOLIO STATISTICS FOR A KELLOGG-XOM PORTFOLIO** | | | |
| 2 | | **K** | **XOM** | |
| 3 | Average, E(r_K) and E(r_XOM) | 6.00% | 11.71% | |
| 4 | Variance, Var(r_K) and Var(r_XOM) | 0.0171 | 0.0267 | |
| 5 | Sigma, s_K and s_XOM | 13.06% | 16.34% | |
| 6 | Covariance of returns, Cov(r_K,r_XOM) | 0.0074 | | |
| 7 | | | | |
| 8 | **Portfolio return and risk** | | | |
| 9 | Percentage in K | 50% | | |
| 10 | Percentage in XOM | 50% | | |
| 11 | | | | |
| 12 | Expected portfolio return, E(r_p) | 8.85% | <-- =B9*B3+B10*C3 | |
| 13 | Portfolio variance, Var(r_p) | 1.47% | <-- =B9^2*B4+B10^2*C4+2*B9*B10*B6 | |
| 14 | Portfolio standard deviation, s_p | 12.10% | <-- =SQRT(B13) | |
| 15 | | | | |
| 16 | | | | |

Portfolio Returns: Expected Return $E(r_p)$ and Standard Deviation $\sigma_p$

Portfolio standard deviation (12.10%) and expected return (8.85%) from a portfolio invested 50% in K and 50% in XOM.

The point here is that you don't need to do an extensive calculation of annual portfolio returns—it's enough to know the return statistics for each stock, the portfolio proportions, and the covariance of the stock returns.

## Another Portfolio—Increasing the Weight of MSFT, Decreasing GM

Now suppose we graph another portfolio—this time a portfolio invested 25% in Kellogg and 75% in Exxon.

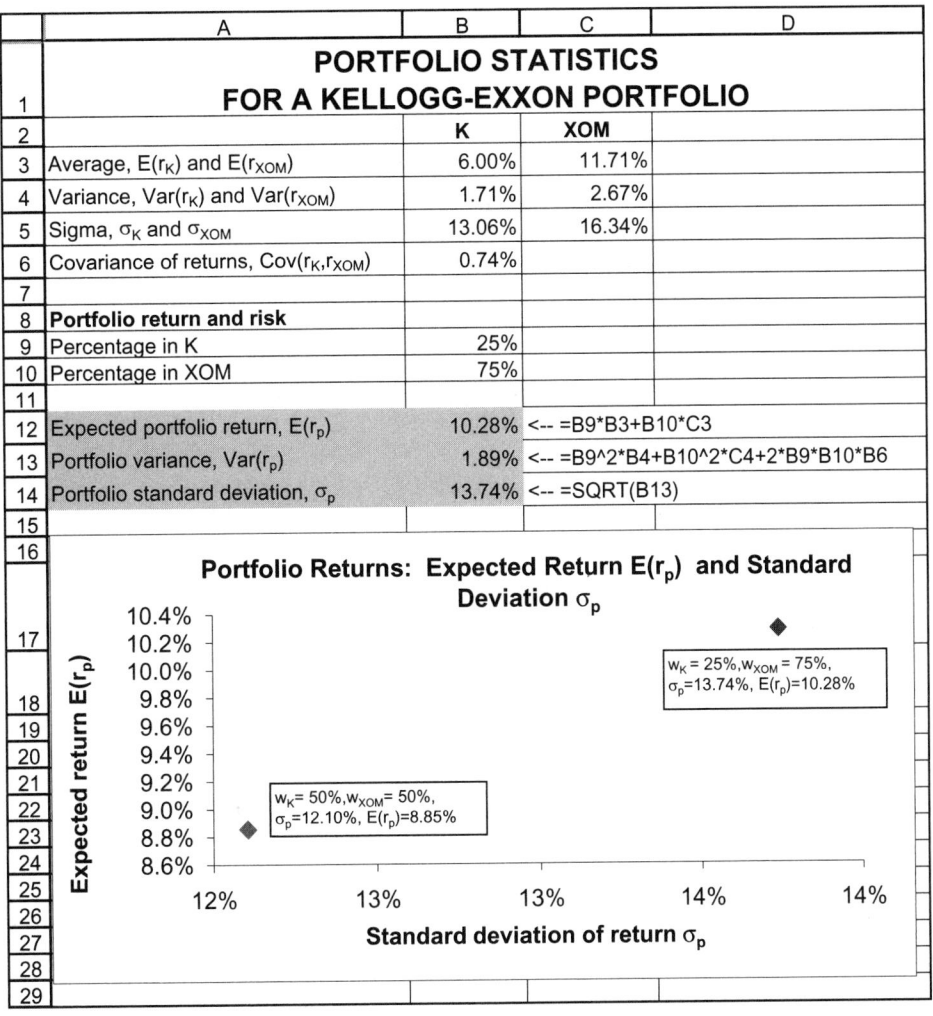

| | A | B | C | D |
|---|---|---|---|---|
| 1 | **PORTFOLIO STATISTICS FOR A KELLOGG-EXXON PORTFOLIO** | | | |
| 2 | | **K** | **XOM** | |
| 3 | Average, $E(r_K)$ and $E(r_{XOM})$ | 6.00% | 11.71% | |
| 4 | Variance, $Var(r_K)$ and $Var(r_{XOM})$ | 1.71% | 2.67% | |
| 5 | Sigma, $\sigma_K$ and $\sigma_{XOM}$ | 13.06% | 16.34% | |
| 6 | Covariance of returns, $Cov(r_K,r_{XOM})$ | 0.74% | | |
| 7 | | | | |
| 8 | **Portfolio return and risk** | | | |
| 9 | Percentage in K | 25% | | |
| 10 | Percentage in XOM | 75% | | |
| 11 | | | | |
| 12 | Expected portfolio return, $E(r_p)$ | 10.28% | <-- =B9*B3+B10*C3 | |
| 13 | Portfolio variance, $Var(r_p)$ | 1.89% | <-- =B9^2*B4+B10^2*C4+2*B9*B10*B6 | |
| 14 | Portfolio standard deviation, $\sigma_p$ | 13.74% | <-- =SQRT(B13) | |
| 15 | | | | |

**Portfolio Returns:  Expected Return $E(r_p)$  and Standard Deviation $\sigma_p$**

$w_K = 25\%, w_{XOM} = 75\%$, $\sigma_p = 13.74\%$, $E(r_p) = 10.28\%$

$w_K = 50\%, w_{XOM} = 50\%$, $\sigma_p = 12.10\%$, $E(r_p) = 8.85\%$

Note that the new portfolio's performance is to the "northeast" of the first portfolio—it has both higher returns and higher standard deviation. The new portfolio gives you greater expected return, but has higher risk. This is what you would expect—higher return is achieved at the price of higher risk. As you will see in the next subsection, this may not always be the case.

## Varying the Portfolio Composition—Graphing All Possible Portfolios

Suppose we vary the composition of the portfolio, letting the percentage of K vary from 0 to 100%. In cells G19:H29 below we generate a table of portfolio returns $E(r_p)$ and standard deviations $\sigma_p$.

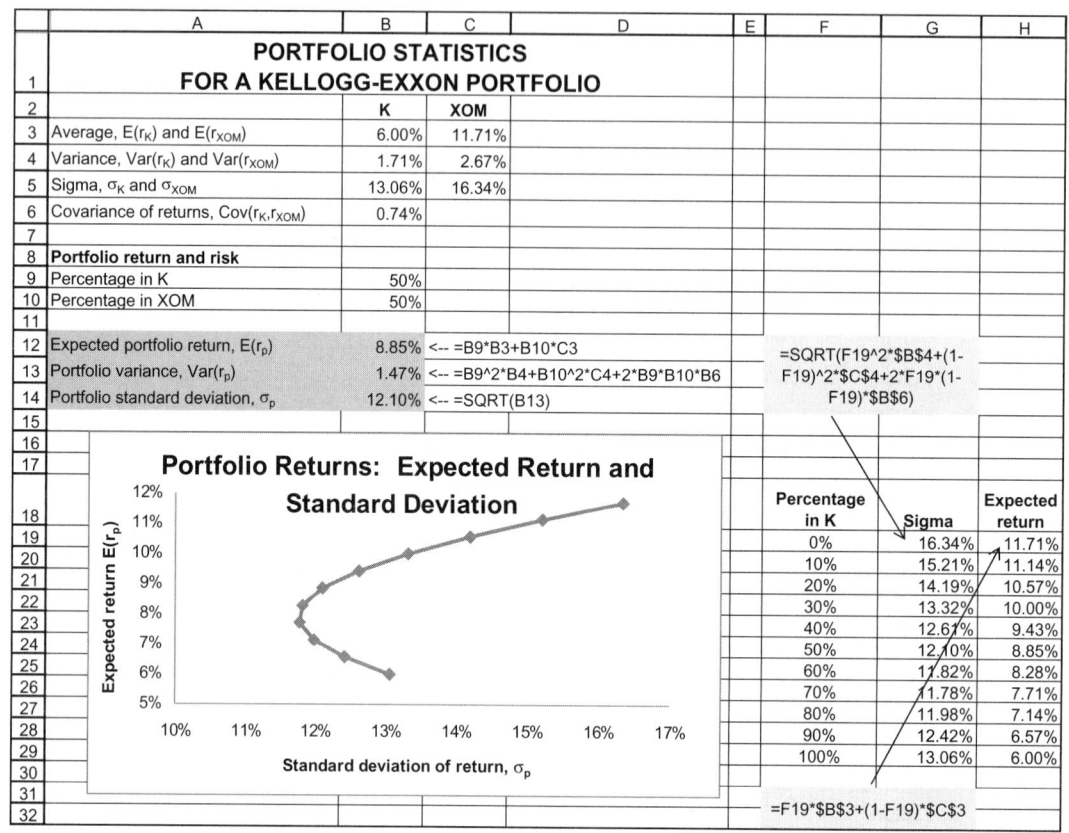

|  | A | B | C | D | E | F | G | H |
|---|---|---|---|---|---|---|---|---|
| 1 | PORTFOLIO STATISTICS FOR A KELLOGG-EXXON PORTFOLIO | | | | | | | |
| 2 |  | K | XOM |  |  |  |  |  |
| 3 | Average, $E(r_K)$ and $E(r_{XOM})$ | 6.00% | 11.71% |  |  |  |  |  |
| 4 | Variance, $Var(r_K)$ and $Var(r_{XOM})$ | 1.71% | 2.67% |  |  |  |  |  |
| 5 | Sigma, $\sigma_K$ and $\sigma_{XOM}$ | 13.06% | 16.34% |  |  |  |  |  |
| 6 | Covariance of returns, $Cov(r_K,r_{XOM})$ | 0.74% |  |  |  |  |  |  |
| 7 |  |  |  |  |  |  |  |  |
| 8 | Portfolio return and risk |  |  |  |  |  |  |  |
| 9 | Percentage in K | 50% |  |  |  |  |  |  |
| 10 | Percentage in XOM | 50% |  |  |  |  |  |  |
| 11 |  |  |  |  |  |  |  |  |
| 12 | Expected portfolio return, $E(r_p)$ | 8.85% | <-- =B9*B3+B10*C3 |  |  | =SQRT(F19^2*$B$4+(1-F19)^2*$C$4+2*F19*(1-F19)*$B$6) | | |
| 13 | Portfolio variance, $Var(r_p)$ | 1.47% | <-- =B9^2*B4+B10^2*C4+2*B9*B10*B6 |  |  |  |  |  |
| 14 | Portfolio standard deviation, $\sigma_p$ | 12.10% | <-- =SQRT(B13) |  |  |  |  |  |
| 15 |  |  |  |  |  |  |  |  |
| 16 |  |  |  |  |  |  |  |  |
| 17 |  | Portfolio Returns:  Expected Return and Standard Deviation | | | | | | |
| 18 |  |  |  |  |  | Percentage in K | Sigma | Expected return |
| 19 |  |  |  |  |  | 0% | 16.34% | 11.71% |
| 20 |  |  |  |  |  | 10% | 15.21% | 11.14% |
| 21 |  |  |  |  |  | 20% | 14.19% | 10.57% |
| 22 |  |  |  |  |  | 30% | 13.32% | 10.00% |
| 23 |  |  |  |  |  | 40% | 12.67% | 9.43% |
| 24 |  |  |  |  |  | 50% | 12.10% | 8.85% |
| 25 |  |  |  |  |  | 60% | 11.82% | 8.28% |
| 26 |  |  |  |  |  | 70% | 11.78% | 7.71% |
| 27 |  |  |  |  |  | 80% | 11.98% | 7.14% |
| 28 |  |  |  |  |  | 90% | 12.42% | 6.57% |
| 29 |  |  |  |  |  | 100% | 13.06% | 6.00% |
| 30 |  |  |  |  |  |  |  |  |
| 31 |  |  |  |  |  |  |  |  |
| 32 |  |  |  |  |  | =F19*$B$3+(1-F19)*$C$3 | | |

# EXCEL NOTE: USING DATA TABLE TO SIMPLIFY THE CALCULATIONS

The table in cells G19:H29 above was generated using formulas for the standard deviation and expected return. Each cell contains a formula (note the use of absolute and relative cell references in these formulas). You can simplify the building of the table using the **Data table** technique discussed in Chapter 27. **Data table** is not an easy technique to master, but it makes building tables much easier. Here's an example.

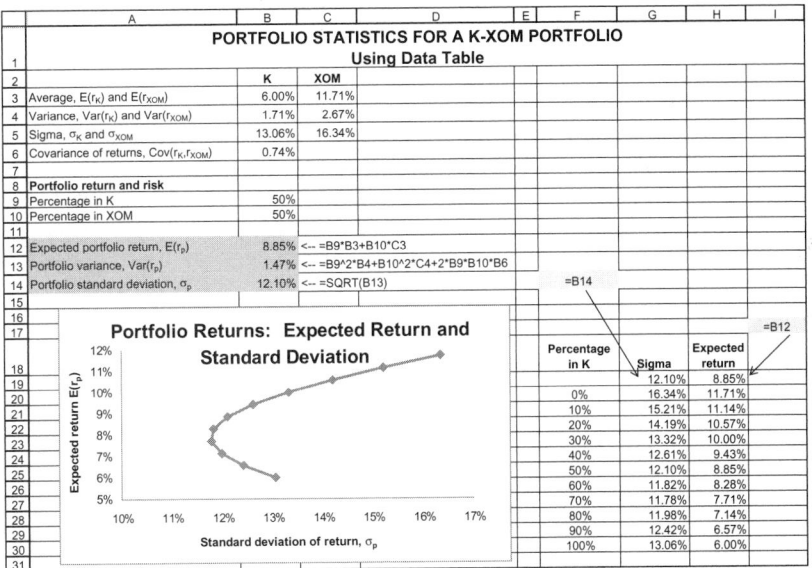

You create the data table by marking the cells F18:H29. The command **Data|What-If Analysis|Table** brings up the dialog box to which you add the appropriate cell reference.

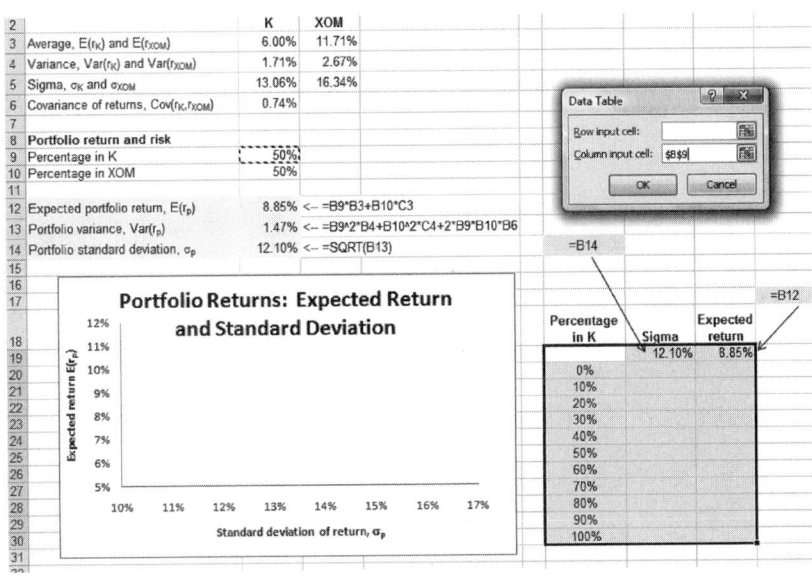

## Better Portfolios...Worse Portfolios...

Take a careful look at the graph in the preceding spreadsheet—it shows the standard deviation $\sigma_p$ of the portfolio returns on the *x*-axis and the corresponding expected portfolio return $E(r_p)$ on the *y*-axis. Looking at the graph it is easy to see that some portfolios are better than others. Consider, for example, the portfolio invested 90% in K and 10% in XOM (this portfolio is circled in the graph below). By investing in the portfolio indicated by the arrow, you can improve the expected return without increasing the riskiness of the return. Thus, the circled portfolio is not optimal. In fact, none of the portfolios on the bottom part of the graph is optimal: Each is dominated by a portfolio on the top part of the graph that has the same standard deviation $\sigma_p$ and higher expected return $E(r_p)$.

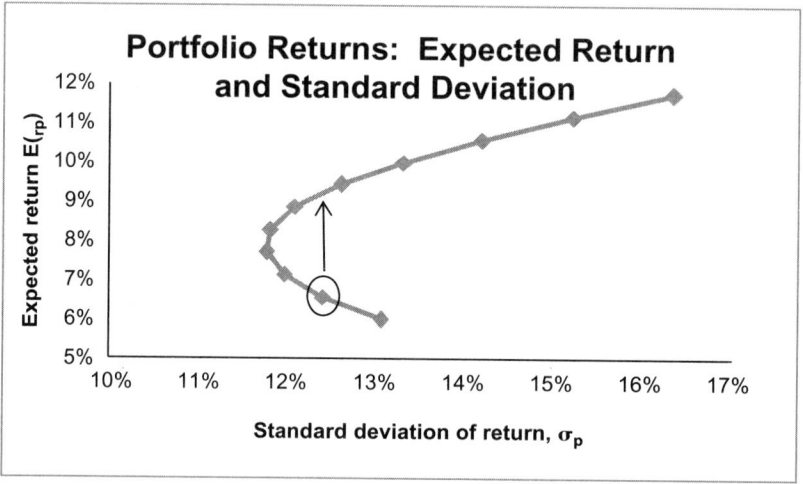

On the other hand, consider the two portfolios circled below.

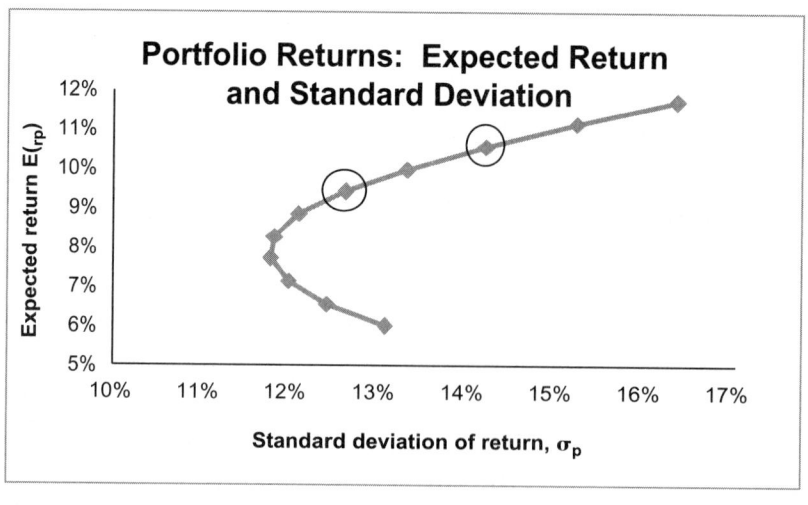

There is a clear risk–return trade-off between these two portfolios—it is impossible to say that one is unequivocally better than the other. The portfolio with the higher return also has the higher standard deviation of returns. All of the portfolios on the top part of the graph have this property. The top part of the graph is called the *efficient frontier*. The efficient frontier is the area of hard portfolio choices—along the efficient frontier, portfolios with greater expected return require you to undertake greater risk.

The efficient frontier slopes upward from left to right. What this means is that the choice between any two portfolios on the efficient frontier involves a trade-off between higher expected portfolio return, $E(r_p)$, and higher risk as indicated by a higher standard deviation of the return, $\sigma_p$. An investor choosing only risky portfolios would choose a portfolio on the efficient frontier.

In the next section we investigate some of the properties of the efficient frontier.

## 10.4. The Efficient Frontier and the Minimum Variance Portfolio

The *efficient frontier* is the set of all portfolios that are on the upward-sloping part of the preceding graph. "Upward-sloping" means that portfolios on the efficient frontier involve difficult choices—increasing expected portfolio return $E(r_p)$ has the cost of increasing portfolio standard deviation $\sigma_p$. If you are choosing investment portfolios that are a mix of K and XOM stock, then clearly the only portfolios you would be interested in are those on the efficient frontier. These portfolios are the only ones that have a "northeast" risk–return relation.

To calculate the efficient frontier, we have to find its starting point, the portfolio with the minimum standard deviation of returns. In the jargon of finance, this portfolio is (somewhat confusingly) called the *minimum-variance portfolio*; just recall that if the portfolio has minimum variance it also has minimum standard deviation. The minimum variance portfolio is the portfolio in the left-hand corner of the efficient frontier; the graph below indicates its approximate location.

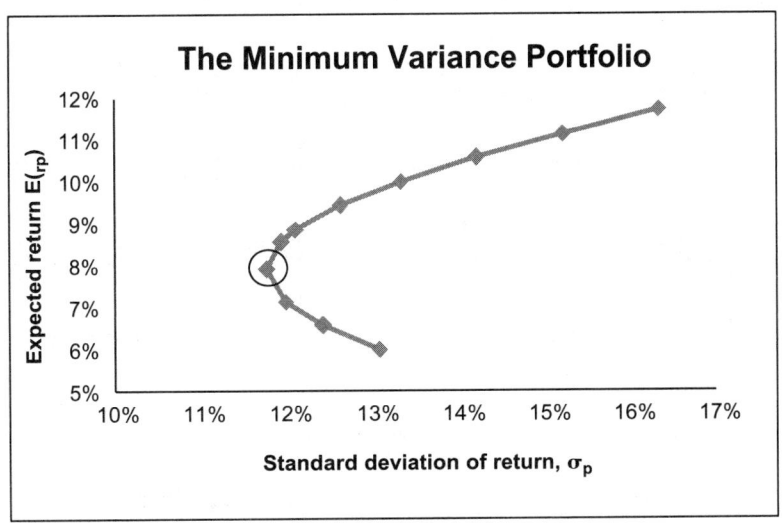

We can find the minimum variance portfolio in two ways—either using the **Solver** or using a bit of mathematics. We illustrate both methods.

## The Minimum Variance Portfolio Using Excel's Solver

Using the **Solver** (see Chapter 28), we can calculate the percentage of Kellogg in a portfolio that has minimum variance. The screen below shows the **Solver** dialog box. In this box, we've asked **Solver** to minimize the portfolio variance (cell B13) by changing the percentage of Kellogg stock in the portfolio (cell B9).

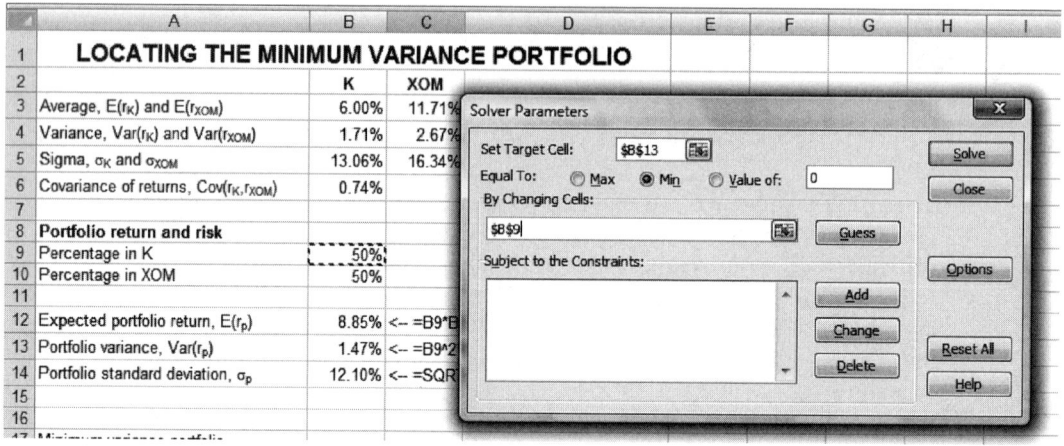

Clicking on **Solve** gives the following.

|  | A | B | C | D |
|---|---|---|---|---|
| 1 | **LOCATING THE MINIMUM VARIANCE PORTFOLIO** | | | |
| 2 |  | **K** | **XOM** |  |
| 3 | Average, $E(r_K)$ and $E(r_{XOM})$ | 6.00% | 11.71% |  |
| 4 | Variance, $Var(r_K)$ and $Var(r_{XOM})$ | 1.71% | 2.67% |  |
| 5 | Sigma, $\sigma_K$ and $\sigma_{XOM}$ | 13.06% | 16.34% |  |
| 6 | Covariance of returns, $Cov(r_K, r_{XOM})$ | 0.74% |  |  |
| 7 |  |  |  |  |
| 8 | **Portfolio return and risk** |  |  |  |
| 9 | Percentage in K | 66.68% |  |  |
| 10 | Percentage in XOM | 33.32% |  |  |
| 11 |  |  |  |  |
| 12 | Expected portfolio return, $E(r_p)$ | 7.90% | <-- =B9*B3+B10*C3 | |
| 13 | Portfolio variance, $Var(r_p)$ | 1.38% | <-- =B9^2*B4+B10^2*C4+2*B9*B10*B6 | |
| 14 | Portfolio standard deviation, $\sigma_p$ | 11.77% | <-- =SQRT(B13) | |
| 15 |  |  |  |  |
| 16 | Minimum variance portfolio using formula | 66.68% | <-- =(C4-B6)/(B4+C4-2*B6) | |

Thus, the minimum variance portfolio has 66.68% in Kellogg and 33.32% in Exxon.[8]

## Minimum Variance Portfolios Using Calculus

There's actually a formula for the minimum variance portfolio:

$$w_K = \frac{Var(r_{XOM}) - Cov(r_K, r_{XOM})}{Var(r_K) + Var(r_{XOM}) - 2Cov(r_K, r_{XOM})}$$

The use of this formula is illustrated in cell B16 in the preceding spreadsheet. Using this formula, which is derived in Appendix 10.1, is simpler than using **Solver**.

## The Efficient Frontier and the Minimum Variance Portfolio

Now that we know the minimum variance portfolio, we can plot the efficient frontier, the set of all portfolios with an economically meaningful return–risk trade-off. "Economically meaningful return–risk tradeoff" means that along the efficient frontier additional portfolio return $E(r_p)$ is achieved at the cost of additional portfolio standard deviation $\sigma_p$. The efficient frontier is all portfolios that are to the right of the minimum variance portfolio.

|   | A | B | C | D | E | F | G | H | I | J | K |
|---|---|---|---|---|---|---|---|---|---|---|---|
| 1 | | | THE EFFICIENT FRONTIER | | | | | | | | |
| 2 | | | K | XOM | | | | | | | |
| 3 | Average, $E(r_K)$ and $E(r_{XOM})$ | | 6.00% | 11.71% | | | | | | | |
| 4 | Variance, $Var(r_K)$ and $Var(r_{XOM})$ | | 1.71% | 2.67% | | | | | | | |
| 5 | Sigma, $\sigma_K$ and $\sigma_{XOM}$ | | 13.06% | 16.34% | | | | | | | |
| 6 | Covariance of returns, $Cov(r_K, r_{XOM})$ | | 0.74% | | | | | | | | |
| 7 | | | | | | | | | | | |
| 8 | Minimum variance portfolio--analytic formula | | | | | | | | | | |
| 9 | Percentage in K | 66.68% | <-- =(D4-C6)/(C4+D4-2*C6) | | | | | | | | |
| 10 | Percentage in XOM | 33.32% | <-- =1-B9 | | | | | | | | |
| 11 | | | | | | | | | | | |
| 12 | Expected portfolio return, $E(r_p)$ | 7.90% | <-- =B9*C3+B10*D3 | | | | | | | | |
| 13 | Portfolio variance, $Var(r_p)$ | 0.0138 | <-- =B9^2*C4+B10^2*D4+2*B9*B10*C6 | | | | | | | | |
| 14 | Portfolio standard deviation, $\sigma_p$ | 11.77% | <-- =SQRT(B13) | | | | | | | | |
| 15 | | | | | | | | Percentage in K | Sigma | Expected return | Efficient frontier points |
| 16 | | | | | | | | | | | |
| 17 | | | | | | | | 0.00% | 16.34% | 11.71% | 11.71% |
| 18 | | | | | | | | 10.00% | 15.21% | 11.14% | 11.14% |
| 19 | | | | | | | | 20.00% | 14.19% | 10.57% | 10.57% |
| 20 | | | | | | | | 30.00% | 13.32% | 10.00% | 10.00% |
| 21 | | | | | | | | 40.00% | 12.61% | 9.43% | 9.43% |
| 22 | | | | | | | | 50.00% | 12.10% | 8.85% | 8.85% |
| 23 | | | | | | | | 66.68% | 11.77% | 7.90% | 7.90% |
| 24 | | | | | | | | 70.00% | 11.78% | 7.71% | |
| 25 | | | | | | | | 80.00% | 11.98% | 7.14% | |
| 26 | | | | | | | | 90.00% | 12.42% | 6.57% | |
| 27 | | | | | | | | 100.00% | 13.06% | 6.00% | |
| 28 | | | | | | | | This is the portfolio percentage in K that gives the minimum variance portfolio. | | | |
| 29 | | | | | | | | | | | |
| 30 | | | | | | | | | | | |
| 31 | | | | | | | | | | | |
| 32 | | | | | | | | | | | |

Expected Return and Standard Deviation of Portfolio Return--Showing Efficient Frontier

Expected portfolio return, $E(r_p)$ vs. Standard deviation of portfolio return, $\sigma_p$

---

[8]Although—as explained in Chapter 28—**Solver** and **Goal Seek** are in many cases interchangeable, this is a calculation that **Solver** does easily, but that cannot be done in **Goal Seek**.

## EXCEL TRICK

The graph of the efficient frontier just shown is an **XY Scatter plot**. The *x*-data are the data for sigma in I17:I27. Cells J17:J27 give the data for the portfolio expected returns, and cells K17:K27 give data for the expected returns *only for efficient portfolios*. The two data series, J17:J27 and K17:K27, constitute the *y*-data for the XY scatter plot. Where they coincide, Excel superimposes them, creating the effect seen in the graph.

To create the graph, mark the three columns I17:K27. Then go to the **Insert** tab and pick XY (Scatter) as shown below. Proceed from there to build the graph.

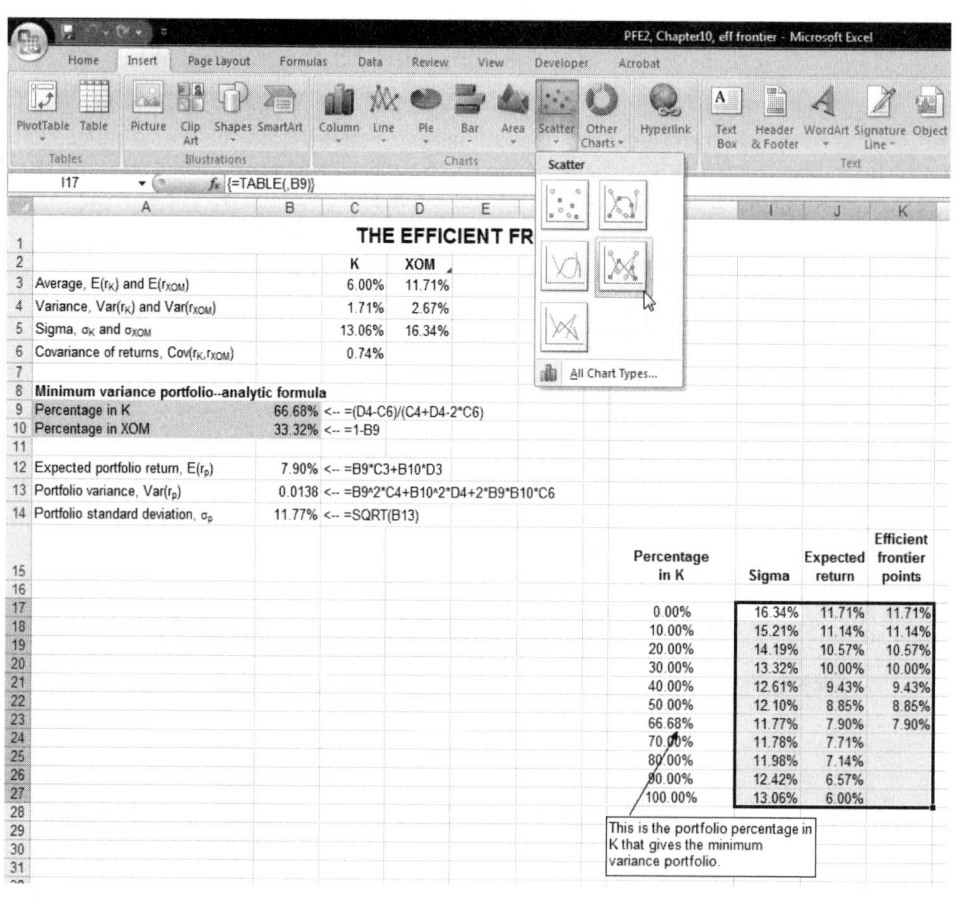

## 10.5. The Effect of Correlation on the Efficient Frontier

When we looked at the "coin-flip" economy of Section 10.1, we concluded that the correlation between asset returns made a big difference. In this section we examine the effect of stock return correlation on portfolio returns, repeating the correlation experiment of Section 10.1 for a more "real-world" example.

First, recall what we concluded in Section 10.1:

- When the two coins have a perfect negative correlation of −1, we can create a risk-free asset using combinations of the two assets. In this section you'll see that a similar conclusion is true for stock portfolios: Perfectly negatively correlated stock returns allow you to create a risk-free asset.

- When the two coins have a perfect positive correlation of +1, it's impossible to diversify away any risk. You will see that a similar conclusion holds for stock portfolios.

- When the two coins have correlation between −1 and +1, some of the risk can be eliminated through diversification. Again, this is true for stock portfolios.

In our example we use some of the same numbers used in our Kellogg–Exxon example, but we'll allow the correlation between the returns on the two stocks to vary. We start with the following example, in which the correlation coefficient between K and XOM is $\rho_{K,XOM} = 0.5$.

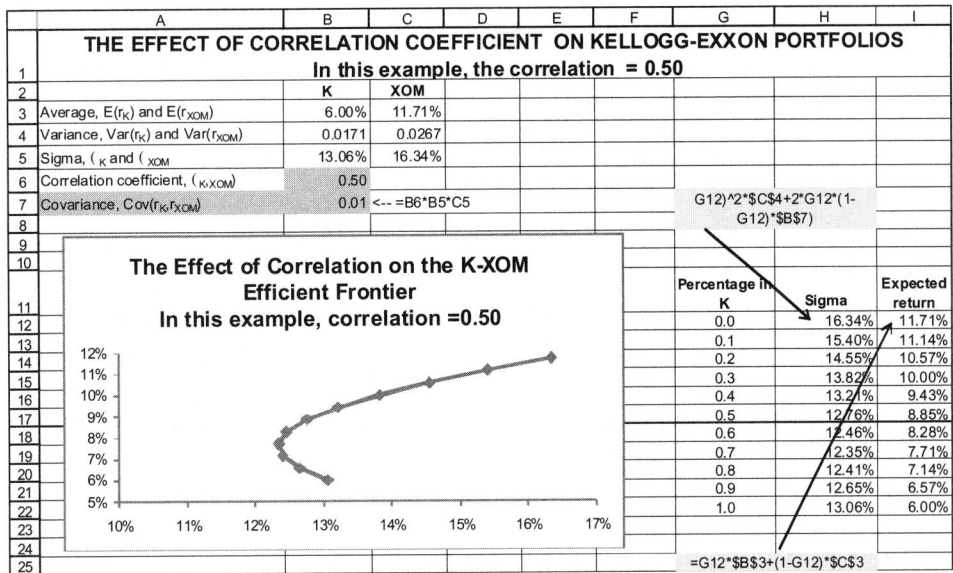

## Correlation Coefficient = −1—Perfect Negative Correlation

When the correlation coefficient $\rho_{GM,MSFT} = -1$, we can use our portfolio to create a riskless asset. This was the message in the simple "coin toss" example with which we started this chapter (Section 10.1), and it is still true here:

Perfect negative correlation between two risky assets allows the creation of a portfolio that is risk free.

Here's our example in Excel.

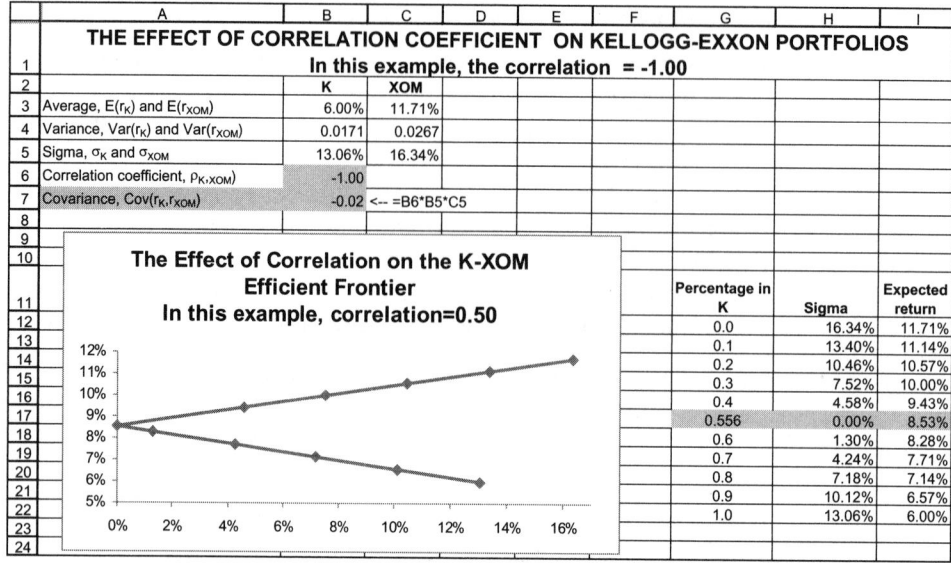

| | A | B | C | D | E | F | G | H | I |
|---|---|---|---|---|---|---|---|---|---|
| 1 | THE EFFECT OF CORRELATION COEFFICIENT ON KELLOGG-EXXON PORTFOLIOS | | | | | | | | |
| | In this example, the correlation = -1.00 | | | | | | | | |
| 2 | | K | XOM | | | | | | |
| 3 | Average, E(r$_K$) and E(r$_{XOM}$) | 6.00% | 11.71% | | | | | | |
| 4 | Variance, Var(r$_K$) and Var(r$_{XOM}$) | 0.0171 | 0.0267 | | | | | | |
| 5 | Sigma, σ$_K$ and σ$_{XOM}$ | 13.06% | 16.34% | | | | | | |
| 6 | Correlation coefficient, ρ$_{K,XOM}$ | -1.00 | | | | | | | |
| 7 | Covariance, Cov(r$_K$,r$_{XOM}$) | -0.02 | <-- =B6*B5*C5 | | | | | | |
| 8 | | | | | | | | | |
| 9 | | | | | | | | | |
| 10 | | | | | | | | | |
| 11 | | | | | | | Percentage in | | Expected |
| 12 | | | | | | | K | Sigma | return |
| 13 | | | | | | | 0.0 | 16.34% | 11.71% |
| 14 | | | | | | | 0.1 | 13.40% | 11.14% |
| 15 | | | | | | | 0.2 | 10.46% | 10.57% |
| 16 | | | | | | | 0.3 | 7.52% | 10.00% |
| 17 | | | | | | | 0.4 | 4.58% | 9.43% |
| 18 | | | | | | | 0.556 | 0.00% | 8.53% |
| 19 | | | | | | | 0.6 | 1.30% | 8.28% |
| 20 | | | | | | | 0.7 | 4.24% | 7.71% |
| 21 | | | | | | | 0.8 | 7.18% | 7.14% |
| 22 | | | | | | | 0.9 | 10.12% | 6.57% |
| 23 | | | | | | | 1.0 | 13.06% | 6.00% |
| 24 | | | | | | | | | |

The minimum variance portfolio (highlighted in cells G17:I17) is achieved when the proportion in Kellogg is 55.6%. When the correlation between the two stocks is −1, the minimum variance portfolio is riskless—the portfolio's return of 8.53% is achieved with zero standard deviation.

A little mathematics explains this result. The portfolio variance for this case can be written

$$Var(r_p) = w_K^2 Var(r_K) + w_{XOM}^2 Var(r_{XOM}) + 2w_K w_{XOM} \rho_{K,XOM} \sigma_K \sigma_{XOM}$$
$$= w_K^2 \sigma_K^2 + w_{XOM}^2 \sigma_{XOM}^2 - 2w_K w_{XOM} \sigma_K \sigma_{XOM}$$
$$= w_K^2 \sigma_K^2 + (1 - w_K)^2 \sigma_{XOM}^2 - 2w_K (1 - w_{XOM}) \sigma_K \sigma_{XOM}$$
$$= (w_K \sigma_K - (1 - w_K) \sigma_{XOM})^2$$

This means that we can—by choosing the appropriate weights $w_K$ and $w_{XOM}$—set the portfolio variance equal to zero:

$$Var(r_p) = (w_K \sigma_K - (1 - w_K) \sigma_{XOM})^2 = 0$$
$$when \ w_K = \frac{\sigma_{XOM}}{\sigma_K + \sigma_{XOM}}$$

In our case, this means that

$$w_K = \frac{\sigma_{XOM}}{\sigma_K + \sigma_{XOM}} = \frac{0.0267}{0.0171 + 0.0267} = 0.5557$$

This value is given in cell G18.

## Correlation Coefficient = +1. The Case of Perfect Positive Correlation

When the correlation coefficient $\rho_{K,XOM} = +1$, diversification does not reduce risk.

Perfect positive correlation between two risky assets means that risk is not reduced in a portfolio context.

Here's our example in Excel.

| | A | B | C | D | E | F | G | H | I |
|---|---|---|---|---|---|---|---|---|---|
| 1 | THE EFFECT OF CORRELATION COEFFICIENT ON KELLOGG-EXXON PORTFOLIOS<br>In this example, the correlation = 1.00 | | | | | | | | |
| 2 | | K | XOM | | | | | | |
| 3 | Average, $E(r_K)$ and $E(r_{XOM})$ | 6.00% | 11.71% | | | | | | |
| 4 | Variance, $Var(r_K)$ and $Var(r_{XOM})$ | 0.0171 | 0.0267 | | | | | | |
| 5 | Sigma, $\sigma_K$ and $\sigma_{XOM}$ | 13.06% | 16.34% | | | | | | |
| 6 | Correlation coefficient, $\rho_{K,XOM}$ | 1.00 | | | | | | | |
| 7 | Covariance, $Cov(r_K, r_{XOM})$ | | 0.02 | <-- =B6*B5*C5 | | | | | |
| 8 | | | | | | | | | |
| 9 | | | | | | | | | |
| 10 | | | | | | | | Percentage in K | Sigma | Expected return |

The Effect of Correlation on the K-XOM Efficient Frontier
In this example, correlation=1.00

| Percentage in K | Sigma | Expected return |
|---|---|---|
| 0.00 | 16.34% | 11.71% |
| 0.10 | 16.01% | 11.14% |
| 0.20 | 15.68% | 10.57% |
| 0.30 | 15.36% | 10.00% |
| 0.40 | 15.03% | 9.43% |
| 0.50 | 14.70% | 8.85% |
| 0.60 | 14.37% | 8.28% |
| 0.70 | 14.04% | 7.71% |
| 0.80 | 13.72% | 7.14% |
| 0.90 | 13.39% | 6.57% |
| 1.00 | 13.06% | 6.00% |

Note what we mean by "portfolios do not reduce risk": The risk–return combinations for this case are on a straight line. In the previous two cases (correlation = 0.50 and correlation = −1) the portfolio frontier had a "northwest" portion; on a "northwest" portion of the frontier, we reduce risk and increase return. For this case the frontier only has a "northeast portion"—there is no way to reduce risk and increase return.

When the correlation between the two assets' returns is +1, the standard deviation of the portfolio return for this case is the weighted average of the asset standard deviations. A little mathematics explains this result. The portfolio variance for this case can be written

$$Var(r_p) = w_K^2 Var(r_K) + w_{XOM}^2 Var(r_{XOM}) + 2w_K w_{XOM} \rho_{K,XOM} \sigma_K \sigma_{XOM}$$
$$= w_K^2 \sigma_K^2 + w_{XOM}^2 \sigma_{XOM}^2 + \underbrace{2w_K w_{XOM} \sigma_K \sigma_{XOM}}_{\substack{\text{The correlation coefficient} \\ \rho_{K,XOM}=1}}$$
$$= \left(w_K \sigma_K + (1 - w_K)\sigma_{XOM}\right)^2$$

This means that the standard deviation of the portfolio is the weighted average of the asset standard deviations:

$$\sigma(r_p) = w_K \sigma_K + (1 - w_K)\sigma_{XOM}$$

Thus, there is no real gain from diversification.

# Summary

In this chapter we have discussed the importance of diversification for portfolio returns and risks. We showed how to calculate the mean and variance and standard deviation of a portfolio's return. The *efficient frontier* is the set of those portfolios that offer the highest expected return for a given standard deviation. We discussed this frontier and how it is affected by the correlation between the asset returns.

## EXERCISES

**Note**: Data for the problems are on the CD-ROM that accompanies the book.

1. The table below presents the year-end prices for the shares of Ford and PPG from 1989 to 2001.

| | A | B | C |
|---|---|---|---|
| 1 | PRICES FOR FORD AND PPG STOCK | | |
| 2 | Date | Ford stock price | PPG stock price |
| 3 | 31-Dec-89 | 11.813 | 14.024 |
| 4 | 31-Dec-90 | 7.210 | 17.229 |
| 5 | 31-Dec-91 | 7.617 | 19.138 |
| 6 | 31-Dec-92 | 11.612 | 25.721 |
| 7 | 31-Dec-93 | 17.469 | 30.518 |
| 8 | 31-Dec-94 | 15.100 | 30.736 |
| 9 | 31-Dec-95 | 15.642 | 38.980 |
| 10 | 31-Dec-96 | 17.472 | 49.007 |
| 11 | 31-Dec-97 | 26.310 | 51.040 |
| 12 | 31-Dec-98 | 31.807 | 53.172 |
| 13 | 31-Dec-99 | 28.895 | 58.626 |
| 14 | 31-Dec-00 | 22.470 | 44.867 |
| 15 | 31-Dec-01 | 15.720 | 51.720 |

a. Calculate the following statistics for these two shares: average return, variance of returns, standard deviation of returns, covariance of returns, and correlation coefficient.

b. If you invested in a portfolio composed of 50% Ford and 50% PPG, what would be the portfolio expected return? The standard deviation?

c. Comment on the following statement: "Ford has lower returns and higher standard deviation of returns than PPG. Therefore, any rational investor would invest in PPG only and would leave Ford out of her portfolio."

2. You invest $500 in a stock for which the return is determined by a coin flip. If the coin comes up heads the stock returns 10%, and if it comes up tails the investment returns −10%. What is the average return, the return variance, and the return standard deviation of this investment if you flip the coin one time?

3. You have $500 to invest. You decide to split it into two parts. The return on each $250 will be determined by a coin toss, and the results of the two tosses are not correlated. If the coin comes up heads the investment will return 10% and if it comes up tails it will return −10%. What is the average return, the return variance, and the return standard deviation of this investment?

4. The previous question assumes that the correlation between the coin flips is 0. Repeat this question with the following correlations:

a. If the first coin flip is heads, then the second coin flip will be heads as well and vice versa (correlation of 1).

b. If the first coin flip is heads, then second coin flip will be tails and vice versa (correlation of −1).

c. If the first coin flip is heads, then the second coin flip will be heads with a probability of 0.8. If the first coin flip is tails, then the second coin flip will be tails with a probability of 0.6.

d. What can you conclude about the connection between the variance of the return from the coin flips and the correlation between the flips?

5. Consider the following statistics for a portfolio composed of shares of companies *A* and *B*.

| | A | B | C | D | E | F |
|---|---|---|---|---|---|---|
| 1 | | Company A stock | Company B stock | | | |
| 2 | Average return | 25% | 48% | | | |
| 3 | Variance | 0.0800 | 0.1600 | | | |
| 4 | Sigma | 28.28% | 40.00% | | | |
| 5 | | | | | | |
| 6 | Covariance of returns | 0.00350 | | | | |
| 7 | Correlation of returns | 0.03094 | <-- =B6/(B4*C4) | | | |
| 8 | | | | | | |
| 9 | Portfolio | | | | | |
| 10 | Proportion of A | 0.9 | | | | |
| 11 | Proportion of B | 0.1 | | | | |
| 12 | Portfolio average return | 27.30% | <-- =B10*B2+C2*B11 | | | |
| 13 | Portfolio standard deviation | 25.89% | <-- =SQRT(B10^2*B3+B11^2*C3+2*B10*B11*B6) | | | |

6. Calculate the average return and the variance of a portfolio composed of 30% GM and 70% MSFT stocks, using the data described from page 323.

| | A | B | C |
|---|---|---|---|
| 1 | **GM AND MSFT RETURN STATISTICS, 1990-1999** | | |
| 2 | Date | GM return | MSFT return |
| 3 | 31-Dec-90 | -11.54% | 72.99% |
| 4 | 31-Dec-91 | -11.35% | 121.76% |
| 5 | 31-Dec-92 | 16.54% | 15.11% |
| 6 | 31-Dec-93 | 72.64% | -5.56% |
| 7 | 30-Dec-94 | -21.78% | 51.63% |
| 8 | 29-Dec-95 | 28.13% | 43.56% |
| 9 | 31-Dec-96 | 8.46% | 88.32% |
| 10 | 31-Dec-97 | 19.00% | 56.43% |
| 11 | 31-Dec-98 | 21.09% | 114.60% |
| 12 | 31-Dec-99 | 21.34% | 68.36% |

a. Suggest a portfolio combination that improves return while maintaining the same level of risk.

b. Calculate the minimum variance portfolio for the portfolio composed of the two assets described above.

7. During the decade 1990–1999, General Motors and Microsoft were negatively correlated (see data in Exercise 6). Find the following two portfolios:

a. The minimum variance portfolio.

b. The efficient portfolio having an expected return of 4%.

8. The following spreadsheet presents data for stocks A and B.

| | A | B | C |
|---|---|---|---|
| 1 | RETURN STATISTICS OF A AND B STOCK | | |
| 2 | | Stock A | Stock B |
| 3 | Average return | 34% | 25% |
| 4 | Variance | 0.12 | 0.07 |
| 5 | Standard deviation | 34.64% | 26.46% |
| 6 | | | |
| 7 | Covariance of return, $Cov(r_A, r_B)$ | 0.0160 | |
| 8 | Correlation of return | 0.1746 | <-- =B7/(B5*C5) |

a. What are the return and the standard deviation of a portfolio composed of 30% of stock A and 70% of stock B?

b. What are the return and the standard deviation of an equally weighted portfolio of stocks A and B?

9. Suppose that the return statistics for A and B stock are given below. What is the standard deviation of the portfolio minimum variance? (The answer requires only one calculation.)

10. ABC and XYZ are two stocks with the following return statistics.

| | A | B | C |
|---|---|---|---|
| 1 | RETURN STATISTICS OF A AND B STOCK | | |
| 2 | | Stock A | Stock B |
| 3 | Average return | 25% | 15% |
| 4 | Variance | 0.16 | 0.0484 |
| 5 | Standard deviation | 40.00% | 22.00% |
| 6 | | | |
| 7 | Covariance of return, $Cov(r_A, r_B)$ | -0.0880 | |

a. Compute the expected return and standard deviation of a portfolio composed of 25% ABC and 75% XYZ.

| | A | B | C |
|---|---|---|---|
| 1 | | Expected return | Standard deviation of return |
| 2 | ABC | 15% | 33% |
| 3 | XYZ | 25% | 46% |
| 4 | Covariance(ABC,XYZ) | 0.0865 | |
| 5 | Correlation(ABC,XYZ) | 0.5698 | |

b. Compute the returns of all portfolios that are combinations of ABC and XYZ with the proportion of ABC being 0, 10, ..., 90, 100%. Graph these returns.

c. Compute the minimum variance portfolio.

11. Melissa Jones wants to invest in a portfolio composed of stocks ABC and XYX (from Question 10), that will yield a return of 19%. What is the weight of each stock in such a portfolio, and what is the portfolio's standard deviation? Answer the question both using Excel's **Goal Seek** or **Solver** and using the mathematical formulas in the chapter (page 322).

12. Your client asks you to create a two-asset portfolio having an expected return of 15% and return standard deviation of 12%. The client specifies that the portfolio includes 60% of the stock Merlyn (named for her beloved mother) that has an expected return of 13% and a standard deviation of 10%.

a. What should be the return statistics of the second stock you'll combine in this portfolio, assuming the stocks have zero correlation?

b. What should be the return statistics of the second stock you'll combine in this portfolio, assuming the stocks have covariance of 0.01?

13. What will be the weights, the expected return, the variance, and the standard deviation of a minimum-variance portfolio combining the stocks below, using the mathematical way?

14. This question relates to the data in Exercise 13.

a. Calculate and graph the efficient frontier of the stock portfolios composed of stocks X and Y in Exercise 13.

|  | A | B | C | D |
|---|---|---|---|---|
| 1 | RETURN STATISTICS OF X AND Y STOCK | | | |
| 2 |  | X | Y |  |
| 3 | Mean return | 21.00% | 14.00% |  |
| 4 | Variance | 0.11 | 0.045 |  |
| 5 | Sigma | 33.17% | 21.21% |  |
| 6 |  |  |  |  |
| 7 | Covariance of returns | -0.0020 |  |  |
| 8 | Correlation of returns | -0.0284 |  |  |

b. Calculate and graph the efficient frontier of the stock portfolios composed of stocks X and Y in Exercise 13, assuming the correlation between the two stocks is –1.

15. Consider the data for stock A and Stock B below. A portfolio composed of 90% of Stock A and 10% Stock B stock has expected return of 19.1% and standard deviation of 20.78%. Find another portfolio with the same standard deviation and a higher return. (You can do this by trial and error, but you can also use **Solver**.)

|  | A | B | C |
|---|---|---|---|
| 1 |  | Stock A | Stock B |
| 2 | Expected return | 14.25% | 62.72% |
| 3 | Variance | 6.38% | 14.43% |
| 4 | Sigma | 25.25% | 37.99% |
| 5 | Covariance of returns | -5.52% |  |

16. John and Mary are considering investing in a combination of ABC stock and XYZ stock. The return on ABC is determined by a coin flip: If the coin is heads the return is 35% and if the coin is tails the return on ABC is 10%. The return on XYZ stock is similarly determined, but by a *separate coin flip.*

a. Compute the mean, variance, and standard deviation of the returns on ABC and XYZ.

b. What is the correlation of the returns? (Nothing to compute here, just think!)

c. John has decided to invest in a portfolio composed of 100% XYZ stock. Mary, on the other hand, is investing in a portfolio composed of 50% ABC and 50% XYZ. Whose portfolio is better? Why?

17. Elizabeth and Sandra are considering investing in a combination of ABC stock and XYZ stock. The return on both stocks is determined by a single coin flip: If the coin is heads the return on both stocks is 35% and if the coin is tails the return is 10%.

a. Compute the mean, variance, and standard deviation of the returns on ABC and XYZ.

b. What is the correlation of the returns? (Nothing to compute here, just think!)

c. Elizabeth has decided to invest in a portfolio composed of 100% XYZ stock. Sandra, on the other hand, is investing in a portfolio composed of 50% ABC and 50% XYZ. Whose portfolio is better?

# APPENDIX 10.1: DERIVING THE FORMULA FOR THE MINIMUM VARIANCE PORTFOLIO

IN THIS APPENDIX WE DERIVE THE FORMULA FOR the minimum variance portfolio. Recall the formula for variance of the portfolio:

$$Var(r_p) = w_K^2 Var(r_K) + w_{XOM}^2 Var(r_{XOM}) + 2w_K w_{XOM} Cov(r_K, r_{XOM})$$

Substituting in $w_{XOM} = 1 - w_K$, this equation becomes

$$Var(r_p) = w_K^2 Var(r_K) + (1 - w_K)^2 Var(r_{XOM}) + 2w_K(1 - w_K)Cov(r_K, r_{XOM})$$

Setting the derivative of this equation equal to zero will give the formula for the minimum variance portfolio:

$$\frac{dVar(r_p)}{dw_K} = 2w_K Var(r_K) - 2(1 - w_K)Var(r_{XOM}) + Cov(r_K, r_{XOM})(2 - 4w_K) = 0$$

$$\Rightarrow w_K = \frac{Var(r_{XOM}) - Cov(r_K, r_{XOM})}{Var(r_K) + Var(r_{XOM}) - 2Cov(r_K, r_{XOM})}$$

# APPENDIX 10.2: PORTFOLIOS WITH THREE AND MORE ASSETS

IN THIS APPENDIX WE LOOK AT PORTFOLIOS AND their efficient frontiers when there are more than two assets. The main points we make are as follows:

- In the multiasset context we can still calculate the efficient frontier, and it still has its characteristic shape.
- The more risky assets there are, the more the portfolio variance is influenced by the covariances between the assets.

We start by considering a three-asset problem. To describe three assets, we need to know the expected return, the variance, and all the *pairs* of covariances. These data are described below.

|   | A | B | C | D | E |
|---|---|---|---|---|---|
| 1 | **A THREE-ASSET PORTFOLIO PROBLEM** | | | | |
| 2 |  | **Stock A** | **Stock B** | **Stock C** | |
| 3 | Mean | 10% | 12% | 15% | |
| 4 | Variance | 15% | 22% | 30% | |
| 5 | | | | | |
| 6 | Cov($r_A$,$r_B$) | 0.03 | | | |
| 7 | Cov($r_B$,$r_C$) | -0.01 | | | |
| 8 | Cov($r_A$,$r_C$) | 0.02 | | | |

Suppose we form a portfolio of risky assets composed of proportion $x_A$ in asset $A$, $x_B$ in asset $B$, and $x_C$ in asset $C$. Because the portfolio is fully invested in risky assets, it follows that $x_C = 1 - x_A - x_B$.

**Portfolio return statistics**: The expected return of the portfolio is given by

$$E(r_p) = x_A E(r_A) + x_B E(r_B) + x_C E(r_C)$$

The calculation of the portfolio's variance of return requires both the variances and the covariances:

$$Var(r_p) = x_A^2 Var(r_A) + x_B^2 Var(r_B) + x_C^2 Var(r_C) +$$
$$2x_A x_B Cov(r_A, r_B) + 2x_A x_C Cov(r_A, r_C) + 2x_B x_C Cov(r_B, r_C)$$

Note that there are three *variances* and three *covariances*. When—at the end of this section—we show you the formula for a four-asset problem, there will be four variances and six covariances. As the number of assets grows, so does the number of covariances (in fact their number grows much faster than the number of variances). This is the meaning of the second bullet at the beginning of this section—for multiasset portfolio problems, the portfolio variance is increasingly influenced by the covariances.

Here's an example of the mean return and variance calculation for our three-asset portfolio: The portfolio statistics are calculated in cells B16:B18.

| | A | B | C | D | E | F | G | H | I | J |
|---|---|---|---|---|---|---|---|---|---|---|
| 1 | A THREE-ASSET PORTFOLIO PROBLEM | | | | | | | | | |
| 2 | | Stock A | Stock B | Stock C | | | | | | |
| 3 | Mean | 10% | 12% | 15% | | | | | | |
| 4 | Variance | 15% | 22% | 30% | | | | | | |
| 5 | | | | | | | | | | |
| 6 | Cov(r_A,r_B) | 0.03 | | | | | | | | |
| 7 | Cov(r_B,r_C) | -0.01 | | | | | | | | |
| 8 | Cov(r_A,r_C) | 0.02 | | | | | | | | |
| 9 | | | | | | | | | | |
| 10 | Portfolio proportions | | | | | | | | | |
| 11 | x_A | 0.2500 | | | | | | | | |
| 12 | x_B | 0.3500 | | | | | | | | |
| 13 | x_C | 0.4000 | <-- =1-B12-B11 | | | | | | | |
| 14 | | | | | | | | | | |
| 15 | Market portfolio statistics | | | | | | | | | |
| 16 | Mean | 0.1270 | <-- =B11*B3+B12*C3+B13*D3 | | | | | | | |
| 17 | Variance | 0.0908 | <-- =B11^2*B4+B12^2*C4+B13^2*D4+2*B11*B12*B6+2*B11*B13*B8+2*B12*B13*B7 | | | | | | | |
| 18 | Sigma | 0.3013 | <-- =SQRT(B17) | | | | | | | |

## Calculating the Efficient Frontier with Three Assets

We can use Excel to calculate and graph the efficient frontier for this case.[9] We'll make use of Excel's **Solver**.

**Step 1**: We use Solver to find the minimum variance portfolio.

---

[9] The procedure we're about to explain is somewhat long-winded—for a much shorter though mathematically more complicated procedure, see my book *Financial Modeling* (3rd edition, MIT Press, 2008).

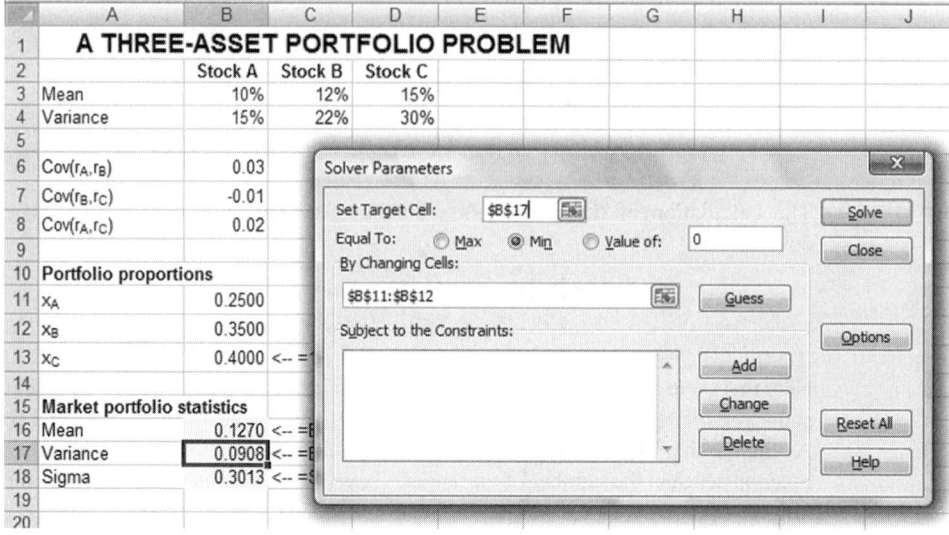

Here's the result.

| | A | B | C | D | E | F | G | H | I | J |
|---|---|---|---|---|---|---|---|---|---|---|
| 1 | A THREE-ASSET PORTFOLIO PROBLEM | | | | | | | | | |
| 2 | | Stock A | Stock B | Stock C | | | | | | |
| 3 | Mean | 10% | 12% | 15% | | | | | | |
| 4 | Variance | 15% | 22% | 30% | | | | | | |
| 5 | | | | | | | | | | |
| 6 | Cov($r_A$,$r_B$) | 0.03 | | | | | | | | |
| 7 | Cov($r_B$,$r_C$) | -0.01 | | | | | | | | |
| 8 | Cov($r_A$,$r_C$) | 0.02 | | | | | | | | |
| 9 | | | | | | | | | | |
| 10 | Portfolio proportions | | | | | | | | | |
| 11 | $x_A$ | 0.4370 | | | | | | | | |
| 12 | $x_B$ | 0.3151 | | | | | | | | |
| 13 | $x_C$ | 0.2479 | <-- =1-B12-B11 | | | | | | | |
| 14 | | | | | | | | | | |
| 15 | Market portfolio statistics | | | | | | | | | |
| 16 | Mean | 0.1187 | <-- =B11*B3+B12*C3+B13*D3 | | | | | | | |
| 17 | Variance | 0.0800 | <-- =B11^2*B4+B12^2*C4+B13^2*D4+2*B11*B12*B6+2*B11*B13*B8+2*B12*B13*B7 | | | | | | | |
| 18 | Sigma | 0.2828 | <-- =SQRT(B17) | | | | | | | |

**Step 2**: We now specify sigma and use **Solver** to find a portfolio with the maximum return. We do this by first adding a cell ("Target sigma," cell B20) to the spreadsheet.

| | A | B | C | D | E | F | G | H | I | J |
|---|---|---|---|---|---|---|---|---|---|---|
| 1 | **A THREE-ASSET PORTFOLIO PROBLEM** | | | | | | | | | |
| 2 | | **Stock A** | **Stock B** | **Stock C** | | | | | | |
| 3 | Mean | 10% | 12% | 15% | | | | | | |
| 4 | Variance | 15% | 22% | 30% | | | | | | |
| 5 | | | | | | | | | | |
| 6 | Cov($r_A,r_B$) | 0.03 | | | | | | | | |
| 7 | Cov($r_B,r_C$) | -0.01 | | | | | | | | |
| 8 | Cov($r_A,r_C$) | 0.02 | | | | | | | | |
| 9 | | | | | | | | | | |
| 10 | **Portfolio proportions** | | | | | | | | | |
| 11 | $x_A$ | 0.2500 | | | | | | | | |
| 12 | $x_B$ | 0.3500 | | | | | | | | |
| 13 | $x_C$ | 0.4000 | <-- =1-B12-B11 | | | | | | | |
| 14 | | | | | | | | | | |
| 15 | **Market portfolio statistics** | | | | | | | | | |
| 16 | Mean | 0.1270 | <-- =B11*B3+B12*C3+B13*D3 | | | | | | | |
| 17 | Variance | 0.0908 | <-- =B11^2*B4+B12^2*C4+B13^2*D4+2*B11*B12*B6+2*B11*B13*B8+2*B12*B13*B7 | | | | | | | |
| 18 | Sigma | 0.3013 | <-- =SQRT(B17) | | | | | | | |

Note that—starting from row 24—we've begun to build a table of the results. The first row of this table is the minimum sigma portfolio. Now we'll use Solver to add another row to this table.

We do this by adding a *constraint* to Solver.

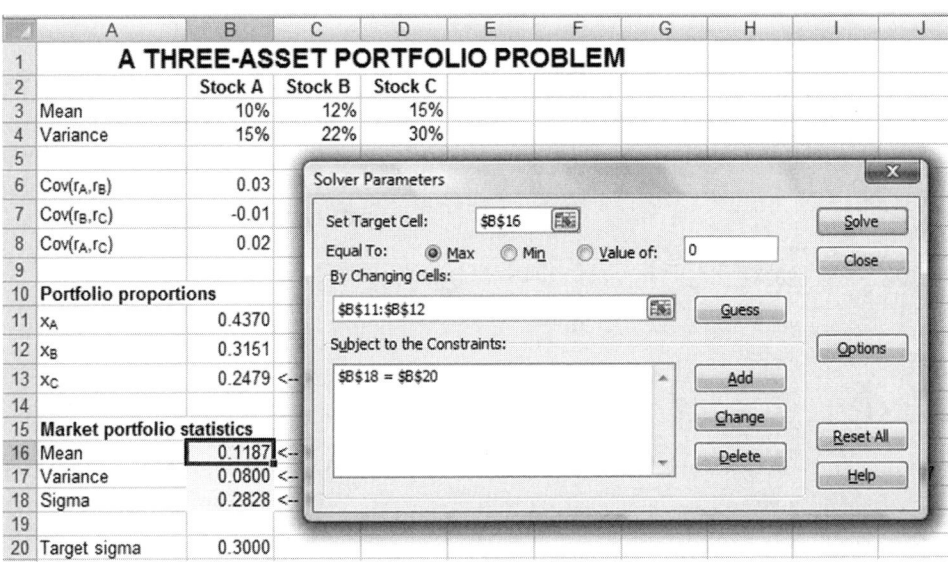

The constraint was added by clicking **Add** in the lower portion of the **Solver** dialog box.

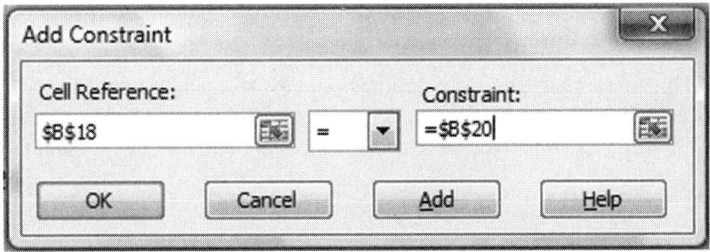

Here's the result.

| | A | B | C | D | E | F | G | H | I | J | K |
|---|---|---|---|---|---|---|---|---|---|---|---|
| 1 | A THREE-ASSET PORTFOLIO PROBLEM | | | | | | | | | | |
| 2 | | Stock A | Stock B | Stock C | | | | | | | |
| 3 | Mean | 10% | 12% | 15% | | | | | | | |
| 4 | Variance | 15% | 22% | 30% | | | | | | | |
| 5 | | | | | | | | | | | |
| 6 | Cov(r_A,r_B) | 0.03 | | | | | | | | | |
| 7 | Cov(r_B,r_C) | -0.01 | | | | | | | | | |
| 8 | Cov(r_A,r_C) | 0.02 | | | | | | | | | |
| 9 | | | | | | | | | | | |
| 10 | Portfolio proportions | | | | | | | | | | |
| 11 | x_A | 0.2533 | | | | | | | | | |
| 12 | x_B | 0.3544 | | | | | | | | | |
| 13 | x_C | 0.3923 | <-- =1-B12-B11 | | | | | | | | |
| 14 | | | | | | | | | | | |
| 15 | Market portfolio statistics | | | | | | | | | | |
| 16 | Mean | 0.1267 | <-- =B11*B3+B12*C3+B13*D3 | | | | | | | | |
| 17 | Variance | 0.0900 | <-- =B11^2*B4+B12^2*C4+B13^2*D4+2*B11*B12*B6+2*B11*B13*B8+2*B12*B13*B7 | | | | | | | | |
| 18 | Sigma | 0.3000 | <-- =SQRT(B17) | | | | | | | | |
| 19 | | | | | | | | | | | |
| 20 | Target sigma | 0.3000 | | | | | | | | | |

If we repeat this calculation many times for many target sigmas, we get the efficient frontier.

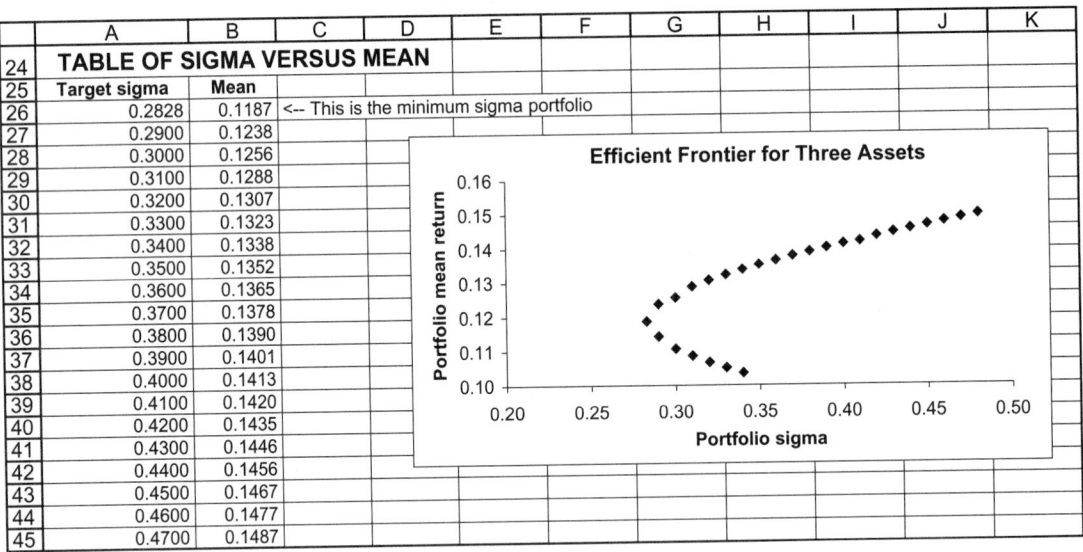

| | A | B | C | D | E | F | G | H | I | J | K |
|---|---|---|---|---|---|---|---|---|---|---|---|
| 24 | TABLE OF SIGMA VERSUS MEAN | | | | | | | | | | |
| 25 | Target sigma | Mean | | | | | | | | | |
| 26 | 0.2828 | 0.1187 | <-- This is the minimum sigma portfolio | | | | | | | | |
| 27 | 0.2900 | 0.1238 | | | | | | | | | |
| 28 | 0.3000 | 0.1256 | | | | | | | | | |
| 29 | 0.3100 | 0.1288 | | | | | | | | | |
| 30 | 0.3200 | 0.1307 | | | | | | | | | |
| 31 | 0.3300 | 0.1323 | | | | | | | | | |
| 32 | 0.3400 | 0.1338 | | | | | | | | | |
| 33 | 0.3500 | 0.1352 | | | | | | | | | |
| 34 | 0.3600 | 0.1365 | | | | | | | | | |
| 35 | 0.3700 | 0.1378 | | | | | | | | | |
| 36 | 0.3800 | 0.1390 | | | | | | | | | |
| 37 | 0.3900 | 0.1401 | | | | | | | | | |
| 38 | 0.4000 | 0.1413 | | | | | | | | | |
| 39 | 0.4100 | 0.1420 | | | | | | | | | |
| 40 | 0.4200 | 0.1435 | | | | | | | | | |
| 41 | 0.4300 | 0.1446 | | | | | | | | | |
| 42 | 0.4400 | 0.1456 | | | | | | | | | |
| 43 | 0.4500 | 0.1467 | | | | | | | | | |
| 44 | 0.4600 | 0.1477 | | | | | | | | | |
| 45 | 0.4700 | 0.1487 | | | | | | | | | |

## Four Assets

This section has gone into depth about how to calculate returns and variances for a three-asset portfolio. If we have four assets, we can do the same kinds of calculations (we leave this as an exercise). What you have to know for this case is how to calculate the portfolio return and variance.

Call the assets $A$, $B$, $C$, and $D$, and denote the portfolio weights by $x_A, x_B, x_C, x_D$.

**Portfolio return statistics:** The expected return of the portfolio is given by

$$E(r_p) = x_A E(r_A) + x_B E(r_B) + x_C E(r_C) + x_D E(r_D)$$

The calculation of the portfolio's variance of return requires both the variances and the covariances:

$$Var(r_p) = x_A^2 Var(r_A) + x_B^2 Var(r_B) + x_C^2 Var(r_C) + x_D^2 Var(r_D)$$
$$2x_A x_B Cov(r_A, r_B) + 2x_A x_C Cov(r_A, r_C) + 2x_A x_D Cov(r_A, r_D)$$
$$+2x_B x_C Cov(r_B, r_C) + 2x_B x_D Cov(r_B, r_D)$$
$$+2x_C x_D Cov(r_C, r_D)$$

Note that there now there are four *variances* and six *covariances*.

## EXERCISES FOR APPENDIX 10.2

All three problems relate to the following statistics for stocks ABC, QPD, and XYZ.

| | A | B | C | D |
|---|---|---|---|---|
| 1 | **RETURN STATISTICS FOR THREE STOCKS** | | | |
| 2 | | ABC | QPD | XYZ |
| 3 | Average return | 22.00% | 17.50% | 30.00% |
| 4 | Variance | 0.2 | 0.05 | 0.17 |
| 5 | Standard deviation | 44.72% | 22.36% | 41.23% |
| 6 | | | | |
| 7 | Correlations | | | |
| 8 | Corr(ABC,QPD) | 0.05 | | |
| 9 | Corr(ABC,XYZ) | -0.1 | | |
| 10 | Corr(QPD,XYZ) | 0.5 | | |

A1. Find the average return and standard deviation of a portfolio composed of 50% stock ABC, 20% stock QPD, and 30% stock XYZ.

A2. Find the minimum variance portfolio and its statistics.

A3. Find the portfolio having maximum return given that the portfolio standard deviation is 30%.

# 11 The Capital Asset Pricing Model and the Security Market Line

## CHAPTER CONTENTS

## Overview

In this chapter we discuss two powerful results about returns and risks in capital markets. One result, termed the *capital market line* (CML), gives investors advice about how to invest. The CML says that the best investment portfolio for any investor is a combination of two assets—a risk-free asset such as a savings account and a risky asset that is representative of the risks of the overall stock market (the S&P 500 index is often used as an example). The choice about which proportion to invest in the risk-free asset and which proportion to invest in the risky asset depends on the investor's willingness to bear risks.

A second result, called the *security market line* (SML), links the return of any asset to its market risk (also termed the asset's *systematic* risk). The SML states that the expected return of any asset depends on the asset's sensitivity to the market. This sensitivity is termed beta and is often written with the Greek letter $\beta$. Assets with higher $\beta$'s have higher risks and will earn higher expected returns.

In this chapter we develop the concepts of the CML and SML. In Chapter 10 we discussed the risk and return combinations offered by a portfolio of risky assets. In this chapter we add a risk-free asset to the portfolio problem discussed in Chapter 10. Adding this asset gives investors new possibilities because it allows them to buy an asset that gives a nonrisky return: They can invest in stocks, in the risk-free asset, or in some combination of the two. A portfolio composed of risky assets and the risk-free asset allows investors to achieve returns that are greater than the returns offered by only a portfolio of risky assets.

The addition of a risk-free asset to the portfolio of risky assets leads to four new concepts:

- The *market portfolio* (denoted by the letter $M$) is the best portfolio of risky assets available to all investors.
- The capital market line (CML) is the set of all optimal investment portfolios for an investor. The CML contains an important piece of investment advice: It tells us that every investor's optimal investment portfolio should be a combination of the risk-free asset and the market portfolio.
- The beta ($\beta$) of a stock is a measure of the stock's market risk.
- The security market line (SML) describes the relation between the expected returns of any stock and its $\beta$.

Because the material in this chapter is not easy, we start the chapter with a summary of its main results. At some point you might want to skip ahead to Chapters 12 and 13 to see how the concepts are used in practice.

## Finance Concepts Used

- Portfolios, risk-free asset
- Capital market line (CML)
- $\beta$, security market line (SML)
- Sharpe ratio

## Excel Functions Used

- **Varp**, **Stdevp**, **Sqrt**
- Sophisticated graphing
- **Solver**

# 11.1. Summarizing the Chapter

Much of the material in this chapter is technical and somewhat harder than that in other chapters in this book. To ease your understanding of the chapter materials, we start with a summary of the chapter's main results.

The big "takeaways" from this chapter are two concepts: the capital market line (CML) and the security market line (SML). The CML tells us how an investor should optimally split his investment between risky and nonrisky assets. The SML tells us how the expected return of any asset is related to its risk and how this risk should be measured. In the next two subsections we give examples of the use of the CML and the SML.

In discussing the CML and the SML it is helpful to have two pieces of notation. We denote by $r_f$ the return of a risk-free asset; you can think of this as the interest rate paid by banks on their savings accounts or as the interest paid by money-market funds.[1] We denote by $E(r_M)$ the *expected return on the market*, the rate of return on a portfolio of stocks that is representative of the riskiness of the whole stock market. Suppose, for example, that the risk-free rate in the United States—a representative rate paid by banks on savings—is $r_f = 3\%$. At the same time, the consensus of stock market analysts is that over the next 5 years the U.S. stock market will have an annual return of $E(r_M) = 8\%$. In the examples below we will use both $r_f = 3\%$ and $E(r_M) = 8\%$ to illustrate the capital market line (CML) and the security market line (SML).

## The Capital Market Line (CML)

The CML says that an investor's optimal investment strategy is to split your capital between two assets: a risk-free asset earning $r_f$ and a risky asset representing the risks of the overall market. The CML states that the expected return of such a portfolio is given by the equation

$$CML:\ \ Expected\ return\ of\ an\ optimal\ portfolio$$
$$E\left(r_p\right) = r_f + \left(\%\ invested\ in\ Market\ portfolio\right) * \left[E\left(r_M\right) - r_f\right]$$

Here's how you might use the CML: Suppose your friend Benjamin says to you: "I've got $10,000 to invest. You're a finance major. Help me pick some stocks."

You should start by telling Benjamin not even to try to pick stocks! Much financial research has shown that stock picking is largely futile; on average, even experienced "stock pickers" do not earn superior returns. Instead of picking stocks, the CML advises you to ask Benjamin what proportion of his money he wants to put at risk and what proportion he needs to keep absolutely safe. There's a trade-off here: The risky part of his investment will, on average, earn more than the riskless part.

Suppose Benjamin answers that he's willing to put 30% of his money at risk and wants the remaining 70% in a safe investment. At that point you can give him the following good advice, based on the CML:

- Invest the $7,000 in a money-market fund such as the Fidelity Cash Reserves Fund. Money-market funds invest in very short-term bonds and earn interest virtually without risk. They are very liquid (meaning you can withdraw your money at any time), and they are very safe.

- Invest the $3,000 that he's willing to put at risk in a mutual fund that represents the average risk of the market. A typical fund might be Fidelity's Spartan 500 Index Fund.

---

[1] A money-market fund is a mutual fund that invests in a highly diversified portfolio of very short-term bonds issued by the U.S. Treasury or by U.S. corporations that have high credit ratings. The bonds bought by a money-market fund typically mature within 7–20 days, meaning that the fund is lending out its money for a very short time in a highly liquid market. The return of a money market fund is representative of the risk-free interest rate in the economy. For a more in-depth explanation, look at http://www.fool.com/savings/shortterm/03.htm.

This fund invests only in the stocks of the S&P 500 index—an index that is broadly representative of the riskiness of the American stock market.[2]

- The CML states that Benjamin's expected portfolio return is related to the risk-free rate $r_f$ and to the percentage of his investment in the market. Suppose that $r_f = 3\%$ and suppose that $E(r_M) = 8\%$. Then Benjamin can expect an annual portfolio return of 4.5%:

$$CML: \textit{ Expected return of an optimal portfolio}$$
$$E(r_p) = r_f + (\% \textit{ invested in Market portfolio})*\left[E(r_M) - r_f\right]$$
$$= 3\% + 30\% * [8\% - 3\%] = 4.5\%$$

Benjamin's 70–30% strategy shows that he's fairly risk averse. His risk aversion leads Benjamin to an investment strategy that puts most of his money in a riskless investment and only a small part in a risky investment. Benjamin will not be putting much of his money at risk, but on the other hand he will earn less than he would if he undertook more risk.

Now suppose your parents ask you how to invest their $1,000,000 of savings. They suggest to you that they're investing for the long run and can bear more risks. Because they can bear more risk than Benjamin, you might ask them what they think of a 20–80% investment strategy. You might suggest to them that they invest $200,000 in Fidelity Cash Reserves and the remaining $800,000 in the Spartan Index 500 Fund. In the long run they will earn more from their investments, but they will undertake more risks. The CML predicts that your parents will earn 7%:

$$CML: \textit{ Expected return of an optimal portfolio}$$
$$E(r_p) = r_f + (\% \textit{ invested in Market portfolio})*\left[E(r_M) - r_f\right]$$
$$= 3\% + 80\% * [8\% - 3\%] = 7\%$$

As you can see, the CML simplifies investment strategies by concentrating only on the split between a riskless and a risky investment asset. It also predicts the expected return of the portfolio.[3] To sum up the investment advice contained in the CML:

- The *best* investment portfolios involve a simple split between the risk-free asset and the market portfolio. These portfolios whose return–risk configuration is given by the CML are the best portfolios available to the investor: Beyond the portfolios that are on the CML, there aren't portfolios that offer a superior return–risk combination.
- Beyond the simple choice of the investor's split between a risk-free asset and the market portfolio, there's *no point* in thinking further! Investors cannot improve the performance of their investment portfolios by the judicious picking of stocks. Neither can investment managers.

## The Security Market Line (SML)

The CML deals only with the composition of optimal investment portfolios. But there are many assets in the market—what about them? The SML says that the expected return of *any stock or portfolio* is related to three factors:

1. The risk-free rate in the market $r_f$.

---

[2] The relevant URLs for the two funds mentioned can be found at the Fidelity Web site: http://www.fidelity.com. Note that almost all mutual fund companies have money-market and index funds, so that the use of the Fidelity funds is merely illustrative.

[3] Anticipating the results of Section 11.3, the CML also suggests that the standard deviation of the returns of the optimal investment strategy are given by $\sigma_P = \%$ *invested in Market portfolio* $*\sigma_M$.

2. The stock's market risk. A stock's risk is measured by a number called beta ($\beta$) that measures the sensitivity of the stock's return to the return of the market. If a stock has a high $\beta$, then when the market goes up, the stock goes up even more (and of course, the opposite: When the market goes down, the stock goes down even more). The price movements of a low $\beta$ stock exhibit less sensitivity to variations in the market.

3. The expected return of the market, $E(r_M)$.

The SML states that the expected return of any asset is determined by the equation

$$SML: \text{ Expected return of any asset} = E\left(r_{Asset}\right) = r_f + \beta_{Asset} * \left[E\left(r_M\right) - r_f\right]$$

Here are two examples of the use of the SML. Suppose that the risk-free rate $r_f = 3\%$ and that the market expected return is $E(r_M) = 8\%$. What's are the expected returns of AMD and Kellogg (stock symbol K) stock? A look at Yahoo! (see Figure 11.1) shows that AMD's $\beta$ is $\beta_{AMD} = 1.81$ and that Kellogg's $\beta$ is $\beta_K = 0.44$. Applying the SML shows that the market expects Microsoft's return to be 9.40% and Merck's return to be 5.08%:

$$AMD's \text{ expected return, } E\left(r_{AMD}\right) = r_f + \beta_{AMD} * \left[E\left(r_M\right) - r_f\right]$$
$$= 3\% + 1.81 * \left[8\% - 3\%\right] = 12.05\%$$
$$Kellogg's \text{ expected return, } E\left(r_K\right) = r_f + \beta_K * \left[E\left(r_M\right) - r_f\right]$$
$$= 3\% + 0.44 * \left[8\% - 3\%\right] = 5.20\%$$

| | A | B | C |
|---|---|---|---|
| 1 | COMPUTING THE RETURNS ON KELLOGG (K) AND AMD | | |
| 2 | Risk-free rate, $r_f$ | 3% | |
| 3 | Expected market return, $E(r_M)$ | 8% | |
| 4 | | | |
| 5 | AMD beta, $\beta_{AMD}$ | 1.81 | |
| 6 | AMD expected return, $E(r_{AMD})$ | 12.05% | <-- =$B$2+B5*($B$3-$B$2) |
| 7 | | | |
| 8 | Kellogg beta, $\beta_K$ | 0.44 | |
| 9 | Kellogg expected return, $E(r_K)$ | 5.20% | <-- =$B$2+B8*($B$3-$B$2) |

You might ask yourself whether AMD's higher expected return means that AMD is a better investment than Kellogg. The answer is no—AMD has a higher expected return because it is riskier than Kellogg; the higher expected return reflects this higher risk.

## Where Do We Go from Here?

This section has summarized the main results from this chapter. In the two succeeding chapters we discuss the uses of these results for evaluating investments (Chapter 12) and for measuring the cost of capital (Chapter 13). In the remainder of this chapter, we derive the CML and the SML. The discussion is (unavoidably) somewhat technical, and you may decide to skip ahead to Chapters 12 and 13.

FIGURE 11.1  Screen clips from Yahoo! showing $\beta$ for AMD and Kellogg. The results can be obtained by going to http://finance.yahoo.com, choosing the stock, and then going to **Key Statistics**.

## 11.2. Risky Portfolios and the Riskless Asset

Now that we've reviewed the main results of the chapter, here's the nitty-gritty. We start by considering a portfolio problem of the kind dealt with in Chapter 10. We will assume that there are two risky assets, Stock A and Stock B, and also a *risk-free asset*—an asset that gives an annual interest payment with *certainty*. You can think of this asset as being a savings account in a bank a government bond or a money-market fund. In the examples of this section, we'll suppose that the risk-free asset gives a 2% annual return, and we will denote the return on the risk-free asset by $r_f$. The first few lines of the following spreadsheet give you all the details.

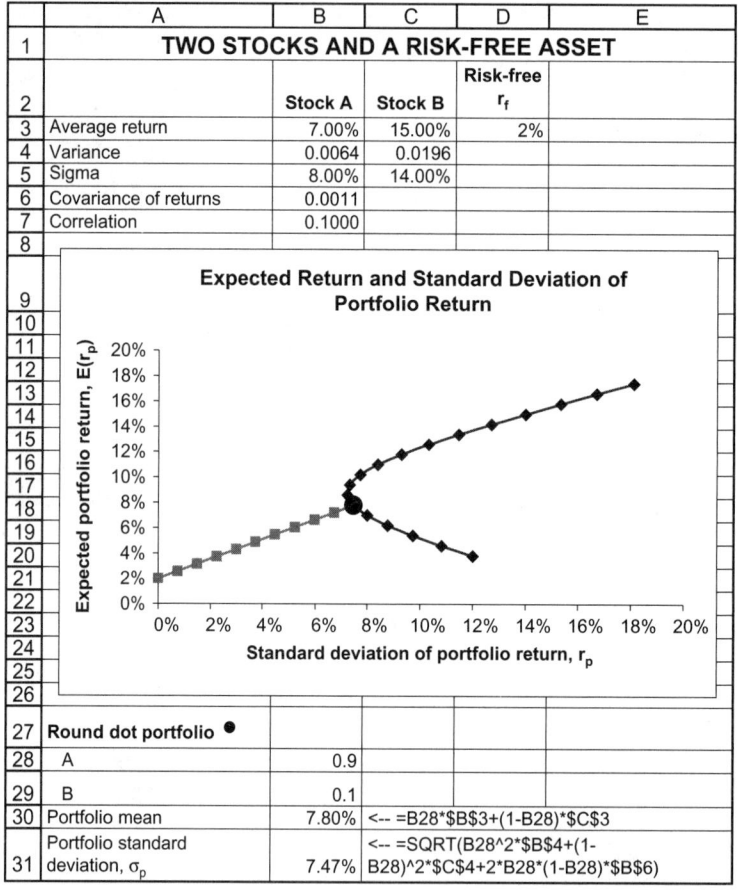

| | A | B | C | D | E |
|---|---|---|---|---|---|
| 1 | \multicolumn{5}{c}{**TWO STOCKS AND A RISK-FREE ASSET**} | | | | |
| 2 | | **Stock A** | **Stock B** | **Risk-free** $r_f$ | |
| 3 | Average return | 7.00% | 15.00% | 2% | |
| 4 | Variance | 0.0064 | 0.0196 | | |
| 5 | Sigma | 8.00% | 14.00% | | |
| 6 | Covariance of returns | 0.0011 | | | |
| 7 | Correlation | 0.1000 | | | |
| 8 | | | | | |
| 27 | **Round dot portfolio** ● | | | | |
| 28 | A | 0.9 | | | |
| 29 | B | 0.1 | | | |
| 30 | Portfolio mean | 7.80% | <-- =B28*$B$3+(1-B28)*$C$3 | | |
| 31 | Portfolio standard deviation, $\sigma_p$ | 7.47% | <-- =SQRT(B28^2*$B$4+(1-B28)^2*$C$4+2*B28*(1-B28)*$B$6) | | |

The curved line shows the portfolio mean $E(r_P)$ and standard deviation ("sigma-p") $\sigma_p$ of combinations of Stock A and Stock B.[4] The straight line shows the mean and standard deviation of portfolio combinations of the risk-free asset (which returns $r_f = 2\%$) and a specific portfolio of risky assets, denoted by round dot ● ).

---

[4]This was illustrated in Chapters 8 and 10.

Rows 28–31 give information about the round dot portfolio •. It is composed of 90% Stock A and 10% Stock B, and it has expected return $E(r_p) = 7.8\%$ and standard deviation of return $\sigma_p = 7.47\%$.

## Computing a Point on the Straight Line

In the spreadsheet below we indicate two points on the straight line that connects the risk-free rate $r_f$ and the round dot portfolio •. Each point represents an investment portfolio that is partly invested in the risk-free asset and partly in the portfolio •. Take a look, and then after the spreadsheet we'll show you how to calculate the mean and standard deviation of the points on the line.

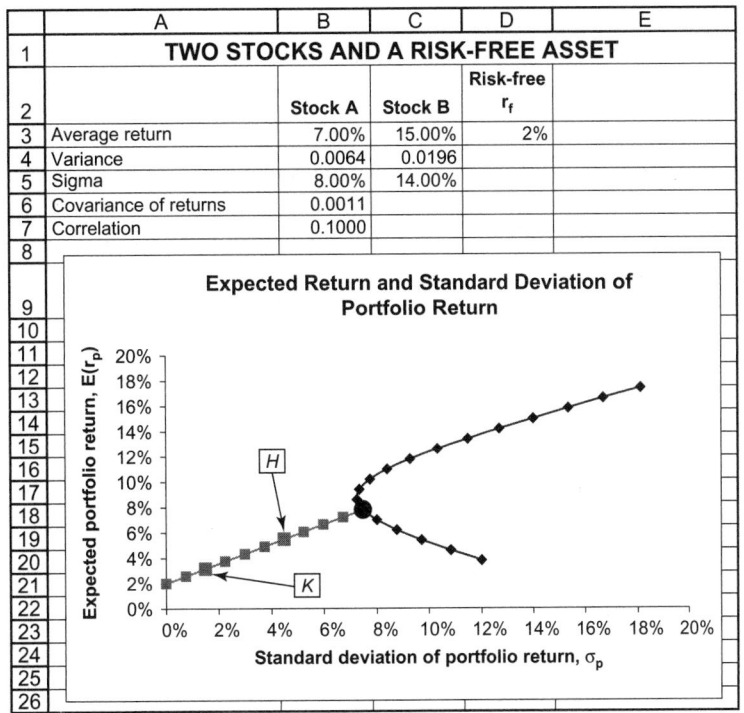

| | A | B | C | D | E |
|---|---|---|---|---|---|
| 1 | TWO STOCKS AND A RISK-FREE ASSET | | | | |
| 2 | | Stock A | Stock B | Risk-free $r_f$ | |
| 3 | Average return | 7.00% | 15.00% | 2% | |
| 4 | Variance | 0.0064 | 0.0196 | | |
| 5 | Sigma | 8.00% | 14.00% | | |
| 6 | Covariance of returns | 0.0011 | | | |
| 7 | Correlation | 0.1000 | | | |
| 8 | | | | | |

Expected Return and Standard Deviation of Portfolio Return

The "round-dot portfolio" • is composed of an investment 90% in A and 10% in B. What about portfolio H? H is a portfolio invested 60% in the "round-dot portfolio" and 40% in the risk-free asset. To compute the returns of this portfolio, we use the following equations:

$$E(r_H) = \underbrace{x}_{\substack{\text{Percent in} \\ \text{"round-dot"} \\ \text{portfolio}}} E(r_{round-dot}) + \underbrace{(1-x)}_{\substack{\text{Percent in} \\ \text{risk-free asset}}} * r_f = 60\% * 7.8\% + 40\% * 2\% = 5.48\%$$

$$\sigma_H = \underbrace{x}_{\substack{\text{Percent in} \\ \text{"round-dot"} \\ \text{portfolio}}} \sigma_{round-dot} = 60\% * 7.47\% = 4.48\%$$

In a similar fashion portfolio $K$—invested 20% in the round-dot portfolio and 80% in the risk-free asset—has statistics

$$E(r_K) = \underset{\substack{\uparrow \\ \text{Percent in} \\ \text{"round-dot"} \\ \text{portfolio}}}{x}\; E(r_{round-dot}) + \underset{\substack{\uparrow \\ \text{Percent in} \\ \text{risk-free asset}}}{(1-x)}\; * r_f = 20\% * 7.8\% + 80\% * 2\% = 3.16\%$$

$$\sigma_K = \underset{\substack{\uparrow \\ \text{Percent in} \\ \text{"round-dot"} \\ \text{portfolio}}}{x}\; \sigma_{round-dot} = 20\% * 7.47\% = 1.49\%$$

## A STATISTICAL NOTE

The equations used in the last calculation follow from our lessons in portfolio statistics in Chapter 9. Suppose the investor invests a percentage of her wealth $x$ in a portfolio $A$ of risky assets that has expected return $E(r_A)$ and standard deviation of return $\sigma_A$. Suppose she invests the rest of her wealth $1 - x$ in a risk-free asset that has expected return $r_f$ and standard deviation of return $0$. By the formula given in Chapter 10, the portfolio's expected return is its weighted-average return:

$$E(r_p) = xE(r_A) + (1-x)r_f \;.$$

The portfolio's return variance is

$$Var(r_p) = x^2 Var(r_A) + (1-x)^2 \underset{\substack{\uparrow \\ = 0, \text{ since} \\ \text{the risk-free} \\ \text{asset is risk-free} \\ \text{(duh!)}}}{Var(r_f)} + 2 * x * (1-x) * \underset{\substack{\uparrow \\ = 0, \text{ since} \\ \text{the risk-free} \\ \text{asset is} \\ \text{risk-free} \\ \text{(duh!)}}}{Cov(A, r_f)} \;.$$

$$= x^2 Var(r_A) = x^2 \sigma_A^2$$

This means that the standard deviation of the portfolio's return is $\sigma_p = \sqrt{Var(r_p)} = x\sigma_A$.

## Improving the Risk–Return Relation

We can choose portfolios that have a better risk–return relation than those on the line connecting $r_f$ and the round-dot portfolio ● by choosing another portfolio on the efficient frontier. The line connecting the risk-free asset and the "big square" portfolio below is an improvement on the line of the previous section.

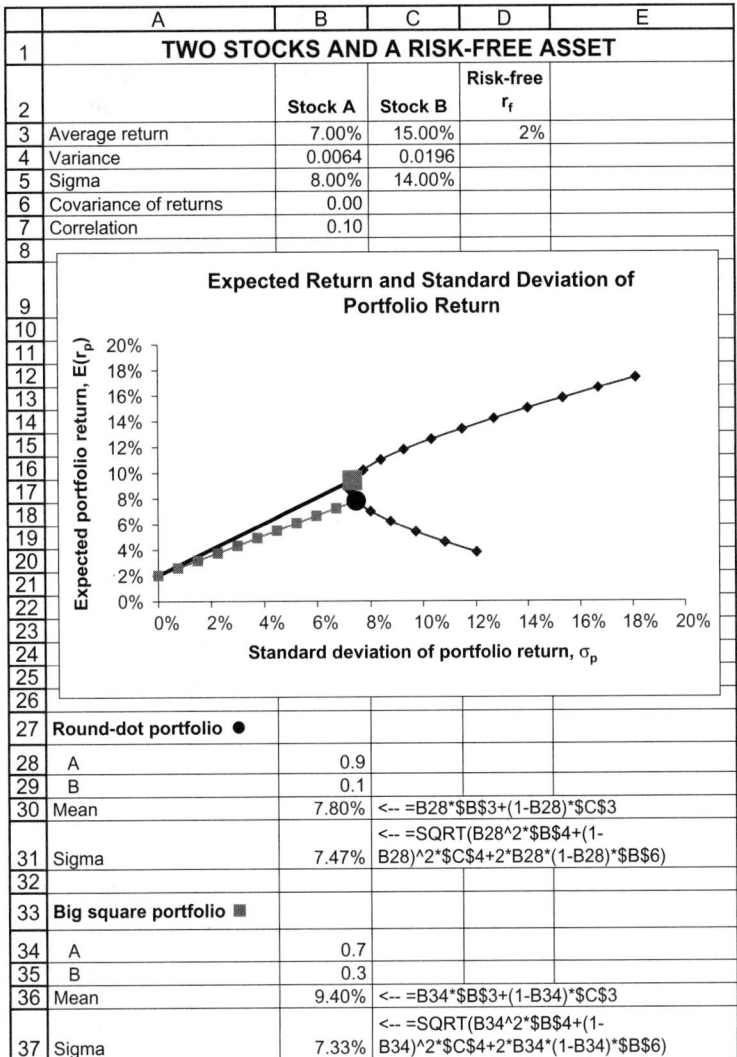

| | A | B | C | D | E |
|---|---|---|---|---|---|
| 1 | **TWO STOCKS AND A RISK-FREE ASSET** | | | | |
| 2 | | **Stock A** | **Stock B** | **Risk-free** $r_f$ | |
| 3 | Average return | 7.00% | 15.00% | 2% | |
| 4 | Variance | 0.0064 | 0.0196 | | |
| 5 | Sigma | 8.00% | 14.00% | | |
| 6 | Covariance of returns | 0.00 | | | |
| 7 | Correlation | 0.10 | | | |
| 8 | | | | | |
| 9 | | | | | |
| 10 | | | | | |
| 11 | | | | | |
| 12 | | | | | |
| 13 | | | | | |
| 14 | | | | | |
| 15 | | | | | |
| 16 | | | | | |
| 17 | | | | | |
| 18 | | | | | |
| 19 | | | | | |
| 20 | | | | | |
| 21 | | | | | |
| 22 | | | | | |
| 23 | | | | | |
| 24 | | | | | |
| 25 | | | | | |
| 26 | | | | | |
| 27 | **Round-dot portfolio ●** | | | | |
| 28 | A | 0.9 | | | |
| 29 | B | 0.1 | | | |
| 30 | Mean | 7.80% | <-- =B28*$B$3+(1-B28)*$C$3 | | |
| 31 | Sigma | 7.47% | <-- =SQRT(B28^2*$B$4+(1-B28)^2*$C$4+2*B28*(1-B28)*$B$6) | | |
| 32 | | | | | |
| 33 | **Big square portfolio ■** | | | | |
| 34 | A | 0.7 | | | |
| 35 | B | 0.3 | | | |
| 36 | Mean | 9.40% | <-- =B34*$B$3+(1-B34)*$C$3 | | |
| 37 | Sigma | 7.33% | <-- =SQRT(B34^2*$B$4+(1-B34)^2*$C$4+2*B34*(1-B34)*$B$6) | | |

Because the new line is higher than the old line, all the points on the line to the big square ■ are better than the points on the line to the black circle ●. For any point on the round-dot line there's always a point on the big square line that gives a higher return but has the same portfolio standard deviation $\sigma_p$.

There must be a *best* line that starts off from the point 2% on the y-axis. This best line, shown next, connects the risk-free rate $r_f = 2\%$ to a point ■ on the efficient frontier.

|  | A | B | C | D | E |
|---|---|---|---|---|---|
| 1 | TWO STOCKS AND A RISK-FREE ASSET<br>The best big square portfolio ■ | | | | |
| 2 |  | Stock A | Stock B | Risk-free $r_f$ | |
| 3 | Average return | 7.00% | 15.00% | 2% | |
| 4 | Variance | 0.0064 | 0.0196 | | |
| 5 | Sigma | 8.00% | 14.00% | | |
| 6 | Covariance of returns | 0.0011 | | | |
| 7 | Correlation | 0.1000 | | | |
| 8 | | | | | |

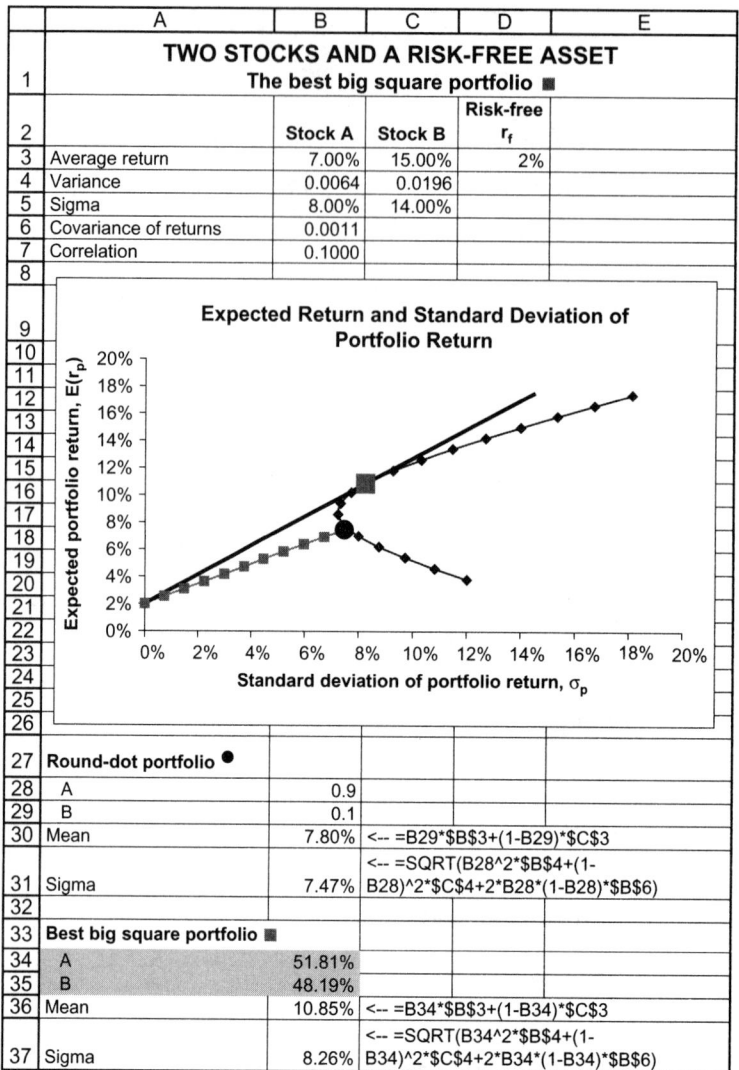

| | | | |
|---|---|---|---|
| 27 | Round-dot portfolio ● | | |
| 28 | A | 0.9 | |
| 29 | B | 0.1 | |
| 30 | Mean | 7.80% | <-- =B29*$B$3+(1-B29)*$C$3 |
| 31 | Sigma | 7.47% | <-- =SQRT(B28^2*$B$4+(1-B28)^2*$C$4+2*B28*(1-B28)*$B$6) |
| 32 | | | |
| 33 | Best big square portfolio ■ | | |
| 34 | A | 51.81% | |
| 35 | B | 48.19% | |
| 36 | Mean | 10.85% | <-- =B34*$B$3+(1-B34)*$C$3 |
| 37 | Sigma | 8.26% | <-- =SQRT(B34^2*$B$4+(1-B34)^2*$C$4+2*B34*(1-B34)*$B$6) |

The line as drawn has several properties:

- It starts from the risk-free rate (2%) on the *y*-axis.
- It goes to (and through) a stock portfolio ■ on the efficient frontier market by the big square. As you can see in cells B35:B38, this portfolio is composed 51.81% of Stock *A* and 48.19% of Stock *B*. It has an expected return of 10.85% and standard deviation of 8.26%. In Section 11.4 we'll describe how we computed this portfolio.

- It is tangent to the efficient frontier—meaning the line touches the efficient frontier only at the big square portfolio and nowhere else. This means that with the exception of the big square portfolio ■, every portfolio on the efficient frontier is below the line.

- Finally (and this is the most important point), because the big square line is above the efficient frontier (except for the one point ■ at which it touches the frontier), all the best investment portfolios are on the line. This point is so important that we explore it in a separate subsection.

The big square portfolio ■ is called the *market portfolio*. The market portfolio is the portfolio of risky assets that allow investors to achieve maximal returns. The equation of the capital market line is

$$E(r_p) = r_f + \sigma_p \left[ \frac{E(r_M) - r_f}{\sigma_M} \right]$$

### The Capital Market Line

To emphasize the optimality, take another look at the "best big square line." Note that the line is above the efficient frontier *everywhere* (except at point of tangency, which we now call the *market portfolio M*). We call this line the capital market line (CML).

The CML is the set of optimal investment portfolios. Each point on the line is:

- A combination of some percentage invested in the risk-free asset
- Another percentage invested in the market portfolio M

In Section 11.4 we show how to compute the market portfolio *M*. In the next section we explore the practical meaning of the CML.

## 11.3. Points on the CML—Exploring Optimal Investment Combinations

What do portfolios on the CML—the line connecting the risk-free rate $r_f$ and the market portfolio *M*—look like? What does the CML mean for an investor? To get a feel for this, we explore several portfolios on the CML.

### Portfolio 1: Investing in the Market Portfolio *M* and in the Risk-Free Asset

Suppose you have $1,000 to invest. You can choose any combination of three assets—the risk-free asset, Stock *A*, or Stock *B*. In Portfolio 1, you choose to invest $500 in the risk-free asset and $500 in the market portfolio *M*—the portfolio composed of 51.81% Stock *A* and 48.19% Stock *B*.

| | A | B | C |
|---|---|---|---|
| 1 | **PORTFOLIO ON THE CAPITAL MARKET LINE (CML)** | | |
| 2 | The market portfolio, *M* | Percent | |
| 3 | Stock A | 51.81% | |
| 4 | Stock B | 48.19% | |
| 5 | Expected return of market portfolio M | 10.85% | |
| 6 | Standard deviation of market portfolio M | 8.26% | |
| 7 | | | |
| 8 | Investor portfolio | | |
| 9 | Invested in risk-free | 50% | |
| 10 | Invested in market portfolio M | 50% | |
| 11 | | | |
| 12 | Portfolio return statistics–point on the CML | | |
| 13 | Expected portfolio return | 6.43% | <-- =B9*I19+B10*B5 |
| 14 | Portfolio standard deviation | 4.13% | <-- =B10*B6 |

This looks a little complicated, but it's really a version of the portfolio calculations we did in Chapter 10. The investment is divided 50% into the risk-free asset and another 50% into portfolio *M*, which has an expected return of 10.85% (cell B5) and standard deviation of 8.26% (cell B6). According to the formula given in Section 11.2, the expected return and the standard deviation of returns are calculated by

$$E(r_p) = xE(r_M) + (1-x)r_f$$
$$\sigma_p = x\sigma_M$$

As you can see in cells B13:B14, this gives $E(r_p) = 6.43\%, \sigma_p = 4.13\%$. This portfolio is indicated in the graph below. Note that the portfolio conforms to the CML equation given at the end of the previous section:

$$E(r_p) = r_f + \sigma_p \left[ \frac{E(r_M) - r_f}{\sigma_M} \right]$$
$$= 2\% + 4.13\% * \left[ \frac{10.85\% - 2\%}{8.26\%} \right] = 6.43\%$$

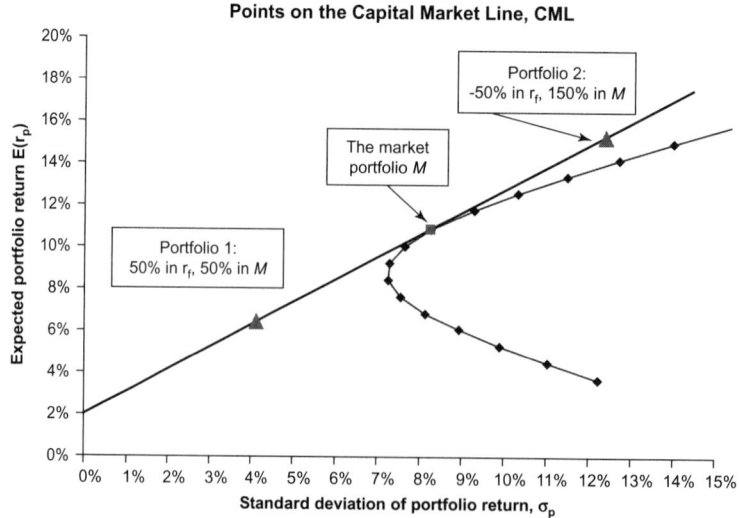

## Portfolio 2: Borrowing at the Risk-Free Rate $r_f$ to Buy More of the Market Portfolio M

In Portfolio 1 you split your investment of $1,000 between the risk-free asset and the market portfolio M. In Portfolio 2 we'll investigate an investment strategy in which you borrow money at the risk-free rate and invest *more than $1,000* in the risky portfolio M. You do this by using borrowed funds to increase your investment in M.

As before, you have $1,000 to invest, and as before you choose to invest some of your money in the risk-free asset and the rest in the market portfolio M, composed of 51.81% Stock A and 48.19% Stock B. However, in Portfolio 2 you choose to *borrow* $500 at the risk-free rate and invest $1500 in the portfolio of Stock A and Stock B. As you can see in cells B13:B14 below, this is a riskier portfolio (it has a standard deviation of 12.40%), but it also has a higher expected return (15.28%).

| | A | B | C |
|---|---|---|---|
| 1 | **PORTFOLIO ON THE CAPITAL MARKET LINE (CML)** | | |
| 2 | The market portfolio, M | **Percent** | |
| 3 | Stock A | 51.81% | |
| 4 | Stock B | 48.19% | |
| 5 | Expected return of market portfolio M | 10.85% | |
| 6 | Standard deviation of market portfolio M | 8.26% | |
| 7 | | | |
| 8 | Investor portfolio | | |
| 9 | Invested in risk-free | -50% | |
| 10 | Invested in market portfolio M | 150% | |
| 11 | | | |
| 12 | Portfolio return statistics–point on the CML | | |
| 13 | Expected portfolio return | 15.28% | <-- =B9*I19+B10*B5 |
| 14 | Portfolio standard deviation | 12.40% | <-- =B10*B6 |

Note that the portfolio conforms to the CML equation given at the end of the previous section:

$$E(r_p) = r_f + \sigma_p \left[ \frac{E(r_M) - r_f}{\sigma_M} \right]$$

$$= 2\% + 12.40\% * \left[ \frac{10.85\% - 2\%}{8.26\%} \right] = 15.28\%$$

## Comparing Portfolio 1 with Portfolio 2

Which portfolio is better—Portfolio 1 or Portfolio 2? Comparing their returns with their standard deviations shows that neither portfolio is better. Portfolio 2 has a much higher expected return than Portfolio 1, but it also has higher risk. The choice between the portfolios depends on how much risk the investor is willing to take.

| | Expected return $E(r_p)$ | Return standard deviation $\sigma_p$ |
|---|---|---|
| **Portfolio 1** | 6.43% | 4.13% |
| **Portfolio 2** | 15.28% | 12.40% |

All the portfolios on the CML incorporate this choice: Each CML portfolio is a combination of an investment in the risk-free asset $r_f$ and the market portfolio $M$. Any portfolio on the CML is optimal in the sense that it could possibly be a rational investor's choice of his best investment portfolio. Figure 11.2 shows some other points on the CML and their return–risk trade-off.

**Portfolio Proportions and Investment Returns on the Capital Market Line (CML)**

| | | |
|---|---|---|
| Percentage invested in market portfolio $M$ | $E(r_p) = \%\ in\ risk\text{-}free * r_f$ <br> $+\%\ in\ market * E(r_M)$ | $\sigma_p = \%\ in\ market * \sigma_M$ |
| 0% (invest all your wealth in risk-free asset $r_f$) | $E(r_p) = 100\% * r_f = 2\%$ | $\sigma_p = 0\% * \sigma_M = 0$ |
| 50% (invest 50% of your wealth in market portfolio $M$ and 50% in risk-free asset) | $E(r_p) = 50\% * r_f + 50\% * E(r_M)$ <br> $= 50\% * 2\% + 50\% * 10.85\%$ <br> $= 6.43\%$ | $\sigma_p = 50\% * \sigma_M$ <br> $= 50\% * 8.26\% = 4.13\%$ |
| 100% (invest all your wealth in market portfolio $M$) | $E(r_p) = 0\% * r_f + 100\% * E(r_M)$ <br> $= 100\% * 10.85\%$ <br> $= 10.85\%$ | $\sigma_p = 100\% * \sigma_M$ <br> $= 100\% * 8.26\% = 8.26\%$ |
| 125% (borrow 25% of your wealth to increase investment in risky assets $M$) | $E(r_p) = -25\% * r_f + 125\% * E(r_M)$ <br> $= -25\% * 2\% + 125\% * 10.85\%$ <br> $= -0.5\% + 13.57\% = 13.06\%$ | $\sigma_p = 125\% * \sigma_M$ <br> $= 125\% * 8.26\% = 10.33\%$ |
| 150% (borrow 50% of your wealth to increase investment in risky assets $M$) | $E(r_p) = -50\% * r_f + 150\% * E(r_M)$ <br> $= -50\% * 1\% + 150\% * 10.85\%$ <br> $= -1\% + 16.28\% = 15.28\%$ | $\sigma_p = 150\% * \sigma_M$ <br> $= 150\% * 8.26\% = 12.39\%$ |
| 200% (borrow 100% of your wealth to increase investment in risky assets $M$) | $E(r_p) = -100\% * r_f + 200\% * E(r_M)$ <br> $= -100\% * 2\% + 200\% * 10.85\%$ <br> $= -2\% + 21.70\% = 19.70\%$ | $\sigma_p = 200\% * \sigma_M$ <br> $= 200\% * 8.26\% = 16.52\%$ |

FIGURE 11.2 Points on the CML. Each point represents a different combination of an investment in the risk-free asset and the market portfolio $M$. As the proportion in the risk-free asset decreases, the proportion invested in the market portfolio $M$ increases. Increasing the proportion invested in $M$ increases the portfolio's expected return $E(r_p)$ but also increases the portfolio's risk $\sigma_p$. The calculations assume that $E(r_M) = 10.85\%$, $r_f = 2\%$, and $\sigma_M = 8.26\%$.

## The CML: Summing Up

The CML indicates that all optimal investment portfolios should be split between a percentage investment in the risk-free asset and a percentage investment in the market portfolio $M$. Suppose we denote these percentages by $x_M$ and $x_{r_f} = 1 - x_M$. Then the investor's portfolio will have:

- Expected return $E(r_p) = x_M E(r_M) + (1 - x_M) r_f$
- Standard deviation of return $\sigma_p = x_M \sigma_M$

Portfolios on the CML are optimal in the sense that investors cannot find investment combinations that have a higher portfolio return $E(r_p)$ given the portfolio risk $\sigma_p$.

## 11.4. Advanced Section: The Sharpe Ratio and the Market Portfolio *M*

In this section we'll show how to compute the market portfolio *M*. In the process we'll introduce a concept called the *Sharpe ratio*—this is one of the standard *return–risk* measures used in capital markets. As you'll see, portfolio *M* is the portfolio that maximizes the Sharpe ratio.

To get some intuition, look at the spreadsheet below. It continues our example of Stocks *A* and *B* and the risk-free rate of 2%. In cells B9:B10 we're looking at a portfolio invested 30% in Stock *A* and 70% in Stock *B*. The expected return of this portfolio is 12.60% and its standard deviation is 10.32% (cells B12:B13).

|  | A | B | C | D | E |
|---|---|---|---|---|---|
| 1 | PORTFOLIO RETURNS WITH A RISK-FREE ASSET | | | | |
|  | THE SHARPE RATIO | | | | |
| 2 |  | **Stock A** | **Stock B** | **Risk-free**<br>$r_f$ |  |
| 3 | Average return | 7.00% | 15.00% | 2.00% |  |
| 4 | Variance of return | 0.64% | 1.96% |  |  |
| 5 | Sigma of return | 8.00% | 14.00% |  |  |
| 6 | Covariance of returns | 0.0011 |  |  |  |
| 7 |  |  |  |  |  |
| 8 | **Portfolio return and risk** |  |  |  |  |
| 9 | Percentage in stock A | 30.00% |  |  |  |
| 10 | Percentage in stock B | 70.00% |  |  |  |
| 11 |  |  |  |  |  |
| 12 | Expected portfolio return | 12.60% | <-- =B9*B3+B10*C3 | | |
| 13 | Portfolio standard deviation | 10.32% | <-- =SQRT(B9^2*B4+B10^2*C4+2*B9*B10*B6) | | |
| 14 |  |  |  |  |  |
| 15 | Risk premium | 10.60% | <-- =B12-D3 | | |
| 16 |  |  |  |  |  |
| 17 | Sharpe ratio | 1.0271 | <-- =(B12-D3)/B13 | | |
| 18 |  |  |  |  |  |
| 19 | The Sharpe ratio is $[E(r_p) - r_f]/\sigma_p$. It denotes the ratio of portfolio **risk premium** to portfolio **risk**. | | | | |

The portfolio's *risk premium* (sometimes called the portfolio *excess return*) is defined as the difference between its expected return and the return of the risk-free asset:

$$portfolio\ risk\ premium = portfolio\ expected\ return - risk\text{-}free\ rate$$
$$= E(r_p) - r_f$$
$$= 12.60\% - 2.00\% = 10.60\%$$

The ratio of this risk premium to the portfolio's standard deviation is called the *Sharpe ratio*:

$$Sharpe\ ratio = \frac{E(r_p) - r_f}{\sigma_p} = \frac{12.60\% - 2.00\%}{10.32\%} = 1.0271 .$$

The Sharpe ratio (named after William Sharpe, one of the developers of modern portfolio theory and winner of the Nobel prize in economics in 1990) is a "return–risk" ratio: The numerator is the extra return (over the risk-free rate) you get from your portfolio, and the denominator is the cost of this extra return—its standard deviation.

If you play a bit with the spreadsheet, you'll see that there are other portfolios with higher Sharpe ratios. Here's an example.

| | A | B | C | D | E |
|---|---|---|---|---|---|
| 8 | **Portfolio return and risk** | | | | |
| 9 | Percentage in stock A | 40.00% | | | |
| 10 | Percentage in stock B | 60.00% | | | |
| 11 | | | | | |
| 12 | Expected portfolio return | 11.80% | <-- =B9*B3+B10*C3 | | |
| 13 | Portfolio standard deviation | 9.28% | <-- =SQRT(B9^2*B4+B10^2*C4+2*B9*B10*B6) | | |
| 14 | | | | | |
| 15 | Risk premium | 9.80% | <-- =B12-D3 | | |
| 16 | | | | | |
| 17 | Sharpe ratio | 1.0557 | <-- =(B12-D3)/B13 | | |

## Calculating the Market Portfolio M—The Portfolio with the *Highest Attainable* Sharpe Ratio

We can use Excel's Solver (see Chapter 28) to calculate the portfolio that gives the highest Sharpe ratio. This portfolio is the *market portfolio M*.

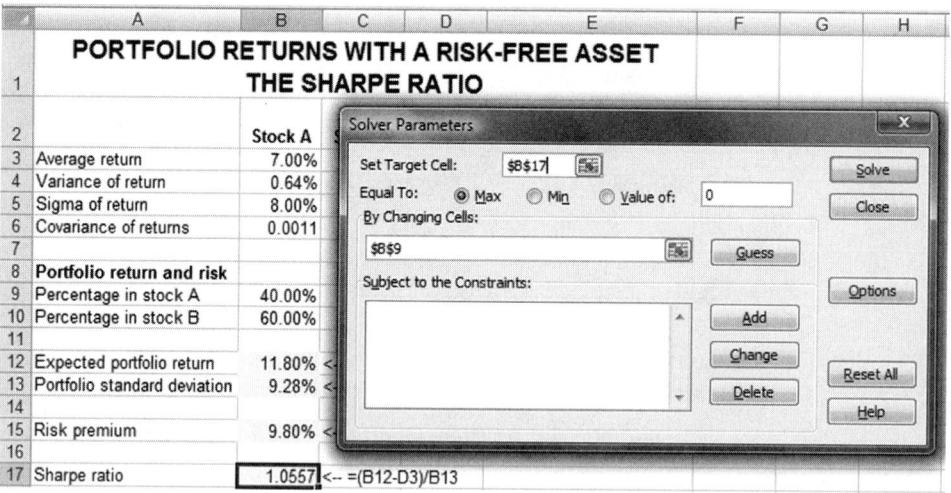

Clicking **Solve** yields the answer.

|  | A | B | C | D | E |
|---|---|---|---|---|---|
| 1 | PORTFOLIO RETURNS WITH A RISK-FREE ASSET THE SHARPE RATIO | | | | |
| 2 |  | Stock A | Stock B | Risk-free $r_f$ |  |
| 3 | Average return | 7.00% | 15.00% | 2.00% |  |
| 4 | Variance of return | 0.64% | 1.96% |  |  |
| 5 | Sigma of return | 8.00% | 14.00% |  |  |
| 6 | Covariance of returns | 0.0011 |  |  |  |
| 7 |  |  |  |  |  |
| 8 | **Portfolio return and risk** |  |  |  |  |
| 9 | Percentage in stock A | 51.81% |  |  |  |
| 10 | Percentage in stock B | 48.19% |  |  |  |
| 11 |  |  |  |  |  |
| 12 | Expected portfolio return | 10.85% | <-- =B9*B3+B10*C3 |  |  |
| 13 | Portfolio standard deviation | 8.26% | <-- =SQRT(B9^2*B4+B10^2*C4+2*B9*B10*B6) |  |  |
| 14 |  |  |  |  |  |
| 15 | Risk premium | 8.85% | <-- =B12-D3 |  |  |
| 16 |  |  |  |  |  |
| 17 | Sharpe ratio | 1.0716 | <-- =(B12-D3)/B13 |  |  |

From now on, we'll denote the portfolio with the maximum Sharpe ratio by *M*:

> Given a risk-free asset and a set of risky assets (in the current example there are only two such assets), the market portfolio M is the portfolio that maximizes the Sharpe ratio: $\dfrac{E(r_M)-r_f}{\sigma_M}$.
> Portfolio M is the best combination of risky assets available to the investor.

# 11.5. The Security Market Line (SML)

The capital market line (CML) shows investors the return–risk relation for their optimal portfolios. The risk–return relation for individual assets is described by a line called the security market line (SML). The SML states that the expected return of an asset or portfolio is determined by the asset's systematic risk (called β), the risk-free rate, and the portfolio that maximizes the Sharpe ratio.

## Summing Up the SML First (Then We'll Explain)

The SML says that *the expected return of any asset i is related to the risk-free rate and the market risk premium through the following relation*:

$$E(r_i) = r_f \; + \; \frac{Cov(r_i,r_M)}{Var(r_M)} \; * \; \left[E(r_M)-r_f\right]$$

$\uparrow$ Risk-free rate  $\qquad$ $\uparrow$ $\beta_i$  $\qquad$ $\uparrow$ $E(r_M)$ is the return on the portfolio that maximizes the Sharpe ratio

Note that in the above equation "asset $i$" (represented by the letter "$i$") can be a lot of things:

- Asset $i$ can be just *one* risky asset. $E(r_i)$ can stand for the return of Stock $A$ or the return of Stock $B$.
- Asset $i$ can be the combination of two risky assets. $E(r_i)$ can stand for the return of a portfolio such as 60% in Stock $A$ and 40% in Stock $B$.
- Asset $i$ can be a combination of the risk-free asset and the two stocks, for example, 25% in the risk-free, 30% in Stock $A$, and 45% in Stock $B$ is a portfolio.

In short, the SML defines the risk–return relation *for all assets in the market*. The SML is an important tool in investment management, and in the next two chapters we examine the uses of the SML for evaluating the performance of portfolio managers (Chapter 12) and for computing the cost of capital for a firm (Chapter 13). In this section we illustrate why the SML holds.

To illustrate the SML, we use a few examples.

## Example 1: The SML Works When Asset i Is Only Stock A

Lines 3–16 of the spreadsheet below repeat facts we've already given. In row 24 we compute the covariance between asset $i$ (in this case Stock $A$) and the market portfolio $M$. We use a general fact about covariance: Suppose that $i$ is composed of a percentage $x_{iA}$ of Stock $A$ and a percentage $x_{iB} = 1 - x_{iA}$ of Stock $B$, and suppose that the market portfolio is composed of a percentage $x_{MA}$ of Stock $A$ and a percentage $x_{MB} = 1 - x_{MA}$ of Stock $B$. Then the covariance between $r_i$ and $r_M$ is

$$Cov(r_i, r_M) = Cov(x_{iA}r_A + x_{iB}r_B, x_{MA}r_A + x_{MB}r_B)$$
$$= x_{iA}x_{MA}Var(r_A) + x_{iB}x_{MB}Var(r_B) + (x_{iA}x_{MB} + x_{iB}x_{MA}) * Cov(r_A, r_B)$$

Now suppose that $x = 1$, so that $i$ refers to Stock $A$.

- Cell B22 indicates that $E(r_i) = 7.00\%$. This is the left-hand side of the SML.
- Cell B24 shows that $Cov(r_i, r_M) = 0.0039$.
- In cell B25 we divide $Cov(r_i, r_M)$ by $Var(r_M)$ to get the $\beta_i = \dfrac{Cov(r_i, r_M)}{Var(r_M)} = 0.5647$.

- Cell B26 shows that $r_f + \beta_i * [E(r_M) - r_f] = 2\% + 0.5647 * [10.85\% - 2\%] = 7.00\%$.

The equality between cells B22 and B26 shows that the SML works for the case where $i$ is only Stock $A$.

Although computed in different ways, cells B22 and B26 give the same result. This is the SML:

$$E(r_A) = r_f + \underset{\underset{\dfrac{Cov(r_A, r_M)}{Var(r_M)}}{\uparrow}}{\beta_A} \left[E(r_M) - r_f\right]$$

$$\underset{\substack{\uparrow \\ \text{SML,} \\ \text{left-hand} \\ \text{side} \\ \text{cell B22}}}{7\%} = \underset{\substack{\uparrow \\ \text{SML,} \\ \text{right-hand side} \\ \text{cell B26}}}{\underline{2\% + 0.5647 * [12\% - 2\%]}}$$

| | A | B | C | D | E |
|---|---|---|---|---|---|
| 1 | THE SECURITY MARKET LINE (SML) ILLUSTRATION | | | | |
| 2 | | Stock A | Stock B | Risk-free $r_f$ | |
| 3 | Average return | 7.00% | 15.00% | 2.00% | |
| 4 | Variance of return | 0.0064 | 0.0196 | | |
| 5 | Sigma of return | 8.00% | 14.00% | | |
| 6 | Covariance of returns | 0.0011 | | | |
| 7 | | | | | |
| 8 | Market portfolio M–this is the portfolio that maximizes the Sharpe ratio | | | | |
| 9 | Proportion of stock A, $x_{MA}$ | 51.81% | | | |
| 10 | Proportion of stock B, $x_{MB} = 1- x_{MA}$ | 48.19% | <-- =1-B9 | | |
| 11 | | | | | |
| 12 | Expected market portfolio return, $E(r_M)$ | 10.85% | <-- =B9*B3+B10*C3 | | |
| 13 | Market portfolio return variance, $\sigma^2_M=Var(r_M)$ | 0.0068 | <-- =B9^2*B4+B10^2*C4+2*B9*B10*B6 | | |
| 14 | Market portfolio standard deviation $\sigma_M$=standard deviation($r_M$) | 8.26% | <-- =SQRT(B13) | | |
| 15 | | | | | |
| 16 | Market excess return $E(r_M)-r_f$ | 8.85% | <-- =B12-D3 | | |
| 17 | | | | | |
| 18 | "Proof" of SML:  $E(r_i) = r_f + \beta_i *[E(r_M) - r_f]$ | | | | |
| 19 | Asset $i$ | | | | |
| 20 | Percentage in stock A, $x_{iA}$ | 100.00% | | | |
| 21 | Percentage in stock B, $x_{iB} = 1- x_{iA}$ | 0.00% | <-- =1-B20 | | |
| 22 | Expected portfolio return $E(r_i)=x_{iA}*E(r_A)+x_{iB}*E(r_B)$ SML, left-hand side | 7.00% | <-- =B20*B3+B21*C3 | | |
| 23 | | | | | |
| 24 | $Cov(r_i,r_M)$ | 0.0039 | <-- =B20*B9*B4+B21*B10*C4+(B20*B10+B21*B9)*B6 | | |
| 25 | Beta $\beta_i$ | 0.5647 | <-- =B24/B13 | | |
| 26 | $r_f+\beta_i*[E(r_M)-r_f]$ SML,right-hand side | 7.00% | <-- =D3+B25*B16 | | |

## Example 2: The SML Works for a Portfolio Composed Only of Stock B

We can repeat the calculations for the case where $i$ is Stock B. As you can see in cell B25 below, Stock B has $\beta_B = 1.4681$. The equality of cells B22 and B26 means that the SML also works for Stock B:

$$E(r_B)=r_f + \underset{\underset{Var(r_M)}{\underset{\uparrow}{Cov(r_A,r_M)}}}{\beta_B} \left[E(r_M)-r_f\right]$$

$$\underset{\substack{\uparrow \\ \text{SML,} \\ \text{left-hand} \\ \text{side} \\ \text{cell B22}}}{15\%} = \underset{\substack{\uparrow \\ \text{SML,} \\ \text{right-hand side} \\ \text{cell B26}}}{2\%+1.4681*\left[12\%-2\%\right]}$$

| | A | B | C | D | E |
|---|---|---|---|---|---|
| 18 | "Proof" of SML:  $E(r_i) = r_f + \beta_i *[E(r_M) - r_f]$ | | | | |
| 19 | Asset $i$ | | | | |
| 20 | Percentage in stock A, $x_{iA}$ | 0.00% | | | |
| 21 | Percentage in stock B, $x_{iB}$ | 100.00% | | | |
| 22 | Expected portfolio return $E(r_i)=x_{iA}*E(r_A)+x_{iB}*E(r_B)$ SML, left-hand side | 15.00% | <-- =B20*B3+B21*C3 | | |
| 23 | | | | | |
| 24 | $Cov(r_i,r_M)$ | 0.0100 | <-- =B20*B9*B4+B21*B10*C4+(B20*B10+B21*B9)*B6 | | |
| 25 | Beta $\beta_i$ | 1.4681 | <-- =B24/B13 | | |
| 26 | $r_f+\beta_i*[E(r_M)-r_f]$ SML,right-hand side | 15.00% | <-- =D3+B25*B16 | | |

## Example 3: The SML Works for Portfolios

In this section asset $i$ is a portfolio composed of 80% Stock $A$ and 20% Stock $B$. As in the previous examples, the equality between cells B22 and B26 means that the SML correctly describes the return–risk relation for the asset.

| | A | B | C | D | E |
|---|---|---|---|---|---|
| 18 | "Proof" of SML: $E(r_i) = r_f + \beta_i*[E(r_M) - r_f]$ | | | | |
| 19 | Asset $i$ | | | | |
| 20 | Percentage in stock A, $x_{iA}$ | 80.00% | | | |
| 21 | Percentage in stock B, $x_{iB}$ | 20.00% | | | |
| 22 | Expected portfolio return $E(r_i)=x_{iA}*E(r_A)+x_{iB}*E(r_B)$  SML, left-hand side | 8.60% | <-- =B20*B3+B21*C3 | | |
| 23 | | | | | |
| 24 | $Cov(r_i, r_M)$ | 0.0051 | <-- =B20*B9*B4+B21*B10*C4+(B20*B10+B21*B9)*B6 | | |
| 25 | Beta $\beta_i$ | 0.7453 | <-- =B24/B13 | | |
| 26 | $r_f+\beta_i*[E(r_M)-r_f]$  SML,right-hand side | 8.60% | <-- =D3+B25*B16 | | |

## βs Add Up

Another way to have done the previous calculation is to use the *portfolio* $\beta$:

The portfolio $\beta$ is the weighted average of the individual $\beta$s, $\beta_p = x_A\beta_A + x_B\beta_B$.

For example, suppose we want to know the expected return from a portfolio invested 80% in Stock $A$ and 20% in Stock $B$. This portfolio will have a $\beta_p$ of

$$\beta_p = x_A\beta_A + x_B\beta_B = 0.8*0.5647 + 0.2*1.4681 = 0.7453,$$

and consequently its expected return should be determined by the SML using the $\beta_p$.

# Summing Up

The capital asset pricing model (CAPM) is a model of portfolio formation and asset pricing. The model shows the following:

- How the expected return and standard deviation of portfolios are affected by the portfolio composition.

- How the addition of a risk-free asset to the choices available to investors changes their risk–return opportunity set.

- How to compute the *market portfolio* M. This is the portfolio that maximizes the Sharpe ratio: $\dfrac{E(r_p)-r_f}{\sigma_p}$.

- How to choose an *optimal portfolio* when you can invest in risky and risk-free assets. This is the capital market line (CML), which states that all optimal portfolios are combinations of the risk-free asset and the market portfolio.

- How to compute the beta ($\beta$) for a stock or portfolio. $\beta$ is a *risk-measure* for an asset. For a portfolio $p$, $\beta_p$ is defined as $\beta_p = \dfrac{Cov(r_p, r_M)}{Var(r_M)}$. (Recall that "portfolio" includes the case of individual assets.)

- How the *expected return of any portfolio* is related to the risk-free rate and the portfolio's β. This is the security market line (SML):

$$E(r_i) = r_f + \beta_i \left[ E(r_m) - r_f \right]$$

In succeeding chapters we explore the implications of this model, using it to examine the performance of portfolio managers and to calculate a firm's cost of capital.

## EXERCISES

**Note**: Data for some of the questions are on the disk that accompanies *Principles of Finance with Excel.*

1. Walking down the street of Spartanburg (your hometown), you encounter two street hustlers. John, the first hustler, is running a coin-toss game, which works like this: You pay John $0.80. He flips a coin. If the coin comes up heads, he pays you $3, and if the coin comes up tails, you pay him $1.

   a. What is your expected return from this game?

   b. What is the standard deviation of your return from playing this game?

2. Still in Spartanburg, you encounter a street hustler named Mary. Her game is more complicated: After you pay Mary $0.80, she throws a die. If the die comes up "1," you pay Mary $2. If it comes up "2," you pay nothing and win nothing. If it comes up "3, 4, 5, 6," Mary pays you $2.

### MARY'S DIE TOSS GAME

| Event | Probability | Winnings |
|-------|-------------|----------|
| 1 | 0.1667 | −2 |
| 2 | 0.1667 | 0 |
| 3 | 0.1667 | 2 |
| 4 | 0.1667 | 2 |
| 5 | 0.1667 | 2 |
| 6 | 0.1667 | 2 |

**picture downloaded from:**
**http://www.turbosquid.com**

   a. What are the expected returns from playing this game?

   b. What is the standard deviation of the returns?

   c. Which game is riskier—Mary's die throw or John's coin toss (previous exercise?).

   d. Which game would you prefer to play? Why?

3. What do Questions 1 and 2 have to do with investing in stocks?

4. Consider a stock with an expected return of 13% and standard deviation of return of 15% and a risk-free asset with a return of 1%. What will be the average return and standard deviation of a portfolio composed of 20% of the risk-free asset and 80% of the stock?

5. You're considering investing in a combination of a stock and the risk-free asset. The stock has an expected return of 17% and standard deviation of return of 11% and a risk-free asset with a return of 3%.

   a. Complete the table below and graph the expected portfolio return as a function of the portfolio standard deviation.

   b. Suppose you're investing $1,000. What is the meaning of a portfolio invested 150% in the risky asset?

| | A | B | C |
|---|---|---|---|
| 1 | Expected stock return | 17% | |
| 2 | Stock standard deviation | 11% | |
| 3 | Risk-free rate | 3% | |
| 4 | | | |
| 5 | | | |
| 6 | Proportion of stock in portfolio | Portfolio standard deviation | Portfolio expected return |
| 7 | 0% | | |
| 8 | 10% | | |
| 9 | 20% | | |
| 10 | 30% | | |
| 11 | 40% | | |
| 12 | 50% | | |
| 13 | 60% | | |
| 14 | 70% | | |
| 15 | 80% | | |
| 16 | 90% | | |
| 17 | 100% | | |
| 18 | 110% | | |
| 19 | 120% | | |
| 20 | 130% | | |
| 21 | 140% | | |
| 22 | 150% | | |

6. Consider the following data of X and Y stocks and a risk-free asset.

| | A | B | C |
|---|---|---|---|
| 1 | RETURNS OF X AND Y STOCKS | | |
| 2 | | X | Y |
| 3 | Average return | 19.00% | 13.00% |
| 4 | Variance | 0.09 | 0.015 |
| 5 | covariance of return | 0.01 | |
| 6 | | | |
| 7 | Risk-free return | 3.00% | |

   a. What are the return and standard deviation of the minimum variance portfolio of X and Y stocks?

   b. What are the return and standard deviation of a portfolio composed of 30% of the minimum variance portfolio and 70% of the risk-free asset? Repeat this question with weights of 50% for the risk-free asset and the minimum variance portfolio.

   c. Mary Jones asks you to create a portfolio composed of the risk-free asset and the minimum variance portfolio. Mary wants an expected return of 9%. What will be the percentage of the portfolio invested in the risk-free asset and in the minimum variance portfolio?

d. Kaid Benfield wants a portfolio composed of the risk-free asset and the minimum variance portfolio. Find a portfolio for Kaid that has a standard deviation of returns of 5%.

7. What is the Sharpe ratio of the minimum variance portfolio of Question 6? Show another portfolio composed of stocks $X$ and $Y$ that has a better Sharpe ratio.

8. Compute the Sharpe ratio for the following portfolios, assuming the risk-free asset is 4%. What is the best portfolio according to the Sharpe ratio?

|  | A | B | C |
|---|---|---|---|
| 1 | **Portfolio statistics** | | |
| 2 | | Average return | Return standard deviation |
| 3 | Portfolio 1 | 19.00% | 9.00% |
| 4 | Portfolio 2 | 13.00% | 1.50% |
| 5 | Portfolio 3 | 25.00% | 10.00% |
| 6 | Portfolio 4 | 32.00% | 15.00% |
| 7 | Portfolio 5 | 14.00% | 2.10% |
| 8 | Portfolio 6 | 22.00% | 3.20% |
| 9 | Portfolio 7 | 17.00% | 5.50% |
| 10 | Portfolio 8 | 12.00% | 0.96% |
| 11 | Portfolio 9 | 40.00% | 20.00% |
| 12 | Portfolio 10 | 23.00% | 23.00% |
| 13 | | | |
| 14 | Risk-free return | 4.00% | |

9. Below are given the end-year prices of the shares of IBM and Coca-Cola. Answer the following questions.

a. For the years 1991–2002, calculate the following statistics for the two shares: annual return, average return for the entire period, variance and standard deviation of returns, covariance of returns, and correlation coefficient.

b. Calculate the returns and standard deviations for portfolios composed of these two stocks.

c. Find the market portfolio using the Sharpe ratio, assuming the risk-free asset return is 5%. Is it the minimum variance portfolio? If not, calculate the Sharpe ratio of the minimum variance portfolio as well.

|  | A | B | C |
|---|---|---|---|
| 1 | **Prices of IBM and Coca-Cola Stock** | | |
| 2 | Date | Coke | IBM |
| 3 | 31-Dec-90 | 13.43 | 28.02 |
| 4 | 31-Dec-91 | 14.91 | 22.07 |
| 5 | 31-Dec-92 | 14.11 | 12.5 |
| 6 | 31-Dec-93 | 29.23 | 14.01 |
| 7 | 30-Dec-94 | 22.01 | 18.23 |
| 8 | 29-Dec-95 | 30 | 22.66 |
| 9 | 31-Dec-96 | 42.65 | 37.58 |
| 10 | 31-Dec-97 | 61.61 | 51.9 |
| 11 | 31-Dec-98 | 52.17 | 91.47 |
| 12 | 31-Dec-99 | 43.78 | 107.03 |
| 13 | 29-Dec-00 | 35.84 | 84.34 |
| 14 | 31-Dec-01 | 36.75 | 120.02 |
| 15 | 31-Dec-02 | 63.94 | 77.21 |

10. In the Golkoland stock market there are only two listed stocks, Xirkind and Yirkind. The risk-free rate of return in Golkoland is 5% and the portfolio of Xirkind and Yirkind stocks that has the highest Sharpe ratio is given here.

|  | A | B | C |
|---|---|---|---|
| 2 |  | **Xirkind** | **Yirkind** |
| 3 | Average return | 19.84% | 15.38% |
| 4 | Variance of returns | 0.1575 | 0.1378 |
| 5 | Standard deviation | 39.68% | 37.12% |
| 6 | Covariance of returns | -1.10% |  |
| 7 | Correlation | -7.47% |  |
| 8 | Risk-free return | 5.00% |  |
| 9 |  |  |  |
| 10 | **Highest Sharpe ratio** |  |  |
| 11 | Weight of Xirkind | 0.546 |  |
| 12 | Weight of Yirkind | 0.454 |  |
| 13 |  |  |  |
| 14 | Portfolio return | 17.81% |  |
| 15 | Portfolio variance | 6.99% |  |
| 16 | Portfolio standard deviation | 26.43% |  |
| 17 | Sharpe ratio | 0.485 |  |

a. What is the market portfolio, $M$, in Golkoland?

b. What is the equation of the CML in Golkoland?

c. What does CML mean and why are we interested in it?

d. What is the expected return and standard deviation of a portfolio composed of 30% risk-free asset and 70% market portfolio?

e. Suppose an investor wants the same return as the above portfolio, but invests only in a portfolio composed of equal weights of Xirkind and Yirkind stocks. What will be the standard deviation of the returns of his portfolio? How do you explain the difference in standard deviations between this question and Question 10d?

11. The market portfolio of the Tierra del Fuego stock market has expected return $E(r_M) = 22\%$ and standard deviation of returns $\sigma_M = 19\%$. The risk-free rate of interest is $r_f = 7\%$.

a. What is the equation of the Tierra del Fuego CML?

b. Compute the following CML portfolios:

- A portfolio composed of 35% risk-free asset and 65% market portfolio.
- A portfolio composed of 120% market portfolio.
- A portfolio that yields a return of 15%.
- A portfolio that yields a return of 23%.
- A portfolio with standard deviation of 35%.
- A portfolio with standard deviation of 5%.

12. Find the equation of the capital market line (CML) for a stock market that has only two stocks. The market portfolio is composed of 37.5% A and 62.5% Z.

|  | A | B | C |
|---|---|---|---|
| 1 | **RETURN STATISTICS OF** | | |
|  | **A AND Z STOCKS** | | |
| 2 |  | **A** | **Z** |
| 3 | Average return | 31.00% | 15.00% |
| 4 | Variance | 0.3 | 0.08 |
| 5 | Covariance of returns | -0.05 |  |
| 6 |  |  |  |
| 7 | Risk-free return | 5.00% |  |

13. Will the market portfolio of Question 12 change if the risk-free asset return is 3%? If yes, explain why and calculate the new market portfolio. Answer this question again assuming the market portfolio is 0%.

14. Below are given the return statistics of X and Y stocks.

| | A | B | C |
|---|---|---|---|
| 1 | RETURN STATISTICS OF X AND Y STOCKS | | |
| 2 | | **X** | **Y** |
| 3 | Average return | 19.00% | 13.00% |
| 4 | Variance | 0.09 | 0.015 |
| 5 | Covariance of returns | 0.01 | |
| 6 | | | |
| 7 | Risk-free return | 3.00% | |

a. Calculate the capital market line (CML) using these data.

b. Find the difference in standard deviation between a portfolio on the CML and a portfolio on the efficient frontier, both with average return of 19%. What will be the weight of the risk-free asset in the CML portfolio?

15. (More difficult exercise.) The Northern Peninsula stock market has only two listed stocks, Big Mining and Shallow Mining. The market portfolio is composed of 40% Big Mining and 60% Shallow Mining. Using the data below, find the $\beta$ of each of the two stocks.

| | A | B | C | D |
|---|---|---|---|---|
| 1 | NORTHERN PENINSULA STOCK MARKET | | | |
| 2 | | **Big Mining** | **Shallow Mining** | |
| 3 | Expected return | 15% | 25% | |
| 4 | Return standard deviation | 25% | 40% | |
| 5 | Covariance of returns | 0.05 | | |

16. Formula and Dormula are two stocks listed on the Chitango stock market. Their $\beta$s are 1.8 and 2.6, respectively. What is the beta ($\beta$) of a portfolio invested 20% in Formula and 80% in Dormula?

17. Consider the following data:

$E(r_m) = 0.18, \; \beta_i = 1.05, \; R_f = 0.07$

What is the expected return of stock $i$?

18. Consider the following data:

$E(r_m) = 0.22, \; E(r_i) = 0.33, \; R_f = 0.09$

What is the $\beta$ of stock $i$?

19. Consider the following data:

$E(r_m) = 0.25, \; \beta_i = 0.85, \; E(r_i) = 0.22$

What is the return of the risk-free asset?

20. Consider the following data:

$E(r_m) = 0.2, \; Cov(r_i, r_m) = 0.1, \; r_f = 0.06, \; \sigma_M^2 = 0.15$

What is the expected return of stock $i$?

21. Consider the following data:

$$E(r_i) = 0.15, \; Cov(r_i, r_m) = 0.067, \; r_f = 0.02, \; \sigma_M^2 = 0.089$$

What is the market return?

22. Consider the following data:

$$E(r_m) = 0.22, \; Cov(r_i, r_m) = 0.27, \; E(r_i) = 0.14, \; \sigma_M^2 = 0.09$$

What is the return of the risk-free asset?

23. Suppose that there are only two stocks, Company A and Company B. The relevant statistics for the portfolio are given below.

| | A | B | C | D |
|---|---|---|---|---|
| 1 | | Company A | Company B | |
| 2 | Expected return | 8.00% | 25.00% | |
| 3 | Variance of return | 0.0200 | 0.0900 | |
| 4 | Standard deviation of return | 14.14% | 30.00% | <-- =SQRT(C3) |
| 5 | | | | |
| 6 | Covariance of returns | -0.03500 | | |
| 7 | Correlation of returns | -0.82496 | <-- =B6/(B4*C4) | |
| 8 | | | | |
| 9 | Portfolio proportions | | | |
| 10 | Company A | 80% | | |
| 11 | Company B | 20% | | |
| 12 | | | | |
| 13 | Portfolio expected return | 11.400% | <-- =B10*B2+B11*C2 | |
| 14 | Portfolio variance | 0.0052 | <-- =B10^2*B3+B11^2*C3+2*B10*B11*B6 | |
| 15 | Portfolio standard deviation | 7.21% | <-- =SQRT(B14) | |

Show that a portfolio invested 80% in Company A and 20% in Company B is not optimal by showing a better portfolio.

24. Using the data provided in the previous question, calculate the market portfolio M, when the risk-free rate of return is 8%. (Recall that the M portfolio is the portfolio that maximizes the Sharpe ratio).

25. On the occasion of your birthday, your wealthy Aunt Hilda sends you a check for $5,000, under the express condition that you invest the money in either (or all) of the following: government bonds, Hilda's Hybrids, Inc., and/or Hilda's Hubby, Inc. The relevant statistics on each of these investments are provided below.

| | A | B | C | D |
|---|---|---|---|---|
| 1 | | Hilda's Hybrids | Hilda's Hubby | Government bond |
| 2 | Expected return | 30.00% | 16.25% | 10.00% |
| 3 | Variance | 28.58% | 2.30% | |
| 4 | Sigma | 53.46% | 15.17% | |
| 5 | | | | |
| 6 | Covariance of returns | 0.0343 | | |
| 7 | Correlation of returns | 0.4224 | <-- =B6/(B4*C4) | |

a. Show the capital market line (CML) (that is, all the combinations of investment in the risk-free asset and the two companies). Provide results in both chart and graph form. Assume that the market portfolio M is composed of equal proportions of the two risky assets.

b. Supposing you decided to invest in the following proportions: 40% in government bonds and 60% in portfolio M. Calculate the expected return and variance of returns for this portfolio.

26. With reference to Exercise 25 above, you are feeling lucky and decide to take on a riskier portfolio. In particular, in addition to your $5,000 gift, you are able to borrow another $1,000 at the risk-free rate of 10%. You decide to invest this total of $6,000 in a portfolio containing a mix of Hilda's Hybrids and Hilda's Hubby.

a. In what proportion will you invest your $6,000 if your objective is to create the "best combination" of these risky assets?

b. What will be the expected return and the expected risk for this more daring portfolio?

27.

a. Consider the data below. Compute the expected return and standard deviation of returns for a portfolio composed of 75% Stock A and 25% Stock B.

|  | Asset A | Asset B |
|---|---|---|
| Mean return | 30% | 13% |
| Return sigma $\sigma$ | 40% | 10% |
| Correlation $\rho_{AB}$ | 0.5 | |

b. Stock C has a $\beta_C$ of 1.3 and the portfolio P composed of 75% C and 25% D has a $\beta_P = 1.8$. What is the $\beta_D$ of Stock D?

28. You have $1,000 to invest. The risk-free rate is $r_f = 6\%$. The market portfolio has expected return $E(r_M) = 15\%$ and $\sigma_M = 20\%$.

a. What is the mean and standard deviation of your investment if you invest $500 in the risk-free asset and $500 in the market portfolio?

b. Your sister also has $1,000 to invest, but wants to borrow another $1,000 to make an investment of $2,000 in the market portfolio M. What will be the mean and standard deviation of her portfolio return?

c. Which portfolio is better, yours or your sister's?

29. The table below provides the annual rates of return on ABC Corp., XYZ Corp., and the market portfolio M.

|  | A | B | C | D |
|---|---|---|---|---|
|  |  | Market | ABC | XYZ |
| 3 | Year | Portfolio | Corp. | Corp. |
| 4 | 1 | 11.90% | 14.40% | 121.20% |
| 5 | 2 | 0.40% | -22.20% | -33.90% |
| 6 | 3 | 26.90% | 47.50% | 3.70% |
| 7 | 4 | -8.60% | 7.70% | 3.10% |
| 8 | 5 | 22.80% | 42.80% | 17.20% |
| 9 | 6 | 16.50% | 30.70% | -16.90% |
| 10 | 7 | 12.50% | 11.40% | -32.80% |
| 11 | 8 | -10.06% | -32.50% | -30.40% |
| 12 | 9 | 23.90% | 30.50% | 114.00% |
| 13 | 10 | 11.10% | 1.80% | -3.70% |
| 14 | 11 | -8.50% | -6.20% | -33.00% |
| 15 | 12 | 3.90% | 22.30% | -33.20% |
| 16 | 13 | 14.30% | 4.30% | 21.60% |
| 17 | 14 | 19.10% | 6.50% | 17.80% |
| 18 | 15 | -14.70% | -37.80% | 7.50% |
| 19 | 16 | -26.50% | -27.60% | -62.30% |
| 20 | 17 | 37.30% | 97.10% | 65.40% |
| 21 | 18 | 23.80% | 45.85% | -28.02% |
| 22 | 19 | -7.15% | -11.25% | -6.33% |
| 23 | 20 | 12.16% | -4.70% | 26.67% |

a. Calculate the $\beta_{XYZ}$ and the $\beta_{ABC}$. Use the formulas

$$\beta_{ABC} = \frac{Covariance(ABC\ returns, market\ returns)}{Variance(market\ returns)}$$

$$\beta_{XYZ} = \frac{Covariance(XYZ\ returns, market\ returns)}{Variance(market\ returns)}$$

b. Which company's returns are better explained by the market's returns? Explain by regressing each company's returns on the market returns (see Chapter 9).

30. Anders Smith proposes to invest in a portfolio of two stocks, $X$ and $Y$. Information about the two stocks is given below.

| | A | B | C |
|---|---|---|---|
| 2 | | Stock X | Stock Y |
| 3 | Expected return | 20% | 14% |
| 4 | Sigma of return | 25% | 15% |
| 5 | Correlation | 0.4 | |
| 6 | | | |
| 7 | General X-Y portfolio | | |
| 8 | Percentage of X | Sigma | Mean |
| 9 | 0% | | |
| 10 | 10% | | |
| 11 | 20% | | |
| 12 | 30% | | |
| 13 | 40% | | |
| 14 | 50% | | |
| 15 | 60% | | |
| 16 | 70% | | |
| 17 | 80% | | |
| 18 | 90% | | |
| 19 | 100% | | |

a. Fill in the highlighted box and compute the mean and standard deviation of each of the indicated portfolios.

b. Plot the portfolios on a mean–standard deviation plot.

c. Suppose that Mr. Smith can also borrow and lend at an interest rate of 6%. Discuss how this alters his investment opportunities. Calculate the portfolio $M$ that maximizes the Sharpe ratio and discuss briefly why Smith will always invest in this portfolio.

31. Assume that there are only three stocks in the market and that the optimal investment proportions in each Stock $A$, $B$, and $C$ is 1/3. Also assume that variance of Stock $A$ is 10%, the variance of Stock $B$ is 8%, and the variance of Stock $C$ is 20%. The covariance between Stock $A$ and $B$ is 0.08, the covariance between Stock $B$ and $C$ is –0.10, and the covariance between Stock $A$ and $C$ is 0.04.

a. Calculate the covariance between each stock and the market portfolio.

b. Calculate the systematic risk beta ($\beta$) for each of the three stocks.

# 12 | Using the Security Market Line to Measure Investment Performance

## CHAPTER CONTENTS

## Overview

This and the next chapter show how to use the SML that was introduced in Chapter 11. The current chapter discusses investment performance, and the next chapter discusses the use of the model to measure the cost of capital.

"Investment performance" is finance jargon for the question "How well did an asset—either a stock or a portfolio—perform?" Often the underlying question is really "How well did my investment manager (or mutual fund manager) do in managing my money?" To determine the investment performance of an asset, we have to account for the asset's risk. Because we

373

anticipate that riskier assets should have higher returns to compensate for their risk, true investment performance measures should take account of the returns that investors earn *in excess* of the returns warranted by the asset risks.

The SML provides us with one of the standard methods of measuring investment performance. Using the SML to measure *risk-adjusted performance*, we can determine whether a particular asset provided performance in excess of its risks (outperformance) or not (underperformance).

In this chapter we show how to use the SML to measure investment performance.

- We show how to compute the $\beta$ ("beta") of a security by regressing the security's excess returns on those of the market portfolio. We often use the S&P 500 as the "market portfolio." $\beta$ measures the riskiness of the security.

- We show how to compute the $\alpha$ ("alpha") of a security. $\alpha$ measures the security's risk-adjusted performance.

- We discuss the difference between *nondiversifiable risk* (also called *market risk)* and *diversifiable risk* (also called *idiosyncratic risk* or *nondiversifiable* risk) and show that combining stocks in a portfolio reduces the diversifiable risk.

## Finance Concepts Discussed

- Security market line (SML)
- $\alpha, \beta, R^2$
- Systematic (nondiversifiable, market) risk
- Nonsystematic (diversifiable) risk
- Performance evaluation

## Excel Functions Used

- **Average, Stdevp, Varp, Covar**
- **Intercept**, **Slope**, **Rsq**
- **Trendline** (Excel's regression tool)

# 12.1. Jack and Jill's Investment Argument

To understand the issues behind performance measurement, we start with the story of Jack and Jill. Sometime in August 2003, Jack and Jill were arguing about their investment strategies. They had been together a long time, and like many couples they often had the same argument/discussion. The one about investment strategies was one they'd replayed many times.

Jill started off: "I invested in the NASDAQ in May 1990," she said to Jack. "If you'd followed my advice and invested in the NASDAQ instead of investing in that stodgy Fidelity Puritan Fund, you'd be a lot better off. For every dollar I put into the NASDAQ, I've now got $3.60, whereas you've only got $2.70 for each dollar you put into Puritan. The NASDAQ simply *outperforms* Puritan."

This line of argument infuriated Jack. Ever since he'd met Jill in their MBA program at Squash Hill College, she'd insisted—in her typical incautious way—that she was much better with money than he. It risked spoiling their otherwise lovely relationship. She claimed to

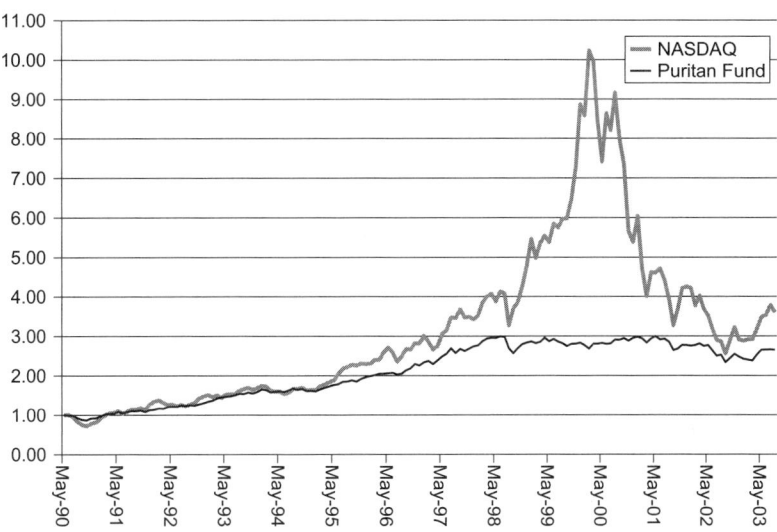

FIGURE 12.1 The growth of $1 invested in the NASDAQ and the Puritan Fund in the period from May 1990 to August 2003. $1 invested in the NASDAQ grew over the period to $3.60, whereas $1 invested in Fidelity's Puritan Fund grew to $2.70.

be able to pick investments that outperform the market, even though she had a difficult time defining this concept.[1]

If you consider the whole period from 1990 to 2003 (Figure 12.1), Jill had indeed done better than Jack. Even though the NASDAQ was subject to bigger fluctuations than Puritan, an investor like Jill who'd stuck with the NASDAQ throughout the period would have been ahead of an investor like Jack who'd stuck with Puritan. An investor who had invested $1 in the NASDAQ in May 1990 would have had $3.60 in August 2003, whereas an investor who had invested $1 in the Puritan fund in May 1990 would have ended up with $2.70 in August 2003.

But Jack also had a valid point. "Listen, dear," he said snootily to Jill. "Look what a bumpy ride the NASDAQ took you on. Remember how cocky you were in late 1999 and what a bundle of nerves you were in 2001? This outperformance stuff is a crock of spam." He showed Jill the wild gyrations of the NASDAQ between May 1999 and May 2001 (Figure 12.1).

"Also," he reminded her, "the supposed outperformance of the NASDAQ hasn't always held. When we got our bonuses in December 1999, you put yours in the NASDAQ and I—OK, I'm more conservative than you—put mine in Puritan. Then the market took a downward turn and we both lost money, but in the downturn you lost a lot more than I." He showed her Figure 12.2. "For every dollar I put in at the end of 1999, I've now got 94 cents, whereas you've got only 41 cents per dollar."

"What comes down will go up again," said Jill, ever the optimist.[2] "I'll bet you a Philadelphia steak sandwich that sometime in the future I'll be ahead."

---

[1] She hadn't read this chapter!

[2] One of the lessons of market efficiency is that past stock price performance doesn't predict future stock prices. Perhaps Jill should read Chapter 14, in which this is explained.

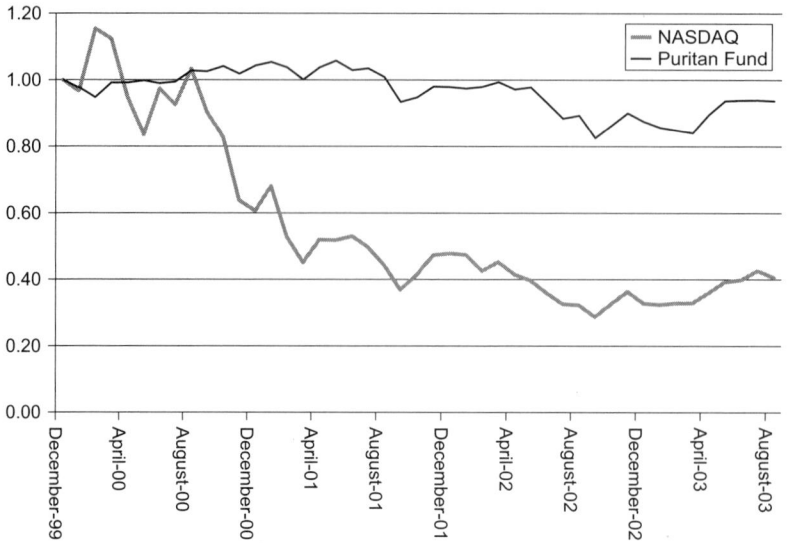

FIGURE 12.2 The growth of $1 invested in the NASDAQ and the Puritan Fund in the period from December 1999 to August 2003. Actually "growth" is a euphemism—both investments went down over the period. $1 invested in the NASDAQ was worth $0.41 by August 2003, and $1 in the Puritan was worth $0.94.

"Of course you'll be ahead once in a while—the NASDAQ is riskier than Puritan. It bounces around more, so at some point you're bound to be ahead. But 'slow and steady' is my motto. The Puritan Fund isn't as risky, and because I'm not into risk, I'm happy with its lower return. Remember how Professor Simons at Squash Hill College was always hammering home the relation between risk and return?"

At this point Jill got tired of the argument. Both she and Jack had made their points, and Jill sat back to read that day's *Wall Street Journal*.

## The Real Question

Jack and Jill's argument about risk, return, performance, and outperformance is typical of the pointless discussions in which many investors engage. Their discussion is misfocused because they've ignored the risks of their investments. In finance we believe that investment performance is related to the riskiness of the assets invested in—assets that are riskier should, on average, provide greater returns to compensate investors for their risk. Thus, we are not surprised that Jill did better with the NASDAQ (a risky investment) and that Jack had to settle for lower returns with his Puritan Fund (a much less risky asset). The real question is whether the NASDAQ returns were commensurate with the riskiness of the NASDAQ and the Puritan returns were commensurate with the riskiness of Puritan.

So the problem with Jack and Jill's argument is that they're not asking the right question. Let's start with Jill's argument that she's made more money than Jack since 1990. She's right, of course, but a glance at Figure 12.1 will show you that the NASDAQ was much riskier than the Puritan Fund—the variations in returns are much greater for the NASDAQ than for Puritan. If the NASDAQ is riskier, then Jill's greater earnings could just be her reward for undertaking more risk.

The same point can be made about Figure 12.2. If the NASDAQ is riskier than the Puritan Fund, it's not surprising that in periods when the market goes down, the NASDAQ goes down even more. When Jack says that he's done better with the Puritan Fund in a down period, we're also not surprised.

So neither Jack nor Jill is asking the right question: The real question is *whether the NASDAQ performance is commensurate with the NASDAQ risk and whether Puritan Fund performance is commensurate with the Puritan Fund risk.* In the language of the CAPM, the question is whether a security has *risk-adjusted underperformance or overperformance.*

This chapter will show you how to answer this question. We will use the SML to answer questions about performance versus risk. In Section 12.6 we return to Jack and Jill and answer the question about who actually did better.

## 12.2. Measuring the Investment Performance of Fidelity's Magellan Fund

In this section we illustrate the use of the SML for measuring investment performance by using it to measure the investment performance of Fidelity's Magellan Fund (stock symbol FMAGX). We will show that over the decade 1999–2008, Magellan outperformed the market on a risk-adjusted basis.

We start by summarizing the SML. The SML shows the relation between an asset's risk and its expected return. An asset's risk is measured by its $\beta$, which shows how sensitive the asset's return is to changes in the market return. The higher the asset's $\beta$, the higher the return investors expect from the asset.

In equation form the SML states that an asset's expected return $E(r_i)$ is given by the equation

$$E(r_i) = r_f + \beta_i \left[ E(r_M) - r_f \right]$$
$$\text{where } \beta_i = \frac{Cov(r_i, r_M)}{\sigma_M^2}$$

The letter "$i$" is used in $E(r_i)$ to indicate that the SML is a risk–return relation for *all* risky assets. Thus the $i$ can stand for any asset, whether a stock, a bond, or a portfolio. In this chapter we use $i$ to represent either stocks or mutual funds (large diversified portfolios of stocks or bonds).

The following spreadsheet contains the data necessary to measure the performance of Magellan:

- Annual return data for Magellan (cells B4:B13) and the S&P 500 index (cells C4:C13) and for the 10-year period from 1999 to 2008.[3] The returns include dividends; the annual return in year $t$ is calculated by assuming that the investor bought the stock at the end of year $t-1$ and held it until the end of year $t$:

$$return_t = \frac{StockPrice_t - StockPrice_{t-1} + Dividend_t}{StockPrice_{t-1}}$$

---

[3] The stock data in this chapter come from Yahoo!. The interest rate data is based on a Web site maintained by the St. Louis Federal Reserve Bank (http://research.stlouisfed.org/fred2/).

- Annual risk-free rate data (cells D4:D13). Because we are looking at annual data, the risk-free rate is taken to be the return on a 1-year U.S. Treasury Bill.[4]

- Excess return data: The "excess return" is the difference between the return on the security (be it the Magellan or the S&P) and the risk-free rate for the same period. For example, someone who owned the S&P 500 Index throughout 1998 would have made 30.54% on his investment (cell C4); in the same period he could have earned 5.66% by holding a riskless U.S. Treasury security. Thus, over this period, the S&P Index returned 24.88% more than the risk-free rate. This 24.88% is the *excess return* for the S&P for the period. As you can see in columns F and G of the spreadsheet, during much of this period both Magellan and the S&P had hefty positive excess returns.

| | A | B | C | D | E | F | G | H |
|---|---|---|---|---|---|---|---|---|
| 1 | | | FIDELITY'S MAGELLAN FUND (FMAGX) AND THE S&P500, 1999–2008 | | | | | |
| 2 | | | | | | Excess returns | | |
| 3 | Year ending | FMAGX return | S&P500 return | Risk-free interest | | FMAX minus risk-free | S&P minus risk-free | |
| 4 | 4-Jan-99 | 39.24% | 30.54% | 5.66% | | 33.58% | 24.88% | <-- =C4-$D4 |
| 5 | 3-Jan-00 | 12.31% | 8.97% | 4.61% | | 7.70% | 4.36% | <-- =C5-$D5 |
| 6 | 2-Jan-01 | -1.54% | -2.04% | 6.34% | | -7.88% | -8.38% | |
| 7 | 2-Jan-02 | -17.13% | -17.26% | 4.78% | | -21.91% | -22.04% | |
| 8 | 2-Jan-03 | -23.35% | -24.29% | 3.17% | | -26.52% | -27.46% | |
| 9 | 2-Jan-04 | 30.00% | 32.19% | 1.70% | | 28.30% | 30.49% | |
| 10 | 3-Jan-05 | 4.14% | 4.43% | 1.88% | | 2.26% | 2.55% | |
| 11 | 3-Jan-06 | 13.63% | 8.36% | 3.18% | | 10.45% | 5.18% | |
| 12 | 3-Jan-07 | 5.49% | 12.36% | 4.33% | | 1.16% | 8.03% | |
| 13 | 2-Jan-08 | 5.19% | -4.15% | 4.76% | | 0.43% | -8.91% | |
| 14 | | | | | | | | |
| 15 | Average | 6.80% | 4.91% | 4.04% | | 2.76% | 0.87% | <-- =AVERAGE(G4:G13) |
| 16 | Standard deviation | 17.97% | 17.20% | 1.45% | | 18.09% | 17.46% | <-- =STDEVP(G4:G13) |
| 17 | | | | | | | | |
| 18 | Alpha | 0.0189 | <-- =INTERCEPT(F4:F13,G4:G13) | | | | | |
| 19 | Beta | 1.0011 | <-- =SLOPE(F4:F13,G4:G13) | | | | | |
| 20 | | 1.0011 | <-- =COVAR(F4:F13,G4:G13)/VARP(G4:G13) | | | | | |
| 21 | R-squared | 0.9330 | <-- =RSQ(F4:F13,G4:G13) | | | | | |

Regressing Magellan's Excess Return on the S&P 500, 1998–2008

$y = 1.0011x + 0.0189$
$R^2 = 0.9330$

---

[4] Finance researchers often use monthly or even weekly return data, but annual data are often easier to visualize. When we return to Jack and Jill in Section 12.6, we use monthly data.

During the period Magellan clearly had higher performance than the S&P 500: The average return on Magellan was 6.80% (B15), whereas the average return on the S&P was 4.91% (cell C15). The question we answer is whether Magellan had *risk-adjusted outperformance.*

To answer this question, we regress Magellan's excess returns on the excess returns of S&P 500. To perform this regression, we estimate the best line that passes through the points on the graph.[5] In essence, we are trying to explain the excess returns of Magellan as a linear function of the excess returns of the S&P:

$$\text{Regression line:} \quad \underbrace{r_{Magellan,t} - r_{f,t}}_{\substack{\text{Magellan's excess} \\ \text{return in period t}}} = \text{}_{Magellan} + \beta_{Magellan} * \underbrace{\left[ r_{S\&P,t} - r_{f,t} \right]}_{\substack{\text{S\&P 500 excess} \\ \text{return in period t}}}$$

The actual regression line that we compute is

$$\text{Magellan excess return} = \underbrace{1.89\%}_{\substack{\text{This is Magellan's} \\ \text{alpha (}_{Magellan}\text{)--its} \\ \text{performance over and} \\ \text{above the S\&P index}}} + \underbrace{1.0011}_{\substack{\text{This is Magellan's} \\ \text{beta (}\beta_{Magellan}\text{)--its} \\ \text{riskiness versus} \\ \text{the S\&P index}}} * S\&P \text{ excess return}, \quad \underbrace{R^2 = 93.3\%}_{\substack{\text{The "r-squared" is} \\ \text{a measure of how} \\ \text{well Magellan's excess} \\ \text{returns are explained} \\ \text{by the S\&P excess returns.}}}$$

The regression calculation requires three statistics:

**Statistic 1, Magellan's $\beta_{Magellan}$ ($\beta$):** $\beta_{Magellan}$ measures the sensitivity of Magellan's excess returns to the S&P 500's excess returns. $\beta$ is the most common measure of a security's market-related risk. In the spreadsheet $\beta_{Magellan}$ is computed in three ways: In cells B19 and B20 and on the graph.[6] All three methods give $\beta_{Magellan}$ = 1.0011.

The $\beta$ is the most common *risk measure* for a stock. Magellan's $\beta_{Magellan}$ =1.0011 shows that Magellan's excess returns were roughly equally as risky as the S&P 500 excess returns: on average a 1% increase in the S&P excess return was accompanied by a 1.0011% increase in the excess return on Magellan stock. In the parlance of investment analysts, Magellan is a *market-neutral* asset; moving very much in tandem with the S&P 500. In the same parlance, an asset whose $\beta < 1$ is termed a *defensive* asset and an asset whose $\beta > 1$ is termed an *aggressive* asset. We give examples of both defensive and aggressive assets below.

**Statistic 2, Magellan's $\alpha_{Magellan}$ (*alpha*):** $\alpha_{Magellan}$ is a measure of the extra performance of Magellan. Magellan's *alpha*, $\alpha_{Magellan}$, is 1.89%. In the spreadsheet $\alpha_{Magellan}$ is computed in two ways: in cell B18 and on the graph. To understand the importance of $\alpha_{Magellan}$, take another look at the regression line:

$$\text{Magellan excess return} = \underbrace{1.89\%}_{\substack{\text{Magellan's alpha (}_{Magellan}\text{)}}} + \underbrace{1.0011}_{\substack{\text{Magellan's beta (}\beta_{Magellan}\text{)}}} * S\&P \text{ excess return}$$

---

[5] For details on how to perform a regression in Excel, see the discussion in Section 4 of Chapter 9 or the Excel note that follows this section.

[6] See the Excel note on the next page for a further explanation of how to compute $\beta$.

Suppose that in a particular year the S&P 500 returns 10% in excess of the risk-free rate. Then the regression predicts that Magellan would return 11.901%:

$$\text{Magellan excess return} = \underbrace{1.89\%}_{\substack{\text{This is "free"}\text{—} \\ \text{the annual return} \\ \text{on Magellan after accounting} \\ \text{for the movements} \\ \text{of the S\&P index}}} + 1.0011 * \underbrace{S \& P \text{ excess return}}_{\substack{\text{Is 10\%}}}$$

$$10.011\% \text{ is the risk-adjusted} \\ \text{return on Magellan stock}$$

$$= 1.89\% + 1.011\% = 11.901\%$$

$\alpha_{Magellan}$ tells you that if Magellan's stock returns behave as predicted by this equation, you will, on average, earn 1.89% annually *more* than the market risk-adjusted excess return. This means that Magellan is a market-outperforming mutual fund![7]

**Statistic 3, Magellan's $R^2$ ("$R$-squared")**: The Magellan returns were very highly correlated with the S&P 500 returns: 93.3% of the variability in the Magellan returns was explained by variations in the S&P 500. This number (known as the $R^2$ of the regression) is calculated by the Excel function **Rsq(y-range,x-range)** in cell B21 and also appears on the graph.[8] Another interpretation of $R^2$ is that it measures the degree to which the stock "tracks" the S&P 500.

Magellan tracks the S&P highly, but most stocks don't track the market index nearly as well. In Sections 12.2 and 12.3 we will show that a diversified portfolio's tracking of the market index is generally much better than the tracking of the individual portfolio components.

---

## EXCEL NOTE: COMPUTING THE THREE STATISTICS $\alpha$, $\beta$, AND $R^2$

The spreadsheet shows several ways of computing each of the statistics $\alpha$, $\beta$, and $R^2$:

- You can use an Excel XY chart and then use the Excel regression function **Trendline** (see Chapter 9, page 289). The trendline equation (printed on the Excel chart) is *Magellan annual return* $= 1.0011 * S\&P$ *annual return* $+ 0.0189$, $R^2 = 0.933$. 1.011 is Magellan's $\beta$ ($\beta_{Magellan}$) and 1.89% is called Magellan's $\alpha$ ($\alpha_{Magellan}$).

- You can use the Excel functions **Intercept(y-range,x-range)**, **Slope(y-range,x-range)**, **Rsq(y-range,x-range)** to compute $\alpha_{Magellan}$, $\beta_{Magellan}$, and $R^2$, respectively. This is illustrated in cells B18, B19, and B21.

- You can use the Excel functions **Covar** and **Varp** to compute the $\beta_{Magellan}$:

$$\beta_{Magellan} = \frac{\text{Covar}(r_{Magellan}, r_{SP})}{\text{Varp}(r_{SP})}.$$

---

[7]Or *was a great fund*—we're making the strong assumption here that historical performance over the 1999–2008 period will predict future performance.

[8]As you will see in some of the other chapter examples, an $R^2$ of 90%, although not unusual for a highly diversified mutual fund, is unusually high for a regression of the SML type, when the data in question describe a single stock. It is much more usual for the $R^2$ of a single stock to be around 10–40%.

## ADVANCED EXCEL HINT:

In the cell formulas below the three statistics $\alpha$, $\beta$, and $R^2$ are calculated directly, without computing the excess returns. For example, the Excel expression B3:B12-D3:D12 can be written in the formulas for the excess return of the S&P 500. Similarly, B3:B12-D3:D12 is understood by Excel to be the excess returns for Magellan. We use this method in the next section.

| | A | B | C | D | E |
|---|---|---|---|---|---|
| 1 | VANGUARD'S MAGELLAN FUND AND THE S&P500, 1999–2008 Computing the regression coefficients without a direct computation of the excess returns | | | | |
| 2 | Date | FMAGX return | S&P500 return | Risk-free interest | |
| 3 | 4-Jan-99 | 39.24% | 30.54% | 5.66% | |
| 4 | 3-Jan-00 | 12.31% | 8.97% | 4.61% | |
| 5 | 2-Jan-01 | -1.54% | -2.04% | 6.34% | |
| 6 | 2-Jan-02 | -17.13% | -17.26% | 4.78% | |
| 7 | 2-Jan-03 | -23.35% | -24.29% | 3.17% | |
| 8 | 2-Jan-04 | 30.00% | 32.19% | 1.70% | |
| 9 | 3-Jan-05 | 4.14% | 4.43% | 1.88% | |
| 10 | 3-Jan-06 | 13.63% | 8.36% | 3.18% | |
| 11 | 3-Jan-07 | 5.49% | 12.36% | 4.33% | |
| 12 | 2-Jan-08 | 5.19% | -4.15% | 4.76% | |
| 13 | | | | | |
| 14 | Alpha | 0.0189 | <-- | =INTERCEPT(B3:B12-D3:D12,C3:C12-D3:D12) | |
| 15 | Beta | 1.0011 | <-- | =SLOPE(B3:B12-D3:D12,C3:C12-D3:D12) | |
| 16 | R-squared | 0.9330 | <-- | =RSQ(B3:B12-D3:D12,C3:C12-D3:D12) | |

## 12.3. Aggressive versus Defensive Stocks

In this section we repeat the analysis of the previous section for three more stocks. To compute the regression statistics we use the method illustrated in the Excel box on page 380.

### Kimberly-Clark

During the decade from 1998 to 2007, Kimberly-Clark (stock symbol KMB):

- Outperformed the market: KMB's $\alpha = 2.25\%$, indicating that on an annual basis, KMB earned 2.25% more than its risk-adjusted return would have warranted.
- Was a defensive stock: KMB's $\beta = 0.6301$, indicating that a 1% increase/decrease in the S&P 500 index led to a 0.63% increase/decrease in KMB's stock.

The $R$-squared of KMB ($R^2 = 40.15\%$) indicates that 40% of KMB's stock price variation was caused by market movements. The remaining 60% of the variability was presumably caused by variables uniquely related to Kimberly-Clark. This is what you would expect for an average

| | A | B | C | D | E |
|---|---|---|---|---|---|
| 1 | **KIMBERLY-CLARK (KMB) AND THE S&P500, 1998–2007** | | | | |
| | **Computing the regression coefficients without a direct computation of the excess returns** | | | | |
| 2 | Date | KMB return | S&P500 return | Risk-free interest | |
| 3 | 4-Jan-99 | -0.41% | 30.54% | 5.66% | |
| 4 | 3-Jan-00 | 29.47% | 8.97% | 4.61% | |
| 5 | 2-Jan-01 | 6.87% | -2.04% | 6.34% | |
| 6 | 2-Jan-02 | -5.18% | -17.26% | 4.78% | |
| 7 | 2-Jan-03 | -21.60% | -24.29% | 3.17% | |
| 8 | 2-Jan-04 | 30.99% | 32.19% | 1.70% | |
| 9 | 3-Jan-05 | 15.60% | 4.43% | 1.88% | |
| 10 | 3-Jan-06 | -10.30% | 8.36% | 3.18% | |
| 11 | 3-Jan-07 | 25.39% | 12.36% | 4.33% | |
| 12 | 2-Jan-08 | -2.48% | -4.15% | 4.76% | |
| 13 | | | | | |
| 14 | Alpha | 0.0225 | <-- =INTERCEPT(B3:B12-D3:D12,C3:C12-D3:D12) | | |
| 15 | Beta | 0.6301 | <-- =SLOPE(B3:B12-D3:D12,C3:C12-D3:D12) | | |
| 16 | R-squared | 0.4015 | <-- =RSQ(B3:B12-D3:D12,C3:C12-D3:D12) | | |

stock—most of the variability of the stock's return is not *systematic* (capital market jargon for market-related risk) but *idiosyncratic* or *nonsystematic* (stock-specific risk). As we will see in the next section, this idiosyncratic risk can be decreased through portfolio diversification.

## General Electric

During the same decade, General Electric (GE) both outperformed the stock market (it had an $\alpha = 3.18\%$ annually) and was an aggressive stock, being riskier than the stock market ($\beta_{GE} = 1.3063$). In addition, GE closely tracked the S&P 500, with an $R$-squared of 86%.

| | A | B | C | D | E |
|---|---|---|---|---|---|
| 1 | **GENERAL ELECTRIC AND THE S&P500 1999–2008** | | | | |
| | **Computing the regression coefficients without a direct computation of the excess returns** | | | | |
| 2 | Date | GE return | S&P500 return | Risk-free interest | |
| 3 | 4-Jan-99 | 37.26% | 30.54% | 5.66% | |
| 4 | 3-Jan-00 | 29.35% | 8.97% | 4.61% | |
| 5 | 2-Jan-01 | 4.11% | -2.04% | 6.34% | |
| 6 | 2-Jan-02 | -17.93% | -17.26% | 4.78% | |
| 7 | 2-Jan-03 | -36.10% | -24.29% | 3.17% | |
| 8 | 2-Jan-04 | 49.35% | 32.19% | 1.70% | |
| 9 | 3-Jan-05 | 10.01% | 4.43% | 1.88% | |
| 10 | 3-Jan-06 | -6.94% | 8.36% | 3.18% | |
| 11 | 3-Jan-07 | 13.36% | 12.36% | 4.33% | |
| 12 | 2-Jan-08 | 1.09% | -4.15% | 4.76% | |
| 13 | | | | | |
| 14 | Alpha | 0.0318 | <-- =INTERCEPT(B3:B12-D3:D12,C3:C12-D3:D12) | | |
| 15 | Beta | 1.3063 | <-- =SLOPE(B3:B12-D3:D12,C3:C12-D3:D12) | | |
| 16 | R-squared | 0.8635 | <-- =RSQ(B3:B12-D3:D12,C3:C12-D3:D12) | | |

## Dupont: Not Every Stock Is an Outperformer!

Lest you think that every stock outperforms the market, take a look at the somewhat less-than-happy history of Dupont over the decade 1999–2008.

| | A | B | C | D | E |
|---|---|---|---|---|---|
| 1 | **DUPONT (DD) AND THE S&P500, 1999–2008**<br>**Computing the regression coefficients without**<br>**a direct computation of the excess returns** | | | | |
| 2 | **Date** | **DD return** | **S&P500 return** | **Risk-free interest** | |
| 3 | 4-Jan-99 | -7.68% | 30.54% | 5.66% | |
| 4 | 3-Jan-00 | 17.80% | 8.97% | 4.61% | |
| 5 | 2-Jan-01 | -23.70% | -2.04% | 6.34% | |
| 6 | 2-Jan-02 | 4.36% | -17.26% | 4.78% | |
| 7 | 2-Jan-03 | -11.44% | -24.29% | 3.17% | |
| 8 | 2-Jan-04 | 19.99% | 32.19% | 1.70% | |
| 9 | 3-Jan-05 | 11.91% | 4.43% | 1.88% | |
| 10 | 3-Jan-06 | -14.98% | 8.36% | 3.18% | |
| 11 | 3-Jan-07 | 31.03% | 12.36% | 4.33% | |
| 12 | 2-Jan-08 | -5.95% | -4.15% | 4.76% | |
| 13 | | | | | |
| 14 | Alpha | | -0.0225 | <-- =INTERCEPT(B3:B12-D3:D12,C3:C12-D3:D12) | |
| 15 | Beta | | 0.3949 | <-- =SLOPE(B3:B12-D3:D12,C3:C12-D3:D12) | |
| 16 | R-squared | | 0.1571 | <-- =RSQ(B3:B12-D3:D12,C3:C12-D3:D12) | |

Dupont's $\alpha = -2.25\%$ indicates that in the absence of market movement, the return on Dupont is 2.25% lower than the S&P. Dupont was a defensive stock, with a $\beta = 0.3949$. Looking at the $r$-squared of the regression, we see that only about 16% of the movement in Dupont stock was explained by market movements.

# 12.4. Diversification Pays

In the previous section we measured the risk-adjusted performance of three stocks by regressing their excess returns on the excess returns of the S&P 500. In this section we repeat this exercise for a portfolio of stocks—regressing the portfolio's excess returns on those of the S&P 500. Doing this enables us to make two points:

- First, we can use the regression to measure the risk-adjusted underperformance or over-performance of a portfolio. This is similar to what we did for single stocks in the previous section.

- Second, we can use the regression to show that diversification pays by increasing the $R^2$ of the regression—meaning that there is less nonsystematic risk in a diversified portfolio: More of the returns are explained by the market portfolio (in this case the S&P 500).

In the example below we repeat annual return data for the Kimberly-Clark, General Electric, Dupont, and the S&P 500. We also show, in cells B3:B5, the composition of a portfolio of these stocks. Using the Excel functions described earlier, we calculate the $\alpha$ and $\beta$ for each of the stocks and the $R^2$ of the regression that determines them (rows 19–21). As you will see, one of the benefits of portfolio diversification is that in general a portfolio has a higher $R^2$ than the assets composing it.

| | A | B | C | D | E | F | G | H | I |
|---|---|---|---|---|---|---|---|---|---|
| 1 | **A PORTFOLIO OF THREE STOCKS:** <br> **Kimberly Clark (KMB), General Electric (GE), Dupont (DD), 1999–2008** <br> **The $R^2$ of the portfolio is significantly higher than the average $R^2$ of the assets** | | | | | | | | |
| 2 | Portfolio composition | | | | | | | | |
| 3 | KMB | 33% | | | | | | | |
| 4 | GE | 33% | | | | | | | |
| 5 | DD | 33% | <-- =1-B3-B4 | | | | | | |
| 6 | | | | | | | | | |
| 7 | Date | KMB return | GE return | DD return | S&P500 return | Risk-free interest | | Portfolio returns | |
| 8 | 4-Jan-99 | -0.41% | 37.26% | -7.68% | 30.54% | 5.66% | | 9.72% | <-- =$B$3*B8+$B$4*C8+$B$5*D8 |
| 9 | 3-Jan-00 | 29.47% | 29.35% | 17.80% | 8.97% | 4.61% | | 25.54% | |
| 10 | 2-Jan-01 | 6.87% | 4.11% | -23.70% | -2.04% | 6.34% | | -4.24% | |
| 11 | 2-Jan-02 | -5.18% | -17.93% | 4.36% | -17.26% | 4.78% | | -6.25% | |
| 12 | 2-Jan-03 | -21.60% | -36.10% | -11.44% | -24.29% | 3.17% | | -23.05% | |
| 13 | 2-Jan-04 | 30.99% | 49.35% | 19.99% | 32.19% | 1.70% | | 33.44% | |
| 14 | 3-Jan-05 | 15.60% | 10.01% | 11.91% | 4.43% | 1.88% | | 12.51% | |
| 15 | 3-Jan-06 | -10.30% | -6.94% | -14.98% | 8.36% | 3.18% | | -10.74% | |
| 16 | 3-Jan-07 | 25.39% | 13.36% | 31.03% | 12.36% | 4.33% | | 23.26% | |
| 17 | 2-Jan-08 | -2.48% | 1.09% | -5.95% | -4.15% | 4.76% | | -2.45% | |
| 18 | | | | | | | | | |
| 19 | Alpha | 0.0225 | 0.0318 | -0.0225 | 0.0000 | | | 0.0106 | <-- =INTERCEPT(H8:H17-$F$8:$F$17,$E$8:$E$17-$F$8:$F$17) |
| 20 | Beta | 0.6301 | 1.3063 | 0.3949 | 1.0000 | | | 0.7771 | <-- =SLOPE(H8:H17-$F$8:$F$17,$E$8:$E$17-$F$8:$F$17) |
| 21 | R-squared | 0.4015 | 0.8635 | 0.1571 | 1.0000 | | | 0.5994 | <-- =RSQ(H8:H17-$F$8:$F$17,$E$8:$E$17-$F$8:$F$17) |
| 22 | | | | | | | | | |
| 23 | Check | | | | | | | | |
| 24 | Portfolio alpha is the weighted average of stock alphas? | | | | | | | 0.0106 | <-- =$B$3*B19+$B$4*C19+$B$5*D19 |
| 25 | Portfolio beta is the weighted average of stock betas? | | | | | | | 0.7771 | <-- =$B$3*B20+$B$4*C20+$B$5*D20 |
| 26 | Portfolio r-squared is the weighted average of stock r-squareds? **NO!!!** | | | | | | | 0.4740 | <-- =$B$3*B21+$B$4*C21+$B$5*D21 |

Now suppose we form a portfolio composed of equal proportions of KMB, GE, and DD. The portfolio proportions are described in cells B3:B5, and the portfolio returns appear in cells H8:H17.

In cells H19:H22 we compute the regression of the portfolio excess returns on the S&P 500 excess returns. The portfolio returns are described by the regression:

$$\textit{Portfolio excess return}_t = \underset{\substack{\uparrow \\ \text{this is the} \\ \text{portfolio } p}}{0.0106} + \underset{\substack{\uparrow \\ \text{this is the} \\ \text{portfolio } \beta_P}}{0.7771} * S \& P \, \textit{Excess return}_t, R^2 = 0.5994$$

Here are some things to note about this regression:

- The portfolio $\alpha_P$ and $\beta_P$ are the weighted average $\beta$ of the individual stock $\beta$s. In the spreadsheet the $\beta$ is calculated twice: In cell H20 the portfolio $\beta_P$ is calculated using Excel's **Slope** function, and in cell H25 $\beta_P$ is calculated using the weighted average of each of the individual stock $\beta$s. If we denote the portfolio weights by $x_{KMB}$, $x_{GE}$, and $x_{DD}$, then, for example, the portfolio $\beta$ (either cell H20 or cell H25) $\beta_P$ is given by $\beta_P = x_{KMB}\beta_{KMB} + x_{GE}\beta_{GE} + x_{DD}\beta_{DD}$. In the particular example illustrated, this formula gives a portfolio $\beta$, $\beta_P = 0.7545$:

$$\beta_P = \underset{\substack{\uparrow \\ \text{Portfolio} \\ \text{weight of} \\ \text{Kimberly-Clark,} \\ x_{KMB}}}{0.3333} * 0.6301 + \underset{\substack{\uparrow \\ \text{Portfolio} \\ \text{weight of} \\ \text{General Electric,} \\ x_{GE}}}{0.3333} * 1.3063 + + \underset{\substack{\uparrow \\ \text{Portfolio} \\ \text{weight of} \\ \text{Dupont,} \\ x_{DD}}}{0.3333} * 0.3949 = 0.7771$$

The same goes for $\alpha_P$, which can be calculated either using Excel's **Intercept** function (cell H19) or as an average of the individual stock $\alpha$s (cell H24).

- Whereas a portfolio's $\alpha$ ($\alpha_P$) and $\beta$ ($\beta_P$) are the weighted average of individual asset $\alpha$s and $\beta$s, the portfolio $R^2$ is *larger* than the average $R^2$. In our example, the $R^2$ of the three-asset portfolio, computed using the **Rsq** function in cell H21, is 59.94%, whereas the portfolio weighted-average $R^2$ of the three stocks (cell H26) is 47.4%. This almost always true: *The $R^2$ of a well-diversified portfolio is higher than the weighted average $R^2$ of the portfolio assets.* What this means is that much more of the return of a well-diversified portfolio is explained by the market return than is the return of the individual portfolio components. In other words, diversification pays by reducing the *nonmarket, nonsystematic, idiosyncratic risks* associated with a portfolio. (Note that all three of these italicized words are synonyms; in addition, the term *diversifiable risk* is also often used for this concept.)

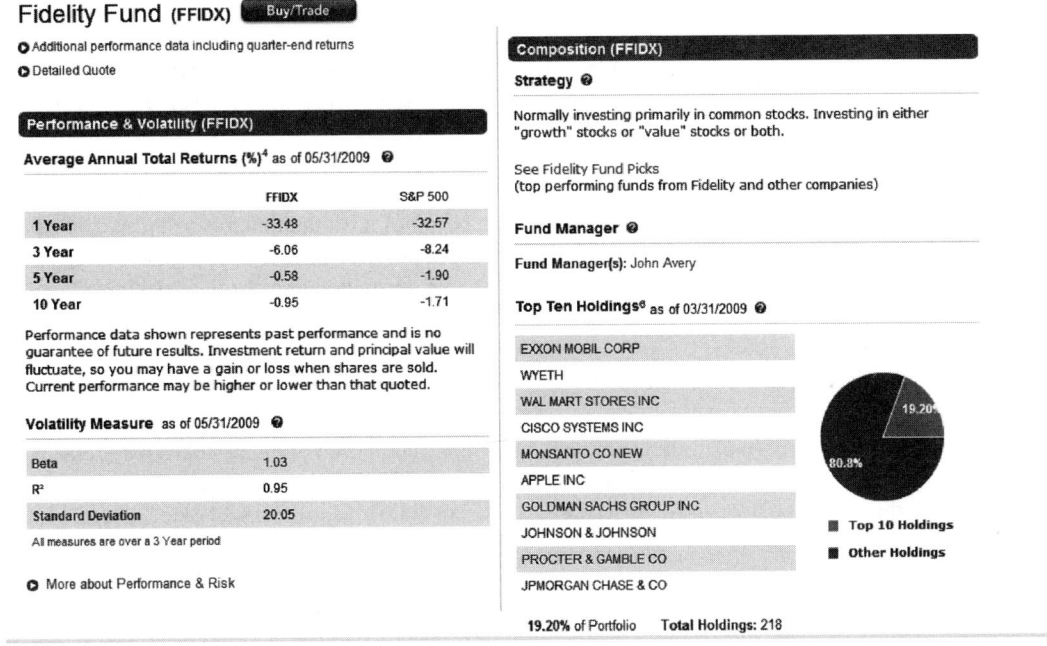

FIGURE 12.3 The Fidelity Fund has 218 stocks in its portfolio. The fund's $\beta = 1.03$, which indicates that it approximately tracks the returns of the S&P 500; on average a 1% increase in the S&P excess return was accompanied by a 1.03% increase in the Fidelity Fund's excess return (and of course, a 1% decrease in the S&P excess return meant a 1.03% decrease in the Fidelity Fund). The Fidelity Fund's $R^2$ is 95%, which means that 95% of the variability in the Fund's returns is explained by the S&P 500. Fidelity's Web site does not give information about the Fidelity Fund's $\alpha$.

Source: http://personal.fidelity.com/products/funds/mfl_frame.shtml?316153105

## Intermediate Summary

By looking at the regressions we have illustrated in the previous two sections, we can distinguish between two kinds of risk.

**Market risk:** Also called *nondiversifiable* or *systematic* risk. This is the risk measured by the $\beta$—the sensitivity of an asset's returns to the returns of the market portfolio. In the case of General Electric we saw that its $\beta_{GE} = 1.3063$, meaning that GE's stock returns were very sensitive to the excess returns on the S&P 500. The $R^2 = 86.35\%$ indicates that 86% of the variability in GE's stock returns is caused by variability in the returns of the S&P 500. Because most stocks are correlated with the market (meaning when the market goes up, the general tendency of the most stock returns is also to rise and vice versa), market risk is well nigh inevitable. The relatively low $R^2$ of Kimberly-Clark means that only about 40% of the risk of the stocks is attributable to the market risk (and for Dupont $R^2 = 15.71\%$ means that 84% of the stock's variability is due to nonmarket factors).

**Idiosyncratic stock risk:** Also called *diversifiable* or *nonsystematic* risk. This is the return riskiness that is not attributable to the market return. GE's idiosyncratic risk is very low (86% of its return variation comes from the market), but the idiosyncratic risk for KMB and DD is much higher: For these individual stocks the $R^2$ is fairly low, which means that the nonmarket components of return riskiness are much higher. Because the portfolio $R^2$ of the equally weighted portfolio is much higher than the average $R^2$, the portfolio's idiosyncratic risk is much lower than the average idiosyncratic risk of the three individual assets. This is one of the benefits of diversification—the portfolio returns "track" much better on the market return, meaning that much more of the portfolio's return is predictable by the market than is the case for the individual asset returns.

What our three-stock example shows is that when you diversify (that is, invest in a portfolio of three stocks instead of one stock), the portion of returns caused by market risk increases and the idiosyncratic portfolio risk of the portfolio becomes less than that for the individual stocks. To put this another way, for a well-diversified portfolio, the portfolio $\beta_P$ is a good description of the portfolio riskiness, *even if* the individual stocks' $\beta$s do not describe their riskiness.

---

### HOW BIG IS A WELL-DIVERSIFIED PORTFOLIO?

For a portfolio of stocks to be well diversified, it should be composed of many stocks with relatively small proportions for each stock. How many? Usually 20–30 stocks suffice to give a high $R^2$. When the $R^2$ is high (say, above 70%), most of the portfolio's risk is market risk.

---

## 12.5. What Does Academic Financial Research Tell Us about Investment Performance?

The *efficient markets hypothesis* (Chapter 14) tells us that it's very difficult to make money using only publicly available information. Thus, there's no reason to believe that investment managers can provide better investment performance than you would get in an otherwise well-diversified portfolio put together by someone (like yourself) with no "investment expertise." In fact, there are two reasons for believing that investment managers may provide worse results:

- They charge fees. (To be fair—investing on your own also involves the payment of brokerage fees, not to mention the opportunity costs of the time you would need to spend gathering information.) In the case of the two Fidelity funds we researched in this chapter, the fees are 0.40%, but mutual fund fees can go from as low as 0.05% to as high as 1.5 or even 2%.

- Many investment managers like to turn over their portfolios. This, in turn, incurs costs for the mutual fund investors and lowers returns.

For these reasons, many knowledgeable academics (and a lot of other "streetwise" types) prefer investing in index funds like the Vanguard Index 500 Fund, which we've used as an example in this chapter. The aim of these index funds is to closely match the composition of a market index like the S&P 500. These funds are able to provide a highly diversified portfolio with low costs and minimal interference in the investment decision by a portfolio manager.

A considerable amount of academic research bears out our conclusions. The average $\alpha$ of mutual funds is negative, and there is little evidence that mutual funds are able to provide superior investment performance.[9]

## Other Index Funds

Lest this chapter sound too much like an advertisement for Fidelity and Vanguard Funds, we hasten to point out that the American investor has many index funds available. Here are just a few examples (a search in Yahoo! finds at least 75 such funds).

| SOME REPRESENTATIVE S&P 500 INDEX FUNDS | | | | | |
|---|---|---|---|---|---|
| Stock symbol | Provider | Fund name | Annual expense ratio | Assets under management (June 2009) | Minimum initial investment |
| FUSVX | Fidelity | Spartan U.S. Equity Fund | 0.07% | 4.53 B | $100,000 |
| VFIAX | Vanguard | Vanguard 500 Index Admiral | 0.08% | 23.35 B | $100,000 |
| VFINX | Vanguard | Vanguard 500 Index Investor | 0.16% | 40.27 B | $3,000 |
| USSPX | USAA Investment | USAA S&P 500 Index Member | 0.23% | 1.51 B | $3,000 |
| ADIEX | RiverSource | RiverSource S & P 500 Index Fund | 0.34% | 93.95 M | $2,000 |
| PEOPX | Dreyfus | Dreyfus S&P 500 Index | 0.50% | 2.02B | $2,500 |
| SXPBX | DWS Investments | DWS S&P 500 Index Fund | 1.42% | 2.07 M | $1,000 |
| PWSPX | UBS | UBS S&P 500 Index Fund | 1.45% | 15.23 M | $1,000 |
| SNPBX | State Farm | State Farm S&P 500 Index Fund | 1.49% | 10.23 M | $250 |
| RYSOX | Rydex Investment | Rydex S&P 500 Fund | 1.51% | 29.57 M | $2,500 |

FIGURE 12.4 Some S&P 500 Index funds available to the investor. All the funds are basically alike, tracking the S&P 500 Index. Not surprisingly, the largest funds tend to be those with the lowest expense ratios.

## 12.6. Back to Jack and Jill—Who's Right?

In the preceding sections we've shown how we can measure under- or overperformance by regressing an asset's excess returns on the market's excess returns. Now let's go back to Jack and Jill. Recall that Jack was investing in the "stodgy" Puritan Fund, whereas Jill was a "go-go" investor in the NASDAQ. Over the period 1990–2003, Jill has done better than Jack, but over the period 1999–2003, she's done a lot worse.

Who's done better? Who's right?

Running the regressions of the monthly excess returns of each portfolio on the S&P 500 shows that each portfolio has earned returns commensurate with its risks. The Puritan Fund is much less risky than the NASDAQ ($\beta_{NASDAQ}$ = 1.4346, $\beta_{Puritan}$ = 0.5632). However,

---

[9] For a good academic reference on this topic, try reading "Returns from Investing in Equity Mutual Funds 1971–1991," by Burton G. Malkiel, *Journal of Finance*, June 1995.

neither investment has an $\alpha$ that is significantly different from zero, so there is no under- or overperformance.

Both Jack and Jill are getting what they're paying for—the correct risk-adjusted return. That's the nature of capital markets.

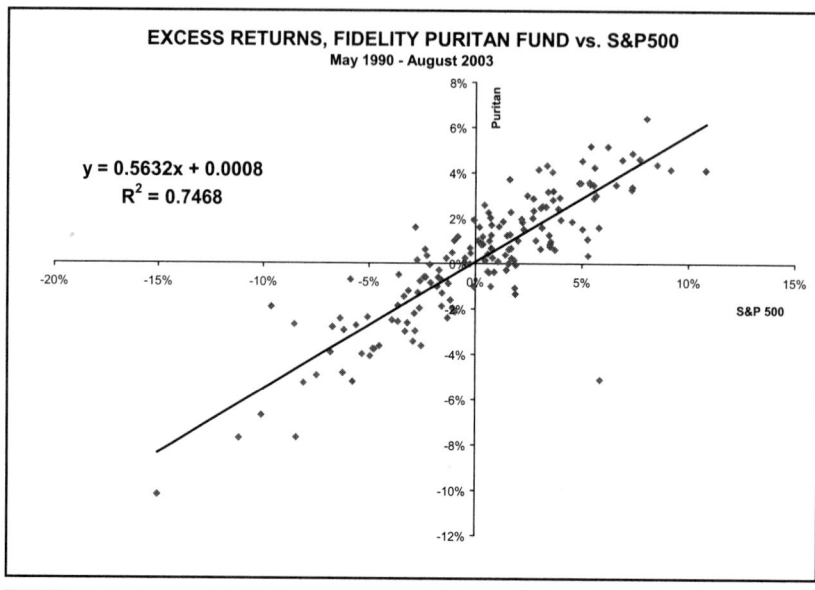

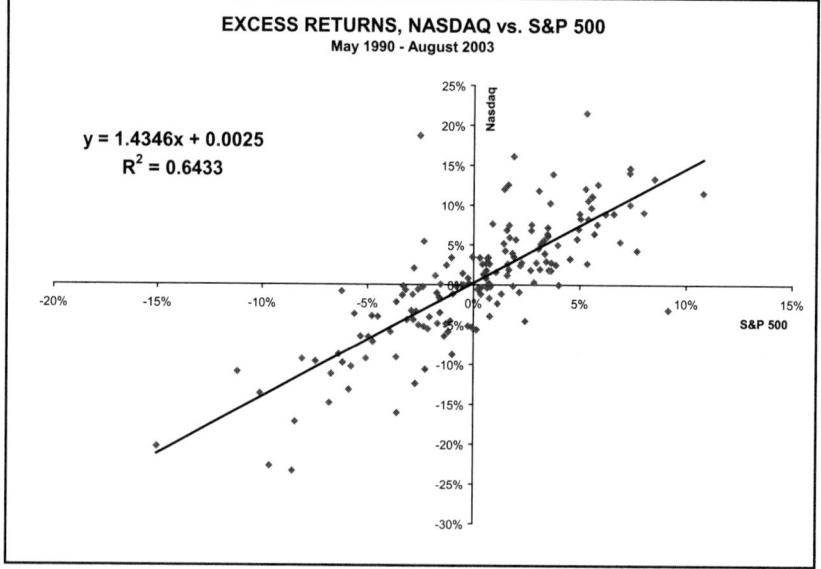

FIGURE 12.5 Analyzing the excess returns on the Puritan Fund and the NASDAQ reveals that over the period 1990–2003, the NASDAQ is almost three times as risky as Puritan ($\beta_{NASDAQ}$ = 1.4346, $\beta_{Puritan}$ = 0.5632). Neither regression reveals $\alpha$s that are significantly different from zero. In other words, both Jack and Jill are getting returns commensurate with the risk they're undertaking. There is no excess performance in either of these investments. The lower $R^2$ for the NASDAQ as opposed to Puritan (64% versus 78%) indicates that the NASDAQ has somewhat more idiosyncratic risk.

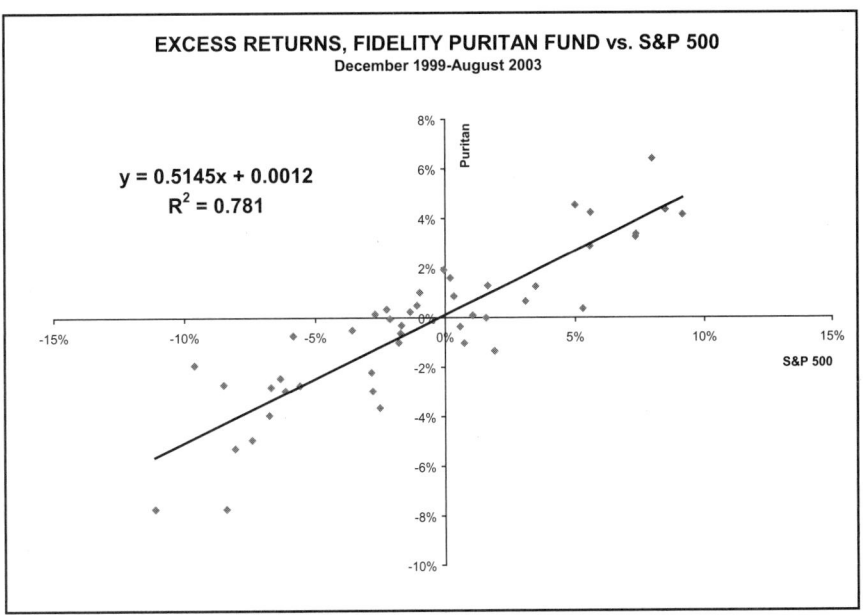

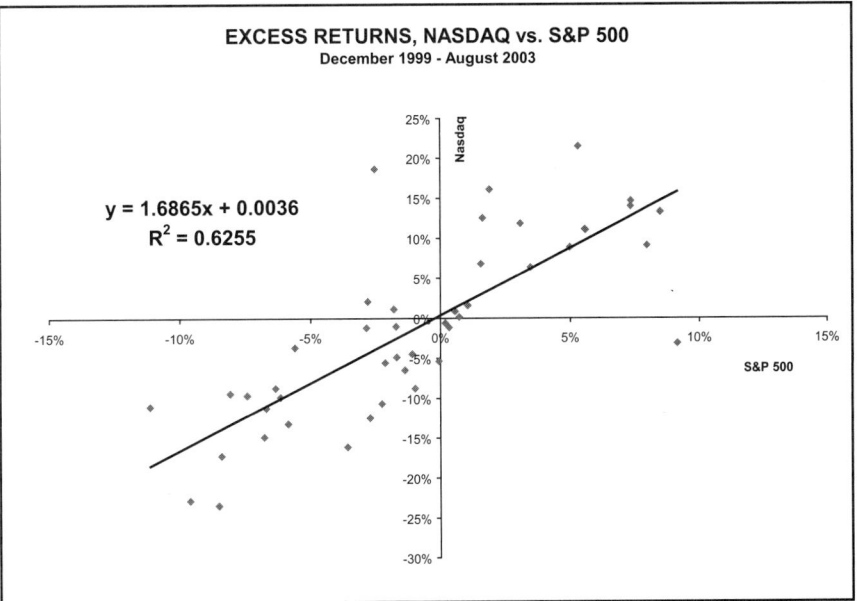

FIGURE 12.6 An analysis of the excess returns on the Puritan Fund and the NASDAQ over the period 1999–2003 reveals no substantial change in our previous conclusion. Although there are minor changes in $\beta$ and $\alpha$, neither investment exhibits excess performance or underperformance.

## Updating Jack and Jill to 2009

We originally met Jack and Jill in 2003. Six years later the author of this book is happy to report that they are still together (in fact they've married and now have two young children). They still maintain separate investment accounts, with Jill invested in the NASDAQ index and more conservative Jack invested in the Puritan Fund.

The chart below shows that our qualitative conclusions with respect to the NASDAQ versus Puritan fund haven't changed:

- Regressing the NASDAQ and Puritan returns on the S&P 500 shows that NASDAQ has become somewhat less risky ($\beta_{NASDAQ}$ has decreased from 1.687 to 1.152 over the period 2003–2009) and that Puritan has become somewhat more risky ($\beta_{Puritan}$ has increased from 0.514 to 0.706).

- There is still no evidence of outperformance for either of the funds: The $\alpha$ of the regressions is indistinguishable from zero.

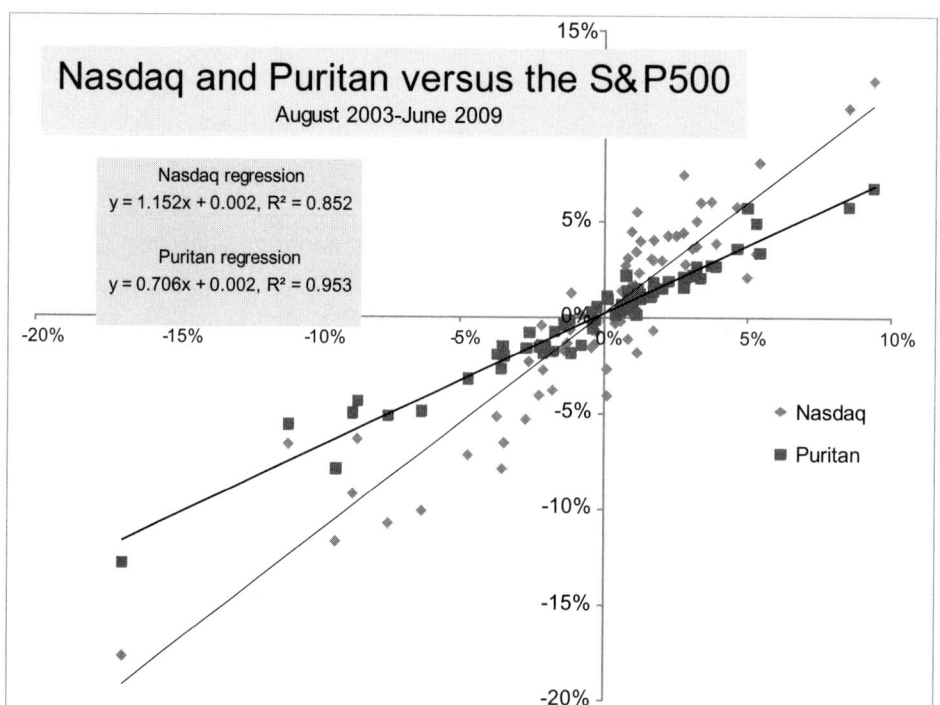

# Summary

In this chapter we have shown how to find the beta ($\beta$) and the alpha ($\alpha$) of a security and of a portfolio. We've defined the concepts of market risk (nondiversifiable risk) and idiosyncratic risk (diversifiable risk), and we've shown how forming a portfolio reduces the idiosyncratic risk. Using the $\alpha$ to measure the investment performance, we've explored the performance of various mutual funds and related this important issue to fund fees and the efficient markets hypothesis.

In Chapter 13, we'll show how the security market line (SML) can be used to compute the cost of capital for a firm.

## EXERCISES

**Note**: Data for the problems can be found on the disk that accompanies *Principles of Finance with Excel*.

1. Find the $\beta_i$ for stock $i$ based on the following data: $E(r_M) = 15\%$, $E(r_i) = 12\%$, $r_f = 7\%$.
2. Suppose that for asset $i$, $\beta_i = 1$, $E(r_i) = 21\%$. What is the market return $E(r_M)$?
3. Suppose that for asset $i$, $E(r_M) = 21\%$, $\beta_i = 0.7$, $E(r_i) = 25\%$. What is the return of the risk-free asset?
4. Consider the following data: $E(r_M) = 25\%$, $Cov(r_i, r_M) = 0.07$, $r_f = 8\%$, $Var(r_M) = 0.1$. What is the expected return of stock $i$, $E(r_i)$?
5. Consider the following data: $E(r_i) = 15\%$, $Cov(r_i, r_M) = 0.06$, $\sigma_M^2 = 0.06$. What is $E(r_M)$, the expected market return?
6. Consider the following data: $E(r_M) = 10\%$, $Cov(r_i, r_M) = 0.2$, $E(r_i) = 18\%$, $Var(r_M) = 0.09$. What is the return of the risk-free asset, $r_f$?
7. Consider the following data concerning S&P 500, FedEx, and the return on 1-year U.S. Treasury Bills.

| | A | B | C | D |
|---|---|---|---|---|
| 1 | \multicolumn{4}{c|}{FEDEX AND S&P 500} |
| 2 | Year | S&P Total return | FedEx return | 1-year T-bill |
| 3 | 1990 | -3.10% | -4.46% | 7.89% |
| 4 | 1991 | 30.47% | 24.18% | 5.86% |
| 5 | 1992 | 7.62% | 9.19% | 3.89% |
| 6 | 1993 | 10.08% | 10.67% | 3.43% |
| 7 | 1994 | 1.32% | -3.61% | 5.32% |
| 8 | 1995 | 37.58% | 24.04% | 5.94% |
| 9 | 1996 | 22.96% | 8.76% | 5.52% |
| 10 | 1997 | 33.36% | 25.95% | 5.63% |
| 11 | 1998 | 28.58% | 14.01% | 5.05% |
| 12 | 1999 | 21.04% | 30.89% | 5.08% |
| 13 | 2000 | -9.10% | -4.26% | 6.11% |
| 14 | 2001 | -11.89% | -7.20% | 3.49% |
| 15 | 2002 | -22.10% | -21.27% | 2.00% |

   a. Compute the excess returns for S&P 500 and for FedEx.
   b. Show by graphing the excess return of FedEx against that of S&P 500. Use Excel to compute the regression line and the $R^2$.
   c. Is FedEx stock an aggressive or defensive stock?
8. Consider the following data concerning S&P 500, IBM, and the return on 1-year U.S. Treasury Bills.
   a. Compute the excess returns for the S&P 500 and for IBM.
   b. Show by graphing the excess return of IBM against that of the S&P 500. Use Excel to compute the regression line and the $R^2$.
   c. Does IBM have excess performance over S&P 500?
   d. Is IBM an aggressive or defensive stock?

|   | A | B | C | D |
|---|---|---|---|---|
| 1 | **IBM AND S&P500** | | | |
| 2 | Year | **S&P Total return** | **IBM Return** | **1-year T-bill** |
| 3 | 1990 | -3.10% | 17.46% | 7.89% |
| 4 | 1991 | 30.47% | -23.87% | 5.86% |
| 5 | 1992 | 7.62% | -56.85% | 3.89% |
| 6 | 1993 | 10.08% | 11.40% | 3.43% |
| 7 | 1994 | 1.32% | 26.33% | 5.32% |
| 8 | 1995 | 37.58% | 21.75% | 5.94% |
| 9 | 1996 | 22.96% | 50.59% | 5.52% |
| 10 | 1997 | 33.36% | 32.28% | 5.63% |
| 11 | 1998 | 28.58% | 56.67% | 5.05% |
| 12 | 1999 | 21.04% | 15.71% | 5.08% |
| 13 | 2000 | -9.10% | -23.83% | 6.11% |
| 14 | 2001 | -11.89% | 35.28% | 3.49% |
| 15 | 2002 | -22.10% | -44.11% | 2.00% |

9. Using the data from Exercises 7 and 8, assume you invested in a portfolio composed of 30% IBM stock and 70% FedEx stock.

   a. Compute the excess return of the portfolio.

   b. Compute the portfolio $\beta_P$. Show three different ways to calculate the portfolio $\beta_P$:
   - Using Excel's **Slope** function.
   - Using the formula $\beta_P = Cov(r_P, r_M)/Var(r_M)$.
   - By averaging the $\beta$s of the two portfolio components, IBM and FedEx.

   c. Compute the portfolio $\alpha_P$. Show two different ways to calculate the portfolio $\alpha_P$:
   - Using Excel's **Intercept** function.
   - By taking the weighted average of the $\alpha$s of the two portfolio components IBM and FedEx.

10. Consider the data of another stock—3M Corp.

|   | A | B | C | D |
|---|---|---|---|---|
| 2 | Year | **S&P return** | **3M return** | **1-year T-bill** |
| 3 | 2001 | -0.85% | 19.23% | 5.78% |
| 4 | 2002 | -17.78% | 2.43% | 4.46% |
| 5 | 2003 | -26.25% | 13.52% | 1.85% |
| 6 | 2004 | 29.55% | 25.84% | 1.16% |
| 7 | 2005 | 5.90% | 8.23% | 1.21% |
| 8 | 2006 | 9.76% | -12.65% | 2.80% |
| 9 | 2007 | 13.40% | 4.49% | 4.55% |
| 10 | 2008 | -2.43% | 9.27% | 4.84% |
| 11 | 2009 | -48.82% | -36.46% | 2.62% |
| 12 | 2010 | 28.64% | 43.63% | 0.28% |

   a. Does 3M have excess performance?

   b. Graph the excess returns of 3M against those of S&P 500. Use Excel to compute the regression line and the $R^2$.

11. Using the data for S&P 500, FedEx, IBM, and 3M from Exercises 7, 8, and 10 above, compute the portfolio alpha, $\alpha_p$, and the portfolio beta, $\beta_p$, of a portfolio composed of 30% 3M stock, 50% FedEx stock, and 20% IBM stock. Explain the diversification advantages of this portfolio.

12. Consider the following data regarding 10 stocks, the S&P 500, and the annual risk-free rate. Your friend who works in an investment bank tells you that an equally weighted portfolio composed of these 10 stocks yields risk-adjusted excess returns when compared to the S&P 500. Check whether she's right.

| | A | B | C | D | E | F | G | H | I | J | K | L | M |
|---|---|---|---|---|---|---|---|---|---|---|---|---|---|
| 1 | ANNUAL RETURN DATA FOR TEN STOCKS, S&P500, AND RISK-FREE RATE | | | | | | | | | | | | |
| 2 | Year | Johnson & Johnson | Apple | Bank of America | PepsiCo | Reebok | Kellogg | Gillette | FedEx | IBM | 3M | S&P 500 | 1-year T-bill |
| 3 | 1990 | 21.09% | 19.90% | -66.07% | 19.75% | -48.20% | 11.50% | 24.51% | -4.46% | 17.46% | 11.03% | -3.10% | 7.89% |
| 4 | 1991 | 48.39% | 27.09% | 61.57% | 26.47% | 106.99% | 54.42% | 58.11% | 24.18% | -23.87% | 14.04% | 30.47% | 5.86% |
| 5 | 1992 | -10.76% | 5.82% | 26.73% | 20.29% | 3.60% | 2.09% | 1.36% | 9.19% | -56.85% | 8.81% | 7.62% | 3.89% |
| 6 | 1993 | -9.34% | -71.48% | -1.44% | -1.51% | -11.53% | -16.23% | 4.69% | 10.67% | 11.40% | 10.85% | 10.08% | 3.43% |
| 7 | 1994 | 22.27% | 28.80% | -4.51% | -12.05% | 28.36% | 2.37% | 22.80% | -3.61% | 26.33% | 1.49% | 1.32% | 5.32% |
| 8 | 1995 | 46.47% | -20.16% | 46.87% | 43.30% | -32.59% | 28.44% | 33.10% | 24.04% | 21.75% | 25.03% | 37.58% | 5.94% |
| 9 | 1996 | 16.63% | -42.32% | 36.74% | 4.58% | 40.34% | -16.30% | 39.99% | 8.76% | 50.59% | 25.04% | 22.96% | 5.52% |
| 10 | 1997 | 29.51% | -46.31% | 24.12% | 21.46% | -37.53% | 41.37% | 25.60% | 25.95% | 32.28% | 1.20% | 33.36% | 5.63% |
| 11 | 1998 | 25.43% | 113.64% | 1.29% | 12.02% | -66.07% | -37.45% | -4.92% | 14.01% | 56.67% | -11.70% | 28.58% | 5.05% |
| 12 | 1999 | 11.77% | 92.07% | -15.09% | -14.82% | -59.71% | -10.20% | -14.90% | 30.89% | 15.71% | 34.43% | 21.04% | 5.08% |
| 13 | 2000 | 13.31% | -123.96% | -4.61% | 34.07% | 120.54% | -16.02% | -12.09% | -4.26% | -23.83% | 20.79% | -9.10% | 6.11% |
| 14 | 2001 | 13.10% | 38.65% | 35.56% | -1.77% | -3.12% | 13.69% | -5.59% | -7.20% | 35.28% | -1.92% | -11.89% | 3.49% |
| 15 | 2002 | -8.20% | -42.41% | 13.59% | -14.26% | 10.38% | 12.97% | -7.50% | -21.27% | -44.11% | 4.22% | -22.10% | 2.00% |

13. Consider the following annual data regarding Fidelity Balanced Fund (FBALX), the S&P 500 stock index fund, and the T-bill rate. Did the fund manager outperform the market?

| | A | B | C | D | E | F | G |
|---|---|---|---|---|---|---|---|
| 1 | RETURN DATA FOR FBALX FUND, S&P500 AND THE RISK-FREE RATE | | | | | | |
| 2 | Year | FBALX return | S&P return | 1-year T-bill | | S&P 500 excess return | FBALX excess return |
| 3 | 2001 | 10.65% | -1.04% | 5.78% | | -6.82% | 4.88% |
| 4 | 2002 | -1.32% | -17.85% | 4.46% | | -22.30% | -5.78% |
| 5 | 2003 | -9.75% | -26.47% | 1.85% | | -28.31% | -11.59% |
| 6 | 2004 | 28.14% | 29.53% | 1.16% | | 28.37% | 26.98% |
| 7 | 2005 | 7.37% | 5.86% | 1.21% | | 4.66% | 6.17% |
| 8 | 2006 | 15.38% | 9.71% | 2.80% | | 6.92% | 12.59% |
| 9 | 2007 | 8.54% | 13.33% | 4.55% | | 8.77% | 3.99% |
| 10 | 2008 | 2.45% | -2.47% | 4.84% | | -7.32% | -2.39% |
| 11 | 2009 | -37.04% | -48.89% | 2.62% | | -51.51% | -39.66% |
| 12 | 2010 | 26.86% | 28.60% | 0.28% | | 28.32% | 26.57% |

# The Security Market Line and the Cost of Capital

## CHAPTER CONTENTS

## Overview

This is the second of two chapters that show the use of the security market line (SML). In Chapter 12 we discussed the use of the SML for performance measurement, and in this chapter we discuss how to use the SML to calculate the cost of capital for a firm.[1]

---

[1] If you need a lightning review of the SML, look at the first section of Chapter 12.

The weighted average cost of capital (WACC) is the minimum return that a firm must earn to satisfy its shareholders and bondholders. As discussed in Section 6.6, the WACC has two major uses:

- Using WACC in capital budgeting: When evaluating a project whose risk is comparable to the riskiness of the company's current activities, the WACC is the appropriate discount rate for the project's cash flows.
- Using WACC to value a company: The value of a company is based on the PV of its future FCFs discounted at the WACC.

In this book we previously discussed the WACC in Chapter 6, where we used the Gordon model to calculate the cost of equity. In this chapter we use the SML to calculate the cost of equity. These two models—the Gordon model and the SML—are the major approaches to computing the cost of equity for a firm.

## Finance Concepts Discussed in This Chapter

- The use of security market line (SML) to calculate the cost of equity $r_E$ for a firm.
- Calculating the firm's weighted average cost of capital (WACC). Note that the computation of the WACC was also discussed in Chapter 6, where we used the Gordon model to calculate the firm's cost of equity $r_E$.
- Calculating the market value of the firm's debt and equity, the firm's tax rate $TC$, and the firm's cost of debt $r_D$. Our discussion of these issues in this chapter is in many ways a repeat of a similar discussion in Chapter 6.
- The concept of *asset beta*, $\beta_{Assets}$, and its use as an alternative method to calculate the firm's WACC.

Throughout this chapter we assume that you know how to calculate the $\beta$ of a stock (this issue was discussed in the previous chapter). In actual fact, you often don't have to compute the $\beta$ of a firm's shares—the information is publicly available (in this chapter, for example, we use data on $\beta$ provided by Yahoo!).

## Excel Functions Used

- **NPV**
- **Average**

## 13.1. The CAPM and the Firm's Cost of Equity—An Initial Example

Abracadabra, Inc. is considering a new project, which has the following free cash flows (FCF).[2]

---

[2] An extended discussion of the free cash flow (FCF) is given in Chapters 6 and 7. Figure 13.1 reviews the concept in tabular form.

| | A | B |
|---|---|---|
| 2 | **Year** | **FCF** |
| 3 | 0 | -1,000 |
| 4 | 1 | 1,323 |
| 5 | 2 | 1,569 |
| 6 | 3 | 3,288 |
| 7 | 4 | 1,029 |
| 8 | 5 | 1,425 |
| 9 | 6 | 622 |
| 10 | 7 | 3,800 |
| 11 | 8 | 3,800 |
| 12 | 9 | 3,800 |
| 13 | 10 | 2,700 |

To decide whether to accept or reject the project, the company needs to calculate the risk-adjusted discount rate for these cash flows. The company decides that the riskiness of the new project is very much like the riskiness of Abracadabra's current activities; the financing for the project is also similar to that of the firm. In this case the appropriate discount rate is the weighted

| Defining the Free Cash Flow (FCF) | |
|---|---|
| Profit after taxes | This is the basic measure of the profitability of the business, but it is an accounting measure that includes financing flows (such as interest), as well as noncash expenses such as depreciation. Profit after taxes does not account for either changes in the firm's working capital or purchases of new fixed assets, both of which can be important cash drains on the firm. |
| + Depreciation | This noncash expense is added back to the profit after tax. |
| + After-tax interest payments (net) | FCF is an attempt to measure the cash produced by the business activity of the firm and available to both equity and debtholders. To neutralize the effect of interest payments on the firm's profits, we<br>Add back the after-tax cost of interest on debt (*after-tax* because interest payments are tax deductible),<br>Subtract out the after-tax interest income on cash and marketable securities. |
| – Increase in current assets | When the firm's sales increase, more investment is needed in inventories, accounts receivable, etc. This increase in current assets is not an expense for tax purposes (and is therefore ignored in the profit after taxes), but it is a cash drain on the company. |
| + Increase in current liabilities | An increase in sales often causes an increase in financing related to sales (such as accounts payable or taxes payable). This increase in current liabilities—when related to sales—provides cash to the firm. Because it is directly related to sales, we include this cash in the FCF calculations. |
| – Increase in fixed assets at cost | An increase in fixed assets (the long-term productive assets of the company) is a use of cash, which reduces the firm's FCF. |
| FCF = sum of the above | |

FIGURE 13.1 The free cash flow (FCF) is the amount of cash generated by a firm's business activities. Discounting the FCFs at a firm's weighted average cost of capital (WACC) gives the enterprise value of the firm. The concept of FCF was introduced in Chapter 6. It appears in several other places in this book: In the context of accounting and financial planning models, we used the FCF in Chapter 7 to value a firm. In Chapter 16 we return to the concept of FCF in the context of stock valuation.

average cost of capital (WACC); this is the average cost of financing the firm's activities. Assuming that Abracadabra has both equity and debt, the formula for the WACC is given by

$$WACC = r_E * \frac{E}{E+D} + r_D * (1-T_C) * \frac{D}{E+D}$$

$$= \begin{pmatrix} r_E = \\ \text{cost of} \\ \text{equity} \end{pmatrix} * \begin{pmatrix} \text{proportion} \\ \text{of firm} \\ \text{financed by} \\ \text{equity} \end{pmatrix} + \begin{pmatrix} r_D = \\ \text{cost of} \\ \text{debt} \end{pmatrix} * \begin{pmatrix} 1-T_C = \\ 1-\text{corporate} \\ \text{tax rate} \end{pmatrix} * \begin{pmatrix} \text{proportion} \\ \text{of firm} \\ \text{financed by} \\ \text{debt} \end{pmatrix}$$

We can use the SML to calculate the cost of equity for Abracadabra. Here are our assumptions for this problem:

- The firm's stock has beta $\beta = 1.4$.
- The expected market return is $E(r_M) = 10\%$.
- The risk-free rate $r_f = 4\%$.
- Abracadabra's equity has a market value $E = \$10,000$.
- Abracadabra's debt has a market value $D = \$15,000$.
- Abracadabra can borrow new funds at a cost of $r_D = 6\%$.
- Abracadabra's corporate tax rate is $T_C = 40\%$.

The first three assumptions mean that Abracadabra's cost of equity $r_E$ as given by the SML is 12.4%:

$$r_E = r_f + \beta * \left[ E(r_M) - r_f \right]$$
$$= 4\% + 1.4 * \left[ 10\% - 4\% \right] = 12.4\%$$

Then Abracadabra's weighted average cost of capital (WACC) is

$$WACC = r_E * \frac{E}{E+D} + r_D * (1-T_C) * \frac{D}{E+D}$$
$$= 12.4\% * \frac{10,000}{10,000+15,000} + 6\% * (1-40\%) * \frac{15,000}{10,000+15,000}$$
$$= 7.12\%$$

The WACC of 7.12% is the discount rate we will use to determine whether Abracadabra should undertake the project.

The following spreadsheet shows our calculations for the WACC (rows 20–36) and the NPV calculation for the project (rows 2–16).

| | A | B | C |
|---|---|---|---|
| 1 | VALUING ABRACADABRA'S INVESTMENT<br>we calculate the WACC using the SML to<br>compute the cost of equity $r_E$ | | |
| 2 | Year | FCF | |
| 3 | 0 | -1,000 | |
| 4 | 1 | 1,323 | |
| 5 | 2 | 1,569 | |
| 6 | 3 | 3,288 | |
| 7 | 4 | 1,029 | |
| 8 | 5 | 1,425 | |
| 9 | 6 | 622 | |
| 10 | 7 | 3,800 | |
| 11 | 8 | 3,800 | |
| 12 | 9 | 3,800 | |
| 13 | 10 | 2,700 | |
| 14 | | | |
| 15 | Weighted average cost of capital, WACC | 7.12% | <-- =B36 |
| 16 | Project NPV | 14,424 | <-- =NPV(B15,B4:B13)+B3 |
| 17 | | | |
| 18 | | | |
| 19 | Computing Abracadabra's Weighted Average Cost of Capital (WACC) | | |
| 20 | Market value of equity, E | 10,000 | |
| 21 | Market value of debt, D | 15,000 | |
| 22 | Market value of equity + debt, E+D | 25,000 | |
| 23 | | | |
| 24 | Corporate tax rate, $T_C$ | 40% | |
| 25 | | | |
| 26 | Abracadabra's stock beta, β | 1.4 | |
| 27 | | | |
| 28 | Facts about market | | |
| 29 | $E(r_M)$ | 10% | |
| 30 | $r_f$ | 4% | |
| 31 | | | |
| 32 | Abracadabra's cost of capital | | |
| 33 | Cost of equity using SML, $r_E$ | 12.40% | <-- =B30+B26*(B29-B30) |
| 34 | Cost of debt, $r_D$ | 6.00% | |
| 35 | | | |
| 36 | Weighted average cost of capital (WACC) | 7.12% | <-- =B20/B22*B33+B21/B22*B34*(1-B24) |

When the project free cash flows are discounted at the WACC, the net present value is $14,424 (cell B16). Because the NPV is positive, Abracadabra should undertake the project.

## Comparing the SML and the Gordon Model for Calculating the WACC

The weighted average cost of capital is the most widely used discount rate for computing the value of corporate projects and for computing the value of the firm. The WACC depends critically on the cost of equity $r_E$. In this chapter we compute the cost of equity using the security market line (SML), whereas in Chapter 6 we computed the cost of equity using the Gordon dividend model.

The Gordon dividend model and the SML are only two practical ways of calculating the cost of equity.[3] Both models have their advantages and disadvantages—the Gordon model is simple to calculate but is very sensitive to assumptions about the firm's equity payout—the total dividends plus stock repurchases of the firm. The SML requires relatively more calculations, but is more widely used. The SML also requires us to make assumptions about the expected return on the market $E(r_M)$. This problem is discussed in the next section.

So which model should you use in practice? The best answer is to *use both models* and to compare the results. This way each model can serve as a "reality check" on the other. We apply this logic in Chapter 16, which discusses stock valuation. There we apply both models and compare the results to see whether we have arrived at an appropriate WACC.

## 13.2. Using the SML to Calculate the Cost of Capital— Calculating the Parameter Values

The Abracadabra example of the previous section gives the broad outlines of calculating the cost of capital using the SML, but it leaves a number of questions unanswered:

- How do we calculate the market value of a firm's equity, $E$?
- How do we calculate the expected return on the market $E(r_M)$?
- How do we calculate the risk-free rate, $r_f$?
- How do we calculate the market value of a firm's debt, $D$?
- How do we calculate the firm's cost of borrowing, $r_D$?
- How do we calculate the firm's corporate tax rate $T_C$?

We discuss each of these questions in turn. Although we occasionally provide an illustration, we save a full-blown example for the following section.

### The Market Value of a Firm's Equity, E

This is easy: For a firm whose shares are sold on the stock market, the market value of the equity ($E$ in our WACC equation) is the number of shares times the market value per share.

### The Expected Return on the Market $E(r_M)$

There are two ways to calculate the expected return on the market: (1) We can use the *historical* market return or (2) we can use a version of the Gordon dividend model to derive $E(r_M)$ from current market data. Neither method is perfect, although we prefer the latter.

### $E(r_M)$ Using the Historic Returns

A standard technique is to use a broad-based index—usually the S&P 500 Index—to proxy for the market portfolio. To do this, you need some data. Below we show you the returns on Vanguard's 500 Index Fund. This is an index mutual fund that is invested in the S&P 500 Index.[4] The average return on the S&P is 8.70% for the period 1994–2008 (cell F20). This

---

[3] The academic finance literature has come up with other models for calculating the cost of equity, but in practice these models are very difficult to apply and are rarely used.
[4] We discuss index funds in Chapter 12, Section 12.4.

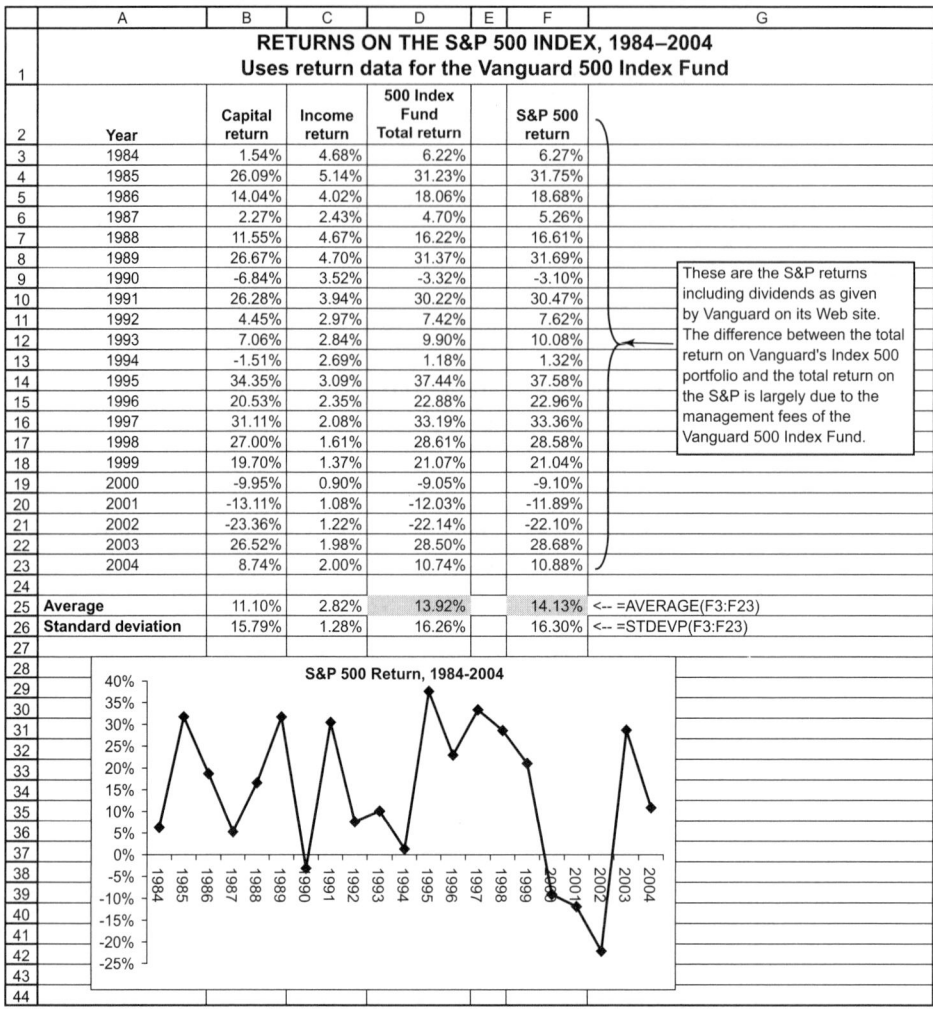

| | A | B | C | D | E | F | G |
|---|---|---|---|---|---|---|---|
| 1 | | | | **RETURNS ON THE S&P 500 INDEX, 1984–2004** | | | |
| | | | | **Uses return data for the Vanguard 500 Index Fund** | | | |
| 2 | Year | Capital return | Income return | 500 Index Fund Total return | | S&P 500 return | |
| 3 | 1984 | 1.54% | 4.68% | 6.22% | | 6.27% | |
| 4 | 1985 | 26.09% | 5.14% | 31.23% | | 31.75% | |
| 5 | 1986 | 14.04% | 4.02% | 18.06% | | 18.68% | |
| 6 | 1987 | 2.27% | 2.43% | 4.70% | | 5.26% | |
| 7 | 1988 | 11.55% | 4.67% | 16.22% | | 16.61% | |
| 8 | 1989 | 26.67% | 4.70% | 31.37% | | 31.69% | |
| 9 | 1990 | -6.84% | 3.52% | -3.32% | | -3.10% | These are the S&P returns including dividends as given by Vanguard on its Web site. The difference between the total return on Vanguard's Index 500 portfolio and the total return on the S&P is largely due to the management fees of the Vanguard 500 Index Fund. |
| 10 | 1991 | 26.28% | 3.94% | 30.22% | | 30.47% | |
| 11 | 1992 | 4.45% | 2.97% | 7.42% | | 7.62% | |
| 12 | 1993 | 7.06% | 2.84% | 9.90% | | 10.08% | |
| 13 | 1994 | -1.51% | 2.69% | 1.18% | | 1.32% | |
| 14 | 1995 | 34.35% | 3.09% | 37.44% | | 37.58% | |
| 15 | 1996 | 20.53% | 2.35% | 22.88% | | 22.96% | |
| 16 | 1997 | 31.11% | 2.08% | 33.19% | | 33.36% | |
| 17 | 1998 | 27.00% | 1.61% | 28.61% | | 28.58% | |
| 18 | 1999 | 19.70% | 1.37% | 21.07% | | 21.04% | |
| 19 | 2000 | -9.95% | 0.90% | -9.05% | | -9.10% | |
| 20 | 2001 | -13.11% | 1.08% | -12.03% | | -11.89% | |
| 21 | 2002 | -23.36% | 1.22% | -22.14% | | -22.10% | |
| 22 | 2003 | 26.52% | 1.98% | 28.50% | | 28.68% | |
| 23 | 2004 | 8.74% | 2.00% | 10.74% | | 10.88% | |
| 24 | | | | | | | |
| 25 | Average | 11.10% | 2.82% | 13.92% | | 14.13% | <-- =AVERAGE(F3:F23) |
| 26 | Standard deviation | 15.79% | 1.28% | 16.26% | | 16.30% | <-- =STDEVP(F3:F23) |
| 27 | | | | | | | |

S&P 500 Return, 1984-2004

*historical average return* is often used as a proxy for the *expected market return* in the SML. The Vanguard 500 Index Fund data show the breakdown of these returns between capital gains (6.77% per year) and dividends (1.84% annually).

## $E(r_M)$ Using Current Market Data

This technique is less widely used, although we prefer it.[5] The technique is based on the Gordon dividend model that gives the expected return on a stock as a function of the stock's current equity payout $Div0$, the current market value of the firm's equity $P0$, and the expected growth rate of $g$ of the equity payout. The equity payout is defined as the sum of the firm's dividends and its stock repurchases (see Chapter 6, page 198, for a full explanation):

---

[5] The technique was first published in *Corporate Finance: A Valuation Approach* by Simon Benninga and Oded Sarig, McGraw–Hill, 1997.

*Gordon Dividend Model*

$$r_E = \frac{Div_0(1+g)}{P_0} + g$$

where

$Div_0$ = current equity payout of firm (total dividends + stock repurchases)

$P_0$ = current market value of equity

$g$ = anticipated equity payout growth rate

To use the Gordon model to calculate the expected return on the market, we restate the model in terms of the price-earnings ratio: Assume that every year the firm pays out a percentage *b* of its earnings to its shareholders, in the form of both dividends and stock repurchases. Then we can rewrite the formula above as

$$r_E = \frac{Div_0(1+g)}{P_0} + g = \frac{b * EPS_0(1+g)}{P_0} + g$$

where $EPS_0$ is the firm's current earnings per share

Manipulating this formula a bit, we get

$$r_E = \frac{b*(1+g)}{\underbrace{P_0 / EPS_0}} + g$$

this is the firm's
P/E (price-earnings)
ratio

We now apply this logic to the market as a whole. We regard a market index such as the S&P 500 (symbolized by *M*) as a stock having its own payout ratio *b* and growth rate of equity payouts *g*. We then use the above formula to compute the expected market return $E(r_M)$.[6] Here's an example using data for the S&P 500 Index on 30 September 2009. We have had to "guesstimate" the estimated growth of dividends and the dividend payout ratio. We also show the historical series for the price-earnings data; the average over 1988–2009 is 19.41.

---

[6]A sensitive reader may note that there's some confusion of symbols here. The formula $r_E = \frac{b*(1+g)}{P_0 / EPS_0} + g$ uses $r_E$ to stand for the cost of equity for a stock. Because the "cost of equity" is a synonym for the "expected return from equity," when we apply the formula to the market portfolio *M* (in this case, the S&P 500), by logic we should have called this $r_M$. Instead, we use $E(r_M)$. Our excuse is that the symbol $E(r_M)$ is so widely used that we cannot give it up.

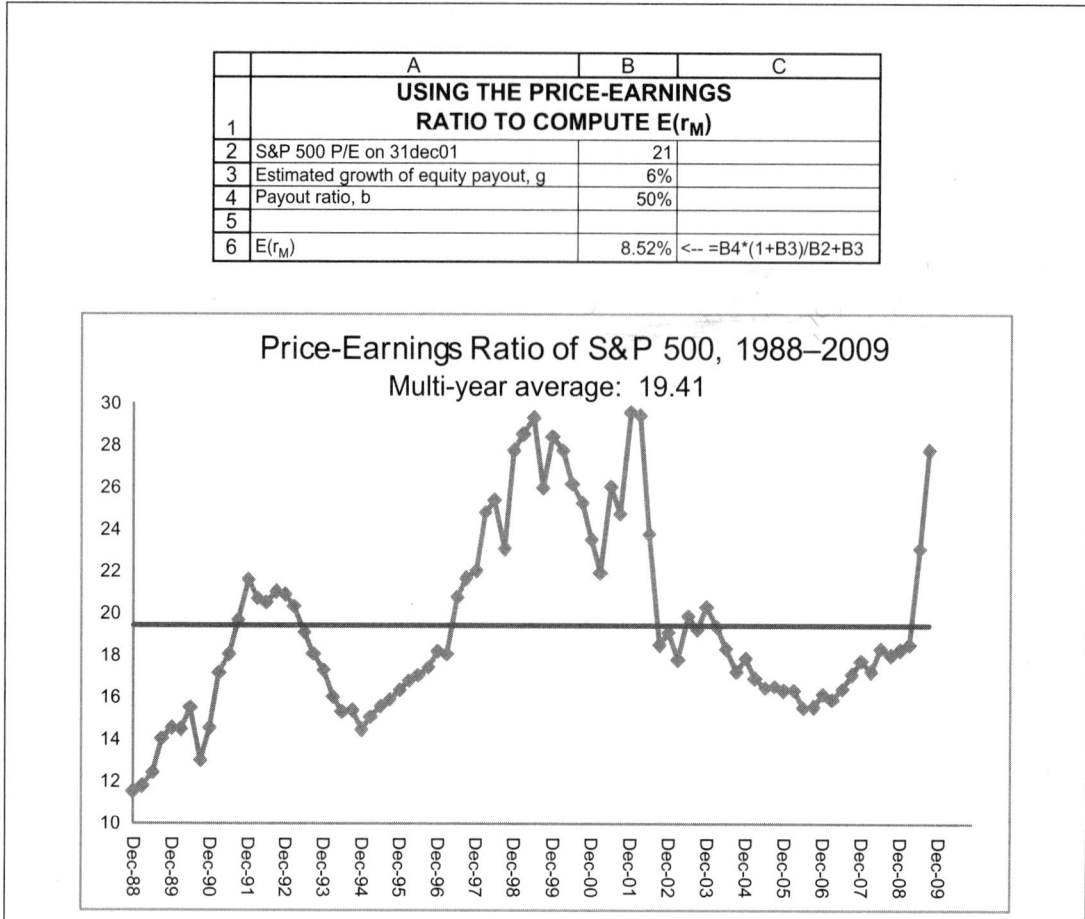

| | A | B | C |
|---|---|---|---|
| 1 | USING THE PRICE-EARNINGS RATIO TO COMPUTE E(r$_M$) | | |
| 2 | S&P 500 P/E on 31dec01 | 21 | |
| 3 | Estimated growth of equity payout, g | 6% | |
| 4 | Payout ratio, b | 50% | |
| 5 | | | |
| 6 | E(r$_M$) | 8.52% | <-- =B4*(1+B3)/B2+B3 |

FIGURE 13.2 The Excel example shows how to use the P/E ratio of the S&P 500 to compute $E(r_M)$. The graph (source: www.marketattributes.standardandpoors.com ) shows the P/E of the S&P 500 from 1988-2009.

*Source*: www.marketattributes.standardandpoors.com

**Dividend payout** is defined as the total expended by firms on both cash dividends and repurchases of shares (we discussed this topic a bit in Chapter 6, when calculating the cost of equity for Courier Corp. using the Gordon model). Although the cash dividends are a matter of record, the amount of repurchases is more debatable. Current estimates put the sum of dividends and repurchases at around 50% of corporate earnings. Figure 13.3, for example, is a graph showing the relation between share repurchases and dividends for the S&P 500 Index through 2005.

**Dividend growth** is the market anticipation of the growth of total dividends (broadly defined as cash dividends plus repurchases) for the future. If we assume that dividends will grow at the rate of growth of the economy, 6% is a reasonable long-term estimate.

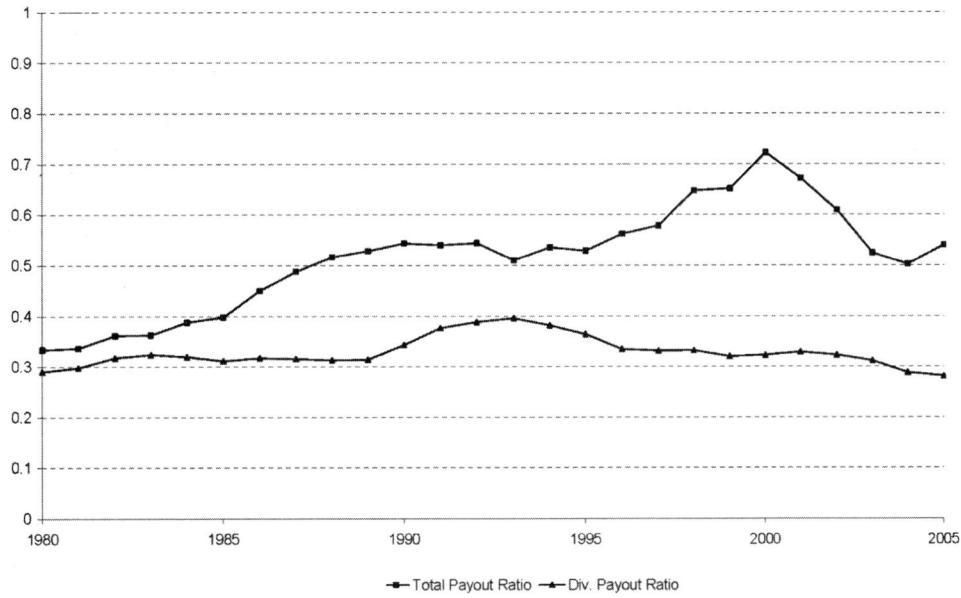

FIGURE 13.3  The dividend payout ratio (lower line) and the total payout ratio (dividends + repurchases) in the United States.
*Source*: Douglas Skinner, "The Evolving Relation Between Earnings, Dividends, and Stock Repurchases," *Journal of Financial Economics*, March 2008.

## Computing the Risk-Free Rate $r_f$

The risk-free rate $r_f$ should be the short-term Treasury rate. This rate is available from a variety of places, including Yahoo! (see example in next section).

## Computing the Value of the Firm's Debt, D

In principle, *D* should be the *market value* of the firm's debt. However, in practice, this value is usually very difficult to calculate. Standard practice is to use the book value of the firm's debt *minus* the value of its cash reserves; we refer to this concept as *net debt*.

## Computing the Firm's Borrowing Rate, $r_D$

The rate $r_D$ used in the WACC formula ought to be the firm's *marginal cost of borrowing*, the rate at which it can borrow additional funds through sales of bonds or from banks. In many cases, however, the marginal cost of borrowing is very difficult to calculate. Two common "quick fixes" are as follows:

- Compute $r_D$ from the firm's average borrowing rate.
- Compute $r_D$ by "eyeballing" the firm's current borrowing rate from information given in the financial statements.

Both approaches are illustrated in Section 13.3.

## Computing the Corporate Tax Rate, $T_C$

The tax rate $T_C$ used in the WACC formula ought to be the firm's *marginal tax rate*, the rate the firm would have to pay on an addition dollar of income. This rate is very difficult to determine, and two "quick fixes" are common:

- In many cases the firm's average tax rate is an acceptable proxy for $T_C$. This is the case for Hilton Hotels in Section 13.3.

- In some cases we might prefer to use information about the average corporate tax rate in the economy. This rate is approximately 37%.[7] For a firm whose own historical tax rate is not a good predictor of its future tax rate, this number might be a preferable substitute.

# 13.3. A Worked-Out Example—Hilton Hotels

We illustrate the approach to calculating the WACC using data for Hilton Hotels Corp. (symbol HLT). As discussed previously, we need seven parameters to calculate the WACC for this (or any other) company:

- $E$, the market value of the company's equity today. This is simply the number of shares times the current stock price.
- $D$, the market value of the company's debt today. We will use the *book value* (that is, the accounting value) of the company's debt as a proxy for this number.
- $r_E$, the cost of equity for the company. In this chapter we use the SML to calculate the cost of equity. Using the SML means that the cost of equity is dependent on the following:
  - The $\beta$ of the firm's equity. In the previous chapter we computed this $\beta$. In practice, it is often available without computation (as in this example; read on).
  - $r_f$, the risk-free rate.
  - $E(r_M)$, the expected return on the market.
- $r_D$, the cost of debt for the company. In principle, this should be the marginal cost (the company's cost of obtaining new debt). In practice, we often use the company's average cost of existing debt.
- $T_C$, the company's tax rate. In principle, this should be the company's marginal tax rate (the rate on an additional dollar of earnings). In practice we often use the company's average tax rate.

Much of the data are available on Yahoo!; Figure 13.4 shows the Yahoo! screen leading to Hilton Hotel's "key statistics," which are shown in Figure 13.5.

---

[7] The Federal tax rate in the United States is 35% (see Chapter 2). Because companies also pay state and local taxes, the tax rate for most companies is somewhere between 35 and 40%.

F<small>IGURE</small> 13.4 The Yahoo! screen, indicating the **Key Statistics**. This choice gives the updated financial information for the firm used below. (Yahoo!'s presentation of financial materials changes occasionally, so that you may have to look elsewhere for the financial profile.)

From Yahoo!'s Profile, here are some data for Hilton as of 21 January 2005. From these data we learn the following:

- Hilton's equity $\beta_E = 0.956$.

- The current value of a share of Hilton is $22.49. The number of shares outstanding is 386.03 million. The market value of Hilton's equity is the product of these two numbers, giving E = $8.68 billion.

- The book value of Hilton's debt is D = $3.743 billion. With a bit of work, this number can be calculated from Yahoo!: According to Yahoo!:

    - The book value of equity per share is $6.388.

    - The debt/equity ratio of Hilton is 1.518. This is the ratio of the book value of the firm's debt to the book value of its equity.

Because Hilton has 386.03 million shares outstanding, its total book value of equity is $386.03 * 6.388 = 2,466$. Multiplying this number by the debt-to-equity ratio gives the total debt of Hilton as $3,743. From this number we subtract the $219 million in cash held by the company to arrive at net debt $D = \$3,524$.[8]

---

[8] Cash is subtracted from the firm's debt because Hilton could, in principle, use the cash to pay off some of its debt.

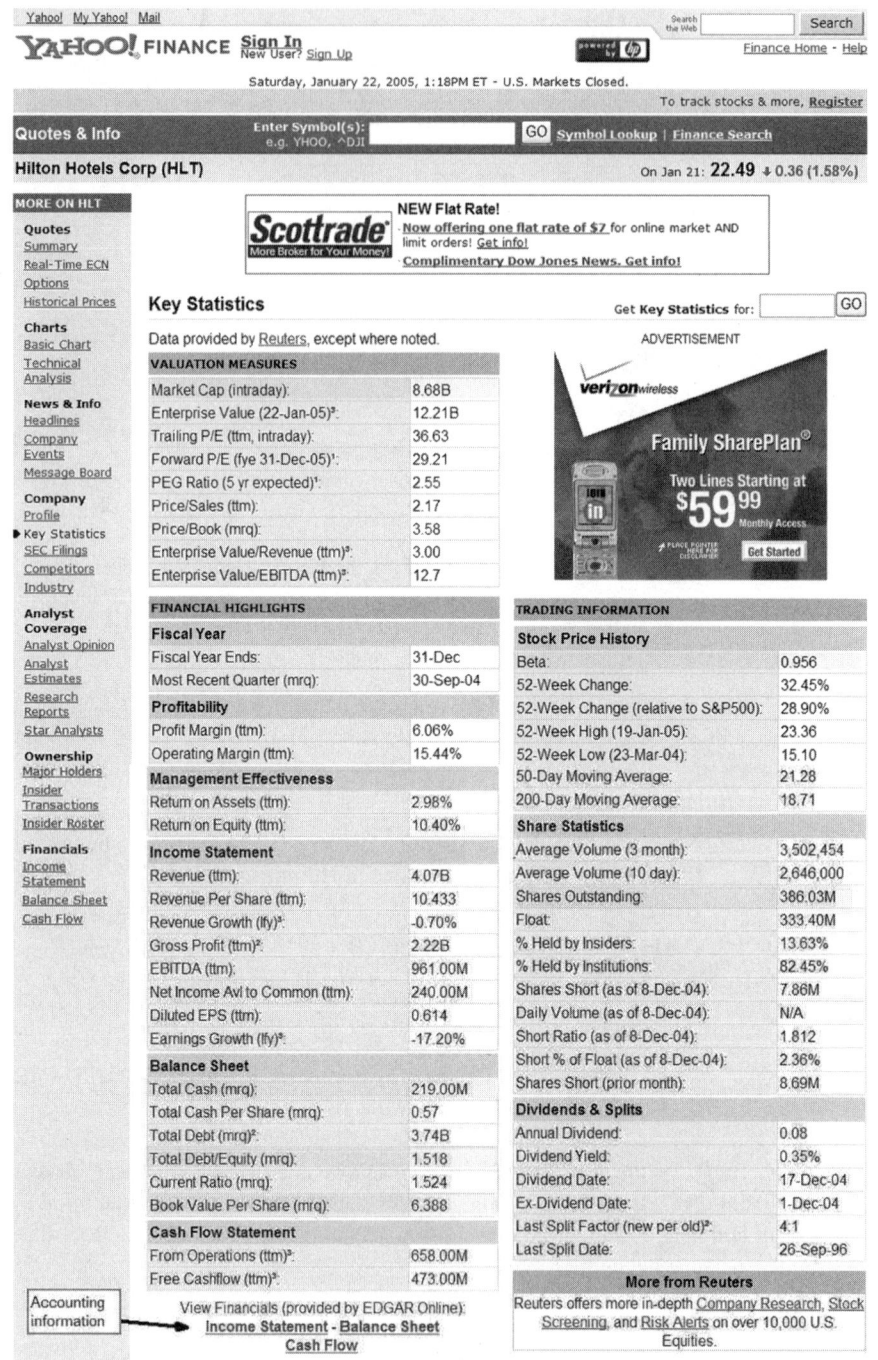

FIGURE 13.5  Yahoo!'s profile for Hilton Hotels. Highlighted numbers are used in the computation of Hilton's WACC.

| | A | B | C |
|---|---|---|---|
| 1 | **HILTON HOTELS CORPORATION (HLT)** <br> **using Yahoo! for much of the information** | | |
| 2 | Equity beta | 0.956 | <-- Yahoo |
| 3 | | | |
| 4 | Shares outstanding (million) | 386.03 | <-- Yahoo |
| 5 | Market value per share | 22.49 | <-- Yahoo |
| 6 | Market value of equity ($ million), E | 8,682 | <-- =B5*B4 |
| 7 | | | |
| 8 | Book value of equity per share | 6.388 | <-- Yahoo |
| 9 | Total book value of equity | 2,466 | <-- =B8*B4 |
| 10 | Debt/Equity ratio | 1.518 | <-- Yahoo |
| 11 | Book value of debt | 3,743 | <-- =B10*B9 |
| 12 | Cash on hand | 219 | <-- Yahoo |
| 13 | Net debt ($ million), D | 3,524 | <-- =B11-B12 |

We still need the two firm-related parameters $(r_D, T_C)$ and two market parameters $(r_f, E(r_M))$. For these, we'll have to work a bit. We can access the Hilton financial statements by clicking on the accounting information at the bottom of the first column of Figure 13.5. The quarterly income statements and balance sheets thus obtained are shown in Figure 13.6.

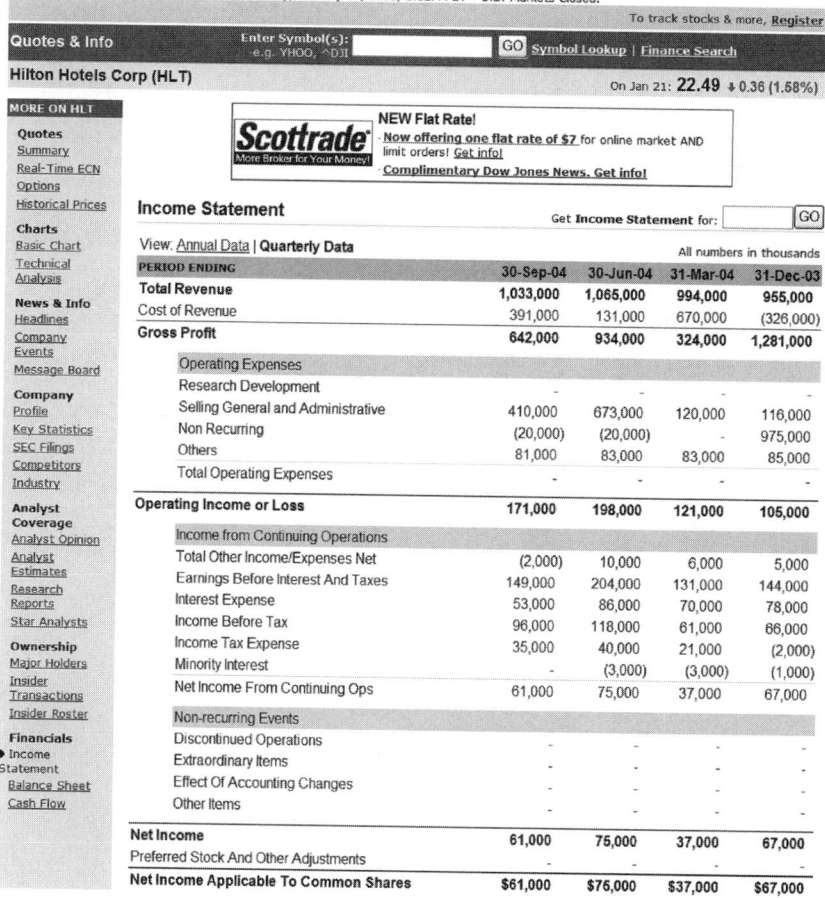

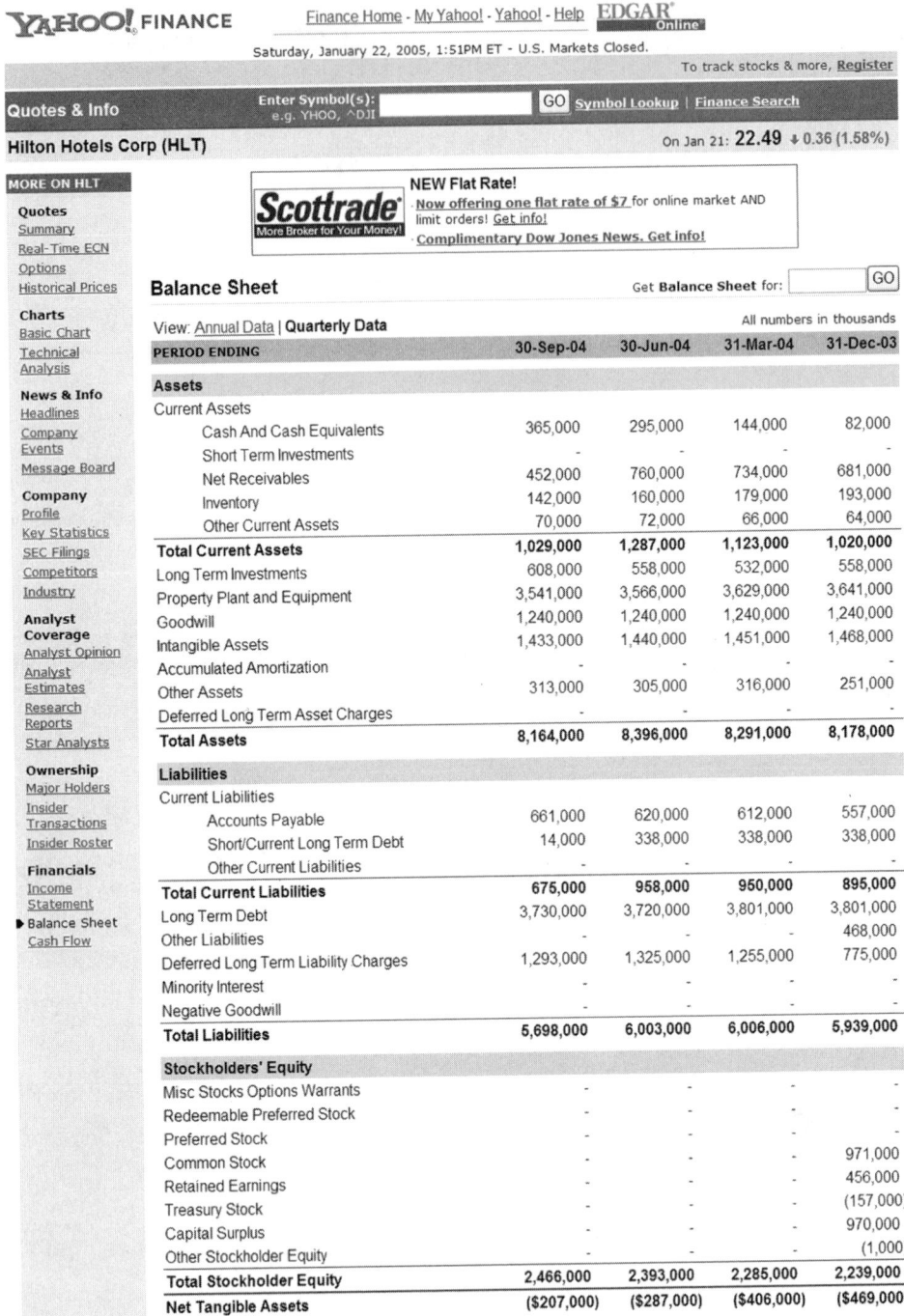

**Hilton Hotels Corp (HLT)**    On Jan 21: **22.49** ↓ 0.36 (1.58%)

**Balance Sheet**    Get **Balance Sheet** for:  **GO**

View: Annual Data | **Quarterly Data**    All numbers in thousands

| PERIOD ENDING | 30-Sep-04 | 30-Jun-04 | 31-Mar-04 | 31-Dec-03 |
|---|---|---|---|---|
| **Assets** | | | | |
| Current Assets | | | | |
|     Cash And Cash Equivalents | 365,000 | 295,000 | 144,000 | 82,000 |
|     Short Term Investments | - | - | - | - |
|     Net Receivables | 452,000 | 760,000 | 734,000 | 681,000 |
|     Inventory | 142,000 | 160,000 | 179,000 | 193,000 |
|     Other Current Assets | 70,000 | 72,000 | 66,000 | 64,000 |
| **Total Current Assets** | 1,029,000 | 1,287,000 | 1,123,000 | 1,020,000 |
| Long Term Investments | 608,000 | 558,000 | 532,000 | 558,000 |
| Property Plant and Equipment | 3,541,000 | 3,566,000 | 3,629,000 | 3,641,000 |
| Goodwill | 1,240,000 | 1,240,000 | 1,240,000 | 1,240,000 |
| Intangible Assets | 1,433,000 | 1,440,000 | 1,451,000 | 1,468,000 |
| Accumulated Amortization | - | - | - | - |
| Other Assets | 313,000 | 305,000 | 316,000 | 251,000 |
| Deferred Long Term Asset Charges | - | - | - | - |
| **Total Assets** | 8,164,000 | 8,396,000 | 8,291,000 | 8,178,000 |
| **Liabilities** | | | | |
| Current Liabilities | | | | |
|     Accounts Payable | 661,000 | 620,000 | 612,000 | 557,000 |
|     Short/Current Long Term Debt | 14,000 | 338,000 | 338,000 | 338,000 |
|     Other Current Liabilities | - | - | - | - |
| **Total Current Liabilities** | 675,000 | 958,000 | 950,000 | 895,000 |
| Long Term Debt | 3,730,000 | 3,720,000 | 3,801,000 | 3,801,000 |
| Other Liabilities | - | - | - | 468,000 |
| Deferred Long Term Liability Charges | 1,293,000 | 1,325,000 | 1,255,000 | 775,000 |
| Minority Interest | - | - | - | - |
| Negative Goodwill | - | - | - | - |
| **Total Liabilities** | 5,698,000 | 6,003,000 | 6,006,000 | 5,939,000 |
| **Stockholders' Equity** | | | | |
| Misc Stocks Options Warrants | - | - | - | - |
| Redeemable Preferred Stock | - | - | - | - |
| Preferred Stock | - | - | - | - |
| Common Stock | - | - | - | 971,000 |
| Retained Earnings | - | - | - | 456,000 |
| Treasury Stock | - | - | - | (157,000) |
| Capital Surplus | - | - | - | 970,000 |
| Other Stockholder Equity | - | - | - | (1,000) |
| **Total Stockholder Equity** | 2,466,000 | 2,393,000 | 2,285,000 | 2,239,000 |
| **Net Tangible Assets** | ($207,000) | ($287,000) | ($406,000) | ($469,000) |

FIGURE 13.6  Income statement and balance sheet information for Hilton.

## Hilton's Cost of Debt, $r_D$, is 5.55%

We compute the cost of Hilton's debt $r_D$ by taking its interest payments and dividing by the average debt over the quarter and then annualizing. We download from Yahoo! information about the company's quarterly balance sheets and income statements (Figure 13.6). In the last quarter for which there are reports, the company paid $53,000 in interest. The debt at the end of this quarter was $3,744,000 and the debt at the end of the previous quarter was $4,058,000. This gives a quarterly interest rate of 1.36% (cell B8 below) and an annualized interest rate of 5.55%:

$$Quarterly\ interest\ paid = \frac{53,000}{Average\,(3,744,000\ and\ 4,058,000)} = 1.36\%$$

$$Annualized\ interest\ rate = r_D = (1+1.36\%)^4 - 1 = 5.55\%$$

| | A | B | C | D | E |
|---|---|---|---|---|---|
| 1 | HILTON'S COST OF DEBT, r<sub>D</sub> | | | | |
| 2 | Quarter | 30-Sep-04 | 30-Jun-04 | 31-Mar-04 | |
| 3 | Interest expense | 53,000 | 86,000 | 70,000 | |
| 4 | Long-term debt | 3,730,000 | 3,720,000 | 3,801,000 | |
| 5 | Short-term debt and current portion of long-term debt | 14,000 | 338,000 | 338,000 | |
| 6 | Debt at end of quarter | 3,744,000 | 4,058,000 | 4,139,000 | <-- =D5+D4 |
| 7 | | | | | |
| 8 | Quarterly interest expense | 1.36% | 2.10% | <-- =C3/AVERAGE(C6:D6) | |
| 9 | Annualized | 5.55% | 8.66% | <-- =(1+C8)^4-1 | |

Note that Hilton's interest rate has decreased from the previous quarter, in which the annualized interest rate was 8.66%. In the previous quarter the company had much more expensive short-term debt.

## Hilton's Tax Rate $T_C$ Is Approximately 35%

From the income statements in Figure 13.6 we can also compute the company's tax rate. The average quarterly tax rate for the last three quarters is 34.93%. This is the rate we will use for $T_C$.

| | A | B | C | D | E |
|---|---|---|---|---|---|
| 1 | HILTON'S TAX RATE T<sub>C</sub> | | | | |
| 2 | Quarter | 30-Sep-04 | 30-Jun-04 | 31-Mar-04 | |
| 3 | Earnings before tax | 96,000 | 118,000 | 61,000 | |
| 4 | Provision for taxes | 35,000 | 40,000 | 21,000 | |
| 5 | Tax rate | 36.46% | 33.90% | 34.43% | <-- =D4/D3 |
| 6 | | | | | |
| 7 | Average tax rate, T<sub>C</sub> | | 34.93% | <-- =AVERAGE(B5:D5) | |

## The Risk-Free Rate in the Economy, $r_f$, is 2.21%

We get this number from Yahoo!, as shown in Figure 13.7.

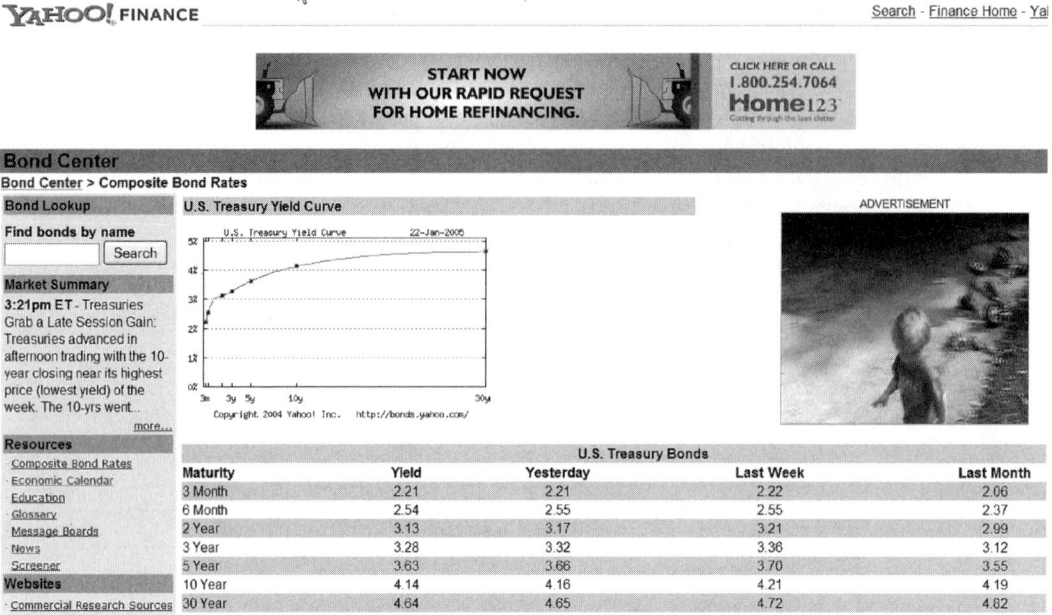

FIGURE 13.7  Yahoo! screen with interest rates. The $r_f$ for use in the SML is the short-term Treasury bond rate, 2.21%.

## The Expected Return on the Market $E(r_M)$ Is Approximately 8.52%

We use the method illustrated in Section 13.3, using the S&P 500 P-to-E ratio for 30 September 2004. We further assume that the growth of the equity payout is 7% and that the payout ratio of dividends plus repurchases is 50%. This gives $E(r_M) = 10.1\%$.

| | A | B | C |
|---|---|---|---|
| 1 | **COMPUTING $E(r_M)$ FOR 30SEP04** | | |
| 2 | S&P 500 P/E on 30Sep2004 | 17.25 | |
| 3 | Estimated growth of equity payout, g | 7% | |
| 4 | Payout ratio, b | 50% | |
| 5 | | | |
| 6 | $E(r_M)$ | 10.10% | <-- =B4*(1+B3)/B2+B3 |

## So What's Hilton's WACC?

The WACC for Hilton is 7.98%. The computations are summarized below:

| | A | B | C |
|---|---|---|---|
| | **HILTON HOTELS CORPORATION (HLT)** | | |
| 1 | **Using Yahoo for much of the information** | | |
| 2 | Equity beta | 0.956 | <-- Yahoo |
| 3 | | | |
| 4 | Shares outstanding (million) | 386.03 | <-- Yahoo |
| 5 | Market value per share | 22.49 | <-- Yahoo |
| 6 | Market value of equity ($ million), E | 8,682 | <-- =B5*B4 |
| 7 | | | |
| 8 | Book value of equity per share | 6.388 | <-- Yahoo |
| 9 | Total book value of equity | 2,466 | <-- =B8*B4 |
| 10 | Debt/Equity ratio | 1.518 | <-- Yahoo |
| 11 | Book value of debt | 3,743 | <-- =B10*B9 |
| 12 | Cash on hand | 219 | <-- Yahoo |
| 13 | Net debt ($ million), D | 3,524 | <-- =B11-B12 |
| 14 | | | |
| 15 | Risk-free rate, $r_f$ | 2.21% | |
| 16 | Expected market return, $E(r_M)$ | 10.10% | |
| 17 | | | |
| 18 | **Computation of WACC** | | |
| 19 | Percentage of equity, E/(E+D) | 0.7113 | <-- =B6/(B6+B13) |
| 20 | Percentage of debt, D/(E+D) | 0.2887 | <-- =1-B19 |
| 21 | Cost of equity, $r_E$ | 9.75% | <-- =B15+B2*(B16-B15) |
| 22 | Cost of debt, $r_D$ | 5.55% | |
| 23 | Tax rate, $T_C$ | 34.93% | |
| 24 | WACC | 7.98% | <-- =B19*B21+(1-B23)*B20*B22 |

## 13.4. Computing the WACC Using an Asset $\beta$, $\beta_{Asset}$

A somewhat different approach to computing the WACC is to use the *asset* $\beta$ approach. In this approach we need both the equity $\beta$, $\beta_E$, and the $\beta_D$ for Hilton. The asset $\beta$ is defined as the weighted average $\beta$ of the debt and equity $\beta$s:

$$\beta_{Asset} = \beta_E \ * \ \frac{E}{E+D} \ + \ \beta_D \ * \ (1-T_C) \ * \ \frac{D}{E+D}$$

$$= \binom{equity}{beta} * \begin{pmatrix} proportion \\ of\ equity \\ in\ firm \\ value \end{pmatrix} + \binom{debt}{beta} * \begin{pmatrix} 1 - \begin{array}{c} corporate \\ tax\ rate \end{array} \end{pmatrix} * \begin{pmatrix} proportion \\ of\ debt \\ in\ firm \\ value \end{pmatrix}$$

Having computed the $\beta_{Asset}$, we now compute the WACC using the SML:

$$WACC = r_f + \beta_{Asset} * \left[ E(r_M) - r_f \right]$$

To illustrate this approach for Hilton, we note that all the necessary calculations have been done in the previous section—with the exception of the computation of the debt $\beta_D$. We compute this $\beta$ by assuming that the SML holds for debt as well as equity:

$$cost\ of\ debt = r_D = r_f + \underset{\substack{\uparrow \\ \text{This is the} \\ \text{beta of} \\ \text{Hilton's debt}}}{\beta_D} * \left[ E(r_M) - r_f \right]$$

$$\Rightarrow \beta_D = \frac{r_D - r_f}{E(r_M) - r_f}$$

In the spreadsheet below you can see that Hilton's debt $\beta$ is 0.528 (cell B8).[9] This means that its asset $\beta$ is 0.78 (cell B15), which gives the WACC as 8.20% (cell B17).

| | A | B | C |
|---|---|---|---|
| 1 | **HILTON HOTELS CORPORATION (HLT)** **Computing the WACC with the asset beta** | | |
| 2 | Equity beta, $_E$ | 0.956 | <-- Yahoo |
| 3 | | | |
| 4 | Risk-free rate, $r_f$ | 2.21% | |
| 5 | Expected market return, $E(r_M)$ | 10.10% | |
| 6 | | | |
| 7 | Cost of debt | 5.55% | |
| 8 | Debt beta, $_D$ | 0.423 | <-- =(B7-B4)/(B5-B4) |
| 9 | | | |
| 10 | Corporate tax rate | 34.93% | |
| 11 | | | |
| 12 | Percentage of equity, E/(E+D) | 0.7113 | |
| 13 | Percentage of debt, D/(E+D) | 0.2887 | |
| 14 | | | |
| 15 | Asset beta, $_{Asset}$ | 0.76 | <-- =B2*B12+(1-B10)*B13*B8 |
| 16 | | | |
| 17 | WACC | 8.20% | <-- =B4+B15*(B5-B4) |

# 13.5. Don't Read This Section!

A final question that may have occurred to you: Why is it that we get a different cost of capital using the traditional WACC approach and using the asset $\beta$ ($\beta_{Asset}$) approach? We're going to answer this question in this section, but we warn you that reading the section may be bad for your health.[10]

Still here? The answer is that for cost of capital purposes, you should adjust the SML for corporate taxes. In addition, there are two SMLs—one for equity and one for debt. Here are the appropriate formulas:

$$\text{Equity SML: } r_E = r_f * (1 - T_C) + \beta_E * \left[ E(r_M) - r_f * (1 - T_C) \right]$$
$$\text{Debt SML: } r_D = r_f + \beta_D * \left[ E(r_M) - r_f * (1 - T_C) \right]$$

Note that the two SMLs have the same tax-adjusted market risk premium $\left[ E(r_M) - r_f * (1 - T_C) \right]$ but have different intercepts—the equity SML has intercept $r_f * (1 - T_C)$, whereas the debt SML has intercept $r_f$.[11]

If we apply this approach to Hilton, and if we assume that the cost of debt is $r_D = 5.55\%$, then we get the debt $\beta_D$ as

$$\beta_D = \frac{r_D - r_f}{E(r_M) - r_f * (1 - T_C)} = \frac{5.55\% - 2.21\%}{10.10\% - 2.21\% * (1 - 34.93\%)} = 0.3851$$

---

[9] Hilton's $\beta_D = 0.423$ may seem high, especially when compared to its equity beta $\beta_E = 0.956$. Clearly the market thinks that Hilton's debt is quite risky.

[10] And—in all honesty—the difference between the two calculations in the previous part of the chapter is not big enough to make much of a difference.

[11] The two-SML model is derived in *Corporate Finance: A Valuation Approach* by Simon Benninga and Oded Sarig, McGraw–Hill, 1997.

Now, as you can see in the spreadsheet below, the WACC is the same, whether you compute it with the traditional method or with the asset $\beta_{Asset}$.

| | A | B | C |
|---|---|---|---|
| | **HILTON HOTELS CORPORATION (HLT)** | | |
| 1 | **Using the two-SML model** | | |
| 2 | Risk-free rate, $r_f$ | 2.21% | |
| 3 | Expected market return, $E(r_M)$ | 10.10% | |
| 4 | Corporate tax rate | 34.93% | |
| 5 | | | |
| 6 | **WACC using traditional method** | | |
| 7 | Equity beta | 0.956 | <-- Yahoo |
| 8 | Cost of equity | 9.72% | <-- =B2*(1-B4)+B7*(B3-B2*(1-B4)) |
| 9 | Cost of debt | 5.55% | |
| 10 | | | |
| 11 | Percentage of equity, E/(E+D) | 0.7113 | |
| 12 | Percentage of debt, D/(E+D) | 0.2887 | |
| | | 7.96% | <-- =B11*B8+B12*(1-B4)*B9 |
| | | | |
| | beta and the two-SML model | | |
| | | 0.956 | |
| | | 0.3851 | <-- =(B9-B2)/(B3-B2*(1-B4)) |
| | | 0.7523 | <-- =B11*B16+B17*(1-B4)*B12 |
| | | 7.96% | <-- =B2*(1-B4)+B18*(B3-B2*(1-B4)) |

$- T_C) + \varepsilon*[E(r_M) - (1-T_C)*r_f]$ and
he method is more theoretically correct; it also produces
ditional WACC approach and the asset beta approach.

s the differences between this method and that illustrated
re usually not significant.

e cost of capital (WACC) is critical for corporate valua-
the importance of the WACC in Chapter 6.[12]
our estimate of the cost of equity $r_E$. There are only
ng the cost of equity—the Gordon dividend model,
.. This chapter has dealt in great detail with using
and the resulting WACC. We've illustrated the use
st of equity $r_E$. We have also shown how you can
$\beta_E$, the debt $\beta_D$, and the asset $\beta_{Asset}$ to compute the
WACC.

Through the use of a detailed example for Hilton Hotels, we have shown where to get the data required to make all these calculations.

---

[12] The issue of stock valuation is discussed in somewhat more detail in Chapter 16, which sums up the various approaches to this important topic.

## EXERCISES

1. Consider the following data concerning ASAP Company:

$$Debt, D = 500,000$$
$$Equity, E = 300,000$$
$$Cost\ of\ debt,\ r_D = 6\%$$
$$Cost\ of\ equity,\ r_E = 11\%$$
$$Corporate\ tax,\ T_C = 25\%$$

   Find ASAP's weighted average cost of capital.

2. Consider the following data, concerning Elizabeth company:

$$E(r_m) = 21\%$$
$$Cost\ of\ debt,\ r_D = 8\%$$
$$Corporate\ tax\ rate,\ T_c = 25\%$$
$$\beta_{Elizabeth\ stock} = 0.7$$
$$Debt, D = 1,000,000$$
$$Value\ of\ equity, E = 1,000,000$$
$$Risk\text{-}free\ rate,\ r_f = 4\%$$

   Find the company's WACC.

3. Consider the following data concerning Abby Company. Abby's stock is not currently listed on a stock exchange.

$$E(r_M) = 20\%$$
$$Cost\ of\ debt,\ r_D = 10\%$$
$$Corporate\ tax\ rate,\ T_C = 30\%$$
$$Cov(r_{Abby}, r_M) = 0.13$$
$$Value\ of\ debt, D = 1,500,000$$
$$r_f = 7\%$$
$$Var(r_M) = 0.11$$
$$Value\ of\ equity, E = 3,000,000$$

   a. Find Abby's WACC.
   b. Suppose Abby issues its stock in an initial public offering (IPO). After the IPO the company has 3,500,000 shares, worth $2.50 each. What is its WACC after the IPO?

4. Consider the following data concerning Ever-Lasting Company:

$$E(r_M) = 18\%$$
$$Cost\ of\ debt,\ r_D = 7.5\%$$
$$Corporate\ tax\ rate,\ T_C = 30\%$$
$$\beta_{EverLasting} = 1$$
$$Market\ value\ of\ debt, D = 1,250,000$$
$$Market\ value\ of\ equity, E = 2,000,000$$

   Find the company's WACC.

5. Consider the following data:

$$EPS_0 = \$0.55$$
$$P_0 = \$22$$
$$g = 0.06$$
$$b = 45\% \ (\textit{dividend payout ratio})$$

Find the price-to-earnings ratio (P/E) and the cost of equity using the Gordon model.

6. Consider the following data:

$$r_D = 10\%$$
$$T_C = 30\%$$
$$D = 2,500,000$$
$$E = 2,000,000$$
$$EPS_0 = \$2.5$$
$$P_0 = \$16$$
$$g = 0.075$$
$$b = 55\% \ (\textit{dividend payout ratio})$$

Find the P/E ratio and the company's WACC.

7. Use the following data to compute the WACC for Cobra, Inc. at year-end 2002:

- Cobra has 1,500,000 shares. The share price at the end of 2002 was $12.00.
- Cobra's debt at year end 2002 is $44,500,000 and its debt at year end 2001 was $35,000,000. The amount of interest paid in 2002 by the company was $400,000.
- Cobra's corporate tax rate is 36%.
- The risk-free rate of interest at the end of 2002 is $rf = 2.16\%$.

Data for the S&P 500 (the market portfolio in this case) and for Cobra returns are given below (these data are on the disk that comes with *Principles of Finance with Excel*).

|    | A | B | C | D |
|----|---|---|---|---|
| 1 | Calculating Cobra's WACC | | | |
| 2 | Year | S&P 500 return | Cobra return | Risk-free rate |
| 3 | 1990 | -3.10% | -16.00% | 7.92% |
| 4 | 1991 | 30.47% | 89.12% | 6.64% |
| 5 | 1992 | 7.62% | 25.33% | 4.15% |
| 6 | 1993 | 10.08% | 28.95% | 3.50% |
| 7 | 1994 | 1.32% | -12.34% | 3.54% |
| 8 | 1995 | 37.58% | 102.33% | 7.05% |
| 9 | 1996 | 22.96% | 51.98% | 5.09% |
| 10 | 1997 | 33.36% | 25.61% | 5.61% |
| 11 | 1998 | 28.58% | 5.05% | 5.24% |
| 12 | 1999 | 21.04% | 50.25% | 4.51% |
| 13 | 2000 | -9.10% | -15.33% | 6.12% |
| 14 | 2001 | -11.89% | -18.22% | 4.81% |
| 15 | 2002 | -22.10% | -38.00% | 2.16% |

8. Use the Yahoo! profile for Microsoft (MSFT) (given below).
   a. What is Microsoft's P/E ratio, its $\beta$, and its debt-to-equity ratio? (Use the trailing P/E ratio.[13])

---

[13] The trailing P/E ratio is the ratio of today's price to the previous year's earnings per share. The "forward P/E" is the ratio of today's price to anticipated future earnings per share.

b. Find MSFT's recent stock price and its number of shares and use them to compute MSFT's market equity value. Does this accord with the Yahoo! computation?

c. Assume that $rf = 3\%$ and the $E(r_M) = 8\%$. Compute MSFT's cost of equity $r_E$.

9. Use the Yahoo! profile for Tyson Food's (TSN) (given below). Compute Tyson's WACC using the company's $\beta$ and other information you find on the profile. Assume that $r_f = 3\%$ and $E(r_M) = 8\%$.

Last year the company paid $186,000 in taxes on $523,000 of pretax income. Its cost of debt $r_D = 7.76\%$.

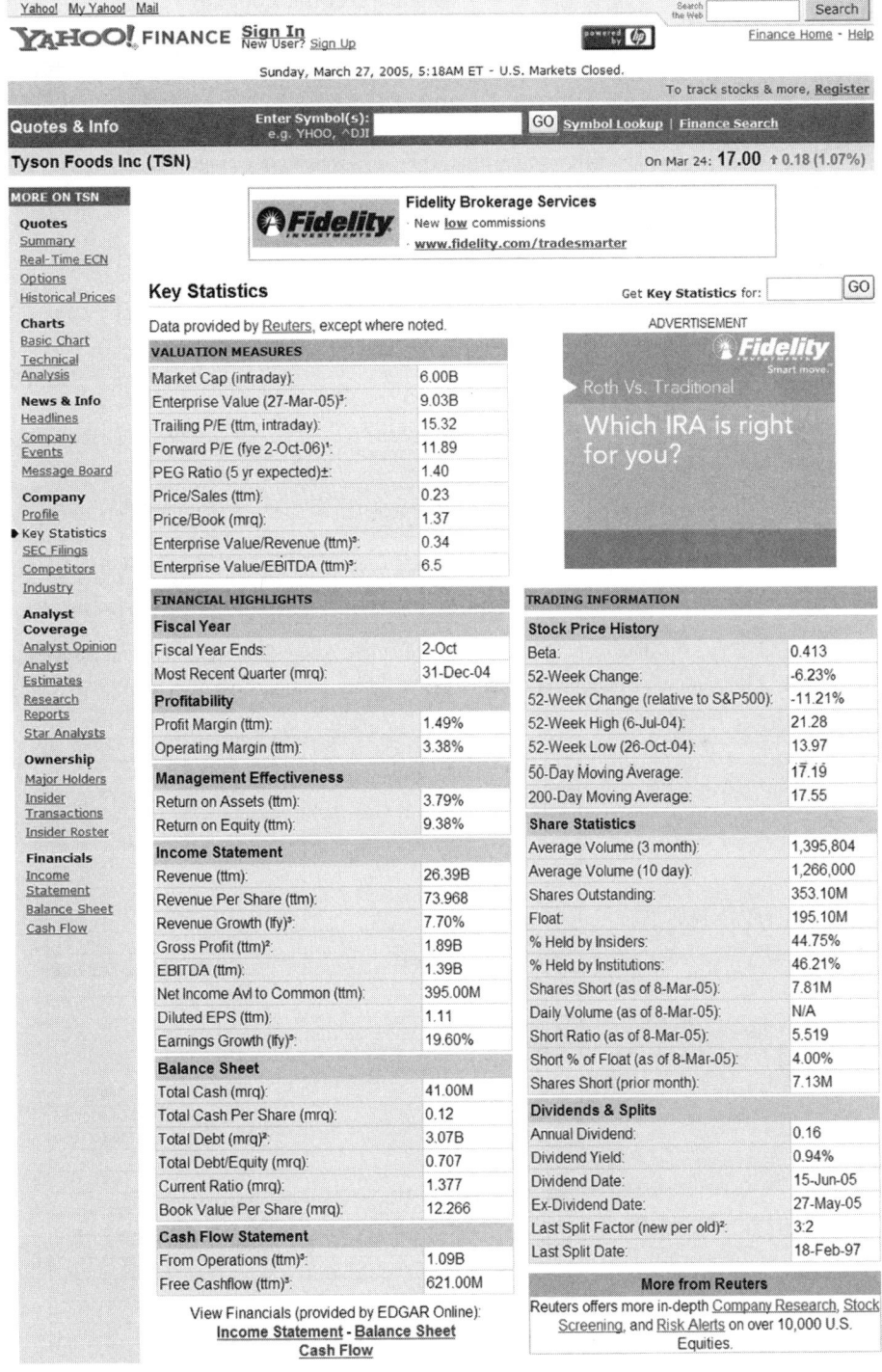

10. Calculate General Electric's tax rate for 2002, 2003, and 2004, using the data below.

|  | A | B | C | D |
|---|---|---|---|---|
| 1 | | GENERAL ELECTRIC COMPANY | | |
| | | Income statements, 2002-2004 | | |
| 2 | | 2002/12/31 | 2003/12/31 | 2004/12/31 |
| 3 | Total Operating Revenue | $132,226,000,000 | $134,641,000,000 | $152,866,000,000 |
| 4 | Cost of Goods Sold | $52,856,000,000 | $51,206,000,000 | $61,759,000,000 |
| 5 | Interest Expense | $10,151,000,000 | $10,892,000,000 | $12,036,000,000 |
| 6 | Income Before Tax | $18,972,000,000 | $20,291,000,000 | $20,480,000,000 |
| 7 | Net Income | $14,167,000,000 | $15,236,000,000 | $16,819,000,000 |

11. Use the data below to calculate Amgen's weighted average cost of capital (WACC) for year-end 2002. Assume that $E(r_M) = 8\%$ and $r_f = 4\%$.

|  | A | B |
|---|---|---|
| 1 | **Calculating Amgen's WACC** | |
| 2 | $E(r_M)$ | 8.00% |
| 3 | $r_f$ | 2.00% |
| 4 | Tax rate | 44.74% |
| 5 | Beta | 0.82 |
| 6 | Stock price, end-2002 | 58.34 |
| 7 | | |
| 8 | Outstanding shares | 1,290,000,000 |
| 9 | Book value per share | 14.70 |
| 10 | Total book value of equity | 18,963,000,000 |
| 11 | Debt to equity ratio (book) | 16.07% |
| 12 | Amgen's debt | 3,047,700,000 |
| 13 | Amgen's total value | 3,047,700,058 |
| 14 | | |
| 15 | Interest paid, 2002 | 44,200,000 |
| 16 | Debt, end-2002 | 3,047,700,000 |
| 17 | Debt, end-2001 | 223,000,000 |

12. Use the data from Question 11 to calculate Amgen's WACC using an asset $\beta_{asset}$.

13. Compute Boeing's year end 2002 weighted average cost of capital (WACC) using the following template.

|  | A | B | C |
|---|---|---|---|
| 1 | **Calculating Boeing's WACC** | | |
| 2 | $E(r_M)$ | 7.50% | |
| 3 | $r_f$ | 3.00% | |
| 4 | Stock price | 53.92 | |
| 5 | Stock beta | 0.72 | |
| 6 | Market value of equity | | |
| 7 | | | |
| 8 | Outstanding shares | 840,900,000 | |
| 9 | Book value per share | $8.28 | |
| 10 | Book value of equity | | |
| 11 | Debt to equity ratio | 2.09 | |
| 12 | Boeing's debt | | |
| 13 | Market value, debt + equity | | |
| 14 | | | |
| 15 | | 2002 | 2001 |
| 16 | Income before tax | 3,180,000,000 | 3,564,000,000 |
| 17 | Income tax expense | 861,000,000 | 738,000,000 |
| 18 | Annual tax rate | 27.08% | 20.71% |
| 19 | | | |
| 20 | Interest paid, 2002 | 730,000,000 | |
| 21 | Debt, end-year 2002 | 12,589,000,000 | |
| 22 | Debt, end-year 2001 | 10,866,000,000 | |
| 23 | Average debt, 2001-2002 | | |
| 24 | Boeing's cost of debt | | |
| 25 | | | |
| 26 | Boeing's cost of equity | | |
| 27 | | | |
| 28 | Boeing's WACC | | |

14. Use the data above to calculate Boeing's WACC using an asset $\beta_{asset}$.

15. The current risk-free rate is $r_f = 4\%$ and the expected rate of return on the market portfolio is $E(r_M) = 10\%$. The Brandywine Corp. has two divisions of equal market value. The debt-to-equity ratio of the company is 3/7, and the company's bonds are risk free. For the past few years, the Brandy division has been using a discount rate of 12% in capital budgeting decisions and the Wine division a discount rate of 10%. You have been asked by their managers to report on whether these discount rates are properly adjusted for the risk of the projects in the two divisions.

   a. What are the betas of typical projects implicit in the discount rates used by the two divisions?

   b. You estimate that the stock beta of Brandywine is $\beta = 1.6$. Is this consistent with the stock $\beta$ implicit in the discount rates used by the two divisions?

   c. You estimate that the stock $\beta$ of the Korbell Brandy Corp. is 1.8. Korbell is purely in the brandy business, its debt-to-equity ratio is 2/3, and its bond $\beta$ is 0.2. Based on this information (and on your estimate of Brandywine's stock $\beta$), what discount rate would you recommend for projects in the Brandy and in the Wine divisions of Brandywine?

16. Sun, Inc. has an equity beta of 0.5. Its capital structure consists of equal amounts of equity and risk-free debt. The debt has a pretax yield of 6% and the expected rate of return on the market index is 18%. Sun, Inc. is considering expanding into Snow, Inc. This new business is expected to generate an after-tax internal rate of return of 25%. Vacation, Inc. is already in this new business; its equity beta is 2.0 and it uses a blend of 10% (risk-free) debt and 90% equity in its capital structure. If the new project is to be funded with 50% debt, should Sun, Inc. enter the Snow, Inc. business? Assume that both companies have a marginal tax rate of 50% and that the business risk of Vacation, Inc. is comparable to the risk of Sun, Inc.'s venture.

17. A company is deciding whether to issue stock to raise money for an investment project that has the same risk as the market and an expected return of 15%. If the risk-free rate is 5% and the expected return on the market is 12%, the company should proceed with the investment.

   a. This is false. The company should not take this project.

   b. Regardless of the company's $\beta$.

   c. Unless the company's $\beta$ is greater than 1.25.

   d. Unless the company's $\beta$ is less than 1.25.

18. The project whose cash flows are given below has a $\beta = 1.6$. If the market return $E(r_M) = 15\%$ and the risk-free rate $r_f = 7\%$, should the firm undertake the project?

| | A | B |
|---|---|---|
| 1 | Year | Cash flow |
| 2 | 0 | -100 |
| 3 | 1 | 60 |
| 4 | 2 | 50 |
| 5 | 3 | 40 |

19. A share of a stock with a $\beta = 0.75$ now sells for $50. Investors expect the stock to pay a year-end dividend of $3. The T-bill rate is 4%, and the market risk premium is 8%. What is the investors' expectation of the price of the stock at the end of the year?

20. Reconsider the stock in Exercise 19. Suppose investors actually believe the stock will sell for $54 at year end. Is the stock a good or bad buy? What will investors do? At what point will the stock reach an equilibrium at which it again is perceived as fairly priced?

# VALUING SECURITIES

Two of the three chapters of Part 3 of *Principles of Finance with Excel* look at how to value bonds (Chapter 15) and stocks (Chapter 16).

Section 3 starts with Chapter 14, which examines market efficiency. Roughly speaking, market efficiency is a group of concepts which look at how information is incorporated in financial markets. Does the bundling of assets into one package affect their prices? This question is known as price additivity, and when you read Chapter 14, you'll see that the answer to this question is not trivial. Does the knowledge of the price history of a stock affect your ability to predict the future price of the stock (market efficiency says "no")?

The market efficiency discussed in Chapter 14 provides you with the necessary background for the valuation of bonds and stocks. Details specific to bond markets are given in Chapter 15; this chapter also discusses preferred stocks, which are very similar to bonds.

In Chapter 16 we apply the concepts of cash flow discounting and market efficiency to the valuation of stocks. Chapter 16 discusses and compares the four most commonly-used techniques for stock valuation.

# 14 Efficient Markets—Some General Principles of Security Valuation

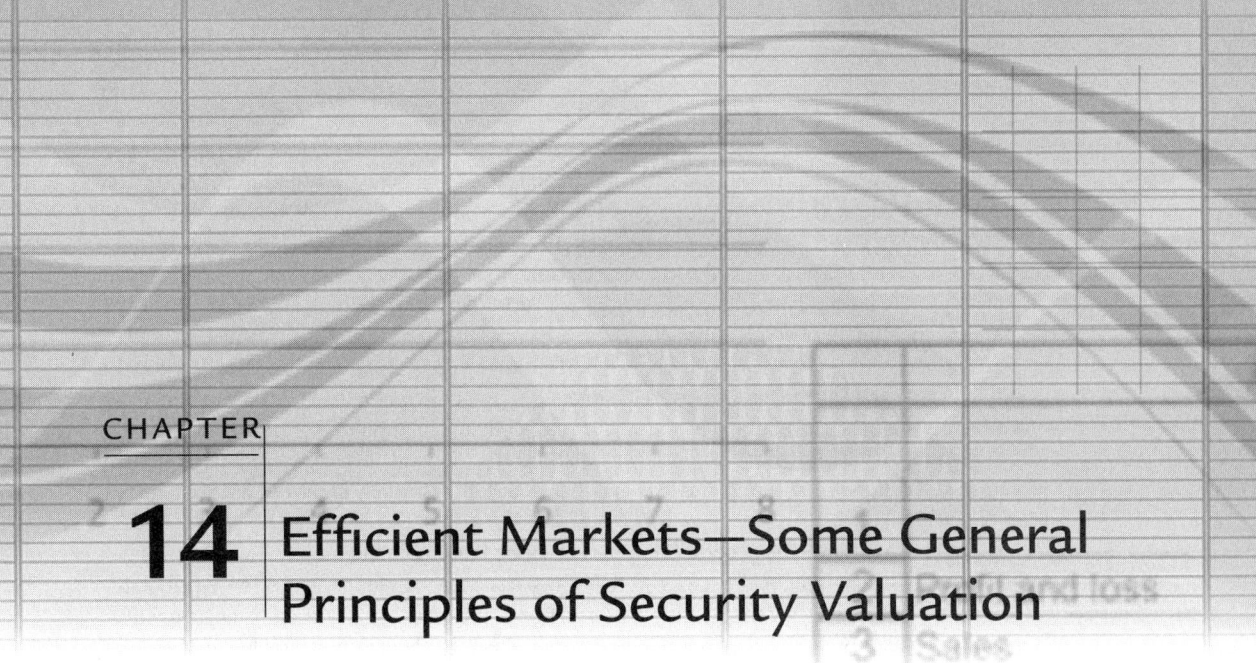

## CHAPTER CONTENTS

## Overview

Finance often requires a lot of calculation, which is why this book concentrates on solving financial problems with a powerful tool like Excel. But sometimes understanding the way that financial markets work requires only wisdom and very little calculation. This chapter discusses some general principles of valuation that can save you from a lot of nonsense and in many cases require almost no calculation. Having discussed these very important general principles, we then move on to deal with the valuation of bonds (Chapter 15) and stocks (Chapter 16).

Here's an example of the kind of nonsense that you'll learn to avoid by reading and understanding this chapter: Your college roommate Clarence has just given you a "hot tip" on Federated Underwear (FU) stock : Clarence is sure that you should immediately buy the stock.

"It's going to go up. I know it," he says excitedly. "My father says that FU has been fluctuating between $15 and $25 for the past year. Every time it gets close to $15, it goes up, and when it gets close to $25, it goes down again. Yesterday FU closed at $15.05. Buy it and wait—the stock is sure to go up, and then you'll sell it at $25 and make a killing."

After reading this chapter, you'll know to tell Clarence: "My friend, your advice is a perfect example of a *technical trading rule*. And Chapter 17 of my college finance textbook, *Principles of Finance with Excel*, explains that these rules are a clear violation of the principle of weak-form market efficiency, which almost always holds. If you want to bet your money on such foolishness, go ahead. I'm going to spend my hard-earned cash on a night out at the Efficient Markets Disco."

In the broadest sense the general principles discussed in this chapter all deal with the role of information in determining asset prices. When translated into simple language, these principles sound pretty dumb. They say things like: "Information is important." "Transaction costs matter." "One plus one equals two." When applied to asset markets the valuation principles discussed in this chapter often enable you to make surprising statements about what things are worth.

Here are four basic principles of valuation discussed in this chapter.

**Efficient Markets Principle 1.** *Single price for a single good.* In financial markets equivalent financial assets have the same price. Section 14.1 uses cross-listed stocks—stocks that trade in two financial markets, like IBM stock on the New York Stock Exchange and IBM stock on the Pacific Stock Exchange—as a nontrivial example of this principle.

**Efficient Markets Principle 2.** *Price additivity* The price of a bundle of securities should be the sum of the prices of each of the securities. It is difficult to overestimate the importance of this principle. One of its predictions is that there are no "money machines"—it costs money to make money. Another prediction is that knowing the prices of the *components* of a financial asset will help you price the whole asset.

**Efficient Markets Principle 3.** *Information is critical.* Finding out previously unknown information can be a very profitable exercise. Conversely, it is difficult to make money from facts that everyone knows. The more widely information is known, the less you can make money from the information. Principle 3 is usually split into three parts:

- The principle of *weak-form efficiency*: Market prices incorporate all current and past price information. If this principle holds (and almost all economists believe that it does), then it is not possible to make money based on the pattern of past prices of a traded security. This means that "money making" rules that are based on price patterns—"buy a stock if it's gone up 3 days in a row, sell it if it's gone down 3 days running"—are futile. The weak-form version of the efficient markets hypothesis should make you skeptical about a lot of investment strategies. An example is investment advisors who claim to be able to tell market trends from price patterns. These so-called "technical traders" are giving advice that violates the weak-form efficient markets hypothesis, and this advice should be ignored.

- The principle of *semistrong form efficiency*: Market prices incorporate all publicly known information. Financial markets are awash in publicly available information. Can you make money by carefully reading the financial statements of IBM? Probably not— IBM has many shareholders and is followed by hundreds of stock analysts. If the analysts are doing their job even moderately well, the information that can be gleaned from the IBM financial statements is already incorporated in the company's stock price. Most economists believe that markets are more or less semistrong efficient. As you'll see in this chapter, it depends on how difficult it is to derive the information and how many investors carefully follow a particular stock.

- The principle of *strong form efficiency*: Market prices incorporate *all information* that exists (public or private) about a security. In addition to IBM's publicly available financial statements and the analyses of stock analysts, there's also lots of *private* information about the company. For example, people working for the company know a lot about the sales, production, and costs of their individual units. Is this information also incorporated in IBM's stock price? Almost no economists believe this. This means that knowing privately available information can provide you with profits.[1] Markets are not strong form efficient.

**Efficient Markets Principle 4.** *Transaction costs are important and can screw up everything.* This is an important truth about markets. Transaction costs—by this we mean not only the costs of buying and selling securities, but also the cost of ferreting out information—make it more difficult to trade. And it's trade—the buying and selling of financial assets like stocks and bonds—that makes market prices reflect the true value of assets.

## Finance Concepts Discussed in This Chapter

- Efficiency
- Additivity
- Short sales
- Open-end and closed-end mutual funds

## Excel Functions Used

- This chapter has some Excel, but nothing sophisticated.

# 14.1. Efficient Markets Principle 1: Competitive Markets Have a Single Price for a Single Good

A *competitive market* is a market with a large number of buyers and sellers, none of whom can influence the price of the goods bought and sold in the market. Financial markets are good examples of competitive markets: There are a large number of buyers and sellers for most stocks sold on major stock exchanges, there are many banks competing for your bank accounts and for your mortgage, and so on.

The principle that *competitive markets have a single price for a single good* is basic to economics and is drilled home in most introductory economics courses. Under some circumstances, this principle seems to be ridiculously obvious. For example, in the Asheville, North Carolina, farmer's market (the author's home town), there are many stands selling apples. Many of the vendors sell Granny Smith (GS) apples. The GS apples sold by the vendors are of approximately the same size and quality. The result: The price of apples of the same type is approximately the same at all the stands. Why? Suppose one vendor deviates from the equilibrium price of GS apples by selling below the price of the other vendors. Then he'll attract a lot of buyers. Being competitive, he will raise his

---

[1] Beware: Stock trading on the basis of insider information is also illegal.

price and the other GS vendors (also competitive) will lower their prices until, equilibrium being restored, the market price for GS apples is the same at all GS stands.

### Cross-Listed Stocks—An Application of the One-Price Principle

The one-good, one-price principle also has applications in stock markets. Here's an example: IBM stock is traded both on the New York Stock Exchange (NYSE) and the Pacific Stock Exchange (PSE). When both exchanges are open, the prices of IBM stock are basically the same in both exchanges. This isn't surprising: If the price of IBM in New York is $120 and its price is $118 in San Francisco, brokers would obviously try to *arbitrage* (that is, make money from unreasonable differences in prices) by buying IBM stock in San Francisco and selling it in New York. Because transaction costs are very low and because trade in stocks is instantaneous, this will drive the prices together.[2]

There's more to this than meets the eye: The NYSE opens before the PSE, but the PSE stays open later. This means that information about IBM that arrives late in the day will be incorporated in the PSE stock price but will hit the NYSE price only the next morning. In some cases this phenomenon is even more extreme—for example, there's a large group of Israeli shares that is traded both in Tel Aviv and on the NASDAQ in the United States. The trading overlap between the two markets is only 1 hour per day (between 9:30 and 10:30 am Eastern time, both NASDAQ and Tel Aviv are open—after this, Tel Aviv closes and all trading in the dual-listing stocks is on the NASDAQ ). During this trading overlap, cross-listed stocks have the same price in both markets, but when only one market is open this need not be so.

## 14.2. Efficient Markets Principle 2: Bundles Are Priced Additively

Prices are *additive* when the market price of A + B is equal to the market price of A plus the market price of B. This sounds so obvious that it's hard to believe that it could be interesting (and, indeed, once you understand it, it's pretty boring!).

For an initial example, we go back to the Asheville farmer's market. Our previous example dealt with Granny Smith apples, but some of the vendors also sell Red Delicious (RD) apples. As we speak, the price of GS apples is $2 per pound and the price of RD apples is $3 per pound. Simon, a somewhat peculiar vendor, sells bags of apples containing both GS and RD apples: Each bag weighs 2 pounds and contains 1 pound of GS and 1 pound of RD apples. How should he price these bags? Obviously at $5 per bag.

Why? Not so trivial, actually. Suppose Simon prices the bags at $4.50. Then anyone wanting 1 pound of GS and 1 pound of RD will obviously buy with Simon. If Simon is sensitive to supply and demand, he'll note the demand for his mixed bags of apples and raise the price; at the same time, other apple stands—seeing their demand weaken—will lower the prices of their apples.

Furthermore, if Simon persists in selling his bags of apples at $4.50, Sharon—a sharp cookie (or should we say "sharp apple"?)—will buy bags of apples from Simon. She'll then take the apples out of the bag and sell them at her apple stand for the market price of $2 for GS and

---

[2] Note how we've already slipped in the importance of *transaction costs* ("Principle 4: Transaction costs are important"). The sentence in the text suggests that transaction costs may include not only the direct cost of buying and selling (commissions, labor costs, etc.), but also the time involved in transporting a good from one market to another. Luckily for this example, stock markets have pretty low transaction costs, especially for brokers and dealers.

$3 for RD. In the language of finance—Sharon is *arbitraging the price*. In the language of her grandmother, Sharon is buying cheap and selling dear.

On the other hand, suppose Simon prices the bags at $5.50. People will probably stop buying with him, even if they want bags with equal combinations of GS and RD—they can buy them cheaper elsewhere. Eventually Simon will have to lower his price. If, contrary to expectations, it turns out that Simon does a brisk business in apple bags for $5.50, then other smart apple stand owners will start selling their own bags of apples; because they can put together a bag for less than what Simon charges, the price of the mixed bags will go back down.

There might actually be room for Simon to sell his apple bags for $5.05 because he's saving his customers the trouble of going to two apple stands. In the language of finance, he's saving them the *transactions cost* of buying the apples separately. They ought to be willing to pay him for this service.

The principle of price additivity is often summed up by the statement that *there are no money machines* in financial markets: You cannot simply make money by buying a complex financial asset (like Simon's bags of apples), taking it apart (separate bags of GS and RD), and selling the separate bags. The converse is also true: The "money machine" of combining GS and RD apples into one bag won't work.[3]

Now that you understand the principle of additivity as applied to the Asheville farmer's market, here are some nontrivial finance applications.

## RICHARD GERE THE ARBITRAGEUR

In the movie *Pretty Woman* (1990), Richard Gere plays an "arbitrageur": Gere buys up companies and then breaks them up and sells the parts for a profit. To quote a Web site that discusses this movie, "This is presented in the movie, as such things are in the press generally, as a useless, evil thing, that destroys jobs and wrecks business—the 'greed' of the 80's. In the movie, Julia Roberts even compares it to stealing cars and selling the parts. In fact, it is a useful thing, which easily creates jobs and increases production. A company can be broken up and sold for a profit only if it is worth less than what the sum of what its parts are worth individually. But if a company is worth less than the sum of its parts, then breaking up the company frees capital that can be used for other investment purposes, including creating jobs in other companies or industries." (http://www.friesian.com/trade.htm)

### Additivity, Example 1: The Term Structure Prices Bonds

The principle of bundle pricing is often applied to the pricing of bonds. A bond gives you a series of payments over time. Each of these payments is a separate financial package. If we can price each financial package, then we should be able to price the bond. For the moment we confine ourselves to a simple bond example, saving more complicated ones for the next chapter.

---

[3] In a broader sense, all of the efficient markets principles in this chapter say that there are no easy ways to make money on financial markets. If you want to make money, you'll have to do some meaningful work.

Here's an example. Suppose there are two bonds in the financial market, Bond *A* and Bond *B*:

- Bond *A* sells today for $100 and pays off $110 in 1 year. The bond's IRR is

$$10.00\% = \frac{110}{100} - 1 \quad .$$

- Bond *B* also sells today for $100. This bond has a payoff only at the end of 2 years, at

which point it pays $125. The IRR of the bond is $11.80\% = \left(\frac{125}{100}\right)^{1/2} - 1$.

Now suppose that you're trying to price a Bond *C*, which has a payoff of $23 in 1 year and $1,023 in 2 years. The price-additivity principle says that the way to price this bond is to apply the IRRs calculated above separately to each year's bond payment. In a formula,

$$Bond\ price = \frac{23}{1.10} + \frac{1,023}{(1.1180)^2} = 839.31$$

In this formula we've discounted the first bond payment of $23 by the market interest rate on the 1-year bonds, and we've discounted the second bond payment of $1,023 by the IRR derived from Bond *B*. Here's the spreadsheet.

|  | A | B | C | D |
|---|---|---|---|---|
| 1 | PRICE ADDITIVITY IN BONDS | | | |
| 2 | **Bond A: maturity in one year** | | | |
| 3 | Price today | 100 | | |
| 4 | Payoff in one year | 110 | | |
| 5 | IRR | 10.00% | <-- =B4/B3-1 | |
| 6 | | | | |
| 7 | **Bond B: maturity in two years** | | | |
| 8 | Price today | 100 | | |
| 9 | Payoff in one year | 0 | | |
| 10 | Payoff in two years | 125 | | |
| 11 | IRR | 11.80% | <-- =(B10/B8)^(1/2)-1 | |
| 12 | | | | |
| 13 | | | | |
| 14 | **Bond C:  A bond with payments at end of year 1 and year 2** | | | |
| 15 | **Date** | **Payment** | **Present value of payment** | |
| 16 | 1 | 23 | 20.91 | <-- =B16/(1+B5) |
| 17 | 2 | 1023 | 818.40 | <-- =B17/(1+B11)^2 |
| 18 | **Bond price?** | | **839.31** | <-- =SUM(C16:C17) |

Figure 14.1 presents the logic in a picture.

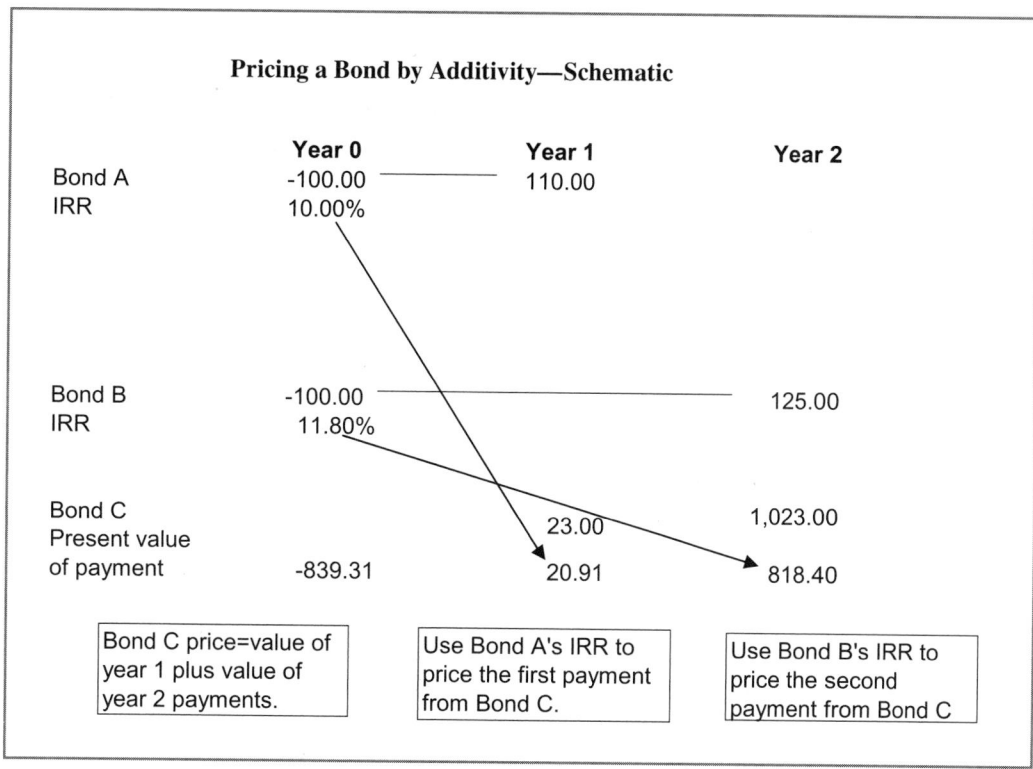

FIGURE 14.1.  Bond C is priced by taking the IRR of Bond A and applying it to the first-year payment of C and by taking the IRR of Bond B and applying it to the second-year payment of Bond C. In the jargon of bond markets, both Bond A and Bond B are known as zero-coupon bonds. A zero coupon bond is a bond with only two cash flows: the initial price of the bond and the final payoff. See Chapter 15 for more details.

To sum up, we've used market discount rates derived from bonds with only one payment to additively price a bond with multiyear payments.

## Additivity, Example 2: Open-End Mutual Funds

The Web page of the U.S. Securities and Exchange Commission (SEC) defines a *mutual fund* as follows:

> A mutual fund is a company that brings together money from many people and invests it in stocks, bonds or other assets. The combined holdings of stocks, bonds or other assets the fund owns are known as its *portfolio*. Each investor in the fund owns shares, which represent a part of these holdings.
> http://www.sec.gov/investor/tools/mfcc/mutual-fund-help.htm

Figure 14.2 gives some more information from the SEC about mutual funds.

# MUTUAL FUNDS

A mutual fund is a company that pools money from many investors and invests the money in stocks, bonds, short-term money-market instruments, or other securities. Legally known as an "open-end company," a mutual fund is one of three basic types of <u>investment company</u>. The two other basic types are <u>closed-end funds</u> and <u>Unit Investment Trusts (UITs)</u>.

Here are some of the traditional and distinguishing characteristics of mutual funds:

- Investors purchase mutual fund shares from the fund itself (or through a broker for the fund), but are not able to purchase the shares from other investors on a secondary market, such as the New York Stock Exchange or NASDAQ Stock Market. The price investors pay for mutual fund shares is the fund's per share <u>net asset value (NAV)</u> plus any <u>shareholder fees</u> that the fund imposes at purchase (such as sales loads).

- Mutual fund shares are "redeemable." This means that when mutual fund investors want to sell their fund shares, they sell them back to the fund (or to a broker acting for the fund) at their approximate NAV, minus any fees the fund imposes at that time (such as deferred sales loads or redemption fees).

- Mutual funds generally sell their shares on a continuous basis, although some funds will stop selling when, for example, they become too large.

- The investment portfolios of mutual funds typically are managed by separate entities known as "<u>investment advisers</u>" that are registered with the SEC.

Mutual funds come in many varieties. For example, there are <u>index funds</u>, <u>stock funds</u>, <u>bond funds</u>, <u>money market funds</u>, and more. Each of these may have a different investment objective and strategy and a different investment portfolio. Different mutual funds may also be subject to different risks, volatility, and <u>fees and expenses</u>.

All funds charge management fees for operating the fund. Some also charge for their distribution and service costs, commonly referred to as "<u>12b-1" fees</u>. Some funds may also impose <u>sales charge or load</u>s when you purchase or sell fund shares. In this regard, a fund may offer different "<u>classes</u>" of shares in the same portfolio, with each class having different fees and expenses.

FIGURE 14.2 Description of mutual funds from the SEC Web site.
*Source:* http://www.sec.gov/answers/mutfund.htm

Does it matter if you *bundle* securities together in a mutual fund? How should the price of such a fund be determined? The principle of pricing additivity gives us a way to handle this problem—it suggests that the price of a mutual fund should be determined by the market prices of all of the fund's assets.

As a simple example, suppose you start a new company, the Super-Duper Fund, that sells a mutual fund of a very specific type.

- Super-Duper currently has 10,000 shareholders, each of whom has invested $100—so that the total assets of the company are $1,000,000.

- Super-Duper's money is currently invested 50% in shares of IBM (currently trading at $100 and 50% in shares of Intel (currently trading at $50). The Super-Duper fund currently owns 5,000 shares of IBM and 10,000 shares of Intel.

- The number of shares in the fund is *flexible*.[4] Right now, there are 10,000 shares, but this number can go up or down:
  - If a shareholder wants to sell, you promise to liquidate his proportional part of the fund's assets. So if Uncle Joe from Winona, who owns one Super-Duper share worth $100, wants to sell his share in the company, Super-Duper will sell ½ share of IBM and 1 share of Intel and repay him his $100. Now the fund will have $999,900 in assets, still invested 50% in IBM and 50% in Intel.
  - If any new shareholders want to join, Super-Duper will buy—per $100 of new funds that come into the company—$50 of IBM and $50 of Intel.[5]

Suppose that today no one sells or buys shares in the fund. The asset value of the Super-Duper fund today is $1,000,000. Now suppose that tomorrow the price of IBM is $110 and the price of Intel is $48. Then the value of a fund share is $103 (cell C14 below).

|  | A | B | C | D |
|---|---|---|---|---|
| 1 | SUPER-DUPER OPEN END MUTUAL FUND | | | |
| 2 | | Today | Tomorrow before new fundholders | |
| 3 | Number of Super-Duper shares | 10,000 | 10,000 | |
| 4 | | | | |
| 5 | **Portfolio** | | | |
| 6 | Price of IBM | 100 | 110 | |
| 7 | Price of Intel | 50 | 48 | |
| 8 | | | | |
| 9 | Portfolio composition | | | |
| 10 | Shares of IBM | 5,000 | 5,000 | |
| 11 | Shares of Intel | 10,000 | 10,000 | |
| 12 | | | | |
| 13 | Total fund value | 1,000,000 | 1,030,000 | <-- =C10*C6+C11*C7 |
| 14 | Value of 1 fund share | 100 | 103 | <-- =C13/C3 |
| 15 | | | | |
| 16 | Tomorrow: after new fundholders | | | New shares are created at the current fund share price, so the fund is now worth 10,500*$103=$1,081,500 . |
| 17 | Number of Super-Duper shares | 10,500 | | |
| 18 | Total fund value | 1,081,500 | <-- =B17*C14 | |
| 19 | | | | |
| 20 | Portfolio composition | | | |
| 21 | Shares of IBM | 4,915.91 | <-- =B18*50%/C6 | |
| 22 | Shares of Intel | 11,265.63 | <-- =B18*50%/C7 | |

---

[4] In the jargon of mutual funds, this makes it an *open-end* fund. Our next example considers a closed-end fund.

[5] Actually, Super-Duper Fund does all this at the end of the day. So if Uncle Joe wants to sell his share and Aunt Maude wants to invest an additional $100, Super-Duper has a *wash*, and it can save on the transaction costs of buying and selling. Every penny helps!

Now suppose that at the close of the day tomorrow another 500 individuals buy shares of the fund. This means that they pay 500 * $103 = $51,500 to buy shares in the fund. Assuming that the fund sticks to its current policy of splitting its investment equally between IBM and Intel, the total fund value of $1,081,500 (cell B18 above) will now be invested in 4,915.91 shares of IBM and 11,265.63 shares of Intel.

In an *open-end mutual fund* the number of shares is flexible. New shareholders buy into the fund at the per-share value of the fund, and shareholders in the fund who want to cash out cash out at the per-share value of the fund. At any point in time, the per-share value of the fund is given by the formula

$$\textit{open-end fund per-share value} = \frac{\textit{fund net asset value (NAV)}}{\textit{number of shares in fund}}$$
$$= \frac{\textit{market value of fund's portfolio} - \textit{fund expenses}}{\textit{number of shares in fund}}$$

Note that we've introduced a new bit of jargon: A mutual fund's net asset value (NAV) is the market value of the fund's portfolio minus fund expenses.

The additivity principle applied to open-end mutual funds means: *An open-end mutual fund is priced at the sum of the values of the share portfolio held by the fund.*

## Mutual Fund Costs: Some Technical Details

The fund has some expenses that are charged to the fund holders and deducted from the value of the fund. These include the costs of buying and selling shares. Another fund cost is the cost of paying the managers: Typically fund managers charge their clients a percentage cost. If your fund charges 1% (in the United States this is typical), then this cost ($10,000 per year in our example) has to be taken out of the value of the fund.

Our Super-Duper Fund doesn't charge shareholders to buy or sell shares in the fund. However, an important class of mutual funds charge shareholders to buy shares in their funds. These so-called *front-end load* mutual funds are more expensive than *no-load* funds. Suppose, for example, that Super-Super-Duper were to charge a 7% front-end load. Then you would pay $107 (=$100 + 7% front-end load) to buy a share of the fund. Front-end loads are obviously expensive; mutual fund salespeople sometimes justify these extra charges as an appropriate price to pay for the expertise of better fund management, but there is almost no evidence to show that this is true.[6]

## Example 3: Closed-End Mutual Funds—When Additivity Fails

Value-additivity doesn't always work. In this subsection we give an example of *closed-end mutual funds*. A closed-end mutual fund is an investment company with a fixed number of shares. Like open-end mutual funds, closed-end mutual funds invest in a portfolio of stocks. As

---

[6] Recall that in Chapter 12 we discussed a technique for judging mutual fund performance using the CAPM. Finance researchers employing this and more sophisticated techniques find little evidence that front-load mutual funds outperform no-load mutual funds.

opposed to an open-end mutual fund, however, where the number of shares can be expanded or contracted, a closed-end mutual fund has a fixed number of shares that are sold on the stock market. The company issues no more new shares, and the market price fluctuates with supply and demand for the fund's shares. Closed-end funds are investment companies for which value additivity usually fails.

Here's an example. The Chippewa Fund is a closed-end fund that looks a lot like the Super-Duper Fund. Like Super-Duper, Chippewa has 10,000 shares. Chippewa's share portfolio currently consists of $500,000 of IBM stock and $500,000 of Intel stock, and its shares are registered on the Chippewa Stock Exchange. The fund has no other assets.

What should be the price of a Chippewa Fund share? It seems that it should be equal to the per-share value of the fund's assets—in our case $100 per share (as you saw in our discussion of open-end mutual funds, the finance jargon is the *net asset value* of the Chippewa Fund is $100 per share). But checking the newspapers, you find that the share price of the Chippewa Fund is $90, below its NAV. A back check of the prices of the Chippewa Fund shows you that Chippewa almost always sells for less than its NAV. In fact, a finance-knowledgeable friend has told you that almost all closed-end funds sell for less than their NAV.

The reasons why closed-end funds sell at a discount are not well understood.[7] What is well understood, however, is that it is difficult to arbitrage a closed-end fund discount—meaning that it is difficult for investors to make money out of the discount and, by making money, cause the discount to disappear. Suppose, for example, that shares of Chippewa fund trade below $100 net asset value, say at $90. Then both existing and potential fund shareholders have a problem: On the one hand, the existing shareholders are holding $100 market-value shares worth only $90. If the closed-end fund were to break up, existing shareholders would get the NAV of $100. So all the shareholders would in principle favor breaking up the fund, but no individual shareholder would want to sell his individual shares before such a breakup. A potential new shareholder is faced with the same problem: He gets $100 (market value) of shares for $90, but he has no guarantee that the value of the closed-end fund will ultimately get back to the market value.

This whole scenario may sound somewhat improbable, but in fact there are many closed-end mutual funds. Figure 14.3 gives an actual example: Tri-Continental Corp. is a closed-end fund registered on the New York Stock Exchange. On 23 November 2001 the fund's shares were worth 11.18% less than the market value of the fund's portfolio. This *closed-end fund discount* is pervasive throughout the closed-end fund industry.

---

[7] A readable survey of closed-end fund discounts is a paper by Elroy Dimson and Carolina Minua-Paluello, "The Closed-End Fund Discount," which is available on the Web. In their introduction, they write, "Closed-end funds are characterized by one of the most puzzling anomalies in finance: the closed-end fund discount. Shares in American funds are issued at a premium to net asset value (NAV) of up to 10 percent, while British funds are issued at a premium amounting to at least 5 percent. This premium represents the underwriting fees and start-up costs associated with the flotation. Subsequently, within a matter of months, the shares trade at a discount, which persists and fluctuates.... Upon termination (liquidation or 'open-ending') of the fund, share price rises and discounts disappear."

## Tri-Continental Corporation—A Closed-End Fund

**PERFORMANCE DATA**

E-MAIL / ARCHIVE / REGISTRATION / ABOUT CEFA / LEGAL INFO

**Tri-Continental Corporation (TY / NYSE)**
as of 11/23/2001

MORE INFO ON    help

### Contact Information

Advisor: Seligman, J.W. & Co., Inc.
Phone: (800) 221-7844
Website: http://www.tricontinental.com

### Portfolio Mgr., Tenure

Charles Smith, 12/1/1994

### Summary Information as of 6/30/2001

Category: Growth & Income
Inception Date: 12/31/1965
Outstanding Shares: 131,077,105
Admin Fees: N/A
Expense Ratio: 0.6
Portfolio Turnover: 38%
Total Net Assets: $3,207.64 (Millions)

### Description

Tri-Continental Corporation is a diversified, closed-end management investment company. The Fund seeks growth of capital while producing reasonable current income. The assets will primarily be invested in common stock. However, the Fund may invest its assets in a variety of asset classes. The Fund's capital structure includes both common and preferred stocks, as well as warrants.

### Price Information as of 11/23/2001

| | |
|---|---|
| NAV: | 22.89 ← Net asset value |
| Net chg: | 0.20 |
| Prior Day: | 22.69 |
| 52-Week NAV Ret: (as of 11/23/2001) | -16.57% |
| Mkt Price: | 20.33 ← Market price on 23 November 2001 |

### Average Annual Total Return as of 10/31/2001

| | MARKET PRICE | NAV |
|---|---|---|
| YTD: | -8.7% | -16.59% |
| 1 yr: | -14.29% | -21.09% |
| 5 yr: | 9.03% | 7.15% |
| 10 yr: | 9.6% | 10.34% |
| Since Inception: | N/A | N/A |

### Premium / Discount as of 10/31/2001

| | |
|---|---|
| Current (as of 11/23/2001): | -11.18% |
| YTD Min: | -13.46% |
| YTD Max: | -10.27% |
| YTD Avg: | -11.22% |
| 5-yr Avg: | -16.38% |
| 10-yr Avg: | -14.57% |

### Top 10 Holdings as of 6/30/2001

| | |
|---|---|
| Microsoft Corporation | 4.2% |
| General Electric Company | 3.9% |
| St Jude Medical Inc | 3% |
| United Technologies Corporation | 3% |
| Citigroup Inc | 2.7% |
| Pitney Bowes Inc | 2.6% |
| Baxter International Inc | 2.6% |
| American International Group Inc | 2.5% |
| Exxon Mobil Corporation | 2.4% |
| Pfizer Inc | 2.3% |

### Top 10 Sectors as of 4/30/2001

| | |
|---|---|
| Technology | 25.3% |
| Financials | 18.2% |
| Cyclicals | 10.6% |
| Health | 9.5% |
| Energy | 8.6% |
| Staples | 8.5% |
| Services | 8.3% |
| Retail | 5.7% |
| Utilities | 3.1% |
| Durables | 2.1% |

FIGURE 14.3 Tri-Continental Corp. is a closed-end fund whose shares are registered on the New York Stock Exchange. On 23 November 2001, Tri-Continental's assets—the market value of the shares contained in its portfolio—totaled $3,207,840,000. Because the fund has 131,077,105 shares, this works out to a net asset value (NAV) per share of

$$NAV = \frac{3,207,840,000}{131,077,105} = \$22.89$$

However, on the same date, the fund's shares sold for $20.33, *a discount* of 11.18%. The Tri-Continental discount is pervasive. In the past 10 years the discount has averaged 14.57%.
*Source*: http://www.closed-endfunds.com

### Summing Up Additivity

As long as market participants can freely arbitrage, we expect value additivity to hold: The value of a basket of goods or financial assets should equal the sum of the values of the components. Arbitrage in this case means the ability of market participants to create and sell their own bundles of goods or assets or to break up existing bundles and sell the components. This is true whether we're discussing the cost of a bag of apples in the Asheville farmers' market or the price of an open-end mutual fund. But there are also situations, like a closed-end fund, where arbitrage is difficult. For these cases, like the closed-end funds just discussed, we would not expect value additivity to hold.

We're not quite done with additivity: In the next section we discuss an interesting case where value additivity was clearly violated, but where—eventually—market prices came to reflect value additivity.

## 14.3. Additivity Is Not Always Instantaneous: The Case of Palm and 3Com

During the 1990s, 3Com developed the Palm Pilot, a handheld personal information manager that became a raging success. In March 2000, 3Com sold 5.7% of its Palm subsidiary to the public. After this "equity carveout" there were separate stock market listings for Palm (still 94.3% owned by 3Com) and for the parent company 3Com. On 3 March 2000, the closing stock price for Palm was $80.25 per share and the closing stock price for 3Com was $83.06 per share. As you'll see, this situation represents an interesting violation of the principle of value additivity.

In the spreadsheet below we calculate the market value of Palm (cell B5) and of 3Com (cell B10).

| | A | B | C |
|---|---|---|---|
| 1 | **3COM AND PALM**<br>**This spreadsheet reflects market prices on**<br>**3 March 2000, the day after the issue of 5.7%**<br>**of Palm stock held by 3Com** | | |
| 2 | **Palm** | | |
| 3 | Price per share | 80.25 | |
| 4 | Number of shares outstanding | 562,258,065 | |
| 5 | Market value | 45,121,209,716 | <-- =B4*B3 |
| 6 | | | |
| 7 | **3Com** | | |
| 8 | Price per share | 83.06 | |
| 9 | Number of shares outstanding | 349,354,000 | |
| 10 | Market value | 29,017,343,240 | <-- =B9*B8 |
| 11 | | | |
| 12 | Value of Palm stock held by 3Com (94.3%) | 42,549,300,762 | <-- =94.3%*B5 |
| 13 | Value of non-Palm 3Com activities | -13,531,957,522 | <-- =B10-B12 |

If you look at these numbers you'll see a startling *failure* of value additivity:

- 3Com owns most of Palm, but Palm's value is bigger than 3Com's! To be more precise, the 94.3% of Palm stock still owned by 3Com is worth $42.5 billion (cell B12), but all of 3Com is worth only $29.0 billion (cell B10).

- Using these numbers, the market seems to value all of the non-Palm activities of 3Com at a *negative* $13.5 billion!!!! The only way this would be possible is if these activities were big money losers (which wasn't the case).

Why did additivity fail in this big way? Why didn't market participants arbitrage the 3Com and Palm stock prices so that additivity would be restored (below we explain how such an arbitrage would work)? One possible reason is that markets are (temporarily) relatively stupid: The enthusiasm for the initial public offering (IPO) of Palm at the beginning of March 2000 was so overwhelming that investors (temporarily, as you'll see below) forgot that 3Com still owned most of Palm. So they mispriced the relative values of Palm and 3Com, producing the weird case shown above. If they had thought a bit, they would have realized that a share of 3Com should be worth at least 1.52 times the price of a share of Palm.

| | A | B | C |
|---|---|---|---|
| 16 | **Minimum logical value of 3Com shares, compared to Palm** | | |
| 17 | Number of shares of Palm held by 3Com | 530,209,355 | <-- =94.3%*B4 |
| 18 | Number of 3Com shares | 349,354,000 | |
| 19 | Number of Palm shares per 3Com share | 1.52 | <-- =B17/B18 |

Actually, if they knew how to read a balance sheet, they would conclude that the price of a 3Com share should be even more. In 3Com's last quarterly statement, just 1 week before the Palm IPO, its balance sheet showed almost $3 billion in cash and short-term investments. Assuming that these items were not needed for production of 3Com's products, they are worth $8.53 per 3Com share.

| | A | B | C |
|---|---|---|---|
| 22 | **On 25 Feb 2000, from 3Com's balance sheet** | | |
| 23 | Cash and equivalents | 1,812,503,000 | |
| 24 | Short-term investments | 1,166,026,000 | |
| 25 | | 2,978,529,000 | <-- =B24+B23 |
| 26 | | | |
| 27 | Cash and investments per 3Com share | 8.53 | <-- =B25/B9 |

So the minimum value for a 3Com share should have been

*3Com share price* $\geq 1.52 *$ *Palm share price* $+ \$8.53$

## Short-Selling as a Way of Correcting Market Mispricing

Short-selling is a technique of borrowing a stock, selling it, and repaying it later.[8] Suppose you could freely short-sell Palm stock. Then you could make money from the above situation by shorting Palm stock and buying 3Com stock. We'll explain the arbitrage technique in a second, but the logic is as follows: Palm stock is overpriced (relative to 3Com stock) and 3Com stock is underpriced

---

[8] The actual procedures for implementing a short sale are not simple. A well-written academic survey is a recent paper by Gene D'Avolio, "The Market for Borrowing Stock," http://papers.ssrn.com/sol3/papers. cfm?abstract_id=305479. There's also a wonderful article in the 1 December 2003 issue of the *New Yorker Magazine* by James Surowiecki. Entitled "Get Shorty," the article can be found on the Web at http:// newyorker.com/talk/content/?031201ta_talk_surowiecki.

(relative to Palm stock), so you should buy the cheap stock (3Com) and sell the overpriced stock (Palm).

The arbitrage with which an investor could profit from the market mispricing is as follows:

- Borrow a share of Palm stock and sell it. Selling borrowed stock is called *short-selling*. In the example below, an arbitrageur short-sells one share of Palm for $80.25.

- Buy the equivalent value of 3Com stock. At the time of the arbitrage we explore below, 3Com was selling for $83.06 per share. The arbitrageur—having just shorted Palm for $80.25, spends this money to buy 0.966 shares of 3Com (0.966 * $83.06 = $80.25).

If you're right about the mispricing of the Palm versus 3Com shares, you should make money under any price scenario. In the example below the arbitrageur shorted 1 share of Palm on 3 March and used the proceeds to buy 0.966 shares of 3Com. Suppose that the arbitrageur undid his position on 10 March (meaning he bought 1 share of Palm and sold 0.966 shares of 3Com). If on 10 March the prices of Palm and 3Com were in line with her additive valuation, then the arbitrageur would make money. In the example below, the share price of Palm on 10 March is $99 and the share price of 3Com is $159.01. As you can see, the arbitrageur makes $60.01.

| | A | B | C |
|---|---|---|---|
| 1 | **3COM AND PALM:  ARBITRAGING THE MISPRICING** | | |
| 2 | 3 March 2000—short-sell 1 Palm share and buy $ 80.25/$83.06 = 0.9662  3 Com shares | | |
| 3 | Cash flow | 0.00 | <-- =80.25-0.9662*83.06 |
| 4 | | | |
| 5 | 10 March 2000—buy 1 Palm share and sell $ 80.25/$83.06 = 0.9662  3 Com shares | | |
| 6 | Suppose Palm price is | 99.00 | |
| 7 | Logical *minimum* 3Com price | 159.01 | <-- =1.52*B6+8.53 |
| 8 | Profit | 60.01 | <-- =B7-B6 |

If you play with the spreadsheet, you'll see that as long as you're right about the *price relation* between Palm and 3Com, you'll make money—whether the price of Palm goes up (as in the previous example) or down. For example, suppose that shares of Palm go down in price and that they sell for $60 on 10 March.

| | A | B | C |
|---|---|---|---|
| 1 | **3COM AND PALM:  ARBITRAGING THE MISPRICING** | | |
| 2 | 3 March 2000—short-sell 1 Palm share and buy $80.25/$83.06 = 0.9662  3Com shares | | |
| 3 | Cash flow | 0.00 | <-- =80.25-0.9662*83.06 |
| 4 | | | |
| 5 | 10 March 2000— buy 1 Palm share and sell $80.25/$83.06 = 0.9662  3Com shares | | |
| 6 | Suppose Palm price is | 60.00 | |
| 7 | Logical *minimum* 3Com price | 99.73 | <-- =1.52*B6+8.53 |
| 8 | Profit | 39.73 | <-- =B7-B6 |

As you can see from this arbitrage example, short-selling is essential to making the prices "behave" in an additive way. Because short-selling involves selling borrowed stock, one explanation of the lack of additivity in 3Com–Palm prices is that initially there were just too few Palm shares around for arbitrageurs to sell.

## What Happened Later?

The graph below shows the relation between Palm's stock price and 3Com's (column C of the spreadsheet calculates the ratio $\frac{3Com's\ stock\ price}{Palm's\ stock\ price}$). As you can see, the ratio climbed in the days following the Palm IPO, reaching the 1.52 point on 9 May 2000. From then until the end of July 2000, the ratio remained above this ratio—presumably the word had gotten out and enough investors understood the intricacies of the 3Com–Palm relationship to force the prices into an appropriate pattern.

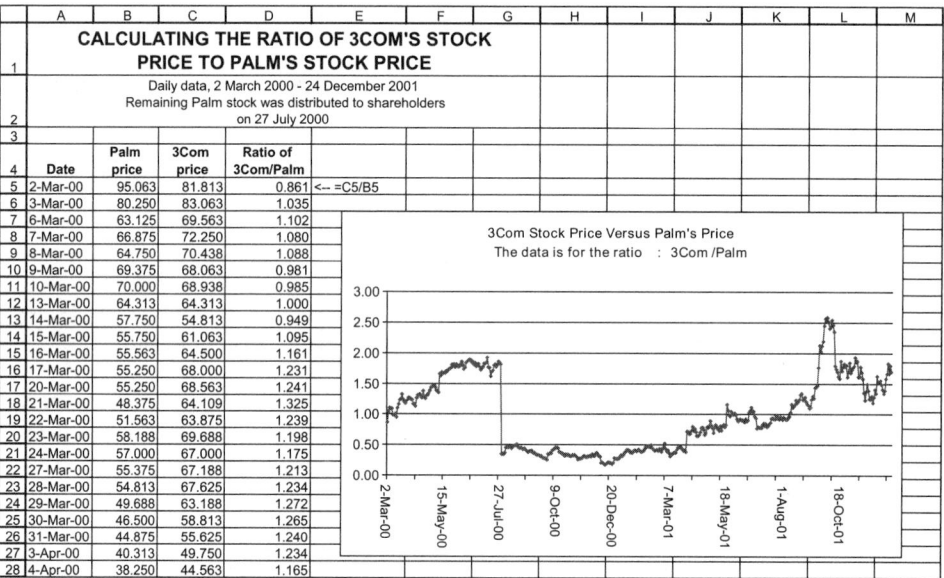

| | A | B | C | D | E |
|---|---|---|---|---|---|
| 1 | | | | | CALCULATING THE RATIO OF 3COM'S STOCK PRICE TO PALM'S STOCK PRICE |
| 2 | | | | | Daily data, 2 March 2000 - 24 December 2001 Remaining Palm stock was distributed to shareholders on 27 July 2000 |
| 3 | | | | | |
| 4 | Date | Palm price | 3Com price | Ratio of 3Com/Palm | |
| 5 | 2-Mar-00 | 95.063 | 81.813 | 0.861 | <-- =C5/B5 |
| 6 | 3-Mar-00 | 80.250 | 83.063 | 1.035 | |
| 7 | 6-Mar-00 | 63.125 | 69.563 | 1.102 | |
| 8 | 7-Mar-00 | 66.875 | 72.250 | 1.080 | |
| 9 | 8-Mar-00 | 64.750 | 70.438 | 1.088 | |
| 10 | 9-Mar-00 | 69.375 | 68.063 | 0.981 | |
| 11 | 10-Mar-00 | 70.000 | 68.938 | 0.985 | |
| 12 | 13-Mar-00 | 64.313 | 64.313 | 1.000 | |
| 13 | 14-Mar-00 | 57.750 | 54.813 | 0.949 | |
| 14 | 15-Mar-00 | 55.750 | 61.063 | 1.095 | |
| 15 | 16-Mar-00 | 55.563 | 64.500 | 1.161 | |
| 16 | 17-Mar-00 | 55.250 | 68.000 | 1.231 | |
| 17 | 20-Mar-00 | 55.250 | 68.563 | 1.241 | |
| 18 | 21-Mar-00 | 48.375 | 64.109 | 1.325 | |
| 19 | 22-Mar-00 | 51.563 | 63.875 | 1.239 | |
| 20 | 23-Mar-00 | 58.188 | 69.688 | 1.198 | |
| 21 | 24-Mar-00 | 57.000 | 67.000 | 1.175 | |
| 22 | 27-Mar-00 | 55.375 | 67.188 | 1.213 | |
| 23 | 28-Mar-00 | 54.813 | 67.625 | 1.234 | |
| 24 | 29-Mar-00 | 49.688 | 63.188 | 1.272 | |
| 25 | 30-Mar-00 | 46.500 | 58.813 | 1.265 | |
| 26 | 31-Mar-00 | 44.875 | 55.625 | 1.240 | |
| 27 | 3-Apr-00 | 40.313 | 49.750 | 1.234 | |
| 28 | 4-Apr-00 | 38.250 | 44.563 | 1.165 | |

On 28 July 2000, the ratio dropped precipitously, from 1.815 to 0.347. What happened? After markets closed on 27 July, 3Com *distributed all remaining Palm shares to its shareholders*. There was no longer any compelling reason for 3Com's share price to be related to Palm's. As you can see in the graph above, since that time the ratio of the prices has been all over the place.

|   | A | B | C | D | E | F | G |
|---|---|---|---|---|---|---|---|
| 1 | **CALCULATING THE RATIO OF 3COM'S STOCK PRICE TO PALM'S STOCK PRICE** | | | | | | |
| 2 | Daily data, 2 March 2000 - 24 December 2001<br>Note that remaining Palm stock was distributed to shareholders<br>on 27 July 2000 | | | | | | |
| 3 | | | | | | | |
| 4 | **Date** | **Palm** | **3Com** | **Ratio of 3Com/Palm** | | | |
| 99 | 17-Jul-00 | 39.500 | 66.813 | 1.691 | Palm's stock price | | |
| 100 | 18-Jul-00 | 37.313 | 64.063 | 1.717 | | | |
| 101 | 19-Jul-00 | 34.875 | 62.750 | 1.799 | | | |
| 102 | 20-Jul-00 | 36.750 | 66.625 | 1.813 | 3Com's stock price | | |
| 103 | 21-Jul-00 | 38.313 | 68.000 | 1.775 | | | |
| 104 | 24-Jul-00 | 36.625 | 66.188 | 1.807 | 3Com sells for 1.815 times Palm | | |
| 105 | 25-Jul-00 | 36.563 | 67.938 | 1.858 | | | |
| 106 | 26-Jul-00 | 36.688 | 67.875 | 1.850 | | | |
| 107 | 27-Jul-00 | 35.563 | 64.563 | 1.815 | <-- =C107/B107 | | |
| 108 | 28-Jul-00 | 37.250 | 12.938 | 0.347 | <-- =C108/B108 | | |
| 109 | 31-Jul-00 | 39.000 | 13.563 | 0.348 | | | |
| 110 | 1-Aug-00 | 39.375 | 13.688 | 0.348 | | | |
| 111 | 2-Aug-00 | 39.125 | 14.438 | 0.369 | | | |

## What Happened on 27 July 2000?

On 27 July 2000 (the divestiture of all Palm stock by 3Com), the price of 3Com dropped precipitously. By that date investors—well informed about the coming divestiture of Palm—realized that the divestiture of the stock by 3Com would lower 3Com's value. And so it did.

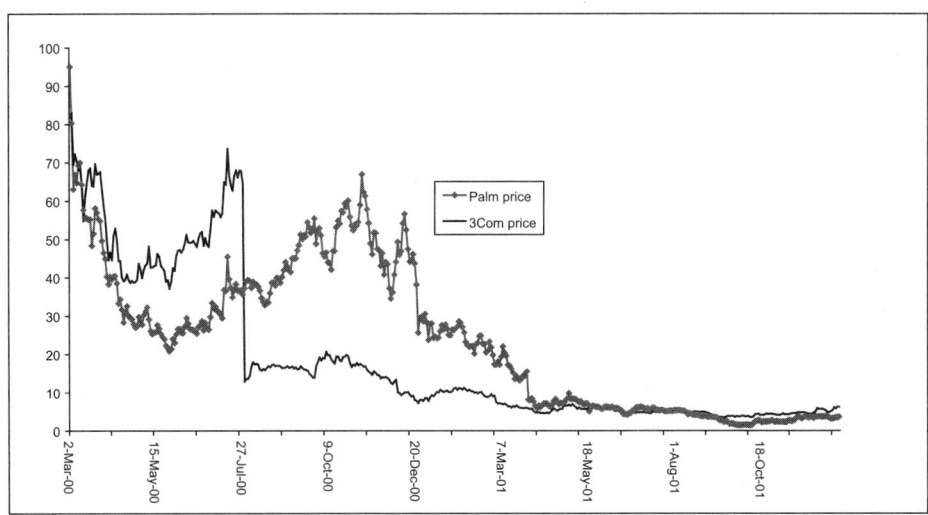

FIGURE 14.4 The prices of 3Com and Palm stock, 2 March 2000–24 December 2001. A partial spin-off of Palm was initiated by 3Com on 3 March 2000 and completed on 27 July 2000 (on this date there was a precipitous decline in 3Com's stock price).

## Palm and 3Com—What's the Point?

Additivity is a basic efficiency feature of financial markets. As in the case of closed-end funds, it may not hold where the structural features of the funds make arbitrage difficult, or—as in the case of Palm and 3Com—it may take some time for markets to figure out what's happening and to initiate the arbitrage that will lead to additivity. One fundamental way to correct nonadditivity is to short-sell, but sometimes (as discussed on page 436) a short-sale may be difficult. Difficulties in short-selling can lead to failure of additivity.

# 14.4. Efficient Markets Principle 3: Cheap Information Is Worthless

Financial markets are awash in information, and it is important for you to have some opinions about how this information affects market prices. In this section we discuss three hypotheses that relate to how information is incorporated into financial markets. The finance jargon for these hypotheses is as follows: Weak-form efficiency, semistrong form efficiency, and strong form efficiency.

In one form or another all three of these hypotheses state that information is important and that cheap and easily accessible information is likely to be worthless. The cheaper and more easily accessible the information, the less it's worth.

Read the previous paragraph again. It sounds contradictory!

- Information is important? This seems obvious. Whether it's the cost of a bank loan or information about whether Upward Slopes Ski Site is making money, the more informed you are about a financial asset, the more you should be able to judge its worth.

- Cheap and easily accessible information is likely to be worthless? If it's so important, why isn't it worth anything? The reason is that many people think that it's important, and so they're all trying to figure out what the information is and how it affects the value of the asset. With so much energy expended on finding out the effect of the information and with the information so cheap, you're likely to find that the whole price impact of the information has already been extracted and is already reflected in the market price.

## Weak-Form Efficiency: Almost Always True

The hypothesis of weak-form efficiency says that you cannot predict the future price of a financial asset by carefully examining the asset's past prices and its current price. Because *everyone* has easy and cheap access to the past prices of IBM stock, there's nothing left to be learned from these prices—all possible information contained in these prices is already incorporated in the *current market price* of IBM. Everyone knows past prices and, therefore, if you could make a profitable prediction based on a stock's price history, so could everyone else. In trying to implement this profitable information, you and other investors would drive its profitability out of existence. This sounds obvious (and it is), but it's a principle often overlooked by investors.

## Technical Analysis—Do Previous Prices Predict Future Prices?

Its proponents claim that *technical analysis* is the art or science of using historical stock price patterns to predict the future stock price. Finance professors think that technical analysis is neither an art nor a science, but simply voodoo. They base this belief on the weak-form efficient markets hypothesis and on tons of academic research.

Here's a simple example of technical analysis: Based on an analysis of ABC's historical stock price, you've concluded that it fluctuates in a band between $25 and $35. When the price gets close to $25 it inevitably goes up, and when the price gets close to $35 the stock price goes down. This leads you to develop the following money-making strategy:

- Buy ABC when the price gets to $25.50; because this is very close to $25, the price will have a very high probability of moving up. In any case you'll have little to lose because the price can't go below $25.

- Sell ABC when the price gets to $34.50; because this is very close to $35, the price has a very high probability of moving down. In any case at $34.50 you have very little to gain.

This sounds like a money-making strategy, but on the other hand it's self-defeating: If all investors try to implement this strategy (and why shouldn't they, because your analysis is based on publicly available information?), then the "price band" will narrow—no one will want to buy ABC stock when it gets close to $34.50 or to sell it when it gets close to $25.50. Now everyone will try to implement a profit strategy based on the new price band. And so on and so on....

The conclusion: There is no price band! It may be that ABC's share price has been between $25 and $35 in the past, but this says nothing about its share price in the future.

In fact, you could make a broader conclusion: As long as there are many people trading in a market, a strategy based only on past and current prices cannot be profitable.

## Technical Trading Rules—Another Violation of Weak-Form Efficiency

A technical trading strategy is a rule for buying and selling a stock based on the stock's previous price movements.[9] The weak-form efficiency hypothesis says that technical trading rules won't work.

The ABC example above (where ABC's stock was assumed to trade in a band between $25 and $35) is a simple example of a technical trading rule. Figure 14.5 gives a more sophisticated example.

The down trendline explains the downturn in Budget Group's stock price by connecting four "price peaks." The prediction and the associated trading rule is as follows:

- When the stock price of Budget Group gets close to the down trendline, it will move down. To exploit this information, you should buy when the price is below the trendline and sell when it is above the line.

- *If* the stock price of Budget Group *breaks through* the down trendline, "a change of trend could be imminent." This is the technical analyst's escape hatch—the information contained in the prices is true except when it's not true.

## Semistrong Form Efficiency: Sometimes True

Semistrong form efficiency predicts that not just past prices, but all publicly available information, is incorporated in current security prices. This suggests, for example, that the

---

[9] There are lots of good Web sites on technical trading. Here are a couple: http://technicaltrading.com/ and http://www.stockcharts.com/education/What/TradingStrategies/MurphysLaws.html.

**Down Trendline**

A down trendline has a negative slope and is formed by connecting two or more high points. The second high must be lower than the first for the line to have a negative slope. Down trendlines act as resistance and indicate that net-supply (supply less demand) is increasing even as the price declines. A declining price combined with increasing supply is very bearish and shows the strong resolve of the sellers. As long as prices remain below the down trendline, the downtrend is considered solid and intact. A break above the down trendline indicates that net-supply is decreasing and a change of trend could be imminent.

FIGURE 14.5 Technical analysis of Budget stock.
http://www.stockcharts.com:85/education/What/ChartAnalysis/trendlines.html

analysis of a firm's financial statements is not going to help you make better investment decisions.

Semistrong market efficiency seems to be true...*occasionally*. It's a lot of work to understand *all* the publicly available information about a stock, and it's quite common to see cases where information existed, but it wasn't incorporated into the stock price. The 3Com–Palm story discussed in Section 14.3 is a case in point. Only after some rigorous analysis of the relation between 3Com and Palm and analysis of the cash reserves of 3Com could we conclude that Palm was overpriced relative to 3Com. There has to be a lot at stake to motivate investors to engage in this kind of research. If it's worthwhile, then we would expect semistrong efficiency to prevail.

## Strong Form Efficiency: Usually Not True

The strong form efficient markets hypothesis says that *all* information is incorporated into securities prices. Hardly anyone believes that this is true. In fact, it's often illegal because *all* information includes proprietary information and inside knowledge—by law, insiders are forbidden to trade on their information if it hasn't been revealed to the public.

## 14.5. Efficient Markets Principle 4: Transaction Costs Are Important

*Transaction costs* are all the various costs of buying and selling a security and also the costs (monetary or otherwise) of *understanding* a security. When you buy a stock for $50, you pay a brokerage commission. In the United States this commission is typically ½ percent. So the purchase of a share of stock costs you $50.25 and its sale delivers you $49.75.

|   | A | B | C |
|---|---|---|---|
| 3 | Buy commission | 0.50% | |
| 4 | Sell commission | 0.50% | |
| 5 | | | |
| 6 | Stock price | $50.00 | |
| 7 | | | |
| 8 | Purchase price | 50.25 | <-- =B6*(1+B3) |
| 9 | Selling price | 49.75 | <-- =B6*(1-B4) |

The result: If you think that the stock is worth $50.15, it won't be worth your while to buy it: Even though the stock's price today is $50, less than what you think it's worth, transaction costs make it more expensive to buy the stock ($50.25) than you think it's worth.

Similarly, suppose you own a share of the stock and suppose you think it's worth only $49.80. In the absence of transaction costs, it would be logical to sell the stock, but with a ½ percent transactions cost, you would be getting less than you think the stock is worth.

Here's a more interesting example: Below are the prices of sugar in London and in New York on 25 July 2003.

|    | A | B | C |
|----|---|---|---|
| 1  | **COMPARING SUGAR PRICES IN LONDON AND NEW YORK** | | |
| 2  | New York (dollars/pound) | 0.0693 | |
| 3  | London (dollars/tonne) | 208.30 | |
| 4  | pounds per tonne | 2,200 | |
| 5  | London (dollars/pound) | 0.0947 | <-- =B3/B4 |
| 6  | | | |
| 7  | **One container of sugar** | | |
| 8  | Contains 21 tons | | |
| 9  | in pounds | 46,200 | <-- =21*B4 |
| 10 | "Arbitrage profit" | 1,172.64 | <-- =(B5-B2)*B9 |

New York sugar is selling for 6.93 cents per pound, whereas sugar in London is selling for $208.30 per "tonne." Could there be an opportunity here to make money? In comparing the prices, you have to make sure the units are the same; for example—a tonne is a *metric ton*, 1,000 kilograms (which equals 2,200 pounds). As you can see, the London price translates to 9.47 cents per pound.

It looks like there's an arbitrage opportunity here: If we buy sugar in New York and sell it in London, we can make over 2.5 cents per pound. Because a 20-foot container can hold 21 tons of sugar (or 46,200 pounds; see cell B9 above), it looks like we could make almost $1,173 profit per container. And because a ship can hold hundreds of containers, this must be a surefire way to get rich!

But hold on—this couldn't be. We must have forgotten the transaction costs:

- It *costs money* to ship sugar from New York to London. It costs approximately $1,000 to ship a container of sugar from New York to London. This alone would almost eliminate the arbitrage profit.

- It *takes time* to ship sugar from New York to London—somewhere between 10 days and 3 weeks, depending on the availability of shipping. So even if the freight costs are less than $1,173, this isn't an arbitrage—it's a kind of educated gamble on the price differentials between the two cities.[10]

So, there might be a profit here, but it's not certain. The transaction costs, the cost and the time needed to ship the sugar from New York to London, will eat up most of the profits. Of course, this is what you would expect in an efficient market: You can't make money from things that are easy to do.

# Conclusion

Financial economists use the words "efficient markets" to describe a variety of rules about financial asset prices that are so simple that they almost always have to be true. In this chapter we've explored several of these asset pricing rules:

- One price for one asset. In an efficient financial market, assets that are the same ought to have the same value and price.

- Price additivity of asset bundles: In an efficient market bundling two or more assets together—whether it's different kinds of apples in a bag or stocks in a mutual fund—doesn't change their value.

- Informational effects on prices: Generally known information cannot be worth much, and the more widely the information is known, the less it is worth. We explored three versions of this principle. The weak-form efficiency principle says that the future asset price cannot be predicted from knowledge of historical asset prices and the current asset price. The semistrong form efficiency principle says that publicly known information—not just prices, but published accounting data and other information that can (with some work) be derived from the information—is worthless. Economists believe that semistrong efficiency holds frequently but not always. The strong form efficiency principle, which almost no one believes, says that *all* information—whether public or not—is worthless.

- Transaction costs: These pesky critters can screw up the previous three principles because they interfere with arbitrage. Arbitrage, the buying and selling of assets with a riskless profit, is the mechanism by which the three above principles are forced to hold. Transaction costs, the cost of buying and selling an asset, or the cost of finding out information about the asset can make it more difficult to arbitrage and hence cause market inefficiencies.

# EXERCISES

1. One of the earliest tests of market efficiency was to examine the returns of stocks around the publication of their earnings reports. The following graph below the price of XYZ stock 7 days before and after the earnings announcement date (date = 0). Assume that the only new information during

---

[10] What we need is a forward or a futures contract: These are contracts that enable us to fix a price today for sugar delivered in London at some point in the future. Such contracts exist, but they're beyond the scope of this book. For a good text, see John Hull, *Options, Futures, and other Derivatives*, 7th edition, Prentice Hall, 2008.

this period is the publication of the earnings report showing higher profits than expected. Does the price pattern of XYZ stocks support the concept of market efficiency?

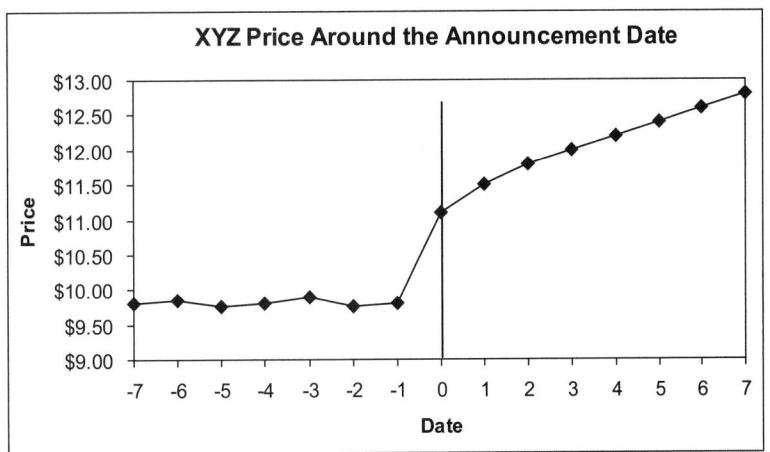

2. In the three graphs below, are the principles of market efficiency violated? If so, which principle and why?

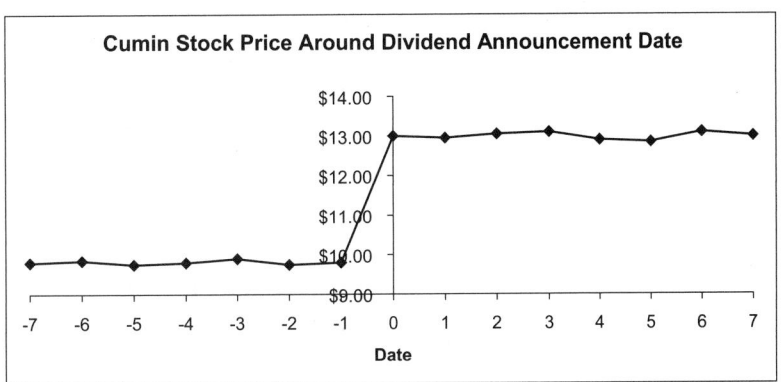

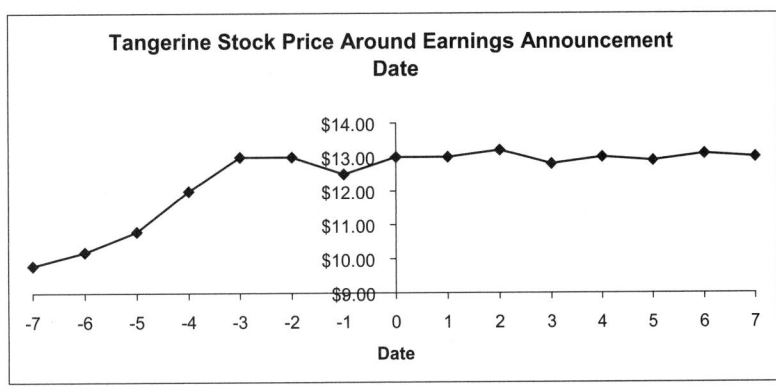

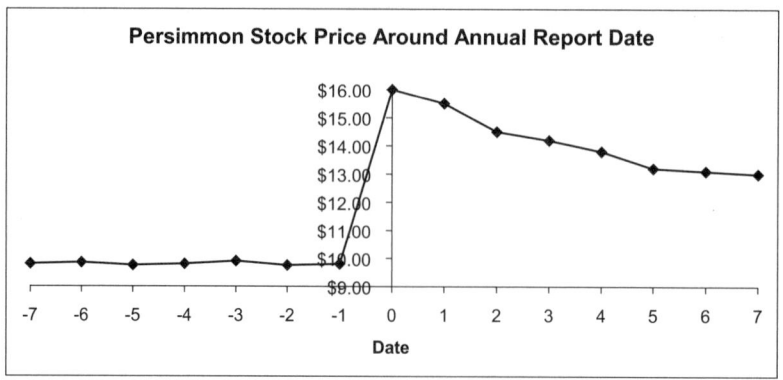

3. Which of the following results support/contradict market efficiency?

    a. Stocks that perform best in January perform worst in February.

    b. Only 35% of mutual funds earned higher returns than the S&P 500.

    c. Firms that announce a dividend cut continue to underperform similar stocks 6 months after the announcement date.

    d. When the founder of a company unexpectedly retires from his management position the firm's stocks tends to go up.

    e. During the month of January stocks earn higher returns than in other months.

4. Are the following statements true or false? Explain.

    a. Studying a company is a waste of effort because all information is incorporated in the company's stock prices.

    b. A price drop of 60% in 1 day implies that the market is inefficient.

    c. Arbitrageurs are key players in preserving market efficiency.

    d. The higher the transaction costs, the more mispricing is expected.

5. On 27 October an arbitrageur in London was following the exchange rates in Asheville. At that time $1 was traded for €0.8051 and £0.4111 (you can't change directly pounds into Euros and vice versa at Asheville). At the same time in London €1 was traded for €1.9608 and $2.4390.

    a. Show a strategy that will enable the arbitrageur to make arbitrage profits.

    b. Assume that the arbitrageur invests £100,000 in the strategy. How much money will he gain from implementing it?

6. Continuing with the previous problem: If the transaction costs in London are 0.25% per transaction and 0.5% in Asheville, is the strategy still profitable? What is the maximum transaction cost (assuming that they are twice as much in Ashville as in London) that will make the strategy break even?

7. Teva is a pharmaceutical company traded both on the Tel Aviv stock exchange and on the NASDAQ. At 9:30 Eastern time (when both exchange markets are open) Teva was traded for $25.75 on the NASDAQ and for 112 New Israeli Shekel (NIS) in Tel Aviv. At the same time $1 was traded for 4.48 NIS. Show a strategy that enables arbitrageurs to earn profits. When do you think that the profit opportunities will cease to exist?

8. On 17 July 2010 ABC Corp. reported an increase of 2 cents in earnings per share (EPS). Nevertheless, the price of the stock dropped by $1.50. In contrast, on the same day, the DEF company reported a decrease of 3 cents in its EPS, but the stock price rose by $2.20. A journalist wrote

that "since this is the only new information received on 17 July about ABC and DEF, this proves that the stock market is inefficient." Is the journalist's statement is correct?

9. In February 2022 a messenger arrived in Lower Fantasia and gave the correct prices of all stocks that traded in the country. A journalist argued that the accurate price disclosure eliminates all risk in investing in stocks; hence, their returns should be equal to the risk-free rate. Assume that the messenger did not know the future, but "only" the average future FCFs and the appropriate discount rate. Is the journalist right in his assessment? Discuss.

10. The chief executive officer (CEO) of Monkey Business Corp. (MBC) and his nephew were arrested after it was found that the nephew bought $1,000,000 worth of MBC stocks shortly before the price of the stocks jumped by 45%. Assuming that the allegations are true, what type of market efficiency does the above contradict?

11. The workers of a large factory in Michigan received information according to which the price of the Monkey Business Corp. stock is about to rise by more than 50%. According to the rumors, the source of the information is the nephew (not the one that was arrested) of the CEO. Your sister is working in that factory and advised you to buy MBC stocks. Would you follow her advice? Explain.

12. Two years after the MBC Company went public, it was found that the company tampered with the accounting reports. As a result of this finding, the price of the company's stocks fell by 80% the next day. Does the sharp fall in price violate market efficiency?

13. One of the puzzling phenomena of financial markets is the "weekend effect." According to this phenomena, stock returns on Monday are lower than every other day of the week. The following graph presents the returns of the stock market dependent on the day of the week.

    a. Do the results contradict market efficiency?

    b. Do you have a reasonable explanation as to why the anomaly persists and does not disappear as a result of the arbitrageurs' actions?

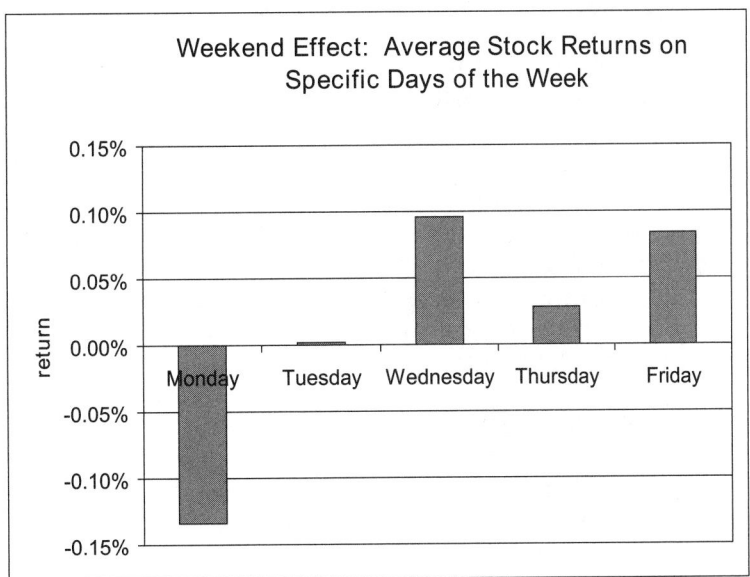

14. "Beat the Market" (BTM) is an open mutual fund. The fund's portfolio consists of 10,000 Yahoo!, Inc. stocks traded for $36.14, 15,000 stocks of Google, Inc. traded for $191.94, and 20,000 stocks of General Electric traded for $33.95. There are currently 32,000 BTM shares.

a. If the price of a BTM share is $122.48 does the price additivity rule hold?

b. The following day the price of Google drops by 5%, the price of General Electric drops by 2%, and the price of Yahoo! remains the same. The price of BTM was $117. Does the price additivity rule hold?

15. The DEF company recruited one of the best CEOs in the country to its service in an unanticipated move. However, the price of the DEF stocks fell once the company announced the change in management. Assume that the new CEO was the only new information about the company (and that he is indeed better than the old CEO). Does the fall of stock prices indicate market inefficiency?

16. Assume that markets are efficient. Do you expect that the average return of mutual funds will be higher, lower, or equal to the market return?

17. "Due to the unexpected positive earnings report the price of GLZ shares rose on each trading day in the past week."

a. Explain why this sentence contradicts market efficiency

b. What type of market efficiency does the sentence contradict? Try to distinguish between two possibilities.

c. What should have been the market response if market efficiency holds?

18. In country A short-selling is allowed, whereas in country B it is illegal. If all other things are equal where do you anticipate more frequent mispricing? Explain.

19. In Upper Fantasia a well-known professor showed that during the past 50 years stocks whose prices rose for 3 consecutive days will tend to go down on the fourth day. Assuming that the professor's finding is true, what do you expect will happen after the publication of this result?

20. The "new issue puzzle" is a phenomenon according to which the returns from investing in firms that issue stocks is lower than other stocks 5 years after the date of the issue. Ritter (who originally reported the phenomenon) argues that it is because investors are too optimistic about the performance of issuing stocks.

a. Is Ritter's explanation consistent with market efficiency?

b. Can you think about an explanation that is consistent with market efficiency that will explain the new issue puzzle?

21. An entrepreneur is marketing new software that estimates the prices of stocks according to a new model.

a. Do you think that brokerage houses should buy the new software?

b. What would you advise the entrepreneur to do with his software?

22. One pound of apples is sold for $2.50 in Asheville and for $4.20 in Alaska. Does this fact violate the one-price rule?

23. Recent research in Lower Fantasia found that companies whose stocks register a large increase in prices in a given quarter tend to have an increase in profits after 6 months. Does this fact contradict market efficiency?

24. The same research conducted in Upper Fantasia found that stocks that have high increase in their profits tend to have low returns in the year after the announcement date. Try to give a reasonable explanation for this finding; does your explanation contradict market efficiency?

25. One of the puzzling results of recent academic literature is that stocks with high $\beta$ do not earn higher returns than stocks with low $\beta$. Does this fact contradict market efficiency?

26. A recent finding shows that low-rated bonds have earned lower returns in the past 60 years than government bonds. Does this fact contradict market efficiency?

# CHAPTER

# 15 | Bond Valuation

## CHAPTER CONTENTS

## Overview

When businesses, governments, or municipalities borrow money, they issue *bonds*. The fundamental characteristic that distinguishes a bond from other kinds of securities such as stocks, preferred stock, and options is that the borrower is very specific about the promised payments on the bond. All bonds specify the precise dates and the amounts that the issuer/borrower *promises* to repay the bond's purchaser/lender.

In this chapter we apply the discounting techniques discussed in Chapters 1 and 2 to value bonds. In the remainder of this overview to Chapter 15 we'll show you some examples of various kinds of bonds and acquaint you with some basic bond terminology.

## The XYZ Corp. Bond

To get the bond terminology straight, Figure 15.1 gives some details for an imaginary bond offering by XYZ Corporation, a highly reliable borrower.

---

**XYZ CORPORATION**

## Offer to sell $10,000,000 of bonds

---

Date of sale: December 15, 2009
*Offer price*: $1,000 (bonds sold at *par value*)
*Face value*: $1,000
Bond *maturity date*: December 15, 2016
*Coupon rate*: 7%, paid annually on December 15 (meaning *coupon payments* of $70 on December 15 of 2010, 2011, ... , 2016)
*Principal repayment*: December 15, 2016
*Tricky details, covenants and other conditions*: See *boilerplate* on other side

---

FIGURE 15.1 On December 15, 2009, XYZ Corp. sold $10 million of bonds paying a 7% coupon. The italicized terms are explained in the text.

The terminology (underlined) is as follows:

- The XYZ bond has a *face value* and a *coupon rate*. The $10 million of bonds issued by XYZ Corp. are issued as individual bonds of $1,000 face value; each such bond pays a coupon rate of 7%. The periodic interest payments are based on the product of the coupon rate and the face value. The XYZ bonds pay interest only once a year; because the coupon rate is 7% and the face value is $1,000, this means that the *coupon payments* are $70 annually. (As you will see in Section 15.1, most corporate bonds pay interest semi-annually; if this were true for the XYZ bonds, they would pay $35 on December 15 and June 15 of each year.)

- The XYZ bond has a *principal repayment* on the last day of the bond's maturity (the bond's *maturity date*). On this day, December 15, 2016, a $1,000 face-value XYZ bond will pay its holder a final repayment of principal of $1,000 in addition to the interest payment of $70 due for 2019.

- The bond's *offer price* is the initial price at which it is sold to the public. The XYZ bonds are offered *at par*, meaning that the initial sale price is equal to the bond's face value.
- *Tricky details, covenants, and other conditions*: XYZ promises to make a set of contractual payments in exchange for the loan of $1,000 made to it by the purchaser. Often the bond-issuing company agrees to abide by certain restrictions on its behavior; these restrictions, termed *bond covenants*, might specify that XYZ will pay no dividends until the bond issue is redeemed or perhaps that it will refrain from certain other actions.[1] The "*boilerplate*" in which all these conditions are specified also specifies what happens if XYZ defaults, that is, if it fails to keep its promises. The boilerplate also specifies what constitutes default.[2]

## Some Other Corporate Bonds

Figure 15.2 shows you some of the corporate bonds issued in the week of 21 July 2003. By looking at the table, you can learn the following facts about bonds:

- Not all the bonds are issued at par. The GMAC bonds, for example, are issued at $107.25 for every $100 of face value. In Section 15.1 we discuss the effect of issuance not at par on the analysis of the bond.
- Bonds differ in their *ratings*. Bonds are rated according the credit worthiness of their issuers. Figure 15.3 shows you the ratings used by the two primary bond-rating agencies, Moody's and Standard and Poors. The ratings are based on the agency's estimation of the issuing company's ability to pay off the bonds and play an important role in determining the interest rate that the company pays on its bonds. The "investment grade" bonds in the top half of Figure 15.2 are issued by companies whose ability to repay the funds borrowed is highly regarded by the rating agencies. The "high yield bonds" (often called "junk bonds") in the bottom half of the table are issued by companies whose credit ratings are lower.
- Some bonds are *callable*. A bond is callable if the issuer has the right to refund the bond's principal before maturity. For example: The Bank of America bonds in Figure 15.2 promise to pay 6.85% interest annually until 15 May 2026. However, these bonds are callable after 15 May 2006: After this date, Bank of America can refund the bonds by forcing bondholders to return their bonds to the company for their face value. We discuss callable bonds in Section 15.5.
- The price, coupon, and maturity of the bond affect the internal rate of return (IRR) of the bond holder. In bond markets the jargon for IRR is *yield to maturity* (YTM). If the bond is callable, we can also calculate a *yield to call* (YTC). These concepts are discussed in Sections 15.1 and 15.5.

---

[1] A detailed example of covenants is given in Section 15.6 where we discuss the Giant Industries bonds.
[2] This is not as trivial as it might sound. If a coupon payment is late by 2 days, does this violation of the contract automatically mean bankruptcy? Suppose one of the bond covenants is violated? Do bond holders have recourse (can they do something if the covenants are violated)?

## Corporate Bond Watch

### Investment Grade Bonds

Corporate Bonds rated BBB / Baa or higher. These bond will fluctuate in value and if sold prior to maturity may be worth more or less than their original cost.

| Description | Rating | Coupon | Maturity | Price | YTM / YTC |
|---|---|---|---|---|---|
| GMAC | BBB | 6.75 | 1/15/06 | 107.25 | 3.65 |
| GE Capital | AAA | 2.85 | 1/3/06 | 102.5 | 1.82 |
| Sears Roebuck Acct | BBB | 5.8 | 2/15/06 | 106.75 | 3.03 |
| Bristol Myers | AA | 4.75 | 10/1/06 | 108.5 | 1.98 |
| Ford Motor Credit | BBB | 6.5 | 1/25/07 | 106 | 4.62 |
| Countrywide | A | 5.5 | 2/1/07 | 110 | 2.51 |
| John Deere Capital | A- | 4.5 | 8/22/07 | 106.5 | 2.8 |
| Merrill Lynch | A+ | 4 | 11/15/07 | 104.75 | 2.82 |
| CIT Group | A | 4 | 5/8/08 | 103.25 | 3.26 |
| Household Finance | A | 5.875 | 2/1/09 | 111 | 3.65 |
| Morgan Stanley | A+ | 4.25 | 5/15/10 | 103.25 | 3.7 |
| Credit Suisse FB | A+ | 6.125 | 11/15/11 | 111.925 | 4.39 |
| Walt Disney | BBB+ | 6.375 | 3/1/12 | 113.375 | 4.48 |
| Alcan | A- | 4.5 | 5/15/13 | 100.325 | 4.45 |
| GMAC | BBB | 7.4 | 2/15/21 | 102.795 | 7.11 / 5.5 |
| Household Finance | A | 6 | 4/15/23 | 104.25 | 5.64 / 5 |
| Bank of America | A | 6.85 | 5/15/26 | 106.806 | 6.28 / 4.25 |
| General Motors | BBB | 8.375 | 7/15/2033 | 101.375 | 8.25 |

### High Yield Bonds

Corporate Bonds rated below BBB / Baa. These bonds may have large fluctuations in value and if sold prior to maturity may be worth more or less thatn their original cost.

| Description | Rating | Coupon | Maturity / Call | Price | YTM / YTC |
|---|---|---|---|---|---|
| Sprint Capital | BBB- | 7.9 | 3/15/05 | 109.5 | 2.05 |
| Royal Caribbean | BB+ | 8.25 | 4/1/05 | 106.25 | 4.13 |
| Sprint Capital | BBB- | 7.125 | 1/30/06 | 110.5 | 2.77 |
| JC Penney | BB+ | 7.6 | 4/1/07 | 105.5 | 5.91 |
| TXU Corp | BBB- | 6.375 | 1/1/08 | 107.25 | 4.55 |
| Williams Hld Del | B+ | 6.5 | 12/1/08 | 98.25 | 6.89 |
| JC Penney | BB+ | 8 | 3/1/10 | 105.75 | 6.89 |
| Xerox | B+ | 7.125 | 6/15/2010 | 100.5 | 7.03 |
| Liberty Media | BBB- | 5.7 | 5/15/13 | 99.25 | 5.8 |
| Xerox | B+ | 7.625 | 6/15/13 | 100.5 | 7.55 / 7.53 |
| Royal Caribbean | BB+ | 7.25 | 3/15/2018 | 96 | 7.7 |
| Georgia Pacific | BB+ | 9.625 | 3/15/2022 | 101.25 | 9.47 / 9.4 |
| Tyco International | BBB- | 6.875 | 1/15/2029 | 102.5 | 6.66 |

FIGURE 15.2 A partial list of corporate bonds issued in the third week of July 2003.

| **Long-Term Senior Debt Ratings** | | | | | |
| --- | --- | --- | --- | --- | --- |
| Investment-Grade Ratings | | | Speculative-Grade Ratings | | |
| S&P | Moody's | Interpretation | S&P | Moody's | Interpretation |
| AAA | Aaa | Highest quality | BB+<br>BB<br>BB- | Ba1<br>Ba2<br>Ba3 | Likely to fulfill obligations; ongoing uncertainty |
| AA+<br>AA<br>AA- | Aa1<br>Aa2<br>AA3 | High quality | B+<br>B<br>B- | B1<br>B2<br>B3 | High-risk obligations |
| A+<br>A<br>A- | A1<br>A2<br>A3 | Strong payment capacity | CCC+<br>CCC<br>CCC- | Caa | Current vulnerability to default |
| BBB+<br>BBB<br>BBB- | Baa1<br>Baa2<br>Baa3 | Adequate payment capacity | C<br>D | Ca<br>D | In bankruptcy or default or with other marked shortcomings |

FIGURE 15.3  Standard and Poors (S&P) and Moody bond-rating classifications.

## U.S. Government Debt

The market for U.S. government debt is without question the largest and most important bond market in the world. In June 2009, the U.S. Treasury had $11.4 *trillion* in outstanding bonds (see Figure 15.4). Almost every week the U.S. Treasury sells stupendous amounts of debt to the public (see Figure 15.5 for a fairly standard weekly announcement, in which the government sells $34 billion of short-term debt).

The U.S. Treasury classifies its debt into three main categories: bills, notes, and bonds.

- *Treasury bills* are short-term bonds sold by the government. Treasury bills have no explicit interest rate; they are sold at a discount. For example, a 1-year Treasury bill with a $100 face value might be sold for $90. The Treasury bill has no explicit interest rate: The purchaser of this bill pays $90 today and gets back $100 in 1 year. We discuss the pricing of T-bills in Section 15.2.

- The U.S. Treasury uses the word *notes* to describe coupon bonds that have maturities up to 10 years. It uses the word *bonds* to describe coupon bonds that have greater maturities. Because there is no analytical difference between U.S. Treasury notes and bonds—both refer to bonds that have coupon payments—we will analyze them together in Section 15.3.

| **UNITED STATES GOVERNMENT DEBT** | | | |
| --- | --- | --- | --- |
| Date | Debt Held by the Public | Intragovernmental Holdings | Total Public Debt Outstanding |
| 31-Dec-01 | 3,394,398,958,214 | 2,549,039,605,223 | 5,943,438,563,436 |
| 31-Dec-02 | 3,647,939,770,384 | 2,757,767,686,464 | 6,405,707,456,848 |
| 31-Dec-03 | 4,044,243,829,240 | 2,953,720,418,579 | 6,997,964,247,818 |
| 31-Dec-04 | 4,408,389,327,643 | 3,187,753,474,781 | 7,596,142,802,424 |
| 30-Dec-05 | 4,714,821,211,003 | 3,455,603,330,310 | 8,170,424,541,314 |
| 29-Dec-06 | 4,901,046,516,368 | 3,779,177,863,718 | 8,680,224,380,086 |
| 31-Dec-07 | 5,136,302,727,073 | 4,092,869,932,146 | 9,229,172,659,218 |
| 31-Dec-08 | 6,369,318,869,477 | 4,330,485,995,136 | 10,699,804,864,612 |
| 1-Jun-09 | 7,097,861,677,672 | 4,282,104,511,903 | 11,379,966,189,575 |

FIGURE 15.4  The debt of the U.S. government. On 1 June 2009, the U.S. government had $7.1 trillion of debt outstanding in the form of bonds owned by the public. A further $4.3 trillion dollars of debt comprised debts of one government agency to another. The total government debt was $11.4 trillion.
*SOURCE*: http://www.treasurydirect.gov/NP/BPDLogin?application=np.

DEPARTMENT OF THE TREASURY

**TREASURY** N E W S

OFFICE OF PUBLIC AFFAIRS • 1500 PENNSYLVANIA AVENUE, N.W. • WASHINGTON, D.C. • 20220 • (202) 622-2960

EMBARGOED UNTIL 11:00 A.M.             CONTACT:     Office of Financing
March 6, 2003                                        202/691-3550

TREASURY OFFERS 13-WEEK AND 26-WEEK BILLS

The Treasury will auction 13-week and 26-week Treasury bills totaling $34,000 million to refund an estimated $27,010 million of publicly held 13-week and 26-week Treasury bills maturing March 13, 2003, and to raise new cash of approximately $6,990 million. Also maturing is an estimated $20,000 million of publicly held 4-week Treasury bills, the disposition of which will be announced March 10, 2003.

FIGURE 15.5 On March 6, 2003, the U.S. Treasury announced the sale of $34 *billion* of Treasury bills. Similar sales are generally held weekly. Note that $27 billion of the proceeds will go toward refunding existing debt.

## What Do We Do in This Chapter?

In this chapter you will learn to analyze a bond based on its yield to maturity (YTM). The YTM is a concept much like the internal rate of return (IRR) discussed first in Chapters 2 and 3. You will learn to analyze the different kinds of bonds: Treasury bills, Treasury bonds, corporate bonds, and callable bonds. We end the chapter with a brief discussion of preferred stock, a security that—despite its name—is very much like a bond.

## Finance Concepts

- Basic definitions, example of bond value, and YTM
- U.S. Treasury markets: discussion of the types of bonds and yield conventions
  - Discussion of T-bills
  - Treasury bonds
  - Strips
- The U.S. Treasury yield curve
- Corporate bond markets: Example of Giant Industries
- Callable bonds
- Preferred stock

## Excel Functions and Concepts

- **IRR**
- **XIRR**
- **Rate**
- **Yield**

## 15.1. Computing the Yield To Maturity (YTM) of a Bond

The most common tool for the analysis of bonds is the YTM. YTM of the bond is the IRR of the bond's cash flows. Suppose we observe the bond's market price $P$ and we know its stream of future promised payments $C_1, C_2, \ldots, C_N$. Then the YTM is defined as the internal rate of return (IRR) of the bond price and its future payments, which is the rate of return that sets the present value of the bond's future promised payments equal to its current price:

$$P = \frac{C_1}{(1+YTM)} + \frac{C_2}{(1+YTM)^2} + \frac{C_3}{(1+YTM)^3} + \ldots + \frac{C_N}{(1+YTM)^N}$$

In this section we illustrate how to compute the YTM. In addition to the **IRR** function that you already know, the Excel **XIRR** and **Yield** functions enable you to compute the YTM in more complicated cases. We use the XYZ Corp. bond from the previous section as our example.

### Back to the XYZ Bond

Suppose that it's the morning of 15 December 2009, and you have been asked to value the XYZ bond illustrated in the overview to this chapter (page 450). Using Excel's **IRR** function, you determine that the YTM of the bond is 7.00%.

|  | A | B | C |
|---|---|---|---|
| 1 | **YIELD TO MATURITY** | | |
| 2 | Market price of bond | 1,000.00 | |
| 3 | | | |
| 4 | Date | Bond cash flow | |
| 5 | 15-Dec-09 | -1,000.00 | |
| 6 | 15-Dec-10 | 70.00 | |
| 7 | 15-Dec-11 | 70.00 | |
| 8 | 15-Dec-12 | 70.00 | |
| 9 | 15-Dec-13 | 70.00 | |
| 10 | 15-Dec-14 | 70.00 | |
| 11 | 15-Dec-15 | 70.00 | |
| 12 | 15-Dec-16 | 1,070.00 | |
| 13 | | | |
| 14 | YTM of bond | 7.00% | <-- =IRR(B5:B12) |

Are the XYZ bonds a good buy? This depends on whether the market interest rate on *equivalently risky* bonds is bigger or smaller than 7%. If the market is paying more than 7% for bonds of companies that—in terms of risk—are like XYZ Corp., then the XYZ bonds are not a good buy. On the other hand, if the market is paying less than 7%, they are a good buy.[3]

---

[3] Having read Chapter 14 on efficient markets, you naturally suspect that the market price pretty much reflects the risk-adjusted return on the XYZ bonds.

Just for the sake of argument, suppose that on 15 December 2009, the market interest rate for bonds like the XYZ Corp. bond is 6.5%. You can use the NPV of the future payments on the bond to determine how much you should be willing to pay for them.

| | A | B | C | D | E | F | G |
|---|---|---|---|---|---|---|---|
| 1 | | | VALUING THE XYZ CORPORATION BONDS | | | | |
| 2 | Market interest rate | 6.50% | | | | | |
| 3 | | | | | | | |
| 4 | Year | Bond cash flow | | | Market interest rate | Bond value | |
| 5 | 1 | 70 | | | 0.00% | 1,490.00 | <-- =NPV(E5,$B$5:$B$11) |
| 6 | 2 | 70 | | | 1.00% | 1,403.69 | <-- =NPV(E6,$B$5:$B$11) |
| 7 | 3 | 70 | | | 2.00% | 1,323.60 | <-- =NPV(E7,$B$5:$B$11) |
| 8 | 4 | 70 | | | 3.00% | 1,249.21 | <-- =NPV(E8,$B$5:$B$11) |
| 9 | 5 | 70 | | | 4.00% | 1,180.06 | |
| 10 | 6 | 70 | | | 5.00% | 1,115.73 | |
| 11 | 7 | 1,070 | | | 6.00% | 1,055.82 | |
| 12 | | | | | 7.00% | 1,000.00 | |
| 13 | Value of the bond | 1,027.42 | <-- =NPV(B2,B5:B11) | | 8.00% | 947.94 | |
| 14 | | | | | 9.00% | 899.34 | |
| 15 | | | | | 10.00% | 853.95 | |
| 16 | | | XYZ Bond Value | | 11.00% | 811.51 | |
| 17 | | | | | 12.00% | 771.81 | |
| 18 | | | | | 13.00% | 734.64 | |
| 19 | | | | | 14.00% | 699.82 | |
| 20 | | | | | | | |
| 21 | | | | | | | |
| 22 | | | | | | | |
| 23 | | | | | | | |
| 24 | | | | | | | |
| 25 | | | | | | | |
| 26 | | | | | | | |
| 27 | | | | | | | |
| 28 | | | | | | | |
| 29 | | | | | | | |
| 30 | | | | | | | |

If the market values the bond using the 6.5% interest rate, then it would be worth $1,030.44. If you could buy the bond for $1,000, you should do so. Making a table (cells E5:F19) in Excel shows that the bond is worth more than $1,000 if the market interest rate is less than 7% and vice versa.

As you can see, the basics of bond analysis using the YTM are very similar to standard IRR analysis and quite simple. However, for bonds there are three factors that sometimes complicate the pricing calculations. In the rest of this section we discuss these factors.

## Complicating Factor 1: Uneven Spacing of Bond Payments

The calculation of both the PV of the bond's future payments and the YTM can be complicated by the fact that the payments are not evenly spaced. Suppose, for example, that you buy the XYZ bond on 15 May 2010 and that its market price on that date is $1,050. To compute the YTM of the bond, we have to compute the IRR of its payments. But the problem is that the payments are not evenly spaced. As you can see in Figure 15.6, the time between the purchase date of the bond and the first coupon payment is 214 days, whereas all the other payments are 365 or 366 days.

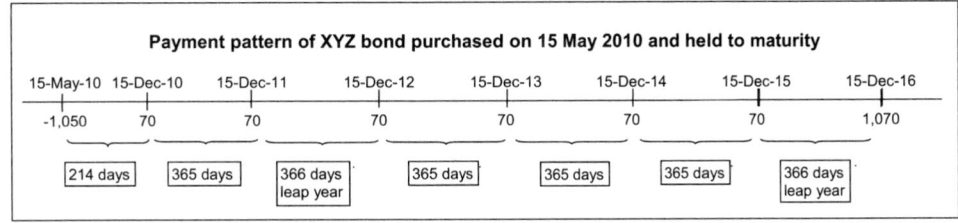

FIGURE 15.6 If you buy the XYZ bond on 15 May 2010, the first coupon payment will be received in 214 days. Subsequent coupon payments will be received with spacing of 1 year. Excel's **XIRR** function computes the YTM for the bond.

Excel's **IRR** function will not correctly compute the YTM of this bond—**IRR** assumes that all the payments are spaced at equal intervals, whereas in our example the first interval (214 days) is very different from the subsequent payment intervals. Fortunately Excel has a function called **XIRR** that correctly computes the IRR for uneven spacing of payments. The use of this function is discussed in a separate Excel box below.[4] Here is its implementation for our problem.

|  | A | B | C |
|---|---|---|---|
| 1 | YIELD TO MATURITY<br>For uneven date spacing | | |
| 2 | Market price of bond | 1,050.00 | |
| 3 | | | |
| 4 | Date | Bond cash<br>flow | |
| 5 | 15-May-01 | -1,050.00 | |
| 6 | 15-Dec-01 | 70.00 | |
| 7 | 15-Dec-02 | 70.00 | |
| 8 | 15-Dec-03 | 70.00 | |
| 9 | 15-Dec-04 | 70.00 | |
| 10 | 15-Dec-05 | 70.00 | |
| 11 | 15-Dec-06 | 70.00 | |
| 12 | 15-Dec-07 | 1,070.00 | |
| 13 | | | |
| 14 | YTM of bond | 6.58% | <-- =XIRR(B5:B12,A5:A12) |

As you can see, when you buy the bond on 15 May 2010, the YTM is 6.58% annually.

---

[4] For more information on dates and date functions in Excel, see Chapter 29.

## EXCEL NOTES: THE XIRR FUNCTION

To use **XIRR**, you have to put in the dates on which the payments are received. In the previous example, cells A5:A12 contain these dates. Once you've got the dates in, you can use **XIRR** as illustrated below (the **XIRR** function computes the effective *annual* YTM).

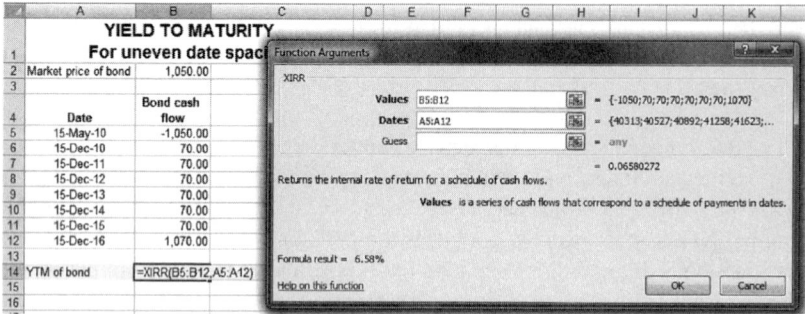

You may not see **XIRR** in your list of Excel functions. In this case,

- Go to the Excel 2007 office button and click **Excel options** and then **Add-Ins.**

- In the drop-down box at the bottom of the **Add-Ins** page indicate
Manage: Excel Add-ins ▾ Go... and click **Go.**

- Click on the **Analysis ToolPak** box.

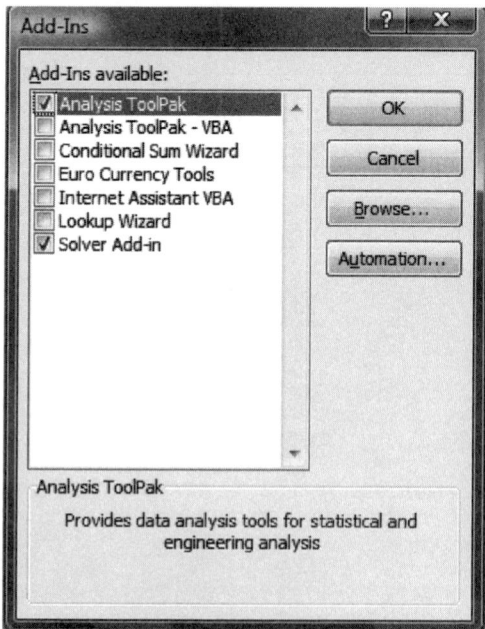

## Complicating Factor 2: Semiannual Interest

Corporate and government bonds often pay interest twice a year rather than annually. We are thus faced with a problem of *annualizing the interest rate on the bond*. This corresponds to the concept of effective annual interest rate (EAIR) discussed in Chapter 3.

Here is an example. Suppose that the ABC Corp. issues a bond at the same time as XYZ Corp. Like the XYZ bond, ABC's bond pays a 7% coupon on its face value of $1,000, is issued on 15 December 2009, and matures on 15 December 2016. The only difference between the two bonds is that ABC's interest payment is *semiannual*: Instead of paying $70 once a year, the ABC bond pays $35 twice a year, on 15 June and 15 December.

We can use either **IRR** or **XIRR** to compute the YTM of the ABC bond.

| | A | B | C |
|---|---|---|---|
| 1 | **YTM WITH SEMIANNUAL COUPON PAYMENTS** | | |
| 2 | Market price of bond | 1000.00 | |
| 3 | | | |
| 4 | **Date** | **ABC bond cash flow** | |
| 5 | 15-Dec-09 | -1,000.00 | <-- =-B2 |
| 6 | 15-Jun-10 | 35.00 | |
| 7 | 15-Dec-10 | 35.00 | |
| 8 | 15-Jun-11 | 35.00 | |
| 9 | 15-Dec-11 | 35.00 | |
| 10 | 15-Jun-12 | 35.00 | |
| 11 | 15-Dec-12 | 35.00 | |
| 12 | 15-Jun-13 | 35.00 | |
| 13 | 15-Dec-13 | 35.00 | |
| 14 | 15-Jun-14 | 35.00 | |
| 15 | 15-Dec-14 | 35.00 | |
| 16 | 15-Jun-15 | 35.00 | |
| 17 | 15-Dec-15 | 35.00 | |
| 18 | 15-Jun-16 | 35.00 | |
| 19 | 15-Dec-16 | 1,035.00 | |
| 20 | | | |
| 21 | Semiannual IRR | 3.50% | <-- =IRR(B5:B19) |
| 22 | Annualized IRR This is the YTM! | 7.12% | <-- =(1+B21)^2-1 |
| 23 | | | |
| 24 | YTM using XIRR | 7.12% | <-- =XIRR(B5:B19,A5:A19) |

In cell B21 we use **IRR** to calculate the internal rate of return of the bond price and its payments. Because the basic period is a half year, the annualized IRR is $(1+3.50\%)^2-1=7.12$ (cell B22). In cell B24 we use the **XIRR** function to compute the annualized YTM directly.

## Complicating Factor 3: Accrued Interest

In U.S. bond markets the "price" quoted for a bond is usually not the amount you will be asked to pay for the bond because it doesn't include the interest that has accrued on the bond. Sound confusing? Here's an example.

Suppose you're going to buy the XYZ bond on 3 April 2010. You call a bond dealer, who quotes you a price of $1,050 for the bond. To this quoted price is added the bond's *accrued interest*, the proportional part of the bond's annual coupon payment (see Figure 15.7).

|   | A | B | C | D | E |
|---|---|---|---|---|---|
| 1 | **ACCRUED INTEREST AND YTM COMPUTATIONS** | | | | |
| 2 | Bond purchase date | 3-Apr-01 | | | |
| 3 | Previous coupon date | 15-Dec-00 | Number of days since last coupon | 109 | <-- =B2-B3 |
| 4 | Next coupon date | 15-Dec-01 | Number of days between coupons | 365 | <-- =B4-B3 |
| 5 | Coupon payment over the period | 70.00 | | | |
| 6 | | | | | |
| 7 | Quoted bond price | 1050.00 | | | |
| 8 | Accrued interest | 20.90 | <-- =B5*D3/D4 | | |
| 9 | Actual bond price paid | 1070.90 | <-- =B7+B8 | | |
| 10 | | | | | |
| 11 | Year | Bond cash flow | | | |
| 12 | 3-Apr-01 | -1,070.90 | | | |
| 13 | 15-Dec-01 | 70.00 | | | |
| 14 | 15-Dec-02 | 70.00 | | | |
| 15 | 15-Dec-03 | 70.00 | | | |
| 16 | 15-Dec-04 | 70.00 | | | |
| 17 | 15-Dec-05 | 70.00 | | | |
| 18 | 15-Dec-06 | 70.00 | | | |
| 19 | 15-Dec-07 | 1,070.00 | | | |
| 20 | | | | | |
| 21 | YTM of bond, using **XIRR** | 6.06% | <-- =XIRR(B12:B19,A12:A19) | | |
| 22 | YTM of bond, using **Yield** | 6.06% | <-- =YIELD(A12,A19,7%,105,100,1,3) | | |

In the spreadsheet above, the accrued interest is $20.90 (cell B8). This is computed as 109/365 times the annual bond coupon of $70. The actual price paid for the bond is $1,070.90 (cell B9), and using **XIRR** we can compute the bond's YTM as 6.06% (cell B21).

In cell B22 we illustrate **Yield**, yet another Excel function that computes the YTM. This function is explained in the Excel box on the next page. **Yield** is somewhat more complicated to use than **XIRR**, but its advantage is that it does the accrued interest calculation automatically.

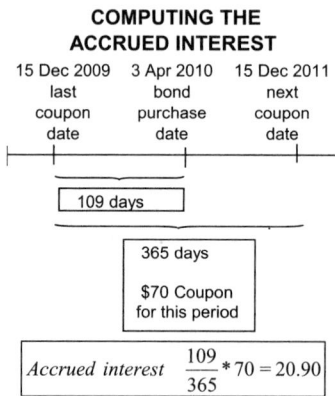

**COMPUTING THE ACCRUED INTEREST**

FIGURE 15.7 Computing the accrued interest. The *accrued interest* is jargon for the unpaid part of the bond coupon since the last interest payment. In U.S. bond markets, the accrued interest is added to the quoted bond price to compute the amount actually paid for the bond. In most European bond markets, there is no separate accrued interest calculation and the quoted bond price is the actual price paid for the bond.

## EXCEL NOTES: THE YIELD FUNCTION

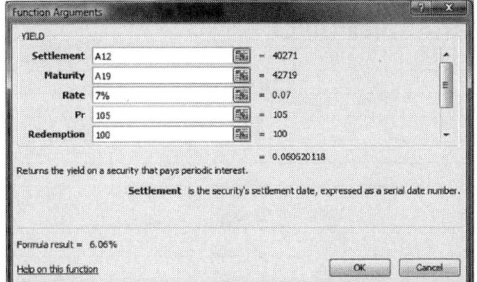 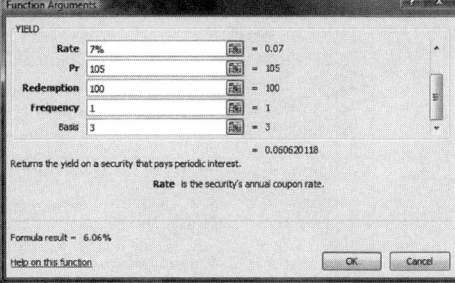

The **Yield** function contains seven cells to fill (**Settlement, Maturity, Rate, Pr, Redemption, Frequency,** and **Basis**). Excel's dialog box for this function can't accommodate all the arguments on one screen, so it includes a "slider" so you can navigate between the arguments. The two screens above show all the arguments.

The yield function used in B22.

- The **Settlement** is the date that the bond is purchased (cell A12). Note that Excel translates this date to 36984; to understand this translation, refer to Chapter 29.
- **Maturity** is the maturity date of the bond.
- **Rate** is the *annual* coupon rate on the bond.
- **Pr** is the price per $100 face value. In our example a $1,000 face-value ABC bond is selling for $1,050; this is $105 for each $100 of face value.
- **Redemption** is the redemption value per $100 face value.
- **Frequency** is the number of coupon payments per year.
- **Basis** is the number of days in a year (sounds stupid, but there are different conventions). The answer of "3" used here tells Excel to use the actual number of days

## 15.2. U.S. Treasury Bills

U.S. government bonds are variously defined as *Treasury bills, Treasury notes,* and *Treasury bonds.* In this section we analyze U.S. Treasury bills, and in the next section we examine U.S. Treasury bonds and notes.[5]

Treasury bills are short-term securities sold by the U.S. Treasury. T-bills mature in 1 year or less from their issue date. They have no coupon payments. Instead, you pay less than the face value and get the face value at maturity. Here's an example: Suppose you purchase a 26-week T-bill with face value $10,000 for $9,750. In 26 weeks (182 days) you will get $10,000. The following spreadsheet illustrates two methods for computing the YTM of the T-bill. (The discussion of these two methods follows the spreadsheet.) Remember that the YTM is nothing more

---

[5] There's a very good Web site operated by the U.S. government that explains more about Treasury securities: http://www.treasurydirect.gov/instit/research/faqs/faqs_basics.htm.

than the annualized IRR; thus these calculations are very reminiscent of our discussion of the effective annual interest rate (EAIR) in Chapter 3.

| | A | B | C |
|---|---|---|---|
| 1 | COMPUTING THE YIELD TO MATURITY (YTM) ON TREASURY BILLS | | |
| 2 | Purchase price | 9,750.00 | |
| 3 | Face value | 10,000.00 | |
| 4 | Time to maturity (days) | 182 | <-- =26*7 |
| 5 | Time to maturity (years) | 0.49863 | <-- =B4/365 |
| 6 | | | |
| 7 | Method 1:  Compound the daily return | | |
| 8 | Daily interest rate | 0.0139% | <-- =(B3/B2)^(1/B4)-1 |
| 9 | YTM--the annualized rate | 5.2086% | <-- =(1+B8)^365-1 |
| 10 | | | |
| 11 | Method 2:  Calculate the continuously compounded return | | |
| 12 | Continuously compounded | 5.0775% | <-- =LN(B3/B2)*(1/B5) |
| 13 | | | |
| 14 | Future value *in one year* using each method | | |
| 15 | Method 1 | 10,257.84 | <-- =B2*(1+B9) |
| 16 | Method 2 | 10,257.84 | <-- =B2*EXP(B12) |

## Method 1: YTM of the Treasury Bill Is the Compounded Daily Return

One way to calculate the T-bill YTM is to compound the *daily interest rate* paid by the T-bill. To do this, we first find the daily interest rate paid by the T-bill: $10,000 = 9,750 * (1 + r_{daily})^{182}$.

Solving this equation gives $1 + r_{daily} = \left(\dfrac{10,000}{9,750}\right)^{1/182}$, which solves to give $r_{daily} = 0.0139\%$.

Compounding this rate to give an annual rate shows that the T-bill pays 5.2086% annually: $(1 + 0.0139\%)^{365} - 1 = 5.2086\%$.

## Method 2: YTM of the Treasury Bill Is the Continuously Compounded Return

This is the method preferred by most finance academics and by many finance professionals.[6] We assume that the purchase price grows at continuously compound rate $r$:

$$10,000 = 9,750 * e^{(182/365)r} = 9,750 * e^{0.49863r}$$
$$\Rightarrow e^{0.49863r} = \frac{10,000}{9,750}$$
$$\Rightarrow r = \frac{\ln\left(\dfrac{10,000}{9,750}\right)}{0.49863} = 5.0775\%$$

## Which Method Is Correct?

Both methods are correct! We know this is confusing, but then so are many other things in life. The principle is that *any method that gives the same future value using the annualized interest* is a valid periodic interest rate. In the spreadsheet cells B14:B15 you can see that both methods indeed give the same FV.

---

[6] Continuous compounding and discounting was explained in Section 2.6. If you're not comfortable with continuous discounting and compounding, just skip Method 2

## 15.3. U.S. Treasury Bonds and Notes

Treasury bonds and notes have a coupon rate and a fixed maturity date at which the bond's principal is repaid.[7] Here's an example: On 15 August 2008 the United States Treasury issued a 10-year, 4% Treasury note.[8] The notes were sold at a price of 99.389034, so that if you bought $1,000 face value of this security at issue you would have paid $993.89034. You would expect to be paid a $20 coupon every half year (15 February 2009, 15 August 2009, 15 February 2010,...) until, on the bond's maturity date of 15 August 2018, you would be paid $1,020 (the repayment of the bond's principal plus the last half year's coupon payment).

If you bought the bond at issue and intended to hold it until maturity, your anticipated cash flows would be as follows.

Cell B32 gives the semiannual IRR for the bond, 2.0375%. When we annualize this semiannual IRR, we find the yield to maturity (YTM) (cell B33).

| | A | B | C |
|---|---|---|---|
| 1 | UNITED STATES TREASURY BOND, 4.075% MATURING 15 AUGUST 2018 Bought at issue date | | |
| 2 | Face value of bonds bought | 1,000.00 | |
| 3 | Price | 993.89 | |
| 4 | Coupon rate | 4.000% | |
| 5 | Issue date | 15-Aug-08 | |
| 6 | Maturity date | 15-Aug-18 | |
| 7 | | | |
| 8 | Cash flows to purchaser at bond issue | | |
| 9 | Date | Cash flow | |
| 10 | 15-Aug-08 | -993.89 | <-- =-B3 |
| 11 | 15-Feb-09 | 20.00 | <-- =$B$4*$B$2/2 |
| 12 | 15-Aug-09 | 20.00 | <-- =$B$4*$B$2/2 |
| 13 | 15-Feb-10 | 20.00 | |
| 14 | 15-Aug-10 | 20.00 | |
| 15 | 15-Feb-11 | 20.00 | |
| 16 | 15-Aug-11 | 20.00 | |
| 17 | 15-Feb-12 | 20.00 | |
| 18 | 15-Aug-12 | 20.00 | |
| 19 | 15-Feb-13 | 20.00 | |
| 20 | 15-Aug-13 | 20.00 | |
| 21 | 15-Feb-14 | 20.00 | |
| 22 | 15-Aug-14 | 20.00 | |
| 23 | 15-Feb-15 | 20.00 | |
| 24 | 15-Aug-15 | 20.00 | |
| 25 | 15-Feb-16 | 20.00 | |
| 26 | 15-Aug-16 | 20.00 | |
| 27 | 15-Feb-17 | 20.00 | |
| 28 | 15-Aug-17 | 20.00 | |
| 29 | 15-Feb-18 | 20.00 | |
| 30 | 15-Aug-18 | 1,020.00 | <-- =$B$4*$B$2/2+B2 |
| 31 | | | |
| 32 | IRR (semiannual interest) | 2.0375% | <-- =IRR(B10:B30) |
| 33 | Annualizing the semiannual IRR | 4.1165% | <-- =(1+B32)^2-1 |
| 34 | YTM using XIRR | 4.1139% | <-- =XIRR(B10:B30,A10:A30) |

---

[7] The nomenclature for interest-paying Treasury securities distinguishes between "Treasury Notes" and "Treasury Bonds." Notes have an initial maturity of 10 years or less, whereas Bonds have an initial maturity longer than 10 years. Because there is no analytical difference between the two, we shall refer to them both as "bonds" (with a lowercase "b").

[8] The notes, issued on 15 December 2008, mature on 15 November 20018, so that the actual maturity is 9 years, 11 months.

$$YTM \ of \ T\text{-}bond = \left(1 + semi\text{-}annual \ IRR\right)^2 - 1 = \left(1 + 2.0375\%\right)^2 - 1 = 4.1165\%$$

We can also compute the YTM on the T-bond directly using **XIRR** (cell B33).[9]

## Time Moves On—Purchasing the 4% T-Note on 16 December 2008

Suppose you purchased $1,000 face value of the bond on 16 December 2008. In this case you would have paid $1,072.98 for the bond (this price, as shown in the Excel spreadsheet below, includes the accrued interest). Had you intended to hold the bond to maturity, you would anticipate getting the following:

- $20 on 15 February 2009, 15 August 2009, 15 February 2010, ..., 15 February 2018.
- $1,020 on 15 August 2018.

In the spreadsheet that follows we calculate the YTM of the bond using three calculations (cells B31:B33):

Cell B33 shows that the YTM computed with the **XIRR** function is 3.301%. Cell B34 shows that Excel's **Yield** function computes the YTM as 3.275%. This is different from cell B31, because **Yield** follows the conventions of the U.S. bond markets in computing the *semiannual*

| | A | B | C | D | E | F |
|---|---|---|---|---|---|---|
| 1 | UNITED STATES TREASURY BOND, 6%, MATURING 15 AUGUST 2009 Bought on 16 December 2008 | | | | | |
| 2 | Face value of bonds bought | 1,000.00 | | | | |
| 3 | Coupon rate | 4.00% | | | | |
| 4 | | | | Today's date | 16-Dec-08 | |
| 5 | Market price | 1,059.61 | | Last coupon date | 15-Aug-08 | |
| 6 | Accrued interest | 13.37 | <-- =E12 | Next coupon date | 15-Feb-09 | |
| 7 | | | | | | |
| 8 | Actual price paid | 1,072.98 | <-- =B5+B6 | Days since last coupon | 123 | <-- =E4-E5 |
| 9 | | | | Days between coupons | 184 | <-- =E6-E5 |
| 10 | Date | Cash flow | | | | |
| 11 | 16-Dec-08 | -1,072.98 | <-- =-B8 | Semiannual coupon | 20 | <-- =B3/2*B2 |
| 12 | 15-Feb-09 | 20.00 | <-- =$B$3*$B$2/2 | Accrued interest | 13.37 | <-- =E8/E9*E11 |
| 13 | 15-Aug-09 | 20.00 | | | | |
| 14 | 15-Feb-10 | 20.00 | | | | |
| 15 | 15-Aug-10 | 20.00 | | | | |
| 16 | 15-Feb-11 | 20.00 | | | | |
| 17 | 15-Aug-11 | 20.00 | | | | |
| 18 | 15-Feb-12 | 20.00 | | | | |
| 19 | 15-Aug-12 | 20.00 | | | | |
| 20 | 15-Feb-13 | 20.00 | | | | |
| 21 | 15-Aug-13 | 20.00 | | | | |
| 22 | 15-Feb-14 | 20.00 | | | | |
| 23 | 15-Aug-14 | 20.00 | | | | |
| 24 | 15-Feb-15 | 20.00 | | | | |
| 25 | 15-Aug-15 | 20.00 | | | | |
| 26 | 15-Feb-16 | 20.00 | | | | |
| 27 | 15-Aug-16 | 20.00 | | | | |
| 28 | 15-Feb-17 | 20.00 | | | | |
| 29 | 15-Aug-17 | 20.00 | | | | |
| 30 | 15-Feb-18 | 20.00 | | | | |
| 31 | 15-Aug-18 | 1,020.00 | | | | |
| 32 | | | | | | |
| 33 | XIRR (annualized IRR) | 3.301% | <-- =XIRR(B11:B31,A11:A31) | | | |
| 34 | Excel's Yield function | 3.275% | <-- =YIELD(A11,A31,B3,B5/10,100,2,3) | | | |
| 35 | Excel's Yield annualized | 3.302% | <-- =(1+B34/2)^2-1 | | | |

*yield doubled.* Cell B35 translates the **Yield** result to a true annualized interest rate:

---

[9] **XIRR** gives a slightly different answer than the calculation in cell B32 because it takes account of the actual days between each payment. See Chapter 26 for more details.

$$\text{Cell B35:} \left(1 + \frac{Excel's \; \textbf{Yield} \; \text{from cell B34}}{2}\right)^2 - 1 = \left(1 + \frac{3.275\%}{2}\right)^2 - 1 = 3.302.$$

The very small difference between cells B35 and B33 is attributable to the fact that **XIRR** is based on the daily interest rate (see Footnote 9).

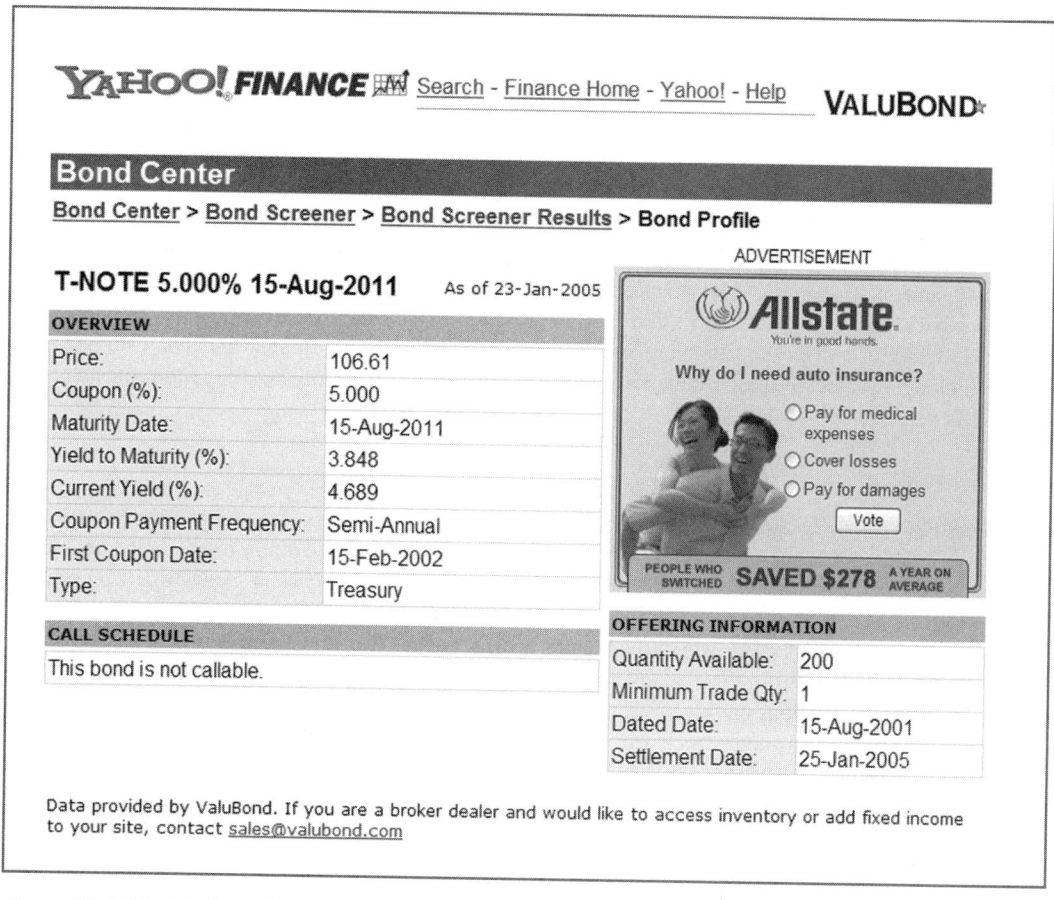

FIGURE 15.8 Much information about bonds is available on http://bonds.yahoo.com/. The Treasury Note reported above pays $2.50 interest on 15 August and 15 February until the 15 August 2011 maturity date. The price of the bond of $106.61 does not include accrued interest. The *current yield* is the annual bond coupon divided by the bond price:
$5/106.61 = 4.689\%$ .

## 15.4. A Corporate Bond Example: Giant Industries

In this section we present a case example of a corporate bond. Giant Industries (stock symbol GI) is a petroleum refiner and marketer in the American Southwest. The firm's shares are listed on the New York Stock Exchange. Here's what the company had to say about the bonds in its 1999 annual report.

## GIANT INDUSTRIES

The following paragraph (mildly edited) appears in GI's 1999 annual report. The "Lexicon" explains some of the terminology.

The Company's capital structure includes $150,000,000 of 9% senior subordinated notes due 2007 (the "9% Notes") and $100,000,000 of 9 3/4% senior subordinated notes due 2003 (the "9 3/4% Notes," and collectively with the 9% Notes, the "Notes"). The Indentures supporting the Notes contain restrictive covenants that, among other things, restrict the ability of the Company and its subsidiaries to create liens, to incur or guarantee debt, to pay dividends, to repurchase shares of the Company's common stock, to sell certain assets or subsidiary stock, to engage in certain mergers, to engage in certain transactions with affiliates, or to alter the Company's current line of business. On December 31, 1999, the Company was in compliance with the restrictive covenants relating to these Notes.

The Company had been precluded from making restricted payments from the third quarter of 1998 until June 30, 1999, because it did not satisfy a financial ratio test contained in one of the covenants relating to the 9 3/4% Notes. This included the payment of dividends and the repurchase of shares of the Company's common stock. The terms of the Indenture also had restricted the amount of money the Company could otherwise borrow during this period. The Company is no longer subject to these restrictions, as the Company currently satisfies the requirements of the covenant's financial ratio test.

### LEXICON:

*Senior unsecured obligations*: The debt in question has first claim on the company's assets in case of default. On the other hand, debt payment is not secured by a claim to a specific set of the company's assets (this would be the case if the company had borrowed money using one of its refiners as security).

*Indenture*: The terms under which the bond is issued. In the GI bond case, this will be a sizable document available from the company or its investment bankers.

*Covenants*: Restrictions on the company's actions.

*Preferred stock*: Corporate stock whose holders are guaranteed payment of dividends and a share of asset distribution before the holders of common stock. Preferred stock typically has a guaranteed annual dividend. It may be *cumulative preferred stock*, in which case the company has to make up any dividends missed.

*Retirement of capital stock*: The repurchase of stock (whether common or preferred) from shareholders.

*Transactions with affiliates*: Purchases or sales between subsidiaries of the company.

*Interest in arrears:* Interest payments missed by the company.

FIGURE 15.9   How Giant Industries reported its 9% senior subordinated notes.

Summarizing:

- The face value of the bonds is $150 million. The bonds were issued 1 September 1997. After deducting expenses, the company netted $146.8 million from the bond issue. The bonds mature on 1 September 2007.

- The coupon rate on the bonds is 9%. This interest is paid semiannually. Thus the purchaser of $1,000 face value of bonds would get two payments per year of $\frac{9\%}{2}*1{,}000 = 45.00$.

## What Did the Bonds Cost the Company?

We start by considering the effective annual interest rate (EAIR) of the bond issue to GI. We do this by setting up a table of GI cash flows from the bonds.

| | A | B | C |
|---|---|---|---|
| 1 | GIANT INDUSTRIES 9% BONDS ISSUER PERSPECTIVE 1 Sept. 1997 (issue date) | | |
| 2 | Principal amount ($ million) | 150.0 | |
| 3 | Net received by Giant Industries | 146.8 | |
| 4 | Coupon rate | 9.00% | |
| 5 | Maturity date | 1-Sep-07 | |
| 6 | Issue date | 1-Sep-97 | |
| 7 | | | |
| 8 | Date | Cash flow to GI | |
| 9 | 1-Sep-97 | 146.8 | <-- =B3 |
| 10 | 1-Mar-98 | -6.75 | <-- =-$B$4*$B$2/2 |
| 11 | 1-Sep-98 | -6.75 | <-- =-$B$4*$B$2/2 |
| 12 | 1-Mar-99 | -6.75 | |
| 13 | 1-Sep-99 | -6.75 | |
| 14 | 1-Mar-00 | -6.75 | |
| 15 | 1-Sep-00 | -6.75 | |
| 16 | 1-Mar-01 | -6.75 | |
| 17 | 1-Sep-01 | -6.75 | |
| 18 | 1-Mar-02 | -6.75 | |
| 19 | 1-Sep-02 | -6.75 | |
| 20 | 1-Mar-03 | -6.75 | |
| 21 | 1-Sep-03 | -6.75 | |
| 22 | 1-Mar-04 | -6.75 | |
| 23 | 1-Sep-04 | -6.75 | |
| 24 | 1-Mar-05 | -6.75 | |
| 25 | 1-Sep-05 | -6.75 | |
| 26 | 1-Mar-06 | -6.75 | |
| 27 | 1-Sep-06 | -6.75 | |
| 28 | 1-Mar-07 | -6.75 | |
| 29 | 1-Sep-07 | -156.75 | <-- =-$B$4*$B$2/2-B2 |
| 30 | | | |
| 31 | Semiannual IRR of payments | 4.67% | <-- =IRR(B9:B29) |
| 32 | YTM--annualized semiannual IRR | 9.55% | <-- =(1+B31)^2-1 |
| 33 | YTM computed with **XIRR** | 9.55% | <-- =XIRR(B9:B29,A9:A29) |

We've written down the semiannual cash flows for the whole bond issue. Excel's **IRR** function shows that the IRR (we could also call this the semiannual yield to maturity) of the bonds is 4.67% (cell B31). The *compounded effective annual cost* of the bonds to GI is given in cell B32: 9.55%. The YTM as computed by Excel's **XIRR** function (cell B33) is the same.

## The Bonds from the Buyer's Perspective

The previous subsection analyzed the GI bonds from the perspective of the issuing company and showed that when we account for the issuing costs of $3.2 million, the bonds cost the company 9.55% annually. We now examine the yield from the perspective of a buyer of the bonds.

Suppose you had bought $1,000 face value of the bonds at issue.[10] As the next spreadsheet shows (cells B30:B32), you would have expected to earn an annualized interest rate of 9.20% on your bonds if: (1) you anticipated holding them to maturity and (2) GI did not default on the bonds.

| | A | B | C |
|---|---|---|---|
| 1 | GIANT INDUSTRIES 9% BONDS BUYER PERSPECTIVE 1 Sept. 1997 (issue date) | | |
| 2 | Face value of bonds bought | 1,000.00 | |
| 3 | Coupon rate | 9.00% | |
| 4 | Maturity date | 1-Sep-07 | |
| 5 | Issue date | 1-Sep-97 | |
| 6 | | | |
| 7 | Date | Cash flow | |
| 8 | 1-Sep-97 | -1,000.00 | <-- =-B2 |
| 9 | 1-Mar-98 | 45.00 | <-- =$B$3*$B$2/2 |
| 10 | 1-Sep-98 | 45.00 | <-- =$B$3*$B$2/2 |
| 11 | 1-Mar-99 | 45.00 | |
| 12 | 1-Sep-99 | 45.00 | |
| 13 | 1-Mar-00 | 45.00 | |
| 14 | 1-Sep-00 | 45.00 | |
| 15 | 1-Mar-01 | 45.00 | |
| 16 | 1-Sep-01 | 45.00 | |
| 17 | 1-Mar-02 | 45.00 | |
| 18 | 1-Sep-02 | 45.00 | |
| 19 | 1-Mar-03 | 45.00 | |
| 20 | 1-Sep-03 | 45.00 | |
| 21 | 1-Mar-04 | 45.00 | |
| 22 | 1-Sep-04 | 45.00 | |
| 23 | 1-Mar-05 | 45.00 | |
| 24 | 1-Sep-05 | 45.00 | |
| 25 | 1-Mar-06 | 45.00 | |
| 26 | 1-Sep-06 | 45.00 | |
| 27 | 1-Mar-07 | 45.00 | |
| 28 | 1-Sep-07 | 1,045.00 | <-- =$B$3*$B$2/2 |
| 29 | | | |
| 30 | Semiannual IRR of payments | 4.50% | <-- =IRR(B8:B28) |
| 31 | YTM--annualized semiannual IRR | 9.20% | <-- =(1+B30)^2-1 |
| 32 | YTM computed with XIRR | 9.20% | <-- =XIRR(B8:B28,A8:A28) |

Note that there's a spread between what the bonds cost the company (9.55% YTM) and what they yield to the purchaser (9.20% YTM). The difference in the YTMs reflects the fact that it cost Giant Industries $3.2 million to issue the bonds, so that its costs are higher than the yield received by investors in the bonds.

## Buying the Bonds on the Open Market after Issue

Thus far we have only considered the purchase of the bonds at issue. We now suppose that the date is 7 December 2000, and that you purchase $1,000 (face value) of the bonds on the open market. Looking on a Web site that reports bond prices, you see that the price of the bonds on this date was $932.50; to this price, we have to add the accrued interest:

$$Actual\ price\ paid = 932.50 + accrued\ interest$$
$$= 932.50 + \frac{days\ between\ Sept.\ 1, 2000\ and\ Dec.7,2000}{days\ between\ Sept.\ 1, 2000\ and\ March\ 1, 2001} * semi-annual\ bond\ coupon$$
$$= 932.50 + \frac{97}{181} * 45.00 = 932.50 + 24.12 = 956.62$$

---

[10] Our example assumes that you paid no commissions or other transactions costs to buy the bonds. Typically these costs would be $25–$50 for a $1,000 bond purchase.

Because the time between the bond payments is unevenly spaced, the computation of the YTM requires the use of **XIRR**. Using this function shows that the YTM is 10.68% (cell B26 below).

|  | A | B | C | D | E | F |
|---|---|---|---|---|---|---|
| 1 | GIANT INDUSTRIES 9% BONDS<br>BUYER PERSPECTIVE<br>7 Dec. 2000 |  |  |  |  |  |
| 2 | Face value of bonds bought | 1,000.00 |  | **Accrued interest calculation** |  |  |
| 3 | Coupon rate | 9.00% |  |  |  |  |
| 4 |  |  |  | Today's date | 7-Dec-00 |  |
| 5 | Quoted price | 932.50 |  | Last coupon date | 1-Sep-00 |  |
| 6 | Accrued interest | 24.12 | <-- =E12 | Next coupon date | 1-Mar-01 |  |
| 7 | Actual price paid | 956.62 |  |  |  |  |
| 8 |  |  |  | Days since last coupon | 97 | <-- =E4-E5 |
| 9 | **Date** | **Cash flow** |  | Days between coupons | 181 | <-- =E6-E5 |
| 10 | 12/7/2000 | -956.62 | <-- =-B7 |  |  |  |
| 11 | 3/1/2001 | 45.00 | <-- =$B$3*$B$2/2 | Semiannual coupon | 45.00 | <-- =B3/2*B2 |
| 12 | 9/1/2001 | 45.00 |  | Accrued interest | 24.12 | <-- =E8/E9*E11 |
| 13 | 3/1/2002 | 45.00 |  |  |  |  |
| 14 | 9/1/2002 | 45.00 |  |  |  |  |
| 15 | 3/1/2003 | 45.00 |  |  |  |  |
| 16 | 9/1/2003 | 45.00 |  |  |  |  |
| 17 | 3/1/2004 | 45.00 |  |  |  |  |
| 18 | 9/1/2004 | 45.00 |  |  |  |  |
| 19 | 3/1/2005 | 45.00 |  |  |  |  |
| 20 | 9/1/2005 | 45.00 |  |  |  |  |
| 21 | 3/1/2006 | 45.00 |  |  |  |  |
| 22 | 9/1/2006 | 45.00 |  |  |  |  |
| 23 | 3/1/2007 | 45.00 |  |  |  |  |
| 24 | 9/1/2007 | 1,045.00 | <-- =$B$3*$B$2/2+B2 |  |  |  |
| 25 |  |  |  |  |  |  |
| 26 | YTM using XIRR | 10.68% | <-- =XIRR(B10:B24,A10:A24) |  |  |  |
| 27 | YTM using Excel's Yield function | 10.41% | <-- =YIELD(A10,A24,B3,B5/10,100,2,3) |  |  |  |
| 28 | Excel's Yield annualized | 10.68% | <-- =(1+B27/2)^2-1 |  |  |  |

Note that Excel's **Yield** function in cell B27 gives the doubled semiannual yield as it is often reported in U.S. bond markets. As in the Treasury bond example in Section 15.3, annualizing this yield (cell B28) gives the same answer as the YTM reported by **XIRR**.

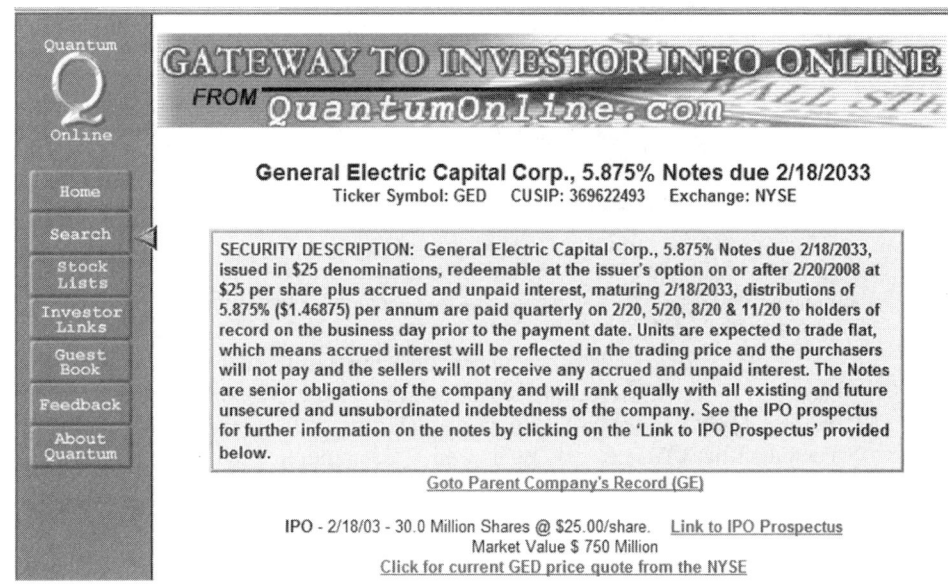

FIGURE **15.11** A description of a callable bond issued by General Electric.
*Source*: http://www.quantumonline.com.

## 15.5. Callable Bonds

Many bonds are *callable*. This means that the bond issuer has the right to refund the bonds after a given date. As an example of a callable bond, we consider the notes (remember that "notes" is just another word for "bond") issued by General Electric that are described in Figure 15.11.

The GE notes pay interest of 5.875%. This interest is paid quarterly, so that per $25 of par value, the bonds pay annual interest of $1.46875 (= 5.875%*$25); this works out to $0.3672 quarterly. The notes are callable at par on or after 20 February 2008. The notes mature on 18 February 2033.

Below we compute the IRR on these bonds, assuming that they are sold on 18 August 2003 for $27.00 and held until maturity. (Note that the Excel clip hides rows 19–122; see Chapter 7, pages 228–9, for instructions on how to do this.)

| | A | B | C |
|---|---|---|---|
| 1 | **GENERAL ELECTRIC BONDS** | | |
| 2 | Face value | 25.00 | |
| 3 | Coupon rate | 5.875% | |
| 4 | Maturity date | 18-Feb-33 | |
| 5 | Current date | 18-Aug-03 | <-- The date the bonds are sold |
| 6 | First call | 20-Feb-08 | |
| 7 | Bond price on current date | 27.00 | |
| 8 | | | |
| 9 | **Computing the Yield to (First Call (YTC)** | | |
| 10 | Date | Cash flow | |
| 11 | 18-Aug-03 | -27.00 | <-- =-B7 |
| 12 | 18-Nov-03 | 0.3672 | <-- =$B$3*$B$2/4 |
| 13 | 18-Feb-04 | 0.3672 | <-- =$B$3*$B$2/4 |
| 14 | 18-May-04 | 0.3672 | |
| 15 | 18-Aug-04 | 0.3672 | |
| 16 | 18-Nov-04 | 0.3672 | |
| 17 | 18-Feb-05 | 0.3672 | |
| 18 | 18-May-05 | 0.3672 | |
| 123 | 18-Aug-31 | 0.3672 | |
| 124 | 18-Nov-31 | 0.3672 | |
| 125 | 18-Feb-32 | 0.3672 | |
| 126 | 18-May-32 | 0.3672 | |
| 127 | 18-Aug-32 | 0.3672 | |
| 128 | 18-Nov-32 | 0.3672 | |
| 129 | 18-Feb-33 | 25.3672 | <-- =$B$3*$B$2/4+B2 |
| 130 | | | |
| 131 | Using XIRR | 5.44% | <-- =XIRR(B11:B129,A11:A129) |
| 132 | Annualizing the quarterly IRR | 5.44% | <-- =(1+IRR(B11:B129,3%))^4-1 |
| 133 | | | |
| 134 | Using Yield | 5.34% | <-- =YIELD(B5,B4,B3,B7*4,B2*4,4,3) |
| 135 | 4 times the YTM | 5.34% | <-- =4*IRR(B11:B129,3%) |

The spreadsheet shows several ways of computing the notes' yield. Using the **XIRR** function (cell B131) gives a yield of 5.44%. Using the **Yield** function, the notes' yield is 5.34% (cell B134).

Each of these numbers can be derived using Excel's **IRR** function. Because the bond payments are quarterly, **IRR** computes the quarterly interest rate on the bonds. Cell B132 annualizes this quarterly rate by calculating $(1 + quarterly\ IRR)^4 - 1$; this is equivalent to the yield computed by **XIRR** in cell B131. Cell B135 multiplies the quarterly IRR by 4 to get the same number as computed by **Yield**.

Here are two comments on this spreadsheet:

1. The EAIR paid by the GE notes is the number computed by **XIRR** and not the number computed by **Yield**. So why do we use **Yield**? Because the *convention* in American bond markets is to compute annual rates of return by multiplying the periodic rates as in cell

B135. If you're going to understand how bond rates are quoted in the United States, you have to understand the difference between the rates computed by **XIRR** and that computed by **Yield**.

2. The equivalence between cells B131 and B132 and between cells B134 and B135 works so nicely because our example starts on 18 August 2003, which is exactly the start of a quarter. For other starting dates, the equivalence would not work exactly. In this case **XIRR** always gives the correct EAIR.

To see the effect of the call provision of the bond, we calculate the *YTC*. This is the YTM, assuming that the bond is actually called by GE at the first call date. The spreadsheet below shows the calculations.[11]

| | E | F | G |
|---|---|---|---|
| 9 | **Computing the Yield to First Call (YTC)** | | |
| 10 | **Date** | **Cash flow** | |
| 11 | 18-Aug-03 | -27.00 | <-- =-B7 |
| 12 | 18-Nov-03 | 0.3672 | <-- =$B$3*$B$2/4 |
| 13 | 18-Feb-04 | 0.3672 | <-- =$B$3*$B$2/4 |
| 14 | 18-May-04 | 0.3672 | |
| 15 | 18-Aug-04 | 0.3672 | |
| 16 | 18-Nov-04 | 0.3672 | |
| 17 | 18-Feb-05 | 0.3672 | |
| 18 | 18-May-05 | 0.3672 | |
| 19 | 18-Aug-05 | 0.3672 | <-- =$B$3*$B$2/4 |
| 20 | 18-Nov-05 | 0.3672 | |
| 21 | 18-Feb-06 | 0.3672 | |
| 22 | 18-May-06 | 0.3672 | |
| 23 | 18-Aug-06 | 0.3672 | |
| 24 | 18-Nov-06 | 0.3672 | |
| 25 | 18-Feb-07 | 0.3672 | |
| 26 | 18-May-07 | 0.3672 | |
| 27 | 18-Aug-07 | 0.3672 | |
| 28 | 18-Nov-07 | 0.3672 | |
| 29 | 20-Feb-08 | 25.3672 | |
| 30 | | | |
| 31 | Using XIRR | 3.97% | <-- =XIRR(F11:F29,E11:E29) |
| 32 | Annualizing the quarterly IRR | 3.99% | <-- =(1+IRR(F11:F29))^4-1 |
| 33 | | | |
| 34 | Using Yield | 3.93% | <-- =YIELD(B5,B6,B3,B7*4,100,4,3) |
| 35 | 4 times the YTM | 3.93% | <-- =4*IRR(F11:F29) |

# 15.6. Preferred Stock

In addition to shares and bonds, companies sometimes issue preferred stock. Preferred stock is a security that promises a fixed payment to the shareholders. Although it is called "stock," preferred has many of the properties of a bond—the dividend is fixed and resembles the coupon payments on bonds. In addition, preferred stock can be callable.

---

[11] The slight difference between cell F31 and cell F32 has to do with the fact that **XIRR** is based on daily interest rates, whereas **IRR** assumes that all quarters are of equal length.

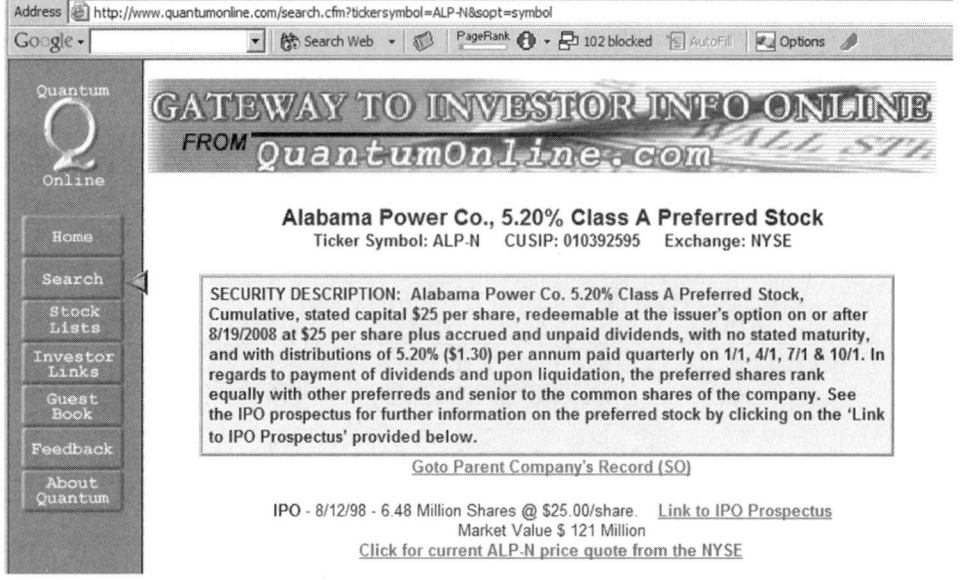

FIGURE 15.12 A description of Alabama Power Company's 5.20% preferred stock.
*SOURCE*: http://www.quantumonline.com.

In this section we analyze the preferred stock issued by Alabama Power Company (Figure 15.12). The 5.20% preferred stock issued by the Alabama Power Company has the following features:

- The par value of the stock is $25.00.
- The preferred stock's dividend is 5.20% of its par value, which is 5.20% * 25 = $1.30 annually. One quarter of this annual dividend, $0.325, is paid four times a year, on 1 January, 1 April, 1 July, and 1 October.
- The preferred stock is listed on the New York Stock Exchange. The price varies with market interest rates and the market's estimation of Alabama Power's credit worthiness—its ability to make good its promise to pay the dividends on the preferred stock. The market price of the preferred stock on 1 July 2003 was $26.10.

## Computing the Yield Assuming No Call

An investor who buys the Alabama Power preferred stock on 1 July 2003 pays the market price of $26.10 and gets a quarterly dividend of $0.325. If the investor assumes that the stock will never be called—that is, that the dividend will be paid forever—then the annualized yield on the stock is 5.07%:

| | A | B | C |
|---|---|---|---|
| 1 | ALABAMA POWER PREFERRED STOCK | | |
| | annualized yield assuming no call | | |
| 2 | Annual dividend | 1.30 | <-- =5.2%*25 |
| 3 | Quarterly dividend | 0.325 | <-- =B2/4 |
| 4 | Market price, 1 July 2003 | 26.10 | |
| 5 | | | |
| 6 | Quarterly yield | 1.25% | <-- =B3/B4 |
| 7 | Annualized yield | 5.07% | <-- =(1+B6)^4-1 |

Cell B6 computes the quarterly yield of 1.25%. In cell B7 we annualize this yield as explained in Chapter 2.

## Computing the Yield to First Call (YTC)

Although in principle the preferred stock will pay its dividends indefinitely, Alabama Power Company can call the stock at any time starting 19 August 2008. If the stock is called, the company is obliged to pay the preferred stockholders the par value of $25 plus the *accrued preferred dividend*. This concept is very much like the concept of the accrued interest discussed in Section 15.1 (page 455). For example, if the Alabama Power Company calls the preferred on 19 August 2008, it has to pay the preferred holders $25.17:

$$\underset{\substack{\uparrow \\ \text{Par} \\ \text{value}}}{\$25} + \underbrace{\frac{\textit{Days between } 19 \textit{ Aug } 2008 \textit{ and } 1 \textit{ July } 2008}{\textit{Days between } 1 \textit{ Oct } 2008 \textit{ and } 1 \textit{ July } 2008}}_{\substack{\uparrow \\ \text{Percentage of the quarter between} \\ \text{call date and last dividend date}}} * \underset{\substack{\uparrow \\ \text{Quarterly} \\ \text{dividend}}}{\$0.325} =$$

$$\$25 + \frac{49}{92} * \$0.325 = \$25.17$$

Suppose that the investor believes that Alabama Power will call the preferred stock at the first legal call date. Then his anticipated yield is 4.30%, as shown below in cell B37.

| | A | B | C |
|---|---|---|---|
| 1 | ALABAMA POWER PREFERRED STOCK<br>computing the yield to first call | | |
| 2 | Call date | 19-Aug-08 | |
| 3 | Last dividend date | 1-Jul-08 | |
| 4 | Next dividend date | 1-Oct-08 | |
| 5 | Par value | 25.00 | |
| 6 | Quarterly dividend | 0.325 | <-- =(5.2%*25)/4 |
| 7 | | | |
| 8 | Days since last dividend | 49 | <-- =B2-B3 |
| 9 | Days between last dividend and next dividend | 92 | <-- =B4-B3 |
| 10 | Accrued dividend on call date | 0.173 | <-- =B8/B9*B6 |
| 11 | Paid by company to shareholders at call | 25.17 | <-- =B5+B10 |
| 12 | | | |
| 13 | **Date** | **Cash flow** | |
| 14 | 1-Jul-03 | -26.10 | |
| 15 | 1-Oct-03 | 0.325 | |
| 16 | 1-Jan-04 | 0.325 | |
| 17 | 1-Apr-04 | 0.325 | |
| 18 | 1-Jul-04 | 0.325 | |
| 19 | 1-Oct-04 | 0.325 | |
| 20 | 1-Jan-05 | 0.325 | |
| 21 | 1-Apr-05 | 0.325 | |
| 22 | 1-Jul-05 | 0.325 | |
| 23 | 1-Oct-05 | 0.325 | |
| 24 | 1-Jan-06 | 0.325 | |
| 25 | 1-Apr-06 | 0.325 | |
| 26 | 1-Jul-06 | 0.325 | |
| 27 | 1-Oct-06 | 0.325 | |
| 28 | 1-Jan-07 | 0.325 | |
| 29 | 1-Apr-07 | 0.325 | |
| 30 | 1-Jul-07 | 0.325 | |
| 31 | 1-Oct-07 | 0.325 | |
| 32 | 1-Jan-08 | 0.325 | |
| 33 | 1-Apr-08 | 0.325 | |
| 34 | 1-Jul-08 | 0.325 | |
| 35 | 19-Aug-08 | 25.17 | <-- =B11 |
| 36 | | | |
| 37 | Yield to first call | 4.30% | <-- =XIRR(B14:B35,A14:A35) |

# 15.7. Deriving the Yield Curve from Zero-Coupon Bonds

A *zero-coupon* bond is a bond that makes no coupon payments between the time of the bond's issue and the bond's maturity. For example, the Treasury bills discussed in Section 15.1 are zero-coupon bonds. Zero coupons have the pleasant property that they allow us to identify the time-specific discount for each payment. Here's an example that is similar to that given in Section 17.2.

|  | A | B | C | D |
|---|---|---|---|---|
| 1 | USING ZERO-COUPONS TO DETERMINE BOND DISCOUNT RATES | | | |
| 2 | Zero-coupon bond A: maturity in one year | | | |
| 3 | Price today | 100 | | |
| 4 | Payoff in one year | 105 | | |
| 5 | IRR | 5.00% | <-- =B4/B3-1 | |
| 6 | | | | |
| 7 | Zero-coupon bond B: maturity in two years | | | |
| 8 | Price today | 99 | | |
| 9 | Payoff in two years | 110 | | |
| 10 | IRR | 5.41% | <-- =(B9/B8)^(1/2)-1 | |
| 11 | | | | |
| 12 | Zero-coupon bond C: maturity in three years | | | |
| 13 | Price today | 101 | | |
| 14 | Payoff in three years | 122 | | |
| 15 | IRR | 6.50% | <-- =(B14/B13)^(1/3)-1 | |
| 16 | | | | |
| 17 | Coupon bond D: A bond with payments at end of years 1, 2, 3 | | | |
| 18 | Date | Payment | Present value of payment | |
| 19 | 1 | 50 | 47.62 | <-- =B19/(1+B5) |
| 20 | 2 | 50 | 45.00 | <-- =B20/(1+B10)^2 |
| 21 | 3 | 1,050 | 869.26 | <-- =B21/(1+B15)^3 |
| 22 | Bond price | | 961.88 | <-- =SUM(C19:C21) |

Bonds *A*, *B*, and *C* have no intermediate payments. The IRR of each bond is thus the discount rate for a specific payment at time *t*. For example: $100 paid out in 2 years would be discounted by 5.41%, the rate determined by Bond *B*.

Now look at Bond *D*. This bond is a regular coupon bond—it pays $50 at dates 1 and 2 and at date 3 it pays $1,050 (the face value plus the interest). In cells A19:C22 we use the *zero-coupon yield curve* to determine the price of the bond as $961.88.

Suppose $961.88 is indeed the market price of Bond *D*. Note that the bond's yield to maturity will be different from each of the pure-discount yields determined above.

|  | A | B | C |
|---|---|---|---|
| 24 | Determining the yield to maturity (YTM) of bond D | | |
| 25 | Date | Payment | |
| 26 | 0 | -961.88 | |
| 27 | 1 | 50.00 | |
| 28 | 2 | 50.00 | |
| 29 | 3 | 1,050.00 | |
| 30 | YTM | 6.44% | <-- =IRR(B26:B29) |

## U.S. Treasury Strips

In the United States brokers often split up the payments on U.S. Treasury bonds and sell them off separately. The bonds created in this way are zero-coupon bonds and are referred to as *strips*. As an example, suppose a broker bought Bond *D* from the previous example. She could sell off the year 1 coupon of $50 as a separate security, the year 2 coupon of $50 as a separate security, and the year 3 payment of $1050 as a separate security. Each of these zero-coupon "strip securities" would have a separate price.

Zero-coupon strips allow customers with specialized payment needs to buy a security that makes a payment on a specific date. For example, if you know that you have to make a payment in 2 years, then you could buy 2-year Treasury strips. This eliminates all intermediate interest rate risks.

We can use strip prices to identify a *yield curve*. This is a graph that shows the zero-coupon interest rate on bonds for each date. Using Treasury strip data from 12 June 2009, here's an example of zero-coupon Treasury yield curve.

| | A | B | C | D | E | F |
|---|---|---|---|---|---|---|
| 1 | PRICES AND YIELDS OF U.S. TREASURY STRIPS | | | | | |
| 2 | Current date | 12-Jun-09 | | | | |
| 3 | | | | | | |
| 4 | Maturity | Price | Days till maturity | | Annual yield | |
| 5 | 15-Aug-09 | 100.02 | 64 | <-- =A5-$B$2 | -0.1140% | <-- =(100/B5)^(365/C5)-1 |
| 6 | 15-Nov-09 | 100.08 | 156 | <-- =A6-$B$2 | -0.1869% | |
| 7 | 15-Feb-10 | 99.86 | 248 | | 0.2064% | |
| 8 | 15-Aug-11 | 98.26 | 794 | | 0.8102% | |
| 9 | 15-May-12 | 96.72 | 1068 | | 1.1463% | |
| 10 | 15-Aug-12 | 95.69 | 1160 | | 1.3959% | |
| 11 | 15-Aug-12 | 94.87 | 1160 | | 1.6709% | <-- =(100/B11)^(365/C11)-1 |
| 12 | 15-Feb-13 | 94.38 | 1344 | | 1.5832% | |
| 13 | 15-Feb-13 | 93.77 | 1344 | | 1.7623% | |
| 14 | 15-Aug-13 | 92.95 | 1525 | | 1.7652% | |
| 15 | 15-Nov-13 | 92.27 | 1617 | | 1.8326% | |
| 16 | 15-Nov-13 | 91.02 | 1617 | | 2.1466% | |
| 17 | 15-Feb-14 | 90.65 | 1709 | | 2.1187% | |
| 18 | 15-Feb-14 | 90.85 | 1709 | | 2.0706% | |
| 19 | 15-May-14 | 89.73 | 1798 | | 2.2242% | |
| 20 | 15-Aug-14 | 88.53 | 1890 | | 2.3807% | |
| 21 | 15-Nov-15 | 83.55 | 2347 | | 2.8345% | |
| 22 | 15-Feb-16 | 82.13 | 2439 | | 2.9900% | |
| 23 | 15-Nov-16 | 78.69 | 2713 | | 3.2768% | |
| 24 | 15-May-17 | 76.28 | 2894 | | 3.4739% | |
| 25 | 15-Feb-18 | 72.80 | 3170 | | 3.7229% | |
| 26 | 15-Aug-18 | 71.27 | 3351 | | 3.7580% | |
| 27 | 15-Nov-18 | 70.28 | 3443 | | 3.8096% | |
| 28 | 15-Aug-19 | 67.09 | 3716 | | 3.9983% | |
| 29 | 15-Feb-20 | 64.90 | 3900 | | 4.1291% | |
| 30 | 15-May-20 | 63.91 | 3990 | | 4.1805% | |
| 31 | 15-Aug-20 | 62.83 | 4082 | | 4.2431% | |
| 32 | 15-Aug-20 | 62.87 | 4082 | | 4.2372% | |

TREASURY STRIP YIELD CURVE

The graph gives actual prices and maturities for Treasury strips on 12 June 2009. The maturities (column C) are calculated in days. (There are many rows of data that we haven't shown but that are on the CD-ROM that comes with this book.) Here's a sample calculation (cells A8:D8): On 12 June 2009 a zero-coupon Treasury strip with maturity 15 August 2012 sells for $94.87. This bond promises $100 on maturity. There are 1,160 days between 12 June 2009 and 15 August 2012. To compute the annualized yield for the bond, we find 1 plus the daily interest rate, $\left(\dfrac{100}{94.87}\right)^{1/1}$. Raising this number to the power 365 (the number of days per year) and subtracting 1 gives the annualized yield in cell E11:

$$yield\ to\ maturity = \left(\frac{100}{94.87}\right)^{365/1160} - 1 = 1.6709\%$$

# Conclusion

This chapter discusses the pricing bonds and the determination bond yield to maturity (YTM). Pricing a bond is largely an exercise in applying the present value concepts discussed in Chapters 1–4. The yield on a bond is the annualized internal rate of return of its payments.

Bond pricing and yield computations are also applicable to callable bonds and to preferred stock. We have given examples of each of these securities. Finally, the chapter discussed zero-coupon securities.

## EXERCISES

1. On 1 August 2001, you are offered the following bond:

   - Face value: $1,000.00
   - Coupon rate: 12%
   - Coupon payments: Once a year on August 1, 2002, 2003,..., 2012
   - Bond price: $1,252.00
   - Bond's face value repaid on last coupon date

   Use Excel's IRR function to compute the bond's yield to maturity (YTM).

2. On 10 September 2001, you are offered the following bond:

   - Face value: $1,000.00
   - Coupon rate: 12%
   - Coupon payments: Once a year on August 1, 2002, 2003,..., 2012
   - Bond price: $1,252.00
   - Bond's face value repaid on last coupon date

   Use Excel's XIRR function to compute the bond's yield to maturity (YTM).

3. Consider the following two bonds.

| Bond A | Bond B |
|---|---|
| Term to maturity: 10 years from today | Term to maturity: 20 years from today |
| Face value: $1,000 | Face value: $1,000 |
| Coupon: 10%, interest payments to be made in 1 year from today, 2 years from today, . . . , 10 years from today | Coupon: 10%, interest payments to be made in 1 year from today, 2 years from today, . . . , 20 years from today |
| Repayment of bond: On last coupon date | Repayment of bond: On last coupon date |

Make a table comparing the bond prices when the market interest rate varies from 5, 6,..., 17%. Use the template provided here, which is on the CD-ROM that accompanies *Principles of Finance with Excel*. In the template you see that when the market interest rate is 10%, both bonds are valued at $1,000.

Can you conclude that "the longer-term bond's price is more sensitive to changes in the market interest rate?" Explain using a graph.

|   | A | B | C | D | E | F | G |
|---|---|---|---|---|---|---|---|
| 1 | **COMPARING TWO BONDS** | | | | | | |
| 2 | | Bond A | Bond B | | Market interest rate | 10% | |
| 3 | Coupon rate | 10% | 10% | | Price of Bond A | $1,000.00 | <-- =NPV(F2,B8:B17) |
| 4 | Maturity | 10 | 20 | | Price of Bond B | $1,000.00 | <-- =NPV(F2,C8:C27) |
| 5 | Face value | 1,000.00 | 1,000.00 | | | | |
| 6 | | | | | | | |
| 7 | Year | Bond A | Bond B | | **Data table: Effect of market interest rate on bond prices** | | |
| 8 | 1 | 100.00 | 100.00 | | Interest rate | Bond A price | Bond B price |
| 9 | 2 | 100.00 | 100.00 | | | | |
| 10 | 3 | 100.00 | 100.00 | | 0% | | |
| 11 | 4 | 100.00 | 100.00 | | 1% | | |
| 12 | 5 | 100.00 | 100.00 | | 2% | | |
| 13 | 6 | 100.00 | 100.00 | | 3% | | |
| 14 | 7 | 100.00 | 100.00 | | 4% | | |
| 15 | 8 | 100.00 | 100.00 | | 5% | | |
| 16 | 9 | 100.00 | 100.00 | | 6% | | |
| 17 | 10 | 1,100.00 | 100.00 | | 7% | | |
| 18 | 11 | | 100.00 | | 8% | | |
| 19 | 12 | | 100.00 | | 9% | | |
| 20 | 13 | | 100.00 | | 10% | | |
| 21 | 14 | | 100.00 | | 11% | | |
| 22 | 15 | | 100.00 | | 12% | | |
| 23 | 16 | | 100.00 | | 13% | | |
| 24 | 17 | | 100.00 | | 14% | | |
| 25 | 18 | | 100.00 | | 15% | | |
| 26 | 19 | | 100.00 | | 16% | | |
| 27 | 20 | | 1,100.00 | | 17% | | |

4. You have been offered a U.S. Treasury bill. The face value of the bill is $10,000 and the price is $8,925. The bill matures in ½ year. Compute the YTM of the bill using both discrete and continuously compounded interest.

5. You have been offered a U.S. Treasury bill. The bill has face value of $10,000 and price of $9,456. It matures in 210 days. Compute: (a) the daily interest rate and the corresponding annualized interest rate and (b) the continuously compounded interest rate.

6. On 20 February 2001 you are offered a U.S. Treasury note. Here are the terms of the note:

- The note has face value of $100,000 and a 6.5% coupon rate. The note matures on 15 October 2006.

- The semiannual interest on the note (that is, $\dfrac{6.5\%*100,000}{2} = \$3,250$) is paid on 15 April and 15 October of each year. The last interest payment was 15 October 2000 and the next interest payment is on 15 April 2001.

- Other interest payments are on 15 October 2001, 15 April 2002,..., 15 October 2006. On this last date the bond's principal of $100,000 is also returned.

- On 20 February 2001 the bond was priced at $109,477.71. This price was computed as follows:

$$\underbrace{\$107,152.00}_{\substack{\text{In the jargon of}\\\text{bond markets this is}\\\text{called the "bond price"}}} + \text{Accrued Interest of } \$2,285.71 = \underbrace{\$109,477.71}_{\substack{\text{In the jargon of}\\\text{bond markets this is}\\\text{called the "invoice price"}}}$$

a. Confirm the calculation of the accrued interest.

b. Use **XIRR** calculate the annualized yield to maturity (YTM).

**Note**: Use the following template.

|  | A | B | C |
|---|---|---|---|
| 1 | **TREASURY BOND CALCULATION** | | |
| 2 | **Computing the accrued interest** | | |
| 3 | Current date | 20-Feb-01 | |
| 4 | Previous interest payment date | 15-Oct-00 | |
| 5 | Next interest payment date | 15-Apr-01 | |
| 6 | Semiannual coupon | 3,250.00 | |
| 7 | | | |
| 8 | Days since last coupon date | | |
| 9 | Days between last coupon date and next coupon date | | |
| 10 | | | |
| 11 | Accrued interest | | |
| 12 | | | |
| 13 | **Computing the YTM** | | |
| 14 | Bond price | 107,152.00 | |
| 15 | Accrued interest | | |
| 16 | Invoice price (bond price + accrued) | | |
| 17 | | | |
| 18 | **Date** | **Bond cash flow** | |
| 19 | 20-Feb-01 | | |
| 20 | 15-Apr-01 | | |
| 21 | 15-Oct-01 | | |
| 22 | 15-Apr-02 | | |
| 23 | 15-Oct-02 | | |
| 24 | 15-Apr-03 | | |
| 25 | 15-Oct-03 | | |
| 26 | 15-Apr-04 | | |
| 27 | 15-Oct-04 | | |
| 28 | 15-Apr-05 | | |
| 29 | 15-Oct-05 | | |
| 30 | 15-Apr-06 | | |
| 31 | 15-Oct-06 | | |
| 32 | | | |
| 33 | YTM | | |

7. On 26 February 2001 a UtilityCorp 8.2% bond maturing 15 January 2007 is priced at 103.790 per $100 of face value (this price does not include the accrued interest). The bond was originally issued in 1992. The bond pays interest semiannually, on 15 January and 15 July of each year. Compute the accrued interest and the YTM of the bond.

8. You are given the following information on three traded bonds making annual coupon payments.

|  | A | B | C | D | E |
|---|---|---|---|---|---|
| 1 | Bond | Face value | Coupon rate | Maturity | Yield to maturity |
| 2 | A | $1,000 | 0.00% | 1 | 5.00% |
| 3 | B | $1,000 | 5.00% | 2 | 5.85% |
| 4 | C | $1,000 | 10.00% | 2 | 6.00% |

a. What are the prices of the above three bonds?

b. What is the zero-coupon bond yield for a 1-year bond?

c. What is the zero-coupon bond yield for a 2-year bond based on the price of Bond *B*?

d. What is the zero-coupon bond yield for a 2-year bond based on the price of Bond *C*?

e. **Challenge question**: Create an arbitrage strategy from buying and/or selling a combination of the three bonds.

9. Use the data in the following table to create two graphs. The data are on the disk that comes with the book.

- A graph of the yields on 10-year U.S. Treasury bonds, AAA corporate, Baa corporate from 1976–2009.

- A graph of the risk premium over 10-year Treasury bonds for the AAA and Baa bonds for each year.

| | A | B | C | D |
|---|---|---|---|---|
| 1 | | **BOND YIELDS: 10-YEAR TREASURY BONDS, AAA CORPORATES, Baa CORPORATES, 1976–2009** | | |
| 2 | | **10-Year Treasury** | **AAA** | **Baa** |
| 3 | 1976 | 7.61% | 8.43% | 9.75% |
| 4 | 1977 | 7.42% | 8.02% | 8.97% |
| 5 | 1978 | 8.41% | 8.73% | 9.49% |
| 6 | 1979 | 9.43% | 9.63% | 10.69% |
| 7 | 1980 | 11.43% | 11.94% | 13.67% |
| 8 | 1981 | 13.92% | 14.17% | 16.04% |
| 9 | 1982 | 13.01% | 13.79% | 16.11% |
| 10 | 1983 | 11.10% | 12.04% | 13.55% |
| 11 | 1984 | 12.46% | 12.71% | 14.19% |
| 12 | 1985 | 10.62% | 11.37% | 12.72% |
| 13 | 1986 | 7.67% | 9.02% | 10.39% |
| 14 | 1987 | 8.39% | 9.38% | 10.58% |
| 15 | 1988 | 8.85% | 9.71% | 10.83% |
| 16 | 1989 | 8.49% | 9.26% | 10.18% |
| 17 | 1990 | 8.55% | 9.32% | 10.36% |
| 18 | 1991 | 7.86% | 8.77% | 9.80% |
| 19 | 1992 | 7.01% | 8.14% | 8.98% |
| 20 | 1993 | 5.87% | 7.22% | 7.93% |
| 21 | 1994 | 7.09% | 7.97% | 8.63% |
| 22 | 1995 | 6.57% | 7.59% | 8.20% |
| 23 | 1996 | 6.44% | 7.37% | 8.05% |
| 24 | 1997 | 6.35% | 7.27% | 7.87% |
| 25 | 1998 | 5.26% | 6.53% | 7.22% |
| 26 | 1999 | 5.65% | 7.05% | 7.88% |
| 27 | 2000 | 6.03% | 7.62% | 8.37% |
| 28 | 2001 | 5.02% | 7.08% | 7.95% |
| 29 | 2002 | 4.61% | 6.49% | 7.80% |
| 30 | 2003 | 4.01% | 5.66% | 6.76% |
| 31 | 2004 | 4.27% | 5.63% | 6.39% |
| 32 | 2005 | 4.29% | 5.23% | 6.06% |
| 33 | 2006 | 4.80% | 5.59% | 6.48% |
| 34 | 2007 | 4.63% | 5.56% | 6.48% |
| 35 | 2008 | 3.66% | 5.63% | 7.44% |
| 36 | 2009 | 3.26% | 5.31% | 7.29% |

10. On 15 August 2006, Corporate Junk issues $100 million of 10-year bonds. The bonds have a coupon of 10%, payable semiannually on 15 February and 15 August of each year. They are issued at par. Corporate Junk's expenses related to the bond issue are $4 million. Compute the annualized yield to the bond investors and the annualized cost to the company.

11. On 18 October 2006 the Corporate Junk bond issue (see previous exercise) is selling for $103. Use **XIRR** to compute the investor's yield to maturity of the bonds.

12. On 15 August 1996 the U.S. Treasury issued a bond maturing on 15 February 2026. The bond has a coupon rate of 6%, payable semiannually on 15 February and 15 August. If a $100 face-value bond is selling for $117.25 on 23 January 2005, compute the bond's yield to maturity.

13. On 15 May 1985 the U.S. Treasury issued a bond maturing 15 November 2014. The bond had a coupon rate of 11.75%, payable semiannually on 15 November and 15 May. On 23 January 2005 a $1,000 face-value bond was selling for $1356.20. This price does not include the accrued interest. The bond is callable at par starting 15 November 2009. Compute the following:

    a. The bond's yield to maturity (YTM).

    b. The bond's yield to first call (YTC).

14. Consolidated Edison's 4.65% Series C cumulative preferred stock trades on the New York Stock Exchange. The stock has face value $100 and pays its dividend four times per year, on the first of February, May, July, and November. The stock is not redeemable. If the share price on 2 February 2005 is $85, what is the preferred stock's yield?

### Consolidated Edison Co. of NY, 4.65% Series C Cumul Preferred Stock

Ticker Symbol: ED-C    CUSIP: 209111301    Exchange: NYSE
Security Type: Preferred Stock

SECURITY DESCRIPTION: Consolidated Edison Co. of New York Inc., 4.65% Series C, Cumulative Preferred Stock, liquidation preference $100 per share, redeemable any time at the company's option at $101.00 per share plus accrued and unpaid dividends, not subject to mandatory redemption, and with distrbutions of 4,65% ($4.65) per annum paid quarterly on 2/1, 5/1, 8/1 & 11/1. Consolidated Edison Co. of New York Inc. is a wholly-owned subsidary of Consolidated Edison Inc. (NYSE: ED).

| Stock Exchange | Cpn Rate Ann Amt | LiqPref CallPrice | Call Date Matur Date | Moodys/S&P Dated | Distribution Dates | 15% Tax Rate |
|---|---|---|---|---|---|---|
| NYSE Chart | 4.65% $4.65 | $100.00 $101.00 | any time None | A3 / BBB+ 7/05/04 | 2/1, 5/1, 8/1 & 11/1 Click for Ex-Div Date | Yes |

15. Reconsider the Consolidated Edison preferred in Exercise 14. Suppose that the stock trades for $87.50 on 3 January 2005. What is its yield? (Don't forget that the price does not include the accrued dividend.)

16. Genworth Financial's 5.25% Series A cumulative preferred stock has a par value of $50 and interest rate of 5.25% payable quarterly on the first day of March, June, September, and December. The stock is callable at par from 1 June 2011. If the stock trades at $45.50 on 2 June 2005, what is its yield to first call (YTC)?

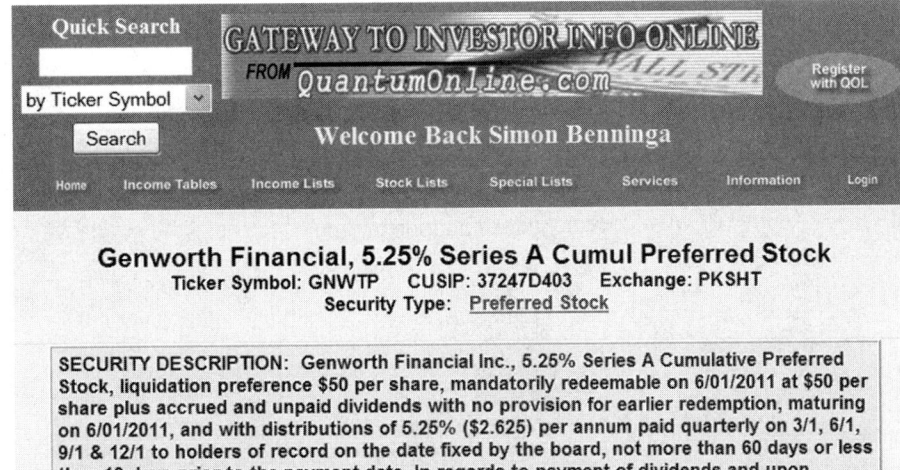

**Genworth Financial, 5.25% Series A Cumul Preferred Stock**
Ticker Symbol: GNWTP    CUSIP: 37247D403    Exchange: PKSHT
Security Type:  Preferred Stock

SECURITY DESCRIPTION:  Genworth Financial Inc., 5.25% Series A Cumulative Preferred Stock, liquidation preference $50 per share, mandatorily redeemable on 6/01/2011 at $50 per share plus accrued and unpaid dividends with no provision for earlier redemption, maturing on 6/01/2011, and with distributions of 5.25% ($2.625) per annum paid quarterly on 3/1, 6/1, 9/1 & 12/1 to holders of record on the date fixed by the board, not more than 60 days or less than 10 days prior to the payment date. In regards to payment of dividends and upon liquidation, the preferred shares rank equally with other preferreds and senior to the common shares of the company. The prospectus (P306) states that the stock should be eligible for the 15% tax rate. See the IPO prospectus for further information on the preferred stock by clicking on the 'Link to IPO Prospectus' provided below.

| Stock Exchange | Cpn Rate Ann Amt | LiqPref CallPrice | Call Date Matur Date | Moodys/S&P Dated | Distribution Dates | 15% Tax Rate |
|---|---|---|---|---|---|---|
| PKSHT Chart | 5.25% $2.625 | $50.00 $50.00 | 6/01/2011 6/01/2011 | Baa1 / BBB+ 11/13/04 | 3/1, 6/1, 9/1 & 12/1 Click for Ex-Div Date | Yes |

Goto Parent Company's Record (GNW)

17. On the disk with this book is the file below.

    a. Complete the file to derive the continuous yields of the zero coupon Treasury strips. Graph the yields to derive the yield curve on 21 January 2005.

    b. Why do you think that the yields of very short-term zero strips (the first two) are negative?

| | A | B | C | D | E | F |
|---|---|---|---|---|---|---|
| 1 | **U.S. TREASURY STRIP DATA** | | | | | |
| | **21 January 2005** | | | | | |
| 2 | | | | | | |
| 3 | Current date | 21-Jan-05 | | | | |
| 4 | **Price** | **Maturity** | **Yahoo! yield** | **Days to maturity** | **Years to maturity** | **Continuous yield** |
| 5 | 100.17 | 15-Feb-05 | -2.956% | | | |
| 6 | 100.15 | 15-Feb-05 | -2.642% | | | |
| 7 | 99.57 | 15-May-05 | 1.421% | | | |
| 8 | 99.56 | 15-May-05 | 1.457% | | | |
| 9 | 98.8 | 15-Aug-05 | 2.188% | | | |
| 10 | 98.85 | 15-Aug-05 | 2.087% | | | |
| 11 | 98.04 | 15-Nov-05 | 2.481% | | | |
| 12 | 98.04 | 15-Nov-05 | 2.477% | | | |
| 13 | 97.33 | 15-Feb-06 | 2.572% | | | |
| 14 | 97.35 | 15-Feb-06 | 2.554% | | | |
| 15 | 97.34 | 15-Feb-06 | 2.563% | | | |
| 16 | 96.52 | 15-May-06 | 2.736% | | | |
| 17 | 96.57 | 15-May-06 | 2.696% | | | |
| 18 | 95.73 | 15-Aug-06 | 2.820% | | | |

18. Be ambitious! Go to Yahoo!, download the zero-coupon data for a recent date, and repeat the previous exercise.

CHAPTER

# 16 | Valuing Stocks

## CHAPTER CONTENTS

## Overview

In Chapter 15 we discussed the valuation of bonds. The current chapter deals with the valuation of stocks. Whereas the valuation of bonds is a relatively straightforward matter of computing the yield to maturity, the valuation of stocks is much more difficult. The difficulty lies both in the greater uncertainty about the cash flows that need to be discounted to arrive at a stock valuation and in the computation of the correct discount rate.

In this chapter we discuss four basic approaches to stock valuation:

- **Valuation method 1, the efficient markets approach.** In its simplest form the *efficient markets* approach states that the current stock price is correct. A somewhat more sophisticated use of the efficient markets approach to stock valuation is that a stock's value is the sum of the values of its components. We explore the implications of these statements in Section 16.1.

- **Valuation method 2, discounting the future free cash flows (FCF).** Sometimes called the discounted cash flow (DCF) approach to valuation, this method values the firm's debt and its equity together as the present value of the firm's future FCFs. The discount rate used is the weighted average cost of capital (WACC). This method is the valuation approach favored by most finance academics. We discuss this approach in Section 16.2 and the calculation of the WACC in Section 16.6. In this chapter we do not discuss the concept or the computation of the FCF—this was done previously in Chapters 6 and 7.

- **Valuation method 3, discounting the future equity payouts.** A firm's shares can also be valued by *discounting the stream of anticipated equity payouts* at an appropriate cost of equity $r_E$. The concept of equity payout (the sum of a firm's total dividends plus its stock repurchases) was previously discussed in Chapter 6.

- **Valuation method 4, multiples.** Finally we can value a firm's shares by a *comparative valuation based on multiples*. This very common method involves ratios such as the P/E ratio, earnings before interest, taxes, depreciation, and amortization (EBITDA) multiples, and more industry-specific multiples such as value per square foot of storage space or value per subscriber.

With the exception of the multiple method 4, almost all of the material in this chapter is also discussed elsewhere in this book. The efficient markets approach to valuation is also discussed in Chapter 14. Discounting free cash flows (FCFs) is discussed in Chapters 6 and 7. The Gordon dividend model (which values a firm's equity by discounting its anticipated dividend stream) is also discussed in Chapter 6. WACC computations are found in Chapters 6 and 13. The purpose of this chapter is to bring together these dispersed materials into a (hopefully coherent) whole.

## Finance Concepts Discussed in This Chapter

- Discounted cash flow (DCF), free cash flow (FCF)
- Cost of capital, cost of equity, cost of debt, weighted average cost of capital (WACC)
- Equity premium
- Beta ($\beta$), equity beta $\beta_E$, asset beta $\beta_{Asset}$
- Two-stage growth models

### Excel Functions Used

- **Sum**, **NPV**, **If**
- **Data table**

## 16.1. Valuation Method 1: The Current Market Price of a Stock Is the Correct Price (the Efficient Markets Approach)

The simplest stock valuation is based on the efficient markets approach (Chapter 14). This approach says that the *current market price of a stock is the correct price*. In other words, the market has already done the difficult job of stock valuation, and it's done this correctly, incorporating all of the relevant information There's a lot of evidence for this approach, as you saw in Chapter 14.

This valuation method is very simple to apply:

- *Question*: "IBM looks a bit expensive to me—its price has been going up for the last 3 months. What do you think: Is IBM's stock price currently underpriced or overpriced?"

- *Answer*: "At Podunk U., we learned that markets with a lot of trading are in general efficient, meaning that the current market price incorporates all of the readily available information about IBM. So I don't think IBM is either underpriced or overpriced. It's actually correctly priced."

Here's another example of the use of this approach.

- *Question*: "I've been thinking of buying IBM, but I've been putting it off. The price has gone up lately, and I'm going to wait until it comes down a bit. It seems a bit high to me right now." What do you think?

- *Answer*: "At Podunk U. we would call you a *contrarian*. You believe that if the price of a stock has gone up, it will go back down (and the opposite). But this technical approach (see Chapter 14) to stock valuation doesn't seem to work very well. So if you want to buy IBM, go ahead and do so now. There's nothing in the price runup of the last couple of months that indicates that there will now be a price rundown."

### Some More Sophisticated Efficient Markets Methods

Efficient markets valuations don't always have to be as simplistic as the above examples. In Chapter 14 we looked at *additivity*, a fundamental principal of efficient markets. The principle of additivity says that the value of a basket of goods or financial assets should equal the sum of the values of the components. Additivity can often be used to value stocks.

Here's a very simple example: ABC Holding Corp., a publicly traded company, owns shares in two publicly traded companies. Besides owning these subsidiaries, ABC does little else.

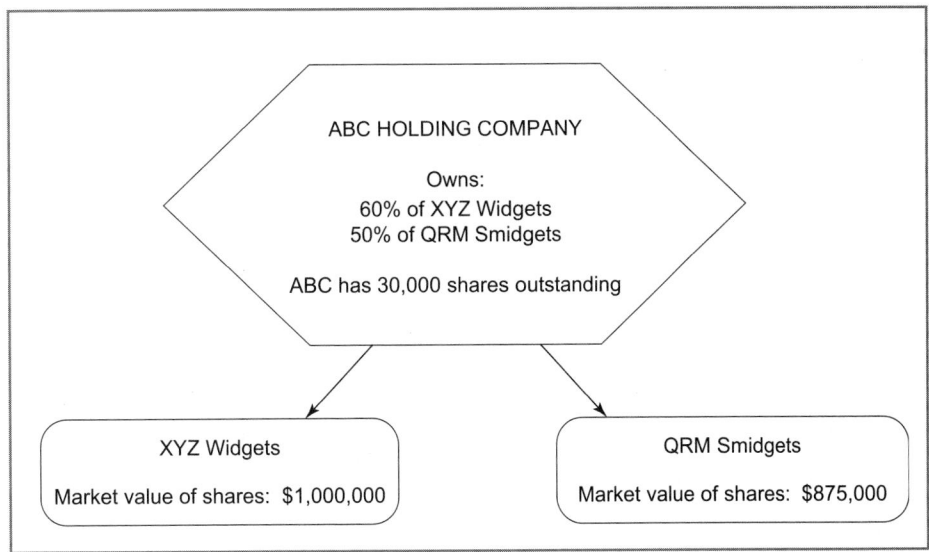

F<small>IGURE</small> 16.1  Ownership structure of ABC Holding Company.

What should be the value of a share of ABC Holding? The obvious way to determine the value is in the following spreadsheet, which computes the share value of ABC to be $34.58.

| | A | B | C | D | E |
|---|---|---|---|---|---|
| 1 | **ABC HOLDING COMPANY** | | | | |
| 2 | Number of ABC shares | 30,000 | | | |
| 3 | | | | | |
| 4 | **ABC owns shares in** | **Percentage of shares owned by ABC** | **Market value** | **Market value of ABC holdings in company** | |
| 5 | XYZ Widgets | 60% | 1,000,000 | 600,000 | <-- =B5*C5 |
| 6 | QRM Smidgets | 50% | 875,000 | 437,500 | <-- =B6*C6 |
| 7 | Total value of ABC holdings | | | 1,037,500 | <-- =D6+D5 |
| 8 | | | | | |
| 9 | Per share value of ABC Holdings | | | 34.58 | <-- =D7/B2 |

Note what this model *is* and *is not* telling you:

- *Is* telling you: If the market values of XYZ and QRM are correct, then the market value of ABC should be $1,037,500. In per-share terms,

$$\frac{ABC\ share}{price} = \frac{60\% * [XYZ\ value] + 50\% * [QRM\ value]}{number\ of\ ABC\ shares} = \$34.58$$

- *Is not* telling you: The formula tells you a relation among the three share prices. It tells you whether the share prices are *relatively correct*, but it does not tell you whether they are *absolutely correct*. As an example, after doing much work and research and applying the methods of the previous section, you come to the conclusion that, although the market valuation of QRM is correct, the market value of XYZ ought to be $1,600,000. Then you would conclude that the share price of ABC ought to be $46.58.

| | A | B | C | D | E |
|---|---|---|---|---|---|
| 1 | **ABC HOLDING COMPANY** | | | | |
| 2 | Number of ABC shares | 30,000 | | | |
| 3 | | | | | |
| 4 | ABC owns shares in | Percentage of shares owned by ABC | Market value | Market value of ABC holdings in company | |
| 5 | XYZ Widgets | 60% | 1,600,000 | 960,000 | <-- =B5*C5 |
| 6 | QRM Smidgets | 50% | 875,000 | 437,500 | <-- =B6*C6 |
| 7 | Total value of ABC holdings | | | 1,397,500 | <-- =D6+D5 |
| 8 | | | | | |
| 9 | Per share value of ABC Holdings | | | 46.58 | <-- =D7/B2 |

Note that if ABC has some of its own overheads and if it doesn't always pass through all the dividends of its subsidiaries, its market value will be *lower* than the sum of the values of XYZ and QRM, because the market price of ABC will reflect not only the cost of the shares of its subsidiaries, but also its own overheads. This looks a lot like the *closed-end fund* valuation problem discussed in Chapter 14.

# 16.2. Valuation Method 2: The Price of a Share Is the Discounted Value of the Future Anticipated FCFs

Valuation method 1 of the previous section says that there is nothing to be gained by second-guessing market valuations. In many cases, however, the finance expert (you!) will want to do a basic valuation of a company and derive the value of a share from the discounted value of the future anticipated free cash flows (FCFs). This method, often called the discounted cash flow (DCF) method of valuation, was discussed and illustrated in Chapters 6 and 7. Figure 16.2 reminds you of the definition of FCF and Figure 16.3 gives a flow diagram of the FCF valuation method.

| Defining the Free Cash Flow (FCF) | |
|---|---|
| Profit after taxes | This is the basic measure of the profitability of the business, but it is an accounting measure that includes financing flows (such as interest), as well as noncash expenses such as depreciation. Profit after taxes does not account for either changes in the firm's working capital or purchases of new fixed assets, both of which can be important cash drains on the firm. |
| + Depreciation | This noncash expense is added back to the profit after tax. |
| + After-tax interest payments (net) | FCF is an attempt to measure the cash produced by the business activity of the firm. To neutralize the effect of interest payments on the firm's profits, we<br>• Add back the after-tax cost of interest on debt (*after-tax* because interest payments are tax deductible),<br>• Subtract out the after-tax interest payments on cash and marketable securities. |
| – Increase in current assets | When the firm's sales increase, more investment is needed in inventories, accounts receivable, etc. This increase in current assets is not an expense for tax purposes (and is therefore ignored in the profit after taxes), but it is a cash drain on the company. |
| + Increase in current liabilities | An increase in the sales often causes an increase in financing related to sales (such as accounts payable or taxes payable). This increase in current liabilities—when related to sales—provides cash to the firm. Because it is directly related to sales, we include this cash in the FCF calculations. |
| – Increase in fixed assets at cost | An increase in fixed assets (the long-term productive assets of the company) is a use of cash that reduces the firm's FCF. |
| FCF = sum of the above | |

FIGURE **16.2** Defining the free cash flow (FCF). We have previously discussed FCFs and their use in valuation in Chapters 6 and 7.

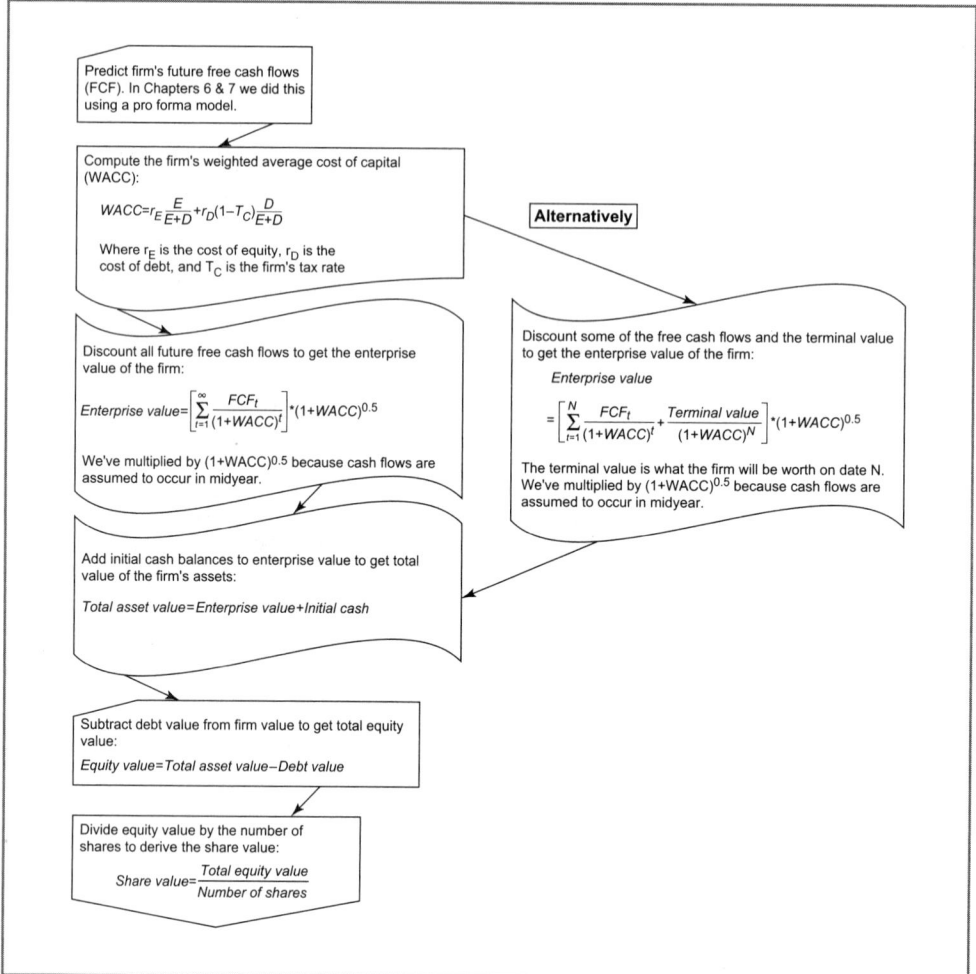

FIGURE 16.3 Flow diagram for a FCF valuation: Calculating a firm's share value.

## Valuation 2: Example 1—A Basic Example

It is 31 December 2010 and you are trying to value Arnold Corp, which finished 2010 with a FCF of $2 million. The company has debt of $10 million and cash balances of $1 million. You estimate the following financial parameters for the company:

- The future anticipated growth rate of the FCF is 8%.
- The WACC of Arnold is 15%.
- Arnold Corp. has 1,000,000 shares outstanding.

You can now estimate the value of Arnold: The *enterprise value* of Arnold is the present value of future anticipated FCFs discounted at the WACC:

$$\text{Enterprise value} = \left[ \sum_{t=1}^{\infty} \frac{FCF_t}{(1+WACC)^t} \right] * \underbrace{(1+WACC)^{0.5}}_{\substack{\text{This factor "corrects"} \\ \text{for the fact that FCFs occur} \\ \text{throughout the year.}}}$$

This is the PV
formula, assuming that
FCFs occur at year-end

$$= \left[ \sum_{t=1}^{\infty} \frac{FCF_{2010}(1+g)^t}{(1+WACC)^t} \right] * (1+WACC)^{0.5}$$

Future FCFs are expected
to grow at rate *g*.

$$= \left[ \frac{FCF_{2010}(1+g)}{WACC-g} \right] * (1+WACC)^{0.5}$$

This formula was
given in Chapter 2

Doing the computations in an Excel spreadsheet shows that the enterprise value of Arnold Corp. is $33,090,599 and that the estimated per-share value is $24.09.

| | A | B | C |
|---|---|---|---|
| 1 | **VALUING ARNOLD CORP.** | | |
| 2 | 2003 FCF (base year) | 2,000,000 | |
| 3 | Future FCF growth rate | 8% | |
| 4 | WACC | 15% | |
| 5 | End-2003 debt | 10,000,000 | |
| 6 | End-2003 cash | 1,000,000 | |
| 7 | Number of shares outstanding | 1,000,000 | |
| 8 | | | |
| 9 | Enterprise value | 33,090,599 | <-- =B2*(1+B3)/(B4-B3)*(1+B4)^0.5 |
| 10 | Add cash | 1,000,000 | <-- =B6 |
| 11 | Subtract debt | -10,000,000 | <-- =-B5 |
| 12 | Value of equity | 24,090,599 | <-- =SUM(B9:B11) |
| 13 | Share value | 24.09 | <-- =B12/B7 |

## Valuation Method 2: Example 2—Two FCF Growth Rates

In the valuation of Arnold Corp. in the previous subsection we assumed a FCF growth rate that is unchanging over the future. This assumption is often suitable for a mature, stable company, but it may not be appropriate for a company that is currently experiencing very high growth rates. In this subsection we show how to perform an FCF valuation of a company for which we assume *two* FCF growth rates—a high FCF growth rate for a number of years followed by a subsequent lower FCF growth rate.

Xanthum Corp. has just finished its 2010 financial year. The company's 2010 FCF was $1,000,000. Xanthum has been growing very fast; you anticipate that for the coming 5 years the annual FCF growth rate will be 35%. After this time, you anticipate that the FCF growth will slow to 10% per year, because the market for Xanthum's products will become mature.

Xanthum has 3,000,000 shares outstanding and a WACC of 20%. It currently has $500,000 of cash on hand that is not needed for operations; Xanthum also has $3,000,000 of debt. To value the company, we apply the same valuation scheme as before, but this time we use the two FCF growth rates.

$$Enterprise\ value = \left[ \underbrace{\sum_{t=1}^{5} \frac{FCF_t}{(1+WACC)^t}}_{\substack{\uparrow \\ \text{The PV of the "high} \\ \text{growth" FCFs}}} + \underbrace{\sum_{t=6}^{\infty} \frac{FCF_t}{(1+WACC)^t}}_{\substack{\uparrow \\ \text{The PV of the "normal} \\ \text{growth" FCFs}}} \right] * \underbrace{(1+WACC)^{0.5}}_{\substack{\uparrow \\ \text{This factor "corrects"} \\ \text{for the fact that FCFs occur} \\ \text{throughout the year.}}}$$

There's a valuation formula that can be derived using techniques described in the appendix to Chapter 2:

$Enterprise\ value =$

$$\left[ \underbrace{\frac{FCF_{2010}(1+g_{high})}{1+WACC} \left( \frac{1 - \left(\frac{1+g_{high}}{1+WACC}\right)^5}{1 - \frac{1+g_{high}}{1+WACC}} \right)}_{\substack{\uparrow \\ \text{In the spreadsheet this is called} \\ \text{"term 1" and } \frac{1+g_{high}}{1+WACC} \text{ is called "term1 factor"}}} + \underbrace{FCF_{2010}\left(\frac{1+g_{high}}{1+WACC}\right)^5 \left( \frac{1+g_{normal}}{WACC - g_{normal}} \right)}_{\substack{\uparrow \\ \text{In the spreadsheet this is called} \\ \text{"term 2"}}} \right] * (1+WACC)^{0.5}$$

The spreadsheet below shows that Xanthum's enterprise value is \$29,621,547 (cell B15) and that its per-share value is \$9.04 (cell B21).

| | A | B | C |
|---|---|---|---|
| 1 | **VALUING XANTHUM CORP.** | | |
| 2 | 2003 FCF (base year) | 1,000,000 | |
| 3 | | | |
| 4 | High growth rate, $g_{high}$ | 35% | |
| 5 | Normal growth rate, $g_{normal}$ | 10% | |
| 6 | Number of high growth years | 5 | |
| 7 | Term 1 factor: $(1+g_{high})/(1+WACC)$ | 113% | <-- =(1+B4)/(1+B9) |
| 8 | | | |
| 9 | WACC | 20% | |
| 10 | End-2003 debt | 3,000,000 | |
| 11 | End-2003 cash | 500,000 | |
| 12 | | | |
| 13 | Term 1: PV of high-growth cash flows | 7,218,292 | <-- =B2*B7*(1-B7^B6)/(1-B7) |
| 14 | Term 2: PV of normal-growth cash flows | 19,822,357 | <-- =B2*B7^B6*(1+B5)/(B9-B5) |
| 15 | Enterprise value | 29,621,547 | <-- =SUM(B13:B14)*(1+B9)^0.5 |
| 16 | Add cash | 500,000 | <-- =B11 |
| 17 | Subtract debt | -3,000,000 | <-- =-B10 |
| 18 | Value of equity | 27,121,547 | <-- =SUM(B15:B17) |
| 19 | | | |
| 20 | Number of shares, end 2003 | 3,000,000 | |
| 21 | Share value | 9.04 | <-- =B18/B20 |

## Valuation Method 2: Example 3—Using the Terminal Value in a Real-Estate Project

In the previous two examples we discounted an infinitely lived stream of cash flows. Sometimes it makes more sense to discount a finite number of cash flows and then attribute a terminal value to the project.

Here's an example: Your Aunt Sarah has quite a bit of money. She's been offered a share in a partnership that is being set up by a local real estate agent. The partnership will buy an existing building, called the Station Building, for $20 million. The agent is selling 25 shares, for $800,000 each $\left( \$800,000 = \dfrac{\$20,000,000}{25} \right)$. Aunt Sarah has asked you to do some financial analysis to determine whether this is a fair price for a partnership share in the Station Building.

Here's what you discover:

- All income from the Station Building partnership will flow through to the shareholders, who will pay taxes on the income at their personal tax rates. Aunt Sarah's tax rate is 40%.

- Station Building will be depreciated over 40 years, giving an annual depreciation of $500,000 per year.

- The building is fully rented out and brings up annual rents of $7 million. You do not anticipate that these rents will increase over the next 10 years.

- Maintenance, property taxes, and other miscellaneous expenses for Station Building cost about $1 million per year.

- The agent who is putting together the partnership has proposed selling Station Building after 10 years. He estimates that the market price of the building will not change much over this period—meaning that the market price of Station Building in year 10 is anticipated to be $20 million, like its price today.

- A reliable financial consultant has told you that the appropriate discount rate for cash flows from buildings like Station Building is 18%. You decide to use this as your WACC for discounting the cash flows.

In your valuation of the Station Building shares, you see that the annual free cash flow (FCF) to Aunt Sarah is $152,000 (cell B16 in the spreadsheet below). This FCF will be available to her in years 1–10 and is based on the building's profit before taxes of $5,500,000, which will be spread equally among the partners.

The terminal value of the building is $20,000,000, which on a per-share basis is $800,000 (cell B19). At the time the building is sold in year 10, its accumulated depreciation is $5,000,000, so that its book value is $15,000,000. To compute Aunt Sarah's cash flow from this terminal value, we deduct the per-share book value of the building ($600,000, cell B20) from the sale price to arrive at taxes of $80,000 on the profit from the sale of the building (cell B22). The cash flow from the sale is the $800,000 sale price minus the taxes, or $720,000, as shown in cell B23.

| | A | B | C | D | E | F | G |
|---|---|---|---|---|---|---|---|
| 1 | | | STATION BUILDING PARTNERSHIP—SHARE VALUATION | | | | |
| 2 | Building cost | 20,000,000 | | | | | |
| 3 | Depreciable life (years) | 40 | | | | | |
| 4 | Annual rents | 7,000,000 | | | | | |
| 5 | Annual expenses | 1,000,000 | | | | | |
| 6 | Annual depreciation | 500,000 | <-- =B2/B3 | | Profit and loss, Station Building as a whole | | |
| 7 | Aunt Sarah's tax rate | 40% | | | Annual rent | 7,000,000 | |
| 8 | WACC | 18% | | | Minus annual expenses | -1,000,000 | |
| 9 | Shares issued | 25 | | | Minus annual depreciation | -500,000 | |
| 10 | Share price | 800,000 | | | Anticipated annual building profit before taxes | 5,500,000 | <-- =SUM(F7:F9) |
| 11 | | | | | | | |
| 12 | **Profit and loss, Aunt Sarah's share** | | | | | | |
| 13 | Anticipated annual building profit before taxes | 220,000 | <-- =F10/B9 | | Terminal value, year 10, Station Building as a whole | | |
| 14 | Profit after taxes | 132,000 | <-- =(1-B7)*B13 | | Anticipated building market price | 20,000,000 | <-- =B2 |
| 15 | Building depreciation, per share | 20,000 | <-- =B6/B9 | | Accumulated depreciation, year 10 | 5,000,000 | <-- =B6*10 |
| 16 | Free cash flow | 152,000 | <-- =B14+B15 | | Book value of building, year 10 | 15,000,000 | <-- =B2-F15 |
| 17 | | | | | | | |
| 18 | **Terminal value, year 10, Aunt Sarah's share** | | | | | | |
| 19 | Anticipated building market price | 800,000 | <-- =F14/B9 | | | | |
| 20 | Book value in year 10, per share | 600,000 | <-- =F16/B9 | | | | |
| 21 | Profit from sale of building | 200,000 | <-- =B19-B20 | | | | |
| 22 | Tax on profit | 80,000 | <-- =B7*B21 | | | | |
| 23 | Terminal value: cash flow from sale | 720,000 | <-- =B19-B22 | | | | |
| 24 | | | | | | | |
| 25 | Year | Aunt Sarah's anticipated FCF | | | | | |
| 26 | 1 | 152,000 | <-- =$B$16 | | | | |
| 27 | 2 | 152,000 | | | | | |
| 28 | 3 | 152,000 | | | | | |
| 29 | 4 | 152,000 | | | | | |
| 30 | 5 | 152,000 | | | | | |
| 31 | 6 | 152,000 | | | | | |
| 32 | 7 | 152,000 | | | | | |
| 33 | 8 | 152,000 | | | | | |
| 34 | 9 | 152,000 | | | | | |
| 35 | 10 | 872,000 | <-- =$B$16+B23 | | | | |
| 36 | | | | | | | |
| 37 | Share value: Present value of Aunt Sarah's free cash flows | $820,667.53 | <-- =NPV(B8,B26:B35) | | | | |

Cells B26:B35 show Aunt Sarah's anticipated FCFs from the building partnership, including the terminal value. Discounting these cash flows at the WACC of 18% values a partnership share at $820,667.53. Conclusion: Aunt Sarah should invest in the building!

## Valuation Method 2: Example 4—Using the Terminal Value to Get around Large FCF Growth Rates

Our second example of using the terminal value involves the Formanis Corp. Formanis is in a growth industry and has had formidable FCF growth rates for the past several years, and you anticipate that these rates will continue for years 1–5. However, after year 5 you anticipate a big slowdown in Formanis's FCF growth, as its industry matures.

Here are the relevant facts about Formanis:

- The company's FCF for the current year is $1,000,000.
- You anticipate that the FCF for years 1–5 will grow at a rate of 25% per year.
- You anticipate a growth rate of FCFs of 6% per year for years 6, 7,... (termed the "long-term growth rate" in the following spreadsheet).
- The company has 5 million shares outstanding.
- The appropriate WACC = 15%.

The valuation formula is

$$Formanis\ value = \frac{FCF_1}{(1+WACC)} + \frac{FCF_2}{(1+WACC)^2} + \frac{FCF_3}{(1+WACC)^3} + \frac{FCF_4}{(1+WACC)^4} + \frac{FCF_5}{(1+WACC)^5}$$
$$+ \frac{1}{(1+WACC)^5} * \underbrace{\frac{FCF_5 * (1+long\text{-}term\ growth\ rate)}{(WACC-long\text{-}term\ growth\ rate)}}$$

This is the terminal value: an explanation is given in Chapter 6

To value Formanis, we first predict the FCFs for years 1–5 (cells B9:B13 of the spreadsheet). The present value of these FCFs is $6,465,787 (cell B20). The terminal value represents the year-5 present value of the Formanis cash flows for years 6, 7,.... To compute the terminal value, we assume that Formanis's cash flows for these years grow at the long-term growth rate:

$$Terminal\ value = year\text{-}5\ PV\ of\ Formanis\ FCFs,\ years\ 6,7,...$$

$$= \frac{FCF_6}{(1+WACC)} + \frac{FCF_7}{(1+WACC)^2} + \frac{FCF_8}{(1+WACC)^3} + ...$$

$$= \frac{FCF_5*(1+long\text{-}term\ growth\ rate)}{(1+WACC)} + \frac{FCF_5*(1+long\text{-}term\ growth\ rate)^2}{(1+WACC)^2}$$

$$+ \frac{FCF_5*(1+long\text{-}term\ growth\ rate)^3}{(1+WACC)^3} + ...$$

$$= \frac{FCF_5*(1+long\text{-}term\ growth\ rate)}{(WACC - long\text{-}term\ growth\ rate)}$$

In cell B17 below the terminal value—assuming a long-term FCF growth rate of 6%—is $35,942,925.

|   | A | B | C |
|---|---|---|---|
| 1 | **FORMANIS CORPORATION** | | |
| 2 | Current FCF | 1,000,000 | |
| 3 | Anticipated growth rate, years 1-5 | 25% | |
| 4 | WACC | 15% | |
| 5 | Long-term growth rate, after year 5 | 6% | |
| 6 | Number of shares outstanding | 5,000,000 | |
| 7 | | | |
| 8 | **Year** | **Anticipated FCF** | |
| 9 | 1 | 1,250,000 | <-- =$B$2*(1+$B$3) |
| 10 | 2 | 1,562,500 | <-- =B9*(1+$B$3) |
| 11 | 3 | 1,953,125 | <-- =B10*(1+$B$3) |
| 12 | 4 | 2,441,406 | |
| 13 | 5 | 3,051,758 | |
| 14 | | | |
| 15 | **Terminal value calculation** | | |
| 16 | FCF in year 5 | 3,051,758 | <-- =B13 |
| 17 | Terminal value | 35,942,925 | <-- =B16*(1+B5)/(B4-B5) |
| 18 | | | |
| 19 | **Valuing Formanis Corporation** | | |
| 20 | Present value of FCFs, years 1-5 | 6,465,787 | <-- =NPV(B4,B9:B13) |
| 21 | Present value of terminal value | 17,869,986 | <-- =B17/(1+B4)^5 |
| 22 | Value of Formanis | 24,335,774 | <-- =B21+B20 |
| 23 | Per share value | $4.87 | <-- =B22/B6 |

The value of Formanis (cell B22) is $14,930,518. The per-share value of Formanis is $2.99 (cell B23).

The terminal value method illustrated for Formanis is often used:

- It allows the stock analyst to distinguish between short-term growth and long-term growth. Often short-term growth is a function of market performance, whereas long-term growth is determined by macroeconomic factors. For example, in a new and rapidly developing market, we might anticipate high short-term growth rates. But we would also anticipate that as the market matures and becomes more saturated, the long-term growth rates would approximate the growth of the economy as a whole.

- From an Excel point of view, the terminal value method allows us to do interesting sensitivity analysis. For example, here is the per-share value of Formanis for a variety of long-term growth rates and WACCs; we use the **Data Table** technique described in Chapter 27.

| | A | B | C | D | E | F |
|---|---|---|---|---|---|---|
| | **Sensitivity analysis: Per-share value of Formanis with different WACC and long-term growth.** | | | | | |
| 26 | **Year 1-5 growth rate = 25%.** | | | | | |
| 27 | =B23 | | Long-term growth rate ↓ | | | |
| 28 | | | $4.87 | 0% | 2% | 4% | 6% |
| 29 | WACC → | 15% | 3.32 | 3.67 | 4.16 | 4.87 |
| 30 | | 20% | 2.36 | 2.52 | 2.73 | 2.99 |
| 31 | | 25% | 1.80 | 1.89 | 1.99 | 2.12 |
| 32 | | 30% | 1.44 | 1.49 | 1.55 | 1.62 |

Varying the year 1–5 growth rate gives different values. In the table below, for example, we've assumed that year 1–5 growth is 20%.

| | A | B | C | D | E | F |
|---|---|---|---|---|---|---|
| | **Sensitivity analysis: Per-share value of Formanis with different WACC and long-term growth.** | | | | | |
| 26 | **Year 1-5 growth rate = 20%.** | | | | | |
| 27 | =B23 | | Long-term growth rate ↓ | | | |
| 28 | | | $4.05 | 0% | 2% | 4% | 6% |
| 29 | WACC → | 15% | 2.79 | 3.08 | 3.48 | 4.05 |
| 30 | | 20% | 2.00 | 2.13 | 2.30 | 2.51 |
| 31 | | 25% | 1.54 | 1.61 | 1.69 | 1.80 |
| 32 | | 30% | 1.24 | 1.28 | 1.33 | 1.38 |

# 16.3. Valuation Method 3: The Price of a Share Is the PV of Its Future Anticipated Equity Cash Flows Discounted at the Cost of Equity

In the previous section we "backed into" the equity valuation of the firm by first calculating the value of the firm's assets (the enterprise value plus initial cash balances) and then subtracting from this number the value of the firm's debts. In this section we present another method for calculating the value of the firm's equity—we directly discount the value of the firm's anticipated payouts to its shareholders.

As an example consider Haul-It Corp., which has a steady record of paying dividends and repurchasing shares. The company has 10 million shares outstanding. Here's a spreadsheet with the valuation model.

| | A | B | C | D | E | F | G |
|---|---|---|---|---|---|---|---|
| 1 | HAUL-IT CORPORATION—EQUITY PAYOUT HISTORY AND SHARE VALUATION | | | | | | |
| 2 | | 1998 | 1999 | 2000 | 2001 | 2002 | |
| 3 | Repurchases | $1,440,000 | $2,410,000 | $3,500,000 | $6,820,000 | $4,830,000 | |
| 4 | Dividends | $3,950,000 | $3,997,000 | $4,238,000 | $4,875,000 | $5,100,000 | |
| 5 | Total cash paid to equity holders | $5,390,000 | $6,407,000 | $7,738,000 | $11,695,000 | $9,930,000 | |
| 6 | | | | | | | |
| 7 | Compound annual growth, 1998-2002 | 16.50% | <-- =(F5/B5)^(1/4)-1 | | | | |
| 8 | | | | | | | |
| 9 | Haul-It's cost of equity, $r_E$ | 25.00% | | | | | |
| 10 | | | | | | | |
| 11 | Valuation | | | | | | |
| 12 | Current equity payout | $9,930,000 | <-- =F5 | | | | |
| 13 | Anticipated future growth | 16.50% | | | | | |
| 14 | | | | | | | |
| 15 | Value of total equity | 136,164,862 | <-- =B12*(1+B13)/(B9-B13) | | | | |
| 16 | Number of shares outstanding | 10,000,000 | | | | | |
| 17 | Value per share | 13.62 | <-- =B15/B16 | | | | |

Haul-It Corporation—Payouts to Equity Holders

Between 1998 and 2002, Haul-It's payouts to its equity holders have increased at an impressive rate of 16.50% per year (cell B7). The company's cost of equity $r_E$ is 25% (cell B9).[1] Assuming that future equity payout growth equals historical growth, Haul-It is valued at $136 million (cell B15), which gives a per-share value of $13.62.

The equity value of the company is the discounted value of the future anticipated equity payouts:

---

[1] At this point we do not discuss how we arrived at this cost of equity. For a recapitulation of cost of capital techniques, see Chapters 6 and 13.

$$Equity\ value = \frac{Equity\ payout_{2003}}{1+r_E} + \frac{Equity\ payout_{2004}}{\left(1+r_E\right)^2} + \frac{Equity\ payout_{2005}}{\left(1+r_E\right)^3} + ....$$

$$= \frac{Equity\ payout_{2002}\left(1+g\right)}{1+r_E} + \frac{Equity\ payout_{2002}\left(1+g\right)^2}{\left(1+r_E\right)^2} + \frac{Equity\ payout_{2002}\left(1+g\right)^3}{\left(1+r_E\right)^3} + ....$$

$$= \frac{Equity\ payout_{2002}\left(1+g\right)}{r_E - g} = \frac{9,930,000\left(1.165\right)}{25.00\% - 16.50\%} = 136,164,862$$

Dividing the equity value by the number of shares outstanding gives the estimated value per share:

$$Value\ per\ share = \frac{Equity\ value}{Shares\ outstanding} = \frac{136,164,862}{10,000,000} = 13.62$$

### Why Do Finance Professionals Shun Direct Equity Valuation?

Valuation method 3, the direct valuation of equity, is so simple that it may surprise you that it is rarely used. There are several reasons for this, none of which we can fully explain at this point in the book:

- The direct equity valuation method depends on projected equity payouts (that is, dividends plus share repurchases), whereas method 2 depends on projected FCFs. Whereas a firm's equity payouts are a function of management decisions about dividends and stock repurchases, FCFs are a function of the firm's operating environment—its sales, costs, capital expenditures, and so on. Because many components of the FCFs are determined by the firm's operating environment rather than management decisions about dividends, analysts are generally more comfortable predicting FCFs.

- The FCF method 2 discounts future FCFs at the firm's weighted average cost of capital (WACC). The equity payout method 3 discounts future equity payouts at the firm's cost of equity $r_E$. For reasons we will explain in Chapters 17 and 18, the cost of equity $r_E$ is very sensitive to the firm's debt-to-equity ratio, whereas the WACC is not as sensitive to the debt-to-equity ratio.[2]

## 16.4. Valuation Method 4, Comparative Valuation: Using Multiples to Value Shares

The last valuation technique we discuss is based on a comparison of financial ratios for different companies. This valuation technique is often referred to as using "multiples." The technique is based on the logic that financial assets that are similar in nature should be priced the same way.

### A Simple Example: Using the Price/Earnings (P/E) Ratio for Valuation

The *P/E ratio* is the ratio of a firm's stock price to its earnings per share:

$$P/E = \frac{stock\ price}{earnings\ per\ share}.$$

---

[2] For reasons explained in Chapters 17 and 18, the WACC may in fact be completely invariant to a firm's leverage. If this is so, we can value a firm based on method 2 without worrying about its leverage.

When we use the P/E for valuation, we assume that similar firms should have similar P/E ratios.

Here's an example: Shoes for Less (SFL) and Lesser Shoes (LS) are both shoe stores located in similar communities. Although SFL is bigger than LS, having double the sales and double the profits, the companies are in most relevant respects similar—management, financial structure, etc. However, the market valuation of the two companies does not reflect their similarity: The P/E ratio of SFL is significantly lower than that of LS, as can be seen in the spreadsheet below.

Based on the similarity between the two companies, SFL appears underpriced relative to LS—its P/E ratio is less. A market analyst might recommend that anyone interested in investing in the shoe store business should invest in SFL rather than LS.[3]

| | A | B | C | D |
|---|---|---|---|---|
| 1 | SHOES FOR LESS (SFL) AND LESSER SHOES (LS) comparing P/E ratios | | | |
| 2 | | SFL: Shoes for Less | LS: Lesser Shoes | |
| 3 | Sales | 30,000 | 15,000 | |
| 4 | Profits | 3,000 | 1,500 | |
| 5 | Number of shares | 1,000 | 1,000 | |
| 6 | Share price | 24 | 18 | |
| 7 | Equity value | 24,000 | 18,000 | <-- =C6*C5 |
| 8 | EPS: Earnings per share | 3 | 1.5 | <-- =C4/C5 |
| 9 | P/E: Price-earnings ratio | 8.00 | 12.00 | <-- =C6/C8 |

## Kroger (KR) and Safeway (SWY)

Both of these firms are in the supermarket business. Some of the data from these profiles are in the spreadsheet below, which shows five multiples for these two firms.

| | A | B | C | D | E | F |
|---|---|---|---|---|---|---|
| 1 | SAFEWAY (SWY) AND KROGER (KR)—COMPARISON BASED ON MULTIPLES Based on Yahoo! Profiles, 12 September 2002 | | | | | |
| 2 | | KR | SWY | | Who's more highly valued? | |
| 3 | Stock price | 18.09 | 26.91 | <-- Yahoo | | |
| 4 | Earnings per share (EPS) | 1.37 | 2.60 | <-- Yahoo | | |
| 5 | Price/Earnings (P/E) ratio | 13.20 | 10.35 | <-- =C3/C4 | | |
| 6 | | | | | Kroger | <-- =IF(B5>C5,"Kroger","Safeway") |
| 7 | Book value of equity per share | 4.79 | 11.41 | <-- Yahoo | | |
| 8 | Equity market to book ratio | 3.78 | 2.36 | <-- =C3/C7 | | |
| 9 | | | | | Kroger | <-- =IF(B8>C8,"Kroger","Safeway") |
| 10 | Number of shares outstanding (million) | 788.8 | 466.5 | <-- Yahoo | | |
| 11 | Market value of equity (billion) | 14.27 | 12.55 | <-- =C10*C3/1000 | | |
| 12 | | | | | | |
| 13 | Debt/Equity (based on book values) | 2.22 | 1.32 | <-- Yahoo | | |
| 14 | Debt (billion) this number is not in Yahoo | 8.39 | 7.03 | <-- =C10*C7*C13/1000 | | |
| 15 | Cash (billion) | 0.185 | 0.051 | <-- Yahoo | | |
| 16 | Net debt | 8.20 | 6.98 | <-- =C14-C15 | | |
| 17 | | | | | | |
| 18 | Book value of equity + debt (billion) - cash (book value of enterprise) | 11.98 | 12.30 | <-- =C10*C7/1000+C14-C15 | | |
| 19 | Market value of equity + debt (billion) - cash (market value of enterprise) | 22.47 | 19.53 | <-- =C11+C14-C15 | | |
| 20 | Enterprise value, market to book | 1.88 | 1.59 | <-- =C19/C18 | | |
| 21 | | | | | Kroger | <-- =IF(B20>C20,"Kroger","Safeway") |
| 22 | Earnings before interest, taxes, depreciation and amortization (EBITDA) in billion$ | 3.53 | 2.64 | <-- Yahoo | | |
| 23 | Market enterprise value to EBITDA | 6.37 | 7.40 | <-- =C19/C22 | | |
| 24 | | | | | Safeway | <-- =IF(B23>C23,"Kroger","Safeway") |
| 25 | Sales | 50.7 | 34.7 | <-- Yahoo | | |
| 26 | Market enterprise value to Sales | 0.44 | 0.56 | <-- Yahoo | Safeway | <-- =IF(B26>C26,"Kroger","Safeway") |

[3] A more radical strategy might be to *buy* shares of SFL and to *short* shares of LS. See Chapter 14 and its discussion of Palm and 3Com shares for a discussion of this strategy.

- **P/E ratio**: This is the most common multiple used. Based on this ratio of the stock price to the EPS, KR is more highly valued than SWY. The problem with using this multiple is that it is influenced by many factors, including the firm's leverage. We prefer *enterprise value* ratios such as the following.
- **Equity market-to-book ratio**: This is the ratio of the market value of the firm's equity to the book value (its accounting value). If the book value accurately measures the cost of the assets, then a higher equity market-to-book value reflects a greater valuation of the equity. However, the accounting numbers are heavily influenced by the age of the assets, the depreciation, and other accounting policies, so that this ratio is not so accurate.
- **Enterprise value-to-book ratio**: The *enterprise value* is the value of the firm's equity plus its net debt (defined as book value of debt minus cash). Row 18 above measures the firm's net debt by subtracting the cash balances from the book value of the debt. The enterprise market to book ratio shows that KR is valued more highly than SWY.
- **Enterprise value-to-EBITDA ratio**: Earnings before interest, taxes, depreciation, and amortization (EBITDA) is a popular Wall Street measure of the ability of a firm to produce cash. In spirit it is similar to the free cash flow (FCF) concept discussed in this chapter, although it ignores changes in net working capital and capital expenditures. The market enterprise value-to-EBITDA ratio shows that SWY is actually more highly valued than KR.
- **Market enterprise value-to-sales ratio**: This one of the many other ratios we could use to compare these two firms. As a percentage of its sales, SWY is more highly valued than KR; this perhaps reflects SWY's ability to extract more cash for its shareholders from each dollar of sales. Or perhaps it reflects greater shareholder optimism about the future sales growth rate.

### Using Multiples to Value Firms—Summary

The multiple method of valuation is a highly effective way of comparing the values of several companies, *as long as the companies being compared are truly comparable.* Comparability is complicated, however, and you should be careful: Truly comparable firms will have similar operational characteristics such as sales and costs, as well as similar financing.[4]

## 16.5. Intermediate Summary

In Sections 16.1–16.4 we've examined four stock valuation methods:

- Valuation method 1, the efficient markets approach, is based on the assumption that market prices are correct.

---

[4] We're getting ahead of ourselves, as we did in the previous footnote. The point is that it doesn't make sense to compare the stock price of two operationally similar firms if one firm is financed with a lot of debt and the other firm is financed primarily with equity. This point is a result of the discussion in Chapters 17 and 18. For more details see Chapter 10 of *Corporate Finance: A Valuation Approach* by Simon Benninga and Oded Sarig, McGraw–Hill, 1997.

- Valuation method 2, the free cash flow (FCF) approach, values the firm by discounting the future anticipated FCFs at the weighted average cost of capital (WACC). Sections 16.6 and 16.7 show several methods of determining the WACC.

- Valuation method 3, the equity payout approach, values all of the firm's shares by discounting the future anticipated payouts to equity. The discount rate is the firm's cost of equity $r$E.

- Valuation method 4, the multiples approach, gives a comparative valuation of firms based on ratios such as the price/earnings (P/E) ratio.

In the next sections we discuss some issues related to valuation methods 2 and 3: We discuss the computation of the WACC) and the cost of equity $r$E (Sections 16.6 and 16.7).

## 16.6. Computing Target's WACC, the SML Approach

Valuation method 2 depends on the WACC, which was previously discussed in Chapters 6 and 13. In this section we briefly repeat some of the things said in Chapter 13 and show how to compute the firm's WACC using the SML.

The basic WACC formula is

$$WACC = \frac{E}{E+D}r_E + \frac{D}{D+E}r_D\left(1-T_C\right)$$

To estimate the WACC we need to estimate the following parameters:

$r_E$ = the cost of equity
$r_D$ = the cost of the firm's debt
$E$ = market value of the firm's equity
   = *number of shares * current market value per share*
$D$ = market value of the firm's debt
   this is usually approximated by the *book value* of the firm's debt
$T_C$ = the firm's marginal tax rate

To illustrate the computation of the WACC, we use data for Target Corp., a large discount retailer. Figure 16.4 gives the relevant financial information for Target. Using the Target data, we devote a short subsection to each of the WACC parameters, leaving the cost of equity $r_E$ until last because it is the most complicated.

| | A | B | C |
|---|---|---|---|
| 1 | **TARGET CORPORATION** | | |
| 2 | **Income statement** | **2001** | **2002** |
| 3 | Revenues | 39,826 | 43,917 |
| 4 | Cost of sales | 27,143 | 29,260 |
| 5 | Selling, general and administrative expenses | 8,461 | 9,416 |
| 6 | Credit card expense | 463 | 765 |
| 7 | Depreciation | 1,079 | 1,212 |
| 8 | Interest expense | 473 | 588 |
| 9 | Earnings before taxes | 2,207 | 2,676 |
| 10 | Income taxes | 839 | 1,022 |
| 11 | Net earnings | 1,368 | 1,654 |
| 12 | | | |
| 13 | **Balance sheet** | | |
| 14 | **Assets** | **2001** | **2002** |
| 15 | Cash and cash equivalents | 499 | 758 |
| 16 | Accounts receivable | 3,831 | 5,565 |
| 17 | Inventory | 4,449 | 4,760 |
| 18 | Other current assets | 869 | 852 |
| 19 | Total current assets | 9,648 | 11,935 |
| 20 | | | |
| 21 | Land, plant, property, and equipment | | |
| 22 | At cost | 18,442 | 20,936 |
| 23 | Accumulated depreciation | 4,909 | 5,629 |
| 24 | Net land, plant, property and equipment | 13,533 | 15,307 |
| 25 | | | |
| 26 | Other assets | 973 | 1,361 |
| 27 | Total assets | 24,154 | 28,603 |
| 28 | | | |
| 29 | **Liabilities and shareholder equity** | | |
| 30 | Accounts payable | 4,160 | 4,684 |
| 31 | Accrued liabilities | 1,566 | 1,545 |
| 32 | Income taxes payable | 423 | 319 |
| 33 | Current portion of long-term debt and notes payable | 905 | 975 |
| 34 | Total current liabilities | 7,054 | 7,523 |
| 35 | | | |
| 36 | Long-term debt | 8,088 | 10,186 |
| 37 | Deferred income taxes | 1,152 | 1,451 |
| 38 | Shareholders equity | | |
| 39 | Common stock | 1,173 | 1,332 |
| 40 | Accumulated retained earnings | 6,687 | 8,111 |
| 41 | Total equity | 7,860 | 9,443 |
| 42 | Total liabilities and shareholder equity | 24,154 | 28,603 |
| 43 | | | |
| 44 | **Other relevant information** | | |
| 45 | Shares outstanding | | 908,164,702 |
| 46 | Stock beta | | 1.16 |
| 47 | Stock price, 1 February 2003 | | 28.21 |

FIGURE 16.4 Financial information for Target Corp. We use this information to determine Target's cost of equity $r_E$ and its weighted average cost of capital (WACC).

## Computing the Market Value of Target's Equity, E

Target has 908,164,702 shares outstanding (cell C45, Figure 16.4). On 1 February 2003, the day of the company's annual report for its 2002 financial year, the stock price of Target was $28.21 per share. Thus the market value of the company's equity is 908,164,702 * $28.21 = $25,619,326,243. We will use this market value of equity in our computation of Target's WACC (see next spreadsheet).

## Computing the Market Value of Target's Debt, D

The Target balance sheets differentiate between short-term debt ("current portion of long-term debt and notes payable"—row 33 of Figure 16.4) and long-term debt (row 36). For purposes of computing the debt for a WACC computation, both of these numbers should be added together. This gives debt for Target as follows.

| | A | B | C | D |
|---|---|---|---|---|
| 6 | | **2002** | **2001** | |
| 7 | Current portion of long-term debt and notes payable | 975 | 905 | |
| 8 | Long-term debt in 2002 and 2001 (columns B and C) | 10,186 | 8,088 | |
| 9 | Total debt, D | 11,161 | 8,993 | <-- =C8+C7 |

## Estimating the Cost of Debt, $r_D$

A simple method to compute the cost of debt $r_D$ is to calculate the *average interest cost* over the year. In 2002 Target paid $588 interest (cell B8, Figure 16.4) on average debt of $10,077. This gives $r_D = 5.84\%$.

| | A | B | C | D |
|---|---|---|---|---|
| 13 | Interest paid, 2002 | 588 | | |
| 14 | Average debt over 2002 | 10,077 | <-- =AVERAGE(B9:C9) | |
| 15 | Interest cost, $r_D$ | 5.84% | <-- =C13/C14 | |

## Target's Income Tax Rate, $T_C$

In 2002 Target paid taxes of $1,022 on earnings of $2,676 (cells B10 and B9, respectively, of Figure 16.4). Its income tax rate was therefore 38.19%.

| | A | B | C |
|---|---|---|---|
| 17 | Earnings before taxes, 2002 | 2,676 | |
| 18 | Income taxes | 1,022 | |
| 19 | Corporate tax rate, $T_C$ | 38.19% | <-- =C18/C17 |

## Computing Target's Cost of Equity, $r_E$, Using the SML

The SML equation for computing Target's cost of equity $rE$ is given by

$$r_E = r_f + \beta_E * \left[ E(r_M) - r_f \right],$$

Yahoo! gives Target's β as 1.16. In February 2003, the risk-free rate $r_f$ was 2% and the expected return on the market $E(r_M)$ was 9.68%.[5] This gives Target's cost of equity as $r_E = 10.91\%$.

| | A | B | C | D |
|---|---|---|---|---|
| 21 | Equity beta, $\beta_E$ | 1.16 | | |
| 22 | Risk-free rate, $r_f$ | 2% | | |
| 23 | Expected market return, $E(r_M)$ | 9.68% | | |
| 24 | Cost of equity, $r_E$ | 10.91% | <-- =B22+B21*(B23-B22) | |

## Putting It All Together

Now that we've done all the calculations, we can compute Target's WACC:

$$WACC = \frac{E}{E+D}r_E + \frac{D}{D+E}r_D(1-T_C)$$
$$= \frac{25,619}{25,619+11,161}10.91\% + \frac{11,161}{25,619+11,161}5.84\%(1-38.19\%)$$
$$= 8.69\%$$

[5] To see how $E(r_M)$ was derived, see the boxed discussion on page 502.

Here it is in a spreadsheet.

| | A | B | C | D |
|---|---|---|---|---|
| 1 | TARGET CORP.'S WACC USING SML FOR COST OF EQUITY | | | |
| 2 | Number of shares (million) | 908 | | |
| 3 | Market value per share, 1 February 2002 | 28.21 | | |
| 4 | Market value of equity 1 February 2002, E | 25,619 | <-- =B3*B2 | |
| 5 | | | | |
| 6 | | 2001 | 2002 | |
| 7 | Current portion of long-term debt and notes payable | 905 | 975 | |
| 8 | Long-term debt in 2002 and 2001 (columns B and C) | 8,088 | 10,186 | |
| 9 | Total debt, D | 8,993 | 11,161 | <-- =C8+C7 |
| 10 | | | | |
| 11 | Market value of Target, E+D | | 36,780 | <-- =C9+B4 |
| 12 | | | | |
| 13 | Interest paid, 2002 | | 588 | |
| 14 | Average debt over 2002 | | 10,077 | <-- =AVERAGE(B9:C9) |
| 15 | Interest cost, $r_D$ | | 5.84% | <-- =C13/C14 |
| 16 | | | | |
| 17 | Earnings before taxes, 2002 | | 2,676 | |
| 18 | Income taxes | | 1,022 | |
| 19 | Corporate tax rate, $T_C$ | | 38.19% | <-- =C18/C17 |
| 20 | | | | |
| 21 | Equity beta, $\beta_E$ | | 1.16 | |
| 22 | Risk-free rate, $r_f$ | | 2% | |
| 23 | Expected market return, $E(r_M)$ | | 9.68% | |
| 24 | Cost of equity, $r_E$ | | 10.91% | <-- =C22+C21*(C23-C22) |
| 25 | | | | |
| 26 | WACC | | 8.69% | <-- =B4/C11*C24+(1-C19)*C9/C11*C15 |

## Computing the Expected Return on the Market, $E(r_M)$

The most controversial part of estimating the cost of capital using the CAPM is the estimation of the expected return on the market $E(r_M)$. We discussed this issue and some methods of estimation in Chapter 13. To recapitulate, we advocate using a P/E multiple model for estimating the equity premium. This model, presented in Chapter 13 and briefly reviewed in the box below, gives us $E(r_M) = 9.68\%$.

## P/E MULTIPLE MODEL FOR ESTIMATING $E(r_M)$

We start with the payout form of the Gordon dividend model:

$$r_E = \underbrace{\frac{D_0(1+g)}{P_0} + g}_{\text{Gordon dividend model}} = \underbrace{\frac{b*EPS_0(1+g)}{P_0} + g}_{\substack{b \text{ is the dividend payout} \\ \text{ratio, } EPS_0 \text{ is the current} \\ \text{firm earnings per share}}}$$

$$= \frac{b*(1+g)}{P_0/EPS_0} + g$$

This model is now used to measure the $E(r_M)$ using current market data:

$$E(r_M) = \frac{b*(1+g)}{P_0/EPS_0} + g$$

where

b = *market payout ratio* (in U.S. around 50%)

g = *growth rate of market earnings* (educated guess)

$P_0/EPS_0 = $ *market price/earnings ratio*

Here's an Excel example.

|   | A | B | C |
|---|---|---|---|
| 1 | **ESTIMATING $E(r_M)$ USING THE P/E RATIO** | | |
| 2 | Market P/E ratio | 20.00 | |
| 3 | Market dividend payout ratio, *b* | 50% | |
| 4 | Estimated growth of market earnings, *g* | 7% | |
| 5 | | | |
| 6 | $E(r_M)$ | 9.68% | <-- =B3*(1+B4)/B2+B4 |
| 7 | Risk-free rate, $r_f$ | 2.00% | |
| 8 | Market risk premium, $E(r_M) - r_f$ | 7.68% | <-- =B6-B7 |

We use these values—representative of market parameters in the United States in early 2003—in our determination of the Target Corp. cost of equity $r_E$.

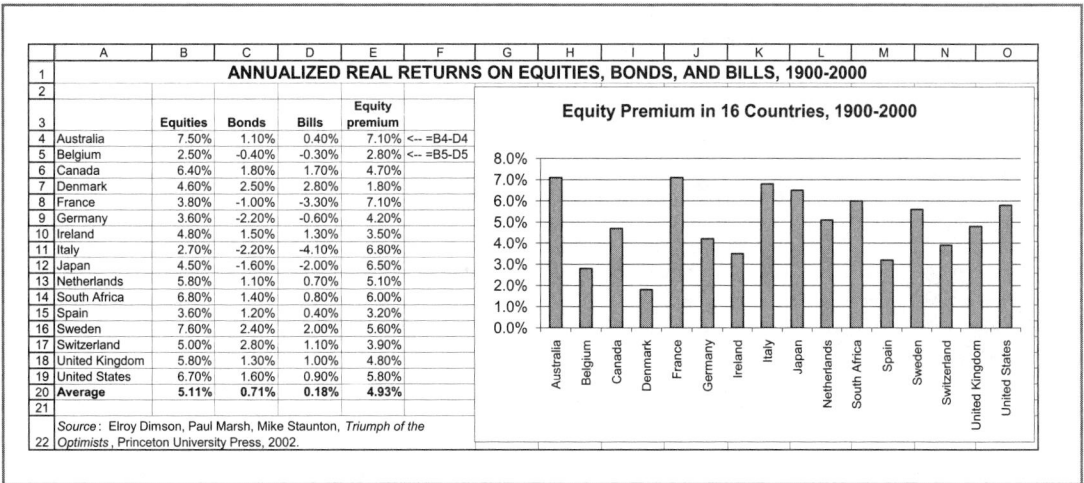

FIGURE 16.5  The equity premium is defined as the difference between the stock market rate of return and the return on risk-free bonds. In our SML-based computation of Target's weighted average cost of capital (WACC), we used the market price/earnings (P/E) as the basis for the equity risk premium $E(r_M)-r_f$. The historic equity premium is often used instead of this market-based equity premium.

# 16.7. Computing Target's Cost of Equity, $r_E$, with the Gordon Model

An alternative to the CAPM for computing the cost of equity $r_E$ is the Gordon model, which we've previously discussed in Chapter 6. The Gordon model says that the equity value is the discounted value of future anticipated dividends. The standard version of the Gordon model is

$$r_E = \frac{Div_0\left(1+g\right)}{P_0} + g$$

where
$Div_0$ = current equity payout of firm (total dividends + stock repurchases)
$P_0$ = current market value of equity
$g$ = anticipated equity payout growth rate

For reasons explained in Chapter 6, we think the Gordon model should be used with the *total equity payout*, defined as total dividends plus stock repurchases. Below is the calculation for Target Corp.'s WACC using the Gordon model. The spreadsheet is the same as that of the previous section, except for the following:

- Rows 32–36 show Target's equity payouts—the sum of its dividends and share repurchases—in each of the past 5 years. The compound annual growth rate of the equity payouts is 8.89% per year (cell D38).

- Rows 22–25 show the Gordon model calculation of the cost of equity $r_E$. This is computed as

$$r_E = \frac{Div_0\left(1+g\right)}{P_0} + g = \frac{232*\left(1+8.89\%\right)}{25,619} + 8.89\% = 9.88\%$$

where
$Div_0$ = current equity payout
$P_0$ = current market value of equity
$g$ = anticipated equity payout growth rate

| | A | B | C | D | E |
|---|---|---|---|---|---|
| 1 | TARGET CORP.'S WACC USING GORDON MODEL FOR COST OF EQUITY | | | | |
| 2 | Number of shares (million) | 908 | | | |
| 3 | Market value per share, 1 February 2002 | 28.21 | | | |
| 4 | Market value of equity 1 February 2002, E | 25,619 | <-- =B3*B2 | | |
| 5 | | | | | |
| 6 | | 2002 | 2001 | | |
| 7 | Current portion of long-term debt and notes payable | 975 | 905 | | |
| 8 | Long-term debt | 7,523 | 7,054 | | |
| 9 | Total debt, D | 8,498 | 7,959 | <-- =C8+C7 | |
| 10 | | | | | |
| 11 | Market value of Target, E+D | 34,117 | <-- =B9+B4 | | |
| 12 | | | | | |
| 13 | Interest paid, 2002 | 588 | | | |
| 14 | Average debt over 2002 | 8,229 | <-- =AVERAGE(B9:C9) | | |
| 15 | Interest cost, $r_D$ | 7.15% | <-- =B13/B14 | | |
| 16 | | | | | |
| 17 | | 2002 | | | |
| 18 | Earnings before taxes | 2,676 | | | |
| 19 | Income taxes | 1,022 | | | |
| 20 | Corporate tax rate, $T_C$ | 38.19% | <-- =B19/B18 | | |
| 21 | | | | | |
| 22 | Current equity value | 25,619 | | | |
| 23 | Current equity payout, $Div_0$ | 232 | <-- =D36 | | |
| 24 | Growth rate of equity payout | 8.89% | <-- =D38 | | |
| 25 | Cost of equity, $r_E$, using Gordon model | 9.88% | <-- =B23*(1+B24)/B22+B24 | | |
| 26 | | | | | |
| 27 | WACC | 8.52% | <-- =B4/B11*B25+(1-B20)*B9/B11*B15 | | |
| 28 | | | | | |
| 29 | | | | | |
| 30 | Dividends and stock repurchases | | | | |
| 31 | Year | Dividends | Repurchases | Total equity payout | |
| 32 | 1998 | 165 | 0 | 165 | |
| 33 | 1999 | 178 | 0 | 178 | |
| 34 | 2000 | 190 | 585 | 775 | |
| 35 | 2001 | 203 | 20 | 223 | |
| 36 | 2002 | 218 | 14 | 232 | |
| 37 | | | | | |
| 38 | | | Growth rate | 8.89% | <-- =(D36/D32)^(1/4)-1 |

Using the Gordon model estimate of the cost of equity, Target's WACC is 8.52% (cell B27).

# Summing Up

This chapter has discussed a grab-bag of share valuation methods. Three of these methods could be termed "fundamental valuations." Valuation method 1, the simplest of the fundamental valuation methods, is based on the assumption of market efficiency and says that a firm's stock is worth its current market price. Simple as it is, this approach has a lot of power and support in the academic community: If market participants have done their work, then the current price of a share reflects all publicly available information, and there's nothing else to do.

Valuation method 2, discounted cash flow (DCF) valuation, is the method preferred by most finance academics and many finance practitioners. This method is based on discounting the firm's projected future free cash flows (FCFs) at an appropriate weighted average cost of capital (WACC). The discounted value arrived at in this way is called the firm's *enterprise value*. To arrive at the valuation of the firm's equity, we add cash and marketable securities to the enterprise value and subtract the value of the firm's debt. Dividing by the number of shares gives the per-share valuation.

Valuation method 3, the *direct equity valuation*, discounts the projected payouts to equity holders (defined as the sum of dividends plus share repurchases) by the firm's cost of equity $r_E$. The resulting present value is the value of the firm's equity. Although it appears simpler and more direct than the FCF valuation, direct equity valuation is usually shunned by finance professionals. This is primarily because the cost of equity is heavily dependent on a firm's debt-to-equity financing mix, whereas the WACC is not nearly as dependent (and perhaps independent) on the debt-to-equity mix.

Valuation method 4, *multiple valuation*, is widely used. This method of valuation arrives at a relative valuation of the firm by comparing a set of relevant multiples for comparable firms. When used correctly, multiple valuations can be a powerful tool, but it is often difficult to arrive at a correct "peer group" for a particular firm.

## EXERCISES

1. OwnItAll (OIA) is a holding company whose sole business is to own a portfolio of shares. The company has 200 million shares outstanding, listed on the PSE.
   a. Given the current portfolio of OIA, what should be its share price? (There's a template on the disk that comes with the book.)

|  | A | B | C |
|---|---|---|---|
| 1 | **OIA PORTFOLIO** | | |
| 2 | **Stock** | **Number of shares** | **Share price** |
| 3 | IBM | 1,500,000 | 92.89 |
| 4 | Ahold | 5,250,000 | 8.23 |
| 5 | Kellogg | 385,259 | 45.29 |
| 6 | General Motors | 12,000,000 | 36.64 |
| 7 | Microsoft | 1,000,000 | 26.18 |
| 8 | AT&T | 98,000,000 | 19.89 |
| 9 | SBC | 12,000,000 | 23.42 |
| 10 | Merck | 15,000,000 | 28.02 |
| 11 | Nicor | 2,000,000 | 36.42 |
| 12 | Duke Power | 25,000,000 | 26.14 |

   b. The actual market price of OIA's shares is $25 per share. What can you conclude from this fact?

2.
   a. Walters, Inc. has an anticipated next-year FCF of $10 million. This cash flow is anticipated to grow at an annual rate of 5%. If the FCFs occur at year end and if the WACC of Walters is 15%, what is the enterprise value of the company?
   b. How would your answer change if the cash flows occur mid-year?

3.
   a. Houda Motors has just announced results that show that the FCF for the past year is $23 million. An experienced analyst believes that the growth rate of the FCF for the next 10 years will be 25% per year and that after 10 years the growth rate will be 7% annually. Houda's WACC is 18%, and the company has 100 million shares outstanding. Value the shares assuming that the FCFs occur at year end. Houda has no debt and no excess cash reserves.
   b. Suppose that the FCFs occur mid-year. What would your answer be now?

4. You are considering buying a building in downtown Asheville. The building is selling for $10 million, and you anticipate an annual FCF of $1 million. At the end of 10 years, the building will be half depreciated, and at this point you think you can sell the building for $15 million. If your cost of capital is 17%, does the building have positive NPV? Assume a 20% capital gains tax on the

sale of the building in 10 years; income taxes and depreciation tax shields have been included in the annual FCF of $1 million.

5. You are considering buying a 500-unit apartment complex in suburban Springfield. The current owner of the apartment complex is asking $25 million. Use the facts below to value the apartment complex:

   • On average, each unit produces $15,000 of pretax income per year.

   • The vacancy rate in Springfield averages 8%.

   • Operating expenses per unit are $2,000 annually. These expenses are incurred regardless of whether the units are occupied.

   • Income and expenses occur at year end.

   • Your tax rate is 40% on pretax income and 20% on capital gains.

   • Your discount rate is 18%.

   • Real-estate prices in the Springfield area have been increasing at 6% per year, and you antici-pate that this rate will continue for the foreseeable future. You anticipate selling the apartment complex at the end of 10 years.

6. In the previous problem, suppose that the cash flows from rentals (including expenses and depre-ciation) occur mid-year. Suppose that the resale cash flow of the complex occurs at the end of 10 years. Recalculate the NPV.

7. Consider the Springfield apartment complex once more (Exercises 5 and 6). Suppose that:

   • Cash flows from rentals (including expenses and depreciation) occur mid-year.

   • Next year's anticipated rental per unit is $15,000 and expenses are $2,000. In years 2–9 these numbers are expected to increase by 2% annually.

   • Other facts about the complex are unchanged.

   a. What is the NPV of the purchase?

   b. Create a **Data Table** for the NPV as a function of the annual rent/expense increase (0, 1, 2,..., 5%) and the discount rate (8, 10, 12,..., 24%).

8. Hectoritis Corp. currently has an FCF of $13 million. A reputable analyst estimates that this FCF is anticipated to increase by 12% per year for the next 5 years. The analyst esti-mates that at the end of 5 years the company's terminal value will be based on the year-5 FCF and a long-term FCF growth rate of 4%. Suppose the Hectoritis $\beta= 1.5$, the $r_f = 3\%$, the market risk premium $E(r_M) - r_f = 14\%$, and Hectoritis has 8 million shares outstanding. How should the analyst value the shares of the company? Assume all cash flows occur at year end.

9. Challenge problem: The past 5 years' results for Niccair Corp. are given below. Value the compa-ny's stock based on a model of FCF growth of your own design and the following additional facts. (This is not an easy problem and it has no explicit answer—valuation is often like that!)

   • Niccair's 2003 year-end debt is $750 million.

   • Niccair's 2003 year-end cash is $50 million.

   • The company has a cost of debt of $r_D = 5\%$.

   • The company has 44,080,000 shares outstanding; the end-2003 share price is $37.

   • Niccair's share $\beta = 0.437$, $r_f = 3\%$, and $E(r_M) = 12\%$.

| | A | B | C | D | E | F |
|---|---|---|---|---|---|---|
| 1 | | NICCAIR CORPORATION, 1999 – 2003 | | | | |
| 2 | | 31-Dec-03 | 31-Dec-02 | 31-Dec-01 | 31-Dec-00 | 31-Dec-99 |
| 3 | Net income | $105,300,000 | $128,000,000 | $122,100,000 | $35,800,000 | $116,300,000 |
| 4 | Depreciation | $161,700,000 | $155,000,000 | $148,800,000 | $145,100,000 | $141,600,000 |
| 5 | Changes in net working capital | (12,600,000) | 268,300,000 | 491,300,000 | 233,000,000 | 213,400,000 |
| 6 | Capital expenditures | (181,300,000) | (192,500,000) | (185,700,000) | (158,400,000) | (154,000,000) |
| 7 | Net interest paid before taxes | (41,100,000) | (34,600,000) | (46,900,000) | (50,600,000) | (45,500,000) |
| 8 | Tax rate | 37.84% | 31.03% | 32.62% | 16.94% | 34.56% |

10. Go to Yahoo! and look up your two favorite drug store chains. Compare the following multiples for the two companies: P/E and Sales/Market Cap. Is one of the chains underpriced vis-à-vis the other?

11. (Challenge). The table below (which appears on the disk that accompanies *Principles of Finance with Excel*) shows P/E ratios and other information for the retail industry.

a. In rows 25–27 use Excel to run a regression of the P/E ratio as the *y*-variable versus each of the columns as the *x*-variable. One of the regressions is shown:

$$P/E = a + b * Market\ cap$$
$$= 21.390 + 0.009 * Market\ cap, R^2 = 0.003$$

Now run regressions of P/E on ROE, long-term debt to equity,....

b. Which regression has the most explanatory power? Do you have an explanation?

| | A | B | C | D | E | F | G |
|---|---|---|---|---|---|---|---|
| 1 | | P/E | Market cap (billion $) | ROE % | Long-Term Debt to Equity | Price to Equity Book Value | Year-on-year revenue growth (%) |
| 2 | Wal-Mart Stores, Inc. (WMT) | 22.89 | 222 | 22.72 | 0.75 | 4.95 | 9.88 |
| 3 | Target Corporation (TGT) | 23.52 | 44.3 | 16.73 | 0.77 | 3.57 | 11.01 |
| 4 | Kohl's Corporation (KSS) | 23.75 | 15.7 | 15.26 | 0.31 | 3.34 | 14.62 |
| 5 | (WMMVY.PK) | 30.56 | 15 | 13.02 | 0 | 3.85 | 12.69 |
| 6 | J.C. Penney Company, Inc. (JCP) | 21.46 | 11.9 | 10.76 | 0.97 | 2.35 | 2.98 |
| 7 | Sears, Roebuck & Co. (S) | 30.74 | 10.8 | 5.97 | 0.73 | 1.77 | -8.37 |
| 8 | May Department Stores (MAY) | 17 | 9.8 | 14.4 | 1.64 | 2.33 | 17.04 |
| 9 | Federated Department Str. (FD) | 14.25 | 9.3 | 12.24 | 0.7 | 1.68 | 0.14 |
| 10 | Coles Myer Ltd. (ADR) (CM) | 20.47 | 8.9 | 14.24 | 0.24 | 2.81 | 25.9 |
| 11 | Kmart Holding Corporation (KMRT) | 8.75 | 8.4 | 45.84 | 0.13 | 2.74 | -13.75 |
| 12 | Neiman-Marcus Group, (NMGA) | 15.08 | 3.2 | 16.11 | 0.33 | 2.21 | 10.89 |
| 13 | Dollar Tree Stores, Inc. (DLTR) | 17.4 | 3 | 17.12 | 0.25 | 2.8 | 8.83 |
| 14 | Dillard's, Inc. (DDS) | 36.34 | 2.1 | 2.69 | 0.81 | 0.96 | -3.59 |
| 15 | Grupo Elektra S.A. de C.V (EKT) | 11.12 | 2 | 30.85 | 2.78 | 3.09 | 22.21 |
| 16 | Saks Incorporated (SKS) | 41.19 | 1.9 | 2.37 | 0.77 | 0.99 | 0.99 |
| 17 | Tuesday Morning Corporati (TUES) | 19.68 | 1.2 | 45.22 | 0.51 | 7.39 | 7.04 |
| 18 | ShopKo Stores, Inc. (SKO) | 13.37 | 0.5282 | 6.72 | 0.76 | 0.88 | -1.59 |
| 19 | Bon-Ton Stores, Inc. (BONT) | 14.15 | 0.2487 | 7.62 | 1.12 | 1.06 | 65 |
| 20 | Retail Ventures, Inc. (RVI) | 22.26 | 0.2252 | 4.74 | 1.8 | 1.04 | 2.81 |
| 21 | Gottschalks Inc. (GOT) | 19.73 | 0.1047 | 5.17 | 1.34 | 0.99 | 1.76 |
| 22 | Duckwall-ALCO Stores, Inc (DUCK) | 28.95 | 0.0832 | 2.61 | 0.2 | 0.74 | 1.32 |
| 23 | | | | | | | |
| 24 | Regression: P/E = a + b*other | | | | | | |
| 25 | a, intercept | | 21.390 | | | | |
| 26 | b, slope | | 0.009 | | | | |
| 27 | R² | | 0.003 | | | | |
| 28 | | | | | | | |
| 29 | Key | | | | | | |
| 30 | Market cap = (number of shares)*(price per share) | | | | | | |
| 31 | ROE = Return on Equity = (Net income)/(Book value of Equity) | | | | | | |
| 32 | Long-term debt to equity = (Book value of debt)/(Book value of equity) | | | | | | |
| 33 | Price to equity book value = (Market cap)/(Book value of equity) | | | | | | |
| 34 | Year-on-year revenue growth = growth rate of sales, most recent quarter versus same quarter one year ago | | | | | | |

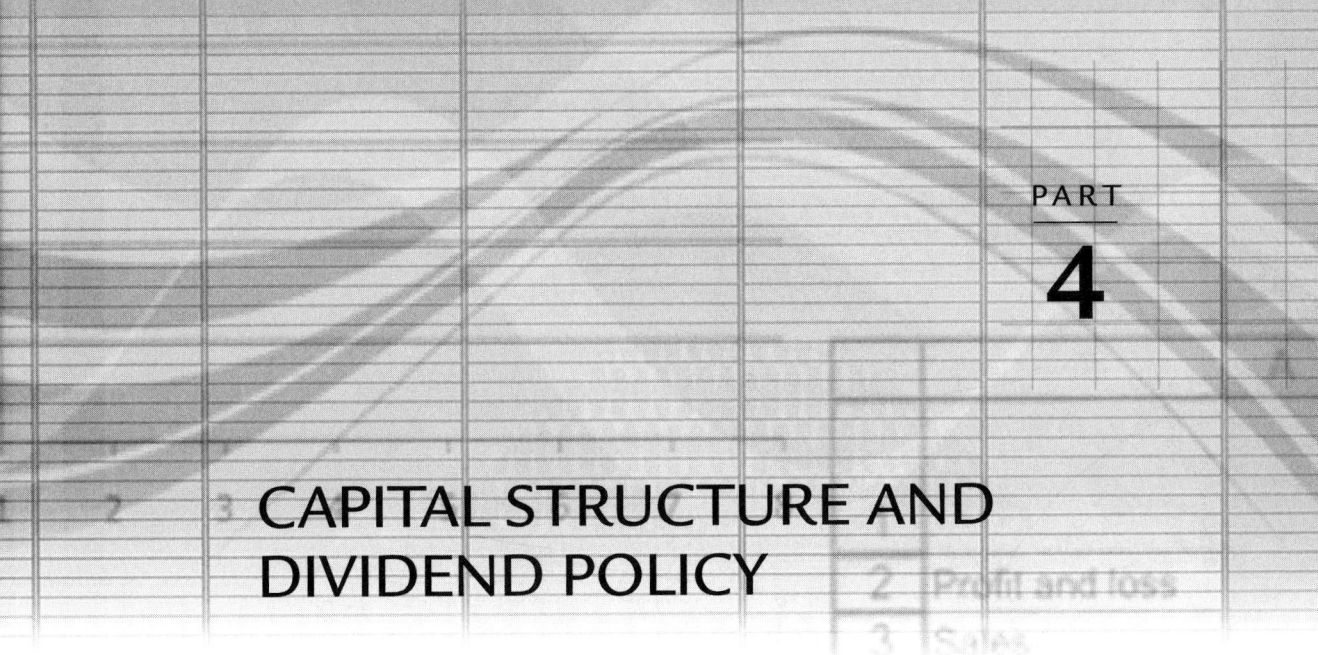

PART

4

# CAPITAL STRUCTURE AND DIVIDEND POLICY

A COMPANY CAN FINANCE ITSELF WITH EITHER MONEY RAISED from its shareholders (equity) or with money borrowed from banks or financial markets (debt). Does the mix of financing affect the value of the company? Chapters 17 and 18 examine this thorny question, which has been the subject of much debate in the finance profession. As these chapters show, the valuation effects of capital structure depend primarily on the taxes that the company and its shareholders pay. Chapter 17 explores this question in detail, using a series of simple examples. Chapter 18 summarizes the results and tells you what to think.

Capital structure is closely related to a firm's dividend policies. When a firm pays more dividends, it uses shareholder cash and implicitly increases the debt to equity ratio of the firm. But there's more to dividends than just debt/equity. Many corporate managers believe that their dividends impart important information to shareholders and the market about the health and the prospects of the company. Chapter 19 examines these questions to come up with an answer to the question: Does dividend policy matter?

# 17 Capital Structure and the Value of the Firm

## CHAPTER CONTENTS

# Overview

"Capital structure" is finance jargon for how a firm should be financed—what mixture of debt and equity should be used by the shareholders of a firm to finance the firm's activities. To start you off thinking about this tricky question, we offer the example of Mortimer and Joanna, who are competing to buy the same supermarket.

## The Fair City Supermarket—Does Financing Affect the Price?

Mortimer and Joanna live in Fair City. Each heads a group of investors that wants to buy a supermarket located in the center of town. Both Mortimer and Joanna have superb records as supermarket managers. As manager of a supermarket, they're pretty much the same—meaning that the supermarket they manage will have the same sales, cost of goods sold, etc. However, although the management aspect of Mortimer's group and Joanna's group is pretty much the same, there's a big financial difference between the two competing groups: Mortimer's investors want to borrow 50% of the money needed to purchase the supermarket, whereas Joanna's investors hate debt and have decided to put up the whole cost of purchasing the supermarket without borrowing a penny.

The question: Which group of investors—Mortimer's or Joanna's—can afford to make the higher bid for the supermarket? This is the question examined in this chapter. At this point in the chapter we offer no answers to this question, but merely want to give you insight into how possible answers might look.

## Example 1: Both Groups Make the Same Bid

Suppose that both Mortimer and Joanna's groups bid $1 million for the supermarket. In this case the balance sheets would look like this.

| Mortimer's Supermarket Group Half equity (50%) and half debt (50%) | | | |
|---|---|---|---|
| Supermarket | $1,000,000 | Debt | $500,000 |
| | | Equity | $500,000 |
| **Total assets** | **$1,000,000** | **Total debt and equity** | **$1,000,000** |

| Joanna's Supermarket Group Only equity (100%) | | | |
|---|---|---|---|
| Supermarket | $1,000,000 | Debt | $0 |
| | | Equity | $1,000,000 |
| **Total assets** | **$1,000,000** | **Total debt and equity** | **$1,000,000** |

Why would both groups make a similar bid for the supermarket? The line of reasoning that might lead to this conclusion is the following:

A supermarket is a supermarket is a supermarket, no matter how it's financed. If Mortimer's group think the supermarket is worth $1 million, then so will Joanna's group (and vice versa). The fact that one group finances with debt and equity whereas the other group finances only with equity is irrelevant to their valuation of the supermarket.

## Example 2: Mortimer's Group Bids More

Is it possible that Mortimer's group should rationally decide that—because of the group's greater proportion of debt financing—the supermarket is worth more than what Joanna's group is willing to pay? One of Mortimer's investors thinks that their group can afford to bid more for the supermarket than Joanna. His line of reasoning is as follows:

> The fact that we're financing with debt means that it's cheaper for us to finance the supermarket. The interest paid on debt is an expense for tax purposes, which means that debt is cheaper than equity. In addition, because equity is more risky than debt, equity holders in any case want a higher return than debtholders. So our greater use of debt means that we can afford to pay more for the supermarket.

If this logic is correct, then it's possible that Mortimer's group would bid $1,200,000 for the supermarket, whereas Joanna's group would only bid $1,000,000. In this case the two balance sheets would look like this.

| Mortimer's Supermarket Group Half equity (50%) and half debt (50%) | | | |
|---|---|---|---|
| Supermarket | $1,200,000 | Debt | $600,000 |
| | | Equity | $600,000 |
| **Total assets** | **$1,200,000** | **Total debt and e`quity** | **$1,200,000** |

| Joanna's Supermarket Group Only equity (100%) | | | |
|---|---|---|---|
| Supermarket | $1,000,000 | Debt | $0 |
| | | Equity | $1,000,000 |
| **Total assets** | **$1,000,000** | **Total debt and equity** | **$1,000,000** |

Of course there's no question what would happen in this case: The sellers of the supermarket would prefer to sell to Mortimer's group, which is offering a higher price.

## Which Example Is More Representative? Example 1 or Example 2?

As you'll see in the chapter, both examples could be representative of how things actually work in the world. In this chapter we frame the capital structure question (Example 1 versus Example 2) primarily in terms of the following two questions:

- Does the choice of financing affect the total cash that can be extracted from the firm? If Mortimer's group, with its higher proportion of debt financing, can extract more cash from the supermarket, then it might be logical for them to be willing to pay more for the supermarket.

- Should the choice of financing affect the discount rate the firm uses to evaluate projects? This is where *risk*, the magic word in finance, comes into play.[1] In simple words, is the correct discount rate to be used for the supermarket by Mortimer's group different from

---

[1] Recall the opening words of Chapter 8: "Risk is the magic word in finance. Whenever finance people can't explain something, we try to look confident and say 'it must be the risk.'"

that which should be used by Joanna's group? Does the choice of a financing mix affect the weighted average cost of capital (WACC)?

As you will see in this chapter, the answers to both these questions relate primarily to taxation. It will turn out that depending on the tax system, either Example 1 or Example 2 could be a representation of how things work.[2]

## Finance Concepts in This Chapter

- Debt versus equity financing
- Valuation effects of leverage
- Corporate versus personal taxation
- Modigliani–Miller model
- Miller's "Debt and Taxes"

## Excel Functions Used

- **If**
- **NPV**

# 17.1. Capital Structure When There Are Corporate Taxes—ABC Corp.

We start our exploration of the effects of capital structure by examining the story of ABC Corp. This well-known company is located in Lower Fantasia. Lower Fantasia has an unusual tax code: In Lower Fantasia, whereas companies are taxed on their corporate income, individuals are not taxed on their personal income.

Our hero, Arthur ABC, is trying to figure out: (a) whether to buy ABC Corp., a well-known company in Lower Fantasia, and (b) if he buys the company, how to finance the purchase.

## Buying ABC Corp. Using Only Equity

This turns out to be fairly simple. ABC has an expected annual FCF of $1,000 per year; this free cash flow (FCF) is anticipated to recur, year after year, at the same level. Arthur—who has an MBA from Eastern Lower Fantasia State University (their football team is called the "elfs")—has computed the cost of capital for the purchase as $r_U = 20\%$. The symbol "U" as a subscript for the discount rate $r_U$ stands for "unlevered" and is meant to remind you that in this case $r_U$ is the discount rate appropriate for the case where Arthur buys ABC Corp. with only equity (meaning his own money, without borrowing).

---

[2]It's even possible that another variant of Example 2 would hold in which Mortimer's group would bid less than Joanna's. This is pretty unlikely, as you'll see in the remainder of the chapter.

This $r_U = 20\%$ is a cost of capital that reflects only the business ri... purchased only with equity, therefore, the company is thus worth 1,000/20% follows we will use the symbol $V_U$ for the "unlevered value of the firm." $V_U$ is ... is worth if it is financed only with equity. In our case,

$$V_U = \sum_{t=1}^{\infty} \frac{FCF_t}{\left(1+r_U\right)^t} = \sum_{t=1}^{\infty} \frac{\$1,000}{\left(1+20\%\right)^t} = \frac{\$1,000}{20\%} = \$5,000.$$

## Buying ABC Using Debt

Arthur has a wonderful source of debt financing: his mother. This wealthy old lady is in fact his business partner, but their joint deals are structured so that she's always the lender and Arthur the equity owner. There's another unusual feature to the old lady's lending—she gives out *perpetual debt*—her loans require only an annual payment of interest, but no repayment of principal.[4] The cost of debt to Arthur, denoted by $r_D$, is the interest rate charged by his mother on her loans to him. In this case $r_D = 8\%$.

Together, Arthur and his mom are exploring two alternative financing arrangements:

- In Alternative *A*, Arthur buys ABC Corp. for cash; immediately thereafter, the company borrows $3,000 from Mom and repays it to Arthur. (Corporate finance deals in Lower Fantasia are a bit complicated!) In this case ABC Corp. is a *levered* company. ("Leverage" in this context means that the company has debt on its balance sheets.)

- In Alternative *B*, Arthur borrows $3,000 from Mom and then buys ABC Corp. for cash. In this case, ABC Corp. is an *unlevered* "all-equity" company (no debt on its balance sheets) and Arthur is levered.

The fundamental difference between these two alternatives is that the Lower Fantasia tax code has a corporate income tax but no personal income taxes. Under the tax code, interest paid by corporations is an expense for tax purposes, but this is not true for interest paid by individuals, who aren't taxed on their personal income.

From Figure 17.1 you can see that the *total family income* produced by Alternative *A* is more than that produced by Alternative *B*.

---

[3] The FCF is already *after* corporate taxes, and the discounted FCF value of the firm is thus

$$\sum_{t=1}^{\infty} \frac{FCF}{\left(1+20\%\right)^t} = \frac{FCF}{20\%}$$

[4] Throughout this chapter you'll note that we often assume that cash flows have infinite duration. This makes the valuations easier, but doesn't affect the principles.

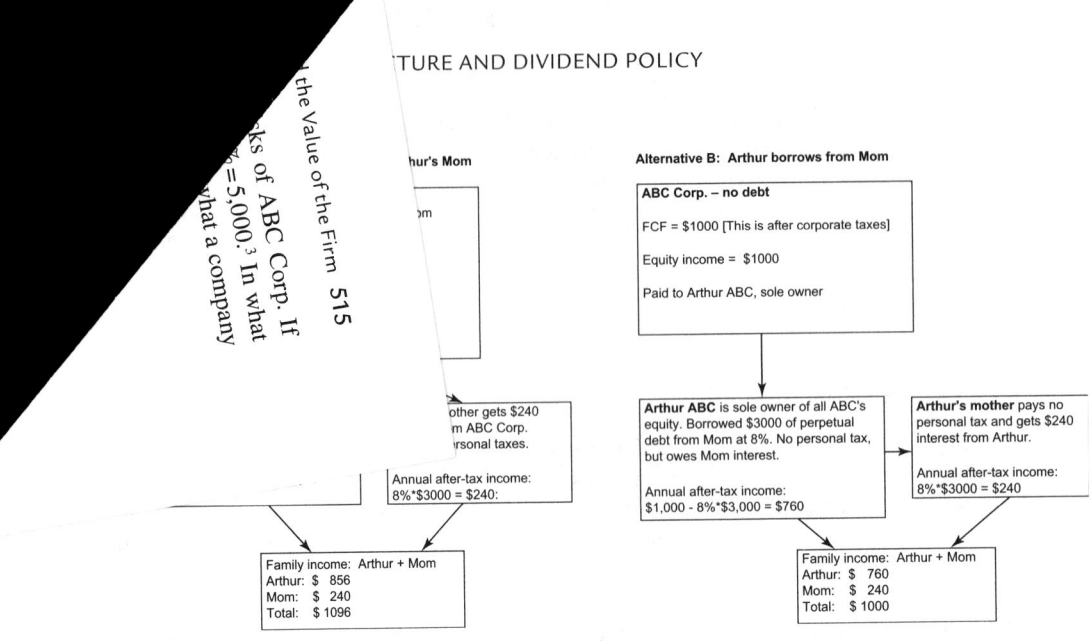

FIGURE 17.1 Financing Arthur's purchase of ABC Corp.: Cash flows resulting from two methods of financing the purchase. The tax code in Lower Fantasia provides for a corporate tax rate $T_C = 40\%$. There are no taxes on personal income.

From the family point of view, it is clear that the first alternative is better than the second. In this alternative the family (Arthur + Mom) has an annual income of $1,096, as opposed to the $1,000 in the second alternative. A little thought will reveal why the first alternative is preferable—ABC Corp. has a tax advantage over Arthur with respect to borrowing. It can deduct its interest expenses from its income taxes, so that its net income taxes are only $8\% * 3,000 * (1 - 40\%) = \$144$. This compares with Arthur's cost for the same loan of $8\% * 3,000 = 240$.

To flesh this out a bit, let's write out some equations:

$$Total \; family \; income \; from \; ABC \; (Arthur + Mom)$$
$$= cash \; produced \; by \; firm = FCF - \underbrace{r_D * Debt * (1 - T_C)}_{\substack{\text{Cost of debt} \\ \text{to ABC Corp}}} + \underbrace{r_D * Debt}_{\substack{\text{Income from} \\ \text{debt to Mom}}}$$

$$= FCF + r_D * Debt * T_C$$

Thus, the total cash produced by the firm for its stockholders and bondholders increases with the amount of debt the firm has. Note that the total cash produced by the firm does not increase if Arthur borrows the money from his mother.[5]

---

[5] Looking at Figure 17.1, it's clear why this is so—when Arthur borrows from Mom, the interest is a *wash*: Arthur has an interest expense of $240 and Mom has interest income of $240, for a net $0. When the company borrows from Mom, the company has an interest expense of *(1—40%) * 8% * 3,000 = $144*, but Mom has interest income of $240, for a net of $96.

## 17.2. Valuing ABC Corp.—The Effect of Leverage When There Are Corporate Taxes

Recall that we stated in Section 17.1 that ABC Corp's FCFs are worth $5,000 if the company has no leverage:

$$V_U = Unlevered\ value\ of\ ABC$$
$$= PV\left(future\ FCFs,\ discounted\ @\ unlevered\ discount\ rate\right)$$
$$= \sum_{t=1}^{\infty} \frac{1,000}{(1.20)^t} = \frac{Annual\ FCF}{r_U} = \frac{1,000}{20\%} = 5,000$$

So how much is the levered version of ABC Corp worth (this is the company that borrows $3,000 from Arthur's mom)? We use the *additivity principle* explained in Chapter 14:

$$V_L = Levered\ value\ of\ ABC$$
$$= Unlevered\ value\ of\ ABC + PV\left(additional\ debt\text{-}related\ CFs\right)$$
$$= 5,000 + \sum_{t=1}^{\infty} \frac{8\% * 3,000 * 40\%}{(1.08)^t} = 5,000 + \frac{96}{0.08}$$
$$= 5,000 + 1,200 = 6,200$$

### THE ADDITIVITY PRINCIPLE IN THIS CONTEXT

The additivity principle (Chapter 14) says that *the value of the sum of two cash flow streams is the sum of their values.* In the context of this problem, the two cash flow streams are: (1) the stream of FCFs that derive from the firm's business activities and (2) the stream of tax shields on the interest paid by the firm.

To value these streams using the additivity principle, we discount each at its appropriate risk-adjusted discount rate. The rate for the FCFs is $r_U$ and the rate for the tax shields—which we assume to be riskless—is the interest rate on the debt $r_D$.

ABC Corp is worth more as a levered firm than as an unlevered firm because it produces more cash for its owners. The additional cash produced—generated by the fact that the company can deduct the cost of its interest payments from its taxes, whereas Arthur cannot—is worth $1,200. In symbols,

$$V_L = V_U + PV\left(additional\ debt\text{-}related\ CFs\right)$$

$$= \begin{cases} V_U = \sum_{t=1}^{\infty} \dfrac{FCF_t}{(1+r_U)^t} = \sum_{t=1}^{\infty} \dfrac{1,000}{(1.20)^t} = \dfrac{1,000}{20\%} = 5,000 \\[4pt] \text{The unlevered value of the firm is} \\ \text{the present value of its free cash flows} \\ \text{discounted at an appropriate (unlevered)} \\ \text{cost of capital } r_U \end{cases}$$

$$+ \begin{cases} PV\left(\begin{matrix} Interest\ tax \\ shields \end{matrix}\right) = \sum_{t=1}^{\infty} \dfrac{T_C * Interest_t}{(1+r_D)^t} = \sum_{t=1}^{\infty} \dfrac{8\% * 3,000 * 40\%}{(1.08)^t} = \dfrac{96}{8\%} = 1,200 \\[4pt] \text{The tax shields created} \\ \text{by the debt are discounted at the interest} \\ \text{rate.} \end{cases}$$

$$= 6,200$$

## The Cost of Equity, $r_E(L)$, and the Weighted Average Cost of Capital with Leverage

The *cost of equity* is the discount rate for the cash flows accruing to shareholders. In Chapters 6 and 13 we discussed the derivation of the cost of equity, stressing its relation to the riskiness of the equity cash flows. In this chapter we use the symbol $r_E(L)$, with the "L" showing that that the cost of equity is related to the leverage of the firm. As you will see, greater leverage leads to a larger $r_E(L)$; the reason for this is that the equity cash flows are riskier when shareholders have promised larger amounts to debtholders.

We now proceed to the computation of $r_E(L)$ for ABC Corp. The levered version of ABC Corp. is worth \$6,200, of which $D = \$3,000$ is debt. Thus the equity of the company is worth \$3,200. We denote the market value of the equity by $E$. To calculate the firm's cost of equity $r_E(L)$, we first compute the cash flows that the equity owners receive:

$$Annual\ equity\ cash\ flow = FCF - after\text{-}tax\ interest\ paid\ by\ ABC$$
$$= 1,000 - 8\% * 3,000 * (1 - 40\%) = 856$$

The discounted value of this annual equity cash flow of \$856 is the value of the equity; this defines the cost of equity $r_E(L)$:

$$E = Equity\ value = \sum_{t=1}^{\infty} \frac{equity\ cash\ flow_t}{(1+r_E)^t}$$

$$3,200 = \sum_{t=1}^{\infty} \frac{856}{(1+r_E)^t} = \frac{856}{r_E}$$

$$\Rightarrow r_E(L) = \frac{856}{3,200} = 26.75\%$$

With a little mathematical flimflammery, we can show that

$$r_E(L) = r_U + \left[r_U - r_D\right]\frac{D}{E}(1-T_C)$$

$$= \underbrace{20\%}_{\substack{\uparrow \\ r_U \text{ is the discount} \\ \text{rate for the FCFs,} \\ \text{which represents} \\ \text{the firm's business} \\ \text{risk}}} + \underbrace{[20\% - 8\%]\frac{3,000}{3,200}(1-40\%)}_{\substack{\uparrow \\ \text{When ABC borrows, its shareholders} \\ \text{bear an additional } \textit{financial risk}\text{. The} \\ \text{term above represents the financial risk} \\ \text{premium for the equity holders}} = 26.75\%$$

We can now compute the WACC:

$$WACC = r_E(L)\frac{E}{E+D} + r_D(1-T_C)\frac{D}{E+D}$$

$$= 26.75\%\frac{3,200}{3,200+3,000} + 8\%(1-40\%)\frac{3,000}{3,200+3,000}$$

$$= 16.13\%$$

With a little more flimflammery we can show that discounting the FCFs at the WACC gives the total value of the firm:

$$\sum_{t=1}^{\infty} \frac{FCF_t}{(1+WACC)^t} = \sum_{t=1}^{\infty} \frac{1,000}{(1+16.13\%)^t} = \frac{1,000}{16.13\%} = 6,200$$

Here's all of this summarized in a spreadsheet. Note from the title of the spreadsheet that we've given this model a name; we've called it the "Modigliani–Miller model with only corporate tax." To see why the name, refer to the box "Some history of finance (1)" on page 521.

| | A | B | C |
|---|---|---|---|
| 1 | **COMPUTING THE WACC IN MODIGLIANI-MILLER MODEL WITH ONLY CORPORATE TAXES** | | |
| 2 | Annual FCF | 1,000 | |
| 3 | $r_U$, unlevered cost of capital | 20% | |
| 4 | D, debt (perpetual) | 3,000 | |
| 5 | $r_D$, the cost of debt (interest rate) | 8% | |
| 6 | $T_C$, corporate tax rate | 40% | |
| 7 | | | |
| 8 | **Value of firm** | | |
| 9 | $V_U$, unlevered value = $FCF/r_U$ | 5,000.00 | <-- =B2/B3 |
| 10 | Value of tax shield on interest = $T_C*r_D*D/r_D = T_C*D$ | 1,200.00 | <-- =B6*B4 |
| 11 | $V_L$, levered value of firm = $V_U + T_C*D$ | 6,200.00 | <-- =B10+B9 |
| 12 | | | |
| 13 | E, value of equity = $V_L$ - D | 3,200.00 | <-- =B11-B4 |
| 14 | | | |
| 15 | Cash flow to equity = FCF - $(1-T_C)$*interest | 856.00 | <-- =B2-(1-B6)*B5*B4 |
| 16 | Return on equity, $r_E(L)$= [FCF - $(1-T_C)$*interest]/E | 26.75% | <-- =B15/B13 |
| 17 | | | |
| 18 | WACC = $r_E(L)*E/(E+D) + r_D*(1-T_C)*D/(E+D)$ | 16.13% | <-- =B16*B13/B11+(1-B6)*B5*B4/B11 |
| 19 | | | |
| 20 | **Two checks** | | |
| 21 | Return on equity, $r_E(L)$= $r_U + (r_U - r_D)*[D/E]*(1-T_C)$ | 26.75% | <-- =B3+(B3-B5)*B4/B13*(1-B6) |
| 22 | Value of firm, $V_L$ = FCF/WACC | 6,200.00 | <-- =B2/B18 |

We complete this section by restating its major conclusions. If only corporate income is taxed, leverage (borrowing) increases the value of the firm. This increase in value, represented by the present value of the tax shields on the debt, increases the cost of equity $r_E$ and decreases the WACC. The present value of the debt tax shields accrues to the firm's equity holders: In the above example, if the corporate tax rate were $T_C = 0\%$, debt of \$3,000 would have decreased the value of the equity to \$2,000. Instead, with $T_C = 40\%$, the value of the equity is decreased by the value of the debt but increased by the value of the debt tax shields:

$$Equity\ value\ of\ levered\ firm = V_L - D = V_U - D + T_C D$$

A summary table is given in Figure 17.2.

## SUMMARY TABLE—CORPORATE VALUATION WHEN ONLY CORPORATE INCOME IS TAXED

| Item | Formula | Why |
|---|---|---|
| $V_U$ = value of unlevered firm | $V_U = \sum_{t=1}^{\infty} \dfrac{FCF_t}{(1+r_U)^t}$ | The value of the unleveraged firm is the PV of future FCFs discounted at $r_U$, the unlevered cost of capital. |
| | $V_L = V_U + PV(\textit{interest tax shields})$ $= V_U + \sum_{t=1}^{N} \dfrac{T_C * interest_t}{(1+r_D)^t}$ | The value of the leveraged firm is $V_U$ plus the present value of future interest tax shields. The cell to the left contains the formula for the value of the leveraged firm when there are $N$ interest payments on the debt. |
| $V_L$ = value of levered firm | $V_L = V_U + PV(\textit{interest tax shields})$ $= V_U + \sum_{t=1}^{\infty} \dfrac{T_C * interest}{(1+r_D)^t}$ $= V_U + T_C * D$ | The cell to the left contains the formula for the leveraged firm when the firm issues perpetual debt. |
| $E$ = value of equity | $V_U - (1 - T_C) * D$ | The equity value of the levered firm is the value of the levered firm minus the value of the firm's debt: $E = V_L - D = V_U + D*T_C - D = V_U - (1 - T_C)D$ |
| $D$ = value of debt | $D$ | The value of the debt is the value of the debt. (OK, this ain't so original!) |
| $r_E(L)$ = cost of equity of the leveraged firm | $r_E(L) = r_U + [r_U - r_D]\dfrac{D}{E}(1 - T_C)$ | The cost of equity $r_E$ is the discount rate for equity cash flows. In a leveraged firm it includes a *financial risk premium*: $[r_U - r_D]\dfrac{D}{E}(1 - T_C)$ |
| WACC = weighted average cost of capital | $WACC = \dfrac{FCF}{V_L}$ | You can correctly value the *whole firm* by discounting its FCFs at the WACC. This is the valuation principle employed in Chapters 6, 7, and 13. |

FIGURE 17.2 Corporate value and cost of capital corporate income is taxed at rate $T_C$ and when there are no personal taxes.

### SOME HISTORY OF FINANCE (1)

The valuation model summarized in Figure 17.2 is often called the *Modigliani–Miller* model, after Professors Franco Modigliani and Merton Miller, both winners of the Nobel Prize in Economics. In two path-breaking articles published in 1958 and 1963, Modigliani and Miller showed that the value of the firm would not be affected by the method in which the firm was financed, except where the tax code explicitly favors one form of financing. In the example of ABC Corp. in Section 17.2, the tax code gives corporations a tax break on debt financing, whereas individuals (who are untaxed) get no such break; it is therefore optimal for the firm to finance with more debt and less equity.

Students of finance know this result as the "MM model." It has been widely studied and even more widely misunderstood.

In Section 17.7 we consider a variation of the MM model that takes account of not only corporate taxes but also personal taxes. Although the logic is the same, the conclusions are very different. This model—less widely studied and even more misunderstood—is known as the Miller model, after Merton Miller, who expounded it in a famous academic article that appeared in the *Journal of Finance* in 1977. (See the box "Some History of Finance (2)" on page 534.

## 17.3. Why Debt Is Valuable in Lower Fantasia—Buying a Turfing Machine

It's easier to understand the theory of the previous section by looking at some numerical examples. In this and the following two sections we discuss several such examples. Each of these examples makes the point that under the Lower Fantasia tax regime—in which corporate income is taxed at a rate $T_C$, but in which there are no taxes on personal income—companies that finance with debt can increase their market value.

The tax regime in Lower Fantasia is characterized by a tax on corporate income but no other taxes. In the previous section we showed that this tax regime means that the value of companies in Lower Fantasia is increased when they lever themselves.

We start with an example that shows the effect of financing on a capital budgeting decision.

### Buying a Machine

Wonderturf Corp., a company in Lower Fantasia, is considering purchasing a new turfing machine. The turfing machine costs $100,000; it has a 10-year life, during which it is straight-line depreciated to zero salvage value. In each of the 10 years of the machine's life, it will produce sales of $40,000. These sales will cost $15,000 to produce. The result is that the machine has an annual free cash flow (FCF) of $19,000 per year (see cell B10 below):

$$\begin{aligned} Annual\ Wonderturf\ FCF &= (1-T_C)*(Sales - Expenses - Depreciation) + Depreciation \\ &= (1-40\%)*(40,000 - 15,000 - 10,000) + 10,000 \\ &= \$19,000 \end{aligned}$$

| | A | B | C |
|---|---|---|---|
| 1 | **THE WONDERTURF TURFING MACHINE** | | |
| 2 | $T_C$, corporate tax rate | 40% | |
| 3 | | | |
| 4 | Machine cost, year 0 | 100,000 | |
| 5 | | | |
| 6 | Free cash flow (FCF) calculation | | |
| 7 | Additional sales, annually | 40,000 | |
| 8 | Additional annual cost of sales | 15,000 | |
| 9 | Annual depreciation | 10,000 | <-- =B4/10 |
| 10 | Annual FCF, years 1-10 | 19,000 | <-- =(1-B2)*(B7-B8-B9)+B9 |
| 11 | | | |
| 12 | $r_U$, discount rate for machine FCFs | 15% | |
| 13 | | | |
| 14 | Year | Machine FCF | |
| 15 | 0 | -100,000 | <-- =-B4 |
| 16 | 1 | 19,000 | <-- =$B$10 |
| 17 | 2 | 19,000 | |
| 18 | 3 | 19,000 | |
| 19 | 4 | 19,000 | |
| 20 | 5 | 19,000 | |
| 21 | 6 | 19,000 | |
| 22 | 7 | 19,000 | |
| 23 | 8 | 19,000 | |
| 24 | 9 | 19,000 | |
| 25 | 10 | 19,000 | |
| 26 | | | |
| 27 | Machine NPV | -4,643 | <-- =B15+NPV(B12,B16:B25) |

The Wonderturf financial wizards have determined that an appropriate risk-adjusted discount rate for the turfing machine's free cash flows is $r_U = 15\%$. Discounting the machine's FCFs at this rate shows that it has a negative NPV of −$4,643 (cell B27). Thus, the conclusion is that Wonderturf should not acquire the turfing machine.

However, there's more to this story—read on!

## Wonderturf Gets a Loan to Buy the Machine

Having heard from Wonderturf that they don't intend to buy the machine, the turfing machine's manufacturer offers the company a loan of $50,000. The loan's conditions are as follows:

- Interest on the loan is $r_D = 8\%$. This is also the market interest rate.

- The loan's payments in years 1–9 consist of interest only: 8% * 50,000 = 4,000. This interest is an expense for tax purposes for Wonderturf, so that the after-tax cost of the interest to the company is (1–40%) * 4,000 = $2,400.

- At the end of year 10, Wonderturf must repay the loan principal. In this year, the after-tax cost of the loan to the company is therefore $52,400 (the loan principal plus the after-tax interest).

The Excel table below shows that the loan to Wonderturf has a positive NPV of $10,736.

| | D | E | F |
|---|---|---|---|
| 12 | Loan to buy machine | 50,000 | |
| 13 | $r_D$, loan interest rate | 8% | |
| 14 | | Loan CFs | |
| 15 | | 50,000 | <-- =E12 |
| 16 | | -2,400 | <-- =-(1-$B$2)*$E$13*$E$12 |
| 17 | | -2,400 | |
| 18 | | -2,400 | |
| 19 | | -2,400 | |
| 20 | | -2,400 | |
| 21 | | -2,400 | |
| 22 | | -2,400 | |
| 23 | | -2,400 | |
| 24 | | -2,400 | |
| 25 | | -52,400 | <-- =-(1-$B$2)*$E$13*$E$12-E12 |
| 26 | | | |
| 27 | Loan NPV | 10,736 | <-- =E15+NPV(E13,E16:E25) |

The Wonderturf financial wizards now conclude that *it is worthwhile buying the turfing machine if Wonderturf takes the loan.* Their logic is as follows:

$$Value(Wonderturf\ machine + financing) = Value(Wonderturf\ machine) + Value(financing)$$
$$= \quad -\$4,643 \quad + \quad \$10,736$$
$$= \$6,093$$

Here's a spreadsheet that shows their calculations.

| | A | B | C | D | E | F |
|---|---|---|---|---|---|---|
| 1 | THE WONDERTURF TURFING MACHINE | | | | | |
| 2 | $T_C$, corporate tax rate | 40% | | | | |
| 3 | | | | | | |
| 4 | Machine cost, year 0 | 100,000 | | | | |
| 5 | | | | | | |
| 6 | Free cash flow (FCF) calculation | | | | | |
| 7 | Additional sales, annually | 40,000 | | | | |
| 8 | Additional annual cost of sales | 15,000 | | | | |
| 9 | Annual depreciation | 10,000 | <-- =B4/10 | | | |
| 10 | Annual FCF, years 1-10 | 19,000 | <-- =(1-B2)*(B7-B8-B9)+B9 | | | |
| 11 | | | | | | |
| 12 | $r_U$, discount rate for machine FCFs | 15% | | Loan to buy machine | 50,000 | |
| 13 | | | | $r_D$, loan interest rate | 8% | |
| 14 | Year | Machine FCF | | | Loan CFs | |
| 15 | 0 | -100,000 | <-- =-B4 | | 50,000 | <-- =E12 |
| 16 | 1 | 19,000 | <-- =$B$10 | | -2,400 | <-- =-(1-$B$2)*$E$13*$E$12 |
| 17 | 2 | 19,000 | | | -2,400 | |
| 18 | 3 | 19,000 | | | -2,400 | |
| 19 | 4 | 19,000 | | | -2,400 | |
| 20 | 5 | 19,000 | | | -2,400 | |
| 21 | 6 | 19,000 | | | -2,400 | |
| 22 | 7 | 19,000 | | | -2,400 | |
| 23 | 8 | 19,000 | | | -2,400 | |
| 24 | 9 | 19,000 | | | -2,400 | |
| 25 | 10 | 19,000 | | | -52,400 | <-- =-(1-$B$2)*$E$13*$E$12-E12 |
| 26 | | | | | | |
| 27 | Machine NPV | -4,643 | <-- =B15+NPV(B12,B16:B25) | Loan NPV | 10,736 | <-- =E15+NPV(E13,E16:E25) |
| 28 | | | | | | |
| 29 | NPV: Machine + Loan | 6,093 | <-- =B27+E27 | | | |

As you can see in cell B29, the total value of the machine + loan combination is $6,093.

## Where Does the Positive Loan NPV Come From?

The preceding analysis shows that the loan to Wonderturf has an NPV of $10,736. If we analyze this number, we will see that this is exactly the *PV of the tax shields on the loan interest*:

$$NPV(loan) = 50,000 - \frac{(1-40\%)*4,000}{1.08} - \frac{(1-40\%)*4,000}{(1.08)^2} - \cdots$$
$$- \frac{(1-40\%)*4,000}{(1.08)^9} - \frac{(1-40\%)*4,000 - 50,000}{(1.08)^{10}}$$

We now split this expression into two parts:

$$NPV(loan) = 50,000 - \frac{4,000}{1.08} - \frac{4,000}{(1.08)^2} - \cdots - \frac{4,000}{(1.08)^9} - \frac{4,000 - 50,000}{(1.08)^{10}}$$
$$+ \frac{40\%*4,000}{1.08} + \frac{40\%*4,000}{(1.08)^2} + \cdots + \frac{40\%*4,000}{(1.08)^9} + \frac{40\%*4,000}{(1.08)^{10}}$$

The first line above has value 0 (recall from Chapter 5 that a loan and all its repayments have zero NPV when the discount rate is the loan-borrowing rate). The second line above is the PV of the tax shields on the loan interest. Their value is $10,736:

$$NPV(loan) = 10,736 = \frac{40\%*4,000}{1.08} + \frac{40\%*4,000}{(1.08)^2} + \cdots + \frac{40\%*4,000}{(1.08)^9} + \frac{40\%*4,000}{(1.08)^{10}}$$

Thus the NPV of the loan is the *present value of the tax shields on the loan interest payments*.

## The Wonderturf Result Is Not Surprising!

The formulas above state that the value of a levered company is the sum of the value of the unlevered company *plus* the value of the debt tax shields:

$$V_L = V_U + PV(interest\ tax\ shields)$$
$$= V_U + \sum_{t=1}^{\infty} \frac{T_C * Interest_t}{(1+r_D)^t}$$

This is precisely what we've done with our analysis of the Wonderturf turfing machine. For this machine,

$$V_L = the\ value\ of\ the\ machine\ when\ purchased\ with\ a\ loan$$
$$= \underbrace{V_U}_{\substack{\text{The value of} \\ \text{the machine's} \\ \text{cash flows}}} + \underbrace{\sum_{t=1}^{\infty} \frac{T_C * Interest_t}{(1+r_D)^t}}_{\substack{\text{The value of the} \\ \text{tax shields from the} \\ \text{loan interest}}}$$
$$= -4,643 + 10,736 = 6,093$$

# 17.4. Why Debt Is Valuable in Lower Fantasia—Relevering Potfooler, Inc.

For our second example of the effect of financing on firm value, we use a question from a Finance 101 final exam at Eastern Lower Fantasia State University. As you'll see it's a fairly long question, with many interrelated parts.[6]

Here's the question: Potfooler, Inc. is a well-known Lower Fantasia company. Here are some facts about the company:

- Potfooler expects to have an annual free cash flow (FCF) of $2 million at the end of years 1, 2, 3,... forever. Recall that the FCF is the after-tax amount of cash that the company generates from its business activities.

- Potfooler currently has 100,000 shares outstanding on the Lower Fantasia stock exchange. The Potfooler share price is $100 per share.

- Potfooler currently has no debt. However, a financial analyst has suggested that the company issue $3,000,000 of perpetual debt and use the proceeds to repurchase shares. The analyst explains that perpetual debt is debt that has only an annual interest payment and has no return of principal.[7] He suggests that this would be worthwhile for the company, because of the relation $V_L = V_U + T_C D$. The current interest rate on debt in Lower Fantasia is 8%, and the interest payments on the debt will be made annually.

Students on the finance exam were asked to answer the following questions.

***Question 1:*** What is the current market value of Potfooler?

*Answer:* Potfooler currently has 100,000 shares outstanding, each of which is worth $100. Thus the company's equity value is currently $10,000,000 = $100 * 100,000. Because the company has no debt, this is also its market value. In short, $V_U = \$10,000,000$.

***Question 2:*** After Potfooler issues $3,000,000 of debt, what will be its market value?

*Answer:* Because Lower Fantasia has only a corporate income tax, the relation $V_L = V_U + T_C D$ holds. This means that after the company issues its debt, its market value will be

$$V_L = V_U + T_C D = 10,000,000 + 40\% * 3,000,000 = 11,200,000.$$

***Question 3:*** After Potfooler issues debt of $3,000,000 and uses the proceeds to repurchase shares, what will be the company's total equity value, E?[8]

*Answer:* After Potfooler issues the debt and repurchases the shares, the total value of its equity, E, plus the total value of its debt, D, have to sum to the company's total market value $V_L$. In short,

$$V_L = E + D = 11,200,000$$
But $D = \$3,000,000$, and therefore:
$$E = V_L - D = 11,200,000 - 3,000,000 = 8,200,000$$

---

[6] The author's colleagues at Eastern Lower Fantasia State University love this question because it's easy to grade. If a student makes a mistake on any part of the question, then the answers on all subsequent parts of the question will also be wrong.

[7] Such debt is sometimes called a *consol*. Consols are easy to value, because a bond with a perpetual annual payment of C is worth $C/r$ when the discount rate is $r$.

[8] Note that up to this point in the exam, we haven't stated the price at which Potfooler repurchases the shares. This comes later.

*Question 4*: At what price will Potfooler repurchase its shares?

*Answer*: By issuing $3 million of debt, Potfooler has raised its total market value by $1,200,000 (from $10 million to $11.2 million). This increase in value belongs to all the shareholders. Because there are 100,000 shares outstanding before the share repurchase, this means that each share's price increases by $1,200,000/100,000=$12. Thus the answer to this question is that the share price for repurchase is $112: Of this amount $100 is the share price before the repurchase, and $12 is the increase in the share price as a result of the debt issue.

*Question 5*: How many shares will Potfooler repurchase?

*Answer*: According to the previous question, Potfooler will repurchase its shares at $112 per share. Because the company has issued $3 million in debt to repurchase the shares, this means that it will repurchase $3,000,000/$112=26,785.71.

*Question 6*: What was Potfooler's cost of equity before the repurchase of shares?

*Answer*: Potfooler has an annual FCF of $2,000,000. Thus its unlevered cost of equity,

$$r_E(U) = \frac{FCF}{V_U} = \frac{2,000,000}{10,000,000} = 20\%.$$

*Question 7*: What is Potfooler's cost of equity after the repurchase of the shares on the open market?

*Answer*: Potfooler issues $3 million in 8% debt to repurchase shares. Thus its annual interest bill is 8% * 3,000,000 = $240,000. Because interest is an expense for tax purposes, the company's shareholders will have an annual expected cash flow of

$$Annual\ equity\ cash\ flow,\ after\ debt\ issuance = FCF - (1 - T_C) * interest$$
$$= 2,000,000 - (1 - 40\%) * 240,000$$
$$= 1,856,000$$

The value of the equity after the share repurchase is $8,200,000, so that the cost of equity of the levered company is

$$r_E(L) = \frac{1,856,000}{8,200,000} = 22.63\%.$$

*Question 8:* What is Potfooler's WACC before the repurchase of the shares?

*Answer*: Recall the definition of the WACC:

$$WACC = r_E * \frac{E}{E+D} + r_D * (1 - T_C) * \frac{D}{E+D}.$$

The answer to Question 8 is easy: Because Potfooler, before the share repurchase, has only equity, its WACC = $r_U$ = *20%*.

***Question 9:*** What is Potfooler's WACC after the repurchase of the shares?

*Answer:*

$$WACC = r_E(L) * \frac{E}{E+D} + r_D * (1-T_C) * \frac{D}{E+D}$$

$$= 22.63\% * \frac{8,200,000}{8,200,000 + 3,000,000} + 8\% * (1-40\%) \frac{3,000,000}{8,200,000 + 3,000,000} = 17.86\%$$

***Question 10:*** Why is $r_E(L) > r_U$ ?

*Answer:* Before Potfooler issued its bonds, the only risk borne by shareholders was the *business risk* inherent in the company's FCF. After the company issues its bonds, shareholders have to bear two kinds of risk: business risk *and* financial risk. Thus $r_E(L)$ represents a discount rate for cash flows that are riskier than the discount rate for the FCFs, $r_U$. Because riskier cash flows have higher discount rates, it follows that $r_E(L) > r_U$.

***Question 11:*** Why does the market value of Potfooler increase after the issuance of the debt and repurchase of the equity?

*Answer:* By issuing the debt, the shareholders of Potfooler get an additional annual cash flow—the tax shield on the debt interest. This tax shield is riskless, and its value is

$$Present\ value\ interest\ tax\ shield = \sum_{t=1}^{\infty} \frac{T_C * Interest\ payment}{(1+r_D)^t}$$

$$= \frac{T_C * Interest\ payment}{r_D} = \frac{T_C * r_D * D}{r_D} = T_C * D$$

The PV of the tax shield accounts for the increase in Potfooler's market value:

$$V_L = \underbrace{V_U}_{\substack{\text{Potfooler's value} \\ \text{before the debt} \\ \text{issuance}}} + \underbrace{T_C D}_{\substack{\text{The PV of} \\ \text{additional} \\ \text{interest tax} \\ \text{shields}}} .$$

***Question 12:*** Why does the WACC decrease after the repurchase?

*Answer:* After the company issues its debt, it gains an additional cash flow (the tax shield on the interest). This cash flow is riskless. Thus the *average risk* of the company's total cash flows—its FCF plus the interest tax shield—decreases. Because the WACC represents the average riskiness of the company, it decreases.

# 17.5. Potfooler Exam Question, Second Part

Having answered the long exam question of the previous section, students at Eastern Lower Fantasia State University were asked to put the calculations for Questions 1–9 into an Excel spreadsheet. Here's the answer.

| | A | B | C |
|---|---|---|---|
| 1 | POTFOOLER-DEBT ISSUED TO REPURCHASE SHARES | | |
| 2 | **Unlevered company** | | |
| 3 | Annual free cash flow (FCF) | $2,000,000 | |
| 4 | Number of shares | 100,000 | |
| 5 | Price per share | $100 | |
| 6 | Total equity value | $10,000,000 | <-- =B5*B4 |
| 7 | | | |
| 8 | Question 1: $V_U$, unlevered value of Potfooler | $10,000,000 | <-- =B6 |
| 9 | | | |
| 10 | **Levered company** | | |
| 11 | Debt issued | $3,000,000 | |
| 12 | Interest rate on debt | 8% | |
| 13 | $T_C$, Lower Fantasia corporate tax rate | 40% | |
| 14 | Question 2: $V_L$, levered value of Potfooler, $V_L = V_U + T_C{}^*D$ | $11,200,000 | <-- =B8+B13*B11 |
| 15 | Question 3: Equity value after share repurchase, $E = V_L - D$ | $8,200,000 | |
| 16 | Incremental firm value from exchanging equity by debt = $V_L - V_U = T_C{}^*D$ | $1,200,000 | <-- =B13*B11 |
| 17 | Incremental firm value on a per-share basis | $12 | <-- =B16/B4 |
| 18 | Question 4: New share value, after repurchase | $112 | <-- =B5+B17 |
| 19 | | | |
| 20 | Question 5: Number of shares repurchased = [debt used for repurchase]/[new share value] | 26,785.71 | <-- =B11/B18 |
| 21 | Number of shares remaining after repurchase = original number of shares minus number of shares repurchased | 73,214.29 | <-- =B4-B20 |
| 22 | **Check:** Market value of remaining shares = number of remaining shares * new share value | $8,200,000 | <-- =B21*B18 |
| 23 | | | |
| 24 | Question 6: Potfooler's cost of equity when unlevered, $r_U=FCF/V_U$ | 20.00% | |
| 25 | | | |
| 26 | Annual interest costs, before taxes | $240,000 | <-- =B11*B12 |
| 27 | Annual equity cash flow, after interest = FCF - (1-TC)*interest | $1,856,000 | <-- =B3-(1-B13)*B26 |
| 28 | Question 7: Potfooler's cost of equity when levered, $r_E(L)=[FCF-(1-T_C)^*interest]/[value of equity, E]$ | 22.63% | <-- =B27/B22 |
| 29 | | | |
| 30 | Question 8: Potfooler's WACC before the debt issuance = $r_U$ | 20.00% | |
| 31 | | | |
| 32 | Question 9: Potfooler's WACC after the debt issuance = $r_E(L)^*E/(E+D)+r_D{}^*(1-T_C)^*D/(E+D)$ | | |
| 33 | Percentage of equity in Potfooler = E/(E+D) | 73.21% | <-- =B22/B14 |
| 34 | Percentage of debt in Potfooler = D/(E+D) | 26.79% | <-- =B11/B14 |
| 35 | WACC = $r_E(L)^*E/(E+D)+r_D{}^*(1-T_C)^*D/(E+D)$ | 17.86% | <-- =B28*B33+B12*(1-B13)*B34 |

This spreadsheet enables us to do some interesting analysis.

## What Happens If the Corporate Tax Rate $T_C$ = 0%?

When $T_C = 0$, leverage doesn't change the value of the firm. If you put $T_C = 0\%$ into cell B13 of the previous spreadsheet, you'll get a demonstration of this. The spreadsheet is given next, and the analysis follows after the spreadsheet.

| | A | B | C |
|---|---|---|---|
| 1 | **POTFOOLER–DEBT ISSUED TO REPURCHASE SHARES, corporate tax rate = 0%** | | |
| 2 | **Unlevered company** | | |
| 3 | Annual free cash flow (FCF) | $2,000,000 | |
| 4 | Number of shares | 100,000 | |
| 5 | Price per share | $100 | |
| 6 | Total equity value | $10,000,000 | <-- =B5*B4 |
| 7 | | | |
| 8 | Question 1: $V_U$, unlevered value of Potfooler | $10,000,000 | <-- =B6 |
| 9 | | | |
| 10 | **Levered company** | | |
| 11 | Debt issued | $3,000,000 | |
| 12 | Interest rate on debt | 8% | |
| 13 | $T_C$, Lower Fantasia corporate tax rate | 0% | |
| 14 | Question 2: $V_L$, levered value of Potfooler, $V_L = V_U + T_C{}^*D$ | $10,000,000 | <-- =B8+B13*B11 |
| 15 | Question 3: Equity value after share repurchase, $E = V_L - D$ | $7,000,000 | |
| 16 | Incremental firm value from exchanging equity by debt = $V_L - V_U = T_C{}^*D$ | $0 | <-- =B13*B11 |
| 17 | Incremental firm value on a per-share basis | $0 | <-- =B16/B4 |
| 18 | Question 4: New share value, after repurchase | $100 | <-- =B5+B17 |
| 19 | | | |
| 20 | Question 5: Number of shares repurchased = [debt used for repurchase]/[new share value] | 30,000.00 | <-- =B11/B18 |
| 21 | Number of shares remaining after repurchase = original number of shares minus number of shares repurchased | 70,000.00 | <-- =B4-B20 |
| 22 | **Check:** Market value of remaining shares = number of remaining shares * new share value | $7,000,000 | <-- =B21*B18 |
| 23 | | | |
| 24 | Question 6: Potfooler's cost of equity when unlevered, $r_U = FCF/V_U$ | 20.00% | |
| 25 | | | |
| 26 | Annual interest costs, before taxes | $240,000 | <-- =B11*B12 |
| 27 | Annual equity cash flow, after interest = FCF - (1-TC)*interest | $1,760,000 | <-- =B3-(1-B13)*B26 |
| 28 | Question 7: Potfooler's cost of equity when levered, $r_E(L) = [FCF-(1-T_C)^*interest]/[value\ of\ equity,\ E]$ | 25.14% | <-- =B27/B22 |
| 29 | | | |
| 30 | Question 8: Potfooler's WACC before the debt issuance = $r_U$ | 20.00% | |
| 31 | | | |
| 32 | Question 9: Potfooler's WACC after the debt issuance = $r_E(L)^*E/(E+D)+r_D{}^*(1-T_C)^*D/(E+D)$ | | |
| 33 | Percentage of equity in Potfooler = E/(E+D) | 70.00% | <-- =B22/B14 |
| 34 | Percentage of debt in Potfooler = D/(E+D) | 30.00% | <-- =B11/B14 |
| 35 | WACC = $r_E(L)^*E/(E+D)+r_D{}^*(1-T_C)^*D/(E+D)$ | 20.00% | <-- =B28*B33+B12*(1-B13)*B34 |

- The total value of the company doesn't change (cell B14) when the amount of debt (cell B11) changes. In a formula,

$$V_L = V_U + \underbrace{T_C D}_{\substack{\uparrow \\ \text{When } T_C = 0\%, \\ \text{this term is zero}}} = V_U$$

- The company's equity becomes more risky. That is, $r_E(L) > r_U$. You can see this in cell B28: $r_E(L) = 25.14\%$ after the debt is issued as opposed to $r_U = 20\%$.

- The company's share price doesn't change. After the issuance of the debt and the repurchase of the equity, the share price is still $100 (cell B18).

- The company's WACC doesn't change. The *average riskiness* of the company's cash flows remains the same:

$$WACC = r_E(L)* \frac{E}{E+D} + r_D*(1-T_C)* \frac{D}{E+D}$$

$$= 25.14\% * \frac{7,000,000}{7,000,000+3,000,000} + 8\% * \underbrace{(1-0\%)}_{\substack{\text{Remember that} \\ \text{in this version of the} \\ \text{question } T_C=0\%}} \frac{3,000,000}{7,000,000+3,000,000}$$

$$= 20\% = r_U$$

## Relate the Company's Value to Different Levels of Debt

By making a **Data Table** (see Chapter 27), we can make the following table and graph.

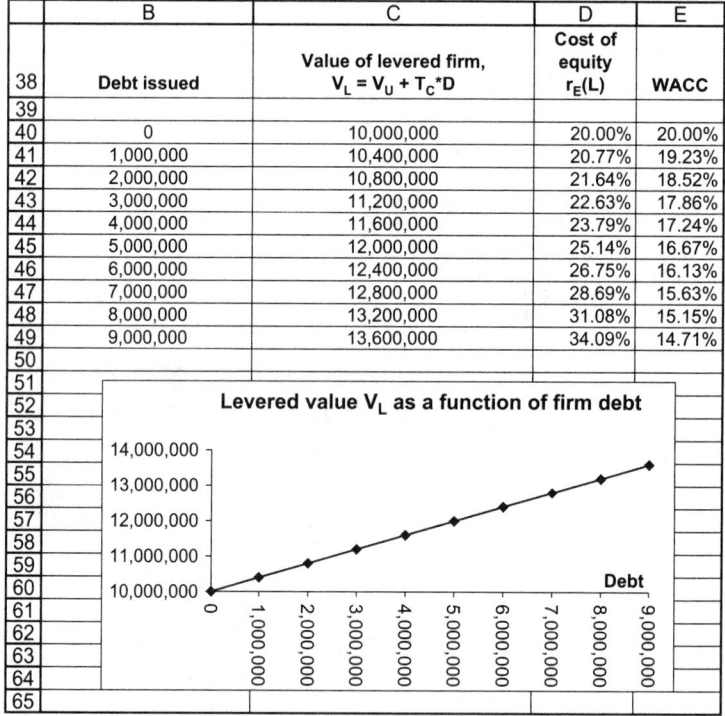

|  | B | C | D | E |
|---|---|---|---|---|
|  |  |  | Cost of equity |  |
| 38 | Debt issued | Value of levered firm, $V_L = V_U + T_C*D$ | $r_E(L)$ | WACC |
| 39 |  |  |  |  |
| 40 | 0 | 10,000,000 | 20.00% | 20.00% |
| 41 | 1,000,000 | 10,400,000 | 20.77% | 19.23% |
| 42 | 2,000,000 | 10,800,000 | 21.64% | 18.52% |
| 43 | 3,000,000 | 11,200,000 | 22.63% | 17.86% |
| 44 | 4,000,000 | 11,600,000 | 23.79% | 17.24% |
| 45 | 5,000,000 | 12,000,000 | 25.14% | 16.67% |
| 46 | 6,000,000 | 12,400,000 | 26.75% | 16.13% |
| 47 | 7,000,000 | 12,800,000 | 28.69% | 15.63% |
| 48 | 8,000,000 | 13,200,000 | 31.08% | 15.15% |
| 49 | 9,000,000 | 13,600,000 | 34.09% | 14.71% |

Levered value $V_L$ as a function of firm debt

# 17.6. Considering Personal as Well as Corporate Taxes—The Case of XYZ Corp.

In our story about ABC Corp. (Section 17.2), the capital structure decision mattered because Lower Fantasia taxes corporations but not individuals. The result is that shareholders (like Arthur) benefit from having companies borrow instead of doing the borrowing themselves.

In this section we tell the story of Upper Fantasia, a country very much like Lower Fantasia, but with a somewhat different tax system. Upper Fantasia has three kinds of taxes:

- Corporations are subject to a 40% corporate tax rate. We denote this tax rate by $T_C$.
- Individual income derived from shares (this refers to dividends and capital gains on shares—in the jargon of the Upper Fantasia tax code, this is called "equity income") is subject to a 10% tax rate. The equity tax rate is denoted by $T_E$.
- All *ordinary income* (this term includes individual income derived from bonds; however, it does not include equity income) is subject to a 30% tax rate. We denote this tax rate by $T_D$. When individuals *pay interest*, they get to deduct the interest payments from their ordinary income.

As before, our mythical entrepreneur, Arthur XYZ, is trying to figure out how to finance his purchase of XYZ Corp. His mom (bless her!) is always available to lend him money. The questions about the debt are the same as before:

- Should the purchase of the company be financed with debt?
- If so, who should borrow—the company or Arthur?

Figure 17.3 explains the cash flows.

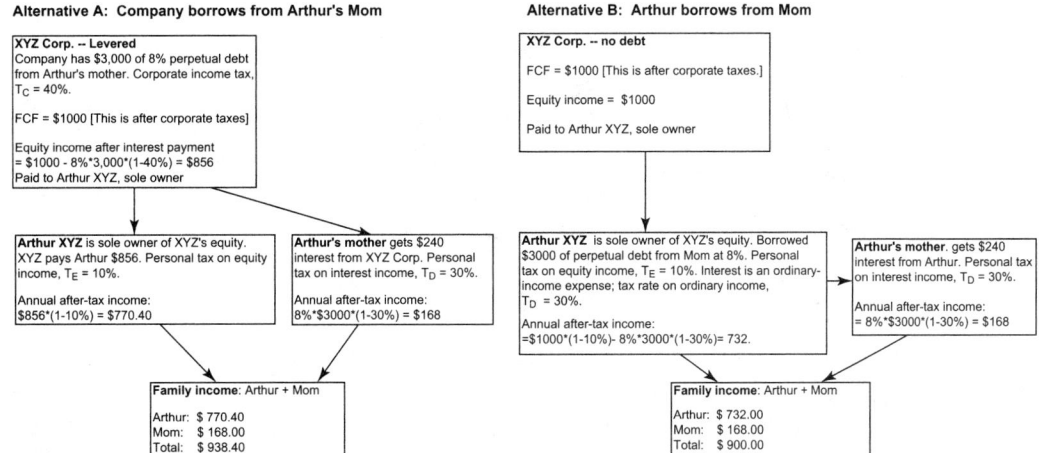

**Alternative A: Company borrows from Arthur's Mom**

> **XYZ Corp. -- Levered**
> Company has $3,000 of 8% perpetual debt from Arthur's mother. Corporate income tax, $T_C$ = 40%.
>
> FCF = $1000 [This is after corporate taxes]
>
> Equity income after interest payment
> = $1000 - 8%*3,000*(1-40%) = $856
> Paid to Arthur XYZ, sole owner

> **Arthur XYZ** is sole owner of XYZ's equity. XYZ pays Arthur $856. Personal tax on equity income, $T_E$ = 10%.
>
> Annual after-tax income:
> $856*(1-10%) = $770.40

> **Arthur's mother** gets $240 interest from XYZ Corp. Personal tax on interest income, $T_D$ = 30%.
>
> Annual after-tax income:
> 8%*$3000*(1-30%) = $168

> **Family income**: Arthur + Mom
> Arthur: $ 770.40
> Mom: $ 168.00
> Total: $ 938.40

**Alternative B: Arthur borrows from Mom**

> **XYZ Corp. -- no debt**
>
> FCF = $1000 [This is after corporate taxes.]
>
> Equity income = $1000
>
> Paid to Arthur XYZ, sole owner

> **Arthur XYZ** is sole owner of XYZ's equity. Borrowed $3000 of perpetual debt from Mom at 8%. Personal tax on equity income, $T_E$ = 10%. Interest is an ordinary-income expense; tax rate on ordinary income, $T_D$ = 30%.
>
> Annual after-tax income:
> =$1000*(1-10%)- 8%*3000*(1-30%)= 732.

> **Arthur's mother**. gets $240 interest from Arthur. Personal tax on interest income, $T_D$ = 30%.
>
> Annual after-tax income:
> = 8%*$3000*(1-30%) = $168

> **Family income**: Arthur + Mom
> Arthur: $ 732.00
> Mom: $ 168.00
> Total: $ 900.00

FIGURE 17.3 Financing Arthur's purchase of XYZ Corp.: The tax code in Upper Fantasia has a corporate income tax rate $T_C$ = 40%, a personal tax rate on equity income $T_E$ = 10%, and a personal tax rate on all other income $T_D$ = 30%.

When the company borrows the money, the total family income is $938.40. This compares to the total income of $900 when Arthur borrows the money from Mom. So it's better in this case for the company to borrow the money.

To understand what's happening, we create a spreadsheet. We'll have more to say about this spreadsheet (and the economics underlying it) later, but in the meantime, we stress its final conclusion:

- Because the total family income (the combined income of Arthur XYZ and his mom) is larger when the company borrows than when Arthur borrows (cell B27 versus cell C27), the company should lever itself and not Arthur.
- The advantages of corporate borrowing are considerably less in this case than in the previous case of ABC Corp. In the previous case corporate leverage of $3,000 added $96 to the family cash flows each year; in the current case it adds only $38.40. The difference is, of course, the fact that we now have taxes on personal income, which were absent in the ABC Corp. example.

| | A | B | C | D |
|---|---|---|---|---|
| 1 | **FINANCING ARTHUR'S PURCHASE OF XYZ**<br>Upper Fantasia tax code: Corporate income tax, $T_C$ = 40%,<br>Personal taxes: Tax on equity income, $T_E$ = 10%,<br>tax on all other income, $T_D$ = 30% | | | |
| 2 | **Computing the family income** | | | |
| 3 | $T_C$, corporate tax rate | 40% | | |
| 4 | $T_E$, personal equity tax rate | 10% | | |
| 5 | $T_D$, personal debt tax rate on ordinary income | 30% | | |
| 6 | $r_D$, interest rate | 8% | | |
| 7 | D, Debt | 3,000 | | |
| 8 | FCF, free cash flow (already after corporate taxes) | 1,000 | | |
| 9 | | | | |
| 10 | | Company borrows | Arthur borrows | |
| 11 | FCF, after personal tax | 1,000.00 | 1,000.00 | |
| 12 | Corporate debt | 3,000.00 | 0.00 | |
| 13 | Corporate pre-tax interest payment | 240.00 | 0.00 | |
| 14 | Corporate after-tax interest payment | 144.00 | 0.00 | <-- =C13*(1-$B$3) |
| 15 | Payout to equity owners | 856.00 | 1,000.00 | <-- =C11-C14 |
| 16 | | | | |
| 17 | Arthur's income | | | |
| 18 | Pre-tax equity income from XYZ | 856.00 | 1,000.00 | <-- =C15 |
| 19 | Post-tax equity income from XYZ | 770.40 | 900.00 | <-- =C18*(1-$B$4) |
| 20 | Arthur's debt | 0.00 | 3,000.00 | |
| 21 | Arthur's pre-tax interest payment | 0.00 | 240.00 | <-- =$B$6*C20 |
| 22 | Arthur's after-tax interest payment | 0.00 | 168.00 | |
| 23 | Arthur's post-tax income | 770.40 | 732.00 | <-- =C19-C22 |
| 24 | | | | |
| 25 | Mom's pre-tax income | 240.00 | 240.00 | <-- =C20*B6 |
| 26 | Mom's post-tax income | 168.00 | 168.00 | <-- =C25*(1-$B$5) |
| 27 | Total family income | 938.40 | 900.00 | <-- =C23+C26 |
| 28 | | | | |
| 29 | Who should borrow--Arthur or company? | Company | | <-- =IF(B27>C27,"Company",IF(B27<C27,"Arthur","Indifferent")) |
| 30 | | | | |
| 31 | **Net advantage of corporate debt** | | | |
| 32 | $(1-T_D)-(1-T_E)*(1-T_C)$ | 0.16 | | |

To understand this better, we need some equations:

$$\textit{Total cash produced by firm} = \underbrace{\left[FCF - r_D * Debt * (1-T_C)\right]}_{\substack{\uparrow \\ \text{Dividend to Arthur}}} * (1-T_E) + \underbrace{r_D * Debt * (1-T_D)}_{\substack{\uparrow \\ \text{Income from} \\ \text{debt to Mom}}}$$

$$\underbrace{\phantom{xxxxxxxxxxxxxxxxxxxxxxxxxxxxxxxxxxxxxx}}_{\substack{\uparrow \\ \text{Arthur's after-tax dividend}}}$$

$$= FCF * (1-T_E) + r_D * Debt * \underbrace{\left[(1-T_D) - (1-T_E) * (1-T_C)\right]}_{\substack{\uparrow \\ \text{Net tax corporate tax-advantage of debt}}}$$

$$\textit{In this case} = (1-T_D) - (1-T_C) * (1-T_E) = (1-30\%) - (1-10\%) * (1-40\%) = 16\%$$

The term that makes all the difference is

$$\underbrace{(1-T_D)}_{\substack{\uparrow \\ \text{After-tax} \\ \text{ordinary income} \\ \text{(including interest)}}} - \underbrace{(1-T_E)}_{\substack{\uparrow \\ \text{After-tax} \\ \text{equity income}}} \underbrace{(1-T_C)}_{\substack{\uparrow \\ \text{After-tax} \\ \text{corporate income}}}$$

$$\underbrace{\phantom{xxxxxxxxxxxxxxxxxxxxxxx}}_{\substack{\uparrow \\ \text{Net after-tax personal} \\ \text{income from pre-tax corporate} \\ \text{cash flows}}}$$

If this term is positive, as in the previous example (see cell B32), then XYZ Corp. should borrow; if it's negative—as in the next example (in which the corporate tax rate is $T_C = 20\%$), then Arthur should borrow and not the firm.

| | A | B | C | D |
|---|---|---|---|---|
| 1 | **FINANCING ARTHUR'S PURCHASE OF XYZ**<br>**Upper Fantasia tax code: Corporate income tax, $T_C$ = 20%**<br>**(instead of 40% in previous example)**<br>**Personal taxes: Tax on equity income, $T_E$ = 10%,**<br>**Tax on all other income, $T_D$ = 30%** | | | |
| 2 | **Computing the family income** | | | |
| 3 | $T_C$, corporate tax rate | 20% | | |
| 4 | $T_E$, personal equity tax rate | 10% | | |
| 5 | $T_D$, personal debt tax rate on ordinary income | 30% | | |
| 6 | $r_D$, interest rate | 8% | | |
| 7 | D, Debt | 3,000 | | |
| 8 | FCF, free cash flow (already after corporate taxes) | 1,000 | | |
| 9 | | | | |
| 10 | | Company borrows | Arthur borrows | |
| 11 | FCF, after personal tax | 1,000.00 | 1,000.00 | |
| 12 | Corporate debt | 3,000.00 | 0.00 | |
| 13 | Corporate pre-tax interest payment | 240.00 | 0.00 | |
| 14 | Corporate after-tax interest payment | 192.00 | 0.00 | <-- =C13*(1-$B$3) |
| 15 | Payout to equity owners | 808.00 | 1,000.00 | <-- =C11-C14 |
| 16 | | | | |
| 17 | Arthur's income | | | |
| 18 | Pre-tax equity income from XYZ | 808.00 | 1,000.00 | <-- =C15 |
| 19 | Post-tax equity income from XYZ | 727.20 | 900.00 | <-- =C18*(1-$B$4) |
| 20 | Arthur's debt | 0.00 | 3,000.00 | |
| 21 | Arthur's pre-tax interest payment | 0.00 | 240.00 | <-- =$B$6*C20 |
| 22 | Arthur's after-tax interest payment | 0.00 | 168.00 | |
| 23 | Arthur's post-tax income | 727.20 | 732.00 | <-- =C19-C22 |
| 24 | | | | |
| 25 | Mom's pre-tax income | 240.00 | 240.00 | <-- =C20*B6 |
| 26 | Mom's post-tax income | 168.00 | 168.00 | <-- =C25*(1-$B$5) |
| 27 | Total family income | 895.20 | 900.00 | <-- =C23+C26 |
| 28 | | | | |
| 29 | Who should borrow--Arthur or company? | Arthur | | <-- =IF(B27>C27,"Company",IF(B27<C27,"Arthur","Indifferent")) |
| 30 | | | | |
| 31 | **Net advantage of corporate debt** | | | |
| 32 | $(1-T_D)-(1-T_E)*(1-T_C)$ | -0.02 | | |

## SOME HISTORY OF FINANCE (2)

The Modigliani–Miller model dates from two articles published in 1958 and 1963. In 1977 Merton Miller (half of the MM team) reconsidered the problem of capital structure. He still focused on taxation, but this time considered the case where both corporate and personal income were taxed.

Miller's reasoning, incorporated in our example of XYZ Corp., was that the corporate tax rate $T_C$ gives an advantage to corporations wishing to finance with debt. On the other hand, for individuals equity income is generally taxed at a lower rate $T_E$ than the tax rate $T_D$ on debt income. The primary reason for this is that the major part of income from equity is received by shareholders as capital gains; not only are these taxed at a lower tax rate, but also the taxes on capital gains are *postponable* (as a shareholder, you can decide when to sell your shares and realize your capital gains). This postponability lowers the $T_E$ below the statutory rate (see some discussion in Chapter 21). Thus, Miller reasoned, there is a trade-off:

- On the corporate level, the deductibility of interest means that corporations produce higher before-personal-tax payouts to stakeholders (bondholders and shareholders) when they have more debt financing.

- On the personal level, giving stakeholders (bondholders and shareholders) more interest income instead of equity income means taxing them at higher personal rates.

This trade-off is summarized in the expression $(1-T_D)-(1-T_C)(1-T_E)$:

$$\underbrace{(1-T_D)}_{\uparrow} \quad - \quad \underbrace{(1-T_C)*(1-T_E)}_{\uparrow}$$

Payments to debtholders are only taxed at the personal tax of the debtholder, since the firm makes these payments out of pre-tax income

Equity income is taxed twice: once at the firm level (since payments to shareholders are paid out of after-tax earnings), and then again at the personal level

On the other hand, $T_E < T_D$, so that there is a trade-off ...

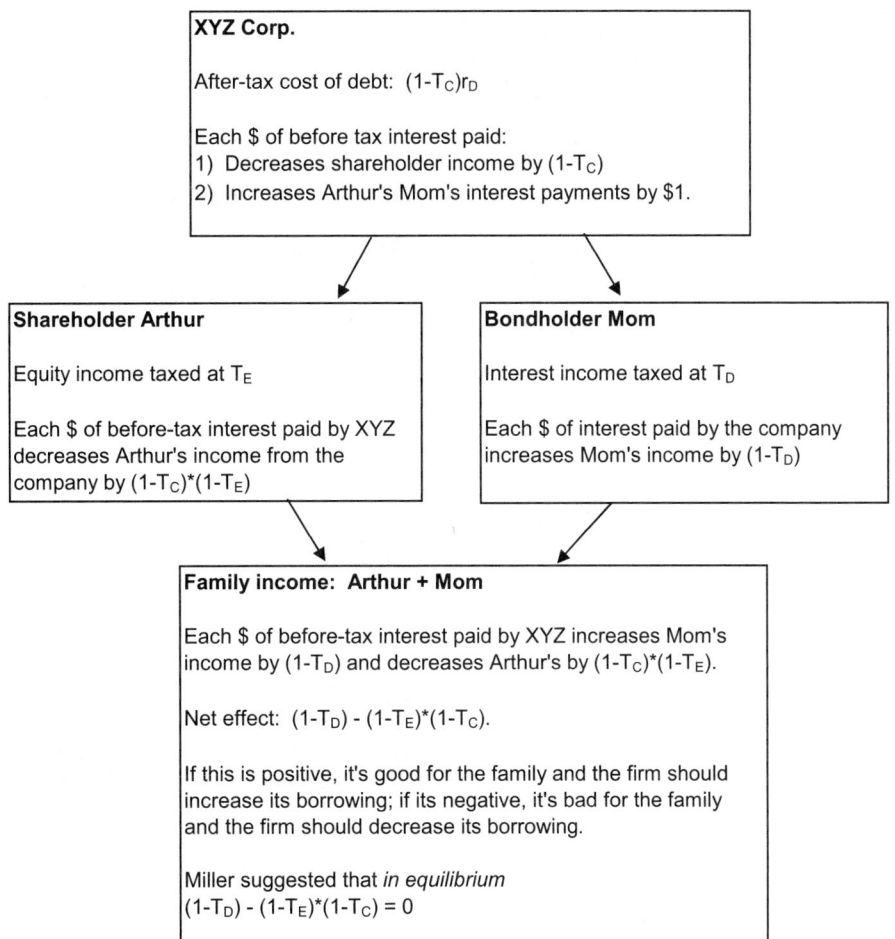

FIGURE 17.4 Cash flows of Arthur + Mom's family income. In this flow diagram, Arthur is the shareholder of XYZ Corp., and Mom is the bondholder of XYZ (meaning she lends the company money). Each $1 of interest income paid to Mom by XYZ Corp. changes the family income by $(1 - T_D) - (1 - T_E) * (1 - T_C)$. If this term is positive, then XYZ Corp.'s borrowing from Mom

adds to the family income; if it is negative, then XYZ Corp.'s borrowing detracts from the family income.

## 17.7. Valuing XYZ Corp.—The Effect of Leverage When There Are Corporate and Personal Taxes

We redo the calculations in Section 17.2, but this time use all the taxes—the corporate tax rate $T_C$, the personal tax rate on equity income $T_E$, and the personal tax rate on ordinary income (including interest) $T_D$. Without leverage XYZ Corp.'s FCFs are worth \$5,000:

$$V_U = Unlevered\ value\ of\ XYZ$$
$$= PV\left(future\ FCFs, discounted\ @\ unlevered\ discount\ rate\right)$$
$$= \sum_{t=1}^{\infty} \frac{1,000}{(1.20)^t} = \frac{Annual\ FCF}{r_U} = \frac{1,000}{20\%} = 5,000$$

We use the additivity principle to value the levered version of XYZ Corp.:

$$V_L = V_U + PV\left(additional\ debt\text{-}related\ CFs\right)$$

$$= \begin{cases} V_U = \sum_{t=1}^{\infty} \frac{FCF_t}{(1+r_U)^t} = \sum_{t=1}^{\infty} \frac{1,000}{(1.20)^t} = \frac{1,000}{20\%} = 5,000 \\[4pt] \text{The unlevered value of the firm is} \\ \text{the present value of its free cash flows} \\ \text{discounted at an appropriate (unlevered)} \\ \text{cost of capital } r_U \\[6pt] + \begin{cases} PV\left(\begin{array}{c} Interest\ tax \\ shields \end{array}\right) = \sum_{t=1}^{\infty} \frac{\left[(1-T_D)-(1-T_C)*(1-T_E)\right]*Interest_t}{\left(1+(1-T_D)r_D\right)^t} \\[6pt] \qquad\qquad\qquad = \sum_{t=1}^{\infty} \frac{8\%*3,000*16\%}{\left(1+8\%*(1-30\%)\right)^t} = \frac{38.4}{5.6\%} = 685.71 \\[6pt] \qquad\qquad \text{The tax shields created} \\ \qquad\qquad \text{by the debt are discounted at the} \\ \qquad\qquad \text{consumer's after-tax interest rate.} \end{cases} \end{cases}$$

$$= 5,685.71$$

XYZ Corp. is worth more as a levered firm than as an unlevered firm because it produces more cash for its owners when it is levered. The additional cash produced—generated by the fact that the company has a cheaper cost of debt than Arthur—is worth \$685.71, which is the present value of the future tax shields on the interest:

$$PV\left(\begin{array}{c} Interest\ tax \\ shields \end{array}\right) = \sum_{t=1}^{\infty} \frac{\left[(1-T_D)-(1-T_C)*(1-T_E)\right]*Interest}{\left(1+(1-T_D)r_D\right)^t}$$

$$= \frac{\left[(1-T_D)-(1-T_C)*(1-T_E)\right]}{(1-T_D)r_D}*Interest$$

$$= \frac{\left[(1-T_D)-(1-T_C)*(1-T_E)\right]}{(1-T_D)}*\frac{Interest}{r_D}$$

$$= \frac{\left[(1-T_D)-(1-T_C)*(1-T_E)\right]}{(1-T_D)}*D$$

We use the letter $T$ to denote the *debt-valuation factor:*  $T = \dfrac{\left[(1-T_D)-(1-T_C)*(1-T_E)\right]}{(1-T_D)}.$

$T$ is the capitalized advantage of debt.[9]

## What About the Cost of Capital—$r_E$ and WACC with Leverage?

The levered version of XYZ Corp. is worth $5,685.71, of which $3,000 is debt. Subtracting the value of the debt from the total worth of the company, we see that the equity of the company is worth $2,685.71. To calculate the firm's cost of equity $r_E$ , we first compute the after-tax cash flows accruing to the equity owners:

$$\begin{aligned} annual\ after\text{-}corporate\text{-}tax\ equity\ cash\ flow &= \left[FCF - after\text{-}tax\ interest\ paid\ by\ XYZ\right] \\ &= \left[1,000 - 8\%*3,000*(1-40\%)\right] = 856.00 \end{aligned}$$

The discounted value of this annual equity cash flow of $856.00 is the value of the equity; this defines the cost of equity $r_E$:

$$Equity\ value = \sum_{t=1}^{\infty} \frac{equity\ cash\ flow_t}{(1+r_E)^t}$$

$$2,685.71 = \sum_{t=1}^{\infty} \frac{856.00}{(1+r_E)^t} = \frac{856.00}{r_E}$$

$$\Rightarrow r_E = \frac{856.00}{2685.71} = 31.87\%$$

With a little mathematical flimflammery, we can show that

$$r_E = r_U + \left[r_U*(1-T)-r_D*(1-T_C)\right]\frac{D}{E}$$

$$= \underset{\substack{\uparrow \\ r_U \text{ is the discount} \\ \text{rate for the FCFs,} \\ \text{which represents} \\ \text{the firm's business} \\ \text{risk}}}{20\%} + \underset{\substack{\uparrow \\ \text{When XYZ borrows, its shareholders} \\ \text{bear an additional } \textit{financial risk}. \text{ The} \\ \text{term above represents the financial risk} \\ \text{premium for the equity holders}}}{\left[20\%(1-22.86\%)-8\%(1-40\%)\right]\frac{3,000}{2,685.71}} = 31.87\%$$

We can now compute the WACC:

$$WACC = r_E \frac{E}{E+D} + r_D(1-T_C)\frac{D}{E+D}$$

$$= 31.87\% \frac{2,685.71}{2,685.71+3,000} + 8\%(1-40\%)\frac{3,000}{2,685.71+3,000}$$

$$= 17.59\%$$

With a little more flimflammery we can show that discounting the FCFs at the WACC gives the total value of the firm:

$$\sum_{t=1}^{\infty} \frac{FCF_t}{(1+WACC)^t} = \sum_{t=1}^{\infty} \frac{1,000}{(1+17.59\%)^t} = \frac{1,000}{17.59\%} = 5,685.71$$

---

[9] To relate this to the previous case with only corporate taxes, note that when $T_E = T_D = 0$, $T = T_C$.

Here's all of this summarized in a spreadsheet.

| | A | B | C |
|---|---|---|---|
| 1 | **COMPUTING THE WACC IN THE MILLER MODEL**<br>**with corporate and personal taxes** | | |
| 2 | FCF, annual free cash flow (already after corporate taxes) | 1,000 | |
| 3 | $r_U$, unlevered cost of capital | 20% | |
| 4 | D, Debt | 3,000 | |
| 5 | $r_D$, interest rate | 8% | |
| 6 | $T_C$, corporate tax rate | 40% | |
| 7 | $T_E$, personal equity tax rate | 10% | |
| 8 | $T_D$, personal debt tax rate on ordinary income | 30% | |
| 9 | | | |
| 10 | Tax advantage of debt, $(1-T_D)-(1-T_C)*(1-T_E)$ | 16.00% | <-- =(1-B8)-(1-B6)*(1-B7) |
| 11 | $T= [(1-T_D)-(1-T_C)*(1-T_E)]/(1-T_D)$, tax factor | 22.86% | <-- =B10/(1-B8) |
| 12 | | | |
| 13 | **Value of firm** | | |
| 14 | $V_U$, unlevered value | 5,000.00 | <-- =B2/B3 |
| 15 | Value of tax shield on interest | 685.71 | <-- =B10*B5*B4/((1-B8)*B5) |
| 16 | $V_L$, levered value of firm | 5,685.71 | <-- =B15+B14 |
| 17 | | | |
| 18 | E, value of equity | 2,685.71 | <-- =B16-B4 |
| 19 | | | |
| 20 | Cash flow to equity | 856.00 | <-- =B2-(1-B6)*B5*B4 |
| 21 | Return on equity, $r_E(L)$ | 31.87% | <-- =B20/B18 |
| 22 | | | |
| 23 | WACC | 17.59% | <-- =B21*B18/B16+(1-B6)*B5*B4/B16 |
| 24 | | | |
| 25 | **Three checks** | | |
| 26 | Return on equity, $r_E(L) = r_U+ [r_U*(1-T) - r_D*(1-T_C)]*D/E$ | 31.87% | <-- =B3+(B3*(1-B11)-B5*(1-B6))*B4/B18 |
| 27 | Value of firm, $V_L$ = FCF/WACC | 5,685.71 | <-- =B2/B23 |
| 28 | Value of firm, $V_L = V_U + T*D$ | 5,685.71 | <-- =B14+B11*B4 |

## Summarizing This Section

We complete this section by restating its major conclusions. If corporate income is taxed and if the tax system differentiates between income derived from equity and ordinary income, then leverage (borrowing) may increase or decrease the value of the firm, depending on the sign of the tax factor $(1-T_D)-(1-T_E)*(1-T_C)$.

A summary table is given in Figure 17.5.

## SUMMARY TABLE—CHANGING LEVERAGE WHEN CORPORATE AND PERSONAL INCOME ARE TAXED

Symbols: Corporate tax rate $T_C$, personal tax rate on equity income $T_E$, personal tax rate on ordinary income $T_D$

Tax advantage of debt $= (1 - T_D) - (1 - T_C) * (1 - T_E)$; Tax factor $T = \dfrac{(1 - T_D) - (1 - T_C) * (1 - T_E)}{(1 - T_D)}$

| Item | Formula | Why |
|---|---|---|
| $V_U$ = value of unleveraged firm | $V_U = \displaystyle\sum_{t=1}^{N} \frac{FCF_t}{(1 + r_U)^t}$ | The value of the unleveraged firm is the PV of future FCFs discounted at $r_U$, the unleveraged cost of capital. |
| $V_L$ = value of the leveraged firm | $V_L = V_U + PV(\text{net interest tax shields})$ $= V_U + \displaystyle\sum_{t=1}^{N} \frac{[(1 - T_D) - (1 - T_E)(1 - T_C)] * interest_t}{(1 + r_D(1 - T_D))^t}$ Another way to write this is $V_L = V_U + T * D$, where $T = \dfrac{(1 - T_D) - (1 - T_E) * (1 - T_C)}{1 - T_D}$ | The value of the leveraged firm is $V_U$ plus the present value of future interest tax shields. When there are both corporate and personal taxes, the PV of the tax shields is given by $\displaystyle\sum_{t=1}^{N} \frac{[(1 - T_D) - (1 - T_E)(1 - T_C)] * interest_t}{(1 + r_D(1 - T_D))^t}$ |
| | $V_L = V_U + PV(\text{net interest tax shields})$ $= V_U + \displaystyle\sum_{t=1}^{N} \frac{[(1 - T_D) - (1 - T_E)(1 - T_C)] * interest}{(1 + r_D(1 - T_D))^t}$ $= V_U + T * D$, where $T = \dfrac{(1 - T_D) - (1 - T_E)(1 - T_C)}{(1 - T_D)}$ | The cell to the left contains the formula for the value of the leveraged firm when the firm issues perpetual debt. This formula is the same as the parallel formula in Figure 17.2 for the case where $T_E = T_D = 0$. In the general case where personal taxes are perhaps not zero, $T = \dfrac{(1 - T_D) - (1 - T_E)(1 - T_C)}{(1 - T_D)}$ can be positive, negative, or zero. |
| $E$ = value of equity | $E = V_U - (1 - T)D$ | The equity value of the leveraged firm $= E = V_L - D = V_U - (1 - T)D$ |
| $D$ = value of debt | $D$ | |
| $r_E(L)$ = cost of equity of the leveraged firm | $r_E(L) = r_U + [r_U(1 - T) - r_D(1 - T_C)]\dfrac{D}{E}$ | |
| $WACC$ = weighted average cost of capital | $WACC = \dfrac{FCF}{V_L}$ | |

FIGURE 17.5 Corporate value and cost of capital when corporate income is taxed at rate $T_C$, personal ordinary income is taxed at rate $T_D$, and personal equity income is taxed at rate $T_E$.

# 17.8. Buying a Sturfing Machine in Upper Fantasia

In this section and the next we return to the examples of Sections 17.3 and 17.4. This time we do these examples for a company in Upper Fantasia, where, as you will recall, there are three tax rates:

- In Upper Fantasia corporate income is taxed at the rate $T_C = 40\%$.
- Personal income from equity (meaning dividends and capital gains) is taxed at rate $T_E = 10\%$.
- Personal income from all other sources is taxed at rate $T_D = 30\%$.

### Sonderturf Considers Buying a Sturfing Machine

Sonderturf Corp., a company in Upper Fantasia, is considering purchasing a new sturfing machine. The sturfing machine costs $100,000; it has a 10-year life, during which it is straight-line depreciated to zero salvage value. In each of the 10 years of the machine's life, it will pro-duce sales of $40,000. These sales will cost $15,000 to produce. The result is that the machine has an annual FCF of $19,000 per year.

The Sonderturf financial wizards have determined that an appropriate risk-adjusted dis-count rate for the sturfing machine's FCFs is $r_U = 15\%$. Discounting the machine's FCFs at this rate shows that it has a negative NPV of −$4,643. Thus the conclusion is that Sonderturf should not acquire the sturfing machine. (For details of these calculations, refer to Section 17.3, page 521.)

### Sonderturf Gets a Loan to Buy the Machine

Having heard the bad news from Sonderturf, the sturfing machine's manufacturer offers the company a loan of $50,000. The loan's conditions are exactly the same as those of the loan in Section 17.3 that was offered to Sonderturf in Lower Fantasia: In years 1–9, Sonderturf will pay only interest ($4,000), and in year 10 it will pay interest of $4,000 as well as repay the loan principal.

It follows from Figure 17.4 that the value of the loan is

$$PV\begin{pmatrix} \text{loan in Upper Fantasia, where there are corporate income} \\ \text{taxes } T_C, \text{taxes on equity income } T_E, \\ \text{and taxes on ordinary income } T_D \end{pmatrix} =$$

$$PV\left(\text{net interest tax shields}\right) = \sum_{t=1}^{10} \frac{\left[\left(1-T_D\right)-\left(1-T_E\right)\left(1-T_C\right)\right] * Interest_t}{\left(1+r_D\left(1-T_D\right)\right)^t}$$

$$= \sum_{t=1}^{10} \frac{\left[\left(1-30\%\right)-\left(1-10\%\right)\left(1-40\%\right)\right] * \$4,000}{\left(1+r_D\left(1-30\%\right)\right)^t} = \$4,801$$

The Sonderturf financial wizards conclude that the company should now purchase the machine, taking the loan to finance part of the purchase. They calculate that

$$NPV\,(machine + loan) = NPV\,(machine) + NPV\,(loan)$$
$$= NPV\,(machine) + PV\,(\underline{loan\ interest\ tax\ shields}$$

In Upper Fantasia the tax shield
takes account of corporate as well as
personal taxes:

$$\sum_{t=1}^{10} \frac{\left[(1\text{-}T_D)\text{-}(1\text{-}T_E)(1\text{-}T_C)\right]*Interest_t}{\left(1+(1\text{-}T_D)*r_D\right)^t}$$

$$= -\$4{,}643 \qquad + \qquad \$4{,}801$$
$$= \$158$$

The calculations are shown in the following Excel spreadsheet.

| | A | B | C | D | E | F |
|---|---|---|---|---|---|---|
| 1 | | | THE SONDERTURF STURFING MACHINE | | | |
| 2 | $T_C$ corporate tax rate | 40% | | | | |
| 3 | $T_E$ personal tax rate on equity | 10% | | | | |
| 4 | $T_D$ personal tax rate on debt | 30% | | | | |
| 5 | | | | | | |
| 6 | Machine cost, year 0 | 100,000 | | | | |
| 7 | | | | | | |
| 8 | Free cash flow (FCF) calculation | | | | | |
| 9 | Additional sales, annually | 40,000 | | | | |
| 10 | Additional annual cost of sales | 15,000 | | | | |
| 11 | Annual depreciation | 10,000 | <-- =B6/10 | | | |
| 12 | Annual FCF, years 1-10 | 19,000 | <-- =(1-B2)*(B9-B10-B11)+B11 | | | |
| 13 | | | | | | |
| 14 | Discount rate for machine FCFs | 15% | | Loan to buy machine | 50,000 | |
| 15 | | | | $r_D$, loan interest rate | 8% | |
| 16 | | | | Net annual advantage of debt financing, $(1\text{-}T_D)\text{-}(1\text{-}T_E)*(1\text{-}T_C)$ | 16% | <-- =(1-B4)-(1-B3)*(1-B2) |
| 17 | | | | | | |
| 18 | Year | Machine FCF | | | Tax advantage of interest | |
| 19 | 0 | -100,000 | <-- =-B6 | | | |
| 20 | 1 | 19,000 | <-- =$B$12 | | 640 | <-- =$E$16*$E$15*$E$14 |
| 21 | 2 | 19,000 | | | 640 | <-- =$E$16*$E$15*$E$14 |
| 22 | 3 | 19,000 | | | 640 | |
| 23 | 4 | 19,000 | | | 640 | |
| 24 | 5 | 19,000 | | | 640 | |
| 25 | 6 | 19,000 | | | 640 | |
| 26 | 7 | 19,000 | | | 640 | |
| 27 | 8 | 19,000 | | | 640 | |
| 28 | 9 | 19,000 | | | 640 | |
| 29 | 10 | 19,000 | | | 640 | |
| 30 | | | | | | |
| 31 | Machine NPV | -4,643 | <-- =B19+NPV(B14,B20:B29) | Loan NPV | 4,801 | <-- =E19+NPV(E15*(1-B4),E20:E29) |
| 32 | | | | | | |
| 33 | NPV: Machine + Loan | 158 | <-- =B31+E31 | | | |

## In Upper Fantasia Debt Is Not Always Valuable!

The Lower Fantasia tax system—which has only a corporate tax $T_C$ but no other taxes on personal income—*always makes it more valuable to finance with debt.* You can see this from the following formula drawn from Figure 17.2, which holds in Lower Fantasia:

$$V_L^{Lower\ Fantasia} = V_U + PV\,(interest\ tax\ shields) = V_U + \sum_{t=1}^{\infty} \frac{T_C * Interest_t}{\left(1+r_D\right)^t} > V_U.$$

The same formula in Upper Fantasia—with its more complicated (but more realistic) tax system that combines a corporate income tax $T_C$ with a personal tax on equity income $T_E$ and a personal tax on ordinary income $T_D$—is given by

$$V_L^{Upper\ Fantasia} = V_U + PV\,(interest\ tax\ shields) = V_U + \sum_{t=1}^{N} \frac{\left[(1-T_D)-(1-T_E)*(1-T_C)\right]*Interest_t}{\left(1+(1-T_D)r_D\right)^t}$$

The last expression need not always be positive. For example,

$$\sum_{t=1}^{N} \frac{\left[(1-T_D)-(1-T_E)*(1-T_C)\right]*Interest_t}{\left(1+(1-T_D)r_D\right)^t} > 0 \quad if \quad (1-T_D)-(1-T_E)*(1-T_C) > 0$$

$$\sum_{t=1}^{N} \frac{\left[(1-T_D)-(1-T_E)*(1-T_C)\right]*Interest_t}{\left(1+(1-T_D)r_D\right)^t} = 0 \quad if \quad (1-T_D)-(1-T_E)*(1-T_C) = 0$$

$$\sum_{t=1}^{N} \frac{\left[(1-T_D)-(1-T_E)*(1-T_C)\right]*Interest_t}{\left(1+(1-T_D)r_D\right)^t} < 0 \quad if \quad (1-T_D)-(1-T_E)*(1-T_C) < 0$$

The conclusion is that in Upper Fantasia, financing with debt need not make a project more valuable. Suppose, for example, that $T_C = 40\%$, $T_E = 3\%$, and $T_D = 50\%$. Then the spreadsheet below shows that financing the sturfing machine with debt *decreases* the NPV.

| | A | B | C | D | E | F |
|---|---|---|---|---|---|---|
| 1 | | | THE SONDERTURF STURFING MACHINE different taxes make debt disadvantageous! | | | |
| 2 | $T_C$, corporate tax rate | 40% | | | | |
| 3 | $T_E$, personal tax rate on equity | 3% | | | | |
| 4 | $T_D$, personal tax rate on debt | 50% | | | | |
| 5 | | | | | | |
| 6 | Machine cost, year 0 | 100,000 | | | | |
| 7 | | | | | | |
| 8 | Free cash flow (FCF) calculation | | | | | |
| 9 | Additional sales, annually | 40,000 | | | | |
| 10 | Additional annual cost of sales | 15,000 | | | | |
| 11 | Annual depreciation | 10,000 | <-- =B6/10 | | | |
| 12 | Annual FCF, years 1-10 | 19,000 | <-- =(1-B2)*(B9-B10-B11)+B11 | | | |
| 13 | | | | | | |
| 14 | Discount rate for machine FCFs | 15% | | Loan to buy machine | 50,000 | |
| 15 | | | | $r_D$, loan interest rate | 8% | |
| 16 | | | | Net annual advantage of debt financing, $(1-T_D)-(1-T_E)*(1-T_C)$ | -8% | <-- =(1-B4)-(1-B3)*(1-B2) |
| 17 | | | | | | |
| 18 | Year | Machine FCF | | | Tax advantage of interest | |
| 19 | 0 | -100,000 | <-- =-B6 | | | |
| 20 | 1 | 19,000 | <-- =$B$12 | | -328 | <-- =$E$16*$E$15*$E$14 |
| 21 | 2 | 19,000 | | | -328 | <-- =$E$16*$E$15*$E$14 |
| 22 | 3 | 19,000 | | | -328 | |
| 23 | 4 | 19,000 | | | -328 | |
| 24 | 5 | 19,000 | | | -328 | |
| 25 | 6 | 19,000 | | | -328 | |
| 26 | 7 | 19,000 | | | -328 | |
| 27 | 8 | 19,000 | | | -328 | |
| 28 | 9 | 19,000 | | | -328 | |
| 29 | 10 | 19,000 | | | -328 | |
| 30 | | | | | | |
| 31 | Machine NPV | -4,643 | <-- =B19+NPV(B14,B20:B29) | Loan NPV | -2,660 | <-- =E19+NPV(E15*(1-B4),E20:E29) |
| 32 | | | | | | |
| 33 | NPV: Machine + Loan | -7,304 | <-- =B31+E31 | | | |

# 17.9. Relevering Smotfooler, Inc., an Upper Fantasia Company

In Section 17.4 we offered a question from a Finance 101 exam at Eastern Lower Fantasia State University. This section offers a similar question from an exam at Upper Fantasia University (their football team is called the Ufus).

Here's the question: Smotfooler, Inc. is a well-known Upper Fantasia company. Here are some facts about the company:

- Smotfooler expects to have an annual FCF of $2 million at the end of years 1, 2, 3,... forever. Recall that the FCF is the after-tax amount of cash that the company generates from its business activities.

- Smotfooler currently has 100,000 shares outstanding on the Upper Fantasia stock exchange. The Smotfooler share price is $100 per share.
- Smotfooler currently has no debt. However, a financial analyst has suggested that the company issue $3,000,000 of perpetual debt and use the proceeds to repurchase shares. The current interest rate on debt in Upper Fantasia is 8%, and the interest payments on the debt will be made annually.
- Tax rates in Upper Fantasia are $T_C = 40\%$, $T_D = 30\%$, $T_E = 10\%$.

Students on the finance exam were asked to answer the following questions.

***Question 1***: What is the current market value of Smotfooler?

*Answer*: Smotfooler currently has 100,000 shares outstanding, each of which is worth $100. Thus the company's equity value is currently $10,000,000 = $100 * 100,000. Because the company has no debt, this is also its market value. In short, $V_U = \$10,000,000$.

***Question 2***: After Smotfooler issues $3,000,000 of debt, what will be its market value?

*Answer*: Because Upper Fantasia has a corporate income tax and personal income taxes, the relation $V_L = V_U + T\,D$ holds, where

$$T = \frac{(1-T_D)-(1-T_C)*(1-T_E)}{(1-T_D)} = \frac{(1-30\%)-(1-40\%)\,(1-10\%)}{(1-30\%)} = 22.86\%.$$

(See also cell B7 on the following spreadsheet.)

This means that after the company issues its debt, its market value will be

$$V_L = V_U + T\,D = 10,000,000 + 22.86\% * 3,000,000 = 10,685,714.$$

***Question 3***: After Smotfooler issues debt of $3,000,000 and uses the proceeds to repurchase shares, what will be the company's total equity value, $E$?

*Answer*: After Smotfooler issues the debt and repurchases the shares, the total value of its equity, $E$, plus the total value of its debt, $D$, have to sum to the company's total market value $V_L$. In short,

$$V_L = 10,685,714 = E + D$$
But $D = \$3,000,000$, and therefore:
$$E = 10,685,714 - 3,000,000 = 7,685,714$$

***Question 4***: At what price will Smotfooler repurchase its shares?

*Answer*: By issuing $3 million of debt, Smotfooler has raised its total market value by $685,714 (from $10 million to $10,685,714). This increase in value belongs to all the shareholders. Because there are 100,000 shares outstanding before the share repurchase, this means that each share's price increases by $685,714/100,000=$6.86. Thus the answer to this question is that the share price for repurchase is $106.86. Of this amount, $100 is the share price before the repurchase and $6.86 is the increase in the share price as a result of the debt issue.

***Question 5***: How many shares will Smotfooler repurchase?

*Answer*: According to the previous question, Smotfooler will repurchase its shares at $106.86 per share. Because the company has issued $3 million in debt to repurchase the shares, this means that it will repurchase $3,000,000/$106.86=28,074.87.

***Question 6:*** What was Smotfooler's cost of equity before the repurchase of shares?

*Answer:* Smotfooler has an annual FCF of \$2,000,000. Thus its unlevered cost of equity,

$$r_E(U) = r_U = \frac{FCF}{V_U} = \frac{2,000,000}{10,000,000} = 20\%.$$

***Question 7:*** What is Smotfooler's cost of equity after the repurchase of the shares on the open market?

*Answer:* Smotfooler issues \$3 million in 8% debt to repurchase shares. Thus its annual interest bill is 8% * \$3,000,000 = \$240,000. Because interest is an expense for tax purposes, the company's shareholders will have an annual expected cash flow of

$$Annual\ equity\ cash\ flow, after\ debt\ issuance = FCF - (1 - T_C)* interest$$
$$= 2,000,000 - (1 - 40\%)* 240,000$$
$$= 1,856,000$$

The value of the equity after the share repurchase is \$7,685,714, so that the cost of equity of the levered company is

$$r_E(L) = \frac{1,856,000}{7,685,714} = 24.15\%.$$

Note from Figure 17.4. that there's another way to do this calculation:

$$r_E(L) = r_U + \left[r_U(1-T) - r_D(1-T_C)\right]\frac{D}{E} =$$
$$= 20\% + \left[20\%(1-22.86\%) - 8\%(1-40\%)\right]\frac{3,000,000}{7,685,714} = 24.15\%$$

***Question 8:*** What is Smotfooler's WACC before the repurchase of the shares?

*Answer:* Recall the definition of the WACC:

$$WACC = r_E(L)*\frac{E}{E+D} + r_D*(1-T_C)*\frac{D}{E+D}.$$

The answer to Question 8 is easy: Because Smotfooler, before the share repurchase, has only equity, its WACC = $r_U$ = 20%.

***Question 9:*** What is Smotfooler's WACC after the repurchase of the shares?

*Answer:*

$$WACC = r_E(L)*\frac{E}{E+D} + r_D*(1-T_C)*\frac{D}{E+D}$$
$$= 24.15\% * \frac{7,685,714}{7,685,714 + 3,000,000} + 8\% * (1-40\%)\frac{3,000,000}{7,685,714 + 3,000,000} = 18.72\%$$

***Question 10***: Why is $r_E(L) > r_U$?

*Answer*: Before Smotfooler issued its bonds, the only risk borne by shareholders was the *business risk* inherent in the company's FCF. After the company issues its bonds, shareholders have to bear two kinds of risk: business risk *and* financial risk. Thus $r_E(L)$ represents a discount rate for cash flows that are riskier than the discount rate for the FCFs, $r_U$. Because riskier cash flows have higher discount rates, it follows that $r_E(L) > r_U$.

***Question 11***: Why does the market value of Smotfooler increase after the issuance of the debt and repurchase of the equity?

*Answer*: By issuing the debt, Smotfooler increases the amount of cash it produces by $\left[(1-T_D)-(1-T_C)*(1-T_E)\right] * Interest\ payment$ for 3every year in which it has debt. This additional cash flow is riskless. Because the holders of riskless cash flows in Upper Fantasia use a discount rate of $(1-T_D)*r_D$ to value the cash flows, it follows that

$$Value\ of\ additional\ debt\text{-}related\ cash\ flows = \sum_{t=1}^{\infty} \frac{\left[(1-T_D)-(1-T_C)*(1-T_E)\right] * Interest\ payment}{\left(1+(1-T_D)r_D\right)^t}$$

$$= \frac{(1-T_D)-(1-T_C)*(1-T_E)}{(1-T_D)r_D} Interest\ payment$$

$$= \frac{(1-T_D)-(1-T_C)*(1-T_E)}{(1-T_D)r_D} * r_D D = \underset{\underset{T=\ \frac{(1-T_D)-(1-T_C)*(1-T_E)}{(1-T_D)}}{\uparrow}}{T} * D$$

The PV of the tax shield accounts for the increase in Smotfooler's market value:

$$V_L = \underset{\underset{\substack{\text{Smotfooler's value}\\\text{before the debt}\\\text{issuance}}}{\uparrow}}{V_U} + \underset{\underset{\substack{\text{The PV of}\\\text{additional}\\\text{debt-related}\\\text{cash flows}}}{\uparrow}}{TD} .$$

***Question 12***: Does debt always increase corporate value in Upper Fantasia?

*Answer*: No. It depends on the sizes of the three tax rates $T_C$, $T_D$, and $T_E$. In the following example, there is a net *tax disadvantage* to debt—by issuing debt, Smotfooler *lowers* its market value and *raises* its WACC.

| | A | B | C |
|---|---|---|---|
| 1 | **SMOTFOOLER—DEBT ISSUED TO REPURCHASE SHARES**<br>**Smotfooler is located in Upper Fantasia** | | |
| 2 | **Upper Fantasia tax system** | | |
| 3 | $T_C$, Upper Fantasia corporate tax rate | 40% | |
| 4 | $T_E$, Upper Fantasia personal tax rate on equity income | 10% | |
| 5 | $T_D$, Upper Fantasia personal tax rate on ordinary income | 30% | |
| 6 | Annual debt advantage: $(1-T_D)-(1-T_E)^*(1-T_C)$ | 16% | <-- =(1-B5)-(1-B4)*(1-B3) |
| 7 | PV of debt advantage: $T = [(1-T_D)-(1-T_E)^*(1-T_C)]/(1-T_D)$ | 22.86% | <-- =B6/(1-B5) |
| 8 | | | |
| 9 | **Unlevered company** | | |
| 10 | Annual free cash flow (FCF) | $2,000,000 | |
| 11 | Number of shares | 100,000 | |
| 12 | Price per share | $100 | |
| 13 | Total equity value | $10,000,000 | <-- =B12*B11 |
| 14 | | | |
| 15 | Question1: $V_U$, unlevered value of Smotfooler | $10,000,000 | <-- =B13 |
| 16 | | | |
| 17 | **Levered company** | | |
| 18 | Debt issued | $3,000,000 | |
| 19 | Interest rate on debt | 8% | |
| 20 | Question 2: $V_L$, levered value of Smotfooler, $V_L = V_U + T^*D$ | $10,685,714 | <-- =B15+B7*B18 |
| 21 | Question 3: Equity value after share repurchase, $E = V_L - D$ | $7,685,714 | |
| 22 | Incremental firm value from exchanging<br>equity by debt = $V_L - V_U = T^*D$ | $685,714 | <-- =B20-B15 |
| 23 | Incremental firm value on a per-share basis | $7 | <-- =B22/B11 |
| 24 | Question 4: New share value, after repurchase | $106.86 | <-- =B12+B23 |
| 25 | | | |
| 26 | Question 5: Number of shares repurchased =<br>[debt used for repurchase]/[new share value] | 28,074.87 | <-- =B18/B24 |
| 27 | Number of shares remaining after<br>repurchase = original number of shares<br>minus number of shares repurchased | 71,925.13 | <-- =B11-B26 |
| 28 | **Check:** Market value of remaining shares =<br>number of remaining shares * new share value | $7,685,714 | <-- =B27*B24 |
| 29 | | | |
| 30 | Question 6: Smotfooler's cost of equity when unlevered,<br>$r_U = FCF/V_U$ | 20.00% | |
| 31 | | | |
| 32 | Annual interest costs, before taxes | $240,000 | <-- =B18*B19 |
| 33 | Annual equity cash flow, after interest = FCF - $(1-T_C)^*$interest | $1,856,000 | <-- =B10-(1-B3)*B32 |
| 34 | Question 7: Smotfooler's cost of equity when levered,<br>$r_E(L)=[FCF-(1-T_C)^*interest]/[value of equity, E]$ | 24.15% | <-- =B33/B28 |
| 35 | Note: See formula in row 44 below for another<br>way to compute the levered cost of equity | | |
| 36 | | | |
| 37 | Question 8: Smotfooler's WACC before the debt issuance = rU | 20.00% | |
| 38 | | | |
| 39 | Question 9: Smotfooler's WACC after the debt issuance<br>$= r_E(L)^*E/(E+D)+r_D^*(1-TC)^*D/(E+D)$ | | |
| 40 | Percentage of equity in Smotfooler = $E/(E+D)$ | 71.93% | <-- =B28/B20 |
| 41 | Percentage of debt in Smotfooler = $D/(E+D)$ | 28.07% | <-- =B18/B20 |
| 42 | WACC = $r_E(L)^*E/(E+D)+r_D^*(1-T_C)^*D/(E+D)$ | 18.72% | <-- =B34*B40+B19*(1-B3)*B41 |
| 43 | | | |
| 44 | Additional formula: $r_E(L)=r_U+[r_U^*(1-T)-r_D^*(1-T_C)]^*D/E$ | 24.15% | <-- =B30+(B30*(1-B7)-B19*(1-B3))*B18/B21 |

## 17.10. Is There Really an Advantage to Debt?

In this chapter we've laid out the theory of capital structure. We can answer the question of the importance of capital structure in several ways.

### Method 1: What are the relevant tax rates $T_C$, $T_D$, and $T_E$?

As you can see, the value of XYZ Corp. is critically dependent on two factors:

- $r_U$, the risk-adjusted rate of return for the FCFs. This rate is unaffected by the capital structure, because the FCFs are operating cash flows and do not depend on the financing of the firm.

- $(1-T_D)-(1-T_C)(1-T_E)$—the relative after-tax costs of debt versus equity income.

Looking at this second parameter, we examine several cases. In the case below, the anticipated dividend yield of 2% is taxed at 40%, whereas the anticipated capital gains yield of 6% is taxed at 10%. The equity tax rate is 17.5%, and the net tax advantage of debt over equity is 8.02%:

| | A | B | C |
|---|---|---|---|
| 1 | **WHAT ARE THE RELATIVE TAX EFFECTS** | | |
| 2 | Corporate tax rate, $T_C$ | 37% | |
| 3 | | | |
| 4 | Anticipated equity tax | | **Tax rate** |
| 5 | Dividend yield | 2.00% | 40% |
| 6 | Capital gains yield | 6.00% | 10% |
| 7 | | | |
| 8 | Net after-tax yield | 6.60% | <-- =B5*(1-C5)+B6*(1-C6) |
| 9 | Before tax yield | 8.00% | <-- =B5+B6 |
| 10 | | | |
| 11 | Personal tax rate on equity income, $T_E$ | 17.50% | <-- =1-B8/B9 |
| 12 | Personal tax rate on ordinary income, $T_D$ | 40.00% | |
| 13 | | | |
| 14 | Tax advantage of debt over equity:  $(1-T_D)-(1-T_C)*(1-T_E)$ | 8.02% | <-- =(1-B12)-(1-B2)*(1-B11) |

With a somewhat different yield and tax configuration there is actually a net tax *disadvantage* to debt.

| | A | B | C |
|---|---|---|---|
| 1 | **WHAT ARE THE RELATIVE TAX EFFECTS** | | |
| 2 | Corporate tax rate, $T_C$ | 37% | |
| 3 | | | |
| 4 | Anticipated equity tax | | **Tax rate** |
| 5 | Dividend yield | 0.00% | 40% |
| 6 | Capital gains yield | 6.00% | 0% |
| 7 | | | |
| 8 | Net after-tax yield | 6.00% | <-- =B5*(1-C5)+B6*(1-C6) |
| 9 | Before tax yield | 6.00% | <-- =B5+B6 |
| 10 | | | |
| 11 | Personal tax rate on equity income, $T_E$ | 0.00% | <-- =1-B8/B9 |
| 12 | Personal tax rate on ordinary income, $T_D$ | 40.00% | |
| 13 | | | |
| 14 | Tax advantage of debt over equity:  $(1-T_D)-(1-T_C)*(1-T_E)$ | -3.00% | <-- =(1-B12)-(1-B2)*(1-B11) |

| | A | B | C |
|---|---|---|---|
| 1 | **WHAT ARE THE RELATIVE TAX EFFECTS** | | |
| 2 | Corporate tax rate, $T_C$ | 37% | |
| 3 | | | |
| 4 | Anticipated equity tax | | **Tax rate** |
| 5 | Dividend yield | 5.00% | 0% |
| 6 | Capital gains yield | 0.00% | 0% |
| 7 | | | |
| 8 | Net after-tax yield | 5.00% | <-- =B5*(1-C5)+B6*(1-C6) |
| 9 | Before tax yield | 5.00% | <-- =B5+B6 |
| 10 | | | |
| 11 | Personal tax rate on equity income, $T_E$ | 0.00% | <-- =1-B8/B9 |
| 12 | Personal tax rate on ordinary income, $T_D$ | 0.00% | |
| 13 | | | |
| 14 | Tax advantage of debt over equity: $(1-T_D)-(1-T_C)*(1-T_E)$ | 37.00% | <-- =(1-B12)-(1-B2)*(1-B11) |

Below you will see a third case in which only corporate income is taxed. In this case there is an overwhelming advantage to debt financing.

## Method 2: What's the Evidence in Firm Behavior?

Instead of asking whether tax rates support a net tax advantage, we can also look at different firms. We can ask whether in a particular industry there is a consistent behavior toward debt. The answer is no, as you will see in Chapter 18. We interpret this "inconsistent" behavior as evidence in favor of the argument that there is no net tax advantage to debt—that is, that firm financial policy does not affect its market value.

## Method 3: What Does Sophisticated Finance Research Say?

Chapter 18 looks at the latest academic research on the capital structure question. Our reading of this research is that the importance of debt over equity financing has been heavily overemphasized in finance textbooks. There may be a small advantage of debt over equity, but it is overwhelmed by the overall uncertainty of valuing a firm.

# Summary and Conclusion—United Widgets Corp.

United Widgets is a new company set up by John and Cindy, who are pondering the effect of the equity-to-debt financing mix. The question they have in mind is does it matter whether the company is financed with share capital (equity) or with money borrowed from a bank (debt)? The risk–return trade-off between the two financing alternatives is complex:

- The providers of equity financing are promised a share of the firm's profits (if there are any). If there are no profits, then shareholders will not get any dividends; although they will surely be disappointed, they cannot use the nonpayment of dividends to force the firm into bankruptcy.

- The providers of debt financing are promised a series of fixed payments. If United Widgets cannot keep the commitment of making the fixed payments, then the company may become insolvent. Bankruptcy will affect the shareholders of the company, denying them their share in United Widgets.

- Debt financing is generally cheaper than equity financing: The riskiness of the interest payments promised by United Widgets to its lenders is less than the riskiness of the dividend payments promised by the company to its shareholders. In addition, interest is a tax-deductible expense for United Widgets, whereas dividends have to be paid out of after-tax income. Shareholders, being at greater risk than lenders, will therefore demand a *higher expected return* than debtholders. The relative cheapness of debt versus equity appears to make debt preferable as a financing mechanism. But:

- Debt financing makes equity financing even more risky. The risky dividend stream that comes from the company is endangered even further when shareholders promise debtholders a series of future payments. The higher the amount of debt the firm has, the more risky the equity financing becomes.[10]

Realizing all these factors, John and Cindy ask themselves the following questions:

- Does the debt-to-equity mix affect the amount of cash that can be extracted from United Widgets?

- Does the mix of equity and debt affect the discount rate that United Widgets should use for discounting project cash flows? As we have seen in Chapters 6, 14, and 16, the relevant discount rate is the weighted average cost of capital (WACC).

- Does the debt-to-equity mix affect the cost of equity?

The next pages give schematic answers to these questions.

Chapter 18 explores some empirical results and tries to give you a "take" on how to apply the theoretical answers developed in this chapter.

---

[10] John and Cindy briefly considered financing their firm with *only debt*. But this is impossible!

# Financing United Widgets—Capital Structure and Its Effects on Cost of Capital and Firm Valuation

## UNITED WIDGETS

John and Cindy set up a new company—United Widgets, Inc. They decide to buy a widget machine because financial analysis shows that the NPV of the machine's cash flows is positive.

United Widgets is financed with equity (meaning money put up by John and Cindy and their friends) and debt (money borrowed from the bank).

Does the debt–equity financing mix change the discount rate used to evaluate widget machines?

Does the debt–equity financing mix change the *total cash* extracted from the company?

## EFFECT OF DEBT/EQUITY MIX ON WEIGHTED AVERAGE COST OF CAPITAL (WACC)

1. If there are no taxes, the debt–equity mix does not affect the widget machine discount rate.

2. If there are only corporate taxes and no personal taxes, then more debt means that the widget discount rate decreases.

3. If both personal and corporate incomes are taxed, widget machine discount rates can increase/decrease/stay the same when the debt–equity mix changes.

## EFFECT OF DEBT/EQUITY MIX ON TOTAL CASH EXTRACTED FROM COMPANY

1. If there are no taxes, the debt–equity mix does not affect the total amount of cash extracted from the company.

2. If there are only corporate taxes and no personal taxes, then more debt means more cash extracted from the company; happens because the tax system subsidizes debt (interest is an expense for tax purposes).

3. If both personal and corporate incomes are taxed, the cash extracted from the company can go up or down: Companies enjoy a tax subsidy on their interest payments (since interest is an expense for tax purposes). But shareholders pay lower taxes on earnings from equity (because of an advantageous capital gains tax) than on interest earnings from debt.

# EFFECT OF DEBT/EQUITY MIX ON COST OF EQUITY AND WACC

More debt in the debt–equity mix *always* makes equity riskier! The equity owners have to pay debtholders before they pay themselves and this increases their risk.

The effect of capital structure on WACC depends on the mix of corporate and personal taxes:

1. If there are no taxes, WACC is unaffected by capital structure: the increase in the cost of equity as the debt–equity mix increases exactly offsets the savings of cheaper debt.

2. If there are only corporate taxes, WACC decreases when more debt is used to finance the firm.

3. If there are both corporate and personal taxes, WACC can increase/decrease/stay the same. Empirical evidence (Chapter 18) seems to indicate that it doesn't change much.

$$WACC = r_E(L)\frac{E}{E+D} + r_D(1 - T_C)\frac{D}{E+D}$$

where:

$r_E(L)$ = cost of equity (increase when debt–equity ratio ↑)

$r_D$ = cost of debt

$E$ = market value of firms equity

$D$ = market value of firms debt

$T_C$ = corporate tax rate

FIGURE 17.6  Summarizing the effects of capital structure on the cost of capital and valuation.

## EXERCISES

1. Go back to the supermarket example from the beginning of the chapter. Assume that the supermarket after-tax operating income is $120,000 each year. If Mortimer's group took a $500,000 loan at a 9% annual interest rate and its tax rate is 30%, what will be the return on equity (ROE) for Mortimer's group and Joanne's group, $\left( ROE = \dfrac{Profit\ after\ tax}{Equity} \right)$?

| Mortimer's Supermarket Group Half equity (50%) and half debt (50%) | | | |
|---|---|---|---|
| Supermarket | $1,000,000 | Debt | $500,000 |
| | | Equity | $500,000 |
| Total assets | $1,000,000 | Total debt and equity | $1,000,000 |

| Joanna's Supermarket Group Only equity (100%) | | | |
|---|---|---|---|
| Supermarket | $1,000,000 | Debt | $0 |
| | | Equity | $1,000,000 |
| Total assets | $1,000,000 | Total debt and equity | $1,000,000 |

2.
   a. Repeat Exercise 1 with the following balance sheets (assume that the debt still bears a 9% interest rate).
   b. Show in a **Data Table** and an Excel chart the sensitivity of the ROE to the equity-to-debt ratio.

| Half equity (50%) and half debt (50%) | | | |
|---|---|---|---|
| Supermarket | $1,200,000 | Debt | $600,000 |
| | | Equity | $600,000 |
| Total assets | $1,200,000 | Total debt and equity | $1,200,000 |

| Joanna's Supermarket Group Only equity (100%) | | | |
|---|---|---|---|
| Supermarket | $1,000,000 | Debt | $0 |
| | | Equity | $1,000,000 |
| Total assets | $1,000,000 | Total debt and equity | $1,000,000 |

3. You are interested in buying a warehouse for your firm. The warehouse costs $350,000 and using it will save the firm $50,000 annually forever. The firm can borrow any amount of money at an 8% annual interest rate; all money borrowed is "perpetual debt"—meaning that the firm pays only the annual interest payment and never returns the debt principal. The firm's tax rate is 40%.

   What will be the firm's additional annual income and its return on equity (ROE) on the investment in the following four cases?

   a. The firm finances the purchase with equity only.
   b. The firm finances the purchase with 75% equity and 25% debt.
   c. The firm finances the purchase with 50% equity and 50% debt.
   d. The firm finances the purchase with 20% equity and 80% debt.

4.
   a. Repeat Exercise 3 and show the total annual amounts received by the firm's shareholders and debt holders.
   b. Show in a **Data Table** and an Excel chart the change in the total amount received by the firm's shareholders and debtholders as a function of the equity invested in the project.

5. Eddy is the sole owner of his firm. He now wishes to purchase the company next door for $600,000. His calculations show that the annual income before tax from the purchase is $80,000.

   He is considering two financing alternatives: The first is to ask for a personal loan of $300,000 and pay the remaining amount from his savings. The second alternative is to finance the purchase by having his firm take the $300,000 loan. Assuming the interest rate on the loan is 9% (for infinite duration) and the corporate tax rate is 40%, what will be the total amount received by the firm's shareholders and debtholders in each scenario, assuming that only the interest paid by Eddy's firm is an expense for tax purposes?

6. Returning to the previous exercise, what is the value of the firm Eddy wishes to buy under the two financing alternatives?

7. Annie owns a "shell firm"—a firm that is incorporated but has no activity whatsoever. Annie's shell firm is about to buy another firm for $900,000. The firm she is purchasing has an annual free cash flow (FCF) of $120,000 each year.

   a. Annie's bank is willing to give her a perpetual loan equal to half of the purchase amount at 8% interest. Assuming Annie's firm has no debt and its tax rate is $T_C = 30\%$, what will be her firm's value after the purchase in the following scenarios?

      • In case it will finance the purchase with equity only.

      • In case it takes the loan.

   b. What will be the firm's value in case the loan is repaid in 20 equal repayments?

8. Section 17.3 gives two formulas for the cost of equity $r_E(L)$ of a levered firm for the case when there are only corporate taxes:

$$r_E(L) = \frac{Annual\ equity\ cash\ flow}{Value\ of\ equity}$$

$$r_E(L) = r_U + [r_U - r_D]\frac{D}{E}(1 - T_C)$$

   Use both of these formulas to find the cost of equity $r_E(L)$ for the following cases:

   a. The cost of equity $r_E(L)$ for the firm Eddy is buying in Exercise 5.

   b. The cost of equity $r_E(L)$ of Amadeus Supermarket in Exercise 1.

   c. The cost of Equity $r_E(L)$ of Annie's firm from Exercise 7.

9. Section 17.3 gives two formulas for the weighted average cost of capital (WACC) of a levered firm for the case when there are only corporate taxes:

$$WACC = r_E(L)\frac{E}{E + D} + r_D(1 - T_C)\frac{D}{E + D}$$

$$WACC = \frac{FCF}{V_L}$$

   Use both of these formulas to find the WACC for the following cases:

   a. The WACC for the firm Eddy is buying in Exercise 5.

   b. The WACC of Amadeus Supermarket in Exercise 1.

   c. The WACC of Annie's firm from Exercise 7.

10. Sandy-Candy, a hot new chewing gum company, is for sale for $2,000,000. Henry is interested in buying the company and is exploring various financing alternatives. He knows that the interest rate on debt is $r_D = 9\%$, the corporate tax rate is $T_C = 36\%$, and the cost of capital of the purchase is $r_U = 12\%$. Henry estimates that Sandy-Candy has a free cash flow (FCF) of $300,000 each year.

   a. What will be the market value of Sandy-Candy if Henry does not take a loan?

b. What will be the market value of Sandy-Candy if Henry takes a $1,200,000 loan? Assume that the loan is paid for out of Sandy-Candy's earnings and that the interest is an expense for tax purposes.

c. What will be Sandy-Candy's cost of equity $r_E$ for the two cases above?

d. What will be Sandy-Candy's WACC for the two cases above?

11. Debby, the owner of Oxford Corp., has decided that it's time to make some changes to the firm's capital structure. She estimates that Oxford's FCF is $150,000 each year and that this FCF can be expected to recur annually forever. The company has no debt and 30,000 shares outstanding, each of which is currently worth $50.

Debby wants Oxford to borrow $600,000 of perpetual debt and use the proceeds to repurchase shares. Assuming the interest rate on debt is $r_D = 6\%$ and the corporate tax rate is $T_C = 30\%$, calculate the following changes.

a. What is Oxford's market value before it issued debt?

b. What is Oxford's market value after it issued debt?

c. What will be Oxford share price after the debt issuance?

d. How many shares will be repurchased?

e. What is Oxford's equity value after the repurchase of the shares?

f. What is Oxford's cost of equity after the repurchase and dividend payment?

g. What is Oxford's WACC after the repurchase and dividend payment?

12. XYZ Corp. is about to borrow $100,000. The terms of the loan specify an annual equal repayment of principal in each of the next 8 years. The loan rate is $r_D = 8\%$, and XYZ has a corporate tax rate of $T_C = 40\%$. If the loan interest is an expense for tax purposes for XYZ and if there are no other taxes besides corporate taxes, what will be the increase in XYZ's market value?

13. Go back to the exercise of buying the turfing machine (Section 17.3). Repeat the exercise assuming the loan is repaid in 10 equal payments. What is the NPV of the investment now?

14.

a. According to a recent tax reform in Lower Fantasia, the personal tax rate on all ordinary income except capital gains from stocks was changed from 0 to 25%. Capital gains will henceforth be taxed at 15%. The Lower Fantasia corporate tax rate remains unchanged at 40%. Assuming you plan to take a loan, what will be better—to borrow using your firm or take a personal loan? Show the net advantage of corporate debt in this case.

b. Will your answer to Exercise 14a change if the corporate tax rate becomes 20%?

15.

a. Eddy, from Exercise 5, needs your help again. He didn't purchase the firm because the bank didn't approved him the loan, but now his dad is willing to step in and help him by loaning him the same amount ($300,000). In addition, after the recent elections he's now facing a personal tax rate of 40% (equal to the corporate tax rate) and a 15% tax on equity income. What should he do—finance the purchase using a firm or take a personal loan? Calculate the total amount received by the stakeholders (shareholders and debtholders).

b. Assuming Eddy purchases the firm next door using his own firm, calculate the value of the firm, his cost of equity, and the WACC (assume his unlevered discount rate is 12%).

16. Assume that the corporate tax rate is $T_C = 30\%$ and the equity income tax rate is $T_E = 10\%$. What is the ordinary income tax rate $T_D$ for which an investor will be indifferent between choosing a personal loan or a loan using a firm?

17.

a. Repeat Exercise 11 (Oxford Corp.) assuming the ordinary income tax rate is $T_D = 34\%$ and the personal equity tax rate is $T_E = 15\%$.

b. For this case calculate the "net advantage of corporate debt" and calculate the expression

$$T = \frac{(1-T_D)-(1-T_E)(1-T_C)}{(1-T_D)}.$$

18. You are interested in buying a machine that will produce sales of $50,000 in each of the next 6 years. The machine costs $120,000 and has a 6-year life. It is straight-line depreciated to a zero salvage value. In addition, the machine activity costs $18,000 annually. The discount rate you decided to use for the machine's FCF is 12%.

    You are considering taking a 9%, 6-year loan to finance the purchase of the machine. The loan amount will be $70,000. The loan terms specify annual payments of interest only in years 1–5 and the repayment of the whole principal in year 6. Assuming that the corporate tax rate is $T_C = 40\%$, the personal tax rate (on ordinary income) is $T_D = 22\%$, and the equity tax rate is $T_E = 15\%$, answer the following questions.

    a. What is the machine FCF?
    b. What is the NPV of the machine if it is financed with equity only?
    b. Calculate the "net advantage of corporate debt," $T$.
    c. What is the NPV of the machine if it is financed with a mix of equity and debt?

19.

    a. Fill in the following Excel sheet.

| | A | B | C |
|---|---|---|---|
| 1 | FILL IN THE TAX EFFECTS | | |
| 2 | Corporate tax rate, $T_C$ | 36% | |
| 3 | | | |
| 4 | Anticipated equity tax | | Tax rate |
| 5 | Dividend yield | 2.50% | 40% |
| 6 | Capital gains yield | 5.00% | 10% |
| 7 | | | |
| 8 | Net after-tax yield | ?? | |
| 9 | Before tax yield | ?? | |
| 10 | | | |
| 11 | Personal tax rate on equity income, $T_E$ | ?? | |
| 12 | Personal tax rate on ordinary income, $T_D$ | ?? | |
| 13 | | | |
| 14 | Tax advantage of debt over equity: $(1-T_D)-(1-T_C)*(1-T_E)$ | ?? | |

    b. Show in a graph the change in "net advantage of corporate debt" as a function of the personal tax rate.

# 18 The Evidence on Capital Structure

## CHAPTER CONTENTS

## Overview

In this chapter we discuss whether the capital structure of a company—with what mix of equity and debt it finances itself—affects the company's weighted average cost of capital (WACC). Chapter 17 discussed the theory of capital structure, which concerns itself with the effects of financing on the valuation of assets. Capital structure theory asks whether firms that are more highly leveraged are worth more than firms with less leverage, all other factors being the same.

In Chapter 17 we suggested that the importance of capital structure depends on how it affects the ability of the corporation to extract cash from its operating and its financial activities. If, by increasing its leverage, a corporation can increase the total amount of cash it pays to its shareholders and bondholders, then it should do so. If, on the other hand, increasing leverage does not change the amount of cash paid to shareholders and bondholders, then increased leverage is not worthwhile.

In Chapter 17 we related the corporate ability to extract cash from a corporation's activities to the trade-off between personal and corporate taxation: Corporate borrowing is tax deductible (because interest is an expense for tax purposes); this tends to favor corporations with more rather than less debt in their capital structures. On the other hand, a corporation with more debt in its capital structure channels more of its income to bondholders rather than to shareholders, and bondholders have a higher tax rate on their interest income than do shareholders on their equity income.

To see why the Chapter 17 discussion of leverage is important, suppose for a moment that firms with more debt are worth more than similar but less-levered firms. Then we would suggest the following steps to corporate managers:

- Corporate managers should strive to increase the amount of debt used in financing corporate activities. If, for example, a firm builds a new plant, then it should try to borrow the maximum amount it can to build the plant.

- Corporate managers should minimize the amount of cash they have on hand (subject, of course, to operational and safety considerations). If leverage (that is, paying interest on debt) adds to value, then holding cash (that is, having an asset that earns interest) is a detriment to value.

- Corporate managers should increase the corporate dividend payments. By paying out dividends, managers decrease the amount of cash on hand and thus increase the effective leverage of the firm.

- For the same reason, corporate managers should increase share repurchases, which decrease the amount of cash on hand and thus increase effective leverage.

The bullets above tell a manager how she should operate if leverage is a positive value driver. If, on the other hand, leverage is a negative value driver—meaning that more leverage decreases corporate value—then the manager should take the opposite actions. And if—as we suggested at the end of Chapter 17—leverage is a neutral value drive because the tax benefits of corporate leverage are offset by the tax disadvantages of leverage at the personal taxation level, then none of the above matters.

As you can see, leverage theory can have significant operative implications.

## WHAT'S THE CONCLUSION?

To anticipate the conclusions of this chapter, we see no evidence that leverage adds value to a firm. Nor do we find significant evidence that a firm's weighted average cost of capital (WACC) is affected by its financing mix of debt versus equity. The operative conclusions are as follows:

- Firms should proceed as if the financing mix of their assets cannot add or subtract value.

- The WACC is unaffected by leverage.

- The best way to measure the WACC is by taking the *average WACC* of a firm's industry.

## What Do We Do in This Chapter?

Chapter 17 was largely theoretical. In this chapter, on the other hand, we discuss the market evidence on capital structure. We ask whether we see—in market prices, cost of capital, and market risk measures—evidence for or against the positive effects of more debt on the value of firms. In Section 18.1 we summarize the results of Chapter 17. The upshot of these results is that the effects of financing on valuation depend largely on the tax system. Roughly speaking, if firms, by borrowing, can increase the total cash flow available to shareholders and bondholders, then the firms should move toward a more leveraged capital structure.

The remaining sections of the chapter present some empirical evidence of the effects of capital structure on the cost of capital. As you will see, the evidence seems to indicate that there is little significant effect of capital structure on the WACC.

### Finance Concepts Discussed

- What are some facts about capital structure (how do firms capitalize)?
- Does capital structure affect the value of the firm?
- Does capital structure affect the cost of capital?
- Are there other important considerations, such as bankruptcy costs or control?
- How do you measure the firm's unlevered cost of capital $r_U$?
- How do you compute the WACC for an *industry*?

### Excel Functions Used

- **Average**
- **Stdev**
- **Regression (trendline)**

# 18.1. Summarizing the Theory

The theory of capital structure outlined in the previous chapter says that the effect of capital structure on the value of the firm is primarily caused by tax considerations. Very roughly speaking, if firms enjoy interest tax deductibility that is unavailable to their shareholders, then firms should borrow and increase their debt-to-equity ratios. This theory—the Modigliani–Miller theory (Chapter 17, Sections 17.3–17.5)—should be contrasted with the Miller model (Chapter 17, Sections 17.6–17.9), which postulates that the advantage of corporate debt is to some extent offset by the tax advantage of equity to investors.

These are complex concepts that we illustrated with two examples (Arthur ABC and Arthur XYX) in the previous chapter. We sum up the conclusions of Chapter 17.

1. Leverage adds value to a firm if the *capitalized value of the interest tax shields* is positive:

$$V_L = V_U + PV\left(Capitalized\ interest\ tax\ shields\right)$$

$$= PV\left(FCFs, discounted\ at\ r_U\right) + \sum_{t=1}^{\infty} \frac{\left[\left(1-T_D\right)-\left(1-T_E\right)*\left(1-T_C\right)\right]*Interest_t}{1+\left(1-T_D\right)r_D}$$

Here,

$$FCF = the\ firm's\ free\ cash\ flows$$
$$r_U = the\ firm's\ unlevered\ cost\ of\ equity$$
$$r_D = the\ firm's\ cost\ of\ debt$$
$$T_C = the\ corporate\ tax\ rate$$
$$T_E = the\ personal\ tax\ rate\ on\ equity\ income$$
$$T_D = the\ personal\ tax\ rate\ on\ ordinary\ income\ (including\ interest)$$

2. Assuming that a firm is contemplating a permanent change $\Delta Debt$ in its capital structure, the value of the additional tax shields produced by the debt are given by the equation

$$
\begin{aligned}
PV\ (Capitalized\ interest\ tax\ shields) &= \sum_{t=1}^{\infty} \frac{\left[(1-T_D)-(1-T_E)*(1-T_C)\right]* Interest}{1+(1-T_D)r_D} \\
&= \frac{\left[(1-T_D)-(1-T_E)*(1-T_C)\right]* r_D * \Delta Debt}{(1-T_D)r_D} \\
&= \frac{\left[(1-T_D)-(1-T_E)*(1-T_C)\right]* \Delta Debt}{(1-T_D)} = T * \Delta Debt
\end{aligned}
$$

$$where\ T = \frac{\left[(1-T_D)-(1-T_E)*(1-T_C)\right]}{(1-T_D)}$$

3. In the classic Modigliani–Miller theory, which invokes only corporate taxes, $T = T_C$, so that debt always adds to value. In Miller's more complex model, which takes into account both personal and corporate taxes, $T$ can be positive, negative, or zero, depending on the sign of $(1-T_D)-(1-T_E)(1-T_C)$. Miller hypothesized that $(1-T_D)-(1-T_E)(1-T_C)=0$; if this is so, then there would be no advantage to debt over equity financing.

4. Leverage affects both the WACC and the cost of equity $r_E$. In the table below we give some formulas for the WACC, the cost of equity $r_E$, and the cost of capital of an unlevered firm $r_U$:

| Weighted average cost of capital | $WACC = \dfrac{E + D*(1-T)}{E+D} * r_U$ | If debt adds value (i.e., $T > 0$), leverage decreases the WACC |
|---|---|---|
| Cost of equity of a levered firm, $r_E$ | $r_E = r_U + \left[r_U*(1-T)-r_D*(1-T_C)\right]\dfrac{D}{E}$ | More debt *always* makes equity more risky and increases the cost of equity $r_E$. The amount by which the equity becomes more risky depends on the relative sizes of $T$ and $T_C$. |
| Cost of unlevered capital, $r_U$ | $r_U = \dfrac{r_D*D*(1-T_C)+r_E*E}{E+D*(1-T)}$ | Often we estimate a firm's cost of equity $r_E$; this formula lets you back out what would be the cost of capital $r_U$ of the firm if it had no leverage. |

5. Contrary to the formula in Conclusion 2 above, the value of debt interest tax shields is not the only factor in determining the effect on firm value of a change in debt. Three other prominent factors discussed by academics and practitioners are bankruptcy costs, the costs of financial control (change name), and the option effects associated with debt. These costs are difficult to quantify, but they certainly exist:

   a. Costs of financial distress ("bankruptcy costs"): Increasing a firm's leverage also makes it more likely that a firm will have a greater future probability of getting into financial trouble. The present value of the costs of getting out of this trouble (they should be called "costs of financial distress," but they are usually call termed bankruptcy costs) should be deducted from the benefits of additional leverage.[1]

   b. Costs of financial control. Borrowers will usually lend the firm more money only if they can exercise more control. Often this control involves debt covenants. These are restrictions imposed by the lender on the firm. For example, the Giant Industries bond issue discussed in Section 15.4 (page 466) has the following covenants:

   "The Indentures . . . contain restrictive covenants that, among other things, restrict the ability of the Company and its subsidiaries to create liens, to incur or guarantee debt, to pay dividends, to repurchase shares of the Company's common stock, to sell certain assets or subsidiary stock, to engage in certain mergers, to engage in certain transactions with affiliates or to alter the Company's current line of business."

   c. Option effects of debt: The shareholders in a heavily indebted firm have less to lose than those in a low-leverage firm. They may thus feel free to take more risks. Increased leverage may thus affect the riskiness of the firm's free cash flow (FCF). As an example, Bob and Jerry each own a similar building; the market value of each of their buildings is $100,000. The buildings are in need of a very expensive repair. Bob owns his building outright, whereas Jerry has a $99,000 mortgage on his building. Bob is much more likely to do the repairs because he has more to lose; Jerry might well reason that in the worst case if something happens to his building, he'll default on his mortgage and let the bank take care of the problems.[2]

6. Finally, it may be that firms are limited in their borrowing by the kinds of assets they own. If lenders require loan collateral, then firms with many fixed assets may be more easily able to borrow than firms with more "ephemeral" assets. Thus, even if Modigliani and Miller are right, and firms want to borrow as much as possible, it may be that software firms (with fewer tangible assets) are less able to borrow than real estate firms.

## 18.2. How Do Firms Capitalize?

One way to think about capital structure is to look the actual capital structures for different companies and industries. As an example, consider Abbott Laboratories, a major American

---

[1] Empirical research in finance estimates bankruptcy costs as generally less than 10% of the face value of debt at the time of bankruptcy. If the Modigliani–Miller full tax shield on debt were to hold, it is unlikely that bankruptcy costs of this magnitude would retard corporate desires for more leverage. A recent paper (Timothy Fisher and M. Jocelyn Martel, "On Direct Bankruptcy Costs and the Firm's Bankruptcy Decision". http://ssrn.com/abstract=256128) gives interesting information on the size of bankruptcy and liquidation costs in Canada.

[2] Lenders know all about option effects. It causes them to restrict their lending and also to impose covenants on the borrowers.

pharmaceutical firm: On 20 March 2002, Abbott's balance sheets showed debt of approximately $8.7 billion and equity of $10.7 billion. Using these book values debt and equity, Abbott had a book value debt-to-equity ratio of 0.81:

$$Abbott\ Labs, book\ value, debt\text{-}equity\ ratio = \frac{Debt}{Equity} = \frac{8.7}{10.7} = 0.81$$

The book value of Abbott's equity understates its market value. On 20 March 2002, Abbott had 1,563,436,372 shares outstanding; the market price per share was $51.80. Multiplying these two numbers together gives the market value of Abbott's equity as $81 billion, so that Abbott had a market value debt-to-equity ratio of 0.108:

$$Abbott\ Labs, market\ value, debt\text{-}equity\ ratio = \frac{Debt}{Equity} = \frac{8.7}{81.0} = 0.108$$

Finance professionals uniformly prefer market values to book values, so that this is our estimate for Abbott's debt-to-equity ratio.

## The Debt-to-Equity Ratio of Pharmaceutical Firms

In the spreadsheet below we calculate the debt-to-equity ratio in both book and market values for major pharmaceutical companies.

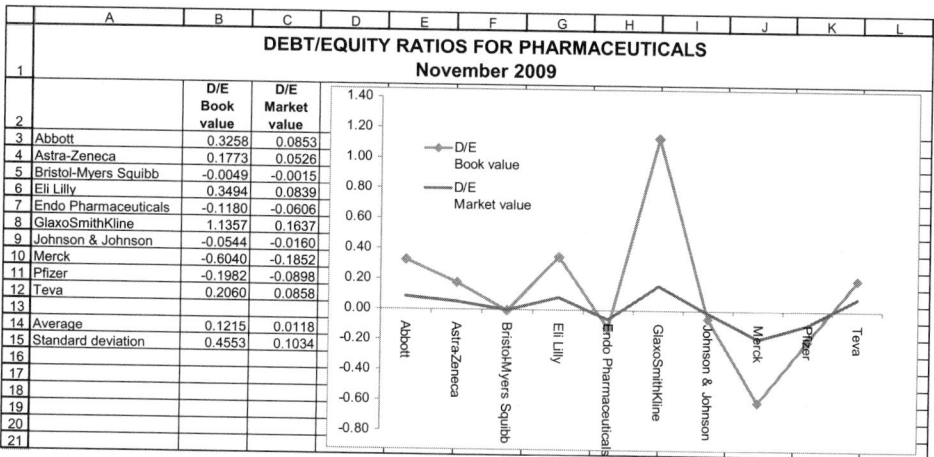

Several things are clear from these data:

- The average market debt-to-equity ratio for these firms is approximately zero. If there is a value advantage to debt over equity, it appears that the pharmaceuticals have not realized this advantage.

- The variability in book debt-to-equity ratios is very large. It does not appear that drug companies appear to be striving for a common book debt-to-equity ratio.

Can we learn something from these data for pharmaceutical firms? To the author of this book, it appears that there is no evidence that pharmaceuticals are striving for any target debt-to-equity ratio. If, as we showed in Chapter 17 and Section 18.1, firm targeting of debt-to-equity ratios depends on the tax system, then the lack of a clear debt-to-equity pattern for pharmaceuticals indicates that the tax effects of debt-to-equity ratios are relatively neutral. In a word, the debt-to-equity ratios of the pharmaceutical sector are consistent with Merton Miller's hypothesis that $(1-T_D)-(1-T_E)*(1-T_C)=0$, so that there are no net tax benefits to either maximizing or minimizing the corporate debt-to-equity ratio.

## The Debt-to-Equity Ratio of Other Industries

How does the pharmaceutical industry compare with retail grocery stores? As the graph below shows, grocery chains appear to have much higher debt-to-equity ratios than pharmaceutical firms. Having said this, the variation in debt-to-equity ratios for groceries is enormous. However, for grocery stores as for drug companies, there appears to be no evidence of a general trend.

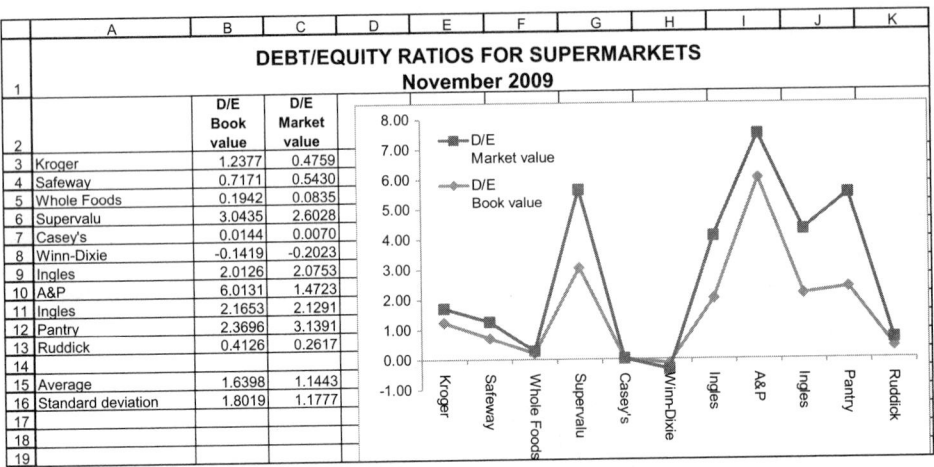

Here are similar data for steel manufacturers.

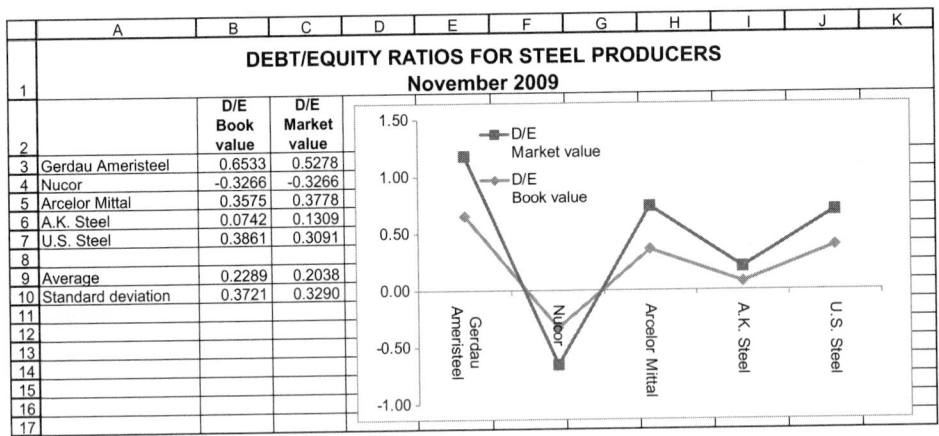

In short, as viewed from the data, there does not appear to be a trend in debt-to-equity ratios, whether measured in book or in market values. This is evidence in favor of *tax neutrality* with respect to debt-to-equity policy and against theories (like the Modigliani–Miller theory of capital structure with only corporate taxes) that claim that debt financing enhances firm value.

# 18.3. Measuring a Firm's Asset Beta ($\beta_{Asset}$) and WACC: An Example

In the previous section we concluded that there is little in actual firm financing patterns to indicate a preference for debt. This seeming indifference to debt raises doubts as to whether debt actually makes a difference in the valuation of the firm. Another way to measure the valuation effects is to look at the firm's *asset beta* and to ask whether this $\beta_{Assets}$ is affected by the firm's debt-to-equity ratio.

In this section we show how we measure the asset $\beta_{Assets}$ for Ford Motor Company. As discussed in Section 16.4, we use this $\beta_{Assets}$ to compute the Ford's WACC using the formula

$$WACC = r_f + \beta_{Assets} * \left[ E(r_M) - r_f \right].$$

Our primary interest in this section is not the WACC, however. Rather, we want to carefully show you how to use public sources of information (in this case Yahoo!) to compute a firm's debt $\beta$, debt-to-equity ratio, and asset beta

## Ford's Cost of Debt and Debt beta, $\beta_D$

At the end of the third quarter of 2009, Ford reported the following numbers for its cash, its debt, and its net interest expenses. From the numbers, we conclude that the average interest rate paid by the company is 6.39%.

| | A | B | C | D |
|---|---|---|---|---|
| 1 | COMPUTING THE ASSET BETA FOR FORD<br>December 2009<br>(most numbers are in $billion) | | | |
| 2 | | 30-Sep-09 | 30-Jun-09 | |
| 3 | Cash and equivalents | 48.37 | 24.01 | |
| 4 | Short-term debt | 15.21 | 0.00 | |
| 5 | Long-term debt | 132.02 | 133.07 | |
| 6 | Net debt | 98.86 | 109.06 | <-- =C5+C4+-C3 |
| 7 | | | | |
| 8 | Quarterly net interest exper | 1.62 | | |
| 9 | Implied annual interest rate | 6.39% | <-- =(1+B8/AVERAGE(B6:C6))^4-1 | |

Yahoo! gives Ford's equity $\beta_E$ as 2.77. To compute Ford's debt $\beta_D$, we use the computation

$$cost\ of\ debt = r_D = r_f + \beta_D * \left[ E(r_M) - r_f \right]$$

$$\beta_D = \frac{r_D - r_f}{E(r_M) - r_f}$$

This is the SML for debt. Because we know that $r_D = 6.39\%$, we can solve for $\beta_D$. In December 2009 the short-term U.S. Treasury rate was $r_f = 0.25\%$ and $E(r_M) - r_f = 8.75\%$. Thus the above equation solves for $\beta_D = 0.70$.

| | A | B | C | D |
|---|---|---|---|---|
| 12 | Risk-free rate | 0.25% | <-- Short-term Treasury rate | |
| 13 | Market risk premium<br>E(r$_M$) - r$_f$ | 8.75% | | |
| 14 | Debt beta | 0.70 | <-- =(B9-B12)/B13 | |

## Ford's Tax Rate

The quarterly income statements for 30 September 2009 report income before taxes of $1.22 billion and taxes of $140 million. Thus Ford's tax rate is 11.44%.

|   | A | B | C |
|---|---|---|---|
| 16 | Income before taxes | 1.22 | |
| 17 | Taxes | 0.14 | |
| 18 | Tax rate | 11.44% | <-- =B17/B16 |

## Computing Ford's Asset beta, $\beta_{Asset}$

The formula for the asset $\beta_{Asset}$ is

$$\beta_{Asset} = \beta_E * \frac{E}{E+D} + \beta_D * (1 - T_C) * \frac{D}{E+D}$$

where

$\beta_E = equity\ beta$

$\beta_D = debt\ beta$

$\frac{E}{E+D} = percent\ of\ equity; \frac{D}{E+D} = percent\ of\ debt$

This computation is implemented below and gives Ford's asset $\beta$ as 1.19.

|   | A | B | C | D |
|---|---|---|---|---|
| 21 | Cash and equivalents | 48.37 | | |
| 22 | Debt | 132.02 | | |
| 23 | | | | |
| 24 | Net debt | 83.65 | <-- =B22-B21 | |
| 25 | Market value of equity | 29.86 | | |
| 26 | Equity + net debt | 113.51 | <-- =B24+B25 | |
| 27 | | | | |
| 28 | Tax rate | 11.44% | | |
| 29 | Equity beta, $\beta_E$ | 2.77 | <-- Reported by Yahoo | |
| 30 | Debt beta, $\beta_D$ | 0.70 | <-- =B14 | |
| 31 | Asset beta, $\beta_{Asset}$ | 1.19 | <-- =B29*B25/B26+B30*(1-B28)*B24/B26 | |

# 18.4. Computing the Asset beta, $\beta_{Asset}$, for the Grocery Industry

In the previous section we showed how to calculate the $\beta_{Asset}$ for Ford. Below we show the results of calculations for the grocery chain industry. The average asset $\beta$ for this industry is almost 1, and there is no significant relation between the asset $\beta$s and the firms' leverage.

## ASSET BETA AND LEVERAGE IN THE GROCERY SECTOR
## Data: November 2009

| | E/(E+D) | D/(E+D) | Equity beta $\beta_E$ | Debt beta $\beta_D$ | Tax rate | Asset beta | |
|---|---|---|---|---|---|---|---|
| Kroger | 67.76% | 32.24% | 0.35 | 0.79 | 34.64% | 0.40 | |
| Safeway | 64.81% | 35.19% | 0.65 | 0.69 | 36.07% | 0.58 | |
| Whole Foods | 92.29% | 7.71% | 1.17 | 1.39 | 35.09% | 1.15 | |
| Supervalu | 27.76% | 72.24% | 1.06 | 0.74 | -2.16% | 0.84 | |
| Casey's | 99.30% | 0.70% | 0.48 | 0.76 | 34.12% | 0.48 | |
| Winn-Dixie | 125.36% | -25.36% | 0.98 | -0.03 | 7.80% | 1.24 | |
| Ingles | 40.45% | 59.55% | 0.94 | 0.96 | 34.18% | 0.76 | |
| A&P | 40.45% | 59.55% | 2.15 | 2.77 | 0.00% | 2.52 | |
| Pantry | 24.16% | 75.84% | 0.33 | 1.31 | 0.00% | 1.07 | |
| Ruddick | 79.26% | 20.74% | 0.67 | 0.51 | 38.46% | 0.60 | |
| | | | | | | | |
| | | | | | Average | 0.9628 | <-- =AVERAGE(G3:G12) |
| | | | | | Sigma | 0.6168 | <-- =STDEV(G3:G12) |

Grocery: Asset Beta versus D/(D+E)

For the grocery industry, we can conclude that the asset $\beta$ is not affected by the capital structure. This is Miller's position:

- If the Modigliani–Miller results are representative, then the WACC will decrease when the amount of debt increases. The effect on the $\beta_{Assets}$ will be that $\beta_{Assets}$ should decrease as leverage increases.

- If the Miller results are representative, then the WACC will be unaffected by the amount of debt. The effect on the $\beta_{Assets}$ will be that $\beta_{Assets}$ should stay constant as leverage increases.

In the event, $\beta_{Assets}$ seem to be unaffected by the debt-to-assets ratio. So, at least for the grocery industry, Miller's theory seems to do better at explaining things than the MM theory.

# 18.5. Academic Evidence

In the previous section we've looked at a specific example—the U.S. auto–truck industry—to try to gauge whether capital structure affects the asset $\beta_{Asset}$ of these firms. Our conclusion is that, for this industry, they don't: The asset $\beta_{Asset}$, and hence the WACC, is not affected by the capital structure.

Recent academic research seems to come to the same conclusion.[3]

- When Eugene Fama and Kenneth French regress firm value on leverage, they conclude that leverage doesn't matter.[4]

- John Graham, in a survey published in 2001, concludes that "at the margin the tax costs and tax benefits [of leverage] might be of similar magnitude."[5] To show you how confusing this is, Graham concludes that—using another method—the tax benefit of debt is approximately 9% for the years 1995–1999.[6] This probably represents the costs of bankruptcy.

- Ivo Welch, in a paper written in 2002, finds no evidence whatsoever that firms look for an optimal structure.[7] He finds that firms tend to make few changes in their debt, so that the actual capital structure (i.e., the ratio of debt to the market value of equity) is largely driven by the market prices of the firm's shares. There is little evidence, according to Welch, of any optimizing in the debt decision.

# Summing Up

The theory of capital structure suggests that the capital structure decision is largely driven by the differential taxation of debt and equity. The empirics of capital structure suggest that it doesn't matter very much in determining the value of the firm.

For practical purposes,

- You can assume that the weighted WACC of a firm is invariant to the firm's capital structure.

- This means that the WACC of a firm can be measured by taking the *average WACC* of the firm's industry. It also means that the $\beta_{Asset}$ of a firm's industry is representative of the industry's overall risks and is not a function of the capital structure of the industry.

- The best way to value a firm is to use the WACC to discount the firm's anticipated future FCFs (recall that these are operating cash flows and do not include interest and other financing). We have illustrated this approach in a number of chapters of this book: Chapters 6, 7, and 13.

---

[3] Be warned that this is still controversial. Every finance professor seems to have an opinion on this matter! If you want a good grade in the course, disagree with the book and not with your professor.
[4] "Taxes, Financing Decisions, and Firm Value," *Journal of Finance* 1998, pp. 819–843.
[5] "Taxes and Corporate Finance: A Review," *Review of Financial Studies*, 2003.
[6] Ibid, pages 26–27.
[7] Ivo Welch, "Columbus' Egg: The Real Determinants of Capital Structure," Yale School of Management working paper, 2002.

CHAPTER CONTENTS

## Overview

When John started his college finance course in the fall semester of 2004, his grandmother gave him 100 shares of General Motors (GM) stock. "Owning shares is the best way to understand the stock market," she said to him. "When you own a stock, you'll start following the company." The succeeding months proved her right—stock ownership was very educational. John started to follow both the stock market and GM. Some of the fruits of his learning are in this introduction.

The present of 100 GM shares was a substantial gift: At the time his grandmother gave John the stock, a share of GM was trading for $41.10, so that Grandma's present was worth $4,110. During the months following the gift, GM's stock price went as high as $43.14 on 8 September

2004 and as low as $37.04 on 25 October 2004 (Figure 19.1). John also followed the news about the company, which was mostly depressing (Figure 19.2).

Then on 29 October 2004, John read that GM had declared a $0.50 dividend per share (Figure 19.3). Because he owned 100 shares, he realized that this meant that he was about to get $50 from GM. Reading the announcement, John saw that he had to learn some new terminology:

- The *dividend payment date* was 10 December 2004. This is the date on which the dividend would actually be paid out to the GM shareholders.

- The dividend is payable to *holders of record* as of 8 November 2004. This means that only shareholders listed with GM on this date got the dividend.

- Because it takes 2 business days to register a change in ownership of a share, the dividend is actually only paid to shareholders who own the stock at the close of trading on 4 November 2004.[1] This date is referred to as the *ex-dividend date* of the stock.

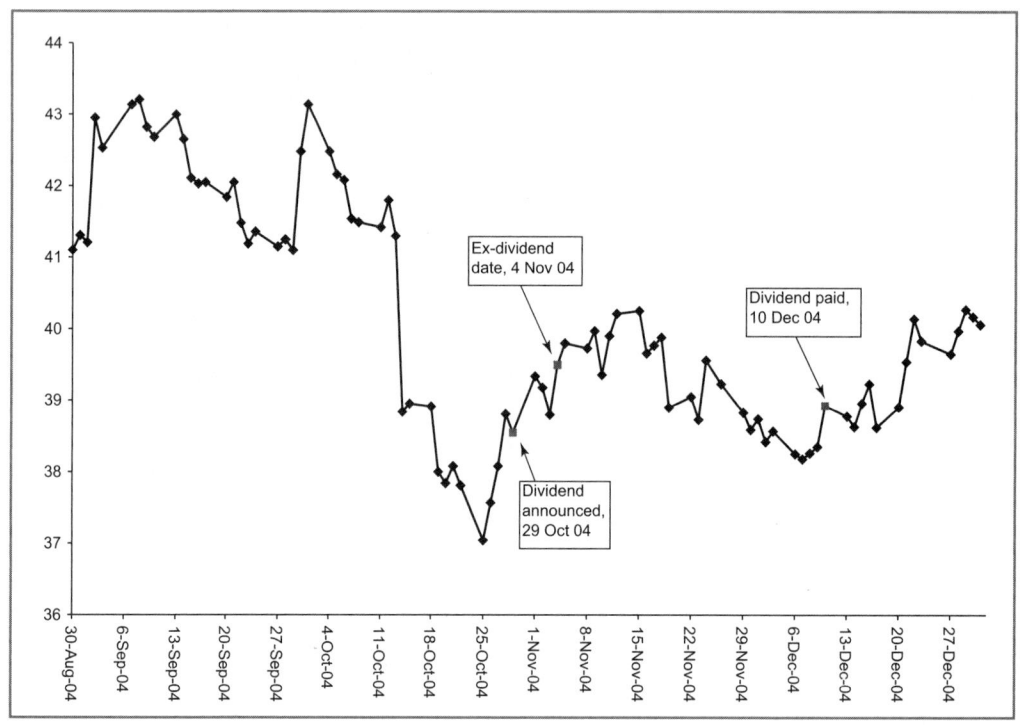

FIGURE 19.1 GM's stock price, September–December 2004.

John spent some time thinking about the whether the dividend was a good thing or a bad thing. He soon realized that there were a considerable number of factors. In succeeding subsections we show John's thinking about the various factors affecting the dividend.

## The Dividend as Information

During the fall of 2004, the news about GM was almost unremittingly bad (see Figure 19.2). The company's sales were dropping, its health care costs were 10 times those of Honda, its bonds

---

[1] 8 November 2004 was a Monday. Two business days before this Monday was Thursday, 4 November 2004.

were rumored to be downgraded, and it was forced to offer enormous rebates and incentives to potential car buyers.

The dividend did not do much to counteract this pessimism about the company. Looking back over the dividend history of GM, John saw that the company had paid a $0.50 per share dividend each February, May, August, and November going back to 1997. Had GM raised its dividend, John would have perhaps been able to interpret the dividend as a piece of positive information about GM. And had the company cut its dividend, this might have been interpreted as bad news. But keeping the dividend steady could hardly be interpreted as a meaningful signal about the company.

## The Dividend and Ordinary Income Taxes

The GM dividend would be part of John's taxable income. As a relatively low-income student, John's income tax rate was only 15%, but still this meant that John would have to pay 15% * $50 = $7.50 in taxes on the dividend, so that his net receipts from the dividend would be $42.50 instead of $50. John realized that for his grandmother, whose tax rate was 40%, the dividend would be much more costly—had she received the dividend, it would have cost her $20 in taxes, so that she would receive only $30 in net dividends.

On the other hand, John saw on Yahoo! (Figure 19.4) that 77% of GM stock was owned by pension funds and mutual funds, which do not directly pay income taxes on their dividend income. So perhaps, he thought, GM's dividend policy is based on the assumption that for most shareholders, taxes on dividends are irrelevant.

## The Dividend and Capital Gains Taxes: Dividend Reinvestment versus Retention by the Company

John actually planned to reinvest his dividends into GM stock. This meant that on receiving the dividend on 10 December 2004, he would spend his after-tax dividend of $42.50 on buying new shares of GM. Because the GM share price on 10 December was $38.93, John would buy $42.50/$38.93 = 1.0917 shares of GM stock.

John contrasted his reinvestment of dividends with the alternative of GM not paying out dividends at all. If GM had not paid out a dividend and retained the income, he assumed that the stock price should increase by $0.50 per share. In this case he would have been better off in at least two ways:

- First of all, if the company had not paid out the dividend, John would have netted $0.50 per share instead of the $0.425 per share he actually got after income taxes. The company would have saved him the ordinary income taxes on his dividends.

- Had GM not paid out the dividends and had John ultimately sold his shares of GM, the gain of $0.50 per share would be taxed as a capital gain instead of as ordinary income. Because capital gains tax rates are lower than ordinary tax rates, John would have benefited a second way from the dividend retention.

Combining these three factors—information, income taxes, and capital gains taxes—John realized that he needed some financial theory to help him understand dividends. The remainder of this chapter explores this theory.

## Finance Concepts Discussed

- Dividends
- Retained earnings
- Capital gains versus ordinary income

## Excel Functions Used

We use a lot of Excel spreadsheets to put order in things, but truth to tell, this chapter uses hardly any sophisticated Excel concepts. The one function used is **Sum**.

---

### NEWS ABOUT GENERAL MOTORS—A SELECTION OF HEADLINES

*Cadillac: Better But Not Best Yet,* **at Forbes.com** (Tue, Dec 14)

*Ford, GM Earnings Outlooks Trimmed,* **at Forbes.com** (Mon, Dec 13)

*GM Signs up its One Millionth XM Satellite Radio Subscriber,* **PR Newswire** (Mon, Dec 13)

*Delphi Hurt By Lower GM Output, Troubled Suppliers,* **at Forbes.com** (Fri, Dec 10)

*General Motors bonds fall on word of job cuts,* **at MarketWatch** (Thu, Dec 9)

*GM to cut 12,000 jobs in Europe,* **at MarketWatch** (Thu, Dec 9)

*GM recalling 640 Saab 9-3 cars for free repair,* **at Forbes.com** (Thu, Dec 9)

*Open Letter to General Motors' CFO,* **at RealMoney by TheStreet.com** (Thu, Dec 9)
GM should refinance at least half its 2005 and 2006 maturities while rates remain low. The company's future is threatened by any increase in bond yields.

*GM's Desperation Gets Noisier,* **Motley Fool** (Thu, Dec 9)
Yesterday, **General Motors** (NYSE: *GM - News*) beat its own previous personal best for crazy sales incentives (read about those *here*) and went for broke, instituting a *"Red Tag"* sale and bumping incentives on some 2004 models up to—better sit down for this—$7,500. And this is not just some gimmick to move the last few 2004 models off the lot, either. The company is apparently also offering rebates of up to $4,500 on select 2005 models as well—considerably more than the average $3,500 in incentives (on both 2004 and 2005 models) the company offered in *November*.

*GM Sputters Toward 2005 Breakdown,* **at RealMoney by TheStreet.com** (Thu, Dec 9)

*GM Beefs Up Incentives After Poor Nov.,* **Associated Press** (Thu, Dec 9)

*GM Europe Pledges to Avoid Plant Closures,* **Associated Press** (Wed, Dec 8)

*Saturn sees improved view,* **at MarketWatch** (Wed, Dec 8)

*Fiat may force GM to buy struggling unit,* **at FT.com** (Mon, Dec 6)

*Automakers Telling the Same Tale,* **Motley Fool** (Fri, Dec 3)

*SUV registrations slowing across country,* **at MarketWatch** (Thu, Dec 2)

*Ford, GM to Lower Production in 2005,* **Associated Press** (Wed, Dec 1)

*GM Sales Fall 13.1 Percent in November,* **Associated Press** (Wed, Dec 1)

*NEWS: Commentary: Sorry Detroit. The Garage Is Full* **at BusinessWeek Online** (Wed, Dec 1)
Why the gloom? For the past three years, as auto makers have thrown ever better deals at buyers, sales have remained essentially flat at around 16.7 million vehicles. Even if sales hit about 16.8 million, as analysts expect, that won't be enough to help Detroit. Ford and General Motors (*GM*) are already having a tough time making money selling cars, while Chrysler (*DCX*) has only recently gotten a lift from some hot models.

*GM to Lay Off About 1,000 at N.J. Plant,* **Associated Press** (Tue, Nov 30)

*2004 Was Record Year for Auto Recalls,* **Associated Press** (Tue, Nov 30)

*Junk Alert* **at Forbes.com** (Mon, Nov 29)
The way things are trending lately, I believe that at least one rating agency will downgrade the auto giants to junk by this time next year. But don't let that stop you from buying Ford's and GM's bonds, with their nice yields. What's gone wrong with the big two car companies? Just about everything: loss of market share, humongous retiree costs, union difficulties, restructuring, rising raw materials prices, excessive inventory, lackluster new products. And what's right with them? They are big car companies, and they won't disappear. Ford and GM are two of the largest corporate bond issuers, with $168 billion and $284 billion, respectively, in consolidated debt (that is, with finance arms included). That means almost every sizable public pension fund and bond mutual fund holds their paper. A downgrade to junk would disqualify some of these investors, and they would have to sell their bonds eventually. But they will not be forced to do so suddenly. Prices, after a brief downdraft, will rebound. Someone buying now and holding for years (better still, to maturity) can afford to shrug off the downgrade.

*Automakers Rein In Growth As Downgrades Loom,* **at Forbes.com** (Wed, Nov 24)

*GM prepares for healthcare cost inflation,* **at FT.com** (Thu, Nov 11)

*US carmakers set to launch new incentives,* **at FT.com** (Mon, Nov 8)

*Ford, GM October Sales Skid,* **at TheStreet.com** (Wed, Nov 3)

*GM Stuck in Reverse,* **at TheStreet.com** (Thu, Oct 14)

*Can't Ignore GM's Side of Economy,* **at RealMoney by TheStreet.com** (Thu, Oct 14)
The national implications of the hapless auto industry must somehow get on the national agenda, pronto.
*General Motors axes 12,000 jobs in Europe,* **at FT.com** (Thu, Oct 14)

*Big Autos Lag Other Transports,* **RealMoney by TheStreet.com** (Tue, Oct 5)

*Interest rates push US drivers into cheaper cars,* **at FT.com** (Sun, Oct 3)

*Auto Sales Mixed as Ford Raises Incentives,* **at TheStreet.com** (Fri, Oct 1)

*GM aims for further cost cuts across company,* **at FT.com** (Wed, Sep 29)

*Welcome to the Bankruptcy Economy,* **at TheStreet.com** (Wed, Sep 22)
At General Motors . . . the average cost of providing health care and pension benefits is around $1,360 a car.
That's more per car than General Motors spends for steel. At Honda's U.S. operations, the health care and
pension-benefit cost is only $107 a car.

*Ford, GM Have Low Reliability Ratings,* **at RealMoney by TheStreet.com** (Wed, Sep 15)

*Tough Month for Automakers,* **at TheStreet.com** (Wed, Sep 1)

FIGURE 19.2 Some headlines about GM, September–December 2004. During the fall of 2004, most of
the news about the company was bad. The company went bankrupt on 1 June 2009.
*SOURCE*: http://finance.yahoo.com.

**News**
*General Motors*
GM Communications
media.gm.com

**FOR RELEASE:** 2004-10-29

**CONTACTS**

## GM Declares Quarterly Dividend

**DETROIT** - General Motors Corp. (NYSE: GM) today announced a fourth-quarter dividend of
$0.50 per share on GM common stock. The dividend is payable Dec. 10, 2004, to holders of
record as of Nov. 8, 2004. The dividend rate is unchanged from the previous quarter.

General Motors, the world's largest vehicle manufacturer, designs, builds and markets cars
and trucks worldwide, and has been the global automotive sales leader since 1931. More
information on GM can be found at www.gm.com.

FIGURE 19.3 GM's dividend press release, 29 October 2004.

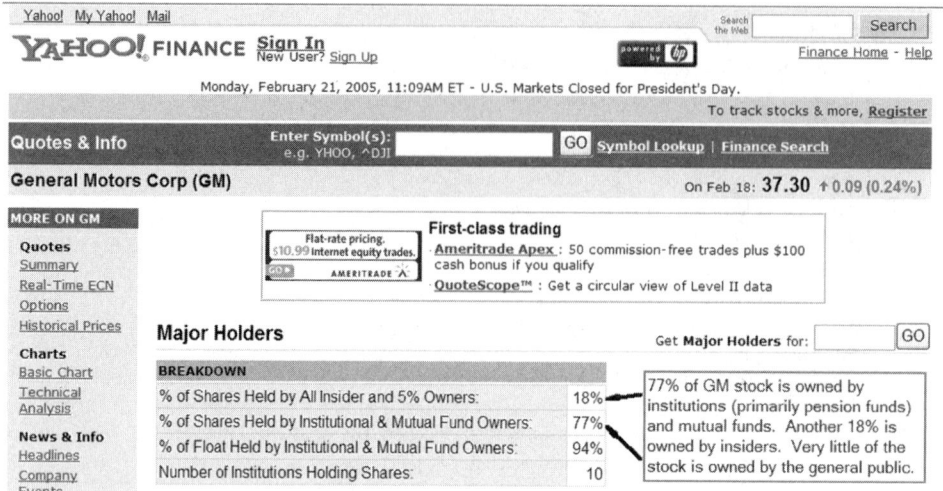

FIGURE 19.4  77% of GM stock is owned by pension funds and mutual funds that do not directly pay taxes on their income, so that tax considerations in the payment of dividends for GM may not be critical.

# 19.1. The Financial Theory of Dividends

To help us consider the pure financial theory of dividends, we consider the story of John and Mary, both of whom own wholly identical taxi companies that differ only in their dividend policies. Each company owns the same number of taxis and has the same income and expenses. Here are the balance sheets for the two companies.

| JOHN'S TAXI COMPANY, MARY'S TAXI COMPANY | | | |
|---|---|---|---|
| **Assets** | | **Liabilities and equity** | |
| Cash | 5,000 | Debt | 10,000 |
| Taxis | 20,000 | Equity | |
| | | Stock | 5,000 |
| | | Accumulated retained earnings | 10,000 |
| **Total assets** | **25,000** | **Total liabilities and equity** | **25,000** |

## John Pays Himself a Dividend

Suppose that John wants some cash and decides to declare a dividend of $3,000. Here's the way his balance sheet looks (Mary's balance sheet is unchanged).

| JOHN'S TAXI COMPANY—after dividend | | | |
|---|---|---|---|
| **Assets** | | **Liabilities and equity** | |
| Cash | 2,000 | Debt | 10,000 |
| Taxis | 20,000 | Equity | |
| | | Stock | 5,000 |
| | | Accumulated retained earnings | 7,000 |
| **Total assets** | **22,000** | **Total liabilities and equity** | **22,000** |

There are two changes in John's balance sheet:

- The cash balances decrease from $5,000 to $2,000, reflecting the dividend paid.

- The accumulated retained earnings decrease from $10,000 to $7,000. This is what is meant by the expression that "dividends are paid out of retained earnings." We don't like this expression, because dividends are paid out of cash; the decrease in retentions simply reflects the matching change made in the balance sheet.

Here are some questions you could ask about this situation.

*Question 1*: What are the valuation effects of the dividend?

Did the dividend paid by John change the value of his taxi business vis-à-vis Mary's business? Obviously not—they both still have the same number of taxis, and Mary has just kept her cash in the business instead of, as John did, pulling it out. A good way to see this is to write the balance sheets in terms of net debt—subtracting the cash from the debt.

| JOHN'S or MARY'S TAXI COMPANY—net debt | | | |
|---|---|---|---|
| **Assets** | | **Liabilities and equity** | |
| | | Net debt = Debt - cash | 5,000 |
| Taxis | 20,000 | Equity | |
| | | Stock | 5,000 |
| | | Accumulated retained earnings | 10,000 |
| **Total assets** | **20,000** | **Total liabilities and equity** | **20,000** |

| JOHN'S TAXI COMPANY—after dividend | | | |
|---|---|---|---|
| **Assets** | | **Liabilities and equity** | |
| | | Net debt = Debt - cash | 8,000 |
| Taxis | 20,000 | Equity | |
| | | Stock | 5,000 |
| | | Accumulated retained earnings | 7,000 |
| **Total assets** | **20,000** | **Total liabilities and equity** | **20,000** |

The asset side of the balance sheet is still worth the same, whether or not the dividend has been paid. On the other hand, the liabilities and equity side of the balance sheet is different—John has more debt and less equity than Mary.

*Question 2*: Perhaps it's just a capital structure question?

The above balance sheets for the two companies show that although they are both the same on the asset side, the dividend has changed the capital structure of the companies. So perhaps the dividend question is related to the capital structure problem discussed in Chapters 17 and 18. If so, this suggests the following:

- Dividends might matter if capital structure matters: An after-dividend company (like John's) will have a higher debt-to-equity ratio than a before-dividend company (like Mary's).

- If companies with a higher debt-to-equity ratio have a higher valuation, then companies should pay dividends.

Now this book takes a definite stand on this question: In the previous chapters we've suggested that the capital structure question is ultimately a question of balancing personal against corporate taxation. We've also suggested that the economic evidence suggests that on balance the taxes are pretty much of a wash, so that capital structure doesn't matter.

Although this argument suggests that dividends do not affect the valuation of a company, there's another tax aspect to this question—the trade-off between ordinary income taxes and capital gains taxes. We discuss this in the next section.

In the meantime, as long as Mary and John's taxi companies aren't taxed and as long as Mary and John aren't taxed on a personal level, the debt-to-equity aspects of the dividend decision shouldn't affect the valuation of their companies.

*Question 3*: Does the dividend affect the enterprise value?

Here's another way of thinking about this question: Suppose that both John and Mary are thinking about selling their taxi companies. Suppose that the "taxi part" of the business is valued at $40,000, which is, of course, more than its value on the balance sheet, and suppose that this valuation doesn't include the cash balances on the books. John and Mary have slightly different strategies about how to sell the business: John intends to first pay himself a dividend and then sell the business, whereas Mary intends to sell the business first without taking a dividend. Here are the calculations.

| | A | B | C | D | E | F | G |
|---|---|---|---|---|---|---|---|
| 1 | Mary sells her taxi company for $40,000 | | | | John sells his taxi company for $40,000 | | |
| 2 | Sale price | 40,000 | | | Sale price | 40,000 | |
| 3 | Pay back net debt | 5,000 | | | Pay back net debt | 8,000 | |
| 4 | Net to equity | 35,000 | <-- =B2-B3 | | Net to equity | 32,000 | <-- =F2-F3 |
| 5 | Book value of equity | 15,000 | | | Book value of equity | 12,000 | |
| 6 | Taxable gain | 20,000 | <-- =B4-B5 | | Taxable gain | 20,000 | <-- =F4-F5 |
| 7 | Taxes on gain (0%) | 0 | <-- =0*B6 | | Taxes on gain (0%) | 0 | <-- =0*F6 |
| 8 | Net to Mary from sale | 35,000 | <-- =B4-B7 | | Net to John from sale | 32,000 | <-- =F4-F7 |
| 9 | | | | | | | |
| 10 | Add back dividend | 0 | | | Add back dividend | 3,000 | |
| 11 | Taxes on dividend (0%) | 0 | <-- =0%*B10 | | Taxes on dividend (0%) | 0 | <-- =0%*F10 |
| 12 | Total | 35,000 | <-- =B8+B10-B11 | | Total | 35,000 | <-- =F8+F10-F11 |

The bottom line on these two calculations is the same—John and Mary each make a total of $35,000 on the sale, so that it doesn't matter whether they pay themselves a dividend.[2] Note the differences:

- Mary has less net debt to repay (John has taken out $3,000 in a dividend, so he has less cash left in the business).

- Mary' book value of equity is greater. When we add capital gains taxes (next example), this will mean that Mary has lower taxable gains. But with a 0% tax rate, it doesn't matter.

---

[2]Although, to anticipate the next section, the assumption that there are no taxes is critical to this argument.

---

### WHO CARES WHERE THE MONEY IS AS LONG AS IT'S THERE?

This is really what it's all about—who cares whether the money is in the taxi company or in the individual bank account of the owner? Of course you can think of several answers to this question that make it appear that it *does* matter:

- Taxes: If the company and its owners pay different tax rates, perhaps dividends are worthwhile. If capital gains taxes are lower than ordinary income taxes, perhaps—as suggested in the overview to this chapter—companies should retain the dividend and not pay it out.
- Trust: If there are multiple owners of the company, maybe you want the money in *your hands* as opposed to leaving it in the company. Economists call this "agency costs"—an agent being someone you've hired to do your work for you (that is, the manager). The agency cost argument for paying dividends suggests that you and your manager may have different goals; if the manager's goal includes wasting your money, then maybe you should get the money out of his hands by paying a dividend.

---

## 19.2. Taxes Can Make a Big Difference!

In Section 19.1 we looked at dividend policy in a world with no taxes. Using John and Mary's taxi businesses, we made two points:

- The value of the taxi part of the business—the enterprise value—is not affected by the dividend policy of John and Mary's taxi business.
- The proceeds—dividends plus gains from selling the business—to John and Mary are exactly the same, independent of their dividend policy.

Now look at the second point again, and suppose that we introduce taxes. We'll assume that dividends are taxed as "ordinary income" at a rate of 30% and that the gains from selling the business are taxed at a capital gains tax rate of 15%.

We'll start with Mary, who sells her taxi company for $40,000. As the following calculation shows, Mary's net from the sale of the company is $32,000.

|  | A | B | C | D |
|---|---|---|---|---|
| 1 | MARY'S TAXI COMPANY | | | |
| 2 | Assets | | Liabilities and equity | |
| 3 | | | Net debt = Debt - cash | 5,000 |
| 4 | Taxis | 20,000 | Equity | |
| 5 | | | Stock | 5,000 |
| 6 | | | Accumulated retained earnings | 10,000 |
| 7 | Total assets | 20,000 | Total liabilities and equity | 20,000 |
| 8 | | | | |
| 9 | Capital gains tax | 15% | | |
| 10 | Ordinary income tax rate | 30% | | |
| 11 | | | | |
| 12 | Mary sells her taxi company for $40,000 | | | |
| 13 | Sale price | 40,000 | | |
| 14 | Pay back net debt | 5,000 | | |
| 15 | Net to shareholders (Mary) | 35,000 | <-- =B13-B14 | |
| 16 | Book value of equity | 15,000 | <-- =SUM(D5:D6) | |
| 17 | Taxable gain | 20,000 | <-- =B15-B16 | |
| 18 | Taxes on capital gain (15%) | 3,000 | <-- =$B$9*B17 | |
| 19 | Net to Mary from sale | 32,000 | <-- =B15-B18 | |
| 20 | | | | |
| 21 | Add back dividend | 0 | | |
| 22 | Taxes on dividend (30%) | 0 | <-- =$B$10*B21 | |
| 23 | Total | 32,000 | <-- =B19+B21-B22 | |

Now John: He also sells his company, but he has first paid himself a dividend. His net is lower.

|  | F | G | H | I |
|---|---|---|---|---|
| 1 | JOHN'S TAXI COMPANY—after dividend | | | |
| 2 | Assets | | Liabilities and equity | |
| 3 | | | Net debt = Debt - cash | 8,000 |
| 4 | Taxis | 20,000 | Equity | |
| 5 | | | Stock | 5,000 |
| 6 | | | Accumulated retained earnings | 7,000 |
| 7 | Total assets | 20,000 | Total liabilities and equity | 20,000 |
| 8 | | | | |
| 9 | Capital gains tax | 15% | | |
| 10 | Ordinary income tax rate | 30% | | |
| 11 | | | | |
| 12 | John sells his taxi company for $40,000 | | | |
| 13 | Sale price | 40,000 | | |
| 14 | Pay back net debt | 8,000 | | |
| 15 | Net to equity | 32,000 | <-- =G13-G14 | |
| 16 | Book value of equity | 12,000 | <-- =SUM(I5:I6) | |
| 17 | Taxable gain | 20,000 | <-- =G15-G16 | |
| 18 | Taxes on capital gain (15%) | 3,000 | <-- =$G$9*G17 | |
| 19 | Net to John from sale | 29,000 | <-- =G15-G18 | |
| 20 | | | | |
| 21 | Add back dividend | 3,000 | | |
| 22 | Taxes on dividend (30%) | 900 | <-- =$G$10*G21 | |
| 23 | Total | 31,100 | <-- =G19+G21-G22 | |

The reason for the difference between John's net of $31,100 and Mary's net of $32,000 is that dividends are taxed at a higher rate than capital gains. By not paying herself a dividend, Mary has saved herself $900 = 30% * 3,000 of taxes on her dividends.[3]

This analysis suggests that *dividends might matter* if there is both a dividend tax and a capital gains tax: If the dividend tax is higher than the capital gains tax, the firm shouldn't pay dividends.[4]

## What If John Really Needs the Money? Solution 1: Pay a Bonus

Suppose for some reason John really needs the money **now**. Then he should pay himself a bonus, which is a tax-deductible expense for the company. When John pays himself a bonus, it comes out of cash but gets tax deductibility. Here's what happens to the cash balances.

| | | |
|---|---|---|
| Initial cash balances | $5,000 | |
| After-tax cost of bonus to company | $1,800 | The company pays John a $3,000 bonus, which is an expense for tax purposes. At the company's 40% corporate tax rate, the after-tax cost of the bonus is $(1-40\%)*3,000.$ |
| Cash on hand after bonus | $3,200 | |

Figure 19.5 shows how the profits for John come out with a dividend and with a bonus. We've assumed that John pays a 25% ordinary income tax on both the dividend and the bonus.

| | A | B | C | D | E | F | G | H | I |
|---|---|---|---|---|---|---|---|---|---|
| 1 | **JOHN'S TAXI COMPANY—after dividend** | | | | | **JOHN'S TAXI COMPANY—after bonus** | | | |
| 2 | Assets | | Liabilities and equity | | | Assets | | Liabilities and equity | |
| 3 | Cash | 2,000 | Debt | 10,000 | | Cash | 3,200 | Debt | 10,000 |
| 4 | Taxis | 20,000 | Equity | | | Taxis | 20,000 | Equity | |
| 5 | | | Stock | 5,000 | | | | Stock | 5,000 |
| 6 | | | Accumulated retained earnings | 7,000 | | | | Accumulated retained earnings | 8,200 |
| 7 | Total assets | 22,000 | Total liabilities and equity | 22,000 | | Total assets | 23,200 | Total liabilities and equity | 23,200 |
| 8 | | | | | | | | | |
| 9 | Corporate tax rate | 40% | | | | Corporate tax rate | 30% | | |
| 10 | Capital gains tax | 15% | | | | Capital gains tax | 15% | | |
| 11 | Ordinary income tax rate | 25% | | | | Ordinary income tax rate | 25% | | |
| 12 | | | | | | | | | |
| 13 | | John sells his taxi company for $40,000 | | | | | John sells his taxi company for $40,000 | | |
| 14 | Sale price | 40,000 | | | | Sale price | 40,000 | | |
| 15 | Pay back net debt | 8,000 | <-- =D3-B3 | | | Pay back net debt | 6,800 | <-- =I3-G3 | |
| 16 | Net to equity | 32,000 | <-- =B14-B15 | | | Net to equity | 33,200 | <-- =G14-G15 | |
| 17 | Book value of equity | 12,000 | <-- =SUM(D5:D6) | | | Book value of equity | 13,200 | <-- =SUM(I5:I6) | |
| 18 | Taxable gain | 20,000 | <-- =B16-B17 | | | Taxable gain | 20,000 | <-- =G16-G17 | |
| 19 | Taxes on capital gain (15%) | 3,000 | <-- =$B$10*B18 | | | Taxes on capital gain (15%) | 3,000 | <-- =$B$10*G18 | |
| 20 | Net to John from sale | 29,000 | <-- =B16-B19 | | | Net to John from sale | 30,200 | <-- =G16-G19 | |
| 21 | | | | | | | | | |
| 22 | Add back dividend | 3,000 | | | | Add back bonus | 3,000 | | |
| 23 | Taxes on dividend (25%) | 750 | <-- =$B$11*B22 | | | John's taxes on bonus (25%) | 750 | <-- =$G$11*G22 | |
| 24 | Total | 31,250 | <-- =B20+B22-B23 | | | Total | 32,450 | <-- =G20+G22-G23 | |

FIGURE **19.5** John's cash flow (cells B24 and G24) with a dividend and with a bonus. Because dividends, corporate income, and capital gains are taxed at different rates, John is better off paying himself a bonus instead of paying himself a dividend.

---

[3] In any case, both John and Mary are going to pay the same capital gains taxes. This is because a dividend, paid out of cash, *reduces* the firm's equity and *increases* the firm's net debt. The result, as you can confirm from the examples, is that the capital gain to the firm's shareholders is independent of the dividend.

[4] Of course this assumes that you trust the firm to guard shareholder money wisely. If the "agency costs" are too high, shareholders would prefer to get their money as fast as possible, even if in the form of more highly taxed dividends.

This little trick (the tax deductibility of the bonus) is actually more profitable than Mary's not paying a dividend at all (compare John's net of $32,450 to Mary's net of $32,000). However, whether a bonus is better than no bonus depends on the corporate versus the ordinary income tax rate. In the example below, John's ordinary income tax rate is 45%, which is more than his corporate tax rate. At these rates he'd be better off by not paying himself a bonus (or a dividend) and selling the company.

| | F | G | H | I |
|---|---|---|---|---|
| 1 | JOHN'S TAXI COMPANY—after bonus | | | |
| 2 | Assets | | Liabilities and equity | |
| 3 | Cash | 3,200 | Debt | 10,000 |
| 4 | Taxis | 20,000 | Equity | |
| 5 | | | Stock | 5,000 |
| 6 | | | Accumulated retained earnings | 8,200 |
| 7 | Total assets | 23,200 | Total liabilities and equity | 23,200 |
| 8 | | | | |
| 9 | Corporate tax rate | 30% | | |
| 10 | Capital gains tax | 15% | | |
| 11 | Ordinary income tax rate | 45% | | |
| 12 | | | | |
| 13 | John sells his taxi company for $40,000 | | | |
| 14 | Sale price | 40,000 | | |
| 15 | Pay back net debt | 6,800 | <-- =I3-G3 | |
| 16 | Net to equity | 33,200 | <-- =G14-G15 | |
| 17 | Book value of equity | 13,200 | <-- =SUM(I5:I6) | |
| 18 | Taxable gain | 20,000 | <-- =G16-G17 | |
| 19 | Taxes on capital gain (15%) | 3,000 | <-- =$B$10*G18 | |
| 20 | Net to John from sale | 30,200 | <-- =G16-G19 | |
| 21 | | | | |
| 22 | Add back bonus | 3,000 | | |
| 23 | John's taxes on bonus (45%) | 1,350 | <-- =$G$11*G22 | |
| 24 | Total | 31,850 | <-- =G20+G22-G23 | |

## What If John Really Needs the Money?
## Solution 2: Repurchase Stock

Maybe John needs the money but can't for some reason pay himself a bonus. In this case, he should—instead of paying himself a dividend—get the company to repurchase some stock from him. Suppose that John convinces the management of the company (himself!) to buy back $3,000 of stock. Suppose that after this repurchase of equity, John sells the company. Finally, suppose that all of the $3,000 repurchase of stock is taxed to John as a capital gain (this is very unlikely—read the note that follows the spreadsheet). In this case, John would still be better off than if he had paid himself a dividend.

| | F | G | H | I |
|---|---|---|---|---|
| 1 | | JOHN'S TAXI COMPANY—after repurchase | | |
| 2 | **Assets** | | **Liabilities and equity** | |
| 3 | Cash after repurchase | 2,000 | Debt | 10,000 |
| 4 | Taxis | 20,000 | Equity | |
| 5 | | | Stock | 5,000 |
| 6 | | | Accumulated retained earnings | 10,000 |
| 7 | **Total assets** | 22,000 | **Total liabilities and equity** | 25,000 |
| 8 | | | | |
| 9 | Corporate tax rate | 30% | | |
| 10 | Capital gains tax | 15% | | |
| 11 | Ordinary income tax rate | 45% | | |
| 12 | | | | |
| 13 | John sells his taxi company for $40,000 | | | |
| 14 | Sale price | 40,000 | | |
| 15 | Pay back net debt | 8,000 | <-- =I3-G3 | |
| 16 | Net to equity | 32,000 | <-- =G14-G15 | |
| 17 | Book value of equity | 15,000 | <-- =SUM(I5:I6) | |
| 18 | Taxable gain | 17,000 | <-- =G16-G17 | |
| 19 | Taxes on capital gain (15%) | 2,550 | <-- =$B$10*G18 | |
| 20 | Net to John from sale | 29,450 | <-- =G16-G19 | |
| 21 | | | | |
| 22 | Add back repurchase of stock | 3,000 | | |
| 23 | John's taxes on repurchase (15%) | 450 | <-- =$G$10*G22 | |
| 24 | Total | 32,000 | <-- =G20+G22-G23 | |

**Note**: To minimize taxes, John should consult his accountant before repurchasing the stock. It is highly unlikely that the whole repurchase would be taxed as a dividend. It could be structured as a payout of capital (in which case there would be no taxes). The accountant might also be able to value John's *basis* in the stock (what he originally paid for it, plus the accumulated capital gains). Here's an example.

| | F | G | H |
|---|---|---|---|
| 27 | | Accountant reasoning? | |
| 28 | **Assets** | | **Liabilities and equity** |
| 29 | | | Net debt |
| 30 | Enterprise value | 40,000 | Equity, market value |
| 31 | **Total assets** | 40,000 | **Total liabilities and equity** |
| 32 | | | |
| 33 | Amount spent on repurchase | 3,000 | |
| 34 | As a percent of market value of equity | 8.57% | <-- =G33/I30 |
| 35 | | | |
| 36 | Book value of equity | 15,000 | |
| 37 | basis = 8.57% of book equity | 1,286 | <-- =G34*G36 |
| 38 | | | |
| 39 | Taxable gain on repurchase | 1,714 | <-- =G33-G37 |
| 40 | Taxes on gain at capital gains tax | 257 | <-- =G10*G39 |
| 41 | Net from repurchase | 2,743 | <-- =G33-G40 |
| 42 | | | |
| 43 | | | |
| 44 | | John sells his taxi company for $40,000 | |
| 45 | Sale price | 40,000 | |
| 46 | Pay back net debt | 8,000 | <-- =I29+G33 |
| 47 | Net to equity | 32,000 | <-- =G45-G46 |
| 48 | Book value of equity | 13,714 | <-- =G36-G37 |
| 49 | Taxable gain | 18,286 | <-- =G47-G48 |
| 50 | Taxes on capital gain (274286%) | 2,743 | <-- =$B$10*G49 |
| 51 | Net to John from sale | 29,257 | <-- =G47-G50 |
| 52 | | | |
| 53 | Total: net from sale + net from repurchase | 32,000 | <-- =G51+G41 |

The accountant reckons as follows:

- Before the payout of cash, the company is worth $40,000, which makes the market value of the equity $35,000.

- By paying out $3,000 in cash for stock in the company, John has effectively repurchased 8.57% of the company's equity. Because the book value of the company's equity is $15,000, John has a capital gain of $1,714 (= 3,000−8.57% * 15,000) on the repurchase. This capital gain will be taxed at 15% (= $257), so that John will net $2,743 from the repurchase.

- Now when John sells the company for $40,000, he will first have to pay off its net debt of $8,000 (the repurchase used $3,000 of cash and raised the net debt from $5,000 to $8,000). This leaves him with a market value of equity of $32,000, which has book value of $13,714 (= $15,000−8.57%*15,000). This gain also gets taxed at the capital gains tax rate of 15%.

- This leaves John with $32,000.

## 19.3. Dividends (Satisfaction Now) versus Capital Gains (Enjoy Later)

Up to this point we've established that if you're going to sell your company, ordinary income taxes on dividends make it unwise to first pay yourself a dividend. But what if you're not going to sell the company right away? Should you leave the money in the company, for that golden day when you're going to sell it and benefit from the lowered capital gains taxes? Or should you pay yourself a dividend?

It all depends, of course, on the level of trust you have in the managers of your company. In the case of John and Mary, this is easy—they manage their own companies, and they wouldn't do anything to harm themselves. In this case they should leave the money in the company, where it can earn the same returns as if they paid it out.

## 19.4. Do Dividends Signal?

Sections 19.1 and 19.2 have developed the theory that from a purely financial point of view, dividends are unnecessary. For investors, the decision on whether a company should pay dividends is at best neutral, and—given the gap between taxes on dividend income and taxes on corporate gains—usually leans toward the nonpayment of dividends. There are two alternatives to dividends, both of which are more financially attractive than the dividend itself:

- The company can choose simply not to pay out the dividend. By retaining the income as cash on its own books, the company translates the potential dividend into a future capital gain for its investors. When ultimately realized by the investor, this capital gain is taxed at a lower rate than ordinary income.

- The company can choose to use the potential dividend cash flow to repurchase its own shares. This translates the dividends into immediate cash gains for those shareholders who sell their shares back to the company (cash gains that are taxed at a favorable capital gains tax rate). Shareholders who do not tender their shares gain an increased proportion of the firm's future earnings.

There remains the possibility that dividends are a signal to the investor about the health of the company. The *signaling theory of dividends* makes two assertions:

- All other things being equal, higher dividends are a signal of more financial strength than lower dividends.
- Changes in dividends are indicative of the future financial health of the company. An increase in dividends is indicative that the future prospects of the firm are improved and vice versa.

## Is a Dividend Increase Always Good News?

On the other hand, not all increases in dividends seem to be good news. When Microsoft announced on 16 January 2003 that it would initiate a dividend, the stock price dropped the next day by 7%. According to a *Business Week* article,

> That may have been mostly because management's outlook for the current quarter was weak, but it's also likely that some investors saw the dividend as a sign that Microsoft had run out of options for growth, says Don Luskin, chief investment officer at research boutique Trend Macrolytics. "The risk is that paying a dividend could signal that tech has matured and is no longer the racy growth sector it once was," says Paul Shread, an analyst at Internet.com.[5]

Current financial research indicates that dividend changes, whether they be increases or decreases, tend to be less informative than once thought. Although stock market analysts interpret a decrease in a company's dividend as a bad signal about the company and an increase in the dividend as a good signal, the actual behavior of profits after a dividend change does not follow this signaling interpretation.[6]

---

[5] http://www.businessweek.com/technology/content/jan2003/tc20030128_1051.htm.
[6] See Chen, Shevlin, and Tong (2004). There is also some evidence that companies that pay dividends outperform those that don't in down markets. See Kathleen Fuller and Michael Goldstein, "Do Dividends Mean More in Declining Markets?" (http://papers.ssrn.com/sol3/papers.cfm?abstract_id=687067). This is discussed in http://www.forbes.com/2003/09/25/cz_vj_0925soapbox.html by Vahan Janjigian.

---

## THE COCA-COLA COMPANY INCREASES ANNUAL DIVIDEND BY 12 PERCENT

### 43rd Consecutive Annual Increase

**Atlanta, February 17, 2005**—The Board of Directors of The Coca-Cola Company today approved the Company's 43rd consecutive annual dividend increase, raising the quarterly dividend 12 percent from 25 cents to 28 cents per common share. This is equivalent to an annual dividend of $1.12 per share, up from $1 per share in 2004.

The dividend is payable April 1, 2005, to shareowners of record as of March 15, 2005.

This reflects the Board's confidence in the Company's long-term cash flow. In 2004, the Company generated $6 billion in cash from operations—a 9-percent increase over 2003. The Company returned more than $4 billion of that to shareowners, through $2.4 billion in dividends and $1.7 billion in share repurchase.

The Coca-Cola Company is the world's largest beverage company. Along with Coca-Cola, recognized as the world's most valuable brand, the Company markets four of the world's top five soft drink brands, including Diet Coke, Fanta and Sprite, and a wide range of other beverages, including diet and light soft drinks, waters, juices and juice drinks, teas, coffees and sports drinks. Through the world's largest beverage distribution system, consumers in more than 200 countries enjoy the Company's beverages at a rate exceeding 1 billion servings each day. For more information about The Coca-Cola Company, please visit our website at www.coca-cola.com.

---

FIGURE 19.6 When Coca-Cola announced a dividend increase on 17 February 2005, the company cited its "confidence in its long-term cash flow." The company was using the dividends to send a signal to the financial markets, but it may not have worked: On the day of the announcement, Coke's stock price fell by 26 cents.

## 19.5. What Do Corporate Executives Think about Dividends?

A long line of financial research indicates that companies are extremely reluctant to change their dividend policy. Corporate executives apparently think that changing a firm's dividend policy is an important signal. In a recent survey of 384 corporate executives, researchers at Duke and Cornell found that they ranked the importance of maintaining the current dividend level on a par with other major corporate investment decisions. Share repurchases, on the other hand, were thought to come out of the residual cash flows after investment and dividend spending. However, the researchers report, "Many managers . . . favor repurchases because they are viewed as being more flexible than dividends and can be used in an attempt to time the equity market or to increase EPS. Executives believe that institutions are indifferent between dividends and repurchases and that payout policies have little impact on their investor clientele. In general, management views provide little support for agency, signaling, and clientele hypotheses of payout policy. Tax considerations play a secondary role."[7]

The way that companies relate to their dividends bears this out. Note the subhead on the Coca-Cola press release notifying the markets of an increase in dividend (Figure 19.6): "43rd Consecutive Annual Increase." Here are two more examples:

- IBM takes great pride in having paid quarterly dividends since 1916 (Figure 19.7). If the company were to change this policy, it would quite naturally be indicative of a major sea change at IBM.

---

[7] "Payout Policy in the 21st Century," Alon Brav, John R. Campbell, John R. Graham, and Roni Michaeli. http://papers.ssrn.com/sol3/papers.cfm?abstract_id=358582.

- GM, with which we started this chapter, is quite reluctant to change its dividend policy, even though the financial health of the company is not good. The company evidently understands that a decrease in the quarterly dividend would be interpreted as bad news by the financial markets.

FIGURE 19.7 Corporations consider dividend maintenance very important. When IBM announced its regular quarterly dividend, the company proudly noted that this it had paid "357 consecutive quarterly dividends, starting in 1916."

## Summing Up

Dividends have a financial and an informational function. If we ignore their informational function, the payment of dividends presents a problem: Given a tax regime in which dividends are taxed at ordinary income tax rates, whereas nonpayment of dividends or stock repurchases are taxed at lower capital gains tax rates, it is difficult to explain why firms pay dividends. Most shareholders would be better off if the dividend payment were either retained in the firm or diverted to share repurchases. As shown in Figure 19.8, this purely financial consideration perhaps explains the increasing role of share repurchases in firm dividend policies.

The informational role of dividends is more complicated. Firms are highly reluctant to change their dividend payout patterns—a company with no dividends tends to continue a no-payout policy, whereas companies with moderate dividend growth strive to continue their growth rates. Both corporate executives and financial markets tend to interpret a change in the dividend payout as having informational content. Most firms believe that dividend increases will be interpreted as good news about future firm prospects and vice versa.

However, we have shown examples in this chapter where dividend changes have contrary effects to expectations: When Microsoft implemented a dividend, the markets interpreted this as a negative signal about the company's future prospects. When Coca-Cola increased its dividend, citing "confidence in its long-term cash flow," the stock price fell.

We can conclude from this that for firms whose shares are traded on stock markets, the dividend decision is a complicated, not totally understood, phenomenon that combines purely financial and tax considerations with complicated signaling and perhaps psychological motives.

Volume 3, Number 9 SEPTEMBER 2002

FORBES

# Growth Investor

ADVICE TO HELP YOU MANAGE YOUR GROWTH PORTFOLIO

www.forbesgrowthinvestor.com

## Share Repurchases Substitute for Dividends

by Vahan Janjigian

The total return on equities is composed of two components: dividends and capital gains. Since the 1980s, however, the proportion coming from dividends has been shrinking. Furthermore, dividend yields (i.e., dividend per share divided by stock price) and payout ratios (i.e., dividend per share divided by earnings per share) have been falling steadily. Many experienced investors take this as prima facie evidence that stocks remain overvalued despite a tremendous two-year sell-off.

Value investors in particular believe that steadily rising cash dividends are an indication of financial health. These investors often shun stocks that lack a long history of dividend payments. But others, such as growth investors, believe dividends are not very meaningful.

A recent article in the Journal of Finance, a leading scholarly publication, provides evidence that the demise of the cash dividend is just an illusion. The authors, Gustavo Grullon and Roni Michaely, argue that focusing only on dividends ignores an increasingly important form of cash payout to stockholders: share repurchases. Cash dividends have been increasing at an annually compounded rate of only 6.3% since 1980. Yet cash spent on share repurchases has been rising at a much more rapid clip of 18.4% compounded annually. Furthermore, cash spent on share repurchases now exceeds that spent on dividends. And total cash paid out (i.e., dividends plus repurchases) as a percentage of earnings has actually been rising during the period studied.

Our tax code explains much of this behavior. When corporations pay dividends, investors are forced to pay taxes. In fact, dividends are taxed at the ordinary rate. But when corporations initiate share repurchases, investors can avoid taxes altogether by choosing not to sell. Yet if they do sell, they are taxed at the capital gains tax rate, which is much lower than the ordinary tax rate.

This was the case thirty years ago as well. So why weren't share repurchases as popular then? Grullon and Michaely argue that share repurchases didn't really start growing in popularity until a 1982 regulatory reform, which made it less likely that repurchasing firms would be accused by the SEC of trying to manipulate their stock prices.

There are a number of lessons to be drawn from this study. First, those who argue that stocks remain overvalued simply because dividend yields or dividend payout ratios are historically low are being shortsighted. They should instead focus on total cash payouts. Second, there should be no doubt that, good or bad, regulatory reforms affect firm behavior. Well-managed firms will do what is best for shareholders. As long as cash dividends are unfavorably taxed, investors will prefer capital gains. And as long as regulators allow it, good corporate boards will deliver what shareholders want.

Which brings us to a very important point. Dividends are paid from after-tax dollars. Taxing investors again for receiving those dividends imposes a very heavy burden. Regulators should eliminate this double taxation. Dividends should either be treated as a tax-deductible expense for corporations, or tax-exempt income for individuals.

FIGURE 19.8 Since the 1980s, cash dividends have been increasing at a much slower rate than share repurchases. The explanation is in the much lower tax rates on capital gains versus ordinary income.

# EXERCISES

1. The following sheet shows the balance sheet for John's Supermarket. John is the sole owner of the supermarket.

| | A | B | C | D |
|---|---|---|---|---|
| 1 | | | **JOHN'S SUPERMARKET** | |
| 2 | **Assets** | | **Liabilities and equity** | |
| 3 | Cash | 500,000 | Debt | 600,000 |
| 4 | | | | |
| 5 | | | Equity | |
| 6 | Supermarket | 1,250,000 | Stock | 800,000 |
| 7 | | | Accumulated retained earnings | 350,000 |
| 8 | **Total assets** | **1,750,000** | **Total debt and equity** | **1,750,000** |

a. Show the supermarket balance sheet in terms of net debt.

b. Assuming John decides to pay himself a $250,000 dividend: Show both the original balance sheet and the net debt balance sheet after the dividend payment.

2. John (from Exercise 1) needs your help again. After paying the dividend of $250,000, he decides to accept an offer to sell the supermarket for $1,800,000. The conditions of the sale are that John gets to keep the cash on the company's books, but that he is responsible for paying back the company's debt.

a. Assuming no taxes of any kind, what will John net from his dividend and from his sale of the company?

b. If John had sold the supermarket for $1,800,000 before the $250,000 dividend, what would have been his net gain?

c. Back to the case of a $250,000 dividend: What will be John's net if there were a 30% tax on the dividend payment and a 20% tax rate on gains from the supermarket sale?

d. With a 30% tax on dividends and a 20% capital gains tax, what would be John's net if he sold the supermarket without first paying a $250,000 dividend?

3. David has a cosmetics shop he's trying to sell for $200,000. The shop's balance sheet is given below. David has a 40% tax on ordinary income (including dividend payments), a 30% corporate tax rate, and a 25% tax rate on capital gains. Before selling the store, he wants to pay himself a dividend of $55,000, equal to his accumulated retained earnings. According to his belief, "My selling price is the same whether I'll pay the dividend (to myself) or not. So why not pay myself a dividend first? I'll have more money that way!"

Is David right? Present the calculations for both the dividend and the nondividend case.

| | A | B | C | D |
|---|---|---|---|---|
| 1 | | | **David's Cosmetics Shop** | |
| 2 | **Assets** | | **Liabilities and equity** | |
| 3 | Cash | 60,000 | Loan from bank | 50,000 |
| 4 | Inventory | 25,000 | | |
| 5 | | | Equity | |
| 6 | Shop | 100,000 | Stock | 80,000 |
| 7 | | | Accumulated retained earnings | 55,000 |
| 8 | **Total assets** | **185,000** | **Total debt and equity** | **185,000** |

4.

a. How will your answer to Exercise 3 change if instead of paying himself a dividend David pays himself a bonus of $55,000?

b. How will your answer to Exercise 4a change if both the corporate tax rate and the ordinary income tax are 40%?

5. How will your answer to Exercise 3 change if instead of paying himself a dividend the shop will repurchase shares from David for $55,000 (assume capital gain tax rate on stock repurchase)?

6. Mallory wants to sell her fishing business. She's trying to decide whether to sell the business as is, to pay herself a dividend of $5,000 combined with a bonus of $10,000, or to repurchase $15,000 of shares. Assuming Mallory will be paid $220,000 anyway, what will you recommend she do?
   The balance sheet of the business is given below.

| | A | B | C | D |
|---|---|---|---|---|
| 1 | | | **Mallory's Fishing Business** | |
| 2 | **Assets** | | **Liabilities and equity** | |
| 3 | Cash | 20,000 | Loan from bank | 25,000 |
| 4 | Inventory | 25,000 | | |
| 5 | | | Equity | |
| 6 | Ship | 100,000 | Stock | 110,000 |
| 7 | Warehouse | 30,000 | Accumulated retained earnings | 40,000 |
| 8 | | | | |
| 9 | **Total assets** | 175,000 | **Total debt and equity** | 175,000 |

7. HighTech.Com is a company whose sales and profits have been steadily increasing. The company has never paid a dividend. The company's management is trying to decide whether to use its large cash balances to pay a dividend to shareholders or to repurchase shares. Can you give them some advice?

8. Simon's Hotels is a company founded in 1995. The company owns a chain of hotels and has thus far not paid dividends, instead using its excess cash to pay down large levels of debt used to buy hotels. The company's debt has now reached acceptable levels. Can you advise management whether it should implement a dividend? How do you think a dividend will be interpreted by the market?

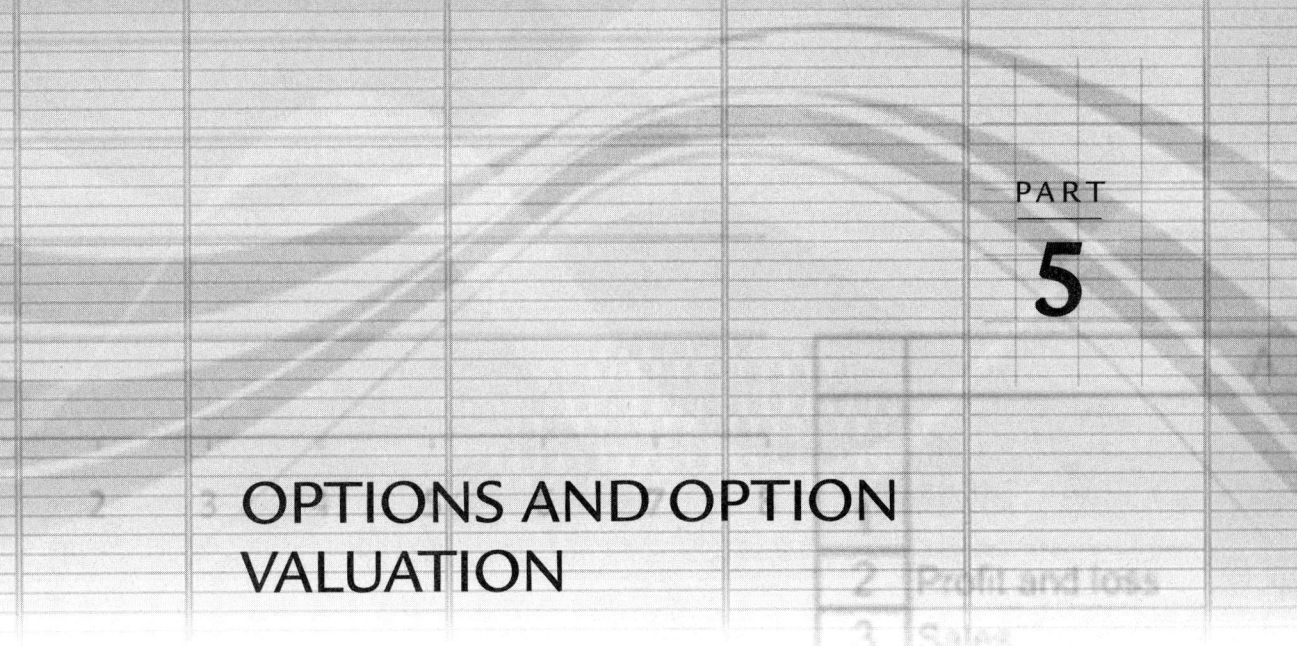

# 5

# OPTIONS AND OPTION VALUATION

THE MARKET FOR OPTIONS HAS GROWN TREMENDOUSLY IN the past two decades, and options form an important component of many capital market investments. In addition *option concepts* are a critical component of much thinking about the way markets work and investments are made. One example is the compensation given to managers in the form of stock options.

Part 5 of *Principles of Finance with Excel* gives an introduction to basic option concepts and valuation. A fuller treatment of these concepts will have to wait for a course dedicated to options, but Part 5 should give you the necessary background.

Chapter 20 introduces basic option concepts and terminology. Using a series of examples, this chapter will tell you about option cash flows, buying and selling options, and the payoffs from option strategies.

Chapter 21 tells you some basic facts about options prices. In more advanced textbooks these go by the name of "arbitrage restrictions" on option prices.

Chapters 22 and 23 discuss two option pricing models. Chapter 22 shows you how to use the Black-Scholes formula, the most famous option pricing model. The mathematics that underlie the Black-Scholes model can be daunting, but we've kept things simple. As Chapter 22 shows, on a mechanical level the Black-Scholes is easy to learn to use.

Chapter 23 discusses the other best-known option pricing model, the binomial model. The binomial model provides good intuitions about how options—as combinations of stocks and bonds—can be priced.

# CHAPTER

# 20 | Introduction to Options

## CHAPTER CONTENTS

## Overview

The financial assets we have discussed so far in this book are bonds (Chapter 15) and stocks (Chapter 16). In Chapters 20–23 we discuss another kind of financial asset—options. As you will see in these chapters, an option is different in many respects from a stock or a bond:

- The value of an option is derived from the value of another asset, usually a stock. For this reason options are sometimes called *derivative assets*.

- The buyer of an option buys upside gains but has only limited downside losses.

- Options are more complicated than bonds or stocks. To understand options we will have to introduce you to some new terminology and some new ways of thinking about financial assets.

## A Simple Example of an Option

To give some meaning to these somewhat mysterious statements, we start with a simple example.[1] It is 1 January 2011, and the price of an ounce of gold is $800. You have a very strong hunch that the price of gold will be $1,200 in 3 months. Your hunches have never failed you, so this must be a sure-fire way to make some money. Taking your total savings of $800, you go to your local jewelry mart to buy some gold. But with your paltry savings you can buy only 1 ounce of gold, and you can make a maximum of only $400—only a 50% return on your initial investment.

However, the jeweler has another offer for you: For $50, he is willing to sell you a contract that gives you the right to buy 1 ounce of gold in 3 months for $800. You realize that this contract—a *call option on gold*—gives you the opportunity of making much more money than actually buying physical gold.

Here's your calculation:

- Using your $800 savings, you can buy 16 call options.
- In 3 months you can use the call options to buy 16 ounces of gold for $800 per ounce. If your hunch is correct, the gold price in 3 months will be $1,200 per ounce, so you can make $400 per ounce of gold purchased.
- Your total profit using the gold call options will be $5,600 = $6,400 – $800—a profit of 700% (= $\frac{6,400}{800} - 1$) on your initial investment. This compares to the profit of 50% you will make if you use your $800 savings to buy 1 ounce of physical gold.

*Downside*: Suppose your hunch is wrong, and the price of gold in 3 months is $600. Now compare the profits of buying 1 ounce of physical gold to the profits of buying 16 call options:

- If you bought 1 ounce of physical gold, you would have lost 25% of your initial $800 investment.
- If you bought 16 options and the price of gold on 31 March 2011 is $600 per ounce, the *options will be worthless*. In this case you would have lost 100% of your initial $800 investment.

### *CALL OPTION ON 1 OUNCE OF GOLD*

**Price on 1 January 2011: $50**

If presented at Asheville Jewelry Mart on or before 31 March 2011, this piece of paper gives you the right to buy 1 ounce of gold for $800. After 31 March 2006, this piece of paper is worthless.

The owner of this piece of paper can sell it to anyone else at any time.

FIGURE 20.1 The gold call option certificates sold by the Asheville Jewelry Mart.

---

[1] Even this simple example is nontrivial. Options are like that!

## Peacemount Stock Options—An Example

Our gold example should convince you that options are an interesting way to make (and lose!) money. In this subsection we give an example of a stock option. Stock options give their holders the right to either buy or sell a stock in the future for a predetermined price. Stock options come in two flavors: A *call option* on a stock allows you to make money if the stock price goes up without losing too much if the stock price goes down. A *put option* on a stock allows you to make money if the stock's price goes down without losing too much if the stock's price goes up.

Take a look at Figure 20.2, which shows a call option (the right to buy a share of stock) on one share of a fictional company called Peacemount. On 26 November 2010 it would cost you $3 to buy this option. Having bought, you then have the right for the next 3 months to buy a share of Peacemount stock for $36.

Why buy this option? By spending $3 now, you lock in $36 as the maximum price Peacemount stock will cost you in the next 3 months. If the price of the stock goes up in the next 3 months, this will save you a lot of money. If, for example, Peacemount stock is selling on 26 February 2011 for $50, then using your call option, you can buy the stock for $36. You will have a profit of $11 (buying the stock for $36 instead of $50 saves you $14; from this amount you have to deduct the $3 cost of the option). If, on the other hand, Peacemount stock declines below $36, then you will not exercise the option but you will only lose your $3 investment. In option market jargon, *the call option offers upside gains but only limited downside losses.*

There's another reason to buy the option: You might be able to sell it at some time during the next 3 months and make a profit. Suppose that in 1 week the price of Peacemount stock is $45. Then the price of the call option should be at least $9, because the owner of the option could immediately make a profit of $9 by exercising it.[2] Note that in this example the price of the stock increases by 25% (from $36 to $45), whereas the price of the option increases by at least 200%. This makes the option a very interesting speculation. In option market jargon, *the call option's market price is very sensitive to the price of the underlying asset (in our case: the price of Peacemount stock).*

In addition to call options, this chapter also discusses *put options*. Whereas a call option is the right to buy a share of stock in the future, a put option is the right to sell a share of stock. An example is given in Figure 20.3: For $2.50 you could, on 26 November 2010, buy the right to sell one share of Peacemount stock for $36 during the next 3 months.

Why might you be interested in buying this put option? One reason is that, for holders of Peacemount stock, the put option places a *floor on your losses.* Suppose you currently own a share of Peacemount stock. On 26 November 2010 shares of Peacemount are selling for $35.50. If you buy the put option today for $2.50, you guarantee yourself that at any point during the next 3 months you will realize at least $33.50 from your stock. To see this, suppose that on 26 February 2004 the price of Peacemount is $20. Instead of selling your share on the open market, you will use ("exercise") the put option to sell the share for $36. Accounting for the cost of the option, your net receipts will be $33.50 ($36 for the share minus the $2.50 cost of the put option).

---

[2]Whoever holds the option can purchase a share of Peacemount for $36. The stock price is now $45, so the immediate realizable profit is $9.

### *CALL OPTION ON PEACEMOUNT STOCK*

**Price on 26 November 2006: $3**

If presented at the Asheville Stock Exchange on or before 26 February 2011, this piece of paper gives you the right to buy one share of Peacemount stock for $36. After 26 February 2011 this piece of paper is worthless. The holder of this piece of paper can sell it to someone else at any time.

Some additional information:

- On 26 November 2010, shares of Peacemount stock sold for $35.50.
- Peacemount's stock price has experienced considerable variations during the past 3 months:

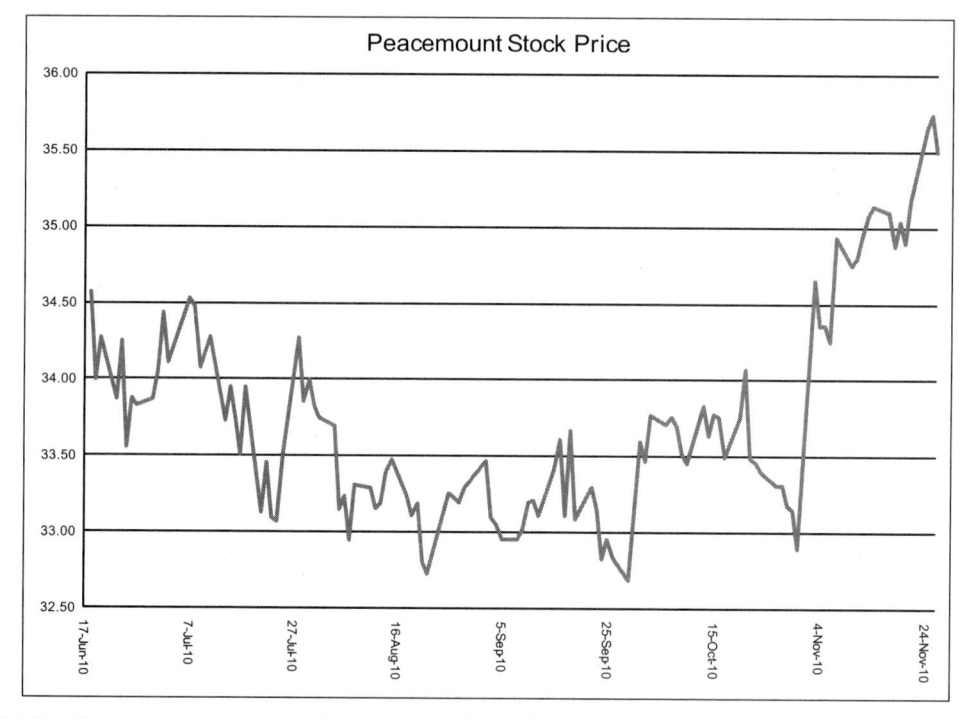

FIGURE 20.2 A call option on Peacemount stock. The option gives the holder the right to buy a share of Peacemount on or before 26 February 2011 for $36. The market price of the option on 26 November 2010 is $3.

---

### *PUT OPTION ON PEACEMOUNT STOCK*

#### Price on 26 November 2010: $2.50

If presented at the Asheville Stock Exchange on or before 26 February 2011, this piece of paper gives you the right to sell one share of Peacemount stock for $36. After 26 February 2011 this piece of paper is worthless. The holder of this piece of paper can sell it to someone else at any time.

---

FIGURE 20.3. A (hypothetical) put option on Peacemount stock. The option gives the holder the right to sell a share of Peacemount on or before 26 February 2011 for $36. The market price of the option on 26 November 2010 is $2.50.

## What's Next?

This chapter shows you basic option definitions and introduces you to option cash flows. In addition, we show you how option strategies—the ability to combine options and stocks in portfolios—can change the payoff patterns available to investors. When you finish this chapter, you will understand why stock options are *really interesting* securities and why you might want to invest in them.

## Finance Concepts Discussed

- Call and put options
- Option strategies: protective puts, spreads, butterflies

| BASIC OPTION TERMINOLOGY AND SYMBOLS | | |
|---|---|---|
| *Name* | *Definition* | *Symbol* |
| Call option | The right to buy a stock or other asset at a predetermined price on or before some future date | $C$ |
| Put option | The right to sell a stock or other asset at a predetermined price on or before some future date | $P$ |
| Exercise price | The predetermined price of the option—the price at which the stock/asset can be purchased in the future; also called the *strike price* | $X$ |
| Exercise date | The last date on which the option can be exercised; past this date the option is worthless | $T$ |
| Underlying asset | The stock or other asset that can be purchased with an option (in our previous examples, gold or one share of Peacemount stock) | $S$ <br> $S_0$: stock price today <br> $S_T$: stock price on the exercise date |

FIGURE 20.4 Option pricing involves a lot of terminology. Here are some very basic terms.

## Excel Functions Used

- **Max**
- **Min**

# 20.1. What's an Option?

A *call option on a stock* is the right to buy a stock on or before a given date at a predetermined price. The spreadsheet below gives prices for options on IBM stock on 8 May 2009, a day on which IBM stock itself sold for $101.49. We will use these prices in the examples that follow.

|  | A | B | C |
|---|---|---|---|
| 1 | 8 MAY 2009: OPTIONS ON IBM, EXPIRING 17 JULY 2009 | | |
| 2 | Exercise price | Call price | Put price |
| 3 | 45 | 60.80 | 0.05 |
| 4 | 55 | 50.80 | 0.10 |
| 5 | 65 | 40.80 | 0.15 |
| 6 | 70 | 35.80 | 0.25 |
| 7 | 75 | 31.30 | 0.40 |
| 8 | 80 | 20.99 | 0.70 |
| 9 | 85 | 16.40 | 1.18 |
| 10 | 90 | 13.30 | 2.05 |
| 11 | 95 | 9.10 | 3.30 |
| 12 | 100 | 6.40 | 5.20 |
| 13 | 105 | 4.00 | 7.70 |
| 14 | 110 | 2.24 | 11.00 |
| 15 | 115 | 1.10 | 15.20 |
| 16 | 120 | 0.52 | 19.70 |
| 17 | 125 | 0.25 | 21.30 |
| 18 | 130 | 0.10 | 29.70 |

Row 12 of the above spreadsheet shows that a call option on IBM with an exercise price of $100 sold on 8 May for $6.40. Suppose you purchased this call option. Figure 20.5 shows the option's cash flow pattern.

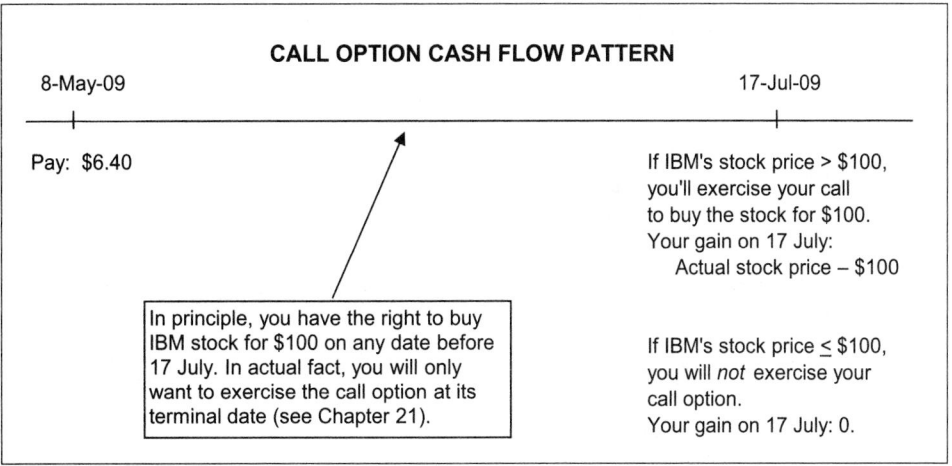

FIGURE **20.5** The cash flows from buying an IBM call option on 8 May 2009 for $6.40 and possibly exercising it on 17 July 2009. The option has exercise price $X = \$100$.

Now let's see what happens on 17 July:

- Suppose the IBM stock price on 17 July is $135. In this case you get to buy one share of IBM for $100. Your gain is $135 – $100 = $35.

- If the IBM stock price on 17 July is $90, you would not exercise your call option to buy a share of IBM for $100 (why should you? you could buy it on the open market for less). The option expires unexercised, and your gain is $0.

## IBM Put Options

What about the IBM put option with an exercise price of $100? It was selling, on 8 May 2009, for $5.20. The put option gives you the right to *sell* a share of IBM on or before the terminal date for its exercise price. The put option's cash flow pattern is shown in Figure 20.6.

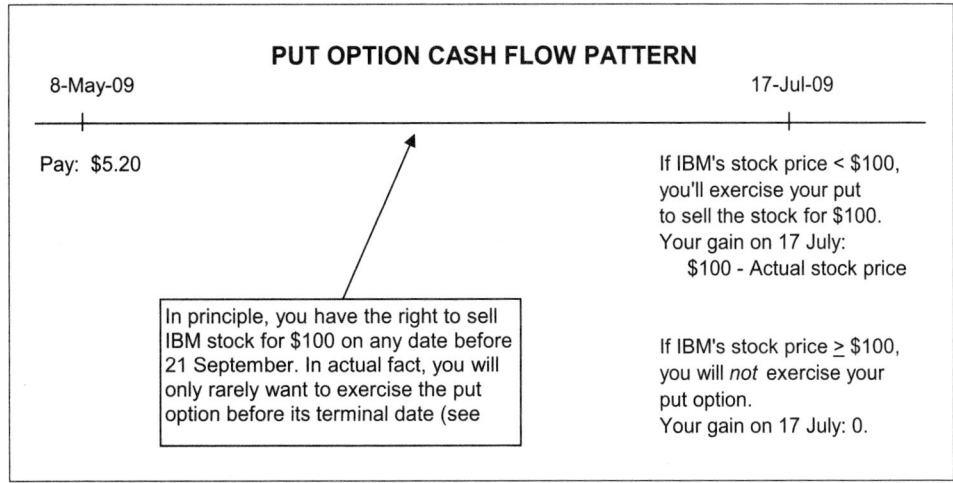

FIGURE **20.6** The cash flows from buying a IBM put option on 8 May 2009 for $5.20 and possibly exercising it on 17 July 2009. The option has exercise price $X = \$100$.

If IBM's stock price on 17 July is $85, you will exercise your put option and sell a share of IBM for $100, thus gaining $15.[3] On the other hand, if IBM's share price on 17 September is $130, you will not exercise the put option (why sell a share using the option for $100 when you can sell it on the open market for $130?).

---

## OPTION WEB SITES

All the data in this chapter were gathered from public sources on the Web. Many of these Web sites have superb data and also educational features. Here are some Web sites we especially enjoy.

- The Web site of the Chicago Board of Options Exchange: http://www.cboe.com
- Yahoo!: http://biz.yahoo.com/opt/

---

### European versus American Options

IBM's stock options are *American* stock options—they can be exercised *on or before* the option maturity date $T$. A *European* stock option can be exercised *only on* its maturity date $T$. Clearly, an American stock option is worth at least as much as a European stock option: American options offer more flexibility than European options.

- Two notes about American versus European stock options: The terminology has nothing to do with geography. Most traded options, whether in the United States, Europe, or Asia, are American and not European.
- A remarkable fact about American call options is the following: In many cases an American call option is worth *exactly* the same as an equivalent European call option. This happens if the stock on which the option is written does not pay a dividend before the option expiration date $T$. We discuss the reasons for this in Chapter 21.

### In the Money, out of the Money, at the Money

A call option is said to be "in the money" if the current stock price is larger than the option's exercise price. Look at the IBM July calls in Figure 20.8. The call with the exercise price of $90 (selling for $13.30) has an exercise price *less* than IBM's current stock price of $101.49. Thus this call is *in the money*—the stock price is greater than the call's exercise price.

The call with exercise price $110 (selling for $2.24) is *out of the money*—its exercise price is more than IBM's current share price. If the call's exercise price is equal to the current stock price, it is termed an *at-the-money* call. The call with an exercise price of $100 is almost at the money, and option traders would refer to it loosely as the at-the-money call.

A put is said to be *in the money* if the put's exercise price is greater than the current stock price. The IBM $120 put (selling for $19.70) is in the money and the $80 put (selling for $0.70) is out of the money. There is no precise at-the-money put, but traders would refer to the $100 exercise put (selling for $5.20) as the *at-the-money* put.

---

[3]What if you don't own a share of IBM on 17 July? No problem: You buy a share on the open market for $85 and use your option to sell it for $100.

| MORE OPTION TERMINOLOGY | |
|---|---|
| Terminology | Definition |
| European option | The option is exercisable *only on* the exercise date $T$. |
| American option | The option is exercisable *on or before* the exercise date $T$. Most options traded on exchanges are American options. Although in principle an American option should be worth more than a European option, in many cases this is not true (see Chapter 21). |
| At-the-money option | An option whose exercise price $X$ is equal to the underlying stock's current stock price $S_0$. "In-the-money" is often loosely used to describe an option whose exercise price $X$ is approximately equal to the current stock price $S_0$. |
| In-the-money option | An option from which money can be made by immediate exercise. A call option is in the money if the current stock price $S_0$ is greater than the option's exercise price $X$. A put option is in the money if the current stock price $S_0$ is less than the option's exercise price $X$. |
| Out-of-the-money option | An option from which no money can be made by immediate exercise. A call option is out of the money if $X > S_0$. A put option is out of the money if $S_0 > X$. |

FIGURE 20.7 Option pricing involves a lot of terminology. Here are some basic terms.

## 20.2. Why Buy a Call Option?

Here are two simple reasons why you might want to buy a call option.

**Reason 1: A call option allows you to delay the purchase of a stock**: It's 8 May 2009, and you're thinking about buying a share of IBM for its current market price of $101.49. As an alternative, you can buy a July call option with $X = \$100$. This option will cost you $6.40. Here's your thinking:

- If, on 17 July 2009, IBM's stock price is > $100.00, you'll exercise the option and purchase the share for $100. If you're careful, you'll realize that there are several "subpossibilities":

  - IBM's 17 July stock price = $130. Now you've made out like a bandit: You spent $6.40 for the option, but you bought the stock for $100, saving $30.00. Your net profit is $23.60 ($30.00 – $6.40 cost of the option).

  - If IBM's 17 July stock price = $105.00, you'll still exercise the option and purchase the stock for $100.00. You've saved $5.00 on the purchase price of the stock, but this time you will have lost a bit of money, because the option cost you $6.40. Your net profit will be –$1.40.

- If on 17 July IBM's stock is selling for less than $100, you will not exercise your call option. If you still want to purchase the stock, you'll buy it on the open market. In all cases, you will have lost only the $6.40 cost of the option.

**Reason 2:** A call option allows you to make a bet on the stock price going up. This bet is: (a) low cost, (b) high upside potential, and (c) one sided.

## ANALYZING THE PROFIT FROM A CALL OPTION

| Price of IBM on 17 July 2009 | Exercise the option? | Your profit or loss | In percentage |
|---|---|---|---|
| $90 | No—the option gives you the right to buy IBM for $100, but the market price is less, so you would *not* exercise the option | −$6.40 | $\dfrac{Profit\ on\ exercise - option\ cost}{Option\ cost} =$ $\dfrac{-6.40}{6.40} = -100\%$ |
| $100 | Yes/no—doesn't matter (you're buying the stock at its market price) | −$6.40 | $\dfrac{Profit\ on\ exercise - option\ cost}{Option\ cost} =$ $\dfrac{-6.40}{6.40} = -100\%$ |
| $105 | Yes—the option lets you buy the stock for $100, but the market price is $100. So you should exercise (even though you've lost money—see next column) | $Profit\ on\ exercise - option\ cost$ $=(105 - 100) - 6.40 = -1.40$ | $\dfrac{Profit\ on\ exercise - option\ cost}{Option\ cost} =$ $\dfrac{5 - 6.40}{6.40} = -22\%$ |
| $120 | Yes | $Profit\ on\ exercise - option\ cost$ $=(120 - 100) - 6.40 = 13.60$ | $\dfrac{Profit\ on\ exercise - option\ cost}{Option\ cost} =$ $\dfrac{20 - 6.40}{6.40} = 213\%$ |
| $140 | Yes | $Profit\ on\ exercise - option\ cost$ $=(140 - 100) - 6.40 = 33.60$ | $\dfrac{Profit\ on\ exercise - option\ cost}{Option\ cost} =$ $\dfrac{40 - 6.40}{6.40} = 525\%$ |

FIGURE 20.8: Analyzing the profit from a call option. If the stock price is down on 17 July, your loss is limited to $6.40. However, if the price goes above $100, your percentage gains from the option can be very large. The call option is a "one-sided" bet on the stock price going up—if the stock price goes up, you make money; if the stock price goes down, you lose a limited amount of money.

Suppose you buy the IBM call option above: You spend $6.40 on 8 May 2009 to purchase an option that—on 17 July—gives you the right to purchase IBM stock for $100. Your purpose is to bet on the price of IBM stock in July. As you can see in Figure 20.8,

- This bet has a low cost: You've put up only $6.40 to make it.

- You will never lose more than the $6.40. This is what we mean when we say that the bet is one sided: You can only lose a limited amount of money.

- The bet has high upside potential: The profits, both in dollars and as a percentage of the money you put up, rise very rapidly when the stock price in July exceeds $100.

You can summarize all of this in a spreadsheet.

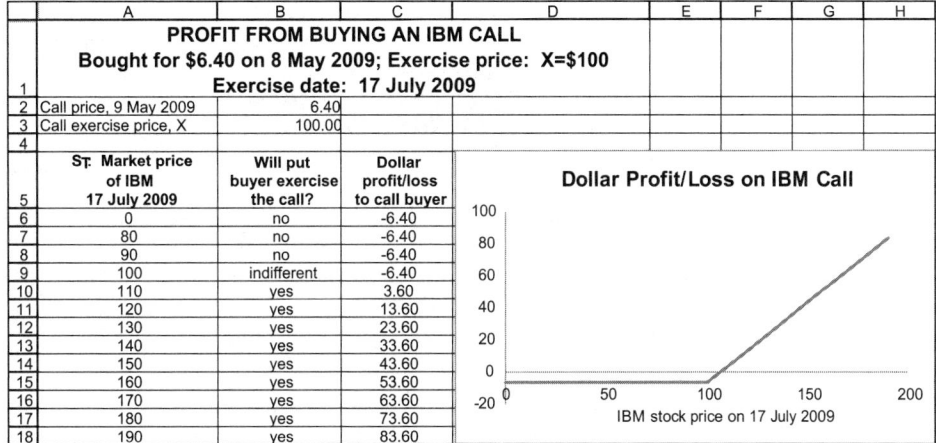

|   | A | B | C | D | E | F | G | H |
|---|---|---|---|---|---|---|---|---|
| 1 | **PROFIT FROM BUYING AN IBM CALL** Bought for $6.40 on 8 May 2009; Exercise price: X=$100 Exercise date: 17 July 2009 | | | | | | | |
| 2 | Call price, 9 May 2009 | 6.40 | | | | | | |
| 3 | Call exercise price, X | 100.00 | | | | | | |
| 4 | | | | | | | | |
| 5 | $S_T$ Market price of IBM 17 July 2009 | Will put buyer exercise the call? | Dollar profit/loss to call buyer | | | | | |
| 6 | 0 | no | -6.40 | | | | | |
| 7 | 80 | no | -6.40 | | | | | |
| 8 | 90 | no | -6.40 | | | | | |
| 9 | 100 | indifferent | -6.40 | | | | | |
| 10 | 110 | yes | 3.60 | | | | | |
| 11 | 120 | yes | 13.60 | | | | | |
| 12 | 130 | yes | 23.60 | | | | | |
| 13 | 140 | yes | 33.60 | | | | | |
| 14 | 150 | yes | 43.60 | | | | | |
| 15 | 160 | yes | 53.60 | | | | | |
| 16 | 170 | yes | 63.60 | | | | | |
| 17 | 180 | yes | 73.60 | | | | | |
| 18 | 190 | yes | 83.60 | | | | | |

## 20.3. Why Buy a Put Option?

As in the case of the call, there are two simple reasons to buy a put.

**Reason 1:** The put option allows you to delay the decision to sell the stock.

It's 8 May 2009, and you own a share of IBM stock. You're considering selling the stock; its current market price is $101.49. As an alternative, you can buy a July put option with $X = $100. This put option will cost you $5.20. Here's your thinking:

- If, on 17 July 2009, IBM's stock price is < $100, you'll exercise the put option and sell the share for $100. As in the case of the call option discussed earlier, there are several "subpossibilities":

  - IBM's 17 July stock price = $50. Now you've made a lot of money: You spent $5.20 for the option, but you sold the stock for $100, which is $50.00 more than its market price. Your net profit is $44.80 ($50.00 – $5.20 cost of the option).

  - If IBM's 17 July stock price = $95.00, you'll still exercise the put option and sell the stock for $100.00. Compared with the market price, you've made $5.00 on the sale of the stock, but this time you will have lost a bit of money, because the option cost you $5.20. Your net profit will be –$0.20.

- If on 17 July IBM's stock is selling for more than $100, you will not exercise your put option. If you still want to sell the stock, you'll sell it on the open market. In all cases, you will be out only the $5.20 cost of the option.

***Reason 2:*** A put option allows you to make a bet on the stock price going down. If you buy a put for \$5.20 and wait until 17 July to exercise, here are your profits:

$$Put\ profits = \begin{cases} 100 - S_T - 5.20 & \begin{array}{l} \textit{IBM stock price on } 17\, Jul09 \le 100 \\ \text{In this case you exercise the put and} \\ \text{make } S_T - 100 \text{ minus the cost of the put} \end{array} \\[2em] -5.20 & \begin{array}{l} \textit{IBM stock price on } 17\, Jul09 \quad 100 \\ \text{In this case you do not exercise the put;} \\ \text{your loss is the cost of the put} \end{array} \end{cases}$$

Here is a summary in a spreadsheet.

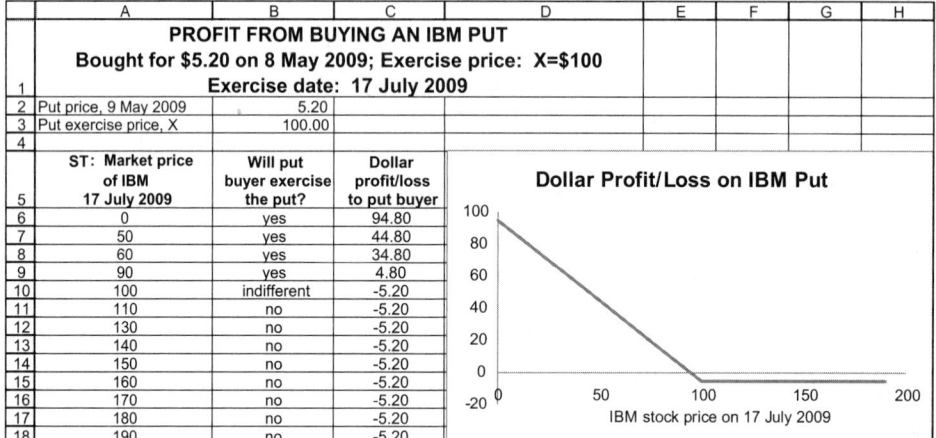

| | A | B | C | D | E | F | G | H |
|---|---|---|---|---|---|---|---|---|
| 1 | | | | | | | | |
| | **PROFIT FROM BUYING AN IBM PUT** | | | | | | | |
| | **Bought for \$5.20 on 8 May 2009; Exercise price: X=\$100** | | | | | | | |
| | **Exercise date: 17 July 2009** | | | | | | | |
| 2 | Put price, 9 May 2009 | 5.20 | | | | | | |
| 3 | Put exercise price, X | 100.00 | | | | | | |
| 4 | | | | | | | | |
| 5 | ST: Market price of IBM 17 July 2009 | Will put buyer exercise the put? | Dollar profit/loss to put buyer | **Dollar Profit/Loss on IBM Put** | | | | |
| 6 | 0 | yes | 94.80 | | | | | |
| 7 | 50 | yes | 44.80 | | | | | |
| 8 | 60 | yes | 34.80 | | | | | |
| 9 | 90 | yes | 4.80 | | | | | |
| 10 | 100 | indifferent | -5.20 | | | | | |
| 11 | 110 | no | -5.20 | | | | | |
| 12 | 130 | no | -5.20 | | | | | |
| 13 | 140 | no | -5.20 | | | | | |
| 14 | 150 | no | -5.20 | | | | | |
| 15 | 160 | no | -5.20 | | | | | |
| 16 | 170 | no | -5.20 | | | | | |
| 17 | 180 | no | -5.20 | | | | | |
| 18 | 190 | no | -5.20 | | | | | |

# 20.4. General Properties of Option Prices

In this section we review three general properties of option prices. We look at the effects of option time to maturity, exercise price, and the stock price. Our discussion is informal and intuitive.

## Property 1: Options with More Time to Maturity Are Worth More

The longer you have to exercise an option, the more it should be worth. The intuition here is clear: Suppose you have a July 2009 call option to buy IBM stock for \$100 and also an October 2009 call option to buy IBM for \$100. Because IBM options are American options, the October call gives you all the opportunities associated with the September call—and then some. Thus the October call should be worth more than the September call.

Here are some data for the IBM options. Note that the prices of the options increase with maturity.

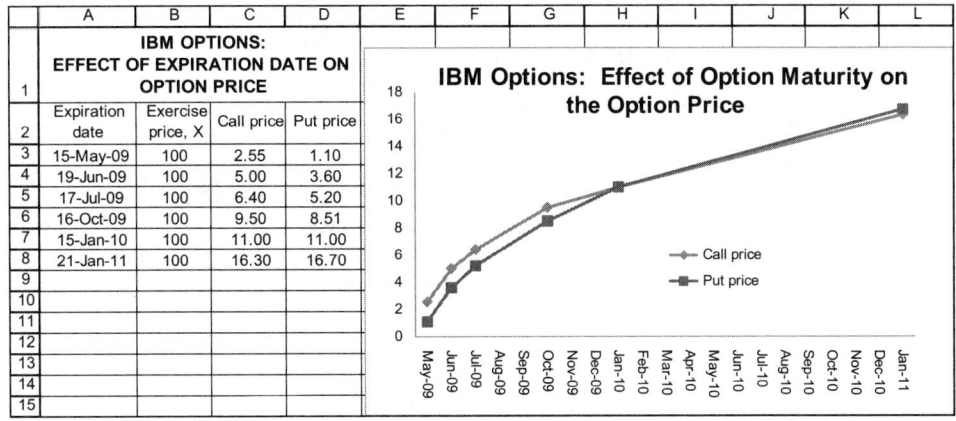

| | A | B | C | D |
|---|---|---|---|---|
| 1 | IBM OPTIONS: EFFECT OF EXPIRATION DATE ON OPTION PRICE | | | |
| 2 | Expiration date | Exercise price, X | Call price | Put price |
| 3 | 15-May-09 | 100 | 2.55 | 1.10 |
| 4 | 19-Jun-09 | 100 | 5.00 | 3.60 |
| 5 | 17-Jul-09 | 100 | 6.40 | 5.20 |
| 6 | 16-Oct-09 | 100 | 9.50 | 8.51 |
| 7 | 15-Jan-10 | 100 | 11.00 | 11.00 |
| 8 | 21-Jan-11 | 100 | 16.30 | 16.70 |

## Property 2: Calls with Higher Exercise Prices Are Worth Less; Puts with Higher Exercise Prices Are Worth More

Suppose you had two October 2009 calls on IBM: One call has an exercise price of $100 and the second call has an exercise price of $120. The second call is worth less than the first. Why? Think about calls as *bets* on the stock price: The first call is a bet that the stock price will go over $100, whereas the second call is a bet that the stock price will go over $120. You're always more likely to win the first bet (IBM will go over $100) than the second bet.

From the table below you can see that IBM's option prices conform to this property.

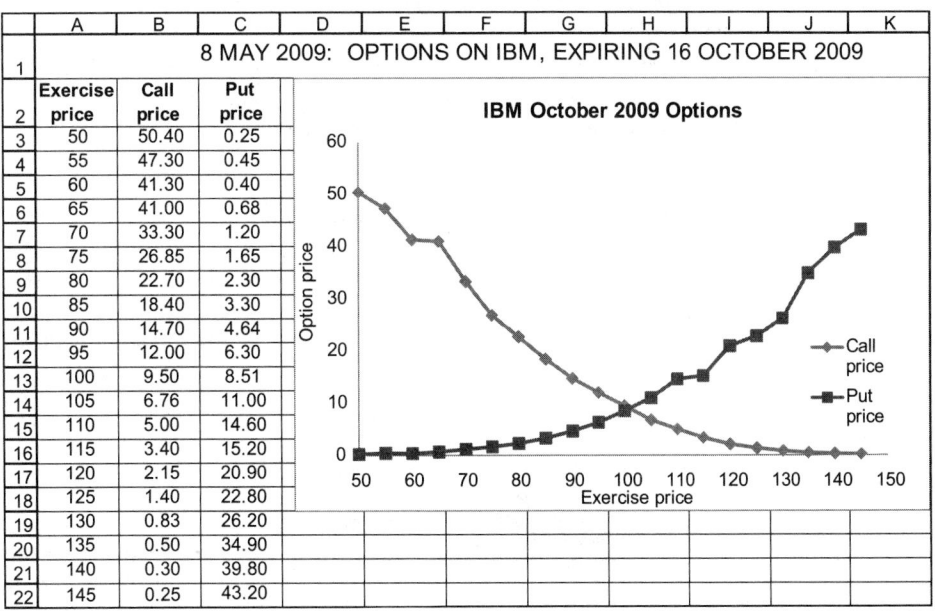

| | A | B | C |
|---|---|---|---|
| 1 | 8 MAY 2009: OPTIONS ON IBM, EXPIRING 16 OCTOBER 2009 | | |
| 2 | Exercise price | Call price | Put price |
| 3 | 50 | 50.40 | 0.25 |
| 4 | 55 | 47.30 | 0.45 |
| 5 | 60 | 41.30 | 0.40 |
| 6 | 65 | 41.00 | 0.68 |
| 7 | 70 | 33.30 | 1.20 |
| 8 | 75 | 26.85 | 1.65 |
| 9 | 80 | 22.70 | 2.30 |
| 10 | 85 | 18.40 | 3.30 |
| 11 | 90 | 14.70 | 4.64 |
| 12 | 95 | 12.00 | 6.30 |
| 13 | 100 | 9.50 | 8.51 |
| 14 | 105 | 6.76 | 11.00 |
| 15 | 110 | 5.00 | 14.60 |
| 16 | 115 | 3.40 | 15.20 |
| 17 | 120 | 2.15 | 20.90 |
| 18 | 125 | 1.40 | 22.80 |
| 19 | 130 | 0.83 | 26.20 |
| 20 | 135 | 0.50 | 34.90 |
| 21 | 140 | 0.30 | 39.80 |
| 22 | 145 | 0.25 | 43.20 |

Here we've looked at all the options that expire on the same date (October 2009). As you can see, the higher the option exercise price, the lower the call price and the higher the put price.

## Property 3: When the Stock Price Goes Up, Call Option Prices Go Up and Put Option Prices Go Down

The reason for this behavior is obvious, if you think of an option as a bet: Suppose you buy a IBM $X = 100$ October 2009 call option. We can view this option as a bet that IBM's stock price in October will be above $100. The probability of your winning this bet is higher if IBM's current stock price is higher and hence so is the call option's price. Thus, for example, if you're willing to pay $9.50 for the $X = 100$ October call when IBM's current stock price is $101.49, you would be willing to pay more for the same call when IBM's stock price is $105.

The logic for puts is the same, although the result is opposite: The higher the stock price, the lower the put option price.

# 20.5. Writing Options, Shorting Stock

Our discussion thus far has been from the point of view of the option purchaser. For example, in Section 20.2 we derived the profit pattern from buying an IBM 100 call for $6.40 on 8 May 2009 and waiting until the call maturity on 17 July 2009. Similarly, in Section 20.3 we looked at the profit from buying an IBM 100 put.

## Writing Calls

There's another side to this story: When you buy a call, someone else sells the call. In the jargon of options markets, the call seller is *writing a call*.

**Call buyer:** On 8 May 2009 buys, for $6.40, the *right* to buy one share of IBM stock for $100 on or before 17 July 2009.

**Call writer:** On 8 May 2009 sells, for $6.40, the *obligation* to sell one share of IBM stock for $100—as per demand of the call option buyer—on or before 17 July 2009.

Here's the way the call writer's profit pattern looks.

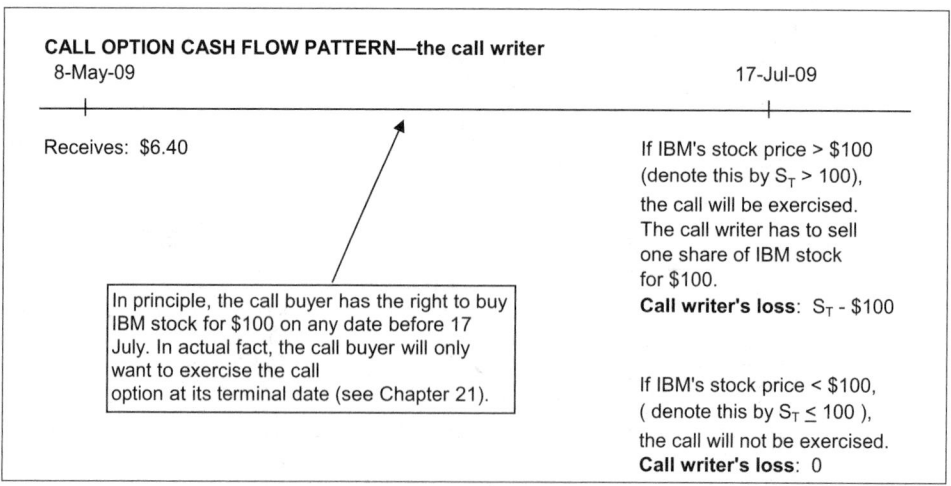

FIGURE 20.9 The cash flows from writing an IBM call option on 8 May 2009 for $6.40 and possibly having it exercised against the writer on 17 July 2009. The option has exercise price $X = \$100$.

Here's the profit graph from writing a call option.

| | A | B | C | D | E | F | G | H |
|---|---|---|---|---|---|---|---|---|
| 1 | PROFIT FROM WRITING AN IBM CALL<br>Sold for $6.40 on 8 May 2009; Exercise price: X=$100<br>Exercise date: 17 July 2009 | | | | | | | |
| 2 | Call price, 9 May 2009 | 6.40 | | | | | | |
| 3 | Call exercise price, X | 100.00 | | | | | | |
| 4 | | | | | | | | |
| 5 | $S_T$: Market price<br>of IBM<br>17 July 2009 | Will call<br>buyer exercise<br>the call? | Dollar<br>profit/loss<br>to call writer | | | | | |
| 6 | 0 | no | 6.40 | | | | | |
| 7 | 80 | no | 6.40 | | | | | |
| 8 | 90 | no | 6.40 | | | | | |
| 9 | 100 | indifferent | 6.40 | | | | | |
| 10 | 110 | yes | -3.60 | | | | | |
| 11 | 120 | yes | -13.60 | | | | | |
| 12 | 130 | yes | -23.60 | | | | | |
| 13 | 140 | yes | -33.60 | | | | | |
| 14 | 150 | yes | -43.60 | | | | | |
| 15 | 160 | yes | -53.60 | | | | | |
| 16 | 170 | yes | -63.60 | | | | | |
| 17 | 180 | yes | -73.60 | | | | | |
| 18 | 190 | yes | -83.60 | | | | | |

Dollar Profit/Loss on IBM Written Call — IBM stock price on 17 July 2009

## Writing Puts

There's a similar story for puts.

*Put buyer:* On 8 May 2009 buys, for $5.20, the *right* to sell one share of IBM stock for $100 on or before 17 July 2009.

*Put writer:* On 8 May 2009 sells, for $5.20, the *obligation* to buy one share of IBM stock for $100—as per demand of the put option buyer—on or before 17 July.

Here's the way the put writer's profit pattern looks.

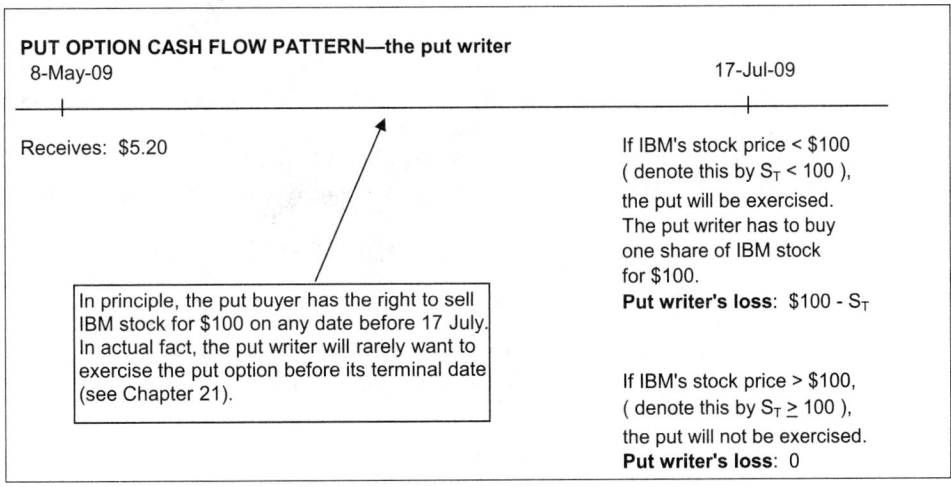

PUT OPTION CASH FLOW PATTERN—the put writer

8-May-09                                                     17-Jul-09

Receives: $5.20

In principle, the put buyer has the right to sell IBM stock for $100 on any date before 17 July. In actual fact, the put writer will rarely want to exercise the put option before its terminal date (see Chapter 21).

If IBM's stock price < $100 ( denote this by $S_T < 100$ ), the put will be exercised. The put writer has to buy one share of IBM stock for $100.
**Put writer's loss:** $100 - $S_T$

If IBM's stock price > $100, ( denote this by $S_T \geq 100$ ), the put will not be exercised.
**Put writer's loss:** 0

FIGURE 20.10 The cash flows from writing an IBM put option on 8 May 2009 for $5.20 and possibly having it exercised against the writer on 17 July 2009. The option has exercise price $X = \$100$.

Here's a graph of the profit pattern from writing a put.

|  | A | B | C | D | E | F | G | H |
|---|---|---|---|---|---|---|---|---|
| 1 | | **PROFIT FROM WRITING AN IBM PUT** Sold for \$5.20 on 8 May 2009; Exercise price: X=\$100 Exercise date: 17 July 2009 | | | | | | |
| 2 | Put price, 9 May 2009 | 5.20 | | | | | | |
| 3 | Put exercise price, X | 100.00 | | | | | | |
| 4 | | | | | | | | |
| 5 | ST: Market price of IBM 17 July 2009 | Will put buyer exercise the put? | Dollar profit/loss to put writer | | | | | |
| 6 | 0 | yes | -94.80 | | | | | |
| 7 | 50 | yes | -44.80 | | | | | |
| 8 | 60 | yes | -34.80 | | | | | |
| 9 | 90 | yes | -4.80 | | | | | |
| 10 | 100 | indifferent | 5.20 | | | | | |
| 11 | 110 | no | 5.20 | | | | | |
| 12 | 130 | no | 5.20 | | | | | |
| 13 | 140 | no | 5.20 | | | | | |
| 14 | 150 | no | 5.20 | | | | | |
| 15 | 160 | no | 5.20 | | | | | |
| 16 | 170 | no | 5.20 | | | | | |
| 17 | 180 | no | 5.20 | | | | | |
| 18 | 190 | no | 5.20 | | | | | |

## Short-Selling a Stock

Short-selling a stock ("shorting") is the stock equivalent of writing an option. Here's how shorting a stock compares to buying a stock.

**Stock buyer:** On 8 May 2009 buys one share of IBM stock, for \$101.49. When you sell the stock—call the date $T$—you'll get the stock price $S_T$. Of course you will have also earned any dividends that IBM will have paid up to and including date $T$. Ignoring the time value of money, your profit from buying the stock is

$$S_T + IBM\ dividends - 101.49$$

**Stock shorter:** On 8 May 2009 contacts his broker and borrows one share of IBM stock, which he then sells, thus receiving \$101.49. At some future date $T$, the short-seller of the stock will purchase a share of IBM on the open market, paying the then-current market price $S_T$. If along the way IBM has paid any dividends, the short-seller will be obliged to pay these dividends to the person he's borrowed the stock from. His total profit will be

$$101.49 - \left(S_T + IBM\ dividends\right)$$

In the option chapters in this book, we will generally assume that stocks don't pay any dividends between the time you buy them and the time you sell them. This means that the profit from buying or shorting a stock can be represented as follows.

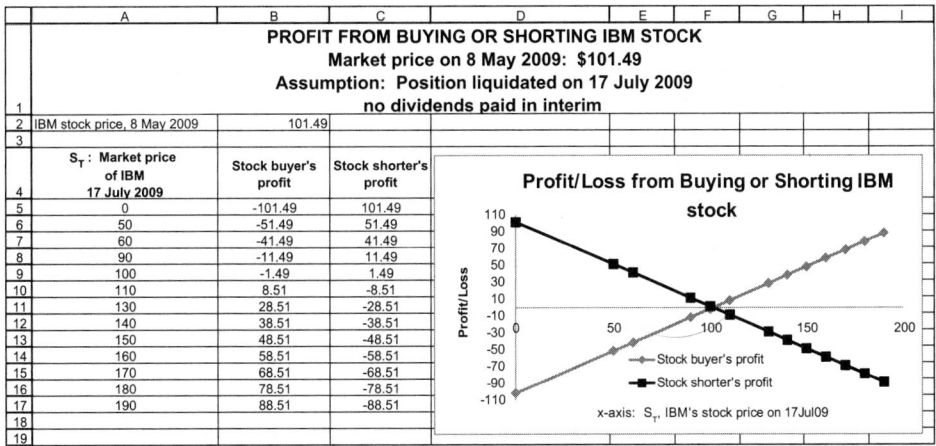

| | A | B | C | D | E | F | G | H | I |
|---|---|---|---|---|---|---|---|---|---|
| 1 | | PROFIT FROM BUYING OR SHORTING IBM STOCK<br>Market price on 8 May 2009:  $101.49<br>Assumption:  Position liquidated on 17 July 2009<br>no dividends paid in interim | | | | | | | | |
| 2 | IBM stock price, 8 May 2009 | 101.49 | | | | | | | |
| 3 | | | | | | | | | |
| 4 | $S_T$: Market price<br>of IBM<br>17 July 2009 | Stock buyer's<br>profit | Stock shorter's<br>profit | | | | | | |
| 5 | 0 | -101.49 | 101.49 | | | | | | |
| 6 | 50 | -51.49 | 51.49 | | | | | | |
| 7 | 60 | -41.49 | 41.49 | | | | | | |
| 8 | 90 | -11.49 | 11.49 | | | | | | |
| 9 | 100 | -1.49 | 1.49 | | | | | | |
| 10 | 110 | 8.51 | -8.51 | | | | | | |
| 11 | 130 | 28.51 | -28.51 | | | | | | |
| 12 | 140 | 38.51 | -38.51 | | | | | | |
| 13 | 150 | 48.51 | -48.51 | | | | | | |
| 14 | 160 | 58.51 | -58.51 | | | | | | |
| 15 | 170 | 68.51 | -68.51 | | | | | | |
| 16 | 180 | 78.51 | -78.51 | | | | | | |
| 17 | 190 | 88.51 | -88.51 | | | | | | |
| 18 | | | | | | | | | |
| 19 | | | | | | | | | |

## SHORT-SELLING

A *long* position in a stock involves buying the stock on a particular date and possibly selling the stock on a later date. When you have a long position in a stock, you can choose to hold on to the stock forever (in this case you will collect the dividends that the stock pays).

A *short* position in a stock involves selling borrowed stock on a particular date and buying the stock on a later date to give the shares back to the stock lender. Buying the stock to return the shares to the lender is called *closing out the short position*. When you have a short position in a stock you must close out the position at some future date.

The profits from short and a long position in a stock are diametrically opposite. When you take a long position in a stock, you will profit if the stock price goes up. When you take a short position in a stock, you profit if the stock price goes down. To see this, suppose that on 31 October 2010, you borrow 100 shares of DipseyDoodle (DD) stock. DD is currently selling for $100 and you anticipate that the share price will drop. Having borrowed the shares, you sell them for $10,000 (100 shares times the current price of $100). One month later, DD stock is selling for $80 a share, and you close out your short position: You purchase 100 shares of DD stock for $8,000 and return the shares to the lender. Your short-selling bet on DD stock's decline has paid off, and you've made $2,000. (Of course, if DD had gone up, you would have lost money.)

Good articles describing short sales can be found at the following Web sites:

- Motley Fool: http://www.fool.com/FoolFAQ/FoolFAQ0033.htm

- "Short (finance):" http://en.wikipedia.org/wiki/Short_(finance)

## 20.6. Option Strategies—More Complicated Reasons to Buy Options

In the previous section we studied the profit and loss from buying and selling calls, puts, and shares. In this and the following two sections we look at the profit involved in more complicated option strategies. "Option strategy" refers to the profits that result from holding a combination of options, shares, and bonds.

## A Simple Option Strategy: Buy a Stock and Buy a Put

We begin with a very simple (but useful) strategy: Suppose we decide, on 8 May 2009, to purchase one share of IBM stock *and* to purchase a July put on the stock with exercise price $100 and expiration date July. The total cost of this strategy is $106.69: $101.49 for the share of IBM and $5.20 for each put.

Such a strategy effectively *insures* your stock returns by guaranteeing that on 17 July you will have at least $100 in hand. Your worst-case net profit will be a loss of $6.69.

| Stock price on 17 July 2009 | Strategy | Cash in hand | Net profit |
|---|---|---|---|
| Less than $100 | Exercise put option and sell your share of IBM for $100. | $100 | $100 − ($101.49 + $5.20) = −$6.69 |
| More than $100 | Let the put option expire (don't use it) | IBM stock price on 17 July, $S_T$ | $S_T − ($101.49 + $5.20) = S_T − $106.69 |

In a spreadsheet, here's the way this strategy looks.

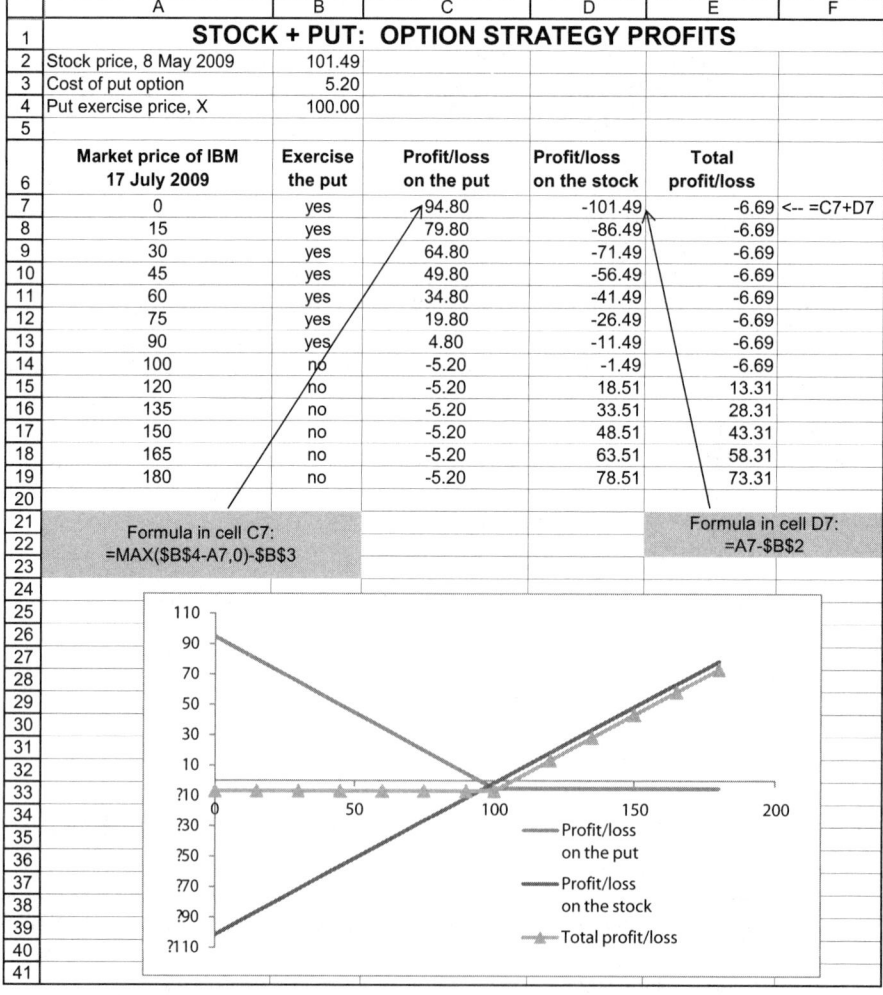

|   | A | B | C | D | E | F |
|---|---|---|---|---|---|---|
| 1 | **STOCK + PUT: OPTION STRATEGY PROFITS** | | | | | |
| 2 | Stock price, 8 May 2009 | 101.49 | | | | |
| 3 | Cost of put option | 5.20 | | | | |
| 4 | Put exercise price, X | 100.00 | | | | |
| 5 | | | | | | |
| 6 | **Market price of IBM 17 July 2009** | **Exercise the put** | **Profit/loss on the put** | **Profit/loss on the stock** | **Total profit/loss** | |
| 7 | 0 | yes | 94.80 | -101.49 | -6.69 | <-- =C7+D7 |
| 8 | 15 | yes | 79.80 | -86.49 | -6.69 | |
| 9 | 30 | yes | 64.80 | -71.49 | -6.69 | |
| 10 | 45 | yes | 49.80 | -56.49 | -6.69 | |
| 11 | 60 | yes | 34.80 | -41.49 | -6.69 | |
| 12 | 75 | yes | 19.80 | -26.49 | -6.69 | |
| 13 | 90 | yes | 4.80 | -11.49 | -6.69 | |
| 14 | 100 | no | -5.20 | -1.49 | -6.69 | |
| 15 | 120 | no | -5.20 | 18.51 | 13.31 | |
| 16 | 135 | no | -5.20 | 33.51 | 28.31 | |
| 17 | 150 | no | -5.20 | 48.51 | 43.31 | |
| 18 | 165 | no | -5.20 | 63.51 | 58.31 | |
| 19 | 180 | no | -5.20 | 78.51 | 73.31 | |
| 20 | | | | | | |
| 21 | Formula in cell C7: | | | | Formula in cell D7: | |
| 22 | =MAX($B$4-A7,0)-$B$3 | | | | =A7-$B$2 | |
| 23 | | | | | | |

Buying a stock or a portfolio *and* buying a put on the stock or portfolio is often called a *portfolio insurance* strategy. Portfolio insurance strategies are very popular among investors. They guarantee a minimum return on the investment in the shares (at an extra cost, of course: you have to buy the puts).

---

## ANTICIPATING A BIT—PUT-CALL PARITY

You'll note that the graph of the stock + put strategy looks a lot like the graph of a call (Section 20.2). This may lead you to surmise that the payoffs of the combination *stock + put* is somehow equivalent to the payoffs of a *call*. However, this isn't quite true, as you'll see in the next chapter. There we discuss the *put–call* parity theorem and show that—for a put and call written on the same stock, with the same expiration date, and having the same exercise price *X*,

$$stock + put = call + PV(X)$$

---

## A More Complicated Strategy: Stock + Two Puts

Suppose you purchased one share of stock and bought two puts, each costing $5.20 and each having an exercise price of $100. Here's what your payoff pattern would look like.

| Stock price on 17 July | Strategy | Cash in hand, 17 July | Net profit |
|---|---|---|---|
| $S_T \leq \$100$ | Exercise both put options. Give someone else your share of IBM for $100. Buy an additional share in the market for $S_T$ and sell it to the put writer for $S_T$. | $2*100 - S_T$ | $2*100 - S_T - (\$101.49 + \$10.40) = \$108.91 - S_T$ |
| More than $100 | Let the put options expire (don't use them) | IBM stock price on 17 July, $S_T$ | $S_T - (\$101.49 + \$10.40) = S_T - \$110.89$ |

If we make an Excel table, here's what it looks like.

| | A | B | C | D | E | F |
|---|---|---|---|---|---|---|
| 1 | **STOCK + 2 PUTS: OPTION STRATEGY PROFITS** | | | | | |
| 2 | Stock price, 8 May 2009 | 101.49 | | | | |
| 3 | Cost of put option | 5.20 | | | | |
| 4 | Put exercise price, X | 100.00 | | | | |
| 5 | | | | | | |
| 6 | **Market price of IBM 17 July 2009** | **Exercise the put** | **Profit/loss on the puts** | **Profit/loss on the stock** | **Total profit/loss** | |
| 7 | 0 | yes | 189.60 | -101.49 | 88.11 | <-- =C7+D7 |
| 8 | 15 | yes | 159.60 | -86.49 | 73.11 | |
| 9 | 30 | yes | 129.60 | -71.49 | 58.11 | |
| 10 | 45 | yes | 99.60 | -56.49 | 43.11 | |
| 11 | 60 | yes | 69.60 | -41.49 | 28.11 | |
| 12 | 75 | yes | 39.60 | -26.49 | 13.11 | |
| 13 | 90 | yes | 9.60 | -11.49 | -1.89 | |
| 14 | 100 | no | -10.40 | -1.49 | -11.89 | |
| 15 | 120 | no | -10.40 | 18.51 | 8.11 | |
| 16 | 135 | no | -10.40 | 33.51 | 23.11 | |
| 17 | 150 | no | -10.40 | 48.51 | 38.11 | |
| 18 | 165 | no | -10.40 | 63.51 | 53.11 | |
| 19 | 180 | no | -10.40 | 78.51 | 68.11 | |
| 20 | | | | | | |
| 21 | Formula in cell C7: | | | | Formula in cell D7: | |
| 22 | =2*(MAX($B$4-A7,0)-$B$3) | | | | =A7-$B$2 | |
| 23 | | | | | | |

Chart: **Stock + 2 Puts** — Profit (y-axis) vs IBM stock price, 17 July 2009 (x-axis)

## Comparing Strategies

What's better as a strategy: buying a share of IBM and buying one put or buying a share of IBM and buying two puts? Look at the graphs of the two strategies.

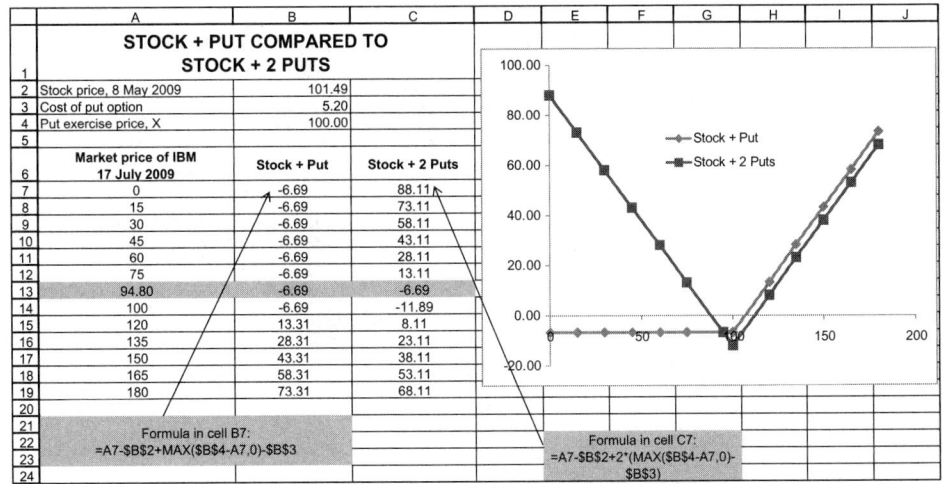

| | A | B | C | D | E | F | G | H | I | J |
|---|---|---|---|---|---|---|---|---|---|---|
| 1 | STOCK + PUT COMPARED TO STOCK + 2 PUTS | | | | | | | | | |
| 2 | Stock price, 8 May 2009 | 101.49 | | | | | | | | |
| 3 | Cost of put option | 5.20 | | | | | | | | |
| 4 | Put exercise price, X | 100.00 | | | | | | | | |
| 5 | | | | | | | | | | |
| 6 | Market price of IBM 17 July 2009 | Stock + Put | Stock + 2 Puts | | | | | | | |
| 7 | 0 | -6.69 | 88.11 | | | | | | | |
| 8 | 15 | -6.69 | 73.11 | | | | | | | |
| 9 | 30 | -6.69 | 58.11 | | | | | | | |
| 10 | 45 | -6.69 | 43.11 | | | | | | | |
| 11 | 60 | -6.69 | 28.11 | | | | | | | |
| 12 | 75 | -6.69 | 13.11 | | | | | | | |
| 13 | 94.80 | -6.69 | -6.69 | | | | | | | |
| 14 | 100 | -6.69 | -11.89 | | | | | | | |
| 15 | 120 | 13.31 | 8.11 | | | | | | | |
| 16 | 135 | 28.31 | 23.11 | | | | | | | |
| 17 | 150 | 43.31 | 38.11 | | | | | | | |
| 18 | 165 | 58.31 | 53.11 | | | | | | | |
| 19 | 180 | 73.31 | 68.11 | | | | | | | |
| 20 | | | | | | | | | | |
| 21 | Formula in cell B7: =A7-$B$2+MAX($B$4-A7,0)-$B$3 | | | | | | | | | |
| 22 | | | | | | | | | | |
| 23 | | | | | Formula in cell C7: =A7-$B$2+2*(MAX($B$4-A7,0)-$B$3) | | | | | |
| 24 | | | | | | | | | | |

The choice between the two strategies involves *trade-offs* (that's the nature of market efficiency: in an efficient market no asset ever completely dominates another asset).

- The stock + put strategy has higher profit when the IBM July stock price > 94.80, but it has a lower profit for IBM $S_T < 94.80$.

- The stock + two put strategy costs more (you can see this by noting that its payoff when $S_T = 100$ is less than that of the stock + put strategy). On the other hand, it has positive profits both for very low and for high $S_T$.

Which strategy should you choose? It depends on your prediction of the future: If you think that IBM is going to make a big move, up or down, then stock + two puts is for you, because this strategy makes profits on "big moves" of the stock price (whether up or down). If you think, on the other hand, that IBM might go up, but you want protection when and if its price goes down (that is, no bets for you), then stock + put is your choice.

## Another Strategy: One Share of Stock + One, Two, Three, or Four Puts

There's almost nothing to say here, except to show you the graphs.

| | A | B | C | D | E | F | G | H |
|---|---|---|---|---|---|---|---|---|
| 1 | STOCK + SEVERAL PUTS PUT: OPTION STRATEGY PROFITS | | | | | | | |
| 2 | Stock price, 8 May 2009 | 101.49 | | | | | | |
| 3 | Cost of put option | 5.20 | | | | | | |
| 4 | Put exercise price, X | 100.00 | | | | | | |
| 5 | | | | | | | | |
| 6 | Market price of IBM 17 July 2009 | Exercise the put | Profit/loss on single put | Profit/loss on the stock | Total profit: 1 put | Total profit: 2 puts | Total profit: 3 puts | Total profit: 4 puts |
| 7 | 0 | yes | 94.8 | -101.49 | -6.69 | 88.11 | 182.91 | 277.71 |
| 8 | 15 | yes | 79.8 | -86.49 | -6.69 | 73.11 | 152.91 | 232.71 |
| 9 | 30 | yes | 64.8 | -71.49 | -6.69 | 58.11 | 122.91 | 187.71 |
| 10 | 45 | yes | 49.8 | -56.49 | -6.69 | 43.11 | 92.91 | 142.71 |
| 11 | 60 | yes | 34.8 | -41.49 | -6.69 | 28.11 | 62.91 | 97.71 |
| 12 | 75 | yes | 19.8 | -26.49 | -6.69 | 13.11 | 32.91 | 52.71 |
| 13 | 90 | yes | 4.8 | -11.49 | -6.69 | -1.89 | 2.91 | 7.71 |
| 14 | 100 | no | -5.2 | -1.49 | -6.69 | -11.89 | -17.09 | -22.29 |
| 15 | 120 | no | -5.2 | 18.51 | 13.31 | 8.11 | 2.91 | -2.29 |
| 16 | 135 | no | -5.2 | 33.51 | 28.31 | 23.11 | 17.91 | 12.71 |
| 17 | 150 | no | -5.2 | 48.51 | 43.31 | 38.11 | 32.91 | 27.71 |
| 18 | 165 | no | -5.2 | 63.51 | 58.31 | 53.11 | 47.91 | 42.71 |
| 19 | 180 | no | -5.2 | 78.51 | 73.31 | 68.11 | 62.91 | 57.71 |

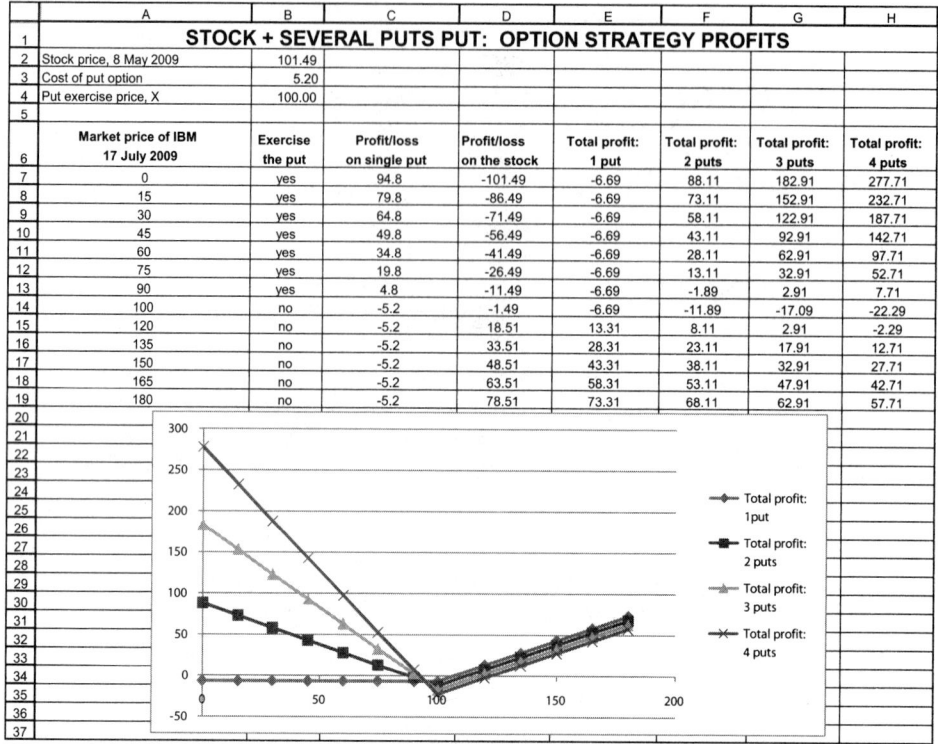

## 20.7. Another Option Strategy: Spread

A spread strategy involves buying one option on a stock and writing another option. In the example below on 8 May 2009,

- We buy one $X = 80$ July call on IBM. This option costs $20.99.
- We write one $X = 110$ July call on IBM. This option costs 2.24; because we're writing the option, this is income on 8 May.

In the following spreadsheet we examine this strategy's payoffs and graph them.

| | A | B | C | D | E | F |
|---|---|---|---|---|---|---|
| 1 | **BULL SPREAD: A MODERATE BET ON STOCK PRICE INCREASE** | | | | | |
| 2 | Cost of July, X=80 call | 20.99 | | | | |
| 3 | Number of X=80 calls purchased | 1 | | | | |
| 4 | | | | | | |
| 5 | Cost of July X=110 call | 2.24 | | | | |
| 6 | Number of X=80 calls purchased | -1 | | | | |
| 7 | | | | | | |
| 8 | **Market price of IBM 17 July 2009** | **Exercise X=80 call?** | **Profit/loss on X=80 bought call** | **Exercise X=110 call?** | **Profit/loss on X=110 written call** | **Total profit** |
| 9 | 0 | no | -20.99 | no | 2.24 | -18.75 |
| 10 | 15 | no | -20.99 | no | 2.24 | -18.75 |
| 11 | 30 | no | -20.99 | no | 2.24 | -18.75 |
| 12 | 45 | no | -20.99 | no | 2.24 | -18.75 |
| 13 | 60 | no | -20.99 | no | 2.24 | -18.75 |
| 14 | 80 | no | -20.99 | no | 2.24 | -18.75 |
| 15 | 90 | yes | -10.99 | no | 2.24 | -8.75 |
| 16 | 100 | yes | -0.99 | no | 2.24 | 1.25 |
| 17 | 110 | yes | 9.01 | no | 2.24 | 11.25 |
| 18 | 120 | yes | 19.01 | yes | -7.76 | 11.25 |
| 19 | 150 | yes | 49.01 | yes | -37.76 | 11.25 |
| 20 | 165 | yes | 64.01 | yes | -52.76 | 11.25 |
| 21 | 180 | yes | 79.01 | yes | -67.76 | 11.25 |

There's another way to think about the strategy profits: On 17 July 2009 (the option expiration date) we will have

$$-20.99 + \underbrace{\underbrace{Max\ S_{IBM,17Jul09} - 80,0}_{\substack{\text{This is the option payoff on 17Jul09} \\ \text{from buying a call with X = \$80}}}}_{\substack{\text{This is the profit from buying} \\ \text{the X = \$80 option}}} + \underbrace{2.24 - \underbrace{Max\ S_{IBM,17Jul09} - 110,0}_{\substack{\text{Writing an option means} \\ \text{taking a loss if IBM's stock} \\ \text{price > \$110}}}}_{\text{This is the profit from writing the X = \$110 option}}$$

$$= -18.75 + \begin{cases} 0 & S_{IBM,17Jul09}\ 80 \\ S_{IBM,17Jul09} - 80 & 80 \le S_{IBM,17Jul09} \le 110 \\ 30 & S_{IBM,17Jul09}\ 110 \end{cases}$$

In this case the spread is a not-too-risky bet on the stock price going up. If it goes up, you profit (moderately); if the stock price goes down, your loss is limited to $18.75. This kind of a spread is called a *bull spread*—you're bullish on the stock (meaning that you think the stock price will go up).

Here's a *bear spread*: In this case we write the $X = 80$ call and buy the $X = 110$ call. As you can see from the graph below, the bear spread is a bet that the stock price will decline.

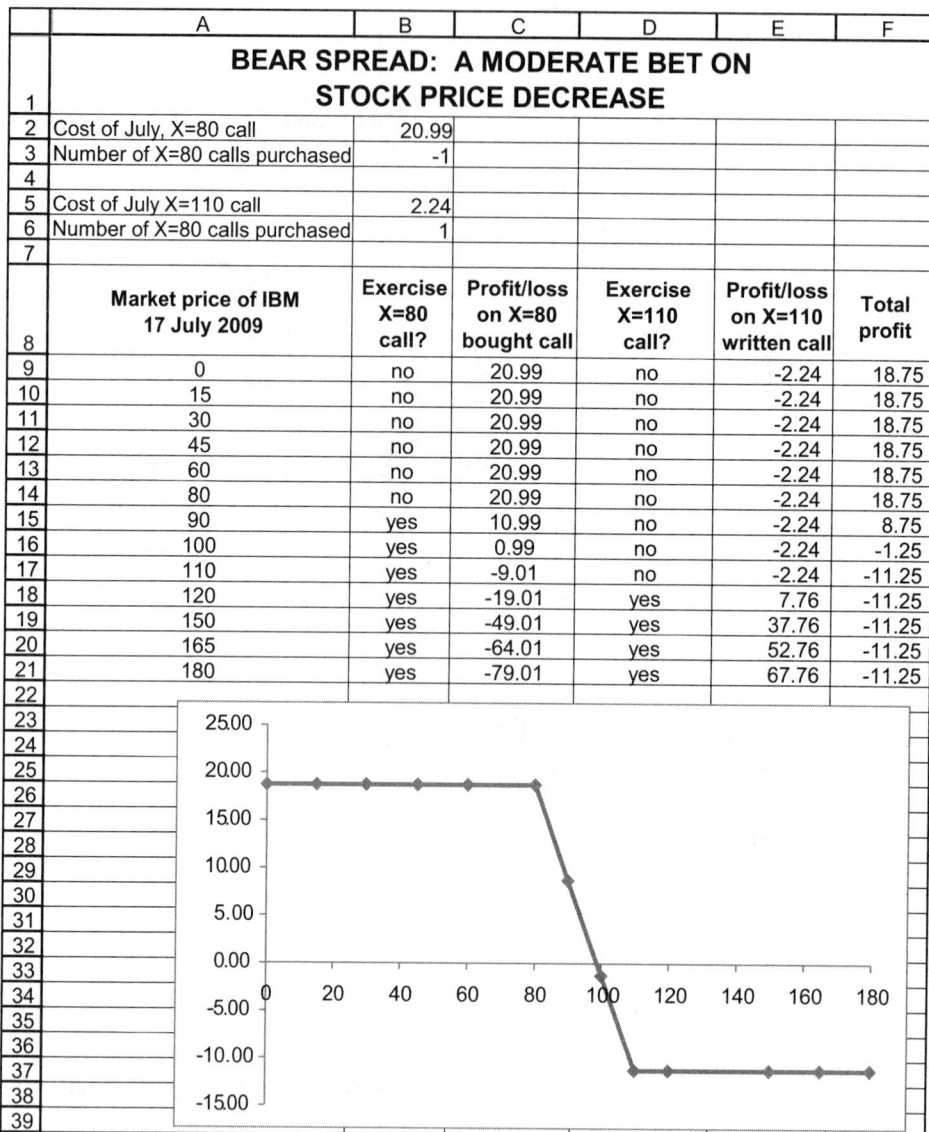

| | A | B | C | D | E | F |
|---|---|---|---|---|---|---|
| 1 | BEAR SPREAD:  A MODERATE BET ON STOCK PRICE DECREASE | | | | | |
| 2 | Cost of July, X=80 call | 20.99 | | | | |
| 3 | Number of X=80 calls purchased | -1 | | | | |
| 4 | | | | | | |
| 5 | Cost of July X=110 call | 2.24 | | | | |
| 6 | Number of X=80 calls purchased | 1 | | | | |
| 7 | | | | | | |
| 8 | Market price of IBM 17 July 2009 | Exercise X=80 call? | Profit/loss on X=80 bought call | Exercise X=110 call? | Profit/loss on X=110 written call | Total profit |
| 9 | 0 | no | 20.99 | no | -2.24 | 18.75 |
| 10 | 15 | no | 20.99 | no | -2.24 | 18.75 |
| 11 | 30 | no | 20.99 | no | -2.24 | 18.75 |
| 12 | 45 | no | 20.99 | no | -2.24 | 18.75 |
| 13 | 60 | no | 20.99 | no | -2.24 | 18.75 |
| 14 | 80 | no | 20.99 | no | -2.24 | 18.75 |
| 15 | 90 | yes | 10.99 | no | -2.24 | 8.75 |
| 16 | 100 | yes | 0.99 | no | -2.24 | -1.25 |
| 17 | 110 | yes | -9.01 | no | -2.24 | -11.25 |
| 18 | 120 | yes | -19.01 | yes | 7.76 | -11.25 |
| 19 | 150 | yes | -49.01 | yes | 37.76 | -11.25 |
| 20 | 165 | yes | -64.01 | yes | 52.76 | -11.25 |
| 21 | 180 | yes | -79.01 | yes | 67.76 | -11.25 |

## 20.8. The Butterfly Option Strategy

The last option strategy we consider in this chapter is a *butterfly*, the combination of three options. In the butterfly illustrated below,

- We buy one IBM, July $X = 80$, call for $20.99.

- We write two IBM, July $X = 100$, calls for $6.40 each.
- We buy one IBM, July $X = 120$, call for $0.52.
- Here's the resulting profit pattern.

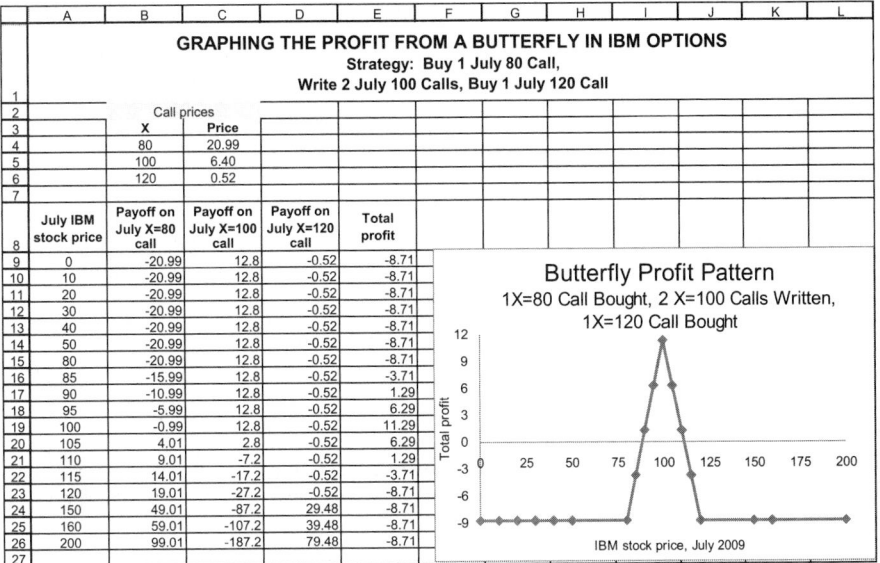

| | A | B | C | D | E | F | G | H | I | J | K | L |
|---|---|---|---|---|---|---|---|---|---|---|---|---|
| 1 | | | | GRAPHING THE PROFIT FROM A BUTTERFLY IN IBM OPTIONS | | | | | | | | |
| | | | | | Strategy: Buy 1 July 80 Call, | | | | | | | |
| | | | | | Write 2 July 100 Calls, Buy 1 July 120 Call | | | | | | | |
| 2 | | Call prices | | | | | | | | | | |
| 3 | | X | Price | | | | | | | | | |
| 4 | | 80 | 20.99 | | | | | | | | | |
| 5 | | 100 | 6.40 | | | | | | | | | |
| 6 | | 120 | 0.52 | | | | | | | | | |
| 7 | | | | | | | | | | | | |
| 8 | July IBM stock price | Payoff on July X=80 call | Payoff on July X=100 call | Payoff on July X=120 call | Total profit | | | | | | | |
| 9 | 0 | -20.99 | 12.8 | -0.52 | -8.71 | | | | | | | |
| 10 | 10 | -20.99 | 12.8 | -0.52 | -8.71 | | | | | | | |
| 11 | 20 | -20.99 | 12.8 | -0.52 | -8.71 | | | | | | | |
| 12 | 30 | -20.99 | 12.8 | -0.52 | -8.71 | | | | | | | |
| 13 | 40 | -20.99 | 12.8 | -0.52 | -8.71 | | | | | | | |
| 14 | 50 | -20.99 | 12.8 | -0.52 | -8.71 | | | | | | | |
| 15 | 80 | -20.99 | 12.8 | -0.52 | -8.71 | | | | | | | |
| 16 | 85 | -15.99 | 12.8 | -0.52 | -3.71 | | | | | | | |
| 17 | 90 | -10.99 | 12.8 | -0.52 | 1.29 | | | | | | | |
| 18 | 95 | -5.99 | 12.8 | -0.52 | 6.29 | | | | | | | |
| 19 | 100 | -0.99 | 12.8 | -0.52 | 11.29 | | | | | | | |
| 20 | 105 | 4.01 | 2.8 | -0.52 | 6.29 | | | | | | | |
| 21 | 110 | 9.01 | -7.2 | -0.52 | 1.29 | | | | | | | |
| 22 | 115 | 14.01 | -17.2 | -0.52 | -3.71 | | | | | | | |
| 23 | 120 | 19.01 | -27.2 | -0.52 | -8.71 | | | | | | | |
| 24 | 150 | 49.01 | -87.2 | 29.48 | -8.71 | | | | | | | |
| 25 | 160 | 59.01 | -107.2 | 39.48 | -8.71 | | | | | | | |
| 26 | 200 | 99.01 | -187.2 | 79.48 | -8.71 | | | | | | | |
| 27 | | | | | | | | | | | | |

Butterfly Profit Pattern
1X=80 Call Bought, 2 X=100 Calls Written, 1X=120 Call Bought

Why buy a butterfly? Looking at the graph, you can see that it's a bet on the stock price not moving very much. If IBM's July stock price is close to $100, we'll make money from our butterfly. If it deviates (up or down) by a lot, we'll lose money, but only moderately.

Of course, if we reverse the option positions in the butterfly, we'll get a bet on the stock price moving a lot (big movements either up or down will lead to profits; small movements in the stock price will lead to losses).

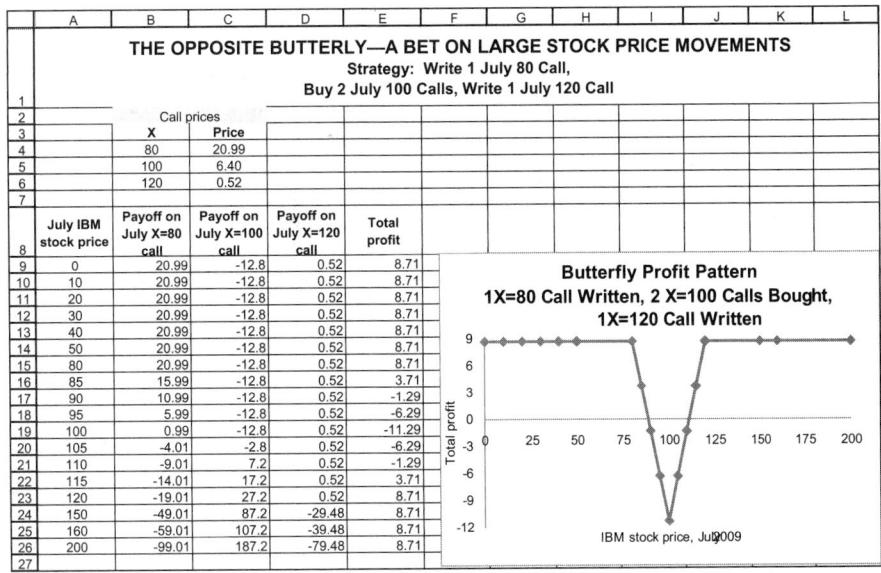

| | A | B | C | D | E | F | G | H | I | J | K | L |
|---|---|---|---|---|---|---|---|---|---|---|---|---|
| 1 | | | | THE OPPOSITE BUTTERFLY—A BET ON LARGE STOCK PRICE MOVEMENTS | | | | | | | | |
| | | | | | Strategy: Write 1 July 80 Call, | | | | | | | |
| | | | | | Buy 2 July 100 Calls, Write 1 July 120 Call | | | | | | | |
| 2 | | Call prices | | | | | | | | | | |
| 3 | | X | Price | | | | | | | | | |
| 4 | | 80 | 20.99 | | | | | | | | | |
| 5 | | 100 | 6.40 | | | | | | | | | |
| 6 | | 120 | 0.52 | | | | | | | | | |
| 7 | | | | | | | | | | | | |
| 8 | July IBM stock price | Payoff on July X=80 call | Payoff on July X=100 call | Payoff on July X=120 call | Total profit | | | | | | | |
| 9 | 0 | 20.99 | -12.8 | 0.52 | 8.71 | | | | | | | |
| 10 | 10 | 20.99 | -12.8 | 0.52 | 8.71 | | | | | | | |
| 11 | 20 | 20.99 | -12.8 | 0.52 | 8.71 | | | | | | | |
| 12 | 30 | 20.99 | -12.8 | 0.52 | 8.71 | | | | | | | |
| 13 | 40 | 20.99 | -12.8 | 0.52 | 8.71 | | | | | | | |
| 14 | 50 | 20.99 | -12.8 | 0.52 | 8.71 | | | | | | | |
| 15 | 80 | 20.99 | -12.8 | 0.52 | 8.71 | | | | | | | |
| 16 | 85 | 15.99 | -12.8 | 0.52 | 3.71 | | | | | | | |
| 17 | 90 | 10.99 | -12.8 | 0.52 | -1.29 | | | | | | | |
| 18 | 95 | 5.99 | -12.8 | 0.52 | -6.29 | | | | | | | |
| 19 | 100 | 0.99 | -12.8 | 0.52 | -11.29 | | | | | | | |
| 20 | 105 | -4.01 | -2.8 | 0.52 | -6.29 | | | | | | | |
| 21 | 110 | -9.01 | 7.2 | 0.52 | -1.29 | | | | | | | |
| 22 | 115 | -14.01 | 17.2 | 0.52 | 3.71 | | | | | | | |
| 23 | 120 | -19.01 | 27.2 | 0.52 | 8.71 | | | | | | | |
| 24 | 150 | -49.01 | 87.2 | -29.48 | 8.71 | | | | | | | |
| 25 | 160 | -59.01 | 107.2 | -39.48 | 8.71 | | | | | | | |
| 26 | 200 | -99.01 | 187.2 | -79.48 | 8.71 | | | | | | | |
| 27 | | | | | | | | | | | | |

Butterfly Profit Pattern
1X=80 Call Written, 2 X=100 Calls Bought, 1X=120 Call Written

# Summary

Stock options are securities that make it possible to bet on an increase in the stock price (calls) or a decrease in the price (puts). In this chapter we've looked at the basics of option markets. We've discussed definitions (calls, puts, American versus European options) and profit patterns of both individual options and combinations of options.

In the next chapter we discuss some facts about stock option prices.

## EXERCISES

**Note**: Templates for many of these problems are on the CD-ROM that comes with this book.

1. On 8 August 2009 Kellogg's stock closed at $52. For $2.90 you can buy a call option on Kellogg's with an exercise price of $45. The option expires 18 December 2009.

   a. What right does this call option give you?

   b. Suppose you buy the call option and hold it until the expiration date. If the price of Kellogg's on 18 December 2009 is $52, will you exercise the option? What will be your profit?

   c. If the price of Kellogg on 18 December 2009 is $38, will you exercise the option? What will be your profit?

2. It is mid-July 2008. Intel stock is currently trading at $30, and you think that the price of the stock will go down by 22 October 2008. For $3 you can buy a put on Intel stock that expires in October and has an exercise price of $25.

   a. What right does this put option give you?

   b. What happens if the stock does not go below $25 by the time your option expires?

   c. Suppose you buy the option and hold it until the expiration date. If the price of Intel on 22 October 2008 is $20, what will be your profit from the option? What if the price is $38?

3. It is 18 July 2009 and you've just bought one call option on ForeverYours stock. The option cost you $6, expires on 18 September 2009, and has an exercise price of $20.

   a. Complete the following Excel table.

   b. Make a graph that shows the profit (column C) on the $y$-axis and the stock price on 18 September 2009 (column A) on the $x$-axis.

|    | A | B | C |
|----|---|---|---|
|    | **ForeverYours stock price, 18 Sep 09—$S_T$** | **Exercise the call option?** | **Profit** |
| 1  |   |   |   |
| 2  | 0 |   |   |
| 3  | 5 |   |   |
| 4  | 10 |   |   |
| 5  | 15 |   |   |
| 6  | 20 |   |   |
| 7  | 25 |   |   |
| 8  | 30 |   |   |
| 9  | 35 |   |   |
| 10 | 40 |   |   |
| 11 | 45 |   |   |
| 12 | 50 |   |   |

4. It is 18 July 2009 and you've just bought one put option on ItStinks stock. The option cost you $3, expires on 13 March 2008, and has an exercise price of $35.

a. Complete the following Excel table.

b. Make a graph that shows the profit (column C) on the *y*-axis and the stock price on 13 March 2008 (column A) on the *x*-axis.

| | A | B | C |
|---|---|---|---|
| | ItStinks stock price, 13 Mar 08—S$_T$ | Exercise the put option? | Profit |
| 1 | | | |
| 2 | 0 | | |
| 3 | 5 | | |
| 4 | 10 | | |
| 5 | 15 | | |
| 6 | 20 | | |
| 7 | 25 | | |
| 8 | 30 | | |
| 9 | 35 | | |
| 10 | 40 | | |
| 11 | 45 | | |
| 12 | 50 | | |

5.

a. On 28 August 2009 Ford's stock price was $7.73 per share. Call options on Ford expiring on 18 September 2009 with an exercise price of $6.00 sold for $1.74. Should a call with an exercise price of $6.00 expiring on 15 January 2009 sell for more than $1.74? Explain.

b. Look at the following table. Is there an option that is clearly mispriced?

| Ford Call Options Expiring 15 Jan10 | |
|---|---|
| Exercise Price X | Call option Price |
| 2.50 | 5.20 |
| 5.00 | 3.90 |
| 7.50 | 2.90 |
| 10.00 | 2.16 |
| 12.50 | 1.20 |
| 15.00 | 1.30 |
| 17.50 | 0.39 |
| 20.00 | 0.26 |
| 22.50 | 0.16 |
| 25.00 | 0.05 |

6.

a. On 1 September 2009 the stock price of Toyota Motor Corp. (TM) was $85.80 per share. Put options on TM expiring on 18 September 2009 with an exercise price of $80 sold for $0.55. Should a put with an exercise price of $80 expiring on the 15 January 2010 sell for more than $0.55? Explain.

b. Look at the following table. Is there an option that is clearly mispriced?

| TM Put Options Expiring 15 Jan 2010 | |
|---|---|
| Exercise price X | Put option price |
| 50.00 | 0.20 |
| 55.00 | 0.30 |
| 60.00 | 0.65 |
| 65.00 | 1.05 |
| 70.00 | 1.60 |
| 75.00 | 2.70 |
| 80.00 | 4.20 |
| 85.00 | 6.30 |
| 90.00 | 8.20 |
| 95.00 | 8.00 |
| 100.00 | 16.20 |
| 105.00 | 21.20 |
| 110.00 | 24.65 |

7. The price of IBM stock on 1 June 2009 was $108.00.

   a. If you purchased the stock on 1 June and sold it on 1 September 2009 for $117.10, what would have been your profit?

   b. If you shorted IBM stock on 1 June and closed out your short position on 1 September 2009, what would have been your profit?

8. It is 15 December 2006, and John is considering buying 100 shares of GoodLuck stock (the stock price is currently $40 per share). On the same date, Mary is considering shorting 100 shares of GoodLuck stock. If both John and Mary intend to close out their positions on 1 April 2007, fill in the following table and graph their profits.

| | A | B | C |
|---|---|---|---|
| 1 | GoodLuck stock price, 15 Dec 06 | $ 40.00 | |
| 2 | | | |
| 3 | GoodLuck stock price on 1 Apr 07 | John's profit from buying 100 shares | Mary's profit from shorting 100 shares |
| 4 | $0.00 | | |
| 5 | $10.00 | | |
| 6 | $20.00 | | |
| 7 | $30.00 | | |
| 8 | $40.00 | | |
| 9 | $50.00 | | |
| 10 | $60.00 | | |
| 11 | $70.00 | | |
| 12 | $80.00 | | |
| 13 | $90.00 | | |
| 14 | $100.00 | | |

9. You've decided to add 100 shares of ABC Corp. to your portfolio. ABC stock is currently trading at $50 a share. As an alternative to buying the shares now, you're considering buying 1,000 call options on ABC. Each option has an exercise price of $50 and expires in 3 months. The options cost $5 each.

   a. Compare the two strategies by filling in the following table and graphing the percentage profits of each strategy against the stock price $S_T$ in 3 months.

   b. Which strategy is riskier?

| | A | B | C | D | E |
|---|---|---|---|---|---|
| 1 | Investment today in buying 100 shares | $ 5,000 | | | |
| 2 | Investment today in buying 1,000 call options | $ 5,000 | | | |
| 3 | | | | | |
| 4 | ABC stock price in 3 months, $S_T$ | Dollar profit from buying 100 shares | Dollar profit from buying 1,000 call options now | Percentage profit from buying 100 shares | Percentage profit from buying 1,000 call options now |
| 5 | 0 | | | | |
| 6 | 10 | | | | |
| 7 | 20 | | | | |
| 8 | 30 | | | | |
| 9 | 40 | | | | |
| 10 | 50 | | | | |
| 11 | 60 | | | | |
| 12 | 70 | | | | |
| 13 | 80 | | | | |
| 14 | 90 | | | | |
| 15 | 100 | | | | |

10. On 1 August 2009 Microsoft (MSFT) stock is trading at $24.4 per share. The price of a call option on MSFT expiring April 2010 is $2.71 for options with $X = $24 and $1.15 for options with $X = $27.

   a. You think that shares of MSFT will rise in price in the future, and you want to speculate in the stock. Compare (graphically) the following two alternatives: purchasing 1,000 MSFT options with an exercise price of $24 versus purchasing 1,000 MSFT options with a strike of $27.

   b. Compare the two strategies. Which is preferable?

   Use the following template.

| | A | B | C |
|---|---|---|---|
| 1 | Exercise price | Call price | |
| 2 | 24 | 2.71 | |
| 3 | 27 | 1.15 | |
| 4 | | | |
| 5 | Investment | | |
| 6 | A: 1000 options, X=24 | 2,710 | <-- =B2*1000 |
| 7 | B: 1000 options, X=27 | 1,150 | <-- =B3*1000 |
| 8 | | | |
| 9 | Stock price on the expiring date, $S_T$ | Percentage profit on strategy A | Percentage profit on strategy B |
| 10 | 0.0 | | |
| 11 | 10.0 | | |
| 12 | 20.0 | | |
| 13 | 22.0 | | |
| 14 | 24.0 | | |
| 15 | 26.0 | | |
| 16 | 27.0 | | |
| 17 | 28.0 | | |
| 18 | 30.0 | | |
| 19 | 35.0 | | |
| 20 | 40.0 | | |
| 21 | 45.0 | | |
| 22 | 50.0 | | |
| 23 | 55.0 | | |
| 24 | 60.0 | | |

11. On 25 September 2009 McDonald's (MCD) stock is trading at $57 per share. The price of a put option on MCD expiring 9 October 2009 is $0.30 for options with $X = $55 and $1.10 for options with $X = $57.5.

a. You think that shares of MCD will fall in price in the immediate future, and you want to speculate on the stock. Compare (graphically) the following two alternatives: purchasing 1,000 MCD options with an exercise price of $55 versus purchasing 1,000 MCD put options with a strike of $57.50.

b. Compare the two strategies. Which is preferable?

Use the following template.

|  | A | B | C |
|---|---|---|---|
| 1 | **Exercise price** | **Put price** | |
| 2 | 55 | 0.3 | |
| 3 | 57.5 | 1.1 | |
| 4 | | | |
| 5 | Investment | | |
| 6 | A: 1000 options, X=55 | 300 | <-- =B2*1000 |
| 7 | B: 1000 options, X=57.50 | 1100 | <-- =B3*1000 |
| 8 | | | |
| 9 | **Stock price in 3 months, S$_T$** | **Percentage profit on strategy A** | **Percentage profit on strategy B** |
| 10 | 0.0 | | |
| 11 | 20.0 | | |
| 12 | 40.0 | | |
| 13 | 45.0 | | |
| 14 | 50.0 | | |
| 15 | 55.0 | | |
| 16 | 56.0 | | |
| 17 | 56.5 | | |
| 18 | 57.0 | | |
| 19 | 57.5 | | |
| 20 | 58.0 | | |
| 21 | 59.0 | | |
| 22 | 60.0 | | |
| 23 | 65.0 | | |
| 24 | 70.0 | | |

12. A put option written on ENERGY-R-US Corp.'s stock is selling for $2.50. The option has an exercise price of $20 and 6 months to expiration. The current market price for a share of ENERGY-R-US is $26. Determine the profit from a strategy of buying the stock and buying the put; graph these profits. Use the following template.

|  | A | B | C | D |
|---|---|---|---|---|
| 1 | Energy-R-Us, stock | 26.00 | | |
| 2 | Put price, X = 20 | 2.50 | | |
| 3 | | | | |
| 4 | **Stock price, S$_T$ in 6 months** | **Profit from put** | **Profit from stock** | **Total profit** |
| 5 | 0 | | | |
| 6 | 5 | | | |
| 7 | 10 | | | |
| 8 | 15 | | | |
| 9 | 20 | | | |
| 10 | 25 | | | |
| 11 | 30 | | | |
| 12 | 35 | | | |
| 13 | 40 | | | |
| 14 | 45 | | | |
| 15 | 50 | | | |

13. Using the data from the previous problem, compare the following three strategies:
    - Purchase one share of stock and one put on the stock.
    - Purchase one share of stock and two puts on the stock.
    - Purchase of one share of stock and three puts on the stock.

14. Using the data and the template below, suppose you bought a Toyota Motors call with exercise (strike) price $X = 50$ and wrote a TM call with exercise price $X = 45$. Graph the profit of this strategy at option expiration. Why might this be an attractive strategy?

|    | A | B | C | D |
|----|---|---|---|---|
| 1  | Call Prices | | | |
| 2  | X | Price | | |
| 3  | 45 | 4.10 | | |
| 4  | 50 | 1.65 | | |
| 5  | | | | |
| 6  | TM stock price, $S_T$ at option expiration | Profit on X=45 call (written) | Profit on X=50 call (bought) | Total profit |
| 7  | 20 | | | |
| 8  | 25 | | | |
| 9  | 30 | | | |
| 10 | 35 | | | |
| 11 | 40 | | | |
| 12 | 45 | | | |
| 13 | 50 | | | |
| 14 | 55 | | | |
| 15 | 60 | | | |
| 16 | 65 | | | |

15. Using the data from the previous problem, compute and graph the profit from a strategy in which you buy a TM call with exercise price $X = 45$ and write a call with exercise price $X = 50$. Explain why this strategy might be attractive.

16. The following options are traded on WOW Corp.'s stock. State the property of option prices that is violated and show that you can design a strategy to profit from this mispricing.[4]

| Option | Exercise Price | Expiration Date | Price |
|--------|---------------|-----------------|-------|
| Call | 40 | 1-Jan-11 | $13.50 |
| Call | 40 | 1-Jan-11 | $12.95 |

17. The following options are traded on Smow Corp.'s stock. State which property of option prices is violated and show that you can design a strategy to profit from this mispricing.

| Option | Exercise Price | Expiration Date | Price |
|--------|---------------|-----------------|-------|
| Put | 50 | 1-Mar-12 | $4.25 |
| Put | 60 | 1-Mar-12 | $4.00 |

18. David wants to buy a call option written on RAIDER Corp. stock. Patrick is willing to sell David a call option on RAIDER Corp. stock with an exercise price of $50 for $8.20. The option will mature in exactly 1 year. The current market price for RAIDER Corp. stock is $50.

---

[4]Such a strategy is called an *arbitrage strategy* and is discussed at length in the next chapter.

a. Determine and graph the payoffs of both David and Patrick's respective positions.

b. For what stock price $S_T$ is the profit of both David and Patrick zero?

19. Portfolio insurance describes a position in which an investor buys put options to insure that the value of his portfolio does not fall below a certain point. Suppose Jerry has a portfolio that consists of 100 shares of RTY stock. The current market price of RTY is $35 per share. The following options are also being traded on RTY stock.

| Call price | 8.20 | |
|---|---|---|
| | | |
| RAIDER stock price at option expiration, $S_T$ | Patrick's profit | David's profit |
| 0 | | |
| 10 | | |
| 20 | | |
| 30 | | |
| 40 | | |
| 50 | | |
| 60 | | |
| 70 | | |
| 80 | | |
| 90 | | |
| 100 | | |

a. What options must Jerry buy if he wants to insure that the value of his portfolio will not drop below $2,000?

b. How much will this cost?

| Expiration date | Exercise price | Call price | Put price |
|---|---|---|---|
| 1-Jun-13 | 20 | 18.00 | 0.10 |
| 1-Jun-13 | 25 | 11.35 | 0.45 |
| 1-Jun-13 | 35 | 3.50 | 3.20 |
| 1-Jun-13 | 40 | 0.75 | 5.65 |

20. A covered call position entails entering into a long position in stock and writing a call option with a high strike price. The purpose of such a position is to finance a portion of the stock purchase from the sale of the call option.

Sam thinks that STF Corp. stock, currently priced at $80/share, will go up in price by about $15 in the next 6 months. He would like to buy 10,000 shares of STF today and cash in on his bullish sentiment. To cut the initial costs of his purchase, he would like to enter into a covered call position. The following options are traded on STF Corp.

Suppose Sam writes 10,000 of the $90 calls. Show Sam's profit. Use the following template.

| Expiration date | Exercise price | Call price |
|---|---|---|
| 1-Aug-11 | 70.00 | 18.95 |
| 1-Aug-11 | 80.00 | 7.65 |
| 1-Aug-11 | 90.00 | 2.70 |
| 1-Aug-11 | 100.00 | 0.50 |

21. Answer the following questions by referring to the facts in the previous problem.

| STF stock price | 80.00 | | |
|---|---|---|---|
| Number of shares purchased | 10,000.00 | | |
| | | | |
| Stock price of STF in 6 months, $S_T$ | Profit from stock position | Profit from option position, 10,000 options with X = $90 | Profit from covered call strategy |
| 50 | | | |
| 60 | | | |
| 70 | | | |
| 80 | | | |
| 90 | | | |
| 100 | | | |
| 110 | | | |
| 120 | | | |

a. Compare the profits from a covered call strategy using the $90 calls with one using the $100 calls.

b. Which of the two covered call strategies would you recommend?

22. Given the three calls below, design a butterfly strategy that pays off if the stock does not make a major move from its current value of $60. Graph the strategy profits. Use the following template.

| Call prices | | | | |
|---|---|---|---|---|
| | X | Price | | |
| | 50 | 22.00 | | |
| | 60 | 15.00 | | |
| | 70 | 10.00 | | |
| | | | | |
| **Payoff and profits** | | | | |
| Stock price at option expiration, $S_T$ | Payoff on X = 50 call | Payoff on X = 60 call | Payoff on X = 70 call | Total profit |
| 30.0 | | | | |
| 35.0 | | | | |
| 40.0 | | | | |
| 45.0 | | | | |
| 50.0 | | | | |
| 52.5 | | | | |
| 55.0 | | | | |
| 57.5 | | | | |
| 60.0 | | | | |
| 62.5 | | | | |
| 65.0 | | | | |
| 67.5 | | | | |
| 70.0 | | | | |
| 72.5 | | | | |
| 75.0 | | | | |
| 80.0 | | | | |
| 85.0 | | | | |
| 90.0 | | | | |

23. Given the data from the previous problem, design a butterfly strategy that pays off if the stock price makes a large move from its current price of $60. Graph the strategy profits.

# 21 Option Pricing Facts

## CHAPTER CONTENTS

## Overview

In Chapter 20 we discussed basic option concepts: definitions of a call and a put, the reasons why you might want to buy or sell an option, and the profits resulting from various options strategies. In this chapter we discuss some basic facts about option pricing. Our emphasis is on a set of propositions known as *arbitrage restrictions* on option prices. These restrictions specify relations between the prices of puts and calls and the prices of either the stock underlying the options or a risk-free asset.

By understanding the option pricing restrictions in this chapter, you can often easily judge whether an option is mispriced. Here's an example: Suppose you're considering buying a call option on Exxon stock, which is currently selling for $S_0 = \$69$ a share. Suppose the option expires in 1 year and has exercise price $X = \$60$. The interest rate is $r = 5\%$. The option is priced at $C_0 = \$10$. Is it a good buy or not? Our first option pricing fact (Section 21.1) will enable you to say that the option is *underpriced* and that it is definitely a good buy. As you will see in Section 21.1, the price of the option should be *at least* $11.86.

---

## NOTATION

Throughout the chapter we use the following notation:

$S$ = The price of the stock. When we want to be precise about the price of the stock on a specific date, we will sometimes write $S_0$ for the price of the stock today (time 0) and $S_T$ for the price of the stock on the option exercise date $T$.

$X$ = The option exercise price

$r$ = The interest rate

$C$ = The call option price. When we want to be precise about the call price on a specific date, we will sometimes write $C_0$ for the price of the stock today (time 0) and $C_T$ for the price of the stock on the option exercise date $T$. Occasionally we will even use the full word, writing $Call_0$.

$P$ = The put option price. When we want to be precise about the call price on a specific date, we will sometimes write $P_0$ for the price of the stock today (time 0) and $P_T$ for the price of the stock on the option exercise date $T$. Occasionally we will even use the full word, writing $Put_0$.

---

Dividends: Throughout the chapter we assume that the stock on which the options are written does not pay dividends before the option maturity date.[1] This is not an overly restrictive assumption: Stocks that pay dividends tend to do so at regular intervals (quarterly, semiannually, or annually). Holders of options on these stocks are thus reasonably sure when the stocks will pay dividends. There are thus long periods of time when market participants can be assured that a stock will not pay a dividend.

For example, Exxon pays a regular quarterly dividend in February, May, August, and November. An investor who purchases an option on Exxon in March with an April maturity knows that in the intervening period no dividends will be paid on the stock.

Many other stocks have never paid a dividend and investors in these stocks' options can be reasonably assured that the dividend pricing restriction imposed in this chapter is not restrictive. Stocks that fall into this category include many of the high-tech stocks whose options tend to attract the most investor interest.

### Finance Concepts Discussed in This Chapter

- Option pricing restrictions
- No early exercise of calls
- Put–call parity
- Early exercise of American puts
- Option price convexity

---

[1] The one exception is Section 21.6, where we briefly discuss the effect of dividends.

Excel Functions Used

- **Max**
- **Sum**
- **If**

## 21.1. Fact 1: Call Price of an Option, $C_0 > Max[S_0 - PV(X),0]$

It's 18 May 2009, and you're considering buying a call option on Exxon (stock symbol XOM). Currently the XOM share itself is selling for $S_0 = \$69$; you want to buy a call on XOM with an exercise price $X = \$60$ and with time to maturity $T = 1$ year. Furthermore, we'll suppose that the option is an *American call option* and can be exercised at any time on or before $T$.

We will examine Fact 1 in two stages. We start with a "dumb fact," something that is obvious once we say it, and then proceed to demonstrate Fact 1 for you.

### Dumb Fact: For an American Call, *Call price,* $C_0 \geq Max[S_0 - X,0]$.

Now it's probably clear to you that the Exxon option should be selling for *at least* $\$9 = S_0 - X = \$69 - \$60$. To see this, suppose that the option is selling for $2. We'll devise an *arbitrage strategy*—a strategy that will make us money risklessly.

Arbitrage strategy to profit from call price $C_0 = \$2$ when stock price is $S_0 = \$69$ and $X = \$60$

| Action taken today | Cash flow (negative numbers indicate costs) |
|---|---|
| Buy the option for price $C_o$ | –$2 |
| Immediately exercise the option, buying the stock for price $S_0$ | –$60 |
| Immediately sell the stock on the open market | +$69 |
| **Arbitrage profit** | **+$7** |

So the "dumb fact"—that an American call option should sell for more than the difference between the stock price and the exercise price—is pretty obvious.

### DEFINITION: ARBITRAGE STRATEGY

An arbitrage strategy is a combination of assets—usually short or long positions in the stock, calls and puts on the stock, and a risk-free security—which produces nonnegative cash flows at all points in time. If you can design an arbitrage strategy for a given set of asset prices (as we do below), it shows that at least one of the prices is *wrong*.

## Smart Fact: *Call price,* $C_0 > Max[S_0 - PV(X),0]$

This is a lot less obvious than the previous fact. It's also a lot more powerful.[2] The dumb fact above says that the option should sell for at least $9. As the spreadsheet below shows, the smart fact says much more; for example, if the interest rate is 9%, then the smart fact says that the option should sell for at least $11.86.

| | A | B | C |
|---|---|---|---|
| 1 | **FACT 1: Lower bound on call price** | | |
| 2 | Exxon stock price, 17 May 2009, $S_0$ | 69 | |
| 3 | Option exercise price, X | 60 | |
| 4 | Option exercise time, T (in years) | 1 | |
| 5 | Interest rate, r | 5% | |
| 6 | | | |
| 7 | Lower bound on call price | | |
| 8 | Dumb fact, call price, $C_0 > Max[S_0 - X,0]$ | 9 | <-- =MAX(B2-B3,0) |
| 9 | Fact 1: call price, $C_0 > Max[S_0 - PV(X),0]$ | 11.86 | <-- =MAX(B2-B3/(1+B5)^B4,0) |

To prove the smart fact, let's assume that you can buy the call for $5. We'll show that there exists an *arbitrage strategy*, and we will therefore conclude that the option price is too low.

The arbitrage strategy involves a set of actions at time 0 (today) and at time $T$ (the option expiration date).

## At time 0 (today):

- Short one share of the stock, get $S_0$.
- Invest in a riskless security paying off the call's exercise price at time $T$. This security will cost its present value, $PV(X)$.
- Buy a call on the option. This will cost $C_0$.

## At time $T$:

- Purchase the stock on the open market at the time-$T$ price to close the short position. Closing the short position will cost $S_T$.
- Collect from our investment in the riskless security. This will give an inflow of $X$.
- Exercise the option if this is profitable. If the stock price $S_T > X$, this will give an inflow of $S_T - X$. If the stock price $S_T < X$, it will not pay to exercise the option.

Here's an example, which assumes that the stock price at time 0 is $S_0 = 69$, the interest rate is $r = 5\%$, the exercise price is $X = 60$, and the time to maturity is $T = 1$. This specific example assumes that the call price at time 0 is $C_0 = 5$. In the spreadsheet below we show the payoffs from the above strategy, assuming that the price of the stock at time $T$ is $S_T = 33$ (cell B17).

---

[2] How smart? Robert Merton, who first established this and lots of other facts about options, subsequently won the Nobel Prize for economics, in part for his work on option pricing.

| | A | B | C |
|---|---|---|---|
| 1 | **ARBITRAGE PROOF OF FACT 1** <br> **Assumes that stock price at time T = $33.00** | | |
| 2 | Exxon stock price, 17 May 2009, $S_0$ | 69.00 | |
| 3 | Option exercise price, X | 60.00 | |
| 4 | Option exercise time, T (in years) | 1 | |
| 5 | Interest rate, r | 5.00% | |
| 6 | | | |
| 7 | **Call price at time 0 (today)** | 5 | Below examine if this price <br> <-- violates the arbitrage restriction |
| 8 | | | |
| 9 | **ARBITRAGE STRATEGY** | | |
| 10 | **Actions at time 0 (today)** | | |
| 11 | Short the stock, get $S_0$ | 69.00 | <-- =B2 |
| 12 | Buy a bond which pays of X at time T, pay PV(X) | -57.14 | <-- =-B3/(1+B5)^B4 |
| 13 | Buy a call, pay $C_0$ | -5.00 | <-- =-B7 |
| 14 | **Total cash flow at time 0** | 6.86 | <-- =SUM(B11:B13) |
| 15 | | | |
| 16 | **Cash flow at time T** | | |
| 17 | $S_T$, stock price at time T | 33.00 | |
| 18 | | | |
| 19 | Repay the shorted stock, pay $S_T$ | -33.00 | <-- =-B17 |
| 20 | Collect money from the bond, get X | 60.00 | <-- =B3 |
| 21 | Exercise the call?  Get Max($S_T$ - X,0) | 0.00 | <-- =MAX(B17-B3,0) |
| 22 | **Total cash flow at time T** | 27.00 | <-- =SUM(B19:B21) |

In cells B19:B22 we calculate the cash flow at time $T=1$ from the strategy. In the example above, Exxon stock at $T$ is selling for $S_T = \$33$. In this case, we would have a positive time $T$ cash flow of $27 (cell B22).

In the example below, we assume that Exxon stock at $T$ is $S_T = \$90$. In this case you exercise the call (giving you a positive cash flow of $30), but the total payoff from the strategy is now $0.

| | A | B | C |
|---|---|---|---|
| 1 | **ARBITRAGE PROOF OF FACT 1** <br> **Assumes that stock price at time T = $90.00** | | |
| 2 | Exxon stock price, 17 May 2009, $S_0$ | 69.00 | |
| 3 | Option exercise price, X | 60.00 | |
| 4 | Option exercise time, T (in years) | 1 | |
| 5 | Interest rate, r | 5.00% | |
| 6 | | | |
| 7 | **Call price at time 0 (today)** | 5 | Below examine if this price <br> <-- violates the arbitrage restriction |
| 8 | | | |
| 9 | **ARBITRAGE STRATEGY** | | |
| 10 | **Actions at time 0 (today)** | | |
| 11 | Short the stock, get $S_0$ | 69.00 | <-- =B2 |
| 12 | Buy a bond which pays of X at time T, pay PV(X) | -57.14 | <-- =-B3/(1+B5)^B4 |
| 13 | Buy a call, pay $C_0$ | -5.00 | <-- =-B7 |
| 14 | **Total cash flow at time 0** | 6.86 | <-- =SUM(B11:B13) |
| 15 | | | |
| 16 | **Cash flow at time T** | | |
| 17 | $S_T$, stock price at time T | 90.00 | |
| 18 | | | |
| 19 | Repay the shorted stock, pay $S_T$ | -90.00 | <-- =-B17 |
| 20 | Collect money from the bond, get X | 60.00 | <-- =B3 |
| 21 | Exercise the call?  Get Max($S_T$ - X,0) | 30.00 | <-- =MAX(B17-B3,0) |
| 22 | **Total cash flow at time T** | 0.00 | <-- =SUM(B19:B21) |

By changing the stock price $S_T$, you can see that our strategy always produces no worse than a zero cash flow at time $T$. This makes it an *arbitrage strategy*:

- At time 0, the cash flow is $\$6.86 > 0$.

- At time $T$, the cash flow is either positive (if the stock price $S_T < 60$) or zero.

You can't lose from this strategy!! In a rational world this means that something is wrong with the asset prices. In this case, it's clear what's wrong—the call price is too low.

To see this, consider the case where the call price is $14. As you can see below (cell B14), this means that the initial cash flow from the arbitrage strategy is negative. If the stock price at time $T$ is less than $60, say $S_T = \$55$, then you will make a future profit (cell B22 below), but this profit is no longer an arbitrage profit (recall that arbitrage occurs when you can *never* lose money—however, in this example, with a $14 call price, you start off with an initial negative cash flow).

|  | A | B | C |
|---|---|---|---|
| 7 | **Call price at time 0 (today)** | **14.00** | Below examine if this price <br> <-- violates the arbitrage restriction |
| 8 |  |  |  |
| 9 |  | **ARBITRAGE STRATEGY** |  |
| 10 | **Actions at time 0 (today)** |  |  |
| 11 | Short the stock, get $S_0$ | 69.00 | <-- =B2 |
| 12 | Buy a bond which pays of X at time T, pay PV(X) | -57.14 | <-- =-B3/(1+B5)^B4 |
| 13 | Buy a call, pay $C_0$ | -14.00 | <-- =-B7 |
| 14 | **Total cash flow at time 0** | -2.14 | <-- =SUM(B11:B13) |
| 15 |  |  |  |
| 16 | **Cash flow at time T** |  |  |
| 17 | $S_T$, stock price at time T | 55.00 |  |
| 18 |  |  |  |
| 19 | Repay the shorted stock, pay $S_T$ | -55.00 | <-- =-B17 |
| 20 | Collect money from the bond, get X | 60.00 | <-- =B3 |
| 21 | Exercise the call?  Get Max($S_T$ - X,0) | 0.00 | <-- =MAX(B17-B3,0) |
| 22 | **Total cash flow at time T** | 5.00 | <-- =SUM(B19:B21) |

The cash flow at $T$ (cell B22) is positive, but the initial cash flow (cell B14) is now negative. This makes more sense: Negative initial cash flows in this arbitrage strategy start when the call price is $ > \$11.86$. If this is true, then you have to invest money today to have a nonnegative cash flow in the future. Note that $11.86 = S_0 - PV(X) = 69 - 60/1.05$.

We've proved our first option pricing fact: *Call price*, $C_0 > Max\left[S_0 - PV(X), 0\right]$. The proof wasn't mathematically difficult, but it involves some sophisticated thinking. Option arbitrage propositions are like that.

# 21.2. Fact 2: It's Never Worthwhile to Exercise a Call Early[3]

Suppose that on 17 May 2009 you bought an Exxon call option for $C_0 = \$14$ (note that this price does not violate Fact 1's price restriction). Furthermore, suppose that the option expires 1 year from today, on 17 May 2010. Recall that the current price of Exxon is $S_0 = \$69$.

---

[3] To be completely accurate, Fact 2 holds when the interest rate is positive and the call is written on a stock that does not pay a dividend before the option maturity date $T$.

Now suppose that after 8 months (approximately 2/3 of a year), you want to get rid of the option. To make the problem interesting, we'll assume that the price of Exxon has risen to $S_t =$ $80. You have two possibilities:

- You could exercise the option. In this case you would collect $20 $= Max[S_t - X,0] = Max[80-60,0]$.

- You could also *sell* the option on the open market. Of course, we don't know what the option's price would be, but Fact 1 tells us that in no case will the price be less than

$$Max\left[S_t - PV(X),0\right] = Max\left[S_t - \frac{X}{(1+r)^{1/3}},0\right]$$

$$= Max\left[80 - \frac{60}{(1+5\%)^{1/3}},0\right] = 20.97$$

The present value $\dfrac{X}{(1+r)^{1/3}}$ expresses the fact that there is 1/3 of a year left before the option's exercise.

What should you do? Clearly, you should *sell* rather than *exercise* the call.

| | A | B | C | D | E | F |
|---|---|---|---|---|---|---|
| 1 | | | FACT 2: No early exercise of calls | | | |
| 2 | Exxon stock price, 17 May 2009, $S_0$ | 69.00 | | | | |
| 3 | Option exercise price, X | 60.00 | | | | |
| 4 | Option exercise time, T (in years) | 1 | | | | |
| 5 | Interest rate, r | 5.00% | | | | |
| 6 | Call price at time 0 | 14.00 | | | | |
| 7 | | | | | | |
| 8 | | | Time line | | | |
| 9 | t=0 | | | t=2/3 | | T=1 |
| 10 | | | | | | |
| 11 | Buy option for $14.00 | | Consider selling the option | | | |
| 12 | | | or exercising it. | | | |
| 13 | | | | | | |
| 14 | | | Stock price, $S_t$ | 80.00 | | |
| 15 | | | | | | |
| 16 | | | Payoff from option exercise | 20.00 | <-- =MAX(D14-B3,0) | |
| 17 | | | Minimum value of option | | | |
| 18 | | | according to Fact 1 | 20.97 | <-- =MAX(D14-B3/(1+$B$5)^(1-2/3),0) | |
| 19 | | | | | | |
| 20 | | | Exercise option or sell it? | sell | <-- =IF(D18>=D16,"sell","exercise") | |

## 21.3. Fact 3: Put–Call Parity, $P_0 = C_0 + PV(X) - S_0$

Put–call parity states that for European options put price is determined by the call price, the stock price, and the risk-free rate of interest.[4] Here's an example: Suppose that we're considering a 1-year put option on the Exxon stock we've been discussing throughout this chapter. Recall that Exxon stock is currently selling for $S_0 =$ $69. Put–call parity tells us the price of a put on Exxon with the same exercise price $X =$ $60 and the same time to maturity $T = 1$.

[4] Again, recall that the assumption is that the stock pays no dividends before the option maturity date $T$.

|   | A | B | C |
|---|---|---|---|
| 1 | **FACT 3: Put–Call Parity** | | |
| 2 | Exxon stock price, 17 May 2009, $S_0$ | 69.00 | |
| 3 | Option exercise price, X | 60.00 | |
| 4 | Option exercise time, T (in years) | 1 | |
| 5 | Interest rate, r | 5.00% | |
| 6 | | | |
| 7 | Call price, $Call_0$ | 15.00 | |
| 8 | Put price, $Put_0$, by put–call parity | 3.14 | <-- =B7+B3/(1+B5)^B4-B2 |

Another interpretation of put–call parity is that the put price plus the stock price always equals the call price plus the present value of the exercise price:

$$Put_0 + S_0 = Call_0 + PV(X).$$

This means that given any three of the following four variables— $Put_0, S_0, Call_0, X$ —the fourth variable is determined.

## An Arbitrage Proof of Put-Call Parity (Can Be Skipped on First Reading)

We can prove put–call parity using arbitrage, as specified in the spreadsheet below. We assume that the stock price is $S_0 = \$69$, the exercise price is $X = \$60$, the time to exercise is $T = 1$ year, the interest rate is $r = 5\%$, and the call price is $Call_0 = \$15$. Given these facts, put–call parity says that the put price should be $Put_0 = \$3.14$ (cell B8).

In cell B11 we suppose that the put price is $1, different from its put–call parity value; we then show that this makes an arbitrage profitable.

|   | A | B | C |
|---|---|---|---|
| 1 | **Arbitrage Proof of Put–Call Parity** | | |
| 2 | Exxon stock price, 17 May 2009, $S_0$ | 69.00 | |
| 3 | Option exercise price, X | 60.00 | |
| 4 | Option exercise time, T (in years) | 1 | |
| 5 | Interest rate, r | 5.00% | |
| 6 | | | |
| 7 | Call price, $Call_0$ | 15.00 | |
| 8 | Put price, $Put_0$, by put–call parity | 3.14 | <-- =B7+B3/(1+B5)^B4-B2 |
| 9 | | | |
| 10 | **Arbitrage proof of put–call parity** | | |
| 11 | Put price today (t=0), $Put_0$ | 1.00 | If this price differs from the price in cell B8, we will show that there is a profitable arbitrage strategy. |
| 12 | | | |
| 13 | **Actions at time 0 (today)** | | |
| 14 | Buy stock, pay $S_0$ | -69.00 | <-- =-B2 |
| 15 | Buy put, pay $Put_0$ | -1.00 | <-- =-B11 |
| 16 | Write call, get $Call_0$ | 15.00 | |
| 17 | Take a loan of PV(X) at risk-free interest, get PV(X) | 57.14 | <-- =B3/(1+B5)^B4 |
| 18 | **Total cash flow at time 0** | 2.14 | <-- =SUM(B14:B17) |
| 19 | | | |
| 20 | **Cash flow at time T** | | |
| 21 | $S_T$, stock price at time T | 90.00 | |
| 22 | | | |
| 23 | Sell stock, get $S_T$ | 90.00 | <-- =B21 |
| 24 | Exercise the put? Get Max(X - $S_T$,0) | 0.00 | <-- =MAX(B3-B21,0) |
| 25 | Cash flow from written call. Pay Max($S_T$ - X, 0) | -30.00 | <-- =-MAX(B21-B3,0) |
| 26 | Repay loan. Pay X | -60.00 | <-- =-B3 |
| 27 | Total | 0.00 | <-- =SUM(B23:B26) |

Here's the arbitrage strategy we designed.

## At time 0 (today):

- Buy one share of Exxon stock for $S_0 = \$69$.
- Buy one put with exercise price $X = \$60$ for $Put_0 = \$1$.
- Write one call with $X = \$60$, collecting (today) $Call_0 = \$15$.
- Take a loan of $PV(X) = \$57.14$; the loan has a 1-year maturity (like the options). At the current interest rate of 5% you will have to pay off $X = \$60$ in 1 year.

## At time *T* we close out all our positions:

- Sell our share of Exxon at the prevailing market price $S_T$.
- Exercise the put, if this is profitable. Exercising the put gives you $Max(X - S_T, 0)$.
- Have the call exercised against us, if this is profitable for the call buyer. As the call writer, you can't make money from having the call exercised. The cash flow to the call writer is $-Max(S_T - X, 0)$.
- Repay the loan. This is a negative cash flow, $-X$.

Our example above shows that the cash flow at $T = 1$ will be zero if $S_T = \$90$. The cash flow will also be zero if $S_T = \$35$.

| | A | B | C |
|---|---|---|---|
| 20 | **Cash flow at time T** | | |
| 21 | $S_T$, stock price at time T | 35.00 | |
| 22 | | | |
| 23 | Sell stock, get $S_T$ | 35.00 | <-- =B21 |
| 24 | Exercise the put? Get Max(X - $S_T$,0) | 25.00 | <-- =MAX(B3-B21,0) |
| 25 | Cash flow from written call. Pay Max($S_T$ - X, 0) | 0.00 | <-- =-MAX(B21-B3,0) |
| 26 | Repay loan. Pay X | -60.00 | <-- =-B3 |
| 27 | Total | 0.00 | <-- =SUM(B23:B26) |

As you can see, no matter what the Exxon stock price in 1 year, the cash flow at $T = 1$ from this strategy will be zero. However, the strategy has a positive initial cash flow of $2.14. Clearly this is an arbitrage!

Symbolically, the future cash flow is given by

$$\underbrace{S_T}_{\text{Stock value}} + \underbrace{Max[X - S_T, 0]}_{\text{Put payoff}} - \underbrace{Max[S_T - X, 0]}_{\substack{\text{Cash flow to call} \\ \text{writer at } T=1}} - \underbrace{X}_{\text{Loan repayment}}$$

$$= \begin{cases} S_T + X - S_T - X & \text{if } S_T < X \\ S_T - (S_T - X) - X & \text{if } S_T \geq X \end{cases}$$

$$= 0$$

A little thought will reveal that—given the stock price $S_0 = 69$, the interest rate $r = 5\%$, the exercise price $X = 60$ of both the put and the call, and the call option price of $15—the put option price must be $3.14 to prevent arbitrage. This follows from the put-price parity relation:

$$Put = Call + PV(X) - S = 15 + \frac{60}{1.05} - 69 = 3.14$$

## 21.4. Fact 4: Bound on an American Put Option Price:
### $P_0 > Max[X - S_0, 0]$

Suppose you're contemplating buying an American put on Exxon stock. The stock's price today is $S_0 = \$69$ and the option exercise price is $X = \$80$. Clearly, the option should sell for at least $11. If not, you could easily devise an arbitrage, as illustrated in the spreadsheet below.

| | A | B | C |
|---|---|---|---|
| 1 | **FACT 4:  Lower bound on *American* put price** | | |
| 2 | Exxon stock price, 17 May 2009, $S_0$ | 69.00 | |
| 3 | Put option exercise price, X | 80.00 | |
| 4 | Option exercise time, T (in years) | 1 | |
| 5 | | | |
| 6 | Fact 4:  Lower bound of American put:  $P_0 > Max[X - S_0, 0]$ | 11.00 | <-- =MAX(B3-B2,0) |
| 7 | | | |
| 8 | **Arbitrage strategy** | | |
| 9 | American put option price | 3.00 | |
| 10 | Buy option, pay $P_0$ | -3.00 | |
| 11 | Buy stock now, pay $S_0$ | -69.00 | |
| 12 | Exercise put option immediately:  deliver stock and get X | 80.00 | |
| 13 | Immediate profit | 8.00 | <-- =SUM(B10:B12) |

If the American put option is mispriced (that is, its price is less than $11), you can make money by buying the option, buying the stock, and exercising the option immediately. This arbitrage profit will not exist if the option's price is greater than $11.

## 21.5. Fact 5: Bounds on European Put Option Prices:
### $P_0 > Max[PV(X) - S_0, 0]$

Fact 5 is the "put parallel" for Fact 1 about calls.[5]

| | A | B | C |
|---|---|---|---|
| 1 | **FACT 5:  Lower bound on *European* put price** | | |
| 2 | Exxon stock price, 17 May 2009, $S_0$ | 69.00 | |
| 3 | Put option exercise price, X | 80.00 | |
| 4 | Option exercise time, T (in years) | 1 | |
| 5 | Interest rate, r | 5.00% | |
| 6 | | | |
| 7 | Lower bound on call price | | |
| 8 | Lower bound of American put:  $P_0 > Max[X - S_0, 0]$ | 11.00 | <-- =MAX(B3-B2,0) |
| 9 | Fact 5:  $P_0 > Max[PV(X) - S_0, 0]$ | 7.19 | <-- =MAX(B3/(1+B5)^B4-B2,0) |

We'll skip the proof of Fact 5. If you're interested, it's on the disk that comes with the book.

---

[5] There's a crucial difference in the parallel between Facts 1 and 5: Fact 1 applies to *all* calls, whether European or American. Fact 5 applies only to European puts. Of course in both cases the assumption is that the stock pays no dividends before option maturity.

---

### AMERICAN VERSUS EUROPEAN PUTS

Fact 5 says that the price of a European put can actually be much lower than the price of an American put. Consider the preceding example, in which we look at the price of a put option on Exxon stock (currently selling for $S_0 = \$69$) with $T = 1$ and $X = 80$. If our put was an American put, then it couldn't sell for less than \$11. On the other hand, a *European put*, which cannot be exercised until date $T$, can sell for anything more than \$7.19.

---

## 21.6. Fact 6: You Might Find It Optimal to Early Exercise an American Put on a Nondividend Paying Stock

Recall that you'll *never* find it optimal to early exercise an American *call* on a nondividend paying stock. But this is not necessarily true for a put option. Here's an example.

Suppose that you're currently holding an option on PFE stock. You bought the option some time ago, when PFE stock's price was still healthy. However, at the current date, the stock has taken a plunge and is selling for \$1 per share. Your American put option has an exercise price of $X = \$100$ and expires in 1 year. The interest rate is 10%. If you exercise the option now, you'll have a net payoff of \$99 (\$100 minus the current value of the stock of \$1), which—if you invest it in bonds with an interest rate of 10%—will be \$99 *1.10 = \$108.90 in 1 year. This is more than anyone would have if they waited for a year until exercise.

Therefore, any rational holder of an American put option will choose to early exercise the option if the current stock price is very low.

## 21.7. Fact 7: Option Prices Are Convex (Somewhat Advanced)

Suppose we have three calls, each with a different exercise price but with the same time to exercise $T$, written on the same stock. Suppose that the exercise price of the first call is $X = \$15$, the exercise price of the second call is $X = \$20$, and the exercise price of the third call is $X = \$25$. Call price convexity says that for three such "equally spaced" calls, the middle call price must be less than the average of the two extreme call prices. In an equation,

$$Call\ price(X = 20) < \frac{Call\ price(X = 15) + Call\ price(X = 25)}{2}$$

To see the meaning of convexity, we return to the butterfly spread example from Chapter 20. Recall that in this example, the convexity relation says that

$$Call\ price(X = 100) < \frac{Call\ price(X = 80) + Call\ price(X = 120)}{2} = \frac{20.99 + 0.52}{2} = 10.76$$

Because the IBM call with $X = \$100$ is selling for \$6.40, it fulfills the convexity relation.

|   | A | B | C |
|---|---|---|---|
| 1 | THREE IBM JULY 2009 CALLS | | |
| 2 | X | Call price | |
| 3 | 80 | 20.99 | |
| 4 | 100 | 6.40 | |
| 5 | 120 | 0.52 | |
| 6 | | | |
| 7 | Convexity: Is the middle call priced less than the average of the high and the low call? | | |
| 8 | Average of high and low call | 10.76 | <-- =(B3+B5)/2 |

## Why Do Call Prices Have To Be Convex?

In this subsection we use the butterfly strategy from Section 20.8 to show you why call prices always have to be convex. Recall that a *butterfly* strategy consists of buying one low-priced and one high-priced call and selling two medium-priced calls.

Suppose that the call option prices for IBM were different from those actually seen in the market. In the example below, we show how our butterfly would have looked had the X = $100 call been priced at $13 instead of $6.40.

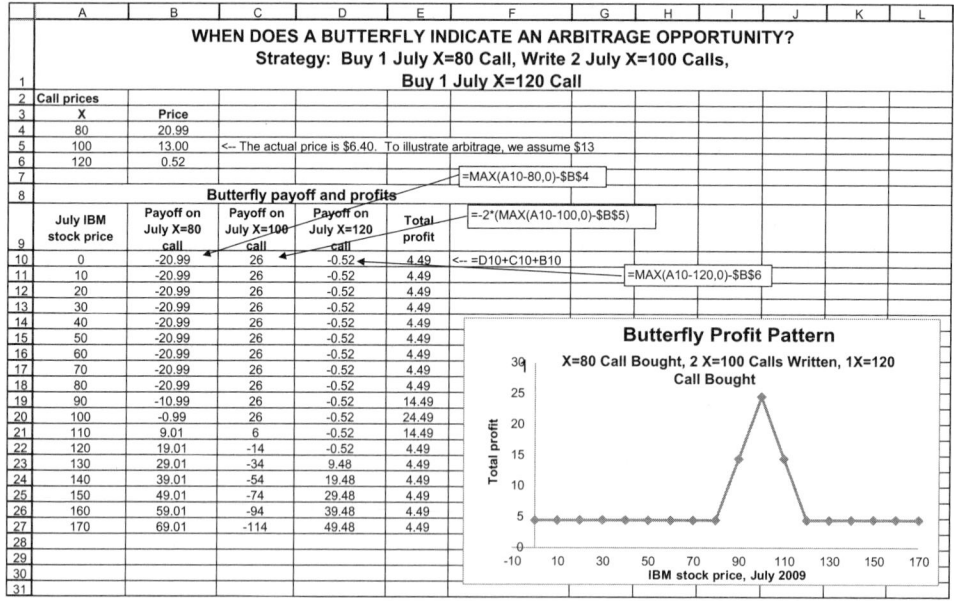

Note that the total profit graph is *completely above the x-axis*. This means that no matter what the stock price in July, you will make a profit. This is clearly not logical—something is wrong with these prices!

You get the same thing if you assume that the $X$ = $80 call option is priced at $10 instead of its actual market price of $20.99.

| | A | B | C | D | E | F | G | H | I | J | K | L |
|---|---|---|---|---|---|---|---|---|---|---|---|---|
| 1 | | | **WHEN DOES A BUTTERFLY INDICATE AN ARBITRAGE OPPORTUNITY?** Strategy: Buy 1 July X=80 Call, Write 2 July X=100 Calls, Buy 1 July X=120 Call | | | | | | | | | |
| 2 | Call prices | | | | | | | | | | | |
| 3 | X | Price | | | | | | | | | | |
| 4 | 80 | 10.00 | <-- The actual price is $20.99.  To illustrate arbitrage, we assume $10 | | | | | | | | | |
| 5 | 100 | 6.40 | | | | | | | | | | |
| 6 | 120 | 0.52 | | | | | | | | | | |
| 7 | | | | | | =MAX(A10-80,0)-$B$4 | | | | | | |
| 8 | | | Butterfly payoff and profits | | | | | | | | | |
| 9 | July IBM stock price | Payoff on July X=80 call | Payoff on July X=100 call | Payoff on July X=120 call | Total profit | =-2*(MAX(A10-100,0)-$B$5) | | | | | | |
| 10 | 0 | -10.00 | 12.8 | -0.52 | 2.28 | <-- =D10+C10+B10 | | | | | | |
| 11 | 10 | -10.00 | 12.8 | -0.52 | 2.28 | | =MAX(A10-120,0)-$B$6 | | | | | |
| 12 | 20 | -10.00 | 12.8 | -0.52 | 2.28 | | | | | | | |
| 13 | 30 | -10.00 | 12.8 | -0.52 | 2.28 | | | | | | | |
| 14 | 40 | -10.00 | 12.8 | -0.52 | 2.28 | | | | | | | |
| 15 | 50 | -10.00 | 12.8 | -0.52 | 2.28 | | | | | | | |
| 16 | 60 | -10.00 | 12.8 | -0.52 | 2.28 | | | | | | | |
| 17 | 70 | -10.00 | 12.8 | -0.52 | 2.28 | | | | | | | |
| 18 | 80 | -10.00 | 12.8 | -0.52 | 2.28 | | | | | | | |
| 19 | 90 | 0.00 | 12.8 | -0.52 | 12.28 | | | | | | | |
| 20 | 100 | 10.00 | 12.8 | -0.52 | 22.28 | | | | | | | |
| 21 | 110 | 20.00 | -7.2 | -0.52 | 12.28 | | | | | | | |
| 22 | 120 | 30.00 | -27.2 | -0.52 | 2.28 | | | | | | | |
| 23 | 130 | 40.00 | -47.2 | 9.48 | 2.28 | | | | | | | |
| 24 | 140 | 50.00 | -67.2 | 19.48 | 2.28 | | | | | | | |
| 25 | 150 | 60.00 | -87.2 | 29.48 | 2.28 | | | | | | | |
| 26 | 160 | 70.00 | -107.2 | 39.48 | 2.28 | | | | | | | |
| 27 | 170 | 80.00 | -127.2 | 49.48 | 2.28 | | | | | | | |
| 28 | | | | | | | | | | | | |
| 29 | | | | | | | | | | | | |
| 30 | | | | | | | | | | | | |
| 31 | | | | | | | | | | | | |

Butterfly Profit Pattern
1 X=80 Call Bought, 2 X=100 Calls Written, 1 X=120 Call Bought

## What's Wrong?

Playing around a bit with the numbers will convince you that a *condition necessary for the butterfly graph to straddle the x-axis* is

$$Call\ price(X_{Middle}) < \frac{Call\ price(X_{Low}) + Call\ price(X_{High})}{2},$$

where $X_{Low}, X_{Middle}, X_{High}$ are three equally spaced exercise prices.

This condition—in the jargon of the options markets referred to as the *convexity property of call prices*—says that for three equally spaced calls, the middle call price must be less than the average of the two extreme call prices. Another way of saying this is that the line connecting two call prices always lies *above* the graph of the call prices.

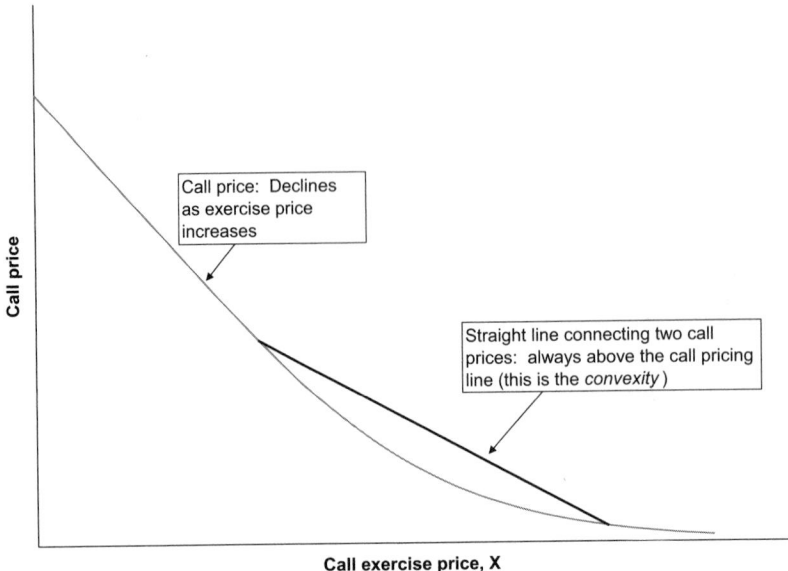

FIGURE 21.1 The curved line illustrates the actual call prices for various exercise prices. Call price convexity means that the line connecting two call prices is always above the actual call pricing curve.

Put prices are also convex.

$$Put\ price\left(X_{Middle}\right) < \frac{Put\ price\left(X_{Low}\right) + Put\ price\left(X_{High}\right)}{2}$$

We leave put butterflies as an exercise and let you prove this on your own. Here's the way put prices look.

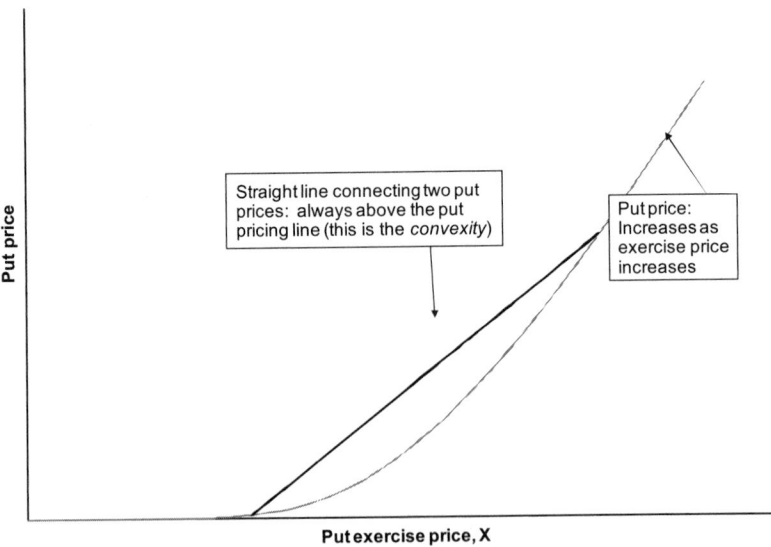

FIGURE 21.2 The curved line illustrates the actual put prices for various exercise prices. Put price convexity means that the line connecting two put prices is always above the actual put pricing curve.

# Summary

In this chapter we have derived restrictions on option prices that stem from their being related to other securities in the market. These arbitrage restrictions help us bound option prices (that is, establish minimum prices for put and call options) as well as establish relations between the prices of various options and the underlying security (as in the case of the put–call parity theorem).

In this chapter we have dealt with seven such option-pricing restrictions, but there are many more that deal with cases involving dividends and transactions costs. Understanding the seven restrictions discussed in this chapter will help you understand not only the pricing of options (we will have more to say on this topic in the next chapter), but also the way option traders think—they are constantly busy trying to figure out how to arbitrage option prices.

## EXERCISES

1. You want to buy one American call option contract on Dell Computer Corp., expiring in 6 months, with a strike price of $25. The current stock price is at $24.80. Can the option price be lower than $0.60? Assume that the interest rate is 8%.

2. Assume that you can buy the above call for $0.50 (which is less than the theoretical minimum). How can you exploit the mispricing to make a riskless gain?

3. Your generous uncle gives you 10,000 units of the above option as a birthday gift. The option expires in 6 months and the interest rate is 8%. The stock price has risen to $28. Will you exercise the option early or rather sell it? Explain.

4. Cash dividends affect option prices through their effect on the underlying stock price. Because the stock price is expected to drop by the amount of the dividend on the ex-dividend date, high cash dividends imply lower call premiums. Suppose you own a call option with a strike price of 90 that expires in 1 week. The stock is currently trading at $100 and is expected to pay a $2.00 dividend tomorrow. The call option has a value of $10. What are you going to do: hold the option or exercise the option early?

5. The Fashion Corp. has stock outstanding that is currently selling for $83 per share. Both a put and a call with a strike price of $80 and an expiration of 6 months are trading. The put option premium is $2.50, and the risk-free rate is 8%. If put–call parity holds, what is the call option premium?

6. The current market price of a 2-month European put option on a non-dividend-paying stock with strike price of $50 is $4. The stock price is $47 and the risk-free interest rate is 6%.

   a. If a 2-month call option with the same strike price is currently selling for $1, what opportunities are there for an arbitrageur? How can you exploit arbitrage?

   b. Would the above market prices still provide an arbitrage opportunity if the option has a 1-month maturity and the stock price is $46.755?

7. In general, what is the problem of using Wall Street Journal prices to search for violations of the put–call parity relationship?

8. Recall from Chapter 20 that a butterfly is an options strategy built on four trades at one expiration date and three different strike prices. For call options, one option each at the high and low strike prices are bought, and two options at the middle strike price are sold. Consider the following spreads:

   • Spread composed of calls: Buy one ABC Jun $180 call for $20, sell two ABC Jun $200 calls each at $10, and buy one ABC Jun $220 call for $5.

   • Spread composed of puts: Buy one ABC Jun $180 put, sell two ABC Jun $200 puts, and buy one ABC Jun $220 put.

Use put–call parity to show that the cost of a butterfly spread created from the calls is identical to the cost of the butterfly spread created from European puts.

9. (Challenge). You have the following information, 25 calendar days before the March 2011 option expiration day.

| Strike | Put/Call | Price |
|--------|----------|-------|
| 1025 | Call | 19.8 |
| 1025 | Put | 14.5 |
| 1040 | Call | 12.5 |
| 1040 | Put | 22.17 |

In the absence of arbitrage, what is the annualized risk-free rate?

10. A European put and call option both expire in 1 year and have the same exercise price of $20. The options are currently traded at the same market price of $3. Assume that the annual interest rate is 8%. What is the current stock price? In general, if a European put and call have the same price and expire at the same time, what can you say about the relationships between the stock price and the exercise price? $S > X$? $S < X$? $S = X$?

11. You consider buying an American put option on Dell Computer Corp., expiring in 6 months, with a strike price of $25. The current stock price is at $18. What is the minimum price the put will sell for? If you can buy the above put for $5 (which is less than the theoretical minimum), how can you exploit the mispricing to make a riskless gain?

12. ABC is a non-dividend-paying stock. Suppose that $S = \$17$, $X = \$20$, and $r = 5\%$ per annum.
    a. Can a **European** put option that expires in 6 months trade at $2.50? Note that a European put option may sometimes be worth less than its intrinsic value.
    b. Consider a situation where the European put option is traded at $2.40. Show how you can gain from arbitrage.

13. Suppose that you are currently holding an American put option on National Australia Bank that has an exercise price of $45. The option expires in 6 months. The share price is currently traded at $23.00.
    a. Consider a situation where the American put option is traded at $21. Show how you can gain from arbitrage.
    b. What is your net payoff if
       i. you exercise the put option today (assume that you invest your proceeds in bonds with an interest rate of 8%)?
       ii. you hold the option until its expiration date?

14. You are trying to decide whether to early exercise a put option you hold that expires in 6 months. The put's exercise price is $X = \$50$ and the interest rate is $r = 20\%$. Consider two cases:
    a. $S = \$20$
    b. $S = \$3$

    In which case are you better off exercising the option?

15. Three calls are written on a stock whose current price is $S = 100$. The $X = 80$ call option has a price of 35 and the $X = 120$ call has a price of 10. What is the maximum price of the $X = 100$ option?

16. A butterfly spread is created using the following put options: The investor buys a put option with a strike price of $55 and pays $10, buys a put with a strike price of $65 and pays $5, and sells two puts with an intermediate strike price of $60.

    a. Use convexity to determine the upper bound for the X = 60 put price.

    b. Assume that the X = 60 put price is $8. Graph the profit pattern at maturity for the butterfly using Excel (let the stock prices at maturity range between $40 and $90). Does the graph indicate an arbitrage opportunity?

17. At the expiration date the put call parity $Put_0(X) = Call_0(X) + PV(X) - S_0$ has the following form: $Put_T(X) = Call_T(X) + X - S_T$ or $S_T = Call_T(X) - Put_T(X) + X$. Verify this equation using Excel: Let ST range from $20 to $100 and the exercise price X = $60. The option values at expiration are $Put(X) = Max(S_T - X, 0)$, $Call(X) = Max(X - S_T, 0)$.

18. Cisco (CSCO) stock sells for $25. The at-the-money CSCO 24 April call sells for $3 3/8 and the at-the-money CSCO 24 April put sells for $1 3/4. The call, the put, and a Treasury Bill all mature in 4 months. Today's price for a Treasury bill that pays off $100 in 4 months is $94.92. Assume that CSCO does not pay dividends in this period. Use the put–call parity relation to find the arbitrage profit today, if exists.

# 22 Option Pricing—The Black–Scholes Formula

## CHAPTER CONTENTS

# Overview

In the two previous chapters on option pricing, we've discussed some facts about options, but we haven't discussed *how to determine the price of an option*. In this chapter we show how to price options using the Black–Scholes formula. The Black–Scholes formula is the most important option-pricing formula. The formula is in wide use in options markets. It has also achieved a certain degree of notoriety, in the sense that even nonfinance people (lawyers, accountants, judges, bankers...) know that options are priced using Black–Scholes. They may not know how to apply it, and they certainly wouldn't know why the formula is correct, but they know that it is used to price options.

In our discussion of the Black–Scholes model, we'll make no attempt whatsoever to give a theoretical background to the model. It's hopeless, unless you know a lot more math than 99% of all beginning finance students will ever know.[1]

The next chapter discusses the other major model for pricing options, the *binomial option-pricing model*. The binomial model gives some insights into how to price an option, and it's also used widely (although not as widely as the Black–Scholes equation). Most books discuss the binomial model—which, in a theoretical sense, underlies the Black–Scholes formula—first and then discuss Black–Scholes. However, because we have no intention of making the theoretical connection between the binomial model and Black–Scholes, we've chosen to reverse the order and deal with the more important model first.

## What Does "Pricing an Option" Mean?

Suppose we're discussing a call option on IBM stock that is sold on 8 May 2009. On this date, IBM's stock price is $S_0 = \$101.49$. Suppose that the call option has an exercise price $X = \$90$ and expires on 17 July 2009. Here is what you have learned so far in this book:

- From Chapter 20, you know the basic option terminology. You know what an exercise price $X$ is, you know the difference between a call and a put, etc.

- From Chapter 20, you also know what the *payoff pattern* and *profit pattern* of the call option looks like—by itself and in combination with other assets.

- From Chapter 21, you know that there are some pricing *restrictions* on the call option. A simple restriction ("Fact 1" from Chapter 21, page 625) says that $Call_0 > Max[S_0 - PV(X),0]$. A more sophisticated restriction ("Fact 3," put–call parity, page 629) says that once we know the price of IBM stock, the call price, and the interest rate, the put price is determined by the relation $Put_0 + S_0 = Call_0 + PV(X)$.

All of these facts are—by themselves—interesting. However, they don't tell us what the *price* of the call option should be. This is the subject of this chapter—the Black–Scholes formula tells us what the market price of the option should be.

## Chapter Notation

We recall the notation we're using throughout Chapters 20–23.

---

[1] A bitter truth, perhaps. But get this—your professor probably can't prove the Black–Scholes equation either (don't ask him, he'll be embarrassed). On the other hand, you know how to drive a car but may not know how an internal combustion engine works, you know how to use a computer but can't make a central processing unit chip,...

---

**NOTATION**

Throughout the chapter we use the following notation:

$S$ = The price of the stock. When we want to be precise about the price of the stock on a specific date, we will sometimes write $S_0$ for the price of the stock today (time 0) and $S_T$ for the price of the stock on the option exercise date $T$.

$X$ = The option exercise price

$r$ = The interest rate

$C$ = The call option price. When we want to be precise about the call price on a specific date, we will sometimes write $C_0$ for the price of the option today (time 0) and $C_T$ for the price of the option on the stock on exercise date $T$. Occasionally we will even use the full word, writing $Call_0$.

$P$ = The put option price. When we want to be precise about the put price on a specific date, we will sometimes write $P_0$ for the price of the put option today (time 0) and $P_T$ for the price of the put on the stock on exercise date $T$. Occasionally we will even use the full word, writing $Put_0$.

---

### Finance Concepts in This Chapter

- Black–Scholes formula
- Put–call parity
- Stock price volatility
- Implied volatility
- Real options

### Excel Functions Used

- **Exp**
- **Date**
- **Ln**
- **Stdevp**
- **Varp**
- **Data Table**

# 22.1. The Black–Scholes Model

In 1973, Fisher Black and Myron Scholes proved a formula for pricing European call and put options on non-dividend-paying stocks. Their model is probably the most famous model of modern finance.[2] The Black–Scholes model uses the following formula to price calls on the stock:

$$C_0 = S_0 N(d_1) - Xe^{-rT} N(d_2),$$
$$where$$
$$d_1 = \frac{\ln(S_0 / X) + (r + \sigma^2/2)T}{\sigma\sqrt{T}}$$
$$d_2 = d_1 - \sigma\sqrt{T}$$

Don't let this formula frighten you! We're going to show you how to use Excel to implement the Black–Scholes formula, and you won't really have to understand the mechanics or the math. However, if you want some explanations, $C_0$ denotes the price of a call, $S_0$ is the current price of the underlying stock, $X$ is the exercise price of the call, $T$ is the call's time to exercise, $r$ is the interest rate, and $\sigma$ is the standard deviation of the stock's return. $N(\ )$ denotes a value of the cumulative standard normal distribution. It is assumed that the stock will pay no dividends before date $T$.

The spreadsheet below prices an option on a stock whose current price is $S_0 = 100$. The option's exercise price is $X = 90$ and its time to maturity is $T = 0.5$ (one-half year). The interest rate is $r = 4\%$, and sigma ($\sigma$, the stock's volatility—a measure of the stock's riskiness; more about this later) is $\sigma = 35\%$.

| | A | B | C |
|---|---|---|---|
| 1 | | **The Black-Scholes Option-Pricing Formula** | |
| 2 | $S_0$ | 100 | Current stock price |
| 3 | X | 90 | Exercise price |
| 4 | T | 0.50000 | Time to maturity of option (in years) |
| 5 | r | 4.00% | Risk-free rate of interest |
| 6 | Sigma | 35% | Stock volatility |
| 7 | | | |
| 8 | $d_1$ | 0.6303 | <-- (LN($S_0$/X)+(r+0.5*sigma^2)*T)/(sigma*SQRT(T)) |
| 9 | $d_2$ | 0.3828 | <-- $d_1$-sigma*SQRT(T) |
| 10 | | | |
| 11 | $N(d_1)$ | 0.7357 | <-- Uses formula NormSDist($d_1$) |
| 12 | $N(d_2)$ | 0.6491 | <-- Uses formula NormSDist($d_2$) |
| 13 | | | |
| 14 | Call price, $C_0$ | 16.32 | <-- $S_0$*N($d_1$)-X*exp(-r*T)*N($d_2$) |
| 15 | Put price, $P_0$ | 4.53 | <-- call price - $S_0$ + X*Exp(-r*T):  by Put-Call parity |
| 16 | | 4.53 | <-- X*exp(-r*T)*N(-$d_2$) - S*N(-$d_1$):  direct formula |

By the put–call parity theorem (see Chapter 21, page 629), a put with the same exercise date $T$ and exercise price $X$ written on the same stock will have price $P_0 = C_0 - S_0 + PV(X)$. Because the Black–Scholes option pricing formula is based on continuous compounding (see Chapter 3 and the note on page 646), we have to write the $PV(X)$ term as $PV(X) = Xe^{-rT}$, so that it becomes $P_0 = C_0 - S_0 + Xe^{-rT}$. We've used this formula in cell B15. Cell B16 includes another version of put pricing—a direct formula that follows from the Black–Scholes formula.

## What Do the Black-Scholes Parameters Mean? How to Calculate Them?

The Black–Scholes option pricing model depends on five parameters:

- $S_0$, the *current price of the stock*. By this we always mean the stock price on the date we're calculating the option price.

- $X$, the *exercise price of the option* (this is also called the *strike price*).

---

[2] The 1997 Nobel Prize for Economics was awarded to Myron Scholes and Robert Merton for their role in developing the option pricing formula. Fisher Black, who died in 1995, would have undoubtedly shared in the prize had he still been alive.

- $T$, the *time to the option's expiration* (sometimes called the *option maturity*). In the Black–Scholes formula, $T$ is always given in *annual terms*—meaning an option with 3 months to expiration has $T = 0.25$ and an option with 51 days until expiration has $T = 51/365 = 0.1397$

You can use Excel's **Date** function (see Chapter 26) to compute the time $T$ to option expiration. In the example below, the current date is 2 February 2010 and the option's expiration date is 19 July 2010. These two dates are entered using Excel's **Date** function (cells B2 and B3). Subtracting the two cells gives the number of days between the dates (cell B4). $T$ is computed in cell B5.

| | A | B | C |
|---|---|---|---|
| 1 | COMPUTING T USING EXCEL DATE FUNCTION | | |
| 2 | Current date | 8-Feb-10 | <-- =DATE(2010,2,8) |
| 3 | Expiration date | 19-Jul-10 | <-- =DATE(2010,7,19) |
| 4 | Days between dates | 161 | <-- =B3-B2 |
| 5 | T, time in years to expiration | 0.4411 | <-- =B4/365 |
| 6 | | | |
| 7 | Note: We formatted cell B4 to give a number, by right-clicking on the cell and then using **Format Cells\|Number\|General** | | |

- $r$, the *risk-free interest rate*. This is also given in annual terms. Meaning, if the interest rate is 6% per year and if an option has $T = 0.25$, then we write $r = 6\%$ in the Black–Scholes formula. We generally use the Treasury bill rate for a maturity that is closest to the option maturity.

- $\sigma$ is a measure of the *riskiness of the stock*. $\sigma$ is an important variable in determining the option price, and it is not a simple concept to explain. We discuss it at length in Sections 22.2 and 22.3. However, here are some facts to help you get your bearings on $\sigma$:

  - If the stock is riskless, then $\sigma = 0\%$. A stock is riskless if its future price is completely predictable.
  - An "average" U.S. stock has $\sigma$ between 10 and 25%.
  - A risky stock may have a $\sigma$ of as much as 80 or 100%.

## 22.2. Historical Volatility: Computing σ from Stock Prices

There are two main ways to compute $\sigma$: One method is to calculate $\sigma$ by looking at the series of past stock returns; this computation is sometimes called the *historical $\sigma$* or the *historical volatility*. Alternatively, we can calculate the *implied $\sigma$* by looking at options prices; this calculation is often called the *implied volatility*. This section describes the computation of the historical volatility, and the next section describes how to compute the implied volatility.

Below we show the annual stock prices for IBM for the decade from 1999–2009. Column C shows the *continuously compounded return* for the prices: $r_t^{continuous} = \ln(P_t/P_{t-1})$. (Continuously compounded interest was first discussed in Chapter 3; for a reminder see the note in this chapter on page 646.) σ is the standard deviation of these annual returns (cell C18). As you can see, the σ computed from these prices is σ = 16.70%.

| | A | B | C | D |
|---|---|---|---|---|
| 1 | **IBM STOCK PRICES AND RETURNS** 1999 – 2009 | | | |
| 2 | Date | Stock price | Annual return | |
| 3 | 4-Jan-99 | 82.78 | | |
| 4 | 3-Jan-00 | 101.89 | 20.77% | <-- =LN(B4/B3) |
| 5 | 2-Jan-01 | 102.14 | 0.25% | |
| 6 | 2-Jan-02 | 98.87 | -3.25% | |
| 7 | 2-Jan-03 | 72.19 | -31.45% | |
| 8 | 2-Jan-04 | 92.31 | 24.59% | |
| 9 | 3-Jan-05 | 87.57 | -5.27% | |
| 10 | 3-Jan-06 | 76.93 | -12.95% | |
| 11 | 3-Jan-07 | 95.08 | 21.18% | |
| 12 | 2-Jan-08 | 104.15 | 9.11% | |
| 13 | 2-Jan-09 | 90.68 | -13.85% | |
| 14 | | | | |
| 15 | Average return | | 0.91% | <-- =AVERAGE(C4:C13) |
| 16 | Return variance | | 2.79% | <-- =VARP(C5:C14) |
| 17 | Return standard deviation | | 16.70% | <-- =STDEVP(C6:C15) |

In the world of option pricing it is not usual to compute σ from annual data. Most traders prefer daily, weekly, or monthly data. The use of nonannual data requires some adjustment to the calculations. We show these adjustments in the example below, where we calculate IBM's σ from monthly data. A discussion of what we did follows the spreadsheet.

| | A | B | C | D |
|---|---|---|---|---|
| 1 | **IBM STOCK PRICES** Monthly data for 2008 | | | |
| 2 | Date | Price | Monthly return | |
| 3 | 2-Jan-08 | 104.15 | | |
| 4 | 1-Feb-08 | 111.14 | 6.50% | <-- =LN(B4/B3) |
| 5 | 3-Mar-08 | 112.39 | 1.12% | <-- =LN(B5/B4) |
| 6 | 1-Apr-08 | 117.82 | 4.72% | |
| 7 | 1-May-08 | 126.85 | 7.38% | |
| 8 | 2-Jun-08 | 116.17 | -8.80% | |
| 9 | 1-Jul-08 | 125.43 | 7.67% | |
| 10 | 1-Aug-08 | 119.77 | -4.62% | |
| 11 | 2-Sep-08 | 115.08 | -3.99% | |
| 12 | 1-Oct-08 | 91.48 | -22.95% | |
| 13 | 3-Nov-08 | 80.74 | -12.49% | |
| 14 | 1-Dec-08 | 83.27 | 3.09% | |
| 15 | 2-Jan-09 | 90.68 | 8.52% | |
| 16 | | | | |
| 17 | **Monthly return statistics** | | | |
| 18 | Average return | | -1.15% | <-- =AVERAGE(C4:C15) |
| 19 | Return variance | | 0.87% | <-- =VARP(C4:C15) |
| 20 | Return standard deviation | | 9.32% | <-- =STDEVP(C4:C15) |
| 21 | | | | |
| 22 | **Annualized return statistics** | | | |
| 23 | Average return | | -13.85% | <-- =12*C18 |
| 24 | Return variance | | 10.43% | <-- =12*C19 |
| 25 | Return standard deviation | | 32.29% | <-- =SQRT(C24) |

The standard deviation of the monthly returns is 9.32% (cell C20). The annualized standard deviation required for the Black–Scholes formula is 32.29% (cell C25). Note that because

$$annual\ variance = 12 * monthly\ variance$$
$$annual\ standard\ deviation = \sqrt{12 * monthly\ variance}$$
$$= \sqrt{12} * monthly\ standard\ deviation$$

In general, if we're calculating from nonannual data,

$$\sigma, annual\ standard\ deviation =$$
$$\sqrt{12} * monthly\ standard\ deviation$$
$$\sqrt{52} * weekly\ standard\ deviation$$
$$\sqrt{260} * daily\ standard\ deviation$$

(The use of 260 in calculating the annualized $\sigma$ from weekly data may be a bit confusing: Because there are 52 weeks per year and 5 business days per week, many traders assume that there are 260 business days per year. However, others use 250 and 365.)

---

## NOTE: CONTINUOUS VERSUS DISCRETE RETURNS—A REMINDER

The Black–Scholes formula uses *continuously compounded* returns, whereas in most of this book we use *discretely compounded returns*. We discussed the difference between these two concepts in Chapter 3. Suppose you have an investment that is worth Pt at time $t$ and worth Pt+1 one period later. There are two ways to define the return on the investment. The *discrete return* is $r_t^{discrete} = \dfrac{P_{t+1}}{P_t} - 1$, and the *continuously compounded return* is $r_t^{continuous} = \ln\left(\dfrac{P_{t+1}}{P_t}\right)$.
The example below shows the difference.

| | A | B | C |
|---|---|---|---|
| 1 | **DISCRETE VERSUS CONTINUOUS RETURNS** | | |
| 2 | Computing the returns from prices | | |
| 3 | $P_t$ | 100 | |
| 4 | $P_{t+1}$ | 120 | |
| 5 | | | |
| 6 | Discrete return | 20.00% | <-- =B4/B3-1 |
| 7 | Continuously compounded return | 18.23% | <-- =LN(B4/B3) |

---

# 22.3. Implied Volatility: Calculating $\sigma$ from Option Prices

In the previous section we computed the annualized standard deviation of returns $\sigma$ from historical stock prices. In this section we compute $\sigma$ from option prices.

When we calculate the implied volatility from option prices, we use the Black–Scholes formula to *find the $\sigma$ that gives a specific options price*. Suppose, for example, that a share of ABC Corp. is currently selling for $S_0 = \$35$ and that a 6-month at-the-money call option on ABC Corp. is selling for $C_0$ = \$5.25. (Recall that an at-the-money option has exercise price $X$ equal to the current stock price $S$.) Suppose the interest rate is 6%. The spreadsheet below shows that $\sigma$ must be greater than 35% (because the call prices increases with $\sigma$ and because $\sigma$ = 35% gives a call price of \$3.94, we'll have to make $\sigma$ larger to get a call price of \$5.25).

|   | A | B | C |
|---|---|---|---|
| 1 | **The Black–Scholes Option-Pricing Formula** | | |
| 2 | $S_0$ | 35 | Current stock price |
| 3 | X | 35 | Exercise price |
| 4 | T | 0.5000 | Time to maturity of option (in years) |
| 5 | r | 6.00% | Risk-free rate of interest |
| 6 | Sigma | 35.00% | Stock volatility |
| 7 | | | |
| 8 | $d_1$ | 0.2450 | <-- (LN(S/X)+(r+0.5*sigma^2)*T)/(sigma*SQRT(T)) |
| 9 | $d_2$ | -0.0025 | <-- $d_1$-sigma*SQRT(T) |
| 10 | | | |
| 11 | N($d_1$) | 0.5968 | <-- Uses formula NormSDist($d_1$) |
| 12 | N($d_2$) | 0.4990 | <-- Uses formula NormSDist($d_2$) |
| 13 | | | |
| 14 | Call price, $C_0$ | 3.94 | <-- S*N($d_1$)-X*exp(-r*T)*N($d_2$) |
| 15 | Put price, $P_0$ | 2.90 | <-- call price - S + X*Exp(-r*T): by Put-Call parity |
| 16 | | 2.90 | <-- X*exp(-r*T)*N(-d2) - S*N(-d1): direct formula |

Using **Goal Seek**, we can compute the $\sigma$ that gives the market price; it turns out to be $\sigma$ = 48.71%. Here's the **Goal Seek** dialog box.

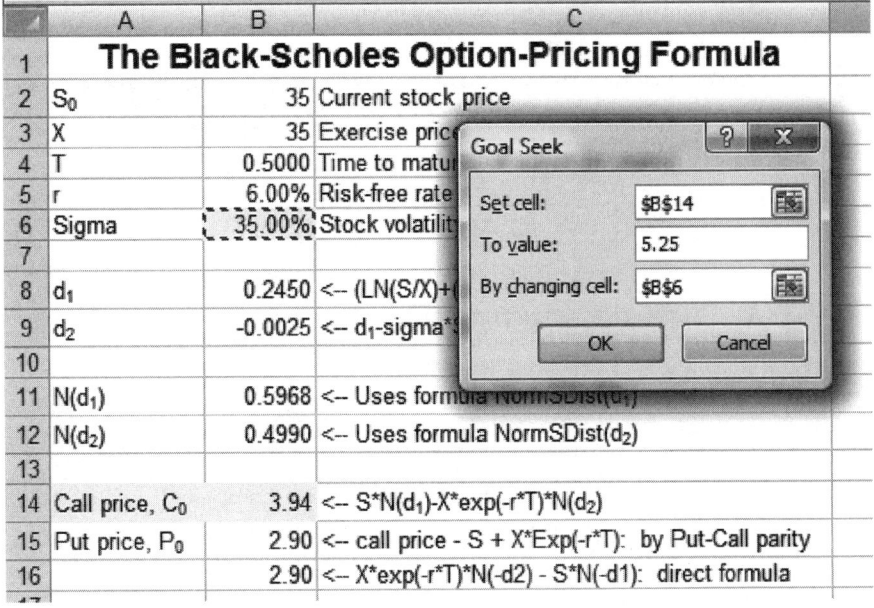

And here's the final result.

| | A | B | C |
|---|---|---|---|
| 1 | | The Black–Scholes Option-Pricing Formula | |
| 2 | $S_0$ | 35 | Current stock price |
| 3 | X | 35 | Exercise price |
| 4 | T | 0.50000 | Time to maturity of option (in years) |
| 5 | r | 6.00% | Risk-free rate of interest |
| 6 | Sigma | 48.71% | Stock volatility |
| 7 | | | |
| 8 | $d_1$ | 0.2593 | <-- (LN(S/X)+(r+0.5*sigma^2)*T)/(sigma*SQRT(T)) |
| 9 | $d_2$ | -0.0851 | <-- $d_1$-sigma*SQRT(T) |
| 10 | | | |
| 11 | $N(d_1)$ | 0.6023 | <-- Uses formula NormSDist($d_1$) |
| 12 | $N(d_2)$ | 0.4661 | <-- Uses formula NormSDist($d_2$) |
| 13 | | | |
| 14 | Call price, $C_0$ | 5.25 | <-- S*N($d_1$)-X*exp(-r*T)*N($d_2$) |

## What's Used in Practice—Implied $\sigma$ or $\sigma$ from Historical Prices?

The answer is a bit of both. Smart traders compare the implied volatility with the historical volatility and try to form estimates of what the stock volatility actually is. There are whole Web sites devoted to this subject and lots of proprietary software.

## 22.4. An Excel Black–Scholes Function

The spreadsheet **PFE2, Chapter22.xlsm** that accompanies this chapter includes two Excel functions that compute the Black–Scholes call and put prices. These functions are not part of the original Excel package; they have been defined by the author. Here's an example of how to use them.

| | A | B | C |
|---|---|---|---|
| 1 | | BLACK–SCHOLES OPTION FUNCTIONS | |
| 2 | | The functions in this spreadsheet—**Calloption** and **Putoption**—were defined by the author. | |
| 3 | $S_0$ | 100 | Current stock price |
| 4 | X | 90 | Exercise price |
| 5 | T | 0.5000 | Time to maturity of option (in years) |
| 6 | r | 4.00% | Risk-free rate of interest |
| 7 | Sigma | 35% | Stock volatility |
| 8 | | | |
| 9 | Call price, $C_0$ | 16.32 | <-- =calloption(B3,B4,B5,B6,B7) |
| 10 | Put price, $P_0$ | 4.53 | <-- =putoption(B3,B4,B5,B6,B7) |

The function **Calloption(stock price, exercise price, time to maturity, interest, sigma)** is a defined macro that is attached to the spreadsheet.[3] When you first open the spreadsheet Excel will display the following message, which asks whether you really want to open this macro.

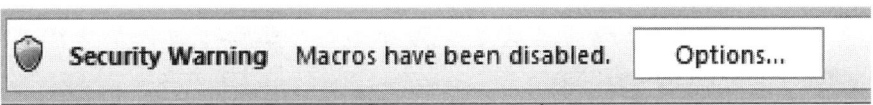

In this case the correct answer is **Enable this content**. More information on enabling macros is given in the document **Adding Getformula to your spreadsheet.docx,** which is on the disk that accompanies *Principles of Finance with Excel.*

The dialog box for these functions is self-explanatory.

---

[3] As you can see in the spreadsheet, **putoption** has the same format for the variables.

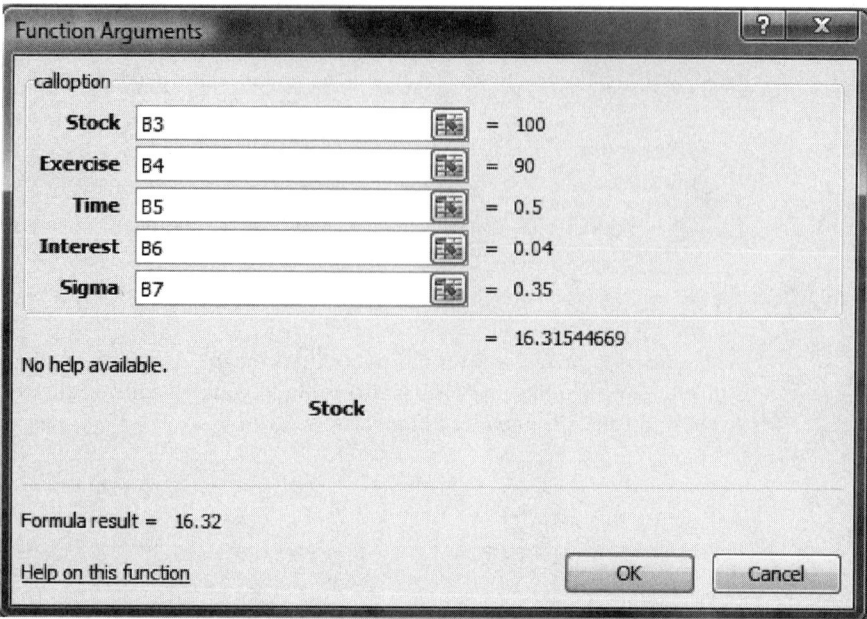

## An Implied Volatility Function

The spreadsheet also comes with two functions that compute the implied volatility for a call and a put option. The function **CallVolatility(stock price, exercise price, option maturity, interest rate, Call_price)** calculates the $\sigma$ that gives the Black–Scholes price given the other parameters. The spreadsheet also includes a function called **PutVolatility,** which computes the implied volatility for a put option.[4] Both functions are illustrated below.

|    | A | B | C |
|----|---|---|---|
| 1 | | **TWO IMPLIED VOLATILITY FUNCTIONS** | |
| 2 | Using CallVolatility to compute the implied volatility for a call | | |
| 3 | $S_0$ | 35 | Current stock price |
| 4 | X | 35 | Exercise price |
| 5 | T | 0.50000 | Time to maturity of option (in years) |
| 6 | r | 6.00% | Risk-free rate of interest |
| 7 | Target | 5.25 | <-- This is the current call price we want to match |
| 8 | Implied call volatility | 48.71% | <-- =CallVolatility(B3,B4,B5,B6,B7) |
| 9 | | | |
| 10 | Using PutVolatility to compute the implied volatility for a call | | |
| 11 | $S_0$ | 35 | Current stock price |
| 12 | X | 35 | Exercise price |
| 13 | T | 1.00000 | Time to maturity of option (in years) |
| 14 | r | 6.00% | Risk-free rate of interest |
| 15 | Target | 3.44 | <-- This is the current put price we want to match |
| 16 | Implied put volatility | 32.49% | <-- =putVolatility(B11,B12,B13,B14,B15) |

---

[4] In the spirit of this chapter, we do not explain how these functions work. For details see my book *Financial Modeling*, 3rd edition (MIT Press, 2008).

## 22.5. Doing Sensitivity Analysis on the Black–Scholes Formula

We can use Excel to do a lot of Black–Scholes sensitivity analysis. In this section we give two examples, leaving other examples for the chapter exercises.

### Example 1: The Sensitivity of the Black–Scholes Call Price to the Current Stock Price S

The following **Data|Table** (see Chapter 27) shows the sensitivity of the Black–Scholes call value to the current stock price $S_0$. It compares the Black–Scholes call value to the call's intrinsic value $Max(S_0-X,0)$.

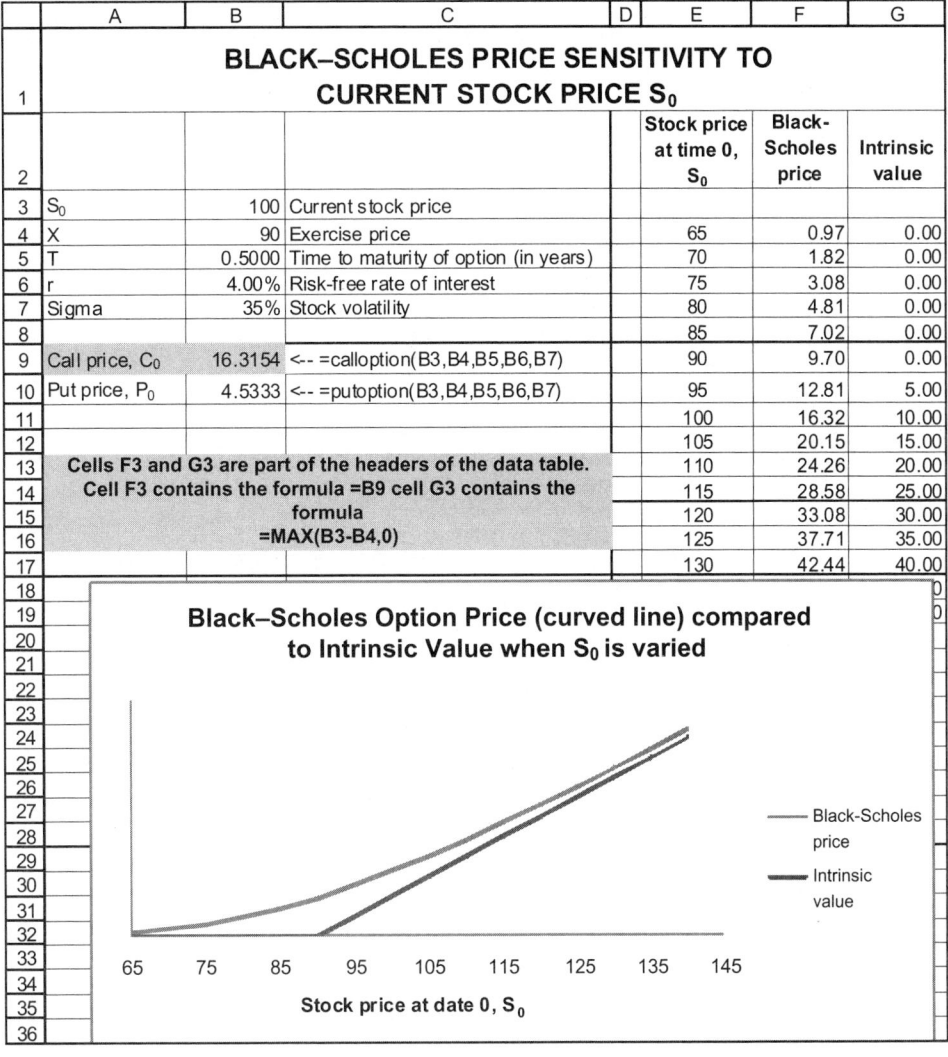

| | A | B | C | D | E | F | G |
|---|---|---|---|---|---|---|---|
| 1 | | | BLACK–SCHOLES PRICE SENSITIVITY TO CURRENT STOCK PRICE $S_0$ | | | | |
| 2 | | | | | Stock price at time 0, $S_0$ | Black-Scholes price | Intrinsic value |
| 3 | $S_0$ | 100 | Current stock price | | | | |
| 4 | X | 90 | Exercise price | | 65 | 0.97 | 0.00 |
| 5 | T | 0.5000 | Time to maturity of option (in years) | | 70 | 1.82 | 0.00 |
| 6 | r | 4.00% | Risk-free rate of interest | | 75 | 3.08 | 0.00 |
| 7 | Sigma | 35% | Stock volatility | | 80 | 4.81 | 0.00 |
| 8 | | | | | 85 | 7.02 | 0.00 |
| 9 | Call price, $C_0$ | 16.3154 | <-- =calloption(B3,B4,B5,B6,B7) | | 90 | 9.70 | 0.00 |
| 10 | Put price, $P_0$ | 4.5333 | <-- =putoption(B3,B4,B5,B6,B7) | | 95 | 12.81 | 5.00 |
| 11 | | | | | 100 | 16.32 | 10.00 |
| 12 | | | | | 105 | 20.15 | 15.00 |
| 13 | | Cells F3 and G3 are part of the headers of the data table. | | | 110 | 24.26 | 20.00 |
| 14 | | Cell F3 contains the formula =B9 cell G3 contains the | | | 115 | 28.58 | 25.00 |
| 15 | | formula | | | 120 | 33.08 | 30.00 |
| 16 | | =MAX(B3-B4,0) | | | 125 | 37.71 | 35.00 |
| 17 | | | | | 130 | 42.44 | 40.00 |
| 18 | | | | | | | |
| 19 | | | | | | | |
| 20 | | | | | | | |
| 21 | | | | | | | |
| 22 | | | | | | | |
| 23 | | | | | | | |
| 24 | | | | | | | |
| 25 | | | | | | | |
| 26 | | | | | | | |
| 27 | | | | | | | |
| 28 | | | | | | | |
| 29 | | | | | | | |
| 30 | | | | | | | |
| 31 | | | | | | | |
| 32 | | | | | | | |
| 33 | | | | | | | |
| 34 | | | | | | | |
| 35 | | | | | | | |
| 36 | | | | | | | |

Black–Scholes Option Price (curved line) compared to Intrinsic Value when $S_0$ is varied

Stock price at date 0, $S_0$

Black-Scholes price

Intrinsic value

The call option's intrinsic value $Max(S_0-X,0)$ shows what it would be worth if exercised immediately. The option's Black–Scholes price shows what the option would be worth on the open market. Note that the Black–Scholes price for the call option is always greater than the intrinsic value—it is not worthwhile to early exercise the call option.

## Example 2: The Sensitivity of the Black–Scholes Price to Different Estimates of $\sigma$

To show the sensitivity of Black–Scholes price to the $\sigma$, we graph below the call prices for two options varying only in their volatility. We let the price of the stock $S_0$ vary and show the price of the call option when $\sigma = 20\%$ and when $\sigma = 50\%$.

| | A | B | C | D | E | F | G |
|---|---|---|---|---|---|---|---|
| 1 | | | **BLACK–SCHOLES PRICE SENSITIVITY TO SIGMA** | | | | |
| 2 | | | | | Stock price at time 0, $S_0$ | Black-Scholes price, sigma = 20% | Black-Scholes price, sigma = 50% |
| 3 | $S_0$ | 90 | Current stock price | | | | |
| 4 | X | 90 | Exercise price | | 10 | 0.00 | 0.00 |
| 5 | T | 1.0000 | Time to maturity of option (in years) | | 20 | 0.00 | 0.01 |
| 6 | r | 4.00% | Risk-free rate of interest | | 30 | 0.00 | 0.15 |
| 7 | Sigma | 20% | Stock volatility | | 40 | 0.00 | 0.77 |
| 8 | | | | | 50 | 0.01 | 2.23 |
| 9 | Call price, $C_0$ | 8.9325 | <-- =calloption(B3,B4,B5,B6,B7) | | 60 | 0.19 | 4.80 |
| 10 | Put price, $P_0$ | 5.4036 | <-- =putoption(B3,B4,B5,B6,B7) | | 70 | 1.16 | 8.53 |
| 11 | | | | | 80 | 3.89 | 13.39 |
| 12 | | | | | 90 | 8.93 | 19.24 |
| 13 | | Cells F3 and G3 are part of the headers of the data table. | | | 100 | 16.06 | 25.93 |
| 14 | | Cell F3 contains the formula =calloption(B3,B4,B5,B6,20%) | | | 110 | 24.61 | 33.30 |
| 15 | | cell G3 contains the formula | | | 120 | 33.96 | 41.24 |
| 16 | | =calloption(B3,B4,B5,B6,50%) | | | 130 | 43.69 | 49.62 |
| 17 | | | | | 140 | 53.50 | 58.34 |
| 18 | | | | | | | 67.34 |
| 19 | | | | | | | 76.56 |

Black-Scholes Option Price when Sigma is Varied

— Black-Scholes price, sigma = 20%
— Black-Scholes price, sigma = 50%

Stock price at date 0, $S_0$

The higher the stock's $\sigma$, the higher the Black–Scholes option price.

## 22.6. Does the Black–Scholes Model Work? Application to Intel Options

In this section we do two experiments to examine whether and how well the Black–Scholes model works. First we compare the Black–Scholes option prices for a set of put and call options on Intel stock to the actual market prices. Then we compare the implied volatilities for the same options.

Our conclusion: Black–Scholes works pretty well!

### Test 1: Comparing Actual Market Prices to Black–Scholes Prices

At the close of trading on 16 October 2009, Intel's stock price was $20.18. An at-the-money call option with expiration date 16 April 2010 was trading at $1.62 and an at-the-money put was trading at $1.67. Our "test" of Black–Scholes consists of the following:

- We compute the implied volatility for these two options (cells B10 and B11) below.
- We then use these implied volatilities to compute the prices of all traded options.
- We compare the pricing using the implied volatility to the actual market prices.

The Black–Scholes model passes this test: It appears to do a good job of pricing options within a reasonable range of the current market price.

| | A | B | C | D | E | F |
|---|---|---|---|---|---|---|
| 1 | \multicolumn{6}{c}{**INTEL OPTION DATA, 16 October 2009**<br>**Call and put pricing using at-the-money implied volatility**} | | | | | |
| 2 | $S_0$, current Intel stock price | 20.18 | | | | |
| 3 | At-the-money X | 20 | | | | |
| 4 | Price of at-the-money call | 1.62 | | | | |
| 5 | Price of at-the-money put | 1.67 | | | | |
| 6 | Current date | 16-Oct-09 | | | | |
| 7 | Expiration date | 16-Apr-10 | | | | |
| 8 | T, time to expiration | 0.4986 | <-- =(B7-B6)/365 | | | |
| 9 | Interest rate | 0.75% | | | | |
| 10 | Implied call volatility | 26.40% | <-- =CallVolatility(B2,B3,B8,B9,B4) | | | |
| 11 | Implied put volatiity | 31.83% | <-- =PutVolatility(B2,B3,B8,B9,B5) | | | |
| 12 | | | | | | |
| 13 | Exercise price | Call option market price | Price call with at-money volatility | | Put option market price | Price put with at-money volatility |
| 14 | 15 | 5.30 | 5.31 | | 0.29 | 0.16 |
| 15 | 16 | 4.50 | 4.40 | | 0.43 | 0.30 |
| 16 | 17 | 3.60 | 3.56 | | 0.64 | 0.52 |
| 17 | 18 | 2.89 | 2.81 | | 0.89 | 0.81 |
| 18 | 19 | 2.19 | 2.16 | | 1.30 | 1.19 |
| 19 | 20 | 1.62 | 1.62 | | 1.67 | 1.67 |
| 20 | 21 | 1.16 | 1.18 | | 2.28 | 2.23 |
| 21 | 22 | 0.82 | 0.84 | | 2.90 | 2.88 |
| 22 | 23 | 0.57 | 0.59 | | 3.60 | 3.59 |
| 23 | 24 | 0.37 | 0.40 | | 4.01 | 4.37 |

## Test 2: Comparing Implied Volatilities for All Puts and Calls

In this test we use the market prices of traded options and compute the implied volatility for each option.

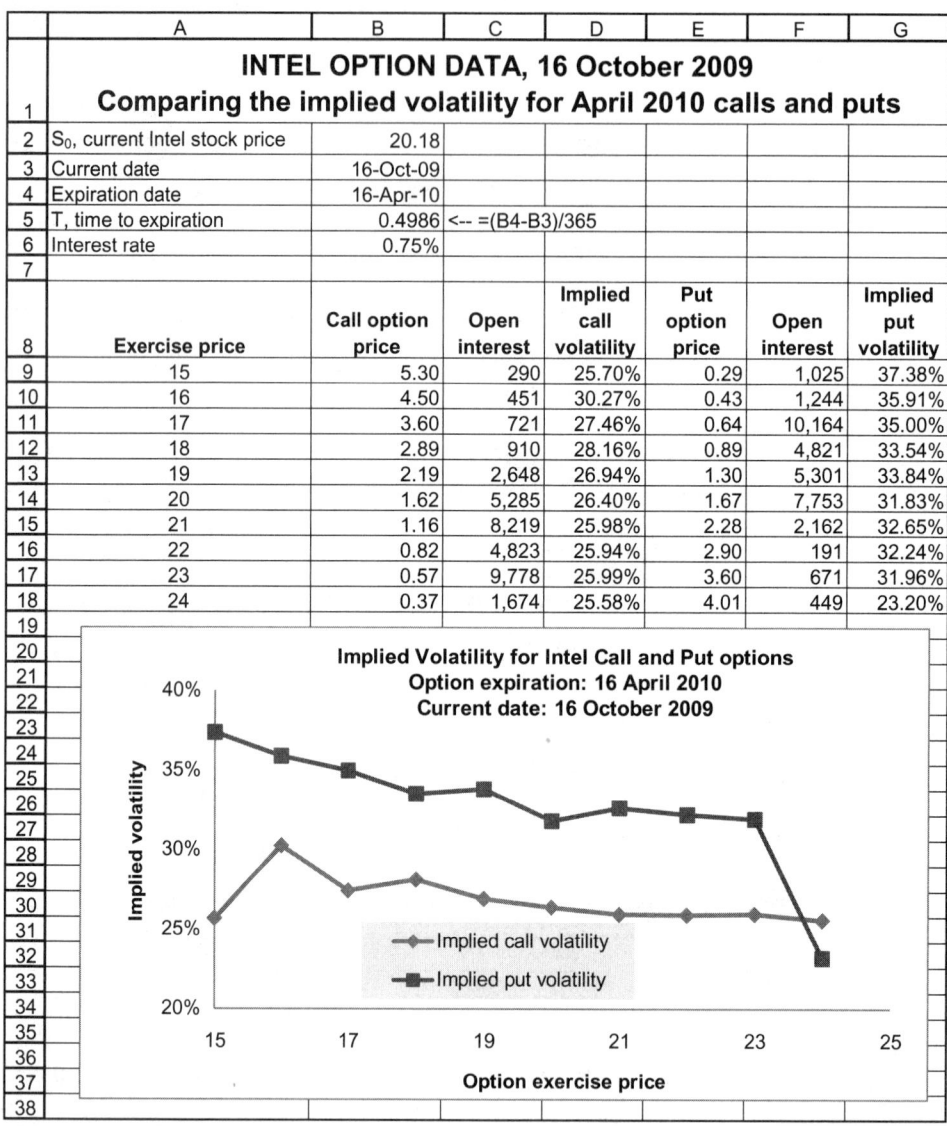

| | A | B | C | D | E | F | G |
|---|---|---|---|---|---|---|---|
| 1 | INTEL OPTION DATA, 16 October 2009 — Comparing the implied volatility for April 2010 calls and puts | | | | | | |
| 2 | S₀, current Intel stock price | 20.18 | | | | | |
| 3 | Current date | 16-Oct-09 | | | | | |
| 4 | Expiration date | 16-Apr-10 | | | | | |
| 5 | T, time to expiration | 0.4986 | <-- =(B4-B3)/365 | | | | |
| 6 | Interest rate | 0.75% | | | | | |
| 7 | | | | | | | |
| 8 | Exercise price | Call option price | Open interest | Implied call volatility | Put option price | Open interest | Implied put volatility |
| 9 | 15 | 5.30 | 290 | 25.70% | 0.29 | 1,025 | 37.38% |
| 10 | 16 | 4.50 | 451 | 30.27% | 0.43 | 1,244 | 35.91% |
| 11 | 17 | 3.60 | 721 | 27.46% | 0.64 | 10,164 | 35.00% |
| 12 | 18 | 2.89 | 910 | 28.16% | 0.89 | 4,821 | 33.54% |
| 13 | 19 | 2.19 | 2,648 | 26.94% | 1.30 | 5,301 | 33.84% |
| 14 | 20 | 1.62 | 5,285 | 26.40% | 1.67 | 7,753 | 31.83% |
| 15 | 21 | 1.16 | 8,219 | 25.98% | 2.28 | 2,162 | 32.65% |
| 16 | 22 | 0.82 | 4,823 | 25.94% | 2.90 | 191 | 32.24% |
| 17 | 23 | 0.57 | 9,778 | 25.99% | 3.60 | 671 | 31.96% |
| 18 | 24 | 0.37 | 1,674 | 25.58% | 4.01 | 449 | 23.20% |

The results are both encouraging and discouraging:

- The implied volatilities for the calls are pretty close together, as are the implied volatilities for the puts. This is good news.

- On the other hand, the implied volatilities for the puts are uniformly larger than the implied volatilities for the calls. This is strange, because in the Black–Scholes formulation, the implied volatility refers to the volatility of the stock's return and hence has nothing to do with whether we're discussing a put or a call option. One interpretation of this difference in volatilities is that option purchasers were more interested in insurance (buying puts) than in speculating positively on the future price of Intel (buying calls).

- On the third hand,[5] the actual difference between the implied volatilities for the calls and the puts is not that great (about 6%).

This is not the place to summarize the vast finance literature on implied volatilities. For our purposes, the Black–Scholes model works pretty well. That's enough!

## 22.7. Real Options (Advanced Topic)

Thus far in this chapter we have discussed the use of the Black–Scholes model to price call or put options on shares. Such options are sometimes termed *financial options* because the option is written on a stock, which is a financial asset. A growing field in finance discusses *real options*. A real option is an option that becomes available as the result of an investment opportunity. Here are some examples of real options:

- Caulk Shipping is considering the purchase of a license to operate a ferry service from Philadelphia to Camden. The license requires the company to operate one boat on the ferry line, but allows Caulk Shipping the possibility of operating as many as 10 ferry boats on the line. This possibility—the *option to expand* the ferry service—should be taken into account when Caulk Shipping evaluates the economics of buying the license.

- Jones Oil is considering the purchase of a plot that is known to contain a large quantity of oil. Tom Shale, the company's financial analyst, has computed the NPV of the lease—he assumes that once the oil drilling equipment is in place, the company will pump the oil out of the ground at the maximum feasible rate. However, Tom also realizes that the financial analysis of the plot purchase should include an important *real option*: If the future oil price is low, Jones Oil can stop pumping the oil and wait until the price gets higher. This *option to delay* has obvious value.

- Merrill Widgets is considering the purchase of six new widget machines to replace machines that are currently in place. The new machines employ an innovative production technology and are much more sophisticated than the old machines. Simona Mba, the company's financial analyst, has determined that the NPV of replacing a single machine is negative and thus recommends against the replacement. Roberta Merrill, the company's owner, has a slightly different logic: She wants to purchase one widget machine to learn about the machine's possibilities; after a year she will then decide whether to buy the remaining five widget machines. The purchase of a single new widget machine gives Merrill Widgets the *option to learn*. The company's financial analysis should value this option. Below we return to this case and show how to value the option to learn.

---

[5] Harry Truman is reported to have gotten so sick of hearing economists say "On the one hand, . . . But on the other hand, . . ." that he asked his chief of staff to get him a "one-handed economist." History does not record whether he succeeded. The economist in this section's bullets has at least three hands. Harry Truman would not have liked him.

## A Simple Example of the Option to Learn

In the rest of this section we will show how the Black–Scholes model can be used to value Merrill Widget's option to learn. Recall that the company is considering replacing each of its existing six widget machines with new machines. The new machines cost $1,000 each and have a 5-year life. Simona Mba, the company's financial analyst, has estimated the expected per-machine cash flows; these flows are defined as the incremental cash flow of replacing a single old machine by a new machine and include the after-tax savings from introducing new machines, the tax shield on incremental depreciation from replacing an old by a new machine, and the sale of the old machine. It is important to emphasize that management does not know the exact realization of these annual cash flows, but only their expected values. The expected cash flows for the new machine are given below.

| | A | B | C | D | E | F | G |
|---|---|---|---|---|---|---|---|
| | | 0 | 1 | 2 | 3 | 4 | 5 |
| 3 | Year | | | | | | |
| 4 | CF of single machine | -1000 | 220 | 300 | 400 | 200 | 150 |

Simona estimates the risk-adjusted cost of capital for the project at 12%. Using the expected cash flows and a cost of capital of 12% for the project; Simona has concluded that the replacement of a single old machine by a new machine is unprofitable because the NPV is negative:

$$-1,000 + \frac{220}{1.12} + \frac{300}{(1.12)^2} + \frac{400}{(1.12)^3} + \frac{200}{(1.12)^4} + \frac{150}{(1.12)^5} = -67.48$$

Now comes the (real options) twist. Roberta Merrill, the company's owner, says, "I want to try one of the new machines for a year and learn the true realization of its cash flows. At the end of the year, if the experiment is successful, I want to replace five other similar machines on the line with the new machines. If I do not try one of the new machines, I will never know their true cash flows."

Does this change our previously negative conclusion about replacing a single machine? The answer is yes. To see this, we now realize that what we have is a package:

- Replacing a single machine today. This has a NPV of –67.48.
- The *option* of replacing five more machines in 1 year. We can view each such option as a call option on an asset that has current value of

$$S = \frac{220}{1.12} + \frac{300}{(1.12)^2} + \frac{400}{(1.12)^3} + \frac{200}{(1.12)^4} + \frac{150}{(1.12)^5} = 932.52$$

and an exercise price $X = 1,000$. Of course these call options can be exercised only if we purchase the first machine now; in effect the real options model will be pricing the learning costs.

Let's suppose that the Black–Scholes option pricing model can price this call option. We further suppose that the risk-free rate is 6% and the standard deviation of the cash flows is $\sigma = 40\%$. The equation below shows that the value of the each of the options to acquire one machine in 1 year is $143.98. It now follows that the value of the whole project is $652.39 (cell B11):

$$Project\ value = NPV\ of\ first\ machine + 5\ options\ to\ acquire$$
$$= -67.48 + 5 * 143.98 = 652.39$$

| | A | B | C | D | E | F | G |
|---|---|---|---|---|---|---|---|
| 1 | MERRILL WIDGET—THE OPTION TO LEARN | | | | | | |
| 2 | Year | 0 | 1 | 2 | 3 | 4 | 5 |
| 3 | CF of single machine | -1000 | 220 | 300 | 400 | 200 | 150 |
| 4 | | | | | | | |
| 5 | Discount rate for machine cash flows | 12% | | | | | |
| 6 | Riskless discount rate | 6% | | | | | |
| 7 | NPV of single machine | -67.48 | | | | | |
| 8 | | | | | | | |
| 9 | Number of machines bought next year | 5 | | | | | |
| 10 | Option value of single machine purchased in one more year | 143.98 | <-- =B24 | | | | |
| 11 | NPV of total project | 652.39 | <-- =B7+B9*B10 | | | | |
| 12 | | | | | | | |
| 13 | **Black-Scholes Option Pricing Formula** | | | | | | |
| 14 | $S_0$ | 932.52 | <-- =NPV(B5,C3:G3), PV of machine CFs | | | | |
| 15 | X | 1000.00 | Exercise price = Machine cost | | | | |
| 16 | r | 6.00% | Risk-free rate of interest | | | | |
| 17 | T | 1 | Time to maturity of option (in years) | | | | |
| 18 | Sigma | 40% | <-- Volatility | | | | |
| 19 | $d_1$ | 0.1753 | <-- (LN(S/X)+(r+0.5*sigma^2)*T)/(sigma*SQRT(T)) | | | | |
| 20 | $d_2$ | -0.2247 | <-- $d_1$ - sigma*SQRT(T) | | | | |
| 21 | $N(d_1)$ | 0.5696 | <--- Uses formula NormSDist($d_1$) | | | | |
| 22 | $N(d_2)$ | 0.4111 | <--- Uses formula NormSDist($d_2$) | | | | |
| 23 | Option value = BS call price | 143.98 | <-- S*N($d_1$)-X*exp(-r*T)*N($d_2$) | | | | |

Thus, buying one machine today, and in the process acquiring the option to purchase five more machines in 1 year, is a worthwhile project.

One critical element here is the volatility. The lower the volatility (i.e., the lower the uncertainty), the less worthwhile this project is. By building a data table we can examine the relation between the standard deviation σ and the project value.

| | B | C | D | E | F | G | H | I |
|---|---|---|---|---|---|---|---|---|
| 26 | **Data Table** | | | | | | | |
| 27 | σ | 652.39 | <-- =B11, Table header | | | | | |
| 28 | 1% | -63.48 | | | | | | |
| 29 | 10% | 97.16 | | | | | | |
| 30 | 20% | 283.09 | | | | | | |
| 31 | 30% | 468.40 | | | | | | |
| 32 | 40% | 652.39 | | | | | | |
| 33 | 50% | 834.59 | | | | | | |
| 34 | 60% | 1014.54 | | | | | | |
| 35 | 70% | 1191.81 | | | | | | |
| 36 | | | | | | | | |
| 37 | | | | | | | | |
| 38 | | | | | | | | |
| 39 | | | | | | | | |
| 40 | | | | | | | | |

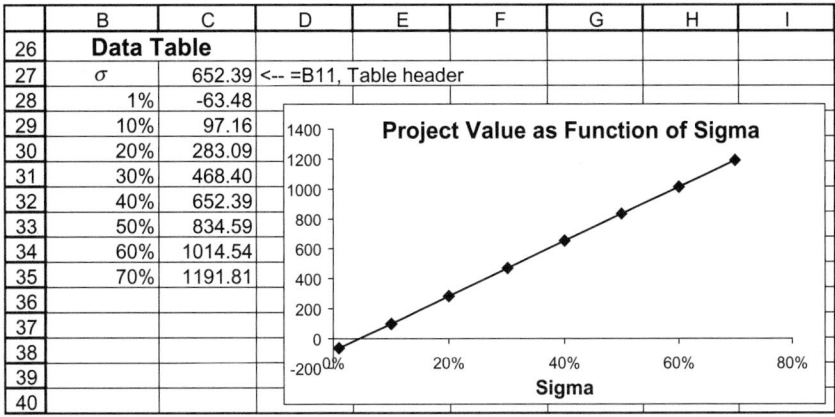

The value of the project as a whole comes from our uncertainty about the actual cash flows 1 year from now. The less this uncertainty is (measured by σ), the less valuable the project. In this particular example a very low uncertainty (σ > 4.75%) with respect to the machine cash flow returns is sufficient to justify its purchase.[6]

---

[6] Estimating the σ for real option cash flows is problematic because little market data exist (similar to stocks) to guide us. Many authors use estimates in the range of 30–50% for the standard deviation of real option returns; this is somewhat higher than the average standard deviation of U.S. market returns for equity, which are in the range of 15–30%. To explore this issue, consult one of the three leading books in the area: Lenos Trigeorgis, *Real Options: Managerial Flexibility and Strategy in Resource Allocation*, MIT Press, 1996; Martha Amram and Nalin Kulik, *Real Options*, Harvard Business School, 1998; or Tom Copeland and Vladimir Antikarov, *Real Options: A Practitioner's Guide*, Texere, 2001.

Real Options: Where Do We Go from Here?

Real options are increasingly used in finance to value corporate investments. The example of Merrill Widgets given earlier is only a small example of the use of the real options technique. For deeper discussions, we suggest you consult one of the books mentioned in Footnote 6.

# Summary

This chapter has given you a quick and hopefully practical insight into how to use the Black–Scholes model. The Black–Scholes model is remarkably good at pricing options and is widely used. It is also easy to use, provided you don't get too hung up on the details of where the formula comes from (in this chapter we've left these hang-ups behind us and concentrated exclusively on implementational details).

# EXERCISES

1. Use the Black–Scholes model to price the following:
   - A call option on a stock whose current price is $S = 50$, with exercise price $X = 50$, $T = 0.5$, $r = 10\%$, $\sigma = 25\%$.
   - A put option with the same parameters.

2. A call option on a stock is priced at $5.35. The option has an exercise price of $X = \$40$. The current stock price $S = \$33$, the option's time to maturity is 6 months, and the interest rate $r = 6\%$. Use the Black–Scholes model to determine the implied volatility, the $\sigma$ used to price the option. (Excel hint: use **Goal Seek**, Chapter 28.)

3. A put option on a stock is priced at $5. The option has an exercise price of $X = \$25$. The stock's current price is $S = \$25$, the option's time to maturity is 1 year, and the interest rate is $r = 5\%$. Use the Black–Scholes model to determine the option's implied volatility, the $\sigma$ used to price the option. (Excel hint: use **Solver**, Chapter 28.)

4. A call option with one-half year to maturity is written on a stock whose current price is $40. The option's exercise price is $38, the interest rate is 4%, and the stock's volatility is 30%.
   a. Find the call option price using the Black–Scholes model.
   b. Make a table showing the option's price for volatilities ranging from 10, 20,…, 60%. (Excel hint: by far the easiest way to do this is to use **Data Table**, explained in Chapter 27.)

5. A put option with one-half year to maturity is written on a stock whose current price is $40. The option's exercise price is $38, the interest rate is 4%, and the stock's volatility is 30%.
   a. Find the put option price using the Black–Scholes model.
   b. Make a table showing the option's price for maturities ranging from $T = 0.2, 0.4,…, 2.0$. (Excel hint: by far the easiest way to do this is to use **Data Table**, explained in Chapter 27.)

6. Use the data from Exercise 1 and **Data|Table** to produce graphs that show the following:
   - The sensitivity of the Black–Scholes call price to changes in the initial stock price $S$.
   - The sensitivity of the Black–Scholes put price to changes in $\sigma$.
   - The sensitivity of the Black–Scholes call price to changes in the time to maturity $T$.
   - The sensitivity of the Black–Scholes call price to changes in the interest rate $r$.
   - The sensitivity of the put price to changes in the exercise price $X$.

7. Consider the data below. Produce a graph comparing a call's *intrinsic value* (defined as $Max(S-X,0)$) and its Black–Scholes price for $S = 20, 25,…, 70$. From this graph you should be able to deduce that it is never optimal to exercise early a call priced by the Black–Scholes.

|   | A | B | C |
|---|---|---|---|
| 3 | S | 50 | Current stock price |
| 4 | X | 50 | Exercise price |
| 5 | T | 0.50000 | Time to maturity of option (in years) |
| 6 | r | 10.00% | Risk-free rate of interest |
| 7 | Sigma | 25% | Stock volatility |

8. Produce a graph comparing a put's intrinsic value (= *Max(X-S,0)*) and its Black–Scholes price. From this graph you should be able to deduce that it may be optimal to early exercise a put priced by the Black–Scholes formula.

9. Use the Excel **Solver** to find the stock price for which the maximum difference exists between the Black–Scholes call option price and the option's intrinsic value. Use the following values: $S = 45$, $X = 45$, $T = 1$, $\sigma = 40\%$, $r = 8\%$.

10. The table below gives June option prices for Pfizer (PFE) on 4 March 2005. On this date PFE's stock price was $26.85 and the interest rate was 2.60% annually. Compute the implied volatility for all traded puts and calls using the functions **Callvolatility** and **Putvolatility**. (If no price is given, the option was not traded.)

|   | A | B | C | D |
|---|---|---|---|---|
| 1 | PFIZER (PFE) OPTION PRICES, 4 MARCH 2005 | | | |
| 2 | Stock price | 26.85 | | |
| 3 | Current date | 4-Mar-05 | | |
| 4 | Interest rate | 2.60% | | |
| 5 | | | | |
| 6 | **Expiration** | **Exercise** | **Call** | **Put** |
| 7 | 17-Jun-05 | 22.50 | 4.70 | 0.25 |
| 8 | 17-Jun-05 | 25.00 | 2.55 | 0.65 |
| 9 | 17-Jun-05 | 27.50 | 1.00 | 1.60 |
| 10 | 17-Jun-05 | 30.00 | 0.30 | 3.50 |
| 11 | 17-Jun-05 | 32.50 | 0.05 | |
| 12 | 17-Jun-05 | 37.50 | | 10.70 |

11. As shown in Chapter 21 and in Exercise 7 above, the call option value is always greater than its immediate exercise value $(S - X)$ for $S > X$. However, the value of the European put is sometimes less that its intrinsic value $(X - S)$ for $S < X$. Use the put option pricing model to find such an example.

12. The probability that a European call option on the stock will be exercised is $N(d_2)$ (same expression as in Black–Scholes option pricing formula). What is the probability that a European call option on a stock with an exercise price of $40 and a maturity date in 6 months will be exercised? The current stock price is at $38, the interest rate is at 5%, and the stock return volatility is at 25%.

13. Consider a European put and a European call, both traded on a stock whose current price is $80 per share. The stock's return has volatility $\sigma = 40\%$, the time to maturity of both options is 9 months, and the interest rate $r = 6\%$. For what exercise price $X$ are the Black–Scholes put and call prices equal?

14. A put option with 1 year to maturity is written on a stock. The current underlying stock price is $20. The option's exercise price is $18, the interest rate is 3.74%, and the stock's volatility is 32.7%. The price of a call option written on the same stock with the same exercise price and time to maturity is $4.30. Use the Black–Scholes model to determine whether put–call parity holds.

15. The stock price of ABC Corp. is currently $S = \$50$. What is the price of a European call option that expires in 2 months and has an exercise price of $60? Assume the yearly interest rate is 5.5%, and the *monthly* volatility of the stock prices is 7.8%.

16. The price of a share of ABC Corp. stock is currently $S = \$55$. Assume that the yearly interest is 2%, and the stock's volatility is 0.4.

    a. Determine the prices of European call and put options with a exercise price of $55 and expiration in 3 months.

    b. Verify put–call parity.

17. A 1-month European call option is currently selling for $3.00. The exercise price of the option is $40, and the current stock price is $S = \$43$. The monthly interest rate is 0.5% and the monthly volatility of the stock return is at 7%. According to the Black–Scholes formula, is the market price correct?

18. Consider an option trading on a stock with a year to maturity. The implied volatility of the option at the opening is 25% and at closing it is 22%. Assume that the stock price hasn't changed. What do you conclude about the option price? Has it increased or decreased?

19. If the volatility of a stock is 30% and assuming 250 trading days a year, what is the standard deviation of the return in 1 trading day?

## APPENDIX: GETTING OPTION INFORMATION FROM YAHOO!

Yahoo! finance (http://finance.yahoo.com) has excellent facilities for getting option prices.

1. Go to Yahoo! finance and put in the stock symbol for which you want prices. In the example below we've put in AT&T, whose symbol is T. Click **Get Quotes**.

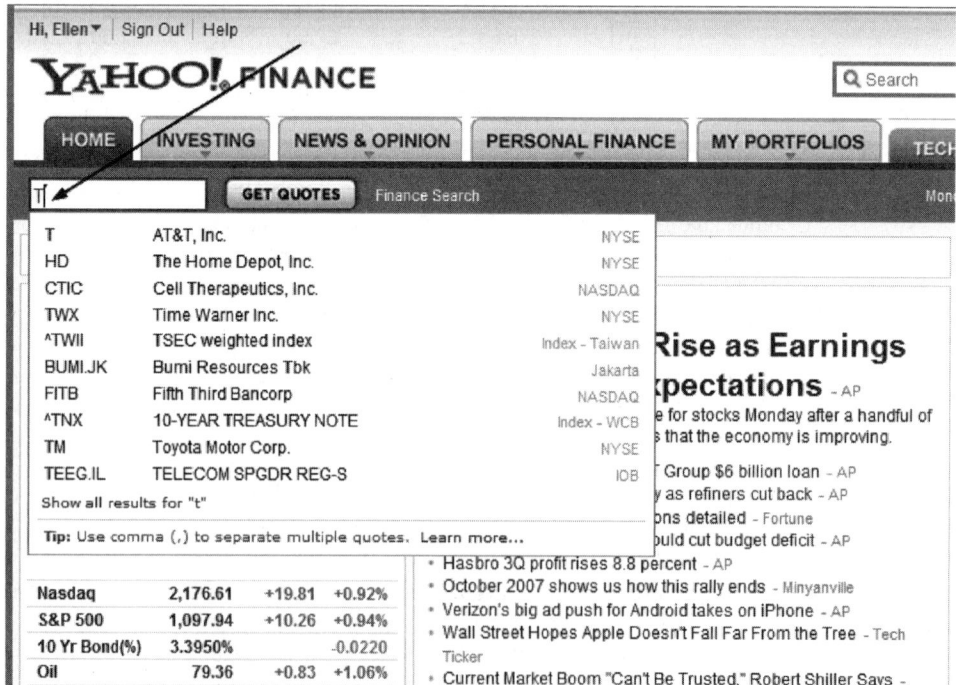

2. When you're on the AT&T page, pick **Options**.

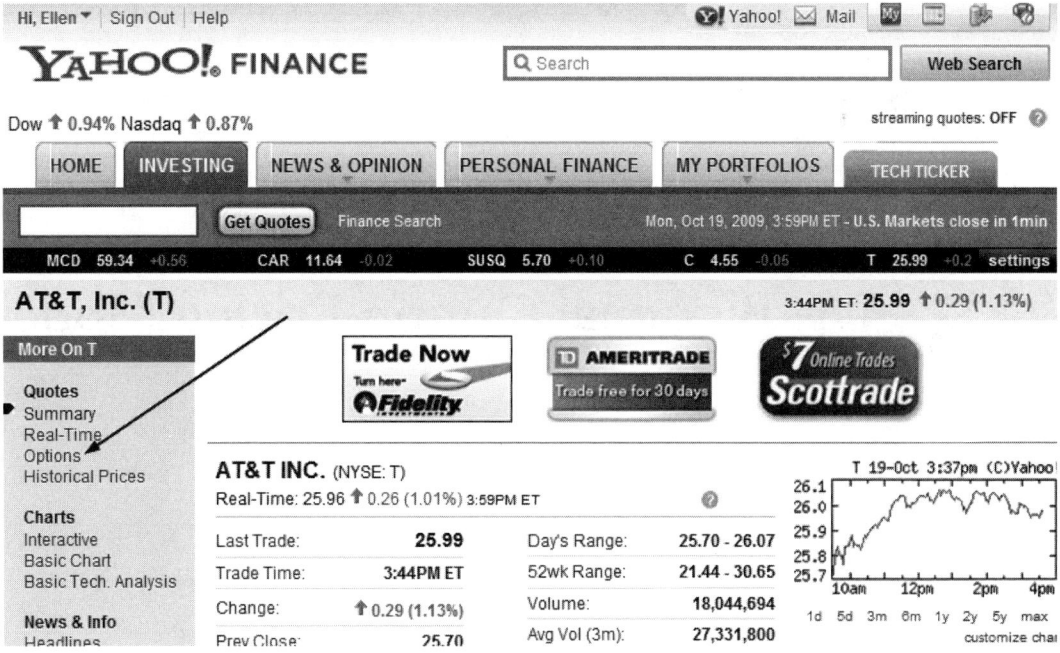

3. Yahoo! gives all the options by expiration date (note the exact expiration date, marked with the arrow).

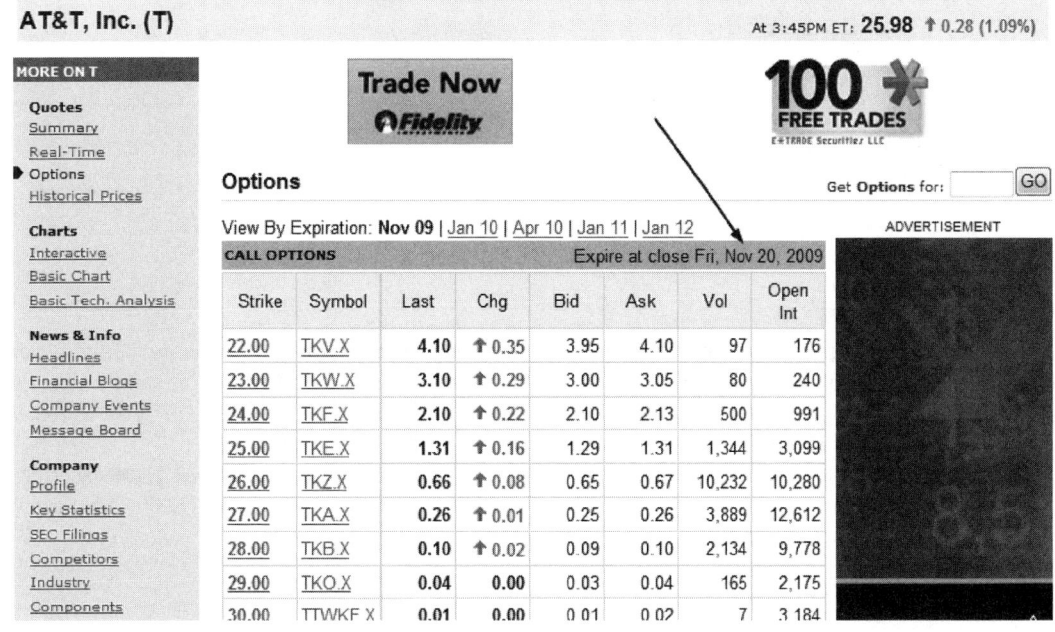

## CHAPTER CONTENTS

## Overview

In Chapter 22 we discussed the Black–Scholes formula, the most common method for pricing options. In this chapter we discuss the other major technique for determining option prices, the *binomial option-pricing model*. This model gives some insights into how to price an option, and it's also used widely (although not as widely as the Black–Scholes equation).

The basis of the binomial model is a very simple description of stock price uncertainty. Here's an example: Suppose the current stock price of MicroDigits (MD) is $100. What can you say about the MD stock price 1 year from now? The *binomial model* assumes that the price of the stock in 1 year will either go *up* by a certain percentage or *down* by a certain percentage. Here's an example.

| | A | B | C | D |
|---|---|---|---|---|
| 1 | BINOMIAL MODEL FOR MICRODIGITS (MD) STOCK PRICE | | | |
| 2 | Up | | 30% | |
| 3 | Down | | -10% | |
| 4 | | | | |
| 5 | MD stock price one year from now | | | |
| 6 | | | 130 | <-- =100*(1+B2) |
| 7 | | 100 | | |
| 8 | | | 90 | <-- =A7*(1+B3) |
| 9 | | | | |
| 10 | Date 0 today | | Date1 one year from now | |
| 11 | | | | |
| 12 | MD stock price *returns* | | | |
| 13 | | | 0.3 | <-- =C6/A7-1 |
| 14 | | | | |
| 15 | | | -0.1 | <-- =C8/A7-1 |
| 16 | Date 0 today | | Date1 one year from now | |

In the example above the MD stock price will either go up by 30% or down by 10% 1 year from today. This means that the *return* on the stock will be either 30 or −10% (cells C13 and C15).

It is difficult to believe that such a simple description of stock price uncertainty could be useful. However, if we extend the model to more periods, it turns out that the binomial model can describe a wide range of stock price behavior. In the example below we assume that the price of MD stock goes up in each of the next 2 years by 30% or goes down by 10%. This means that there are three possible outcomes for the stock price at Date 2: It can be either $169, $117, or $81.

| | A | B | C | D | E | F |
|---|---|---|---|---|---|---|
| 1 | TWO-PERIOD BINOMIAL MODEL FOR MICRODIGITS (MD) STOCK PRICE | | | | | |
| 2 | Up | | 30% | | | |
| 3 | Down | | -10% | | | |
| 4 | | | | | | |
| 5 | | | | | 169 | <-- =C6*(1+B2) |
| 6 | | | 130 | | | |
| 7 | | 100 | | | 117 | <-- =C6*(1+B3) |
| 8 | | | 90 | | | |
| 9 | | | | | 81 | <-- =C8*(1+B3) |
| 10 | Date 0 today | | Date 1 one year from now | | Date 2 two years from now | |

If we extend the model to more periods, we'll get a wide range of possible prices and returns. In the following spreadsheet we look at stock prices after 10 periods.

|    | A | B | C | D | E | F | G | H | I | J | K |
|----|---|---|---|---|---|---|---|---|---|---|---|
| 1 | **MULTIPERIOD BINOMIAL MODEL FOR MICRODIGITS (MD) STOCK PRICE** | | | | | | | | | | |
| 2 | Up | 30% | | | | | | | | | |
| 3 | Down | -10% | | | | | | | | | |
| 4 | | | | | | | | | | | |
| 5 | Date | | | | | | | | | | |
| 6 | 0 | 1 | 2 | 3 | 4 | 5 | 6 | 7 | 8 | 9 | 10 |
| 7 | | | | | | | | | | | 1378.58 |
| 8 | | | | | | | | | | 1060.45 | |
| 9 | | | | | | | | | 815.73 | | 954.40 |
| 10 | | | | | | | | 627.49 | | 734.16 | |
| 11 | | | | | | | 482.68 | | 564.74 | | 660.74 |
| 12 | | | | | | 371.29 | | 434.41 | | 508.26 | |
| 13 | | | | | 285.61 | | 334.16 | | 390.97 | | 457.44 |
| 14 | | | | 219.70 | | 257.05 | | 300.75 | | 351.87 | |
| 15 | | | 169.00 | | 197.73 | | 231.34 | | 270.67 | | 316.69 |
| 16 | | 130.00 | | 152.10 | | 177.96 | | 208.21 | | 243.61 | |
| 17 | 100.00 | | 117.00 | | 136.89 | | 160.16 | | 187.39 | | 219.24 |
| 18 | | 90.00 | | 105.30 | | 123.20 | | 144.15 | | 168.65 | |
| 19 | | | 81.00 | | 94.77 | | 110.88 | | 129.73 | | 151.78 |
| 20 | | | | 72.90 | | 85.29 | | 99.79 | | 116.76 | |
| 21 | | | | | 65.61 | | 76.76 | | 89.81 | | 105.08 |
| 22 | | | | | | 59.05 | | 69.09 | | 80.83 | |
| 23 | | | | | | | 53.14 | | 62.18 | | 72.75 |
| 24 | | | | | | | | 47.83 | | 55.96 | |
| 25 | | | | | | | | | 43.05 | | 50.36 |
| 26 | | | | | | | | | | 38.74 | |
| 27 | | | | | | | | | | | 34.87 |

If you plot the stock return and the probabilities of the returns after 10 years, you get a graph such as the one below.[1]

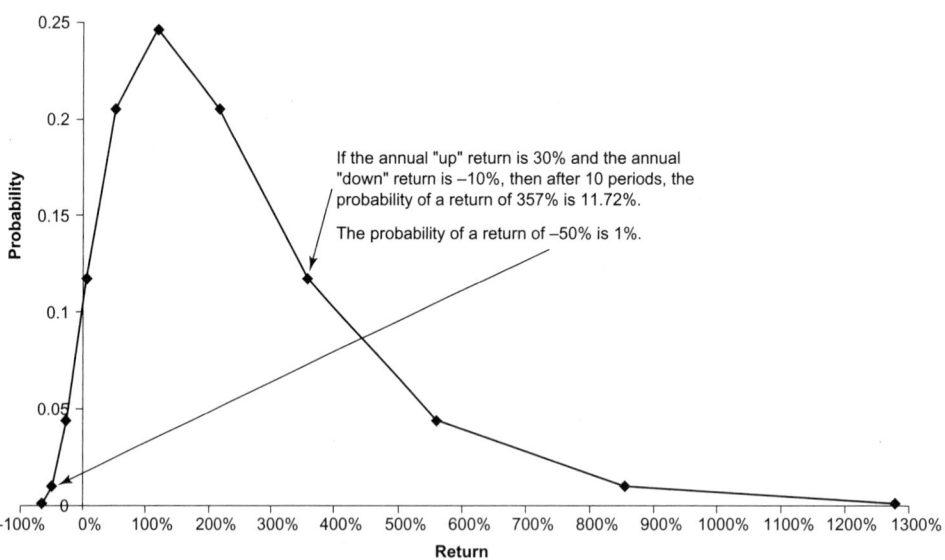

If the annual "up" return is 30% and the annual "down" return is –10%, then after 10 periods, the probability of a return of 357% is 11.72%.

The probability of a return of –50% is 1%.

---

[1] The mathematics required to produce such a graph are outside the scope of this book. For further details see my book *Financial Modeling*, 3rd edition (MIT Press, 2008).

## A Pedagogical Note

Most finance books first discuss the binomial option model and then discuss Black–Scholes. Their reasoning is that this order is logical because in principle the Black–Scholes pricing formula can be derived from the binomial model. In this book we've reversed the order, because we despair of telling you exactly how Black–Scholes is derived from the binomial. Instead, we've treated the two models as entirely different topics with different pedagogical goals: Black–Scholes is the most commonly used option-pricing model; as a finance person you should be familiar with this model and understand how to manipulate it (note that we haven't said that you need to understand it!). The binomial model is more educational but less useful (at least on the level of this book): It gives some insights into how options are priced through a process of replication. It can also be used to understand topics such as the pricing of American options and real options.

One of the uses we show for the binomial option pricing model is the use of the model to price American options (Section 23.4). These options cannot be priced using the Black–Scholes formula, which prices only European options. In an advanced options course you will learn to use the binomial option pricing model to price other, more complicated options.

### Finance Concepts in This Chapter

- Binomial model
- Replicating portfolio

### Excel Functions Used

- **Max**

# 23.1. The Binomial Pricing Model

To illustrate the use of the binomial model, we start with the following very simple example:

- You're trying to calculate the value of a call option on ABC stock. The option expires in 1 year and has an exercise price of $110.
- ABC stock sells today for $100. A wise person has informed you that in 1 year, the price of the stock will either be $130 or $90.[2] We will refer to these possibilities as the "up" and the "down" states.
- The 1-year interest rate is 6%. You can borrow or lend at this rate.

Here's a spreadsheet picture that incorporates all of this information (the spreadsheet also shows the payoffs on a put written on ABC stock—we'll get to that in a moment).

---

[2] This wise person forgot to tell you the probabilities attached to these two events, but it turns out not to matter. Surprised? You should be. But read on.

|   | A | B | C | D | E | F | G | H | I | J |
|---|---|---|---|---|---|---|---|---|---|---|
| 1 | PRICING OPTIONS ON ABC STOCK—THE BINOMIAL MODEL | | | | | | | | | |
| 2 | Up | 30% | | | | | | | | |
| 3 | Down | -10% | | | | | | | | |
| 4 | | | | | | | | | | |
| 5 | Initial stock price | 100 | | | | | | | | |
| 6 | Interest rate | 6% | | ABC's stock price in the "up" state | | | | | | |
| 7 | Exercise price | 110 | | | | | | | | |
| 8 | | | | | | | | | | |
| 9 | | ABC's stock price | | | | | Bond price | | | |
| 10 | | | | 130 | <-- =$B$11*(1+B2) | | | | 1.06 | <-- =$G$12*(1+$B$7) |
| 11 | | 100 | | | | | 1 | | | |
| 12 | | | | 90 | <-- =$B$11*(1+B3) | | | | 1.06 | <-- =$G$12*(1+$B$7) |
| 13 | | ABC's stock price in the "down" state | | | | | | | | |
| 14 | | | | | | | | | | |
| 15 | | | | | Call payoff in the "up" state | | | | | |
| 16 | | Call option payoffs | | | | | Put option payoffs | | | |
| 17 | | | | 20 | <-- =MAX(D10-$B$7,0) | | | | 0 | <-- =MAX($B$7-D10,0) |
| 18 | | ??? | | | | | ??? | | | |
| 19 | | | | 0 | <-- =MAX(D12-$B$7,0) | | | | 20 | <-- =MAX($B$7-D12,0) |
| 20 | | | | | Call payoff in the "down" state | | | | | |
| 21 | | | | | | | | | | |
| 22 | | | | | | | | | | |

We're going to price the call option by showing that there is a *combination of the bonds and stocks that gives exactly the same payoffs as the call option*. To show this, we use some basic high school algebra: Suppose we buy a portfolio of $A$ shares of the stock and buy $B$ bonds. Then the payoff of the portfolio in the up state is $130A + 1.06B$ and the payoff of the portfolio in the down state is $90A + 1.06B$. Now let's find $A$ and $B$ so that these two payoffs equal the call option payoffs:

$$130A + 1.06B = 20$$
$$90A + 1.06B = 0 \quad .$$

This system of equations solves to give

$$130A + 1.06B = 20$$
$$90A + 1.06B = 0$$
$$A = \frac{20 - 0}{130 - 90} = 0.5, \quad B = \frac{0 - 90A}{1.06} = \frac{-90 * 0.5}{1.06} = -42.4528$$

So now we know that buying half a share of ABC (cost $50) and borrowing $42.4528 will give you payoffs in 1 year that are exactly the same as the payoffs of the call option. The expenditure on this portfolio of {buy one-half share, borrow $42.4528} should be the same as the expenditure on the call option. Thus the call option's price should be $7.5472:

$$\text{call option price} = \underbrace{0.5 * 100}_{\substack{\text{the cost of the} \\ \text{stock in the} \\ \text{"replicating} \\ \text{portfolio"}}} - \underbrace{42.4528}_{\substack{\text{the financing} \\ \text{provided by} \\ \text{borrowing in the} \\ \text{"replicating} \\ \text{portfolio"}}} = \underbrace{7.5472}_{\substack{\text{the market price} \\ \text{of the call} \\ \text{option}}}$$

## THE REPLICATING PORTFOLIO

The portfolio we just derived—$A = 0.5$ shares and $B = -\$42.4528$ borrowed—gives the same payoffs as the call option. For this reason it is often called the *replicating portfolio*.

## What's Going On?—Market Efficiency at Work

Option pricing in the binomial model is a wonderful example of the first two principles of efficient markets discussed in Chapter 17. The first principle ("Competitive markets have a single price for a single good") implies that the combination of the stock + borrowing (which in terms of payoffs has exactly the payoffs of the call option) should be priced like the call option. The second principle, price additivity ("The price of a bundle of securities should be the sum of the prices of each of the securities") is also illustrated here—the price of the call option is the cost of the stock ($45) minus the borrowing to finance this cost.

For option-pricing theorists this method of pricing options is an example of *arbitrage*—the principle that if you can construct an asset's payoffs in two ways, each of these ways should have the same market value (which is, of course, Chapter 17's first principle of efficiency).

It can all be summed up as follows.

| | A | B | C | D | E | F | G | H | I | J |
|---|---|---|---|---|---|---|---|---|---|---|
| 1 | | | PRICING OPTIONS ON ABC STOCK—THE BINOMIAL MODEL | | | | | | | |
| 2 | Up | 30% | | | | | | | | |
| 3 | Down | -10% | | | | | | | | |
| 4 | | | | | | | | | | |
| 5 | Initial stock price | 100 | | | | | | | | |
| 6 | Interest rate | 6% | | ABC's stock price | | | | | | |
| 7 | Exercise price | 110 | | in the "up" state | | | | | | |
| 8 | | | | | | | | | | |
| 9 | | ABC's stock price | | | | | Bond price | | | |
| 10 | | | | 130 | <-- =$B$11*(1+B2) | | | | 1.06 | <-- =$G$12*(1+$B$7) |
| 11 | | 100 | | | | | 1 | | | |
| 12 | | | | 90 | <-- =$B$11*(1+B3) | | | | 1.06 | <-- =$G$12*(1+$B$7) |
| 13 | | ABC's stock price | | | | | | | | |
| 14 | | in the "down" state | | | Call payoff in | | | | | |
| 15 | | | | | the "up" state | | | | | |
| 16 | | Call option payoffs | | | | | Put option payoffs | | | |
| 17 | | | | 20 | <-- =MAX(D10-$B$7,0) | | | | 0 | <-- =MAX($B$7-D10,0) |
| 18 | | ??? | | | | | ??? | | | |
| 19 | | | | 0 | <-- =MAX(D12-$B$7,0) | | | | 20 | <-- =MAX($B$7-D12,0) |
| 20 | | | | | Call payoff in the | | | | | |
| 21 | | | | | "down" state | | | | | |
| 22 | | | | | | | | | | |
| 23 | The call replicating portfolio | | | | | | | | | |
| 24 | Stock, A | 0.5000 | <-- =(D17-D19)/(D10-D12) | | | | | | | |
| 25 | Bonds, B | -42.4528 | <-- =(D19-D12*B24)/(1+B6) | | | | | | | |
| 26 | Call price | 7.5472 | <-- =B24*B5+B25 | | | | | | | |

## Using the Binomial Model to Price a Put on ABC Stock

We now use the binomial model to price a put on ABC with an exercise price of $110. The put payoffs are shown below.

| | G | H | I | J |
|---|---|---|---|---|
| 14 | | | | Put payoff in the "up" state |
| 15 | | | | |
| 16 | Put option payoffs | | | |
| 17 | | | 0 | <-- =MAX($B$7-D10,0) |
| 18 | | ??? | | |
| 19 | | | 20 | <-- =MAX($B$7-D12,0) |
| 20 | | | | Put payoff in the "down" state |
| 21 | | | | |
| 22 | | | | |

The replicating portfolio is:

$$130A + 1.06B = 0$$
$$90A + 1.06B = 20 \ .$$

These equations solve to give

$$A = \frac{-20}{130-90} = -0.5, \quad B = \frac{-130A}{1.06} = \frac{-130*(-0.5)}{1.06} = 61.3208$$

The solution to the replicating portfolio indicates that short-selling $A = -0.5$ shares and investing in $B = \$61.3208$ bonds gives the same payoffs as the put option. This means that the price of the put is \$11.3208:

$$put \ option \ price = \underset{\substack{\uparrow \\ \text{cash provided by} \\ \text{the short sale of} \\ \text{stock in the} \\ \text{"replicating} \\ \text{portfolio"}}}{-0.5*100} + \underset{\substack{\uparrow \\ \text{cash used to buy} \\ \text{bonds in the} \\ \text{"replicating} \\ \text{portfolio"}}}{61.3208} = \underset{\substack{\uparrow \\ \text{the market price} \\ \text{of the put} \\ \text{option}}}{11.3208}$$

## Put–Call Parity—Another Way of Pricing the Put

In Chapter 21 we learned the put–call parity principle:

$$Put \ price + Stock \ price = Call \ price + PV\left(Exercise \ price\right)$$

Applying this principle in our problem, we get

$$Put \ price = Call \ price + PV\left(Exercise \ price\right) - Stock \ price$$
$$= 7.5472 + \frac{110}{1.06} - 100 = 11.3208$$

Here's the whole spreadsheet, one more time.

|    | A | B | C | D | E | F | G | H | I | J |
|----|---|---|---|---|---|---|---|---|---|---|
| 1 | | | | PRICING OPTIONS ON ABC STOCK—THE BINOMIAL MODEL | | | | | | |
| 2 | Up | 30% | | | | | | | | |
| 3 | Down | -10% | | | | | | | | |
| 4 | | | | | | | | | | |
| 5 | Initial stock price | 100 | | | ABC's stock price | | | | | |
| 6 | Interest rate | 6% | | | in the "up" state | | | | | |
| 7 | Exercise price | 110 | | | | | | | | |
| 8 | | | | | | | | | | |
| 9 | | ABC's stock price | | | | | Bond price | | | |
| 10 | | | | 130 | <-- =$B$11*(1+B2) | | | | 1.06 | <-- =$G$12*(1+$B$7) |
| 11 | | 100 | | | | | 1 | | | |
| 12 | | | | 90 | <-- =$B$11*(1+B3) | | | | 1.06 | <-- =$G$12*(1+$B$7) |
| 13 | | | | | | | | | | |
| 14 | | ABC's stock price | | | | | | | Put payoff in the | |
| 15 | | in the "down" state | | | | | | | "up" state | |
| 16 | | Call option payoffs | | | | | Put option payoffs | | | |
| 17 | | | | 20 | <-- =MAX(D10-$B$7,0) | | | | 0 | <-- =MAX($B$7-D10,0) |
| 18 | | ??? | | | | | ??? | | | |
| 19 | | | | 0 | <-- =MAX(D12-$B$7,0) | | | | 20 | <-- =MAX($B$7-D12,0) |
| 20 | | | | | | | | | Put payoff in the | |
| 21 | | | | | | | | | "down" state | |
| 22 | | | | | | | | | | |
| 23 | The call replicating portfolio | | | | | | | | | |
| 24 | Stock, A | 0.5000 | <-- =(D17-D19)/(D10-D12) | | | | | | | |
| 25 | Bonds, B | -42.4528 | <-- =(D19-D12*B24)/(1+B6) | | | | | | | |
| 26 | Call price | 7.5472 | <-- =B24*B5+B25 | | | | | | | |
| 27 | | | | | | | | | | |
| 28 | The put replicating portfolio | | | | | | | | | |
| 29 | Stock, A | -0.5000 | <-- =(I17-I19)/(D10-D12) | | | | | | | |
| 30 | Bonds, B | 61.3208 | <-- =(I17-D10*B29)/(1+B6) | | | | | | | |
| 31 | Call price | 11.3208 | <-- =B29*B11+B30 | | | | | | | |
| 32 | | | | | | | | | | |
| 33 | Pricing the put by put-call parity | | | | | | | | | |
| 34 | Call price | 7.5472 | <-- =B26 | | | | | | | |
| 35 | PV(exercise) | 103.7736 | <-- =B7/(1+B6) | | | | | | | |
| 36 | Stock price | 100 | <-- =B5 | | | | | | | |
| 37 | Put price | 11.3208 | <-- =B34+B35-B36 | | | | | | | |

## 23.2. What Can You Learn from the Binomial Model?

The binomial option-pricing model is very instructive. It is an easy way to price options, and it can also tell you something about a more complicated option-pricing model. Here are a few lessons you can learn from the binomial model.

- A call "looks like" a portfolio composed of the purchase of a stock and the short sale of a bond. The call's replicating portfolio is

$$A * S_{Up} + B * (1+r) = Call\ payoff_{Up}$$
$$A * S_{Down} + B * (1+r) = Call\ payoff_{Down}$$

where:

$S_{Up}$ and $S_{Down}$ are the stock prices in the "up" and "down" states

$Call\ payoff_{Up}$ and $Call\ payoff_{Down}$ are the call payoffs

In terms of the call's replicating portfolio, it turns out that $A$ (the stock) is always positive and $B$ (the bond) is always negative. This indicates the purchase of a stock financed by borrowing. In a sense the Black–Scholes formula has the same property:

$$BS \ call \ price = \underbrace{S * N(d_1)}_{\substack{\uparrow \\ \text{Purchase of} \\ \text{stock} \\ \text{(positive number)}}} - \underbrace{Xe^{-rT} N(d_2)}_{\substack{\uparrow \\ \text{Borrowing at} \\ \text{the risk free rate} \\ \text{(negative number)}}}$$

- A put looks like a portfolio composed of the short sale of a stock and the purchase of a bond. The put's replicating portfolio is

$$A * S_{Up} + B * (1 + r) = Put \ payoff_{Up}$$
$$A * S_{Down} + B * (1 + r) = Put \ payoff_{Down}$$
where:
$S_{Up}$ and $S_{Down}$ are the stock prices in the "up" and "down" states
$Put \ payoff_{Up}$ and $Put \ payoff_{Down}$ are the put payoffs

In terms of the put's replicating portfolio, it turns out that $A$ (the stock) is always negative and $B$ (the bond) is always positive. This indicates the purchase of bonds financed by a short sale of the stock. In a sense, the Black–Scholes formula has the same property:

$$BS \ put \ price = \underbrace{-S * N(-d_1)}_{\substack{\uparrow \\ \text{Short sale of} \\ \text{stock} \\ \text{(negative number)}}} + \underbrace{Xe^{-rT} N(-d_2)}_{\substack{\uparrow \\ \text{Investing at} \\ \text{the risk free rate} \\ \text{(positive number)}}}$$

- The probabilities of the up and the down states don't appear explicitly in the calculation of the option price. To see what this means, look at the way we solved for the call option price at the beginning of this chapter:

$$130A + 1.06B = 20$$
$$90A + 1.06B = 0$$

These equations solve to give:
$$A = \frac{20 - 0}{130 - 90} = 0.5, \quad B = \frac{0 - 90A}{1.06} = \frac{-90 * 0.5}{1.06} = -42.4528$$

The resulting call option price:

$$call \ option \ price = \underbrace{0.5 * \$100}_{\substack{\uparrow \\ \text{Cost of the} \\ \text{stock in the} \\ \text{"replicating} \\ \text{portfolio"}}} - \underbrace{\$42.4528}_{\substack{\uparrow \\ \text{Financing} \\ \text{provided by} \\ \text{borrowing in the} \\ \text{"replicating} \\ \text{portfolio"}}} = \underbrace{7.5472}_{\substack{\uparrow \\ \text{Market price} \\ \text{of the call} \\ \text{option}}}$$

This calculation of the call option price when the option exercise price is \$110 relies on three facts: (i) the current stock price is \$100, (ii) the stock price next period is either 130 or 90, and

(iii) the interest rate is 6%. Nowhere in this calculation have we made any reference to the *probabilities* that the stock price will be $130 or $90.[3]

- The binomial model is *extendible*—it can be used to price many options in a multiperiod setting. In the next section we show a multiperiod binomial model.

## 23.3. Multiperiod Binomial Model

The binomial model can be extended to multiple periods. Here's an example that extends the previous example.

| | A | B | C | D | E | F | G | H | I | J | K | L |
|---|---|---|---|---|---|---|---|---|---|---|---|---|
| 1 | | | | | THREE-DATE BINOMIAL OPTION PRICING | | | | | | | |
| 2 | Up | 30% | | | | | | | | | | |
| 3 | Down | -10% | | | | | | | | | | |
| 4 | | | | | | | | | | | | |
| 5 | Initial stock price | 100 | | | | | | | | | | |
| 6 | Interest rate | 6% | | | | | | | | | | |
| 7 | Exercise price | 110 | | | | | | | | | | |
| 8 | | | | | | | | | | | | |
| 9 | Stock price | | | | | | Bond price | | | | | |
| 10 | | | | | 169.00 | | | | | | 1.1236 | |
| 11 | | | 130 | | | | | | 1.06 | | | |
| 12 | | 100 | | | 117.00 | | 1 | | | | 1.1236 | |
| 13 | | | 90 | | | | | | 1.06 | | | |
| 14 | | | | | 81.00 | | | | | | 1.1236 | |
| 15 | Date 0 | | Date 1 | | Date 2 | | Date 0 | | Date 1 | | Date 2 | |
| 16 | | | | | | | | | | | | |
| 17 | | | | | | | | | | | | |
| 18 | Call option price | | | | | | Put option price | | | | | |
| 19 | | | | | 59.00 | <-- =MAX(E10-$B$7,0) | | | | | 0.00 | <-- =MAX($B$7-E10,0) |
| 20 | | | ???-1 | | | | | | ???-1 | | | |
| 21 | | ???-0 | | | 7.00 | <-- =MAX(E12-$B$7,0) | ???-0 | | | | 0.00 | <-- =MAX($B$7-E12,0) |
| 22 | | | ???-2 | | | | | | ???-2 | | | |
| 23 | | | | | 0.00 | <-- =MAX(E14-$B$7,0) | | | | | 29.00 | <-- =MAX($B$7-E14,0) |
| 24 | Date 0 | | Date 1 | | Date 2 | | Date 0 | | Date 1 | | Date 2 | |

In this example, the stock price goes up by 30% or down by 10% in each period. Starting with a stock price of $100 at Date 0, the stock price at Date 1 will be either $130 or $90, and the stock price at Date 2 will be $169, $117, or $81.

- $169: This happens if it goes up twice—that is, $169 = 100*(1.30)(1.30)$.
- $117: This happens if the stock price goes up once and down once—that is, $117 = 100*(1.30)*(0.90)$. Note that it doesn't matter if the stock price goes up first and then down or the reverse.
- $81: This happens if the stock price goes down twice—that is, $81 = 100*(0.90)(0.90)$.

In each period the risk-free interest rate is 6%, so that $1 invested in the bond will grow to $1.1236 at date 2.

---

[3] Of course you could quibble a bit and insist that the stock price today must incorporate these probabilities in some sense, and you'd be right. But even here you have to be careful—for example, it would be wrong to say that the stock price is the discounted expected future payoff of the stock. To explain this all would take us too far afield—suffice it to say that if investors are risk averse, they'll price the stock *below* its expected future discounted payoff. The amount of this discount depends on the risk aversion.

## The Call Option's Terminal Payoffs

At the end of the second period, the option's payoffs are given by

$$Max(stock\ price\ at\ date\ 2-110,0)=\begin{cases} Max(169-110,0)=59 \\ Max(117-110,0)=7 \\ Max(81-110,0)=0 \end{cases}$$

We now have to value the option. We proceed by doing three valuations—these are labeled in the diagram as "???-1," "???-2," and "???-0." The put option has the same labels—we'll figure out in a while how to price these.

## Determining "???-1" for the Call

We proceed as we did for the one-period binomial option-pricing model. Setting up the one-period stock and bond prices and option payoffs, we get the following.

| | A | B | C | D | E | F | G | H |
|---|---|---|---|---|---|---|---|---|
| 26 | Finding ???-1 for the call | | | | | | | |
| 27 | | | | | | | | |
| 28 | | Stock price | | | | Bond price | | |
| 29 | | | | 169.00 | | | | 1.1236 |
| 30 | | 130 | | | | 1.06 | | |
| 31 | | | | 117.00 | | | | 1.1236 |
| 32 | | | | | | | | |
| 33 | | Call option price | | | | | | |
| 34 | | | | 59.00 | | | | |
| 35 | | ???-1 | | | | | | |
| 36 | | | | 7.00 | | | | |
| 37 | | | | | | | | |
| 38 | The call replicating portfolio | | | | | | | |
| 39 | Stock, A | 1.0000 | <-- =(D34-D36)/(D29-D31) | | | | | |
| 40 | Bonds, B | -97.8996 | <-- =(D36-B39*D31)/H29 | | | | | |
| 41 | Call price | 26.2264 | <-- =B39*B30+B40*F30 | | | | | |

Setting up the equations (we use $A$ to denote the number of shares and $B$ to denote the bonds in the replicating portfolio),

$$169A+1.1236B=59$$
$$117A+1.1236B=7$$

Solution:

$$A=\frac{59-7}{169-117}=1$$
$$B=\frac{7-117*A}{1.1236}=-97.8996$$

$Call\ option\ price=130*A+1.06*B=26.2264$

These calculations are done in cells B39:B41.

## Determining "???-2" for the Call

Again we proceed as we did for the one-period binomial option-pricing model. Setting up the one-period stock and bond prices and option payoffs, we get the following.

| | A | B | C | D | E | F | G | H |
|---|---|---|---|---|---|---|---|---|
| 44 | Finding ???-2 for the call | | | | | | | |
| 45 | | | | | | | | |
| 46 | | Stock price | | | | Bond price | | |
| 47 | | | | 117.00 | | | | 1.1236 |
| 48 | | 90 | | | | 1.06 | | |
| 49 | | | | 81.00 | | | | 1.1236 |
| 50 | | | | | | | | |
| 51 | | Call option price | | | | | | |
| 52 | | | | 7.00 | | | | |
| 53 | | ???-2 | | | | | | |
| 54 | | | | 0.00 | | | | |
| 55 | | | | | | | | |
| 56 | The call replicating portfolio | | | | | | | |
| 57 | Stock, A | 0.1944 | <-- =(D52-D54)/(D47-D49) | | | | | |
| 58 | Bonds, B | -14.0174 | <-- =(D54-B57*D49)/H47 | | | | | |
| 59 | Call price | 2.6415 | <-- =B57*B48+B58*F48 | | | | | |

## Determining "???-0" for the Call

Once more, we set up a simple binomial model, but this time we use the two values derived above—the prices of the call option at date 1.

| | A | B | C | D | E | F | G | H |
|---|---|---|---|---|---|---|---|---|
| 62 | Finding ???-0 for the call | | | | | | | |
| 63 | | | | | | | | |
| 64 | | Stock price | | | | Bond price | | |
| 65 | | | | 130.00 | | | | 1.0600 |
| 66 | | 100 | | | | 1 | | |
| 67 | | | | 90.00 | | | | 1.0600 |
| 68 | | | | | | | | |
| 69 | | Call option price | | | | | | |
| 70 | | | | 26.2264 | | | | |
| 71 | | ???-0 | | | | | | |
| 72 | | | | 2.6415 | | | | |
| 73 | | | | | | | | |
| 74 | The call replicating portfolio | | | | | | | |
| 75 | Stock, A | 0.5896 | <-- =(D70-D72)/(D65-D67) | | | | | |
| 76 | Bonds, B | -47.5703 | <-- =(D72-B75*D67)/H65 | | | | | |
| 77 | Call price | 11.3919 | <-- =B75*B66+B76*F66 | | | | | |

The result—we've calculated the option price today as $11.3919.

## Pricing the Put—The Long Way

As you can see from the diagram, the put has date 2 payoffs as follows.

| | G | H | I | J | K | L |
|---|---|---|---|---|---|---|
| 18 | Put option price | | | | | |
| 19 | | | | | 0.00 | <-- =MAX($B$7-E10,0) |
| 20 | | | ???-1 | | | |
| 21 | ???-0 | | | | 0.00 | <-- =MAX($B$7-E12,0) |
| 22 | | | ???-2 | | | |
| 23 | | | | | 29.00 | <-- =MAX($B$7-E14,0) |
| 24 | Date 0 | | Date 1 | | Date 2 | |

We can use the same logic (and even the same equations) to price the put. The results, shown below with no explanations, show that the put price at date 0 is 9.2916.

| | A | B | C | D | E | F | G | H |
|---|---|---|---|---|---|---|---|---|
| 80 | **PRICING THE PUT** | | | | | | | |
| 81 | **Finding ???-1 for the put** | | | | | | | |
| 82 | | | | | | | | |
| 83 | | **Stock price** | | | | **Bond price** | | |
| 84 | | | | 169.00 | | | | 1.1236 |
| 85 | | 130 | | | | 1.06 | | |
| 86 | | | | 117.00 | | | | 1.1236 |
| 87 | | | | | | | | |
| 88 | | **Put option price** | | | | | | |
| 89 | | | | 0.00 | | | | |
| 90 | | ???-1 | | | | There's actually no need to do any calculations for ???-1: The price ???-1 is the value of a security which has <u>zero payoffs</u> one period hence. By any logic this price should be zero. | | |
| 91 | | | | 0.00 | | | | |
| 92 | | | | | | | | |
| 93 | **The put replicating portfolio** | | | | | | | |
| 94 | Stock, A | 0.0000 | <-- =(D89-D91)/(D84-D86) | | | | | |
| 95 | Bonds, B | 0.0000 | <-- =(D91-B94*D86)/H84 | | | | | |
| 96 | Put price | 0.0000 | <-- =B94*B85+B95*F85 | | | | | |
| 97 | | | | | | | | |
| 98 | | | | | | | | |
| 99 | **Finding ???-2 for the put** | | | | | | | |
| 100 | | | | | | | | |
| 101 | | **Stock price** | | | | **Bond price** | | |
| 102 | | | | 117.00 | | | | 1.1236 |
| 103 | | 90 | | | | 1.06 | | |
| 104 | | | | 81.00 | | | | 1.1236 |
| 105 | | | | | | | | |
| 106 | | **Put option price** | | | | | | |
| 107 | | | | 0.00 | | | | |
| 108 | | ???-2 | | | | | | |
| 109 | | | | 29.00 | | | | |
| 110 | | | | | | | | |
| 111 | **The put replicating portfolio** | | | | | | | |
| 112 | Stock, A | -0.8056 | <-- =(D107-D109)/(D102-D104) | | | | | |
| 113 | Bonds, B | 83.8822 | <-- =(D109-B112*D104)/H102 | | | | | |
| 114 | Put price | 16.4151 | <-- =B112*B103+B113*F103 | | | | | |
| 115 | | | | | | | | |
| 116 | | | | | | | | |
| 117 | **Finding ???-0 for the put** | | | | | | | |
| 118 | | | | | | | | |
| 119 | | **Stock price** | | | | **Bond price** | | |
| 120 | | | | 130.00 | | | | 1.0600 |
| 121 | | 100 | | | | 1 | | |
| 122 | | | | 90.00 | | | | 1.0600 |
| 123 | | | | | | | | |
| 124 | | **Put option price** | | | | | | |
| 125 | | | | 0.0000 | | | | |
| 126 | | ???-0 | | | | | | |
| 127 | | | | 16.4151 | | | | |
| 128 | | | | | | | | |
| 129 | **The put replicating portfolio** | | | | | | | |
| 130 | Stock, A | -0.4104 | <-- =(D125-D127)/(D120-D122) | | | | | |
| 131 | Bonds, B | 50.3293 | <-- =(D127-B130*D122)/H120 | | | | | |
| 132 | Put price | 9.2916 | <-- =B130*B121+B131*F121 | | | | | |

### Pricing the Put Using Put–Call Parity

We can also use put–call parity to price the put. As discussed in Section 21.3, put–call parity says:

$$Put\ price + Stock\ price = Call\ price + PV(Exercise\ price)$$

Applying this principle to the two-date option, we get

$$Put\ price = Call\ price + PV(Exercise\ price) - Stock\ price$$
$$= 11.3919 + \frac{110}{(1.06)^2} - 100 = 9.2916$$

| | A | B | C | D | E | F |
|---|---|---|---|---|---|---|
| 135 | **Pricing the put with put-call parity** | | | | | |
| 136 | Initial stock price | 100 | | | | |
| 137 | Interest rate | 6% | | | | |
| 138 | Exercise price | 110 | | | | |
| 139 | Call price | 11.3919 | | | | |
| 140 | Put price | 9.2916 | <-- =B139+B138/(1+B137)^2-B136 | | | |

# 23.4. Advanced Topic: Using the Binomial Model to Price an American Put

The binomial model is cute and easy to understand. But why do we need it? The answer is complex and mostly beyond the scope of this book:

- Whereas the Black–Scholes formula prices only European options, the binomial model can be used to price American options. This use of the binomial model is illustrated in the next subsection.

- Properly implemented, the binomial model can help us prove the Black–Scholes formula. This use of the binomial model is too advanced for this book.

- The binomial model can be used to price more complex options than those priced with Black–Scholes, which prices only European options. For example, we can use the binomial model to price options where the exercise price changes over time or where the interest rate varies.

- We can also use the binomial model to price options where the "up" and the "down" movements of the stock price vary over time. Many finance people believe, for example, that the volatility of the stock price return varies with the price itself—that the percentage up and the down movements for a stock are larger when the stock price is small. This can be handled by the binomial model, but not by Black–Scholes.

## "WEIRD" OPTIONS AND THE BINOMIAL MODEL

The binomial model is especially useful in determining the price of weird options. Here are two examples of such options.

An *Asian option* is an option whose payoff is determined by the average price of the stock over a certain period before the option's maturity. One specification of an Asian call option might be as follows:

- On 29 January 2005 you buy an Asian call option on IBM with a maturity of 1 year. The option's payoff on 29 January 2006 is the difference between the average daily closing IBM stock price in the 30 days preceding the option's maturity and the option's exercise price $X = \$120$. This option cannot be priced using the Black–Scholes model, but it can be priced using the binomial model.

A *barrier option* is an option whose payoff depends on whether the stock price reaches a certain point during the life of the option. Here's an example:

- On 29 January 2005 you buy a 1-year *knock-in barrier* option on IBM, which is currently selling at $93. The option specifies that you have the right to buy a share of IBM on 29 January 2006 for an exercise price of $100, provided that at some point during the year IBM's stock price exceeds $130 (this is the "knock-in barrier"). If the price of IBM during the coming year does not exceed $130, your option is worthless. Barrier options cannot be priced using the Black–Scholes model, but they can be priced using the binomial model.

There are many more of these weird options. A good place to start for some background is http://www.risk-glossary.com.

## Using the Binomial Model to Price American Options

To illustrate one more sophisticated use of the binomial model, we'll show you how it can be used to price an American put option. Recall that American options can be exercised early. We go back to our two-date example and focus on the put price (highlighted).

| | A | B | C | D | E | F | G | H | I | J | K | L |
|---|---|---|---|---|---|---|---|---|---|---|---|---|
| 1 | | THREE-DATE BINOMIAL OPTION PRICING—American options | | | | | | | | | | |
| 2 | Up | 30% | | | | | | | | | | |
| 3 | Down | -10% | | | | | | | | | | |
| 4 | | | | | | | | | | | | |
| 5 | Initial stock price | 100 | | | | | | | | | | |
| 6 | Interest rate | 6% | | | | | | | | | | |
| 7 | Exercise price | 110 | | | | | | | | | | |
| 8 | | | | | | | | | | | | |
| 9 | Stock price | | | | | | Bond price | | | | | |
| 10 | | | | | 169.00 | | | | | | 1.1236 | |
| 11 | | | 130 | | | | | | 1.06 | | | |
| 12 | | 100 | | | 117.00 | | 1 | | | | 1.1236 | |
| 13 | | | 90 | | | | | | 1.06 | | | |
| 14 | | | | | 81.00 | | | | | | 1.1236 | |
| 15 | | | | | | | | | | | | |
| 16 | Call option price | | | | | | Put option price | | | | | |
| 17 | | | | | 59.00 | <-- =MAX(E10-$B$7,0) | | | | | 0.00 | <-- =MAX($B$7-E10,0) |
| 18 | | | ???-1 | | | | | | ???-1 | | | |
| 19 | | ???-0 | | | 7.00 | <-- =MAX(E12-$B$7,0) | ???-0 | | | | 0.00 | <-- =MAX($B$7-E12,0) |
| 20 | | | ???-2 | | | | | | ???-2 | | | |
| 21 | | | | | 0.00 | <-- =MAX(E14-$B$7,0) | | | | | 29.00 | <-- =MAX($B$7-E14,0) |

We'll price the put just as we did the call in the previous section. However, this time we assume that the put is an *American put*—meaning that it can be exercised early.[4]

We start by pricing the put at the up-state of date 1 (this is marked "???-1" in the spreadsheet). This is actually fairly simple: At ???-1 the put owner has future payoffs of zero, no matter what happens. This means that the put should be worth zero, and that's exactly what the spreadsheet tells us.

| | A | B | C | D | E | F | G | H |
|---|---|---|---|---|---|---|---|---|
| 24 | Finding ???-1 for the put | | | | | | | |
| 25 | | | | | | | | |
| 26 | | Stock price | | | | Bond price | | |
| 27 | | | | 169.00 | | | | 1.1236 |
| 28 | | 130 | | | | 1.06 | | |
| 29 | | | | 117.00 | | | | 1.1236 |
| 30 | | | | | | | | |
| 31 | | Put option price | | | | | | |
| 32 | | | | 0.00 | | There's actually no need to do any calculations for ???-1: The price ???-1 is the value of a security which has zero payoffs one period hence. By any logic this price should be zero. | | |
| 33 | | ???-1 | | | | | | |
| 34 | | | | 0.00 | | | | |
| 35 | | | | | | | | |
| 36 | The put replicating portfolio | | | | | | | |
| 37 | Stock, A | 0.0000 | <-- =(D32-D34)/(D27-D29) | | | | | |
| 38 | Bonds, B | 0.0000 | <-- =(D34-B37*D29)/H27 | | | | | |
| 39 | Put price ???-1 | 0.0000 | <-- =B37*B28+B38*F28 | | | | | |

At ???-2 the situation is more complicated. The put has a future payoff that is positive. We can use the binomial model to solve for the put price.

| | A | B | C | D | E | F | G | H |
|---|---|---|---|---|---|---|---|---|
| 42 | Finding ???-2 for the put | | | | | | | |
| 43 | | | | | | | | |
| 44 | | Stock price | | | | Bond price | | |
| 45 | | | | 117.00 | | | | 1.1236 |
| 46 | | 90 | | | | 1.06 | | |
| 47 | | | | 81.00 | | | | 1.1236 |
| 48 | | | | | | | | |
| 49 | | Put option price | | | | | | |
| 50 | | | | 0.00 | | | | |
| 51 | | ???-2 | | | | | | |
| 52 | | | | 29.00 | | | | |
| 53 | | | | | | | | |
| 54 | The put replicating portfolio | | | | | | | |
| 55 | Stock, A | -0.8056 | <-- =(D50-D52)/(D45-D47) | | | | | |
| 56 | Bonds, B | 83.8822 | <-- =(D52-B55*D47)/H45 | | | | | |
| 57 | European put price ???-2 | 16.4151 | <-- =B55*B46+B56*F46 | | | | | |
| 58 | American put price ???-2 | 20.0000 | <-- =MAX(B7-B46,B55*B46+B56*F46) | | | | | |

But now the early exercise feature of the put comes in (remember—it's an American put). The put value of $16.4151 (cell B57 above) is the value of a put that has payoffs only next period. Instead of waiting until next period, we can exercise the put today: The stock price is $90 and the put exercise is $110, which means we can collect $20 immediately if we early

---

[4]There is usually no problem pricing American call options: Recall from Chapter 21 that the price of an American call on a non-dividend-paying stock is the same as the price of a European call. So the real problem in pricing American options relates to puts.

exercise the put. So the actual put value—given the early exercise feature—is $20 and not $16.4151 (cell B58):

Using this value of $20, we can price the put at date 0.

| | A | B | C | D | E | F | G | H |
|---|---|---|---|---|---|---|---|---|
| 60 | Finding ???-0 | | | | | | | |
| 61 | | | | | | | | |
| 62 | | Stock price | | | | Bond price | | |
| 63 | | | | 130.00 | | | | 1.0600 |
| 64 | | 100 | | | | 1 | | |
| 65 | | | | 90.00 | | | | 1.0600 |
| 66 | | | | | | | | |
| 67 | | Put option price | | | | | | |
| 68 | | | | 0.0000 | | | | |
| 69 | | ???-0 | | | | | | |
| 70 | | | | 20.0000 | | | | |
| 71 | | | | | | | | |
| 72 | The put replicating portfolio | | | | | | | |
| 73 | Stock, A | -0.5000 | <-- =(D68-D70)/(D63-D65) | | | | | |
| 74 | Bonds, B | 61.3208 | <-- =(D70-B73*D65)/H63 | | | | | |
| 75 | American put price ???-0 | 11.3208 | <-- =MAX(B7-B64,B73*B64+B74*F64) | | | | | |

In Section 23.3 we priced a European put with the same exercise price $X = \$110$. There we concluded (page 671) that the value of the European put is $9.2916. When we reprice the put as an American put, we see that its price is $11.3208, *higher* than the European put price. This happens because we will want to *early exercise* the put at ???-2.

# Conclusion

The binomial option pricing model can be used to price options under more general conditions than those that hold for the Black–Scholes model. This chapter has revealed only the tip of this financial iceberg, showing you how to implement the model in a one-date and a two-date framework. We've also indicated how the model can be used to price American options and weird options such as Asian options or barrier options.

# EXERCISES

1. A stock selling for $25 today will, in 1 year, be worth either $35 or $20. If the interest rate is 8%, what is the value today of a 1-year European call option on the stock with exercise price $30?

2. In Exercise 1, calculate the value today of a 1-year European put option on the stock with exercise price $30. Show that put–call parity holds: That is, using your answer from this problem and the previous problem, show that

$$call\ price + \frac{X}{1+r} = stock\ price\ today + put\ price$$

3. In a binomial model a European put option is written on a stock selling today for $30. The exercise price of the put option is 40. The put option's payoffs are 20 and 5. The price of the put is $9.50. What is the riskless interest rate? Assume that the basic period is 1 year.

4. All reliable analysts agree that a share of ABC Corp., selling today for $50, will be priced at either $65 or $45 1 year from now. They further agree that the probabilities of these events are 0.6 and

0.4, respectively. The market risk-free rate is 6%. What is the value of a call option on ABC whose exercise price is $50 and that matures in 1 year?

5. A stock is currently selling for $60. The price of the stock at the end of the year is expected either to increase by 25% or decrease by 20%. The riskless interest rate is 5%. Calculate the price of a European put on the stock with exercise price $55. Use the binomial option pricing model.

6. Fill in all the cells labeled ??? in the following spreadsheet.

| Up | 30% | | | | | | | |
|---|---|---|---|---|---|---|---|---|
| Down | -10% | | | | | | | |
| | | | | | | | | |
| Initial stock price | 60 | | | | | | | |
| Interest rate | 6% | | | | | | | |
| Exercise price | 70 | | | | | | | |
| | | | | | | | | |
| **Stock price** | | | | | **Bond price** | | | |
| | | | | ??? | | | | ??? |
| | | ??? | | | | | ??? | |
| 60 | | | | ??? | 1 | | | ??? |
| | | ??? | | | | | ??? | |
| | | | | ??? | | | | ??? |
| Date 0 | | Date 1 | | Date 2 | Date 0 | | Date 1 | Date 2 |
| | | | | | | | | |
| **Call option price** | | | | | **European Put option price** | | | |
| | | | | ??? | | | | ??? |
| | | ??? | | | | | ??? | |
| ??? | | | | ??? | #REF! | | | ??? |
| | | ??? | | | | | ??? | |
| | | | | ??? | | | | ??? |
| Date 0 | | Date 1 | | Date 2 | Date 0 | | Date 1 | Date 2 |
| | | | | | | | | |
| **American Put option price** | | | | | | | | |
| | | | | ??? | | | | |
| | | ??? | | | | | | |
| ??? | | | | ??? | | | | |
| | | ??? | | | | | | |
| | | | | ??? | | | | |
| Date 0 | | Date 1 | | Date 2 | | | | |

7. Consider the following two-period binomial model, in which the annual interest rate is 9% and in which the stock price goes up by 15% per period or down by 10%:

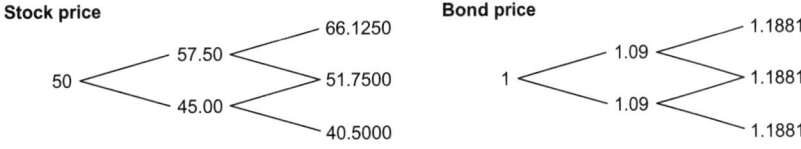

a. Price a European call on the stock with exercise price 60.
b. Price a European put on the stock with exercise price 60.
c. Price an American call on the stock with exercise price 60.
d. Price an American put on the stock with exercise price 60.

8. Consider the following two-period binomial model:
   - In each period the stock price either goes up by 30% or decreases by 10%.
   - The one-period interest rate is 25%

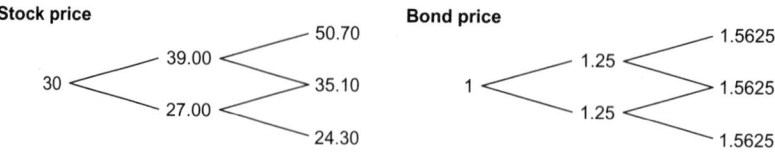

a. Consider a European call with $X = 30$ and $T = 2$. Fill in the blanks in the tree.

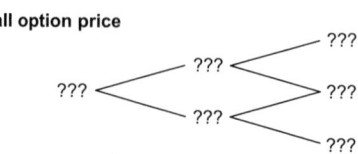

b. Price a European put with $X = 30$ and $T = 2$.
c. Now consider an American put with $X = 30$ and $T = 2$. Fill in the blanks in the tree.

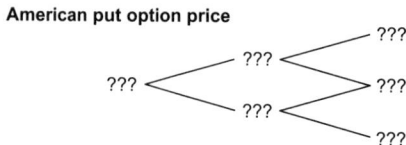

9. A prominent securities firm recently introduced a new financial product. This product, called "The Best of Both Worlds" (BOBOW for short), costs $10. It matures in 5 years, at which point it repays the investor the $10 cost *plus* 120% of any positive return in the S&P 500 Index. There are no payments before maturity.

   For example, if the S&P 500 is currently at 1,500, and if it is at 1,800 in 5 years, a BOBOW owner will receive back $12.40 = $10 * [1 + 1.2 * (1,800/1,500 − 1)]. If the S&P is at or below 1,500 in 5 years, the BOBOW owner will receive back $10.

   Suppose that the annual interest rate on a 5-year, continuously compounded, pure-discount bond is 6%. Suppose further that the S&P 500 is currently at 1,500 and that you believe that in 5 years it will be at either 2,500 or 1,200. Use the binomial option-pricing model to show that BOBOWs are worth more than their current price of $10.

10. A call option is written on a stock whose current price is $50. The option has maturity of 2 years, and during this time the annual stock price is expected to increase by 25% or to decrease by 10%. The annual interest rate is constant at 6%. The option is exercisable at date 1 at a price of $55 and at date 2 for a price of $60. What is its value today? Will you ever exercise the option early?

11. A stock is currently selling for $60. A put option has maturity of 2 years, and during this time the annual stock price is expected to increase by 30% or to decrease by 10%. The riskless interest annual rate is 6%. The put option is currently selling for $9. Is the option more likely an American or a European put option? Use the binomial option pricing model to determine.

12. A call option is written on a stock whose current price is $100. The option has maturity of 2 years, and during this time the annual stock price is expected to increase by 30% or to decrease by 10%. The annual interest rate is constant at 6%. The option's exercise price is $110. Extend the binomial option pricing to incorporate a $3.00/share dividend that will be paid out in period 2. In other words, all of the period 2 stock prices will be reduced by $3.00. Determine the current prices of the call. Compare with the nondividend case that appears in this chapter.

13. A 2-year American put option is written on a stock whose current price is $42. You expect that in each year the stock price either goes up by 15% or decreases by 5%. The one-period interest rate is 5%. The option's exercise price is $45. Will you ever exercise the option early?

# BACKGROUND TO EXCEL

$P$RINCIPLES OF FINANCE WITH EXCEL USES EXCEL THROUGHOUT as the tool to understanding and implementing financial analysis. Part 6 serves two purposes:

- It serves as an introduction and reminder of the basics of Excel.
- It reviews the principal Excel techniques used in the book.

Section 6 starts off with Chapter 24, which reviews Excel basics. These are all the things that you probably knew all along but might have forgotten. Topics include opening Excel, saving your work, copying (both relative and absolute), and basic graphing.

Chapter 25 gets into more detail on graphs in Excel. After reading this chapter, you'll know how to make Excel charts look better, how to graph non-contiguous data, and how to make graph titles that change when the inputs change, and more.

Chapter 26 has brief discussions on most of the functions used in *Principles of Finance with Excel*.

Excel's **Data Table**, the topic of Chapter 27, is a fabulous technique to do sensitivity analysis. **Data Table** is a bit complicated, but once you master it, you'll never understand how you functioned without it.

Chapter 28 discusses **Goal Seek** and **Solver**. These are two very useful Excel tools to find model solutions. Most students are aware of **Goal Seek**, but many Excel users are not aware that **Solver** is almost as easy to use and more useful. Chapter 28 shows you how to use both of these tools.

Chapter 29 discusses dates in Excel. Topics include the manipulation of dates and times in Excel and the use of Excel's date functions in financial analysis.

# 24 Introduction to Excel

## CHAPTER CONTENTS

## Overview

This chapter introduces you to Excel and shows you how to do the most important initial operations. Excel is not difficult to learn to use, provided you're willing to make many mistakes along the way and you take an occasional look at the online Help (press function key F1).

## Contents of This Chapter

- Turning Excel on
- Saving, creating a new directory
- Copying—relative versus absolute
- Formatting numbers
- Making a graph
- Fiddling with the default settings for Excel
- Using a few functions
- Printing

# 24.1. Getting Started

You've started your computer and clicked the Excel icon  Excel 2007 on your desktop (or maybe it's not on your desktop—maybe you got there through the Office button ). You're facing a blank spreadsheet, and you want to play. Let's write a spreadsheet describing how $1,000 deposited in the bank at 15% will grow over time.

|    | A    | B            | C |
|----|------|--------------|---|
| 1  | **COMPOUND INTEREST** | | |
| 2  | Year | Bank balance | |
| 3  | 0    | 1000         | |
| 4  | 1    |              | |
| 5  | 2    |              | |
| 6  | 3    |              | |
| 7  | 4    |              | |
| 8  | 5    |              | |
| 9  | 6    |              | |
| 10 | 7    |              | |
| 11 | 8    |              | |
| 12 | 9    |              | |
| 13 | 10   |              | |

After you've finished typing in the above, put the cursor in cell B4. We're going to make a formula that describes how much money will be in the bank at the end of year 1. When you're in cell B4, type in the following formula and then press [Enter] (no spaces, please!):

$$=B3*(1+15\%)$$

Here's what the spreadsheet should look like.

|    | A | B | C |
|----|---|---|---|
| 1  | COMPOUND INTEREST | | |
| 2  | Year | Bank balance | |
| 3  | 0 | 1000 | |
| 4  | 1 | 1150 | |
| 5  | 2 | | |
| 6  | 3 | | |
| 7  | 4 | | |
| 8  | 5 | | |
| 9  | 6 | | |
| 10 | 7 | | |
| 11 | 8 | | |
| 12 | 9 | | |
| 13 | 10 | | |

If you put the cursor on cell B4 and look at the *formula bar* (next to the *fx* symbol), you'll see what you've written in the spreadsheet.

| B4 | | | $fx$ =B3*(1+15%) | |
|----|---|---|---|---|
|    | A | B | C | Formula Bar E |
| 1  | COMPOUND INTEREST | | | |
| 2  | Year | Bank balance | | |
| 3  | 0 | 1000 | | |
| 4  | 1 | 1150 | | |
| 5  | 2 | | | |
| 6  | 3 | | | |
| 7  | 4 | | | |
| 8  | 5 | | | |
| 9  | 6 | | | |
| 10 | 7 | | | |
| 11 | 8 | | | |
| 12 | 9 | | | |
| 13 | 10 | | | |

## Copying the Formula

So, if you deposit $1,000 in the bank today and the bank gives you 15% interest, you'll have $1,150 at the end of year 1. If you've read Chapter 2 of this book, you know that at the end of year 2 you'll have 1,150 * (1 + 15%) in the bank. Instead of typing in this formula, we'll use

Excel's *copy* ability to put it in cell B5:

- The lower right-hand corner of the frame around cell B4 has a little black square; we call this the "handle" of the cell.

| B4 | | $f_x$ =B3*(1+15%) | | |
|---|---|---|---|---|
| | A | B | C | D |
| 1 | | **COMPOUND INTEREST** | | |
| 2 | Year | Bank balance | | |
| 3 | 0 | 1000 | | |
| 4 | 1 | 1150 | | |
| 5 | 2 | | | |
| 6 | 3 | | The "handle" | |
| 7 | 4 | | | |
| 8 | 5 | | | |
| 9 | 6 | | | |
| 10 | 7 | | | |
| 11 | 8 | | | |
| 12 | 9 | | | |
| 13 | 10 | | | |

- Put the cursor on the handle of cell B4. Hold down the left mouse button and drag down until you get to cell B13. At this point your spreadsheet will look like this.

| B4 | | $f_x$ =B3*(1+15%) | | |
|---|---|---|---|---|
| | A | B | C | D |
| 1 | | **COMPOUND INTEREST** | | |
| 2 | Year | Bank balance | | |
| 3 | 0 | 1000 | | |
| 4 | 1 | 1150 | | |
| 5 | 2 | | | |
| 6 | 3 | | | |
| 7 | 4 | | | |
| 8 | 5 | | | |
| 9 | 6 | | | |
| 10 | 7 | | | |
| 11 | 8 | | | |
| 12 | 9 | | | |
| 13 | 10 | | | |
| 14 | | | + | |

Release the left mouse button.

|   | A | B | C |
|---|---|---|---|
| 1 | **COMPOUND INTEREST** | | |
| 2 | Year | Bank balance | |
| 3 | 0 | 1000 | |
| 4 | 1 | 1150 | |
| 5 | 2 | 1322.5 | |
| 6 | 3 | 1520.875 | |
| 7 | 4 | 1749.00625 | |
| 8 | 5 | 2011.357188 | |
| 9 | 6 | 2313.060766 | |
| 10 | 7 | 2660.01988 | |
| 11 | 8 | 3059.022863 | |
| 12 | 9 | 3517.876292 | |
| 13 | 10 | 4045.557736 | |

Note how Excel copied the cell formulas:

- The formula in cell B4 says: "Take the contents of the cell above and multiply by (1 + 15%)."

- When we *drag down* the cell formula in B5 says "Take the contents of the cell above and multiply by (1 + 15%)."

This kind of copying is called *relative copying* in Excel: The cell formulas change in the direction of the copy (that is, in the direction that you dragged the cell handle). There's also *absolute copying*, which we'll explain in Section 24.4.

## EXCEL HINT

Instead of dragging cell B4, there's an even simpler way to copy. If you put your cursor on the handle and double-click with the left mouse button, the formula in cell B4 will be copied through the last row of the adjacent filled column, in this case from cell B5 through B13.

## Entering Formulas by Pointing (a Better Way)

So far we've written the formula in cell B4. But it's usually a better idea to use the mouse and *point* at the relevant cells. Pointing and clicking formulas avoids a lot of mistakes. In the previous example,

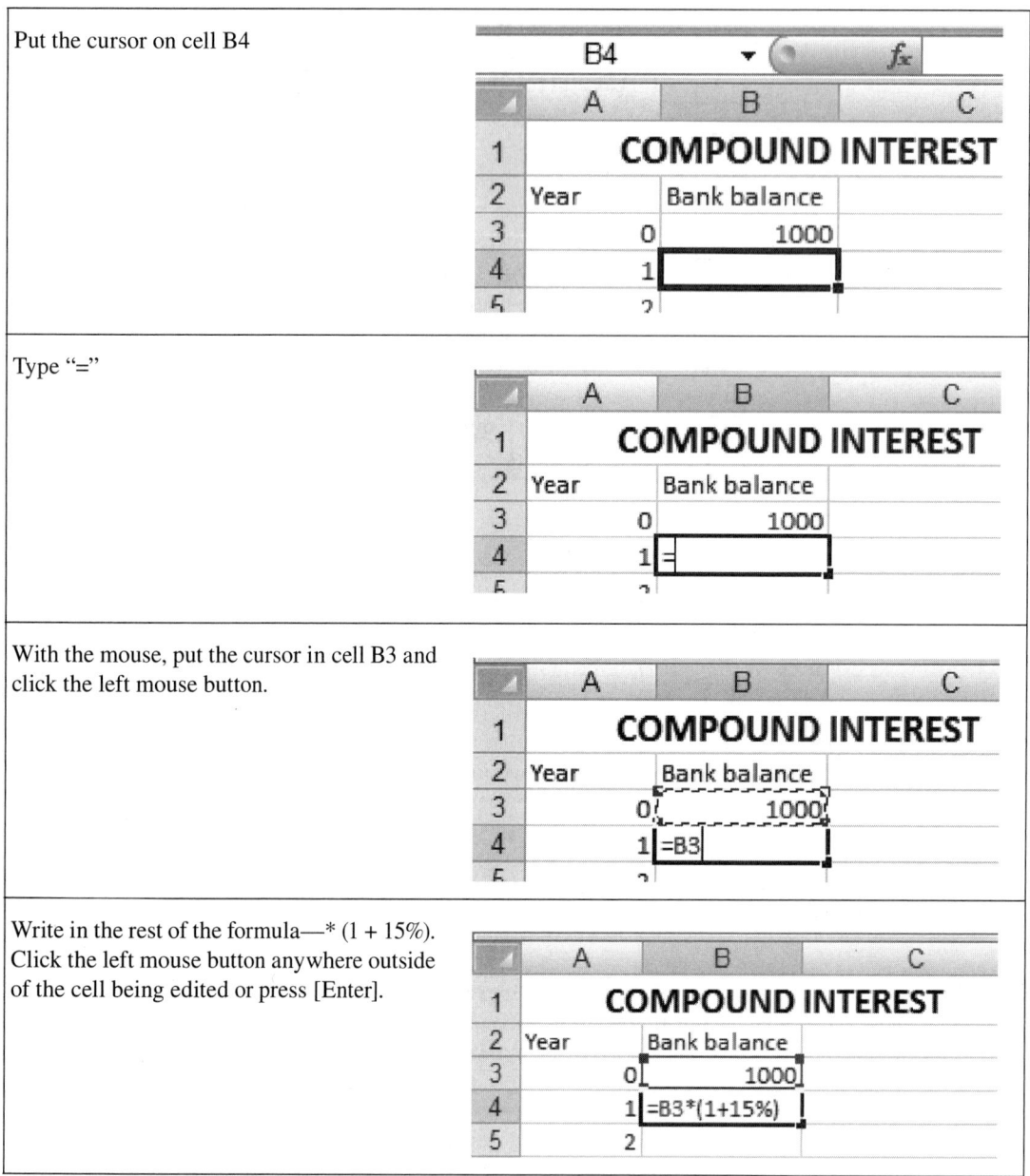

| | Put the cursor on cell B4 | Type "=" | With the mouse, put the cursor in cell B3 and click the left mouse button. | Write in the rest of the formula—* (1 + 15%). Click the left mouse button anywhere outside of the cell being edited or press [Enter]. |

## 24.2. Formatting the Numbers

The spreadsheet we've constructed so far is cute but ugly. Why do we need so many decimal places? Why aren't there commas in the numbers? How about indicating that these are *dollar* amounts?

We can make all these changes using Excel's extensive *formatting* facilities.

## FORMATTING NUMBERS IN EXCEL

Before: Mark the numbers to be formatted.

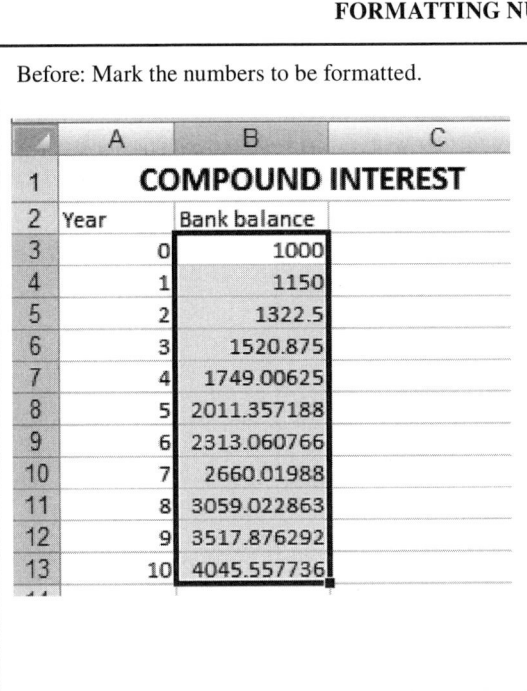

Click the right mouse button and choose **Format Cells**. Here's what we chose.

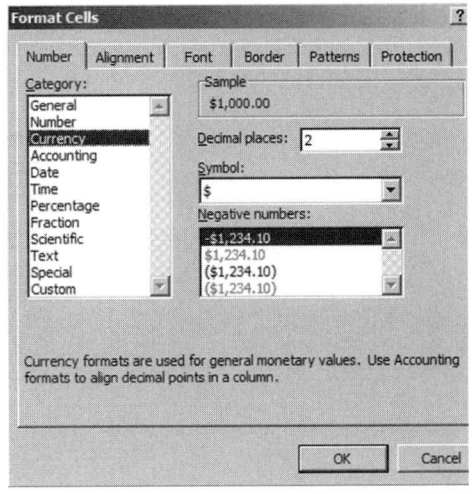

After the formatting, here's how the numbers look.

|    | A | B | C |
|----|------|---------------|---|
| 1  | COMPOUND INTEREST | | |
| 2  | Year | Bank balance | |
| 3  | 0 | $1,000.00 | |
| 4  | 1 | $1,150.00 | |
| 5  | 2 | $1,322.50 | |
| 6  | 3 | $1,520.88 | |
| 7  | 4 | $1,749.01 | |
| 8  | 5 | $2,011.36 | |
| 9  | 6 | $2,313.06 | |
| 10 | 7 | $2,660.02 | |
| 11 | 8 | $3,059.02 | |
| 12 | 9 | $3,517.88 | |
| 13 | 10 | $4,045.56 | |

In other chapters we'll use the **Format Cells** command to change the way dates and text and fonts appear in Excel. The important thing to note about this command is that *it changes the way cell contents appear, but not the actual cell contents.* For example, suppose your cell contents read 3287.65898992; now suppose that you made them look like dollars with a comma and two decimal places, so that the cell reads $3,287.66. The actual contents of the cell haven't changed—there are still eight decimal places, but it only shows two of them.

## 24.3. Copying with Absolute References—Building a More Sophisticated Model

The spreadsheet of the previous section is cute, but it doesn't allow us to change the interest rate at which the money accumulates. We fix this by writing the following spreadsheet; in this spreadsheet we've got a separate cell (B2) to indicate the interest rate. By changing this cell we'll change all the accumulations.

|     | A        | B          | C |
| --- | -------- | ---------- | - |
| 1   | **COMPOUND INTEREST** | | |
| 2   | Interest | 7%         | |
| 3   |          |            | |
| 4   | Year     |            | |
| 5   | 0        | $1,000.00  | |
| 6   | 1        |            | |
| 7   | 2        |            | |
| 8   | 3        |            | |
| 9   | 4        |            | |
| 10  | 5        |            | |
| 11  | 6        |            | |
| 12  | 7        |            | |
| 13  | 8        |            | |
| 14  | 9        |            | |
| 15  | 10       |            | |

Go to cell B6 . Type the formula "=B5*(1+$B$2)" in this cell. The dollar signs on $B$2 indicate that when we copy this formula, this particular cell reference will not change. In the jargon of Excel: $B$2 is an *absolute reference*, whereas B5 is a *relative reference*—it will change to B6, B7,... as we go down the column.

|     | A        | B          | C |
| --- | -------- | ---------- | --------------- |
| 1   | **COMPOUND INTEREST** | | |
| 2   | Interest | 7%         | |
| 3   |          |            | |
| 4   | Year     |            | |
| 5   | 0        | $1,000.00  | |
| 6   | 1        | $1,070.00  | <-- =B5*(1+$B$2) |
| 7   | 2        |            | |
| 8   | 3        |            | |
| 9   | 4        |            | |
| 10  | 5        |            | |
| 11  | 6        |            | |
| 12  | 7        |            | |
| 13  | 8        |            | |
| 14  | 9        |            | |
| 15  | 10       |            | |

Copying as we did in the previous section (click on B6, put the cursor on the B6 handle and drag), we obtain the following.

|   | A | B | C |
|---|---|---|---|
| 1 | **COMPOUND INTEREST** | | |
| 2 | Interest | 10% | |
| 3 | | | |
| 4 | Year | | |
| 5 | 0 | $1,000.00 | |
| 6 | 1 | $1,100.00 | <-- =B5*(1+$B$2) |
| 7 | 2 | | Cursor |
| 8 | 3 | | |
| 9 | 4 | | |

The result is a table much like that of the previous section.

|   | A | B | C |
|---|---|---|---|
| 1 | **COMPOUND INTEREST** | | |
| 2 | Interest | 7% | |
| 3 | | | |
| 4 | Year | | |
| 5 | 0 | $1,000.00 | |
| 6 | 1 | $1,070.00 | <-- =B5*(1+$B$2) |
| 7 | 2 | $1,144.90 | <-- =B6*(1+$B$2) |
| 8 | 3 | $1,225.04 | <-- =B7*(1+$B$2) |
| 9 | 4 | $1,310.80 | <-- =B8*(1+$B$2) |
| 10 | 5 | $1,402.55 | <-- =B9*(1+$B$2) |
| 11 | 6 | $1,500.73 | <-- =B10*(1+$B$2) |
| 12 | 7 | $1,605.78 | <-- =B11*(1+$B$2) |
| 13 | 8 | $1,718.19 | <-- =B12*(1+$B$2) |
| 14 | 9 | $1,838.46 | <-- =B13*(1+$B$2) |
| 15 | 10 | $1,967.15 | <-- =B14*(1+$B$2) |

(We've formatted the numbers as currency.)

The difference between this spreadsheet and the previous one is that we can change the interest rate simply by changing the contents of cell B2. In this example the interest rate is 10%:

|   | A | B | C |
|---|---|---|---|
| 1 | **COMPOUND INTEREST** | | |
| 2 | Interest | 10% | |
| 3 | | | |
| 4 | Year | | |
| 5 | 0 | $1,000.00 | |
| 6 | 1 | $1,100.00 | <-- =B5*(1+$B$2) |
| 7 | 2 | $1,210.00 | <-- =B6*(1+$B$2) |
| 8 | 3 | $1,331.00 | <-- =B7*(1+$B$2) |
| 9 | 4 | $1,464.10 | <-- =B8*(1+$B$2) |
| 10 | 5 | $1,610.51 | <-- =B9*(1+$B$2) |
| 11 | 6 | $1,771.56 | <-- =B10*(1+$B$2) |
| 12 | 7 | $1,948.72 | <-- =B11*(1+$B$2) |
| 13 | 8 | $2,143.59 | <-- =B12*(1+$B$2) |
| 14 | 9 | $2,357.95 | <-- =B13*(1+$B$2) |
| 15 | 10 | $2,593.74 | <-- =B14*(1+$B$2) |

---

**EXCEL HINT**

Never use a number if you can use a cell reference! Compare the previous example with this one: If, as in the previous section, you "hard-wire" the 15% interest rate in cells B6:B15, you have to change each of these cells to change the interest rate assumption. On the other hand, if you put the interest rate in a cell (as in this section's example), you need only change the contents of that cell to recalculate the whole spreadsheet.

In Excel, numbers are always inferior to formulas!

---

## Pointing and Using the F4 Key

Let's go back to the stage in this example where we were putting the formula "=B5*(1+$B$2)" into cell B5. We've already suggested that it's better to enter formulas by pointing and clicking than by typing. Now we'll teach you another little trick, the use of the F4 key to "dollarize" cell references—that is, to make them absolute references instead of relative references. Here's what you do:

- Put the cursor in cell B6. Type "=" and point at cell B5 (the one that contains $1,000). You can either point with the mouse (clicking when you're on B5) or you can point with the arrow keys.

| | A | B | C |
|---|---|---|---|
| 1 | **COMPOUND INTEREST** | | |
| 2 | Interest | 10% | |
| 3 | | | |
| 4 | Year | | |
| 5 | 0 | $1,000.00 | |
| 6 | 1 | =B5 | |
| 7 | 2 | | |

- Now type an asterisk, an opening parenthesis, a 1, and a + : *(1+ . Then point at cell B2 containing the interest rate and click.

| SUM | | X ✓ $f_x$ | =B5*(1+B2 |
|---|---|---|---|

| | A | B | C |
|---|---|---|---|
| 1 | **COMPOUND INTEREST** | | |
| 2 | Interest | 10% | |
| 3 | | | |
| 4 | Year | | |
| 5 | 0 | $1,000.00 | |
| 6 | 1 | =B5*(1+B2 | |
| 7 | 2 | | |

- Next press function key **F4**. This puts the dollar signs into the cell reference B2 in cell B6.

| SUM | ▾ ⊙ × ✓ ƒ | =B5*(1+$B$2 |
|---|---|---|

| | A | B | C |
|---|---|---|---|
| 1 | **COMPOUND INTEREST** | | |
| 2 | Interest | 10% | |
| 3 | | | |
| 4 | Year | | |
| 5 | 0 | $1,000.00 | |
| 6 | 1 | =B5*(1+$B$2 | |
| 7 | | 2 | |

- Finally, close the parentheses by typing a ")". Press [Enter].
- Copy cell B6 as before.

## Correcting Errors—Editing the Cell

Suppose you made a mistake and forgot to "dollarize" the B2 cell reference, so that the contents of cell B6 are "=B5*(1+B2)." This isn't good—the cell contents should read "=B5*(1+$B$2)." To make the appropriate change, we edit the formula in cell B6 and we use the F4 key:

- Put the cursor on B6 and press the left mouse button twice. This opens the formula for editing.

| | ▾ ⊙ × ✓ ƒ | =B5*(1+B2) |
|---|---|---|

| | A | B | C |
|---|---|---|---|
| 1 | **COMPOUND INTEREST** | | |
| 2 | Interest | 10% | |
| 3 | | | |
| 4 | Year | | |
| 5 | 0 | $1,000.00 | |
| 6 | 1 | =B5*(1+B2) | |
| 7 | | 2 | |

- Move the cursor until it's somewhere on the B2 in the formula (it doesn't matter where). Press the F4 key and your cell reference will be "dollarized."

| | ▾ ⊙ × ✓ ƒ | =B5*(1+$B$2) |
|---|---|---|

| | A | B | C | |
|---|---|---|---|---|
| 1 | **COMPOUND INTEREST** | | | |
| 2 | Interest | 10% | | |
| 3 | | | | |
| 4 | Year | | | |
| 5 | 0 | $1,000.00 | | |
| 6 | 1 | =B5*(1+$B$2) | | |
| 7 | | 2 | | |

- Now press [Enter] and copy as before.

## THREE EXCEL HINTS ABOUT EDITING

1. You can also edit the cell contents by putting the cursor on the cell and pressing the **F2** function button.

2. If you can't edit the formula in the cell, someone may have changed the default settings on your Excel spreadsheet. Go to the Office button , click **Excel Options|Advanced,** and check the "Allow editing directly in cells" box.

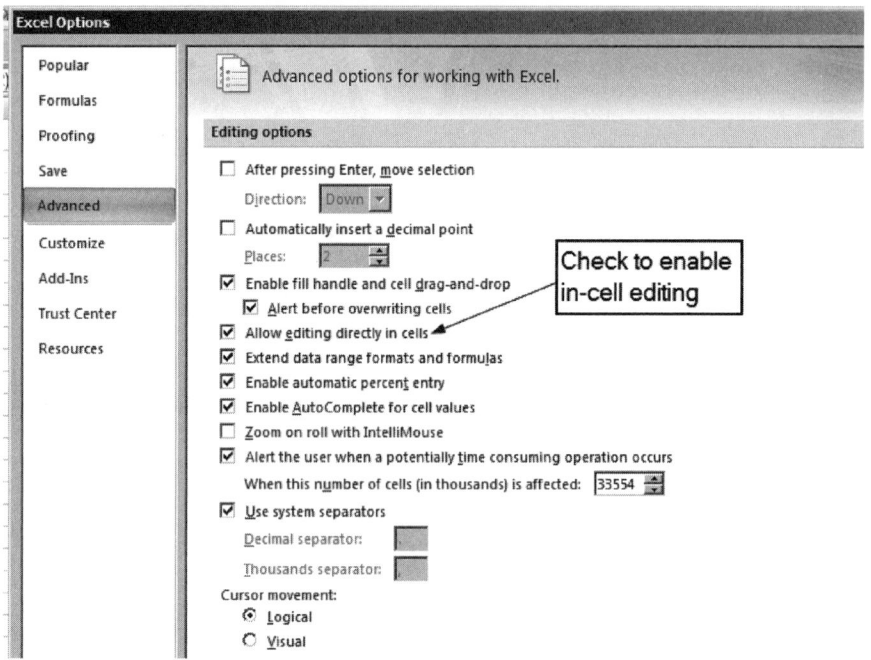

3. You can always edit a cell formula in the formula bar.

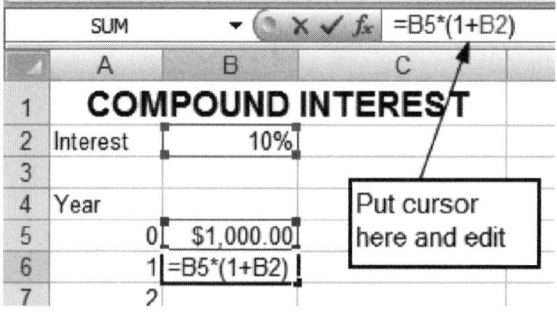

## 24.4. Saving the Spreadsheet

What's the next step? We suggest that you *save* the spreadsheet.[1] An appropriate place to save it is in that **Junk** directory that you're going to create right now.

- Click the Office button and then click **Save.**

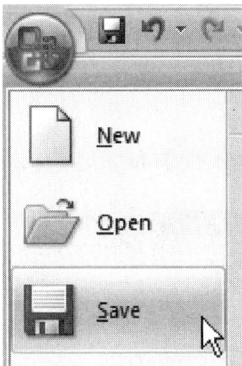

- Excel will probably suggest a directory called **Documents**.

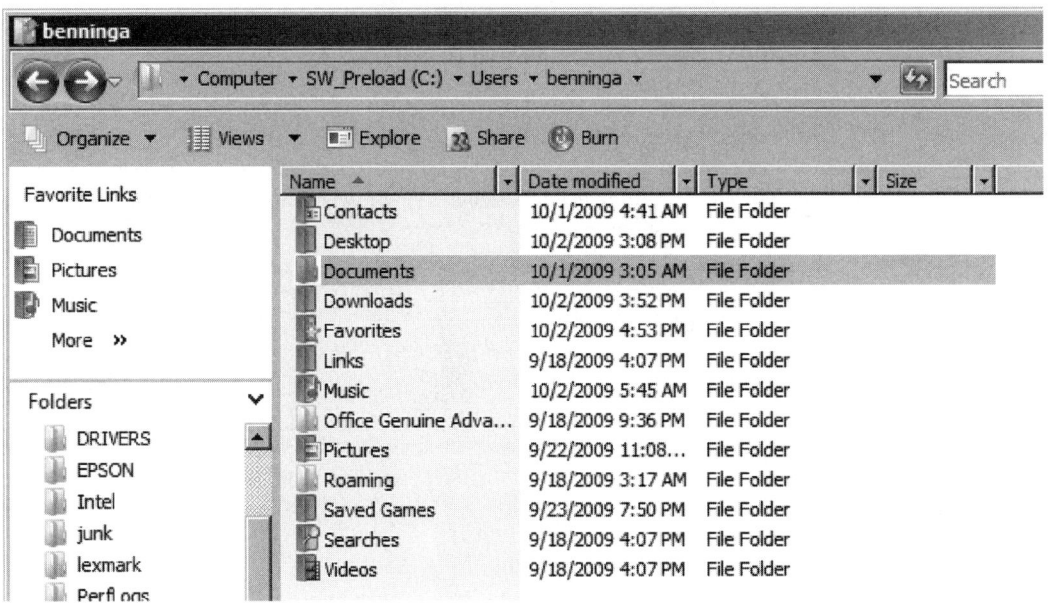

---

[1]As a rule of thumb, we suggest that you save *all the time*. Someday, your computer is going to crash *right after* you've spent a long time working and *before* you've saved your work.

- Click **My documents**, and then click the **New Folder** icon that looks like this.

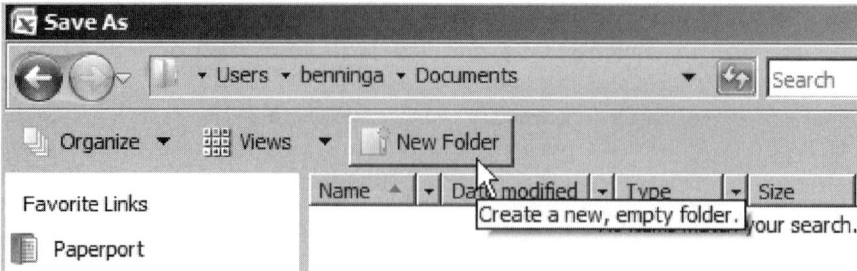

- When you click **New Folder**, you'll get the opportunity to name your new folder.

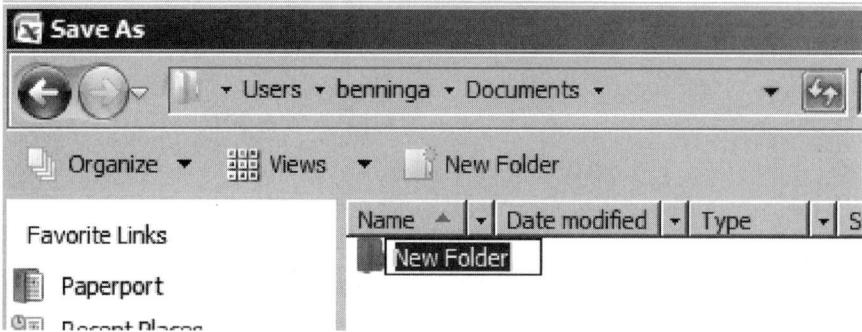

In the Name box, type "junk." The author's computer always has a directory called "junk"—it's the directory containing all the files that you can get rid of without thinking twice (a file called "junk" in the junk directory is a double whammy—absolutely worthless!). Now you'll find yourself in the junk subdirectory.

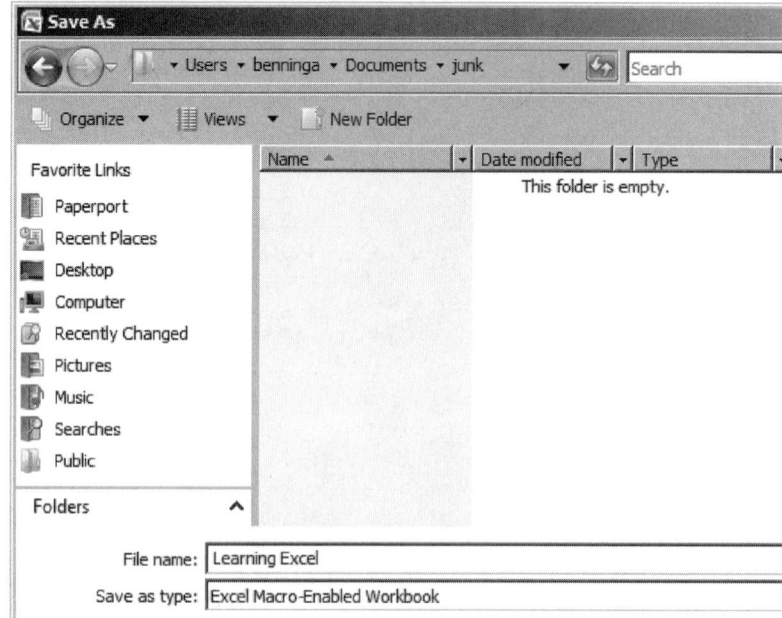

Type something informative in the box called **File Name**. We'll call our spreadsheet "Learning Excel."

Now you'll see the name of the spreadsheet on the top of the sheet.

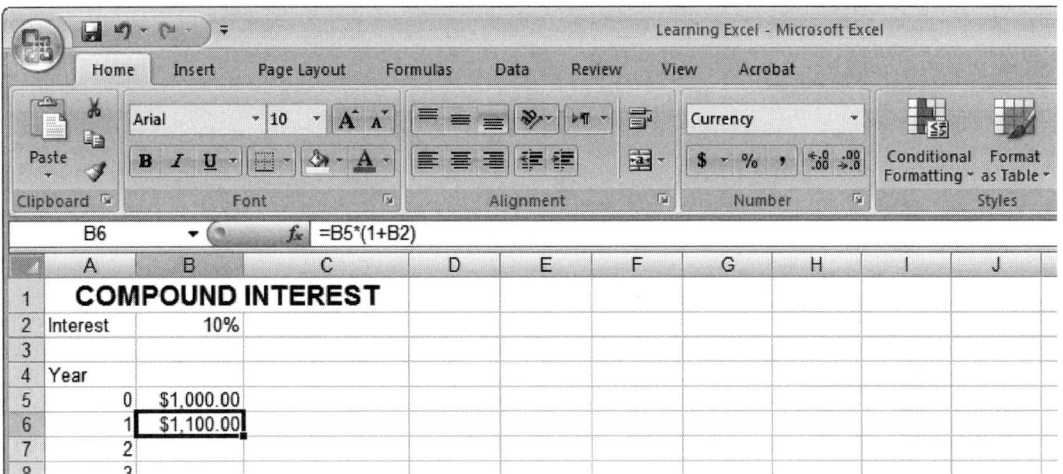

Every time you subsequently save the workbook (either by **Office button|Save** or by pressing [Ctrl] + S or by clicking the save icon in the form of the little disk ), the workbook with all its changes will be saved under the same name in the same place.

## 24.5. Your First Excel Graph

You're going to want to graph the compound interest example. Take your mouse, put it in cell A5; click the left button, and move down until you get to cell B15.

|    | A | B | C |
|----|---|---|---|
| 1  | COMPOUND INTEREST | | |
| 2  | Interest | 10% | |
| 3  |  |  | |
| 4  | Year | | |
| 5  | 0 | $1,000.00 | |
| 6  | 1 | $1,100.00 | |
| 7  | 2 | $1,210.00 | |
| 8  | 3 | $1,331.00 | |
| 9  | 4 | $1,464.10 | |
| 10 | 5 | $1,610.51 | |
| 11 | 6 | $1,771.56 | |
| 12 | 7 | $1,948.72 | |
| 13 | 8 | $2,143.59 | |
| 14 | 9 | $2,357.95 | |
| 15 | 10 | $2,593.74 | |
| 16 |  |  | |

Now go to **Insert|Scatter** and choose one of the chart types there. Our favorite chart (used most in this book) is **Scatter with straight lines and markers**.

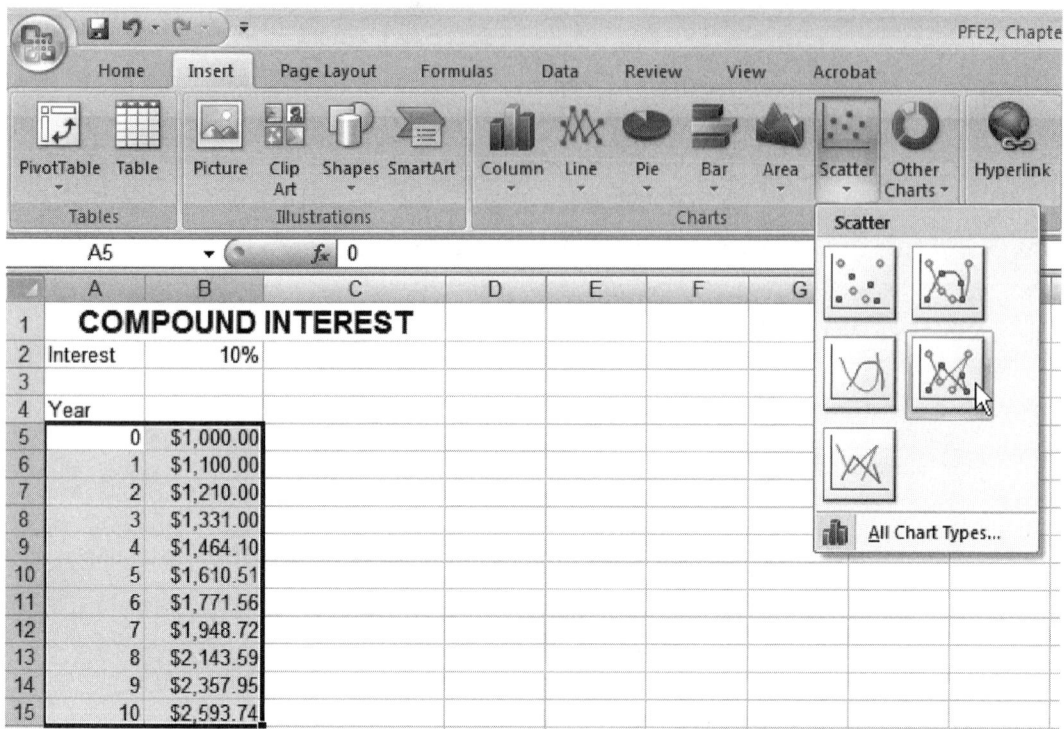

Having pressed this button, you'll get a chart on your spreadsheet.

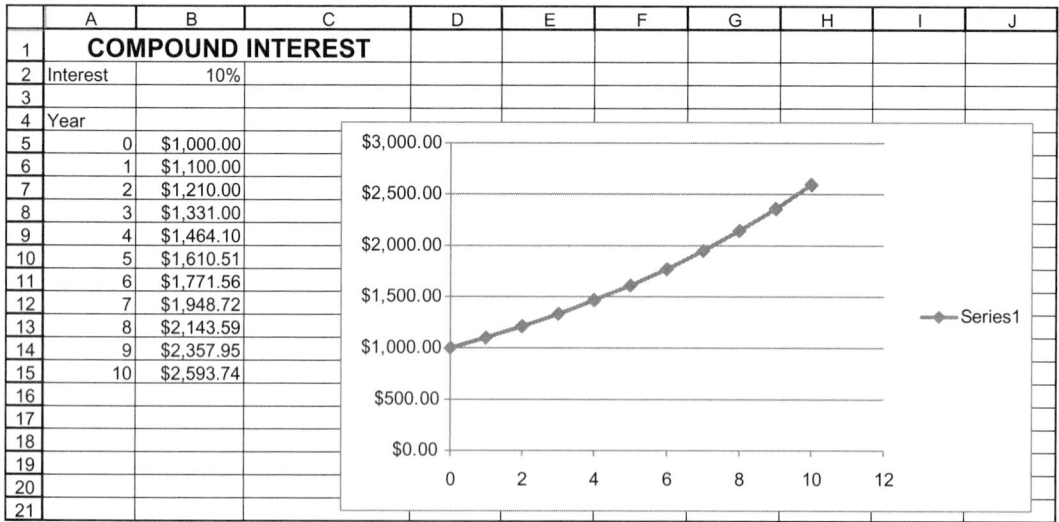

This graph has lots of features we don't like, but they can all be fixed (Chapter 28 again). Instead of fixing things, *play* with the spreadsheet—change the interest rate and see what happens.

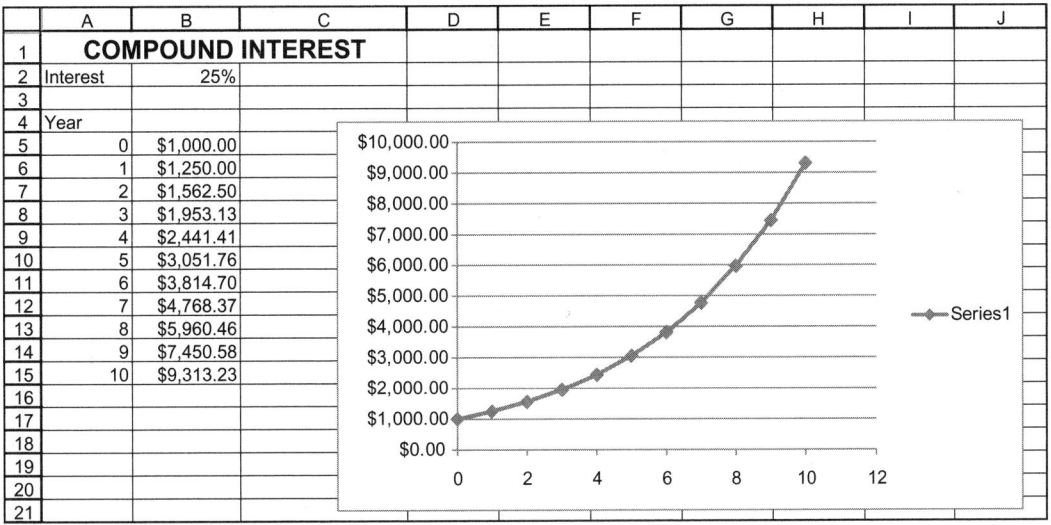

| | A | B | C | D | E | F | G | H | I | J |
|---|---|---|---|---|---|---|---|---|---|---|
| 1 | COMPOUND INTEREST | | | | | | | | | |
| 2 | Interest | 25% | | | | | | | | |
| 3 | | | | | | | | | | |
| 4 | Year | | | | | | | | | |
| 5 | 0 | $1,000.00 | | | | | | | | |
| 6 | 1 | $1,250.00 | | | | | | | | |
| 7 | 2 | $1,562.50 | | | | | | | | |
| 8 | 3 | $1,953.13 | | | | | | | | |
| 9 | 4 | $2,441.41 | | | | | | | | |
| 10 | 5 | $3,051.76 | | | | | | | | |
| 11 | 6 | $3,814.70 | | | | | | | | |
| 12 | 7 | $4,768.37 | | | | | | | | |
| 13 | 8 | $5,960.46 | | | | | | | | |
| 14 | 9 | $7,450.58 | | | | | | | | |
| 15 | 10 | $9,313.23 | | | | | | | | |
| 16 | | | | | | | | | | |
| 17 | | | | | | | | | | |
| 18 | | | | | | | | | | |
| 19 | | | | | | | | | | |
| 20 | | | | | | | | | | |
| 21 | | | | | | | | | | |

## 24.6. Initial Settings

Before you make intensive use of Excel, it's worthwhile to change a few of the initial settings to suit your needs and preferences. In this section we'll show you our suggestions (they're all reversible).

### Make Excel Less Jumpy

The default installation of Excel has the cursor go down one cell each time you press [Enter].

| | A | B |
|---|---|---|
| 1 | | |
| 2 | | |
| 3 | | |
| 4 | you put in some junk here, pressed [Enter] and ... | |
| 5 | YOU'RE HERE!! | |
| 6 | | |

This is great for accountants, who have to enter lots of data. But we're finance people, and we make lots of mistakes! We want to stay on the cell we just entered, so we can correct it, and so we want to turn this feature off.

How? Press **Office Button|Excel Options|Advanced**. Clear the **Move selection after enter** box. In the picture below, this box is still clicked (this is the default).

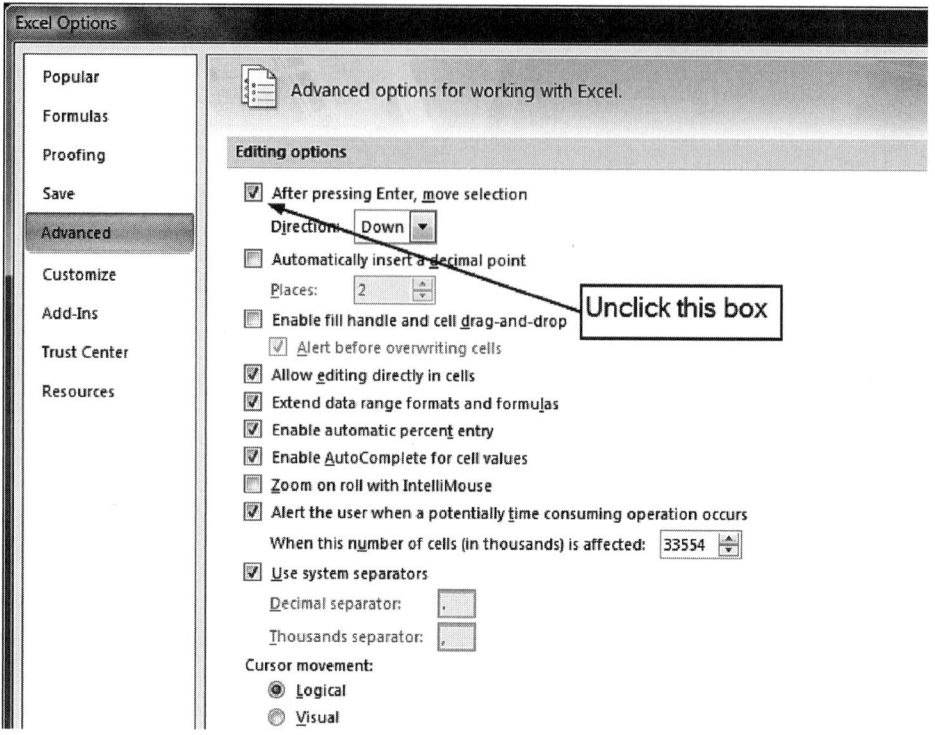

## The Number of Sheets in a Workbook

The default installation for Excel starts each new workbook with three spreadsheets.[2] This means that the bottom of your screen looks like this.

---

[2] Nomenclature: Microsoft calls an Excel file (the thing you saved as "Learning Excel.xls") a *workbook*. The individual sheets of the workbook are called *spreadsheets* or *worksheets*. Like many Excel users, we often mix up this nomenclature.

These three sheets (you can even add more by clicking on the fourth tab, the one after **Sheet3**) can be very handy. But the fact remains that most users use only one sheet per workbook. We suggest that you change the defaults so that Excel starts a new workbook with only one spreadsheet (you can always add more). To do this, go **Office Button|Excel Options|Popular** and click on **Include this many sheets**:

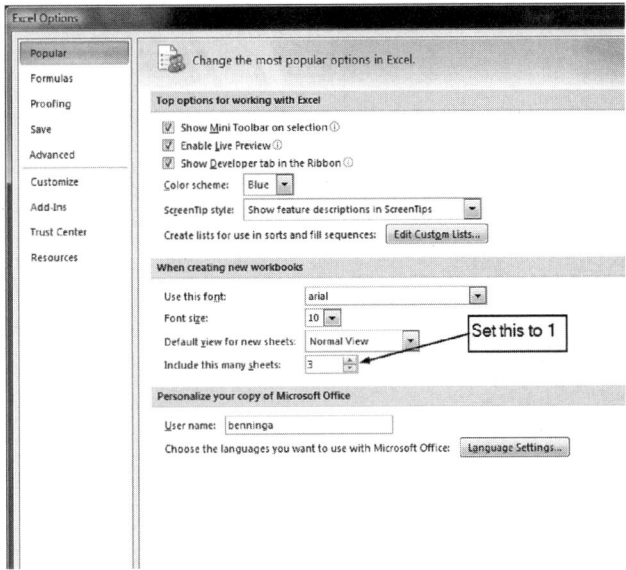

In the picture above we've changed the **Sheets in new workbook** to "1."

## Naming a Sheet

To name a sheet, double-click on the sheet tab. You can now type in the name you want for the sheet.

| Before | After |
|---|---|
| 27 | |
| 28 | 28 |
| 29 | 29 |
| 30 | 30 |
| 31 | 31 |
| 32 | 32 |
| 33 | |
| ⏮ ◀ ▶ ⏭  **Sheet1** | ⏮ ◀ ▶ ⏭  **Compound interest** |

## Adding More Sheets

To add more sheets, right-click on a tab and choose **Insert** and then choose to insert a new worksheet.

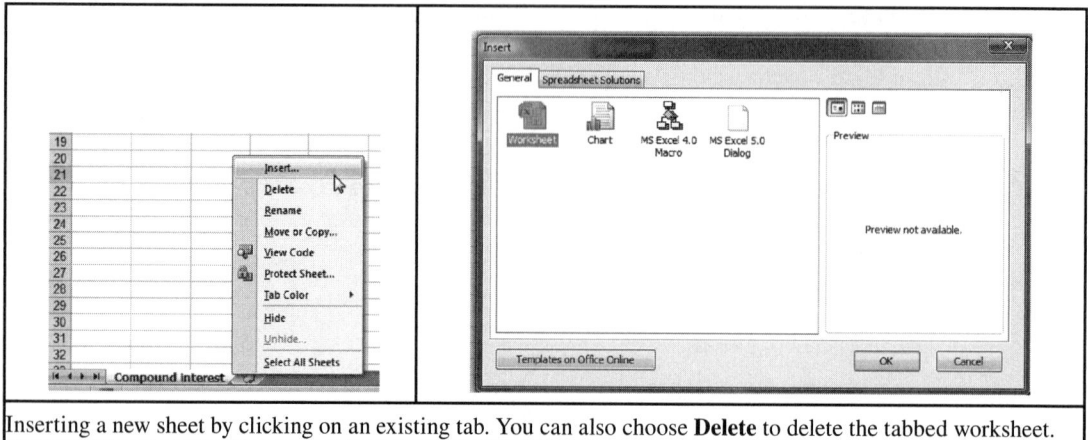

Inserting a new sheet by clicking on an existing tab. You can also choose **Delete** to delete the tabbed worksheet.

You can also delete a sheet by right-clicking on a tab and choosing **Delete**. This is an *irreversible* action, so we suggest you save the workbook before doing this.

## 24.7. Using a Function

Excel contains many functions. In this section we illustrate a few of these.[3] We'll go back to the spreadsheet in Section 24.3. In cell B17 we'll calculate the average value of the cells B5:B15 (this has very little economic meaning...). The final product will look like this.

| | A | B | C |
|---|---|---|---|
| 1 | COMPOUND INTEREST | | |
| 2 | Interest | 7% | |
| 3 | | | |
| 4 | Year | | |
| 5 | 0 | $1,000.00 | |
| 6 | 1 | $1,070.00 | <-- =B5*(1+$B$2) |
| 7 | 2 | $1,144.90 | <-- =B6*(1+$B$2) |
| 8 | 3 | $1,225.04 | <-- =B7*(1+$B$2) |
| 9 | 4 | $1,310.80 | <-- =B8*(1+$B$2) |
| 10 | 5 | $1,402.55 | <-- =B9*(1+$B$2) |
| 11 | 6 | $1,500.73 | <-- =B10*(1+$B$2) |
| 12 | 7 | $1,605.78 | <-- =B11*(1+$B$2) |
| 13 | 8 | $1,718.19 | <-- =B12*(1+$B$2) |
| 14 | 9 | $1,838.46 | <-- =B13*(1+$B$2) |
| 15 | 10 | $1,967.15 | <-- =B14*(1+$B$2) |
| 16 | | | |
| 17 | Average | $1,434.87 | <-- =AVERAGE(B5:B15) |

To do this, perform the following steps:

- In cell A17 we type "Average." This is known as "annotating the spreadsheet." In simple English, tell yourself what you're doing, because otherwise you'll forget.

---

[3]The discussion in this section is really preliminary and intended to give you a taste of how Excel functions work. In this book we use many Excel functions. Chapter 26 discusses most of the functions used in the book and Chapter 29 discusses Excel's date functions.

In cell B17, we type "**=Average(**", and then click the *f*x sign on the toolbar:

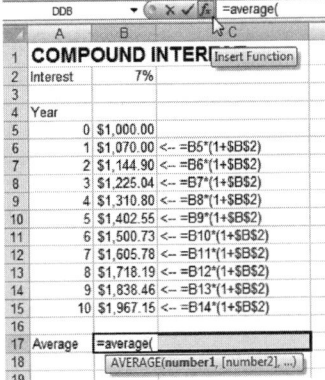

You'll see a *function dialog box.*

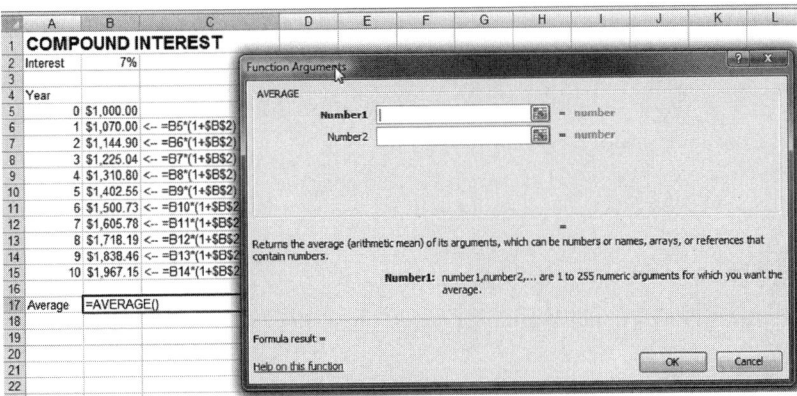

Your cursor is already in a box labeled **Number1**. Put the mouse on cell B5, click the left mouse button, and drag the cursor to B15. When you release the mouse button, here's what you'll see.

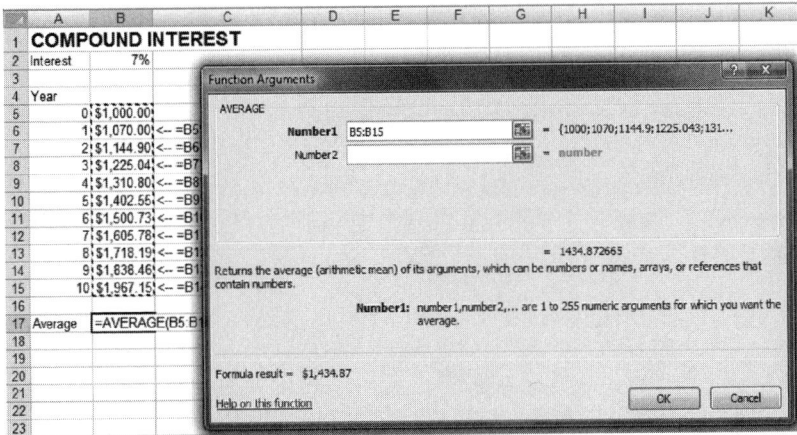

Now press **OK** in the dialog box. Here's the result.

|    | A        | B          | C                        |
|----|----------|------------|--------------------------|
| 1  | **COMPOUND INTEREST** | | |
| 2  | Interest | 7%         |                          |
| 3  |          |            |                          |
| 4  | Year     |            |                          |
| 5  |        0 | $1,000.00  |                          |
| 6  |        1 | $1,070.00  |                          |
| 7  |        2 | $1,144.90  |                          |
| 8  |        3 | $1,225.04  |                          |
| 9  |        4 | $1,310.80  |                          |
| 10 |        5 | $1,402.55  |                          |
| 11 |        6 | $1,500.73  |                          |
| 12 |        7 | $1,605.78  |                          |
| 13 |        8 | $1,718.19  |                          |
| 14 |        9 | $1,838.46  |                          |
| 15 |       10 | $1,967.15  |                          |
| 16 |          |            |                          |
| 17 | Average  | $1,434.87  | <-- =AVERAGE(B5:B15)     |

Suppose you didn't want to average all the numbers, but only those from years 5 to 10. There are two ways to do this:

- You can double-click on cell B17 and change the range in the formula to **=Average(B10:B15)**.
- You can also click on cell B17 and click the *fx* sign on the toolbar and make the appropriate changes in the dialog box.

### Practice Makes Perfect

The exercises to this chapter let you practice with a few functions that work like **Average**.

## 24.8. Printing

You've just completed your beautiful first spreadsheet and you want to print it. Go to **Office Button|Print**. This brings up a screen with a printer name.

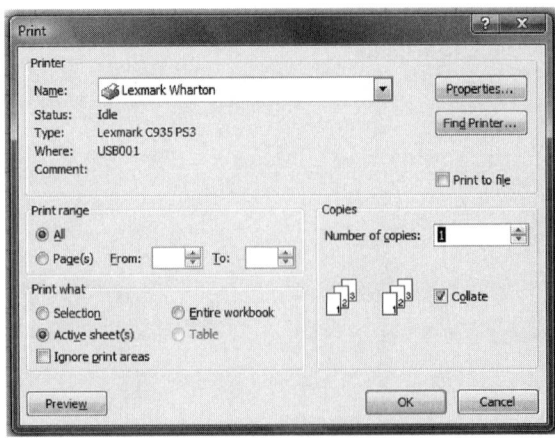

Before printing, click the **Preview** button. On the **Sheet** tab, you can choose to print the spreadsheet using **Gridlines** and **Row and column headings** (these are the settings we've used for most of the spreadsheets in this book).

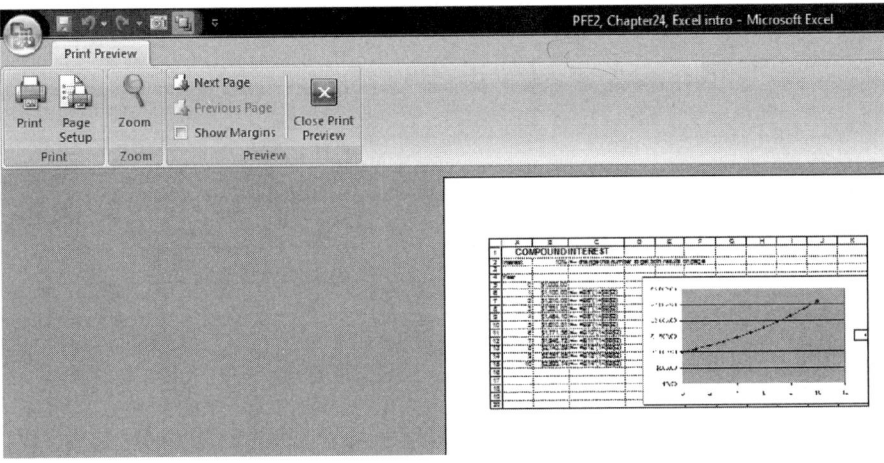

Click **Print** to print your spreadsheet.

## Summary

In this chapter we've explored the preliminaries of Excel—how to set up a spreadsheet, save it, type in a formula, use a function, and print your results. The following chapters explore more advanced Excel techniques.

## EXERCISES

1. Excel has a function called **Sum**, which works like **Average**. Set up the spreadsheet below and use

|   | A | B |
|---|---|---|
| 1 | 28 | |
| 2 | 15 | |
| 3 | 22 | |
| 4 | | <-- Use **Sum** to add the numbers |

it to add the numbers in cells A1:A3.

2. In a new spreadsheet, follow the instructions below.

|   | A | B |
|---|---|---|
| 1 | 28 | |
| 2 | 15 | |
| 3 | 22 | |
| 4 | | <-- Use **Sum(A1:A3)/3** to find the average |

3. In another spreadsheet, show that you can use the function **Average** to get the same result.

|   | A | B |
|---|---|---|
| 1 | 28 | |
| 2 | 15 | |
| 3 | 22 | |
| 4 | | <-- Use **Sum(A1:A3)/3** to find the average |
| 5 | | |
| 6 | | <-- Use **Average(A1:A3)** |

4. The Excel function **Count** counts the number of cells containing numbers. Use this function in the spreadsheet below.

|   | A | B |
|---|---|---|
| 1 | 15 | |
| 2 | -11 | |
| 3 | John | |
| 4 | 23 | |
| 5 | | <-- Use **Count(A1:A4)** |

5. The Excel function **CountA** counts the number of all the cells in the a given range. Experiment with this function in the spreadsheet below.

|   | A | B |
|---|---|---|
| 1 | 15 | |
| 2 | -11 | |
| 3 | John | |
| 4 | 23 | |
| 5 | | <-- Use **CountA(A1:A4)** |

6. Below are some statistics on the monthly rainfall in the city of Dunedin, New Zealand (the numbers are on the disk that comes with the book). Use **Sum** and **Average** to compute the total annual and average monthly rainfall.

| | A | B | C | D | E | F | G | H | I | J | K | L | M | N | O |
|---|---|---|---|---|---|---|---|---|---|---|---|---|---|---|---|
| 1 | | | | | MONTHLY RAINFALL IN THE CITY OF DUNEDIN, NEW ZEALAND (in centimeters) | | | | | | | | | | |
| 2 | | Jan | F eb | Mar | A pr | May | Jun | Jul | Aug | Sep | Oct | Nov | Dec | Total annual | Average monthly |
| 3 | 1980 | 115 | 79 | 83 | 74 | 57 | 195 | 72 | 89 | 39 | 56 | 117 | 45 | 1021 | |
| 4 | 1981 | 17 | 47 | 107 | 40 | 20 | 142 | 163 | 49 | 49 | 62 | 24 | 82 | | |
| 5 | 1982 | 142 | 48 | 37 | 45 | 68 | 39 | 33 | 47 | 32 | 147 | 42 | 140 | | |
| 6 | 1983 | 99 | 65 | 113 | 78 | 140 | 78 | 84 | 35 | 81 | 64 | 38 | 93 | | |
| 7 | 1984 | 107 | 22 | 126 | 33 | 83 | 36 | 69 | 59 | 86 | 38 | 52 | 77 | | |
| 8 | 1985 | 28 | 17 | 29 | 23 | 35 | 35 | 89 | 39 | 29 | 63 | 51 | 85 | | |
| 9 | 1986 | 41 | 179 | 101 | 49 | 60 | 79 | 75 | 48 | 22 | 69 | 89 | 83 | | |
| 10 | 1987 | 59 | 89 | 150 | 24 | 136 | 88 | 25 | 21 | 71 | 47 | 47 | 67 | | |
| 11 | 1988 | 147 | 90 | 25 | 38 | 60 | 44 | 62 | 40 | 13 | 27 | 40 | 61 | | |
| 12 | 1989 | 55 | 48 | 81 | 31 | 39 | 95 | 39 | 35 | 20 | 96 | 64 | 100 | | |
| 13 | 1990 | 34 | 44 | 18 | 62 | 48 | 21 | 34 | 137 | 19 | 96 | 42 | 55 | | |
| 14 | 1991 | 77 | 178 | 49 | 99 | 33 | 52 | 38 | 124 | 54 | 41 | 45 | 68 | | |
| 15 | 1992 | 52 | 88 | 26 | 65 | 52 | 39 | 56 | 123 | 88 | 80 | 68 | 112 | | |
| 16 | 1993 | 126 | 35 | 79 | 62 | 94 | 25 | 21 | 47 | 72 | 41 | 73 | 109 | | |
| 17 | 1994 | 140 | 69 | 170 | 23 | 42 | 115 | 99 | 14 | 45 | 13 | 78 | 57 | | |
| 18 | 1995 | 41 | 37 | 91 | 12 | 41 | 121 | 42 | 40 | 97 | 92 | 72 | 61 | | |
| 19 | 1996 | 56 | 52 | 33 | 108 | 55 | 75 | 58 | 61 | 14 | 143 | 132 | 95 | | |
| 20 | 1997 | 120 | 117 | 44 | 122 | 48 | 20 | 60 | 43 | 30 | 62 | 88 | 85 | | |
| 21 | 1998 | 10 | 101 | 60 | 52 | 66 | 24 | 26 | 44 | 58 | 109 | 33 | 66 | | |
| 22 | 1999 | 42 | 12 | 65 | 43 | 17 | 58 | 83 | 32 | 52 | 41 | 59 | 80 | | |

7. Referring to the Dunedin rainfall data from the previous exercise:

    a. Use the Excel function **Max** to compute the largest monthly rainfall in each of the years 1980–1999.

    b. Compute the largest monthly rainfall for *all* of the months in the table.

8.

    a. Complete the following spreadsheet, showing how much will be in your bank account if you deposit an initial deposit (cell B2) today and it draws annual interest given in cell B1.

    b. Graph the results of the bank account.

|    | A | B |
|----|---|---|
| 1  | Interest | 8% |
| 2  | Initial deposit | $155 |
| 3  | | |
| 4  | Year | In bank account |
| 5  | 0 | |
| 6  | 1 | |
| 7  | 2 | |
| 8  | 3 | |
| 9  | 4 | |
| 10 | 5 | |

## Overview

In this short chapter, we'll discuss the basics of Excel graphing, assuming that—by and large—you already know how to make a chart in Excel.[1] We will also discuss some less well-known techniques that have to do with charts:

- Making a graph with noncontiguous data series

---

[1] In "Excelese," graphs are called "charts." We will use both words interchangeably.

- Changing the axis parameters of a chart
- Making a chart where the title changes when the data changes

## 25.1. The Basics of Excel Charts

Every Excel chart has its origins in the data on a spreadsheet.

| | A | B | C | D |
|---|---|---|---|---|
| 1 | MERCK & CO. 1991–2000 | | | |
| 2 | | Dividends | Purchase of treasury stock | Proceeds from exercise of stock options |
| 3 | 1991 | 893 | 184 | 48 |
| 4 | 1992 | 1,064 | 863 | 52 |
| 5 | 1993 | 1,174 | 371 | 83 |
| 6 | 1994 | 1,434 | 705 | 139 |
| 7 | 1995 | 1,540 | 1,571 | 264 |
| 8 | 1996 | 1,729 | 2,493 | 442 |
| 9 | 1997 | 2,040 | 2,573 | 413 |
| 10 | 1998 | 2,253 | 3,626 | 490 |
| 11 | 1999 | 2,590 | 3,582 | 323 |
| 12 | 2000 | 2,798 | 3,545 | 641 |

To create a graph that shows the dividends paid each year, we mark the relevant data and then go to **Insert|Charts|Scatter**.

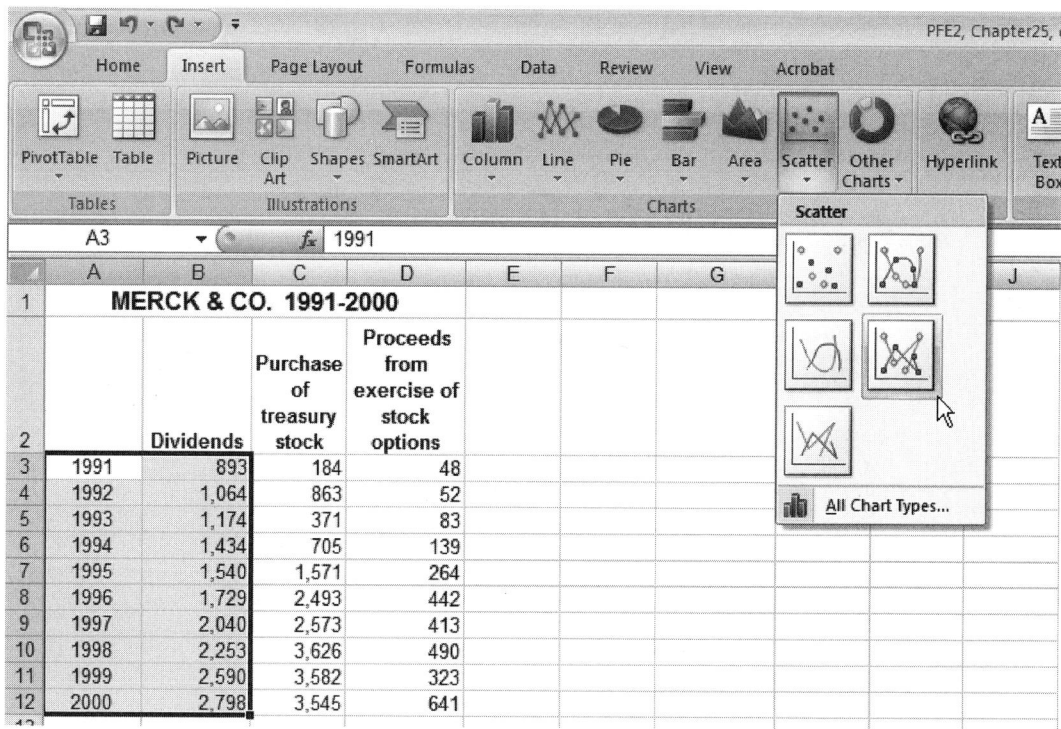

We've chosen the XY Scatter Chart option that connects the data with lines. Clicking this option creates our chart.

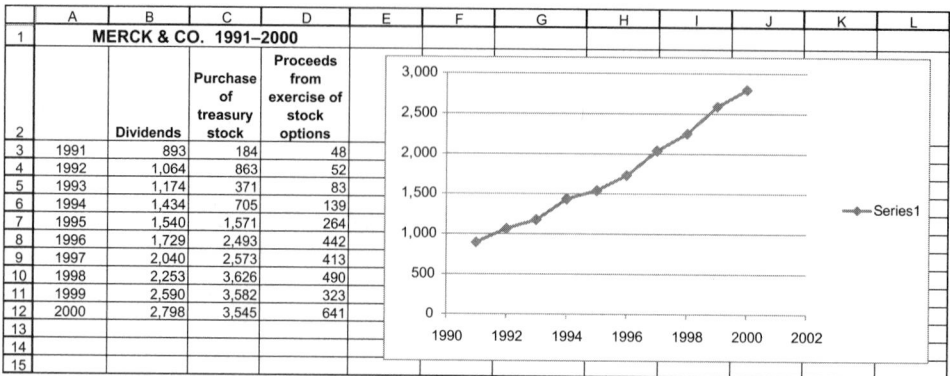

This isn't bad, but we want to make a few additions and corrections:

- We'll get rid of the "Series 1" legend by simply clicking on it and deleting.
- We want to adjust the *x*-axis so that it goes from 1991 to 2000 and not—as in the case above—from 1990 to 2002.
- We want to add titles to the axes and a title to the chart as a whole.

We start by double-clicking on the chart itself. This brings up the **Chart Tools** toolbar. From this toolbar we choose the circled option.

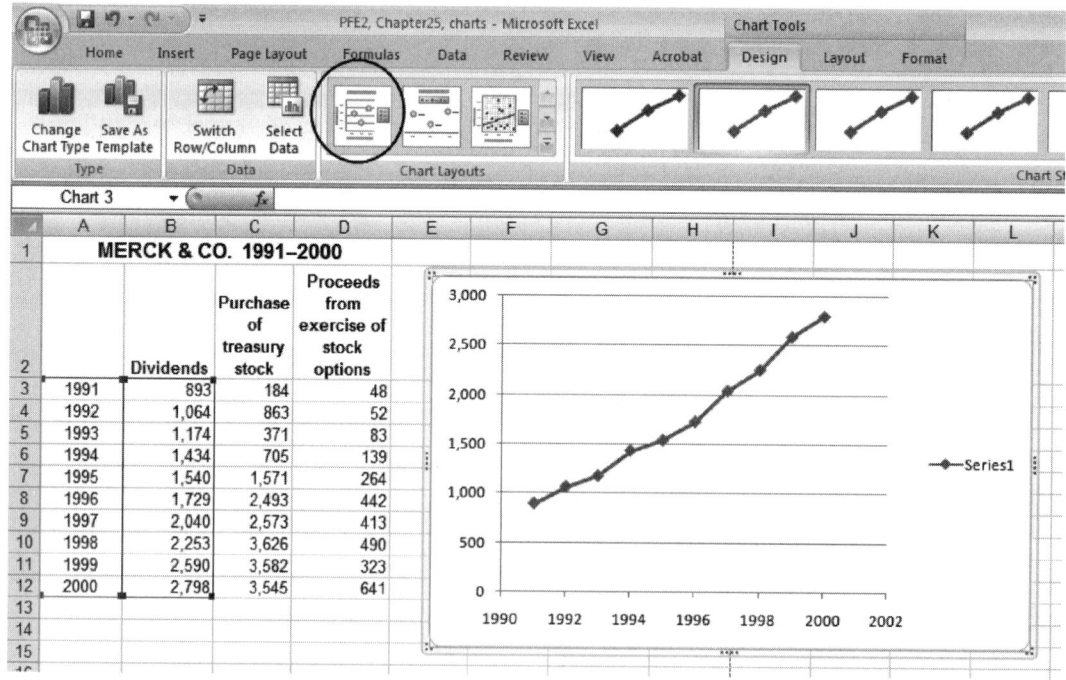

This makes the chart look like this.

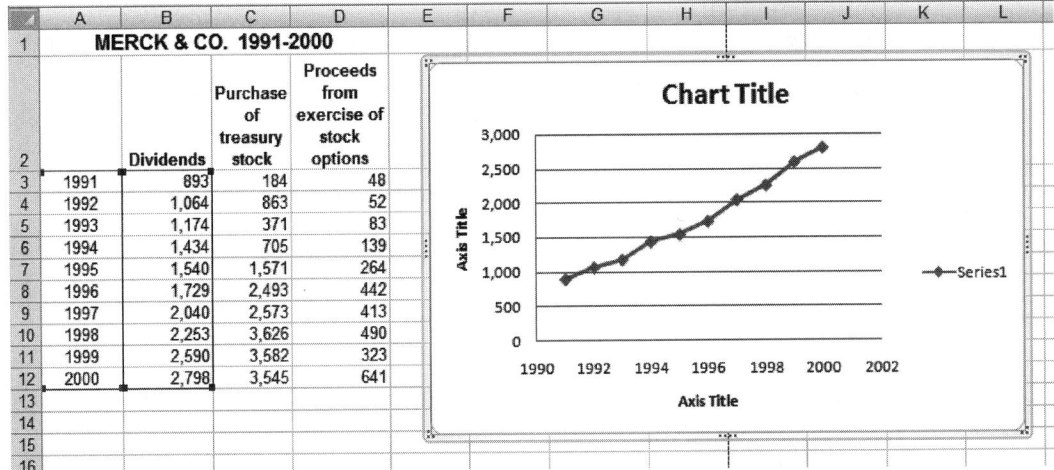

You can now click on all the titles and change them appropriately (while you're at it, get rid of the **Series 1** legend).

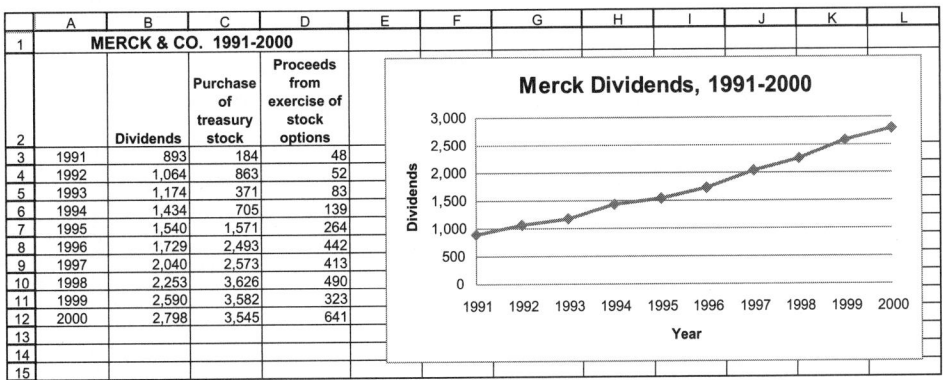

To change the format of the *x*-axis, click on the axes numbers (note the box around the axis numbers in the illustration below). Then right-click on the box and choose **Format Axis**.

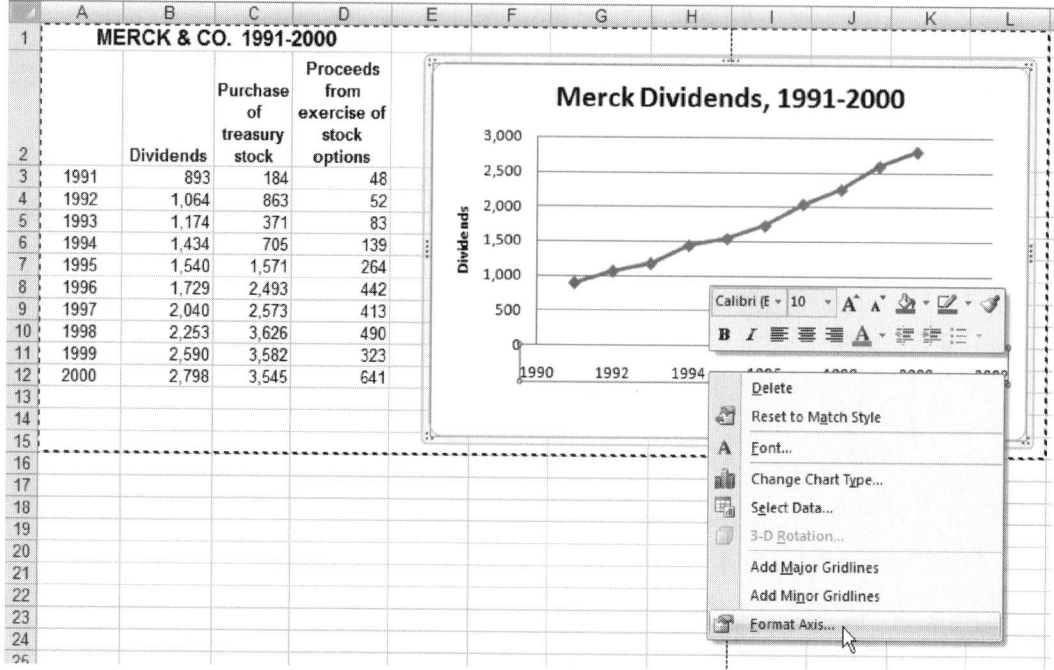

This brings up the following menu, to which we've already made the changes we want—changing the axes years from 1991 to 2000:

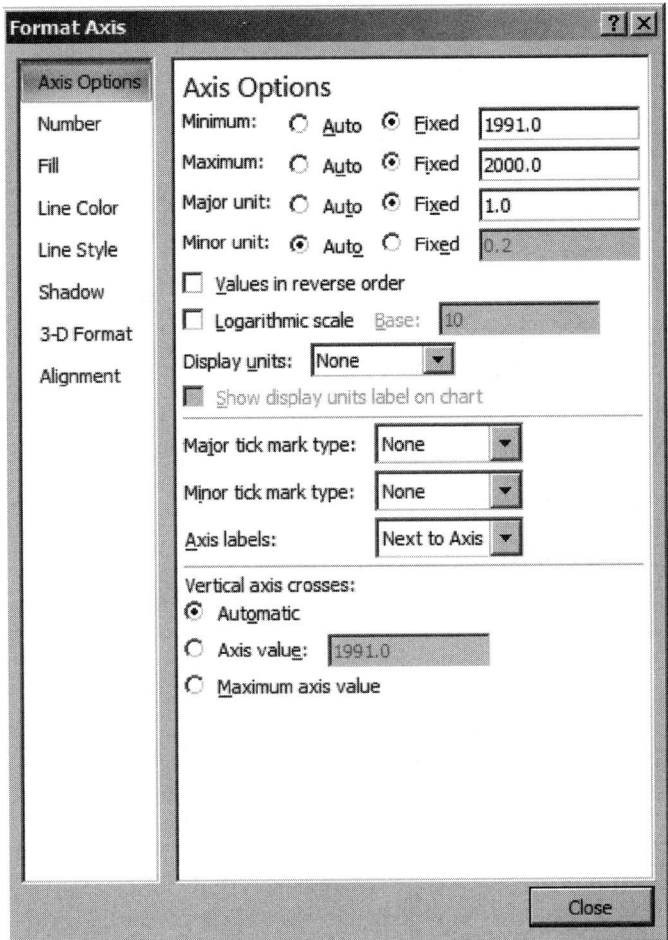

Here's the resulting chart.

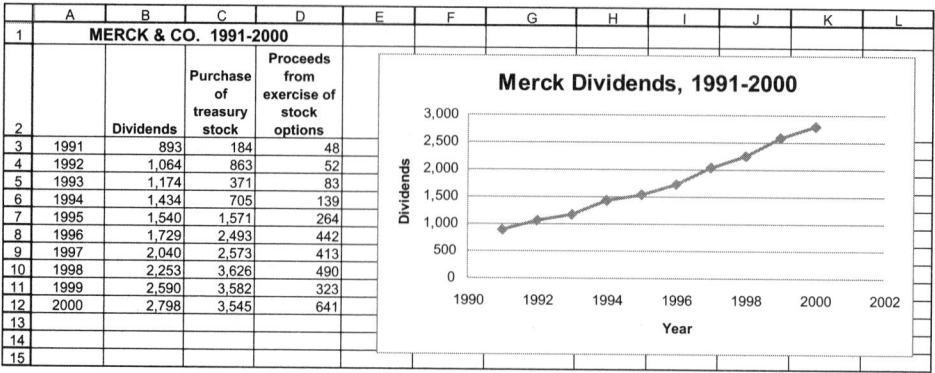

| | A | B | C | D | E | F | G | H | I | J | K | L |
|---|---|---|---|---|---|---|---|---|---|---|---|---|
| 1 | MERCK & CO. 1991-2000 | | | | | | | | | | | |
| 2 | | Dividends | Purchase of treasury stock | Proceeds from exercise of stock options | | | | | | | | |
| 3 | 1991 | 893 | 184 | 48 | | | | | | | | |
| 4 | 1992 | 1,064 | 863 | 52 | | | | | | | | |
| 5 | 1993 | 1,174 | 371 | 83 | | | | | | | | |
| 6 | 1994 | 1,434 | 705 | 139 | | | | | | | | |
| 7 | 1995 | 1,540 | 1,571 | 264 | | | | | | | | |
| 8 | 1996 | 1,729 | 2,493 | 442 | | | | | | | | |
| 9 | 1997 | 2,040 | 2,573 | 413 | | | | | | | | |
| 10 | 1998 | 2,253 | 3,626 | 490 | | | | | | | | |
| 11 | 1999 | 2,590 | 3,582 | 323 | | | | | | | | |
| 12 | 2000 | 2,798 | 3,545 | 641 | | | | | | | | |
| 13 | | | | | | | | | | | | |
| 14 | | | | | | | | | | | | |
| 15 | | | | | | | | | | | | |

There are many options left, but we trust that you'll figure these out for yourself.

## 25.2. Creative Use of Legends

If you build your XY chart with data that includes legends, then Excel will generally transfer them in the proper way to the graph. Here's an example: We've marked the data to include the column headings.

| | A | B | C | D | E |
|---|---|---|---|---|---|
| 1 | MERCK & CO. 1991-2000 | | | | |
| 2 | | Dividends | Purchase of treasury stock | Proceeds from exercise of stock options | |
| 3 | 1991 | 893 | 184 | 48 | |
| 4 | 1992 | 1,064 | 863 | 52 | |
| 5 | 1993 | 1,174 | 371 | 83 | |
| 6 | 1994 | 1,434 | 705 | 139 | |
| 7 | 1995 | 1,540 | 1,571 | 264 | |
| 8 | 1996 | 1,729 | 2,493 | 442 | |
| 9 | 1997 | 2,040 | 2,573 | 413 | |
| 10 | 1998 | 2,253 | 3,626 | 490 | |
| 11 | 1999 | 2,590 | 3,582 | 323 | |
| 12 | 2000 | 2,798 | 3,545 | 641 | |
| 13 | | | | | |
| 14 | | | | | |

Here's the resulting graph after a little massaging.

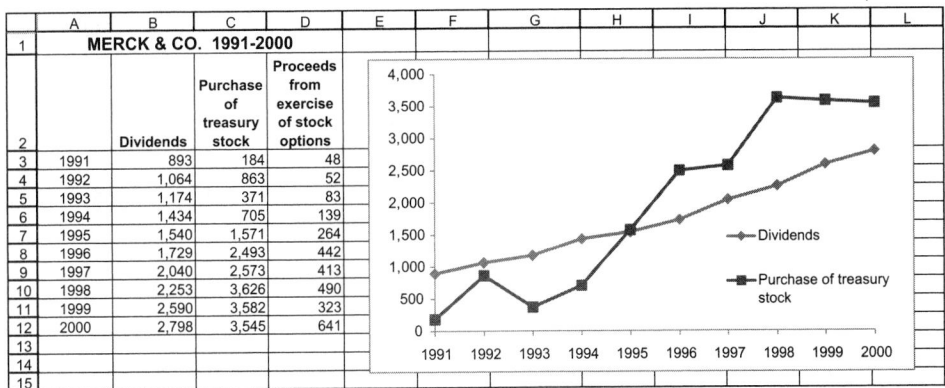

| | A | B | C | D | E | F | G | H | I | J | K | L |
|---|---|---|---|---|---|---|---|---|---|---|---|---|
| 1 | MERCK & CO. 1991-2000 | | | | | | | | | | | |
| 2 | | Dividends | Purchase of treasury stock | Proceeds from exercise of stock options | | | | | | | | |
| 3 | 1991 | 893 | 184 | 48 | | | | | | | | |
| 4 | 1992 | 1,064 | 863 | 52 | | | | | | | | |
| 5 | 1993 | 1,174 | 371 | 83 | | | | | | | | |
| 6 | 1994 | 1,434 | 705 | 139 | | | | | | | | |
| 7 | 1995 | 1,540 | 1,571 | 264 | | | | | | | | |
| 8 | 1996 | 1,729 | 2,493 | 442 | | | | | | | | |
| 9 | 1997 | 2,040 | 2,573 | 413 | | | | | | | | |
| 10 | 1998 | 2,253 | 3,626 | 490 | | | | | | | | |
| 11 | 1999 | 2,590 | 3,582 | 323 | | | | | | | | |
| 12 | 2000 | 2,798 | 3,545 | 641 | | | | | | | | |
| 13 | | | | | | | | | | | | |
| 14 | | | | | | | | | | | | |
| 15 | | | | | | | | | | | | |

# 25.3. Graphing Noncontiguous Data

Suppose you want to make a graph of columns A, C, and D of the Merck data. To mark these three columns:

- Mark the first column (that is, click the left mouse button and "paint" cells A3:A12).
- Press the [Ctrl] key and mark columns C and D (again, clicking the left mouse button).

At this point your spreadsheet looks like this.

| | A | B | C | D |
|---|---|---|---|---|
| 1 | MERCK & CO. 1991-2000 | | | |
| 2 | | Dividends | Purchase of treasury stock | Proceeds from exercise of stock options |
| 3 | 1991 | 893 | 184 | 48 |
| 4 | 1992 | 1,064 | 863 | 52 |
| 5 | 1993 | 1,174 | 371 | 83 |
| 6 | 1994 | 1,434 | 705 | 139 |
| 7 | 1995 | 1,540 | 1,571 | 264 |
| 8 | 1996 | 1,729 | 2,493 | 442 |
| 9 | 1997 | 2,040 | 2,573 | 413 |
| 10 | 1998 | 2,253 | 3,626 | 490 |
| 11 | 1999 | 2,590 | 3,582 | 323 |
| 12 | 2000 | 2,798 | 3,545 | 641 |
| 13 | | | | |

You can now follow the regular graphing procedure to create the following chart.

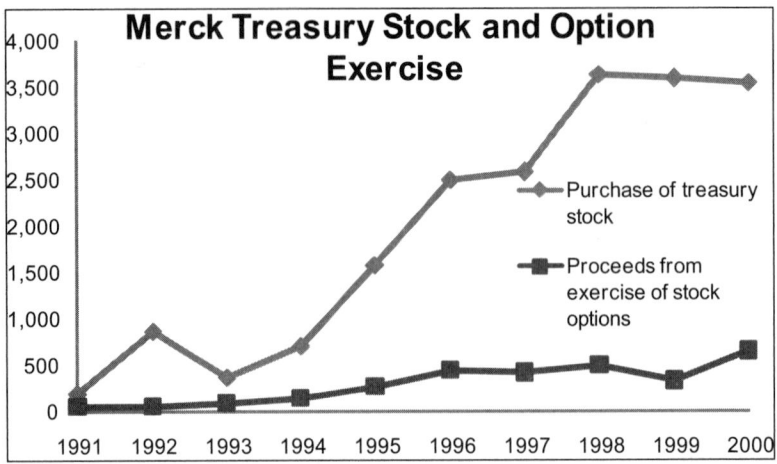

## 25.4. Line Charts with Titles on the *x*-Axis

Excel offers a bewildering variety of chart types. In this section we will show you the **line chart**, leaving other variations for you to explore. We will use data for the average minimum and maximum temperatures in New York City. We want to create a chart with the month labels on the *x*-axis.

| | A | B | C | D | E | F | G | H | I | J | K | L | M |
|---|---|---|---|---|---|---|---|---|---|---|---|---|---|
| 1 | | AVERAGE MONTHLY MAXIMUM AND MINIMUM TEMPERATURES—NEW YORK CITY | | | | | | | | | | | |
| 2 | | Jan | Feb | Mar | Apr | May | Jun | Jul | Aug | Sep | Oct | Nov | Dec |
| 3 | Avg max temp (F) | 38 | 40 | 50 | 61 | 72 | 80 | 85 | 84 | 76 | 65 | 54 | 43 |
| 4 | Avg min temp (F) | 25 | 27 | 35 | 44 | 54 | 63 | 68 | 67 | 60 | 50 | 41 | 31 |
| 5 | | | | | | | | | | | | | |
| 6 | | | | | | | | | | | | | |
| 7 | | | | | | | | | | | | | |
| 8 | | | | | | | | | | | | | |
| 9 | | | | | | | | | | | | | |
| 10 | | | | | | | | | | | | | |
| 11 | | | | | | | | | | | | | |
| 12 | | | | | | | | | | | | | |
| 13 | | | | | | | | | | | | | |
| 14 | | | | | | | | | | | | | |
| 15 | | | | | | | | | | | | | |
| 16 | | | | | | | | | | | | | |
| 17 | | | | | | | | | | | | | |
| 18 | | | | | | | | | | | | | |
| 19 | | | | | | | | | | | | | |
| 20 | | | | | | | | | | | | | |
| 21 | | | | | | | | | | | | | |
| 22 | | | | | | | | | | | | | |
| 23 | | | | | | | | | | | | | |

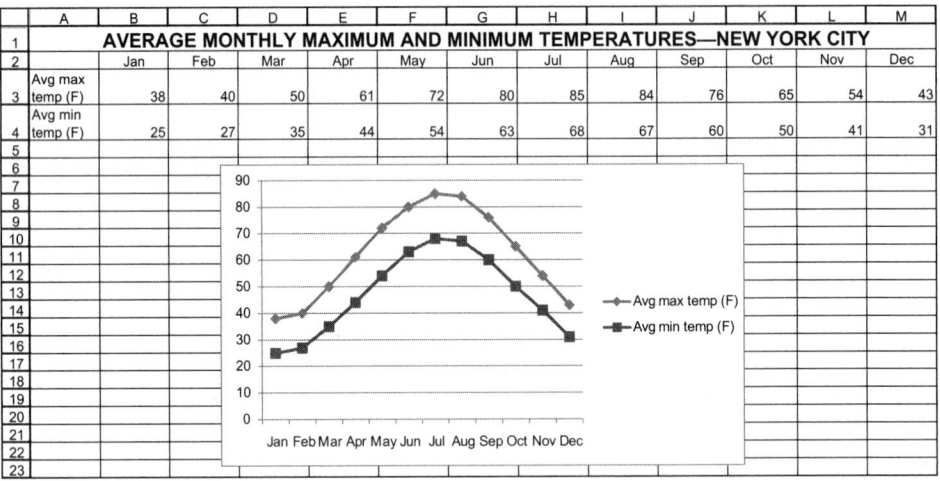

To construct the chart, first mark the data you want to graph, including the *x*-axis data and the months. Then go to **Insert|Charts|Line** and choose the appropriate type of graph.

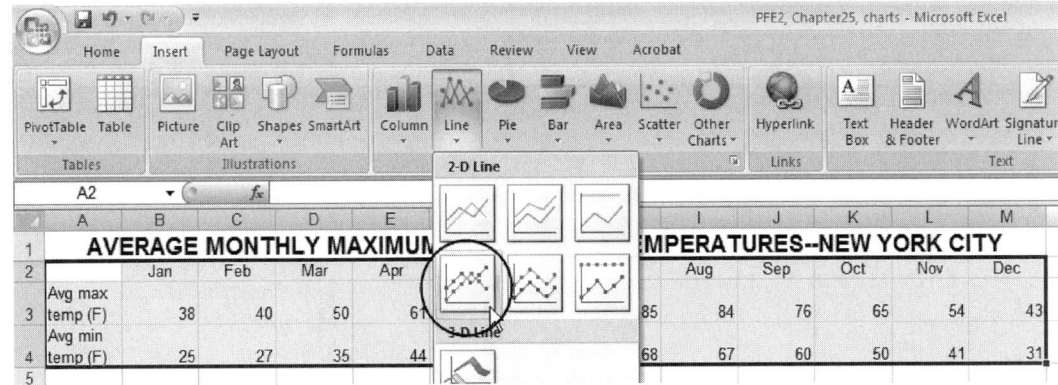

Clicking the left mouse button does the rest.

## What's the Difference between a Line Chart and an XY (Scatter) Chart?

Line charts use equal spacing for the *x*-axis legend, whereas XY charts space the *x*-axis legend depending on the distance between the points. The following example explains this perhaps obscure sentence.

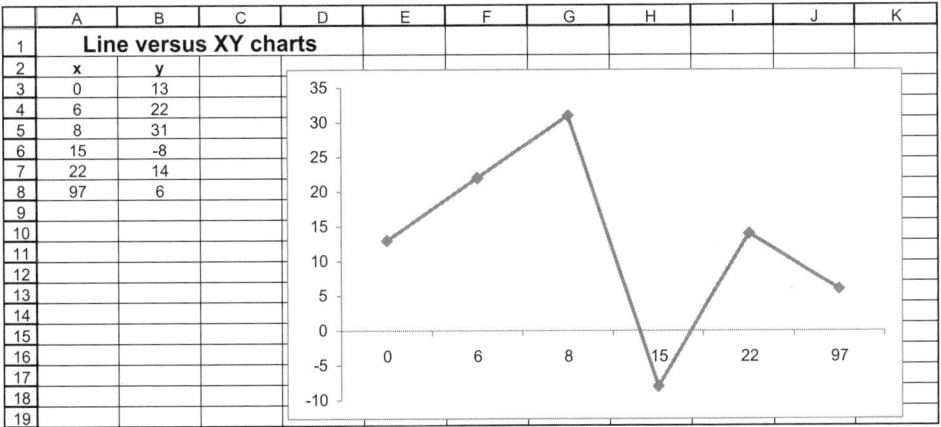

Note that even though the *x*-axis values are very unevenly spaced (0, 6, 8, 15, 22, 97), the line chart puts them at equal intervals on the *x*-axis. It is only the XY (Scatter) chart that spaces the *x*-axis labels according to their values.

## Creating the Previous Chart

There are two ways to create the previous chart.

The "tricky way" is to eliminate the "*x*" in cell A2 and to mark the range A2:B8. Going to **Insert|Charts|Line** does the rest.

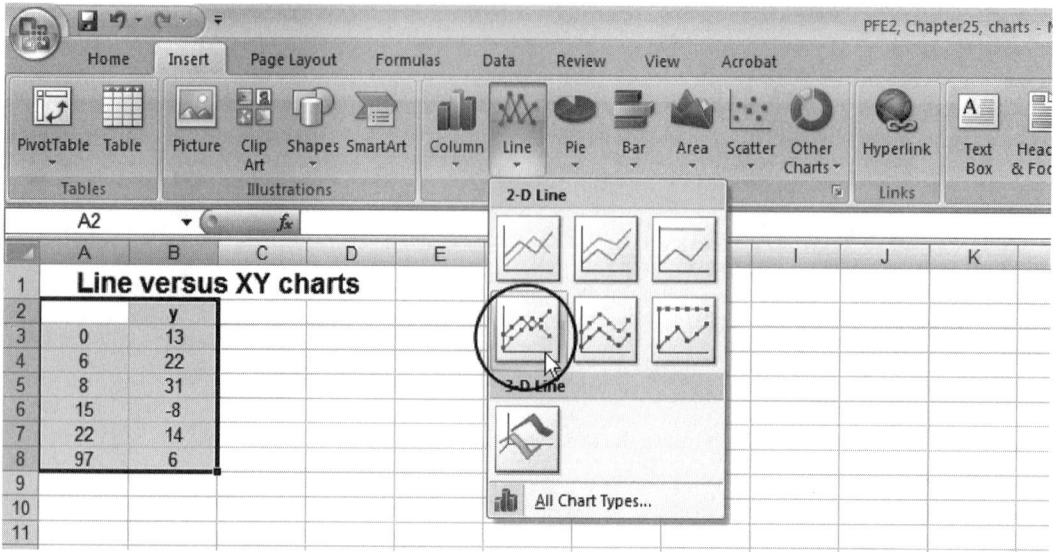

The nontricky way is to first choose only the y data in B3:B8. Creating the line chart in the usual fashion gives you the following.

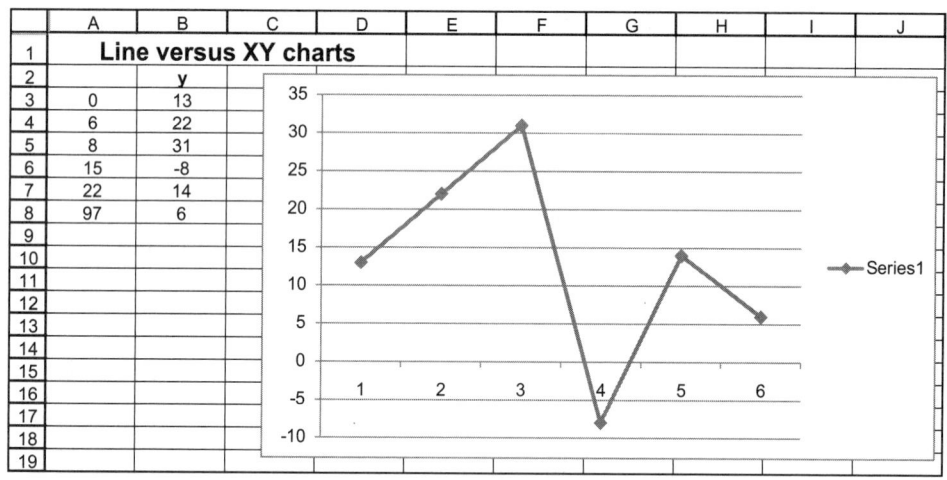

Now double-click the chart and go to **Select Data**.

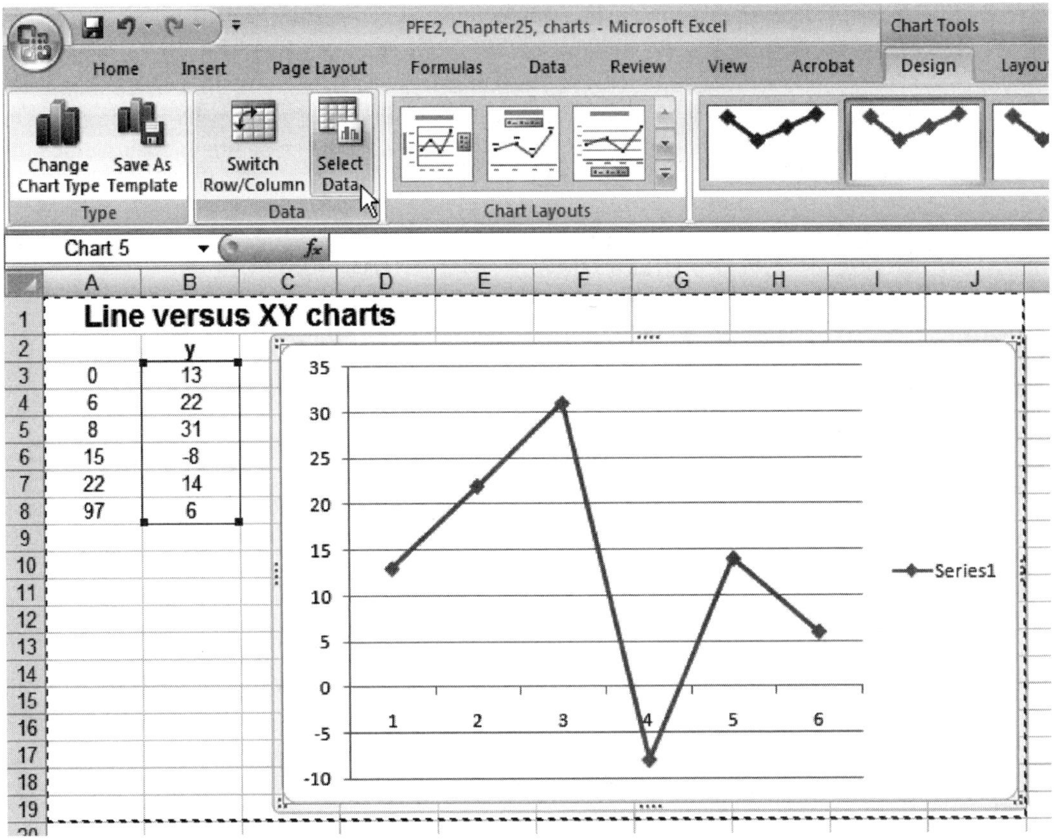

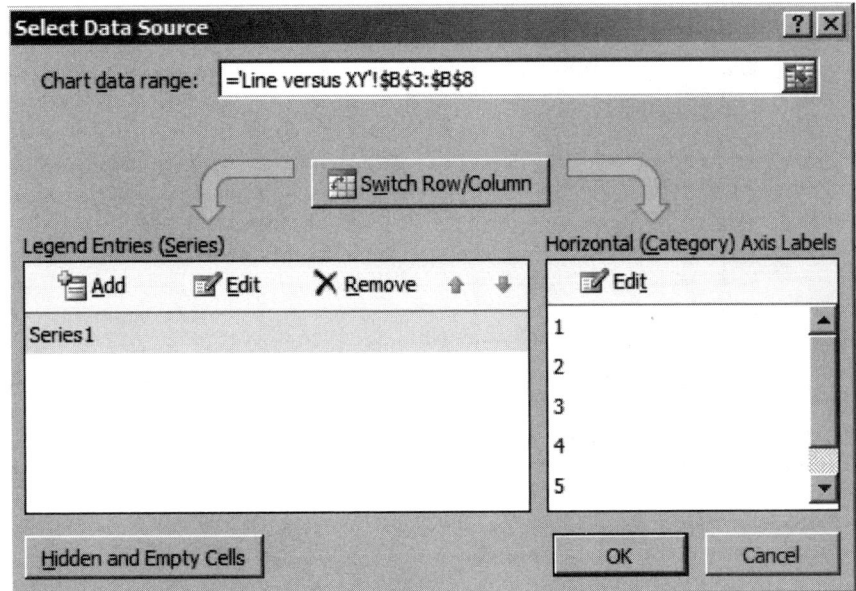

In the resulting dialog box, choose to edit the *x*-axis labels and introduce the data in A2:A8.

## 25.5. Graph Titles That Update

This slightly more advanced section makes use of the **Text** function, which is discussed in Chapter 26. You want to have the graph title change when a parameter on the spreadsheet changes. For example, in the next spreadsheet, you want the graph title to indicate the growth rate.

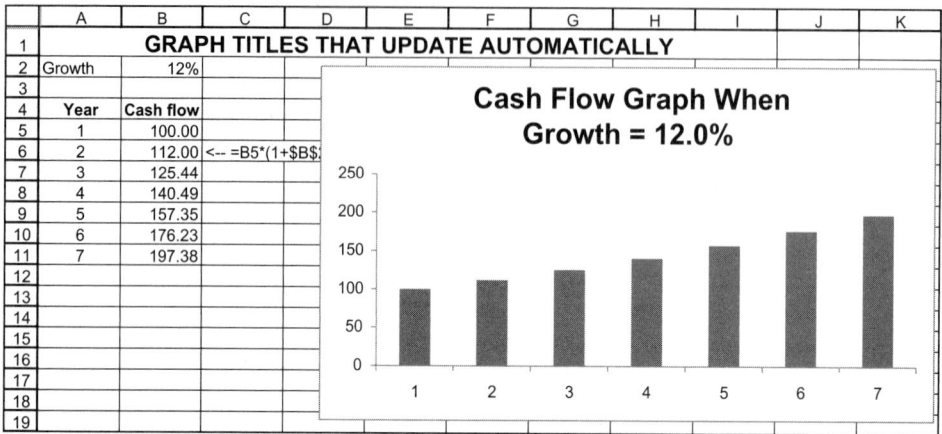

Once we have completed the necessary steps explained below, a change in the growth rate will change both the graph *and* its title.

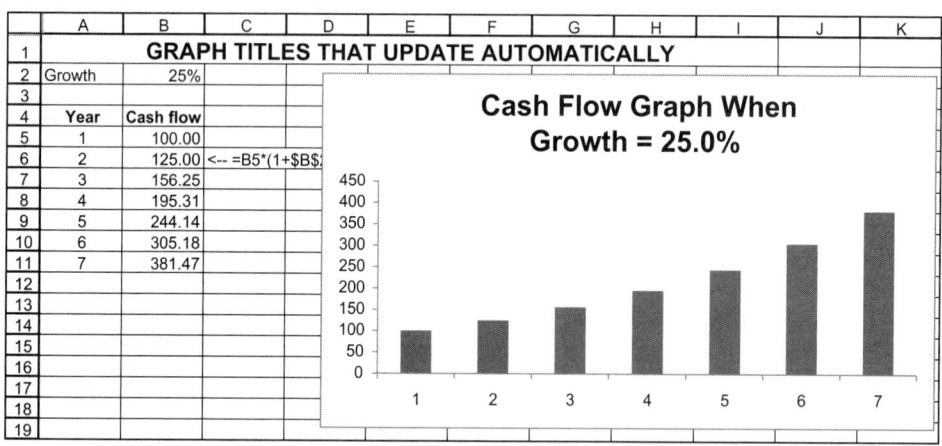

To make graph titles update automatically, carry out the following steps:

- Create the graph you want in the format you want it. Give the graph a "proxy title." (It makes no difference what; you're going to eliminate it soon.) At this stage your graph might look like this.

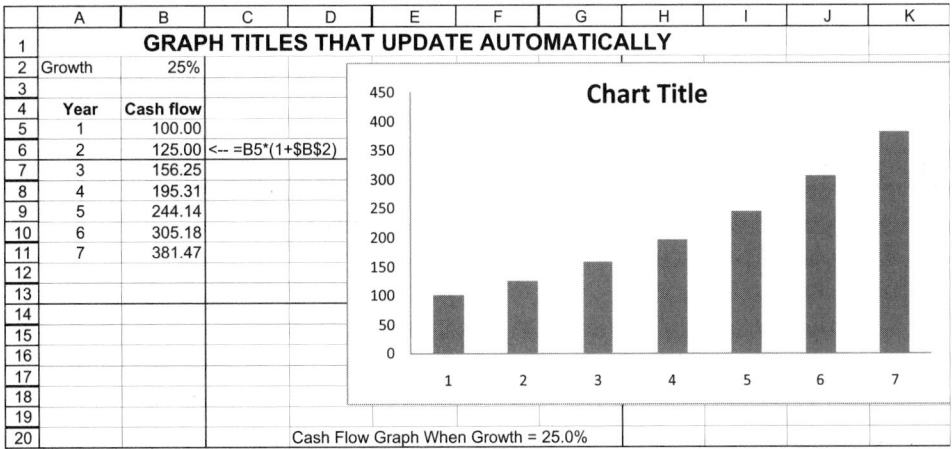

- Create the title you want in a cell. In the example above, cell D20 contains the formula: =“Cash Flow Graph when Growth = ”&TEXT(B2,”0.0%”).
- Click on the graph title to mark it, and then go to the formula bar and insert an equals sign to indicate a formula. Then **point** at cell D20 with the formula and click [Enter]. In the picture below, you see the chart title highlighted and in the formula bar “=Titles that update!$D$20” indicating the title of the graph. Note that “Titles that update” is the name of the spreadsheet.

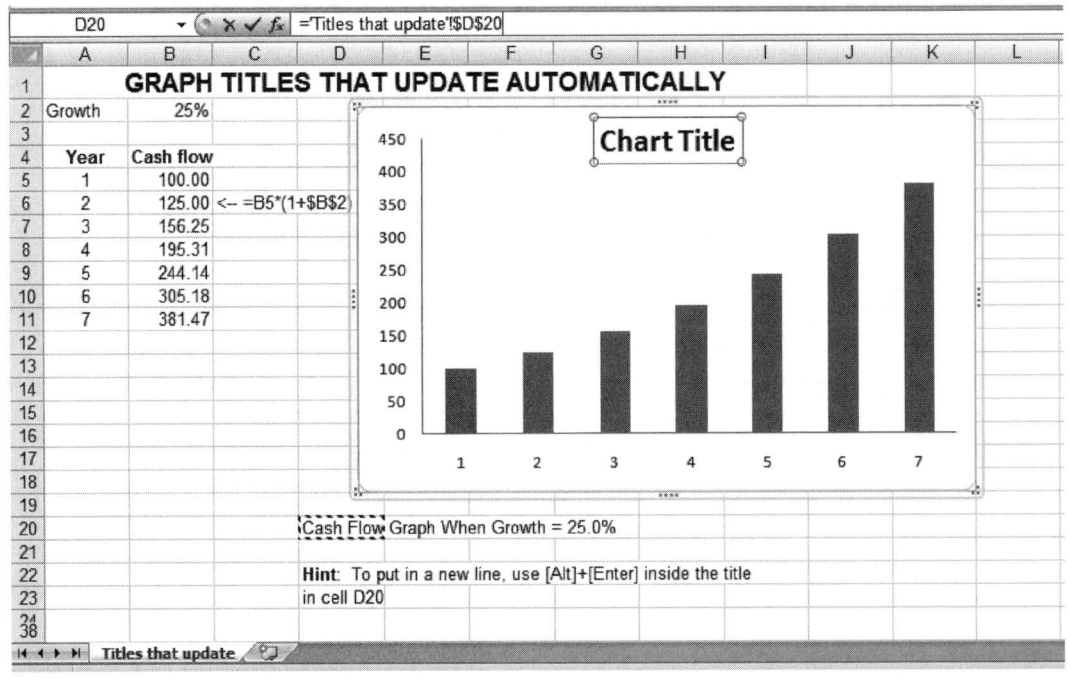

# Summary

There's lots more you can do with Excel charts, but we've covered the essentials. The exercises to this chapter will show you some more variations.

## EXERCISES

**Note**: All data for the exercises are on the CD-ROM that accompanies *Principles of Finance with Excel*.

1. The CD gives the monthly prices for the Dutch grocery chain Ahold from April 1991 through August 2004. Graph these prices so that the resulting spreadsheet looks like the following spreadsheet.

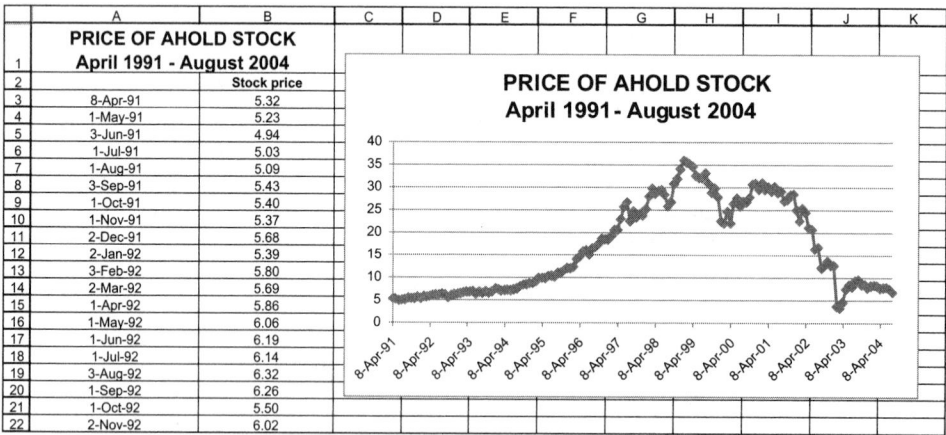

2. Using the data for Ahold from the previous exercise, determine the monthly stock returns and graph them. The monthly return for a stock that has price $P_t$ in month $t$ and price $P_{t-1}$ in month $t-1$ is $(P_t / P_{t-1}) - 1$ (When you compute the returns, you'll have "noncontiguous data," so you'll have to use the technique described in Section 25.3).

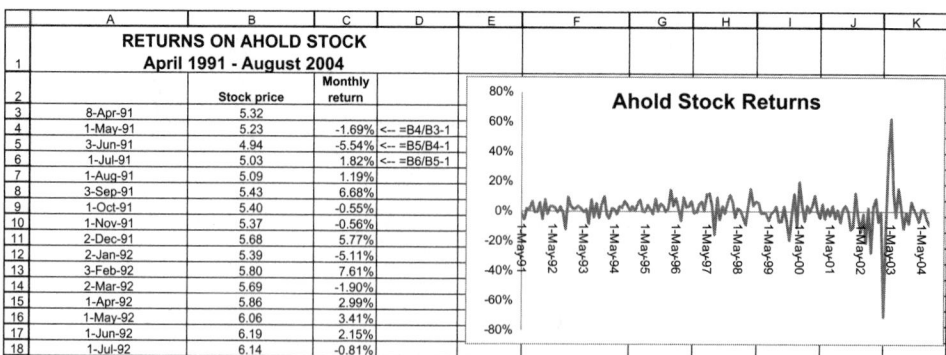

3. The CD with the book gives the prices for Ahold and for the S&P 500. Use these data to produce the following graph (see note following the graph).

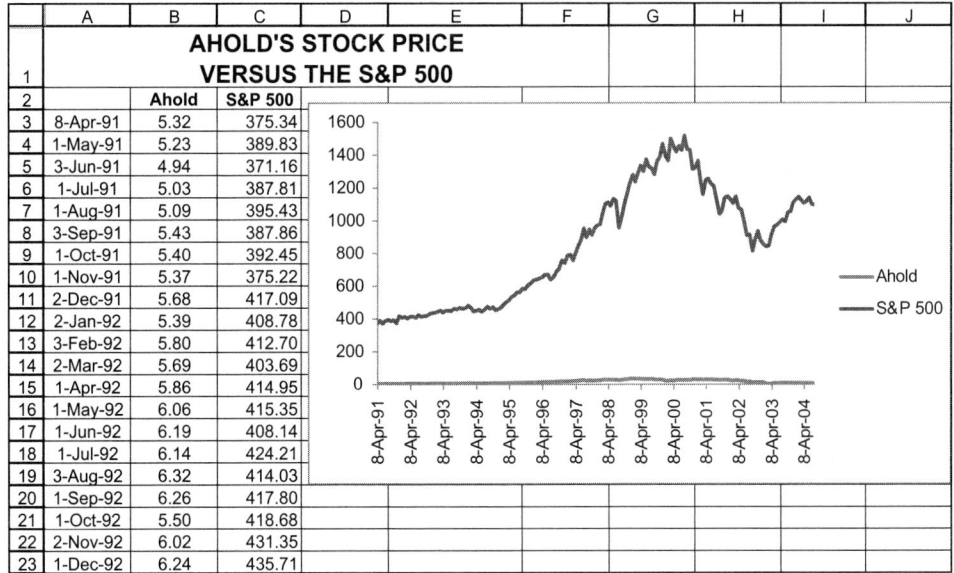

|   | A | B | C | D | E | F | G | H | I | J |
|---|---|---|---|---|---|---|---|---|---|---|
| 1 |   | **AHOLD'S STOCK PRICE** | | | | | | | | |
|   |   | **VERSUS THE S&P 500** | | | | | | | | |
| 2 |   | **Ahold** | **S&P 500** | | | | | | | |
| 3 | 8-Apr-91 | 5.32 | 375.34 | | | | | | | |
| 4 | 1-May-91 | 5.23 | 389.83 | | | | | | | |
| 5 | 3-Jun-91 | 4.94 | 371.16 | | | | | | | |
| 6 | 1-Jul-91 | 5.03 | 387.81 | | | | | | | |
| 7 | 1-Aug-91 | 5.09 | 395.43 | | | | | | | |
| 8 | 3-Sep-91 | 5.43 | 387.86 | | | | | | | |
| 9 | 1-Oct-91 | 5.40 | 392.45 | | | | | | | |
| 10 | 1-Nov-91 | 5.37 | 375.22 | | | | | | | |
| 11 | 2-Dec-91 | 5.68 | 417.09 | | | | | | | |
| 12 | 2-Jan-92 | 5.39 | 408.78 | | | | | | | |
| 13 | 3-Feb-92 | 5.80 | 412.70 | | | | | | | |
| 14 | 2-Mar-92 | 5.69 | 403.69 | | | | | | | |
| 15 | 1-Apr-92 | 5.86 | 414.95 | | | | | | | |
| 16 | 1-May-92 | 6.06 | 415.35 | | | | | | | |
| 17 | 1-Jun-92 | 6.19 | 408.14 | | | | | | | |
| 18 | 1-Jul-92 | 6.14 | 424.21 | | | | | | | |
| 19 | 3-Aug-92 | 6.32 | 414.03 | | | | | | | |
| 20 | 1-Sep-92 | 6.26 | 417.80 | | | | | | | |
| 21 | 1-Oct-92 | 5.50 | 418.68 | | | | | | | |
| 22 | 2-Nov-92 | 6.02 | 431.35 | | | | | | | |
| 23 | 1-Dec-92 | 6.24 | 435.71 | | | | | | | |

*Note:* This graph is obviously unsatisfactory—Ahold's price is so much less than the S&P's that the Ahold price series appears to be zero. See the next exercise for one solution to this problem.

4. Transform the S&P and Ahold price data so that the beginning price of each is 100 and graph these series.

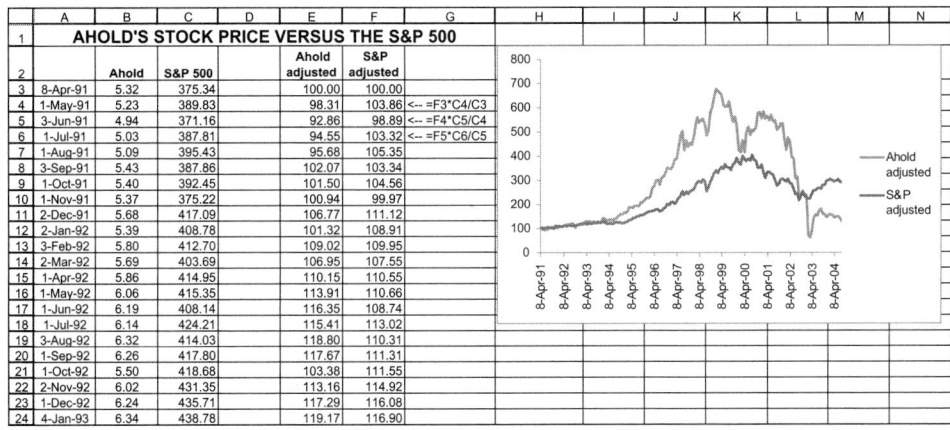

|   | A | B | C | D | E | F | G | H | I | J | K | L | M | N |
|---|---|---|---|---|---|---|---|---|---|---|---|---|---|---|
| 1 | **AHOLD'S STOCK PRICE VERSUS THE S&P 500** | | | | | | | | | | | | | |
| 2 |   | **Ahold** | **S&P 500** | | **Ahold adjusted** | **S&P adjusted** | | | | | | | | |
| 3 | 8-Apr-91 | 5.32 | 375.34 | | 100.00 | 100.00 | | | | | | | | |
| 4 | 1-May-91 | 5.23 | 389.83 | | 98.31 | 103.86 | <-- =F3*C4/C3 | | | | | | | |
| 5 | 3-Jun-91 | 4.94 | 371.16 | | 92.86 | 98.89 | <-- =F4*C5/C4 | | | | | | | |
| 6 | 1-Jul-91 | 5.03 | 387.81 | | 94.55 | 103.32 | <-- =F5*C6/C5 | | | | | | | |
| 7 | 1-Aug-91 | 5.09 | 395.43 | | 95.68 | 105.35 | | | | | | | | |
| 8 | 3-Sep-91 | 5.43 | 387.86 | | 102.07 | 103.34 | | | | | | | | |
| 9 | 1-Oct-91 | 5.40 | 392.45 | | 101.50 | 104.56 | | | | | | | | |
| 10 | 1-Nov-91 | 5.37 | 375.22 | | 100.94 | 99.97 | | | | | | | | |
| 11 | 2-Dec-91 | 5.68 | 417.09 | | 106.77 | 111.12 | | | | | | | | |
| 12 | 2-Jan-92 | 5.39 | 408.78 | | 101.32 | 108.91 | | | | | | | | |
| 13 | 3-Feb-92 | 5.80 | 412.70 | | 109.02 | 109.95 | | | | | | | | |
| 14 | 2-Mar-92 | 5.69 | 403.69 | | 106.95 | 107.55 | | | | | | | | |
| 15 | 1-Apr-92 | 5.86 | 414.95 | | 110.15 | 110.55 | | | | | | | | |
| 16 | 1-May-92 | 6.06 | 415.35 | | 113.91 | 110.66 | | | | | | | | |
| 17 | 1-Jun-92 | 6.19 | 408.14 | | 116.35 | 108.74 | | | | | | | | |
| 18 | 1-Jul-92 | 6.14 | 424.21 | | 115.41 | 113.02 | | | | | | | | |
| 19 | 3-Aug-92 | 6.32 | 414.03 | | 118.80 | 110.31 | | | | | | | | |
| 20 | 1-Sep-92 | 6.26 | 417.80 | | 117.67 | 111.31 | | | | | | | | |
| 21 | 1-Oct-92 | 5.50 | 418.68 | | 103.38 | 111.55 | | | | | | | | |
| 22 | 2-Nov-92 | 6.02 | 431.35 | | 113.16 | 114.92 | | | | | | | | |
| 23 | 1-Dec-92 | 6.24 | 435.71 | | 117.29 | 116.08 | | | | | | | | |
| 24 | 4-Jan-93 | 6.34 | 438.78 | | 119.17 | 116.90 | | | | | | | | |

5. You want to graph the function $y = ax^3 - 2x^2 + x - 16$. The variable $a$ can take on a variety of values (in the example below, $a = 0.4$). Make a graph of this function with a title that indicates the value of $a$, as illustrated below. (You may want to refer to Section 25.4.)

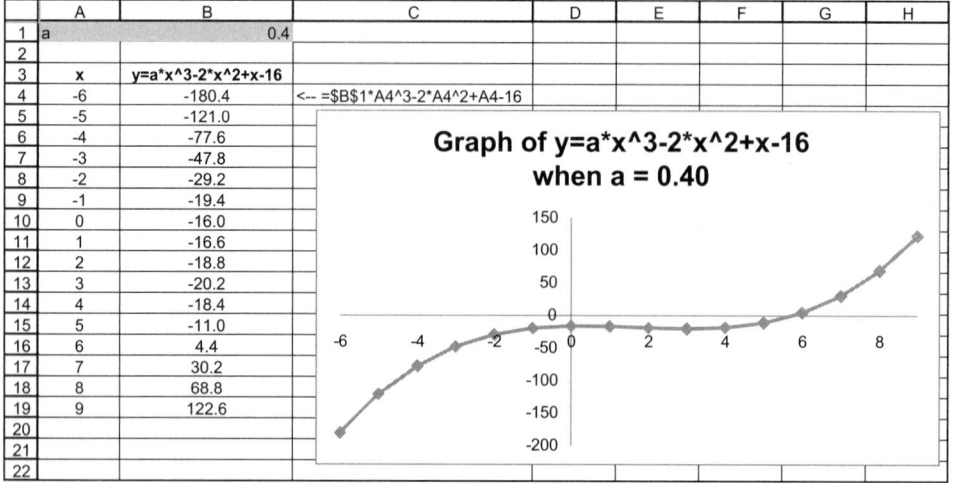

|    | A | B | C | D | E | F | G | H |
|----|---|---|---|---|---|---|---|---|
| 1  | a | 0.4 | | | | | | |
| 2  | | | | | | | | |
| 3  | x | y=a*x^3-2*x^2+x-16 | | | | | | |
| 4  | -6 | -180.4 | <-- =$B$1*A4^3-2*A4^2+A4-16 | | | | | |
| 5  | -5 | -121.0 | | | | | | |
| 6  | -4 | -77.6 | | | | | | |
| 7  | -3 | -47.8 | | | | | | |
| 8  | -2 | -29.2 | | | | | | |
| 9  | -1 | -19.4 | | | | | | |
| 10 | 0 | -16.0 | | | | | | |
| 11 | 1 | -16.6 | | | | | | |
| 12 | 2 | -18.8 | | | | | | |
| 13 | 3 | -20.2 | | | | | | |
| 14 | 4 | -18.4 | | | | | | |
| 15 | 5 | -11.0 | | | | | | |
| 16 | 6 | 4.4 | | | | | | |
| 17 | 7 | 30.2 | | | | | | |
| 18 | 8 | 68.8 | | | | | | |
| 19 | 9 | 122.6 | | | | | | |
| 20 | | | | | | | | |
| 21 | | | | | | | | |
| 22 | | | | | | | | |

Graph of y=a*x^3-2*x^2+x-16 when a = 0.40

6. The CD that comes with this book contains a spreadsheet with monthly rainfall in San Diego from 1850 to 2008. Create the graph shown below.

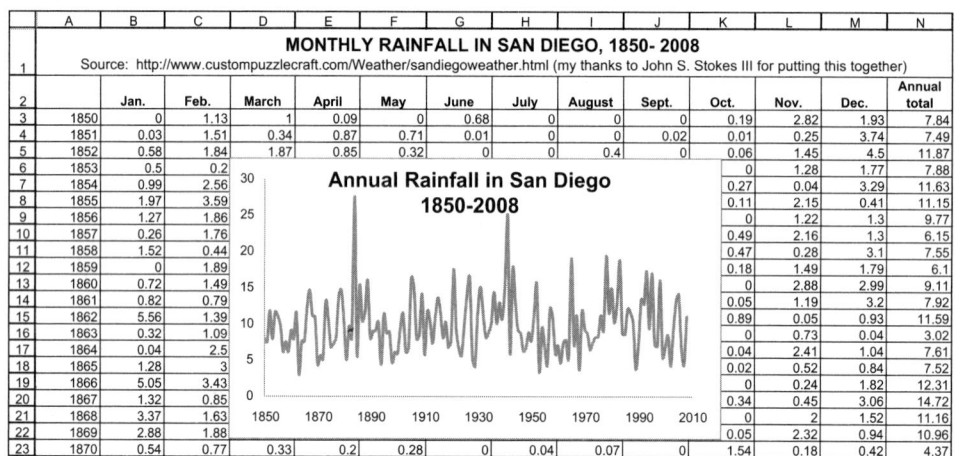

| | A | B | C | D | E | F | G | H | I | J | K | L | M | N |
|---|---|---|---|---|---|---|---|---|---|---|---|---|---|---|
| 1 | MONTHLY RAINFALL IN SAN DIEGO, 1850- 2008 Source: http://www.custompuzzlecraft.com/Weather/sandiegoweather.html (my thanks to John S. Stokes III for putting this together) | | | | | | | | | | | | | |
| 2 | | Jan. | Feb. | March | April | May | June | July | August | Sept. | Oct. | Nov. | Dec. | Annual total |
| 3 | 1850 | 0 | 1.13 | 1 | 0.09 | 0 | 0.68 | 0 | 0 | 0 | 0.19 | 2.82 | 1.93 | 7.84 |
| 4 | 1851 | 0.03 | 1.51 | 0.34 | 0.87 | 0.71 | 0.01 | 0 | 0 | 0.02 | 0.01 | 0.25 | 3.74 | 7.49 |
| 5 | 1852 | 0.58 | 1.84 | 1.87 | 0.85 | 0.32 | 0 | 0 | 0.4 | 0 | 0.06 | 1.45 | 4.5 | 11.87 |
| 6 | 1853 | 0.5 | 0.2 | | | | | | | | 0 | 1.28 | 1.77 | 7.88 |
| 7 | 1854 | 0.99 | 2.56 | | | | | | | | 0.27 | 0.04 | 3.29 | 11.63 |
| 8 | 1855 | 1.97 | 3.59 | | | | | | | | 0.11 | 2.15 | 0.41 | 11.15 |
| 9 | 1856 | 1.27 | 1.86 | | | | | | | | 0 | 1.22 | 1.3 | 9.77 |
| 10 | 1857 | 0.26 | 1.76 | | | | | | | | 0.49 | 2.16 | 1.3 | 6.15 |
| 11 | 1858 | 1.52 | 0.44 | | | | | | | | 0.47 | 0.28 | 3.1 | 7.55 |
| 12 | 1859 | 0 | 1.89 | | | | | | | | 0.18 | 1.49 | 1.79 | 6.1 |
| 13 | 1860 | 0.72 | 1.49 | | | | | | | | 0 | 2.88 | 2.99 | 9.11 |
| 14 | 1861 | 0.82 | 0.79 | | | | | | | | 0.05 | 1.19 | 3.2 | 7.92 |
| 15 | 1862 | 5.56 | 1.39 | | | | | | | | 0.89 | 0.05 | 0.93 | 11.59 |
| 16 | 1863 | 0.32 | 1.09 | | | | | | | | 0 | 0.73 | 0.04 | 3.02 |
| 17 | 1864 | 0.04 | 2.5 | | | | | | | | 0.04 | 2.41 | 1.04 | 7.61 |
| 18 | 1865 | 1.28 | 3 | | | | | | | | 0.02 | 0.52 | 0.84 | 7.52 |
| 19 | 1866 | 5.05 | 3.43 | | | | | | | | 0 | 0.24 | 1.82 | 12.31 |
| 20 | 1867 | 1.32 | 0.85 | | | | | | | | 0.34 | 0.45 | 3.06 | 14.72 |
| 21 | 1868 | 3.37 | 1.63 | | | | | | | | 0 | 2 | 1.52 | 11.16 |
| 22 | 1869 | 2.88 | 1.88 | | | | | | | | 0.05 | 2.32 | 0.94 | 10.96 |
| 23 | 1870 | 0.54 | 0.77 | 0.33 | 0.2 | 0.28 | 0 | 0.04 | 0.07 | 0 | 1.54 | 0.18 | 0.42 | 4.37 |

Annual Rainfall in San Diego 1850-2008

CHAPTER

# 26 | Excel Functions

## CHAPTER CONTENTS

## Overview

In this chapter we discuss the principal Excel functions a financial analyst needs to know. There is some overlap between the discussion here and in other chapters (for example, the **NPV** function is discussed in Chapter 2). We also discuss some functions that are not used in this book, but that are so handy that we include them for reference.

A word about nomenclature: To differentiate an Excel function from the surrounding text, we usually (although not in the table above!) denote it with boldface type. Most Excel functions depend on some variable, but we do not always indicate these variables. For example, the variables for the **NPV** function are the interest rate and the range to be discounted; when we want to make this explicit, we write **NPV(interest,range)**.

One more note: The functions in each class are not always discussed alphabetically. Where there's a logical order, we use this (for example, we discuss **NPV** before **IRR**).

# 26.1. Financial Functions

## NPV( )

This function is extensively discussed in Chapter 2. The Excel definition of **NPV( )** differs somewhat from the standard finance definition. In the finance literature, the NPV of a sequence of cash flows $C_0, C_1, C_2, \ldots, C_n$ at a discount rate $r$ refers to the expression

$$\sum_{t=0}^{n} \frac{C_t}{(1+r)^t} \text{ or } C_0 + \sum_{t=1}^{n} \frac{C_t}{(1+r)^t}.$$

The term $C_0$ typically represents the cost of the asset purchased and is therefore negative.

The Excel definition of **NPV( )** always assumes that the first cash flow occurs after one period. The user who wants the standard finance expression must therefore calculate **NPV(r,{C_1,..., C_n}) + C_0**. Here is an example.

| | A | B | C | D | E | F | G |
|---|---|---|---|---|---|---|---|
| 1 | | | EXCEL'S NPV FUNCTION | | | | |
| 2 | Discount rate | 10% | | | | | |
| 3 | Year | 0 | 1 | 2 | 3 | 4 | 5 |
| 4 | Cash flow | -100 | 35 | 33 | 34 | 25 | 16 |
| 5 | | | | | | | |
| 6 | NPV | $11.65 | <-- =NPV(B2,C4:G4)+B4 | | | | |

## IRR( )

The IRR of a sequence of cash flows $C_0, C_1, C_2, \ldots, C_n$ is an interest rate $r$ such that the NPV of the cash flows is zero:

$$\sum_{t=0}^{n} \frac{C_t}{(1+r)^t} = 0.$$

The Excel syntax for the **IRR( )** function is **IRR(cash flows, guess)**. Here **cash flows** represents the whole sequence of cash flows, including the first cash flow $C_0$, and **guess** is a starting point for the algorithm that calculates the IRR.

First a simple example—consider the cash flows given above.

| | A | B | C | D | E | F | G |
|---|---|---|---|---|---|---|---|
| 8 | | | EXCEL'S IRR FUNCTION | | | | |
| 9 | Year | 0 | 1 | 2 | 3 | 4 | 5 |
| 10 | Cash flow | -100 | 35 | 33 | 34 | 25 | 16 |
| 11 | | | | | | | |
| 12 | IRR | 15.00% | <-- =IRR(B10:G10,0) | | | | |
| 13 | | 15.00% | <-- =IRR(B10:G10) | | | | |

Note that **guess** is not necessary when there is only one IRR. Thus in cell B13 (where we haven't indicated a **guess**) we get the same answer as in cell B12 (**guess** = 0).

The choice of **guess** can, however, make a difference when there is more than one IRR. Consider, for example, the following cash flows.

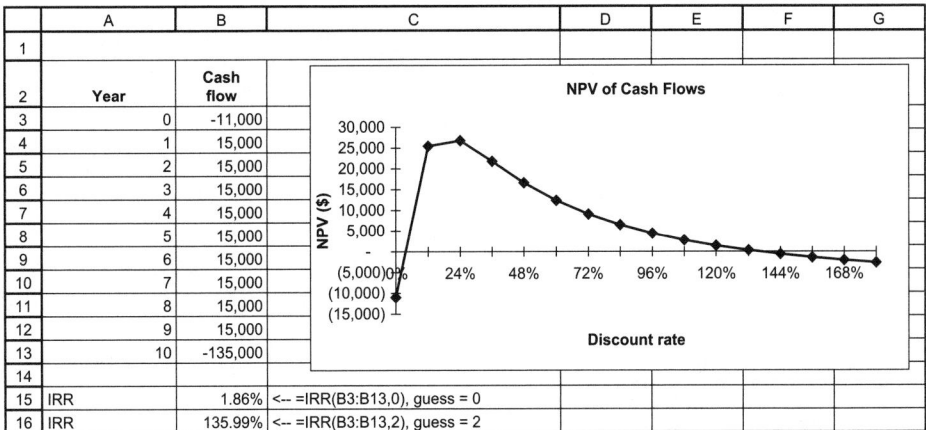

| | A | B | C | D | E | F | G |
|---|---|---|---|---|---|---|---|
| 1 | | | | | | | |
| 2 | Year | Cash flow | | | | | |
| 3 | 0 | -11,000 | | | | | |
| 4 | 1 | 15,000 | | | | | |
| 5 | 2 | 15,000 | | | | | |
| 6 | 3 | 15,000 | | | | | |
| 7 | 4 | 15,000 | | | | | |
| 8 | 5 | 15,000 | | | | | |
| 9 | 6 | 15,000 | | | | | |
| 10 | 7 | 15,000 | | | | | |
| 11 | 8 | 15,000 | | | | | |
| 12 | 9 | 15,000 | | | | | |
| 13 | 10 | -135,000 | | | | | |
| 14 | | | | | | | |
| 15 | IRR | 1.86% | <-- =IRR(B3:B13,0), guess = 0 | | | | |
| 16 | IRR | 135.99% | <-- =IRR(B3:B13,2), guess = 2 | | | | |

The graph (created from table that is not shown) shows that there are two IRRs because the NPV curve crosses the $x$-axis twice. To find both IRRs, we have to change the **guess** (although the precise value of guess is still not critical). In the example below we have changed both guesses, but still get the same answer.

| | A | B | C |
|---|---|---|---|
| 15 | IRR | 1.86% | <-- =IRR(B3:B13,0.1) |
| 16 | IRR | 135.99% | <-- =IRR(B3:B13,0.8) |

**Note:** A given set of cash flows typically has more than one IRR if there is more than one change of sign in the cash flows—in the above example, the initial cash flow is negative, and $CF_1$–$CF_9$ are positive (this accounts for one change of sign); but then $CF_{10}$ is negative, making a second change of sign. If you suspect that a set of cash flows has more than one IRR, the first thing to do is to use Excel to make a graph of the NPVs, as we did above. The number of times that the NPV graph crosses the $x$-axis identifies the number of IRRs (and also their approximate values).[1]

# FV( )

The *FV* function, **FV**, calculates the FV of a series of deposits. Below we discuss several cases of this function. For a finance discussion of this function and the meaning of the numbers it produces, you should refer to Chapter 2 (page 18).

## The Future Value of a Series of Annual Investments: Using FV and the Type Parameter

Suppose you intend to make five annual deposits of $1,000 each to a 5% savings account. The first deposit is made today. How much will you have at the end of 5 years? In the following spreadsheet, we do this computation in two ways (cells C13 and C14).

---

[1] For more examples of multiple IRRs, see Chapter 4.

| | A | B | C | D |
|---|---|---|---|---|
| 1 | SAVING FOR THE FUTURE<br>FV Type PARAMETER = 1 | | | |
| 2 | Annual deposit to savings | 1,000 | | |
| 3 | Interest rate | 5% | | |
| 4 | | | | |
| 5 | Year | Deposit | Value at end<br>of year 5 | |
| 6 | 0 | 1,000 | 1,276.28 | <-- =B6*(1+$B$3)^(5-A6) |
| 7 | 1 | 1,000 | 1,215.51 | |
| 8 | 2 | 1,000 | 1,157.63 | |
| 9 | 3 | 1,000 | 1,102.50 | |
| 10 | 4 | 1,000 | 1,050.00 | |
| 11 | 5 | | | |
| 12 | | | | |
| 13 | Total at end of 5 years | | 5,801.91 | <-- =SUM(C6:C11) |
| 14 | | | 5,801.91 | <-- =FV(B3,5,-B2,,1) |

In the table in cells A6:C11, we take each annual deposit of $1,000 and compute its future value at the end of year 5. Summing these values (cell C13) gives $5,801.91.

In cell C14 we use the **FV** function. Here's the dialog box, with an explanation of the use of **Type**.

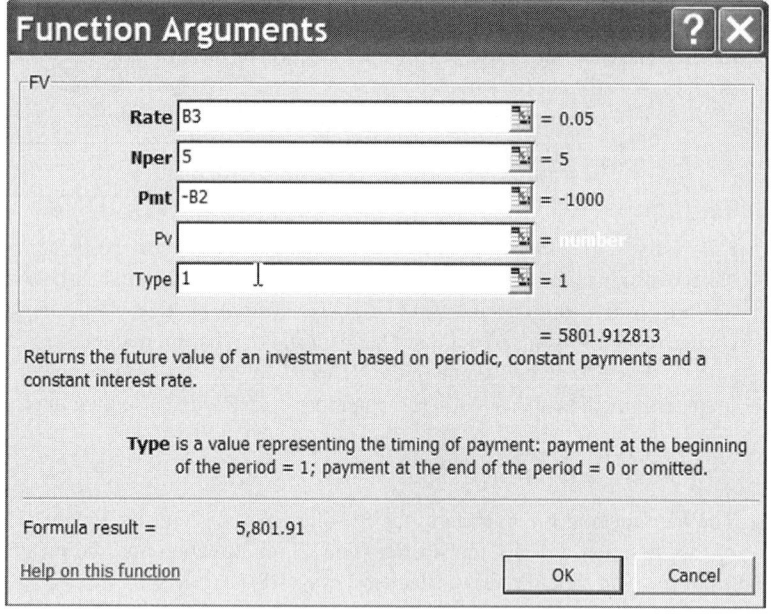

Note that we've set **Type** equal to 1: The five payments are made *at the beginning of the period*: today and in each of years 1, 2, 3, and 4.

The **FV** function allows **Type** to be 0 when the payments are made at the end of the period. To illustrate this, suppose you intend to make five annual deposits of $1,000 each to a 5% savings account, with the *first deposit to be made 1 year from now*. How much will you have at the end of 5 years? In the spreadsheet below, we again do this computation in two ways (cells C13 and C14).

| | A | B | C | D |
|---|---|---|---|---|
| 1 | | SAVING FOR THE FUTURE<br>FV Type PARAMETER = 0 | | |
| 2 | Annual deposit to savings | 1,000 | | |
| 3 | Interest rate | 5% | | |
| 4 | | | | |
| 5 | Year | Deposit | Value at end<br>of year 5 | |
| 6 | 0 | 0 | 0.00 | <-- =B6*(1+$B$3)^(5-A6) |
| 7 | 1 | 1,000 | 1,215.51 | <-- =B7*(1+$B$3)^(5-A7) |
| 8 | 2 | 1,000 | 1,157.63 | |
| 9 | 3 | 1,000 | 1,102.50 | |
| 10 | 4 | 1,000 | 1,050.00 | |
| 11 | 5 | 1,000 | 1,000.00 | |
| 12 | | | | |
| 13 | Total at end of 5 years | | 5,525.63 | <-- =SUM(C6:C11) |
| 14 | | | 5,525.63 | <-- =FV(B3,5,-B2,,0) |

To end this discussion, here are two additional points:

- If you don't enter a value for the **Type** in the **FV** function, Excel assumes that **Type** equals 0 (meaning the deposits are made at the end of the period).

- It is easy to confuse the "beginning" and "end" of period distinction and blind use of the **FV** function can lead to errors. The obvious way to avoid such errors is to build an extensive Excel table as illustrated above.

One final note: The **FV** function also allows for an optional **Pv** parameter. This parameter allows you to use the **FV** function to compute loan payments. We prefer not to use this parameter—if we need to compute loan payments, we use the **PMT** function illustrated later.[2]

# PV( )

The Excel **PV** function calculates the PV of an annuity (a series of fixed periodic payments). Here is an example.

| | A | B | C |
|---|---|---|---|
| 1 | THE PV FUNCTION | | |
| 2 | Payments made at the end of the period | | |
| 3 | Rate | 10% | |
| 4 | Number of periods | 10 | |
| 5 | Payment | 100 | |
| 6 | Present value | (614.46) | <-- =PV(B3,B4,B5) |

---

[2] The use of the **Pv** parameter of the **FV** function is nicely illustrated in note by Linda Johnson on the following Web site: http://pubs.logicalexpressions.com/pub0009/LPMArticle.asp?ID=385.

Thus $\$614.46 = \sum_{t=1}^{10} \dfrac{100}{(1.10)^t}$. Here are two things to note about the **PV( )** function:

- Writing **PV(B3,B4,B5)** assumes that payments are made at dates $1, 2, \ldots, 10$. If the payments are made at dates $0, 1, 2, \ldots, 9$, you should write the following.

|    | A | B | C |
|----|---|---|---|
| 8  | **Payments made at the beginning of the period** | | |
| 9  | Rate | 10% | |
| 10 | Number of periods | 10 | |
| 11 | Payment | 100 | |
| 12 | Present value | (675.90) | <-- =PV(B9,B10,B11,,1) |

- Irritatingly, when the payments are positive as in the above example, the **PV( )** function (and the **PMT( )** function—see below) gives the PV as a negative number (there is a logic here, but it's not worth explaining). To get a positive PV in cell B12, we would either write - **PV(B3,B4,B5)** or let the payment be negative by writing **PV(B3,B4,-B5)**.

## PMT( )

This function calculates the payment necessary to pay off a loan with equal payments over a fixed number of periods. For example, the first calculation below shows that a loan of $1,000, to be paid off over 10 years at an interest rate of 8%, will require equal annual payments of interest and principal of $149.03. The calculation performed is the solution of the following equation:

$$\sum_{t=1}^{n} \frac{X}{(1+r)^t} = \text{initial loan principal},$$

Where $X$ is the payment

|    | A | B | C |
|----|---|---|---|
| 1  | **THE PMT FUNCTION** | | |
| 2  | **Payments made at the end of the period** | | |
| 3  | Rate | 8% | |
| 4  | Number of periods | 10 | |
| 5  | Principal | 1000 | |
| 6  | Payment | ($149.03) | <-- =PMT(B3,B4,B5) |
| 7  | | | |
| 8  | **Payments made at the beginning of the period** | | |
| 9  | Rate | 8% | |
| 10 | Number of periods | 10 | |
| 11 | Principal | 1000 | |
| 12 | Payment | ($137.99) | <-- =PMT(B9,B10,B11,,1) |

Loan tables can be calculated using the **PMT( )** function. These tables—explained in detail in Chapter 2—show what part of each payment is interest and what part is repayment of the loan principal. In each period, the payment on the loan (calculated with **PMT( )**) is split:

- We first calculate the interest owing for that period on the principal outstanding at the beginning of the period. In the table below, at the end of year 1, we owe $80 (= 8% * $1,000) of interest on the loan principal outstanding at the beginning of the year.

- The remainder of the payment (for year 1, $69.03) goes to reduce the principal outstanding.

| | A | B | C | D | E |
|---|---|---|---|---|---|
| 1 | | LOAN TABLE | | | | |
| 2 | Interest | 8% | | | |
| 3 | Number of periods | 10 | | | |
| 4 | Principal | 1,000 | | | |
| 5 | Annual payment | 149.03 | <-- =-PMT(B2,B3,B4) | | |
| 6 | | | | | |
| 7 | | | | Split of payment between | |
| 8 | Year | Principal at beginning of year | Payment | Interest | Repayment of principal |
| 9 | 1 | 1,000.00 | 149.03 | 80.00 | 69.03 |
| 10 | 2 | 930.97 | 149.03 | 74.48 | 74.55 |
| 11 | 3 | 856.42 | 149.03 | 68.51 | 80.52 |
| 12 | 4 | 775.90 | 149.03 | 62.07 | 86.96 |
| 13 | 5 | 688.95 | 149.03 | 55.12 | 93.91 |
| 14 | 6 | 595.03 | 149.03 | 47.60 | 101.43 |
| 15 | 7 | 493.60 | 149.03 | 39.49 | 109.54 |
| 16 | 8 | 384.06 | 149.03 | 30.73 | 118.30 |
| 17 | 9 | 265.76 | 149.03 | 21.26 | 127.77 |
| 18 | 10 | 137.99 | 149.03 | 11.04 | 137.99 |

Note that the repayment of principal at the end of year 10 is exactly equal to the principal outstanding at the beginning of the year (i.e., the loan has been paid off).

## Using the IPMT and PPMT to Compute the Interest and Principal Payments of the Loan Table

Columns D and E of the loan table in the previous example can be computed by these two functions. In the following example we compute the interest and principal components in year 4.

| | A | B | C |
|---|---|---|---|
| 1 | | USING IPMT AND PPMT | |
| 2 | Interest | 8% | |
| 3 | Number of periods | 10 | |
| 4 | Principal | 1,000 | |
| 5 | Annual payment | 149.03 | <-- =PMT(B2,B3,-B4) |
| 6 | | | |
| 7 | Year | 3 | |
| 8 | Interest payment | 68.51 | <-- =IPMT(B2,B7,B3,-B4) |
| 9 | Principal payment | 80.52 | <-- =PPMT(B2,B7,B3,-B4) |

## Using the FV Parameter of the PMT Function

The **PMT** function can also compute the periodic payment necessary to achieve a given *FV*. Here's an example: Suppose you want make 10 annual payments into your savings account so that you have $10,000 in 10 years. Suppose the interest rate is 6%. What should your annual payment be? In the spreadsheet below we show two ways of solving this problem.

| | A | B | C | D |
|---|---|---|---|---|
| 1 | SAVING FOR THE FUTURE | | | |
| 1 | Using the PMT function to compute a _future_ value | | | |
| 2 | Annual deposit to savings account | $ 715.74 | | |
| 3 | Interest rate | 6% | | |
| 4 | | | | |
| 5 | Year | Deposit to account | Total in account | |
| 6 | 0 | $ 715.74 | $ 715.74 | <-- =B6 |
| 7 | 1 | $ 715.74 | $ 1,474.42 | <-- =B7+C6*(1+$B$3) |
| 8 | 2 | $ 715.74 | $ 2,278.63 | <-- =B8+C7*(1+$B$3) |
| 9 | 3 | $ 715.74 | $ 3,131.09 | |
| 10 | 4 | $ 715.74 | $ 4,034.69 | |
| 11 | 5 | $ 715.74 | $ 4,992.51 | |
| 12 | 6 | $ 715.74 | $ 6,007.81 | |
| 13 | 7 | $ 715.74 | $ 7,084.01 | |
| 14 | 8 | $ 715.74 | $ 8,224.79 | |
| 15 | 9 | $ 715.74 | $ 9,434.02 | |
| 16 | 10 | $ - | $ 10,000.06 | <-- =B16+C15*(1+$B$3) |
| 17 | | | | |
| 18 | Using PMT to do the calculation | | $715.74 | <-- =PMT(B3,10,,-10000,1) |

The table in cells A6:C16 shows you exactly what's happening: By using trial and error or **Goal Seek** (Chapter 28) you can compute the number in cell B2: You need $715.74 deposited today and in each of the next 9 years to achieve your goal of $10,000 at the end of 10 years.

The **PMT** function in cell B18 can do the same calculation. Here's the way the dialog box for this function looks. Note the use of **Type** = 1, because the payments are made at the beginning of each year. Note also that we haven't put any entry into the **Pv** box.

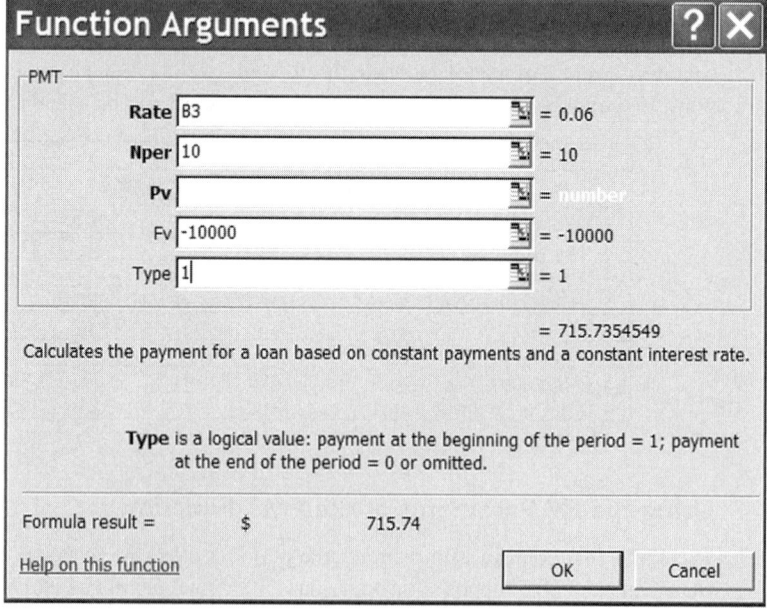

# RATE( )

**RATE** calculates the IRR of a series of constant payments. In the example below **RATE(B4,B5,-B3)** in cell B6 computes 10.56%, which is the IRR:

$$-600 + \frac{100}{(1.1056)} + \frac{100}{(1.1056)^2} + \ldots + \frac{100}{(1.1056)^{10}} = 0$$

| | A | B | C | D |
|---|---|---|---|---|
| | | **THE RATE FUNCTION** | | |
| 1 | | **Compare to IRR** | | |
| 2 | RATE used for payments made at the end of the period | | | |
| 3 | Initial payment | 600 | | |
| 4 | Number of periods | 10 | | |
| 5 | Annual payment | 100 | | |
| 6 | Rate of return | 10.56% | <-- =RATE(B4,B5,-B3) | |
| 7 | | | | |
| 8 | RATE used for payments made at the beginning of the period | | | |
| 9 | Initial payment | 600 | | |
| 10 | Number of periods | 10 | | |
| 11 | Annual payment | 100 | | |
| 12 | Rate of return | 13.70% | <-- =RATE(B10,B11,-B9,,1,20%) | |
| 13 | | | | |
| 14 | What does RATE do?  Computing the IRR | | | |
| 15 | Year | **Payment at end of period** | **Payment at beginning of period** | |
| 16 | 0 | -600 | -500 | |
| 17 | 1 | 100 | 100 | |
| 18 | 2 | 100 | 100 | |
| 19 | 3 | 100 | 100 | |
| 20 | 4 | 100 | 100 | |
| 21 | 5 | 100 | 100 | |
| 22 | 6 | 100 | 100 | |
| 23 | 7 | 100 | 100 | |
| 24 | 8 | 100 | 100 | |
| 25 | 9 | 100 | 100 | |
| 26 | 10 | 100 | | |
| 27 | | | | |
| 28 | **IRR** | 10.56% | 13.70% | <-- =IRR(C16:C26) |

Like **PV** and **PMT**, **Rate** gives the possibility of specifying whether the cash flows occur at the end of the period (the default) or at the beginning. If you look in cell B12, **Rate(B10,B11,-B9,,1,20%)** computes 13.70%; this is the IRR of an initial payment of $600 and 10 payments of $100 *made at the beginning of the period* (the beginning of the period is indicated by the "1" at the end of the formula. The **20%** in the function is a **Guess** like that which is also allowed in the IRR function.

Here's the dialog box that created this result.

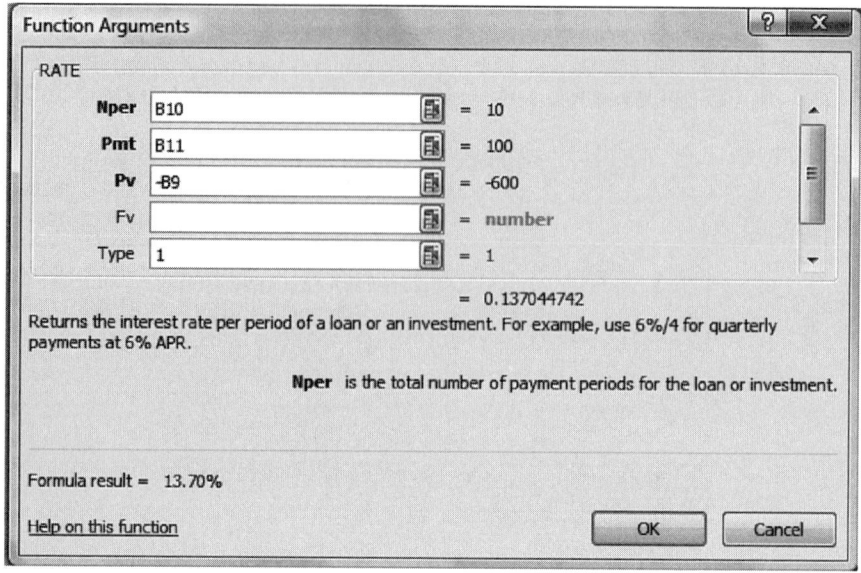

Think for a second what this means for an IRR:

$$-600 + \underbrace{100}_{\substack{\text{First payment} \\ \text{made at "beginning"} \\ \text{of period--meaning,} \\ \text{made at time 0}}} + \frac{100}{(1.1370)} + \frac{100}{(1.1370)^2} + \frac{100}{(1.1370)^3} + \ldots + \frac{100}{(1.1370)^9} = 0$$

Effectively, then **RATE(B10,B11,-B9,,1,20%)** refers to an initial payment of $500 and nine subsequent payments of 100.

## RATE versus IRR

If you look at the above example, you will see (rows 16–28) that **IRR** and **RATE** give the same values. There are, of course, trade-offs:

- **RATE** is shorter; **IRR** requires you to specify all the cash flows.
- On the other hand, **IRR** can handle cash flows that vary over time.

## NPER( )

This function calculates the number of periods to repay a loan given a fixed amount. For example, you borrow $1,000 from the bank, which charges you a 10% annual interest rate. You intend to repay the loan with $250 per year. How long will it take you to repay the loan?

| | A | B | C | D | E |
|---|---|---|---|---|---|
| 1 | | **HOW LONG TO PAY OFF THIS LOAN?** | | | |
| 2 | Loan amount | 1,000.00 | | | |
| 3 | Interest rate | 10% | | | |
| 4 | Annual payment | 250 | | | |
| 5 | How long to pay off the loan? | 5.3596 | <-- =NPER(B3,B4,-B2) | | |
| 6 | | | | | |
| 7 | Year | Principal at beginning of year | Payment at end of year | Interest | Repayment of principal |
| 8 | 1 | 1,000.00 | 250.00 | 100.00 | 150.00 |
| 9 | 2 | 850.00 | 250.00 | 85.00 | 165.00 |
| 10 | 3 | 685.00 | 250.00 | 68.50 | 181.50 |
| 11 | 4 | 503.50 | 250.00 | 50.35 | 199.65 |
| 12 | 5 | 303.85 | 250.00 | 30.39 | 219.62 |
| 13 | 6 | 84.24 | 250.00 | 8.42 | 241.58 |

As you can see from the loan table, it takes somewhere between 5 and 6 years to repay the loan.[3] **NPER(B3,B4,-B2)** gives the exact number of periods as 5.3596.

## 26.2. Math Functions

### Using Exp to Calculate FVs

Suppose you invest $100 at 10% for 3 years. As explained in Chapter 2, if interest is compounded annually, the FV after 3 years will be as follows.

| | A | B | C |
|---|---|---|---|
| 1 | | **ANNUAL COMPOUNDING** | |
| 2 | Initial investment | 100 | |
| 3 | Years invested, t | 3 | |
| 4 | Interest rate, r | 10% | |
| 5 | Future value, FV | 133.1 | <-- =B2*(1+B4)^B3 |

Suppose the 10% is compounded semiannually (meaning: you get 5% each half year). Then there will be six compounding periods—3 years * 2 periods/year. Your FV will be *Initial Investment* * $(1 + 5\%)^6 = 134.0096$.

| | A | B | C |
|---|---|---|---|
| 7 | Initial investment | 100 | |
| 8 | Years invested, t | 3 | |
| 9 | Compounding periods per year, n | 2 | |
| 10 | Interest rate, r | 10% | |
| 11 | Future value, FV | 134.0096 | <-- =B7*(1+B10/B9)^(B8*B9) |

Denote the number of years by $t$, the interest rate by $r$, and the number of compounding periods per year by $n$. As the number of compounding periods increases, the FV tends toward $100 * e^{r*t}$, where $e$ is the number 2.71828.[4] In Excel this is written 100 * **Exp(r * t)**. This is illustrated in the table and graph below.

---

[3] Why? At the end of year 5 (which is also the beginning of year 6), there's still $84.24 of principal outstanding. But if you pay back $250 at the end of year 6, then you've paid back too much.

[4] In mathematical notation: $\lim_{n \to \infty}\left(1 + \dfrac{r}{n}\right)^{nt} = e^{rt}$.

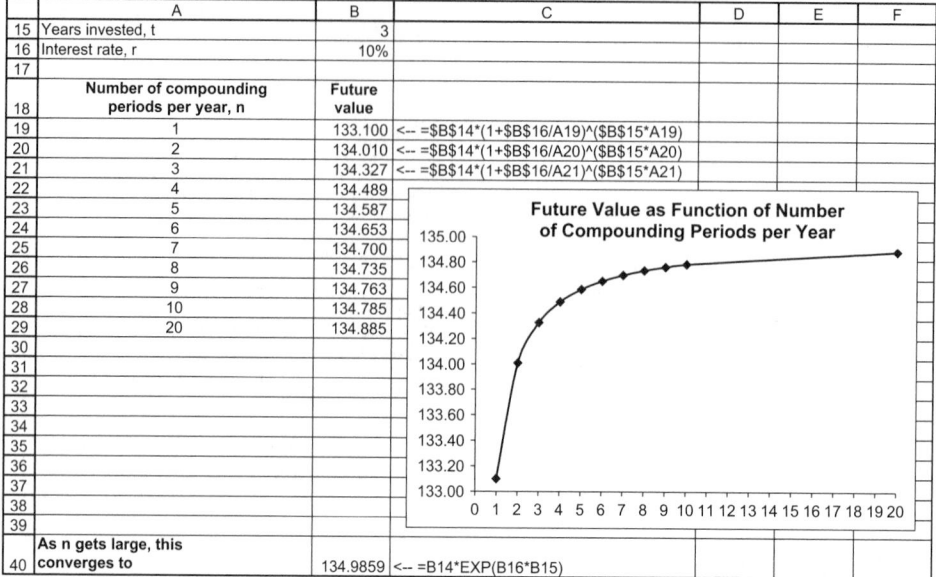

| | A | B | C | D | E | F |
|---|---|---|---|---|---|---|
| 15 | Years invested, t | 3 | | | | |
| 16 | Interest rate, r | 10% | | | | |
| 17 | | | | | | |
| 18 | Number of compounding periods per year, n | Future value | | | | |
| 19 | 1 | 133.100 | <-- =$B$14*(1+$B$16/A19)^($B$15*A19) | | | |
| 20 | 2 | 134.010 | <-- =$B$14*(1+$B$16/A20)^($B$15*A20) | | | |
| 21 | 3 | 134.327 | <-- =$B$14*(1+$B$16/A21)^($B$15*A21) | | | |
| 22 | 4 | 134.489 | | | | |
| 23 | 5 | 134.587 | | | | |
| 24 | 6 | 134.653 | | | | |
| 25 | 7 | 134.700 | | | | |
| 26 | 8 | 134.735 | | | | |
| 27 | 9 | 134.763 | | | | |
| 28 | 10 | 134.785 | | | | |
| 29 | 20 | 134.885 | | | | |
| 30 | | | | | | |
| 31 | | | | | | |
| 32 | | | | | | |
| 33 | | | | | | |
| 34 | | | | | | |
| 35 | | | | | | |
| 36 | | | | | | |
| 37 | | | | | | |
| 38 | | | | | | |
| 39 | | | | | | |
| 40 | As n gets large, this converges to | 134.9859 | <-- =B14*EXP(B16*B15) | | | |

**Nomenclature:** When the number of compounding periods becomes infinite, the investment is said to be *continuously compounded*. Otherwise (that is, when there are a finite number of compounding periods per year), the investment is said to be *discretely compounded*.

## Using Exp to Calculate PVs

Earlier we illustrated how $100 grows to 100 * **Exp(r * t)** when it is compounded continuously for $t$ years at interest rate $r$. Suppose you're going to get $100 in 3 years. What is the PV of this $100 if the relevant interest rate is $r$? The answer depends on the number of compounding periods:

- If the investment is discretely compounded $n$ times per year, then its PV is

$$\frac{100}{\left(1+\frac{r}{n}\right)^{n*t}} = 100 * \left(1+\frac{r}{n}\right)^{-n*t}$$

- If the investment will be continuously compounded, then its PV is

$$\frac{100}{\exp(r*t)} = 100 * \exp(-r*t)$$

Here is an Excel spreadsheet.

| | A | B | C |
|---|---|---|---|
| 1 | DISCRETE VERSUS CONTINUOUS DISCOUNTING | | |
| 2 | Future value | 100 | |
| 3 | What year received, t | 3 | |
| 4 | Compounding periods per year, n | 2 | |
| 5 | Interest rate, r | 10% | |
| 6 | | | |
| 7 | Present value, discrete discounting | 74.62154 | <-- =B2/(1+B5/B4)^(B4*B3) |
| 8 | | | |
| 9 | Present value, continuous discounting | 74.08182 | <-- =B2*EXP(-B5*B3) |

You can use the above spreadsheet to show that as *n* gets very large, the two values in B56 and B58 converge. For example, when *n = 100*, we obtain the following.

| | A | B | C |
|---|---|---|---|
| 1 | DISCRETE VERSUS CONTINUOUS DISCOUNTING | | |
| 2 | Future value | 100 | |
| 3 | What year received, t | 3 | |
| 4 | Compounding periods per year, n | 100 | |
| 5 | Interest rate, r | 10% | |
| 6 | | | |
| 7 | Present value, discrete discounting | 74.09293 | <-- =B2/(1+B5/B4)^(B4*B3) |
| 8 | | | |
| 9 | Present value, continuous discounting | 74.08182 | <-- =B2*EXP(-B5*B3) |

## LN

This function (the "natural logarithm" to differentiate it from the "logarithm base 10" that you learned in high school) is often used to calculate continuously compounded rates of return.[5] Suppose you invest in a stock that is worth \$25 and suppose that 1 year later the stock is worth \$40. What rate of return *r* have you earned? If you use *discrete compounding*, the rate of return is $r = \dfrac{P_1}{P_0} - 1 = \dfrac{40}{25} - 1 = 60\%$ .

Now suppose that your alternative is to earn *continuously compounded interest r.* Then the rate of return has to solve the equation

$$P_0 \exp(r) = P_1 \Rightarrow \exp(r) = \frac{P_1}{P_0} .$$

The function that solves this equation is the natural logarithm ln:

$$r = \ln\left(\frac{P_1}{P_0}\right).$$

The following spreadsheet shows an example using Excel.

---

[5] In this book we've used it extensively in the option chapters, Chapters 20–24.

| | A | B | C |
|---|---|---|---|
| 1 | **USING LN TO COMPUTE CONTINUOUSLY COMPOUNDED RATES OF RETURN** | | |
| 2 | Price of stock, t=0 | 25 | |
| 3 | Price of stock, t=1 | 40 | |
| 4 | Discretely compounded rate of return, r | 60.00% | <-- =B3/B2-1 |
| 5 | Continously compounded rate of return, r | 47.00% | <-- =LN(B3/B2) |

When $t \neq 1$, the problem looks like this:

$$P_0 \exp(r*t) = P_t \Rightarrow \exp(r*t) = \frac{P_t}{P_0}$$

has solution:

$$r = \frac{1}{t} \ln\left(\frac{P_t}{P_0}\right)$$

For example, suppose you invested in Intel stock on 25 October 1999, buying the stock for its closing price of \$38.6079, and suppose you sold it at the end of the day, 24 July 2000, for \$64.4379. As the calculation below shows, you would have earned a continuously compounded return of 68.49% on your stock.

| | A | B | C | D |
|---|---|---|---|---|
| 7 | **Intel stock** | | | |
| 8 | Purchase date and price | 25-Oct-99 | 38.6079 | |
| 9 | Sale date and price | 24-Jul-00 | 64.4379 | |
| 10 | | | | |
| 11 | Elapsed time, t | 0.7479 | <-- =(B9-B8)/365 | |
| 12 | Continuously compounded rate of return, r | 68.49% | <-- =1/B11*LN(C9/C8) | |

Note that this calculation is easier than the calculation of the *annualized daily return*—it has one fewer step.

| | A | B | C | D |
|---|---|---|---|---|
| 14 | **Daily return, annualized** | | | |
| 15 | Purchase date and price | 25-Oct-99 | 38.6079 | |
| 16 | Sale date and price | 24-Jul-00 | 64.4379 | |
| 17 | | | | |
| 18 | Elapsed days | 273 | <-- =(B16-B15) | |
| 19 | Daily return | 0.1878% | <-- =(C16/C15)^(1/B18)-1 | |
| 20 | Annualized | 98.35% | <-- =(1+B19)^365-1 | |

## A Short Finance Note

We can't resist a short finance note on the difference between the continuously compounded annual return of 68.49% and the discretely compounded annual return of 98.35%.

- Both of these returns cause \$38.6079 to grow over a period of 273 days to \$64.4379. So they're both—in an economic sense—the same number.

- The *daily* returns are very close: The continuously compounded daily return is calculated by $\dfrac{annual\ continuously\ compounded\ return}{365}$ and the discretely compounded daily return is calculated by $\left(\dfrac{Stock\ price,\ day\ 273}{Stock\ price,\ day\ 0}\right)^{1/273}-1$. These numbers are very close.

| | A | B | C |
|---|---|---|---|
| 22 | **Note** | | |
| 23 | Daily, continuously compounded return | 0.1876% | <-- =B12/365 |
| 24 | Daily, discretely compounded return | 0.1878% | <-- =B19 |

However, when you compound them for 365 days, the differences are very large.

## Round, RoundDown, RoundUp, Trunc

The Excel functions **Round**, **RoundDown**, and **RoundUp** do exactly what they say. All three functions require you to specify the number of decimal places to which you want to round off the number. The function **Trunc** cuts off a number after a specified number of places (if you do not specify, **Trunc** gives you the integer part of a number). Here are examples using the Excel function **Pi** as a basis.

| | A | B | C |
|---|---|---|---|
| 1 | ROUNDING NUMBERS IN EXCEL | | |
| 2 | Number | 3.1415926535898 | <-- =PI() |
| 3 | | | |
| 4 | Round, no decimal places | 3.00000000 | <-- =ROUND(B2,0) |
| 5 | Round, 3 decimal places | 3.14200000 | <-- =ROUND(B2,3) |
| 6 | | | |
| 7 | RoundDown, no decimal places | 3.00000000 | <-- =ROUNDDOWN(B2,0) |
| 8 | RoundDown, 3 decimal places | 3.14100000 | <-- =ROUNDDOWN(B2,3) |
| 9 | | | |
| 10 | RoundUp, no decimal places | 4.00000000 | <-- =ROUNDUP(B2,0) |
| 11 | RoundUp, 4 decimal places | 3.14160000 | <-- =ROUNDUP(B2,4) |
| 12 | | | |
| 13 | Truncate, no decimal places | 3.00000000 | <-- =TRUNC(B2) |
| 14 | Truncate, 5 decimal places | 3.14159000 | <-- =TRUNC(B2,5) |

There's a difference between using these functions and merely formatting a number so that it looks rounded or truncated. Here's an example.

| | A | B | C |
|---|---|---|---|
| 16 | Number | 4.5632 | |
| 17 | Rounded to 2 decimals | 4.56 | <-- =ROUND(B16,2) |
| 18 | Formatted to 2 decimals | 4.56 | <-- =B16 |
| 19 | | | |
| 20 | 10 times cell B20 | 45.6 | <-- =10*B17 |
| 21 | 10 times cell B21 | 45.632 | <-- =10*B18 |

In cell B18 we used the "decrease decimal" button 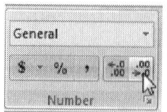 on the **Home** tab to change the representation of the number. However, as you can see in cell B21, this button does not change the number, whereas **Round** actually changes the number.[6]

## Sqrt

This function calculates the square root of a number. In this book, we've used square roots to calculate the standard deviation (see Chapter 12) of returns.

|   | A | B | C |
|---|---|---|---|
| 1 | | **SQRT** | |
| 2 | Number | 3 | |
| 3 | Square root | 1.732051 | <-- =SQRT(B2) |
| 4 | Equivalent way | 1.732051 | <-- =B2^(1/2) |

Note that you can use the carat (^) as an alternative way of calculating the square root. In Excel's notation, $a \wedge b$ raises $a$ to the power $b$ (meaning $a \wedge b = a^b$). Because a square root is equivalent to the power ½, you can also use this notation (see cell B4 above).

## Sum

The Excel function **Sum** adds numbers in a range of cells.

|   | A | B |
|---|---|---|
| 1 | | **SUM** |
| 2 | 1 | |
| 3 | 2 | |
| 4 | 3 | |
| 5 | 4 | |
| 6 | 5 | |
| 7 | 15 | <-- =SUM(A2:A6) |

## SumIf

**SumIf** allows you to add only numbers that fulfill a specific condition. Here's an example in which we add only those scores that are greater than 30.

|   | A | B |
|---|---|---|
| 9 | **Score** | |
| 10 | 30 | |
| 11 | 50 | |
| 12 | 80 | |
| 13 | 90 | |
| 14 | 20 | |
| 15 | 220 | <-- =SUMIF(A10:A14,">30") |

---

[6] Excel also has functions **Roundup** and **Rounddown** that do what their names suggest. We'll leave you to explore these functions on your own.

The function **SumIf** also allows you to have the conditional column some other place. In the following example, we add the numbers in D10:D14 for which the corresponding number in E10:E14 is greater than 40 (highlighted here).

|    | D       | E       | F |
|----|---------|---------|---|
| 9  | **Score 1** | **Score 2** |   |
| 10 | 30      | 55      |   |
| 11 | 50      | 89      |   |
| 12 | 80      | 22      |   |
| 13 | 90      | 65      |   |
| 14 | 20      | 35      |   |
| 15 | 170     | <-- =SUMIF(E10:E14,">40",D10:D14) | |

The function wizard really helps when you use this function. Here it is for the above example. You'll note that **Range** is the column of criteria ("Score 2") and **Sum_range** is the column to be added. If you don't specify **Sum_range**, Excel assumes that it's the same as **Range**.

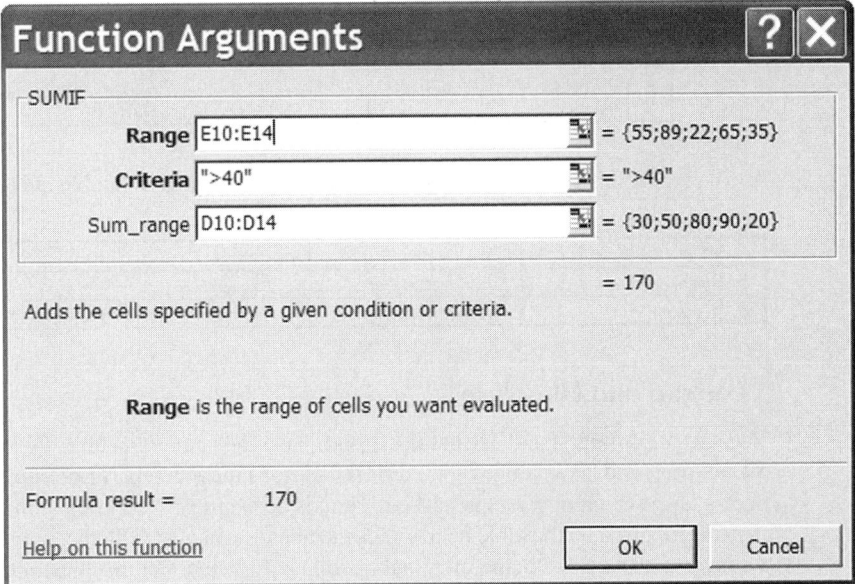

## SumProduct

This function pairwise multiplies the entries in two columns and adds the results. It's sometimes useful in statistics (do we have an example?). Here's a simple example that calculates the expected return of a portfolio. There are four assets, each with a different expected return. To calculate the expected portfolio return, we have to multiply the expected return in column B by the portfolio proportion of each asset (column C). **SumProduct** does this nicely.

|    | A | B | C | D | E | F |
|----|---|---|---|---|---|---|
| 18 | **Asset** | **Expected return** | **Portfolio proportion** | | | |
| 19 | 1 | 20% | 15% | | | |
| 20 | 2 | 8% | 22% | | | |
| 21 | 3 | 15% | 38% | | | |
| 22 | 4 | 12% | 25% | | | |
| 23 | | | | | | |
| 24 | | Expected portfolio return | 13.46% | <-- =SUMPRODUCT(B19:B22,C19:C22) | | |

## 26.3. Conditional Functions

**If( )**, **VLookup( )**, and **HLookup( )** are three functions that allow you to put in conditional statements.

The syntax of Excel's **If** statement is **If(condition,output if condition is true, output if condition is false)**. In the example below, if the initial number in B3 < 3, then the desired output is 15. If B3 > 3, then the output is 0.

|   | A | B | C |
|---|---|---|---|
| 1 | | **THE IF FUNCTION** | |
| 2 | Initial number | | 2 |
| 3 | If statement | | 15 <-- =IF(B2<=3,15,0) |

You can make **If** print text also, by enclosing the desired text in double quotes.

|   | A | B | C |
|---|---|---|---|
| 5 | Initial number | 2 | |
| 6 | If statement | Less than or equal to 3 | <-- =IF(B5<=3,"Less than or equal to 3","More than 3") |

### VLookup and HLookup

Because **VLookup( )** and **HLookup( )** both have the same structure, we will concentrate on **VLookup( )** and leave you to figure out **HLookup( )** for yourself. **VLookup( )** is a way to introduce a table search in your spreadsheet. Here is an example: Suppose the marginal tax rates on income are given by the table below—for income less than $8,000, the marginal tax rate is 0%; for income above $8,000, the marginal tax rate is 15%, etc. Cell B9 illustrates how the function **VLookup** is used to look up the marginal tax rate.

|   | A | B | C |
|---|---|---|---|
| 1 | | **VLOOKUP FUNCTION** | |
| 2 | **Income** | **Tax rate** | |
| 3 | 0 | 0% | |
| 4 | 8,000 | 15% | |
| 5 | 14,000 | 25% | |
| 6 | 25,000 | 38% | |
| 7 | | | |
| 8 | Income | 15,000 | |
| 9 | Tax rate | 25% | <-- =VLOOKUP(B8,A3:B6,2) |

The syntax of this function is **VLookup(lookup_value,table,column)**. The first column of the lookup table, A3:A6, must be arranged in ascending (increasing) order. The **lookup_value** (in this case the income of 15,000) is used to determine the applicable row of the **table**. The row is the first row whose value is < the **lookup_value**; in this case, this is the row that starts with 14,000. The **column** entry determines from which column of the applicable row the answer is taken; in this case the marginal tax rates are in column 2.

Here's the Excel function wizard for this table.

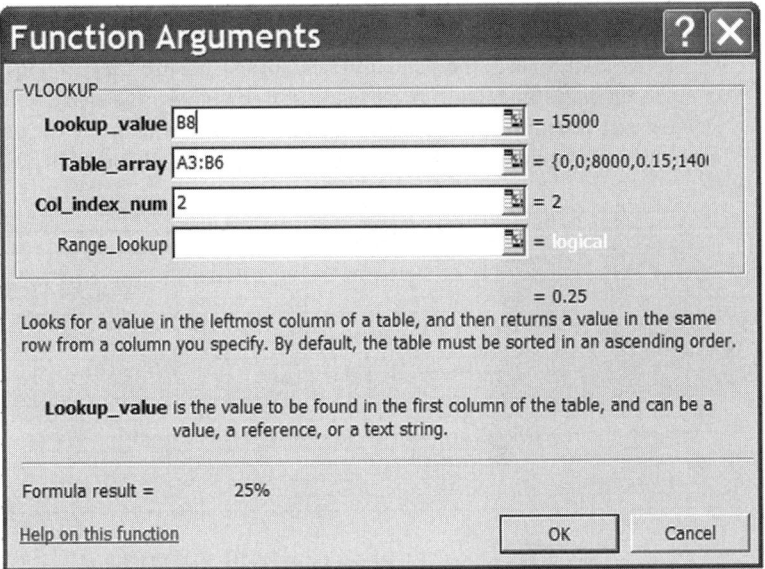

## The First Column of VLookup Must Be Sorted

The first column of the **VLookup** table must be *sorted*, meaning it must be in increasing order (either numerical or alphabetical). To see what this means, we have a slightly complicated example: The data in columns A and B below were imported from a database; column A gives the date and column B gives an interest rate on a particular date.

| | A | B | C | D | E | F |
|---|---|---|---|---|---|---|
| 1 | | FIRST COLUMN OF VLOOKUP MUST BE SORTED | | | | |
| 2 | Date | Interest rate | | Month | Day | Year |
| 3 | JAN. 07,1991 | 6.721 | | JAN | 07 | 1991 |
| 4 | FEB. 07,1991 | 6.145 | | Feb | 07 | 1991 |
| 5 | FEB. 11,1991 | 6.03 | | FEB | 11 | 1991 |
| 6 | MAR. 04,1991 | 6.287 | | MAR | 04 | 1991 |
| 7 | APR. 01,1991 | 5.985 | | APR | 01 | 1991 |
| 8 | JUN. 08,1991 | 5.777 | | JUN | 08 | 1991 |
| 9 | AUG. 15,1991 | 5.744 | | AUG | 15 | 1991 |
| 10 | OCT. 22,1991 | 5.868 | | OCT | 22 | 1991 |
| 11 | | | | | | |
| 12 | | | | | | |
| 13 | | =LEFT(A10,3) | | =MID(A10,6,2) | =RIGHT(A10,4) | |

We would like to give each date a standard Excel value. That is, instead of "Jan. 07, 1991," we'd like to write the following.

| | A | B |
|---|---|---|
| 18 | **Standard Excel date format** | **Number equivalent** |
| 19 | 7-Jan-91 | 33245 |

(The equivalence between Excel dates and numbers is discussed in Chapter 29.)

To write the date in the standard Excel format, we use the functions **Left**, **Mid**, and **Right** to *parse* the dates in column A into month, day, and year (see next section). We now need to identify each month with its number (i.e., Jan = 1, Feb = 2, etc.). We can use **VLookup** to do this, but only if the **VLookup** table has its left column in alphabetical order.

| | A | B | C | D | E | F | G | H | I | J | K |
|---|---|---|---|---|---|---|---|---|---|---|---|
| 1 | | FIRST COLUMN OF VLOOKUP MUST BE SORTED | | | | | | | | | |
| 2 | Date | Interest rate | | Month | Day | Year | | Which month? | | Date value | |
| 3 | JAN. 07,1991 | 6.721 | | JAN | 07 | 1991 | | 1 | <-- =VLOOKUP(D3,$J$6:$K$17,2) | 1/7/1991 | <-- =DATE(F3,H3,E3 |
| 4 | FEB. 07,1991 | 6.145 | | Feb | 07 | 1991 | | 2 | | | |
| 5 | FEB. 11,1991 | 6.03 | | FEB | 11 | 1991 | | 2 | | VLookup table | |
| 6 | MAR. 04,1991 | 6.287 | | MAR | 04 | 1991 | | 3 | | Apr | 4 |
| 7 | APR. 01,1991 | 5.985 | | APR | 01 | 1991 | | 4 | | Aug | 8 |
| 8 | JUN. 08,1991 | 5.777 | | JUN | 08 | 1991 | | 6 | | Dec | 12 |
| 9 | AUG. 15,1991 | 5.744 | | AUG | 15 | 1991 | | 8 | | Feb | 2 |
| 10 | OCT. 22,1991 | 5.868 | | OCT | 22 | 1991 | | 10 | | Jan | 1 |
| 11 | | | | | | | | | | Jul | 7 |
| 12 | | | | | | | | | | Jun | 6 |
| 13 | | =LEFT(A10,3) | | =MID(A10,6,2) | =RIGHT(A10,4) | | | | | Mar | 3 |
| 14 | | | | | | | | | | May | 5 |
| 15 | | | | | | | | | | Nov | 11 |
| 16 | | | | | | | | | | Oct | 10 |
| 17 | | | | | | | | | | Sep | 9 |

This gives a rather strange-looking table (cells J6:K17), but you can convince yourself that this works.

# 26.4. Text Functions

Excel distinguishes between numbers and *text*. To sound dense, you can add, subtract, etc. numbers, but you can't do this for text. On the other hand, Excel allows you to *concatenate* text (if this sounds mysterious, read on).

## Concatenation: Combining Text from Several Cells

In the example below, we've written "twelve" in cell A2 and "cows" in cell B2. In cell A4, we tried to write **=A3+B3**; we intended this to come out "Twelvecows", but Excel won't accept this, because neither the contents of A2 ("Twelve") nor those of B2 ("cows") is a number. We can combine the text as in cell A5, by writing **=A3&B3**.

| | A | B |
|---|---|---|
| 2 | Twelve | cows |
| 3 | | |
| 4 | #VALUE! | <-- =A2+B2 |
| 5 | Twelvecows | <-- =A2&B2 |
| 6 | | |
| 7 | Twelve blue cows | <-- =A2&" blue "&B2 |

In cell A7, we've added the word "blue" plus some spaces, putting the additional text/spaces inside quotation marks.

## Text

Now look at the example below.

| | A | B | C |
|---|---|---|---|
| 10 | Number of cows | 1200 | |
| 11 | | | |
| 12 | Text | 1200 cows | <-- =TEXT(B10,"0")&" cows" |
| 13 | | | |
| 14 | | 1200.00 cows | <-- =TEXT(B10,"0.00")&" cows" |
| 15 | | 1,200.0 cows | <-- =TEXT(B10,"0,000.0")&" cows" |
| 16 | | 120,000.00% cows | <-- =TEXT(B10,"0,000.00%")&" cows" |

In cell B12 we want to create a text that contains the number of cows (cell B10) and the word "cows". The Excel function **Text(B10,"0")** turns the number 1200 into a text form that can then be used in the formula in cell B12. The second part of the **Text** function—where we've currently written "0"—is used to indicate the appearance of the text. Cells B14:B16 give some other examples.

## Left, Right, Mid, Len

The first three functions allow you to pick out parts of texts. In the example below, we've used these functions to pick out parts of the text in cell A18.

| | A | B |
|---|---|---|
| 18 | 15 pink flamingos went to the zoo | |
| 19 | | |
| 20 | 15 | <-- =LEFT(A18,2) |
| 21 | pink flamingos | <-- =MID(A18,4,14) |
| 22 | zoo | <-- =RIGHT(A18,3) |
| 23 | | 33 <-- =LEN(A18) |

The function **=Left(A19,2)** picks out the 2 leftmost characters of cell A19. The function **=Mid(A19,4,14)** picks out the 14 characters of cell A19, starting with the 4th character. And the function **=Right(A19,3)**, well...you'll figure that one out yourself.

As illustrated in cell A23, the function **Len** tells you the number of characters in the text.

You might ask why a finance book needs to consider these functions. The following data give prices for some options on General Motors and were downloaded from the Web site of the Chicago Board of Options Exchange. When we downloaded the data, here's what they looked like.

| | A | B | C | D |
|---|---|---|---|---|
| 1 | GENERAL MOTORS OPTION DATA<br>Downloaded from Chicago Board of Options Exchange<br>Web Site | | | |
| 2 | Calls | Last Sale | Puts | Last Sale |
| 3 | 01 Aug 60.00 (GM HL-E) | 3.5 | 01 Aug 60.00 (GM TL-E) | 0.5 |
| 4 | 01 Aug 60.00 (GM HL-A) | 3.4 | 01 Aug 60.00 (GM TL-A) | 0.4 |
| 5 | 01 Aug 60.00 (GM HL-P) | 3 | 01 Aug 60.00 (GM TL-P) | 0.4 |
| 6 | 01 Aug 60.00 (GM HL-X) | 2.9 | 01 Aug 60.00 (GM TL-X) | 0.6 |
| 7 | 01 Aug 60.00 (GM HL-8) | 3.4 | 01 Aug 60.00 (GM TL-8) | 0.5 |
| 8 | 01 Aug 65.00 (GM HM-E) | 0.45 | 01 Aug 65.00 (GM TM-E) | 2.85 |
| 9 | 01 Aug 65.00 (GM HM-A) | 0.45 | 01 Aug 65.00 (GM TM-A) | 1.8 |
| 10 | 01 Aug 65.00 (GM HM-P) | 0.45 | 01 Aug 65.00 (GM TM-P) | 2.4 |
| 11 | 01 Aug 65.00 (GM HM-X) | 1.15 | 01 Aug 65.00 (GM TM-X) | 2.25 |
| 12 | 01 Aug 65.00 (GM HM-8) | 0.4 | 01 Aug 65.00 (GM TM-8) | 2.7 |
| 13 | 01 Aug 70.00 (GM HN-E) | 0.05 | 01 Aug 70.00 (GM TN-E) | 7.9 |
| 14 | 01 Aug 70.00 (GM HN-A) | 0.05 | 01 Aug 70.00 (GM TN-A) | 6.3 |
| 15 | 01 Aug 70.00 (GM HN-P) | 0.05 | 01 Aug 70.00 (GM TN-P) | 0 |
| 16 | 01 Aug 70.00 (GM HN-X) | 0.2 | 01 Aug 70.00 (GM TN-X) | 7.5 |
| 17 | 01 Aug 70.00 (GM HN-8) | 0.05 | 01 Aug 70.00 (GM TN-8) | 6.8 |
| 18 | | | | |
| 19 | | | | |
| 20 | | | Other information | |
| 21 | | | | |
| 22 | Option expiration year and month | | | |
| 23 | | | Option exercise price | |

The information in columns A and C gives information about the option, including the expiration year and month, the exercise price, and a parenthetical item that shows you the stock on which the option is written, the option symbol, and the exchange on which the option traded. For example,

GM HN-E   a General Motors call option with exercise price 70 expiring in August 2001 and trading on the Chicago Board of Options Exchange

GM TL-A   the stock symbol for a General Motors put option with exercise price 60, expiring in August 2001 and trading on the American Stock Exchange

Now suppose we want to separate the dates, the option's symbol, and the exchange on which the option traded.

| | C | D | E | F | G | H | I | J | K |
|---|---|---|---|---|---|---|---|---|---|
| 2 | Puts | Last Sale | | Date | Symbol | Exchange | | | |
| 3 | 01 Aug 60.00 (GM TL-E) | 0.5 | | 01Aug | TL | E | | | |
| 4 | 01 Aug 60.00 (GM TL-A) | 0.4 | | | | | | | |
| 5 | 01 Aug 60.00 (GM TL-P) | 0.4 | | | | | | | |
| 6 | 01 Aug 60.00 (GM TL-X) | 0.6 | | =LEFT(C3,2)&MID(C3,4,3) | | | | | |
| 7 | 01 Aug 60.00 (GM TL-8) | 0.5 | | | | | =MID(C3,LEN(C3)-4,2) | | |
| 8 | 01 Aug 65.00 (GM TM-E) | 2.85 | | | | | | | |
| 9 | 01 Aug 65.00 (GM TM-A) | 1.8 | | | | | | | |
| 10 | 01 Aug 65.00 (GM TM-P) | 2.4 | | | | | | | |
| 11 | 01 Aug 65.00 (GM TM-X) | 2.25 | | | =MID(C3,LEN(C3)-1,1) | | | | |
| 12 | 01 Aug 65.00 (GM TM-8) | 2.7 | | | | | | | |
| 13 | 01 Aug 70.00 (GM TN-E) | 7.9 | | | | | | | |

In Chapter 29 (which explains how to use times and dates in Excel), we use this information to design a function that gives us the option's expiration date.

# 26.5. Statistical Functions

Many of Excel's statistical functions have already been discussed in previous chapters.

| Average | Finds the average of a range of cells | Chapters 8 and 9 |
|---|---|---|
| Covar | The covariance of two sets of data | Chapter 9 |
| Correl | The correlation coefficient of two sets of data | Chapter 9 |
| Frequency | An array function that computes the frequency distribution | Chapter 8 |
| Intercept, Slope, Rsq | Compute the intercept, slope, and $R^2$ of a regression | Chapters 9 and 12 |
| Max, Min | The maximum and minimum of a set of numbers | Chapter 8, Chapters 20–23 |
| Stdev, StdevP | The standard deviation | Chapters 8 and 9 |
| Var, VarP | The variance | Chapters 8 and 9 |

## Median, Large, and Rank

In this subsection we discuss three more statistical functions: **Median**, **Large**, and **Rank**. We illustrate the following example, which gives the grades for 11 students.

| | A | B | C |
|---|---|---|---|
| 1 | **Median, Large, Rank** | | |
| 2 | Student | Grade | |
| 3 | 1 | 100 | |
| 4 | 2 | 50 | |
| 5 | 3 | 75 | |
| 6 | 4 | 32 | |
| 7 | 5 | 98 | |
| 8 | 6 | 86 | |
| 9 | 7 | 72 | |
| 10 | 8 | 63 | |
| 11 | 9 | 41 | |
| 12 | 10 | 88 | |
| 13 | 11 | 92 | |
| 14 | | | |
| 15 | Average | 72.45 | <-- =AVERAGE(B3:B13) |
| 16 | Median | 75 | <-- =MEDIAN(B3:B13) |
| 17 | Large | 92 | <-- =LARGE(B3:B13,3) |
| 18 | Rank | 7 | <-- =RANK(B9,B3:B13) |

The median is the grade that splits the list in two: There are five grades higher than 75 and five lower. The median is different from the average, as you can see.

The Excel function **Large** tells you the $k$th largest number in the set of grades.

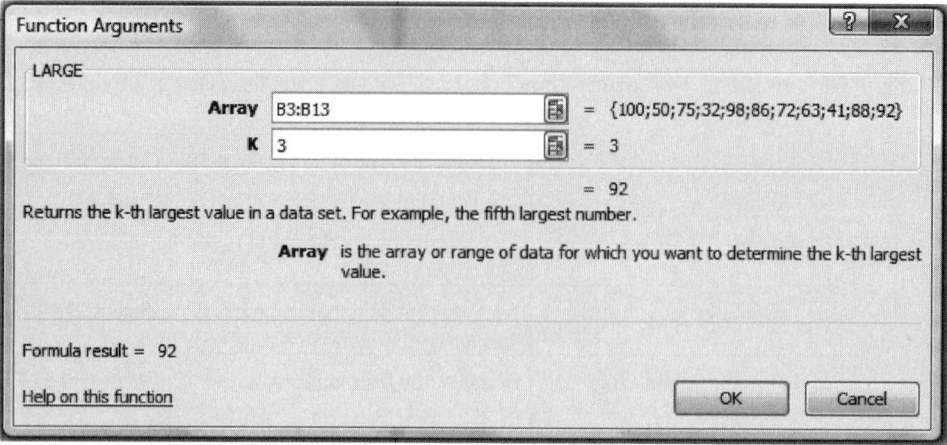

The Excel function **Rank** tells you where a particular number places in the range of grades. In the example given the grade 72 is the seventh among the set of grades in B3:B13.

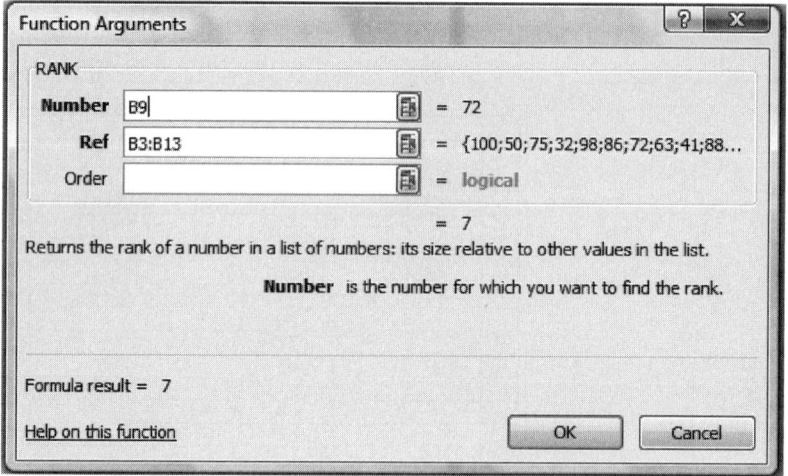

## Count, CountIf, CountA

All three of these functions *count* cells. The difference (we'll illustrate) is that:

- **Count** counts the number of cells that contain values and ignores the cells that contain text.
- **CountA** counts all nonblank cells in a range, whether they contain values or text.
- **CountIf** counts cells that fulfill a particular condition.

Now we'll illustrate.

|   | A | B | C |
|---|---|---|---|
| 1 | COUNT, COUNTIF, COUNTA | | |
| 2 | List | | |
| 3 | 1 | | |
| 4 | 2 | | |
| 5 | 3 | | |
| 6 | 4 | | |
| 7 | Terry | | |
| 8 | Oliver | | |
| 9 | Noah | | |
| 10 | Sara | | |
| 11 | Zvi | | |
| 12 | | | |
| 13 | Count | 4 | <-- =COUNT(A3:A11) |
| 14 | CountA | 9 | <-- =COUNTA(A3:A11) |
| 15 | CountIf | 2 | <-- =COUNTIF(A3:A11,">2") |

# 26.6. Match and Index

We use these functions in a minor way in Chapter 8 to locate the specific dates on which McDonald's stock achieved its maximum and minimum price.

## Using Index to Locate a Value in an Array

In the example below, we use **Index** to locate the value in row 5 and column 6 of an 8 x 8 array.

|   | A | B | C | D | E | F | G | H |
|---|---|---|---|---|---|---|---|---|
| 1 | USING INDEX TO LOCATE A NUMBER IN AN ARRAY | | | | | | | |
| 2 | 34 | 43 | 90 | 19 | 60 | 16 | 83 | 10 |
| 3 | 85 | 52 | 89 | 56 | 9 | 21 | 17 | 10 |
| 4 | 66 | 6 | 48 | 18 | 19 | 20 | 36 | 64 |
| 5 | 20 | 96 | 70 | 18 | 16 | 73 | 55 | 9 |
| 6 | 38 | 10 | 68 | 52 | 63 | 97 | 62 | 40 |
| 7 | 38 | 19 | 90 | 85 | 46 | 62 | 38 | 11 |
| 8 | 25 | 35 | 58 | 55 | 91 | 25 | 77 | 79 |
| 9 | 73 | 59 | 82 | 49 | 55 | 10 | 67 | 88 |
| 10 | | | | | | | | |
| 11 | Row | 5 | | | | | | |
| 12 | Column | 6 | | | | | | |
| 13 | Number? | 97 | <-- =INDEX(A2:H9,B11,B12) | | | | | |

## Using Match to Find Where a Specific Value Occurs

The data below are the price of Citicorp on the first trading day of September 2007–September 2009. The minimum price over this period was $1.50. Using **Match(Lookup_value,Lookup_array,MatchType)** we can locate this value on row 18 of the set of prices.

| | A | B | C | D | E | F |
|---|---|---|---|---|---|---|
| 1 | | | | USING MATCH TO LOCATE A VALUE IN AN ARRAY | | |
| 2 | Date | Citicorp closing price | | | | |
| 3 | 4-Sep-07 | 43.55 | | | | |
| 4 | 1-Oct-07 | 39.10 | | Minimum price | 1.5 | <-- =MIN(B3:B27) |
| 5 | 1-Nov-07 | 31.48 | | Maximum price | 43.55 | <-- =MAX(B3:B27) |
| 6 | 3-Dec-07 | 27.83 | | | | |
| 7 | 2-Jan-08 | 26.94 | | Where is the minimum? | 18 | <-- =MATCH(E4,B3:B27,0) |
| 8 | 1-Feb-08 | 22.67 | | Where is the maximum? | 1 | <-- =MATCH(E5,B3:B27,0) |
| 9 | 3-Mar-08 | 20.48 | | | | |
| 10 | 1-Apr-08 | 24.16 | | Date of the minimum price? | 2-Feb-09 | <-- =INDEX(A3:A27,E7) |
| 11 | 1-May-08 | 21.20 | | | 2-Feb-09 | <-- =INDEX(A3:A27,MATCH(E4,B3:B27,0)) |
| 12 | 2-Jun-08 | 16.23 | | | | |
| 13 | 1-Jul-08 | 18.41 | | Date of the maximum price? | 4-Sep-07 | <-- =INDEX(A3:A27,E8) |
| 14 | 1-Aug-08 | 18.71 | | | | |
| 15 | 2-Sep-08 | 20.21 | | | | |
| 16 | 1-Oct-08 | 13.62 | | | | |
| 17 | 3-Nov-08 | 8.27 | | | | |
| 18 | 1-Dec-08 | 6.69 | | | | |
| 19 | 2-Jan-09 | 3.55 | | | | |
| 20 | 2-Feb-09 | 1.50 | | | | |
| 21 | 2-Mar-09 | 2.53 | | The syntax of **Match** is Match(Lookup_value,Lookup_array,MatchType). | | |
| 22 | 1-Apr-09 | 3.05 | | | | |
| 23 | 1-May-09 | 3.72 | | A note on the third parameter of **Match** (called **MatchType**): | | |
| 24 | 1-Jun-09 | 2.97 | | If **MatchType** = 0 or is omitted, then **Match** finds the exact match of the **LookupValue**. | | |
| 25 | 1-Jul-09 | 3.17 | | If **MatchType** = 1 , then **Match** finds the smallest number larger than  the **LookupValue**. | | |
| 26 | 3-Aug-09 | 5.00 | | If **MatchType** = -1 , then **Match** finds the smallest number larger than the **LookupValue**. | | |
| 27 | 1-Sep-09 | 4.57 | | | | |

## Combining Match and Index

On what date did the minimum price for Citicorp occur? We can combine **Index** and **Match** as shown in the example above to determine 2 February 2009 as the date of the minimum price for Citicorp.

# Summary

Excel has hundreds of functions. This chapter has illustrated the major functions used in this book (and then some). We rely on you, as an educated reader, to figure the rest out for yourself.

## EXERCISES

1.

   a. Use **NPV** to compute the present value of the project below.

| | A | B |
|---|---|---|
| 1 | Discount rate | 15% |
| 2 | | |
| 3 | Year | Cash flow |
| 4 | 1 | 100 |
| 5 | 2 | 200 |
| 6 | 3 | 300 |
| 7 | 4 | 400 |
| 8 | 5 | 500 |

   b. Suppose the project costs $600. What is its net present value?

2.

    a. Use **NPV** to compute the net present value for the project below.

| | A | B |
|---|---|---|
| 1 | Discount rate | 15% |
| 2 | | |
| 3 | Year | Cash flow |
| 4 | 0 | -600 |
| 5 | 1 | 100 |
| 6 | 2 | 200 |
| 7 | 3 | 300 |
| 8 | 4 | 400 |
| 9 | 5 | 500 |

    b. Use **Data Table** (see Chapter 27) to compute the present value of the project for discount rates of 0%, 4%,..., 48%. Graph the results and estimate the project's IRR.

3. Use the IRR function to compute the internal rate of return of the project in the previous problem.

4. Use the **FV** function in the following exercises.

    a. What is the value at the end of 10 years of $200 deposited in the bank today and at the beginning of each of the next 9 years at an annual interest rate of 3%?

    b. What is the future value at the end of 10 years of $200 deposited in the bank at the end of years 1, 2,..., 10. Assume a 3% interest rate.

5. You're 25 years old, and you want to save for the future. You intend to deposit $1,000 in the bank today. In each of the next 44 years you intend to make a similar deposit. If the interest rate is 5% annually, how much will you have when you reach the age of 70?

6. Your mom is 50 and wants to put away some money for retirement. She would like to make monthly deposits in the bank, starting today and at the beginning of every month between now and the month before her retirement at age 70. (To save you irritation, the total number of deposits is 15 * 20 = 300.) If the interest rate is 6% annually (0.5% per month), how much should she save each month to have $200,000 on the day she retires? Use the **FV** function.

7.

    a. Your mom is 50 and wants to put away some money for retirement. She would like to make monthly deposits in the bank, starting today and at the beginning of every month between now and the month before her retirement at age 70. (To save you irritation, the total number of deposits is 15 * 20 = 300.) If the interest rate is 6% annually (0.5% per month), how much should she save each month to have $200,000 on the day she retires? Use the **PMT** function.

    b. Use **Data Table** (Chapter 27) to repeat the above calculation for annual interest rates of 0%, 1%,..., 12%.

8.

    a. You've taken a $60,000, 30-year mortgage to finance the purchase of your new house. The mortgage has an interest rate of 10% annually and requires monthly flat payments of interest and principal (by "flat" we mean that all the payments are equal). Use **PMT** to compute the monthly payment.

    b. Design a loan table showing that the payment you computed in the first part of this problem indeed pays off the mortgage.

9. You are considering buying a bond that pays $112.50 at the end of this and each of the subsequent 10 years. The interest rate is 12%. Use the **PV** function to value the bond.

10. You've offered to finance Joe's purchase of a $20,000 car. Joe offers to repay you $500 per month for the next 48 months.

   a. Use **Rate** to compute the monthly interest rate he's offering. Confirm your answer using **IRR**.

   b. What is the annual interest rate?

11. You are taking a $12,000 loan at 6%. If the maximum annual payment you can make is $2,000, how long will it take you to pay off the loan (hint: use **NPER**)? Build a loan table that confirms your answer.

12. Your money market fund pays 3% interest annually, compounded continuously.

   a. If you deposit $100,000 into the fund today, and if the 3% interest rate holds for the next 10 years, how much will you have in 10 years?

   b. b. What is your effective annual interest rate (EAIR) on the fund? (Although you don't need it to answer this question, you may want to remind yourself what the EAIR is—see Chapter 3.)

13. Your bank account pays 5.2% interest annually, compounded continuously. You have $25,000 in the account today, and you intend to withdraw this amount 3 years and 4 months from today. How much will you have in the account at that time?

14. Compute the continuously compounded present value of the following set of cash flows, using a discount rate of 15%.

|   | A | B |
|---|---|---|
| 1 | Continuously compounded discount rate | 15% |
| 2 |   |   |
| 3 | **Date** | **Cash flow** |
| 4 | 1 | 15,000 |
| 5 | 2 | 22,000 |
| 6 | 3 | 14,750 |
| 7 | 4 | 3,222 |
| 8 | 5 | 6,333 |
| 9 | 6 | 18,000 |
| 10 | 7 | 280,000 |

15. Compute the continuously compounded PV of the following set of cash flows, using a discount rate of 15%. (This problem requires some familiarity with dates in Excel—see Chapter 29.)

|   | A | B |
|---|---|---|
| 1 | Continuously compounded discount rate | 15% |
| 2 | Date today | 1-Jan-06 |
| 3 | **Date** | **Cash flow** |
| 4 | 31-Jan-06 | 15,000 |
| 5 | 31-Jan-07 | 22,000 |
| 6 | 17-Jul-07 | 14,750 |
| 7 | 31-Dec-07 | 3,222 |
| 8 | 14-Mar-08 | 6,333 |
| 9 | 11-Nov-08 | 18,000 |
| 10 | 13-Mar-09 | 280,000 |

16. You've been offered a financial asset that costs $1,000 today and pays back $1,100 in 1 year.

   a. Compute the discretely compounded rate of return on the asset.

   b. Compute the continuously compounded rate of return on the asset.

17. The CD-ROM that accompanies this book contains a spreadsheet with IBM stock prices and dividends from February 1990 through August 2004. Part of this spreadsheet is given below; note that column D of the spreadsheet shows the stock return for the period over which the dividend is paid (usually this period is a quarter). Use SumIf to find the total of all dividends paid during periods when the stock return was greater than 25%.

| | A | B | C | D | E |
|---|---|---|---|---|---|
| 1 | Date | IBM Dividends | IBM Stock price | Stock return | |
| 2 | Feb-90 | | 103.87 | | |
| 3 | May-90 | 1.21 | 120.00 | 15.53% | <-- =C3/C2-1 |
| 4 | Aug-90 | 1.21 | 101.87 | -15.11% | <-- =C4/C3-1 |
| 5 | Nov-90 | 1.21 | 113.62 | 11.53% | <-- =C5/C4-1 |
| 6 | Feb-91 | 1.21 | 128.75 | 13.32% | <-- =C6/C5-1 |
| 7 | May-91 | 1.21 | 106.12 | -17.58% | |
| 8 | Aug-91 | 1.21 | 96.87 | -8.72% | |
| 9 | Nov-91 | 1.21 | 92.50 | -4.51% | |
| 10 | Feb-92 | 1.21 | 86.87 | -6.09% | |

18. Use SumProduct to compute the return of the portfolio given below. The portfolio is composed of three stocks with weights as indicated.

| | A | B | C |
|---|---|---|---|
| 1 | Stock | Percentage of portfolio | Stock return |
| 2 | A | 40% | 15% |
| 3 | B | 25% | 22% |
| 4 | C | 35% | 13% |

19. The end-semester grades for Finance 101 are given below.

| | A | B | C |
|---|---|---|---|
| 1 | Student | Number grade | Letter grade |
| 2 | Mary | 85 | |
| 3 | John | 68 | |
| 4 | Jennifer | 72 | |
| 5 | Mo | 100 | |
| 6 | Simon | 57 | |
| 7 | Noah | 91 | |
| 8 | Terry | 78 | |
| 9 | Sara | 81 | |
| 10 | Zvi | 45 | |
| 11 | George | 93 | |

The professor for the course has to assign each student a letter grad based on his or her average. The professor's grading key is as follows.

| Grade range | |
|---|---|
| $\geq 0$ and $< 50$ | F |
| $\geq 50$ and $< 60$ | D |
| $\geq 60$ and $< 70$ | C |
| $\geq 70$ and $< 85$ | B |
| $\geq 85$ | A |

Use **VLookup** to assign grades to each student.

20. On the CD-ROM that comes with the book is a list of companies in the Dow Jones 30 Industrials (DJ30) and their share prices on 27 August 2004. Part of the list is given below.

a. What is the average price of a DJ30 stock?

b. What is the median price?

c. Use **Large** to determine the largest of the stock prices. Do the same using **Max**.

d. Use **Large** to determine the smallest of the stock prices. Do the same using **Min**.

e. Use **Rank** to determine the relative ranking of Microsoft's stock price among the DJ30.

| | A | B |
|---|---|---|
| 1 | **DOW JONES 30 INDUSTRIALS**<br>**Stock prices on 27 August 2004** | |
| 2 | 3M Corporation | 81.63 |
| 3 | Alcoa Inc | 32.99 |
| 4 | Altria Group inc | 49.15 |
| 5 | American Express Company | 50.07 |
| 6 | American Intl Group Inc | 70.96 |
| 7 | Boeing Co. | 52.08 |
| 8 | Caterpillar Inc. | 73.74 |
| 9 | Citigroup, Inc. | 46.75 |
| 10 | E.I. du Pont de Nemours and Company | 42.60 |

21. Using the list of DJ30 companies from the previous exercise, determine the following.

a. Use **CountA** to determine the number of companies in the list in column A.

b. Use **Count** to determine the number of share prices in the list in column B.

c. Use **CountIf** to determine the number of companies whose share price is greater or equal to $30.

# 27 Data Tables

## CHAPTER CONTENTS

## Overview

Data tables are Excel's most sophisticated way of doing sensitivity analysis. They are a bit tricky to implement, but the effort of learning them is well worth it!

## 27.1. A Simple Example

If we deposit $100 today and leave it in a bank drawing 15% interest for 10 years, what will be its future value? As the example below shows, the answer is $404.56.

| | A | B | C |
|---|---|---|---|
| 1 | DATA TABLE EXAMPLE | | |
| 2 | Interest rate | 15% | |
| 3 | Initial deposit | 100 | |
| 4 | Years | 10 | |
| 5 | Future value | $404.56 | <-- =B3*(1+B2)^B4 |

Now suppose we want show the sensitivity of the future value to the interest rate. In cells A10:A16 we have put interest rates varying from 0 to 60%, and in cell B9 we have put **=B5**, which refers to the initial calculation of the future value.

| | A | B | C |
|---|---|---|---|
| 1 | DATA TABLE EXAMPLE | | |
| 2 | Interest rate | 15% | |
| 3 | Initial deposit | 100 | |
| 4 | Years | 10 | |
| 5 | Future value | $404.56 | <-- =B3*(1+B2)^B4 |
| 6 | | | |
| 7 | | | |
| 8 | Interest rate | | |
| 9 | | $404.56 | <-- =B5 |
| 10 | 0% | | |
| 11 | 10% | | |
| 12 | 20% | | |
| 13 | 30% | | |
| 14 | 40% | | |
| 15 | 50% | | |
| 16 | 60% | | |

To use the data table technique we mark the range A9:B16 and then use the command **Data|What-If Analysis|Data Table**.

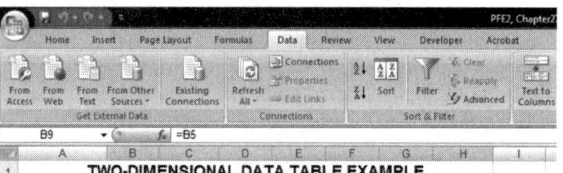

After you click on **Data Table**, here's the way the screen looks.

The dialog box asks whether the parameter to be varied is in a *row* or a *column* of the marked table. In our case, the interest rate to be varied is in column A of the table, so we move the cursor from **Row input cell** to **Column input cell** and indicate *where in the original example the interest rate occurs.*

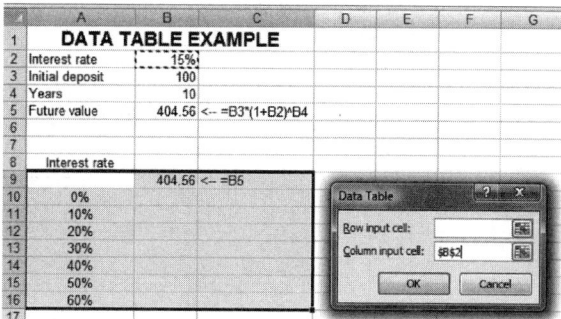

When you click **OK** you get the result.

|   | A | B | C |
|---|---|---|---|
| 1 | DATA TABLE EXAMPLE | | |
| 2 | Interest rate | 15% | |
| 3 | Initial deposit | 100 | |
| 4 | Years | 10 | |
| 5 | Future value | $404.56 | <-- =B3*(1+B2)^B4 |
| 6 | | | |
| 7 | | | |
| 8 | Interest rate | | |
| 9 | | $404.56 | <-- =B5 |
| 10 | 0% | 100 | |
| 11 | 10% | 259.3742 | |
| 12 | 20% | 619.1736 | |
| 13 | 30% | 1378.585 | |
| 14 | 40% | 2892.547 | |
| 15 | 50% | 5766.504 | |
| 16 | 60% | 10995.12 | |

## 27.2. Summary: How to Do a One-Dimensional Data Table

- Create an initial example.
- Set up a range with:
  - Some variable in the initial example that will be changed (like the interest rate in the above example).

|   | A | B | C | D |
|---|---|---|---|---|
| 1 | **DATA TABLE EXAMPLE** | | | |
| 2 | Interest rate | 15% | | |
| 3 | Initial deposit | 100 | | |
| 4 | Years | 10 | | |
| 5 | Future value | $404.56 | <-- =B3*(1+B2)^B4 | |
| 6 | | | | |
| 7 | | | Blank cell when variable is in column | |
| 8 | Interest rate | | | |
| 9 | | $404.56 | <-- =B5 | |
| 10 | 0% | | | |
| 11 | 5% | | | |
| 12 | 10% | | | |
| 13 | 15% | | | |
| 14 | 20% | | | |
| 15 | 25% | | | |
| 16 | 30% | | | |

- A reference to the initial example (like the **=B5** in the above). Note that you will always have a *blank cell* next to this reference. Note the blank cells when the variable is in a column.

Here's the blank cell when the variable is in a row.

|   | E | F | G | H | I | J | K | L |
|---|---|---|---|---|---|---|---|---|
| 6 | | | | | | | | |
| 7 | | Blank cell when variable is in row | | | | | | |
| 8 | | | | | | | | |
| 9 | | 0% | 5% | 10% | 15% | 20% | 25% | 30% |
| 10 | $404.56 | | | | | | | |
| 11 | | | | | | | | |
| 12 | =B5 | | | | | | | |
| 13 | | | | | | | | |

- Bring up the **Data|Table** command and indicate in the dialog box:
  - Whether the variable is in a column or a row.
  - Where in the initial example the variable occurs.

Either way, the result will be a sensitivity table.

| | A | B | C | D | E | F | G | H | I | J | K | L |
|---|---|---|---|---|---|---|---|---|---|---|---|---|
| 1 | | DATA TABLE EXAMPLE | | | | | | | | | | |
| 2 | Interest rate | 15% | | | | | | | | | | |
| 3 | Initial deposit | 100 | | | | | | | | | | |
| 4 | Years | 10 | | | | | | | | | | |
| 5 | Future value | $404.56 | <-- =B3*(1+B2)^B4 | | | | | | | | | |
| 6 | | | | | | | | | | | | |
| 7 | | | Blank cell when variable is in column | | | | Blank cell when variable is in row | | | | | |
| 8 | | Interest rate | | | | | | | | | | |
| 9 | | | $404.56 | <-- =B5 | | | 0% | 5% | 10% | 15% | 20% | 25% | 30% |
| 10 | 0% | 100 | | | $404.56 | 100 | 162.8895 | 259.3742 | 404.5558 | 619.1736 | 931.3226 | 1378.585 |
| 11 | 5% | 162.8895 | | | | | | | | | | |
| 12 | 10% | 259.3742 | | | =B5 | | | | | | | |
| 13 | 15% | 404.5558 | | | | | | | | | | |
| 14 | 20% | 619.1736 | | | | | | | | | | |
| 15 | 25% | 931.3226 | | | | | | | | | | |
| 16 | 30% | 1378.585 | | | | | | | | | | |

## 27.3. Some Notes on Data Tables

### Data Tables are Dynamic

You can change either your initial example or the variables and the table will adjust. Here's an example where we've changed the interest rates we want to vary (compare with the previous example).

| | A | B | C |
|---|---|---|---|
| 1 | DATA TABLE EXAMPLE | | |
| 2 | Interest rate | 15% | |
| 3 | Initial deposit | 100 | |
| 4 | Years | 10 | |
| 5 | Future value | $404.56 | <-- =B3*(1+B2)^B4 |
| 6 | | | |
| 7 | | | |
| 8 | Interest rate | | |
| 9 | | $404.56 | <-- =B5 |
| 10 | 0% | 100 | |
| 11 | 10% | 259.3742 | |
| 12 | 20% | 619.1736 | |
| 13 | 30% | 1378.585 | |
| 14 | 40% | 2892.547 | |
| 15 | 50% | 5766.504 | |
| 16 | 60% | 10995.12 | |

Here's another example: We change the function we're calculating, putting =FV(B2,B4,-B3,,1) in cell B5, as explained in Chapter 2, this function calculates the future value of 10 annual $100 deposits starting today and accumulating interest at 15% for 10 years.[1] Note that we've also changed the text in cell A5 from "initial deposit" to "annual deposit" to reflect what's now happening.

---

[1] As we also explained in Chapters 2 and 26, we put the minus sign before **B3** because otherwise—for reasons beyond logic—Excel produces a negative future value. Note that if we had typed **FV(B2,B4,-B3)** the assumption is that there are 10 deposits starting 1 year from now.

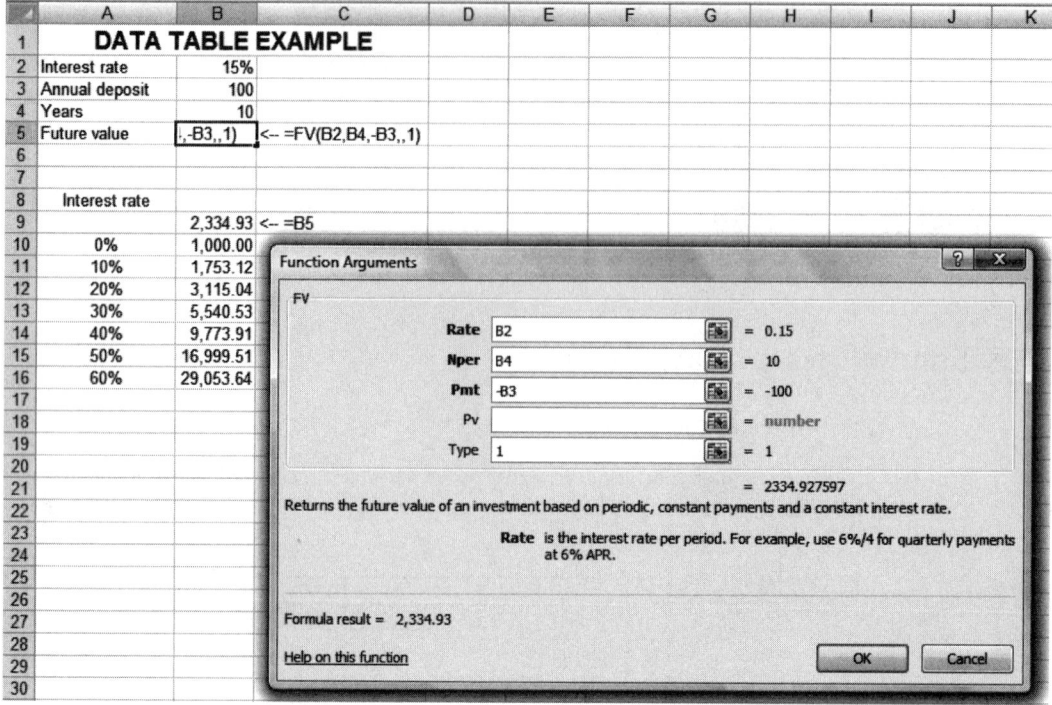

When we click **OK**, both the computation in cell B5 and the data table update.

|   | A | B | C |
|---|---|---|---|
| 1 | DATA TABLE EXAMPLE | | |
| 2 | Interest rate | 15% | |
| 3 | Initial deposit | 100 | |
| 4 | Years | 10 | |
| 5 | Future value | $2,334.93 | <-- =FV(B2,B4,-B3,,1) |
| 6 | | | |
| 7 | | | |
| 8 | Interest rate | | |
| 9 | | 2334.928 | <-- =B5 |
| 10 | 0% | 1000 | |
| 11 | 10% | 1753.117 | |
| 12 | 20% | 3115.042 | |
| 13 | 30% | 5540.535 | |
| 14 | 40% | 9773.913 | |
| 15 | 50% | 16999.51 | |
| 16 | 60% | 29053.64 | |

## You Can Only Erase the Whole Table but You Cannot Erase Part of a Table

If you try to erase part of a data table, you'll get an error message.

## You Can Hide the Cell Header but Not Erase It

The formula at the top of the table's second column (cell B9 in our case, containing the reference to cell B5) is called the "column header." This formula controls what the data table calculates. If you want to print a table, you often want to hide the column header. In the example below, we've put the cursor on cell B9. We right-click on the cell, go the command **Format|Cells**, and go to **Number|Custom**. Typing a semicolon in the **Type** box hides the cell.

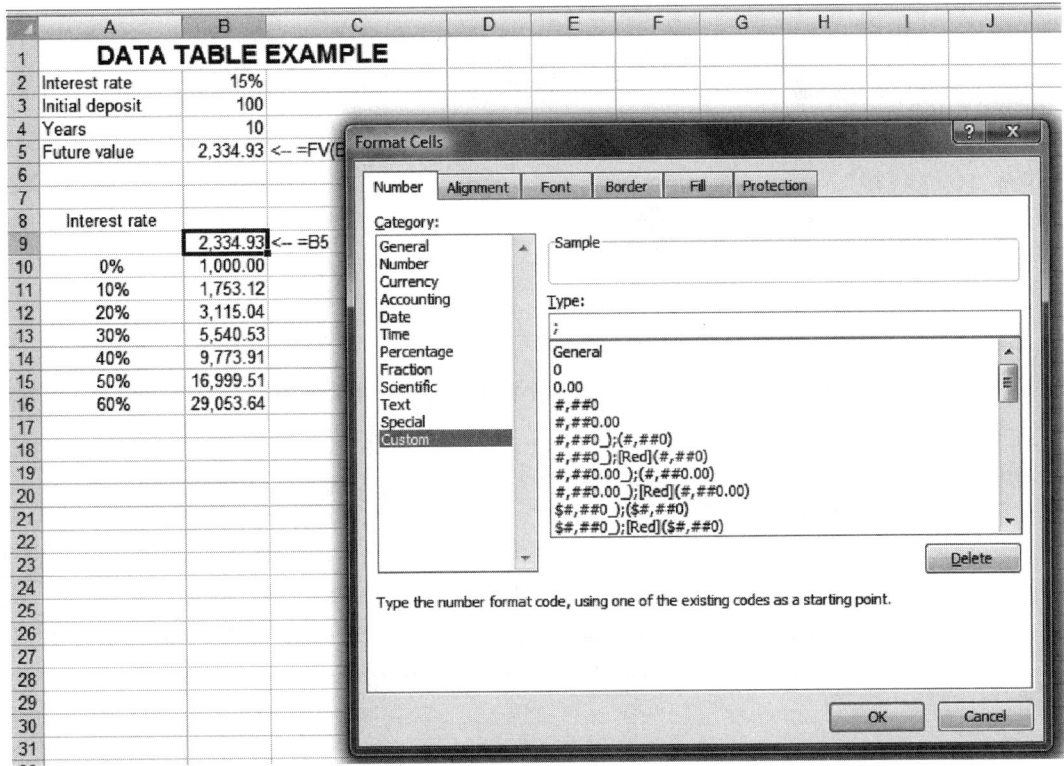

Here's the result.

| | A | B | C |
|---|---|---|---|
| 8 | Interest rate | | |
| 9 | | | <-- =B5 |
| 10 | 0% | 1000 | |
| 11 | 10% | 1753.117 | |
| 12 | 20% | 3115.042 | |
| 13 | 30% | 5540.535 | |
| 14 | 40% | 9773.913 | |
| 15 | 50% | 16999.51 | |
| 16 | 60% | 29053.64 | |

## 27.4. Two-Dimensional Data Tables

In the example below we return to the **FV** example discussed above. We want to vary our initial example with respect to both the interest rate and the initial deposit. The data table is set up in cells B9:H15.

| | A | B | C | D | E | F | G | H | I |
|---|---|---|---|---|---|---|---|---|---|
| 1 | DATA TABLE EXAMPLE | | | | | | | | |
| 2 | Interest rate | 15% | | | | | | | |
| 3 | Annual deposit | 100 | | | | | | | |
| 4 | Years | 10 | | | | | | | |
| 5 | Future value | $2,334.93 | <-- =FV(B2,B4,-B3,,1) | | | | | | |
| 6 | | | | | | | | | |
| 7 | Two-dimensional table, showing sensitivity of future value to both interest rate and deposit size | | | | | | | | |
| 8 | | | | | | | | | |
| 9 | | $2,334.93 | 0% | 5% | 10% | 15% | 20% | 25% | |
| 10 | | 50 | | | | | | | |
| 11 | =B5 | 100 | | | | | | | |
| 12 | | 150 | | | | | | | |
| 13 | | 200 | | | | | | | |
| 14 | | 250 | | | | | | | |
| 15 | | 300 | | | | | | | |

This time we indicate in the **Data|Table** command that there are two variables.

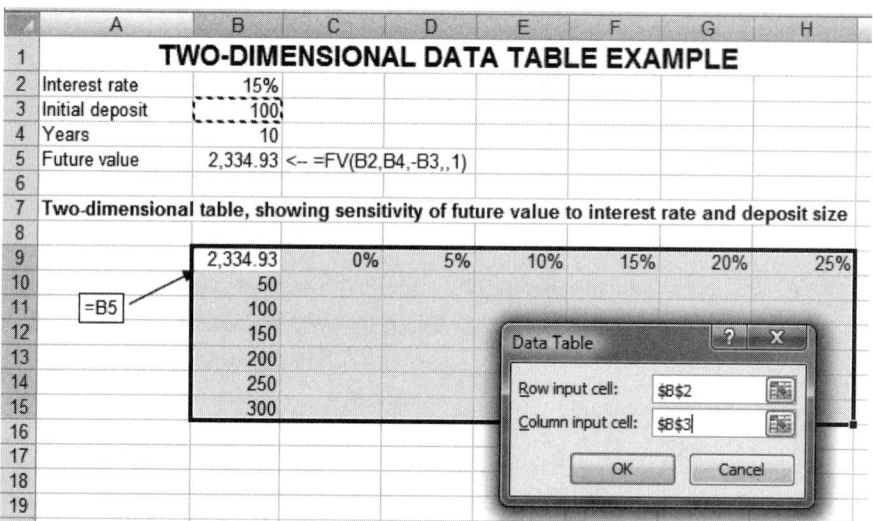

This creates a two-dimensional table.

| | B | C | D | E | F | G | H |
|---|---|---|---|---|---|---|---|
| 9 | $2,334.93 | 0% | 5% | 10% | 15% | 20% | 25% |
| 10 | 50 | 500.00 | 660.34 | 876.56 | 1,167.46 | 1,557.52 | 2,078.31 |
| 11 | 100 | 1,000.00 | 1,320.68 | 1,753.12 | 2,334.93 | 3,115.04 | 4,156.61 |
| 12 | 150 | 1,500.00 | 1,981.02 | 2,629.68 | 3,502.39 | 4,672.56 | 6,234.92 |
| 13 | 200 | 2,000.00 | 2,641.36 | 3,506.23 | 4,669.86 | 6,230.08 | 8,313.23 |
| 14 | 250 | 2,500.00 | 3,301.70 | 4,382.79 | 5,837.32 | 7,787.60 | 10,391.53 |
| 15 | 300 | 3,000.00 | 3,962.04 | 5,259.35 | 7,004.78 | 9,345.13 | 12,469.84 |

# EXERCISES

1. The spreadsheet below shows the value of the function $f(x) = x^2 + 3x - 16$ for $x = 3$. Create the indicated data table and use it to graph the function in the range $(-10,14)$.

|  | A | B | C | D |
|---|---|---|---|---|
| 3 | x | 3 |  |  |
| 4 | f(x) | 2 | <-- =B3^2+3*B3-16 |  |
| 5 |  |  |  |  |
| 6 |  |  |  |  |
| 7 | Data table |  |  |  |
| 8 |  |  | 2 | <-- =B4 |
| 9 | -10 |  |  |  |
| 10 | -8 |  |  |  |
| 11 | -6 |  |  |  |
| 12 | -4 |  |  |  |
| 13 | -2 |  |  |  |
| 14 | 0 |  |  |  |
| 15 | 2 |  |  |  |
| 16 | 4 |  |  |  |
| 17 | 6 |  |  |  |
| 18 | 8 |  |  |  |
| 19 | 10 |  |  |  |
| 20 | 12 |  |  |  |
| 21 | 14 |  |  |  |

2. The example below calculates the NPV and IRR for an investment.

    a. Create a one-dimensional data table showing the sensitivity of the NPV and IRR to the year-1 cash flow (currently $10,000). Use a range of $9,000–12,000 in increments of $500.

    b. Create a two-dimensional data table showing the sensitivity of NPV to the year-1 cash flow and to the discount rate. Use the same range for the cash flow as above and use discount rates from 8 to 20%, with increments of 2%.

|  | A | B | C | D | E |
|---|---|---|---|---|---|
| 3 | Discount rate | 15% |  |  |  |
| 4 | Cost | 50,000 |  |  |  |
| 5 | Cash flow growth | 6% |  |  |  |
| 6 |  |  |  |  |  |
| 7 | Year | Cash flow |  |  |  |
| 8 | 0 | (50,000.00) | <-- =-B4 |  |  |
| 9 | 1 | 10,000.00 |  |  |  |
| 10 | 2 | 10,600.00 | <-- =B9*(1+$B$5) |  |  |
| 11 | 3 | 11,236.00 | <-- =B10*(1+$B$5) |  |  |
| 12 | 4 | 11,910.16 |  |  |  |
| 13 | 5 | 12,624.77 |  |  |  |
| 14 | 6 | 13,382.26 |  |  |  |
| 15 | 7 | 14,185.19 |  |  |  |
| 16 | 8 | 15,036.30 |  |  |  |
| 17 | 9 | 15,938.48 |  |  |  |
| 18 | 10 | 16,894.79 |  |  |  |
| 19 |  |  |  |  |  |
| 20 | NPV | 11,925.54 | <-- =NPV(B3,B9:B18)+B8 |  |  |
| 21 | IRR | 20.41% | <-- =IRR(B8:B18) |  |  |

3. Project *A* and Project *B* cash flows are given in the spreadsheet below. Re-create the **Data Table** in cells A21:C37 and create the graph. Note that the Data Table headers in cells B21:C21 have been hidden (see Section 27.3 for details on how to do this).

What is the crossover point of the two lines? (You can use the data table to do this, but you can also refer to Chapter 4 for a better solution.)

| | A | B | C | D | E | F | G | H | I |
|---|---|---|---|---|---|---|---|---|---|
| 1 | | | | TWO INVESTMENTS AND THEIR NPVs | | | | | |
| 2 | Discount rate | 15% | | | | | | | |
| 3 | | | | | | | | | |
| 4 | Year | Project A cash flow | Project B cash flow | | | | | | |
| 5 | 0 | -1,000 | -1,000 | | | | | | |
| 6 | 1 | 220 | 300 | | | | | | |
| 7 | 2 | 220 | 300 | | | | | | |
| 8 | 3 | 220 | 300 | | | | | | |
| 9 | 4 | 220 | 300 | | | | | | |
| 10 | 5 | 220 | 300 | | | | | | |
| 11 | 6 | 220 | 100 | | | | | | |
| 12 | 7 | 220 | 100 | | | | | | |
| 13 | 8 | 220 | 100 | | | | | | |
| 14 | 9 | 220 | 100 | | | | | | |
| 15 | 10 | 220 | 100 | | | | | | |
| 16 | | | | | | | | | |
| 17 | NPV | 104.13 | 172.31 | <-- =NPV($B$2,C6:C15)+C5 | | | | | |
| 18 | IRR | 17.68% | 20.64% | <-- =IRR(C5:C15) | | | | | |
| 19 | | | | | | | | | |
| 20 | | NPV A | NPV B | | | | | | |
| 21 | | | | <-- The data table headers have been hidden; see Chapter 27 for details | | | | | |
| 22 | 0% | 1,200.00 | 1,000.00 | | | | | | |
| 23 | 2% | 976.17 | 840.95 | | | | | | |
| 24 | 4% | 784.40 | 701.45 | | | | | | |
| 25 | 6% | 619.22 | 578.48 | | | | | | |
| 26 | 8% | 476.22 | 469.55 | | | | | | |
| 27 | 10% | 351.80 | 372.61 | | | | | | |
| 28 | 12% | 243.05 | 285.98 | | | | | | |
| 29 | 14% | 147.55 | 208.23 | | | | | | |
| 30 | 16% | 63.31 | 138.18 | | | | | | |
| 31 | 18% | -11.30 | 74.84 | | | | | | |
| 32 | 20% | -77.66 | 17.37 | | | | | | |
| 33 | 22% | -136.90 | -34.95 | | | | | | |
| 34 | 24% | -189.99 | -82.74 | | | | | | |
| 35 | 26% | -237.74 | -126.51 | | | | | | |
| 36 | 28% | -280.84 | -166.71 | | | | | | |
| 37 | 30% | -319.86 | -203.73 | | | | | | |
| 38 | | | | | | | | | |
| 39 | | | | | | | | | |

4. Finance texts always have tables that give the present value (PV) factor for an annuity:

$$PV \text{ factor for annuity of } \$1 \text{ for } N \text{ years at interest } r = \sum_{t=1}^{N} \frac{1}{(1+r)^t}.$$

As illustrated below in Excel, these present value factors are created with the **PV function**.

| | A | B | C | D | E | F | G | H | I | J | K |
|---|---|---|---|---|---|---|---|---|---|---|---|
| 1 | | | | | ANNUITY TABLE | | | | | | |
| 2 | r, interest | 9% | | | | | | | | | |
| 3 | N, number of periods | 5 | | | | | | | | | |
| 4 | PV factor | 3.8897 | <-- =PV(B2,B3,-1) | | | | | | | | |
| 5 | | | | | | | | | | | |
| 6 | | | | | | | | | | | |
| 7 | Number of periods | | PRESENT VALUE OF AN ANNUITY OF $1 FOR N PERIODS | | | | | | | | |
| 8 | | 1% | 2% | 3% | 4% | 5% | 6% | 7% | 8% | 9% | 10% |
| 9 | 1 | | | | | | | | | | |
| 10 | 2 | | | | | | | | | | |
| 11 | 3 | | | | | | | | | | |
| 12 | 4 | | | | | | | | | | |
| 13 | 5 | | | | | | | | | | |
| 14 | 6 | | | | | | | | | | |
| 15 | 7 | | | | | | | | | | |
| 16 | 8 | | | | | | | | | | |
| 17 | 9 | | | | | | | | | | |
| 18 | 10 | | | | | | | | | | |

Use **Data Table** to create the table in the template above.

5. (Do this example only if you've studied Chapters 20–23 on option pricing.) The Black–Scholes option-pricing model, defined in Chapter 22, prices call and put options based on five parameters:

- $S$, the stock price today
- $X$, the option's exercise price (also called the option's *strike price*)
- $T$, the option's expiration date
- $r$, the interest rate
- $\alpha$, the riskiness of the stock

These inputs and the resulting call and put prices are highlighted below.

**Your assignment**: Use **Data Table** to create tables showing the sensitivity of the call and put prices to the various inputs. Here are some suggestions.

a. Using the parameters shown below, what are the call and put prices given $\sigma = 10\%$, 15%, 20%,..., 80%?

b. Using the parameters shown below, what are the call and put prices when $T = 0.1, 0.2, 0.3,..., 1$?

| | A | B | C |
|---|---|---|---|
| 1 | **The Black-Scholes Option-Pricing Formula** | | |
| 2 | S | 100 | Current stock price |
| 3 | X | 90 | Exercise price |
| 4 | T | 0.50000 | Time to maturity of option (in years) |
| 5 | r | 4.00% | Risk-free rate of interest |
| 6 | Sigma | 35% | Stock volatility |
| 7 | | | |
| 8 | $d_1$ | 0.6303 | <-- (LN(S/X)+(r+0.5*sigma^2)*T)/(sigma*SQRT(T)) |
| 9 | $d_2$ | 0.3828 | <-- $d_1$-sigma*SQRT(T) |
| 10 | | | |
| 11 | $N(d_1)$ | 0.7357 | <-- Uses formula NormSDist($d_1$) |
| 12 | $N(d_2)$ | 0.6491 | <-- Uses formula NormSDist($d_2$) |
| 13 | | | |
| 14 | Call price | 16.32 | <-- S*N($d_1$)-X*exp(-r*T)*N($d_2$) |
| 15 | Put price | 4.53 | <-- call price - S + X*Exp(-r*T): by Put-Call parity |

# 28 Using Goal Seek and Solver

## CHAPTER CONTENTS

## Overview

**Goal Seek** and **Solver** are Excel tools that produce targeted results from your models (the technical jargon is "calibrate your model"). If this sentence sounds a bit dense, read on—you'll see that these tools are extremely useful.

Although **Solver** is a much more sophisticated tool than **Goal Seek**, we won't use many of its more advanced capabilities. For our purposes, **Goal Seek** and **Solver** are thus largely interchangeable—they can both do most of the financial tasks that we require and are not difficult to use. When you get used to them, you'll probably find that **Solver** is preferable, because it "remembers" its arguments (at this stage you won't understand this, but read on).

## 28.1. Installing Solver

Both **Goal Seek** and **Solver** come with the standard Excel package, but **Solver** has to be installed. If it is not on your computer, do the following:

- Open Excel. Click the Office button and go to **Excel Options** and then **Add-Ins**.

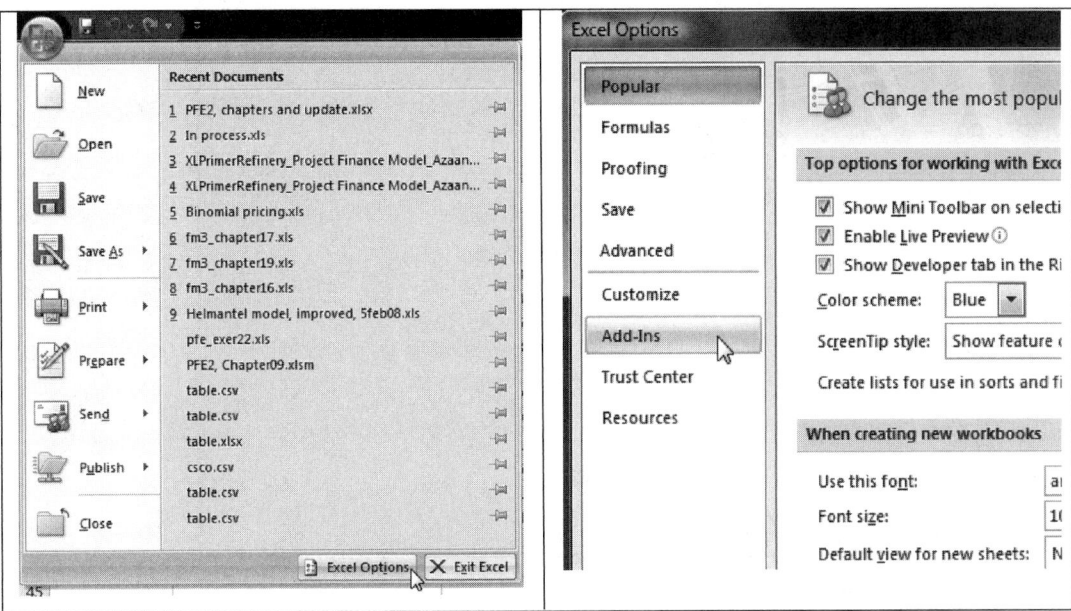

- Having clicked **Add-Ins**, you choose the option **Excel Add-ins** from the drop-down box.

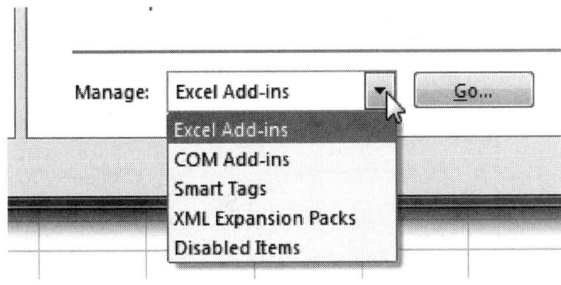

- Scroll down to **Solver Add-in** and click the box. That should do it.

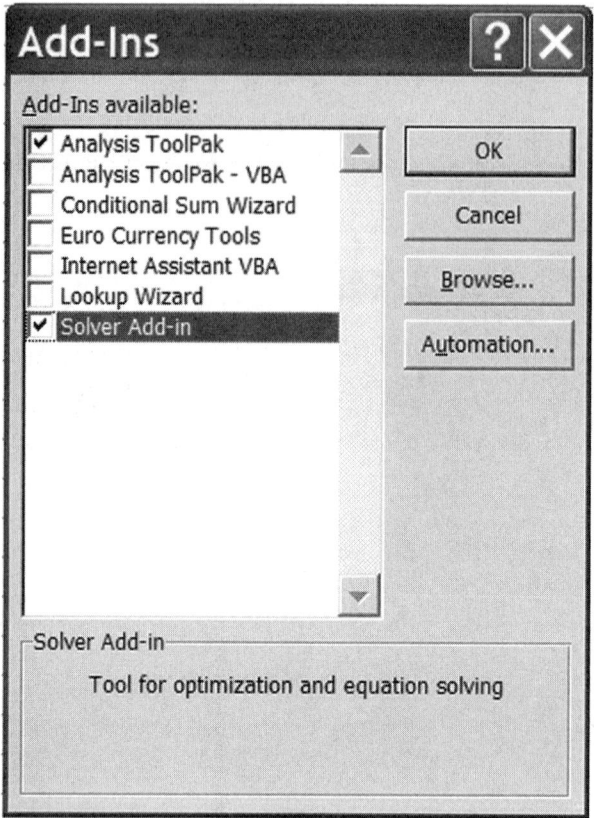

## 28.2. Using Goal Seek and Solver: A Simple Example

We'll start with a high school algebra example: Suppose we're trying to graph the equation $y = -x^3 + 2x^2 - 3x + 121$. We can do this in Excel as follows.

|   | A | B | C | D | E | F | G |
|---|---|---|---|---|---|---|---|
| 1 |   | **SIMPLE EXAMPLE** |   |   |   |   |   |
| 2 | x | 5.166147 |   |   | Table |   |   |
| 3 | y | 21.00001 | <-- =-B2^3+2*B2^2-3*B2+121 |   | x | y |   |
| 4 |   |   |   |   | -9 | 1039 | <-- =-E4^3+2*E4^2-3*E4+121 |
| 5 |   |   |   |   | -8 | 785 | <-- =-E5^3+2*E5^2-3*E5+121 |
| 6 |   |   |   |   | -7 | 583 | <-- =-E6^3+2*E6^2-3*E6+121 |
| 7 |   |   |   |   | -6 | 427 | <-- =-E7^3+2*E7^2-3*E7+121 |
| 8 |   |   |   |   | -5 | 311 |   |
| 9 |   |   |   |   | -4 | 229 |   |
| 10 |   |   |   |   | -3 | 175 |   |
| 11 |   |   | 1500 |   | -2 | 143 |   |
| 12 |   |   |   |   | -1 | 127 |   |
| 13 |   |   | 1000 |   | 0 | 121 |   |
| 14 |   |   |   |   | 1 | 119 |   |
| 15 |   |   | 500 |   | 2 | 115 |   |
| 16 |   |   |   |   | 3 | 103 |   |
| 17 |   |   | 0 |   | 4 | 77 |   |
| 18 |   |   |   |   | 5 | 31 |   |
| 19 |   |   | -500 |   | 6 | -41 |   |
| 20 |   |   |   |   | 7 | -145 |   |
| 21 |   |   | -1000 |   | 8 | -287 |   |
| 22 |   |   | -1500 |   | 9 | -473 |   |
| 23 |   |   |   |   | 10 | -709 |   |
| 24 |   |   |   |   | 11 | -1001 |   |

**Note** that we've put the function in twice: In cells B2:B3, we've got a simple example of the function (one value of $x$ and its corresponding $y$ value); in the table to the right, we've got the table for the graph (many values of $x$ and many values of $y$).

Now we want to find the $x$ such that the corresponding $y$ is 21. You can tell from the table that the value will be somewhere between 5 and 6. To solve for it, we go to the Excel command **Data|What-If Analysis|Goal Seek**.

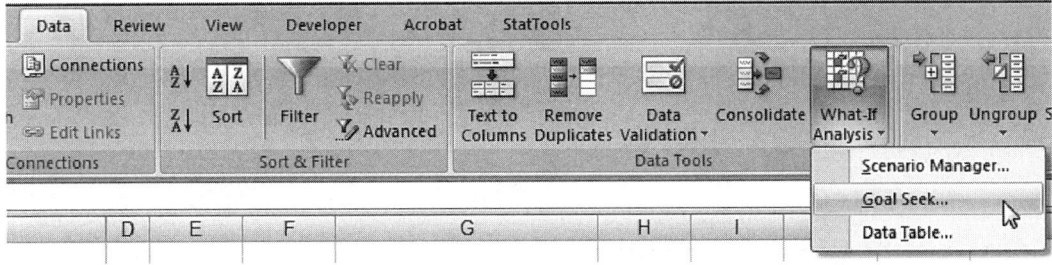

This brings up a dialog box, which we fill in as below.

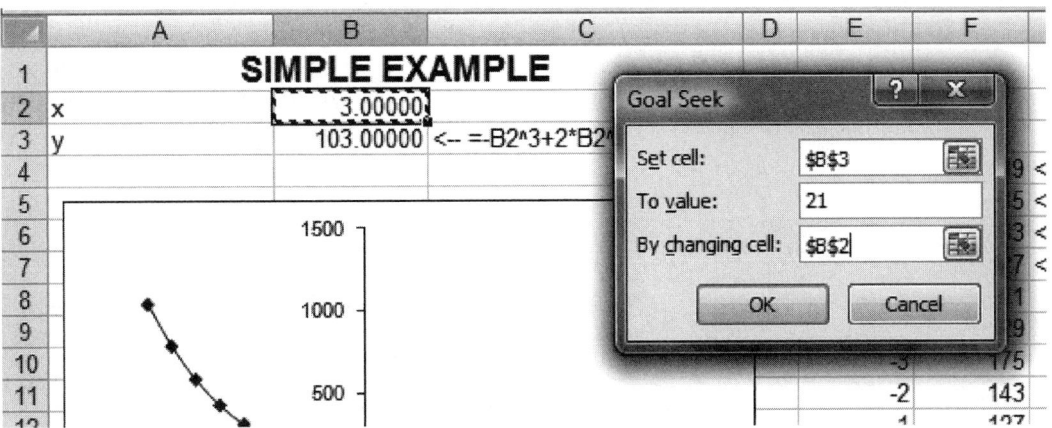

Clicking **OK** indicates that the answer is approximately 5.166147.

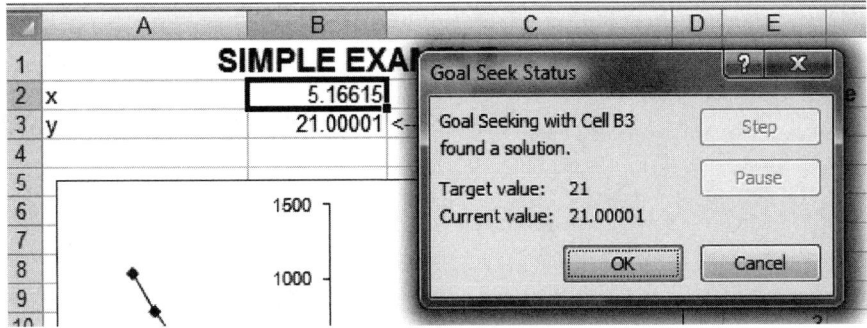

Clicking **OK** again accepts this answer.

|  | A | B | C |
|---|---|---|---|
| 1 |  | **SIMPLE EXAMPLE** |  |
| 2 | x | 5.166147 |  |
| 3 | y | 21.00001 | <-- =-B2^3+2*B2^2-3*B2+121 |

## Doing the Same Thing with Solver

We can do the same calculation with **Solver**. On the same spreadsheet, we go to the command **Data|Solver**.

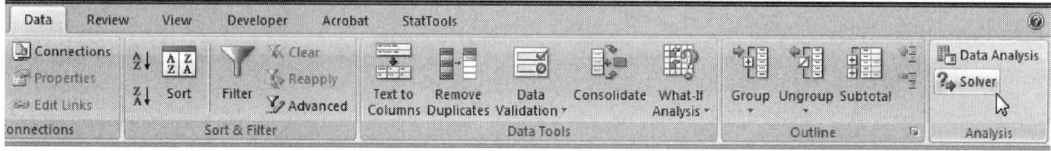

This brings up a dialog box that we fill in as follows (note that we changed the question a bit—this time we're asking for the *x* value that gives a *y* = –58).

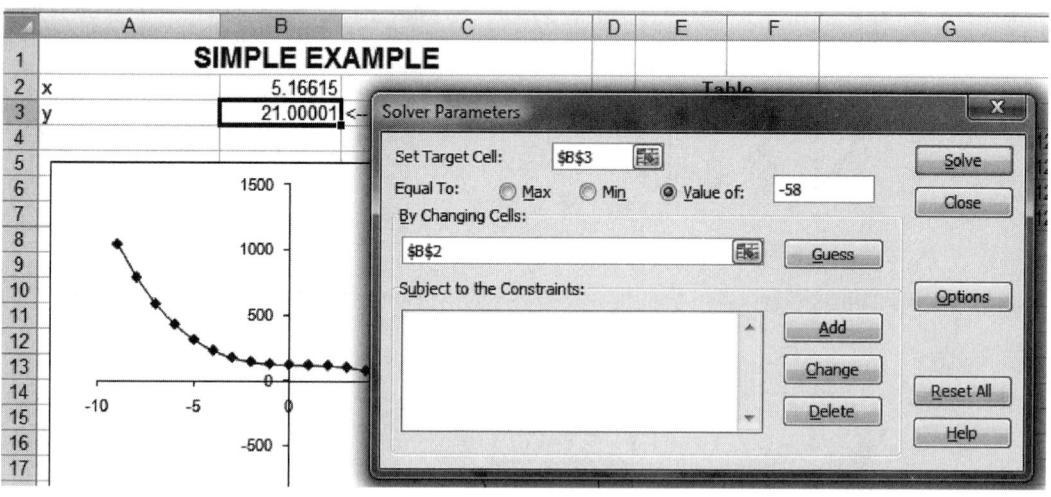

Clicking **Solve** gives the answer.

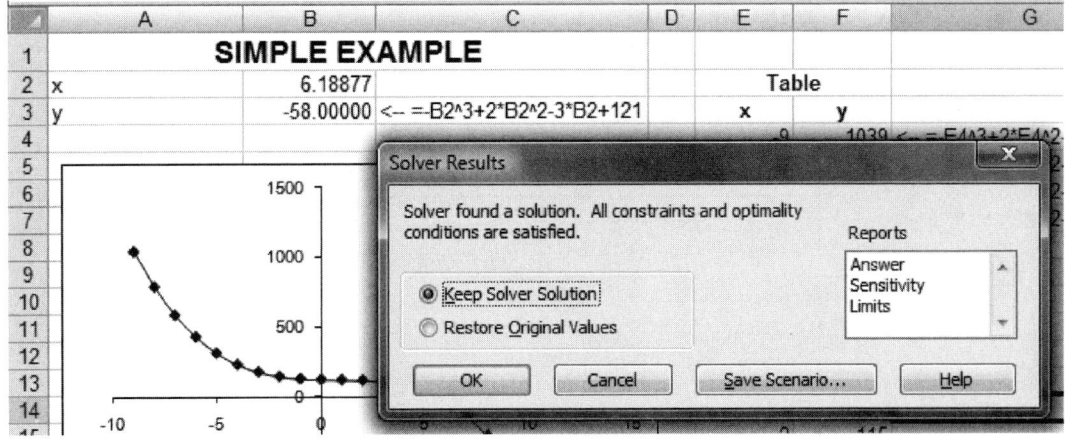

Clicking **OK** accepts the answer.

## 28.3. What's the Difference between Solver and Goal Seek?

**Solver** and **Goal Seek** serve much the same purpose. Nevertheless, there are several differences between them.

### Solver Remembers, Goal Seek Forgets

Suppose you've got another question: For which *x* will *y* = 158? If you use **Goal Seek** to answer this question, you'll have to re-enter all the values into the dialog box. But if you use **Solver**, you'll see that it comes up with the previous set of values—you only have to change the entry into the **Value of** box.

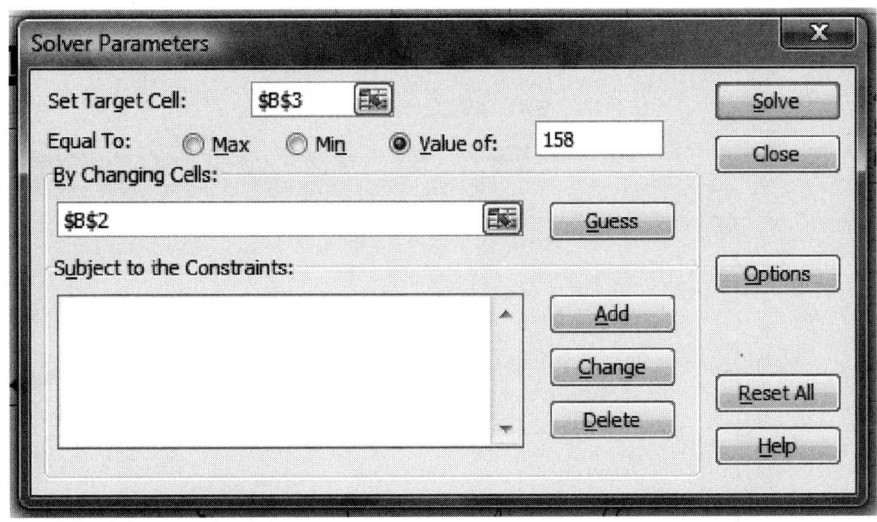

This "memory" of **Solver** carries over even if you save the file and reopen it later.

## Solver Is More Flexible

Again we use an algebra example, but this time we use the function $y = x^2 - 7x - 14$. This function is a simple parabola.

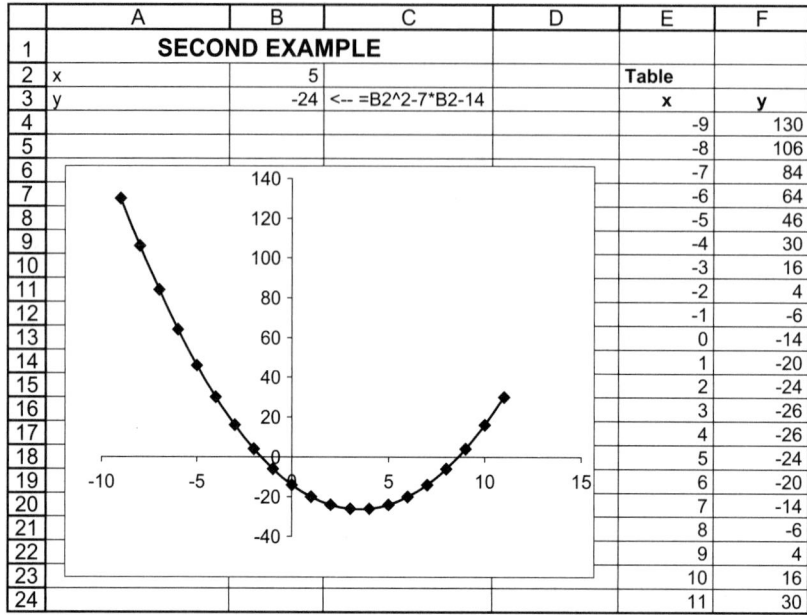

Now suppose we want to find $x$ such that $y = 21$. As you can see above, there are two such $x$'s: One is between −3 and −4, and the other is between 10 and 11. If you use **Goal Seek**, you cannot specify which $x$ to find.

With **Solver**, however, you can specify *constraints* on the variables.

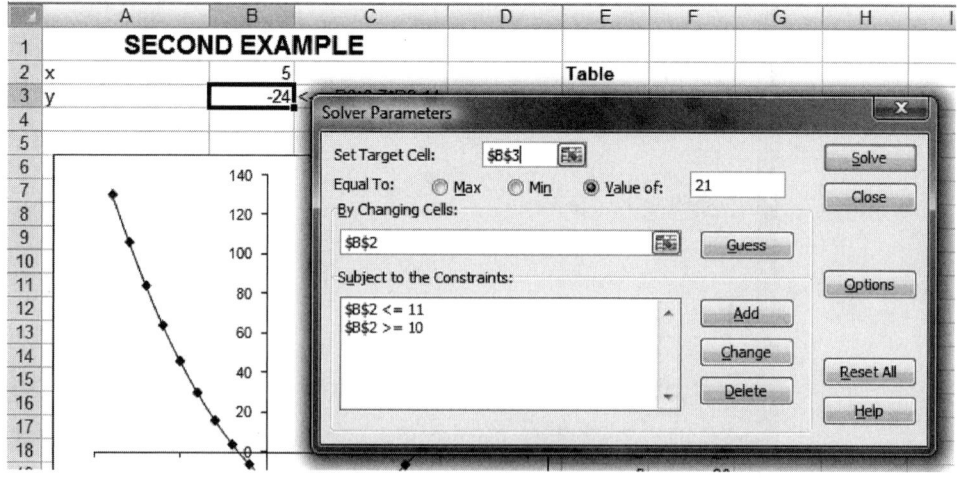

Here we've used **Add** to enter two constraints on $x$. Clicking **Solve** gives the correct answer.

| | A | B | C |
|---|---|---|---|
| 1 | **SECOND EXAMPLE** | | |
| 2 | x | 10.37386 | |
| 3 | y | | 21 | <-- =B2^2-7*B2-14 |

## 28.4. Setting the Accuracy of Solver and Goal Seek

Both **Solver** and **Goal Seek** compute to a given decimal accuracy. You can change this setting in Excel by going to the Office button and pressing **Excel Options|Formulas|Iterative Calculations** and changing the **Maximum Change**.

☑ Enable iterative calculation
Maximum Iterations: 100
Maximum Change: 0.001

## EXERCISES

1. Consider the present value calculation of a financial asset whose cash flows are given below. Use **Goal Seek** to find the discount rate such that the present value of the asset's cash flows is $800.

| | A | B | C |
|---|---|---|---|
| 1 | Discount rate | 12.00% | |
| 2 | | | |
| 3 | Year | Cash flow | |
| 4 | 1 | 100 | |
| 5 | 2 | 200 | |
| 6 | 3 | 300 | |
| 7 | 4 | 400 | |
| 8 | 5 | 500 | |
| 9 | | | |
| 10 | Present value | $1,000.18 | <-- =NPV(B1,B4:B8) |

2. A financial asset costs $500 and produces cash flows in years 1, 2,..., 5. The year-1 cash flow is $100 and subsequent cash flows grow at a rate of 5%. As you can see below, the asset's internal rate of return (IRR) is 3.32%.

Use **Solver** to find a growth rate such that the IRR is 10%.

|   | A | B | C |
|---|---|---|---|
| 1 | Year 1 cash flow | 100.00 | |
| 2 | Cash flow growth rate | 5.00% | |
| 3 | | | |
| 4 | Year | Cash flow | |
| 5 | 0 | -500.00 | |
| 6 | 1 | 100.00 | <-- =B1 |
| 7 | 2 | 105.00 | <-- =B6*(1+$B$2) |
| 8 | 3 | 110.25 | <-- =B7*(1+$B$2) |
| 9 | 4 | 115.76 | |
| 10 | 5 | 121.55 | |
| 11 | | | |
| 12 | Internal rate of return | 3.32% | <-- =IRR(B5:B10) |

3. (This problem requires some knowledge of portfolio calculations covered in Chapter 9.) Below you will find data on the returns, $E(r_A)$ and $E(r_B)$, and standard deviations, $\sigma_A$ and $\sigma_B$, of Stocks A and B. The number $\sigma$ is the correlation coefficient of the returns of A and B.

For a portfolio composed of proportion $x_A$ of Stock A and $x_B$ of Stock B, the portfolio expected return and standard deviation are given by

$$Expected\ portfolio\ return, E(r_P) = x_A E(r_A) + x_B E(r_B)$$
$$Portfolio\ standard\ deviation, \sigma_P = \sqrt{x_A^2 \sigma_A^2 + x_B^2 \sigma_B^2 + 2 x_A x_B \rho \sigma_A \sigma_B}$$

Because the portfolio proportions have to add to 100%, $x_B = 1 - x_B$.

A sample calculation of a portfolio expected return and standard deviation is given in cells B15:B16.

|   | A | B | C |
|---|---|---|---|
| 1 | **Stock A** | | |
| 2 | Expected return, $E(r_A)$ | 12% | |
| 3 | Return standard deviation, $\sigma_A$ | 15% | |
| 4 | | | |
| 5 | **Stock B** | | |
| 6 | Expected return, $E(r_B)$ | 22% | |
| 7 | Return standard deviation, $\sigma_B$ | 25% | |
| 8 | | | |
| 9 | Correlation of A and B returns, $\rho$ | 0.50 | |
| 10 | | | |
| 11 | **Portfolio** | | |
| 12 | Proportion of A, $x_A$ | 25% | |
| 13 | Proportion of B, $x_B$ | 75% | <-- =1-B12 |
| 14 | | | |
| 15 | Portfolio expected return, $E(r_P)$ | 19.500% | <-- =B12*B2+B13*B6 |
| 16 | Portfolio standard deviation, $\sigma_P$ | 20.88% | <-- =SQRT(B12^2*B3^2+B13^2*B7^2+2*B12*B13*B9*B3*B7) |

a. Use **Solver** to compute the proportions $x_A$ and $x_B$ for a portfolio that has the minimum standard deviation $\sigma_P$.

b. Use **Solver** and a constraint to compute the proportions $x_A$ and $x_B$ for a portfolio that has the minimum standard deviation $\sigma_P$ and a return of at least 18%.

4.

a. Graph the function $y = -2x^2 - 2x + 14$ for the $x = -4.0, -3.75, -3.50, \ldots, 3.0$. What are the approximate values of $x$ for which $y = 0$?

b. Using **Goal Seek** on the function, find $x$ such that $y = 0$. Which of the two values of $x$ does **Goal Seek** find?

c. Use **Solve** with an appropriate constraint to find the second value of $x$ for which the function $y = -2x^2 - 2x + 14$ has value 0.

# 29 Working with Dates in Excel

## CHAPTER CONTENTS

## Overview

One of the most powerful features of Excel is its ability to work with dates. We made use of this feature in Chapter 15 on bond calculations and in Chapter 22 on the Black–Scholes model. In this short technical chapter we explain how to use dates in Excel.

### Excel Concepts Covered in This Chapter

- Entering dates and times into spreadsheets
- "Stretching out" dates and times over multiple cells
- Formatting cells for dates
- Functions: **Now**, **Today**, **Month**, **XNPV**, **XIRR**, **Date**, **Weekday**, **VLookup**

## 29.1. Typing Dates in a Spreadsheet

Read the quote from the Excel help in Figure 29.1 on the next page and you will know almost everything you need to know about entering dates into your spreadsheet. The basic fact you need to know is that Excel translates dates into a number. Here's an example: Suppose you decide to type a date into a cell.

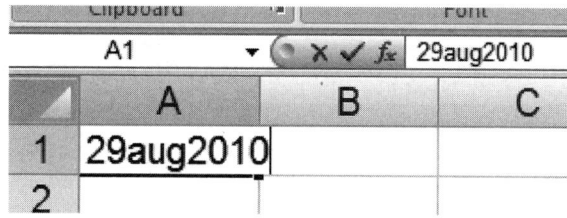

When you hit **Enter**, Excel decides that you've entered a date. Here's the way it appears.

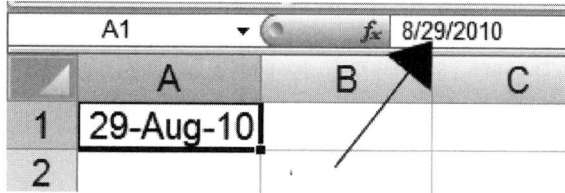

Note that in the formula bar (indicated by the arrow above), Excel interprets the date entered as **8/29/2010**.[1]

Right-click on the cell; go to **Format Cells** and then to **Number|General**.

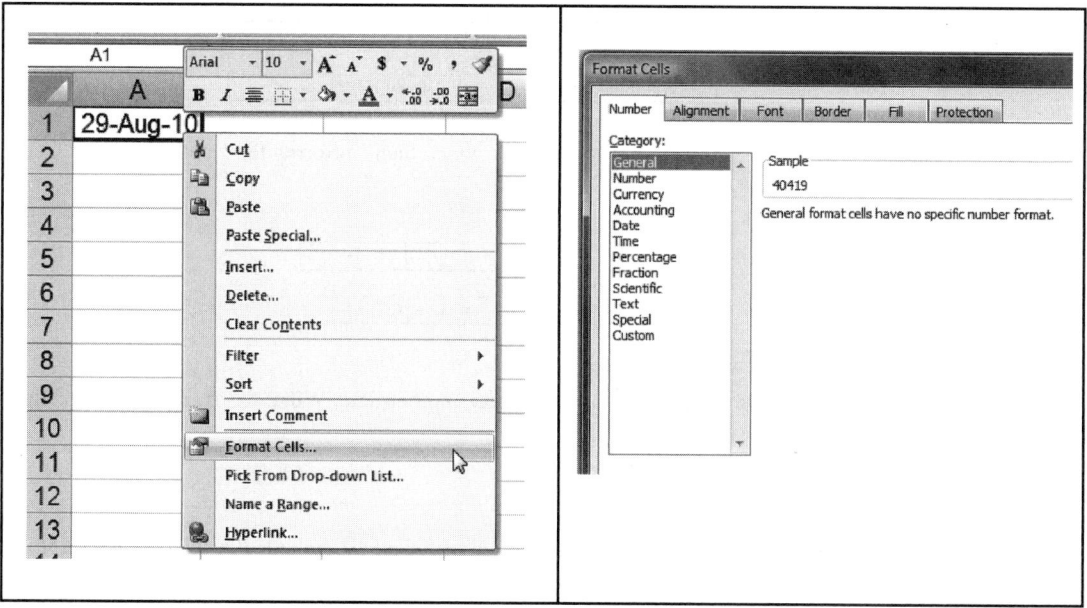

---

[1] The way this appears and is interpreted depends on the Regional Settings entered in the Windows Control Panel. Our settings in this book follow the U.S. conventions.

You see that Excel interprets this date as the number 40419, the number 1 being January 1, 1900.

| | A | B |
|---|---|---|
| 1 | 40419 | |
| 2 | | |

## FROM THE EXCEL HELP: ABOUT DATES AND DATE SYSTEMS

Microsoft Excel stores dates as sequential numbers that are called serial values. By default, January 1, 1900, is serial number 1, and January 1, 2008, is serial number 39448 because it is 39,448 days after January 1, 1900. Excel stores times as decimal fractions because time is considered a portion of a day.

Because dates and times are values, they can be added, subtracted, and included in other calculations. You can view a date as a serial value and a time as a decimal fraction by changing the format of the cell that contains the date or time to General format.

Because the rules that govern the way that any calculation program interprets dates are complex, you should be as specific as possible about dates whenever you enter them. This will produce the highest level of accuracy in your date calculations.

FIGURE 29.1 Excel's Help explains dates.

Spreadsheet dates can be subtracted: In the spreadsheet below we've entered two dates and subtracted them to find the number of days between the dates.

| | B | C | D | E |
|---|---|---|---|---|
| 5 | | 2-Dec-00 | | |
| 6 | | 8-Mar-99 | | |
| 7 | Days between | 635 | <-- =C5-C6 | |

(Cell C7 initially showed a date, but was then reformatted with **Format|Cells|Number|General**.)

| | C | D | E |
|---|---|---|---|
| 11 | 16-Nov-47 | | |
| 12 | 29-Apr-48 | <-- =C11+165 | |

You can also add a number to a date to find another date. What, for example, was the date 165 days after 16 November 1947?

## Stretching out Dates

In the two following cells we've put in two dates and then "stretched" the cells out to add more dates with the same difference between them.

| Write in two dates; mark both cells | Grab the handle (arrow on previous drawing) and pull. | The result: More dates added with same spacing (in this case, 6 months). |
|---|---|---|
| 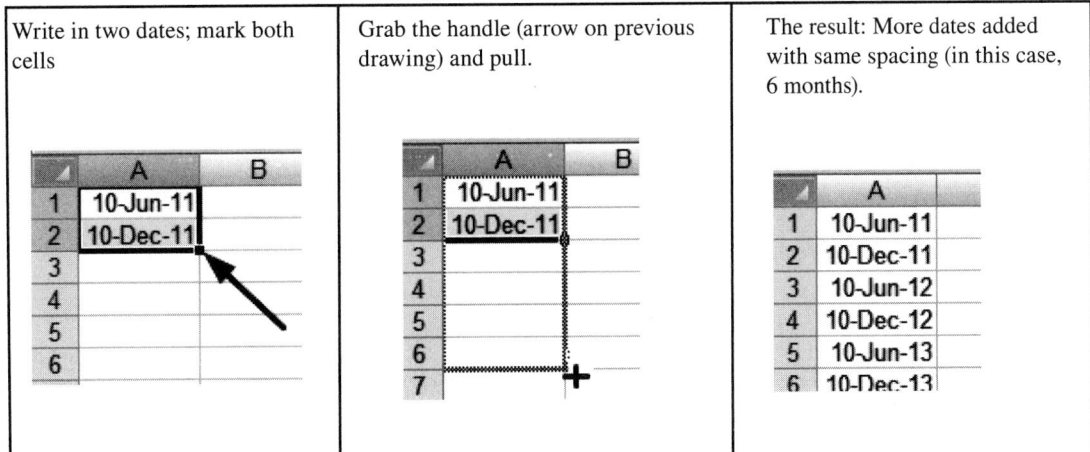 | | |

## 29.2. Times in a Spreadsheet

Hours, minutes, etc., can also be typed into a cell. In the cell below, we've typed in 8:22.

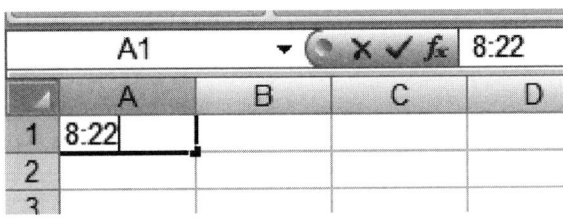

When we hit **Enter**, Excel interprets this as 8:22 AM.

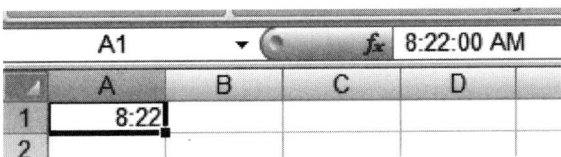

Excel recognizes 24-hour times and also recognizes the symbol **a** for AM and **p** for PM.

| As entered | When you press **Enter** |
|---|---|

Note that the **p** is separated from the time by a space. (Of course AM is represented by an **a**.)

---

**EXCEL RECOGNIZES 24-HOUR CLOCK**

| As entered | When you hit **Enter** |
|---|---|

| A1 | ▼ | × ✓ ƒₓ | 16:22 |
|---|---|---|---|

| | A | B | C | D |
|---|---|---|---|---|
| 1 | 16:22 | | | |
| 2 | | | | |

| A1 | ▼ | ƒₓ | 4:22:00 PM |
|---|---|---|---|

| | A | B | C | D |
|---|---|---|---|---|
| 1 | 16:22 | | | |
| 2 | | | | |

---

You can subtract times just like you subtract dates; cell B5 below tells you that 7 hours and 32 minutes have elapsed between the two times (ignore the "AM" in B5).

| | B | C | D |
|---|---|---|---|
| 3 | 3:48 PM | | |
| 4 | 8:16 AM | | |
| 5 | 7:32 AM | <-- =B3-B4 | |

When you reformat the cells above with **Format|Cells|Number|General**, you can see that times are represented in Excel as fractions of a day.

| | B | C | D |
|---|---|---|---|
| 3 | 0.658333 | | |
| 4 | 0.344444 | | |
| 5 | 0.313889 | <-- =B3-B4 | |

If you type in a date and a time and reformat, you can also see this.

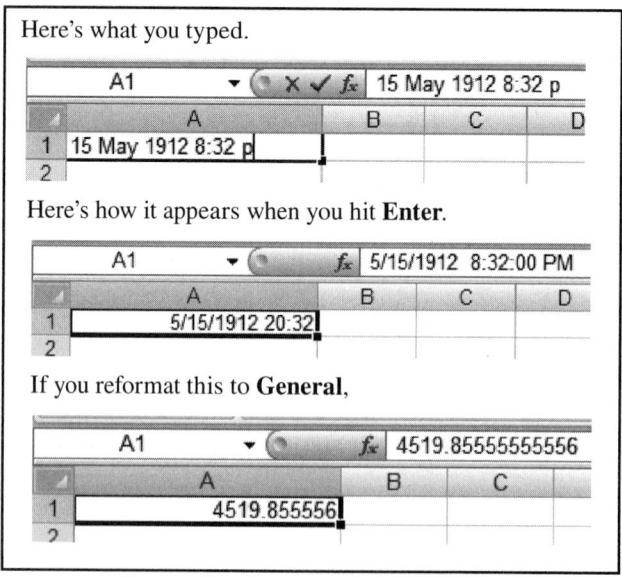

Here's what you typed.

| A1 | ▼ | × ✓ ƒₓ | 15 May 1912 8:32 p |
|---|---|---|---|

| | A | B | C | D |
|---|---|---|---|---|
| 1 | 15 May 1912 8:32 p | | | |
| 2 | | | | |

Here's how it appears when you hit **Enter**.

| A1 | ▼ | ƒₓ | 5/15/1912  8:32:00 PM |
|---|---|---|---|

| | A | B | C | D |
|---|---|---|---|---|
| 1 | 5/15/1912 20:32 | | | |
| 2 | | | | |

If you reformat this to **General**,

| A1 | ▼ | ƒₓ | 4519.85555555556 |
|---|---|---|---|

| | A | B | C |
|---|---|---|---|
| 1 | 4519.855556 | | |
| 2 | | | |

## 29.3. Time and Date Functions in Excel

Excel has a whole set of time and date functions. Here are several functions that we find useful. Note that several of these functions require empty parentheses:

- **Now( )** reads the computer clock and represents the date and the time.
- **Today( )** reads the computer's clock and prints the date.
- **Date(yyyy,mm,dd)** gives the date entered.
- **Weekday( )** gives the day of the week.
- **Month( )** gives the month.

Here are the first three functions in a spreadsheet.

| | A | B | C | D | E |
|---|---|---|---|---|---|
| 2 | **Serial representation** | **Date/time format** | | | |
| 3 | 36944.8493184028000 | 2/22/2001 20:23 | <-- =NOW() | | |
| 4 | 36944 | 2/22/2001 | <-- =TODAY() | | |
| 5 | 36245 | 3/26/1999 | <-- =DATE(1999,3,26) | | |
| 6 | | | | | |
| 7 | **Different formatting of Now( )** | | | | |
| 8 | | February 22, 2001 | <-- =NOW() | | |
| 9 | | 2/22/01 8:23 PM | <-- =NOW() | | |
| 10 | | 8:23 PM | <-- =NOW() | | |
| 11 | | | | | |
| 12 | **When was day 1?** | | | | |
| 13 | 1 | | <-- =DATE(1900,1,1) | | |

The use of **Weekday** and **Month** is self-explanatory.

| | A | B | C |
|---|---|---|---|
| 3 | 3-Nov-01 | 7 | <-- =WEEKDAY(A3) |
| 4 | | 7 | <-- =WEEKDAY("3nov2001") |
| 5 | In **Weekday**, 1=Sunday, 2=Monday, etc. | | |
| 6 | | | |
| 7 | | 11 | <-- =MONTH(A3) |
| 8 | | 12 | <-- =MONTH("22dec2003") |

### Calculating the Difference between Two Dates—The Function DATEDIF

This Excel function computes the difference between two dates in various useful ways.

| | A | B | C |
|---|---|---|---|
| 1 | | **DATEDIF COMPUTES DIFFERENCE BETWEEN TWO DATES** | |
| 2 | Date1 | 3-Apr-47 | |
| 3 | Date2 | 22-Dec-02 | |
| 4 | | | |
| 5 | | | **Explanation** |
| 6 | 55 | <-- =DATEDIF(B2,B3,"y") | Number of years between dates |
| 7 | 668 | <-- =DATEDIF(B2,B3,"m") | Number of months between dates |
| 8 | 20352 | <-- =DATEDIF(B2,B3,"d") | Number of days between dates |
| 9 | 19 | <-- =DATEDIF(B2,B3,"md") | Number of days in excess of full number of months |
| 10 | 8 | <-- =DATEDIF(B2,B3,"ym") | Number of months in excess of full number of years |
| 11 | 263 | <-- =DATEDIF(B2,B3,"yd") | Number of days in excess of full number of years |

If Date1 is the author's birth date and Date2 is today, then the author is currently 62 years and 117 days old (cells A6 and A11).

## 29.4. The Functions XIRR, XNPV

These two functions calculate the IRR and the NPV for a series of cash flows received on specific dates. They are especially useful for calculating IRR and NPV when the dates are unevenly spaced.[2] If you do not have these functions, you will have to activate the **Analysis ToolPak.**

**You do this by going to the Office button** 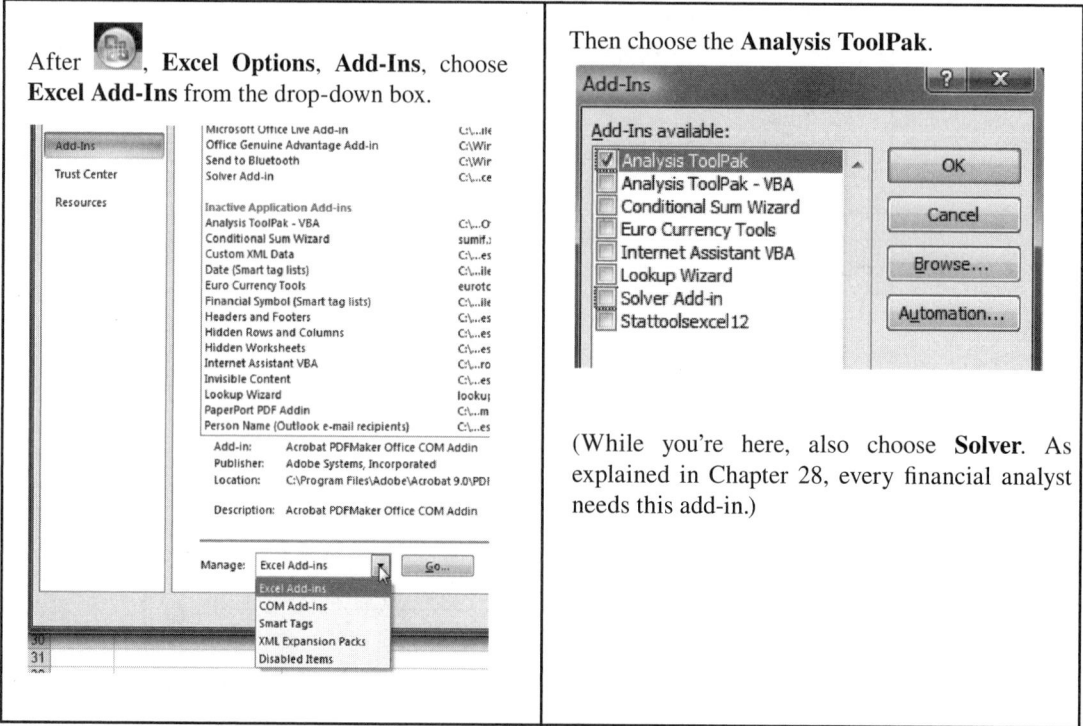, clicking **Excel Options** at the bottom of the box, and then going to **Add-Ins**.

After , **Excel Options**, **Add-Ins**, choose **Excel Add-Ins** from the drop-down box.

Then choose the **Analysis ToolPak**.

(While you're here, also choose **Solver**. As explained in Chapter 28, every financial analyst needs this add-in.)

### XIRR

Here's an example: You pay $600 on 16 February 2001 for an asset that repays $100 on 5 April 2001, $100 on 15 July 2001, and then $100 on every 22 September from 2001 until 2009. The

---

[2] Excel's IRR function assumes that the first cash flow occurs today, the next cash flow occurs one period hence, the following cash flow two periods hence, etc. Excel's NPV function assumes that the first cash flow occurs one period from now, the next cash flow in two periods, etc. We call this "even spacing of cash flows." When this is not the case, you'll need the XIRR and XNPV functions.

dates are not evenly spaced, so that you cannot use **IRR**. With **XIRR** (cell B16 below), you can compute the *annualized internal rate of return (IRR)* (the effective annual interest rate, EAIR, as defined in Chapter 3).

| | A | B | C |
|---|---|---|---|
| 1 | THE EXCEL FUNCTION XIRR | | |
| 2 | Date | Payment | |
| 3 | 16-Feb-01 | -600 | |
| 4 | 05-Apr-01 | 100 | |
| 5 | 15-Jul-01 | 100 | |
| 6 | 22-Sep-01 | 100 | |
| 7 | 22-Sep-02 | 100 | |
| 8 | 22-Sep-03 | 100 | |
| 9 | 22-Sep-04 | 100 | |
| 10 | 22-Sep-05 | 100 | |
| 11 | 22-Sep-06 | 100 | |
| 12 | 22-Sep-07 | 100 | |
| 13 | 22-Sep-08 | 100 | |
| 14 | 22-Sep-09 | 100 | |
| 15 | | | |
| 16 | XIRR | 21.97% | <-- =XIRR(B3:B14,A3:A14) |

The **XIRR** works by discounting each cash flow at the daily rate. In our example the first cash flow of $100 occurs 48 days from now, the second in 149 days, .... The XIRR transforms 21.97% to a daily rate and uses it to discount the cash flows:

$$-600 + \frac{100}{\left(1.2197\right)^{48/365}} + \frac{100}{\left(1.2197\right)^{149/365}} + \ldots + \frac{100}{\left(1.2197\right)^{3140/365}} = 0$$

| | A | B | C | D | E |
|---|---|---|---|---|---|
| 19 | HOW DOES XIRR WORK? | | | | |
| 20 | Date | Payment | Days from initial date | PV | |
| 21 | 16-Feb-01 | -600 | | -600 | |
| 22 | 05-Apr-01 | 100 | 48 | 97 | <-- =B22/(1+$B$34)^(C22/365) |
| 23 | 15-Jul-01 | 100 | 149 | 92 | <-- =B23/(1+$B$34)^(C23/365) |
| 24 | 22-Sep-01 | 100 | 218 | 89 | |
| 25 | 22-Sep-02 | 100 | 583 | 73 | |
| 26 | 22-Sep-03 | 100 | 948 | 60 | |
| 27 | 22-Sep-04 | 100 | 1314 | 49 | |
| 28 | 22-Sep-05 | 100 | 1679 | 40 | |
| 29 | 22-Sep-06 | 100 | 2044 | 33 | |
| 30 | 22-Sep-07 | 100 | 2409 | 27 | |
| 31 | 22-Sep-08 | 100 | 2775 | 22 | |
| 32 | 22-Sep-09 | 100 | =H15-$H$4 ——➤ 3140 | 18 | |
| 33 | | | | | |
| 34 | IRR? | 21.97% | <-- =XIRR(B21:B32,A21:A32) | 0 | <-- =SUM(D21:D32) |

## XNPV

This function computes the NPV for unevenly spaced cash flows. In the following example we use the function to compute the NPV on the same example we used for **XIRR**.

|    | A | B | C |
|----|---|---|---|
| 1  | **THE EXCEL FUNCTION XNPV** | | |
| 2  | **Date** | **Payment** | |
| 3  | 16-Feb-01 | -600 | |
| 4  | 05-Apr-01 | 100 | |
| 5  | 15-Jul-01 | 100 | |
| 6  | 22-Sep-01 | 100 | |
| 7  | 22-Sep-02 | 100 | |
| 8  | 22-Sep-03 | 100 | |
| 9  | 22-Sep-04 | 100 | |
| 10 | 22-Sep-05 | 100 | |
| 11 | 22-Sep-06 | 100 | |
| 12 | 22-Sep-07 | 100 | |
| 13 | 22-Sep-08 | 100 | |
| 14 | 22-Sep-09 | 100 | |
| 15 | | | |
| 16 | Discount rate | 15% | |
| 17 | XNPV | 97.29 | <-- =XNPV(B16,B3:B14,A3:A14) |

Note that **XNPV** requires you to indicate all the cash flows (starting with the initial cash flow), as opposed to **NPV,** which starts from the first cash flow.

## XNPV and NPV Can Give Different Answers

The functions **XNPV** and **NPV** can give slightly different answers. Here's an example.

|    | A | B | C |
|----|---|---|---|
| 1  | **XNPV VERSUS NPV** | | |
| 2  | Discount rate | 12% | |
| 3  | | | |
| 4  | **Date** | **Cash flow** | |
| 5  | 1-Jan-06 | -1,000 | |
| 6  | 1-Jan-07 | 250 | |
| 7  | 1-Jan-08 | 250 | |
| 8  | 1-Jan-09 | 250 | |
| 9  | 1-Jan-10 | 250 | |
| 10 | 1-Jan-11 | 250 | |
| 11 | 1-Jan-12 | 250 | |
| 12 | 1-Jan-13 | 250 | |
| 13 | | | |
| 14 | NPV | 140.94 | <-- =B5+NPV(B2,B6:B12) |
| 15 | XNPV | 140.68 | <-- =XNPV(B2,B5:B12,A5:A12) |

In cell B14 we calculate the NPV using the **NPV** function and in cell B15 we do the same calculation using **XNPV**. Why the different answers? **XNPV** does the calculation using the daily interest rate $(1+12\%)^{(1/365)} - 1 = 0.03105\%$ and based on the number of days between each date. **NPV**, on the other hand, uses the annual interest rate of 12%. Because 2008 and 2012 are leap years, the **XNPV** calculation is slightly lower.[3]

---

[3] For the same reason, **IRR** and **XIRR** can give slightly different results.

## 29.5. A More Sophisticated Example—Calculating Option Expiration Dates

In this section we show how to use several Excel functions to compute the date an option expires (see Chapters 20–22 for why this might be important). The actual option expiration date is the third Friday of the month. The calendar below illustrates what we mean—the relevant day for each month is highlighted.

How do we find this day? We start with Excel's **Weekday** function. This function takes the text form of the date and tells you the day of the week. Similarly, Excel's **Month** function tells you the month of a particular date. Here are some examples.

|   | A | B | C |
|---|---|---|---|
| 1 | 18-Nov-10 | 5 | <-- =WEEKDAY(A1) |
| 2 |  | 5 | <-- =WEEKDAY("18nov2010") |
| 3 | In **Weekday**, 1=Sunday, 2=Monday, etc. |  |  |
| 4 |  |  |  |
| 5 |  | 11 | <-- =MONTH(A1) |
| 6 |  | 12 | <-- =MONTH("22dec2016") |

# 2010

### JANUARY

| S | M | T | W | T | F | S |
|---|---|---|---|---|---|---|
|  |  |  |  |  | 1 | 2 |
| 3 | 4 | 5 | 6 | 7 | 8 | 9 |
| 10 | 11 | 12 | 13 | 14 | 15 | 16 |
| 17 | 18 | 19 | 20 | 21 | 22 | 23 |
| 24 | 25 | 26 | 27 | 28 | 29 | 30 |
| 31 |  |  |  |  |  |  |

### FEBRUARY

| S | M | T | W | T | F | S |
|---|---|---|---|---|---|---|
|  | 1 | 2 | 3 | 4 | 5 | 6 |
| 7 | 8 | 9 | 10 | 11 | 12 | 13 |
| 14 | 15 | 16 | 17 | 18 | 19 | 20 |
| 21 | 22 | 23 | 24 | 25 | 26 | 27 |
| 28 |  |  |  |  |  |  |

### MARCH

| S | M | T | W | T | F | S |
|---|---|---|---|---|---|---|
|  | 1 | 2 | 3 | 4 | 5 | 6 |
| 7 | 8 | 9 | 10 | 11 | 12 | 13 |
| 14 | 15 | 16 | 17 | 18 | 19 | 20 |
| 21 | 22 | 23 | 24 | 25 | 26 | 27 |
| 28 | 29 | 30 | 31 |  |  |  |

### APRIL

| S | M | T | W | T | F | S |
|---|---|---|---|---|---|---|
|  |  |  |  | 1 | 2 | 3 |
| 4 | 5 | 6 | 7 | 8 | 9 | 10 |
| 11 | 12 | 13 | 14 | 15 | 16 | 17 |
| 18 | 19 | 20 | 21 | 22 | 23 | 24 |
| 25 | 26 | 27 | 28 | 29 | 30 |  |

### MAY

| S | M | T | W | T | F | S |
|---|---|---|---|---|---|---|
|  |  |  |  |  |  | 1 |
| 2 | 3 | 4 | 5 | 6 | 7 | 8 |
| 9 | 10 | 11 | 12 | 13 | 14 | 15 |
| 16 | 17 | 18 | 19 | 20 | 21 | 22 |
| 23 | 24 | 25 | 26 | 27 | 28 | 29 |
| 30 | 31 |  |  |  |  |  |

### JUNE

| S | M | T | W | T | F | S |
|---|---|---|---|---|---|---|
|  |  | 1 | 2 | 3 | 4 | 5 |
| 6 | 7 | 8 | 9 | 10 | 11 | 12 |
| 13 | 14 | 15 | 16 | 17 | 18 | 19 |
| 20 | 21 | 22 | 23 | 24 | 25 | 26 |
| 27 | 28 | 29 | 30 |  |  |  |

### JULY

| S | M | T | W | T | F | S |
|---|---|---|---|---|---|---|
|  |  |  |  | 1 | 2 | 3 |
| 4 | 5 | 6 | 7 | 8 | 9 | 10 |
| 11 | 12 | 13 | 14 | 15 | 16 | 17 |
| 18 | 19 | 20 | 21 | 22 | 23 | 24 |
| 25 | 26 | 27 | 28 | 29 | 30 | 31 |

### AUGUST

| S | M | T | W | T | F | S |
|---|---|---|---|---|---|---|
| 1 | 2 | 3 | 4 | 5 | 6 | 7 |
| 8 | 9 | 10 | 11 | 12 | 13 | 14 |
| 15 | 16 | 17 | 18 | 19 | 20 | 21 |
| 22 | 23 | 24 | 25 | 26 | 27 | 28 |
| 29 | 30 | 31 |  |  |  |  |

### SEPTEMBER

| S | M | T | W | T | F | S |
|---|---|---|---|---|---|---|
|  |  |  | 1 | 2 | 3 | 4 |
| 5 | 6 | 7 | 8 | 9 | 10 | 11 |
| 12 | 13 | 14 | 15 | 16 | 17 | 18 |
| 19 | 20 | 21 | 22 | 23 | 24 | 25 |
| 26 | 27 | 28 | 29 | 30 |  |  |

### OCTOBER

| S | M | T | W | T | F | S |
|---|---|---|---|---|---|---|
|  |  |  |  |  | 1 | 2 |
| 3 | 4 | 5 | 6 | 7 | 8 | 9 |
| 10 | 11 | 12 | 13 | 14 | 15 | 16 |
| 17 | 18 | 19 | 20 | 21 | 22 | 23 |
| 24 | 25 | 26 | 27 | 28 | 29 | 30 |
| 31 |  |  |  |  |  |  |

### NOVEMBER

| S | M | T | W | T | F | S |
|---|---|---|---|---|---|---|
|  | 1 | 2 | 3 | 4 | 5 | 6 |
| 7 | 8 | 9 | 10 | 11 | 12 | 13 |
| 14 | 15 | 16 | 17 | 18 | 19 | 20 |
| 21 | 22 | 23 | 24 | 25 | 26 | 27 |
| 28 | 29 | 30 |  |  |  |  |

### DECEMBER

| S | M | T | W | T | F | S |
|---|---|---|---|---|---|---|
|  |  |  | 1 | 2 | 3 | 4 |
| 5 | 6 | 7 | 8 | 9 | 10 | 11 |
| 12 | 13 | 14 | 15 | 16 | 17 | 18 |
| 19 | 20 | 21 | 22 | 23 | 24 | 25 |
| 26 | 27 | 28 | 29 | 30 | 31 |  |

Now suppose we know the month and the year (as in cells B5 and C5 below). In cell D5 we have included a text formula that creates "1Nov2001" from the combination of the month and the year (text formulas are discussed in Chapter 28 on graphs).

| | A | B | C | D | E |
|---|---|---|---|---|---|
| 1 | A FUNCTION THAT LOOKS UP THE OPTION EXPIRATION DATE Looks up the third Friday of the month | | | | |
| 2 | | Month | Year | Month-Year | |
| 3 | | Nov | 2010 | 1Nov2010 | <-- ="1"&B3&TEXT(C3,0) |
| 4 | | | | | |
| 5 | Day of the week of the first day of month | | 2 | <-- =WEEKDAY(D3) | |
| 6 | Key:  1=Sun, 2=Mon, ... 7= Sat | | | | |
| 7 | | | | | |
| 8 | Date of option expiration | | 19 | <-- =VLOOKUP(B5,B12:C18,2) | |
| 9 | | | | | |
| 10 | Lookup table | | | | |
| 11 | Day of the week | Excel's Weekday function | Relevant Friday date | | |
| 12 | Sunday | 1 | 20 | | |
| 13 | Monday | 2 | 19 | | |
| 14 | Tuesday | 3 | 18 | | |
| 15 | Wednesday | 4 | 17 | | |
| 16 | Thursday | 5 | 16 | | |
| 17 | Friday | 6 | 15 | | |
| 18 | Saturday | 7 | 21 | | |

In cell B5 we use **Weekday** to tell us that 1 November 2010 is a Monday. Now it's only a matter of counting: If 1 November is a Monday, so are 8 November and 15 November. So the third Friday of the month is 19 November. Cell B8 uses the **VLookup** function (see Chapter 26) and the table in cells B12:C18 to give us the correct date.

## EXERCISES

1. Enter a series of annual dates into Excel, starting with 31 January 2008 and ending with 31 January 2015. The final product should look like this.

| | A |
|---|---|
| 1 | 31-Jan-08 |
| 2 | 31-Jan-09 |
| 3 | 31-Jan-10 |
| 4 | 31-Jan-11 |
| 5 | 31-Jan-12 |
| 6 | 31-Jan-13 |
| 7 | 31-Jan-14 |
| 8 | 31-Jan-15 |

2. Enter a series of hourly times into Excel, starting with midnight and ending with 11 AM. The final product should look like this.

| | A |
|---|---|
| 1 | 12:00 AM |
| 2 | 1:00 AM |
| 3 | 2:00 AM |
| 4 | 3:00 AM |
| 5 | 4:00 AM |
| 6 | 5:00 AM |
| 7 | 6:00 AM |
| 8 | 7:00 AM |
| 9 | 8:00 AM |
| 10 | 9:00 AM |
| 11 | 10:00 AM |
| 12 | 11:00 AM |

3.

   a. Prof. Smith was born on 15 February 1964. Today is 18 March 2007. Subtract the two dates to compute Prof. Smith's age in days.

   b. Divided by 365 to compute Smith's age in years.

   c. Use **Weekday** to determine the day of the week when Smith was born.

   d. Use **Datedif** to determine the number of months of Smith's age.

4.

   a. On 15 February 2005 a bond of XYZ Corp. is selling for $923. The bond has a $60 coupon payment on 15 May 2005 and each 6 months afterward until 15 November 2008, when it pays

| | A | B |
|---|---|---|
| 1 | Date | Bond cash flow |
| 2 | 15-Feb-05 | -923 |
| 3 | 15-May-05 | 60 |
| 4 | 15-Nov-05 | 60 |
| 5 | 15-May-06 | 60 |
| 6 | 15-Nov-06 | 60 |
| 7 | 15-May-07 | 60 |
| 8 | 15-Nov-07 | 60 |
| 9 | 15-May-08 | 60 |
| 10 | 15-Nov-08 | 1,060 |

   $1,000 plus the $60 coupon. Use **XIRR** to compute the bond's IRR.

   b. On 28 February 2005, the bond's price is $951. What is its IRR now?

5. A project whose discount rate is 13% has the cash flows indicated below. Use **XNPV** to compute the project's net present value.

|   | A | B |
|---|---|---|
| 1 | Discount rate | 13.00% |
| 2 | | |
| 3 | Date | **Project cash flow** |
| 4 | 1-Nov-03 | -1,000.00 |
| 5 | 13-Jan-04 | -523.00 |
| 6 | 18-Jul-04 | -1,500.00 |
| 7 | 31-Dec-04 | 1,500.00 |
| 8 | 17-May-05 | 2,200.00 |
| 9 | 19-Dec-05 | 1,200.00 |
| 10 | 22-Aug-05 | -435.00 |
| 11 | 15-Jan-06 | 2,000.00 |

6. In this exercise you will show how **XNPV** is based on daily interest rates. In the spreadsheet below, fill in all the cells marked ??? and show that the sum of the entries E5:E10 gives the same result as cell B12.

|   | A | B | C | D | E | F |
|---|---|---|---|---|---|---|
| 1 | Discount rate | 8% | | | | |
| 2 | Daily interest rate | ??? | | | | |
| 3 | | | | | | |
| 4 | Date | Cash flow | | **Days between dates** | **Present value based on days from initial date** | |
| 5 | 15-Mar-22 | -1,500 | | | ??? | |
| 6 | 18-Apr-23 | 250 | | ??? | ??? | |
| 7 | 22-Jun-23 | 155 | | ??? | ??? | |
| 8 | 15-Nov-24 | 610 | | ??? | ??? | |
| 9 | 16-Feb-25 | 222 | | ??? | ??? | |
| 10 | 19-Oct-25 | 100 | | ??? | ??? | |
| 11 | | | | | | |
| 12 | NPV | -380.076 | <-- =XNPV(B1,B5:B10,A5:A10) | | ??? | <-- =sum(E5:E10) |

7. Use the number of dates between dates to explain why the calculations of the IRR in cell B12 and in cell B13 are different.

|   | A | B | C |
|---|---|---|---|
| 1 | | **IRR vs. XIRR** | |
| 2 | Date | Cash flow | |
| 3 | 1-Jan-06 | -1,000 | |
| 4 | 1-Jan-07 | 250 | |
| 5 | 1-Jan-08 | 250 | |
| 6 | 1-Jan-09 | 250 | |
| 7 | 1-Jan-10 | 250 | |
| 8 | 1-Jan-11 | 250 | |
| 9 | 1-Jan-12 | 250 | |
| 10 | 1-Jan-13 | 250 | |
| 11 | | | |
| 12 | IRR | 16.327% | <-- =IRR(B3:B10) |
| 13 | XIRR | 16.317% | <-- =XIRR(B3:B10,A3:A10) |

# INDEX